BLACK SHOE CARRIER ADMIRAL

Vice Adm. Frank Jack Fletcher, 17 September 1942.
Courtesy of Yeoman Frank W. Boo, via Dr. Steve Ewing

Black Shoe Carrier Admiral

Frank Jack Fletcher at Coral Sea, Midway, and Guadalcanal

JOHN B. LUNDSTROM

Naval Institute Press
Annapolis, Maryland

This book has been brought to publication
with the generous assistance of Marguerite and Gerry Lenfest.

Naval Institute Press
291 Wood Road
Annapolis, MD 21402

First Naval Institute Press paperback edition published in 2013.
ISBN: 978-1-59114-419-9

The Library of Congress has cataloged the hardcover edition as follows:
Lundstrom, John B.
Black shoe carrier admiral: Frank Jack Fletcher at Coral Sea, Midway, and Guadalcanal / John B. Lundstrom.
p. cm.
Includes bibliographical references and index.
ISBN 1-59114-475-2 (alk. paper)
1. World War, 1939–1945—Campaigns—Pacific Ocean. 2. World War, 1939–1945—Naval operations, American. 3. World War, 1939–1945—Aerial operations, American. 4. Aircraft carriers—United States—History—20th century. 5. Fletcher, Frank Jack. I. Title.
D767.L86 2006
940.54'5973092—dc22

2005037937

∞ This paper meets the requirements of ANSI/NISO z39.48-1992 (Permanence of Paper).
Printed in the United States of America.

21 20 9 8 7 6 5

All maps are courtesy of the author's wife, Sandra Lundstrom.

To Elmer "Pete" Lundstrom, Private First Class, U.S. Army Air Force,
and Bernard R. Weber, Lieutenant, U.S. Naval Reserve,
who did more for me than they ever knew.

Contents

Photographs

Maps

Acknowledgments

The present book, the product of some thirty years of research into the early campaigns of the Pacific War, would not have come to pass without the extraordinary help and encouragement of many individuals and organizations. This simple statement of gratitude that names only a few cannot possibly describe my obligation to all of them.

Given my obvious sympathy for this book's controversial subject, I am greatly concerned not to offer in any way a whitewash of Admiral Fletcher's actions, but to treat them objectively. Thus I am most grateful to four reviewers who read the manuscript specifically with that object in mind: Dr. Steve Ewing, my close friend and coauthor of *Fateful Rendezvous*; the distinguished historian Richard B. Frank, who is also a valued friend; Frank Uhlig Jr. of the Naval War College; and Rear Adm. Kenneth R. Manning, USNR (Ret.). They all contributed excellent comments and advice, pressed me to prove my case, and even urged me on occasion to ratchet up the justified criticism of Fletcher's detractors. Lt. Cdr. Richard H. Best, USN (Ret.), read the chapters up through Midway and offered wonderful comments from his perspective as one of the Navy's most illustrious dive bomber leaders of World War II. I owe a special debt to Edward M. Miller, author of the seminal work *War Plan Orange*, who also read the manuscript. Without his stalwart support this book might not have been published. The errors that remain in the text are solely mine.

Other fine friends and associates eagerly aided my research. James C. Sawruk is a peerless researcher of Pacific War aviation who always seems to find key information when it is needed. Robert J. Cressman and Dr. Jeffrey G. Barlow, superb historians at the Naval Historical Center, provided invaluable assistance, as have Dr. Izawa Yasuho, James T. Rindt, J. Michael Wenger, Mark E. Horan, Mark Peattie, William Vickrey, Charles Haberlein, Ronald Mazurkiewicz, and Craig Smith. Steven L. Roca offered not only friendship but also put me up (and put up with me) during my numerous visits to College Park. Dr. Lloyd J. Graybar generously gave me access to the important and irreplaceable correspondence he generated for his excellent 1980 article on the relief of Wake. Two previous Midway authors, Walter Lord and Dr. Thaddeus V. Tuleja, graciously shared their research with me, as did Dr. Stephen D. Regan, who wrote a biography of Admiral Fletcher. Lt. Cdr. Jozef H. Straczek, RAN, provided excellent information from Australian archives. Although we differ strongly on Fletcher, I am grateful to Dr. Chris Coulthard-Clark for his very useful work on Adm. John G. Crace, RN. In the Milwaukee Public Museum, Dr. William Moynihan, previously president and CEO, and my former boss Carter L. Lupton were extremely supportive of my research.

Through the Internet I gained more help than I could have imagined and made more friends. Jonathan Parshall is a kindred spirit whose perspicacity and breadth of knowledge is amazing. He and coauthor Anthony Tully have written the most important new book on Midway in years. I would also like to thank Benjamin Schapiro, Randy Stone, David Dickson, Sandy Shanks, Jean-François Masson, Allan Alsleben, Allyn Nevitt, Andrew Obluski, and Cheralynn Wilson. The Battle of Midway Roundtable, run by William Price and Ronald Russell, has been an important asset in researching that battle.

Among the many participants and their families who aided my research, I would like to mention Thomas Newsome, George Clapp, Norman Ulmer, and Frank Boo, all of whom served directly with Fletcher in the *Yorktown* and *Saratoga*. Capt. Forrest R. Biard, USN, graciously answered my queries despite knowing that my opinion of his old boss Fletcher is so directly opposite to his own. Rear Adm. William N. Leonard, USN (Ret.), an old friend from my earliest days of research, offered insights into the role of an admiral in his flagship. William F. Surgi, another VF-42 veteran, and his wife Jean greatly facilitated my early research and took me to visit Mrs. Martha Fletcher in 1973 a few months after the admiral's death. Vice Adm. David C. Richardson shared with me his recollections of compiling the Naval War College analyses. Col. William W. Smith, USA (Ret.), gave me full access to the papers of his father, Vice Adm. William Ward Smith. The family of Rear Adm. Oscar Pederson, USN (Ret.), also opened his papers to me. John C. Fitch spoke to me of his father Adm. Aubrey W. Fitch and provided copies of his papers. Harriet L. Houck, daughter of Vice Adm. Spencer S. Lewis, furnished photographs, as did Cdr. Samuel E. Latimer Jr. I would also like to thank the heirs of Adm. Sir John G. Crace, RN, for permission to cite his papers in the Imperial War Museum.

Most of the documents utilized for this book now rest in the National Archives at the Archives II facility in College Park, Maryland. Over the years I have been fortunate to work with outstanding archivists Dr. Gibson B. Smith, Barry Zerbe, and Richard Peuser. At the Operational Archives Branch of Naval Historical Center, Kathy Lloyd, Michael Walker, and John Hodges were equally helpful. Admiral Fletcher's papers are held at the excellent American Heritage Center of the University of Wyoming–Laramie, where Carol L. Bowers and Lori Olson copied everything I required. Dr. Evelyn Cherpak likewise opened to me the many important collections of personal papers the Naval War College is privileged to hold. At the Nimitz Library of U.S. Naval Academy, Alice Creighton made available the Vice Adm. Wilson Brown papers. Steve Nielsen of the Minnesota Historical Society assisted me with Congressman Melvin J. Maas's papers. I am also grateful for the help of Hill Goodspeed of the National Museum of Naval Aviation at NAS Pensacola. My good friend Paul Stillwell furnished numerous histories from the oral history program at the U.S. Naval Institute, which are key sources for this work.

At the Naval Institute Press, I would like to thank Mark Gatlin for overseeing this project and both Donna Doyle and Chris Onrubia for their guidance in preparing the illustrations. My editor, Mary Svikhart, has shown remarkable kindness and patience in dealing expertly with a manuscript of this length.

My wife, Sandy, my dear partner in this as in all my endeavors, learned the mysteries of computer-generated graphics to draw the maps for me when it was no longer practical to do them by hand as she did for the last three books. She and my daughter Rachel gave me unstinting encouragement, understanding how important it was to me to complete this project.

Introduction

During the first nine months of the war against Japan, the U.S. Pacific Fleet clawed its way back from near destruction in one of the swiftest and most remarkable reversals of naval fortune since the Greeks defeated the Persians at Salamis. Shattered by the surprise assault at Pearl Harbor, the Pacific Fleet was outmatched at the outset by the tough and highly skilled Imperial Japanese Navy (IJN). In five months Japan overran the western Pacific and Southeast Asia, gained all its initial strategic goals, and grasped for more. In May and June 1942, in hard-fought aircraft carrier battles in the Coral Sea and off Midway, the Pacific Fleet won victories that not only denied Japan crucial strategic positions, but also inflicted crippling losses. The United States achieved relative parity in naval strength in the Pacific and gained the initiative. On 7 August the Pacific Fleet launched an amphibious counteroffensive in the southwest Pacific. Following seven bitter months, as the advantage seesawed from one side to the other, the Allied victory at Guadalcanal decided the course of the Pacific War

From December 1941 to October 1942 Vice Adm. Frank Jack Fletcher led forces that contributed decisively to the dramatic turnabout, sinking six Japanese carriers for the loss of two U.S. carriers. In the history of those crucial early campaigns, he is second in importance to Adm. Chester W. Nimitz, the beloved commander in chief of the Pacific Fleet. Only Fletcher participated in all the different phases of the Pacific Fleet's strategy during that time period. He took part in the futile attempt of Nimitz's predecessors to hold the vital asset of Wake Island, fought in the early raids, spearheaded Nimitz's dramatic carrier confrontations at Coral Sea and Midway, and supported the invasion of Guadalcanal.

Fletcher was a "black shoe." That color, worn by the majority of U.S. naval officers, was emblematic of the surface navy as a whole, as opposed to the brown shoes brandished by the proud naval aviators. After Pearl Harbor it finally became obvious the ungainly aircraft carrier had supplanted the majestic battleship as the cynosure of sea power. Only other carriers could truly contend with them. However at the outset of the war, Japan outnumbered the United States in that category of warships. The U.S. Navy could only hope to attain decisive superiority in late 1943, after new construction reinforced the fleet. No one could say whether the Pacific Fleet could survive in the meantime. Ideally the admiral who led the U.S. carriers in the first three of the only five carrier battles in history would have been a naval aviator and task commander of vast experience. Instead Fletcher, the non-aviator, happened to be the man on the spot, and thus he bore that awesome responsibility.

Having someone run the show in a new and to him unfamiliar method of warfare would seem the very recipe for disaster. Yet when the odds were never more tilted in favor of the IJN, Fletcher gained three vital carrier victories. In May 1942 the Battle of the Coral Sea prevented the invasion of Port Moresby and handed Japan its first strategic setback of the war. Fletcher's carrier striking force scored decisive success on 4 June in defense of Midway, although the crippling of his flagship *Yorktown* gave the laurels to his talented subordinate Rear Adm. Raymond A. Spruance. In August 1942 Fletcher led the carriers (and nominally the whole expeditionary force) against Guadalcanal. Just surviving the Battle of the Eastern Solomons on 24 August, his third carrier clash in four months, helped forestall a devastating attack on the marine foothold and prevent the Japanese from landing fresh troops. The South Pacific Force thereby earned an essential breather during a critical portion of the Guadalcanal campaign. Frozen out of carrier command in October 1942, Fletcher returned to combat a year later in charge of the North Pacific Area. In September 1945 he accepted the surrender of naval forces in northern Japan.

No other U.S. admiral—and very few flag officers of any nation—came out ahead in three separate pitched battles during World War II. Fletcher retired in 1947 wearing four stars. The destroyer USS *Fletcher* (DD-992) is named in his honor. Yet by 1950 he wore the dubious distinction of most controversial figure in U.S. naval history. For all his hard-won accomplishments in battle, he is scornfully remembered primarily for two incidents: the failure to relieve the marine garrison of Wake Island in December 1941 and the supposed deliberate abandonment of the marine landing force at Guadalcanal, which is said also to have caused the terrible defeat at Savo. Historian Nathan Miller wrote in 1995, "No American admiral has had a worst press in postwar histories than Fletcher and even though he had won the Medal of Honor during the Vera Cruz expedition of 1914, he has been accused of cowardice." A general history of the era, David M. Kennedy's *Freedom from Fear: The American People in Depression and War, 1929–1945*, noted of the withdrawal of the carriers from Guadalcanal, "The fact remains that Fletcher displayed highly questionable judgment and a conspicuous want of courage." The 1999 memoir of noted author Capt. Edward L. Beach condemned Fletcher ("Fueling Jack") as a "peacetime" commander "weak in professional concern for the demands of war," who succumbed to "craven caution from on high" and "his own fears of the unknown." Historians Williamson Murray and marine Col. Allen R. Millett declared in their study of World War II the "very cautious" Fletcher "lacked the character to lead hard-pressed American forces." The most recent analysis of the naval war from Pearl Harbor through Guadalcanal, by a respected Napoleonic-era scholar, astonishingly avowed Fletcher bore the taint of "traitor," and that for his "cowardice" in pulling the carriers out from Guadalcanal, he was "court-martialed" and "relieved of his command." No such court-martial ever took place, and no one else labeled Fletcher a "traitor." Such, though, is the pervasive nature of Fletcher's strongly negative historical reputation, which is based on severely outdated secondary sources.[1]

The image of Fletcher as timid bungler is due in large part to his portrayal in volumes three through five of Rear Adm. Samuel Eliot Morison's enormously influential "semiofficial" *History of United States Naval Operations in World War II.* In 1947 Morison wisely observed in the preface of volume one, "No history written shortly after the event it describes can pretend to be completely objective or even reasonably definitive. Facts that I know not will come to light; others that I discard will be brought out and incorporated in new patterns of interpretation."[2] It is time to heed Morison's admonition and present a major reinterpretation of Fletcher's role in the Pacific Fleet from December 1941 to October 1942. Those who for more than fifty years accepted Morison's relentlessly derogatory portrait of Fletcher must now weigh a mountain of new evidence that demands a fresh verdict for a heretofore maligned naval officer who won his battles at sea, but lost the war of objective evaluation.

The present book has long been in the works. In 1974 Rear Adm. Oscar Pederson, who served on Fletcher's staff in 1942, wrote: "I hope you will be able to do a study on Frank Jack Fletcher. I feel he is a forgotten man and I think he made some hard and tough decisions for which not only did he not receive credit, but was severely criticized."[3] At that time I had just begun my research on the Pacific War and required the next twenty years to complete three books: *The First South Pacific Campaign* (1976), *The First Team* (1984), and *The First Team and the Guadalcanal Campaign* (1994), which analyzed Pacific Fleet strategy and the 1942 carrier battles in great detail. That lengthy apprenticeship developed many additional sources and gave me the background better to understand the command decisions that underlay these complex events. Fletcher once told the celebrated author Walter Lord, "After an action is over, people talk a lot about how the decisions were deliberately reached, but actually there's always a hell of a lot of groping around."[4] In the heat of battle it probably seemed that way, but in fact doctrine and method provided the indispensable framework. The goal of this study is to probe and explain the "groping around," and thereby illustrate just how a carrier task force commander functioned both in battle and in the often mundane but vital preparation for combat. Only in that way can Fletcher's decisions and actions be well and truly judged.

Abbreviations, Acronyms, and Special Terms

AA	antiaircraft
AAF	Army Air Forces
ABDA	American-British-Dutch-Australian Area
Airsopac	Aircraft, South Pacific Force
AK	cargo ship
Alnav	All Navy
Amphibsopac	Amphibious Force, South Pacific
Anzac	Australia and New Zealand
AO	fleet oiler
AP	transport ship
APD	high-speed transport (converted destroyer)
B-17	Boeing B-17 Heavy Bomber (Flying Fortress)
B-25	North American B-25 Medium Bomber (Mitchell)
B-26	Martin B-26 Medium Bomber (Marauder)
bandit	enemy aircraft
Batdiv	battleship division
BB	battleship
Belconnen	radio intelligence unit in Australia
Bleacher	Tongatabu
bogey	unidentified aircraft
Buaer	Bureau of Aeronautics
Bunav	Bureau of Navigation
Buord	Bureau of Ordnance
Bupers	Bureau of Naval Personnel (Bureau of Navigation until May 1942)
Button	Espíritu Santo
CA	heavy cruiser
Cactus	Guadalcanal
CAG	Commander, Air Group
Cardiv	carrier division
Carpac	Carriers, Pacific Fleet
Cast	Combat Intelligence Unit, Sixteenth Naval District
CG	commanding general
Cincaf	Commander in Chief, Asiatic Fleet
Cinclant	Commander in Chief, Atlantic Fleet
Cincpac	Commander in Chief, Pacific Fleet
Cincpoa	Commander in Chief, Pacific Ocean Areas
Cincus	Commander in Chief, U.S. Fleet
CL	light cruiser

CNO	Chief of Naval Operations
CO	commanding officer
Com	Commander, Naval District
Comairbatfor	Commander, Aircraft, Battle Force, Pacific Fleet
Comairpac	Commander, Aircraft, Pacific Fleet
Comairsopac	Commander, Aircraft, South Pacific Force
Comamphibforpac	Commander, Amphibious Force, Pacific Fleet
Comamphibforsopac	Commander, Amphibious Force, South Pacific Area
Comanzac	Commander, Anzac Area
Combatfor	Commander, Battle Force, Pacific Fleet
Comcarpac	Commander, Carriers, Pacific Fleet
Comcru	Commander, Cruisers
Comcrubatfor	Commander, Cruisers, Battle Force, Pacific Fleet
Comcrudiv	Commander, Cruiser Division
Comcrupac	Commander, Cruisers, Pacific Fleet
Comcruscofor	Commander, Cruisers, Scouting Force
Comdesdiv	Commander, Destroyer Division
Comdespac	Commander, Destroyers, Pacific Fleet
Comdesron	Commander, Destroyer Squadron
Cominch	Commander in Chief, U.S. Fleet
comint	communications intelligence
Comnorpac	Commander, North Pacific Area and Force
Compatwing	Commander, Patrol Wing
Comscofor	Commander, Scouting Force, Pacific Fleet
Comserforpac	Commander, Service Force, Pacific Fleet
Comsopac	Commander, South Pacific Area and Force
Comsowespac	Supreme Commander, Southwest Pacific Area
Comsowespacfor	Commander, Southwest Pacific Force
Comsubpacflt	Commander, Submarines, Pacific Fleet
Copek	radio network for intelligence organizations
Crudiv	cruiser division
Crupac	Cruisers, Pacific Fleet
CSCMF	Cincpac Secret and Confidential Message File
CTF	Commander, Task Force
CV	aircraft carrier
CXAM	type of radar
DD	destroyer
Desdiv	destroyer division
Desron	destroyer squadron
DMS	high-speed minesweeper (converted destroyer)
DSM	Distinguished Service Medal
ECM	electrical cipher machine

F2A	Brewster F2A Fighter (Buffalo)
F4F	Grumman F4F Fighter (Wildcat)
FDO	Fighter Director Officer
fish	torpedo
GCT	Greenwich Central Time
HMS	His Majesty's ship
Huddle	Ndeni
Hypo	Combat Intelligence Unit, Fourteenth Naval District
IFF	identification, friend or foe
IJN	Imperial Japanese Navy
JCL	"Johnny come lately," term for naval aviators who qualified as captains or commanders
(jg)	junior grade
Kidō Butai	striking force
MAG	marine air group
Mardiv	marine division
NAS	naval air station
Navsta	naval station
Negat	Op-20-G, Radio Intelligence Unit, Office of the Chief of Naval Operations
NHC	Naval Historical Center
Norpac	North Pacific Area
NWC	Naval War College
NY	navy yard
ONI	Office of Naval Intelligence
Opnav	Office of the Chief of Naval Operations
Op-Ord	operations order
Op-Plan	operations plan
P-40	Curtiss P-40 Fighter (Warhawk)
Pacflt	Pacific Fleet
Patwing	patrol wing
PBY	Consolidated PBY Flying Boat (Catalina)
Pestilence	three-part offensive to seize Rabaul
RAAF	Royal Australian Air Force
RAN	Royal Australian Navy
RG	record group
Ringbolt	Tulagi
RN	Royal Navy
Roses	Efate
SBD	Douglas SBD-2, -3 Scout Bomber (Dauntless)
SC	Sail Cast (a type of radar)
Secnav	Secretary of the Navy

SOC	Curtiss SOC Seaplane (Seagull)
Sopac	South Pacific Area
Sowespac	Southwest Pacific
SWPA	Southwest Pacific Area
TBD	Douglas TBD-1 Torpedo Bomber (Devastator)
TBF	Grumman TBF-1 Torpedo Bomber (Avenger)
TBS	talk-between-ships short range radio
TF	task force
TG	task group
Transdiv	transport division
TS	top secret
TU	task unit
Ultra	ultra secret radio intelligence
USMC	United States Marine Corps
USN	United States Navy
USNA	United States Naval Academy (Annapolis)
USNR	United States Naval Reserve
USS	United States ship
VB	bombing plane, bombing squadron
VF	fighting plane, fighting squadron
VHF	very high frequency
Victor	defensive formation
VMF	marine fighting squadron
VMO	marine observation squadron
VMSB	marine scout-bombing squadron
VP	patrol plane, patrol squadron
VS	scouting plane, scouting squadron
VSB	scout bomber
VT	torpedo plane, torpedo squadron
VTB	torpedo bomber
Watchtower	Task One in Rabaul offensive
YE	homing signal and transmitter
Z	Greenwich time zone; times are given as Z-plus or Z-minus GCT

Black Shoe Carrier Admiral

CHAPTER 1

The World Turned Upside Down

COPING WITH CATASTROPHE

Sunrise on 13 December 1941 revealed Oahu's familiar profile to Rear Adm. Frank Jack Fletcher, the commander of Cruiser Division Six in the U.S. Pacific Fleet. His flagship, heavy cruiser *Astoria*, prepared to enter the cozy confines of Pearl Harbor. After eighteen months' duty in the Hawaiian Islands, going back into base should have been routine, but not on that occasion. Six days before, Japanese aircraft carriers surprised the fleet at Pearl Harbor and opened the Pacific portion of World War II. The task force in which Fletcher served was near Midway and pursued the raiders but fortunately—as it turned out—never caught up with them. Now he was returning for a new assignment. Radio dispatches from Adm. Husband E. Kimmel, commander in chief of the Pacific Fleet (Cincpac), painted a grim picture. Nothing, though, prepared Fletcher for what he saw. First there was a crashed U.S. carrier plane perched in the shallow water, then to starboard gutted Hickam airfield. Aground after her valiant sortie was the battleship *Nevada*, "Her nose in the beach and her bow partly submerged, her deck plates all hogged up from bomb hits." Beyond, in Battleship Row, the sunken *California* rested in the mud, as did the *West Virginia*; the *Oklahoma* presented just her "red bottom and one bronze propeller," and the *Arizona* had blown apart. Only the hurt *Pennsylvania*, *Maryland*, and *Tennessee* remained seaworthy. Hundreds of carrier-based torpedo planes, dive bombers, level bombers, and strafing fighters sank or damaged eighteen ships and ravaged Oahu's airfields of 188 planes. Nearly twenty-four hundred Americans died, but so far as anyone knew, the victory cost Japan a few midget submarines and an insignificant number of aircraft.[1]

The "horrible sight" of the once magnificent battle line reduced to an impotent shambles shook Fletcher to the core. Like Kimmel and nearly all the senior officers, he was a "black shoe," a nickname derived from the color of the footgear most naval officers wore. Black shoes were surface warriors, to whom big-gunned and heavily armored battleships, the "major fighting power of the U.S. Fleet," represented true naval might. Aircraft carriers—the pride of the "brown shoe" naval aviators—they considered secondary to battleships in the navy's prime mission of destroying the enemy battle fleet. Conceding carriers were valuable for reconnaissance, air cover, attacking weakly protected forces, and raiding ground targets, black shoes avowed only battleships could defeat other battleships and win supremacy on the seas. The unfolding Pacific War stood the black-shoe world on its head. Not only did Japan, a despised adversary, demolish the battle line, but also they accomplished that astounding feat by massing carriers to project vast firepower. The successful prosecution of the war now required air supremacy, both from the seagoing airfields and shore bases. Nailing that last point was the almost equally shocking destruction, on 10 December, of the modern British battleship *Prince of Wales* and old battle cruiser *Repulse* by land-based medium bombers. Not caught in harbor like the Italian battleships in 1940 at Taranto and the U.S. battleships at Pearl Harbor, they succumbed at sea to a blizzard of aerial torpedoes and heavy bombs.[2]

Alone among his peers, Adm. Yamamoto Isoroku, commander of the Combined Fleet, recognized carrier air power to be the trump card in modern naval warfare. The Imperial Japanese Navy (IJN) already possessed the strongest such capacity in the world. He resolved to use carriers to open the war in a daring stab to the heart of U.S. naval strength at remote Pearl Harbor. Sinking the Pacific Fleet's battleships and carriers would cover the seizure of the Philippines and Southeast Asia and give Japan vital time to consolidate its defense of newly won gains. To attack Pearl Harbor, Yamamoto created an immensely powerful striking force of no fewer than six aircraft carriers, wielding more than four hundred planes. Vice Adm. Nagumo Chūichi's *Kidō Butai* (literally "mobile force," but the best term in English is "striking force") comprised carriers *Akagi*, *Kaga*, *Sōryū*, *Hiryū*, *Shōkaku*, and *Zuikaku*, two fast battleships, two heavy cruisers, one light cruiser, sixteen destroyers, three submarines, and seven oilers. Seventeen other subs (including five equipped with midget subs) would rampage Hawaiian waters. On 26 November the *Kidō Butai* secretly sortied from northern Japan to venture three thousand miles across the barren, stormy North Pacific bound for a launch point 230 miles north of Oahu. Such an odyssey could only occur because the IJN recently developed the capability to fuel heavy ships under way similar to its principal opponent, the U.S. Navy, and greatly exceeding Britain's Royal Navy. On 7 December (8 December, Tokyo time), Nagumo delivered a crushing assault by 350 aircraft in two waves that nearly annihilated the Pacific Fleet. The cost of such colossal results was only twenty-nine planes (with many others shot up), five midget subs, and sixty-four lives.[3]

One bold and brilliant stroke transformed the entire character of naval warfare, although even Yamamoto did not fully fathom the extent of his revolution. His massing of six powerful carriers was totally unprecedented when all other navies reckoned their carriers in units of ones or twos. Yamamoto's innovation equated to a kind of 1941 atomic bomb. U.S. naval intelligence never understood prior to 7 December that Japan fashioned a single operational task force completely around several carriers, instead of the usual practice of attaching individual carrier divisions to different fleets. Each of the three principal Pacific Fleet task forces included only one carrier, with no immediate plans of operating more than one carrier together. Not having as yet made the huge intellectual leap of thinking of carriers in multiple units, it is hardly surprising that the U.S. Navy brass did not accord their future opponents any more insight in that regard. The high command simply did not believe that a single carrier raid could seriously harm Pearl Harbor. It was truly a miracle the two U.S. carriers in the Hawaiian region, the *Enterprise* and *Lexington*, survived the outbreak of the war intact, while the *Saratoga*, the third, happened to be at San Diego. A few days after the Pearl Harbor attack, Capt. Charles H. "Soc" McMorris, the Pacific Fleet War Plans officer, conceded Japan's failure to destroy the U.S. carriers left Cincpac a "very powerful" weapon, but certainly it was one that neither he nor his boss Kimmel had truly appreciated.[4]

Thus the aircraft carrier supplanted the battleship as the major factor in the Pacific naval war. The same, Fletcher discovered, was more or less true for battleship admirals. Had the massive fleet campaign in the central Pacific unfolded as Kimmel envisioned prior to 7 December, Fletcher, although a well regarded subordinate, would have played only a relatively minor role. Now as the fighting fell to the more junior admirals, Fletcher proved to be in exactly the right place at exactly the right time. Two days after he returned to Pearl Harbor he received a combat mission of great importance—relief of embattled Wake Island two thousand miles west of Oahu. His new task force comprised the *Saratoga*, three cruisers, nine destroyers, a seaplane tender transporting ground reinforcements, and a fleet oiler. Therefore Fletcher, a trusted flag officer who nevertheless totally lacked naval aviation experience, stepped into carrier command that afforded him an extraordinary opportunity to be among the first U.S. admirals to fight a new form of naval war. No one else played a more important role in the crucial 1942 carrier battles that helped turn the tide of war in the Pacific.

A MIDWESTERN SAILOR

Born on 29 April 1885 in Marshalltown, Iowa, the son of a Union veteran, Frank Jack Fletcher grew up in comfortable middle-class circumstances. His uncle Frank Friday Fletcher, an 1875 Naval Academy (USNA) graduate, inspired his naval career. Fletcher himself graduated from Annapolis in 1906, ranked twenty-sixth out of 116 midshipmen. His years at Annapolis overlapped numerous other midshipmen, who some forty years hence played a crucial role in his life as well as the nation's. Fellow members of the class of 1906 included Aubrey W. Fitch, Robert L. Ghormley, John S. McCain, Leigh Noyes, Milo F. Draemel, and John H. Towers. Among other future admirals were William F. Halsey Jr. and Husband E. Kimmel (class of 1904); Chester W. Nimitz, H. Fairfax Leary, and John Henry Newton (class of 1905); Raymond A. Spruance, Robert A. Theobald, and Patrick N. L. Bellinger (class of 1907); and Thomas C. Kinkaid and Richmond Kelly Turner (class of 1908).[5]

Fletcher rose to flag rank in November 1939 after a conventional succession of sea and shore duty postings. His first command, while an ensign in the Asiatic Fleet, was the destroyer *Dale* in 1910. Fletcher thrived. In 1911 the *Dale* placed first among the navy's twenty-two destroyers in spring battle practice and won the gunnery trophy. Capt. Frank Friday Fletcher wrote Frank Jack's father: "I am more proud of his having won this trophy than if I had won it myself." In April 1914 when Rear Adm. Frank Friday Fletcher led the occupation of Veracruz, Lt. Frank Jack Fletcher commanded the chartered mail ship SS *Esperanza* and spirited 350 civilians to safety while under fire. Later he ran the train that brought endangered foreigners from the interior, negotiating safe passage with the mercurial Mexican authorities. Fletcher's able service at Veracruz earned a commendation for gallantry from his uncle, which the navy upgraded in 1915 to the Congressional Medal of Honor.[6]

In November 1917 in the war against Germany, Fletcher undertook a riotous voyage to Britain in the ex-yacht *Margaret* (SP-527) of the Scout Patrol, a motley collection of converted civilian ships aptly known as the "Suicide Fleet." The *Maggie* proved less seaworthy than the craft she was supposed to tow. In 1930 one of her officers reminisced: "[Fletcher] was the kind of officer to say 'orders are orders' and fight a rowboat against a sixteen-inch gun, trusting to his own skill to pull him through. And that skill was superb. Many a time, save for his flawless seamanship, the *Maggie* might have ended her career as a warship a good deal earlier than she did." In mid 1918 Commander Fletcher led the destroyer *Benham* on convoy duty in the North Atlantic, where he got to roll depth charges only four times and never knowingly harmed a U-boat. On 22 July the *Benham* was damaged in a collision with the destroyer *Jarvis*, but a court of inquiry cleared Fletcher of any blame. In 1920, like most wartime ship captains and destroyer skippers, he received the newly instituted Navy Cross, at that time the navy's third highest decoration for gallant and distinguished service.[7]

In the early 1920s while in the Asiatic Fleet, Commander Fletcher commanded in succession the old gunboat *Sacramento* and two submarine tenders, with the additional duty of running the submarine base at Cavite. From 1927 to 1929 he was executive officer of the hard-luck battleship *Colorado* and weathered another collision where a passenger steamer was completely at fault. Thereafter he completed the senior course at the Naval War College and attended the Army War College. Such scholarly duty furnished vital background in strategic thought and operational planning. Captain Fletcher became chief of staff to Adm. Montgomery Meigs Taylor, the doughty commander in chief of the Asiatic Fleet. Japan's invasion of Manchuria in September 1931 and subsequent incursion into southern China gave Fletcher experience in naval diplomacy and a firsthand look at how the Japanese navy functioned in action. The coveted battleship command came in 1936 in the *New Mexico*, rated overall the number one in the Battle Force. With the help of subordinates like Lt. Hyman G. Rickover, the assistant engineer officer, Fletcher further enhanced her reputation as a crack warship. The *New Mexico* received the engineering trophy for the second and third years in a row and also took two of the three top prizes for gunnery. Providing oil to destroyers during a severe storm in the Aleutian Islands earned Fletcher a commendation for refueling in a "smart seamanlike manner." Two of Fletcher's former *New Mexico* officers recalled favorable impressions of their old captain, one calling him a "very, very fine naval officer."[8]

Yet Fletcher bore the taint of having benefited from pull in high places, starting with his uncle, who in September 1914 rose to commander in chief of the Atlantic Fleet. Fletcher joined his staff as aide and flag lieutenant, and thus became known to the navy's senior leaders and the political movers and shakers in Washington. It was during that tour the navy awarded the Medal of Honor to thirty naval officers, including both Fletchers, and nine marine officers for Veracruz. That was in addition to the sixteen medals already presented to enlisted men. Although instituted in 1861, the navy's Medal of Honor was not authorized for officers until March 1915, when it was still the navy's sole decoration both for gallant and distinguished service. Not until 1919 did the navy create other awards for lesser acts of gallantry as part of a "pyramid of honor." By their very number the fifty-five Veracruz Medals of Honor became controversial. Frank Jack Fletcher was always reticent about his award and never flaunted the coveted decoration, although other recipients certainly found it valuable for their advancement. The award also engendered envy.[9]

Another source of envy was Fletcher's status as one of the fabled "Washington Repeaters," whose frequent forays within the corridors of power raised the ire of the less politically connected. According to Adm. James Otto "J. O." Richardson, commander in chief of the U.S. Fleet (Cincus) in 1940–41, duty in the Office of Naval Operations and the Bureaus of Navigation (Bunav) and Ordnance (Buord) offered "a sure way to Flag rank." Fletcher served two tours in Washington in the 1920s. In 1933–36, when President Franklin D. Roosevelt pushed through a strong expansion of the navy, Fletcher was aide to Secretary of the Navy Claude A. Swanson. In 1938 Roosevelt named Richardson chief of the Bureau of Navigation, but scolded: "Now remember, no repeaters in Washington." Richardson responded he must have a few "repeaters" in key positions to run the bureau effectively. Primarily he meant Fletcher, who relieved Capt. Chester Nimitz, another Richardson protégé, as assistant chief.[10]

In November 1939 Fletcher became the eighth member of the class of 1906 "frocked" as rear admiral. He received Cruiser Division (Crudiv) Three, part of Cruisers, Battle Force, U.S. Fleet, based on the West Coast. Crudiv Three comprised four old *Omaha*-class light cruisers, commissioned in the early 1920s. Over the winter he participated in training exercises, drills, and inspections, followed in April 1940 by Fleet Problem XXI in Hawaiian waters under Richardson, the new Cincus. In simulated night combat Fletcher lost his two old crocks to two new *Brooklyn*-class light cruisers. During the second phase he surprised and neutralized the opposing air base on Johnston island, a small atoll seven hundred miles southwest of Oahu. "The unusual thing about this minor operation," Fletcher mused in his report, "was that it worked out almost exactly as planned." A few nights later the opposing fleets blundered into an unplanned major night engagement. Fletcher helped repulse a couple of heavy cruisers attempting to break through the screen to get at the transports. The melee offered a sobering warning of the poor quality of night attack training in the U.S. Fleet, a lesson that went unheeded. The top leaders thought the fleet would enjoy the benefits of radar before ever fighting at night for real, but the Battle of Savo would prove that radar alone was not the answer.[11]

In June 1940 Fletcher stepped up to Crudiv Six, one of three heavy cruiser divisions in the Scouting Force, U.S. Fleet. His new ships were the *New Orleans*, *Astoria*, *Minneapolis*, and *San Francisco*, powerful ten-thousand-ton ships commissioned in 1934. They had a main armament of nine 8-inch guns and eight 5-inch/25 antiaircraft guns. Although designed according to naval treaty restrictions, the *New Orleans* class enjoyed somewhat increased protection, but less fuel and hence considerably less range. Fletcher prepared his four heavy cruisers to fight by supervising their operational readiness and material well-being. Joint exercises and minor fleet problems allowed practice steaming in different formations, night fighting (although Crudiv Six lacked radar), air defense, and other specialized tactics, as well as gunnery and, to a limited extent, underway refueling. Fletcher led task groups and honed his command skills.

Near the end of November 1941 Fletcher learned he would soon relieve Rear Adm. John Henry Newton as Commander, Cruisers, Scouting Force, for administrative charge of all twelve heavy cruisers and direct control of Crudiv Four (*Chicago*, *Louisville*, *Portland*, and *Indianapolis*). The change was to occur about 17 December, when Fletcher's own relief, newly promoted Rear Adm. Thomas Kinkaid, reached Pearl Harbor. Fletcher was delighted with the assignment of Kinkaid, an old friend. His other admiral would be Raymond Spruance, leader of Crudiv Five. In the meantime Fletcher anticipated one more cruise as Commander, Cruiser Division (Comcrudiv) Six on another minor fleet exercise.[12]

On 27 November, however, Kimmel received a sobering dispatch from Adm. Harold R. Stark, the Chief of Naval Operations (CNO). "This is to be considered a war warning," for "an aggressive move by Japan is expected within the next few days." Washington, no less than Kimmel himself, assessed the immediate threat squarely in the Far East. Japanese preparations to strike Malaya, Hong Kong, and the Philippines were obvious. To Kimmel and the few senior officers and staff with whom he shared the message (Fletcher not among them), the initial task was to enhance readiness. Should war break out, the fleet would swiftly sortie and execute diversionary strikes against Japanese bases in the Marshall Islands. Aware that Wake was a likely flashpoint, Kimmel directed Vice Adm. William Halsey to have the carrier *Enterprise* transport a dozen marine Grumman F4F-3 Wildcats to Wake. The two admirals discussed the war warning and the real possibility of encountering hostile forces while on the way there. Halsey resolved to blast anything he found in his way. Any Japanese warships found cutting between Wake and Oahu could be up to no good. Once near Wake he could encounter long-range planes searching northeast out of the Japanese Mandated Islands of Micronesia (commonly known as the Mandates). Halsey's Task Force 8 (TF-8) sailed on 28 November with the *Enterprise*, three heavy cruisers, and nine destroyers. He was to fly the fighters to Wake on 4 December (east longitude date) and return to Pearl on the morning of the seventh. To deliver marine scout bombers to Midway, another vital island outpost 1,130 miles northwest of Pearl, Kimmel formed Task Force 12 (TF-12) under Admiral Newton, with the *Lexington*, three heavy cruisers, and five destroyers, including Fletcher in the *Astoria*, the sole available component of Crudiv Six.[13]

USS *Astoria* (CA-34), 11 July 1941. The cruiser was Admiral Fletcher's flagship in December 1941.
Courtesy of National Archives (19-N-25346), via Jeffrey G. Barlow

A belief that war was imminent persuaded Kimmel to position his two available carriers in support of his outlying bases. Recent sightings in the Far East detailed Japanese forces heading south through the South China Sea toward British Malaya, a provocation that could not be ignored. Early on 5 December, as TF-12 sailed from Pearl, a Japanese intelligence agent on shore reported via the Hawaiian consulate radio that a carrier and five cruisers departed Pearl. The Pacific War was two days off. While continuing special antisubmarine patrols off Oahu, Kimmel allowed many sailors one last liberty night before they got back to work on Sunday, 7 December. By that dawn Halsey, his Wake mission successful, closed within 250 miles of Pearl. Rough seas, though, hindered fueling of his destroyers from the heavy ships and forced him to slow down and delay his arrival until afternoon. At the same time Newton's TF-12 drew within 450 miles of Midway and made ready to launch the marine scout bombers. For his own part Fletcher anticipated a quiet Sunday in flag plot planning for the upcoming exercise. However at 0815, a plain language dispatch from Cincpac shattered the routine. "Air raid on Pearl Harbor. This is not a drill." Tragically for America as well as the Pacific Fleet, Japanese carriers just knocked Kimmel's war plan into a cocked hat, altered naval warfare forever, and gave Fletcher his opportunity to lead carriers.[14]

By December 1941 Frank Jack Fletcher had served thirty-nine of his fifty-six years in the U.S. Navy, including more than twenty-two years at sea. Of medium height, he had a slender, fit build, with straight black hair, a broad, high forehead, "smiling brown eyes," and a weathered, ruddy complexion. "Trigger-quick on repartee," Fletcher maintained a "sunny disposition and a hearty laugh." A proud, confident man who enjoyed company, he was also unassuming and down to earth, without a trace of ego or theatrics. A characteristic anecdote perfectly illuminates his personality. In March 1939 Richardson's acting flag secretary in Bunav, Lt. Cdr. George C. Dyer, tried to keep the endless correspondence flowing smoothly, but he became exasperated when Fletcher did not take immediate action on memoranda that lay on his desk. Dyer boldly braced the assistant chief: "Your problem is you don't work hard enough." Far from taking umbrage, Fletcher was highly amused. He introduced Dyer to a group of fellow senior officers as "the young fellow who tells me I don't work hard enough." As Dyer recalled, Fletcher never let up teasing him about it, and they became "fast friends." Dyer added: "I, of course, got to know him very well, and to like him very much." He thought Fletcher showed "wonderful judgment, but he had a tendency not to do things" (a trait shared with the brilliant Spruance). Never keen on paperwork (exasperating future historians as well as Dyer), Fletcher was too much of an old hand to get immersed in details and lose sight of the big picture. Nor did he unduly interfere with subordinates.[15]

Determining Fletcher's true ability as a commander as revealed in the critical carrier actions of 1941–42 is the central purpose of this book. He never owned the reputation of a naval intellectual or profound theorist. His friend Vice Adm. William Ward "Poco" Smith, who fought under him at Coral Sea and Midway, privately conceded Fletcher was "not the smartest Task Force Commander of the war." Moreover, a former member of Admiral Nimitz's Cincpac staff anonymously described Fletcher as "a big, nice, wonderful guy who didn't know his butt from third base." Such anonymity conceals possible prejudice or bias. Superior intelligence alone is not the sole or often the most important gauge of a successful commander. A practical nature, strong nerves, flexibility, and an open mind are even more essential. Smith understood this, calling Fletcher "a man's man," who "made quick decisions, usually the right ones." Considering the stress under which Fletcher had to function in fighting the desperate 1942 carrier battles, that was high praise. Readers must judge for themselves, based on the evidence, much of which has never before been presented, whether Fletcher indeed measured up to the job.[16]

FLETCHER AND NAVAL AVIATION

In 1914 during the fighting at Veracruz, Lt. Frank Jack Fletcher witnessed the very first American aerial combat missions. It was the first of several occasions in which he was present during key events in the history of naval aviation. The U.S. Navy's love affair with the airplane bloomed in November 1910, when Eugene Ely, a civilian pilot, lifted his primitive biplane off a wooden deck laid on the bow of the cruiser *Birmingham*, the first time an airplane took off from a ship. Ely made the first shipboard landing two months later on a similarly rickety platform installed on the armored cruiser *Pennsylvania*. Shortly thereafter the first U.S. naval officers began flight training, among them Fletcher's classmate Lt. John Towers, who qualified as naval aviator number three. The pioneer naval aviators were a proud bunch, eager to show the rest of the navy the potential of the airplane, but well aware it was a hard sell to skeptical battleship officers. By spring 1914 an aviation detachment equipped with small flying boats trained at Pensacola, the cradle of U.S. naval aviation. Some came south to support the Veracruz landing. Beginning 25 April Lt. Patrick Bellinger reconnoitered Mexican positions, and for his trouble suffered bullet holes in his aircraft.[17]

In 1919 while he had the destroyer *Gridley*, Commander Fletcher took a minor role in another pivotal event of naval aviation, the transatlantic flight of NC flying boats led by Towers. Operating off the Azores, the *Gridley* served as one of the many destroyers stationed all along the route to guide the planes. On 17 May her signals helped direct the NC-4, the only aircraft to reach the Azores. Subsequently while searching for Bellinger's downed NC-1, Fletcher found its crew safe on board a Greek freighter that tried to tow the awkward aircraft. Rough seas prevented transfer of the aviators to the *Gridley*, so Fletcher stayed with the derelict seaplane until relieved. Soon afterward the *Gridley* acted as one of the guard ships for the final leg of the flight of the NC-4 to England.[18]

In early 1928 while executive officer of the *Colorado*, Fletcher endeavored to take his career in a whole new direction by enrolling for flight training. By the mid 1920s naval aviation still suffered the opprobrium of the new gimmick lacking true importance in the navy's overall mission. A "gun club" denizen condescendingly warned one aviator-hopeful to "keep out of the side shows and get back into the main tent." However in September 1925, in the aftermath of the airship *Shenandoah* disaster, President Calvin Coolidge formed a special aviation board chaired by Dwight W. Morrow to examine aviation policy. Retired Rear Adm. Frank Friday Fletcher was the navy's sole representative. The Morrow Board conducted extensive hearings and among other things recommended against an independent air force such as the one in Britain. Its findings led to legislation that strengthened naval aviation. In 1926 Congress not only authorized expansion to one thousand planes in five years, but also restricted command of the growing number of aircraft carriers, seaplane tenders, and naval air stations solely to naval aviators (pilots) or naval aviation observers. Those were the billets long desired by the pioneers like Towers who learned to fly as young officers.[19]

With most aviators still very junior, there was no ready supply of qualified flag officers, captains, and commanders. Aware of the problem, Rear Adm. William A. Moffett, the chief of the Bureau of Aeronautics (Buaer), himself qualified as an observer in 1922 and started recruiting a limited number of line captains and commanders to take flight training. Many pioneer aviators detested these newcomers as opportunists, dubbing them "Johnny come lately" (usefully abbreviated JCL). In 1939 one proud original naval aviator explained, "[Moffett's] idea [was] to induct more rank into the game so that it would 'draw more water' in the service. This caused a bad situation in two ways, it blocked off the possibilities of advancement in billets . . . for the more junior officers who had been here for a moderate or a long time, and secondly it put officers in responsible billets for which they were not qualified by experience." He did not speak for all the younger aviators. H. S. Duckworth (USNA 1922, wings 1924) served as flight instructor for some of the older aviator trainees, and thus knew them well. He "*never* resented their rank or their wings" and "never knew one who tried to tell us how to fly/run our squadrons." Duckworth was "always glad to have their experience running the carriers & the big organizations" and judged the JCLs "willing for our opinions to be heard when we felt our flying experience outweighed their rank & age." The training program lasted until 1937, with some thirty-eight senior officers qualifying as naval aviators or observers. JCLs like Joseph M. Reeves, Ernest King, William Halsey, Aubrey Fitch, John McCain, and Frederick C. Sherman served as powerful advocates for naval aviation and held the fort until the pioneers could lead in their own right.[20]

There is no indication in the surviving sources why Fletcher requested naval aviation. Certainly he consulted his Uncle Frank, who always looked out for his welfare and was well able to offer counsel in that regard. More rapid advancement might have seemed possible in naval aviation than via the crowded battleship route. Fletcher would have been well placed, having already been executive officer of a capital ship. One should not discount the possibility he was genuinely interested in airplanes. It was a glamorous time because of the transoceanic flights. Naval aviation itself had come a long way since the first U.S. carrier, the converted collier *Langley* (CV-1), was commissioned in 1922. Fletcher frequently saw the "covered wagon" exercising with the Battle Fleet. Two far more impressive carriers, reconstructed battle cruiser hulls, were in the offing. At nine hundred feet, the *Lexington* (CV-2) and *Saratoga* (CV-3) were the longest warships in the world. They displaced thirty-three thousand tons with a top speed of thirty-three knots and carried eighty or more planes.[21]

Fletcher's eyesight proved inadequate for pilot training. Again the available sources are silent as to how he responded to his rejection. Clark G. Reynolds charged in his superb biography of Towers that in the late 1930s Fletcher "persistently denigrated naval aviation during cocktail chatter," to which Towers supposedly commented: "[Fletcher] doesn't know what he's talking about. It's no use discussing it." Highly conscious of his role as the pioneer-aviator crown prince, the supersensitive Towers warred not only against non-aviators like Fletcher, but also the despised JCLs. What he considered "denigrating" to naval aviation might simply have been a difference of opinion. Besides, Fletcher was a rival who always seemed one step ahead. The crucial point is that in December 1941, Fletcher found himself thrust into the role of wartime carrier commander without even a veneer of aviation training. The old aviators like Towers never forgave the luck of the draw that gave him the unique opportunity to be the first to take carriers into a naval battle.[22]

THE U.S. CARRIERS AT THE START OF THE WAR

Although not as formidable in numbers and certainly not in combat experience as its Japanese counterpart, the U.S. carrier force also evolved considerably since the late 1920s. Venerable *Langley* was relegated to seaplane tender, but huge *Lexington* and *Saratoga* remained the cornerstone of the carrier fleet. Commissioned in 1934, the *Ranger* (CV-4) proved an unsuccessful transitional concept. However, the 1937 *Yorktown* (CV-5), shorter and smaller than the *Lexington,* was equally fast and capacious, as well as of much more modern design. Her sisters were the 1938 *Enterprise* (CV-6) and the slightly larger *Hornet* (CV-8), commissioned in October 1941. In between, the 1940 *Wasp* (CV-7) was smaller because of naval treaty constraints, and less well protected than the *Yorktown.* As of 7 December 1941 the *Lexington, Saratoga,* and *Enterprise* served in the Pacific Fleet, the rest in the Atlantic. Eleven superb *Essex*-class carriers—twenty-five thousand tons displacement, all of the latest gadgets—were under construction, but the first would not be ready to fight until the middle of 1943.

Instead of the heavy shells and ship-launched torpedoes of surface warships, the bombs and torpedoes of the carrier's aircraft constituted her main battery. Executing highly accurate dive bombing (pioneered by the U.S. Navy and Marine Corps), the two-seat Douglas SBD-2 and SBD-3 Scout Bombers (nicknamed "Dauntless") could tote a powerful 1,000-pound bomb. Robust and long-ranged, if not particularly fast, the SBDs also flew searches and antisubmarine patrol, and served as "smokers" laying smoke screens to shield friendly forces during fleet engagements. Their only real flaw was the lack of folding wings that cost valuable storage space. The three-seat Douglas TBD-1 Torpedo Bomber ("Devastator") lugged either one 2,000-pound Mark XIII aerial torpedo (an abysmal weapon prone to malfunction) or three 500-pound bombs for horizontal bombing. In service since 1937, the TBD was slow, short-ranged, and vulnerable. Its replacement, the excellent Grumman TBF-1 Avenger, existed only as a prototype. The carrier fighting squadrons flew the rugged Grumman F4F-3 and F4F-3A Wildcat fighters (that lacked folding wings), or in the *Lexington,* fragile Brewster F2A-3 Buffaloes. Both fighters featured four powerful .50-caliber machine guns. The excellent gunnery training and superior tactics of their pilots constituted their principal advantage in combat. These carrier planes were all single-engine designs with stubby airframes strengthened for shipboard landings. They were deemed inferior to their sleek land-based counterparts that could fly higher, faster, and farther and carry much larger payloads. Wartime experience quickly showed that carrier-type aircraft were much better suited than typical land planes to destroy warships and provide close air support for amphibious operations. After Taranto, and especially the Pearl Harbor attack, no one doubted carriers could execute raids of strategic importance.

In December 1941 U.S. carrier air groups comprised four aircraft squadrons: bombing (VB), scouting (VS), fighting (VF), and torpedo (VT). The VB and VS squadrons functioned identically. Most VT squadrons numbered twelve torpedo planes, and the VB and VS squadrons eighteen or twenty-one dive bombers. The chronic shortage of aircraft limited VF squadrons to eighteen fighters instead of twenty-seven. Adding the dive bomber flown by the carrier air group commander (CAG) raised the group's total to seventy-three planes.

As of 7 December the authorized aircraft strength of the *Lexington* and *Saratoga* each comprised eighteen fighters, forty-three dive bombers, and twelve torpedo bombers; the *Enterprise* eighteen fighters, thirty-seven dive bombers, and eighteen torpedo bombers. The *Yorktown* and *Hornet* in the Atlantic Fleet were organized in similar fashion to the *Lexington*. In contrast, the *Ranger* and *Wasp* groups each contained two VF squadrons and two VS squadrons, although they operated only one VF squadron at a time. VT squadrons were in the process of being formed for them.

The carrier air group accomplished three basic missions: reconnaissance, attack, and defense. The SBDs flew searches, usually 150 to two hundred miles (in rare exceptions three hundred miles), routinely taking place mornings and afternoons. The accepted maximum strike radius for the SBD was 225 miles with a 500-pound bomb and 175 miles with full 1,000-pound load; the TBD 150 miles with torpedo or 175 miles with bombs. Escort fighters, which lacked auxiliary fuel tanks, ventured no farther than the TBDs. Strikes usually comprised every available SBD and TBD, with at least half the fighters retained for a defensive combat air patrol to protect the task force. Some carriers occasionally supplemented the combat air patrol with SBDs on low-level "anti-torpedo-plane patrol" near the ships. Combat air patrols rotated every two or three hours, so that all the assigned fighters should be fueled and ready in the event of attack. From 1941 onward the great ace in the hole on defense was air search radar that could detect enemy search planes and incoming strike groups far beyond visual sighting distance. That theoretically maximized the capability of the air defense, but effective fighter direction was a complex goal where reality did not always match theory.[23]

Of all the many components of the U.S. naval service, carrier aviation was arguably the best trained and the most prepared to fight. It ranked ahead of the gunnery and torpedo warfare of the surface ships and even the elite submarine force. The carriers superbly accomplished their prime mission of sustaining aircraft afloat, the skills of the individual aviators proved outstanding, and their squadrons functioned well. That superior performance was the major reason behind U.S. carrier aviation's remarkable success in the first year of the war against a superb foe. However, serious flaws existed above the squadron level, due to the lack of coordinating doctrine within air groups and between individual carriers. The latter defect concerned top carrier command that remained in the hands of "Johnny come lately" naval aviators and, increasingly, non-aviator surface admirals. The pioneer naval aviators always considered anyone but themselves grossly unqualified to command carrier task forces, but none had yet achieved that goal. By December 1941 only two pioneers (Towers and Bellinger) made flag rank, but both were mired in the vast aviation shore organization they labored so long to create. Fletcher, the unlikely trailblazer in carrier battle, earned their undying animosity. The pioneers, though, were also part of the problem in that the aerial weapon they forged was not always up to the task.

The administrative boss of the three Pacific Fleet carriers was Vice Adm. William F. Halsey Jr., Commander, Aircraft, Battle Force (Comairbatfor). He was the carrier type commander, and hence the navy's senior carrier admiral. Craggy, outspoken, and thoroughly loyal to his classmate and good friend Kimmel, Halsey was a JCL who earned his wings in 1935 as a fifty-two-year-old captain. He epitomized the navy's aggressive spirit. His two carrier divisions were purely administrative commands. Halsey exercised direct control of Carrier Division Two (Cardiv Two, his flagship *Enterprise* and absent *Yorktown*), while Rear Adm. Aubrey Fitch led Cardiv One (*Saratoga* and *Lexington*). Based ashore at San Diego, Fitch functioned as Halsey's stateside administrative representative, not as an operational commander.[24]

Prior to June 1941 the Pacific Fleet mainly conducted training through the Battle Force and Scouting Force that comprised the ship and aircraft type commands. Fleet problems and other tactical exercises utilized ad hoc task forces of different kinds of ships divided into task groups and task units according to a numeric nomenclature. Kimmel organized the striking power of the Pacific Fleet into three permanent task forces. Vice Adm. William S. Pye (Commander, Battle Force) led Task Force 1 (TF-1) with six battleships, the *Saratoga*, eight light cruisers, and eighteen destroyers. Admiral Halsey's TF-2 comprised three battleships, the *Enterprise*, four heavy cruisers, one light cruiser, and eighteen destroyers. TF-3 under Vice Adm. Wilson Brown (Commander, Scouting Force) controlled the *Lexington*, the other eight heavy cruisers (including Fletcher's Crudiv Six), and nine destroyers, in addition to patrol planes, submarines, minecraft, transports, high-speed transports (converted old destroyers or APDs), and the Second Marine Division. However, separate task forces soon appeared for the subs (TF-7), mining force (TF-8), and patrol planes (TF-9). Even so, these task forces were still too cumbersome for actual combat operations.[25]

The assignment of Fletcher to lead the relief of Wake Island became controversial only much later. At the time it certainly raised no eyebrows. Historian Rear Adm. Samuel Eliot Morison opined that Kimmel "may have doomed his own project by a perfunctory handling of the command assignment." He should have ignored seniority to reach down to Aubrey Wray "Jake" Fitch, a carrier-wise naval aviator who was Fletcher's classmate but junior to him. A JCL who qualified as a pilot in 1930 at age forty-seven, Fitch commanded two carriers, two naval air stations, and a patrol wing before taking over Cardiv One in 1940. He excelled in all. Personable and levelheaded, the short, white-haired Fitch combined sharp ability with strong professionalism. Following refit at Bremerton in Washington State, the *Saratoga* reached San Diego at noon on 7 December to reclaim her air group, take on more planes as cargo, then sail the next day for Pearl as scheduled. Now with the war, Fitch took it upon himself to shift his flag on board and shanghaied three old flush deck destroyers from the sound school to accompany her as antisubmarine escort. With the *Sara* crammed with more than one hundred planes, including Marine Fighting Squadron 221 (VMF-221), Fitch sailed on 8 December and expected to reach Pearl in four days. Sea conditions dictated otherwise. On 10 December Kimmel designated Fitch the commander of Task Force 16 and ordered him to enter Pearl on the afternoon of the thirteenth. Fitch labored through rough seas, forcing Kimmel to postpone his arrival to the next afternoon. The presence of the *Sara* was essential as the centerpiece of Fletcher's Wake relief expedition.[26]

Morison's preference for Fitch was based strictly on hindsight. Kimmel did not care if a naval aviator led the Wake relief force. That was not the prime qualification he or his successors sought in the commander of a task force that included carriers. Admiral Brown, a non-aviator, took over the *Lexington* task force on 8 December from non-aviator Newton.

Non-aviators would routinely lead Pacific Fleet carriers in battle until the last was forced out in November 1942. Fletcher's cruisers comprised the covering force for the Wake relief. Because he had shown himself ready for higher command, the mission was his. However unfairly, Kimmel considered Fitch merely a shore-based administrator. In the past year Fitch had come out to Pearl for only two weeks during one of the *Sara*'s routine shuttle trips. He never joined in any of the battle exercises. In one key prewar map exercise Kimmel gave command of the *Saratoga* task group to a non-aviator, Rear Adm. H. Fairfax Leary, Commander, Cruisers, Battle Force (Comcrubatfor), who led the cruisers allocated to that task group. Kinkaid recalled that Kimmel postponed the Newton-Fletcher-Kinkaid round of musical chairs precisely to give Fletcher the Wake task force. Indeed, Kimmel thought enough of Fletcher to put his name third on the short list of "strong vigorous" men from whom he recommended Stark choose his successor if necessary. Kinkaid would accompany his friend Fletcher in the flagship *Astoria* for a "makie-learn" cruise to Wake before succeeding him as Comcrudiv Six.[27]

CHAPTER 2

"To Retrieve Our Initial Disaster"

GALLANT WAKE

On 9 December Admiral Stark essentially restricted the Pacific Fleet to defense east of the 180th meridian and even questioned its ability to hold Midway, let alone Wake. Capt. Charles H. "Soc" McMorris, head of the Pacific Fleet War Plans Section, acknowledged in a 10 December situation estimate that losing the battleships forced the fleet onto the strategic defensive. He anticipated more enemy raids east of the 180th meridian, with attempts to capture Wake, Midway, and Samoa. Oahu must be held at all costs. Although Admiral Halsey desired all three carriers ferry aircraft from the West Coast to replenish Oahu, McMorris declared that too passive a role. Instead the carriers, soon to be joined by the *Yorktown* from the Atlantic, would remain in the streamlined task forces, each with three heavy cruisers and a destroyer squadron. They should operate "boldly and vigorously on the tactical offensive in order to retrieve our initial disaster" and regain the initiative "at the earliest possible date." McMorris completely missed the vital concept of massing carrier air power, if not on the scale that integrated six carriers into one mighty striking force, at least in pairs. He was far from alone. Long after Pearl Harbor nearly all senior U.S. naval aviators, JCLs and pioneers alike, thought of carriers in terms of single units and much preferred to keep them apart instead of risking all their eggs in one basket. In the spring of 1942 the Pacific Fleet fought its way back on top, the crucial difference being that another Cincpac concentrated his carriers at Coral Sea and Midway. McMorris, however, did not care to wait until 1942, but wished to "regain the initiative" immediately by holding onto Wake. That grew almost into an obsession.[1]

Wake Island was the one bright spot in the doom that threatened to engulf the entire western Pacific. Wake, Midway, Johnston, and Palmyra—four tiny central Pacific atolls located west and southwest of Hawaii—had played an essential role in prewar planning as bases for the far-ranging Consolidated PBY flying boats to detect enemy fleet movements. Midway and Wake proved of particular interest. Wake lay only five hundred to eight hundred miles north of a string of atolls in the Marshalls believed to harbor air bases. Kimmel considered Wake an immediate enemy objective that he must defend not just to deny it to the Japanese, but to profit from its obvious desirability in their eyes. If Wake were strongly held, Japan not only must commit considerable naval strength to take it, but also advance those forces to "where we might be able to get at them." Kimmel intended to contrive, "by every possible means, to get the Japanese to expose naval units." Yet that depended "objectives that require such exposure." A strong Wake would put real teeth into the Marshalls diversions.[2]

In the late summer of 1941 Wake and Midway gained new strategic importance. In a stunning reversal of previous Pacific strategy, the War Department sought to transform the vast Philippine archipelago into a "self-sustaining fortress capable of blockading the South China Sea by air power." Gen. George C. Marshall, Army Chief of Staff, and Maj. Gen. Henry H. "Hap" Arnold, Deputy Chief of Staff for Air, staked everything on long-range heavy bombers and daylight precision bombing, the true capabilities of which they terrifically exaggerated. The quickest means to deploy the bombers to the Philippines was to fly them through Oahu, Midway, Wake, Port Moresby in New Guinea, Darwin in northwest Australia, and finally northward to Luzon. By that circuitous route they hoped to ferry upward of seventy Boeing B-17 Flying Fortresses and Consolidated B-24 Liberators to the Philippines before the end of 1941, and many more soon after. Only in early 1942 would airfields in the South Pacific be ready for bombers to stage from Oahu to the Philippines without passing over or near Japanese-held territory.[3]

"Because of the great importance of continuing to reinforce Philippines with long range Army bombers," Stark ordered Kimmel on 17 October "to take all practical precautions for the safety of airfields at Wake and Midway." Such representations from Washington were music to Kimmel's ears, because they accorded with his plans for strengthening both bases to support fleet operations. He expedited preparations to base a dozen flying boats and a dozen land planes (fighters or scout bombers) at distant Wake, as well as increasing its antiaircraft protection. Midway would also receive the ability to support a second squadron of flying boats and eighteen land planes. On 4 December, as previously related, Halsey's *Enterprise* delivered twelve marine F4F Wildcats to Wake. "We felt," Kimmel later testified, "that if we could keep Wake reasonably defended—and I think it was reasonably defended—it would serve as bait to catch detachments of the Japanese, the Japanese fleet coming down there, and we hoped to be able to meet them out there in sufficient force to handle them."[4]

Because Wake as yet lacked radar, Cdr. Winfield Scott Cunningham, the island commander, lost two-thirds of his fighters on the first day of the war. Thirty-six medium bombers winging north from the Marshalls caught them on the ground. Early on 11 December (tenth, Hawaiian time), Vice Adm. Inoue Shigeyoshi's South Seas Force (Mandates Fourth Fleet) unleashed against Wake what historian Edward Miller aptly called a "scruffy" group of a few old light cruisers, destroyers, auxiliaries, and a small landing force under Rear Adm. Kajioka Sadamichi. Marine coastal guns and the few remaining Wildcats sank two destroyers, prevented the invasion, and sent Kajioka packing. Inoue demanded strong reinforcements before trying Wake again. His only option until then was to continue long distance bombing raids. Wake's heroism won the admiration of the nation. The rout of the attackers refurbished hope that Wake, if reinforced, could still serve as bait to trap and defeat part of the Japanese fleet. It cannot be stressed too strongly that in the days after Pearl Harbor, Kimmel and McMorris remained confident of Wake's ability to hold out in the short run. McMorris recognized that eventually "a stronger [attack] may be considered a certainty," but even an incompletely prepared Wake was a tough nut to crack. Besides, the enemy would not return soon with an amphibious force strong enough to

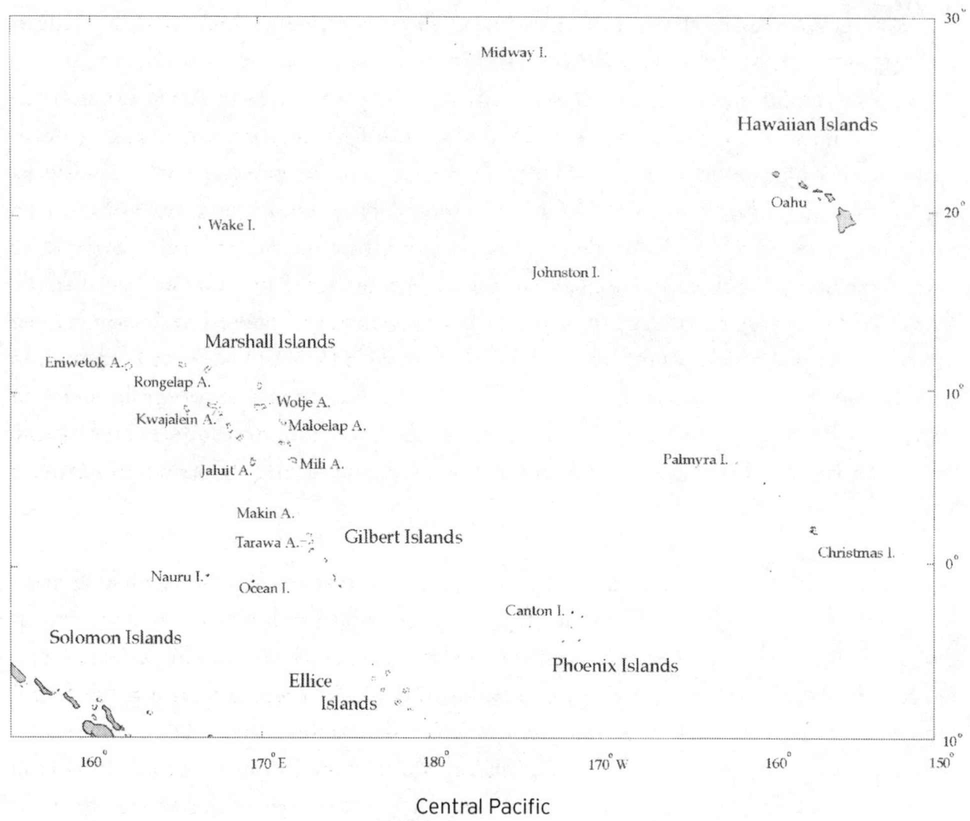

Central Pacific

overwhelm it. Instead, Wake would face air raids "from shore bases," with "possible minor landing attempts," like the one just repulsed.[5]

The first priority was to give Wake the means to prolong its effective defense. If reinforced, Cunningham should be able to hold out an additional one to three months, long enough for something more permanent to be contrived. On 7 December Rear Adm. Claude C. Bloch, the Fourteenth Naval District commandant, recalled an unescorted transport, the *William Ward Burrows*, plodding toward Wake at 8.5 knots while towing a barge. It was particularly unfortunate the *William Ward Burrows* had not left Pearl prior to 29 November, for she carried, along with supplies and munitions, the SCR-270 air search radar and three SCR-268 fire control radars that Wake desperately needed. Cdr. Ross A. Dierdorff only learned of the recall order on the morning of 9 December (Z–12 time; that is, Greenwich Central Time [GCT] minus twelve hours), after a routine retransmission. When he turned back he was only 425 miles east of Wake. On the evening of the tenth, hearing of Wake's troubles, Dierdorff offered to cast loose the barge, reverse course, and reach Wake during the night of 12–13 December. He thought he could evacuate about three hundred men and still get away by the next dawn. "If proposal will help the situation," he radioed Bloch, "am willing to make the attempt." Bloch testily told Dierdorff to follow orders to withdraw and to maintain radio silence. Dierdorff might have got to Wake a day and a half after the abortive invasion had Cincpac wanted to take the risk. Kimmel, however, had in mind sending much more than just the *William Ward Burrows* to Wake.[6]

As a precaution in case the Japanese tried to reprise their Sunday punch, Kimmel endeavored to keep his own flattops away at sea. The *Enterprise* in Halsey's TF-8 entered Pearl after dark on 8 December and only partially refueled before sailing prior to dawn with an air group weakened from losses on the seventh. Kimmel then shifted Halsey north of Oahu as a covering force and promptly ignored him. At the same time TF-12 with the *Lexington* patrolled west of Pearl under Admiral Brown, who joined Newton and Fletcher on 8 December. Kimmel desired Brown to keep close to Oahu, but not in Pearl. Therefore he dispatched the *Neosho*, his only available fast oiler, and nine destroyers to refuel TF-12 on the morning of 11 December about two hundred miles southwest of Oahu. The *Lexington* freed up her deck by releasing the marine scout bombers back to Oahu. (They later flew on their own to Midway.) Cincpac directed Brown, once he completed fueling on the eleventh, to detach the *Astoria* (with Fletcher) and the five original TF-12 destroyers to bring the *Neosho* safely back to Pearl. Kimmel wanted Brown's force ready for a special mission, but to have Fletcher available for another task.[7]

On 10 December McMorris roughed out a plan for the relief of Wake by Brown's TF-12. After loading marines and ammunition at Pearl, the new seaplane tender *Tangier*, escorted by two destroyers, could join TF-12 about 13 December. After fueling, Brown would release the oiler and depart for Wake, gathering the *William Ward Burrows* along the way. After reinforcing Wake and embarking such civilian workers "as may be found expedient without undue exposure of this force," Brown was to fall back and cover a similar bolstering of Midway. Other forces would succor Johnston and Palmyra islands. McMorris's draft operations order (Op-Ord) vaguely declared "if enemy contact is made during any of foregoing operations take offensive action against them and give such instructions to vessels being covered as your judgment dictates." That was certainly no specific blueprint for battle. At that point any plans for the Wake relief were strictly hypothetical. McMorris made no provision for delivering the additional fighters that Wake desperately needed, unless the *Lexington* left most of her own fighters. Equally important, Brown was not to take the oiler along. Halsey's TF-8 went near Wake without an oiler, but only briefly to deliver planes and certainly not to linger or fight.[8]

On the morning of 11 December Brown met the *Neosho* and started fueling. Nothing, however, went as expected. Although the sea was not especially rough, a heavy swell and moderate northeasterly wind prevented proper connection. "Had counted on fueling carrier and destroyers today," Brown explained, but "due to high seas which kept the deck of *Neosho* awash, found it to be impossible." Kimmel instructed him to proceed northwest in the direction of Midway while waiting for the weather to moderate. "Since then," Cdr. Laurence A. Abercrombie, one of the destroyer leaders, later explained, "we have fueled a good many times in weather a lot worse than that, but we couldn't make it jell that day." Underway refueling would prove an unforeseen, but fortunately brief, weakness for the Pacific Fleet. Japan's dramatically demonstrated ability in that regard amazed the U.S. admirals, who wondered how the carrier force managed to fuel while traversing the vast and tempestuous North Pacific. Early on the twelfth Cincpac ordered Brown to attempt recovery of a downed PBY flying boat southwest of Oahu. Fletcher left on this errand with the *Astoria* and destroyer *Drayton*. Brown tried once more to draw oil from the *Neosho*, but similar conditions produced similar results. That afternoon a false alarm of sub torpedoes caused the *Chicago* to break all fuel connections while maneuvering clear of the oiler. She was the only ship to get any oil. Running out of spare fuel hoses, Brown had to radio Pearl, "Damaged gear prevents further fueling today." That failure forced an exasperated Kimmel to recall TF-12 to enter Pearl on the afternoon of 13 December.[9]

Cincpac in fact had much else on his plate other than Wake. On 11 December Secretary of the Navy Frank Knox arrived at Pearl as the president's personal emissary to investigate the surprise attack and, frankly, to size up Kimmel. Nothing he saw reassured him. Understandably Kimmel and his fellow officers appeared quite shaken by events. Capt. Frank E. Beatty, Knox's naval aide, described how "the shock effect of the attack" adversely affected them in proportion to their "authority and responsibility." Admiral Kinkaid, Kimmel's brother-in-law and Fletcher's prospective relief, flew into Oahu on the twelfth and graphically described the scene: "If I had been shocked by the sight of Pearl Harbor from the air I was doubly shocked by the appearance of the members of Cincpac's staff and of the senior officers of the Fleet whom I saw at Headquarters. Each of them looked as though he had not had a wink of sleep in the five days which had elapsed since the Japanese attack. All were in a defiant mood but at the moment none could produce a concrete plan as to how we would 'get those ——.'"

Defiance was one thing, but this crucial juncture demanded clear thinking. During the first meeting between Knox and Kimmel, McMorris urged the relief of Wake despite Stark's declared desire to restrict fleet defense to Midway and eastward. The next day McMorris barged uninvited into another conference to plead his case and perhaps stiffen Kimmel's resolve. His presumptuous persistence paid off. By the time Knox departed on the evening of 12 December, Kimmel finally determined to relieve Wake. He congratulated Cunningham's "splendid work" and told him to "conserve ammunition until arrival replenishments about to be forwarded."[10]

Once Knox left, the staff got down to detailed planning for the relief, but the confused interval between 10 and 12 December undermined much of their original calculations. Amazingly, no one thought to tell Cdr. Clifton A. F. Sprague, the *Tangier*'s captain, to prepare for the new mission. He needed to remove the normal load of bombs and torpedoes to make the room for marine personnel and cargo. That process only began the evening of 12 December, meaning the *Tangier* could not sail before the afternoon of the fourteenth. At noon on the thirteenth, two hundred marines from Col. Harold S. Fassett's 4th Defense Battalion started hauling their gear on board. Lacking artillery, they were little more than a gesture, "a mixed bag." Wake needed constant reinforcements to survive. The *William Ward Burrows* was no longer in the picture after Bloch diverted her on 13 December southeast to Johnston Island. In turn Brown went nowhere except back to Pearl in order to fuel. Kimmel postponed Fitch's arrival with the *Saratoga* to not risk two carriers in port at the same time. McMorris welcomed the delay to allow the fourteen Brewster F2A-3 Buffalo fighters of VMF-221 to shift from the *Sara* to the *Lexington* and eventually join VMF-211 on Wake. On the morning of 14 December the *Saratoga* would be near enough to stage the marine fighters to Ford Island to be hoisted on board the *Lex*. Thus Kimmel could expect Brown to leave for Wake on the evening of 14 December and probably have the *Tangier* there on 21 December, Wake local time—20 December in Hawaii. Whether that would be in time was another matter.[11]

THE DIVERSION

McMorris gauged the principal danger to the Wake relief to be land-based bombers and flying boats from island airfields poised south and southeast of Wake. The arcs of their estimated search radii of seven hundred miles extended north and northeast at least two hundred miles beyond Wake. They also overlapped the last five hundred miles of the direct route from Oahu. Wake's dwindling fighter strength battled almost daily raids by unescorted medium bombers. To McMorris they posed relatively little danger to a mobile carrier covering force. They must locate it at a vast distance from their base and force their way through its own fighters. However, the *Tangier* and her antisubmarine escorts, when pinned down indefinitely at Wake, would be vulnerable. McMorris remembered the atoll's renowned difficulty in handling ships. No channel existed into the inner lagoon. Ships had to stand in the open sea and transfer cargo into boats and barges. Under ideal conditions unloading might be accomplished in two days, but seven to eight days was not unusual if seas were rough. McMorris recalled that rugged weather stretched one ship's unloading to twenty-eight days. Bloch actually proposed to Cunningham that the construction crew continue dredging the ship channel in the midst of the siege, yet another indication of the unrealistic attitude of some at Pearl. Later he relented and told Wake to cease all dredging to conserve fuel.[12]

Thus McMorris worried the *Tangier*, even with carrier protection, would face "considerable danger" from shore-based air attack while unloading. The obvious solution was for those enemy bombers to be somewhere else, and the answer was a powerful diversion. On 13 December McMorris dusted off his Marshalls "Reconnaissance and Raiding Plan," which had been part of his two prewar 1941 fleet plans, WPUSF-44 and WPPac-46. The final version had called for simultaneous, widely separated carrier raids against the northern and southern Marshalls. One carrier group, approaching from the direction of Wake, was to strike the northern bases; the second, after executing a wide detour southeast through the British Gilbert Islands, would hit Jaluit atoll in the southern Marshalls. Now McMorris proposed that Brown's *Lexington* task force strike Jaluit one day before the actual relief force was to arrive off Wake, 850 miles north. That attack would draw off land-based air strength far to the southeast and open, at least briefly, the door to Wake. The Jaluit raid might also deter the forces that just seized Makin and Tarawa in the Gilberts. The *Lexington* was to make only one strike, then at once withdraw to Pearl. Kimmel adopted the plan. "Extensive unloading of men and materiel from ships at Wake in the face of any enemy operation would be impossible." Therefore in place of the *Lex*, the *Saratoga* would go to Wake. She, too, must refuel at Pearl, but could sail on the fifteenth, one day after Brown. Unfortunately the *Enterprise* could not participate. Kimmel had not bothered to recall Halsey from his make-work patrol north of Oahu in time to return to Pearl for fuel and supplies.[13]

The absence of the *Enterprise* to beef up the Wake relief did not deter McMorris. Having assumed only the weak Mandates (Fourth) Fleet, with a few light cruisers and destroyers, threatened Wake, he completely dismissed the danger of carrier opposition. The proposed relief force would be "ample to deal with such surface craft as might reasonably be expected there," making the chances for success at Wake "excellent." Kimmel obviously concurred. Had he foreseen or even desired a major battle, he would have put Admiral Pye, his senior and most trusted battle commander, in charge. Nor would he have had Brown's TF-11 merely raid Jaluit once and retire. In 1951 Vice Adm. Vincent R. Murphy, one of McMorris's war planners in December 1941, recalled that the Wake operation "was conceived as a pure relief expedition," with "never any thought that we might seek an opportunity to engage any important part of the Jap fleet. In fact, this was the last thing we were looking for." Yet that is diametrically different from the way the Wake relief came to be portrayed well after the fact.[14]

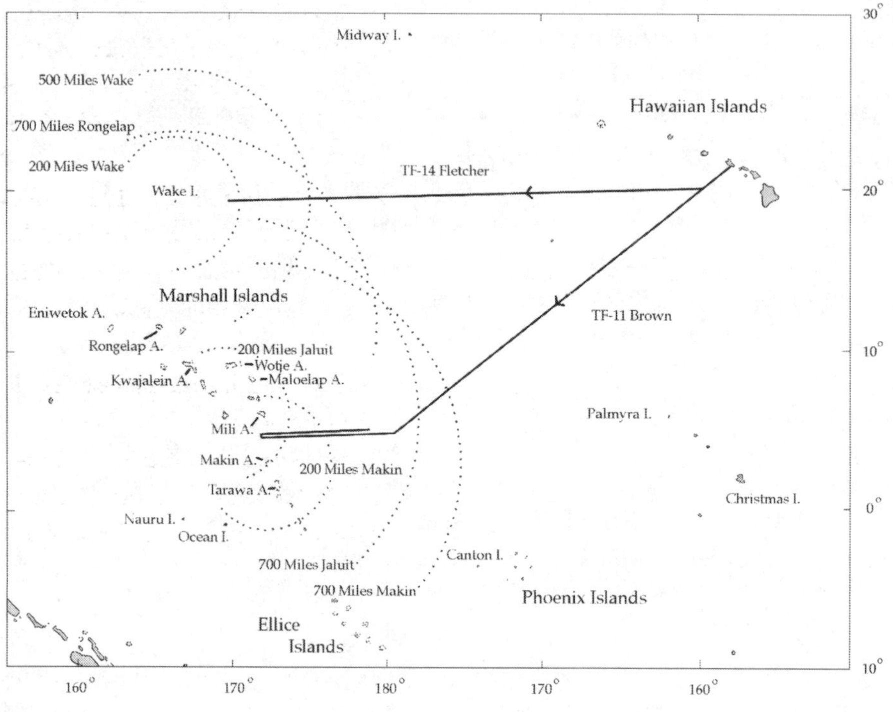

Wake Island relief plan

McMorris was correct that as of that date no Japanese carriers had been committed against Wake, but his thinking and Kimmel's betray an astonishing blindness. No less shell-shocked by the Sunday surprise than their seniors, Cdr. Joseph J. Rochefort of the Fourteenth Naval District's Combat Intelligence Unit ("Hypo") and Lt. Cdr. Edwin T. Layton, the Cincpac intelligence officer, cautiously deduced enemy strength and location from fragmentary radio intercepts, traffic analysis of a few extracted unit call signs, and captured documents. They agreed that six carriers had participated in the Hawaiian operation. Ignoring the firsthand evidence of the devastating effectiveness and mobility of the Japanese carrier force at Pearl Harbor, Kimmel and McMorris blithely assumed that all six carriers would just slink off somewhere and conveniently not bother the central Pacific until after the Pacific Fleet reinforced Wake.[15] Instead, McMorris's 13 December brainstorm threw off the whole schedule for the Wake relief and placed significant forces in terrible danger.

On the morning of 14 December Brown briefly conferred with Kimmel and learned that he would sail that afternoon with a task force renumbered TF-11. He would have the heavy cruisers *Indianapolis* (his flagship), *Chicago* (Newton's flagship), *Portland*, the *Lexington* (with sixty-eight aircraft), nine destroyers, and fleet oiler *Neosho*. The fleet was taking "the offensive." Getting reinforcements to Wake was to be "our main effort for the moment," with the ultimate goal to inflict "as much damage as possible on the Japanese naval forces supporting the [Wake] attack." Cincpac's Operation-Order 40-41 to Brown defined "D-Day," during which the relief force was to reach Wake, as the twenty-four-hour period that would begin at 0000, 22 December, Hawaiian local time (Z+10.5). According to Wake and Jaluit local time (Z−11), that translated to late evening (2130) on 22 December. In turn Brown was to attack Jaluit "as near to local daylight D minus one day as practicable," that is, at dawn on 22 December, Jaluit time, and one day before the relief force was to reach Wake. TF-11 was to execute only *one* air strike, then withdraw directly to Pearl. That single gesture, Brown was assured, would "draw the Japanese Navy to the southward, while [the Wake relief] arrived the next day."[16]

Vice Adm. Wilson Brown had the Scouting Force since February 1941, following three years as superintendent of the Naval Academy. A 1902 Annapolis graduate, he was an intelligent paragon of old school formality, as evidenced by his duty as naval aide for presidents Coolidge, Hoover, Roosevelt, and Truman. A few months shy of his fifty-ninth birthday, the wan, thin, and frail Brown looked every bit of his age and more. A slight head tremor caused young officers to dub him "Shaky," and his stamina was in doubt. The upcoming Jaluit operation was not for the faint of heart. Cincpac lacked detailed information on enemy strength in the mysterious Marshalls, but according to Brown "it was believed to be quite powerful." That was a dramatic difference from the Cincpac chart maneuver in the summer and fall of 1941 to play the opening scenario of WPPac-46. Then Halsey's *Enterprise* task group had simulated the ransacking of northern Marshalls, while Admiral Leary's *Lexington* took care of Jaluit. Now Brown with only one carrier would simply knock on the door not knowing who was home. According to an admittedly cautious Brown, Kimmel seemed "reluctant to risk further naval casualties at this time," and "appears to have consented to the proposed attack only because of the urgent need for the immediate relief of Wake." Thus to the disgust of the vehement McMorris and the *Lex*'s Capt. Frederick C. "Ted" Sherman, he readily assented to Brown's request for discretion to switch targets, or not to attack at all. Perhaps McMorris accepted the risk of widely separating the carrier task forces because it offered at least some opportunity for face-saving offensive action, instead of simply staying on defense. In fairness it must be said other senior officers also judged a foray into the Mandates to be a fine idea. Pye later described himself as its "strongest advocate," but he soon changed his mind.[17]

It is interesting to consider what might have been the impact on Stark, Kimmel, Pye, and McMorris had the *Kidō Butai* gone forward with another raid that Nagumo seriously contemplated. Two destroyers shelled Midway on the night of 7 December to prevent its search planes from harassing the carriers on their way out. As a contingency, Nagumo could also bomb Midway should the attack on Pearl Harbor be particularly successful, or if fuel ran low and he could not risk detouring around it. In either event the 5th Carrier Division (*Shōkaku* and *Zuikaku*) was to hit Midway on 9 December, local time. Furthermore, on 9 December (8 December, local time), Yamamoto ordered Nagumo to pummel Midway,

Rear Adm. Wilson Brown, circa 1945.
Courtesy of Naval Historical Center (NH-51561)

"so as to make the further use of it impossible," but also gave him discretion not to attack if he thought it was impractical. Braving high winds and heavy seas, Nagumo refused to unleash his aerial might against such an insignificant target, a useless "tiny island" according his chief of staff Rear Adm. Kusaka Ryūnosuke. The high command, Kusaka complained, "didn't know the way to treat heroes." The *Kidō Butai* had virtually won the war and must be allowed to go home and reap the reward. Citing horrible weather that hindered refueling, Nagumo managed to delay, and ultimately on 15 December (14 December in Hawaii) cancel the Midway strike. Had hundreds of carrier aircraft pounced on Midway between 11 and 15 December, Cincpac's desire to relieve Wake or venture into the Marshalls would have vanished over fears that Midway, too, was about to be invaded. Washington would almost certainly have insisted any relief expedition sustain Midway instead of the more distant Wake.[18]

Besides grossly dispersing the limited American carrier strength, the Jaluit diversion inflicted two severe handicaps on the Wake relief. Just to get to Jaluit, twenty-three hundred miles southwest of Pearl, a task force had to count on refueling at least once; the same was true for Wake two thousand miles to the west. The prewar supporting plans always provided an oiler for a carrier group transiting such a long distance. As noted, sea conditions at Wake's unprotected anchorage made it highly uncertain how long the *Tangier* had to loiter while requiring carrier air support. That was another powerful reason why a relief force must refuel prior to approaching the atoll. On 14 December Kimmel had available only three fleet oilers: the fast *Neosho* (eighteen knots) and two relics, the fourteen-knot *Neches* and the ten-knot *Ramapo*. Only the *Neosho* was properly equipped and trained for underway refueling. The schedule required for the new diversion plan compelled Brown to take the *Neosho*. It was to be as serious a detriment as failing to concentrate the carriers. The Wake relief force had to make do with the elderly *Neches*, commissioned in 1921 and possessing half the capacity and a fueling rig less capable than the modern *Cimarron*-class fleet oilers. Although rated at fourteen knots, thirteen was the best anyone thought the *Neches* could do these days. The *Tangier* herself could make 16.5 knots, and the combatants, of course, much more, but prior to refueling, the Wake relief expedition could only steam as fast as the *Neches*. The nominal difference of two knots between the *Neches* and a normal speed of advance (fifteen knots) meant forty-eight fewer miles per day out to the refueling point. Moreover just switching the *Saratoga* for the *Lexington* and the *Neches* for the *Neosho* would postpone for one day the departure of the relief force. No one at Pearl comprehended how critical these delays would prove.[19]

The morning of 14 December Fitch sent most of the *Saratoga* Air Group and VMF-221 to Pearl and made ready to enter himself. Then a sub scare in the harbor itself resulted in "conflicting orders," the upshot of which postponed Fitch's arrival until 0900 on the fifteenth. That, of course, set back by still another day the *Sara*'s departure for Wake, although the slower elements of the relief force could go on ahead. On the afternoon of the fourteenth the *Saratoga* re-embarked most of her air group to remain combat-ready and proceeded southwest of Oahu, passing Brown on his way out to sea. That evening Fitch learned the *Saratoga* was critically low on fuel, and that water improperly used as ballast had adulterated the oil remaining in some of the tanks. Only after some anxious moments did her engineers extract just enough fuel oil and diesel oil (used to power emergency generators) to reach port. Coming into Pearl the next morning the *Sara* ran out of usable fuel. As her last two working boilers lost fuel suction, she gratefully moored at Ford Island. Orders awaited Fitch to refuel and load without delay. The VMF-221 ground echelon hastily boarded the *Tangier* just before she sailed, while the *Sara* hoisted the fourteen marine fighters back on board. The last piece necessary for the Wake relief expedition finally seemed in place.[20]

FLETCHER IN COMMAND

On 15 December, the same day the *Saratoga* finally reached Pearl, Kimmel placed Fletcher in charge of Task Force 14, the Wake relief force, of one carrier (eighty-one aircraft including VMF-221), three heavy cruisers, nine destroyers, one seaplane tender, and one fleet oiler. Fletcher would run TF-14 from the *Astoria*. His flag secretary, Lt. Cdr. Samuel E. Latimer (USNA 1924), came with him in 1939 from the Bureau of Navigation. He was also intelligence officer. Tall, debonair Lt. Harry Smith (USNA 1930) was flag lieutenant, handling the admiral's signals and doubling as operations officer. The staff radio officer was Lt. Leland G. Shaffer (USNA 1931). Lt. Cdr. Myron T. Evans, commanding officer of Cruiser Scouting Squadron Six (VCS-6), also served as the staff aviation officer. The Crudiv Six enlisted flag allowance numbered twenty-two bluejackets (yeomen, signalmen, radiomen, cooks, and stewards) and six marines.[21]

It is not known when Kimmel actually brought Fletcher into the picture as prospective Commander, Task Force 14 (CTF-14). The revised Cincpac Op-Ord 39-41 for TF-14 is dated 0900, 15 December, but Fletcher did not get it, or the one previously issued to Brown (Op-Ord 40-41), until that afternoon. In the meantime someone on the Cincpac

Cruiser Division Six staff, 1941. Seated: Admiral Fletcher, Lt. Cdr. Samuel E. Latimer. Standing (*left to right*): Lt. Leland G. Shaffer, Lt. Harry Smith, Lt. Cdr. Myron T. Evans. *Courtesy of Cdr. Samuel E. Latimer Jr.*

staff finally realized that taking the sluggish *Neches* did not permit TF-14 to reach Wake as originally scheduled. Thus the revised Op-Ord 39-41 postponed D-Day for twenty-four hours, resetting its start to 0000, 23 December, Hawaiian local time (2130, 23 December, at Wake). That deferred the *Tangier*'s arrival to during daylight on 24 December (Wake time). The *Tangier* and *Neches*, the slowest ships, were to sail the evening of the fifteenth; the rest of TF-14 the next day. Four destroyers under Capt. Harvey E. Overesch, Commander, Destroyer Squadron (Comdesron) Five, would escort the two auxiliaries to Point Jig, four hundred miles southwest of Oahu, where Fletcher would catch up on the seventeenth. On the evening of 15 December Kimmel radioed the change in schedule to Brown and delayed his Jaluit attack by one day to the dawn of 23 December, Jaluit local time. Thus after subtracting the day lost crossing the date line to westward, Fletcher received a week to cover the two thousand miles to Wake. Once he gathered the *Tangier* and *Neches* at Point Jig, he could only count on thirteen knots—the speed of the *Neches*—until he refueled and detached the oiler. Kimmel also arranged for the *Drayton* to conduct a radio deception mission from 16 to 18 December to mimic a carrier task force loitering three to four hundred miles southwest of Hawaii.[22]

Two hours after the slowpokes sailed, Fletcher and Kinkaid greeted Fitch and Capt. Cornelius W. Flynn (Comdesron Four) in the *Astoria* to hammer out the details of the Wake relief. Fitch and Fletcher were close friends. It rankled Fitch not to lead TF-14, but he never held it against Fletcher. Following the Cincpac operations order, Fletcher divided TF-14 into two task groups: TG-14.1, the escort, led by Fitch, and TG-14.2, the train, under Sprague. The basic assumption was the island would not fall prior to the arrival of TF-14. Thus the objective was to see the *Tangier* safely to Wake, whereupon Sprague would land additional marines, radar, ammunition, and supplies to last the garrison at least another month. The *Tangier* would also take off the wounded and 650 civilian workers, although many more were actually there. That process was expected to take at least two days even if the weather cooperated, perhaps considerably more if it did not. Fitch was to fly VMF-221 to the airstrip on Wake at the earliest opportunity. Although the operations order did not mention total evacuation, Kimmel wisely reserved that option. In one day the *Tangier* could simply embark all personnel after demolishing the installations—if the weather and the Japanese permitted. Kimmel declared later that he had intended to wait until the *Tangier* arrived before deciding whether to remove the garrison. His main source of information was Cunningham's daily radio report. The task force commanders also monitored these messages, which Kimmel in turn rebroadcast with additional comments.[23]

The route that Kimmel and McMorris optimistically dictated to TF-14 followed the direct line from Oahu to Wake, rather than the course ninety to a hundred miles farther north that Halsey took just before the war to avoid search planes. Thus Fletcher could expect to encounter enemy searchers when slightly more than five hundred miles from Wake. A more northerly, but longer, approach like Halsey's would have reduced that risk by three hundred miles. Aside from subs that could appear at any time, Kimmel and McMorris pegged aircraft based in the northern Marshalls as Fletcher's main opposition. Wake reported upward of forty medium bombers that attacked almost daily. Cincpac intelligence remained vague as to exactly where they and the wider-ranging flying boats originated. Rongelap, 475 miles south of Wake, was the most likely site, but other suspected bases included Eniwetok (520 miles southwest) and Kwajalein (620 miles south). Wotje, located 170 miles east of Kwajalein, might also have an airfield. In fact the medium bombers in the Marshalls flew only out of Roi in Kwajalein atoll. The Chitose Air Group, part of the 24th Air Flotilla, numbered thirty-four Mitsubishi G3M2 Type 96 "land attack planes" (later code-named Nell). Rongelap and Eniwetok were not even garrisoned. The Yokohama Air Group comprised thirty-two Kawanishi H6K4 Type 97 four-engine flying boats (code-named Mavis) split among Roi, Wotje, and Jaluit. On 14 December, following the seizure of the Gilberts, three flying boats advanced to Makin, a movement U.S. radio intelligence detected that very day but greatly exaggerated.[24]

Cincpac's Op-Ord 39-41 to Fletcher simply stated: "Fuel from *Oiler* at discretion." On 16 December, though, the "Greybook" (Cincpac War Plans Section war diary) stated that both Brown and Fletcher were to refuel "before beginning active operations," that is, before the risk of being sighted. For Fletcher later was better. He had no idea how long the *Tangier* must loiter off Wake and how much oil his thirsty ships would expend in the interval. Fuel certainly troubled him. After the first Cincpac conference on the fifteenth, he summoned Lt. Cdr. John D. Hayes, the *Astoria*'s engineer officer, to discuss her radius of action. Hayes flatly avowed that despite the endurance figures cooked up by the War Plans Section, the *New Orleans*–class heavy cruisers could not go to Wake and back without refueling. Fletcher's questioning of Hayes stemmed from a crisis brewing in the Cincpac staff. Reports since 7 December showed what Kimmel called "excessive and alarming rates of fuel consumption." In some cases cruising radius was half of what was anticipated. Kimmel called it "a matter of the gravest concern." Indeed the logistical planning that underpinned the vast fleet movements in WPPac-46 seemed in jeopardy. Kimmel blamed "engineering performance" and chided force commanders and captains to be "careful in calling for speed, boiler power and reserve requirements." He was wrong. The theoretical steaming estimates were seriously flawed, and the economies and tricks engineers used in peacetime to win fuel conservation awards availed little during wartime. Just maintaining readiness to go to full power in an emergency consumed considerable oil. Fuel would be a major liability in the upcoming Jaluit and Wake operations.[25]

With all of the subsequent changes in plan, it is difficult to reconstruct the original TF-14 timetable. It appears that Fletcher intended to start fueling at dawn on 22 December (D–2 Day), Wake time, when about five hundred miles east of Wake and near the edge of the enemy's air search. Fueling would take the daylight hours, which meant little if any progress toward Wake or even a loss of distance. With an overnight run, though, he could anticipate closing within four hundred miles of Wake by dawn on 23 December (D–1 Day) and resume fueling if necessary. That day TF-14 would be well within enemy air search range of Rongelap and Wotje, risking detection and a bomber attack that early afternoon. Once fueling was completed the *Neches* and a destroyer would leave for Pearl, while the rest of TF-14 started for Wake at fifteen knots. Upon reaching Point Love (150 miles east of Wake) perhaps an hour prior to sunrise on 24 December (D-Day), the *Saratoga* would launch the fourteen marine fighters and also, presumably at Fitch's suggestion, one of her two dive bombing squadrons with eighteen SBDs. These aircraft would land at Wake shortly after dawn. At the same time Flynn, with the *Tangier* and four destroyers was to advance from Point Love, arrive at Wake that afternoon, and begin unloading. The Wake-based planes would cover his approach. In the meantime Fletcher would leave for Point Roger (one hundred miles north of Wake), from where he could provide air support at a slight hazard of air strikes from distant Rongelap. That he planned to base half his dive bombers at Wake during the *Tangier*'s approach and sojourn offers more dramatic evidence that no one expected real trouble, certainly no carrier battle. Their absence would greatly reduce the *Saratoga*'s own attack strength, because her remaining SBDs must also fly routine searches. After the *Tangier* completed her task (however many days that took), the SBD squadron would rejoin the *Sara* at Point Roger. Afterward TF-14 was to reassemble either at Point Love or eastward and return to Pearl.

Sources confirm this scenario. TF-14 Op-Ord 1-41, issued on 19 December, provides the basic sequence, but it lacked specific times because everything depended on how long the refueling would actually take. In 1948 Fletcher recalled that he was to be at Wake beginning at 0700 on a particular day. Likely that was when the first element, VMF-221, would land there. On 17 December Pearl informed Cunningham that the *Tangier* would arrive during daylight on the twenty-fourth, but cautioned "this is subject to change." VMF-221, though, might show up "prior to that time." Cincpac Op-Ord 42-41, issued on 18 December to Halsey, placed the *Tangier* at Wake "beginning D-Day probably after local noon [24 December]." If the fueling worked out well, however, Fletcher might be ahead of schedule, and could send VMF-221 and the SBDs on the twenty-third.[26]

Kimmel directed TG-14.1 to sail at 1000, 16 December, and overtake the *Neches* and *Tangier* the following morning at Point Jig. Fletcher departed on schedule with the cruisers and destroyers, but at the last minute Fitch reluctantly requested a delay. The *Saratoga* simply lacked time to prepare. Despite having the *Ramapo* alongside pumping for twenty-four hours, she only fueled to roughly 83 percent of full capacity (in terms of usable fuel—radius oil—about 80 percent). Part of the delay was due to having to purge seawater out of some of the fuel tanks.[27] The failure to fuel near to capacity was a serious deficiency, given her propensity to burn oil at a vast rate. Nor was all of her ammunition loaded on board. At noon Fitch's patience came to an end. If he waited any longer, he must waste oil on a high-speed run to reach Jig on time. Accosting Capt. Archibald H. Douglas on the flight deck, he gave the order in "appropriately peremptory fashion" to get under way immediately.[28] Once the *Sara* was clear of the harbor, five destroyers considerately provided by Fletcher slipped into antisubmarine formation to see her safely to the rendezvous. Fitch steamed at twenty knots and, like Fletcher, arrived on the seventeenth at Jig without incident. At noon Fletcher released Overesch's four destroyers to return to Pearl and set course due west toward Wake. Although TF-14 optimistically rang up thirteen knots, 12.75 knots was the most that Cdr. William B. Fletcher Jr. (no relation) could coax out of the *Neches*'s tired power plant. At least that snail's pace conserved oil.

CHAPTER 3

The Wake "Fiasco"

A NEW CINCPAC

The reinforcement of Wake was under way, but soon came under new management. On 15 December, clearly due to Knox's visit, Stark authorized Kimmel to reinforce Wake and Midway. Kimmel enthusiastically replied with a summary of his plans, including the Jaluit diversion, with which Stark "heartily concurred." That evening, however, Kimmel saw press reports that stated the navy was being blamed for not being alert at Pearl Harbor and that he was to be investigated. That was why he had listed possible successors in the previously cited letter to Stark. Even so he was crushed the next morning when Washington advised he would soon be relieved of command. It had been a hope beyond hope that he would be permitted to lead his fleet into battle. That afternoon Kimmel forthrightly recommended he be detached at once to clear the decks for his successor, Rear Adm. Chester Nimitz, chief of the Bureau of Navigation. Stark accommodated him. Kimmel never dreamt of the ordeal in store for him after Roosevelt, Stark, Marshall, and the others refused to acknowledge that they, too, never believed Pearl Harbor in peril of a massive surprise attack. They allowed a political firestorm to destroy an honorable man, who should have been allowed to contribute to the enemy's defeat.[1]

While Nimitz made his way from Washington, Vice Adm. William Pye, next in seniority, became temporary Cincpac on 17 December. A 1901 Annapolis graduate, sixty-one years old, "short in stature, bushy eyebrowed, thoughtful, quietly efficient," Pye was regarded as an outstanding thinker and strategist. A former head of the CNO's War Plans Division, he was an expert on the Pacific theater and also a master tactician never bested in the prewar fleet maneuvers. His classmate and friend Ernest King valued his intelligence but thought he "operated in something of an ivory tower, and was always unable to condense his ideas to reasonable dimensions." Pye relegated Kimmel's chief of staff, Capt. William W. "Poco" Smith, to administration and brought his own Battle Force staff officers to serve alongside Cincpac's staff. The new chief of staff for operations, Rear Adm. Milo F. Draemel (USNA 1906), hitherto senior destroyer flotilla leader in Halsey's TF-2, was a man much like Pye. Having taught at the Naval War College, Draemel likewise was valued as a strategist and planner. He later remarked he was chosen specifically to rein in Soc McMorris.[2]

About the time Pye took over, intelligence provided a fresh, if not always accurate, picture of Japanese fleet deployment. On 16 December Stark listed its strength and location based on his own estimates and British data. The main battle fleet (nine battleships, six carriers, a dozen cruisers, and thirty-seven destroyers) was now thought to have deployed south from home waters to Saipan. Its numbers included the force that assaulted Oahu and believed now back with the main body. Two other carriers were in the Philippines. The Mandates (Fourth) Fleet, based at Jaluit, evidently comprised only three light cruisers, nine destroyers, and sixteen subs—in line with McMorris's optimistic estimate. Commander Rochefort, though, reported that he did not think the commander of the carrier striking force (First Air Fleet) had yet reached the main body, but he could not locate him. Subsequent estimates put the commander in chief of the Combined Fleet in the triangle Bonin Islands–Saipan–Marcus Island, the last only 760 miles northwest of Wake. By 19 December it looked as if carriers and land-based air had reinforced the Marshalls, while Japan tightened its hold on the Gilberts. Pye radioed these vague, conflicting estimates to Brown and Fletcher. Still and all, he reckoned that tough Wake would hold out for the near future despite almost daily air attacks. Although hard-pressed, the atoll appeared in no immediate danger. The same could not be said of Brown and, to a lesser extent, Fletcher. With the ominous buildup in the Marshalls and west of there, Pye and Draemel gloomily reassessed the prospects for success by their widely scattered carrier forces.[3]

Adm. Husband Kimmel, 1 February 1941, the day he became Cincpac.
Courtesy of Tai Sing Loo, via Col. W. W. Smith Jr.

Yamamoto and most of the battleships actually remained in Japan. He carefully considered whether to unleash Nagumo's whole *Kidō Butai* against Wake. Stung by the failure of his 11 December invasion, Admiral Inoue beseeched Combined Fleet for carriers. At the same time Nagumo's brilliant air staff officer, Cdr. Genda Minoru, devised a bold plan to keep the pressure on the crippled Pacific Fleet. On 13 December during the wide circuit around Midway (which he avoided having to raid), Nagumo radioed Yamamoto to propose that he and Inoue combine to finish off Wake, then capture Midway, Johnston, and Palmyra, all to set up the invasion of Hawaii. Worried about seizing the oil-rich Dutch East Indies (which was, after all, why Japan went to war), the Naval General Staff firmly opposed for the time being any renewed advance east of Wake. On 15 December (14 December in Hawaii), Yamamoto ordered the *Kidō Butai* to aid the invasion of Wake with "appropriate force." That day Nagumo decided to bypass Wake and make for Truk, the fleet base in the Carolines 1,140 miles southwest of there. After fueling at Truk on the twenty-second he could sortie against Wake and open the way for Inoue to invade later in December. In that event nothing would stand in the way of Fletcher's Wake relief expedition. The next day, however, Nagumo's own underway fueling woes caused him to release most of his forces to Japan to prepare for operations in the Dutch East Indies. He split off a Wake Island Attack Force under Rear Adm. Abe Hiroaki, commander of the 8th Cruiser Division, with Rear Adm. Yamaguchi Tamon's 2nd Carrier Division (*Sōryū* and *Hiryū*), two heavy cruisers, just two destroyers, and an oiler group. Nagumo cautioned Inoue that Abe would only make a single air strike against Wake around 20 December, then proceed to Japan. In fact Abe did not get away that easily. Now with immediate carrier support, Inoue looked forward to capturing Wake on 23 December (twenty-second Hawaiian time). That was one day before Fletcher was to arrive, although Inoue had no idea he was coming. The brisk radio traffic between Combined Fleet, the *Kidō Butai*, and Inoue at Kwajalein that marked this planning exchange was what led Rochefort to believe something was cooking in the Mandates.[4]

Pye's priorities in addition to the Wake relief were to get Halsey's TF-8 (*Enterprise*) back to sea after its lengthy patrol north of Oahu and to reinforce the other outlying bases. Halsey's TF-8 finally entered Pearl on 16 December after the *Saratoga* sailed. Drawing fuel and provisions, he departed on the nineteenth with the *Enterprise*, three heavy cruisers, and nine destroyers to serve as backstop for TF-11 or TF-14, should either have to run while pursued. However, his initial position west of Johnston island lay far beyond support range of either Brown or Fletcher. Halsey also lacked fuel for long high-speed runs. The old oiler *Sepulga* (ten knots) reached Pearl on 18 December, but she was too slow to go with TF-8. No fast oilers would arrive for six days. On 18 December Overesch's newly formed TF-17 left Pearl with the seaplane tender *Wright* bound for Midway. Other expeditions were being organized to bolster Johnston and Palmyra.[5]

Soon after sailing, Brown grew more uneasy about tackling mysterious Jaluit. Intelligence hinted at expanding strength in the Marshalls, possibly including carriers, and the target itself was reputed to be a large sub base. The approach to Jaluit in the prewar reconnaissance and raiding plan was from the southeast, via the northern Gilberts. That no longer seemed feasible after Cincpac discovered a seaplane tender and some flying boats (actually three, but said wrongly to number as many as forty) had moved into Makin. Other events also eroded Brown's nerve. On 16 December two *Lexington* SBDs mistook a derelict barge for a carrier and bombed, but missed it. Subsequently a strike group could not even find the barge. The next day all the five-inch antiaircraft shells fired by the *Indianapolis* in a test proved duds. TF-11 commenced fueling from the *Neosho* on the morning of 18 December, and as usual did not finish until late the next day. By that time Brown was persuaded that he would surely be spotted long before he ever neared heavily defended Jaluit. His concerns engendered pressure for the *Lexington* Air Group to strike from what the pilots judged excessively long range, "way beyond the airplanes' capability." Instead of Jaluit, Brown resolved to raid Makin and Tarawa in the Gilberts. To clear air searches fanning out from the eastern Marshalls, he intended to continue south to about Tarawa's latitude, then sprint west at twenty-four knots. The attack would go in as scheduled at dawn on 23 December, local time, from a point one hundred miles equidistant from both objectives. As a ruse a destroyer was to sheer off to the northwest to transmit radio messages to imitate a carrier task force threatening the Marshalls.[6]

The first three days that the united TF-14 lurched westward were uneventful, although Fletcher's handling of the force during air operations greatly disconcerted the *Saratoga*. Near dawn on 18 December, the carrier and her plane guard destroyers turned northeast into the wind to launch a routine morning search. Instead of conforming to her movements Fletcher kept the rest of the ships zigzagging westward. That left the *Sara* feeling exposed to subs. She had to lift her skirts and crank on 22 knots to overhaul the others, taking nearly three hours to regain her place in formation. Fletcher in fact conformed to standard doctrine in which the carrier and plane guards broke off to run into the wind ("flying stations"). Despite disapproval in the flattop he had little choice. With the *Neches* present TF-14 plodded like a convoy—far too slow to stay with the *Sara* during air operations. Fletcher counted on the carrier's increased speed during such episodes to hinder sub attacks. Pearl likewise kept Fletcher informed of the sketchy intelligence on Japanese strength and possible movements. Thus on 17 December he learned that cruisers and destroyers and perhaps one or more carriers might have reinforced the Mandates (Fourth) Fleet. The next day new estimates placed the 24th "Air Squadron" at or near Utirik, 160 miles east of Rongelap and one hundred miles north of Wotje, yet another air base that endangered Fletcher's left flank. Actually no forces were there. The *Astoria* intercepted transmissions that appeared to originate north of Utirik, causing Fletcher to wonder if a carrier homed aircraft in its vicinity. On 19 December, despite that concern, he authorized Fitch to break strict radio silence when a squall concealed TF-14 from two dive bombers on search. A short message brought them home.[7]

A CHANGE IN PLAN

Shortly before noon on 20 December (Z+12), when TF-14 was 725 miles due east of Wake, the *Astoria* monitored a message from Wake, announcing that approximately one squadron of carrier dive bombers attacked at 0830, 21 December, local time. Now with at least one carrier confirmed off Wake, Fletcher implemented what was apparently a contingency plan. At 1155 he altered course 20 degrees starboard to veer TF-14 northwest and keep safely clear, for a while, of air searches he thought emanated from Rongelap, Wotje, and possibly Utirik. Had TF-14 continued west on 270 degrees, fueling the next day would have occurred at the edge of or possibly inside the enemy's search umbrella. With one or more Japanese carriers frolicking in the neighborhood, Fletcher did not care to have his location revealed until he had finished that necessary chore.[8]

Earlier the same morning of 20 December (21 December, Wake time), Pye independently ruled out Brown's diversion. The prewar reconnaissance and raiding plan certainly had not envisioned battling carriers in the Marshalls. Given the buildup of aircraft in the Mandates, the possible presence of carriers, subs, and a warning net of local air and picket boat patrols, Brown's chances of surprising Jaluit looked remote. Draemel later characterized the Jaluit foray as the "shot in the dark raid." To lose the *Lex* at this time would jeopardize Hawaii's shaky defense. Therefore Pye resolved to bring TF-11 north to support TF-14. He had already decided, but had yet to announce it, when he received electrifying word of the carrier strike on Wake. Now all bets were off. That afternoon, after advising Washington, Pye transmitted new orders to Brown, Halsey, and Fletcher. Fresh forces reaching the Mandates might now include the "4th Carrier Division" (actually, the 5th—*Shōkaku* and *Zuikaku*) and possibly the 2nd Carrier Division (*Sōryū* and *Hiryū*). Therefore Pye, unaware Brown had substituted Makin and Tarawa for Jaluit, canceled his attack and redeployed TF-11 northward. While retracing his route Brown was to stay at least seven hundred miles from Wotje to avoid being sighted—a substantial detour. Once clear of the Marshalls search zone, TF-11 was to go no farther north than latitude 20° north, roughly Wake's latitude, unless to succor TF-14. To cover the right flank, Pye sent Halsey's TF-8 (*Enterprise*) northwest from near Johnston to north of Midway. He was to remain east of the 180th meridian, unless needed to aid Brown or Fletcher. Pye had restricted the operating areas of TF-11 and TF-8 "to prevent their interference with each other, as both were on radio silence." His alteration merely reduced, but did not eliminate, the huge defect in Kimmel's original plan. No one could actually help Fletcher if he did get into trouble off Wake.[9]

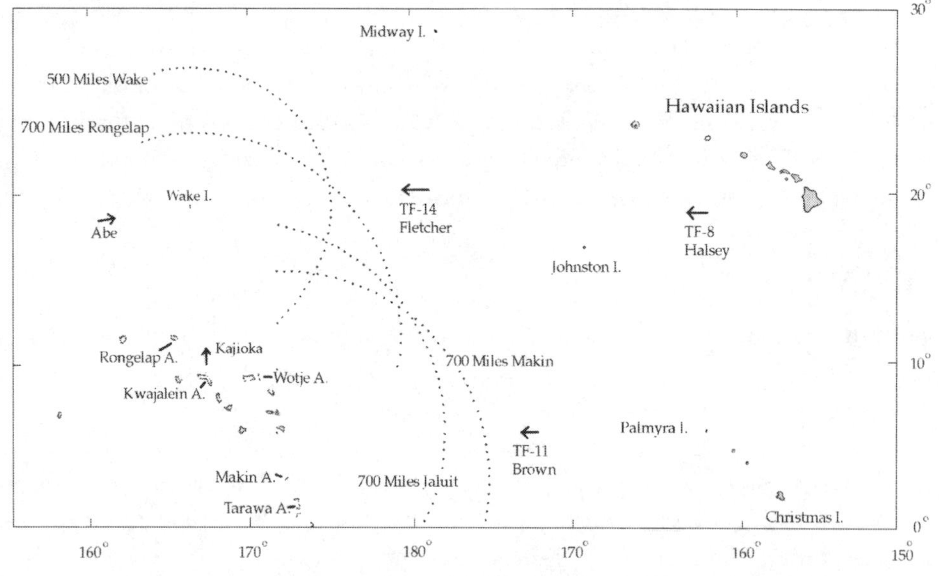

Situation at 1200, 21 December 1941

With a carrier or carriers skulking within striking distance of Wake—a danger Cincpac hitherto disregarded—a fight became a distinct possibility. In message 210157 of December 1941, Pye warned Fletcher to "be prepared for possibility of enemy forces your vicinity," a contingency not previously contemplated. By ordering the *Saratoga* and the three heavy cruisers to stay more than seven hundred miles from Rongelap during daylight, Pye ratified Fletcher's decision to approach Wake from the northeast quadrant. He could still draw as near as 225 miles northeast of Wake, but not take his heavy ships any closer. "When released to approach Wake, *Tangier* proceed without carrier air support." This momentous dispatch reached Fletcher about 1530 on 20 December, just before TF-14 turned its clocks ahead to 21 December upon vaulting to Wake's side of the date line. The directive to leave the *Tangier* without carrier air protection on her last perilous leg shocked him. If she were lost the whole mission became pointless. Pye provided no additional guidance. To Fletcher it seemed that defense now took precedence over seeing the *Tangier* safely to Wake. He was profoundly troubled, later telling Sprague that under the circumstances "he felt like he was putting a pistol to [Sprague's] head." Sprague himself entertained no illusions. He was prepared, if need be, to run the *Tangier* aground to save the supplies and join the defenders. Before it was necessary to do anything drastic, however, Fletcher intended to fuel on the twenty-second.[10]

Brown was about 750 miles northeast of Makin and thirty-six hours short of launching his strike when he learned that Pye canceled the mission. To those in the *Indianapolis* who first saw it, Cincpac's message "felt like a kick in the groin." Frustrated TF-11 staffers even debated whether to show the message to Brown and chief of staff Capt. Marion C. Robertson (uncharitably dubbed "an old woman" by one Young Turk), or just let the raid go ahead. Reason prevailed. Although quite disappointed, Brown had another worry: the voracious expenditure of fuel. Just as Kimmel discovered the week before, the destroyers guzzled 50 percent more oil than expected. Had he gone ahead with the Makin-Tarawa raid, Brown would have had to refuel his destroyers the day after from his heavy ships, no matter the sea conditions or enemy interference. Now while heading north he rang up 16 knots, all that he felt he could spare over the long haul. At that speed he estimated the *Lexington* could first put planes over Wake on D+2 Day (26 December, Wake time), that is, two days after the relief arrived. He even wondered whether he might have to leave his destroyers to follow at a more economical pace or detach them to fuel from the *Neosho*.[11]

In fact Inoue already arranged to seize Wake before the *Tangier* could ever get there. On 21 December Kajioka left Kwajalein with the second invasion force of three old light cruisers, six destroyers, the motley array of auxiliaries and a thousand troops, plus the four heavy cruisers of Rear Adm. Gotō Aritomo's 6th Cruiser Division that came east from Guam to fight in the unlikely event a U.S. surface force showed up. Kajioka planned to storm the atoll before dawn on the twenty-third. U.S. intelligence did not discover the existence of his force, and no one sighted it. Abe's Wake Island Attack Force with the *Sōryū* and *Hiryū* closed Wake from the west, expecting to attack on 22 December, the day before the invasion. However on the twentieth, Inoue implored him to strike early the next day, "if at all possible." Japanese radio intelligence detected hints of U.S. flying boats moving to Wake. Inoue feared they might bomb the approaching transports. (Actually only one PBY Catalina flew to Wake.) Having just refueled, Abe could afford to crank on thirty knots at a colossal expenditure of oil to draw within three hundred miles of Wake at dawn on the twenty-first, dispatch his strike, and close to shorten the return flight. That was a far longer mission than the U.S. carriers could achieve. Far from merely the "squadron" of dive bombers (eighteen planes) that Wake described, forty-nine aircraft (eighteen fighters, twenty-nine dive bombers, and two torpedo bombers) swarmed overhead. After recovering his strike, Abe swung south of the island to protect the advancing invasion force.[12]

THE FUELING CONTROVERSY

Ever since Fletcher departed Pearl, he and his superiors anticipated refueling before approaching Wake. Even McMorris admitted the necessity for TF-14, "particularly the destroyers," to fuel prior to closing Wake. He recognized the "hazards of getting 2,000 or more miles away from the base with the fuel of cruisers as well as destroyers depleted [and] where a strong enemy force might be encountered and high speed required." Not everyone concurred. Morison concluded well after the fact that the fuel present was wholly adequate for Fletcher's needs as *he* conceived them. If the destroyers ran short, the cruisers and capacious *Sara* herself could have provided oil. "It is clear there was no immediate danger of the destroyers going dry unless the force tanker was sunk." After the publication of Morison's account, Fletcher responded that fueling his destroyers at that point was "not merely desirable but absolutely necessary." He contended even the cruisers needed oil.[13]

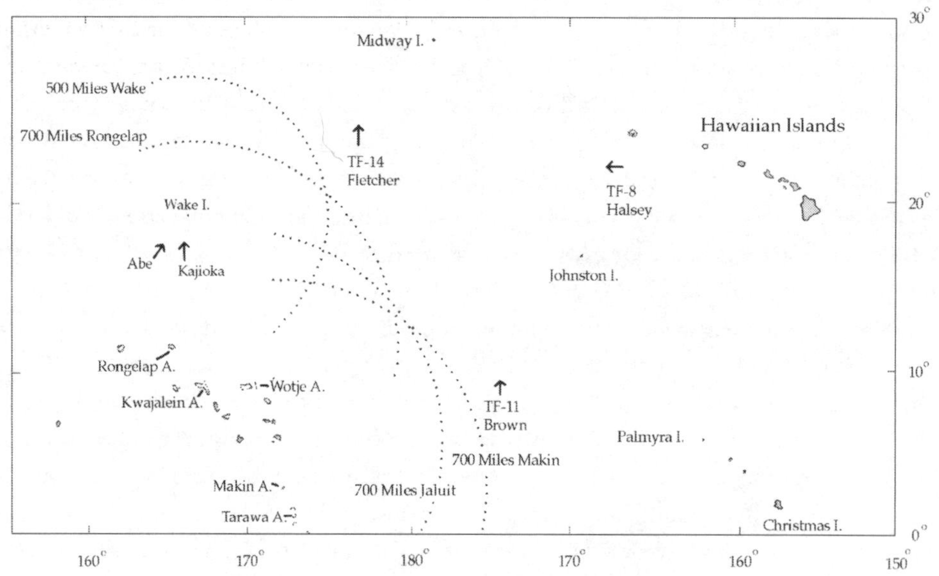

Situation at 1200, 22 December 1941

By 22 December Fletcher's destroyers averaged 63 percent of capacity after steaming slowly for six days at economical speed, mostly thirteen knots. Of course, higher speeds vastly increased fuel consumption. Based on reliable data compiled later in the war, the *Bagley* class of destroyers in Destroyer Squadron (Desron) Four burned roughly 1.8 times the fuel at twenty knots than at fifteen knots, 3.9 times at twenty-five knots, and 8.4 times at thirty knots. High-speed bursts were commonplace during carrier air operations and essential in battle. Task force commanders reckoned available fuel according to estimates of endurance at fifteen knots ("patrol speed") and twenty-five knots, according to the ship with the least fuel. Later, more accurate, calculations showed that Desron Four, with the oil on hand on 22 December, should have been able to steam about 10.5 days at fifteen knots and 2.7 days at twenty-five knots.[14] Fletcher and the other task force commanders lacked exact fuel expenditure tables valid for wartime conditions, instead of unrealistic peacetime exercises. All they knew at the time was their ships burned oil far more quickly than expected. In 1976 Vice Adm. Ralph Earle Jr., who in December 1941 was skipper of the *Ralph Talbot*, averred that refueling on 22 December was "necessary and wise."[15]

The heavy ships could certainly fuel destroyers, but that required quiet daylight hours with decent seas and no enemy pressure—precisely what Fletcher could not guarantee. Averaging 75 percent, the three heavy cruisers were much better off than the destroyers, but as Hayes, the *Astoria*'s engineer, had warned, they still might not have enough oil to ensure getting to Wake and back on their own. The insatiable *Saratoga* was already down to roughly 63 percent (about 57 percent of her radius oil, what she could actually use). That limited the oil she could provide in a pinch. Fletcher had to anticipate a tactical situation that could force him to separate from the slow *Neches*. If a sub did sink her (her fate in January 1942, which compelled another task force to abort a raid on Wake), TF-14 would really have been in a tight spot because no other oiler was available. He could not count on any fuel from Brown unless the *Neosho* was actually present, or from Halsey in the unlikely event he met either. Under the actual tactical circumstances, as opposed to postwar omniscience, it would not have been daring but folly for Fletcher to mount the last lunge for Wake without refueling. A 1945 navy study on war service fuel consumption remarked that after the outbreak of the war, "task forces engaged in operations ran low on fuel appreciably earlier than expected," and that "the actual radius of all ships was appreciably less than originally expected, and in the case of destroyers and some cruisers it was inadequate."[16]

The refueling woes evident earlier smote TF-14. At dawn on the twenty-second with Wake some 515 miles southwest, Fletcher changed course northeast to head into the wind and remain out of enemy search range. Lt. Cdr. George A. Sinclair brought the *Bagley* (at 53 percent the low destroyer) alongside the *Neches*. Nothing went as planned. Twenty-knot northeasterly winds, moderating to fourteen during the day, posed no big problem, but long cross-swells made it difficult for oiler and destroyer to hold proper position alongside. Hoses and occasionally tow lines parted, greatly slowing the process. In 1976 Capt. Richard D. Shepard, former gunnery officer of the *Ralph Talbot*—the second destroyer to fuel that day—recalled: "Many things went wrong. Hoses were not smartly passed. Communications broke down. There were oil spills. Destroyers came alongside the oiler not ready to receive, tanks not consolidated and the like." By sundown (1642, Z–11), only four tin cans had managed to fuel, leaving five more to go and, if time allowed, the *Sara* and the cruisers as well. Even worse, the oiler rapidly exhausted her supply of spare hose sections.[17]

There obviously was a marked failure in underway refueling in all task forces. The U.S. Navy had started refueling destroyers at sea in 1917 and heavy ships in 1939. During

1941 the Pacific Fleet practiced underway refueling, but "rarely, if ever," as historian Thomas Wildenberg wrote, "in anything but a calm sea." As Pye later testified, "When you get out in these broad swells they have here in the broad Pacific it is a difficult job." The elderly *Neches* was poorly equipped for underway refueling, particularly in such a sea. Kimmel had intended her only for harbor use. Her winches were too small and, like all the other oilers, her fuel hoses were the wrong type, too heavy. Moreover, the destroyers were not yet equipped with quick release hose couplings. That was not the whole story. Shepard noted the U.S. Navy in December 1941 was "simply not well trained in fueling at sea, particularly under combat conditions." Capt. Joel C. Ford, who was engineer officer of the *Jarvis*, commented in 1976, "It *is* true that fueling at sea procedures were cumbersome at that time—long slow approaches, all manner of lines across, secured and settled down *before* passing a fuel hose, and then only one hose as a rule. Later it became whip alongside, pass two hoses (never mind the other lines in normal circumstances) pump at high pressure and clear the side." Few destroyer skippers had much experience in underway refueling. The draft of the first standard manual for destroyer refueling was only submitted on 5 December and approved by Pye the day TF-14 first fueled at sea. By early 1942 improved fueling rigs and more experience quickly transformed underway refueling to a great strength for the U.S. Navy.[18]

AN OSCILLATING RESOLVE

At 1601 on 22 December, when the fourth destroyer broke away from the *Neches*, the distance to Wake had increased to about 550 miles, a thirty-five-mile loss. Fletcher turned northwest at the usual 12.75 knots, so by the next dawn [D–1 Day] to draw one hundred miles closer to Wake. There, still beyond enemy air search range, he would complete refueling and proceed with the relief. After sunset he received two messages from Cincpac. Based on radio direction finding, Pye placed the "*Soru* [*sic*]" north of Wake. In fact the *Sōryū* and *Hiryū* were actually south of Wake. The second message recounted more raids that afternoon against Wake by dive bombers and fighters and land-based bombers, but boasted two plucky marine Wildcats downed several attackers. "Material damage" at Wake was said to be "slight."[19] Despite increasing pressure, the outlook for the besieged atoll remained hopeful, but such optimism did not last long.[20]

Later that evening, 21 December in Hawaii, Pye's staff debriefed a weary Ens. James J. Murphy, who had just brought his PBY back from a long solo mission to Wake to deliver the relief plan. His flight was what had troubled Inoue, who thought many more flying boats were involved. Murphy departed Wake just prior to the first carrier raid. He completely contradicted the rosy view that Pearl held of Wake despite its daily radio reports. Wake was "a shambles," and nearly half of VMF-211 was dead. For the first time the Cincpac staff perceived Wake *was* in terrible danger, barely holding on. One War Plans officer, marine Lt. Col. Omar T. Pfeiffer, described the tone of Murphy's revelations as "grim, grim, grim." The news hit Pye like a splash of cold water. Only now, in his words, did circumstances "warrant taking a greater chance to effect [Wake's] reinforcement even at the sacrifice of the *Tangier* and possible damage to some major ships of Task Force 14."[21]

Shortly after midnight, to the vast relief of McMorris and others on the staff, Pye radioed a new battle plan to Halsey, Brown, and Fletcher. For some unknown reason he reduced the number of flattops supposed lurking in the Mandates or off Wake to just one, "possibly *Siryu* [*sic*]." That was wishful thinking to say the least. Therefore he removed all restrictions on Fletcher's movements and authorized him to "furnish *Tangier* air support at discretion." Wake advised the marine fighters arrive after 1500 to escape air raids. Upon reaching the objective the *Tangier* was to land her radar set first of all. That adhered to the schedule created the week before at Pearl, *without* additional orders to hurry the relief. Cincpac likewise rearranged the supporting cast. He lifted the restriction on Brown going no closer than seven hundred miles to Wotje, which entailed a lengthy northern detour before TF-11 could turn west toward Wake. Now Brown need only keep five hundred miles from Rongelap. Pye set the western limit for TF-11 at longitude 172° east, about three hundred miles east of Wake. Hitherto Halsey was not to cross longitude 180° or go south of latitude 20° north, but now Pye likewise authorized him to proceed 480 miles farther west to longitude 172° east. These "area assignments," the order explained, existed "solely to prevent interference between task groups[;] disregard as circumstances dictate."[22]

TOO LATE

Near midnight on the twenty-second after a long and frustrating day, Fletcher read Pye's new orders. He looked forward to resume fueling at dawn about 440 miles northeast of Wake. The *Selfridge*, the destroyer leader wearing Flynn's pennant, would first go alongside the *Neches*. As soon as she got her drink of oil, by 0900 at the latest, Flynn was to proceed with the *Tangier* and three other refueled destroyers directly southwest to Wake. At fifteen knots, Flynn could be there shortly after local noon on 24 December, right "on schedule," as Fletcher noted in his report. Once the remaining four destroyers fueled, the *Neches* and *Helm* would leave for Pearl as ordered, while Fletcher followed Flynn with the *Saratoga*, three heavy cruisers, and four destroyers. Fitch, at least, contemplated having the *Saratoga* in range in time for VMF-221 to fly to Wake before sundown. Even if that were not possible, if fueling took all the daylight on the twenty-third, an overnight run at twenty knots nevertheless would, by dawn on the twenty-fourth, bring Fletcher only a hundred miles astern of the *Tangier* group and 180 miles northeast of Wake. VMF-221 could depart at dawn, while the *Sara* searched for the Japanese carrier and attack if within range. Thus TF-14 confidently looked forward to completing the relief of Wake.[23]

Around 0325, 23 December, Fletcher was surprised by Wake's flash report of "ships to southward and gunfire to northeast." A half hour later another message warned of a "bombardment and apparently landing attack at Wake." Two old destroyers crammed with special landing force sailors had deliberately run aground; more green-jacketed troops splashed ashore from landing barges. Wake's marines put up a terrific defense. To subdue roughly four hundred marine defenders bereft of naval support of their own, Kajioka eventually committed nine hundred men, supported by naval gunfire and, after dawn, by aircraft from the *Sōryū* and *Hiryū*, now west of Wake.[24]

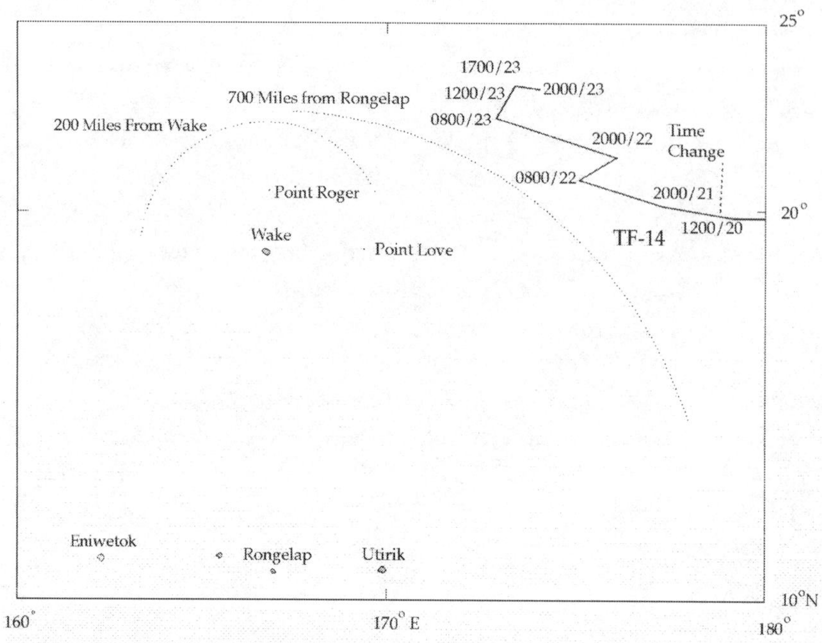

Track chart TF-14, 20–23 December 1941

With endangered Wake still 440 miles distant and far beyond strike range, Fletcher decided he had to stick with the plan and complete fueling as quickly as possible. Sea conditions were little better than the previous day, with swells prodded by a northeasterly wind of twenty knots. He turned due north, keeping as far out of the wind as feasible and still facilitate the fueling. Nineteen minutes before sunrise the *Selfridge* eased alongside the *Neches*. Things looked bad, but if Wake could only hold out, the *Tangier* and her escorts would soon be on their way, followed by the rest of TF-14 after it fueled. Likewise following the grave situation, Brown took seriously his assignment to support TF-14. At 0444, 23 December (Wake local time), he changed course directly toward Wake and upped speed to eighteen knots. A few minutes later he broke radio silence to advise Fletcher that in forty-eight hours (0500, 25 December, Wake time), TF-11 would reach a reference point 180 miles east of Wake. Until then Fletcher was on his own, which again demonstrated the basic flaw of the original Kimmel-McMorris plan.[25]

About 0655 (Z–11) while the *Selfridge* still drew oil, Fletcher read another Cincpac message addressed also to Halsey and Brown: "Relief or evacuation of Wake now impossible. TF-14 and 11 retire on Pearl searching enroute. Report positions when within 700 miles of Pearl. TF-8 retire toward Midway and cover *Wright* now enroute Midway due to arrive about daylight 24 December." Pye had decided to abandon Wake and recall his task forces without a fight.[26]

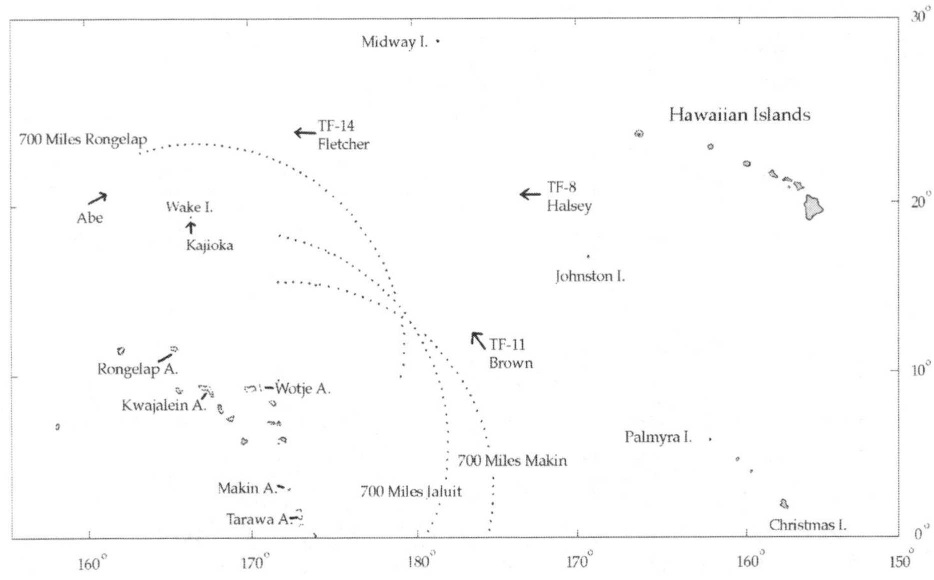

Situation at 0800, 23 December 1941

The first warning from Wake reached Pearl about 0415, 22 December (Hawaii time). Pye, Draemel, and McMorris discussed the grave situation and debated various responses until long after sunrise. By 0530 they realized Wake had probably been invaded. Just a few hours before, Pye had determined to go ahead with the relief even at the risk of severe damage to TF-14. Now with Wake's weakness so evident, he and Draemel were taken aback when Japan struck so quickly without warning. To further complicate matters, the CNO suddenly changed his tune about aggressive action at Wake. About 0645 Pye received a message that Stark sent, not because of the swiftly developing crisis (of which he was not yet aware), but from concern over Pye's newly found—but now rapidly waning—resolve to push the relief. Reverting to his earlier caution, Stark declared: "General considerations and recent developments emphasize that Wake is now and will continue to be a liability." He sanctioned its evacuation "with appropriate demolition" and urged that "efforts to strengthen and hold Midway should continue." He added, "King concurs," in reference to Ernest King, about to become the new Commander in chief of the U.S. Fleet. Busy gearing up for the visit of Prime Minister Winston Churchill, President Roosevelt and Secretary Knox did not know that Stark *and* King had given up on Wake. For his own part Pye was only too aware that he was only a caretaker Cincpac. Who was he to argue with the two top admirals?[27]

At 0700 Draemel questioned whether the relief of Wake was still possible with the Japanese apparently present in strength. They might be laying a trap for TF-14. At the very least, proceeding with the Wake mission boded a major battle that could engulf the Pacific Fleet's scattered carrier groups. Pye declared the time to save Wake was past. "The Wake relief expedition," he explained later that day, "was a desperate move to give reinforcements to the gallant defenders, and I was willing, if no enemy activity other than bombing was in progress, to sacrifice the *Tangier* and several destroyers in the attempt." That situation no longer pertained. The question became whether he should risk a significant portion of TF-14 to retaliate for the invasion and perhaps even trade the *Saratoga* for meaningful damage inflicted on the Combined Fleet. "The offensive spirit shown by our Navy may be worth the sacrifice." However, even that might not be possible. Like Draemel, Pye feared a trap. The timing of the invasion seemed too opportune in view of Fletcher's approach. For the time being, though, he kept open the option of TF-14 (minus the *Tangier* and *Neches*) swiftly closing Wake for one air attack before retiring.[28]

Another Wake message that Pye received around 0730 seemed to signal the end. "Enemy on island. Issue in doubt." The issue was in doubt, too, at Pearl. As usual McMorris favored the aggressive response. At 0800 he submitted a memo entreating Pye to loose TF-14 against ships off Wake, while moving Brown and Halsey up in support. Fletcher could smash the invasion, perhaps even in time to save the garrison. Radio intelligence, McMorris stressed, could only confirm the presence of the carrier *Sōryū*, erroneously thought to displace only ten thousand tons with a capacity of forty-two aircraft. Actually she was sixteen thousand tons with nominally fifty-four planes, not to mention the *Hiryū* was also there. The little lone carrier seemed easy meat for a beefed-up *Saratoga* that included two fighting squadrons instead of one. McMorris thought the odds were "strongly in her favor." (In fact the *Sara* lacked nine of thirty-six fighters McMorris thought she had.) He beseeched Pye not to squander this "golden opportunity," one that was "unlikely to come again soon." No one could dispute his conclusion. "We are in great need of a victory."[29]

Pye called in McMorris, Capt. Lynde D. McCormick, and Cdr. Vincent Murphy from War Plans. He reiterated that Wake, despite its gallant defense, could not be saved and addressed whether the carriers should fight near the embattled atoll as McMorris advocated. "With extreme regret," Pye's answer was no. He feared that Fletcher, even if Brown joined later, might become embroiled with superior forces enjoying shore-based air support. If defeated, they must run a gauntlet and sacrifice any cripples. Black-shoe Pye felt reluctant on general principle to fight a major fleet action far beyond Pearl without battleship support. It is hard to blame him, for Kimmel had long felt the same way. Following Washington's lead, Pye set as top priority the defense of Midway, Hawaii, and Samoa. When Pye announced his decision, McMorris interrupted: "Is that final, Admiral, or may I speak?" Pye replied, "It's final." Leary and Draemel supported his actions, but Poco Smith and McMorris barely contained their fury and contempt. At 0911, 22 December, in Hawaii (0641, 23 December, Wake time), Pye radioed the recall order that so stunned Fletcher and the fleet. Cunningham sent his valedictory at 0652: "Enemy on island. Several ships plus transport moving in. Two DD [destroyers] aground." A half hour later he sought formal surrender. At 1400 the last of the Wake garrison laid down their arms and went into brutal captivity.[30]

Understandably the response to the recall on board the *Astoria* and the rest of TF-14 was bitter. Lt. (jg) Jack E. Gibson, a junior gunnery officer, watched in fascination as Fletcher disgustedly threw his gold-braided cap to the deck. Years later Lt. Harry Smith, staff duty officer, primly (and unconvincingly) denied that such an outburst ever took place. He recalled the admiral never said a thing (which was true), but "simply carried on as usual."

Some of the staff advised Fletcher to find some way to advance toward Wake, but he refused. Morison later insinuated he should have disobeyed Pye's recall, quoting one unidentified cruiser captain, "Frank Jack should have placed the telescope to his blind eye, like Nelson." Indeed Fletcher felt "tempted to disregard orders" and charge the enemy forces off Wake. In 1964 he commented: "My reaction was that as much as I disapproved I had no information which Cincpac did not have and that they probably had some that I did not have, so I had no reason to disobey orders." The fact that Pye was now in charge also played a factor. In 1950 Vice Adm. Poco Smith recalled how Fletcher "and all of us had great confidence in Admiral Pye." Although imperturbable (at least afterward) in front of his juniors, Fletcher let his hair down with a sympathetic Kinkaid. "I could do nothing else, could I?" Without hesitation Kinkaid replied "No."[31]

On the flag bridge high in the *Saratoga*'s island, the blow landed equally hard. In hopes of getting VMF-221 off that day, Fitch was conferring with its senior officers. The Cardiv One staff questioned the decision to turn back with such vehemence that Fitch judged "actually mutinous" their urgent advice to disregard orders. He left the bridge to not "(officially) to hear such talk," and also not to display his own great anger. "Such intense indignation and resentment" raged in the *Sara* as Fitch never before knew in the navy. Everyone hoped to go ahead with the relief, or if that was no longer possible, to get a crack at that "one little carrier" sitting off Wake. Captain Douglas requested Fitch's permission to recommend to Fletcher that the *Sara* make a high-speed run toward Wake, launch searches, and strike anything located. He even wanted to press on without Fletcher's leave, if need be. Although fully in sympathy, Fitch refused. He, too, thought a great opportunity was being wasted to smash the invasion force. Much later he recalled how he wished he could have conferred privately with Fletcher, perhaps to contrive some way to get around the recall order, but that was not possible. It is instructive that the officer whom the critics deemed better fitted for command of TF-14 reacted to Pye's order exactly as did Fletcher, with dismayed obedience, not defiance.[32]

Fletcher's many detractors also ignored that he did not jump at the opportunity to withdraw once the *Selfridge* was done fueling at 0811, but instead steamed slowly north. In fact he hung around all day to fuel all his remaining destroyers and be ready to fight should Cincpac have a change of heart. Turning northeast at 1040 directly into the wind eased sea conditions. The fueling went more smoothly. The *Neches* delivered more oil, but used the last of her fuel hoses. By 1630, fifteen minutes before sundown, TF-14 had increased its distance from Wake by only some seventy-five miles while finishing the destroyer fueling. Only then, after no further word from Pye, did Fletcher finally relent and point his ships eastward. After dark new orders from Cincpac concerned Midway not Wake. Fletcher was to fly VMF-221 to Midway on 25 December and release the *Tangier* and two destroyers to arrive there the day after. On the second 24 December (after recrossing the date line), Fletcher detached Sprague with the *Tangier*, *Ralph Talbot*, and *Blue* northeast to reach Midway on 26 December, while he shaped course for Pearl. The reinforcements that never fought at Wake helped hold Midway the next time the Japanese fleet showed up in the central Pacific.[33]

LOST OPPORTUNITY?

Years later fully informed, unlike Pye and Fletcher, of the intentions and movements of the second Wake invasion force and Abe's carriers, Morison decreed that word alone of a carrier air strike on Wake should have spurred Fletcher to drastic action. On the evening of 21 December Fletcher should have canceled plans to refuel and charged ahead at twenty knots. Supposedly that would have placed him in perfect position at dawn on 23 December to smash the invasion ships. To Morison the failure to act at this time spelled the doom of Wake, and he never ceased to upbraid Fletcher for this perceived dereliction. In his view, Fletcher shirked his duty because he chose to slow down and fuel, a totally unnecessary delay.[34]

Operational plans and orders are, of course, how commanders exercise control over their subordinates and coordinate their activities to accomplish the mission. Such prognostications, though, can never account for every situation that might occur. Also they can be unrealistic and flawed. Circumstances arise when a subordinate is fully justified in altering the plan and proceeding according to his own best judgment. Was that a valid course of action for Fletcher in this particular instance? Morison offered his assessment long after the fact based strictly on hindsight. The key point is that no one on the U.S. side knew of the existence of a force en route to invade Wake. Pye did not feel that a carrier attack alone put Wake in immediate danger. On the contrary, he was even willing to risk the *Tangier*'s final approach without the *Saratoga*'s air support. There is no evidence at all that before Wake was actually invaded anyone at Pearl recommended that Fletcher race ahead and engage the Japanese carrier force.

For the sake of argument, one can speculate what might have happened (aside from severe fuel shortage) had Fletcher pressed ahead on 21 December on his own at twenty knots. That meant disobeying Pye's direct order, just received, to keep the *Saratoga* and the cruisers seven hundred miles beyond Rongelap during daylight. It also would have cast aside the whole plan by isolating TF-14 even further from the support that Pye was mustering. Had Fletcher taken the bit in his teeth and pushed straight to Wake, he would gone on the direct line to southwestward. Even so, the *Sara*'s 22 December afternoon air search would have fallen short of the invasion forces and Abe's carriers coming up from the south. Perhaps the most Fletcher might have accomplished that day was to launch VMF-221 at extreme range to land at Wake before sunset. However, those fighters would have been useless against a predawn invasion, but their absence would gravely weaken TF-14. The *Saratoga*'s own Fighting Squadron Three counted only a dozen operational Grumman Wildcats.[35]

Yet by proceeding directly west toward Wake, TF-14 would have risked running afoul of the Japanese air search on 22 December. Four flying boats left before sunrise to sweep 630 miles north of Wotje. Chances would have been good that at least one might have spotted TF-14 and alerted Abe's carriers. Overnight on 21–22 December Abe closed the Wake Island invasion force approaching from the south. On the twenty-second he turned northward and by mid afternoon was about 150 miles south of Wake. His morning strike numbered six fighters and thirty-three carrier attack planes. VMF-211 downed two bombers, but the escort Zeros finished off the last two Wildcats. If Abe had learned of the existence of TF-14, the advantage would have switched decisively to him for the knock-out blow the morning of the twenty-third. Had neither Fletcher nor Abe discovered each other on 22 December, the dawn of the twenty-third could have found TF-14 only one hundred miles east or northeast of Wake. Overnight Abe moved northwest of Wake. The two carrier forces could have been well within range of each other at sunrise. The odds would have favored the carrier commander who first found his opponent and attacked.[36]

Morison and others wrote exuberantly of Fletcher's chances of crippling or sinking the *Sōryū* and *Hiryū*. Adm. Frederick C. "Ted" Sherman (no Fletcher enthusiast) later speculated, on the basis of Morison's interpretation, that had the *Saratoga* conducted an "adequate air search," the *Sōryū* and *Hiryū* "were open to attack [and] might have been destroyed."[37] He did not explain how the *Saratoga* could have searched "adequately" and retained enough aircraft to ensure sinking those two formidable targets. She wielded about seventy-seven flyable aircraft (twenty-six F4F and F2A fighters, forty SBD dive bombers, and eleven TBD torpedo bombers), as opposed to the ninety-four planes (thirty-four Mitsubishi A6M2 Type 0 "Zero" fighters, twenty-nine Aichi D3A1 Type 99 carrier bombers, and thirty-one Nakajima B5N2 Type 97 carrier attack planes) of the *Sōryū* and *Hiryū*. Except for dive bombers, Japanese aircraft enjoyed a distinct edge in performance over their American counterparts, especially with regard to range. Their aerial torpedoes were vastly superior. Unlike the great 1942 carrier battles, most U.S. carrier planes, like their nimbler opponents, as yet lacked pilot armor and self-sealing fuel tanks. The 2nd Carrier Division comprised superbly trained, battle-hardened aviators who played a lead role at Pearl Harbor. Although well trained, the *Saratoga* flyers lacked combat experience. Even so, McMorris, for one, felt confident of victory should the *Sara* engage an enemy carrier. Rather surprisingly given Japan's brilliant performance at Pearl, he declared on 22 December, "Such indications we have indicate no overwhelming [Japanese] superiority and our carrier people are good themselves."[38] That certainly was true by spring 1942 after the U.S. carriers flexed their muscles against weak targets. Yet in December 1941 American carrier aviation was still woefully green. Defensively TF-14 enjoyed the advantage of the *Sara*'s air search radar, but the cruisers and destroyers lacked radar of their own, whereas Japan excelled in night surface combat. Shipboard antiaircraft in both navies was weak in number and largely ineffective, a state of affairs that the United States rapidly changed for the better in 1942.

For the time being Fletcher would have had to show the wisdom to ignore the Wake invasion until after he dealt decisively with the carriers. His one chance to strike and emerge unscathed was to land the first blow and knock out the enemy flight decks, if not sink the carriers outright. If Wake fell in the meantime, he would have no way to get it back. The tactical situation was such that he had no land-based air support, unlike later at Coral Sea, Midway, and the Eastern Solomons. That crucial deficiency rendered him blind beyond the limited search radius (three hundred miles) of the *Sara*'s dive bombers. However many SBDs the vital, wide-perimeter dawn search absorbed correspondingly reduced the strength of the strike. Perhaps Fletcher could have counted on only twenty SBDs and the eleven TBDs for a first attack wave, with a fighter escort only *if* he had retained VMF-221 on board. Prior to dawn on the twenty-third, Abe dispatched small strikes against Wake. Thus it would have taken time, once he became aware of Fletcher's presence, to regroup, locate the *Saratoga*, and attack. In that interval the 2nd Carrier Division would be especially vulnerable, although with two flight decks as opposed to Fletcher's one, Abe was less likely to be crippled by a lucky hit. The *Sara*'s own search had to perform flawlessly, with clear radio communications and accurate position estimates (which happened rarely even in 1942) to enable her strike to find the target. That attack had better be especially accurate just to give Fletcher a chance to survive. The Japanese enjoyed a far superior search network in the crucial area. An attack in strength by the 2nd Carrier Division, particularly with torpedoes, would imperil the *Saratoga*. Thus the odds definitely favored the *Sōryū* and *Hiryū*. Perhaps the most Fletcher could have accomplished was to trade the *Sara* for one carrier. Admiral Murphy judged in 1951 that the outcome of a fight between the two elite Japanese carriers and the *Saratoga* would have been, "to say the least, very doubtful." Even the addition of the *Lexington* might only "have assured less than an even chance of victory."[39]

Kinkaid later concluded that if Pye and Fletcher really knew ahead of time of a second Wake invasion force, they might have taken "extraordinary steps." Vice Adm. Paul D. Stroop, who in 1941 was Fitch's flag secretary, speculated that had his boss been in charge the night of 22 December he might have taken the *Saratoga* ahead along with some of the fueled destroyers and left the rest to follow with the *Tangier*. The goal would be to get the marine fighters to Wake as early as possible after dawn on the twenty-third, launch a strike on the invaders from two hundred miles out from Wake, then run in to 125 miles to recover those planes. Stroop did not anticipate a carrier battle until the twenty-fourth, an unreasonable surmise given the actual movements of the 2nd Carrier Division. For his own part Kinkaid thought nothing that actually did occur justified a change in plan. He deemed any wild rush toward Wake as pure recklessness.[40]

What if Pye had unleashed Fletcher after the invasion of Wake? When he ordered the recall, he had no clear idea, due to strict radio silence, exactly where two of his three carrier forces were. Based on the plan, which he had every reason to believe Fletcher was following, he assumed TF-14 (*Saratoga*) was five hundred miles northeast of Wake. Actually Fletcher was 440 miles northeast. Pye knew from Brown's message that TF-11 (*Lexington*) steamed northwest just beyond the five-hundred-mile air search arc from Wotje. In fact, Brown was 975 miles southeast of Wake and 660 miles southeast of TF-14 and could draw just within air strike range of Wake at sunrise on 25 December. For Halsey's TF-8 (*Enterprise*), Pye could only go by the operating limits he set. Halsey was about 1,140 miles northeast of Wake and 750 miles east of TF-14. Such long distances, coupled with his lack of a fleet oiler, prevented Halsey from offering support anywhere near Wake. Indeed no task force was within a day's steaming of another. Fitch, on the other hand, "felt convinced that a vigorous move-in to the atoll would result in hitting the Japanese when they could least afford to receive such a blow."[41]

Fitch was correct. If at 0400 on 23 December Fletcher had cast loose the *Tangier* and *Neches* and started in at twenty knots with his fueled destroyers, he would still be too distant for the *Sara*'s aircraft to locate any enemy forces that day or even to search immediately adjacent to Wake. By sunset the main Japanese supporting cast had retired out of range—Abe's carrier force west for a hero's welcome in Japan and Gotō's heavy cruisers south to Kwajalein. TF-14 could not have harmed the enemy on 23 December. Neither could TF-11. Even had Brown raised speed to twenty knots, a long run hurdling the date line would, by dawn on 24 December, have put him no closer to Wake than five hundred miles. Much would have depended on whether air searches spotted either TF-14 or TF-11 on 23 December. That day five land-attack planes based at Roi assumed air search duties around Wake and east of there. They did not fly far enough to sight either TF-14 or TF-11 had Fletcher or Brown continued to advance.[42] The door was wide open for a nasty surprise at Wake on 24 December. Lulled by the devastation at Pearl, Combined Fleet certainly discounted any serious attempt to relieve Wake or to counterattack. A dawn raid on the twenty-fourth by the *Saratoga* would have raised havoc with the light cruisers, destroyers, and transports huddled around Wake and given the Allies a wonderful, though fleeting, Christmas gift. Wake would remain Japanese no matter what Fletcher could have done. Afterward TF-14 should have retired beyond range of any possible counterattack and rejoined the *Neches* well to the northeast. The criticisms of Fitch and the many others over Pye's recall were valid. However in Pye's defense, he could not know the Japanese were so lackadaisical, that their heavy forces would pull out almost immediately and that no bombers were based at Rongelap, which was considerably closer to Wake than the real base at Kwajalein. Most importantly he felt little inclination to gamble with the Pacific Fleet's few remaining assets.

POSTMORTEM

On Christmas morning Adm. Chester Nimitz emerged from a flying boat to meet Capt. William W. Smith waiting in the admiral's barge. He asked about the Wake relief and, when informed of the recall, inquired whether the order came from Washington. Told it had not (which was not entirely true), Nimitz kept his thoughts to himself. Although "disappointed," he considered the failed Wake relief to be "all water over the dam & finished business." He "did not waste time in speculation on *what might have been done* [his emphasis]." TF-14 was understandably embittered over drawing so close to Wake, but not fighting to save it or avenge its fall. To slink away was especially disheartening. Very few knew the whole story. Of those who did, no one faulted Fletcher for following the plan, for being precisely where he was supposed to be, and for obeying direct orders to withdraw. Likewise Stroop noted that Fitch evinced no resentment at all over Fletcher's handling of the relief. Meeting Fletcher and Kinkaid upon their return, Pye apologetically explained that the "heart breaking" decision to recall TF-14 had been difficult but reflected "his best judgment."[43]

In Washington the reaction also was dismay and anger, but never directed at the largely anonymous Fletcher. The president had followed the progress of the Wake relief, even querying his naval aide, Capt. John R. Beardall, about the characteristics of the *Tangier*, too new to be in his naval register. Capt. Frank Beatty, Knox's aide, asked Stark whether he would tell the president of Pye's recall order. The CNO sighed, "No, Frank, I wouldn't have the heart." Knox himself reluctantly took the bad news to the White House and later confided to Beatty that Roosevelt considered not fighting for Wake to be "worse" than Pearl Harbor. Knox commiserated with a sympathetic Churchill, who blandly observed it was "dangerous" to "meddle" with admirals, although that never stopped him. Stark formally requested Pye's reasons for the recall, and in January 1942 the Roberts Pearl Harbor Commission grilled him about the abortive Wake relief. "Perhaps Pye's decision about the relief of Wake was correct," King later commented. "I do not blame him." Roosevelt did not feel as charitable. Pye incurred his lifelong wrath over Wake.[44]

The defense of Wake rightly held the spotlight as an exemplar of U.S., more specifically, Marine Corps heroism. After the war Wake came under new scrutiny by Morison and marine Lt. Col. Robert Debs Heinl, who rode the *Tangier* during the relief and strongly regretted not reaching Wake. Their books colored the image of Fletcher that appeared in most subsequent treatments.[45] Yet they showed no clear understanding of the actual circumstances behind the Wake relief, why it was attempted, and how Cincpac and his task force commanders went about it. Morison and Heinl did not realize that yet again Kimmel's fundamental error was to underestimate the Japanese and continue to act as if he knew their intentions rather than carefully assessing their true capabilities. Despite radically changed conditions, Kimmel and McMorris opted for essentially a reprise of the prewar Marshalls reconnaissance plan. They strongly believed that in the short run Wake could hold out. The Japanese were not going to return in time to interfere with the relief. Inexplicably given how the enemy carriers proved so devastatingly effective in the Pearl Harbor attack, Kimmel and McMorris completely ignored possible carrier opposition off Wake. Despite committing three carriers, the U.S. forces were too far from each other and could be destroyed in detail by a weaker, but concentrated force. Having not discerned this root cause of the relief fiasco, Morison and Heinl compounded their error with a shallow analysis that failed to probe the series of key blunders that proceeded from Cincpac's original misjudgment. Kimmel saw no need to execute the relief with all possible haste. His staff failed to expedite preparation of the *Tangier*. Kimmel then split his limited carrier strength. If he had truly worried about the imminent fall of Wake, he should have immediately sent the *Lexington* and *Tangier*, followed by the *Saratoga* and *Enterprise* in support.[46] Moreover, the Jaluit diversion deprived the relief force of the only available fast oiler, leaving Fletcher with the *Neches* as his ball and chain. Morison and Heinl never examined the reality of the Pacific Fleet's first harsh experiences with underway refueling in wartime and the unsettling discovery that the actual radius of action of all ships proved dramatically less than peacetime experience ever hinted.[47]

The inability of Brown's TF-12 to refuel at sea on 11–12 December and the delay in readying the *Tangier* effectively ended any real chance for aid to get to Wake ahead of another, far more powerful assault. That was not what an embattled Kimmel came to believe. In 1964 he described his relief plan, which was never intended to engage strong enemy forces, as an "attack."[48] Kimmel's partisans deplored the failed Wake relief as a tragically lost opportunity for his vindication. One book incredulously characterized the original relief plan as a "bold and tactically imaginative scheme" to "lure the Japanese into a trap," which, when Kimmel was relieved, the enemy was "preparing to steam right into." Although Kimmel had "disposed his forces for a decisive naval engagement," Pye and Fletcher subsequently spoiled the chances for victory by their timidity—or perhaps even outright cowardice—with Fletcher possibly "intentionally prolonging his refueling."[49] In the same vein Capt. Edward L. Beach, a severe critic of Fletcher as well as a strong Kimmel supporter, recently declared that Kimmel's orders for the relief, "if carried out as planned," would "unquestionably have succeeded." Beach speculated, "Most likely Wake would not have been captured at all," or the garrison would have been "rescued . . . with ease."[50] The reader can judge whether the facts support these suppositions.

Because of Heinl and Morison and those who echo their assertions, Fletcher is cast in folklore as the gutless admiral who "let the Corps down . . . when he had been sent to relieve the beleaguered men on Wake Island and turned back pleading lack of fuel, though his own logs proved he had plenty."[51] Instead, the historiography of the Wake relief is a classic example of the pitfalls of history written by biased contemporaries without the benefit of the whole story. Admiral Murphy's scathing review of Morison's treatment of the Wake relief called it "not even a reasonable facsimile of history," that "does grave injustice to Admiral Fletcher." Murphy was certainly in a position to know the real facts. He judged the "failure to relieve Wake was due, not to poor seamanship and want of decisive action, but to the presence of two Jap first line carriers." Due to postwar rancor, Fletcher unjustly became the scapegoat for the fall of Wake. His detractors refused to realize that in December 1941 the badly wounded Pacific Fleet simply was not capable of functioning properly immediately after such a huge disaster as Pearl Harbor. Someone had to take the blame for Wake, and Fletcher was an altogether too convenient mark.[52]

CHAPTER 4

To Samoa with a Carrier

THE NEW REGIME

After two frustrating weeks at sea, Task Force 14 entered Pearl Harbor on 29 December 1941, having done nothing to save Wake Island or even retaliate for its fall. On the plus side of the ledger, Fletcher could only mark the reinforcement of Midway. Reporting for his arrival call, he learned to his pleasure that Chester Nimitz would take over the Pacific Fleet on the thirty-first.[1] A 1905 Annapolis graduate, the fifty-six-year-old Nimitz possessed a gracious, cheerful personality and optimistic outlook that seemed ideal to restore sagging morale in Hawaii. They knew each other well from their mutual sojourns in Washington, although they were not particularly close. Having seen Nimitz hurdle all of the obstacles raised by the president, Congress, and the Navy Department, Fletcher respected him as an excellent administrator and a calm, resolute, and unflappable leader.

President Roosevelt personally chose Nimitz for Cincpac, but CNO Stark had preferred his own assistant, Rear Adm. Royal E. Ingersoll. Nor did Roosevelt's selection overawe the rest of the navy. An early submariner and expert in diesel propulsion, Nimitz eventually broadened his career to cruisers and battleships. Not since the 1920s, when he studied at the Naval War College and served on the staff of the commander in chief of the U.S. Fleet, had Nimitz moved within the inner councils that formulated fleet strategy and doctrine. Moreover, he never exercised senior leadership in the massive fleet problems that so dominated thinking in the prewar navy. Instead he made his reputation pushing papers during two tours (1935–38 and 1939–41) with the Bureau of Navigation, responsible for personnel. Rivals deplored Bunav denizens like Richardson, Nimitz, and Fletcher, all "Washington Repeaters" who reaped unearned benefit from their proximity to the power brokers. There was truth in this. Much later Nimitz revealed that in January 1941 Knox approached him, certainly at Roosevelt's behest, to offer the post of Cincpac. He declined because he regarded himself too junior. Had Nimitz become Cincpac in January 1941, the uproar would have exceeded even that which greeted Kimmel. Evidently Roosevelt considered Kimmel, with whom he was not well acquainted, just a peacetime taskmaster. According to Fleet Admiral King, Stark stated in the fall of 1941 that in the event of war, King would keep the Atlantic Fleet, Nimitz was to take over the Asiatic Fleet, and Ingersoll would become Cincpac. Events ultimately vindicated the brilliance of Roosevelt's choice, which he based on a close personal knowledge of Nimitz's qualities and talents. Not wedded to any particular faction, Nimitz approached his daunting task with an open mind. No one could have done a better job to revive the reeling Pacific Fleet. His courage, aggressiveness, and superb strategic insight played a major role in the defeat of Japan. But Nimitz acknowledged his intimidating task, writing home on 28 December 1941: "I am not discouraged and will do my best—but everyone must be very, very patient."[2]

Whether the new Cincpac, with his sunny disposition and piercing blue eyes, was really a fighter remained an open question for some senior officers. By contrast, no one who knew Adm. Ernest Joseph King, newly appointed commander in chief of the U.S. Fleet (Cincus), ever doubted his pugnacity. A 1901 Annapolis graduate (fourth in his class), King gravitated to aviation in 1927 as a JCL, earning his wings at age fifty. He held the top aviation administrative post (chief of Buaer) and the top carrier command (Aircraft, Battle Force, U.S. Fleet), but was bitterly disappointed in 1939 not to become the Chief of Naval Operations. A gloomy tour on the General Board boded retirement, but his appointment in late 1940 as commander of the Patrol Force (soon to become the Atlantic Fleet) revived his career. Since the spring of 1941 he waged an awkward undeclared war with German U-boats and raiders in the Atlantic. On 18 December Roosevelt reduced the role of the CNO largely to administration and logistics, in favor of a more powerful commander in chief of the U.S. Fleet. Unlike Kimmel, who was Cincus concurrently with Cincpac merely as a courtesy, King took firm control of all naval forces afloat. There was nothing courteous about King in the line of duty. He immediately changed the dreadful acronym Cincus (pronounced "sink us") to Cominch. Looking and acting younger than his sixty-three years, the intelligent, imperious, abrasive, and demanding King also possessed the moral strength and strategic insight to guide the U.S. Navy to victory in a global naval war. For the time being he worked in uneasy partnership with his colleague Stark, whose prestige with Roosevelt suffered because of the unforeseen dire situation in the Pacific. King also deeply distrusted ex-Bunav officers like Nimitz and Fletcher (protégés of the departed J. O. Richardson), whom he judged political admirals owing their advancement to their Washington connections. He called them "fixers," not in a corrupt sense, but because they always tried to smooth things out and not dispose of failing subordinates. King not only kept Nimitz on a short leash, but also soon sought to curtail much of Cincpac's real power.[3]

LOOKING TO SAMOA

Nimitz's arrival at Pearl coincided with deliberations over the next likely Japanese thrust east across the date line. To Stark, the principal South Pacific island groups appeared in special danger should Japan attempt to sever the lines of communication between the United States and New Zealand–Australia. Yet in that vast expanse of ocean the only significant American base was at Pago Pago on Tutuila in Eastern Samoa, which possessed only a modest marine garrison. New Zealand's defenses in Western Samoa were negligible. On 14 December Stark suggested to Kimmel that a marine regiment and defense battalion be shipped directly from San Diego to Samoa, a voyage of 4,180 miles. For close cover he earmarked the carrier *Yorktown* and four destroyers, expected at San Diego at the end of the year. To this

Adm. Ernest J. King, 1942. Autographed photo given to Admiral Fletcher.
Courtesy of American Heritage Center, University of Wyoming–Laramie

powerful nucleus he proposed to attach two old light cruisers *Richmond* and *Trenton* under Rear Adm. Abel Trood Bidwell, a recent flag selectee who would command the mission.[4]

Kimmel's planners were too preoccupied with potential combat in the Marshalls and at Wake to fret much about Samoa. On 15 December McMorris contemplated a much smaller Samoa reinforcement of only half as many troops and escorted merely by the two old light cruisers and a few destroyers. The *Yorktown* could better haul desperately needed aircraft out to Pearl, then deploy to the central Pacific. Anxious to get another carrier on line, Pye, Kimmel's interim successor, concurred. Stark left the decision to Cincpac, but again advocated the full reinforcement in one trip covered by the *Yorktown*. Pye assented on 28 December. Bidwell was to depart San Diego on 6 January. "Covering or diversion operations" were also contemplated. On 29 December Stark emphasized that the Japanese buildup in the Gilberts threatened both Samoa and the Fiji Islands and again desired some sort of "covering or diversion operations" in connection with the Samoan reinforcement.[5]

On 30 December King fired off his first directive to Cincpac. Stark's prior efforts to include the South Pacific within the Pacific Fleet's prime area of interest were but gentle nudges when compared to King's trumpet calls. Acknowledging the necessity of holding Hawaii and Midway, King decreed that "only in small degree less important" was defending the line of communication between the United States and Australia. Samoa was just the first step in extending fleet control westward to Fiji and beyond. The ultimate objective was to halt the Japanese advance and launch a counteroffensive. In a major reversal of prewar strategic policy, King with great perception and decisiveness postponed the concept of a gradual offensive

South Pacific

through the Marshalls and Truk toward the Philippines. For the next three months he would compel Cincpac to shift more and more of his resources southward to lay the groundwork for his new interim strategy. Nimitz's reluctance stoked his growing displeasure.[6]

The pair of rockets from Washington caused Pearl to rethink Samoa. Suddenly it seemed advisable both to beef up the reinforcement convoy and change commanders. Nimitz knew whom he wanted. He replaced the two aged light cruisers with the heavy cruiser *Louisville* and modern light cruiser *St. Louis*, and in place of the inexperienced Bidwell, assigned a new Task Force 17 and the Samoa mission to Fletcher. The *Yorktown* would not only protect the convoy, but also raid the central Pacific afterward. Thus Fletcher discovered on 30 December he was exchanging TF-14 for the equally important job of CTF-17. The news was not good for his friend Jake Fitch. Admiral Leary, a non-aviator, took over TF-14 with the *Saratoga*. Despite being one of only two carrier admirals in the Pacific Fleet, Fitch regretfully reverted to his role as Halsey's shore representative. With Halsey busy at sea leading the *Enterprise* task force, Nimitz needed a savvy administrator for Aircraft, Battle Force, to coordinate the operations and supply of all carrier aircraft ashore. At the same time Pye and

Rear Adm. Robert A. Theobald (commanding the Battle Force destroyers) joined Fitch as shore-bound planners and administrators, but Nimitz informed Stark he intended to employ them as relief task force commanders "as necessary." In turn Admiral Draemel formally replaced Capt. William W. Smith as Pacific Fleet chief of staff. Nimitz concentrated Draemel's talents on operations. He also desired a second flag officer in each carrier task force to command the cruisers and lead surface attack groups. Rear Adm. Raymond Spruance filled that role for Halsey's TF-8, Admiral Kinkaid was to join Leary's TF-14, while Smith fleeted up to rear admiral to take Newton's place in Brown's TF-11. For the time being, however, Fletcher was on his own until Nimitz could scrounge another cruiser admiral for TF-17.[7]

Fletcher had to get to San Diego as soon as possible to organize the Samoa convoy. On 30 December he hauled down his flag from the *Astoria*. The stalwart flag secretary Sam Latimer and flag lieutenant Harry Smith stayed with him, but his increased responsibilities required the much larger Cruisers, Scouting Force (Cruscofor) staff. They were at sea with Newton in the *Chicago*, part of Brown's TF-11 on an "offensive patrol" southwest of Oahu. Cincpac immediately recalled the *Chicago* to Pearl for the actual change of command on the morning of the thirty-first. At 1000 the *Chicago* moored northeast of Ford Island. At the same time Nimitz assumed command of the Pacific Fleet on the deck of the submarine *Grayling*. He liked to joke privately that a sub was the only ship the Japanese left for him at Pearl Harbor. Wearing his starched whites, Fletcher witnessed the ceremony, as all flag officers at Pearl were invited to attend, then hastened to the *Chicago* for his own change of command with Newton. That afternoon he collected part of his staff and repaired to the seaplane base for an overnight flight in a navy flying boat to San Diego.[8]

Fletcher and the Cruscofor staff certainly knew each other well. Capt. Spencer S. Lewis, Cdr. Gerard F. Galpin, and Lt. Charles B. Brooks Jr. were to accompany Fletcher, Latimer, and Harry Smith on the fourteen-hour flight. Lt. Cdr. Alexander C. Thorington, the assistant operations officer, was loaned to Poco Smith, who cobbled together a cruiser staff in the *Chicago* for TF-11. As befitted the chief of staff of a major command, Spence Lewis was an able, highly experienced senior captain. A 1910 Annapolis graduate, the fifty-three-year-old, short, slender, soft-spoken Texan was renowned for his professional ability, cordial personality, rich sense of humor, and uncanny knack of rolling his own cigarettes no matter how much a ship pitched and heaved. In 1917–18 he commanded the destroyer *Patterson* in combat in European waters, and from June 1939 to January 1941 was captain of the *Cincinnati* in Crudiv Three, where he won Fletcher's high regard. Lewis studied at the Naval War College and served on several staffs. As Fletcher's personal aide and closest advisor, he supervised the preparation of orders and plans and ran the staff. Fletcher also relied heavily on the talents of another Texan, Gerry Galpin (USNA 1921), the operations officer responsible for tactical planning. The near antithesis of Lewis in terms of personality, Galpin was a rather aloof, fussy character, somewhat forbidding for junior members of the staff, but sharp and able. The third member of the trio was Charles Brooks (USNA 1931), the quietly competent radio officer. For the time being the bobtailed TF-17 staff made do without its communication watch officers and the enlisted yeomen, radiomen, signalmen, quartermasters, and marines, as well as the officers' cooks and stewards of the flag mess. In their place, the Naval Receiving Station at San Diego put together a scratch team under experienced chiefs.[9]

MEET THE *YORKTOWN*

On New Year's morning the huge Consolidated PB2Y-2 Coronado flying boat carrying Fletcher's party circled San Diego harbor before setting down at Naval Air Station (NAS) North Island. Dominating the view was the angular outline of a large carrier. A veteran of grueling "neutrality patrols" in the North Atlantic, the *Yorktown* had interrupted a refit in order to go to war in another theater. Ordinarily Fletcher would have hoisted his flag in the *Louisville* in his own Crudiv Four. However, Cincpac decreed the carrier task force commander must be in the carrier, the better to integrate air operations within the basic mission. Therefore Fletcher broke his two-star flag in the *Yorktown* to begin a memorable association. He was the proverbial stranger in a strange land. In place of the pleasing symmetry of a cruiser's triple gun turrets, twin raked funnels, and elegant clipper bow sprawled a vast, flat expanse of weathered timber that resembled the top of a giant raft. Its only protuberance was a high, narrow superstructure located amidships, but perched off center to starboard. The aptly dubbed "island" included the navigating bridge, flag bridge, air control center, a tripod mast with observation post, antiaircraft gun mounts, and a large stack. If a battleship resembled an iceberg with her mass mostly below the waterline, the boxlike carrier rode so high that it seemed the smallest wave could roll her right over. What the *Yorktown* lacked in nautical aesthetics she more than made up in raw firepower. Although commissioned in 1937 as the fifth American aircraft carrier (CV-5), she was the first that could truly be called modern. Displacing 19,800 tons over a length of 809 feet, the *Yorktown* could cut through the waves at an impressive thirty-two knots. As recent events so well demonstrated, the fragile carrier airplanes such as those wielded by the *Yorktown* Air Group now controlled the balance of naval power in the Pacific.[10]

The carrier task force commander allocated the resources of the carrier air group according to the basic mission. He decided the sectors to be searched and by how many planes, the targets to be attacked and the size and composition of the strikes, as well as the number of fighters retained for defense. Equally crucial, he maneuvered the task force during and after the conduct of these flights to facilitate the safe and speedy return of the aircraft. Had Fletcher's eyesight been sufficiently sharp in 1928 for him to earn his wings, he would have accrued the vast experience in fleet aviation his new job required. No longer could he rely on Fitch and the Cardiv One staff to handle the aviation end of task force operations, and his own Crudiv Four staff aviator, Lt. Cdr. Gordon A. McLean, was unavailable. Thus Fletcher desperately needed aviation guidance, and now in the midst of all his other obligations, he imbibed a crash course in the doctrine and tactics of carrier warfare. He naturally looked first to the *Yorktown*'s commanding officer, Capt. Elliott Buckmaster. A tall, dignified 1912 Annapolis graduate, "Buck" Buckmaster displayed an icy reserve that melted on closer acquaintance. After years in destroyers, he completed flight training in 1937 as a forty-seven-year-old commander, the very last "Johnny come lately." Buckmaster became executive officer of the *Lexington* and commanding officer of the naval air station at Pearl Harbor before getting the *Yorktown* in February 1941. Like all JCLs, he had no actual squadron flight duty and little practical aviation experience. That deficiency meant a great deal to his talented but prickly executive officer, Cdr. Joseph J. "Jock" (later "Jocko") Clark (USNA 1918), who declared the "leadership" in the *Yorktown* "left a great deal to be desired." The senior aviator on board in terms of time, having earned his wings eleven years before Buckmaster, Clark was only too eager to tell his neophyte captain how to run his carrier and differed with him on nearly every crucial issue. To make matters more difficult, he was himself promoted to captain in January 1942, but without new orders. As a courtesy to Buckmaster, Clark did not assume the higher rank while in the *Yorktown*.[11]

Although the "fresh-caught" Buckmaster possessed a limited aviation background, he was an able officer who wisely understood he needed expert advice. To Clark's intense displeasure he reached down past his executive officer to the aviators who actually ran his air group: the air officer, group commander, and squadron commanding officers. The pilots naturally favored such an "enlightened approach." They reciprocated their captain's trust and grew to like him once they got to know him. Unburdened by outmoded doctrine, Buckmaster allowed squadrons to experiment with new ideas. Consequently the *Yorktown* Air Group became one of the very best in the fleet. Jock Clark, on the other hand, was a "hard man," haughty, demanding, and at least in the *Yorktown*, lacking a sense of humor or even a smile. He did not seem willing to share the wisdom of his long aviation career, and the pilots could never draw him out from behind his domineering personality. A severe stomach ulcer exacerbated his naturally acerbic disposition.

Fletcher soon discerned the complex politics on board his new flagship, with the strong tension between commanding officer and executive officer. His knowledge of naval aviation lore was far less than Buckmaster's, and his need was equally great. Once he settled in, Fletcher adopted Buckmaster's own solution and regularly consulted the top aviators with the most recent active service, such as air officer Cdr. Henry F. MacComsey and group leader Cdr. Curtis S. Smiley. Indeed, Smiley recalled that Fletcher came to treat him like a member of his staff. Later to learn more about naval aviation (and his men), Fletcher trolled deeper among the air group, often summoning junior pilots to flag plot to ask about their flights. Thus he steered clear of Clark, who would have gladly played Ludendorff to his Hindenburg and taken charge of everything. By his own account Clark later regaled Cominch with his displeasure at both Fletcher and Buckmaster. In fairness it must be said that Clark was an outstanding officer and very highly regarded by the enlisted men. He became one of the navy's finest carrier captains and task force commanders. It seems he just needed to run the show.[12]

OUTFITTING FOR SAMOA

Fletcher's orders specified that he depart San Diego on 6 January and reach Tutuila on the twentieth. He was to transport Brig. Gen. Henry L. Larsen's Second Marine Brigade (forty-eight hundred men) and a recently organized navy scouting detachment of six unassembled float planes, plus all their gear and additional supplies. The fast convoy comprised the ammunition ship *Lassen*, modern fleet oiler *Kaskaskia*, three big Matson liners *Lurline*, *Monterey*, and *Matsonia*, and cargo ship *Jupiter*. Loading began on 1 January, and on the fifth, Fletcher wrote Nimitz that "in spite of numerous obstacles and delays it is expected this force will depart tomorrow" on schedule. He praised the personnel of the naval districts at San Francisco and San Diego, as well as the marines, "who made every effort to get all essential material loaded in time." The combatant portion of TF-17 comprised the *Yorktown*, heavy cruiser *Louisville*, light cruiser *St. Louis*, and the destroyers *Hughes*, *Sims*, *Russell*, and *Walke* of Capt. Frank G. Fahrion's Destroyer Division (Desdiv) Three. In lieu of a separate flag officer, Capt. Elliott B. Nixon of the *Louisville* led the cruiser task unit. Nixon was familiar to Fletcher because his cruiser had served with Crudiv Six during fleet exercises.[13]

The *Yorktown* was not only Fletcher's first carrier, but also his first radar-equipped ship. In October 1940 she received the last of the original six CXAM air search radar sets, the navy's first operational radar. The process had just begun to outfit all of the warships in the fleet with air search and fire control radars. The *Yorktown*'s radar operator was Rad. Elec. Vane M. Bennett, one of the most valued radar specialists in the navy. The arduous North Atlantic neutrality patrols demonstrated radar's great value both for air operations and surface search. Fletcher visited the radar shack to discuss the capabilities of radar and impressed Bennett with his general knowledge of radar and the quality of questions he posed to elicit advice on how best to use radar and forward the information where it was most needed. The tin cans likewise sported air search radars, the newer but less effective SC, nicknamed "Sail Cast." The *Louisville* had no radar whatsoever, but the *St. Louis* was equipped with an early fire control radar with a limited surface search capability. The *Yorktown* and the destroyers had the talk-between-ships (TBS) voice very high frequency (VHF) radios that allowed relatively secure short-range communications, but the cruisers lacked that useful device.[14]

Cincpac's operation order and subsequent intelligence correctly discounted other than a submarine threat to the Samoa reinforcement. Fully occupied in conquering the Far East, Japan could spare only a few subs and two auxiliary cruisers for the South Pacific. The menace to Samoa appeared more theoretical than real, but Nimitz was not about to take any chances. He advised Fletcher that a carrier task force from Pearl might conduct a "covering operation," either a diversionary raid against the Mandates or direct support of TF-17 off Samoa. In turn Fletcher cautioned Nimitz on 5 January not to take Japanese passivity for granted, especially as the "composition and destination of this force is common knowledge." Numerous crates stocked at dockside prominently displayed the address "Supply Officer, Naval Station, Tutuila, Samoa." Even before receiving Fletcher's letter, Nimitz informed King that should the Japanese appear in strength off Samoa, he would redirect the reinforcement convoy to Pearl, unless King desired it farther west at Fiji. Fletcher would remain off Samoa until the convoy completed delivery, and thereafter undertake an offensive task or proceed to Pearl. Nimitz believed unloading would take eight days, but Fletcher had his doubts. The best estimate in San Diego from those knowledgeable about conditions at Samoa was two weeks. Consequently he suggested that Nimitz release TF-17 after the three liners and the *Kaskaskia* had off-loaded. After consulting Buckmaster, Fletcher had the scouting detachment removed from the carrier. To off-load it, the *Yorktown* would have to go into Pago Pago, a risky action Fletcher wanted to avoid. Tutuila lacked an airfield, and it was folly to immobilize a carrier in port with her planes stuck on board. He directed two float planes be assembled and placed on the *St. Louis*, with the rest loaded on the *Jupiter*. The *Yorktown* was already overcrowded with 101 planes: a cargo of thirty-two aircraft (twenty fighters, nine dive bombers, and three J2F-5 utility planes) destined for Pearl in addition to her own air group (eighteen fighters, thirty-nine dive bombers, and twelve torpedo bombers). Because of the congestion, she operated only thirty-one of the SBDs.[15]

On the morning of 6 January just as TF-17 was about to sail, a sudden serious illness consigned Sam Latimer to the San Diego Naval Hospital. Harry Smith assumed the duties of flag secretary as well as flag lieutenant. Fletcher experienced another setback when the master of the *Jupiter* reported her civilian crew refused to sail in protest over the lack of an adequate supply of cigarettes. No doubt wishing the navy rather than the merchant marine manned that ship, an irritated Fletcher enlisted the aid of the Eleventh Naval District authorities. After a "slight delay," the *Jupiter* got under way along with the rest of the convoy. TF-17 cleared the channel, formed up in circular formation, and set course southwest at 15.5 knots, top speed for the *Lassen* and *Jupiter*. On 8 January Nimitz ordered Fletcher to keep to the scheduled arrival date at Samoa, even if he could actually get there earlier. "Unless inadvisable," TF-17 was to pass one hundred miles south of Christmas Island and on the morning of 19 January reach a specific point near Pukapuka northeast of Tutuila. Obviously Cincpac coordinated Fletcher's operations with someone else.[16]

"UNDERTAKE SOME AGGRESSIVE ACTION"

On 2 January barely after settling in, the new Cominch in Washington prodded Nimitz into action. The situation in the Far East demanded earnest effort by the Pacific Fleet to divert Japanese strength away from the Philippines and the Dutch East Indies, just as contemplated in prewar plans. As before, the burden would fall on the few available mobile task forces built around the carriers and cruisers, only now without battleship support. King also had his own reasons for an early offensive move. Wary of the threat to Fiji and Samoa, he ordered Nimitz to raid the Gilberts and also the Ellice Islands should the enemy advance there. These attacks preferably would be in concert with the arrival of the reinforcement convoy at Samoa. "Undertake some aggressive action for effect on general morale," King admonished. Nimitz replied that such operations were "contemplated and under consideration."[17]

McMorris's War Plans Section offered various attack scenarios. To provide a diversion for the Samoa reinforcement (and finally to execute the navy's first offensive move), he suggested on 2 January that Brown's TF-11 (*Lexington*) strike the outer Marshalls (Wotje and Maloelap) on 13 or 14 January and that Halsey's TF-8 (*Enterprise*) hit the Gilberts on the seventeenth. In the meantime Leary's TF-14 (*Saratoga*) would cover Oahu to westward. Evidently not eager as yet to run such risks, Nimitz asked Pye, his closest advisor, to examine the strategic and tactical aspects of the Samoa mission. Pye's study, dated 8 January, recommended that TF-8 be sent south to cover the arrival of TF-17 at Samoa. Disagreeing as usual with McMorris, he declared "unsound" any prior diversionary raid by Halsey against the Marshalls and Gilberts, but called for offensive action by both carrier task forces after the Samoa convoy had safely accomplished its mission. TF-8 should include four extra destroyers to beef up Fletcher's inadequate screen against the threat posed by subs. Pye also recommended that six B-17 bombers and six PBY flying boats fly shuttle searches between Canton in the Phoenix Islands (seven hundred miles north of Samoa) and Suva in Fiji southwest of Samoa. These patrols would cover the front door, so to speak, and warn of enemy surface forces threatening Samoa from the Marshalls. Pye judged the best post-raid targets to be Mili in the southeastern Marshalls and Makin-Tarawa in the Gilberts. Reflecting the prevailing conservatism, he warned these attacks should be made, "if at all," with "a complete understanding of the risk involved in attacking with a carrier within 500 miles of a possible land-based bomber group at Jaluit." Given that Japanese bombers had destroyed the *Prince of Wales* and *Repulse*, his caution is understandable. After simultaneous dawn raids against Mili and the Gilberts, the two carrier task forces should remain within mutual support range (two to three hundred miles) while withdrawing. The air search shuttling between Canton and Fiji should locate and bomb any pursuers.[18]

Nimitz adopted Pye's plan to have Halsey cover Samoa, and then during the first week of February lead TF-8 (*Enterprise*) and TF-17 (*Yorktown*) against Mili, Maloelap, and Wotje in the Marshalls and Makin in the Gilberts. He preferred to delay those attacks until Fletcher could be released from Samoa, "to more positively insure success [for] that expedition and to avoid serious situation that would arise if one carrier were damaged 2,000 miles from base while operating without other carrier support." Nimitz also arranged for his own subs to conduct an extensive reconnaissance of the Marshalls. For his own part Halsey jubilantly described his part of the proposed raids as a "rare opportunity." TF-8 sailed on 11 January with the *Enterprise*, four heavy cruisers (including the *San Francisco* meant for TF-17), twelve destroyers (including three for Tutuila), and the oiler *Platte*. Another Fueling Group (oiler *Sabine* and a destroyer) likewise started south to fuel TF-17 off Samoa. Cincpac Op-Ord 3-42 and Op-Plan 4-42 directed Halsey to be near Samoa prior to 20 January to cover TF-17, then at his discretion arrange for TF-8 and TF-17 to strike the northern Gilberts or the eastern Marshalls or both. Thus Nimitz committed half his carriers to the Samoa mission and post reinforcement raids, while retaining the *Lexington* and *Saratoga* to protect the Midway–Hawaii–Johnston island axis. This contrasted sharply with Kimmel's scattergun response to the attack on Wake.[19]

While Nimitz planned the first U.S. carrier raids, Yamamoto redeployed Nagumo's *Kidō Butai* south from Japan to support the offensives in the Southern Area. On 8 January the *Akagi*, *Kaga*, *Shōkaku*, and *Zuikaku* left for Truk; the *Sōryū* and *Hiryū* started for Palau four days later. Yamamoto had wondered whether the U.S. carriers he missed at Pearl Harbor might attempt retaliatory strikes, perhaps even against the homeland. Should there be such a threat, some carriers might have to remain north to deal with it. Rear Adm. Ugaki Matome, Combined Fleet chief of staff, too, had recognized the potential for mischief on the part of the U.S. mobile forces. On 26 December, though, he judged that unlikely until after the Pacific Fleet could reorganize from the devastating blow it had suffered. Consequently the Japanese carriers went south.[20]

The same day (11 January in Oahu, 12 January in Japan) that Halsey sailed from Pearl, two enemy actions, one trivial and the other profound, caught Nimitz's full attention. Before dawn on 11 January Cdr. Yamada Takashi's *I-20* popped to the surface off Tutuila's north coast and loosed a dozen 14-cm shells into the naval station. Yamada subsequently reported "no significant enemy activity" and went on his merry way to reconnoiter Fiji. Damage was minor, but Nimitz wondered whether the Japanese might have more in mind for Samoa. The second event occurred that evening southwest of Oahu. While Leary's TF-14 steamed at fifteen knots, a torpedo from the *I-6* stove in the *Saratoga*'s port side amidships, flooded three fire rooms, and put her in a bad way. She limped back to Pearl on 13 January. That ended the neat balance Nimitz hoped to effect with two carriers north and two south of the equator. Now only Brown's *Lexington* protected the central Pacific. Dismayed, Nimitz ordered him to depart on 19 January to patrol off Christmas Island eleven hundred miles south of Hawaii. From there he could support Halsey and Fletcher if they got in trouble after the raids. Halsey's TF-8 (*Enterprise*) would move northwest of Samoa about 18 January to cover Fletcher's approach and arrival. His three destroyers should reach Pago Pago on 19 January to beef up antisubmarine defenses. The *Sabine* would loiter southeast of Samoa ready to fuel TF-17 when necessary. Clearly Cincpac committed even stronger forces than anticipated to ensure the safety of the Samoa reinforcement and perhaps to forestall any premature attacks that King might propose for elsewhere. Combined Fleet headquarters received with some skepticism, at least initially, the report from the *I-6* that it had sunk a *Lexington*-class carrier, but it certainly reinforced the impression that the Pacific Fleet must be immobilized for the immediate future.[21]

A few misadventures marked Fletcher's voyage to the South Pacific. From 8 to 14 January three Grumman F4F-3 Wildcats of the *Yorktown*'s Fighting Squadron Forty-two (VF-42) splashed on takeoff, but all the pilots were rescued. On 16 January TF-17 fueled from the *Kaskaskia* six hundred miles northeast of Samoa. The next day while maneuvering alongside the *Yorktown*, the oiler "nearly caused a serious collision and endangered the success of the mission." On the eighteenth the *Jupiter* dropped behind because of condenser problems, but soon rejoined the convoy. The next day with Samoa only 275 miles ahead, Fletcher released the three great Matson liners and two destroyers to proceed ahead at twenty knots and reach Tutuila the following morning. The balance of the convoy was to arrive either late on the twentieth or the next day. Before dawn on 20 January the *Yorktown* sent a Grumman J2F utility amphibian to nearby Pago Pago on Tutuila to deliver official mail. By 1230 it was back bearing welcome tidings. Tutuila advised that the harbor could accommodate all six ships of the train at a time, whereupon Fletcher immediately detached the *Lassen*, *Kaskaskia*, *Jupiter*, and one destroyer. Marking time about one hundred miles northwest of Samoa, Halsey's TF-8 had already provided the three destroyers to patrol off Tutuila for subs. The third and most welcome development was that upon completion of its Samoan duties, TF-17 would join TF-8 to attack the Marshalls and Gilberts.[22]

CHAPTER 5

The First Counterattack

PLANNING THE STRIKES

On 20 January Fletcher gladly read Halsey's orders for simultaneous raids by TF-8 and TF-17 against the Marshalls and Gilberts six days after they left Samoan waters. They could not depart until the troops had disembarked, but Fletcher did not know how long that might take. In the first true demonstration of his boldness as a war leader, Halsey daringly chose Jaluit as his main objective, rather than an outpost atoll. He definitely exceeded Cincpac's original intent, if not his actual orders. U.S. subs poking around the mysterious Marshalls discovered especially heavy activity there and at Kwajalein. Halsey estimated Jaluit might have eighty planes of all types. Just to get within strike range meant penetrating the 170-mile gap between Mili and Makin, which only increased the risk of being spotted the day before the raid. The *Enterprise* and two cruisers would race ahead at twenty-five knots; the destroyers would follow at fifteen knots to save fuel. Jaluit would absorb nearly all the *Enterprise* strike planes and most of the *Yorktown*'s. The rest of the *Yorktown* group was to attack Makin, while the *Enterprise* fighters hit Mili 120 miles east of Jaluit.[1]

Still undecided on the exact attack sequence, Halsey's staff prepared three alternatives. Plan Afirm called for two *Enterprise* dive bombing squadrons (thirty-six SBDs) to depart just prior to sunrise from 175 miles southeast of Jaluit, while six fighters strafed Mili. TF-17, located sixty miles southeast of TF-8 and 170 miles south of Jaluit, was to contribute one dive bombing squadron to the Jaluit strike and send the other squadron southward against Makin. After the launch, both task forces would retire eastward at high speed, recover their planes, and hightail it away. Plan Baker was similar, except that if heavy ships were known to be at Jaluit, Halsey would take both carriers to 150 miles and employ their torpedo squadrons as well. If the weather cooperated, Plan Cast stipulated an earlier arrival at the launch point and spooky moonlit strikes at midnight, either with or without torpedo planes as circumstances dictated. Fletcher prepared for each contingency. Following Halsey's lead, he incorporated his big ships into a "striking group" and the four destroyers as a "support group" to save fuel. After launching the first air attack, the Striking Group would retire at high speed, rejoin the Support Group, and withdraw northeast. Thereafter Fletcher was to take care to stay 150 miles southeast of TF-8. Halsey planned only one flurry of strikes before hauling out northeast for Pearl. On the second morning after the attack, he wanted

Adm. William F. Halsey Jr., circa 1944.
Courtesy of U.S. Navy

to be more than a thousand miles northeast to meet the *Platte*. Fletcher likewise arranged to join the *Sabine* 160 miles southeast of Halsey's own fueling rendezvous.[2]

King waited impatiently for Nimitz's counterblow to unfold. Beginning on 17 January, radio intelligence, based on traffic analysis, detected a possible shift of strength from the Marshalls southwest to Truk. That became more evident on 20 January after the Australians reported about one hundred carrier planes pounded Rabaul on New Britain in the Bismarck Archipelago north of New Guinea. Rabaul indeed fell on 23 January, local time. King did not care for his carriers to linger too long at Samoa. On the twentieth he told Nimitz that merely advancing TF-8 and TF-17 northwest from Samoa "will afford adequate cover," and "the time factor appears paramount." A separate raid against Wake two or three days after the Halsey-Fletcher strikes would forestall any determined pursuit. With powerful forces evidently moving out of the Marshalls, Wake now looked exposed. Despite misgivings about committing all three carriers at once, Nimitz bent to Cominch's will. He arranged for the *Neches* to sail on 22 January and meet Brown six hundred miles west of Johnston. Brown was to bomb Wake and possibly also shell it with his cruisers. On 21 January Nimitz told Halsey and Fletcher it was "essential" to "expedite" the "execution of my Op-Plan 4-42." The carriers now needed only to cover Tutuila until the three big liners got clear, leaving the *San Francisco* and three destroyers to protect the *Lassen* and *Jupiter*. Nimitz also authorized Halsey to select targets in the inner Marshalls chain, namely Kwajalein and Jaluit, and thus belatedly sanctioned what Halsey had already decided.[3]

The fall of Rabaul convinced Capt. Jock Clark, the *Yorktown*'s headstrong executive officer, that TF-17 must attack there rather than the Marshalls. He tried to get Buckmaster not only to recommend the change of objective to Fletcher, but also to break radio silence to secure Nimitz's approval. Buckmaster refused. Clark brazenly went over his head to flag plot. Fletcher told him the plans could not be changed, but Clark loftily declared that "no plan should be absolutely inflexible." No doubt put off by the executive officer's effrontery, Fletcher naturally declined to stir up his superiors, who knew much more about the situation than did he or Clark. Later Clark personally relayed his version of that episode, and a great many other things, to King, who replied that the Cominch staff had briefly thought of that very thing. Of course neither Clark nor King considered the drawbacks of an improvised Rabaul raid, namely daunting logistics and at least two nearby Japanese carriers.[4]

On the evening of 22 January Fletcher flew a message to Tutuila for radio relay to Halsey. Nearly all the troops were ashore. He recommended TF-17 depart Samoa on 24 January. According to Halsey's timetable, the attacks would go in the morning of Sunday, 1 February, local time (Saturday, 31 January, east of the date line). Halsey concurred. On 24 January Fletcher again had Samoa radio advise that he would keep 150 miles astern of TF-8, then fuel and attack as ordered. That evening Halsey and Fletcher shoved off to the northwest toward the Phoenix Islands and the Mandates beyond.[5]

Ironically the nearest Japanese surface force to Halsey and Fletcher approached from the *northeast*. For nearly two months Rear Adm. Takeda Moriharu's 24th Cruiser Division, with the armed merchant cruisers *Hokoku Maru* and *Aikoku Maru*, prowled the southeast Pacific, but only managed to sink two Allied ships. So elusive was Takeda (and to his disgust, his prey) that intelligence bulletins merely offered vague warnings of commerce raiders far to the east near Easter Island. Now Takeda steamed back toward the Mandates through the very same waters Halsey and Fletcher intended to traverse. Fortunately for them, several false alarms slowed Takeda's progress, and squally weather on the twenty-sixth and twenty-seventh discouraged him from flying air searches. Consequently both task forces passed ahead of the oncoming Japanese—TF-17 within two hundred miles, but at night. Neither side was any wiser. Contact would have meant Takeda's swift destruction, but it also would have alerted Combined Fleet to American carriers in the South Pacific.[6]

King's uneasiness over the slow progress of Cincpac's developing raids deepened after 23 January, when a submarine picked off the star-crossed *Neches* 135 miles southwest of Oahu as she plodded without destroyer escort to her rendezvous with TF-11. As Brown lacked the fuel to continue to Wake, and no other oiler was available, Nimitz canceled the mission and recalled him to Pearl. With Rabaul in hand, Japan appeared ready to surge unchecked into the southwest Pacific. More evidence mounted that the Marshalls had been stripped of air and sea power to support the new advance. The U.S. counterstrike must take place as soon as possible. On 25 January Nimitz told his task force commanders that sub reconnaissance of Maloelap and Wotje showed that "all installations could be razed by bombing or bombardment with negligible risk." Two days later King condescending queried Cincpac: "Assume you are aware of serious threat to communications with Australia created by current enemy occupation of points especially Rabaul in Bismark [*sic*] archipelago." It was "inadvisable" to redirect part of Halsey's force westward (so much for Clark's idea to raid Rabaul). Thus, "it is essential that planned attack in Marshalls be driven home." Cominch felt pressured to act before the Japanese got the jump on his evolving South Pacific strategy and beat him to the crucial island groups. "Now is opportunity to destroy enemy forces and installations Gilberts Marshalls," Nimitz told Halsey and Fletcher. It was "essential that attacks be driven home," with "repeated air attacks and ship bombardments" as "feasible." The attacks could extend beyond one day, "if practicable." Although Nimitz's orders were unequivocal and aggressive, he worried about them, writing his wife on 29 January: "I do feel depressed a large part of the time but I always hope for a turn for the better."[7]

In this particular instance King could not complain about a lack of spirit either at Pearl or in the *Enterprise*. Halsey read the new orders just after he crossed the equator west of the Phoenix Islands. Cincpac now demanded a "close-in attack" against the Marshalls that effectively resurrected the old reconnaissance and raiding plan. The TF-8 staff, led by the intelligent but erratic Cdr. Miles R. Browning, recast the attack plans for TF-8 and TF-17. Browning "put a pencil on the chart and indicated the ideal spot from where we could do the most damage." There would be strikes against Wotje, Maloelap, and Kwajalein, now the prime objective. Just to get into range of Kwajalein, the *Enterprise* must launch from only a few miles north of Wotje. "To bring a carrier within visual distance of an enemy-held position," Halsey mused, "is not considered good practice." Even so, he shifted his approach nearly three hundred miles northward to the northern Marshalls and divided TF-8 into three task groups to hit widely separated targets. The first air strike was to go in fifteen minutes prior to sunrise. Spruance would bombard Wotje with two heavy cruisers and one destroyer, while the third heavy cruiser and two destroyers pounded Taroa in Maloelap atoll, also the target of a fighter sweep. Halsey alerted his task force to "be prepared for further attacks as ordered."[8]

As TF-17 fueled from the *Sabine* on 28 January, Halsey delivered new orders by plane to the *Yorktown*. Fletcher likely gave a shake of his head in amazement when he discovered how Halsey intended to rampage the northern Marshalls. TF-17 received the original objectives of Jaluit, Mili, and Makin, with the main effort against Jaluit. Other than decreeing simultaneous strikes timed to coordinate with his own assaults, Halsey left the details to Fletcher. He did suggest using nine SBDs and three torpedo-armed TBDs against Makin, where Cincpac intelligence placed an auxiliary seaplane tender servicing about seven large flying boats, and authorized Fletcher to bombard Mili and also Majuro and Arno atolls (north and northeast of Mili) "at discretion." Fletcher should repeat the attacks "as objectives and developments warrant," report results promptly, and inform him of particularly juicy ship targets. Halsey also promised to let him know when TF-8 pulled out and to tell him when to do the same.[9]

Fletcher retained the tactic of dividing TF-17 into a striking group (the *Yorktown* and two cruisers) and a support group (four destroyers under Captain Fahrion). From Point Ram the evening before the attack, the Striking Group was to sprint the last 215 miles at twenty-five knots west to the launch position. That was Point Bomb, which Fletcher relocated fifty miles northeast of the original launch point in case he decided to shell Mili. Point Bomb was within easy range of all three objectives, the farthest being Jaluit 140 miles northwest. At 0500 on 1 February (Z–12), the Striking Group was to reverse course to the east. The *Yorktown* would dispatch her air attacks and soon after rejoin the Support Group closing at fifteen knots. With sixty flyable aircraft (seventeen fighters, thirty-one dive bombers, and twelve torpedo bombers), the *Yorktown* wielded thirteen fewer planes than the *Enterprise* (eighteen fighters, thirty-seven dive bombers, and eighteen torpedo bombers). There were not enough torpedo planes to split between Jaluit and Mili as Halsey suggested. Fletcher retained his few fighters to protect the task force. He committed to the Jaluit strike Lt. Cdr. Robert G. Armstrong's Bombing Five (seventeen SBDs) and all twelve TBDs of Lt. Cdr. Joe Taylor's Torpedo Five, led by group commander Curt Smiley in an SBD. Jaluit was a large, irregularly shaped atoll, with the principal shore installations on the southeast portion of the rim. Fletcher still had no clear idea what was there, perhaps auxiliary ships, as well as submarines and aircraft. The mixed nature of the targets and the distance led him, on Buckmaster's advice, to arm the TBDs with three 500-pound bombs each instead of torpedoes, at least for the first strike. Scouting Five (Lt. Cdr. William O. Burch Jr.) received the other two targets: Makin located 130 miles south of the launch point and Mili some seventy miles north. Burch with nine SBDs would deal with the seaplane tender and flying boats at Makin, while Lt. Wallace C. Short took five more to Mili, another sizeable atoll. Each SBD carried a single 500-pound bomb.[10]

Fletcher wished to see what his strikes turned up before deciding his next course of action. He did plan one follow-up raid against Jaluit that afternoon, but never seriously considered bombarding Mili, Arno, and Majuro. TF-17 was considerably weaker than Halsey's TF-8. Both his cruisers lacked air search radar, which limited their effectiveness for independent missions. Also, Cincpac's 21 January message advised that a U.S. sub found no evidence of military activity whatsoever at Arno and Majuro. Honoring Halsey's injunction to repeat the attacks if required, Fletcher planned to withdraw east the evening of 1 February to meet his Fueling Group (*Sabine* and *Mahan*) conveniently parked near Point Ocean 440 miles east of Makin. After topping off destroyers, he would again plaster Jaluit and perhaps Makin on the morning of 3 February.[11]

THE APPROACH

U.S. naval intelligence correctly deduced the enemy carriers and most land-based air strength had deployed southwest beyond Truk, thus confirming the splendid opportunity to strike the Mandates. The capture of Rabaul (the "R" Operation) was the only foray into the "Southeast Area" that Imperial General Headquarters included in the first operational phase. Admiral Nagumo's *Akagi*, *Kaga*, *Shōkaku*, and *Zuikaku* supported that invasion while the *Sōryū* and *Hiryū* raided Ambon in the East Indies. By 31 January the *Akagi*, *Kaga*, and *Zuikaku* were anchored at Truk, the *Sōryū* and *Hiryū* returned to Palau, and the *Shōkaku* headed home to pick up aircraft. Admiral Inoue's South Seas Force focused on its offensive southward into the Bismarcks. Only nine of thirty-five medium bombers and nine of twenty-seven flying boats remained in the Marshalls. What is more, the Japanese relaxed their guard. The top commanders failed to heed an intelligence alert of increased U.S. radio activity in the central Pacific that might foreshadow an attack.[12]

On 29 January TF-8 conducted a daring midnight refueling of the *Enterprise* by the *Platte* that aptly illustrated the fleet's improving skills in that regard. It was the first time an oiler fueled a heavy ship in the dark. Afterward Halsey set course northwest at eighteen knots.

By sundown he was less than five hundred miles from the Mandates. At midnight he crossed the date line, skipping 30 January to jump to 31 January (Z–12 time). The longer than anticipated run to the target cost fuel that he must replace. The empty *Platte* and destroyer *Craven* left for Pearl. The oil already on hand might just bring TF-8 back to Pearl, but not if the offensive lasted beyond one day. Via a message later radioed by the *Platte*, Halsey informed Cincpac that if he did not send another oiler, "it will be necessary to withdraw after one day due to fuel requirements." Also on 29 January Fletcher completed fueling TF-17 about 150 miles south of TF-8. He detached the *Sabine* and *Mahan* to proceed to Point Ocean and counted on her fuel to see TF-17 home.[13]

Nimitz acted quickly to succor Halsey. In light of Cominch concern about enemy thrusts beyond Rabaul into the southwest Pacific, Nimitz examined deploying carriers far south of Pearl. Pye strongly recommended that after the Marshalls raid one of Halsey's carrier task forces veer south to Fiji rather than retire to Pearl. At the same time Brown's TF-11 with the *Lexington* would sortie from Pearl to take station west of Samoa. Together these two carriers could check forays toward the New Hebrides or New Caledonia. McMorris, as usual, clashed with Pye, calling the proposed deployment "too eccentric" and complained that it conflicted with the fleet's primary mission of defending Hawaii. McMorris much preferred keeping TF-11 in the central Pacific, either to follow up Halsey's strikes against the Marshalls or hit Wake. Nimitz had hoped to defer any decision regarding TF-11 until after Halsey and Fletcher attacked. Now he advised Halsey that Brown would sail on 31 January with the *Neosho*, the "only available tanker," to meet him two days following the attack one hundred miles northeast of the original fueling rendezvous. Even so, Nimitz gave Halsey the option to curtail the raids after the first day. After delivering the oil, Brown was to patrol southward as far as Canton Island, then return to Pearl around 16 February.[14]

Halsey and Fletcher next faced the hurdle of reaching their launch points undetected. On 31 January (Z–12), less than twenty-four hours before the scheduled attack, Fletcher belatedly discovered that the *Yorktown*'s air search had violated his strict orders not to be seen from land. On the morning of the twenty-seventh two SBDs flew over tiny Howland Island, the small sand spit Amelia Earhart failed to find in July 1937. The pilots now stated they found nothing amiss there, but that did not square with a message from Canton Island that Fletcher monitored on the thirtieth. Air reconnaissance on 28 January revealed that Howland and neighboring Baker Island recently suffered a severe bombing. The culprits were correctly assumed to be Makin-based flying boats. Based on what his pilots said, Fletcher deduced the bombing must have taken place either the afternoon of 27 January or early the following day, when TF-17 cruised only one hundred miles northwest of Howland. Japanese planes could have spotted either the *Yorktown* planes or the task force—a prospect with potentially dire consequences. Fletcher also sweated out daylight on the thirty-first when he might expect search planes from Makin or Jaluit, but nothing appeared on radar. Halsey was even luckier. That day radar detected an intruder within thirty miles of TF-8, but the bogey (an unidentified aircraft) neither changed course nor sparked any urgent messages. Halsey assumed haze hid his ships from view. Now it looked as if both task forces might surprise the enemy. Marine Capt. Bankson T. Holcomb, a Japanese linguist borrowed from Rochefort's ultrasecret Hypo radio intelligence unit, rode the *Enterprise*. Halsey mischievously directed

Holcomb to compose a message in Japanese taunting the search crew for its laxness and ordered hundreds of mimeographed copies be dropped during the next day's raids in the Marshalls. According to Halsey, Nimitz later chuckled at the story, but the episode discloses a casual attitude senior admirals showed at that time toward radio intelligence security. Halsey's joke in truth revealed that the raiders had discovered the searcher and knew it sent no warning.[15]

"THIS SUNDAY IT'S OUR TURN TO SHOOT!"

Reaching Point Ram on Saturday evening, the *Yorktown*, *Louisville*, and *St. Louis* upped speed to 25.5 knots, leaving Captain Fahrion's four destroyers to follow at a sedate fifteen. The weather turned ugly with a thickening overcast. The *Yorktown*'s aerologist, Lt. Cdr. Hubert R. Strange, forecast the next morning would be "sloppy," with a frontal zone hindering visibility over the task force and perhaps the targets as well. Even that unappealing estimate was a great understatement. Before dawn on 1 February a high overcast, punctuated by dark clouds, obscured the horizon that soon became less distinct as the moon set. To the northwest lightning flashes and squalls pointed the way to Jaluit. Figures scuttled around the thirty-two planes (four F4Fs for combat air patrol; the Jaluit strike of seventeen SBDs and eleven TBDs) squatting on the dark flight deck. Soon the deck blossomed with bright blue exhaust flames. Spectators filled "Vulture's Row" on the island catwalks eager to watch the *Yorktown*'s first battle launch. At 0452 the Striking Group turned northeast into the wind at Point Bomb. The planes took off without incident. Fletcher steadied his three ships due east at twenty-six knots, hurrying back the way he had come all night. The *Yorktown* swiftly respotted the flight deck with the second deck load of fourteen VS-5 SBDs destined for Makin and Mili. By 0604 both flights had departed, and Fletcher settled down to wait results. After sunrise at 0649 the cloud cover retained much murkiness. A few minutes later Fletcher welcomed the fine sight of Fahrion's four destroyers closing from the southeast. They maneuvered to form an antiaircraft screen around the carrier group, a timely precaution, when the *Yorktown*'s radar picked up a bogey twenty-five miles northwest. The interloper turned out to be a TBD with a mechanical malady. Its crew reported more horrible weather in the direction of Jaluit.[16]

By 0800 the fourteen Makin and Mili attackers circled overhead. Once on board, Burch briefed Fletcher about the converted seaplane tender and two flying boats moored in Makin lagoon. Though far from ideal, it turned out the weather was not a factor. Burch claimed two hits that set the tender afire, and destruction of both aircraft. In fact one bomb struck the stern of the transport/gunboat *Nagata Maru* (2,900 tons), causing "medium damage." Both flying boats burned. If Makin seemed an unlikely candidate for a second strike, Lieutenant Short judged Mili not even worth the first one. His five SBDs discovered nothing whatsoever of military value, understandable because Mili's garrison comprised merely a lookout post and a construction detail. Fletcher soon relaunched the fourteen dive bombers as a low-level anti-torpedo-plane patrol to help protect TF-17.[17]

With the Makin and Mili attackers safely in the fold, Fletcher concentrated his attention on Jaluit. At 0815 the *Yorktown* copied a radio message from Lt. Harlan T. Johnson, the popular VT-5 executive officer. He and a wingman were about to ditch on the northern fringe of Jaluit, far beyond any help Fletcher could offer. The weather around home plate dramatically worsened. Fletcher tried zigzagging around a series of vicious rain storms, but the squall line was too wide. By 0930 flying conditions deteriorated to the extent that he gave Buckmaster permission to recover all combat air patrol fighters and the fourteen SBDs. They started landing along with the first returning Jaluit attackers. Sheets of rain reduced visibility to a hundred yards, with wind gusts to fifty knots. Nevertheless the *Yorktown* continued recovering planes. Suddenly a VS-5 SBD from the anti-torpedo-plane patrol plowed into the sea close aboard the destroyer *Hughes*, wearing Fahrion's pennant. Fahrion alertly stopped so as not to lose sight of the ditched aviators and detailed the destroyer *Walke* to pick them up. In the midst of the storm, the *Walke*'s whaleboat bravely rescued both pilot and radioman. By 1010 Fletcher knew the *Walke* had on board two aviators, one believed suffering internal injuries.[18]

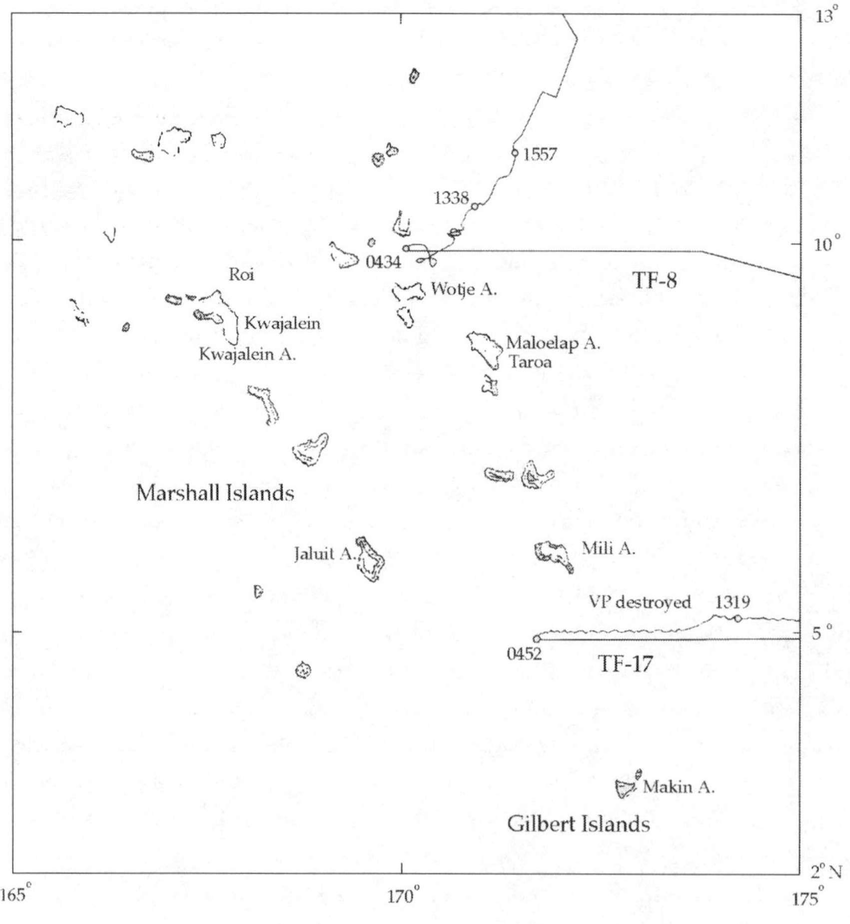

Raids, 1 February 1942

In the meantime Fletcher learned from the first of the Jaluit flyers that weather was causing great difficulty for the flight home. Some pilots radioed to ask the direction of the ship. Luckily the *Yorktown*'s YE radio homer functioned well, but Fletcher also permitted Buckmaster to break radio silence and provide a vector. At 1002, after learning more of the situation, Fletcher sent the destroyer *Russell* ten miles astern to direct lost planes to the task force and recover ditched crews. The wisdom of that decision swiftly became apparent at 1023, when one TBD radioed that another Devastator crew had taken to its raft after ditching twenty miles northwest of the task force. Concerned that the storm boiling westward might foil the rescue, Fletcher told Fahrion to take the *Hughes* and *Sims* and join the *Russell* searching astern of TF-17. Fahrion was to spread the three destroyers into a scouting line, sweep fifteen to twenty miles west, find the downed crew, and do what he could for other returning planes. When the squalls abated for a time, Fletcher also directed the *Walke*, which lacked a doctor, to transfer her hurt VS-5 passengers to the *Louisville* for medical care. Fortunately their injuries proved minor. In the meantime the *Yorktown* and *St. Louis* continued east at reduced speed. Fletcher's willingness to strip the *Yorktown* of nearly her entire destroyer screen and to slow a cruiser to save two aircrew would appear beyond reproach, but even that proved insufficient in Jock Clark's jaundiced view.[19]

By 1040 the last of the attackers were either stowed on board the *Yorktown* or beyond hope. One TBD made it on only two gallons of gasoline. The *Russell* proved invaluable in guiding stragglers toward the task force. Even so the *Yorktown* lost four VT-5 TBDs and two VB-5 SBDs from the Jaluit strike. From the squadron commanding officers, Fletcher and Buckmaster gained a grim sense of what transpired on the Jaluit mission. Neither VB-5 nor VT-5 completed its own rendezvous nor established tactical contact. Taylor, the commanding officer of VT-5, found himself totally alone. Smiley quickly lost control, but Armstrong, VB-5 skipper, got most of the aircraft to follow him. Hoping to assemble more planes, he delayed departure for twenty minutes. On the way out a rain squall forced him down to five hundred feet. Long before 0630, when Armstrong reached the vicinity of Jaluit, the formation broke beyond redemption. To make matters even worse, heavy thunderstorms blanketed Jaluit. From 0700 to 0750 *Yorktown* planes showed up in twos and threes. Perhaps fifteen SBDs and six TBDs actually bombed targets. No one got a clear look at the whole area. The planes either attacked the few visible large ships or settled for shore installations. The low ceiling forced VB-5 to dive bomb from low altitude, while the TBDs attempted abbreviated glide-bombing runs. Lt. William S. Guest of VB-5, the first to attack, apparently scored the only hit. He inflicted minor damage to the 8,600-ton transport *Kantō Maru*. The *Yorktown*ers claimed hitting another auxiliary, but the transport *Daidō Maru* sustained negligible harm. Some SBDs strafed small craft in the harbor or, like the TBDs, bombed sites on shore. One blessing was the paucity of air opposition, despite float planes buzzing the area. The attackers failed to sight three large flying boats moored there. These Japanese planes left Jaluit after the attack to find the U.S. carrier.[20]

ATTEMPTED RETALIATION

While looking for the downed TBD crew west of TF-17, Fahrion's three destroyers ran into snoopers probing the stormy skies. Emerging from clouds, one Type 97 flying boat started a bomb run against the *Russell* at 1109, only to be dissuaded by five-inch antiaircraft bursts. It then dropped a stick of four bombs that exploded harmlessly in the *Sims*'s wake. At 1117 the *Yorktown*'s CXAM radar discovered the bogey thirty-two miles due west about the same time Fahrion requested fighter support. Buckmaster scrambled six fighters in the midst of a rainstorm, but they sighted nothing. In turn the Kawanishi radioed base that two destroyers lurked 230 miles southeast of Jaluit, lost contact around 1145, and withdrew. Meanwhile, Fahrion searched where the hapless TBD went down an hour before. Lookouts in the *Hughes* noted an oil slick and wreckage, but no life raft. Satisfied by 1145 that under the circumstances he did all he could to find the missing aircrew, Fahrion rounded up his three destroyers and rang up thirty-five knots to overtake TF-17 to the east. The TBD crew was never recovered. In his memoirs Clark asserted that Fletcher and Buckmaster deliberately abandoned these aviators despite his urgent entreaty to turn the whole task force around and rescue them. He supposed Fletcher behaved so cravenly because he lacked "confidence in our air protection." Instead, "being masters of the local air situation, we could have easily recovered the three men without any real risk." In Washington the next month Clark related his version of these events to a receptive King and Rear Adm. Jack Towers, the chief of Buaer. It was an unforgivably malicious smear, given that Fletcher indeed sent three destroyers back amid turbulent seas to find this lost crew. Fletcher's career reveals numerous instances of his concern for his aviators.[21]

By noon Fletcher and his staff pondered their next move. He had hoped to unleash a second wave against Jaluit that afternoon. However, the weather was so poor, and the first strike took so long to get back (more than five hours), that any planes sent that afternoon could not reappear until after dark. Such marginal flying conditions made that an undesirable option. Figuring the enemy already knew about where he was, Fletcher broke radio silence at 1240 to transmit a summary to Halsey and Nimitz. TF-17 was "retiring for fuel[;] weather precludes further attack today." Captain Nixon in the *Louisville* inquired whether the *Yorktown* or the *St. Louis* could see one of his Curtiss SOC float planes, aloft since early that morning on antisubmarine patrol. Fletcher replied negative. A few minutes later he allowed Nixon to break radio silence to try to bring the SOC home. The effort failed, and the Seagull was presumed downed in the earlier violent storms. That raised to eight the number of planes lost by TF-17 that dreary morning. With squalls obscuring the horizon, Fletcher radioed Fahrion to follow him to Point Ocean should he not rejoin that afternoon. Actually the destroyers swiftly closed his location.[22]

Shortly after 1300 the *Yorktown* rotated her combat air patrol of six Wildcats. At the same time her radar suddenly detected a bogey thirty-five miles northeast. At 1313 a second Jaluit-based flying boat lurched into view ten miles ahead. Two combat air patrol Wildcats swiftly latched onto the big Kawanishi as it crossed over to port and passed behind the clouds. Four minutes later it exploded in bright flames five miles away. The *Yorktown*'s first aerial victory cheered the whole task force. Ens. E. Scott McCuskey, one of the two fighter pilots, piped up on the fighter radio circuit: "We shot his ass off!" Clark added on the bullhorn for the benefit of the whole ship: "Burn, you son-of-a-bitch, burn!" The destruction of the flying boat greeted Fahrion as he brought the *Hughes*, *Sims*, and *Russell* in sight. The flying boat never had time to radio base before it was lost.[23]

ORDERS TO WITHDRAW

Fletcher again considered whether to launch another air strike or even bombard one of the nearby islands, Mili perhaps or Makin. Given the poor weather conditions, he wondered whether the enemy patrol planes might have airborne radar, so skillfully did they find and track TF-17. Finally he decided to withdraw. The horrible weather already cost eight planes, including two simply trying to stay aloft near the task force. The aerologist forecast continued bad weather for the region. No islands within reach appeared to be worth the effort or possible risk to get at them. In addition a detour at this time would interfere with plans to refuel the destroyers on 2 February. It seemed wiser to resume the attack on Jaluit the day after that, hopefully with better weather. The issue became moot after 1430, when Fletcher received new orders from Halsey. Declaring, "Destruction military objectives this force such that further operations my area not justified," Halsey advised Nimitz and Fletcher that he was retiring northeast while under attack. The TF-8 bluejackets later dubbed the maneuver "Haul ass with Halsey." Heavy cruiser *Chester* had swallowed one bomb but made thirty knots, and plane losses were light. Halsey told Fletcher to "withdraw your force at discretion not later than tonight." Thus the Pacific Fleet's first counterattack was over. Fletcher changed course northeast and arranged for a new fueling rendezvous in the direction of Hawaii. That evening he learned more about what befell TF-8 in the northern Marshalls. Halsey certainly enjoyed much better hunting but confronted a more spirited defense. He claimed "many" transports and auxiliaries sunk or hit by air attack at Kwajalein. Bombing and ship bombardments had beached or damaged more transports at Wotje, while shore installations on Maloelap and Wotje also sustained extensive damage. "Many enemy planes [were] destroyed on ground and in air." The *Chester*'s condition improved, and the *Enterprise* suffered only light damage. All this mayhem cost TF-8 only six planes.[24]

Halsey's great concern, aside from evading further attack, was fuel. That evening he requested Brown, shepherding the *Neosho* southward, to meet him "earliest" along a line projecting southwest of Pearl. Brown obliged, radioing that he now expected to join TF-8 on 3 February (west longitude date) north of Johnston island. The next morning (1 February, west longitude time), Nimitz confirmed the rendezvous between Halsey and Brown. He warned Fletcher that if the *Neosho* were lost, he must provide Halsey oil from the *Sabine*. Happily Halsey decided that he had sufficient fuel to reach Pearl, so Cincpac released Brown to continue south to Christmas Island. Nimitz sent Halsey and Fletcher a satisfying, "Well done from the entire fleet." Now it was just a case of attending to business and getting safely to Pearl. That evening Fletcher met his oiler and fueled the next two days while edging northeast toward Oahu. TF-8 reached Pearl on 5 February to great acclaim. Cheers and whistles sounded throughout the harbor, and a jubilant Nimitz rushed on board the *Enterprise* to greet Halsey. At noon on 6 February as TF-17 entered Pearl, the curious *Yorktown*ers lined up in whites along her flight deck for their first look at the great devastation still evident after two months. The public reception proved considerably more restrained than the one accorded Halsey, but Nimitz's welcome was warm. Fletcher immediately noticed the difference in mood ("like a breath of fresh air") in the month since Nimitz assumed command. "Nimitz brought calmness to the scene and he restored morale."[25]

Halsey claimed sinking or crippling about fifteen ships at Kwajalein and Wotje, including a cruiser, two submarines, several gunboats and tenders, and a flotilla of auxiliaries. He also reported destroying thirty-five planes. For five hours he laid the *Enterprise* alongside Wotje much like an old-time frigate grappling an opponent. Fighting furiously, he got away despite a determined air attack that included a flaming bomber that grazed the *Big E*'s flight deck. Halsey's actual score was far less than thought at the time. Japanese sources later revealed that TF-8 sank three small auxiliary ships; damaged an old minelayer, an old light cruiser, and four transports; and destroyed about fifteen planes. As the Cincpac War Plans diary noted, Fletcher's actually accurate tally of two auxiliaries damaged and three flying boats destroyed added "little" to what TF-8 had supposedly achieved. Following Morison's lead, E. B. Potter wondered if Fletcher's meager results were "perhaps" also due to "excess caution." In retrospect, though, it is hard to see what Fletcher could have done differently other than to sail right up to Jaluit and slug it out. Halsey put it best. "The jinx that had dogged us . . . transferred to [TF-17] during the attack."[26]

Nimitz described the Marshalls-Gilberts raids as "well conceived, well planned and brilliantly executed." He recommended Halsey for an immediate Distinguished Service Medal (DSM), and Browning for promotion to captain. Rightly Halsey got the credit, but if Fletcher did not exactly win plaudits, at least he accomplished his mission. The raids did little to deter the Japanese juggernaut in the Far East, but that did not detract from the real effect of Halsey's success. As he said, no matter what the results, "richer still" was the effect on American morale. The Pacific Fleet finally fought back. On 13 February the Navy Department released details of the raids that swelled a sorely tested national pride. Overnight Bill Halsey became one of the best known officers in the navy. He was an aggressive, down-to-earth warrior whom the press would flamboyantly nickname "Bull." Fletcher was mentioned acting under his orders in attacks on Jaluit and Makin. Combined Fleet reacted to the surprise assault with "acute embarrassment" over the failure to detect the U.S. carriers and a feeble response thought to have just damaged a cruiser. Yamamoto hurled Nagumo's three carriers at Truk in pursuit of the raiders, but on 2 February recalled them when it became evident they got clean away. Japan dismissed the raids as "motivated largely by considerations of American internal politics, public opinion and morale." At least some officers felt secretly relieved Tokyo was not attacked. While the *Akagi* and *Kaga* proceeded to Palau to join the *Sōryū* and *Hiryū* in the Southern Area, the *Zuikaku* left Truk on 9 February for Yokosuka. Thus Yamamoto quietly redeployed the 5th Carrier Division of *Shōkaku* and *Zuikaku* to the homeland. Worry over possible U.S. carrier attacks was at least a factor in keeping them back.[27]

With the *Yorktown*'s much-anticipated return to the Pacific after nearly a year, three carriers reposed within the confines of Pearl Harbor for the first time in many months. Only the *Lexington* was at sea, bound for the remote South Pacific. Growing more confident about the ability of his radio intelligence to predict enemy threats, Nimitz risked temporary immobilization of most of his striking force. The giant *Saratoga* sulked in dry dock number two, the big torpedo gash in her port side patched sufficiently to see her to Bremerton for permanent repairs. However, she could not return to combat until June at the earliest, and a great deal might happen in four months. The *Enterprise* and *Yorktown* would remain at Pearl only a short time for normal upkeep before heading out to fight again. The brief sojourn gave Halsey and Fletcher the chance to evaluate the efficiency of their ships, aircraft, and men in the Pacific Fleet's first counterattack. For the most part the results pleased everyone. Halsey declared the achievement of the *Enterprise* "justifies the highest hopes heretofore held regarding the effectiveness of [carriers] when properly employed." Concerns were raised about ship's gunnery. Antiaircraft, in particular, was slow to get on target and erratic, but radar fire control and better training would cure that. Impressed by the "ferocity" of the enemy's land-based bombers, Halsey felt a sort of perverse pride that Japanese bluejackets flew those planes instead of the Imperial Army Air Force. His attacks ruined by poor weather, Fletcher could add little to the recommendations of his more colorful colleague. He was pleased with Buckmaster's excellent seamanship and could ask for no better men to lead into battle.[28]

CHAPTER 6

To the Southwest Pacific

CREATING THE ANZAC AREA

Fletcher's return to Pearl coincided with round two of the fundamental strategic debate between Cominch and Cincpac over whether the Pacific Fleet should defend Australia as well as the central Pacific. King's attention remained firmly fixed on the southwest Pacific and Far East, where the defense of Singapore and Dutch East Indies rapidly crumbled. The loss of Rabaul posed not only immediate peril to adjacent New Guinea and the Solomons, but also threatened New Caledonia, Fiji, and Samoa. Nimitz, on the other hand, stubbornly placed the main danger squarely to Hawaii and outposts of Midway and Johnston in the central Pacific. Hawaiian defenses were too weak, particularly against raids, to permit any wide dispersion of the carriers.[1]

King worked furiously to create an American presence in the South Pacific beyond Samoa. A line of mutually supporting bases would check the Japanese and support the counteroffensive. He had not only to whip Nimitz into line, but also persuade the War Department to disgorge garrison troops and aircraft for the new island bases. They must be in place before Japan turned eastward into the South Pacific. On 19 January King announced to Nimitz that he was thinking of occupying Funafuti, in the Ellice Islands southeast of the Gilberts, as an "outpost" for Samoa and Fiji and a "linkage post toward the Solomon Islands." The army reluctantly agreed to send units to Bora-Bora, Canton, Christmas, and New Caledonia, but King was far from satisfied. In January following the Arcadia Conference of U.S. and British leaders in Washington, the Combined Chiefs of Staff contemplated a special naval command, Anzac, to secure the seas adjacent to Australia and New Zealand and north as far as New Caledonia and Fiji. It was to be a twin to the multinational ABDA (American-British-Dutch-Australian) command created to defend Malaya, the Philippines, and the Dutch East Indies. The British greatly desired American involvement in Anzac, because the hard-pressed Royal Navy alone could not defend it. An Anzac command fitted King's own strategic agenda, but he was loath to use Pacific Fleet warships to escort convoys all the way to Australia.

The principals hammered out an agreement that placed Anzac under King's direct control through an American subordinate. The Royal Navy was to provide the elderly carrier *Hermes* (refitting in South Africa), and the Pacific Fleet a heavy cruiser and two destroyers. Australia and New Zealand agreed to contribute two heavy and three light cruisers, plus escort ships and auxiliaries. The *Hermes* never reached Australia, so Anzac's naval power was vested in the Australian Squadron (renamed the Anzac Squadron) under Rear Adm. John Gregory Crace, Royal Navy (RN). Born in 1887 in Australia, Crace joined the Royal Navy as a cadet in 1902 and specialized in torpedo and antisubmarine warfare. After commanding a light cruiser and a light cruiser squadron, he received the Australian Squadron in November 1939. The tall, gray-haired Crace carried the well-earned reputation of a fine, aggressive seaman, who was frank, honest, and straightforward. After two frustrating years limited to escort duty and hunting raiders, he found himself in the ticklish spot of having to work with and under the Americans in a multinational command while carefully maintaining his prerogatives.[2]

Rear Adm. John G. Crace, RN, 1940.
Courtesy of Australian War Memorial (Negative Number 305285)

Nimitz was told to nominate the commander of the Anzac Area, subject to approval in Washington. King suggested his friend Admiral Pye. Nimitz assented, but Roosevelt and Knox, still angry over Pye's failure to prevent the fall of Wake (but also perhaps preventing a greater disaster to the Pacific Fleet), would not have it. Nimitz urgently requested reconsideration of Pye, the "most capable and suitable officer available" (that is, he was levelheaded and not dangerously aggressive). If not Pye, then for Commander, Anzac Area (Comanzac), Nimitz desired Rear Adm. H. Fairfax Leary, Comcrubatfor. An able, strict disciplinarian disliked for his argumentative personality and loud, raspy voice, Leary was certainly "available" after the *Saratoga* was torpedoed. According to rumor, Nimitz welcomed an opportunity to ease his truculent Annapolis classmate out of the Pacific Fleet. With Washington unrelenting regarding Pye, King selected Leary on 29 January. He was promoted to vice admiral and left for New Zealand. The *Chicago* would follow to become his flagship. An unforeseen complication was that Leary was junior to Admiral Brown, whom he was to command.[3]

King remained far from satisfied with Nimitz's efforts to engage the enemy and divert his resources away from the Far East. The day after the Marshalls raid, Rochefort's Hypo radio intelligence analysts at Pearl informed Washington of the hubbub in the Mandates, but found "no definite indications forces outside [that] area are to be disturbed." That was not what King hoped to hear. On 5 February he queried Nimitz regarding two distressing alternatives: instantly sending strong reinforcements directly to Anzac or the Far East, or undertaking major aggressive action in the central Pacific "with maximum forces available." By that King meant carriers *and* battleships. On 7 January Nimitz had formed the Pacific Fleet battleships into Task Force 1 under Rear Adm. Walter S. Anderson (Commander, Battleships, Battle Force) and gathered them at San Francisco as they became available. Soon Anderson controlled seven elderly leviathans (*Pennsylvania*, *Tennessee*, *Idaho*, *Mississippi*, *New Mexico*, *Colorado*, and *Maryland*), only one short of the number available on 7 December. Up to that point Nimitz merely used a few battleships to escort convoys between the West Coast and Pearl, which irked Cominch. Now King insisted they be included in any offensive plans. McMorris examined a number of dismal alternatives, even a possible strike against Japan that was rejected because of the seasonal bad weather. With four or more battleships in support, he proposed a combined assault on Truk; if not, perhaps a carrier strike against the Bonin Islands or Saipan in the Marianas or both.[4]

Even before Nimitz could reply, King fired another blast. Japan could now raid all along the line—from Midway to Hawaii to the South Pacific to northeast Australia—and threaten Anzac with an amphibious offensive covered by two carriers. Crace's Anzac Squadron would be greatly outmatched. Conveniently at hand, however, was Brown's TF-11 (*Lexington*), available after Halsey had no need of its oiler. Brown headed for a central position off Canton in the Phoenix Islands but anticipated returning to Pearl in mid February. Once TF-11 dipped south of the equator, though, King would see that it did not return north very soon. On 6 February he directed Brown to proceed "at once" to the Anzac Area, and thus beyond Cincpac's direct control. In addition to the Anzac Squadron, King reinforced TF-11 with heavy cruisers *San Francisco* and *Pensacola* and six destroyers hitherto dispersed on convoy escort duty. Nimitz was to provide "all practicable" navy patrol planes and army heavy bombers in support. To Brown the orders to steam to the remote South Pacific was tantamount to "jumping off into space." Scanning his admittedly inadequate charts, he could find no harbor short of Sydney that could shelter the massive *Lex* if need be.[5]

Aghast at King's command to strip the central Pacific of TF-11 and so many land-based aircraft, Nimitz replied on 7 February that he lacked the strength to respond to the threat with anything but swift raids. Such pinpricks, though, would fail as significant diversions. Displaying a firm grasp of realities, Nimitz discounted the combat effectiveness of the old battleships in the era since December 1941 and assessed them especially ill suited for hit-and-run warfare. They lacked the speed to keep pace with the carriers but could not fight on their own without a proper screen of scarce light cruisers and destroyers. They also consumed a great deal of fuel. Nothing the battleships could accomplish in the short run equaled their possible loss. Nimitz's two remaining carriers were tied up for the next five days for upkeep. He planned to deploy one carrier group toward Fiji and keep the other in reserve near Pearl. It was not wise to execute any more raids at present, "because the probable results do not balance the probable risks." Nimitz suggested that Pye fly immediately to Washington to discuss the situation personally with King. As historian Frank Uhlig Jr. shrewdly commented, while Nimitz wrested for strategic control of the Pacific Fleet, King probably posed a greater hazard to him than Yamamoto. On 9 February, before Pye left for Washington, King confuted virtually all of Nimitz's points. "Pacific Fleet [is] not, repeat not, markedly inferior" to those ships the Japanese could employ against Hawaii if the enemy also tried something bold in the southwest Pacific. "Action by you towards and in Mandates will of itself cover and protect Midway-Hawaii." Cincpac was using the old battleships improperly, King averred, but declined to explain how best to employ the dinosaurs. Nimitz realized their grave limitations far sooner than anyone else and wisely refused to squander them. King also decreed the Pacific Fleet must continue striking the enemy in the central Pacific to provide some relief to the hard-pressed Far East. He mentioned Wake and the northern Marshalls as possible targets.[6]

THE RAID THAT NEVER WAS

Nimitz huddled with Milo Draemel and Soc McMorris to ponder how best to carry out King's edicts. That proved especially difficult after losing the reinforced *Lexington* task force, along with the three oilers necessary to maintain it so far from Pearl. Nimitz found it difficult to select an objective that constituted a meaningful diversion, but posed no inordinate risk. One possibility was for Halsey's *Enterprise* to join Brown in the Anzac Area and raid Rabaul. At the same time Fletcher's *Yorktown* could either remain in reserve or strike Wake. Yet if Cominch got Halsey as well as Brown, he might not give either back. The idea of raiding Tokyo came up again. A successful strike would reap tremendous psychological impact, but aside from strong defenses, the North Pacific's notoriously rough winter weather would impede vital refueling. Little did Nimitz know that the same thought already percolated in King's mind, and nothing trifling like horrifying weather would deter Cominch. Finally on 11 February Nimitz accepted a plan by McMorris for simultaneous carrier strikes against Wake and Eniwetok, located 620 miles southwest of Wake. If Eniwetok proved inappropriate, tiny Marcus Island, 760 miles northwest of Wake and only a thousand miles southeast of Tokyo, would take its place. McMorris cautioned such raids "will not divert much strength from the southwest but it is as strong and aggressive operation as can be undertaken at this time." Intelligence offered reasonable assurance that no carriers prowled the central Pacific. Nimitz informed King of these plans, but temporized with regard to the battleships. He contemplated employing the battlewagons "in support of raids where strong enemy forces are likely to be encountered," but in truth he did not yet intend to *go* against "strong enemy forces."[7]

Halsey incorporated the *Enterprise* and *Yorktown* into one task force of two carrier groups and characteristically reserved for himself Eniwetok, the more distant and presumably more dangerous objective. That left Wake for Fletcher, just fine with him, as he had a personal grudge to settle there. In a thoughtless moment Cincpac not only numbered the new task force thirteen, but also directed Halsey's own TG-13.1 to sail on Friday, 13 February. With mock seriousness Browning, Halsey's chief of staff just promoted to captain for his superb planning of the Marshalls raids, hastened to headquarters to ask an amused McMorris what gives. The Greybook diarist noted how "deference was paid to possible superstitious persons," when later that day Cincpac changed the number to sixteen and postponed Halsey's departure to more felicitous Valentine's Day. Fletcher had to tarry at Pearl until 16 February while his assigned oiler, the *Cimarron*-class *Guadalupe*, finally arrived from the West Coast.[8]

On 12 February Halsey issued his operations order for the upcoming raids. Both carrier task groups were to approach their objectives from the north. His own TG-16.1 (*Enterprise*, two heavy cruisers, seven destroyers, and oiler *Sabine*) was to depart Oahu the evening of 14 February and circle well north of Wake to avoid being spotted. He would begin his run-in on the evening of 24 February from 425 miles north of Eniwetok and 270 miles west of Wake and take the *Enterprise* and Raymond Spruance's cruisers ahead at twenty-five knots, with the destroyers following at fifteen knots. At dawn on 25 February the *Enterprise* SBDs alone would execute a single long distance strike against Eniwetok from 175 miles north. Halsey set aside two days to evade pursuit and retrace his route back around Wake to his second fueling point and be back at Pearl about 4 March. In the event he was sighted on the way, he would either turn west against Marcus or join Fletcher in pummeling Wake. Fletcher's TG-16.2 (*Yorktown*, two heavy cruisers, six destroyers, and an oiler) was to bomb and shell Wake starting at dawn on 25 February in concert with the Eniwetok raid. The *Yorktown* would launch a full strike from one hundred miles northwest of Wake, after which the TF-17 cruisers would bombard the island. These plans were sound, but two developments forced a change. On 12 February the submarine *Cachalot* radioed the results of her survey of both objectives. It jolted the War Plans Section. If Wake seemed pretty quiet, only one small gunboat in evidence, Eniwetok was purely somnolent. The *Cachalot*'s periscope revealed nothing military there at all, not surprising inasmuch as the Japanese never built anything there. McMorris's gang was puzzled, for prior to the war Hypo's radio intelligence pegged Eniwetok as a major air base. Now it "appears to be even less of an *optimum* objective for attack than had been believed before."[9]

Things also heated up in the Anzac Area. King and Leary clashed over how to exercise command. Leary's original orders were to establish his headquarters at Melbourne, but King now wanted him in the *Chicago* leading a "strong and comprehensive offensive" to cover a U.S. Army convoy expected shortly at New Caledonia. Leary preferred Melbourne, from where he could coordinate sea and air operation without worrying about radio silence. He made a good case. On 14 February King grudgingly told Brown, cruising off Fiji, to take direct charge of offensive operations with Crace's Anzac cruiser squadron and available land-based air. The next day Brown proposed raiding Rabaul on 21 February. King heartily approved, as did Leary. Nimitz dug deep for air support. A dozen army B-17 heavy bombers and six PBY-5 flying boats flew south to Fiji. Brown advanced the B-17s all the way to Townsville in northeast Australia from where they could bomb Rabaul. He also moved the PBYs and their tender *Curtiss* to Nouméa on New Caledonia. A disappointed Crace received the "dreary task" of escorting the oiler *Platte* coming out to join TF-11. Brown advised he lacked the fuel to use the Anzac Squadron offensively.[10]

Still expecting to raid Eniwetok, Halsey departed Pearl on 14 February. That day across the date line Singapore surrendered, an appalling if not unforeseen development that eased the pressure for immediate action. On the fifteenth the first fruits of Pye's visit to Washington became manifest, when King allowed that occasional raids against the Mandates would suffice as diversions. He preferred to deploy the Pacific Fleet's mobile forces to meet likely threats and suggested moving either Halsey or Fletcher south to Canton near the equator. From there the carrier task force could range north or south if necessary. That was enough for Nimitz. A raid on an unoccupied Eniwetok would have all the impact of a wet firecracker. Because Halsey was already on his way, he might as well tackle Wake. Halsey attacked on 24 February. Approaching from the northeast, he confidently unleashed Spruance's two heavy cruisers and two destroyers to shell the atoll, while the *Enterprise* launched a full air strike from one hundred miles. Although TF-16 did not inflict severe damage, it certainly drew attention. The *Shōkaku* and *Zuikaku* temporarily remained in Japan in case the United States grew more bold, while Nagumo's other four carriers attacked Port Darwin in northeast Australia on 19 February to cover the pending invasion of Java.[11]

REGROUPING AT PEARL

Fletcher welcomed the stay in port to take care of business regarding TF-17 and the administration of Cruscofor. He exchanged light cruiser *St. Louis* for an old friend, the *Astoria*, wearing the flag of Rear Adm. William W. Smith, the former Cincpac chief of staff. Poco Smith first broke his flag in the *Chicago* in Brown's TF-11, but for only one cruise before Kinkaid and the *Minneapolis* took his place. Then he nearly ended up back on staff duty, but King desired him in cruisers. A 1909 Annapolis graduate, the steady, savvy Smith possessed a mathematician's precise mind and a great sense of humor. The nickname "Poco" started at Annapolis when an upperclassman commented that Smith, with his dark complexion and prominent nose, must have been "the result of some hanky panky between Captain John Smith and Pocahontas." Fletcher respected his intelligence and admired him, and they worked well together. Capt. Charles P. Cecil, Commander, Destroyer Division (Comdesdiv) Eleven, took Fahrion's place in TF-17. Ironically nearly all his destroyers derived from Desron Two, indicative of how the Pacific Fleet's elaborate prewar destroyer organization broke down due to operational necessities.[12]

Fletcher fought to keep his own staff intact. Stark requested Spence Lewis to accompany his former boss John Henry Newton for duty with the Office of the Chief of Naval Operations (Opnav) in Washington. Securing Nimitz's endorsement, Fletcher asked Bunav to cancel Lewis's orders, as he was "urgently needed as my chief of staff and no relief available." To his delight (and Lewis's), the bureau relented. As intended, he secured the services of Newton's old flag secretary, Lt. Cdr. Ira H. Nunn (USNA 1924), an efficient disciplinarian, to take absent Latimer's place. On 10 February nearly all the Cruscofor staff and flag allowance trooped on board the *Yorktown*. Cdr. Harry A. Guthrie (USNA 1921) was the damage control expert, who also handled combat intelligence. His classmate Cdr. Walter G. "Butch" Schindler, the staff gunnery officer, was also a qualified air observer. The rest comprised the four communication watch officers, flag warrant officer, and radiomen, yeomen, signalmen,

Vice Adm. William Ward Smith.
Courtesy of Col. W. W. Smith Jr.

quartermaster, officers' cooks, stewards, and mess attendants. For the time being Commander Thorington, assistant operations officer, remained with Smith in the *Astoria*. Likewise Commander McLean, the staff aviator, advised Kinkaid in the *Minneapolis*, but Fletcher could rely on the *Yorktown* for all aviation counsel he desired.[13]

Lt. Forrest R. "Tex" Biard (USNA 1934), the new assistant combat intelligence officer, was a Japanese linguist with Rochefort's radio intelligence unit. After the Wake relief, Fletcher requested "specially trained radiomen to copy Japanese sending, and specially trained officers to interpret what is being intercepted." He got exactly that. In January marine Captain Holcomb went in the *Enterprise*, but without any radiomen. Thereafter, Nimitz tried to place a radio intelligence team with each carrier task force. Biard "lost" Rochefort's coin toss over Holcomb's relief in the *Enterprise* and to his eventual regret ended up in the *Yorktown* with Fletcher. Able but extremely intense, Biard did not get along well with the admiral and his staff. His primary task was to translate low-level enemy radio transmissions sent in the clear, such as aircraft sighting reports, that could be of great value in the midst of battle. His team also monitored radio frequencies, circuits, and call signs for later traffic analysis by Hypo, but itself possessed only a very limited deciphering capability. Biard did not handle the special intelligence that passed directly from Cincpac to Fletcher.[14]

Another problem facing Fletcher was his burgeoning administrative responsibilities. With Leary leaving for Anzac, Fletcher learned that as of 6 February he was now responsible for the light cruisers as well. In fact, the whole administrative apparatus of the Pacific Fleet fell apart. Most ship type commanders and their staffs served constantly at sea leading task forces under radio silence, making it nearly impossible to process paperwork and render administrative decisions. From 7 December through 5 February, Fletcher himself was at Pearl Harbor only seven days. On 17 January Cincpac ordered the type commanders to establish separate offices ashore, which proved another bureaucratic burden for overworked staffs. Fletcher recommended on 12 February that their administrative functions be merged into a shore office under Cincpac. At the same time a Cincpac adviser proposed abolishing both Cruscofor and Crubatfor to simplify administration. Nimitz called that too radical, but did agree with King that the Base Force (soon designated Service Force) should supervise maintenance of the carriers and cruisers. They looked into overhauling the whole structure of type commands. On 16 February Fletcher set up an administrative office in the Pearl Harbor Navy Yard.[15]

The *Yorktown* herself experienced changes that ultimately enhanced Fletcher's handling of TF-17. Buckmaster detached dissatisfied executive officer Jock Clark, when he found Clark's relief, Cdr. Dixie Kiefer, was at hand. A member of the 1919 Annapolis class (the year after Clark), Kiefer was a more seasoned naval aviator (wings 1922 versus 1925) and, like Clark, highly competent. He was also not apt to second-guess every decision and thus was a great deal easier to live with. His warm personality resonated throughout the ship. When air officer MacComsey left for medical treatment, Buckmaster replaced him with his assistant, Cdr. Murr E. Arnold (USNA 1923), a dynamic, demanding, bantam-sized warrior much respected by his wary pilots, whose eardrums quivered from his orders barked over the bullhorn. A recent commanding officer of VB-5, Arnold was well versed in the present state of carrier doctrine and operations. Fletcher came to rely greatly on him for aviation advice.[16]

DOWN TO CANTON

On 15 February Fletcher learned he was again CTF-17, with new orders to "proceed to area between Canton and Ellice Islands and operate therein awaiting further orders which are dependent on developments." Although not party to the exchanges between King and Nimitz, Fletcher knew of Brown's plans to raid Rabaul and that very likely a voyage to the remote South Pacific also lay in his future. Late the next morning, Fletcher sailed from Pearl with the *Yorktown* (seventeen fighters, thirty-five dive bombers, and twelve torpedo planes), Smith's heavy cruisers *Astoria* and *Louisville*, Cecil's six destroyers, and oiler *Guadalupe*.[17]

During Fletcher's cruise to equatorial waters, the usual stream of messages detailed what happened elsewhere. Thus he learned of Brown's misadventures while attempting to raid Rabaul. On 20 February, one day before the scheduled attack, search planes discovered TF-11 still four hundred miles east of Rabaul. *Lexington* fighters swiftly downed two flying boats, but his cover blown, Brown canceled the raid, despite the urging of the *Lex*'s Capt. Ted Sherman and others to press on. Instead of immediately retiring, however, he continued toward Rabaul for a few hours, accepting the prospect of an afternoon air strike to create more of a diversion. Rabaul eagerly complied, hurling seventeen medium bombers (Mitsubishi G4M1 Type 1 "land attack planes" or "Bettys") against TF-11, but failed to inflict any damage. The Grumman Wildcat fighter pilots were brilliant. The star was Lt. Edward H. "Butch" O'Hare, credited with shooting down five bombers and saving the *Lex*.

Brown thought thirty or more "heavy bombers" attacked TF-11 and lost more than a dozen of their number. In fact only two land attack planes returned to base, a stunning U.S. victory, although the Japanese themselves wrongly believed they crippled the carrier. The *Lex*'s fighters had blasted open the way to Rabaul, but Brown withdrew to refuel prior to resuming the offensive. Reinforcements, though, quickly restored Rabaul's crippled air arm.[18]

On 21 February TF-17 crossed the equator and marked time fighting the weather while maneuvering back and forth west of bleak Canton Island. Meanwhile King, Nimitz, Leary, and Brown were busily determining Fletcher's next mission. Deeply impressed by the excellence of Rabaul's search network and its ferocious riposte, Brown opined, "Any further attempt should be made by two carriers in order to provide force with adequate air protection." A fuel shortage again compelled him to retain Crace's Anzac cruiser squadron between Fiji and New Caledonia, while TF-11 took position southeast of the Solomons "in readiness to contest enemy advance to southeastward or to Port Moresby." Brown essentially shut down in defense mode until reinforced. Leary thought the solution was simply to hustle Fletcher down to join Brown for another jab at Rabaul. On the evening of 24 February Nimitz concurred with Brown that Rabaul required a minimum of two carriers. King speculated that a Rabaul raid would help cover the large convoy of U.S. Army troops set to proceed in early March from Australia to New Caledonia. Nimitz replied that Fletcher could join Brown west of Fiji after both task forces refueled. Logistics were key. TF-11 alone required three *Cimarron*-class oilers shuttling from distant ports. The loss of just one oiler, Nimitz warned, would "seriously jeopardize important ships." Even so, if the two carrier task forces joined, they should strike Rabaul with the support of Leary's land-based air in Australia, but logistics would soon compel at least one carrier task force to withdraw from the South Pacific. Brown became aware, to his intense displeasure, of Leary's push for an immediate two-carrier raid against Rabaul and commenced backpedaling. He radioed King, Nimitz, and Leary that he never intended to advocate a two-carrier attack on Rabaul. "Do not recommend it under present conditions." Events, though, had gone too far for such caution.[19]

On 26 February Fletcher copied a long message from Cominch that disclosed what was in the wind. Brown and Leary were fellow action addressees. King clarified the Anzac command structure. Unquestionably Leary was to run the forces afloat and coordinate land-based air operations from Australia and Port Moresby in New Guinea to support his naval forces. The fluid situation, however, never allowed Leary the measure of strict control over Brown or Fletcher that he so greatly desired. He could only echo the general directives that Cominch passed down to the task force commanders, who exercised great independence because they had to maintain strict radio silence. The important 26 February Cominch message also elucidated King's basic philosophy regarding carrier operations in Anzac. "Whenever circumstances permit," single carrier task forces should not undertake raids without land-based air coverage or execute so-called offensive sweeps that lacked definite objectives. That risked detection that removed the advantage of surprise. Refuting Brown's newly emerging caution, King stressed that present tasks were "not merely protective but also offensive where practicable." However, simply raiding shore bases often were not profitable unless significant naval forces were also present. The best way to safeguard a position was to reduce the enemy's offensive strength by destroying his mobile forces, "particularly carriers, cruisers, loaded transports and long range bombers."[20]

Of direct interest to Fletcher, King's message also directed that either TF-11 or TF-17, but preferably both, should remain in Anzac until the army settled into New Caledonia. Of course to *remain* in the Anzac Area, Fletcher must first *be* there. The summons could not be long in coming. He knew Halsey was enjoying himself, given Nimitz's orders to TF-16 to strike Marcus if possible after plastering Wake. Interesting events, too, were in the offing for TF-17. Pearl warned of a large tropical storm developing north of Fiji and expected to move across the direct route between Canton and the New Hebrides. On 27 February the *Yorktown* copied two messages addressed to Fletcher, one from Cominch, the other from Cincpac, that were transmitted in ciphers the flag communicators could not break. Not being able to read his mail was disconcerting, but enjoined to strict radio silence, he could do little about it. After the weather moderated late that afternoon, he sent the *Hughes* eastward toward Canton where she could safely radio a message asking Cincpac to rebroadcast the dispatches in a cipher that TF-17 held.[21]

In fact King jumped the gun by placing TF-17 in the southwest Pacific. Pye returned to Pearl on 26 February from his conference with Cominch bringing dismaying news that strategic planning in Washington seemed muddled. King still lacked a comprehensive plan other than to create a series of island bases in the southwest and South Pacific. On the twenty-seventh Nimitz, Pye, Draemel, and McMorris deliberated over the necessity of committing strong forces so distant from the central Pacific. "We don't know how 'all-out' our help is to be to Australia," McMorris moaned. Finally Nimitz bowed to the inevitable and sent Fletcher south to Anzac. That evening just as the *Hughes* departed, Fletcher finally received the word he awaited, and happily he could decipher it. Cincpac told him to rendezvous with TF-11 at noon on 6 March three hundred miles north of Nouméa. That was just west of Efate in the New Hebrides and nearly twelve hundred miles southeast of Rabaul. Soon after Fletcher read a long message from Nimitz to King that confirmed his orders. Nimitz acknowledged deteriorating weather might affect the rendezvous. The present state of supply would support both task forces if offensive action against New Britain began "promptly" upon Fletcher's arrival. However, Brown's TF-11 must depart by mid March, and just to reach Pearl it would deplete the store ship *Bridge* at Samoa. Brown considered food almost as serious a problem as oil. He estimated his cruisers and destroyers would run out of dry provisions by 20 March, despite supplemental food from the *Lexington*.[22]

Fletcher saw that he had plenty of time to complete fueling and await the return of the *Hughes* before it became necessary to leave. Fortuitously the weather on the last day of February allowed TF-17 to resume refueling west of Canton. The process took two days. The *Hughes* returned the morning of 1 March from her errand, but Pearl did not rebroadcast the two offending messages or further elucidate them. Fletcher would not know until 6 March, when he met Brown, that the unbreakable Cominch communication contained a fairly accurate estimate of enemy strength in the Bismarcks: a cruiser division, a destroyer flotilla, and about fifty land-based planes at Rabaul. More enemy strength would become available after the Dutch East Indies fell, threatening northeastern Australia, New Caledonia, and Fiji. Even before then, the Japanese might try for Lae and Salamaua on the north coast of

Rear Adm. Spencer S. Lewis, circa 1944.
Courtesy of Harriet L. Houck

Papua, or even Port Moresby on its south coast, and also Tulagi, an important anchorage in the lower Solomons. The evening of 1 March Fletcher departed Canton waters bound for the Ellice Islands and the New Hebrides beyond.[23]

LIFE WITH "THE FLAG"

Flag officers conducted themselves at sea according to an elaborate protocol that evolved to ease the ever-present tension between an admiral and the captain of his flagship. The captain's inherent status as commanding officer of his ship had to be preserved without undue interference from above. By tradition the admiral was merely a guest on board his flagship. Thus before visiting the navigation bridge, he would as a courtesy ask permission of his flag captain. An embarked admiral usually limited his presence to "flag country," the spaces that served as his living quarters and personal command post. In turn ship's company entered flag areas only upon invitation. Led by Cpl. William E. Thompson, the ten elite seagoing marines of the Commander, Cruisers, Scouting Force (Comcruscofor) flag allowance preserved Fletcher's privacy and served as personal aides. One marine orderly accompanied him everywhere on the ship and stood watch beside the door to his cabin. Chief of staff Spence Lewis also had a marine orderly.[24]

The *Yorktown*'s flag quarters were located port side forward on the gallery deck one level beneath the flight deck. There Fletcher enjoyed a lavish suite replete with sitting room, spacious bedroom, and a small personal office. The nearby flag office served as home base for the nine yeomen under Frank W. Boo, Yeoman First Class. Lewis slept in the adjacent cabin, and the staterooms of operations officer Gerry Galpin, flag secretary Ira Nunn, and

Harry Smith, the flag lieutenant, were also nearby. The other staff officers lived with ship's company in "officer's country," and the flag allowance bunked with the crew. Care of the flag quarters was the domain of Luis Motas, Officer's Steward First Class; Melchor Punongbayan, Officer's Cook First Class, supervised the flag galley and pantry. All eight flag stewards, cooks, and mess attendants hailed from Guam or the Philippines. Under the navy's rigid hierarchy the rated stewards and cooks did not get to wear the eagle badge ("crow") and chevrons of equivalent petty officers, although they received the same pay. Fletcher's quarters were sumptuous, but when the situation was the least bit tense he was rarely there except to eat. His customary dining companions were Lewis, Nunn, and Smith, although on occasion the entire staff assembled for a meal. When necessary Fletcher lived in his emergency sea cabin located in the *Yorktown*'s island, where he had a bed, an easy chair, a table, and a shower. Captain Buckmaster led a more cloistered life. His own plush in-port living quarters, office, and galley were situated to starboard across from flag country, but while at sea he stayed in his own sea cabin behind the pilot house on the navigation bridge one level above the flag bridge. Buckmaster ate alone and often had his evening meal before sunset, so he would not need to shine any lights in his emergency cabin that would harm his night vision.[25]

Fletcher ran his task force from the flag bridge, situated two decks up from the flight deck inside the island. The command post was flag plot, the forward compartment on that deck, where the junior members of the staff rotated as duty watch officer. A large chart table abutted the forward bulkhead, upon which the plot displayed the latest known positions of friendly and enemy forces, sighting reports, and other important information meticulously entered by Lloyd V. Sternberg, Quartermaster First Class. The current message files were always handy. Various communication devices, including the new TBS transmitter-receiver (the VHF short-ranged radio used to contact ships of the task force), cluttered the side bulkheads. There was also a speaker that relayed aircraft radio transmissions, internal telephone circuits, and a voice tube to the navigation bridge directly above. A duty yeoman manned the TBS at all times, and Thomas I. Newsome, Yeoman Second Class, a calm, careful speaker, was the designated combat talker. Fletcher generally conducted business from a comfortable brown leather transom couch that rested against the aft bulkhead. A doorway to starboard opened outside to a small, squared-off platform tucked beneath the large overhanging wings of the navigation bridge. There Fletcher enjoyed a swivel chair reserved for his exclusive use. Extending aft alongside the island, the platform connected with ladders leading to the navigation bridge above and the flight deck below. The next compartment aft of flag plot was the small flag radio, which Lewis turned over to Biard's two radiomen. They installed their radio receivers and special typewriters for reproducing Japanese kana syllables. Periodically Biard would emerge from the green-curtained doorway that barred trespassers and rather mysteriously whispered his intelligence reports in the admiral's ear. Fletcher's sea cabin was located beyond flag radio. Between stints in flag plot, he liked to relax there, doffing his khaki shirt for an athletic-style undershirt to help beat the tropical heat. His favorite leisure activity was reading Westerns. Occasional walks on the flight deck offered additional recreation, but he was no hiking fanatic like Raymond Spruance. Fletcher often smoked a corncob pipe (he had a dozen shipped to him at a time) and liked iced coffee delivered from the flag pantry. His middle name and yen for Black Jack licorice gum either inspired or coincided with his navy nickname of "Black Jack."[26]

Boatswain Hubert R. Cooley's eight flag signalmen took over the *Yorktown*'s signal bridge one deck above the navigating bridge. Under the supervision of Harry Smith, they handled visual communications with the rest of the task force by means of flag hoists (the most common means of maneuvering the ships during daylight), blinking lights, and semaphore. Charles Brooks's flag radio team comprised the four communication watch officers and RM1c Henry F. Duggins's ten radio operators. They worked alongside the *Yorktown*'s own communicators in Radio I, one deck below the flag bridge. When the flag radiomen copied a message addressed to CTF-17, the communication watch officer on duty used the navy's electrical cipher machine (ECM) Mark II to decipher it. Admirals were usually provided with additional rotors for the ECM to handle special flag ciphers, but Fletcher did not always have all he needed to read his message traffic. Routine messages were delivered to the staff duty officer in flag plot, but the communication watch officer personally brought those with high priority immediately to Fletcher. To send messages the process was reversed.[27]

The Cruscofor enlisted flag allowance was a quietly competent, tight-knit group conscious of their favored status and proud of their access to the top man. Admirals did not awe them. They soon got to know Fletcher well, and judging from later testimony, they came to like and respect him a great deal. "Very cordial, level-headed and decisive" was Tom Newsome's assessment. He never heard Fletcher raise his voice or use profanity. The only time Newsome ever remembered seeing Fletcher agitated (and that included three battles during which he was the admiral's combat talker) was early one morning in flag plot. "He shook me!" a shirtless Fletcher shouted as he stormed out of his sea cabin after a hapless seaman had blundered onto the flag bridge, slipped past the marine orderly, and thought he was waking someone else for the watch. Fletcher took no disciplinary action for the incident. Frank Boo called Fletcher "the very best officer I ever had the privilege of working for." He was "firm and tough, but fair, sensitive, caring, and emotional." Fletcher took an interest in Boo's family and liked to hear the latest news. Norman W. Ulmer, a signalman, thought Fletcher was "always calm, cool, collected, always pleasant, calm and sure," not one to unduly interfere or try to micromanage a situation. Raymond W. Kerr, one of the marine orderlies, recalled Fletcher as very quiet, almost "deadpan," definitely "no smiler." That stern demeanor reflected the enormous strain Fletcher often endured. However, he loosened up in flag plot, where Kerr would not ordinarily have seen him. Newsome particularly enjoyed hearing Fletcher reminisce about his experiences as an ensign and young destroyer skipper in the old Asiatic Fleet. The design of the tattoo on Fletcher's arm, a souvenir of his early days in the Far East, is still a bone of contention among surviving members of the flag allowance. Some say it was a dragon, others a rose. They are proud of their association with the admiral during some of the darkest but most crucial days of World War II, and they bristle at the criticism of their former leader that has become prevalent in historical treatments of those perilous times.[28]

CHAPTER 7

"The Best Day's Work We Have Had"

BROWN'S UNDERSTUDY

Near noon on 6 March Fletcher sighted TF-11 on schedule one hundred miles west of Efate. On the way south he copied a message King sent on 2 March to Leary and Brown ordering the augmented force to attack ships and bases in the Bismarcks-Solomons area "about" 10 March. The goal was to check the enemy's advance and cover the Australia–New Caledonia convoy slated to arrive at Nouméa two days later. King suggested a multipronged approach of carriers from the east or southeast, while Crace's Anzac Squadron came from the south. Intelligence showed that Rabaul harbor bulged with ships (twenty-four sighted on 2 March alone) gathering for mischief. Brown soon would wield the strongest concentration to date of Allied naval air power in the Pacific and must find the best way to use it. It is unfortunate King mentioned 10 March. Brown took it wrongly as a mandate even though events might compel an earlier attack.[1]

On the morning of 6 March two *Lexington* planes thumped down on the *Yorktown* bearing a sheaf of operational dispatches, battle reports, letters, and Brown's TF-11 Op-Ord 5-42 for his planned 10 March strike against Rabaul. The alert enemy air search ruled out an approach from the northeast or east. That left only the south, where poorly charted, reef-studded waters and chronic rainy weather precluded accurate navigation. Considering it "tactically sounder" to keep his whole force together, Brown rejected King's suggestion of synchronizing attacks from different directions. Instead, the combined assault would be launched from almost due south of Rabaul at a point equidistant from Rabaul and Gasmata on New Britain. Simultaneous air strikes would hit both bases, followed by cruiser bombardments. Brown counted on Leary's aircraft to bomb Rabaul and Gasmata an hour after sunrise on the tenth. With so much U.S. and Australian air strength embroiled in the faltering Dutch East Indies, the B-17s comprised the most powerful land-based air striking force in Australia. Leary also coordinated searches from northeast Australia, Port Moresby, and Tulagi by Royal Australian Air Force (RAAF) Catalina flying boats and Hudson medium bombers. Such weak numbers precluded any comprehensive air coverage south of Rabaul, so Brown could never be certain whether the Japanese might slip past unseen. The six PBYs at Nouméa, where Captain Sprague's *Tangier* recently replaced the *Curtiss*, guarded the approaches to New Caledonia and the New Hebrides. After the attack Brown expected to return TF-11 to Pearl. He named Fletcher his second in command for the current operation (Fletcher would soon discover how little that meant) and assumed that Fletcher would take overall command after he left. The potential complication was Crace's seniority, although King clearly intended the senior U.S. naval officer to be in charge. Crace's date of rank was 1 August 1939; Fletcher's 1 November 1939. Brown described Crace as "most intelligent and co-operative" and "most anxious that his squadron shall operate as an integral part of our force."[2]

TF-11 Op-Ord 5-42 explained how Brown planned to unite TF-11, TF-17, and the Anzac Squadron into one large Task Force 11. The main body would comprise the *Lexington* and *Yorktown* (Task Group 11.5) under the *Lex*'s Capt. Frederick Sherman, Admiral Kinkaid's three heavy cruisers (TG-11.2), and ten destroyers (TG-11.4) under Capt. Alexander R. Early (Comdesron One). Rear Adm. William W. Smith's TG-11.8 (three heavy cruisers, two destroyers) received the unenviable chore of bombarding Rabaul, while Admiral Crace's TG-11.9 (two heavy cruisers, two destroyers) did the honors for Gasmata. Following a cautious, fuel-conserving approach, Brown aimed to traverse the Solomon Sea on the afternoon of 9 March in hopes of avoiding the enemy air search and that evening, when 450 miles southeast of Rabaul, commence a twenty-five-knot gallop overnight to the launch point. The carriers would launch before dawn on 10 March when 125 miles from the two targets, while the two cruiser groups steered for their respective objectives. The carriers would make only one attack and swiftly retire. Meanwhile, Crace and Smith were to go in independently without air cover, complete their bombardments by noon, then withdraw and rejoin the carriers two days later 750 miles southeast of Rabaul. Brown promised to cancel their missions if it was discovered enemy ships already decamped. He also gave Crace and Smith the freedom to attack or withdraw at their discretion. They could quickly get in over their heads if the opposition proved formidable.[3]

Brown's radical rearrangement of the task forces put Fletcher out of a job unless Brown became incapacitated. Despite the highfalutin title "second in command" (CTG-11.1), Fletcher fit nowhere in the chain of command. No one reported directly to him. He was not even accorded the courtesy of an addressee of the operations order. The reason lay in Brown's extraordinary handling of the carriers. Far from retaining the *Lexington* and *Yorktown* in individual task groups, he incorporated them directly in the same screen. "We may be able to iron out the difficulties of working two carriers together in close proximity to each other." That was a radical change over U.S. doctrine. Brown's inspiration was Frederick "Ted" Sherman, the prospective Commander, Air (CTG-11.5). A 1910 Annapolis graduate, Sherman tried his hand at subs and destroyers before earning his wings in 1936 at age forty-seven. Commanding the *Lexington* for nearly two years enhanced her reputation as a highly efficient, well-run warship. Sherman was a "headstrong, outspoken, and a taskmaster," who was "also a fearless, extremely skilled shiphandler and tactician" wrapped in an ego the size of the *Lex* with the ambition to match. The pioneer naval aviator community deeply distrusted him as an uppity JCL, but Sherman proved more farsighted. He was one of the first to realize the importance of concentrating carrier air power. The danger, though, in yoking these two particular flattops involved their disparate tactical (turning) diameters: two thousand yards for the *Lexington* versus the *Yorktown*'s one thousand yards. Not only was the *Lady Lex* about the same size as the RMS *Titanic*, but also, unfortunately, her rudder

Rear Adm. Frederick C. Sherman, 19 December 1942.
Courtesy of National Archives (80-G-34231)

was equally nonresponsive. During evasive maneuvers it might prove impossible to keep the two carriers together, but Sherman accepted that risk to enhance coordination.[4]

On the afternoon of 6 March the *Yorktown* dispatched a boat containing Fletcher, Lewis, and Galpin from the TF-17 staff, as well as Buckmaster and Arnold, to visit the *Lexington*. They conferred with Brown, chief of staff Captain Robertson, Capt. C. Turner Joy (the able TF-11 operations officer), Sherman, and Cdr. H. S. Duckworth (the *Lex*'s fine air officer). It was a brief and awkward gathering. "Very reluctant to make an attack" but unable to "avoid it," Brown deplored having to close within 125 miles to permit the short-ranged torpedo bombers and fighters to participate. Fletcher replied the *Yorktown* experts had set a maximum limit of 175 miles, but that he personally recommended 125 to 150 miles "to be on the safe side." Buckmaster preferred 100 miles. Brown distrusted the "stereotyped" dawn strike and worried he could be ambushed at sunup with the aircraft still on board. Should weather and visibility permit, he hoped to attack three hours prior to sunrise. Buckmaster and Arnold countered that most of the *Yorktown* Air Group had yet to qualify at night and expressed little confidence in the accuracy of night bombing, particularly by only a quarter moon. Fletcher strongly advised against a night strike, so Brown reverted to a dawn launch. That afternoon Sherman drew up his air task group operations order. He allocated fifty-three planes to each target, the *Lexington* group to Rabaul and the *Yorktown* for Gasmata. Some *Yorktown* planes could be diverted to Rabaul if necessary. Ironically given Brown's worries about defense, Sherman aggressively earmarked only a dozen of thirty-two F4F fighters to protect TF-11. To the disgust of their pilots, he equipped the twenty escort fighters with a pair of tiny 30-pound fragmentation bombs to (hopefully) catch enemy fighters on the ground. In another debatable move, he withheld eight SBD dive bombers from the strike for a low level "anti-torpedo-plane patrol" around the carriers.[5]

Such was the bare bones of the plan. Fletcher did not consider it "tactically sound as it risked too much for the objectives to be gained." Poco Smith was livid over the prospects of a lonely dash fifty miles up St. George's Channel to Rabaul harbor possibly under "continuous" air attack, with the additional prospect of unsupported surface action against cruisers. "I could expect no air cover whatsoever." One strike wave by just one carrier air group could only take out a few of the many ships expected at Rabaul and probably not all of the planes either. Crace was pleased his Anzac Squadron would shell Gasmata and not merely protect the carriers. He explained personally to Brown on 7 March that such an aggressive assignment was of the "utmost importance for the morale of his personnel, who felt strongly that they should take an active part in all offensive operations in the Anzac area." According to Crace, Brown had "no intention of making this a bald-headed raid and he proposed to take all precautions to safeguard the carriers," despite the considerable risk to Smith.[6]

A NEW TARGET

Brown and Fletcher prepared for action. On the afternoon of 6 March the *Kaskaskia* had completed fueling TF-11 and Crace's Anzac Squadron. It marked the *Australia*'s first try at underway refueling from an oiler. Crace noticed her Capt. Harold B. Farncomb did not appear "keen" at the prospect, but "after various struggles with hoses [he] got connected up" and in two hours drew nearly fourteen hundred barrels. Fortunately "it was a fine calm day" and fueling "will come much easier the next time." The "Americans have made it a fine art." The *Kaskaskia* and a destroyer withdrew south to safer waters, while the *Guadalupe* and a destroyer left for Suva.[7]

Even as Brown and Fletcher conversed on 6 March, Leary warned of movement westward out of Rabaul toward New Guinea. That evening another Comanzac message placed seven medium transports and a cruiser off Gasmata. The next morning Rochefort's Combat Intelligence Unit (Hypo) in Hawaii advised that the New Britain area was "fairly quiet," but air reconnaissance had detected a shift of forces west toward Salamaua in New Guinea. Busy topping off his ships, Brown could not or would not take immediate action.[8]

Admiral Inoue's South Seas Force had indeed gotten the jump on Anzac. Prewar strategic planning was remarkably ambiguous regarding the course of the Pacific War after Japan attained its initial objectives in the "Southern Area" (Malaya, Philippines, and Dutch East Indies). Within the "Southeast Area" (that is, south and east of the Mandates), planners had envisioned only going as far south as Rabaul and east to the Gilberts to gain linchpins for their defensive perimeter. They worried about Australia as a focus of Allied resistance and a potential source of counteroffensives but doubted they could do much about it. In January 1942, with the Southern Operation going unexpectedly well, the Naval Section of Imperial General Headquarters daringly looked far beyond Rabaul to isolate Australia and knock it out of the war. "British New Guinea" and the Solomon Islands would come first, but even the capture of distant Fiji and Samoa looked feasible. At the same time Admiral Yamamoto's Combined Fleet staff seriously considered the invasion of Hawaii once they defeated the Pacific Fleet. "Victory Disease" rendered the Japanese overconfident to the point of recklessness, but they still had to reckon with the Pacific Fleet. Fletcher would personally figure in determining the outcome.[9]

Inoue's first step, timed for early March, was the SR Operation: the seizure of Salamaua and adjacent Lae in eastern New Guinea 350 miles west of Rabaul. SR represented "Saramoa-Rae," the Japanese rendition of Salamaua and Lae. Lae airfield would facilitate an air offensive against Port Moresby 180 miles southeast on the south Papuan coast. The capture of Port Moresby would follow in early April to secure a keystone in the new defensive perimeter and the "gateway" to Australia. Inoue coveted Tulagi in the southern Solomons for its superb harbor. With those two vital locales safely in hand, he could directly threaten northern Australia and New Caledonia. The severe plane losses suffered on 20 February in Brown's abortive Rabaul strike forced Inoue to postpone the Salamaua-Lae invasion from 3 to 8 March. That significant delay allowed Fletcher to reach the Anzac Area. Despite the demonstrated presence of at least one U.S. carrier and his own lack of carrier support (the light carrier *Shōhō* only transported aircraft), Inoue nonchalantly proceeded with the SR Operation. On the afternoon of 5 March, Admiral Kajioka, the conqueror of Wake, left Rabaul with his SR Invasion Force of one light cruiser, six destroyers, one fast minelayer, one seaplane tender, five transports, and two minesweepers. That evening Admiral Gotō's Support Force (four heavy cruisers, two light cruisers, and three destroyers) sailed to protect his seaward flank. At Rabaul were fifteen fighters, twenty-one medium bombers, and six flying boats, with the *Shōhō* to deliver nineteen more fighters on 9 March. A small number of Zero fighters would move up near Gasmata, two hundred miles from Lae, to provide air cover for the SR Invasion Force and would stage to Lae as soon as the airfield was ready. Bombers pounded Port Moresby, while flying boats ranged the upper Solomons and the northern Coral Sea on alert for Allied warships that might intervene.[10]

On the evening of 7 March as TF-11 proceeded northwest across the Coral Sea, Brown received a long-delayed sighting report of a half-dozen transports discovered that morning west of Gasmata. However, he still did not think that sufficient reason to go faster than the leisurely twelve knots required to remain on schedule for his 10 March attacks. Near to midnight word came of a convoy (six transports escorted by one cruiser and four destroyers) sighted 150 miles southwest of Gasmata and bound for the northeast New Guinea coast. Buna, a mission 140 miles southeast of Salamaua, was a possible destination. Brown instantly abandoned Rabaul-Gasmata in favor of Buna and especially Salamaua, the obvious enemy objective. He exulted "this was the very break we had been hoping for and praying for," the "opportunity to catch Japanese navy and transports away from the concentrated defense of their shore-based planes." Striking before Japan consolidated its hold on eastern New Guinea would "remove any immediate threat to Port Moresby and go far towards checking the enemy's advance." Of course an earlier attack on Rabaul proper might have delayed, if not prevented, the actual leap to New Guinea. Brown headed west at twenty knots. The challenge was to draw sufficiently close (125 miles) for a full carrier strike. With Salamaua and nearby

Lae tucked far up Huon Gulf and the way barred by the east-jutting Papuan peninsula, TF-11 would have to cross the narrow gap of 140 miles between Papua's outlying islands and New Britain in order to approach directly from the east. Should Brown wish to attack there as soon as possible on 9 March, he must run at twenty-five knots for thirty-six hours and consume oil at a prodigious rate, although the destroyers could start with nearly full fuel. However it would be virtually impossible to traverse or even draw near those restricted waters without being sighted on 8 March by air patrols from Rabaul and Gasmata.[11]

At 0200 on 8 March Brown reduced speed to twelve knots. After careful deliberation he chose to launch his attack on Salamaua and Lae from southeast in the Gulf of Papua near Port Moresby. Roused in the middle of the night, Sherman discovered the Rabaul attack was shelved in favor of New Guinea. "This suited Brown to a tee," he recalled, "as he didn't want to get within range of their shore bases but did want to attack their ships from a distance." Brown's proposed launch point, two hundred miles southeast of the target, would be well beyond air strike range for all but the dive bombers. Inasmuch as the charts were totally blank inside the shorelines, Sherman was ignorant of the exact topography along the projected strike route. The aircraft must cross the rugged Owen Stanley mountains, whose cloud-enshrouded peaks were reputed to rise as high as fifteen thousand feet. He argued for reinstating the original Rabaul plan or executing a safer strike from east of Salamaua, but Brown refused.[12]

Before dawn on 8 March two thousand Japanese soldiers stormed ashore at Salamaua and eight hundred naval troops at Lae. Kajioka's ships began the lengthy process of unloading supplies and base equipment. At the same time Gotō's Support Force started eastward back across the Solomon Sea toward Buka to survey the area before returning to Rabaul. Late on the morning of 8 March Brown finally received word that Lae and Salamaua had fallen. He consolidated his forces into the one big TF-11. The two carriers slid into the center, surrounded by Kinkaid's cruisers and Early's destroyers, while Crace and Smith took station four miles ahead. As yet no one outside the *Lexington* knew officially that Brown changed the objective, but the westerly course augured differently. Crace wondered what he was up to, and Fletcher did as well. Finally at 1130 Brown increased speed to twenty knots. In the meantime Sherman studied the proposed launch point. Its distance from the target, two hundred miles, ruled out both torpedo planes and escort fighters, not to mention that the lumbering TBDs could not vault over high mountains. They could rarely top six thousand feet when laden with torpedoes and full tanks. Chronic poor weather over the mountains further jeopardized a safe return, especially at such a distance. Drawing a 125-mile semicircle from Salamaua on the chart, Sherman noticed that it cut across the top of the Gulf of Papua almost directly south of the target area. Perhaps the carriers could proceed farther west and launch from there. He needed expert counsel regarding the mountains south of Salamaua and assurance of sufficient sea room in the Gulf of Papua.[13]

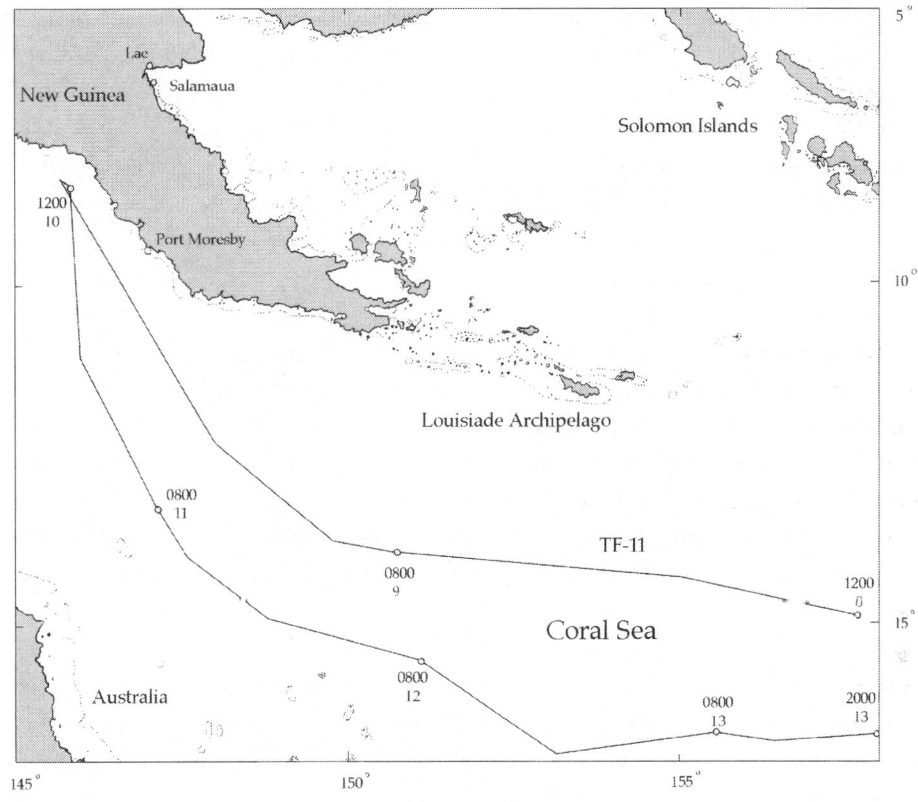

Lae-Salamaua raid, 10 March 1942

Early that afternoon came word of eleven ships off Salamaua, but only near sundown did Brown announce his decision to attack Salamaua from south of Moresby to "check the enemy advance." Crace was to take charge of his own and Smith's cruisers (less the *Pensacola,* to return to Kinkaid) and four destroyers to attack surface forces "when directed." In fact Brown worried about committing TF-11 so far westward out of position to counter threats to New Caledonia. Because one of his prime tasks was to cover the Nouméa convoy, he thought it wise to position Crace's four cruisers east of New Guinea to watch the back door and flank any surface force going after New Caledonia. Crace felt extremely disappointed not to continue with the original plan to attack Rabaul. If that was no longer possible, he wanted to cut through China Strait (a perilous trip due to coral reefs) and race up the northeast coast of Papua to Salamaua. "As Rabaul is the nest [Brown] should have maintained it as his chief objective & let the surface forces go for Salamoa [*sic*] & Lae. If only he had kept on at 20 knots last night & got into the area between New Britain & New Guinea, I'm sure we should have more chances of gaining our objective. I wonder if the last attack shook Brown's nerve." On the other hand Fletcher fully agreed with Brown's decision not to raid Rabaul, although the *Yorktown* aviators much preferred taking on Salamaua from the east.[14]

Before dawn on 9 March as TF-11 drew level with the east tip of New Guinea, Cdr. Walton W. Smith, the staff aviation officer, rode a *Lexington* SBD to the air base at

Townsville in northeastern Australia. He delivered Brown's request for B-17 strikes against Salamaua, Lae, and perhaps even Rabaul on 10 March. Brown soon received an affirmative from Leary, who doubted, though, "much valuable shipping remains Salamaua." Late that evening he notified Brown that eight army B-17s would bomb Salamaua and Lae about noon the next day. Cdr. William B. Ault, the *Lexington* Air Group commander, dropped in on Port Moresby between air raids and brought back invaluable information. A seventy-five-hundred-foot pass through the mountains lay almost on the direct line between the Gulf of Papua and Salamaua, and the mountains themselves were generally free of clouds in the morning. Relieved, Sherman secured permission to attack the morning of 10 March, weather permitting, then issued his operations order. Buckmaster shared it with Fletcher. Of special note Sherman cautiously armed the *Yorktown*'s TBDs for horizontal bombing with two instead of three 500-pound bombs, but risked the *Lex*'s TBDs with 2,000-pound torpedoes to hurdle the mountain pass. Likewise most SBDs carried one 500-pound bomb against ships and two 100-pounders to drop on the airfields, but again six *Lexington* SBDs toted 1,000-pound bombs. Sherman provided a detailed schedule of launches and a series of attacks by squadrons at ten-minute intervals, with the *Yorktown* as a second wave a half hour after the *Lex*.[15]

Also on the morning of the ninth Crace's TG-11.7 (*Australia, Chicago, Astoria, Louisville,* and four destroyers) doubled back toward the Louisiade Archipelago. Crace was to remain beyond six hundred miles of Rabaul, out of air search range, and stand ready should the Japanese move south into the Coral Sea. Brown told him to rejoin on 14 March in the Coral Sea, 350 miles south of Guadalcanal. Crace read his new orders with "great sadness," as he believed his force was being wasted. He judged "unlikely" a Japanese move toward New Caledonia, but just in case, at dawn on 10 March he would be in position southeast of Rossel in the Louisiades.[16]

OVER THE MOUNTAINS

After dawn on 10 March the rugged New Guinea topography loomed uncomfortably close as TF-11 crossed the confined waters at the head of the Gulf of Papua. With Brown's permission Sherman advanced the launch almost three hours to 0745 to take advantage of the customary fine mid-morning weather over the mountains. Unfortunately he failed to pass the word to the *Yorktown* in timely fashion, causing Fletcher and Buckmaster last-minute anxiety. From 0749 to 0850 the carriers lofted two strike groups totaling 104 aircraft (eighteen fighters, sixty-one dive bombers, and twenty-five TBDs). The burly *Lexington*, burdened with only one very slow working flight deck elevator amidships, could only ever commit one true deck load to any strike. In this case Sherman took the highly unusual step of launching his short-legged fighter escorts first along with the combat air patrol F4Fs, followed by all the SBDs and TBDs. When the deck was finally clear he recovered the eight escorts, topped off their tanks, and rushed them off a second time to catch up with the rest of the strike that already departed. Sherman told the *Yorktown* to handle her fighter escort the same way but need not have bothered. CV-5 possessed three fast elevators and thus ready ability to stage planes out the hangar. Buckmaster therefore employed three convenient deck loads: the first of twenty-five planes (thirteen VS-5 SBDs and twelve VT-5 TBDs), the second with seventeen VB-5 SBDs, and last the ten VF-42 escort F4Fs whose higher cruising speed allowed them to overtake the others in an innovative "running rendezvous" en route to the target. The entire launch went smoothly. One *Yorktown* pilot insisted on flying the mission with a balky engine, an indication of the high morale in the air group. That was despite the forbidding terrain and very primitive survival "gear," a meat cleaver and a bottle of aspirin.[17]

From the *Yorktown*'s flag bridge Fletcher watched his squadrons climb bravely toward the dark green mountains and disappear from view. Even before they reached the target, coast-watcher reports relayed via Australia placed about thirteen transports, two cruisers, and three destroyers off Lae. Around 0922 TF-11 copied the first radio messages from attackers over the target. Almost simultaneously Forrest Biard, the TF-17 radio intercept officer, monitored frantic air raid warnings at Salamaua. The radio chatter signaled the aviators were having a field day. Buckmaster relayed the joyous clamor over the *Yorktown*'s loudspeakers. At 1014 eight B-17s passed high over TF-11, and eight RAAF Hudson medium bombers also headed north to Salamaua. A half hour later the first *Lex* strike planes reappeared, eager to come on board and report. Eventually all returned except one SBD downed by antiaircraft fire at Lae. By 1201 all fifty-two *Yorktown* planes landed safely with much happier tidings than on 1 February. Several pilots briefed Fletcher, who was thrilled they surprised so many ships. The weather turned out to be "excellent," antiaircraft was weak, and only two float planes showed up, both of which were swiftly shot down. Luckily poor weather kept a half dozen Zero fighters from advancing on the ninth to Lae.[18]

Lexington aviators first estimated that five transports were sunk or beached, a cruiser and a destroyer also sunk, and one cruiser and two destroyers badly damaged. The *Yorktown* aircrews counted thirteen or fifteen ships off Salamaua-Lae, as well as a seaplane tender and a destroyer twenty-five miles east in Huon Gulf, and an additional transport and destroyer glimpsed at Hanisch Harbor northeast of Lae. They also noted the five sunken transports or cargo ships off Lae and Salamaua, a medium-sized cruiser that swallowed at least four bombs, and two destroyers dead in the water. The VT-5 TBDs bombed the seaplane tender and supposedly left her drifting without power. Returning *Yorktown* aviators warned of "many ships retiring to eastward at high speed." Commander Armstrong, commanding officer of VB-5, and last to leave the target, radioed: "Recommend second attack immediately." Burch of VS-5 personally urged Fletcher to strike again. Biard advised that a preliminary analysis of enemy radio traffic failed to confirm numerous sinkings. Fletcher directed Buckmaster to rearm and refuel the *Yorktown* attack group and to suggest another wave to Brown and Sherman. Buckmaster sent the message at 1316, but Brown refused. "No second attack was made because damage to enemy shipping found in the attack area was considered to be decisive and complete," so "we had accomplished our mission." Brown worried the crucial mountain pass usually filled with clouds in the afternoon, which Fletcher and Buckmaster did not know. Sherman, like Brown, was not eager to test fate again. He speculated had the good visibility disappeared, both carrier air groups might have suffered catastrophic losses recrossing the mountains. "I do not recommend that this kind of an operation for carrier planes be repeated very often." Yet such conditions should not have ruled out the long-ranged, high-flying SBDs from going back again. The *Yorktown*ers disputed the "decisive" nature of the attack and were very disappointed not to go again. They took the measure of the weather and the terrain and were confident they could strike again without difficulty.[19]

Sherman concluded the *Lex* and *Yorktown* planes thrashed fifteen ships off Salamaua and Lae. Some twenty-five miles east another force appeared with at least one cruiser, four destroyers, one seaplane tender, and six transports. Its escorts raced ahead to Salamaua only to encounter more *Yorktown* SBDs, while VT-5 TBDs caught up with the seaplane tender farther out to sea. Sherman knew numerous ships had not been attacked or cripples finished off. Following the carrier strike, the eight B-17s claimed hits on at least two transports and damaging near misses against several warships, including a cruiser, while RAAF Hudsons tallied six hits on large ships left burning. At first it was thought they bombed newly arriving forces, but Leary later conceded they attacked ships that TF-11 had already pounded. Brown's final assessment listed five transports or cargo ships, two heavy cruisers, one light cruiser, and one destroyer sunk, and one auxiliary minesweeper probably destroyed. Two destroyers and one gunboat were "seriously damaged, probably sunk," whereas another gunboat and a seaplane tender were badly damaged. Nimitz believed at least two units of the 6th Cruiser Division sustained heavy damage if not sunk outright, but no heavy cruisers were there. Actually three transports and one converted minesweeper went down; a transport, seaplane tender, fast minelayer, and two destroyers suffered medium damage. This was much less than Brown claimed. Nevertheless, the loss to Inoue's South Seas Force was significant.[20]

TF-11 retired southeast at twenty knots until nightfall, then east at fifteen knots. Events prevented more than a feeble gesture of retaliation. The horde of carrier-type planes over Salamaua certainly horrified the South Seas Force. For a time the high command feared enemy carriers were about to strike Rabaul. At first it was uncertain whether the attacking planes came directly from a carrier or staged through Port Moresby. That question was resolved at 1720, when a flying boat located a *Saratoga*-class carrier and escorts ninety miles east of Port Moresby. Daylight was too fleeting for an air strike, especially with the enemy headed away. Inoue ordered air searches for the next day and held land attack planes in reserve, but in vain, for TF-11 soon retired well out of range. Neither Biard's radio intelligence unit or other radio intelligence analysts in Australia and Hawaii picked up the Japanese sighting report.[21]

Fletcher wrote Brown on 11 March to offer his "personal congratulations for the splendid job your force did yesterday." He fully agreed with shifting the objective from Rabaul and Gasmata to Lae and Salamaua and called it a "fine plan and well executed." However, he revealed his misgivings regarding the original Rabaul-Gasmata attack plan and concurred with a fiery letter (which has not been preserved) that Poco Smith had sent Brown regarding the proposed Rabaul bombardment. Fletcher commended Smith's "moral courage" for writing it. "I do not hesitate to tell you this because it seems probable that you issued the order reluctantly in order to execute the desires of the high command." The next day Brown replied rather icily that he felt he had no choice but to attack Rabaul and Gasmata and affirmed "our plan was the best way to handle it." Fletcher responded: "Your point is well taken and I accept the correction." However, one has the impression that this cruise did not exactly enhance their relationship. Smith subsequently learned that

Sherman had written the original operations order directing the cruiser bombardment and that Turner Joy, Brown's operations officer, had not approved that plan.[22]

Brown exulted that he had stopped the "immediate attack" in New Guinea. Never realizing that TF-11 had been sighted, he thought the Japanese remained mystified over the source of the massive air strike and believed they must stop and regroup before proceeding further. "Any such delay was to our advantage," he later explained. At first Nimitz was surprised to learn that Brown struck New Guinea and not Rabaul, and Soc McMorris opined, "It is doubtful if the enemy will be greatly retarded." However from Brown's additional reports, it seemed apparent at Pearl that the "damage inflicted was really great," a point of view fully shared by Inoue and his army counterparts. Brown inflicted the greatest loss of ships yet suffered by the IJN during World War II and either sank or crippled key amphibious ships needed for several pending invasions, including not only Moresby and Tulagi (the so-called MO Operation), but also Ocean and Nauru islands northeast of the Solomons. Now truly aware he needed carriers, Inoue petitioned Yamamoto for the loan of a carrier division for the MO Operation. However, his request ran afoul of other Combined Fleet commitments, including a foray into the Indian Ocean and ordinary upkeep that would tie up the carriers for the next two months. Therefore Inoue postponed the MO Operation until he could count on strong carrier support. In the meantime he would reorganize and greatly bolster his land-based air, secure the area around Rabaul, and reconnoiter the route to Moresby. In the interval the Allies, too, would grow stronger. Brown's Lae-Salamaua strike had indeed done its job. Roosevelt crowed to Churchill on 17 March that it was "by all means the best day's work we have had." Cominch sent a rare "well done" for all hands in TF-11, not only for the successful raid but also the "seamanship, endurance and tenacity of purpose" of its lengthy cruise that was "inspiration and incentive" for the entire navy.[23]

BROWN SHOVES OFF

On 12 March as TF-11 moved southeast into the Coral Sea, Nimitz offered Brown and Fletcher a hearty "well done." He also instructed Brown to detach the *Pensacola* to TF-17 and retire to Pearl, while Fletcher continued to operate in the Anzac Area. Nimitz reiterated King's message of 7 March for TF-11 to "make good whatever plane and/or armament munitions personnel deficiencies may exist in TF17." Despite Brown's concern about provisions for his return voyage, King told him to dine on "beans and hardtack" instead of drawing upon the few supplies already in the South Pacific. That amused Secretary Knox, but it was no laughing matter for TF-11. The *Lexington* was down mainly to canned spinach and beans, and the cuisine on the cruisers and destroyers was much worse.[24]

At dawn on 14 March Crace's TG-11.7 hove into view. His mission had gone well, with no enemy contacts, but routine searches had cost the U.S. cruisers an appalling five missing Curtiss SOC Seagull float planes. To add to his troubles, two sailors killed a petty officer on board the *Australia*. That crime would eventually alter Crace's plans. On 13 March he had stationed the cruisers ten miles apart to sweep a huge area, but found nothing and left for the next day's rendezvous with Brown. Crace's "signal of sympathy" to Poco Smith elicited "a very nice reply." Smith theorized that a squall had forced the Seagulls to set down on the sea. That morning one of them had radioed for the bearing and course of the ship, but Smith steadfastly refused to break radio silence and risk revealing his position to the Japanese. The SOCs were stout aircraft, he told Crace, and he hoped they would reach land somewhere. Indeed Smith's faith in his cruiser aviators was buoyed when he later learned how that very day TF-11 had retrieved the *San Francisco*'s missing SOC adrift since 7 March.[25]

At noon on 14 March the heavy cruiser *Portland*, oilers *Neosho* and *Kaskaskia*, and four destroyers joined the conclave of ships in the eastern Coral Sea. The *Lexington* transferred six fighters, five dive bombers, and one torpedo plane to the *Yorktown* in return for her two oldest fighters. Before reaching the *Yorktown* one *Lex* Wildcat ditched from engine trouble—an ominous hint of troubles to come. Later that day Brown dissolved the combined task force into its component parts, which returned TF-17 to Fletcher's command. The *Portland* took the *Louisville*'s place in TF-17 to release her for a much-needed West Coast refit. Crace's Anzac Squadron left for Nouméa to fuel from one of Leary's auxiliary fleet oilers and would then come under Fletcher's command. Before going their separate ways, TF-11 and TF-17 greedily drained the two oilers. Finally on the morning of 16 March, Fletcher headed southeast, leaving Brown to complete his fueling and start northeast for home.[26]

Wilson Brown reached Pearl on 26 March to a tumultuous welcome. Nimitz gave him until the twenty-eighth to bask in the glory, then gently informed him he would no longer have either the Scouting Force or TF-11. Instead he was to go to San Diego to form the Amphibious Force of the Pacific Fleet. On 20 February King had directed the Atlantic and Pacific Fleets each to form its own amphibious force. Nimitz proposed Brown as his amphibious commander and that Vice Adm. Bill Pye, another black shoe and even older, relieve him as CTF-11. Given his role in Pacific Fleet amphibious planning in 1941, Brown was the logical choice. His departure from carrier command had nothing to do with any perceived impression of lack of "aggressiveness." He received the DSM for his tenure as CTF-11, and certainly retained the good wishes of King, who after the war rated him "pretty good" and deplored that his health was not better. Indeed King always treated Brown more considerately than he did Fletcher, possibly because he never gained a true picture of Fletcher's accomplishments. The courtly Brown soon passed from the Pacific scene to command a naval district on the East Coast. In early 1943 he happily returned to the White House as FDR's naval aide and served in that capacity until 1945.[27]

Fletcher remained to face a resolute and aggressive enemy in the vast southwest Pacific. If he was alone, at least he was in charge. Up to this point he was one of the supporting cast, but with the spotlight turned directly onto him, the top commanders wondered how he would fare.

CHAPTER 8

Alone in the Coral Sea

EVOLVING A DEFENSIVE STRATEGY

After Wilson Brown's TF-11 departed on 16 March, Fletcher's TF-17 came under the direct operational control of Cominch in Washington. King formally defined Fletcher's mission as "offensive action against enemy activities [in the] New Guinea area and eastward," especially Port Moresby and the Solomon Islands. He gave Fletcher discretion to attack as he saw fit "to cripple and destroy enemy forces." Leary again would coordinate land-based Army Air Forces (AAF) and RAAF bomber support that seemed "so effective" on 10 March at Lae and Salamaua. Despite rosy appraisals of the 10 March counterattack, Japan still held the initiative. Any lull would only be temporary, inasmuch as Java had fallen and the Philippines were completely isolated. The enemy could strike southward from Rabaul whenever he chose to commit the necessary strength.[1]

The prime Japanese objective in the region was Port Moresby, the indispensable Australian air base located on the southeast coast of New Guinea. Geography largely shielded Moresby from direct assault by land and sea. The harsh Owen Stanley mountains appeared virtually impenetrable to troops marching south across Papua. To seaward beyond New Guinea the Louisiade Archipelago, a barrier of islands and reefs, extended nearly 250 miles into the Coral Sea. Although Moresby was 440 air miles southwest of Rabaul, skirting the Louisiades added five hundred more miles to the sea route. Only two true gaps existed: poorly charted Jomard Passage in the center (840 miles) and narrow China Strait off the east tip of New Guinea (670 miles). Because of reefs and fast currents, U.S. planners judged the full detour around the Louisiades the only safe convoy route. Tulagi, a fine harbor in the lower Solomon Islands eight hundred miles east of Moresby and 550 miles southeast of Rabaul, was another logical goal. Although valuable as a flying boat base for searches northward beyond Rabaul, the Australians left Tulagi undefended due to its exposed position. Japanese air power at Tulagi would ease the way for task forces that could threaten not only the rest of the Solomons, but also New Caledonia and the New Hebrides beyond. Its capture would be simpler than Port Moresby. The Japanese already opened a limited bombing campaign against Port Moresby and Tulagi.

Fletcher had to defend both Port Moresby and the Solomons with the *Yorktown*, heavy cruisers *Astoria*, *Portland*, and *Pensacola*, and six destroyers, barely half the strength of the old combined TF-11. Leary directed Crace's Anzac Squadron (heavy cruisers HMAS *Australia*,

USS *Chicago*, and two U.S. destroyers) to operate "as desired by Fletcher," but three weeks would elapse before they would actually be available. Anzac air reconnaissance was poorly organized, and B-17 bombers in northeastern Australia dwindled through attrition. Strong air reinforcements were en route from the United States, but the first of the new AAF groups would not be in place before early April. For additional guidance, Fletcher followed the Cominch general directive of 26 February that deplored "offensive sweeps," intended to deter the enemy by merely allowing the task force to be spotted, and raiding shore bases that lacked significant ship targets.[2]

Perhaps the most dramatic way for Fletcher to delay a brewing southwest Pacific offensive was to revive Brown's original idea of a carrier raid and cruiser bombardment of Rabaul. For his own part Brown now emphasized that growing enemy air power in the region prevented U.S. carriers from operating with impunity. On 16 March he advised King, Nimitz, Leary, and Fletcher that the alert air warning network no longer permitted surprise carrier raids on major bases such as Rabaul. Yet TF-17 simply lacked the strength to bull its way in. The geography that isolated Port Moresby to eastward formed a bottleneck that worked both ways. Starting with the 350-mile gap between the Louisiades and Solomons, access to Rabaul from the south grew more restricted the closer a carrier force neared air strike range. To attack Rabaul from the east beyond the Solomons would entail a radical detour that could uncover distant Moresby. Thus Fletcher ruled out preemptive attack on Rabaul. The necessity of defending both New Guinea and the Solomons constrained him to deploy in the center in the Coral Sea, where the enemy's necessarily long voyage to Port Moresby should offer favorable opportunities for ambush. Likewise ships attacking Tulagi could be vulnerable to a carrier counterstroke.[3]

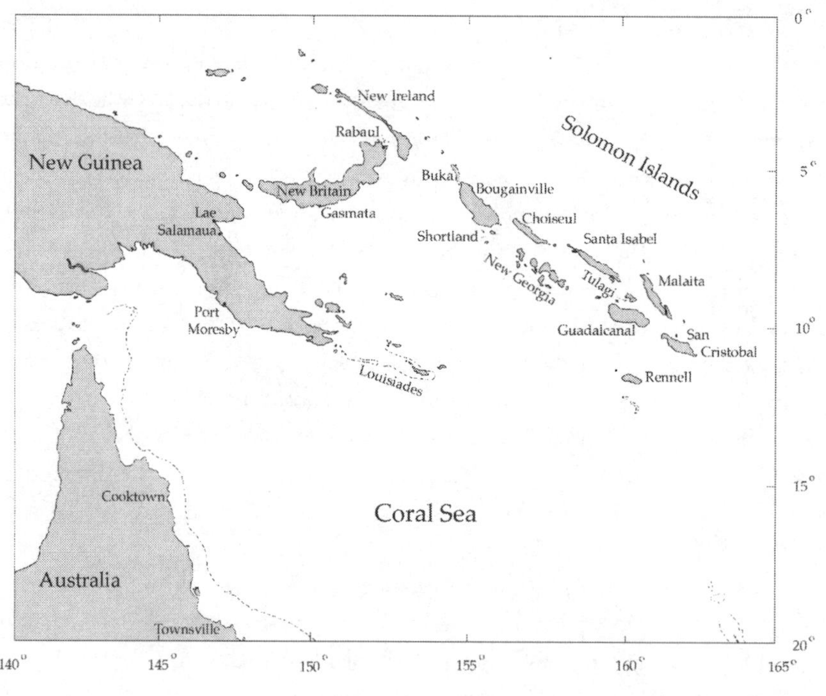

Coral Sea and vicinity

King considered the defense of New Guinea and particularly the Solomons a holding action while he built up a series of South Pacific bases behind them. In February and March he fought his own battles with General Marshall and General Arnold over the allocation of precious resources to the South Pacific. These three top leaders comprised a command body soon to be known as the Joint Chiefs of Staff. King chose Suva in Fiji and Tongatabu (later the name was changed to Tongatapu) in the Tonga Islands as advance bases in the South Pacific, backed up by Auckland in New Zealand as the main operating base. Efate in the New Hebrides was to be the first stepping stone of a projected advance up the New Hebrides and the Solomons to Rabaul itself. That became the cornerstone of King's offensive strategy. In contrast the army sought to restrict its involvement in the South Pacific in favor of an early cross-channel assault in Europe. By mid March Marshall succeeded in limiting troop commitments just to Efate and Tongatabu. King could not afford the delay even to wait for those small army garrisons to arrive from the West Coast. Instead he tapped Nimitz's limited number of marines for Tongatabu, while the army commander on New Caledonia sent a few soldiers to Efate.[4]

SQUARING AWAY TO FIGHT AGAIN

Both communications and logistics seriously constricted Fletcher's role as the first line of defense for King's nascent South Pacific bases. Brown urged that task force commanders be accorded more flexibility to accomplish their missions. They, not Cominch or Comanzac, should decide exactly when and where to attack. The nature of radio communications compelled that essential independence. Strict policy and common sense dictated a commander dare not break radio silence except in an emergency, or else risk alerting his foe of his presence and being located by radio direction finders. The only exceptions were the TBS VHF voice radios, thought undetectable beyond short range, and the much less secure medium-range high-frequency voice radios the carrier fighter director officers used. Instead, cruiser float planes periodically flew outgoing dispatches to the nearest shore base for radio transmission but could do so only if they were within flying range and the weather cooperated. Unavoidable delays in getting the word out caused King and Leary considerable exasperation and colored their perception of Fletcher. As yet Fletcher could not even read all the radio messages addressed to him in the highest flag cipher systems. He asked Cincpac to vet his radio traffic and retransmit those sent in a system he did not hold. Crace, his senior subordinate, did not even possess a U.S. ECM, but depended on the *Chicago* to forward his messages. Nonetheless, Leary refused to issue Crace an ECM because King restricted them to U.S. ships. Crace lamented, "It's a great pity if the U.S. aren't going to trust us completely."[5]

The shaky logistical situation in the remote southwest Pacific forced Fletcher to pay close attention to supply, with fuel always the dominant concern. The next oiler in the rotation was Cdr. Atherton Macondray's venerable *Tippecanoe*, older and at 10.5 knots even slower than the late *Neches*. That and her modest cargo (sixty-five thousand barrels, about 60 percent of a *Cimarron*) severely limited her service to a fast carrier task force. Better news was the expected appearance at Fiji about 26 March of the crack oiler *Platte*, along with

Capt. Gilbert C. Hoover, Comdesron Two, in the destroyer *Morris*. Fletcher calculated that TF-17 expended about fifty-eight hundred barrels of oil per day at patrol speed (fifteen knots). That did not count the Anzac Squadron, whose fuel was to come from the Royal Australian Navy (RAN) fleet auxiliary tankers *Falkefjell* and *Bishopdale* that Leary shuttled between Sydney and New Caledonia. Those slow ships were not equipped or trained for underway refueling. Fletcher knew he might have to provide fuel to Crace's ships in a pinch, but the reverse was also true. He instructed Macondray to join him at Point Moon one hundred miles southwest of Efate. From 19 to 21 March TF-17 would make daily visits to Moon, but if Macondray could not make it he was to proceed instead to Nouméa. No destroyer could accompany the *Tippecanoe* beyond Suva, a calculated risk that a sub would not pick her off. To save time Fletcher instructed Hoover to bypass Fiji and bring the *Platte* straight out to Nouméa.[6]

Indeed Fletcher much preferred Nouméa as a supply base over either Fiji (675 miles from Nouméa) or Samoa (nearly thirteen hundred miles distant), but Nimitz advised that a base at Tongatabu (code name Bleacher) was to be established about 26 March. A thousand miles northeast of Nouméa, Bleacher was almost as inconvenient as Samoa. Now more than a month out of Pearl, TF-17 urgently needed provisions and other supplies. The stores ship *Bridge* and destroyer tender *Dobbin* were at Samoa, with the hospital ship *Solace* expected shortly. Nimitz authorized Fletcher to move them elsewhere, but only in an emergency. For his own part Fletcher desired Leary to run his support ships and make them more accessible, preferably at Nouméa. Samoa was too far from the "probable scene of operations" in the Coral Sea, and he especially needed the *Bridge*'s food. Unwilling to risk valuable auxiliaries more than absolutely necessary, Nimitz allowed them to come forward for limited intervals, provided Fletcher returned them "promptly" to Samoa. A large convoy, TF-13, had just left Pearl to reach Tongatabu on 28 March with supply personnel and a marine defense battalion, but that was too late to do Fletcher any immediate good. He requested the *Bridge* be at Nouméa on 1 April to provision TF-17 and then return to Samoa. Nimitz issued the necessary orders. Fletcher was surprised to learn that the *Tippecanoe* discharged nearly half her cargo into storage facilities at Suva, leaving only thirty-five thousand barrels on board. Although the *Kaskaskia* gave the *Tippecanoe* additional fuel (fourteen thousand barrels, in fact), Fletcher did not know how much. Before conducting any offensive operations, he must be sure of a ready fuel supply, but now he had considerably less than expected. On 19 March he ordered Macondray to proceed directly to Point Moon and advise his earliest time of arrival. If TF-17 was not there, he was to take the *Tippecanoe* northwest an additional four hundred miles into the Coral Sea, then turn around and head southeast for Nouméa. Macondray replied that he would arrive at Moon on 22 March. Fletcher definitely intended to be there.[7]

Fletcher received great news on 19 March that the RAAF discovered safe at Rossel, on the eastern tip of the Louisiades, all five SOC seaplanes lost from Poco Smith's cruisers the week before. That certainly justified Smith's confidence in his sturdy Seagulls. Told the SOCs might be able to fly back to their cruisers, Fletcher factored that contingency into his future plans. On the evening of 21 March as he steamed toward his rendezvous with the *Tippecanoe*, he composed a radio message to inform King, Nimitz, and Leary of his plans to patrol the Coral Sea. After fueling on 22–23 March north of New Caledonia, TF-17 would sail west to approximately longitude 153° east, south of the Louisiades and just beyond air search range (six hundred miles) of Rabaul. To Leary's request for forty-eight hours notice prior to action to arrange bomber strikes, Fletcher promised "as much advance information as possible," but that depended on circumstances. He again cautioned he must soon break off the patrol and reach Nouméa by 1 April to provision ships. TF-17 operated without Crace's Anzac Squadron, which certainly weakened its chances in the event of a surface action. King abruptly decided that the small army detachment at Efate (code name Roses) must be reinforced immediately and had Nimitz redirect the troop convoy from Tongatabu to Efate. That delayed the establishment of the advance base at Tongatabu and forced Nimitz to scramble for an escort to bring TF-13 safely west to Efate. In turn Leary detached the entire Anzac Squadron to that task, which put Crace beyond immediate support of TF-17 until at least early April.[8]

At noon on 22 March Fletcher met the *Tippecanoe* on schedule west of Efate and spent that day and the next fueling while moving slowly northwest into the Coral Sea. He counted on sending cruiser float planes to Nouméa to deliver radio messages, including his plans for the Coral Sea patrol, but a heavy overcast intervened. With engines turning over, two SOCs sat on catapults for a half hour before Fletcher reluctantly called off the flight. Finally that evening he detached Smith with the *Astoria* and a destroyer southeast toward New Caledonia.[9]

"CAPTAIN LOW TO TELL JIMMY TO MOVE ON"

Nimitz anticipated a welcome reinforcement from the Atlantic, the *Hornet*. He would then have four carriers on line for the first time since 11 January. Along with two cruisers, four destroyers, and a fleet oiler, the *Hornet* reached San Diego on 20 March in Task Force 18, led by her Capt. Marc A. "Pete" Mitscher (USNA 1910), a well regarded pioneer naval aviator already selected for rear admiral. As far as Nimitz knew, the *Hornet* needed only to upgrade aircraft and qualify pilots to be ready for battle. He decided to give TF-18 to Rear Adm. John S. McCain, Commander, Aircraft, Scouting Force, who administered the patrol wings from San Diego. A classmate of Fletcher and Fitch, "Slew" McCain, a profane, disheveled warrior, was another JCL latecomer to naval aviation, having qualified in 1936 at the age of fifty-two. Admiral Halsey's TF-16 (*Enterprise*) returned on 10 March to Pearl after the far-flung raids on Wake (24 February) and Marcus (4 March), while Admiral Brown's TF-11 (*Lexington*) was to arrive before the end of March. Admiral Fletcher's TF-17 (*Yorktown*) alone patrolled in the far South Pacific. As noted above, Nimitz desired Admiral Pye, his most trusted strategic advisor, to relieve Brown as CTF-11. For the *Saratoga*, completing repairs in late May, Nimitz penciled in Rear Adm. Leigh Noyes as task force commander. He reached Pearl on 13 March following a stormy tour as director of naval communications.[10]

Nimitz contemplated operating his four available carriers as two pairs, each under a vice admiral. His most pressing problem was to replace Fletcher's *Yorktown* in the Anzac Area. Halsey with the *Enterprise* could depart Pearl on 21 March and relieve TF-17 on station. How Nimitz intended to use McCain and the *Hornet* is not known. McCain could either come out to Pearl or, more likely, proceed directly to the South Pacific, just as the *Yorktown* did in January. He could escort convoys, deliver aircraft, and otherwise support the South Pacific bases before joining Halsey in the Coral Sea. Meanwhile, Pye's *Lexington* would be in the central Pacific, soon to be joined by Fletcher and the *Yorktown*. A brace of carriers each in the South Pacific and central Pacific would achieve the balanced deployment Nimitz sought in January. Whatever plans he had for his carriers soon became superfluous. On 12 March he informed Cominch of his intention to place McCain in charge of TF-18, but King mysteriously replied the *Hornet* was instead to go in Halsey's TF-16, so McCain was out. King also directed Halsey to fly to the West Coast for a conference after the *Hornet* reached San Diego. That certainly ruined Cincpac's timetable for carrier deployment. On the fourteenth Nimitz responded that TF-16 would be ready to sail on 21 March and TF-17 to leave the Anzac Area about 5 April. The proposed conference, however, required him either to delay the departure of TF-16 or assign a new commander in Halsey's place. King told Nimitz to put everything on hold until his personal representative could brief him.[11]

Nimitz finally got his answer (not the one he wanted) on 19 March. Capt. Donald B. Duncan, Cominch air operations officer, arrived at Pearl with King's secret plan to bomb Japan in mid April. After approaching (hopefully undetected) within 450 miles of the enemy homeland, the *Hornet* was to launch army North American B-25 Mitchell medium bombers under Lt. Col. James H. Doolittle for a one-way night mission against Tokyo and other large cities. They were to land in China. King designated the *Enterprise* to protect the *Hornet*, and Halsey, Nimitz's best carrier commander, to lead the combined task force. The raid had been in the works since January. Asked if he thought he could attack Japan, Halsey responded with enthusiastic affirmation. Far from being excited at the prospect of raiding Japan, Nimitz felt "dubious" at best. Such a grandstand play appeared to serve no strategic purpose other than a dramatic gesture of defiance. He fretted about committing so much effort, half his carriers, to a dangerous raid that would also tie them up in the North Pacific for six weeks. The temporary unavailability of the *Lexington* would leave Fletcher without support in the remote South Pacific. No one knew what effect that might have on fleet strategy. Nimitz's chief of staff Draemel was also opposed. Whatever Nimitz's reservations, he could do nothing about the Tokyo raid. "This was not a proposal made for him to consider but a plan to be carried out by him." At Duncan's behest Nimitz radioed King: "Captain Low to tell Jimmy [Doolittle] to move on. Dates we agreed on are OK."[12]

Cincpac sustained yet another body blow on 19 March, when the whole question arose again of employing TF-1, Admiral Anderson's seven old battleships based at San Francisco. King wanted TF-1 brought out to Pearl, then used in some sort of combat operation, perhaps to advance to where search planes could sight them, presumably off the Marshalls or Gilberts. He had received an urgent personal plea from the Royal Navy's First Sea Lord, Admiral of the Fleet Sir Dudley Pound, who cautioned the fall of Java and the assault on Burma left the Indian Ocean and Ceylon wide open. Some sort of powerful diversion in the next few weeks by the Pacific Fleet "may make all the difference." King told Pound he "can depend on us to do all that we find ourselves in any way able to do to keep the enemy interested in the Pacific." King certainly kept the knowledge of the impending Doolittle raid close to the vest, declining to give even Roosevelt and Knox any details, let alone the British.

Thus bringing the old battleships forward to where the Japanese might sight them came to mind. In addition to drawing attention away from the Indian Ocean, TF-1 might usefully support Halsey's withdrawal from Japanese waters. How the slow old battleships could shield Halsey's carriers when their ability to protect even themselves was in doubt, King did not say. The discovery of battleships prowling the central Pacific could be expected to provoke a powerful Japanese response.[13]

While considering his reply to King, Nimitz completely changed his mind over Pye's future assignment. If King was sending the battleships into action, Pye must command them. On 22 March Nimitz named Pye to succeed Anderson as CTF-1, certainly a more suitable appointment than a carrier command. Nimitz even proposed the fleet comprise a "covering force" under Pye and Brown's Amphibious Force. Fitch would take Brown's place as CTF-11 on the thirty-first, and the *Lexington* could not be in better hands. Nimitz counseled on 23 March, in a message that Duncan carried personally to King, that it might be wiser to keep the battleships on the West Coast at least until mid April, when Halsey neared Japan. The last thing he desired was to stir up the central Pacific before bombs actually fell on Japan. The Tokyo raid should provide enough of a diversion for the Indian Ocean. Mid April was also when Nimitz anticipated having Fitch's TF-11 ready to sail from Pearl. Until then he could provide no carrier air cover for the slow battlewagons, protected by only a weak screen of destroyers. Pye could bring TF-1 out toward Pearl later in April and join TF-11 for operations westward "to intensify enemy concern." Nimitz also warned King that if Fletcher remained in Anzac that whole time, TF-17 must rest and refit in a port. He suggested Sydney.[14]

The events of the past few days deeply depressed Nimitz, although characteristically he never betrayed his worries to his subordinates. King's truculent meddling he took for granted, but Secretary Knox (and by inference the president) snubbed him. Nimitz confided to his wife on 22 March: "I'm afraid [Knox] is not so keen for me now as he was when I left—but that is only natural. Ever so many people were enthusiastic for me at the start but when things do not move fast enough—they sour on me. I will be lucky to last six months. The public may demand action and results faster than I can produce." There was powerful reason to doubt Secnav's support. In February Knox secretly formed an "unofficial selection board" of nine senior officers, active duty and retired, to name the forty "most competent" flag officers in the navy. Five or more votes would constitute selection. Stark and King, on the panel, were the only two serving officers exempted and thus automatically included in the magic forty. Among those directly concerned here, Halsey and Robert Ghormley received eight votes; Royal Ingersoll, Fletcher, Fitch, Richmond Kelly Turner, and Mitscher seven; Leary, McCain, and Smith six; and Draemel and Theobald five. Incredibly Nimitz was not selected, having not received five votes. Nor did Pye, Brown, Noyes, Spruance, or Kinkaid. Knox submitted the results to Roosevelt on 9 March. Almost certainly Nimitz learned of the "selection board" via back channels.[15]

On 27 March King backed down regarding TF-1. Using the battleships to cover the Tokyo raiders was now "not contemplated." He approved Nimitz's suggestion to join TF-1 with TF-11 later in April. Fletcher could have a respite in port, but definitely not Sydney. That move "would inspire political demands to keep him in Australian waters." King shrewdly recognized such "political demands" would originate with the Australian government abetted by Gen. Douglas MacArthur. MacArthur arrived there on 17 March from the Philippines eager to carve out a major piece of the Pacific command. In place of Sydney, King offered Nimitz either Tongatabu, where his new advance base was to be established, or even more remote Auckland.[16]

By late March Cominch had much to worry about, not only in the Pacific, but also the Atlantic, where U-boats ravaged American shipping. Halsey's carriers were preparing to leave for the Tokyo raid. In the desperate days of January what was a good idea to avenge Pearl Harbor might not have been so wise in late March. In the interval King had matured a strategy to hold and fight in the South Pacific. If the Japanese got wind of the carriers on the way in, or the raid otherwise miscarried, the results could be catastrophic. Conversely if Doolittle actually bombed Tokyo, American morale would soar, but even a successful raid would prevent the *Enterprise* and *Hornet* from deploying elsewhere until mid May. Even if King agreed, Fitch and the *Lexington* could not reinforce Fletcher in the South Pacific before the end of April. Thus King gambled that the Japanese would remain quiet in the South Pacific until Nimitz could reorient the rest of his carriers southward. That was all the more ironic because that network of South Pacific bases had become the foundation of King's Pacific strategy. Despite his great fear of a Japanese offensive there, he now contrived to leave the door ajar. For a while it appeared the Japanese would not take advantage, but at the end of March they unwittingly gave King a tremendous scare, causing him to vent his nervous anger on the hapless Fletcher.

KING'S WRATH

On the evening of 23 March, Fletcher welcomed Smith back from his pony express run to Nouméa then got on with the patrol. Nothing critical in terms of enemy action appeared imminent. Recent RAAF air searches of the northern Coral Sea were negative. The Pacific Fleet War Plans Section noted on 18 March how "the enemy seems to be occupied in reorganizing." Fletcher's long-delayed 21 March message finally reached Pearl on 23 March (24 March in the Coral Sea). Already perturbed that Fletcher had not hitherto revealed his intentions, Nimitz was surprised he was not attacking anywhere. Doubtless King and Leary reacted the same way. On 25 March Leary advised Fletcher that a bomber group had apparently moved from Rabaul to Gasmata on New Britain's south coast. To avoid its presumed search radius of six hundred miles, Fletcher curtailed his patrol on 26 March a hundred miles short of longitude 153° east. Thereafter TF-17 marked time in the center of the Coral Sea, waiting for the *Tippecanoe* to catch up so she could be emptied and released to refill from a chartered tanker that Nimitz redirected to Samoa.[17]

On the twenty-seventh Fletcher learned that the five SOCs stranded at Rossel would soon be ready to go. Leary planned to fly them out via Port Moresby to Australia but told Fletcher he could alter that plan by sending a plane directly to Rossel. Inasmuch as TF-17 was already in the neighborhood and things were quiet, Fletcher acted to retrieve the SOCs straightaway. That evening he directed Smith to take the *Astoria* and *Russell* northwest to within flying distance of Rossel and fetch the wayward Seagulls. In the meantime the rest of

TF-17 would top off from the *Tippecanoe* and await his return on the morning of 29 March. The daily Cincpac intelligence bulletin reinforced the impression of a quiescent period. "Indications [are] that losses in New Britain area have restricted activity to air patrols and bombing attacks." Also Fletcher received welcome word that the *Platte* and *Morris* were at Nouméa after having made excellent time from Pearl.[18]

The tranquil situation abruptly changed early on 29 March, when Leary broadcast to King, Nimitz, and Fletcher the startling results of the Anzac air search conducted the previous day. Thirty transports crowded Rabaul harbor. Alarm bells sounded in Washington and Pearl Harbor. To make matters worse radio intelligence analysts at Pearl had just got wind of some sort of Japanese offensive they thought might start on 30 or 31 March—a supposition not vouchsafed to Fletcher. Both King and Nimitz understood Anzac's vulnerability. Unless King immediately canceled the Tokyo raid, no additional carrier could reinforce Fletcher before 1 May.[19]

In turn Fletcher, the man on the spot, again considered attacking the concentration of ships at Rabaul. If he immediately bent on twenty knots he could close to 150 miles (carrier strike range) of Rabaul after sunrise on 30 March. Some of his staff recommended that aggressive move. However, he believed that if he rushed north, the alert air search network would sight him on 29 March, just as happened with Brown. Presumably much of the shipping at Rabaul would then scatter out of range, while the Japanese turned the tables and sent bombers to stalk TF-17. The best Fletcher might do was to damage some merchant ships while risking perhaps catastrophic damage and hence the whole Allied position in the South Pacific. He resolved to provision TF-17 at Nouméa as planned, then regroup and hit the Japanese if they came south. On 29 March, right on time, the *Astoria* and *Russell* hove into view. To Fletcher's inquiry about the missing aircraft, Smith replied, "All on board." Fletcher responded, "As I expected." He pointed TF-17 southeast toward Nouméa and the *Bridge*'s long-awaited food. Later that morning he detached the *Tippecanoe* to Samoa with the *Russell* as escort as far as Efate. In the meantime Nimitz queried Leary about the transports sighted the day before and received various estimates based on photographs. By the evening of 29 March Leary settled on thirty-one ships at Rabaul, including four cruisers, five destroyers, perhaps seventeen transports or merchantmen, and other auxiliaries. More significant for Fletcher was Leary's negative for all the other Anzac air searches on the twenty-eighth. Leary vowed six B-17s would strike Rabaul on 30 March. Thereafter, "maximum sustained attack that area . . . will continue."[20]

Shortly after midnight on 30 March as Fletcher drew nearer to New Caledonia, it was his turn to be startled. Leary belatedly notified him that the previous afternoon a search plane placed TF-17 only 228 miles southeast of Rabaul and one hundred miles southwest of Bougainville. That was news to Fletcher. At the time of the purported sighting, he was actually five hundred miles southeast of there and subsequently moved farther away. He did not get unduly excited. "Our experience had been that the Army aviators' reports were apt to be incorrect as to types[,] and I thought it probable that they had sighted an enemy auxiliary with two or three destroyers." (In fact an RAAF Catalina flying boat made the wrong evaluation.) Such a target was too small to alter his plans. Unwilling to break radio silence, he would "clear the situation" that afternoon when within range of Nouméa. Nimitz, for one, was certainly surprised that TF-17 was seen so close to Rabaul, nearly within striking range, meaning Fletcher should have attacked.

In the early afternoon of 30 March, Fletcher dispatched a pair of SOCs to Nouméa with guard mail for the *Tangier*'s radio. Message 292346 of March 1942 gave his correct position on the previous afternoon and restated his intention to arrive at Nouméa on 1 April to provision his ships. He requested Leary to verify the sighting report. "If force reported is enemy heading south I will proceed toward enemy." Should that indeed be the case, he asked that the *Platte* and *Morris* depart Nouméa at once for Point Corn, 325 miles south of Guadalcanal, so he would know where to find them. At this juncture the situation did not seem especially urgent, at least to Fletcher. In the meantime Leary's daily report stated that no RAAF air reconnaissance flights on the twenty-ninth sighted enemy ships. However, at 1535 he offered the first tangible indication that the Japanese might actually be up to something. An RAAF PBY Catalina flying another shuttle search between Port Moresby and Tulagi discovered three cruisers and a transport lurking at Shortland off the southern coast of Bougainville. At 1955 Leary relayed a coast-watcher report that placed a few cruisers, destroyers, and small ships at Shortland that morning. He speculated they were the same ships the Catalina spotted.[21]

In fact Admiral Inoue's South Seas Force had begun a modest, three-pronged operation to occupy positions in and around Buka and Bougainville. It was part of a housekeeping effort to secure the immediate territory around Rabaul, while preparing for the much bigger offensive against Port Moresby and Tulagi that Inoue hoped to reschedule to late May. The Bougainville Invasion Force sailed on 28 March with three destroyers, an ammunition ship, and a few troops. The same evening Admiral Gotō's Support Force left Rabaul with four heavy cruisers, two light cruisers, and three destroyers. His ships were those mistaken for TF-17 on the afternoon of the twenty-ninth. Later that day the Buka Invasion Force of three gunboats departed Rabaul for Buka, only 160 miles to the south, to construct an auxiliary airfield. At dawn on 30 March the Bougainville Invasion Force landed base personnel at Shortland and left by dark for Kieta on Bougainville's east coast. At the same time the Buka force delivered its contingent and promptly returned to Rabaul. At sunrise on the thirtieth Gotō patrolled about 130 miles south of Shortland, then retired north, passing between Bougainville and Choiseul. By the next morning he was north of Buka and inbound to Rabaul. As of 31 March, the Bougainville-Buka operation was over, although the Allies did not know it. All of this, of course, illustrates just how fleeting was the opportunity to catch small detachments of Japanese shipping south or southeast of Rabaul.[22]

Before dawn on 31 March Leary forwarded more coast-watcher reports of cruisers and destroyers seen in Shortland harbor on the thirtieth. Also nine warships (Gotō's Support Force) had gone off to the northeast that evening. Leary's flyers discovered no enemy forces actually south of Bougainville. Thus Fletcher learned of Japanese activities at Shortland. His orders from Cominch dictated offensive action in the event they established bases in the Solomons. The objectives lay well within the Rabaul air umbrella. Fletcher could either turn north immediately and maneuver into attack range or continue to Nouméa. At that time he was more than 750 miles southeast of Shortland. The *Yorktown* could launch a strike late on the afternoon of the thirty-first after a full day's run at twenty-five knots, but risked being sighted that morning and afternoon. A more leisurely twenty knots could mean a dawn strike on 1 April, but again it was likely TF-17 would be detected on the thirty-first. In either case the enemy ships could have moved on. Such a detour also would greatly delay getting TF-17 ready to fight for the long haul. With Nouméa so close, Fletcher carried on with his original plan, but kept a watchful eye should the Japanese keep moving south.[23]

In remote Washington King fretted over the havoc Japan might wreak in the South Pacific. Was TF-17 already fighting? What had Fletcher accomplished? What were his losses? About fifteen hours elapsed from the time Fletcher's 292346 message left TF-17 until Cominch and the others received it. King's temper finally boiled over. At 0630, 31 March (Z–11; Washington local time was 1430, 30 March), he radioed Fletcher, information Nimitz and Leary: "Your 292346 not understood if it means you retiring from enemy vicinity in order to provision." On King's handwritten rough also appears the gibe: "Why not use dry stores and keep after the enemy?" Leary hopped on the Cominch bandwagon by exhorting Fletcher and Crace (who was stuck near Efate covering the convoy): "Jump boys[,] vessels Solomon New Guinea area last two days are enemy." That was not exactly news, but Leary offered no further insight as to the kinds of ships or where they might be going. At noon he noted to King: "Fletcher has been fully informed [of] enemy concentration Rabaul area and of enemy forces located at sea south and west of Bougainville on 29 and 30 Mar." Leary soon admitted that no B-17s in fact bombed Rabaul on 30 March (so much for his promise of air support), but his search planes still sought the ships reported south of Bougainville the last few days.[24]

Fletcher and Poco Smith read Cominch's affront after dawn on 31 March, as TF-17, nearly a thousand miles southeast of Shortland, approached the west coast of New Caledonia. Livid at its tone and the implication that his boss was "fleeing in the face of the enemy," Smith empathized with Fletcher by semaphore: "That is the stinkingest message I have ever read." Fletcher merely responded: "I am not perturbed." For his own part he wondered just what was going on in Washington and Melbourne. He noticed that Leary had not included Cominch as an addressee of the 30 March message that wrongly placed TF-17 just south of Rabaul and surmised that omission caused the "misunderstanding" in King's mind. Actually Cincpac forwarded Leary's dispatch to Cominch as a matter of course. Fletcher was not about to let King's evident "misunderstanding" stampede him into some ill-advised course of action. He did not grasp at the time how the false impression created by the erroneous RAAF sighting report of TF-17 had prejudiced his standing with King and Nimitz. With Nouméa on the horizon, Fletcher directed Smith to go on ahead with the *Astoria*, *Portland*, and two destroyers to fuel, retrieve the goods, and rejoin the main body on 2 April. That afternoon Fletcher composed a number of radio messages for Smith to take in with him. One was a quietly defiant reply to Cominch. Fletcher deemed it "mandatory" to provision some ships that had been at sea since 16 February and again referred to the message he sent to King on 22 March. "Consider fact that no enemy forces moving to southward makes this opportune time to provision. Returning Coral Sea April Second." Smith greatly admired Fletcher's equanimity in the face of such a provocation from King and later cited it as an example of his "strength of character." King, though, neither forgot nor forgave. Fletcher surmised that the acerbic Rear Adm. Richmond Kelly Turner, then Assistant Cominch Chief of Staff for War Plans, composed the offending dispatch, and that mild-mannered Vice Adm. Russell Willson, the chief of staff, wrote a more temperate message sent the next day. The episode still rankled Fletcher in July when he saw Turner and teased him about it. Turner laughed and said no, King had written both messages.[25]

Not informed whether a relief task force headed south from Pearl, Fletcher certainly realized that he would not soon be leaving the South Pacific. Other messages that he vouchsafed to Smith secured his tenuous logistics. He again wheedled Nimitz to keep the *Bridge* at Nouméa. TF-17 would need more provisions by 5 May, and Nouméa was a convenient place to replenish. That issue soon became moot. Fletcher also summoned the *Tippecanoe* to Nouméa after she had refilled at Samoa. At dawn on 1 April Smith entered Nouméa harbor. The *Bridge* soon hove in and opened her ample food lockers. Leary offered nothing further on Japanese movements other than a report of enemy ships seen off Kieta the previous day. The War Plans analysts at Pearl likewise noted such sightings in the Bougainville area, but "nothing definite has developed in that area, nor have the first steps of the other enemy advances been reported."[26]

At the same time, Crace's Anzac Squadron stood off Efate covering the TF-13 convoy. On 31 March the *Australia* fueled a U.S. destroyer for the first time while under way. "She took some time," Crace noted, "but arrangements are good." Captain Farncomb used only one fuel hose, but Crace thought there would be no problem with two the next time. The Australians were receiving a useful introduction to the refueling techniques of the U.S. Navy, though Crace still required a quiet anchorage for his own auxiliary oiler *Falkefjell* to fuel his cruisers. She was to meet the squadron on 4 April at the Uvéa atoll off the northeast coast of New Caledonia and southwest of Efate.[27]

On 31 March, even before he received Fletcher's reply, King ordered TF-17 to replenish at Tongatabu "upon completion current operations" and to prepare for "further operations to northwestward." He then scolded: "The situation in the area where you are operating requires constant activity of a task force like yours to keep the enemy occupied." Because the other carriers were tied up, Fletcher must continue "active operations south of equator" for the time being. Nimitz endorsed King's orders for Tongatabu and gave Fletcher leave to concentrate the auxiliaries there. Because Crace knew Fletcher preferred to replenish in Nouméa, he called "most obscure" King's message directing TF-17 to distant Tongatabu. "I should imagine [Fletcher] was pretty annoyed." Annoyed or not, Fletcher spent the balance of 1 April recalculating all his logistical requirements, now that Tongatabu was to be his advance base rather than Nouméa. He estimated TF-17 could stay in the Coral Sea until about 24 April, when dwindling supplies would compel him to break off to reach Tongatabu around 1 May. Fresh dispatches ordered the *Bridge*, *Dobbin*, *Solace*, *Platte*, and *Tippecanoe* to proceed there. The survey ship *Sumner* relayed welcome news of a good airfield for the *Yorktown* Air Group while the carrier was at anchor.[28]

AN ABORTED ATTACK

On the morning of 2 April with his long-range requirements covered, Fletcher considered his next move in the Coral Sea. As yet he could not decide on a definite target. The situation around Bougainville appeared confused. Leary's latest word was a coast-watcher report sent on 1 April of two cruisers and a transport seen off Kieta the previous afternoon. According to Fletcher's tentative offensive plan later transmitted via the *Tangier* at Nouméa, he would attack "enemy surface forces" somewhere in the "Solomon area" at dawn on 6 April. He could not be more specific because he depended on future sighting reports to determine his objective. Thus it was "essential" beginning 4 April that Leary rebroadcast all enemy contact reports immediately, rather than hold them for a routine daily summary that TF-17 often did not copy until noon the following day. "Radio silence will preclude informing you location my target and details of plan." Fletcher desired, if possible, a simultaneous B-17 strike against the Rabaul airfields, with the hope of catching enemy bombers on the ground. Because the submarine *Tambor* might be patrolling in New Britain–New Ireland waters, he asked that she be instructed to keep clear for the time being. "Will base in Coral Sea and operate against enemy in Solomon area until further notice." During the second the *Platte* refueled the *Yorktown*, *Pensacola*, and three destroyers. Lt. Cdr. Sam Latimer, the previously ill flag secretary, returned to the *Yorktown* for an enthusiastic homecoming. In turn the *Yorktown* sent across to the *Platte* the dispatches Fletcher wished the *Tangier* to radio on his behalf. That evening Smith returned with the *Astoria*, *Portland*, and two destroyers, while Fletcher released the *Platte* to Nouméa. She arrived at 0900 on 3 April, but again it took another day to get the messages through to Washington, Pearl, and Melbourne.[29]

On the evening of 2 April as TF-17 ventured northwest at fifteen knots, it looked as if the only viable ship targets short of Rabaul itself clustered around Bougainville. Fletcher knew from Leary that a small force supported by five warships had occupied Buka on 1 April, whereas four warships were said to have entered Faisi harbor at Shortland only that afternoon. At the same time, McMorris at Pearl wrote that TF-17 "might find some worthwhile objectives" off Bougainville. Fletcher hoped for concrete and timely information on enemy movements, but he was disappointed. News of the RAAF daily search (in this case, negative) still only reached him at noon the following day. On the third Cincpac opined that the enemy continued to mop up the New Britain area with all or parts of the 6th and 18th Cruiser Divisions, the 6th Destroyer Squadron, and auxiliaries. Indications were strong that air units at Rabaul were reorganizing with reinforcements from the Marshalls and the Philippines. Indeed, the Japanese created the headquarters of the 5th Air Attack Force (25th Air Flotilla) at Rabaul and added a fresh fighter group to the bomber and flying boat groups already there. Quoting Lt. Gen. George H. Brett (MacArthur's deputy), King pointedly warned Fletcher that the Japanese could now attack Tulagi and Port Moresby simultaneously, and that they could commit a whole infantry division against Moresby.[30]

On 4 April Leary could reveal no enemy movements to Fletcher. Air reconnaissance was again negative, as were coast-watcher reports. The ships off Bougainville faded away, leaving no worthwhile targets south of Rabaul. It could not even be confirmed whether the Japanese actually left a garrison at Shortland. That afternoon as TF-17 neared Point Corn, Fletcher decided against an attack on 6 April. He prepared a message for King, Nimitz, and Leary informing them that he was postponing his attack "until I have definite location enemy." TF-17 would remain in the vicinity of Corn, so Crace, who completed fueling on 5 April at Uvéa, and also the *Chester*, another reinforcement, would know where to find it.

Roughly halfway between the Solomons and the Louisiades and two hundred miles beyond the Rabaul air search, Corn was as good a place as any to keep watch on the northern Coral Sea. That evening Fletcher detached the *Portland* westward to go within five hundred miles of Townsville and fly the dispatches there. Two SOCs delivered the goods the next afternoon and stayed while the *Portland* rejoined TF-17. Leary went ahead with the Rabaul air attack. On the sixth just one B-17 and six army Martin B-26 Marauder medium bombers bravely bombed the harbor and surrounding airfields. The *Chester* caught up with TF-17 shortly after dawn on the seventh to relieve the *Pensacola*, which Cincpac desired for convoy escort duty. The *Platte* and *Russell* returned soon after. By 8 April Fletcher had patrolled the center of the Coral Sea for three days without incident. No enemy action appeared on the immediate horizon. The Japanese now seemed to be busy securing the northern approaches to New Britain, mainly the Admiralty Islands. The real hot spot was the Bay of Bengal, where Japanese carriers bombed Ceylon and raised havoc with the British Eastern Fleet. Dudley Pound's prognostications sadly came to pass.[31]

Events on 8 April offered more reason to admire the unsung cruiser aviators. The *Astoria* and *Portland* each sent two SOCs on routine dawn patrol in low visibility. TF-17 was supposed to hold its base course until the Seagulls returned, but before the last *Astoria* SOC turned up Fletcher changed course into the wind for a *Yorktown* launch. He quickly made amends by releasing the *Astoria* to look for the overdue aircraft. Smith soon had it on board and rejoined the force that afternoon. Choppy seas and winds up to thirty-nine knots made fueling difficult. Crace brought the *Australia*, *Chicago*, *Perkins*, and *Lamson* to Corn that afternoon. "Glad to have you with us," Fletcher signaled. "Hope you will come on board tomorrow." He had not met—indeed never would meet—his senior subordinate. Crace was curious about him as well. Fletcher designated the Anzac Squadron Task Group 17.3 and stationed it five miles ahead. The seas were no better on the ninth, as TF-17 turned southwest just short of the six-hundred-mile search line from Gasmata. Even so, the *Platte* topped off the *Chicago* and *Australia*.

The weather on the tenth still was not conducive to small boat travel, so Crace sent across a letter asking for permission to return to Nouméa unless Fletcher planned to attack "soon." In fact Crace already arranged for a full-scale court-martial on 14 April of murder suspects in the *Australia* and was determined to hold it. Fletcher responded with what Crace called "a very nice reply," stating that he had hoped to attack ships at Rabaul on 6 April, but called off the raid because of a lack of targets. Now he planned to stay in the Coral Sea until 24 April. Crace thought the court-martial was vital and "a chance I didn't think I should miss because it might not recur." In the spirit of Allied amity, Fletcher acceded to his vigorous entreaty. Technically Crace was senior to him, and their tricky command relationship had yet to be completely defined. Crace's own staff officers actually gave their chief a harder time over his timing of the court-martial, reminding him of Leary's order of 4 April directing the Anzac Squadron to report to TF-17 for an offensive operation. Crace disagreed. Because Fletcher was apparently not going to attack anywhere in the next few days, he felt free to go if released. Further, Leary made no objection. Of course everything would change if the Japanese actually appeared in the Coral Sea.[32]

THE FIGHTER FUEL TANKS GO "SOUR"

Fletcher had much more on his mind than Crace's court-martial or the sad news of the fall of Bataan. On 10 April Buckmaster brought to his attention a potentially disastrous problem with the rubber fuel tanks, actually bladders, fitted in the Grumman F4F-3 Wildcat fighters. They could seal bullet damage and prevent fuel from leaking and igniting, thus offering much greater safety than the plain metal types used by the Japanese. In March some tanks installed in VF-42 F4Fs leaked on their own accord and grounded three F4Fs. Now seven of nineteen *Yorktown* F4Fs showed signs of faulty tanks. Fletcher detailed the problem to Cincpac and requested "urgent air shipment" of more leak-proof tanks. The *Pensacola* had already left for Samoa, so he again deputized the *Portland* to run messages to Townsville and also recover her two SOCs. The cruiser departed at dusk. In addition to the fuel tank dispatch, Fletcher informed his superiors that he would remain on station until 24 April, then leave for Tongatabu. He notified Leary should enemy ships "move to southward [I] will probably be unable to notify you in advance of my attack."[33]

USS *Yorktown* (CV-5), April 1942. The carrier was Admiral Fletcher's flagship from January to June 1942.
Courtesy of National Archives (80-G-640553), via Jeffrey G. Barlow

Almost as an anticlimax, Fletcher received a message on 10 April that implemented the major administrative overhaul of the Pacific Fleet under consideration since February. On 23 March Nimitz had recommended to King to abolish the Battle Force and Scouting Force and organize their ships into individual type commands for administration and training. The Service Force would take over maintenance. Secretary Knox approved on 31 March, and Bunav issued new orders to all concerned commanders. Fletcher now became Commander, Cruisers, Pacific Fleet (Comcrupac), responsible for Cruiser Divisions Three, Four, Five, Six, Nine, and Eleven. Comcrupac represented a promotion over his previous post and again reinforced his status as one of the senior admirals in the Pacific Fleet.[34]

On the evening of the tenth Fletcher was surprised to see "a big crowd of cheering and laughing young sailors parading and frolicking around the flight deck." Guarded by armed marines and serenaded by the band, a host of hopeful celebrants escorted the last five remaining T-bone steaks to be raffled off for charity. Positioned just above the hangar deck, the number two elevator made a handy stage where the band played the latest swing music. Two sailors gave a rousing display of jitterbugging, and a young seaman dolled up as a "buxom waitress" served the steaks to the lucky winners. The spectacle of the *Yorktown*'s "jamboree" gave the crew a great morale boost as they resumed their monotonous diet of "baked beans, canned Vienna sausage, canned corn beef, canned salmon, and chipped beef and rice," while cruising in dangerous waters.[35]

On 11 April while TF-17 continued draining the *Platte*, Fletcher released the *Australia* and *Lamson* to Nouméa but kept the *Chicago* and *Perkins* with him. Soon afterward the *Australia* experienced heavy knocking in the outer starboard propeller shaft. Only in port could divers safely examine the hull and determine the extent of the damage. Two interesting pieces of intelligence reached Fletcher from Leary. The first warned an enemy carrier expected shortly at Truk and that the long-awaited offensive against eastern New Guinea might begin around 21 April. That intelligence, derived from analysis of deciphered radio traffic, was the first definite indication offered to Fletcher of a possible upcoming battle in the Coral Sea. The second message, prefaced "urgent," informed Fletcher that more than twelve hours before, air search had discovered a carrier already at Rabaul. Five B-26s would hit her on the morning of the twelfth, while "all additional planes" advanced from Townsville to Moresby. An hour later Leary described the carrier at Rabaul as *Sōryū*-class, with ten other ships, including three "fairly large" transports, also in harbor. He clearly hoped Fletcher would swiftly strike but again was disappointed. On the twelfth Fletcher marked time in the middle of the Coral Sea watching developments. TF-17 was certainly in no condition to storm Rabaul. Leary now judged the enemy carrier to be the "*Kusuga* (*sic*)" and speculated, correctly, that she transported fighters to Rabaul as part of the general strengthening of land-based air. On 9 April Cincpac warned that eighty bombers and additional fighters were expected to operate there. Leary's B-26s bombed Rabaul on the twelfth and claimed damaging the carrier, which they called the "*Kaga*." Even so, the flattop was last seen disappearing northwest at high speed. Indeed the *Kasuga Maru* had been at Rabaul on the eleventh and twelfth delivering aircraft and supplies. She sustained no damage. The *Portland* rejoined TF-17 on the evening of 13 April, while Crace arrived in Nouméa. Because of a worn shaft bracket, the *Australia* required ten days refit at Sydney. Crace would accompany, but if needed before repairs were finished, he could shift his flag to light cruiser *Hobart* refitting at Sydney after hard times in the Mediterranean and the Far East.[36]

On 14 April as TF-17 topped off just beyond search range from Gasmata, the fighter fuel tank situation worsened. Six F4Fs were no longer usable, gone "sour" according to Fletcher. For the other thirteen it was only a matter of time. Fletcher could no longer consider TF-17 battle worthy. Without reliable fighters it simply could not defend itself from air attack. Should more fighters succumb, he decided he must depart immediately for Tongatabu, where, hopefully, replacement tanks would be waiting. That evening the *Chicago* and *Perkins* left the main body to fly dispatches to Nouméa that updated Cincpac regarding the appalling fighter fuel tank dilemma. Fletcher requested twenty-two new tanks be shipped by air to Fiji from where they could be forwarded to Tongatabu. At least VF-42 now knew why the fuel tanks leaked. Aromatic aviation gasoline actually dissolved the rubber self-sealing layers in that particular model, allowing particles to flake off and clog fuel strainers and gas lines. The effect ranged from a momentary drop in power to complete engine failure that had caused the loss of F4Fs on 14 March and 1 April. The only remedy was to replace all the tanks with an improved version, but none were to be found short of Pearl Harbor. Fletcher's oil supply, at least, seemed secure. He anticipated having the refilled *Tippecanoe* at Nouméa on 18 April, from where she could easily reach the designated rendezvous north of New Caledonia. On her way back south from Pearl, the *Kaskaskia* should be in Nouméa by 20 April. On the morning of the fifteenth Fletcher released the *Platte* and *Hughes* directly to Pearl. That same day Lt. Cdr. Alexander Thorington, the Cruisers, Pacific Fleet (Crupac) assistant operations officer, transferred over from the *Astoria*, finally restoring Fletcher's staff whose workload had increased greatly in the past month. Things were not expected to get any easier.[37]

A "PREDICAMENT" SOLVED

Fletcher's worry over possibly breaking off his Coral Sea patrol because of ailing fighters suddenly dissolved on the morning of 15 April. To his delight he learned that TF-17 had again come under Cincpac's direct control, "effective immediately." Nimitz directed him to Tongatabu for upkeep and told him to prepare to depart there on 27 April for further operations in the Coral Sea. Fletcher could deploy the *Tippecanoe* and *Kaskaskia* as necessary, while Cincpac brought the *Dobbin* and *Solace* to Tongatabu. Fletcher turned southeast to jog south of New Caledonia before swinging northeast for Tongatabu. Ironically on the fifteenth another fighter fuel tank failed, meaning he would have had to leave the Coral Sea in any event. On 17 April Capt. Howard Bode took the *Chicago* and *Perkins* to Nouméa to await the Anzac Squadron. They would stay in Nouméa the next two weeks. TF-17 looked forward to reaching Tongatabu on 20 April. Fletcher welcomed the rest. He was itching for a crack at the enemy under halfway decent conditions.[38]

Fletcher's lone sojourn in the Coral Sea was over, seemingly with little to show for it. King's taunt on 31 March has been noted previously. Nimitz, too, became apprehensive over what appeared to be Fletcher's indecision and lack of an aggressive response to the enemy advance into the Solomons. On 13 April, for example, the War Plans Section noted "no indication that Task Force 17, operating in the Coral Sea, has had any enemy contacts for some time." In late May when Fletcher returned to Pearl he was surprised to learn from Nimitz that his handling of TF-17 from 16 March to 20 April had been impugned. In defense he pointed to the directives he received from Cominch that decried raids on shore bases without significant ship targets present. The nature of the opposition (or lack of it) certainly dictated Fletcher's deployment of TF-17. Unlike Wilson Brown, he found "no definite information of any concentration of enemy ships" that he could "attack under directive contained in Cominch 261630 of February." Thus he chose to wait until the Japanese committed themselves. Once they infiltrated Buka and southern Bougainville at the end of March, however, all the invasion ships swiftly decamped, leaving only a small force ashore that built no installations to speak of. Neither ships nor aircraft yet operated from Shortland or Buka. Of course Inoue only marked time until late in May. Once Nimitz heard Fletcher's personal explanation, his doubts changed to wholehearted support. Fletcher never had the opportunity to put the same case to Cominch. Besides, it is doubtful King would have listened. He was renowned for writing off a subordinate at the first suspicion of irresolution or timidity. It was likely at this point his evident distrust of Fletcher as a "social admiral" well tuned to Washington politics turned into outright animosity.[39]

The fault in this particular instance lay with the peculiar circumstances behind Fletcher's March–April cruise. He suffered under the lack of defined targets and having to conduct a static "offensive" patrol adjacent to enemy-controlled waters on the off chance the Japanese might advance. Ideally a carrier force took shelter in a safe locale until a worthy objective presented itself, struck swiftly and decisively, then speedily withdrew. Fletcher lacked that option. Other than Sydney, or perhaps Nouméa, no such convenient South Pacific refuge yet existed. Nor did he ever wield even half the strength Brown enjoyed in early March. It is obvious that Cominch, especially, desired some belligerent gesture in response to the seizure of southern Bougainville but was unsure what it should have been. If King had wanted Fletcher to raid Shortland, whether or not a suitable target was present, or even to tackle Rabaul, he should have ordered him instead of stewing on the sidelines. That begs the question, however, as to how the Japanese might have reacted had Fletcher actually struck Bougainville or Rabaul simply for the sake of showing some aggressiveness. One wonders if King and Nimitz would have truly desired to provoke them into committing even stronger forces to the South Pacific at a time when the Allied bases there were weak and with no other carriers available to reinforce the *Yorktown.* As will be shown, the strength Combined Fleet did provide the MO Operation against Port Moresby and Tulagi was enough to cause Fletcher enormous trouble in May. His disinclination to reveal the presence of his carrier task force without good reason was extremely wise.

CHAPTER 9

Nimitz Takes Charge

INDIAN OCEAN INTERLUDE

Like Fletcher's lonely vigil in the Coral Sea, the strategic situation in early April for the whole of Nimitz's Pacific Fleet was one of watchful waiting. The few in the know intensely anticipated the Cominch-inspired Tokyo raid. Crammed with sixteen army B-25 medium bombers, the *Hornet* sailed on 2 April from San Francisco as part of Captain Mitscher's TF-18 (one carrier, one heavy cruiser, one light cruiser, four destroyers, and fleet oiler) bound for a distant North Pacific rendezvous with Halsey's TF-16 (*Enterprise*, two heavy cruisers, four destroyers, and fleet oiler) coming out from Pearl. Pye took command of the seven old battleships of TF-1 at San Francisco on 4 April, while Fitch, the new CTF-11, waited until mid month for the *Lexington* to emerge from the Pearl Harbor Navy Yard after necessary upkeep and replacement of her four 8-inch gun mounts with many light automatic antiaircraft weapons.[1]

In early April following the annihilation of the ABDA forces in the Dutch East Indies, two powerful Japanese task forces stormed the Indian Ocean. They included five carriers from Admiral Nagumo's *Kidō Butai* (less the *Kaga* under repair in Japan), light carrier *Ryūjō*, four fast battleships, nine cruisers, and seventeen destroyers. Nagumo set his sights on naval forces and land-based air on Ceylon, while the second force swept the Bay of Bengal of shipping. The newly reconstituted Eastern Fleet under Adm. Sir James Somerville comprised only five old battleships, three carriers (including venerable *Hermes*) with inferior aircraft, seven cruisers, and fourteen destroyers. Radio intelligence warned the wary British of an incursion into the Indian Ocean, but not one of such strength. Somerville expected perhaps two carriers and some cruisers to appear on 1 April. He advanced to meet them but found nothing. When Nagumo's forces finally turned up on 4 April, Somerville had already pulled back. The next day Nagumo raided Colombo on Ceylon and pummeled two heavy cruisers. Somerville bravely positioned his striking force south of Ceylon, but his only viable option was a night carrier torpedo strike. It proved too difficult to move into range without the risk of being pounded in daylight by the Japanese carriers, so he retired southwest to Addu atoll in the southern Maldives. On 9 April Nagumo struck Trincomalee on Ceylon and sank the unfortunate *Hermes* before she could get clear.[2]

Nagumo withdrew on the evening of 9 April well satisfied with the mayhem inflicted at the cost of only seventeen aircraft. The British lost five warships and twenty merchant ships.

Nagumo did not attain his primary objective, the destruction of the Eastern Fleet, but he certainly took the wind out of its sails. The Eastern Fleet withdrew to African waters and for nearly two years only played a modest role in the war against Japan. In turn the Japanese never followed up their success in the Indian Ocean, which could have disrupted the British defense of the Middle East and offered the best chance for an Axis triumph. Conversely, had Admiral Yamamoto committed to the southwest Pacific just a portion of the forces used in the Indian Ocean, Admiral Inoue's South Seas Force would have rolled over Fletcher's TF-17 and swiftly gained all of its objectives. When Japan got around to advancing to Port Moresby and the Solomons, it would not be so easy.

Once the British realized the magnitude of force arrayed against them in the Indian Ocean, they again beseeched Washington for swift action in the Pacific. Churchill chided Roosevelt on 7 April that Nimitz "must be decidedly superior to the enemy Forces in the Pacific" and urged he cash in on this "immediate opportunity." King told Pound that "measures already in hand [are] ordered to be expedited," and that they "should tend to relieve pressure in critical area." However, he was not about to offer any details. King intended Pye's TF-1 to operate in concert with Fitch's TF-11 (*Lexington*) in the central Pacific, but before then, the bombs dropped on Tokyo should yank Japanese attention out of the Indian Ocean. At the same time Fletcher's isolation in the face of the enemy buildup in the southwest Pacific preyed on Nimitz's mind, particularly as all of his other assets were tied up elsewhere. On 2 April he had McMorris's War Plans Section look into using Fitch's TF-11 to reinforce TF-17 in the South Pacific. On the eighth he suggested to King that TF-11 go south rather than chaperone the old battleships off Hawaii. On the way the *Lexington* could deliver marine fighters to Palmyra and Efate, which King greatly desired. Nimitz suggested that TF-1 sail on 14 April from San Francisco, exercise alone north of Hawaii, and then in early May either continue to Pearl or return to the West Coast. This message signaled a significant shift from previous Cincpac policy of retaining carrier strength in the central Pacific, but Nimitz soon ventured far beyond that first step. Concerned Halsey might need support should the enemy pursue the Tokyo raiders, King still wanted to join Pye and Fitch but directed that they meet down in the Palmyra–Christmas Island area a thousand miles south of Pearl. The *Lex* could deliver the planes to Palmyra. Consequently on 10 April Nimitz cut orders for TF-1 (seven battleships, seven destroyers) and TF-11 (*Lexington*, two heavy cruisers, and seven destroyers) to rendezvous on 22 April five hundred miles southeast of Hawaii and train west of the Palmyra-Christmas line. They would stay together until 4 May, after which the battleships, at least, would proceed to Pearl. Nimitz, however, would not drop the issue of getting TF-11 south to the Coral Sea.[3]

BECOMING CINCPOA

On 10 April Fletcher copied as information addressee another puzzling Cominch bolt from the blue. King apprized Nimitz that Vice Adm. Robert Ghormley would command the South Pacific Force. The last Fletcher knew of his classmate was Ghormley's relief after serving briefly as commander of U.S. Naval Forces in Europe. Because Ghormley would need considerable time to take up his distant post, King suggested Fletcher be named acting

South Pacific Area (Sopac) commander. His true intention may have been for Fletcher to go ashore to organize the headquarters and main operating base at Auckland, then fade away once Ghormley showed up. King did not say who would run TF-17 in the meantime, but of course only Poco Smith was available.[4]

Fletcher was unaware of the brawl in Washington, as King wrangled with rivals Marshall and Arnold over reorganizing the Pacific high command. On 2 March King proposed that the Anzac Area be greatly enlarged to include all the South Pacific island bases he needed for his anticipated offensive toward Rabaul. Anzac and its western neighbor ABDA would be integrated into a single command, with the rest of the Pacific divided into northern, central, and southern areas. He did not reveal that he fully expected to take personal command of this enlarged ABDA/Anzac Area. On 4 March he laid out a similar vision of the Pacific for Nimitz, who, at least "initially," was to have only the North, Central, and South Pacific command confined to Fiji and waters north and east of there. King himself would handle ABDA/Anzac and the Southeast Pacific. Finally revealing a streak of independence, Nimitz countered on 6 March, asking for the Anzac, South Pacific, and Central Pacific commands for himself and leaving King the rest. Even before King read Nimitz's emphatic reply, he found himself locked in a real dogfight in Washington. The Australian and New Zealand governments also favored an expanded Anzac Area that not only included their respective nations but also New Guinea and the old ABDA area. However, they had in mind as supreme commander not King, but General Brett, MacArthur's deputy in Australia, who obviously just warmed a chair. Appalled he might lose control over his cherished South Pacific offensive, King complained such an arrangement "would cut across the whole system of command and operations in the Pacific Fleet." In fact he proposed precisely the same thing with regard to Nimitz. Now King thought it imperative to separate Australia and New Zealand into an "Australian Area" and a "Pacific Ocean Area," which would include New Zealand and the New Hebrides.[5]

Marshall watched benignly on 9 March as his own War Plans Division recommended to the Joint Chiefs that a new Southwest Pacific Area absorb not only ABDA but also extend as far eastward as longitude 170° west, gobbling up even Samoa. The respective Allied governments would then decide upon a supreme commander of the Southwest Pacific Area, doubtless MacArthur. Marshall got a rise out of King and gracefully gave in if the Philippines could be included in a much-reduced Southwest Pacific Area under MacArthur. The Pacific concerned Marshall far less than Europe, except to keep the U.S. commitment as low as possible. A greatly relieved King tasked his own War Plans Division to draft the proposal for the new Pacific organization. The Southwest Pacific Area under MacArthur (Supreme Commander, Southwest Pacific Area, or Comsowespac) would absorb the Anzac command, to be designated the Southwest Pacific Force under Leary (Commander, Southwest Pacific Force, or Comsowespacfor), while the navy received the Pacific Ocean Areas. The boundary between the two would cut between the Solomons and the New Hebrides. The president approved the arrangement on 31 March.[6]

On 3 April Nimitz learned to his pleasure he was to become commander in chief of the Pacific Ocean Areas (Cincpoa), made up of the North Pacific, Central Pacific, and South Pacific areas (a command he held concurrently with Cincpac). Given King's reluctance to turn over real power to Cincpac, that alone was a major victory. Aside from defending his region and supporting MacArthur, Nimitz was to "prepare for execution of major amphibious offensives against positions held by Japan initially to be launched from South Pacific and Southwest Pacific Areas." King being King, however, made things difficult and complicated by diluting Cincpac's control over the crucial area. Nimitz received direct control of the North and Central Pacific areas but was to "appoint" the South Pacific commander. "Acting under [Cincpac's] authority and general direction," Commander, South Pacific Area and Force (Comsopac) would "exercise command of combined armed forces which may at any time be assigned that area." Comsopac was a necessary political buffer between Nimitz and the supersensitive MacArthur, although it appears King also did not fully trust Nimitz alone to carry out his offensive. On 4 April King now told Nimitz merely to "nominate" the Comsopac, subject to Washington's approval. Nimitz trotted out Pye, who had just taken over TF-1, and proposed Ghormley relieve Pye with the battleships. Well aware Pye might not be acceptable, he also offered Ghormley as an alternative Comsopac. His prudence was justified when Pye was rejected in favor of Ghormley.[7]

Ghormley was available due to a major command shake-up in Washington. Since 30 December Admiral Stark, the CNO, had worked alongside Cominch with little friction. King himself was willing to serve under him, but Stark wisely realized the perils of divided command. He offered his resignation on 7 March, and five days later Roosevelt combined the posts of CNO and Cominch in the person of King with unprecedented control over the navy. As reward for one of the main architects of the Germany-first strategy, Stark took over the newly established U.S. Naval Forces in Europe. Personally for Ghormley that was a shame. He served ably as special naval observer in Britain and looked forward to the European command. Well respected for his intelligence and diplomatic savvy, Ghormley made flag rank in 1938 as an assistant CNO, then traveled to London in the summer of 1940. Despite rising to vice admiral in October 1941, he had not held an operational post as a flag officer either ashore or at sea except, briefly, the European command. Still smarting over the failed Wake relief, Roosevelt would never agree to Pye as Comsopac. It had to be Ghormley, who was not altogether pleased to leave that theater for the other side of the world. In fact Ghormley was in over his head as Comsopac and might better have remained in Europe or accrued much needed seasoning as CTF-1.[8]

Nimitz also rebuffed King's attempt to put Fletcher on the shelf. On 10 April he declared privately to King that it was "inadvisable repeat inadvisable" to name Fletcher as temporary Comsopac. That would be "incompatible with effectively operating his task force," which "should be ready to counter prospective enemy moves and cover arrival of forces now en route advanced bases." Nimitz also requested personal command of Sopac until Ghormley settled in and questioned the fuzzy command relationship that King set out between Cincpac and Comsopac. Originally Cincpac was to relinquish operational control of Pacific Fleet task forces assigned to Sopac. Nimitz much preferred to do that only when he desired and asked for similar latitude should his ships cross into MacArthur's Southwest Pacific Area. On 14 April King gave Nimitz direct control of Sopac until Ghormley could take command but retained control over the establishment of the South

Pacific bases. Nimitz did not mind. He had far more important things to consider: the safe return of the Tokyo raiders and prospects of a major battle in the Coral Sea.[9]

READING THE ENEMY'S MAIL

Nimitz's firmer grasp of the reins of command coincided with a vast increase in the amount and value of the communications intelligence (comint) available to him. Hitherto the intense efforts to decipher Japanese naval traffic relied largely on traffic analysis—who was talking to whom—and the relative regional intensity of radio transmissions. That, along with old-fashioned combat intelligence (sighting reports, captured documents, and so on), yielded considerable insight into the changing enemy order of battle and facilitated broad estimates as to future activities. King and Nimitz particularly valued comint to forecast where powerful Japanese striking forces were likely to appear, so U.S. carriers could safely raid elsewhere. Such timid strategy would change drastically later in April, when Nimitz began spoiling for a fight.

There were several reasons why Allied radio intelligence improved so dramatically by early April. Foremost among them was the failure of the IJN to institute a timely change of its general purpose fleet cryptographic system, Naval Codebook D. Used in the vast majority of high-level naval radio messages, Codebook D consisted of a printed list of thirty thousand five-digit numbers, each of which stood for a unit designation, technical term, verb, and so on. Separate ciphers for dates, grid locations, and geographic place names also appeared within the messages. Before transmission, another series of five-digit numbers taken from a huge list of up to fifty thousand random numbers (the "random additive table") were added to the original numbers as an enhanced cipher. Such a primitive system contrasted sharply with electrical cipher machines, such as the U.S. ECM (Sigaba) and the German Enigma, but it was formidable nonetheless. To the Allies, the version of Naval Codebook D in use at the start of the war was known as JN-25B. Prior to the war not a single JN-25B message was deciphered. Just prior to the war the IJN implemented another random additive table that caused great consternation for the cryptanalysts who tackled JN-25B after Pearl Harbor. In February, however, they realized it did not constitute a whole new codebook. The IJN originally intended in April 1942 to issue the wholly new Naval Codebook D1. However, delays in distribution postponed the changeover to 1 May and eventually to 27 May, with fatal consequences for Japan.[10]

While the Japanese continued to use an elderly code, the U.S. Navy took advantage by greatly improving its cryptographic efforts. Commander Rochefort's Hypo team concentrated on JN-25B in concert with Station Cast (with Com 16) on Corregidor. In turn Cast spun off a separate cryptographic station (dubbed Belconnen after the Australian naval radio station near Canberra) under Lt. Rudolph J. Fabian, who set up shop in Melbourne in March under Leary's Anzac command. In Washington Cdr. John R. Redman's OP-20-G Radio Intelligence Unit (Negat), in the office of the chief of naval operations, redoubled its efforts against JN-25B and continued monitoring Magic, the Japanese diplomatic cipher. All three stations exchanged data and reviewed findings through a radio network known as Copek. The radio intelligence organizations fed comint to the intelligence officers of the several fleet commands for analysis and to brief their respective chiefs. Lt. Cdr. Edwin Layton handled that duty for the Pacific Fleet, with input from McMorris's War Plans Section. An excellent Japanese linguist, Layton enjoyed a close personal relationship with Rochefort's talented team. In turn Cincpac and Comanzac advised the task force commanders through daily bulletins supplemented with urgent special messages. In March the radio intelligence centers even began piecing together fragmentary texts of intercepted messages. It was tempting, but risky, to fill in all those tantalizing blank spots with informed speculation. Although one authority asserted there was "no indication that erroneous decisions were made based on the partial message texts," inevitable inaccuracies in interpretation certainly occurred and did adversely affect command decisions. Layton recalled, "A message partially decrypted but with blanks in important places grammatically or subject-wise can render an 80% message somewhat less than 40% *reliable in fact*!" Moreover, "This fact is, again, something the reader of this sort of matter just can't understand until he has to make a decision on fragmentary, incomplete intelligence." Indeed the practice of providing interpretations based on incomplete messages for immediate tactical as opposed to strategic purposes proved dangerous and was later curtailed.[11]

Radio intelligence became an incredibly valuable asset for the hard-pressed Pacific Fleet in spring 1942. It negated Japan's great strategic advantages of interior lines and the initiative by allowing the Allies to deploy their weaker forces to best advantage to surprise and blunt enemy offensives. There has been a tendency to regard radio intelligence as the sole factor in the U.S. success (as if the fighting were not important) and to concentrate on its successes and ignore (or cover up) the mistakes. However, comint was not an end in itself, but only a tool for determining enemy intentions. Its true value concerned what it actually furnished to the combat commanders ashore and at sea and what they in turn did with it.

REVEALING AN OFFENSIVE SOUTH OF RABAUL

As of 4 April Inoue confidently anticipated having most of the *Kidō Butai* carriers to support the MO Operation, his late May offensive against Port Moresby and Tulagi. That was wishful thinking on his part, but his delusions quickly evaporated in the wake of a contentious debate between the Naval General Staff and Yamamoto's Combined Fleet over fundamental strategy for the second operational phase. The Naval General Staff strongly urged an anti-Australia strategy through severing the line of communication with the United States. The capture of Port Moresby and the Solomons would open the way that summer to New Caledonia, Fiji, and Samoa. As for the northern theater, the Naval General Staff hoped to seize positions in the western Aleutian Islands, not only to bolster the northern flank, but also to please the army by threatening the line of communication between the United States and the Soviet Union. For his own part Yamamoto, about to take a crack at the Eastern Fleet, proposed shifting the offensive all the way to the central Pacific to destroy his principal opponent, the U.S. Pacific Fleet. He keenly regretted not taking out the U.S. carriers along with the battleships at Pearl Harbor and now would finish the job once and for all in one massive blow in early June. The bait was to be Midway. Yamamoto believed its capture would draw the Pacific Fleet out for annihilation. Victory would deeply demoralize the Americans and open the way for the eventual invasion of the Hawaiian Islands. If the

Pacific Fleet cravenly chose not to play its role in Yamamoto's script by fighting (and losing), Japan would acquire a useful outpost.[12]

Beginning 2 April the proponents of these rival plans dueled in Tokyo. The Naval General Staff pressed its South Pacific strategy. If anything was to be done in the north, the Aleutians must come before Midway. Combined Fleet felt equally adamant about its Midway plan. Neither side gave an inch. On 5 April the Combined Fleet staff representative played his trump card—a telephone call to his chief on board his new flagship, the super battleship *Yamato*. Yamamoto expressed his wholehearted support of the Midway plan. His prestige carried the day. The Naval General Staff had little choice but to accept his Midway stratagem or relieve him of command. Yamamoto compromised by agreeing to conduct the Aleutians (AL) Operation simultaneously with the big assault on Midway (MI Operation). The AL Operation is usually described in Western sources as a diversion for the Midway attack, but that is completely wrong. In fact, the initial carrier strikes against Dutch Harbor and Midway were to go in at dawn of the same day. Also the very idea of such a "diversion" makes no sense given the relative strategic positions of the Aleutians, Midway, and Oahu. Yamamoto brashly counted on having enough strength for both offensive operations at the same time. In truth he seriously dispersed his forces, which meant, in the end, the Aleutians foray only diverted the Combined Fleet.[13]

The MI and AL Operations were to occur in early June after the *Kidō Butai* enjoyed much-needed upkeep in the homeland. Therefore Yamamoto advanced the Port Moresby Operation to *early* May. Inoue's first inkling of the radical change came the day after he announced the MO Operation would take place in late May. On 5 April Combined Fleet promulgated a new task organization, effective 10 April, for the first stage of the second operational phase. For the MO Operation, Inoue's South Seas Force would be loaned the big carrier *Kaga*, light carrier *Shōhō*, and the 5th Cruiser Division, but only until 10 May. These new orders were a great blow to Inoue. Not only did he not get all the carriers he thought he was promised in March, but he also must complete the MO Operation in time to return those borrowed units for Midway. He violently opposed the Midway gambit and made no secret of his distaste for the Combined Fleet brass. But now he had little precious time to complete detailed planning for the MO Operation.[14]

When Combined Fleet cut orders on 5 April assigning the *Kaga* to the South Seas Force, she became an addressee for certain communications concerning the MO Operation that passed between Yamamoto and Inoue. Within a few days messages intercepted by cryptanalysts at Pearl and Melbourne linked an important unit of the Combined Fleet, the *Kaga*, to the Fourth Fleet (South Seas Force) and something called the "RZP Campaign." Intelligence speculated that RZP referred to Port Moresby. The new carrier "*Ryūkaku*" (wrongly thought another big *Shōkaku*-class carrier, but whose call sign was actually the *Shōhō*'s) was already known to be associated with the Fourth Fleet. That implied at least two flattops earmarked for a future southern Pacific offensive. Thus on 10 April McMorris speculated the Japanese might advance south from Rabaul possibly as early as 17–21 April, because Rabaul's reinforced air force should be ready by then. On 11 April Leary likewise warned of an attack against eastern New Guinea by 21 April.[15]

Inoue looked with dismay at only the *Kaga* and *Shōhō* and wanted the 2nd Carrier Division (*Sōryū* and *Hiryū*) as well. Unwilling to commit the 2nd Carrier Division, which had to rest before fighting at Midway, Yamamoto substituted the 5th Carrier Division (*Shōkaku* and *Zuikaku*) for the *Kaga*. The *Kidō Butai*'s most modern carriers, they were the least experienced and would supposedly benefit from a warm-up in the Coral Sea prior to the main event at Midway. On 10 April Yamamoto revised the task organization for the first stage and two days later issued formal orders attaching the 5th Cruiser Division, the 5th Carrier Division, and two destroyer divisions to the South Seas Force, effective 18 April. For the time being U.S. cryptanalysts missed the fact that the *Kaga* was no longer part of the Moresby operation, but their British counterparts at Colombo quickly learned of two new carriers about to appear in the southwest Pacific. They recovered nearly in total a 13 April message to Inoue advising that the 5th Carrier Division, after splitting off from the *Kidō Butai* near Singapore, would stop on 18 April at Bako on Taiwan, then proceed to Truk around 28 April. The Admiralty passed the word to King (one of the first times this was done), who warned Nimitz and Leary on 15 April.[16]

Now it looked to King, Nimitz, and Leary that as many as four enemy carriers would be available by the end of April for an offensive in the southwest Pacific. That was a natural assumption given the general withdrawal of Japanese naval units from the Bay of Bengal. "We are planning opposition," the Pacific Fleet War Plans Section noted on 16 April, although that was not Cincpac's call. Nimitz worried whether Cominch would release the necessary forces, starting with Fitch's TF-11, to give him a fighting chance. So did MacArthur, who on the seventeenth expressed his concern that the carrier task force ordinarily stationed in the Coral Sea had left for Tongatabu. "Consider it necessary that one task force be maintained that area at all times to check further enemy advance." Nimitz quickly explained that TF-17 was being withdrawn due to the length of time it had been at sea and the trouble with its fighters. "Strongly agree desirability maintaining force in Coral Sea and will endeavor to do so," he soothed. "Believe persistent courageous attacks by your aircraft have delayed enemy offensive and that Fletcher will return to area in time to oppose advance involving surface forces." According to his biographer Potter, Nimitz was now "seriously regretting" the Tokyo raid. The fifty-dollar question remained whether Fletcher would have the necessary help. "We are trying to get a force together to oppose," War Plans noted, "TF17 will be ready, TF11 and TF16 are otherwise committed." Nimitz picked away at King regarding Fitch, who sailed on 15 April to meet the old battleships south of Hawaii. On the heels of the MacArthur message, Nimitz braced King privately: "It is my strong conviction that enemy advance should be opposed by force containing not less than two carriers. Again recommend that Fitch proceed Coral Sea where Fletcher will join him after upkeep." Nimitz did not want Pye venturing beyond the Palmyra-Christmas line and desired the battleships to return to San Francisco.[17]

SHUFFLING THE DECK AFTER THE TOKYO RAID

On the evening of 18 April as TF-17 neared Tongatabu, Forrest Biard, the *Yorktown*'s saturnine language officer, emerged from his green-curtained radio room shouting: "They bombed Tokyo, they bombed Tokyo!" He listened to Japanese domestic news broadcasts that he judged more reliable than American, for at this dismal stage of the war the enemy had less to conceal. What he heard cheered him beyond measure. Japanese radio angrily reported air raids against Tokyo, Yokohama, Kobe, and Nagoya. By dawn on the eighteenth Halsey brought the *Enterprise* and *Hornet* within 650 miles of Japan and intended to launch Doolittle's B-25s that afternoon when the range decreased to four hundred miles. The Doolittle flyers would attack Japan that night and proceed on to China. Early that morning, however, TF-16 ran afoul of a line of picket boats, whose alarms Lt. Gilven M. Slonim's radio intelligence team in the *Enterprise* soon intercepted. Therefore Halsey reluctantly dispatched the B-25s from beyond six hundred miles, later apologizing to Doolittle for having to "dump you off at that distance." Expecting only short-ranged carrier planes, Combined Fleet judged any air attack had to be a day away. Yamamoto was astonished that afternoon when fast medium bombers roared over Tokyo and other cities. Physical damage proved slight, and all the B-25s crashed, except one that took refuge in the USSR.[18]

The shock to the Japanese psyche proved as immense as the satisfaction gained among the Allies. Given the growing crisis in the southwest Pacific, the War Plans Section at Pearl delivered a less sanguine private verdict to Nimitz. The *Enterprise* and *Hornet* were sorely missed. Even if King released TF-11 (which must happen quickly), "Cincpac will probably be unable to send enough forces to be *sure* of stopping the expected Jap offensive." At the time Fletcher had only an inkling Halsey executed the raid. Once he learned the details he judged that although the exploit was great for morale, it tied up two carriers urgently needed in the Coral Sea. Yamamoto roused Combined Fleet to chase the U.S. carrier force, but Halsey had too great of a lead. When the Allied cryptanalysts analyzed the many messages that orchestrated the pursuit of Halsey, the raid yielded an unforseen bonus of excellent radio intelligence. The Doolittle raid had no effect on the choice of Midway as the next main objective or the rescheduling of the MO Operation against Port Moresby. Those decisions were already made. It did whet Yamamoto's desire for a full reckoning with the Pacific Fleet.[19]

King waited a day before replying to Nimitz's request for TF-11, perhaps to see if Halsey indeed got clean away. He was relieved to report to Nimitz, Leary, and MacArthur that the reference to 21 April for the start of the Japanese offensive resulted from an error in decryption. Three or 4 May appeared more likely, especially in light of the Admiralty decryption placing two carriers at Truk on 28 April. Port Moresby would be the objective of a seaborne assault and possibly also a land attack. Cominch's next comment likely elicited profanities at Pearl, for King now proposed that "if supply vessels can be gotten there," TF-17 should go to Nouméa for upkeep instead of remote Tongatabu. This marked an abrupt about-face from his vehement insistence on Tongatabu or Auckland, no matter how inconvenient. For MacArthur's benefit he stressed that "in any case we can not repeat not accept commitment to maintain fleet forces continuously in Coral Sea or any other area but must employ them where situation requires." No general would tell Cominch where to deploy his ships. TF-17 was too weak on its own, even with MacArthur's help, to withstand the enemy, so King finally approved Nimitz's request to deploy TF-11 southward. As yet he refused to countenance returning the battleships to the West Coast. Nimitz and MacArthur were to advise as to "maximum concentration of forces of all categories you consider possible to make against enemy New Guinea area first part of May." That evening Nimitz quickly disabused King of the notion of Fletcher refurbishing at Nouméa. "Consider it impracticable to change base for upkeep and that departure Bleacher on 27 April for Coral Sea conforms to present requirements of the situation." He immediately alerted Fitch to start south toward Fiji. The new orders found TF-11 heading northeast toward the TF-1 rendezvous after having flown the marine fighters to Palmyra. Three days later Nimitz issued the actual order for Fitch to meet TF-17 on 1 May (local time) in the eastern Coral Sea, where Fletcher would take command of the assembled force. Nimitz also informed Fletcher of his estimate of the situation and that "reinforcement for Taskfor 17 at later date under consideration."[20]

A RADICAL PROPOSAL

In mid April Nimitz emerged as a leader grown dramatically in confidence and resolve. Earlier he fretted as King shifted the Pacific Fleet's center of gravity southward and in the process took away most of his striking force. The Japanese firmly held the initiative and King, it seemed, most of the cards. Nimitz appeared at times hesitant and indecisive as he fumbled in reaction to events rather than seeking to control them. Speaking much later of that time, Adm. Arthur Davis, in 1942 a captain and Pacific Fleet staff aviation officer, frankly characterized his boss as "scared and cautious." A foreign naval observer who met Nimitz in January uncharitably described him as "an old man, slow and perhaps slightly deaf." King sensed weakness, for he was notorious for bullying subordinates he thought were not tough enough. By the third week of April, however, Nimitz found his sea legs as a theater commander. The Cincpoa directive significantly enhanced his power. Radio intelligence greatly improved. At the same time there was a major change in the personnel immediately around him. Pye, hitherto Nimitz's closest advisor, already departed to become CTF-1, and McMorris left War Plans on 15 April. Their influence on Nimitz certainly was not baleful, but their exit cleared the air and made it easier for him to do what he must. Moreover, Milo Draemel's days as chief of staff were numbered. Earnest and hardworking, he was overtired and stressed by the constant pressure and disagreed with Nimitz's growing eagerness to confront the enemy. Capt. Lynde McCormick (USNA 1915), McMorris's assistant, took over the War Plans Section. As bright in his way as McMorris but not fixated on the central Pacific, he was less domineering and under the circumstances easier for Nimitz to work with and through.[21]

Another key Cincpac personal relationship was with Commander Layton, the Pacific Fleet intelligence officer, who developed an excellent rapport with Nimitz. He described his boss's demeanor as the "coolest, most self-collected [and] sunny at the same time." In April Layton created a daily "score card" (the Cincpac Enemy Activities File) that displayed for Nimitz the location of enemy fleet units and their estimated intentions. Despite the tremendous trust Nimitz demonstrated in radio intelligence in general and in Layton in particular, he could not afford to be completely credulous and uncritical. He assigned a senior War Plans officer to offer his own analysis of the daily intelligence to balance that of Rochefort and Layton. McCormick handled that responsibility until 13 April, when he turned it over to Capt. James M. Steele. Layton deplored "Boob" Steele as especially obtuse and stubborn, but Nimitz considered him an essential brake against over-enthusiasm by Hypo. The physical arrangements in Cincpac headquarters at the Pearl Harbor submarine base also improved in April. Capt. Walter S. DeLany's Operations Section ran the plot room, which featured strategic and tactical displays on large maps with friendly and enemy positions depicted for the whole Pacific. Four newly assigned naval reserve officers, who trained at the Naval War College, became the operations watch officers as part of an expanded system for recording ship and aircraft movements and contacts. A pneumatic tube delivered messages directly from communications so the latest information could be entered immediately. When the situation was at all tense, Nimitz and Draemel kept a close watch on the plot, where they could confer at once with McCormick, DeLany, and Layton.[22]

The rapidly changing strategic situation demanded that Nimitz himself make all the major decisions at fairly short notice. He reserved to the staff, most particularly McCormick's War Plans Section, the task of properly framing and presenting his intentions. That was vital, because he was on the cusp of a stunning reversal of strategic policy. On 20 April Nimitz met informally with McCormick's team to explain his thoughts regarding the threat in the southwest Pacific. He wanted to have, prior to his conference with King later that week in San Francisco, a concrete plan that reflected his ideas. Within two days McCormick prepared a detailed—and sober—estimate of the situation. Three May was the likely starting date of the New Guinea–New Britain–Solomons offensive. Ultimate enemy strength was not yet known, but it was believed that at least five carriers (*Shōkaku*, *Zuikaku*, "*Ryūkaku*," *Kasuga Maru*, and *Kaga* with 306 aircraft) were involved, with indications that Nagumo's flagship *Akagi* (sixty-three aircraft) might also participate. One fast battleship appeared committed, probably along with another, because the Japanese invariably operated their battleships in pairs. Five heavy cruisers with the usual supporting cast of light cruisers and destroyers were also thought en route to the area. Estimates remained vague regarding ground forces, but McCormick believed the Japanese had sufficient troops available to overrun Port Moresby. Nimitz and the planners recognized the enemy had his eye on objectives beyond Rabaul. "Will it only be for Moresby or Moresby and the Solomons at this time or will a direct advance to Nouméa or Suva be attempted?" Past Japanese practice of a step-by-step advance supported by land-based air indicated to McCormick that Port Moresby and the Solomons were the first objective. This by no means precluded carrier raids on New Caledonia and Fiji or Townsville and Horn Island in northern Australia, with very likely a widespread South Pacific offensive to follow. McCormick even warned against possible strikes against Efate, Tongatabu, and Samoa that could seriously disrupt efforts to reinforce those bases in May. He was not certain how the Japanese would employ their carriers, but probably not all would appear in the first wave.[23]

The obvious response was to commit the "full strength of the Pacific Fleet." The 22 April situation report deemed that impractical for many reasons. Despite Cominch's enthusiasm for the old battleships, Nimitz excluded TF-1. He could not support it given tenuous logistics or properly protect it with screening ships and aircraft, especially because those battleships were far too slow to stay with the carriers. Nimitz desired TF-1 to remain on the West Coast. Unlike King he had seen the battleships—huge holes ripped in their sides by aerial torpedoes—resting in the mud at Pearl Harbor. The *Yorktown* and *Lexington* were already committed to the South Pacific, but they alone could not handle five or six flattops. At least one carrier from TF-16 must go south, so why not both? "Nothing appears to be making for Hawaii yet. Other demands do not appear very strong, so we may find a force in the Southwest even larger than listed." Cincpac could ultimately deploy four carriers (three hundred aircraft) for the great South Pacific battle. Expected back on 25 April, Halsey's TF-16 could sail by the end of month and join Fletcher around 14 May (east longitude date). The only concern was whether the *Hornet* had a full complement of planes. The seven available fleet oilers could support both task forces in the South Pacific until about 1 June. Thereafter chartered tankers would have to be diverted from West Coast–Oahu runs to Fiji and Samoa. TF-16 would fight alongside TF-17 and then relieve the *Yorktown* and later the *Lexington* as well. Fletcher should start north around 15 May, because the *Yorktown* desperately required navy yard upkeep. Fitch's *Lexington* force would need to follow about 1 June. The flying boats at Nouméa, serviced by the *Tangier*, should be increased from six to twelve. MacArthur's Southwest Pacific Area would provide land-based air support, a cruiser task force, and a half-dozen submarines. In addition Pearl was sending five subs to patrol the waters around Truk.

Thus Nimitz resolved to hurl all four of his flattops into battle in the South Pacific, not purely for defense, but to seize the initiative. The most effective way was to crush the enemy's strongest asset, his carriers. For months the *Kidō Butai* led the triumphal advance through the western Pacific to the Indian Ocean, while U.S. carriers only essayed pinprick raids on the periphery. To assault the South Pacific bases, the Japanese must expose a substantial part of their carrier fleet, hitherto effectively out of reach, out to where a resourceful defender could counterattack with carriers, land-based air, and subs for a great opportunity to smash them. Nimitz projected an attitude of quiet confidence, not desperation. The Japanese were not as formidable as they seemed. "Because of our superior personnel in resourcefulness and initiative, and the undoubted superiority of much of our equipment, we should be able to accept odds in battle if necessary." The final decision regarding TF-16 had to wait until the Cominch-Cincpac meeting. On the twenty-second Nimitz sent King a list of potential forces available to counter the enemy's South Pacific offensives. In addition to TF-17 and TF-11 (two carriers, five heavy cruisers, thirteen destroyers, and two fleet oilers), TF-16 with two more carriers, four cruisers, eight destroyers, and two fleet oilers could arrive there about 14 May. He again made the pitch for the battleships returning to San Francisco, "after remaining sufficiently long at sea to have effect on enemy dispositions."[24]

MEETING COMINCH

On 23 April Nimitz flew to San Francisco to see King on the twenty-fifth. It was the first time they met since Nimitz left Washington. King arrived fresh from lengthy meetings with First Sea Lord Pound, who flew to Washington on 19 April to discuss fleet commitments in the North Atlantic, the Mediterranean, and the Indian Ocean. Significant Atlantic Fleet units were being deployed to European waters, while the carrier *Wasp* delivered British Spitfires to Malta. Pound questioned King regarding future operations in the Pacific that might ease the pressure on India and the crucial supply lines passing through the western Indian Ocean. He did not consider the Doolittle raid enough of a diversion. King's response deeply disappointed Pound, who told his government that nothing King proposed for the Pacific would be likely to have much of an immediate effect on the critical situation in the Indian Ocean. That was true because King still only projected a buildup of bases in the South Pacific as a prelude to a push perhaps that autumn toward Rabaul. He needed Nimitz to start offering substantial ideas on how and where to commit the fleet to battle.[25]

The long and varied agenda demonstrated that Cominch and Cincpac had much to say to each other. Among the first items discussed was Fletcher's recent Coral Sea cruise. According to the conference minutes, both men "expressed uneasiness," but "decided to take no further action until more information is available." (The same could be said for King's true feelings toward Nimitz.) The two deliberated personnel matters, particularly flag officer assignments. Younger officers needed to qualify for carrier command by means of "makie-learn" cruises. Nimitz preferred not to deal personally with flag officer reassignments, but recommended they proceed through proper channels. He would come to regret that concession. Once these matters were addressed, Nimitz laid out his bold plan to concentrate the four carriers, all the fleet's offensive assets, in the South Pacific by 13 May. Noncommittal as yet, King examined in detail the logistical support that radical redeployment would require. Still obsessed with the old battlewagons, he directed Nimitz to look into stationing Battleship Division (Batdiv) Three (*Idaho*, *Mississippi*, and *New Mexico*) in New Zealand.[26]

On 26 April King lectured Nimitz on the general Allied strategic situation and logistics. Dissecting the Cincpoa directive, he made it clear that once Ghormley was in place, the task forces in the South Pacific would "operate under his suzerainty." Moreover, "when Ghormley drives to northwestward, it is to be expected that MacArthur will conform."[27] King carefully considered whether to authorize Halsey's carriers to go south, a move that would expose the central Pacific. Consequently he asked whether Midway was safe from a "major attempt." Nimitz replied that the island would need direct support from the Pacific Fleet to weather attacks by two or more carriers and promised to look into the matter of Midway's defense. King and Nimitz again debated carrier organization. For "flexibility of assignment and deployment," they settled on five single-carrier task forces, each under its own flag officer and ideally operating in pairs. That was yet more evidence that the U.S. Navy much preferred tactical dispersion for the carriers. King reminded Nimitz to see whether Auckland could support the old battleships and offered him the new battlewagons *North Carolina* and *Washington* when the Atlantic Fleet could spare them, probably in August.[28]

Nimitz left San Francisco on the afternoon of 27 April after a third session without knowing King's final decision regarding his South Pacific battle plan. Upon arriving at Pearl the next morning he was enormously gratified by Cominch's dispatch. "Think TF16 should proceed towards critical area as indicated with *Hornet* Air Group augmented as practicable in Hawaii or from *Yorktown*. Also concur in proposed return of TF17 and any other dispositions appropriate to keeping at least equivalent of TF16 in South Pacific Area." King again directed "full consideration to sending one batdiv preferably Batdiv 3 towards same area with other BBs [battleships] returning to West Coast for time being." Nimitz immediately requested Cominch approval to return all the battleships to the West Coast about 10 May and advised that happily the *Hornet* already had all her aircraft. Thus TF-16 would leave Pearl on

30 April. He breathed a sigh of relief when King concurred with his proposed retirement of all battleships. Cincpac got what he wanted. Now he could fight his carrier battle in the South Pacific. The meeting at San Francisco cleared the air. After faltering in the beginning, Nimitz was obviously on the right path. Reflecting both assurance and an aggressive nature, he presented a comprehensive plan that persuaded a skeptical King to take the enormous risk of finally committing his carrier task forces to battle.[29]

Nimitz conferred with a weary Halsey while TF-16 prepared for a quick return to sea. The far northwest Pacific had proved arduous as well as exhilarating. He outlined the now familiar, nevertheless chilling, estimates of enemy South Pacific objectives that included Port Moresby and the Solomons, as well as Ocean and Nauru islands. Carriers might also raid New Caledonia and Fiji. On the way south Halsey was to reconnoiter Howland and Baker islands and hit the Gilberts, "Whenever information and other conditions indicate that it may be profitably done." Once in the Coral Sea he would command all the carriers briefly to number four before Fletcher departed with the *Yorktown*. Therefore Halsey "should be able to strike the enemy a heavy blow if suitable objectives can be found." Later he should have the three carriers "long enough to complete another offensive operation." Nimitz "strongly hoped that this powerful force can be put to good use" before Fitch, too, had to leave. "If present indications continue," Nimitz stated he would "probably find it desirable" to redeploy the *Yorktown* and *Lexington* to the Coral Sea after they refitted at Pearl. In that event Halsey could again lead the four carriers. In the meantime he should consider sending one carrier at a time to replenish at Nouméa. Halsey sailed on 30 April with two carriers, three heavy cruisers, seven destroyers, and two fleet oilers. A heavy cruiser and a destroyer would follow on 2 May. Nimitz advised MacArthur, Leary, and Fletcher that TF-16 "should arrive your area about 12 May."[30]

On 1 May Rochefort radioed "Hypo's Evaluation of the Picture in the Pacific" to Opnav, Belconnen, and Com 16 on Corregidor. This message offers a very important summary of what he (and hence Nimitz and Layton) was thinking. Enshrined in Midway lore is the notion that Nimitz, when he was planning to fight in the Coral Sea, already knew from radio intelligence about an upcoming attack on Midway. Nothing could be further from the truth. On 1 May Rochefort explained that enemy fleet units in the Bay of Bengal had redeployed to the Pacific. "Their departure indicated a change of plan forced on Japan by us. Suggest movement of Pacflt [Pacific Fleet] TF1 as possible reason." That politic flattery of Cominch showed that he knew of King's partiality toward using the old battleships as a deterrent. As for "MO Campaign now underway," Rochefort pegged southeast New Guinea and the Louisiades as the crucial area. The lineup comprised the 5th Carrier Division, 5th (heavy) and 18th (light) Cruiser Divisions, 6th Destroyer Squadron, 8th Gunboat Division, several aircraft tenders, transports, and possibly a submarine squadron. Available air strength included sixty-five bombers, sixteen flying boats, and an unknown number of fighters. "Crudiv 5 and C-in-C Fourth Fleet [is] in Rabaul region tonight." (They were actually at or near Truk.) Rochefort did not think Australia would be involved despite a message that gave Townsville as a reference point. That soon changed. Rochefort also detailed powerful forces, including the 1st and 2nd Battleship Divisions, the 4th and 6th Cruiser Divisions, and carriers *Kaga* and *Sōryū*, that were "available for offensive-defensive operations." Strong Japanese interest in Palmyra, Samoa, Canton, Howland, and Baker islands led him to speculate that "part or all of above units will cover MO Campaign with possible raids on Samoa and Suva areas." That was the basis behind Nimitz's strong commitment to fight in the South Pacific and again refutes subsequent hallowed assertions that Hypo already fingered Midway as the next likely objective. Rochefort noted the *Kaga*'s link to the Fourth Fleet and wrongly believed she was "scheduled for operations in New Britain area." He judged the Aleutians to be the only other potential hot spot in the Pacific and a possible objective of these forces. "This considered unlikely at this time, but certainly is probable at a later date."[31]

That last part worried King, who took to heart Rochefort's warning of powerful Japanese forces that would soon be available for "offensive-defense operations." On 2 May he admonished Nimitz and MacArthur not to get too wrapped up in the southwest Pacific. Acceptance of Nimitz's strategy "must not be construed as eliminating the possibility that enemy may attack Hawaii-Midway line or launch attacks against our line of communications via Gilbert-Ellice-Samoa line." In that regard the next few weeks would prove quite interesting for Cominch and Cincpac alike.[32]

Comint had provided and would continue to provide vital predictions of the South Pacific onslaught against which King and Nimitz courageously redeployed their forces. Now it was up to Fletcher to deal with the first blow and hopefully still be around to help Halsey smash the second.

Table 9.1 Estimated Japanese Carrier Strength According to an ONI Report

	Name	Completed	Tonnage	Speed	Aircraft[a]			
					VF	VSB	VTB	Total
CV-1	*Hōshō*	1922	7,470	26	9+3	9+3	9+3	36[b]
CV-2	*Akagi*	1927	26,900	28.5	18+3	18+3	18+3	63
CV-3	*Kaga*	1928	26,900	24	18+3	18+3	27+3	72
CV-4	*Ryūjō*	1933	7,100	25	12+4	12+4	0	32
CV-5	*Sōryū*	1937	10,050	30	18+3	18+3	18+3	63
CV-6	*Hiryū*	1938	10,050	30	18+3	18+3	18+3	63
CV-7	*Shōkaku*	1941	15,000	30?	18+3	18+3	18+3	63
CV-8	*Zuikaku*	1941	15,000	30?	18+3	18+3	18+3	63
CV-9	*Koryu*	1941	10,050	30	18+3	18+3	18+3	63[b]
CV-10	*Kasuga*	1941	22,500	23	9+3	18+3	9+3	45[b]
CV-11	*Ryūkaku*	1941	15,000	30?	18+3	18+3	18+3	63[b]
XCV-1	*Nitta Maru*	1939	22,500(?)	22.5	9+3	18+3	9+3	45[b]

Office of Naval Intelligence (ONI) Intelligence Report Serial 44-42 (22 April 1942), in RG-313, Commander, Fleet Air, West Coast (Comfairwest), Box 1003.

Note: "VF" designates fighting planes, "VSB" designates scout bombers, "VTB" designates torpedo bombers, and "CV" designates aircraft carriers.

[a] Smaller figures indicate spare or reserve aircraft (which usually were not present).

[b] Estimated.

Table 9.2 Actual Japanese Carrier Strength 1 May 1942

Name	Completed	Tonnage	Speed	Aircraft[a]			
				VF	VSB	VTB	Total
Hōshō	1922	7,470	25	0	0	6+2	8
Akagi	1927	36,500	31.2	18+3	18+3	18+3	63
Kaga	1928	38,200	28.3	18+3	18+3	27+3	72
Ryūjō	1933	10,600	29	12+4	0	16+4	36
Sōryū	1937	15,900	34.3	18+3	18+3	18+3	63
Hiryū	1939	17,300	34.5	18+3	18+3	18+3	63
Zuihō	1940	11,262	28	9+3	0	9+3	24
Shōkaku	1941	25,675	34	18+3	18+3	18+3	63
Zuikaku	1941	25,675	34	18+3	18+3	18+3	63
Shōhō	1942	11,262	28	9+3	0	9+3	24
Junyō	1942	24,140	25.5	16+4	21+3	0	44
Kasuga Maru	1941	17,830	21	0	0	0	0

Notes: "VF" designates fighting planes, "VSB" designates scout bombers, "VTB" designates torpedo bomber, and "CV" designates aircraft carriers.

[a] Smaller figures indicate spare or reserve aircraft (which usually were not present).

CHAPTER 10

Clearing for Action

A WELCOME REST

On 20 April TF-17 dropped anchor off Nukualofa on the north coast of Tongatabu. Waiting in the spacious harbor were the *Bridge* with fresh food, the *Dobbin* to repair travel-worn ships, particularly the hard-working destroyers, and hospital ship *Solace*. Two shipments of replacement tanks cured the *Yorktown* fighters' fuel tank woes, and within a few days all nineteen VF-42 Grumman Wildcats were ready to fight. The rest of the air group numbered thirty-six SBD Dauntless dive bombers from Bombing Five and Scouting Five and thirteen VT-5 Devastator torpedo bombers. The delights of a genuine tropical South Seas island enticed weary sailors who had not been ashore for more than two months. A true town of three thousand inhabitants, Nukualofa was the capital of Queen Salote Tupou's Kingdom of Tonga, a British protectorate. Fletcher met the British consul and arranged liberty for his crews. On a subsequent courtesy call, he drank coconut juice and reviewed the local militia. Picturesque sights and fresh fruit were plentiful, but the bluejackets discovered to their dismay that in one respect Tonga failed to live up to its familiar name of the "Friendly Islands," when Queen Salote hid all the young women in the hills.[1]

Such an idyllic interlude could only be brief. Even before the *Yorktown*'s anchor clattered into Nukualofa harbor, Fletcher understood the serious threat in the Coral Sea. He learned on 21 April the 5th Carrier Division, carrier "*Ryūkaku*," and a fresh cruiser division were bound for Truk. The next afternoon another Cincpac message declared, "Impending operations centering New Britain area will start very soon." Fletcher was to rendezvous with TF-11 on 1 May (local time) at Point Butternut three hundred miles off the northwest tip of New Caledonia and command the combined force. The directive that Nimitz transmitted to Fletcher is worth quoting in full:

> An enemy offensive in New Guinea dash Solomon Area is at present indicated for first week of May probable primary objective Moresby. May eventually include three or four carriers [and] about 80 heavy bombers and same number of fighters at New Guinea and New Britain air bases. Your task [is to] assist in checking further advance by enemy in above area by seizing favorable opportunities to destroy ships shipping and aircraft. Cincpac will arrange coordination of Souwestpacfor and will keep you fully informed. Comsouwestpac [Leary] is requested to continue present dissemination intelligence that area, to keep

> MacArthur informed of Pacflt plans and operations and to inform me plans for his forces especially those which can support fleet forces. Reinforcement for Taskfor 17 at later date under consideration.

Nimitz requested Fletcher's proposed task organization when it was convenient to transmit without breaking radio silence.[2]

Thus Nimitz provided Fletcher the "when" and "where," but as Morison aptly stated, the "how" was up to him. Indeed Fletcher had contemplated the "how" ever since he began his solitary Coral Sea cruise. His basic mission was the same as before, to cover Port Moresby and the Solomons. With unlocated enemy carriers, a preemptive strike against Rabaul would have been foolhardy. Fletcher wisely decided to resume his stratagem of lying in wait beyond maximum air search range (seven hundred miles) of Rabaul and seek favorable opportunity to ambush, or at least intercept, enemy forces moving across the Coral Sea. He would return to Point Corn, 325 miles south of Guadalcanal, and carefully monitor air sighting reports to see what turned up.[3]

MacArthur's Southwest Pacific Area had the greatest stake in ending the menace. To his chagrin he lacked the air and naval strength to deal with it himself but had to rely on Pacific Fleet carriers he did not control. To his credit MacArthur furnished Fletcher the bulk of his surface forces, the Anzac Squadron recently reorganized as Task Force 44 under Admiral Crace. The *Chicago* and *Perkins* were to join Fletcher on 1 May at Butternut, followed by Crace with heavy cruiser *Australia* and light cruiser *Hobart* on 4 May at a rendezvous 350 miles southwest of Guadalcanal. Rear Adm. Francis W. Rockwell's Task Force 42 could deploy four old subs to the New Guinea–Solomons–Bismarcks in time to patrol behind enemy lines. They had to be very careful not to mistake TF-17 for the enemy, especially because Fletcher could give only a general idea where he expected to operate. He might need to shift without notice and requested to be apprized of the movements of the subs.[4]

Nimitz presumed that the earlier arrangement between Brown and Crace (and confirmed by Cominch) resolved the question of the U.S. carrier admiral being in charge, even if the Royal Australian Navy's cruiser admiral was senior. However on 14 April, he was disturbed to read an Admiralty message declaring "U.S. authorities" agreed that when U.S. and British ships cooperated "tactically," command would be "exercised by that officer of either power who is senior or if both officers of equal rank the one who is longest in rank." That arrangement jeopardized Fletcher's control over TF-17 with Crace present. Nimitz alerted King it was "essential" carrier task forces remain under U.S. flag officers. King asked MacArthur and Leary to confirm with the Australian Commonwealth Naval Board that the original Brown-Crace agreement was still in force. The Australians graciously assented. Nimitz informed his task force commanders on 26 April that the commander of Pacific Fleet carrier task forces would run the show "regardless of rank."[5]

Of all the help MacArthur could offer Fletcher, none was more important than Lieutenant General Brett's Allied Air Forces, Southwest Pacific Area. The long-range B-17 heavy bombers, B-25 and B-26 mediums, and RAAF Catalina flying boats were vital for early warning of enemy movements, particularly carriers. The bombers could also attack ships that ventured within strike range, as well as raid Rabaul and Lae. Fletcher could only count on their support in a strategical, rather than tactical sense. Brett's command structure was in the process of being organized, and control and coordination was weak in the uneasy multinational partnership. Flyable aircraft were few, averaging twelve to fifteen B-17s, sixteen B-26s, nine to fourteen B-25s, ten RAAF Hudsons, and three RAAF PBYs. MacArthur defined the proposed air search areas. Coverage between Rabaul, the western rim of the central Solomons, and the Louisiades appeared acceptable if not ample, but flights over the upper Solomons and farther eastward depended on RAAF Catalina flying boats flying out of vulnerable Tulagi. Neither Nimitz nor Fletcher exercised any control over MacArthur's searches. Nor did they have a clear idea how many aircraft MacArthur had and how many might be available for different missions. Fletcher took what he could get. The 29 March incident, where MacArthur's flyers grossly erred in a sighting report, emphasized the limitations of shore-based search crews with regard to ship identification. That offered another good reason to keep TF-17 well to the south until such search contacts could be amplified. On 23 April Fletcher diplomatically praised the quality of Leary's intelligence summaries. Nimitz concurred. He urged "every effort" be made to furnish "important aircraft reports immediately available to fleet TF commander concerned."[6]

On 25 April Fletcher did take control of one search element "for operations [in] Coral Sea." The *Tangier* tended a brood of six U.S. Navy PBY Catalinas based at Nouméa. Six more PBYs were slated to arrive about 3 May. From Nouméa they could search seven hundred miles to just short of San Cristóbal and Rennell islands in the extreme southern Solomons. That gave Fletcher only limited coverage of his eastern flank. He told the *Tangier* to use the new PBYs "for effective coverage Nouméa and New Hebrides Area north and northwestward to boundary Sowespac [Southwest Pacific] Area" and later specified a daily six-plane search from Nouméa northward to the Sowespac/Sopac border and the Santa Cruz Islands 350 miles southeast of Tulagi. Capt. Richard W. Bates's 1947 Naval War College analysis correctly noted TF-17 lacked adequate air searches, not only of the central and eastern Solomons, but also to the east. However, "this lack of air coverage, particularly to eastward," supposedly gave Fletcher no "undue concern." Bates suggested the *Tangier* should have shifted north to Efate or at least sent her PBYs, although no seaplane base existed on site. In that way the PBYs could have searched beyond Tulagi and part of Malaita. Even better, Bates wrote, PBYs should have advanced to unoccupied Espíritu Santo in the northern New Hebrides 550 miles from Tulagi. That criticism of Fletcher originated purely from a clear understanding of the Japanese plan that Bates gained by hindsight. The Cincpac message that gave Fletcher control of the *Tangier* specifically mentioned the Coral Sea. Rightly or wrongly, the primary focus was there, not east of the Solomons. Given the focus on Port Moresby, it did not occur to Fletcher (or anyone else) that the prime danger to TF-17 might arise in the east.[7]

Another vital aspect of planning for battle in the Coral Sea concerned logistics. The *Kaskaskia* joined TF-17 on its way north to Tongatabu, while the old *Tippecanoe* was en route to Nouméa after refilling at Suva. They were sufficient for Fletcher's normal needs until next oiler rotated south from Pearl, but Fitch's TF-11 (not to mention Halsey's TF-16) forced a radical change in the fueling schedule. Lacking an oiler of his own, Fitch would soon run short of fuel. Nimitz's solution was to have the *Kaskaskia* top off TF-17 at Tongatabu, fuel TF-11 north of Fiji, and then return to Pearl. Fletcher asked permission for Fitch to retain the oiler until 1 May when both task forces could empty her. Cincpac declined. It was more important than ever for the *Kaskaskia* to refill at Pearl. Instead, Pearl provided the *Neosho* to cover Fletcher's long-range requirements and scheduled five fleet oilers to reach Nouméa during the next five weeks: the *Platte* on 13 May, elderly *Cuyama* and *Kanawha* on 17 May, *Kaskaskia* on 23 May, and *Neosho* on 3 June. The *Cuyama* and *Kanawha* were to remain at Nouméa, while the *Platte, Neosho,* and *Kaskaskia* shuttled back and forth to the task forces as "feeders." The *Tippecanoe* would serve as the emergency reserve. Even so, the situation would be extremely tight. To supplement fuel in the crucial area MacArthur graciously offered the cargo (105,500 barrels) of the chartered tanker *E. J. Henry*, due in Sydney on 7 May. She could reach Suva in Fiji on 4 May, "If she receives and complies with diversion signal," or otherwise became available after arriving at Sydney.[8]

On 26 April Fletcher received Cincpac's revised fueling schedule. Together the *Neosho* and *Tippecanoe* provided 153,000 barrels. The *Neosho* could begin fueling TF-17 at the end of April, and the *Tippecanoe* could handle TF-11 at the 1 May rendezvous, although she had to save fourteen thousand barrels for a convoy bound for Efate. At fifteen knots TF-11 and TF-17 together burned about 11,400 barrels per day. After about twelve days (28 April to 10 May), both oilers should be empty and both task forces full. High-speed steaming prior to 10 May, though, might cost an additional thirty-three thousand barrels and advance to 7 May when the oilers could be empty and the task forces full. These figures did not include Crace's TF-44, which was to draw oil from its own Australian oilers, but which Fletcher might likely have to fuel himself. The *E. J. Henry* was to proceed to Nouméa after filling shore tanks at Suva and then restock the *Tippecanoe* on 10 May for Fletcher's emergency reserve. Nimitz alerted Fletcher that the original TF-17 ships might leave for Pearl around 15 May, considerably easing fuel requirements. Fletcher did not need his staff logistical expert Thorington to explain how thin was his fuel supply. The loss of a single oiler or even delay could dislocate everything. At the end of April the slow *Tippecanoe*, on which much depended, would have to come out of Nouméa without destroyer escort. Fletcher believed it essential to top off his ships from the *Neosho* at every convenient opportunity. Later when not with the main body she was to alternate between Point Corn and Point Rye, 180 miles apart, and keep south of the line linking the two points. After refilling on 10 May the *Tippecanoe* was to return to the Coral Sea and likewise meander between Corn and Rye in place of the emptied *Neosho*. For reasons no one foresaw, the locations Fletcher assigned the oilers would prove a major blunder.[9]

TF-17 sailed from Tongatabu on 27 April and the next day met the *Neosho* and destroyer *McCall* three hundred miles southwest. On 29 April Fletcher celebrated his fifty-seventh birthday, the same day as Emperor Hirohito.[10]

PLANNING A CARRIER BATTLE

With the preliminaries out of the way, Fletcher concentrated on how actually to fight a battle against carriers. He had no experience in a real carrier-versus-carrier action, but neither did anyone else. Now with only a jerry-built air search umbrella, he must fight in the far southwest Pacific against a tough, battle-hardened opponent who could strike hard and fast from long range. The situation called for flexible tactics, strong resolution, and a great measure of luck. Fletcher was much encouraged that his close friend Jake Fitch had TF-11 with the *Lexington*. Fitch's vast carrier experience and aviation staff gave Fletcher great confidence, and he would become TF-17 air task group commander to advise on search sectors, the size and composition of strikes, and suitable courses for flight operations.

Fletcher continued to exploit the rich expertise found in the *Yorktown*. Rear Adm. William N. Leonard, a former VF-42 pilot, recalled that Fletcher was at first an "eminence on high," who gradually "warmed up" after the Samoa reinforcement and "took an interest in air operations." Besides consulting Captain Buckmaster, a recent JCL inexperienced in air operations, Fletcher soon summoned pilots to flag plot to brief him about their missions. At first he consulted just the senior aviators, but soon junior pilots as well. Leonard never knew Fletcher to interfere beyond his rightful purview. "We had a happy flagship with no known flag meddling." Fletcher especially relied on the counsel of air officer Murr Arnold and Curt Smiley, the group commander. Arnold became a de facto member of the staff, called upon often to discuss search sectors, the types and numbers of planes to be used, "in fact in all matters concerning flight operations." Arnold felt uneasy, as he found himself advising the flag regarding orders to be issued to the *Yorktown*, in effect telling his own captain what to do. "Buckmaster didn't particularly care for the set-up, and neither did I, but we had no choice." It says much for Buckmaster's strong character that he showed no outward resentment. Arnold judged Fletcher "a fine naval officer, very easy to work with and for, but [who] knew nothing about the capabilities and limitations of carrier aviation. He knew his limitations and was always more than willing to accept advice." Arnold could not remember any occasion when Fletcher disagreed with his recommendations. Before rotating home on 25 April, Smiley also shared his aviation knowledge with the flag, but to a much smaller extent than Arnold. Buckmaster replaced Smiley with Lt. Cdr. Oscar Pederson, commanding officer of VF-42. Like Arnold, "Pete" Pederson became one of Fletcher's most valued aviation advisors. Buckmaster controversially insisted that Pederson remain on board as fighter director officer (FDO) to control the combat air patrol instead of leading his air group in battle. "Very upset," Pederson could do nothing about it. The absence of his leadership aloft would tell in the upcoming battle.[11]

Fletcher took note when Wilson Brown, at the urging of the *Lex*'s Capt. Ted Sherman, placed the *Lexington* and *Yorktown* in the same screen instead of following the standard policy of operating individual carriers well apart. Even though it put him out of a job at Lae-Salamaua, Fletcher approved. He understood the benefits of a concentrated fighter and antiaircraft defense, as well as easier coordination in attack. TF-17 Op-Ord 2-42 (1 May 1942) specified normal daylight ("S") and night ("L") cruising dispositions that incorporated all eight cruisers within the circular screen, whereas Brown had kept Smith's and Crace's cruisers in distinct task groups. In the event of air attack, TF-17 was to assume disposition "V" for Victor, with carriers deployed abreast within a circle of cruisers at the three thousand yards radius and the destroyers at four thousand yards. It was anticipated the carriers, because of their vastly disparate turning radius, would split up when maneuvering radically at high speed to avoid torpedoes and bombs. The cruisers and destroyers were to conform to their movements and form separate screens when necessary.[12]

Fletcher, the navy's senior cruiser commander, sought opportunities for day and night surface actions. He seriously contemplated shifting his flag to a heavy cruiser to lead surface attacks but concluded communication and administrative facilities on board a cruiser were "entirely inadequate" for his needs. Instead he created two separate cruiser-destroyer task groups within TF-17. The Attack Group (TG-17.2) under Admiral Kinkaid (Comcrudiv Six) would include former TF-11 heavy cruisers *Minneapolis* and *New Orleans*, Rear Adm. Poco Smith's *Astoria*, *Chester*, and *Portland*, and Captain Early's five Desron One destroyers. Admiral Crace's Support Group (TG-17.3) would comprise flagship *Australia*, *Chicago*, and light cruiser *Hobart*, screened by the *Perkins* (Cdr. Francis X. McInerney, Comdesdiv Nine) and *Walke*, on loan from Desron Two. Fletcher could detach either or both groups to operate independently of the main body. Fitch, the prospective air task group commander (CTG-17.5), received his own dedicated screen of four destroyers under Captain Hoover (Comdesron Two). This arrangement resembled prewar exercises, where carriers and plane guard destroyers often separated from the rest. Rear Adm. Edward C. Kalbfus, president of the Naval War College, described Fletcher's operations order as an "excellent example of flexible organization."[13]

Op-Ord 2-42 included an annex compiled largely from Cincpac and Comsowespacfor intelligence summaries. Japanese air strikes against Horn Island in northernmost Australia, Port Moresby, and Tulagi presaged an offensive against southeast New Guinea and probably Tulagi. Enemy land-based air might number 102 aircraft (forty-two fighters, thirty-six bombers, twenty flying boats, and four float planes), divided between Rabaul and Lae, with a fresh bomber group expected shortly.[14] Air searches could extend to six hundred miles from Rabaul and from Shortland off the south coast of Bougainville. Gasmata on southern New Britain was in use as an auxiliary field. Fletcher predicted major operations might commence as early as 28 April. The suspected lineup was formidable: first-line carriers *Shōkaku* and *Zuikaku* of the 5th Carrier Division, each with sixty-three planes (twenty-one fighters, twenty-one dive bombers, and twenty-one torpedo bombers, including spares), and the new mystery carrier "*Ryūkaku*" (actually *Shōhō*), which on her own might wield eighty-four planes (twenty-one fighters, forty-two dive bombers, and twenty-one torpedo planes).[15] The converted carrier *Kasuga Maru* (with possibly forty-five aircraft) was believed en route. The supporting cast could comprise two heavy cruisers (5th Cruiser Division), three light cruisers, sixteen destroyers, two converted seaplane tenders, a submarine tender and six subs, eight gunboats, and nineteen transports and auxiliaries. One Cincpac message hinted of two or three battlewagons south of Truk, likely to curb Fletcher's appetite for surface actions. As of 1 May the Allies could pinpoint only a small convoy ninety miles south of New Ireland and bound either for Rabaul or directly into the Solomons. Otherwise the enemy had yet to reveal his hand.[16]

THE JAPANESE PLAN

By mid April Admiral Inoue's South Seas Force planners at Truk fleshed out their MO Operation, the capture of Port Moresby and Tulagi. Assigned forces numbered 282 aircraft of all types (divided almost equally between carrier and shore-based) and sixty-five ships, including two big carriers, a light carrier, six heavy cruisers, three light cruisers, fourteen destroyers, six submarines, and a wide variety of auxiliaries. Most of the ships ended up in Admiral Gotō's MO Attack Force conducting the actual invasions. His daunting task was to see the vulnerable, eight-knot troop convoy safely through the Louisiade Archipelago and assault Port Moresby on X-Day, 10 May. Inoue finally opted for Jomard Passage near the center of the barrier for a voyage of 840 miles from Rabaul. The greatest danger would occur in the two-day passage of 350 miles from Jomard to Moresby. Gotō formed MO Main Force from the four heavy cruisers of his 6th Cruiser Division, the light carrier *Shōhō* (twenty planes), and a destroyer to provide close cover for the invasion convoy while Admiral Kajioka's 6th Destroyer Squadron comprised the actual screen.[17]

Inoue assessed land-based aviation at Port Moresby and northeast Australia as the gravest threat to the MO Operation. The Allies had maintained surprising pressure on Lae and Rabaul despite the big buildup of Japanese air units. Especially worrisome were the Townsville and Cooktown air bases in northeast Australia that could pummel the Moresby convoy on its final leg. Inoue deplored that these two air bases lay beyond the range of his bombers at Lae and Rabaul. Even worse, strong air reinforcements were believed on the way to Australia. Warships and subs in eastern Australia and New Zealand constituted the second hazard to the MO Operation. The big question was whether the *Saratoga*, the carrier believed to have struck Salamaua and Lae on 10 March, was still in the neighborhood. Inoue, for one, thought that unlikely. Thus Fletcher's calculated tactic of masking his presence paid huge dividends in lulling the Japanese. Interestingly, Inoue dreaded land planes far more than those on carriers. A non-aviator, he nevertheless became the Japanese counterpart of Billy Mitchell, preaching the superiority of shore-based air.[18]

Inoue divided the MO Operation into three phases. To extend the air search network, Rear Adm. Marumo Kuninori's Support Force—centered on the two old light cruisers of the 18th Cruiser Division—would build a series of forward seaplane bases progressing southeast from Rabaul through the Solomons. These initial bases would cover the capture of Tulagi by Rear Adm. Shima Kiyohide's Tulagi Invasion Force, and the later ones assist in the capture of Port Moresby. Six flying boats and nine float planes would shift to Shortland on 28 April, followed on 2 May by float planes deploying to Thousand Ships Bay at the south end of Santa Isabel Island. Shima was to begin his assault on Tulagi before dawn on 3 May (X–7 Day), supported after sunrise by planes from the *Shōhō* in Gotō's MO Main Force. Inoue expected weakly defended Tulagi to fall in one day.[19]

From the assets provided by Combined Fleet, Inoue created the MO Striking Force (MO *Kidō Butai*) under Rear Adm. Takagi Takeo, commander of the 5th Cruiser Division (*Myōkō* and *Haguro*). Takagi's force also included Rear Adm. Hara Chūichi's 5th Carrier Division (*Shōkaku* and *Zuikaku* with 124 aircraft), six destroyers, and the oiler *Tōhō Maru*. Takagi's prime mission was to neutralize the Australian air bases and ease final passage of the Port Moresby convoy to the objective. Instead of squeezing the carriers through the narrow triangle of the northern Coral Sea and risk their speedy discovery, Inoue conceived an audacious left hook deep around the Allied flank. Proceeding south from Truk, the MO Striking Force was to pass far to the east of New Britain and parallel the eastern fringe of the Solomons. Following the fall of Tulagi, Takagi would pass westward between San Cristóbal and Espíritu Santo and dash across the Coral Sea. At dawn on 7 May, three days before the landing at Port Moresby, the carriers would surprise the Townsville air base and destroy its planes on the ground.[20]

As part of phase two, flying boats would advance to newly captured Tulagi on 4 May in time to cover Takagi's MO Striking Force sweep around the southern end of the Solomons. On 5 May the search effort would divide. Tulagi-based flying boats would scan the seas around the MO Striking Force as it traversed the Coral Sea toward Townsville. Four submarines (the Eastern Detachment) were to deploy in a line about 450 miles southwest of Guadalcanal to watch for naval forces scurrying north from Brisbane. In the meantime, Gotō's MO Main Force would double back to the north to shield the Port Moresby invasion convoy, set to sail on 4 May from Rabaul. By 6 May (X–4), a seaplane base was to be functioning at Deboyne in the central Louisiades, followed two days later by another at Cape Rodney east of Moresby. After neutralizing Townsville, Takagi would refuel southwest of the Solomons and take station in the center of the Coral Sea to maintain vigil for Allied naval forces that only then should be appearing. Inoue hoped the carriers could also raid Cooktown and Port Moresby itself. The landing force would assault Port Moresby on 10 May (X-Day). Following its capture, elements of Shima's Tulagi Invasion Force and Takagi's MO Striking Force were to cooperate with forces coming south from the Marshalls to seize Ocean and Nauru (the RY Operation) on 15 May (X+5). Situated west of the Gilberts and northeast of the Solomons, those two islands, virtually undefended, would fall whenever Japan chose to make the effort. Afterward, the 5th Carrier Division, the 5th Cruiser Division, and the *Shōhō* were to race north to the homeland in time to join the armada departing near the end of May for Midway.[21]

Inoue's plan depended on Takagi's carriers crippling Townsville's air strength long before any Allied naval forces could react to the unfolding MO Operation. It is vital to understand that despite the assertions of Morison and other Western historians, Inoue never planned to use the *Shōhō* as "bait" for U.S. carriers that he supposed already lurked in the Coral Sea. Instead he conceived the wide left hook around the Solomons merely to enable Takagi to surprise Townsville, while his own land-based air (Base Air Force) covered Rabaul and the Louisiades. Equally important, Inoue expected no carrier opposition until the MO Operation was nearly completed.[22]

It took most of April for Inoue's scattered forces to assemble, delayed in particular because of the fruitless pursuit of the Tokyo raiders. Hara's 5th Carrier Division reached Truk on 25 April, Takagi's 5th Cruiser Division two days later. Promoted to vice admiral effective 1 May, Takagi was a submarine specialist who made the transition to capital ships in 1937. He achieved flag rank in November 1938 at the tender age of forty-six and received the 5th Cruiser Division in September 1941. Victor of the Battle of the Java Sea (27 February–1 March 1942), he was dismayed that Tokyo soon questioned his decisions. Totally inexperienced in carrier operations because his cruisers did not operate with Nagumo's *Kidō Butai*, the careful and unassertive Takagi was a safe, if uninspired, choice to lead MO Striking Force. At age fifty-three the burly Hara was a surface warfare expert. Dubbed "King Kong," he made his reputation as a fiery staff officer in China and with Naval General Staff before rising to rear admiral in November 1939. In September 1941 he formed the 5th Carrier Division and led it against Pearl Harbor, Rabaul, and in the Indian Ocean. Neither Hara nor his carrier captains, Yokogawa Ichihei of the *Zuikaku* and the *Shōkaku*'s Jōjima Takaji, were aviators. The relatively pliant Takagi led MO Striking Force from a cruiser. Lacking staff officers familiar with air operations, he delegated full control of carrier air to Hara, subject to consultation. Thus Hara exerted far more influence on general events in his task force than did Fitch in TF-17.[23]

Hara vehemently protested the planned strikes on Australia, not because he anticipated immediate carrier opposition, but from concern the strong Allied land-based air would certainly detect his approach. He also worried that coral reefs off Australia would severely hamper his mobility and that having only the one fleet oiler would limit the radius of his destroyers. Takagi evidently concurred, but nevertheless included the Townsville scenario in his operation order. Hara's loud complaints, combined with a false sighting on 27 April of a supposed carrier southeast of Rabaul, reopened the debate in Truk and Tokyo over the early presence of U.S. carriers. On 29 April Inoue authorized Takagi to cancel the Townsville strike if he thought he would not achieve surprise. That same day Yamamoto settled the matter by directing MO Striking Force to suspend all attacks on the Australian mainland and instead remain watchful for enemy carriers. Therefore on the thirtieth Inoue reluctantly called off the carrier strikes against Townsville, Cooktown, and Port Moresby and looked to Base Air Force to assume the crucial task of neutralizing enemy land-based air forces. As part of this new policy he directed Takagi to transport nine Zero fighters from Truk to reinforce Rabaul, but Hara must use his own pilots to fly those planes to Rabaul and also retrieve them. That seemingly simple ferry mission, only a footnote to the overall plan, would cause profound repercussions.[24]

By midnight on 30 April–1 May, the stage was set for a major confrontation in the Coral Sea. Aside from the Port Moresby invasion convoy, the principal task forces had either gone to sea or were just about to sail. Japanese auxiliary ships already plied the upper Solomons setting up the initial bases. Shima's Tulagi Invasion Force steamed southeast from Rabaul, while Gotō's MO Main Force departed Truk on the thirtieth. Takagi's MO Striking Force was set to follow on the first. Far to the southeast in the eastern Coral Sea, Fletcher's TF-17 and Fitch's TF-11 were just a few hours apart. Both sides began the battle with illusions that could prove fatal. Inoue serenely assumed he had the jump on the Allies and would have his forces in position before they could react. His MO Operation depended on intricate timing and close coordination of widely separated task forces. An unexpected glitch or surprise attack could disrupt the whole schedule and imperil the individual detachments. Inoue never dreamt that the Allies, warned by a vast breach of radio security, had already deployed two carriers at the entrance to the Coral Sea nearly a week earlier than anticipated. Such powerful adversaries could catch the South Seas Force with its guard down before MO Striking Force completed its sweep south around the Solomons. In turn Fletcher, cued by superb radio intelligence, focused on the Louisiades and the developing threat to Port Moresby but did not appreciate the danger to Tulagi. Lacking an effective shore-based search, he had no inkling of Takagi's "left hook" from east of the Solomons. For his own part, Fletcher had little hope he could avoid the active enemy search network. TF-17 must pitch straight in and fight. The side that survived these initial mistakes and profited most from the other's errors would win the battle.

CHAPTER 11

The Battle of the Coral Sea I
Opening Moves

RENDEZVOUS

Fletcher's TF-17 hustled through the New Hebrides to meet Fitch's TF-11 on the afternoon of 1 May in the Coral Sea at Point Butternut, three hundred miles northwest of New Caledonia and four hundred miles southeast of Guadalcanal.[1] On the evening of 30 April Fletcher read a Cincpac message that confirmed the principal objective was Port Moresby. It identified Deboyne, an atoll strategically placed in the central Louisiades, as site for a rendezvous between the "Saipan Base Force" and two merchantmen ("Marus") about to sail from Rabaul. Japan also showed interest in Samarai at the east tip of New Guinea and Cape Rodney on the south Papuan coast.[2]

Before Fletcher could fight, however, he must assemble his scattered forces and refuel, a process he anticipated might take several days. Cincpac ordered him to unite the task forces at Butternut, but circumstances militated against it. At dawn on 1 May, the *Lexington*'s unmistakable profile materialized a dozen miles west of TF-17. Fletcher took advantage of Fitch's early arrival to send TF-11 alone to Butternut and gather the *Chicago*, *Perkins*, and oiler *Tippecanoe* coming out from Nouméa. Fletcher would join them there at dawn on 2 May. He changed the plan because he hoped to fuel TF-17 from the *Neosho*, not easy given the bad weather that barred fueling on 30 April. May Day likewise shaped up raw and rainy. Rough seas and gusty southeast winds forced TF-17 to steer away from Butternut to ease conditions. Heavy seas smashing over the *Neosho*'s main deck injured several crewmen. It took until almost dark just to fuel the *Yorktown* and *Astoria*, while the *Portland* and *Chester* provided oil to the destroyers. In the meantime, Fitch marked time near Butternut. At noon unescorted *Tippecanoe* hove into view, followed by the *Chicago* and *Perkins*. Fitch did not start immediately fueling TF-11, but had a destroyer shepherd the slow oiler around the area and rejoin the next dawn. According to Poco Smith, Fletcher refused to permit both carriers to refuel simultaneously at low speed in possible sub-infested waters. Fletcher, Fitch, and the *Tippecanoe* group all joined at sunrise on 2 May, where the oilers fueled their respective forces. Fletcher hoped by the evening of the third to get as much fuel as possible out of the *Tippecanoe* before releasing her to Efate and to hold the balance of *Neosho*'s oil in immediate reserve. He constantly worried about uncertain logistics and preferred to keep a fast oiler with him until just before going into action.[3]

Fletcher received no fresh information on 1 May either from intelligence or aircraft sightings, indicating the enemy offensive must still be in an early stage. The next afternoon while fueling he learned of increasing pressure against Tulagi. Leary's summary remarked of "ships sighted afternoon 1 May," as well as raids by shipborne aircraft on Tulagi that had to come from "a possible cruiser or seaplane carrier." The reference to "ships sighted afternoon 1 May" caught Fletcher's attention, for Leary hitherto had said nothing about them. Two ships, types not given, were spotted on the first about thirty-five miles southwest of Gizo in New Georgia, two hundred miles northwest of Tulagi. An RAAF Catalina was to have shadowed them the night of 1–2 May, but Leary offered no updates. He also told Fletcher that Area C (from New Guinea east to Bougainville) and Area E (the east flank of Solomons) were not searched on 1 May. Presumably they would be on the second.[4]

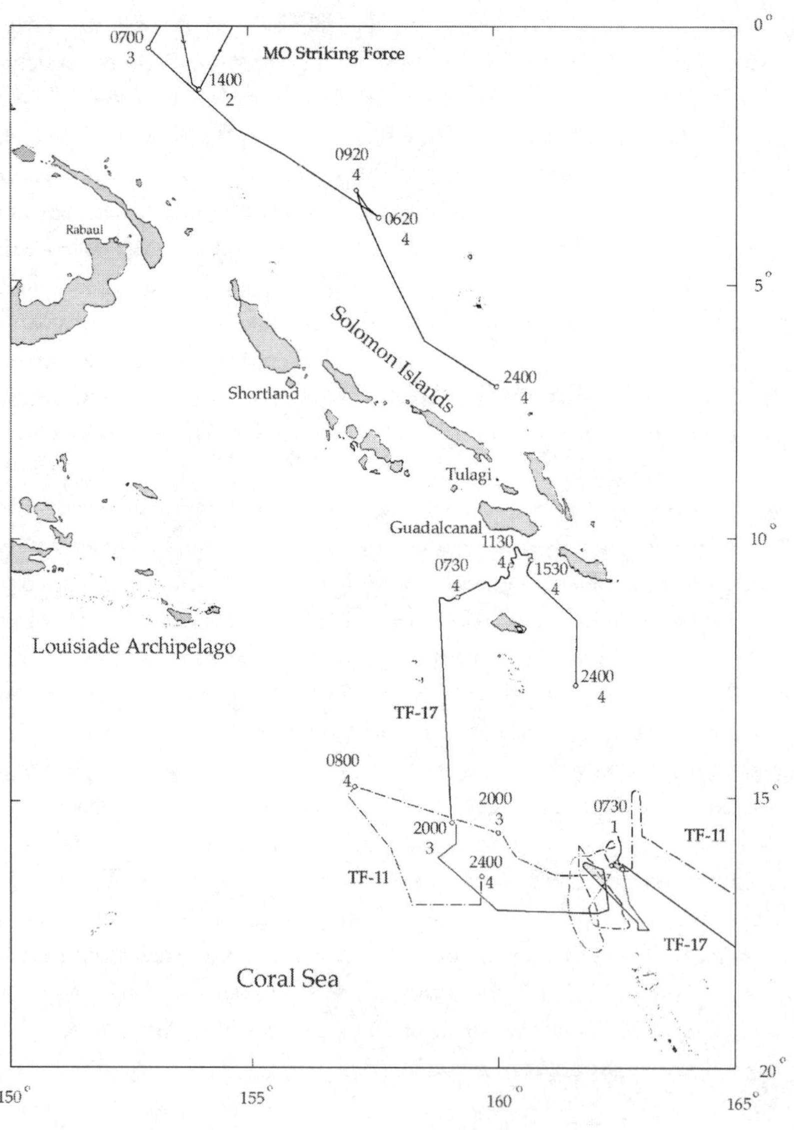

Carrier operations, Coral Sea, 1–4 May 1942

Enemy activity in the Solomons did not as yet appear strong or focused. Unfortunately on the second Fitch's fueling did not go well. He started with his cruisers, and the *Tippecanoe*'s outmoded fueling rig carried away once that afternoon. The *Chicago* did not finish until near to evening, leaving the destroyers and the *Lex*'s vast maw to fill. Fitch ruefully advised Fletcher that he did not expect to wrap up until noon on 4 May. Although "disappointed," Fletcher believed that "reports of enemy forces precluded remaining so far to the southward." He once again separated the carriers, this time for thirty-six hours. TF-17 would head west along with the *Chicago* and *Perkins*. Fitch would continue fueling to southward, release the *Tippecanoe* and a destroyer to Efate, then rejoin TF-17 on the morning of 4 May at the same rendezvous set for Crace's TF-44, which was coming up from Sydney. That was three hundred miles northwest of their present position.[5]

Captain Bates criticized Fletcher for not immediately uniting TF-17 and TF-11, or at least keeping in visual contact. He recognized Fletcher's "desire to be ready for immediate service—his desire for freedom of action should an emergency arise—his anxiety over the developing situation—his desire to be more to the westward and northward." Nevertheless, he should have combined the two task forces. Bates understood it was unwise to loiter in a small fueling area because of subs and speculated that Fletcher could have expedited fueling by swapping oilers with Fitch. Actually the ancient *Tippecanoe* gave Fletcher few options. To stay together greatly restricted mobility, especially considering Fitch's lengthy estimate for fueling. Fletcher could not simply give Fitch the *Neosho*, because he counted on her oil to tide TF-17 over for the next week. Instead, he planned to patrol west of his present position, watching the situation develop to the northwest in the Louisiades. Intelligence pointed to the Rabaul-Louisiade-Moresby axis where the enemy carriers would turn up to support the Invasion Force. Fletcher obviously expected nothing major to break loose until after Fitch rejoined on 4 May.[6]

The Sowespac air search network poorly served Fletcher, but not through the fault of the aviators. The problem lay with higher headquarters not correctly interpreting search results or disseminating them in a timely manner. On 1 May RAAF flying boats shuttling in and out of Tulagi discovered not only "two ships" (which they properly identified as merchant types), but also a convoy of five "merchant vessels" west of New Georgia. One Catalina shadowed the little convoy for five hours and later amplified the contact as one ship of twenty-five hundred tons and numerous armed trawlers. That activity occurred in Area C, which Leary mistakenly said was not even searched. In fact by 2 May Japanese ships dotted the northern and central Solomons. The "two ships" were small converted gunboats from Marumo's Support Force involved in building seaplane bases. He left New Ireland on 29 April with two light cruisers and the seaplane tender *Kamikawa Maru*, stopped at Queen Carola Harbor on Buka, and ventured south on 1 May through Area C. By the next dawn he was in Blanche Channel off southern New Georgia. Shima's Tulagi Invasion Force departed Rabaul on the thirtieth and passed west of the Solomons, again through Area C. The little convoy belatedly reported late on 2 May to Fletcher was Shima's Patrol Force of small minesweepers. The whole force was to be off Tulagi by midnight on 2–3 May. On the evening of 2 May Gotō's MO Main Force (four heavy cruisers, light carrier *Shōhō*, and a destroyer) cut through Bougainville Strait between Bougainville and Choiseul, then turned southeast toward Tulagi. These extensive enemy movements within the area supposedly being searched by Brett's flyers far exceeded the "two ships" relayed to Fletcher.[7]

On the afternoon of 2 May, before TF-17 and TF-11 separated, an SBD dropped a message informing Fletcher of a sub running on the surface twenty-three miles north. Three *Yorktown* TBD torpedo bombers plastered the I-boat with depth charges as it crash-dived. The pilots were so positive about the kill that Fletcher thought it "difficult to understand how the submarine could have escaped." To make sure, he dispatched eleven dive bombers and sent for good measure the *Anderson* and *Sims* with orders to rejoin TF-17 to westward the next dawn. Biard's radio intelligence team heard no contact report from a sub, which again led credence to its destruction. In fact the *I-21* was crossing the Coral Sea to scout Nouméa when two planes forced her to dive. Her lookouts failed to recognize the assailants as carrier-based, nor did her skipper attach importance to the attack, for he was within range of Allied air bases.[8]

The evening of 2 May Fletcher shoved off to the west. No intelligence he received that evening offered any reason to change his plans. Tulagi was again bombed, which indicated "either enemy intention destroy base or preparation for occupation." The Japanese seemed interested also in South Cape on New Guinea and Australian air bases at Cooktown and Townsville. The 6th Destroyer Squadron was believed still en route from Truk to Rabaul, another hint that the offensive had not yet begun. The sighting reports, all from early morning flights on the second, again placed a few merchant ships, mostly small, off New Georgia. As usual those reports only appeared after long delays, especially inexplicable considering one of those Catalinas reached Port Moresby at noon. Early on 3 May Leary advised that the RAAF was evacuating the Tulagi base. By dawn TF-17 was one hundred miles west of TF-11. The *Sims* and *Anderson* reappeared on schedule after finding no trace of the sub bombed the previous afternoon. During the day Fletcher worked his way northwest toward next morning's meeting with Fitch and Crace. By 1530 he had efficiently topped off all seven destroyers from the *Neosho*, in line with his wise policy of keeping TF-17 "in readiness for action on short notice." He endeavored to fuel his destroyers from heavy ships or oilers, "whenever they could receive as much as five hundred barrels of fuel." Mortified by the delay in fueling, Fitch meanwhile ordered the *Tippecanoe* and four destroyers to fuel through the night. Favorable wind and sea conditions facilitated the process. Escorted by the *Worden*, the *Tippecanoe* left for Efate to fuel the convoy after providing TF-11 more than half her oil. At the same time Fitch, having completed fueling twenty-two hours ahead of his revised schedule, proceeded northwest to join TF-17 the next morning.[9]

TULAGI STRIKE

Once again the intelligence provided to Fletcher depicted limited enemy activity. The daily Cincpac bulletin opined, but could not affirm, that Fourth Fleet, with the expected cast of Cardiv 5, Crudiv 5, Crudiv 18, and the 5th Air Attack Corps, had started its offensive against southeast New Guinea and "outlying islands." The *Kaga* was believed to have left Japan, whereas the *Sōryū* was ready to sail in a few days. Unknown to Fletcher, Shima seized undefended Tulagi before dawn on 3 May. The *Shōhō* from Gotō's MO Main Force launched an unneeded air strike from just south of New Georgia and 120 miles west of Tulagi and by noon started back to Bougainville to fuel. The MO Operation appeared to be going very well, but its most important component was out of position. The MO Striking Force (*Shōkaku* and *Zuikaku*) had departed Truk on 1 May. The next day Takagi sent off the ferry flight of nine Zeros and seven carrier attack planes from northeast of Rabaul. Storms compelled their return to the carriers. Because Inoue considered those nine fighters vital to gain air superiority over Moresby, Takagi postponed his advance toward the waters east of Tulagi and maneuvered northward in a wide box to return to the same launching point on the morning of 3 May. Things went no better the second time. Disgusted, Takagi deferred flying off the Zeros to Rabaul until he could do so from the Coral Sea flank of the Solomons. He belatedly resumed his southward advance to the east of the Solomons. This setback would prove extremely detrimental to Japanese fortunes.[10]

At dusk on 3 May Fletcher anticipated an easy overnight run to next morning's rendezvous with Fitch and Crace just 130 miles northwest. At 1830, however, the radio resounded with "the kind of report we had been waiting two months to receive." MacArthur tardily placed five or six ships (the biggest five to eight thousand tons) off southern Santa Isabel Island as of 1630, 2 May—twenty-six hours before—and suggested they might be bound for Tulagi. The source for this intelligence must have been an Australian coast watcher. None of the available aircraft search reports mention this sighting. Fletcher's report noted another message received about that time of two transports unloading troops into barges at Tulagi. Again coast watchers must have provided it, but the details are not clear. With Tulagi less than four hundred miles north, Fletcher considered what, if anything, to do about it. The absence of TF-11 was "regrettable," but he was determined if at all possible to hit such "juicy" targets at dawn. TF-17 would need to work eastward into the prevailing wind to conduct air operations, so Arnold advised approaching Tulagi from the southwest. Fletcher did not believe that the Moresby offensive had yet begun in earnest or that hostile carriers prowled nearby and remained convinced the Japanese were still unaware of his presence. Surprising Tulagi seemed a real possibility. The strength at hand (one carrier, four heavy cruisers, and six destroyers) was adequate for that task. Due to careful husbanding of fuel, TF-17 had oil to spare for high-speed steaming. Fletcher detached the *Neosho* and *Russell* to keep the appointment with Fitch and Crace and redirect them to a new meeting 180 miles east at dawn on 5 May at familiar Point Corn, 325 miles south of Guadalcanal.[11]

Bates again faulted Fletcher for not keeping TF-17 and TF-11 together. Unknown to Fletcher, Fitch had finished refueling well ahead of schedule and at 2000 was only sixty miles east of TF-17. Strict radio silence prevented either admiral from advising the other. Bates likewise questioned Fletcher's decision to set the 5 May rendezvous at Corn, rather than closer to Tulagi, where he could have united the task forces more quickly after the strike. Hindsight gave Bates the advantage of knowing Japanese dispositions and movements, although neither he nor Morison ever actually understood Inoue's plan. The MO Striking Force was to sweep around the Solomons and westward into the Coral Sea right enough, but to attack Townsville, not lurking U.S. carriers. Bates also surmised that the *Shōhō* force was to come down from the north and help trap the U.S. carrier force west of the Solomons. He chided Fletcher for "fail[ing] to discern the Japanese plan of encirclement from the east."

Not only did Bates unjustly focus the lens of hindsight, but he also falsely accused Fletcher of being duped by a crafty plan that never existed. Inoue, in fact, had no clue an enemy carrier was even in the area, and certainly he entertained no plan to "encircle" it. And if Fletcher was lax in not anticipating danger from the east, he was not alone. No one at Pearl or Washington thought the Japanese carriers would use the back door either. Fletcher set the 5 May meeting at Point Corn because he did not want to end up too far to the northeast. He saw sighting reports of seventeen transports waiting in Rabaul and assumed, correctly, the Moresby invasion convoy was about to sail. That evening Leary (echoing a Cincpac message Fletcher could not read) advised that two "marus" with escort were expected to reach Deboyne about noon on 5 May, probably to set up a seaplane base. Indeed Fletcher believed, and with good reason, that Tulagi was peripheral to the main event. If he wanted to attack it, he must do so quickly before defending Port Moresby. The most logical employment of the enemy carriers, which Allied air had yet to spot, was to stick close to the invasion convoy once it sailed from Rabaul and guard against the threat from southward in the Coral Sea.[12]

Fletcher increased speed to twenty-seven knots, hastening toward a dawn launch point southwest of Guadalcanal. Relaxing in the *Astoria*'s flag quarters, Smith happened to be reading a novel when the sudden vibration of the ship startled him. His spirits lifted at the prospective attack. Likewise cheers resounded on the *Yorktown* when Buckmaster announced that the air group would strike Tulagi at dawn. TF-17 soon ran into bad weather caused by a moderate cold front moving slowly northward toward the Solomons—a characteristic Coral Sea weather pattern that time of year. Aerologist Strange forecast generally bad weather on 4 May, with an overcast, squalls, and gusty southeast winds from the cold front stalled on the southern fringe of the Solomons. Fletcher expected no fighter opposition at Tulagi and retained the eighteen F4Fs to defend the task force. That evening Arnold devised the air attack plan for all forty SBDs and TBDs. The *Yorktown*'s first deck load comprised six F4Fs for combat air patrol, thirteen VS-5 SBDs under Commander Burch, and Commander Taylor's twelve TBDs. Lieutenant Short's fifteen VB-5 SBDs were poised on the hangar deck. With group leader Pederson stuck on board as FDO, Arnold directed Burch, the senior squadron commander, to coordinate his dive bombers with Taylor's torpedo strike. Working in darkness, the air department earned praise for efficiently spotting the flight deck and arming each SBD with a 1,000-pound bomb and each TBD with a torpedo. Burch would lead the strike, but not as ranking officer. That night Cdr. Butch Schindler, the Crupac staff gunnery officer, asked Fletcher for permission to ride in the rear seat of an SBD. Qualified in aerial observation, he was eager to study the attacks. Reluctant to risk him, Fletcher finally gave in to his earnest pleas. Fletcher felt dubious about the ability of the aviators to recognize ship types and depended on Schindler's judgment in that regard. Schindler in fact would fly several combat missions with VS-5.[13]

Prior to dawn on 4 May, TF-17 closed within one hundred miles of Guadalcanal and 150 miles southwest of Tulagi. The stormy skies matched Strange's prediction, but the *Yorktown* aviators were eager to go. By 0702 the last attacker was airborne. Continuing northeast to shorten the range to Tulagi, Fletcher prepared for a possible air counterattack. By 0945 the first wave had returned. Burch, the first to land, raced to the bridge to tell Buckmaster they had "hit the Japs but didn't do any good." Like all the SBD pilots, he was extremely frustrated that his windshield and telescopic sight fogged while diving from high altitude into much warmer humid air near the sea. "It's like putting a white sheet in front of you and you have to bomb from memory." Burch wanted to go back and finish the job. "All right," Buckmaster replied, "get in your plane." Fletcher had decided on a second strike well before Burch suggested it. Radio chatter revealed Tulagi crawled with targets. Biard could not decipher the frantic messages, but at least he recognized no obvious sighting reports of TF-17. Nor did the *Yorktown*'s radar detect bogeys that might be enemy searchers. The weather proved an effective shield. The *Yorktown* recovered VS-5 and VT-5 first, struck them below for fuel and ordnance, then landed Short's VB-5 SBDs (the last at 0954) and quickly serviced them on the flight deck. All planes returned safely, and the pilots hastily filled out Burch's account. The skies providentially cleared near Guadalcanal, leaving only patchy clouds over Tulagi harbor. Three cruisers were moored together, and nearby were three transports or cargo ships, a large seaplane tender, four gunboats, and numerous small craft. The nested "cruisers" drew the most attention. Burch reported four "sure" bomb hits and one probable. Taylor, splitting his attack between cruisers and transports, claimed hits on all three merchantmen. Two of the "cruisers" then left port, but the third beached itself. Ten minutes later VB-5 bombed a cargo ship and the large seaplane tender but could not confirm any hits.[14]

The *Yorktown* Air Group spoiled a beautiful morning for the Tulagi Invasion Force. Shima's plans proceeded like clockwork as he regrouped his forces. Three small minesweepers had just left for the Port Moresby Invasion Force, the old destroyers *Kikuzuki* and *Yūzuki* had moored alongside the fast minelayer *Okinoshima* (Shima's flagship) to fuel, and two large transports (*Azumasan Maru* and *Kōei Maru*) were unloading base equipment. Two small patrol craft were under way in the harbor. Only the *Kikuzuki* suffered damage in the first attack. A torpedo in her engine room forced her to go aground before she sank. As flagship light cruiser *Kashima* arrived at Rabaul, Inoue heard Shima's alarm. Shocked a U.S. carrier was already in the area, he ordered Takagi's MO Striking Force and the land-based 5th Air Attack Force to destroy the assailants within two hundred miles of Tulagi. Fearing additional strikes in the meantime, he told Shima to retire north. Fortunately for Fletcher, Takagi was far behind schedule due to the two fruitless attempts to deliver fighters to Rabaul. Instead of 120 miles north of Tulagi, from where he could have provided fighter support and possibly attacked TF-17 that afternoon (if he found it), Takagi languished 350 miles northward and was refueling to boot. Unlike the U.S. Navy, Japanese battleships, carriers, and cruisers did not as yet regularly fuel destroyers, a considerable drawback. Leaving most of his destroyers to finish with the *Tōhō Maru*, Takagi hastened southeast with the rest of his ships. He searched 250 miles ahead in the waters east of the Solomons. Fletcher, of course, was south not east of Tulagi, so Takagi's flyers sighted nothing. The three Shortland flying boats got the word too late to search. That was bad for Inoue, because only they might have actually located TF-17.[15]

Scouting west and north of Guadalcanal for ships fleeing Tulagi, Short's fourteen VB-5 SBDs, leading the second wave, sank three "gunboats," actually the *No. 1* and *No. 2* special duty minesweepers and the *Tama Maru*, which departed Tulagi prior to the first attack. A heavy cruiser or a large seaplane tender proved much more elusive. She was actually the minelayer *Okinoshima*, accompanied by the *Yūzuki*. Her twenty-knot speed and adroit shiphandling snookered not only VB-5 but also Burch's thirteen VS-5 SBDs (which claimed two nonexistent hits) and Taylor's eleven TBDs. The SBDs ran afoul of pugnacious float planes over Tulagi harbor. Buckmaster got wind of trouble and asked permission for a fighter sweep to Tulagi. Nothing hostile appeared in the immediate vicinity, so Fletcher released four F4Fs. In a sharp engagement over Tulagi, they claimed three seaplanes and later strafed the *Yūzuki*.

Mulling the reports, Fletcher considered sending in two cruisers and two destroyers to "mop up damaged ships." Asked by Fletcher to nominate two cruisers for Tulagi, Smith swiftly offered his flagship *Astoria* along with the *Chester*. Although Tulagi was only seventy-five air miles distant, the big island of Guadalcanal blocked the way, meaning no chance to reach there before darkness. He planned to approach from the west, shell Tulagi harbor at sunrise on 5 May, then retire eastward at high speed. Fletcher was not yet ready to unleash Smith but waited to see how the situation developed. At 1330 the *Yorktown* started landing SBDs from the second wave, which claimed sinking two destroyers or small gunboats and possibly a cargo ship. Seeking firsthand information, Fletcher spoke with one of the pilots, Lt. (jg) Floyd E. Moan of VB-5, who described bombing the gunboats and the big seaplane tender. Moan suggested a follow-up attack. Fletcher appeared somewhat skeptical, but by the time Moan got down to the VB-5 ready room, he learned there was to be a third wave. Burch also desired another go. Twenty-one SBDs left at 1400 to deliver the coup de grâce. Likely it was then Fletcher gave up the idea of sending Smith to bombard Tulagi. That was a good thing. Every ship less the stricken *Kikuzuki* and a small auxiliary soon decamped, and Takagi's carriers would have made short work of Smith's cruisers on 5 May. On their third foray Burch's dozen SBDs incorrectly claimed one hit on a cargo ship, although just the blast of near misses harmed the crew of the *Azumasan Maru* and sailors of the Tulagi garrison. Short's nine SBDs took another unsuccessful shot at the *Okinoshima* and *Yūzuki*. With their departure, the Tulagi air battle ended.[16]

The *Yorktown* recovered all but one Devastator missing from the second wave. Two fighters set down on the beach at Cape Henslow on Guadalcanal less than fifty miles north of TF-17. Fletcher acted swiftly to retrieve the downed aviators. He detached the *Perkins* to seek the TBD's crew and the *Hammann* to Cape Henslow. The two destroyers were to rejoin TF-17 at sunrise at Corn 325 miles south of Guadalcanal. The *Perkins* did not find the TBD crew, who luckily fell in with loyal Solomon islanders, but the *Hammann*'s motor whaleboat effected a courageous rescue of the two VF-42 pilots. Morison chose this occasion to give Fletcher "great credit for initiating efforts to rescue aviators downed in combat," but he had already done so on the 1 February raid.[17]

By sunset with all aircraft retrieved, it was high time to leave. Fletcher turned southeast at twenty-three knots toward Point Corn. Morale was high. One SBD pilot wrote in his diary that "the men were proud of the way Admiral Fletcher and Captain Buckmaster ran the affair." After reviewing reports and aerial photographs, *Yorktown* assessed two destroyers, a cargo ship, and four small gunboats (one thousand to fifteen hundred tons) sunk and a light cruiser (possibly *Jintsu*-class) forced aground. One nine-thousand-ton seaplane tender (or perhaps heavy cruiser) sustained heavy damage; a light cruiser and a large cargo ship (eight to ten thousand tons) were also damaged to a lesser degree. *Yorktown* aircraft shot down five small seaplanes and strafed numerous small boats. Australian coast watchers later stated that nine ships went down off Tulagi, including three cruisers (one beached) and three transports. Actual Japanese losses were much less. Only the destroyer *Kikuzuki* (beached at Tulagi) and three small minesweepers (*No. 1*, *No. 2*, and *Tama Maru*) sank, whereas the minelayer *Okinoshima* and the destroyer *Yūzuki* sustained minor damage. Four observation seaplanes were lost.[18]

Even according to the *Yorktown*'s exaggerated claims, the lack of air opposition and heavy antiaircraft certainly rendered the results, to use Nimitz's own word, "disappointing." Only five of twenty-two torpedoes and eleven of seventy-six 1,000-pound bombs were adjudged hits. Fogging of telescopic sights hindered bombing, but Schindler, who flew three missions with VS-5, candidly described overall accuracy as "poor." Peacetime standards of marksmanship, he thought, would have tripled enemy losses. However, Tulagi served as a valuable warm-up for aviators gone stale during a long and quiet, but nonetheless nerve-wracking, cruise. It marked the first time in a year that VT-5 had actually dropped torpedoes. Nimitz praised the "very creditable willingness" of the *Yorktown* aviators to "to keep after their enemy objective until it was destroyed," but diagnosed their obvious need for regular target practice. He enjoined the task force commanders to increase training at sea. Yet the risky strategic situation and the *Yorktown*'s lengthy cruise offered few chances for the kind of elaborate air group practices held off Pearl.[19]

The Cincpac daily intelligence that Fletcher received on the afternoon of 4 May added the *Kaga*, some fast battlewagons, and two more heavy cruisers to the ominous list of reinforcements possibly bound for Truk. The 2nd Carrier Division (*Sōryū* and *Hiryū*) might also come south in mid May. All this conformed to Nimitz's expectation of a widespread offensive in the South Pacific. During 4 May Comsowespac air sighting reports were remarkably sparse. Several search areas were not even covered. That evening Fletcher belatedly learned that at 1135 a U.S. B-25 bomber in Area C spotted a carrier ("probably *Kaga* class") and two battleships or heavy cruisers off the west coast of Bougainville, approximately two hundred miles southeast of Rabaul and more than five hundred miles northwest of TF-17. That sighting did not affect Fletcher's immediate plans. Sowespac still placed twenty to twenty-five transports at Rabaul, obviously the Moresby invasion convoy. Fletcher held off until that convoy and its covering force had moved south. In fact Sowespac finally discovered the light carrier *Shōhō* that for two days crisscrossed the northern Solomons with Gotō's MO Main Force. While returning to Bougainville to fuel, Gotō learned that Shima was in trouble and turned back.[20]

On 4 May Fitch was surprised to find only an oiler and a destroyer waiting at the rendezvous. The *Neosho*'s Capt. John S. Phillips duly advised that Fletcher had gone north to Tulagi and would be at Point Corn, 180 miles east, at dawn on the fifth. Crace arrived on schedule with the *Australia* and *Hobart*. Fitch led the combined force southeast. Crace wondered why that direction instead of east or even northeast toward Tulagi. Later so did Bates, who again scolded both U.S. commanders for keeping TF-17 and TF-11 separated. When Crace joined, TF-11 was nearly three hundred miles southwest of Fletcher, "unable," according to Bates, "to support TF 17 should a sudden need arise." Bates blamed Fletcher.

Yet Fitch steered southeast, "Even though such a course would probably place him in a poor supporting position." Bates thought if Fitch had only turned northeast, he could have been 250 miles nearer to TF-17 by sundown, but still out of enemy search range. Instead he maintained his southeasterly course until sundown, then turned eastward toward dawn rendezvous. Fitch later told Bates that he preferred the southeast because he did not know how Fletcher fared at Tulagi and judged it best to keep TF-11 well south of the rendezvous. Six *Lexington* SBDs searched two hundred miles northwest to ensure TF-11 itself was not being stalked. Fitch had access to the same intelligence sources as Fletcher. Had it seemed Fletcher was in peril, he would not have hesitated to rush to Tulagi. Instead like Fletcher, he anticipated little real danger to the north or northeast. The main threat to Port Moresby must come via the Louisiades.[21]

REUNION

At dawn on 5 May Fitch's TF-11 and Crace's TF-44 made the scheduled meeting at Point Corn. The *Perkins* showed up alone after her fruitless search off Guadalcanal. Crace, for one, thought Fletcher was off chasing the enemy carrier sighted near Bougainville the previous day, but actually TF-17 loomed over the eastern horizon. On 3 May he received another special Cincpac message transmitted in a cipher he did not hold. After dawn on the fifth he broke radio silence—believing he could finally do so safely, for he had certainly revealed his presence if not his exact position—to inform Pearl of his inability to decipher certain systems, a good thing because another unreadable message came through in the interval.[22]

TF-17 emerged from thick overcast only to detect a bogey thirty miles west. Four Wildcats ambushed a Type 97 flying boat low over the water. Both TF-17 and TF-11 noticed the smoke that announced its fiery end, and forty minutes later they sighted each other as well. The Kawanishi went down fifteen miles from TF-11 and twenty-seven miles from TF-17. The victim was one of three flying boats searching out of Shortland; six others flew from Tulagi. It never established radio contact with base, and only later did its absence lead to the conclusion a U.S. carrier prowled south of the Solomons. Soon afterward a *Yorktown* search SBD discovered a sub 150 miles northwest and moving toward TF-17. Fletcher wondered whether it responded to a contact report from the flying boat. Three TBDs hunted the sub without success. Had Fletcher known it was only one of four I-boats of the Eastern Detachment, he would have been more perturbed. They cut through the Solomons bound for a deployment line farther south in the Coral Sea to catch Allied fleet units expected to rush north from Australia. The center of that line was about two hundred miles southwest of Fletcher's current position. On the fifth Inoue instructed the Eastern Detachment to shift 150 miles northeast, but even that fell short of TF-17.[23]

Waiting for the enemy offensive to develop, Fletcher radioed Cincpac a summary of the Tulagi strike and noted the three task forces had now joined. He refueled TF-17 to make up for the past day's high-speed run. Fueling required steaming slowly southeast into the wind during the day, but Fletcher planned to run northwest overnight to regain position. The *Neosho* fueled the *Astoria* and *Yorktown*, while six destroyers drew much-needed oil from the *Chester* and *Portland*. Cincpac promptly responded to Fletcher's report. "Congratulations and well done to you and your force. Hope you can exploit your success with your augmented force." The afternoon was quieter than the morning. At 1341 Leary provided a rare timely sighting report of a seaplane tender discovered at 1313 southwest of New Georgia, though the Sowespac morning search missed the massive Port Moresby invasion convoy that finally departed Rabaul the previous evening. MacArthur did advise Fletcher that he had ordered his aircraft to relay contact reports in plain language on certain frequencies, but that did not solve the problem of passing on information expeditiously. The daily Cincpac bulletin warned that the *Hiryū* might depart Japan soon for Truk and the *Sōryū* might already be on her way there, according to "unconfirmed information."[24]

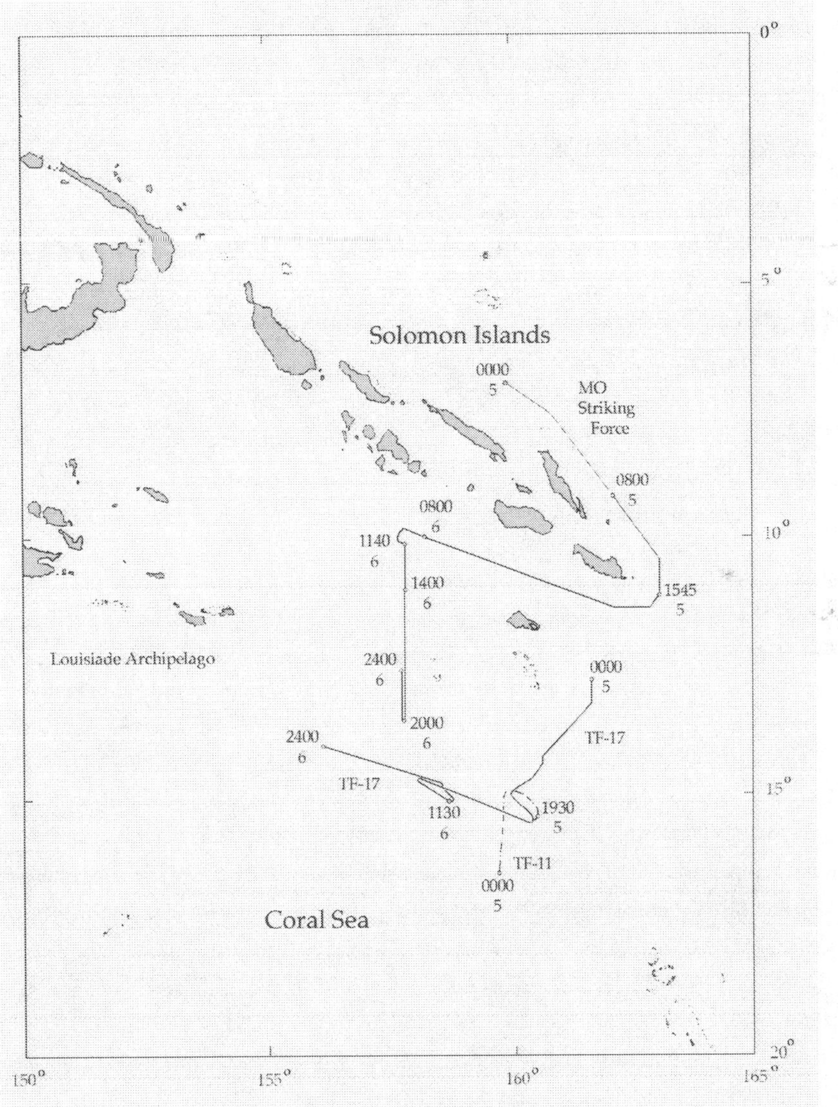

Carrier operations, Coral Sea, 5–6 May 1942

Fitch flew over to the *Yorktown* that afternoon for a brief reunion with Fletcher. Naturally mistaking the stocky man in the back seat of the *Lex* SBD for a radioman, one of the deck crew teased: "Well, chief, you guys kinda missed out on some fun yesterday." Fitch laughed, revealed his two stars, and replied: "Yes, son, I guess we did." Frustrated with shore duty, he was more than ready to fight. Fitch's own brand of dynamic leadership complemented the *Lex*'s fiery Capt. Ted Sherman, himself no shrinking violet. He named Sherman ex officio TF-11 chief of staff for the present cruise and requested the assignment be permanent. Bunav, however, offered its regrets. Sherman was due for promotion and another billet. Like their boss nearly all of Fitch's staff were naval aviators. Confident of their expertise, aviation and otherwise, they were eager to run a carrier battle if Fletcher let them.[25]

Fitch received his copy of TF-17 Op-Ord 2-42 and the job of air task group commander. He also informed Fletcher that on 2 May his own radio intelligence team, led by Lt. Cdr. Ranson Fullinwider, indeed detected a contact report from the bombed sub (*I-21*), along with appropriate reverberations within the enemy theater command. Fletcher relayed these findings to an astonished Biard, who heard nothing from that sub and had advised Fletcher to that effect. Fullinwider was a Japanese language specialist whom Fletcher knew and respected. Of the 2 May incident, Fletcher declared in his action report that the "proximity of the submarine to our surface forces and radio interceptions pointed to the probability of our position having been reported to the enemy," and that "in over two months of operating in the Coral Sea, this was the first definite indication of our presence having become known to the enemy." Biard, though, was completely correct. There was no report of the incident, although it is possible the *I-21* sent some other routine message. The relationship between Fletcher and Biard was already troubled, and according to Biard this only magnified Fletcher's growing distrust.[26]

DANGEROUS ILLUSIONS

By the afternoon of 5 May as Fletcher fueled TF-17, it seemed he eluded any immediate retribution from the Tulagi raid. His dominating concern remained the Japanese carriers. More information from the Sowespac air search reached him that afternoon. For the second time in two days MacArthur's flyers located the *Kaga* or a "*Kaga*" class carrier near Bougainville. The search summary on 5 May placed a *Kaga*-class carrier and a battleship ("*Yamashiro* or *Haruna* type") 125 miles southwest of Bougainville. War Plans at Pearl assumed the presence of warships of that type in the Solomons, and that was now confirmed. Layton, the Cincpac intelligence officer, postulated the carrier sighted on 4 May off the west coast of Bougainville could be one of two Cardiv 5 flattops in the Moresby Striking Force. Comsowespac only reinforced that impression by amending the original report, calling the carrier sighted the previous day "*Ihokauu*" class, a garble for *Shōkaku*. In truth on both days aircraft sighted only the *Shōhō*. On the morning of 5 May the *Shōhō* and destroyer *Sazanami* continued north to cover the invasion convoy, while the 6th Cruiser Division ducked into Shortland to refuel. The 5th Carrier Division was nowhere nearby. On 4 May, as noted above, Shima's cry for help surprised Takagi's MO Striking Force busy fueling well north of the central Solomons. Takagi raced southeast with most of his ships expecting to find the enemy carrier east of

Tulagi but never sighted it. Directed by Inoue to resume the plan of entering the Coral Sea from south of the Solomons, Takagi rescheduled the rendezvous with his oiler to dawn on 6 May in the Coral Sea 180 miles west of Tulagi. On the afternoon of the fifth he circled west around San Cristóbal, too late in the day for the *Tangier*'s flying boats to sight him. Nor did his own search planes peering three hundred miles ahead spot any Allied ships. That night he passed west of Guadalcanal headed for his oiler.[27]

Thus on the afternoon of 5 May TF-17 and MO Striking Force unwittingly drew much closer to each other than either realized. Fletcher based his perception of the situation largely on a series of Cincpac special intelligence messages. The first, sent on 3 May in the wrong cipher and rebroadcast the afternoon of 5 May, noted that "good information indicates following Orange Operation Order for Southwest Pacific offensive now starting." The Japanese would operate "to utmost to restrict Blue fleet movements by attacks on outlying units and various areas along north coast of Australia." They might even occupy Allied air bases "to wipe out shore based aircraft." What Fletcher made of that particular message is not precisely known, except that he could be expected to believe that carrier strikes against air bases was a high Japanese priority. The Cincpac analysts judged its meaning: "To keep our forces from interfering, the Japanese plan to raid such places as Cooktown, Townsville, and Horn Island, and may raid as far east as [Efate], Nouméa, Fiji, and Samoa." That, of course, reflected Nimitz's prediction of a wider Japanese South Pacific offensive and was the main reason he committed Halsey's two carriers along with Fletcher and Fitch. The seizure of Tulagi only heightened that impression. Hypo had extracted this decrypt from a Japanese message that proved "difficult to read due to lack of code groups." In truth Rochefort's assessment of the meaning of that message was *exactly the opposite* of its true intent. It was actually the 29 April signal in which Yamamoto *called off* carrier raids on Australia and directed Takagi to be prepared to hunt down U.S. carriers.[28]

The code breakers provided further erroneous interpretations of partially deciphered Japanese messages. Two additional Cincpac special messages that Fletcher received on the afternoon of 5 May dealt specifically with the "Moresby Striking Force" of the 5th Cruiser and 5th Carrier divisions. According to the first message, "reliable indications on 3 May" showed the Moresby Striking Force had orders to strike Port Moresby on X–3 or X–2 Days apparently from the southeast. Uncertain of X-Day, Pearl correctly guessed 10 May. That meant carrier raids against Moresby could occur on the seventh or eighth. Cincpac asserted to Fletcher, "above attacks [are] to be carried out until successful completion by Orange." For the most part the U.S. cryptanalysts at Pearl and Melbourne recovered the sense of that particular Japanese message but never realized that it was not even relevant. On 3 May Inoue attempted to revive the controversial MO Striking Force raids on troublesome Allied air bases, in this case Port Moresby. He radioed Takagi it had been "agreed informally" that, depending on the enemy air strength, he was to attack Port Moresby on 7 or 8 May from the southeast. Takagi, though, chose to ignore the "informal agreement," as was his right. Unlike the Allied code breakers, he well understood the terms of Yamamoto's 29 April order that canceled carrier raids on shore bases until the U.S. carriers were destroyed. Fletcher's Tulagi strike ended any doubt on that score. Consequently Takagi had no intention of attacking a shore target. However, Cincpac's categorical rendering of the "order" to attack Port Moresby appeared to offer the Japanese carrier commander little discretion. Thus Fletcher learned that the Moresby Striking Force was to bomb Port Moresby either on 7 or 8 May. Geography made the southeast a virtual certainty due to the remote reef-strewn waters northeast of Papua. For the Moresby Striking Force, the voyage westward from the Bougainville Strait via the Louisiades to within strike range (two hundred miles) southeast of Port Moresby would total six hundred miles—thirty hours at a steady twenty knots. To get there on time the Japanese carriers must get cracking through the Louisiades.[29]

The last Cincpac special message vouchsafed Fletcher on 5 May appeared to describe how his Tulagi strike might affect future movements of the enemy carriers. According to Cincpac, the commander of the Moresby Striking Force "indicates 4 May" that if he determines the U.S. carrier force is in the Coral Sea ("questionable location"), he would "proceed north northeast of Bougainville, thence southward." Then at 0630 local time on 5 May, after reaching someplace not known to Cincpac, he would continue in accordance with "further orders." If no further orders were received, the Moresby Striking Force was to make for Tulagi. If it proved necessary to search to the south and some other sector, the 5th Carrier Division was to send its bombers to Tulagi at daybreak. What did Fletcher and the others deduce from this message? At this long remove without specific documentation one can only speculate. One possible rendering is that if the Japanese discovered the U.S. carrier force south of Tulagi, as opposed to east of the Solomons, the Moresby Striking Force was to withdraw northeast of Bougainville, then turn back south. That could keep its carriers clear of Allied land-based air search until the proper moment to resume the southward advance. As for the Moresby Striking Force proceeding to Tulagi if it received no "further orders," one possible explanation is that should the U.S. carrier be found east of the Solomons, the Japanese carrier force was to deploy toward Tulagi to guard the flank. As mentioned before, Fletcher knew of sightings of Japanese carriers in the Bougainville area. He had every reason to think from the supposed sighting of TF-17 and TF-11 on the morning of 5 May that the Japanese well knew he was on the Coral Sea side of Tulagi. That could induce the Moresby Striking Force to mark time a short while northeast beyond Bougainville before advancing southwest toward the Louisiades. Unfortunately U.S. naval intelligence (and thus Nimitz and Fletcher) did not understand this last order never even applied to Takagi's MO Striking Force but instead concerned Gotō's MO Main Force (6th Cruiser Division, *Shōhō*, and destroyer *Sazanami*), the separate existence of which Hypo and Belconnen were totally unaware.[30]

Despite the seemingly comprehensive intelligence, the Allies actually had no clue where the 5th Carrier Division was or where it had been. Fletcher did receive a tangible indication that evening of the apparently reliability of this intelligence. For several days Nimitz and Leary had forecast the arrival at noon on 5 May of two merchant ships ("Marus") at Deboyne near the northern approach to Jomard Passage. That evening Fletcher learned Allied aircraft indeed located "two merchant vessels about 2,000 tons with other units" about one hundred miles northeast of Deboyne and obviously bound there. Although the Japanese ran a bit late, the contact report appeared to give dramatic proof of the astonishing accuracy of Cincpac's prognostications.[31]

THE BATTLE THAT ALMOST WAS

On the evening of 5 May Fletcher instructed Fitch and Crace to keep within ten miles of TF-17 while steaming overnight to the northwest. By dawn on 6 May they were about 150 miles west of Point Corn. Fletcher swung back southeast. The *Lexington* loosed a dozen SBDs for a routine search northward to 275 miles, nearly to the southern Solomons. Fletcher executed Op-Ord 2-42 that merged the three task forces into TF-17, with Kinkaid's Attack Group (TG-17.2), Crace's Support Group (TG-17.3), Fitch's Air Task Group (TG-17.5), Phillips's Fueling Group (TG-17.6) and Cdr. George H. DeBaun's Search Group (TG-17.9) with the *Tangier*. Fletcher predicated his plans for the sixth on his belief, based on the intelligence provided him, that the battle would not break out until at least the next day. He welcomed the lull to replace the oil his two cruisers furnished the TF-17 destroyers and, if time and the enemy permitted, to fuel Crace's cruisers as well. That again meant heading slowly southeast into the prevailing wind. The weather, fine on 5 May, decayed as clouds closed in and the wind picked up. Rough seas hindered fueling all day. The SBDs that searched in the clear weather up near the Solomons filed no contact reports. It was Fletcher's ill fortune they did not locate the MO Striking Force around 0815 as it fueled south of New Georgia. By good luck Takagi loitered just beyond the limit of visibility of the nearest *Lexington* SBD. A sighting would have precipitated a carrier battle, with Fletcher hoping to surprise the enemy as he had at Tulagi. Unfortunately the Sowespac air search concentrated on the Bougainville-Louisiades area, so Fletcher gained no help from that quarter.[32]

The Japanese shore-based search had better luck. About 1015 TF-17 radars discovered an intruder lurking in nearby clouds. *Yorktown* F4Fs failed to trap their quarry, although at least one ship glimpsed it. As a precaution should an enemy strike follow on its heels, Fletcher drew all of TF-17, except the Fueling Group, into the tight "Victor" defensive formation. Nothing showed up, but the bogey did not go away either. It was a near certainty that a snooper was shadowing TF-17, although neither Fullinwider nor Biard intercepted any sighting reports. By noon flying conditions became so bad that the SOC float planes flying antisubmarine patrol over the Fueling Group were soon recalled. The *Chester* finally finished fueling about then, and the *Portland* took her place alongside the oiler. At 1252 radar warned of another contact twenty-eight miles south.[33]

That afternoon as Fletcher warily fueled, he learned from Melbourne and Pearl that the Japanese were indeed tracking something. Cincpac's message quoted a deciphered message warning of "enemy one carrier one BB two cruisers five destroyers and four unidentified vessels course 190 speed 20 at 0830 Item (minus 9) [1030, Z-11]." Unfortunately neither Belconnen nor Hypo could read the position, but Fletcher correctly understood that with Tulagi only four hundred miles north the message must refer to TF-17. At 1030 a Japanese flying boat had revealed a U.S. carrier force 420 miles southwest of Tulagi, but erred in placing it fifty miles south of Fletcher's actual position. It also wrongly reported course and speed as south (190 degrees) at twenty knots, whereas TF-17 slowly fueled on a southeasterly course. Fletcher soon received more evidence of carriers prowling off Bougainville. At 1207 Comsowespac placed a carrier, two cruisers, and two destroyers only thirty miles off the southwest coast of Bougainville and headed south. Forty minutes later MacArthur advised that B-17s sought a carrier in the "Misima" (eastern Louisiades) and "Bougainville areas." Fletcher took the precaution that afternoon of having *Lexington* SBDs again search 275 miles north and northwest.[34]

The TF-17 afternoon search found no enemy ships, but that did not rule out any hiding under the clouds. At 1050 Takagi was again embarrassed to be caught fueling when he received word of the U.S. carrier force discovered 350 miles south and headed almost directly away. At noon he released Hara's 5th Carrier Division and two fueled destroyers to chase the carrier. He soon followed with his two cruisers, leaving the rest of the destroyers behind with the *Tōhō Maru* to continue fueling. Racing southward into increasingly hostile weather, Hara perceived dim prospects for a long-range air strike that afternoon and elected not to launch his own air search to pinpoint the enemy. He was unsure given the poor visibility whether it would be worthwhile, and he most especially did not want to alert the Americans to his presence.[35]

Actually TF-17 was less than three hundred miles away. Because the *Lexington* SBDs missed both the 5th Carrier Division and 5th Cruiser Division in the murk, Fletcher had no idea the scattered elements of MO Striking Force bore down on him from the north. By 1500 the *Neosho* finished fueling the *Portland*. To give Crace's cruisers oil would require continuing southeast during the evening. All day, though, Fletcher copied Sowespac sighting reports of activity north of the Louisiades. Just to draw within striking distance (170 miles) of Deboyne by the next dawn already demanded an overnight run of nearly three hundred miles at twenty-plus knots. Therefore Fletcher brought TF-17 around to the northwest. To Crace, disappointed not to fuel, it looked "like business." Fletcher intended by dawn on 7 May to be 170 miles southeast of Deboyne to strike forces reportedly concentrating off Misima just east of Deboyne in the Louisiade Archipelago. At 1730 he stepped up to twenty-one knots. The *Neosho* and *Sims* peeled off to the south in order to shuttle every other day between Points Corn and Rye. Fletcher committed a major error by failing to modify his operations order after the fall of Tulagi. Corn was only 360 miles south and Rye 440 miles southwest of Tulagi. Both were easily within range of flying boats he knew were now based there. It would have been much wiser to park the Fueling Group beyond the range of any Japanese shore-based aircraft.[36]

Thus by the evening of 6 May Fletcher rated TF-17 ready for battle. His attention to fueling had and would continue to pay huge dividends.[37] The tactical situation he faced was not for the faint of heart. He had no recourse to subterfuge or the luxury of the indirect approach. The enemy air searches blanketing the critical area pinpointed TF-17 on the fifth and the sixth. Once the Invasion Force showed its hand, he might have to bull his way through three carriers, perhaps more, not to mention land-based air. However, he reckoned on one special advantage. Air search reports had located numerous Japanese ships, "practically every type," within the triangle formed by Papua, New Britain, and the Solomon Islands. They appeared "scattered" and to lack a "common direction of movement." Yet the radio intelligence furnished by Nimitz and Leary seemed to reveal where they were going and when they might get there. As early as 7 May the invasion convoy should traverse the center of the Louisiades at Jomard Passage. Aircraft sightings on 6 May of several groups of transports and auxiliaries northeast of Deboyne and farther north off Woodlark further confirmed the Jomard shortcut. That fitted Fletcher's estimate that the final advance on Moresby would commence on the seventh or the eighth. The numerous Sowespac sightings in the Louisiades on 5–6 May included the 18th Cruiser Division (old light cruisers *Tenryū* and *Tatsuta*), the seaplane tender *Kamikawa Maru*, and several auxiliaries from Marumo's Support Force converging on Deboyne to build the seaplane base. As yet the Allies had not seen Port Moresby Invasion Force, except for a few ships coming up from Tulagi.[38]

The convoy was one thing, the carriers another. Fletcher never stated exactly what he made of the enemy carrier deployment other than he anticipated action off the Louisiades on 7 or 8 May. Fitch offered the clearest estimate: "Naval units, including one carrier and the invasion fleet were reported converging on Deboyne Island. It was expected that the enemy would use Jomard Entrance to enter the Coral Sea. Two additional CV's [aircraft carriers], probably Carrier Division Five, were reported in the vicinity of Bougainville Island, on May 6 . . . Carrier Division Five [was expected to] run southward from the vicinity of Bougainville and might be within striking distance on the morning of May 7." Fitch had access to the same special Cincpac intelligence as Fletcher, but Crace only received Comsowespacfor messages. Crace's diary on 6 May placed "about 10 transports off Deboyne Islands & one or possibly two carriers with cruiser or battleship escort to the west of Bougainville Island steering south & presumably acting in support." Thus two senior admirals in TF-17 located Japanese forces, including their carriers, far to the northwest, perhaps four to five hundred miles away.[39]

That assessment was deeply flawed. Of the three carriers, only the *Shōhō* (*Ryūkaku* to the Allies) was or had ever been anywhere near Bougainville. After his cruisers fueled at Shortland, Gotō reassembled MO Main Force on the morning of 6 May west of Bougainville, then steamed southwest to meet the Port Moresby Invasion Force approaching the northern Louisiades. That morning three B-17s bombed a cruiser and then spotted a carrier nearby. At 1800 on 6 May, close to sundown, the *Shōhō* was about 425 miles northwest of TF-17, but Hara's 5th Carrier Division was already only 150 miles north. By turning northwest Fletcher unwittingly increased the rate of closure between himself and Hara. Fortunately for him, Hara still thought his opponent was much farther south. Even so Hara persisted in his pursuit until 1930, some seventy-five minutes after sunset, when he was only sixty or seventy miles north of TF-17, but never knew it. Takagi had long given up and reversed course to reassemble his force. They both decided it would be wiser to abandon their futile pursuit. The U.S. carrier force must be gunning for the invasion convoy and MO Main Force converging on the Louisiades. That seemed to present an excellent opportunity for MO Striking Force to surprise the American carrier from the rear.[40]

Had the air searches of either side been a little sharper, the first carrier clash in the Coral Sea should have occurred on 6 May rather than the seventh. Even so, the results of the day had armed Takagi and Hara with a general notion of where their opponent was and what he might do the next day. That augured well for a devastating ambush. Fletcher enjoyed no similar benefit. He wrongly perceived that his most dangerous adversaries mustered far to the northwest. In the broadest sense the comint furnished to Fletcher was reliable and potentially decisive at the strategic level. Yet for immediate tactical purposes, it created an incomplete and dangerously false portrait. Allied radio intelligence depended on partially decrypted, therefore incomplete, Japanese naval messages. There was the great danger that code breakers and intelligence officers would misinterpret their contents or fail to understand the context in which they were sent. Their errors unwittingly placed TF-17 in grave danger on 6 May and set up the strong possibility of Fletcher being surprised, perhaps fatally, on the morning of 7 May.[41]

CHAPTER 12

The Battle of the Coral Sea II 7 May—Offense

RIVAL BATTLE PLANS

Sunset on 6 May drew the curtain on the last unalloyed strategic success Japan would enjoy in the Pacific War. A thrilled empire learned of the surrender of Corregidor and the end of organized resistance in the Philippines, the last of the original strategic objectives of the brilliantly conducted first operational phase. The MO Operation against eastern New Guinea comprised the first offensive of the second operational phase. Despite the earlier than anticipated appearance of a U.S. carrier in the Coral Sea and the embarrassing raid on Tulagi, Tokyo expected nothing less than complete victory. Admiral Inoue and his top subordinates laid out their battle plan for 7 May. That day the invasion convoy would approach the Louisiades from the northeast, turn the corner at Deboyne, and cut south through Jomard Passage that evening for the final leg of the voyage to Port Moresby. Surprisingly the convoy itself had escaped being sighted, but Inoue knew the Allied air search was bound to find it early on the seventh and call in the carrier force in the Coral Sea. Gotō's MO Main Force (four heavy cruisers, one light carrier with eighteen planes, and a destroyer) drew up near the convoy for direct protection. Float planes from the cruisers and the new seaplane base at Deboyne would scour the waters adjacent to the Louisiades. Likewise, bombers from Rabaul and Tulagi flying boats sought enemy forces south and east of the Louisiades. Inoue's own carriers and land-based bombers would crush the opposition and open the way to Port Moresby. Admiral Takagi, commanding MO Striking Force (two carriers with 111 operational planes, two heavy cruisers, and six destroyers), remained confident. On the sixth he pursued the U.S. carrier that surprised Tulagi but could not overtake it. The seventh would be different. Air searches—his own and the other commands—would surely pinpoint the enemy carrier skulking well southeast of the Louisiades. At the same time Base Air Force at Rabaul planned its own search-and-destroy mission of twelve torpedo-armed land attack planes, while twenty level bombers and a dozen fighters softened up Port Moresby. Inoue positioned the four submarines of the Eastern Detachment far south to harass the remnants once the enemy fled toward Australia. All the bases appeared to be covered.[1]

For Fletcher, closing the Louisiades from the southeast, the prospects of a major battle soon after dawn on 7 May also loomed large. Overnight TF-17 (two carriers with 128 operational planes, seven heavy cruisers, one light cruiser, and eleven destroyers) hastened to take position at dawn one hundred miles south of Rossel in the eastern Louisiades. His job was to prevent a seaborne invasion of Port Moresby and hopefully not lose his shirt in the process. Available long-range air support in Australia and at Port Moresby totaled eighteen B-17 heavy bombers, fourteen B-25 and sixteen B-26 medium bombers, a half-dozen RAAF Hudson medium bombers, and a lone RAAF Catalina.[2]

On the evening of 6 May Fitch, the new TF-17 air task group commander, issued orders for the *Lexington* and *Yorktown* air groups (thirty-six fighters, seventy dive bombers, and twenty-two torpedo bombers) for the seventh. The *Yorktown* as duty carrier was to launch ten SBDs at "earliest dawn" to search 250 miles northwest to northeast (325 to 085 degrees) in the direction of Bougainville. That offered more evidence of the baleful influence of misleading radio intelligence regarding the likely location of the enemy carriers. Fitch reserved half the fighters for combat air patrol and assigned the rest as strike escort. He also held back, certainly at Ted Sherman's urging, seven *Lex* SBDs to fly anti-torpedo-plane patrol instead of augmenting the attack. The strike was to be ready to leave at dawn. To enable the two groups to attack in successive waves, he ordered the *Yorktown* to delay departure of her strike for fifteen minutes after the *Lexington* aircraft left. That was another direct contrast to the Japanese, who adroitly integrated their strikes.[3]

Fitch's order confined the big 1,000-pounders to the bombing squadrons and prescribed one 500-pound and two 100-pound bombs for each VS SBD. The TBDs would have torpedoes. On the evening of 6 May Commander Arnold, the *Yorktown*'s peppery air officer, had already as a matter of routine started loading 1,000-pound bombs on all strike SBDs. He deplored the mixed bomb load that forced the SBDs, despite the threat of defending fighters, to execute multiple dives to drop the 100-pound "fire crackers" for antiaircraft suppression. The *Yorktown* SBDs invariably packed the largest payload when attacking capital ships. Arnold protested the arming order to Buckmaster, who referred him to flag plot. Fletcher agreed things "didn't look quite right," but reluctant to override Fitch regarding aviation matters, he suggested the *Yorktown* question the order. Predictably Fitch rejected the complaint and demanded compliance, but by then it was dark. The *Yorktown*'s flight deck bristled with all thirty-five SBDs (armed with 1,000-pound bombs except for the ten allocated for search) and ten VT-5 TBDs. "Horrified" the only way the SBDs could be rearmed was by extensive use of flashlights, not permissible because of danger of subs, Buckmaster kept the big bombs on VS-5. After the battle Arnold privately queried his friends on Fitch's staff, who blamed Sherman. Contrary to the advice of the staff, Fitch had given into Sherman and approved the same outmoded bomb loading as at Salamaua-Lae. Later in May Sherman became "quite miffed" when he learned all the *Yorktown* SBDs wielded the 1,000-pounders contrary to orders. Fletcher "cooled him off" by explaining that rearming was not feasible and that it was probably better to use "the biggest bombs we had." Nevertheless, Sherman bore a grudge against Fletcher and the *Yorktown* that he voiced to King and others that summer.[4]

On the evening of 6 May the search summary from Comsowespac appeared to confirm Jomard Passage as the enemy's route through the Louisiades. At 1530 planes had seen four transports and two destroyers off Deboyne and bound for Jomard. Earlier other Australia-based aircraft reported additional forces, including a half-dozen transports, four or five cruisers, and six destroyers, north and northwest of Rossel. Around midnight MacArthur advised Fletcher that his B-17s struck out that morning against the carrier forty miles southwest of Bougainville. That was the last word Fletcher received of enemy carriers on 6 May, and it certainly corresponded with his estimates based on radio intelligence. Allied aircraft were to shadow the force off Deboyne throughout the night and report positions every hour in plain language as they neared Jomard, but there is no evidence Fletcher was ever told which frequencies to monitor. After daylight on 7 May three B-17s were to attack shipping at Deboyne and Woodlark, while three B-17s and eight B-26 medium bombers hit Jomard Passage.[5]

Having configured TF-17 with two cruiser striking groups, Fletcher sought to use them independently to achieve his fundamental mission. Now with at least part of the invasion convoy about to traverse Jomard Passage, he perceived a golden opportunity for a separate surface attack. He selected Crace's multinational Support Group (two heavy cruisers, one light cruiser, and two destroyers) for the Jomard mission and reinforced it with the destroyer *Farragut* from Kinkaid's Attack Group. For the past two months Fletcher had carefully pondered the proper tactical employment of the Australian Squadron. In April while at Tongatabu he consulted Poco Smith, who briefly served under Crace in mid March. Smith praised Crace as a "good seaman," who "handled the force very well," but he judged the differences in tactical doctrine, gunnery, and communications between the two navies to be great. Fletcher replied that Smith would not have to serve under Crace again. "Next time I shall give [Crace] an independent command."[6] It is likely that Wilson Brown informed Fletcher of Crace's fervent desire not merely to screen the carriers, but to execute independent attack missions in support of Australian territory. This one definitely filled the bill. At 0538 the *Yorktown* blinkered a message to Crace: "Proceed at daylight with your group to destroy enemy ships reported passing through Jomard Passage and threatening Moresby. Conserve fuel. Fuel destroyers from cruisers. Retire to Townsville when necessary to fuel." The fact that the Australian Squadron had adopted U.S. underway refueling methods allowed Crace the flexibility for such a mission. Fletcher authorized Crace to break radio silence at his discretion to keep Leary informed of his movements. He clearly thought it unlikely that Crace would rejoin him until after the carriers exchanged blows, though he did expect to be nearby as the battle shifted closer to Port Moresby. Crace in turn determined twenty-five knots could see him off Jomard Passage by 1330, leaving five hours of daylight to plug the gap. He assembled his force, took course 315 degrees at twenty-five knots, and disappeared to the northwest.[7]

Fletcher's decision to detach Crace has elicited much controversy. Fletcher explained to Bates at the Naval War College that he feared the opposing carriers would quickly neutralize each other, just as in many prewar tactical exercises. Therefore he positioned a separate cruiser task group to repulse the Port Moresby invasion convoy, whether or not the U.S. flattops could intervene. Bates in turn raked him over the coals for exposing Crace's Support Group without air cover and depriving TF-17 of its antiaircraft defense. Morison sarcastically dubbed the mission "Crace's Chase" and claimed it served no useful purpose. If the Japanese carriers had won the main battle, he argued, they would have easily dealt with Crace, whereas a triumph by Fletcher would also have saved Port Moresby. Morison ignored the fact that carriers, even if not sunk or crippled, might have to withdraw because of battle damage or heavy plane losses. G. Hermon Gill, the official Australian naval historian, and British naval historian H. P. Willmott seconded the opinions of Bates and Morison.[8]

Not everyone agreed with the critics. Crace himself fully supported the Jomard mission. In 1957 he acknowledged Morison's denunciation of dividing TF-17, but added, "Under the circumstances prevailing at the time, I am certain Fletcher was right and the advantage to be gained by possibly catching the Moresby Invasion Group in the Jomard Passage far outweighed that gained by increasing the Anti-Aircraft screen by the ships of my force." In other words Crace recognized that the distilled wisdom of a war's worth of carrier combat was not the yardstick by which to fairly measure the initial pioneers. He was not particularly surprised by these orders, given that he lobbied Brown in February and March for exactly such an aggressive role. Schindler, TF-17 staff gunnery officer and antiaircraft expert, also deprecated the general ineffectiveness of ship antiaircraft fire in the early days of the war. He judged the Support Group's contribution "a very minor consideration as far as AA [antiaircraft] protection was concerned," and worried more about losing three destroyers from the TF-17 antisubmarine screen. Schindler heartily endorsed Fletcher's decision to send Crace to Jomard Passage. "Had the Group made contact it might have well destroyed an important enemy force which couldn't have had air protection." That was a key factor in the original decision. It was believed that with TF-17 between the enemy carriers and Crace, every Japanese plane that could carry a torpedo or a bomb would be gunning for the U.S. carriers, not a cruiser group. As will be shown, a series of complex events rendered that assessment completely invalid on 7 May.[9]

WHAT CARRIERS?

A half hour before dawn on 7 May Fletcher turned TF-17 southeast into the brisk wind to launch the search. The ten *Yorktown* SBDs fanned out north and east. At 0625 Fletcher changed course to 025 degrees at fifteen knots. At that time Rossel was 115 miles due north and Deboyne 170 miles northwest. After the sun rose at 0645, he increased speed to twenty-two knots. Four *Lexington* fighters took off for combat air patrol, and six SBDs flew anti-torpedo-plane patrol. At 0718 Fletcher turned north. During the morning search the tension in TF-17 was almost palpable, with strike planes poised on deck and pilots crowded in the ready rooms. All three enemy carriers could be within striking range. Victory hinged on getting the jump before the enemy could locate TF-17 and land his own blows.

First word from the search reached the *Yorktown* at 0735. Lt. Keith E. Taylor, VB-5 executive officer, radioed the sighting of two heavy cruisers northwest of Rossel and about 170 miles northwest of TF-17. These ships ambled away northwest at twelve knots. A pair of cruisers was small-fry but perhaps indicated an enemy concentration in the neighborhood. To Fletcher, carefully monitoring the situation, northeast still looked where the enemy carriers would likely show, but he hedged his bets. He told Fitch and Kinkaid at 0758 that should a "suitable objective" appear to the northwest, he would move west at 1000. In that event he reckoned the Point Option[10] speed (the average rate of advance) would be eight knots—slow, because the twenty-knot southeasterly wind would require the carriers to turn sharply away to conduct air operations. However, if nothing

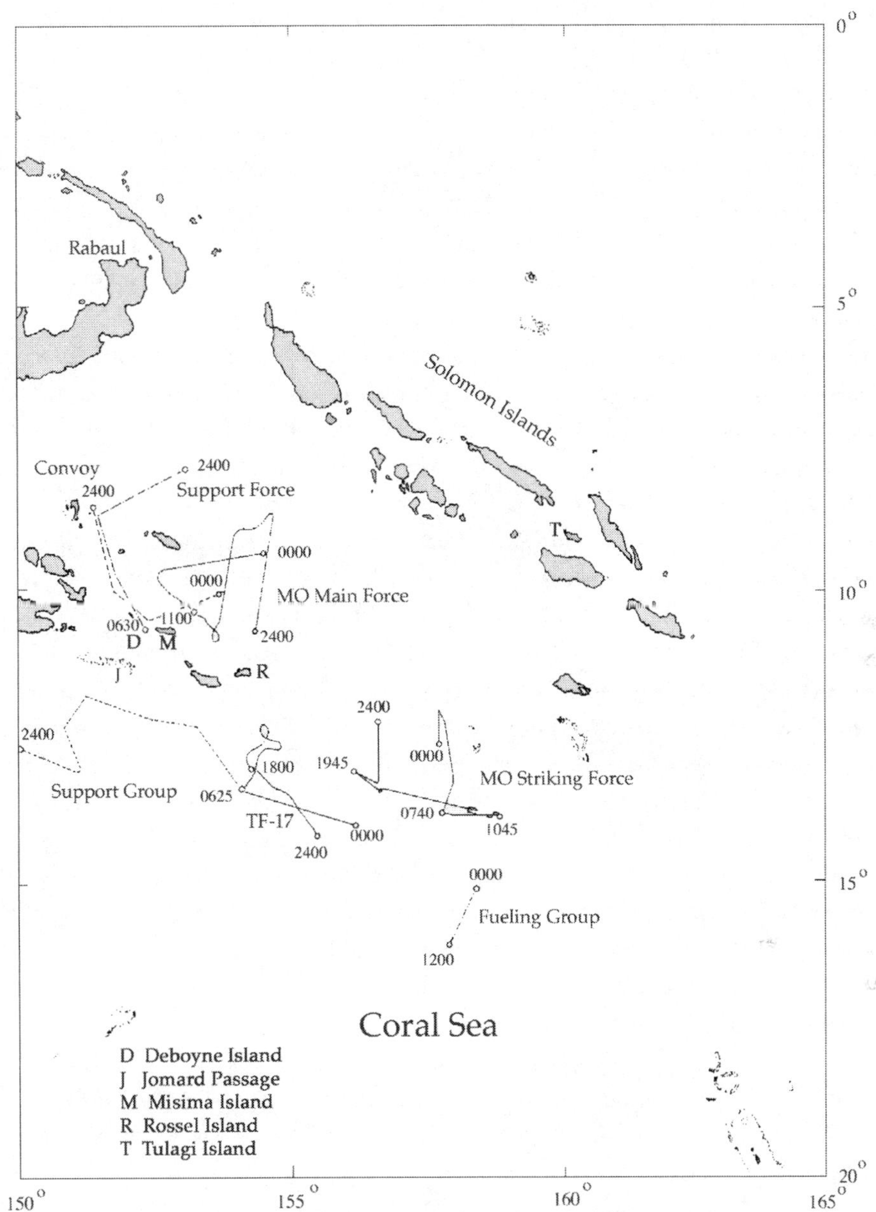

Task force operations, Coral Sea, 7 May 1942

more substantial turned up to the northwest, Fletcher planned to advance northeast with a Point Option speed of ten knots.[11]

At 0815 Fletcher hit the jackpot. Lt. John L. Nielsen, who flew the far western search sector, found two carriers and four heavy cruisers north of Misima, an island located northwest of Rossel and just east of Deboyne. This force steamed southeast at eighteen to twenty knots, that is, almost directly toward TF-17.[12] Fletcher logically assumed this was the Moresby Striking Force with the two big carriers of the 5th Carrier Division. Fitch could strike them.[13] At fully 225 miles northwest of TF-17, the target was perhaps fifty miles beyond the limited radius of the U.S. carrier fighters and torpedo planes. Yet if the enemy maintained course and speed, the distance would shrink to where they might just be able to accompany the dive bombers. Fletcher and Fitch bravely risked waiting an hour while closing the target in order to launch a full strike. This was despite evidence that Japanese search planes already glimpsed TF-17. Lt. Frank F. Gill, the *Lexington* FDO, discovered worrisome contacts soon after 0700. Shortly after 0833 both *Lexington* and *Yorktown* radars picked up a bogey thirty miles west. Gill dispatched combat air patrol fighters in "another heartbreaking" pursuit that the intruders evaded.[14]

At 0915 Fitch finally released Sherman and Buckmaster to attack, "objective enemy CV." With the estimated distance still two hundred miles, Buckmaster asked whether the short-ranged torpedo planes and fighters should go. Fitch replied affirmative. If the enemy persisted in approaching TF-17 at the same reported course and speed, the strike should only need to fly 170 miles to reach the target. At 0921, after consulting with Fitch, Fletcher set the subsequent Point Option course at 290 degrees. He counted on an average rate of advance of fifteen knots to cut down the strike's return leg. TF-17 swung southeast into the wind at 0926, and the first aircraft took off from the *Lexington*'s one huge deck load of ten F4Fs, twenty-eight SBDs, and twelve TBDs. After Fletcher himself got on the bullhorn to exhort the *Yorktown* flyers to get the carriers, Buckmaster followed suit at 0944, three minutes before the last *Lex* TBD waddled into the air. Twenty-five SBDs and ten TBDs comprised the first *Yorktown* deck load. To ensure the planes reached the target together, Pederson devised another innovative "running rendezvous" as employed on 10 March. The TBDs and SBDs left immediately, while the second deck load of eight escort F4Fs, departing at 1013, used their faster cruising speed to catch up. Burch, commanding officer of VS-5, again exercised general supervision of the *Yorktown* strike, while Schindler occupied the rear seat of a VS-5 SBD. At 1024, after the *Yorktown* landed her search SBDs, Fletcher brought TF-17 all the way around to 290 degrees, the designated Point Option course, and rang up twenty-three knots. The skies gradually filled to half cloud cover, and worse weather was on the way.

Several new complications confronted Fletcher in close succession. At 0943 one of the senior TF-17 leaders reported, accurately as it turned out, that the "enemy has our position." Who sent that message is not recorded, but the likeliest possibility is Fitch, utilizing the findings of Fullinwider's radio intelligence unit in the *Lexington*.[15] Although Gill, and Pederson in the *Yorktown*, strongly suspected the presence of snoopers based upon radar, they had not been absolutely certain because no one had yet spotted one. Now Fletcher's fear that the enemy had located TF-17 was confirmed. Everything depended on which side could hit harder.

The next problem arose at 1021 when the *Neosho*, ostensibly out of harm's way, radioed that three planes had bombed the Fueling Group some 325 miles southeast of TF-17. Fletcher later explained his concern that neither the oiler nor the destroyer *Sims* ever identified whether the planes were land-based bombers, carrier planes, or flying boats. Bates and others questioned that judgment, pointing out that the *Neosho* was some 750 miles from Rabaul, the nearest Japanese airfield, and thus supposedly out of range. Thus Fletcher should have realized the attackers must have come from a carrier. However, the critics failed to realize that the Fueling Group's operating area fell within range of flying boats from Tulagi and Shortland. The *Neosho*'s message mentioned only three enemy planes, although in fact her observers *saw* many more aircraft in the area. A mere trio could still mean flying boats. Fletcher's puzzlement was legitimate, but also his own fault due to his serious misjudgment in keeping the Fueling Group within seven hundred miles of Tulagi.[16]

Word of an air attack, source unknown, against the distant Fueling Group troubled Fletcher. What occurred simultaneously proved devastating. When Nielsen returned, he dropped a message on the *Yorktown*'s flight deck stating that he had sighted four light cruisers and two destroyers. When asked, after he landed, about the two enemy carriers his astonished response was in effect: "What carriers?" Investigation established that Nielsen's coding device was misaligned and wrongly enciphered the all-important message. The system was later discarded. According to Biard, Nielsen was immediately hauled up to flag plot to explain, whereupon an irate Fletcher, gesturing violently, supposedly yelled: "Young man, do you know what you have done? You have just cost the United States two carriers!" Nielsen subsequently recounted "catching hell" from someone. Yeoman Thomas Newsome, Fletcher's combat talker, was also present in flag plot but recalled no dramatic outburst.[17] If Fletcher indeed lost his composure (and there is no independent confirmation), it was only briefly. At 1031 he relayed to Fitch the potentially disastrous news that the TF-17 strike had miscarried, having been directed to the wrong target. Other than Keith Taylor and Nielsen, the *Yorktown* search discovered no enemy ships. Thick clouds and squalls to the northeast and east rendered a thorough search impossible. Lt. (jg) Henry M. McDowell flying the 067-degree line to the northeast even turned back after only going 165 miles.[18] Therefore Fletcher could not rule out enemy carriers hiding in the northeast quadrant, where in fact he originally thought they might be. He considered whether to recall the strike now well on its way to the objective or let it press on northwest in the hope it might find a worthy target. Avoiding possibly fatal hesitation, he correctly decided to let the planes continue.[19]

While Fletcher still talked to Nielsen in flag plot, Gerry Galpin appeared holding a vital message that could partially redeem the situation. At 1022 air headquarters at Port Moresby radioed that one carrier, ten transports, and sixteen warships had been located only thirty miles south of the position Nielsen provided for the misidentified carrier force. Fletcher increased speed at 1041 to twenty-five knots on the Point Option course of 290 degrees and probably wished he could, by sheer will alone, bridge the gap to direct his strike planes. Hugely relieved they would at least have a chance to attack one carrier after all, he informed Fitch of the contact at 1045, and at 1053 transmitted a message in the clear to redirect the strike groups toward the new target. Fletcher shot his bolt and could do nothing more in the meantime but wait and hope. He did not know that Takagi, his deadliest opponent, faced the same dilemma after his dawn search also grossly misreported the identity of a target.[20]

Daybreak on 7 May found the eager MO Striking Force 275 miles southeast of Rossel (already too far south for Fletcher's dawn search to find) and moving south. Hara personally believed the U.S. carrier force was no closer to the Louisiades than four hundred miles. Hence beginning at 0600 a dozen carrier attack planes swept across the southwest quadrant to 250 miles. Unknown to Takagi and Hara, TF-17 was 210 miles *west*, much closer to

Rossel than they suspected, and already too far north for their own search to encounter. At 0722 two *Shōkaku* searchers radioed exciting news that American ships lurked only 163 miles south of MO Striking Force. One enemy carrier, one cruiser, and three destroyers headed due north at sixteen knots. Hara felt vindicated. The enemy was just where he thought. By 0815, seventy-eight *Shōkaku* and *Zuikaku* aircraft winged south to end the carrier threat to the MO Operation. As an added bonus, the searchers also reported an oiler and a heavy cruiser about twenty-five miles southeast of the main enemy force.[21]

The happy scenario of Takagi and Hara quickly soured. By dawn virtually all of Gotō's MO Attack Force—Kajioka's Port Moresby Invasion Force, his MO Main Force, and Marumo's Support Force—converged in the Misima-Deboyne area north of Jomard Passage. Seaplanes from Marumo's temporary base at Deboyne and from the heavy cruisers *Furutaka* and *Kinugasa* of the 6th Cruiser Division (temporarily operating east of the main body) combed the waters beyond the Louisiades. Allied planes were also active over the eastern Louisiades. To Gotō's consternation they made contact before his own searchers could report back. Three B-17s led by Capt. Maurice C. Horgan left Port Moresby before sunrise for a search-attack mission toward Deboyne, where the invasion convoy might be expected to pass. At 0748 they sighted Japanese ships and carefully checked out the area. Below was the whole array of ships at and near Deboyne. As Fletcher later attested, Horgan's subsequent sighting report, routed through Port Moresby, was of the highest importance. Shortly thereafter the B-17s bombed the seaplane tender *Kamikawa Maru* but caused only minor damage.[22]

At 0750 Gotō heard the alarming news of an enemy carrier plane seen snooping part of MO Main Force northwest of Rossel. That was Keith Taylor, who inspected the *Furutaka* and *Kinugasa*. With a U.S. carrier obviously nearby, Gotō worried that a strike might follow. Soon afterward Nielsen showed up north of Misima. His unintentionally misleading message reporting two carriers and four heavy cruisers led Fletcher to unleash a full strike. Ironically Nielsen had in truth spotted a carrier force, namely the rest of Gotō's MO Main Force (*Shōhō*, *Aoba*, *Kako*, and *Sazanami*), but never realized it.[23] It is fascinating to contemplate what Fletcher might have done had Nielsen just reported the one carrier, perhaps just what he actually did. Gotō's own searchers offered more daunting news after 0820, when they came upon an American carrier, a battleship, two cruisers, and seven destroyers eighty miles south of Rossel. They shadowed the U.S. force and continued transmitting contact reports, some of which reached Takagi and Hara as well as others, including Hypo at Pearl Harbor and Fullinwider in the *Lex*. Gotō correctly decided on the basis of search reports that the enemy force south of the Louisiades had separated into two groups (Crace heading west and Fletcher moving northeast), but other Japanese commanders failed to perceive that key fact. Their confusion only grew during the day, ultimately to Fletcher's great advantage. Gotō knew from radio traffic that MO Striking Force also found the enemy and was attacking. By 0900 he realized to his vast dismay that Takagi's target was hundreds of miles farther southeast than the one that threatened MO Attack Force. Gotō told Kajioka to retire temporarily north or northwest and girded his reunited MO Main Force for battle. For his own part Hara thought the enemy southern force that he was attacking was the stronger of the two, whereas Takagi desperately wanted to finish up in the south and hasten west to support Gotō.[24]

Takagi's supposedly formidable southern enemy group was merely the unlucky *Neosho* and *Sims*, inexplicably magnified by inept searchers into a whole carrier task force. Hara's strike sifted the target area after 0910, but found only the lowly oiler and its escorting "cruiser." Captain Phillips, in charge of the Fueling Group, thought at first the two search planes had come from TF-17, but after one rudely released a "bomb" (actually a target designator) he realized his error. Beginning at 0935 several high-flying Japanese formations passed overhead unaffected by a 5-inch gun barrage from the *Sims*. Lt. Cdr. Willford M. Hyman, her commanding officer, apparently radioed a contact report, but no one in TF-17 received the message.[25] At 1005 three planes, wrongly supposed to be twin-engine bombers, broke off from yet another Japanese group seemingly for a horizontal bombing run that caused only near misses. Actually they were carrier attack planes lugging torpedoes, and again the "bombs" were target indicators. As noted before, the *Neosho*'s 1021 contact report mentioned only three aircraft, definitely not helpful to Fletcher. Phillips later censured his communications officer for not correctly dispatching contact and position reports.[26]

At 1008 a *Kinugasa* float plane shadower alerted Gotō that the Americans southeast of Rossel were launching a strike. The same searchers later noted the presence of one *Saratoga*-type carrier and another carrier, class not identified. That proved a sharp jolt to the Japanese who had not anticipated facing such a formidable force so early in the MO Operation. Takagi finally got MO Striking Force pointed west at 1042. Watching the situation deteriorate, Inoue ordered his forces to concentrate against the enemy south of Rossel. At 1051 the original searchers from MO Striking Force belatedly confessed they had discovered only an oiler. Thus at 1100 Takagi recalled the strike. Lt. Cdr. Takahashi Kakuichi, the mission leader, required time to gather his scattered squadrons and start the fighters and torpedo planes northward. As soon as that was accomplished he led the thirty-six carrier bombers against the hapless *Neosho* and *Sims*. By 1148 their accurate dive-bombing sank the destroyer and left the mortally wounded oiler drifting without power. But by then Inoue had already lost a carrier.[27]

PARTIAL REDEMPTION

As the situation simultaneously unraveled for both sides, Fletcher sought an accurate picture of Japanese tactical dispositions so he could decide what to do next. At 1059 Leary summarized the Sowespac air contact reports, based mainly on sightings of numerous transports, auxiliaries, and escorting warships starting around 0800 by Horgan's B-17s.[28] Those enemy ships all clustered in the vicinity of Deboyne. Fletcher's big worry remained the actual whereabouts of the Japanese carriers and the immediate threat they posed to TF-17. For the next several hours until his strike groups returned, he was committed to his westerly Point Option course. Even after all the planes landed, an additional hour or more would be required to rearm and refuel them. Therefore TF-17 could not count on launching a second strike before 1400 at the very earliest. At the same time Biard apparently deduced from fragmentary radio intercepts that the other two carriers prowled to the east and were the source of danger to the *Neosho* and *Sims*. His assessment was correct, but it is not possible at this time with the incomplete evidence available to understand precisely how and when he came to his conclusion, or the exact nature of the advice he gave Fletcher.[29] Another bogey on the *Yorktown*'s radar at 1044 served as a reminder the Japanese continued to track TF-17. At 1100 the *Yorktown* combat air patrol shot down a Type 97 flying boat only six miles northeast of the task force. At 1126 the *Yorktown* launched the ten former search SBDs on anti-torpedo-plane patrol. It is not known whether Fletcher ever contemplated sending them or the seven *Lexington* SBDs already on patrol to search for the enemy carriers. Given the low number of available fighters, Fitch obviously considered all seventeen Dauntlesses essential to the defense of TF-17. The poor weather in the sectors where the enemy carriers were thought to be hiding also militated against another try to find them there.

First word from the strike groups reached TF-17 at 1145, when a *Lex* SBD pilot announced he was ditching at Rossel. At 1154 several ships in TF-17 (as well as in Crace's Support Group) heard an unidentified voice exult on the attack radio frequency: "Boy we sure got that carrier good. How about the other one?" Welcome confirmation that a carrier indeed had sunk arrived at 1210, when Lt. Cdr. Robert E. Dixon, the extremely able commanding officer of the *Lex*'s VS-2, sang out: "Scratch one flattop signed Bob." Dixon stayed behind to make sure the carrier sank and sent a prearranged message to that effect.[30] Fletcher's run northwest toward the target lowered the return leg below 150 miles. TF-17 radars picked up friendly strike planes at fifty to sixty miles. Fletcher brought TF-17 around to the southeast into the wind for air operations. The weather had turned vile with deepening overcast and squalls, a taste of things to come. By 1316 the *Lexington* and *Yorktown* recovered ninety strike aircraft. Only three SBDs were missing.

Enthusiastic aviators described finding a task force northeast of Misima and sinking a carrier variously reported as "*Koryu*" or modified "*Ryujo*" class. A cruiser also rolled over and sank after a bomb hit or near miss. Fletcher called the two senior squadron commanders to the flag bridge to brief him and Buckmaster. Asked what he saw, Joe Taylor, the skipper of VT-5, replied: "I'll show you in a minute." Fletcher countered sharply, "Come now, this is no time for joking." Taylor was not kidding around. In a few minutes he produced photographs taken by one of the crewmen that presented a graphic portrait of the destruction of what was soon identified as the "*Ryūkaku*." Taylor recalled that Fletcher and Buckmaster "jumped up and down like a couple of old grads when a last minute touchdown saved the day." They "just threw their arms around Bill Burch and me and hugged us," so "excited and happy" were they. That afternoon Fletcher congratulated Fitch and his aviators for their "splendid performance."[31]

In the haste of getting the air groups ready to fight again, details of the attack only emerged slowly. After crossing over Tagula Island twenty miles west of Rossel, Cdr. Bill Ault's *Lexington* group welcomed rapidly clearing skies. Around 1040, even before Fletcher attempted to redirect the strike groups to Horgan's contact, the *Lex* flyers sighted ship wakes to the northeast beyond Misima. Drawing closer, they recognized a carrier in the midst of a cruiser force. There was no question of bypassing that target. Besides, Ault never received the message that changed their targets from two carriers to one. He stalked the *Shōhō*, which with the rest of Gotō's reunited MO Main Force (the four heavy cruisers and one destroyer) covered the Port Moresby Invasion Force located off to the northwest. The *Shōhō* was preparing a small air strike of five carrier attack planes and three Zero fighters against the U.S. carriers being tracked southeast of Rossel. Only three Zeros flew combat air patrol and two Mitsubishi Type 96 carrier fighters handled antisubmarine patrol. Three more Zeros and two Type 96s were ready to relieve them.[32]

Ault's command section of three SBDs pushed over against the carrier at 1110, followed by the ten of Dixon's VS-2. Adroit shiphandling caused all to miss the *Shōhō*. She also sent three Zeros aloft to reinforce the defense. In contrast to U.S. practice, Gotō spread his ships far apart for independent evasive maneuvering. Nonetheless, the *Shōhō* did not escape a devastating, well-coordinated assault (one of the best of the war) by fifteen VB-2 SBDs under Lt. Cdr. Weldon L. Hamilton and Lt. Cdr. James H. Brett's twelve VT-2 TBDs. Two 1,000-pound bombs set the flight deck and hangars on fire, and five torpedo hits tore open the hull, dooming the ship. Trailing the *Lex* group by fifteen minutes at Fitch's order, Burch's twenty-five *Yorktown* SBDs spotted the MO Main Force around 1100. Unlike Ault, he heard Fletcher's message that relieved him of having to search for another carrier. Nearing the dive point while VT-2 made its attack, Burch saw only a "small" fire break out on the carrier and consequently at 1125 followed up the *Lexington* attack. The *Yorktown* SBDs scored eleven hits according to Japanese sources. Only Ens. Thomas W. Brown of VB-5, the last SBD pilot to dive, elected to shift to another target. Schindler and other *Yorktowners* thought he hit a cruiser that capsized and sank, but the nimble *Sazanami* was undamaged. There was no doubt about the carrier's fate, particularly after the VT-5 TBDs piled on. They claimed hits by all ten torpedoes, and the Japanese confirmed at least two. The *Shōhō* succumbed at 1135 with great loss of life. The eight Japanese fighters aloft shot down one VS-2 SBD and forced another to ditch at Rossel, but the eighteen Wildcat escorts destroyed five of their number. Overkill was the only criticism that could be lodged against the TF-17 strike, after all the aircraft except two SBDs concentrated on the carrier. At least half the *Yorktown* SBDs and all of VT-5 should have diverted to other targets. That lapse could not overshadow the real triumph of annihilating the first major Japanese warship in the war.[33]

The balance of MO Main Force fled north without even stopping to rescue survivors. From just over the horizon Kajioka's Port Moresby Invasion Force heard the explosions that signaled the end of the *Shōhō*. Kajioka kept withdrawing northwest. Once Inoue learned of the fiasco, he suspended the MO Operation until the enemy carrier force could be destroyed. At 1210 he directed the convoy to keep going north temporarily and mustered his forces to counterattack. Takagi was to keep after the U.S. carriers, while Gotō concentrated MO Main Force and Kajioka's 6th Destroyer Squadron for a night surface battle south of Rossel. Land-based air from Rabaul also hunted the Allied task forces.[34]

CHAPTER 13

The Battle of the Coral Sea II 7 May—Defense

NO SECOND STRIKE

At 1338 after recovering the first strike, Fletcher turned southwest in accordance with his belief the battle would shift westward and to reduce the distance to Crace's Support Group racing toward Jomard Passage. The *Yorktown* and *Lexington* required another thirty to forty minutes to finish rearming and refueling planes, leaving a narrow window of opportunity to attack again before sundown. The swiftly deteriorating weather further restricted options. One enemy carrier was gone, but the whereabouts of the other two remained undetermined. Fletcher consulted Fitch, who advised at 1406 that the best he could offer was another go at the Deboyne area, although "target prospects are poor." Should Fletcher authorize the strike, it must depart by 1430. If there were no targets near Deboyne, Fitch recommended it return via Jomard Passage, "if practicable," and "attack any ships trying to squeeze through." Sherman strongly favored this course of action. In the meantime Fletcher asked the senior *Yorktown* aviators whether they wanted to return to Deboyne, keeping in mind that the 5th Carrier Division might be nearby and that it knew where TF-17 was. Burch recalled: "I told them I didn't think so if there were other carriers about." The consensus was the *Yorktown* should keep her strike group on board, ready to go, while other commands located the enemy flattops. Fletcher himself considered the chance of "finding a suitable objective near the scene of the morning attack was not great." That was correct. Nearly all of Gotō's MO Attack Force withdrew far out of attack range. Had Fletcher gone ahead with a second strike to Deboyne, his aviators might only have sighted Kajioka's light cruiser *Yūbari* and five destroyers steaming southeast to reinforce Gotō for a possible night battle off Rossel.[1]

Given the decision to concentrate on the two remaining carriers, the question became what, if anything, Fletcher could or should do to help find and attack them before sundown. Sherman thought the *Yorktown* should search again, but there is no evidence Fitch ever suggested that to Fletcher. For his own part, Biard argued to Fletcher that his reading of the radio intelligence placed the 5th Carrier Division somewhere to the east, and that it had already hit the Fueling Group. He beseeched Fletcher to dispatch a search-and-attack mission to eastward but could offer no specific course to fly or a distance to travel. Again Biard's surmise was correct—at 1338 MO Striking Force was 235 miles southeast of TF-17—but not necessarily his fervent advice. Fletcher declined Biard's recommendations. Nothing further had been heard from the *Neosho* and *Sims*. (Neither ship ever radioed a distress message before one was crippled and the other sunk.) Fletcher also knew from his search pilots that the weather to eastward was poor, while the overcast and frequent squalls blanketed TF-17. The remaining daylight left no time for a separate search and follow-up strike. Lacking a more definite objective, even a straight search-and-attack mission would literally be a dangerous shot in the dark.[2]

At 1429 Fletcher informed Fitch and Kinkaid: "Will hold off awaiting information from Army hoping to repeat in the morning this day's excellent work." He would head southwest until dark, then west, intending by daylight on 8 May to be only eighty-five miles south of China Strait at the east tip of New Guinea. From there he could flank the direct enemy route to Port Moresby and execute another "search and attack." Fletcher requested comment. "Concur," Fitch replied at 1450, "had arrived at same opinion for tomorrow's operation." Sherman certainly did not agree. "We should have either made another attack or sent out a search." Because Fletcher did not allow Fitch to "use his own judgment in running the air operations, nothing was accomplished in the way of either an attack or a search on the afternoon of the 7th." Yet his own action report described the weather as "squally, with about 90% overcast, frequent rain squalls, in which ceiling and visibility were zero." Later Kinkaid, as well as Bates and Morison, declared sound Fletcher's decision to sit tight.[3]

THE SUPPORT GROUP NEEDS SUPPORT

Early on the afternoon of 7 May Fletcher realized the Japanese showed high interest in the waters to the west of TF-17. At 1242 the *Lexington*'s radar disclosed a large group of planes seventy-five miles northwest and headed southwest. This "must have been the Japanese attack group looking for us." Twelve torpedo-armed Type 1 land attack planes from Rabaul, escorted by eleven Zeros from Lae, combed the waters near Rossel for the U.S. carrier force. Nineteen Type 96 land attack planes sortied south from Rabaul on a separate strike seeking Allied ships in the Louisiades. At 1320 Leary radioed the text of an intercepted message that placed a U.S. force (one carrier, four cruisers, and four destroyers) 170 miles southwest (241 degrees) of Rossel. That was nowhere near TF-17. Biard likewise intercepted messages relating to a target that could not be TF-17. One noted, "Sky over enemy clear visibility 100 kilometers," certainly not the darkening skies over TF-17. At 1449 Biard related how a Japanese plane crowed: "Have sunk a battleship." Fletcher's growing concern over the safety of Crace's Support Group certainly figured in his decision to head toward China Strait. Crace justified that worry with a 1526 message announcing that twenty-seven bombers just attacked him. "Consider fighters to be essential if my object is to be attained."[4]

Crace anticipated surface action as he approached the Louisiades that morning.[5] Unlike Fletcher, Crace copied the search summaries broadcast by air headquarters at Townsville and knew an hour earlier that Horgan's B-17s found a large force with a carrier off Misima, only 120 miles northwest of the Support Group. He could not break the *Yorktown*'s enciphered air contact reports and hence did not know of the contacts made by Taylor and Nielsen. Like Fletcher, he realized that the enemy force discovered off Misima could just as easily skip

Jomard Passage in favor of exiting the reef barrier at China Strait at the western end. At 0930 he turned west to steer forty miles south of Jomard Passage, from where he could watch the pass and keep going west should the Japanese make for China Strait. Late that morning he heard the TF-17 plane rejoice, "We got the carrier good," and assumed TF-17 blasted the carrier off Misima. The lack of updated news from Sowespac on Japanese movements in the Louisiades was a great concern. To make sure the convoy did not indeed slip past, he resolved to continue west to cover China Strait.

Unlike the rest of TF-17, the Support Group enjoyed the mixed blessing and danger of clear skies. Continued neglect by the Japanese was too much to expect. At 1345 the *Chicago*'s CXAM radar detected a large bogey twenty-eight miles southeast; twelve minutes later it materialized into about a dozen single-engine planes roaring up from astern at low altitude. The ships fired as they went past on roughly parallel westward course. The intruders were the eleven Zero fighters released from escort duty a few minutes before. They just stumbled on the Support Group, but lacking radios (land-based Zeros had them removed), they could not tell anyone. A few minutes later an orphaned *Yorktown* SBD Dauntless from the strike wandered overhead and flashed a request for the bearing and distance to TF-17. Crace had no idea, so he pointed the way west to Port Moresby.[6]

At 1415, as the Support Group passed forty miles south of Jomard, the *Chicago*'s radar picked up one contact seventy-five miles southwest and closing, and soon afterward another bogey forty-five miles northeast, also inbound. Just as Crace contemplated becoming the meat in a Japanese sandwich, the westerly strike group abruptly arrived. Sunlight reflecting off polished surfaces revealed a dozen twin-engine bombers racing in down low for a whirlwind torpedo attack off the port bow. The strike, conscious of dwindling fuel, settled for the "battleships." Crace turned away as the attackers concentrated on the *Australia* in the center. Antiaircraft fire knocked down the leader and disconcerted the others, who released their fish too far out. The nearest torpedo missed the *Australia* by only ten yards. Sweeping past the ships at close range, the aircraft suffered for their audacity. Allied gunners claimed five bombers and actually splashed four. A fifth later crashed. The attackers showed more heart than head. Crace accurately described their strike as "most determined," but "fortunately badly delivered." The Japanese strike assessment matched its poor execution. The survivors jubilantly claimed a *California*-class battleship sunk and at least two hits on a *Warspite*-class battleship.

At 1443 after the torpedo attack ceased, ship lookouts noticed level bombers high in the skies overhead. The nineteen land attack planes sneaked in from up sun and astern. Many near misses straddled the *Australia*. The aviators thought several bombs left a cruiser in sinking condition, but their attack caused no damage. To cap off an exciting half hour, three more level bombers appeared far above at 1457. Three "friendly" B-17 Fortresses under Capt. John A. Roberts hunted the enemy convoy and thought they found it. They apparently aimed at the *Australia*, but their bombs fell closer to the *Farragut*. Roberts claimed a large transport set on fire. The army flyers compounded their error of ship identification with misleading contact reports that deceived Fletcher and Crace. The last act added a bit of farce to an excellent performance by Crace and his ships in repelling a strong air attack despite lacking fighter cover.[7]

Crace's 1526 message gave his position sixty miles southwest of Jomard Passage. He intended by dawn on 8 May to take station southeast of New Guinea. After 1540 additional information indicated the enemy might have temporarily postponed the Port Moresby operation, or at least given up on Jomard Passage in favor of China Strait. Comsowespac advised that aircraft sighting reports placed nine ships fifty miles north of Deboyne at 1110 and headed northwest. Ten other ships, position not given, steamed in the same direction. Crace evidently knew this even earlier, by 1450, and factored that into his decision to retire south, then southwest during the night. He recognized grave danger for no substantial benefit if he interposed himself between the dueling flattops and preferred to be in position to deal with any forces that might get past Fletcher and threaten Moresby.[8]

The weather around TF-17 further decayed. Squalls repeatedly hid the two carriers from each other and made it rough for the combat air patrol fighters and anti-torpedo-plane SBDs to maintain station. "Twas a rugged afternoon to be flying the wily Wildcat." With Fitch's permission, the two carriers recovered their anti-torpedo SBDs and the cruisers their SOCs on antisubmarine patrol. Fitch likewise rotated his fighters, deploying a dozen Wildcats as combat air patrol and holding the rest ready to scramble. Deep in thought about the next day's prospects, Fletcher told him at 1549 to raise the planned Point Option speed on 8 May from ten to fifteen knots because of the anticipated wind direction. Fitch followed at 1605 with his plans for the next day's air operations. Starting at dawn from Fletcher's designated start position south of China Straits, the *Lex* SBDs were to search 010–100 degrees to three hundred miles, and thus blanket the Louisiades and the waters to the north and east. Obviously Fitch sought carriers north of the reef barrier, but he took precautions if any ventured south of Rossel or its western neighbor Tagula. Once the search located a target, the *Yorktown* was to launch her strike group first, the *Lexington* fifteen minutes later, for the favored "wave attack." Fitch reserved half the fighters for combat air patrol and later told the *Yorktown* to retain eight SBDs for anti-torpedo-plane patrol. Aircraft payloads were to be the same as on the seventh. That raised the same dilemma for Arnold and Buckmaster, with the same result that again all *Yorktown* SBDs (not just VB-5) ended up armed with 1,000-pound bombs in defiance of Fitch's wishes.[9]

Two factors intruded on Fletcher's thinking regarding the probable course of operations on 8 May. At 1518 a station using the *Neosho*'s call sign began sending in plain language the word "Sinking." That was the first heard from her since 1021, when she reported being bombed by three planes. The logical assumption, made by both Nimitz and Fletcher, was that the fatal attack had just occurred. They did not know that it took the crippled oiler three hours to rig the emergency generator to send the distress message. Thus the *Tippecanoe*, busy giving the last of her fuel to the convoy at Efate, became the only fleet oiler available to TF-17. At 1645 Cincpac alerted the *Tippecanoe* that the *Neosho* might have been sunk and warned of a Japanese sub off Nouméa. The *Tippecanoe* was to "take all possible precautions" in carrying out plans to refuel TF-17. "If *Neosho* lost[,] fuel in [the chartered tanker] *E. J. Henry* vital to continued operations." It had just been learned that the *E. J. Henry* only reached Suva that noon, three days later than anticipated. Therefore she would need several days to discharge part of her cargo ashore and come on to Nouméa to refill the *Tippecanoe*. At 1718 the *Neosho* radioed that she had been "heavily bombed," gave a position that was

275 miles southeast of TF-17, and stated she was drifting northwest while sinking. The *Sims* was already gone. Fitch suggested, and Fletcher soon agreed, that a destroyer be detached eastward away from TF-17, both to send important radio messages and succor the *Neosho*. Fletcher then received word of trouble closer at hand. At 1700 Comsowespac warned that at 1435 three warships and three transports were twenty-five miles *southwest* of Jomard Passage. That was only forty-five miles northeast of the position Crace gave after being bombed a few minutes later. Fletcher now wondered whether Crace had been driven off by air attack and that some Japanese ships had got through Jomard after all. At 1721 he informed Fitch: "I expect situation has changed and most of Japs will be through the pass headed for Moresby tomorrow. Therefore propose to head west tonight and suggest you search to northward and that option be west at speed eight." The loss of the *Neosho* "upsets our logistics," making it necessary to slow down and conserve fuel "in order remain on job a few days longer." Fletcher's prudence in fueling certainly proved justified.[10]

Fletcher thought a carrier had to be supporting the Japanese ships discovered south of Jomard Passage. He did not know (at least for a while) that the "enemy" force was actually the Support Group misreported by Roberts's B-17s. Crace likewise assessed reports, including one from Townsville that Fletcher never received, that located enemy ships south of Jomard. He considered whether to force a night battle, intercept nearer to dawn, or just wait until the next morning to find the enemy. Before he settled on one of these unpromising options, he deduced that the report indeed referred to his own force, and that the nearest Japanese ships were safely north of the Louisiade barrier. Crace marveled at the lack of navigational and recognition skills of his land-based air support and hoped they would not pay him a similar visit on the eighth. His own fuel situation was not encouraging, particularly for the *Hobart* and the destroyers. If nothing more turned up by next morning, he intended to fuel destroyers while awaiting developments. Crace heard occasional aircraft-related transmissions from TF-17, but learned nothing of value. "I had received no information from [Fletcher] regarding his position, his intentions or what had been achieved during the day." He assumed that TF-17 was nearby to the east and hoped that Fletcher would find a way the next morning to let him know what was happening. "The attacks we received were probably intended for the Carriers and if this is the case some good had been achieved." Crace did not know the half of it. Japanese blunders prevented both Takagi's MO Striking Force and the Rabaul land-based air from dealing with Fletcher's carriers.[11]

ONE CANNOT ALWAYS DO AS ONE MIGHT WISH

After 1100 the Japanese completely lost touch of Fletcher's carriers in the bad weather southeast of Rossel. Instead they bent all their efforts toward Crace's Support Group that search planes quickly discovered south of the Louisiades and promoted as the enemy main body. The host of shadowers, including float planes from Deboyne, land attack planes from Rabaul, and even a Tulagi-based flying boat, continuously tracked Crace as he steamed west but confused the Japanese commanders with their gross errors. Somehow these searchers placed battleships and even carriers with Crace's group, while shoddy navigational work conveyed the impression that the "main body" itself had split into two groups. As a result

Inoue repeatedly commanded Takagi's MO Striking Force to assail the enemy carrier force off the Louisiades. However, two circumstances restrained Takagi from dashing westward to get within range. First he must turn away to the southeast into the wind to conduct air operations. Second, he had to await the return of the strike wasted against the *Neosho* and *Sims*, and every minute of delay permitted the U.S. carrier force south of the Louisiades to edge farther away. At noon Hara informed Takagi that he could launch a second strike at 1400 for a late afternoon attack. From 1230 to 1300 most of the original morning group landed back on board, but the *Zuikaku* Carrier Bomber Squadron got lost in the bad weather surrounding MO Striking Force. Takagi would wait no longer. He started west at 1330 hoping that radio homing would guide the errant aircraft back.[12]

By 1400 with the *Zuikaku* carrier bombers still floundering in the clouds nearby, Hara shelved the afternoon attack because his planes could not possibly strike the target and return before sunset. Unlike Fletcher he enjoyed some night carrier air capability, so he mulled a night strike by his dive bombers and torpedo planes. Given that most of the aviators had little night carrier flight time, his staff talked him into recommending to Takagi that only the most experienced crews should attack. The erroneous sighting reports placed the enemy battleship group about 380 miles west and the enemy carriers fifty miles beyond, both headed away at twenty knots. That vast distance compelled a chastened Takagi to advise Inoue at 1500 that MO Striking Force would not attack again that day. Unbeknownst to the Japanese, the actual distance between MO Striking Force and Fletcher's carriers was less than 250 miles. A few minutes later Hara learned that one of the Deboyne search planes had radioed: "The enemy has changed course." He reckoned that if the U.S. ships held the new course of 120 degrees for the next several hours (a big "if"), his elite strike group could reach them after dark. Takagi gave his permission. Beginning at 1515 eight carrier attack planes swept two hundred miles west to ensure no previously undiscovered task force lay ahead. They were to return at sundown. After they departed, the missing *Zuikaku* carrier bombers finally landed after a harrowing seven-hour mission. Several exhausted crews learned they were going out again into the murk. At 1600 Hara estimated the distance to the U.S. carrier group (if it had kept coming southeast) had decreased to 360 miles. That could drop to a manageable two hundred miles by 1830 if both sides continued on course and maintained speed. At 1615 Commander Takahashi departed with twelve Type 99 carrier bombers and fifteen Type 97 carrier planes with orders to fly 277 degrees to 280 miles. Takahashi expected to find the U.S. carriers under clear skies but after dark, so there would be no defending fighters. MO Striking Force's lunge to the west should reduce their return leg to well under two hundred miles. Takagi and Hara took a vast risk with their best men.[13]

NIGHTTIME FIREWORKS

The shadowers that bedeviled TF-17 that morning took a break, but at 1623 a new bogey popped up on radar eighteen miles southwest. Combat air patrol fighters could not run it down in the gray skies, even after *Yorktown* lookouts briefly sighted a seaplane. At 1647 the snooper disappeared northward off the screen. Evidently it was a Deboyne-based float plane that never radioed a report, or at least one that was ever logged. Possibly its crew, thinking they had spotted MO Striking Force because the Americans were supposed to be much farther west, chose not to break radio silence. The lack of a report from the search plane proved a tremendous break for Fletcher. Had Takagi and Hara learned of it, they could have warned Takahashi, who unwittingly neared TF-17. At the same time the Japanese carrier search pattern fell just short of contacting Fletcher.[14]

An entry in Lt. Cdr. Phillip F. Fitz-Gerald's diary aptly recorded the attitude in TF-17 as the sun dipped toward the horizon: "We had just about settled in for the night and congratulated ourselves that we had gotten away scot free." At 1745, near to sundown, the *Lexington*'s radar picked up three groups of aircraft twenty-two to twenty-eight miles southeast. Two minutes later the *Yorktown* likewise registered a large contact eighteen miles southeast. At the same time the *Lex* reported another big group forty-eight miles southeast approaching at low altitude. This looked like the long awaited carrier counterattack. The dozen combat air patrol fighters were low on fuel. For a distant intercept Gill, the FDO, selected only those four led by Lt. Cdr. Paul H. Ramsey, the commanding officer of VF-2. Fletcher turned southeast into the wind to scramble the reserve fighters. Beginning at 1750 the *Yorktown* launched twelve and the *Lexington* six Wildcats, raising the combat air patrol to thirty fighters. In the past two weeks Lt. Cdr. James H. Flatley Jr., an outstanding fighter leader who recently became VF-42 executive officer, had not warmed to the stern, rather aloof Buckmaster. He changed his mind that evening when he saw the usually undemonstrative *Yorktown* captain up on the bridge vigorously shaking his fist toward the enemy and exhorting his pilots. Gill dispatched Flatley's seven F4Fs to support Ramsey and jockeyed the fighters southwest out ahead of the enemy group crossing from east to west thirty miles south of TF-17. The weather was hazy with a heavy overcast. At 1803 Ramsey executed a brilliant ambush of nine planes (he thought Zero fighters) caught low over the water and claimed five victories, while Flatley's flight glimpsed two other low-flying enemy groups in the clouds. Two F4Fs broke off to chase some torpedo planes and shot down two. The rest ganged up on a lone dive bomber.[15]

The scattered, but victorious, F4Fs started back toward the ships with the prospect of night carrier landings. Committed to steaming into the wind until all of his fighters were back on board, Fletcher steadied on course 145 degrees at twenty-five knots. He and Fitch knew little of what just transpired other than the pilots excitedly radioed that they scored several kills. However, the radio intelligence teams in the *Yorktown* and *Lexington*, as well as Hypo itself at Pearl, picked up remarkable enemy aircraft radio transmissions sent mostly in plain language. Things obviously were not going well for the Japanese. One crew lamented at 1803: "Attack squadron has been annihilated by enemy fighters." In another instance the pilot was killed and the observer in the middle seat took control of the aircraft. Thinking the target was still far ahead, Takahashi was completely unprepared for fighters swooping into his midst. In a large, one-sided triumph, the combat air patrol splashed seven carrier attack planes (Ramsey's "Zero fighters") and one carrier bomber; another carrier attack plane (the one piloted by the observer) was badly damaged. Out to the west beyond TF-17, a shaken Takahashi aborted the mission, had the survivors drop their payloads, and tried to reassemble the group for the flight home.[16]

At sundown the U.S. carriers started recovering fighters. The process went slowly as several pilots hesitantly made their first night landings. More bogeys appeared on radar. The combat air patrol went looking for them, but without success. Fletcher was wary. Unaware the enemy strike was toothless, he warned TF-17 at 1840, "Be on alert for enemy torpedo plane attack." In the growing darkness the carriers turned on their landing lights, while impatient Wildcats buzzed overhead in the landing circle. Elements of the battered strike group straggled past TF-17. At 1850 three strange aircraft showing running lights flew past the *Yorktown*'s starboard side and used a hand-held light to blink a message in Morse code. In the fading light Lt. (jg) Brainard Macomber of VF-42 recognized them as foes and chased them away. By 1857 the *Lex* had completed recovering all her fighters but one, while a half-dozen *Yorktown* F4Fs still orbited the task force. After the destroyer *Dewey* observed suspicious aircraft with rounded wingtips, Captain Early (Comdesron One in the *Phelps*) queried Fletcher on TBS whether any planes other than square-winged fighters were aloft. Before the *Yorktown* could respond negative, the intruders flashed out another recognition query. Turning on their running lights as if they intended to land, they circled in the direction opposite to the friendly planes. About 1909 some destroyers opened fire, followed by the *Minneapolis* and *Astoria*. As tracers laced through the sky, both Sherman (*Lexington*) and Hoover (Comdesron Two) sternly ordered their ships not to join in. At 1910 the *Yorktown*'s entire starboard antiaircraft battery "went off like a fire cracker," prompting one harassed VF-42 pilot to radio: "What are you shooting at me for? What have I done now?" Fletcher maneuvered radically to avoid attack, but the enemy fled into the darkness. The antiaircraft fire swiftly stopped, and the scattered F4Fs gingerly returned. It was a very bizarre moment that crowned a remarkable day.[17]

With Japanese planes flocking to TF-17 and mistakenly trying to land, at least one enemy carrier, perhaps more, had to be nearby, but where? Seemingly it had to be different from the carrier or carriers that had attacked the *Neosho* and *Sims* that afternoon. Sowespac again reported five transports just south of Jomard Passage, but all other indications were that the rest of the invasion force remained north of the Louisiades. MacArthur also placed the converted carrier *Kasuga Maru* at Queen Carola anchorage off Buka that afternoon. For the time being Fletcher delayed going west. Southeast, where the Japanese strike group was first detected, was as good a direction as any to go temporarily. He kept his options open until the situation cleared, and he could figure how to retaliate either that night with a surface attack or the next dawn with aircraft.[18]

TF-17 resumed landing planes, the last at 1930, but three Wildcats were missing. By an unfortunate coincidence two of the pilots shared the surname Baker: Lt. (jg) Paul G. Baker from VF-2 and Ens. John D. Baker of VF-42. Almost certainly Paul Baker died ninety minutes before during Ramsey's ambush, but John Baker returned to the task force only to be driven off to the northeast by the sudden antiaircraft barrage. By the time John Baker's identity was realized and Gill passed control to Pederson in the *Yorktown*, his F4F had disappeared off the radar screen. Pederson needed to get him back on radar so he could coach him back to the ship. Hearing of Baker's plight, Fletcher went up to air plot. Despite his worry over enemy carriers he gave Pederson permission to use the radio to keep trying to reach Baker. Pederson thought Fletcher "willing to do anything to try to get our pilot back." Unfortunately Pederson never steered the errant F4F back onto radar. Finally at 2028 he had to give Baker the course to the nearest land. "I remember the talker with me was practically in tears when I had to tell the pilot good-bye and Good Luck." John Baker was never found.[19]

In the meantime Biard continued relaying to Fletcher the messages intercepted from the Japanese strike group. In the *Lexington* Fullinwider did the same for Fitch. Lt. Cdr. Clarence C. Ray, the *Yorktown* communications officer, recalled, "The air was full of their conversation trying to get home and aboard." One of Biard's intercepts received at 1903 gave an all too accurate position for TF-17 (bearing 160 degrees and 110 miles from Rossel), so not all enemy aircrew were befuddled. At 1900 another aircraft said it would "arrive" at 1940. Had it been one that buzzed TF-17, its carrier might be seventy to a hundred miles away, direction unknown. That seemed to be that case at 1939, when another plane requested its carrier turn on the lights. At 2003 an aircraft advised: "I see you." A few minutes later the observer piloting his plane requested, then demanded, that a searchlight be shone on the sea so he could try a water landing. The revealing transmissions lasted until about 2130. They appeared to show two carriers differentiated by their call signs. In addition to communicating directly with the aircraft, these ships also used high-frequency transmissions as radio homing beacons, but TF-17 lacked proper receivers capable of taking a bearing on such transmissions. Fletcher and Buckmaster guessed the enemy carriers might be up as far as 140–150 miles either to the east or west. The best that Cincpac could offer later was a bearing (233 degrees) from Oahu, which put the carriers somewhere off to the east. Late that night Pearl also provided a double radio fix (from Oahu and Samoa) that moved the source of the homing signals nearer toward San Cristóbal Island in the southern Solomons. That was too far east of TF-17 to be accurate, but again pointed east. Biard with his characteristic demeaning of Fletcher described that in reply to one of his reports, "The Admiral looked up at me with the most stupidly sheepish look I have ever seen on a naval officer's face and said to me, almost apologetically . . . 'you know—I didn't think they were that aggressive.'" Perhaps Fletcher actually said or meant 'foolhardy,' for Biard and others estimated the enemy might have lost fifteen or twenty aircraft that night.[20]

Not only did Hara's night strike group contact the enemy earlier than anticipated, but defending fighters also made mincemeat of it. Takagi agreed to Hara's recommendation that MO Striking Force assume a special formation to facilitate recovery of the strike. The *Shōkaku* and *Zuikaku* deployed abreast, while ahead off to starboard the two heavy cruisers aimed searchlights across their bows and destroyers on both quarters shined their searchlights forward to demarcate the flanks. Takagi could risk illuminating MO Striking Force for as long as it took to recover his planes, because he (unlike Fletcher) had a pretty good idea of the position of the nearest enemy ships. At 2000 when the first strike plane landed, the two carrier forces were about one hundred miles apart. Thereafter the distance between them increased as Takagi steamed east and Fletcher southeast.[21]

THE "EXCELLENT OPPORTUNITY"

At 2151 Fitch informed Fletcher by TBS: "Presence of enemy planes during recovery of our fighters and analysis of later radar plots indicate enemy carrier or carriers about thirty miles bearing 090 at 1930." He also warned that the Japanese carriers might have "excellent" high frequency radio direction finders. Thirty miles east? The *Lexington*'s radar tracked the strike planes as they circled thirty miles away and seemed to disappear one by one as if landing. The reason why at least some Japanese planes circled was the U.S. fighter director transmissions jammed their radio homing signals. Cued by Fullinwider's findings, Fitch concluded the aircraft had to belong to the 5th Carrier Division, "which until that time had been unaccounted for." Yet Fitch never explained why he waited two-and-a-half hours before forwarding such vital information to Fletcher. Perhaps he thought the *Yorktown*'s radar registered the same activity. Stroop, Fitch's flag secretary, urged that destroyers execute a night torpedo attack, but Fitch believed the enemy was probably already too far away and too hard to find. Sherman reached the opposite conclusion. He strongly regretted the failure to hunt the enemy carriers that night, not only with destroyers, but also the VT-2 TBDs, which were, he wrote, "Fully qualified in night carrier operations" and "capable of making such an attack." In 1950 he complained that had Fletcher given Fitch "complete freedom of action, it is probable such an attack would have been launched, and it might have made a tremendous difference in the next day's events." However, Sherman's later assertions originated from hindsight. There is no evidence he seriously proposed to Fitch to use VT-2 that night. Nothing of the sort appeared in any action reports or, more importantly, in Sherman's reconstructed diary. Nor did Stroop mention it in his oral history. There were also serious practical objections. Simply wringing out the TBDs from the *Lexington*'s crowded flight deck would have been a nightmare. Sherman would have had to launch all the SBDs and some of the fighters just to clear the deck for their takeoffs. The Japanese were actually much farther away than thirty miles, and there is no indication the short-ranged TBDs would have ever found them.[22]

In fact Fitch's belated revelation startled Fletcher. The *Yorktown*'s only radar contact at 1930 was John Baker's missing Wildcat, which disappeared soon afterward. With the enemy striking force apparently so close (or least it was said to be close nearly three hours before), Fletcher considered whether to unleash Kinkaid's cruiser group, or even just the destroyers, to eastward for a night surface attack. TF-17 had five heavy cruisers and eight destroyers. The carriers required at least two or three destroyers as a screen. Those destroyers assigned to the surface attack group would have to spread out ahead of the cruisers in a scouting line hoping to pick up enemy ships on radar. Rejecting a night surface strike, Fletcher resolved to keep his force together to battle the Japanese carriers the next morning. Kinkaid completely concurred. So, later, did Nimitz, who wrote in his endorsement of Fletcher's report that the "decision not to attempt such an attack was sound and that [Fletcher] was correct in not dispersing his forces at that particular time when he did not know the composition of the enemy force." There were several reasons why a night surface attack might not have been wise in that instance. Even if Fitch's surmise was correct, since 1930 the Japanese could have gone seventy-five miles in nearly any direction. They might not be found before dawn, at which time the surface attack group would be isolated and highly vulnerable to air attack. At the same time the carriers might sorely miss their antiaircraft protection. Moreover, high-speed steaming would cost a great deal of fuel oil that TF-17 could not spare after losing the *Neosho*.[23]

Fletcher had not only considered a night surface battle, but also a night air strike. Burch strongly suggested that the SBDs and TBDs attack, but that was rejected because of the group's lack of night flying experience. Much later Vice Adm. Turner Caldwell, the former VS-5 executive officer, recalled, "In view of the weather we recommended against, and [Fletcher] did not insist. It was probably just as well. Some of us would have been surely lost, and at that time we had no doctrine nor training for night combat, although everyone was checked out in night landings." Caldwell also offered a mature appraisal of Fletcher seasoned by his own subsequent command perspective. At the time the young tigers "did not have much respect for Fletcher, as he was indecisive and knew little about aviation, and we thought he could have used us better." However, "I now understand he did his best, and given the experience level of the time did as well as anyone else could have done."[24]

PLANNING FOR 8 MAY

That evening at Rabaul a bemused Inoue tried to fathom the crushing setbacks inflicted on his MO Operation. He bore the shame of losing the first carrier or major warship of any kind. Despite the cunning deployment of the MO Striking Force and a rich harvest of search contacts, decisive victory south of the Louisiades had eluded him. Inoue postponed the Port Moresby landings two days to 12 May (X+2 Day). Yamamoto assented. Because Gotō had miscalculated time and distance, the 6th Cruiser Division and Kajioka's 6th Destroyer Squadron never reached a position from which to execute the night surface attack. Consequently Inoue detached two of Gotō's heavy cruisers to reinforce the MO Striking Force and told him to regroup the rest of MO Attack Force north of the Louisiades. Once the path was clear they could start for Moresby again. Inoue directed Takagi to reach a point 110 miles south-southeast of Rossel at dawn on 8 May. From there MO Striking Force should finally catch and sink the troublesome carriers and open the way to Moresby. From 1945 to 2200 while landing the night strike, Takagi steamed eastward away from the Allied task forces. He never seriously contemplated a night surface attack against the U.S. ships. Remarkably in a great demonstration of Japanese night carrier skill, eighteen of twenty-seven aircraft made it back on board Hara's carriers. But the loss of eight carrier attack planes and their highly experienced crews on a fruitless attack seriously harmed the 5th Carrier Division's capability for effective torpedo attack. Looking ahead to battle on the eighth, Hara recommended to Takagi that MO Striking Force keep well to the east or even head south in order to flank the U.S. carrier force lurking south of the Louisiades. Takagi rejected that advice. Noting that Inoue's prescribed dawn position was quite close to the enemy's last known location, Hara was concerned that insufficient separation would force the 5th Carrier Division to search in nearly all directions. He suggested that the dawn search point be shifted 120 miles northward. The U.S. carriers would never venture so far north, so the search could be concentrated to southward to free up more carrier attack planes for attack. Takagi did agree to that. "This will aid us so that we will not fail to spot the enemy quickly, overtake and destroy him." He set a new dawn position about 140 miles northeast of Rossel and 160 miles northeast of Inoue's original point. The 2nd Section (*Kinugasa* and *Furutaka*) from the 6th Cruiser Division was to join Takagi there soon after dawn.[25]

After the situation finally calmed toward midnight, Fletcher and Fitch laid out their battle plan for the next morning. Fitch signaled: "Agree our mission destruction carriers possibly two carriers in this area one definitely in immediate area." It was not feasible, given that proximity, to guarantee much separation of the two opposing carrier forces during the night. Consequently he recommended a full 360-degree dawn search by SBDs from the *Lexington*, the duty carrier on the eighth. Because the Japanese could maneuver to close aboard in any quadrant during the night, he had no choice in the matter. The tactical situation resembled one in the 1940 Fleet Problem XXI, in which the *Yorktown* was "destroyed" due to the failure to conduct a similar full circle search. Given that TF-17 was moving southward, Fitch thought it adequate to set the northern semicircle at two hundred miles, the southern to 125 miles. He wanted the combat air patrol fighters and anti-torpedo-plane SBDs aloft fifteen minutes before sunrise and the attack groups ready to go. After steaming southeast all evening, Fletcher turned south shortly after midnight. At 0039 he replied to Fitch: "As usual I agree with you thoroughly. I will change course to west. Set your own course and speed Point Option." At 0117 Fletcher came around to the west at fourteen knots. By that time TF-17 was 180 miles south of Rossel and hence some six hundred miles from Rabaul, near the extreme attack range of Japanese bombers. (At that time MO Striking Force was about 130 miles northeast of TF-17 and moving away.) Fletcher intended to proceed west until about sunrise, then move southeast into the prevailing wind and launch the dawn search. Thus he changed his mind about taking station south of the China Strait and preferred to go no farther west than about longitude 154° east, until he dealt once and for all with the Moresby striking force.[26]

Fletcher detailed the *Monaghan*, whose engines were ailing, to rescue the *Neosho* and *Sims* survivors and take them to Nouméa. Once well away from TF-17, the destroyer radioed dispatches on his behalf, necessary because of fears of radio direction finding. One offered Cincpac a succinct summary of the day's action. TF-17 sank a "large" carrier and a cruiser off Misima, while Crace operated east of Moresby. Enemy carrier planes retaliated against TF-17 at dusk but were repulsed after losing about nine planes. Six of his own planes were lost that day. Fletcher placed two enemy carriers "in vicinity," and advised they were aware of "our exact position." He would attack them in the morning, then fuel his destroyers and "continue [to] oppose enemy movement toward Moresby." The loss of the *Neosho*'s fuel would "cripple" his "offensive action and may cause my withdrawal in a few days." That night Leary stepped up by offering his two Royal Australian Navy oilers, the *Bishopdale*, which he said was at Efate, and the smaller *Kurumba*, located at Whitsunday Island off the northeast Australian coast 135 miles south of Townsville. Presumably the *Tippecanoe* could restock from the *Bishopdale* at Efate and bring the oil to Nouméa.[27]

That night Crace steered the Support Group to westward in accordance with what he told Fletcher. He remained concerned about not hearing from Fletcher that day and had no idea what befell TF-17. For his own part Fletcher drew up a message for Crace, evidently for the *Monaghan* to transmit, but there is no evidence it was ever sent. It described the action of Misima and explained: "Was proceeding your vicinity when attacked at sunset by carrier planes." Crace was to "get close to Moresby for fighting protection but use your own discretion." Fletcher also apologized for not joining the Support Group "at once." Fortunately for Crace, the *Kurumba* was not too far away. That night he unwittingly avoided a potential attack due to more mistaken identity on the part of Japanese searchers. Based on the flying boat report of two enemy carriers discovered 185 miles southwest of Rossel, three Type 97 flying boats armed with torpedoes hunted Crace but never found him.[28]

"WE CANNOT BUT SHUDDER AT THIS REPEATED FAILURE"

On 7 May Admiral Ugaki, chief of staff of the Combined Fleet, tried to follow the battle in the Coral Sea from the many radio dispatches sent by Inoue and his principal subordinates. Surprised and depressed by the turn of events, he lamented in his diary why, "when we were able to foretell the enemy's attack, could we not have contrived to more closely coordinate our forces?" It took time before the reason behind the failures of the seventh became apparent. In 1943 a committee of Japanese naval officers compiling battle lessons for the first year of the war analyzed in detail the reports of the land-based and carrier air searches rendered on 7 May. "Not only was it extremely difficult to assess them at the time," they concluded, "but even today they are confusing." The committee enumerated numerous gross errors in relating the numbers and types of ships present, as well as the navigation that determined their positions. "We cannot but shudder at this repeated failure." The senior commanders were poorly served by the search effort that very likely prevented a decisive victory. Analysts and historians subsequently affirmed that verdict. Nimitz and Potter declared in their account of the Battle of the Coral Sea that the Japanese "failed to attack Fletcher on the 7th only because of a series of errors which by evening reached the fantastic." In 1972 Vice Adm. H. S. Duckworth, the former *Lexington* air officer, asserted after reading the Japanese official account, "Without doubt, May 7 1942, vicinity of Coral Sea, was the most confused battle area in world history. A list of errors (by both sides) together with *lucky* decisions would be interesting." The many errors (mostly Japanese) have been enumerated above. Fletcher's "lucky" decisions were detaching Crace and keeping TF-17 in the bad weather southeast of Rossel. Neither luck nor the weather would cooperate on 8 May.[29]

CHAPTER 14

The Battle of the Coral Sea III
A Costly Victory

FINDING THE ENEMY

During the predawn hours of 8 May a weary TF-17 steamed west while keeping 180 miles from the southeast fringe of the Louisiades. The skies cleared, and moonlight bathed the ships. Fletcher intended to continue west until just before sunrise, then pivot southeast into the prevailing trade winds to dispatch his dawn search. The two carriers of the Moresby striking force were on the prowl nearby, and he must locate them and attack as quickly as possible. The previous morning his aircraft destroyed the third carrier, "*Ryūkaku*" (*Shōhō*), and drove off, at least temporarily, the Port Moresby invasion force. At the same time Fletcher's two detached forces, Crace's Support Group and Phillips's Fueling Group, sustained strong air attacks. Crace skillfully avoided damage, but the *Sims* was sunk and the *Neosho* still afloat, although a total loss. The victor of the Battle of the Coral Sea would emerge only after the carriers traded blows.[1]

Seven May exhausted aircrews and ships' company alike. Such sleep as Fletcher secured came between 0130 and 0430. Morison sneered that Fletcher awoke the morning of 8 May "in somewhat more than his usual fighting mood." Dawn found Crace's Support Group (TG-17.3) about 130 miles south of the New Guinea coast, steaming northwest through the position that Crace gave Fletcher the previous evening. Crace was disappointed not to see a destroyer or an aircraft there to advise him of Fletcher's intentions. In the absence of further orders, he decided to stay southeast of Port Moresby that morning to see what turned up. If it was quiet he would fuel the three destroyers from the cruisers.[2]

Fitch and his staff likewise rose early to plan their air battle with the 117 operational planes (thirty-one fighters, sixty-five dive bombers, and twenty-one torpedo planes) remaining in the *Lexington* and *Yorktown*. Deducting the eighteen SBDs necessary to conduct the full 360-degree search, the available striking force shrank to seventy-five aircraft. A dozen VS-2 Dauntlesses were to search the crucial northern semicircle to two hundred miles and six from VB-2 scan the southern sector to one hundred miles. Instead of relaunching the search SBDs as a follow-up strike, Fitch would use them to reinforce the eight *Yorktown* SBDs on anti-torpedo-plane patrol. He reserved sixteen fighters, eight from each carrier, for the combat air patrol. Beginning at 0635 the *Lexington* turned southeast into the wind to launch four combat air patrol fighters and the eighteen search SBDs.

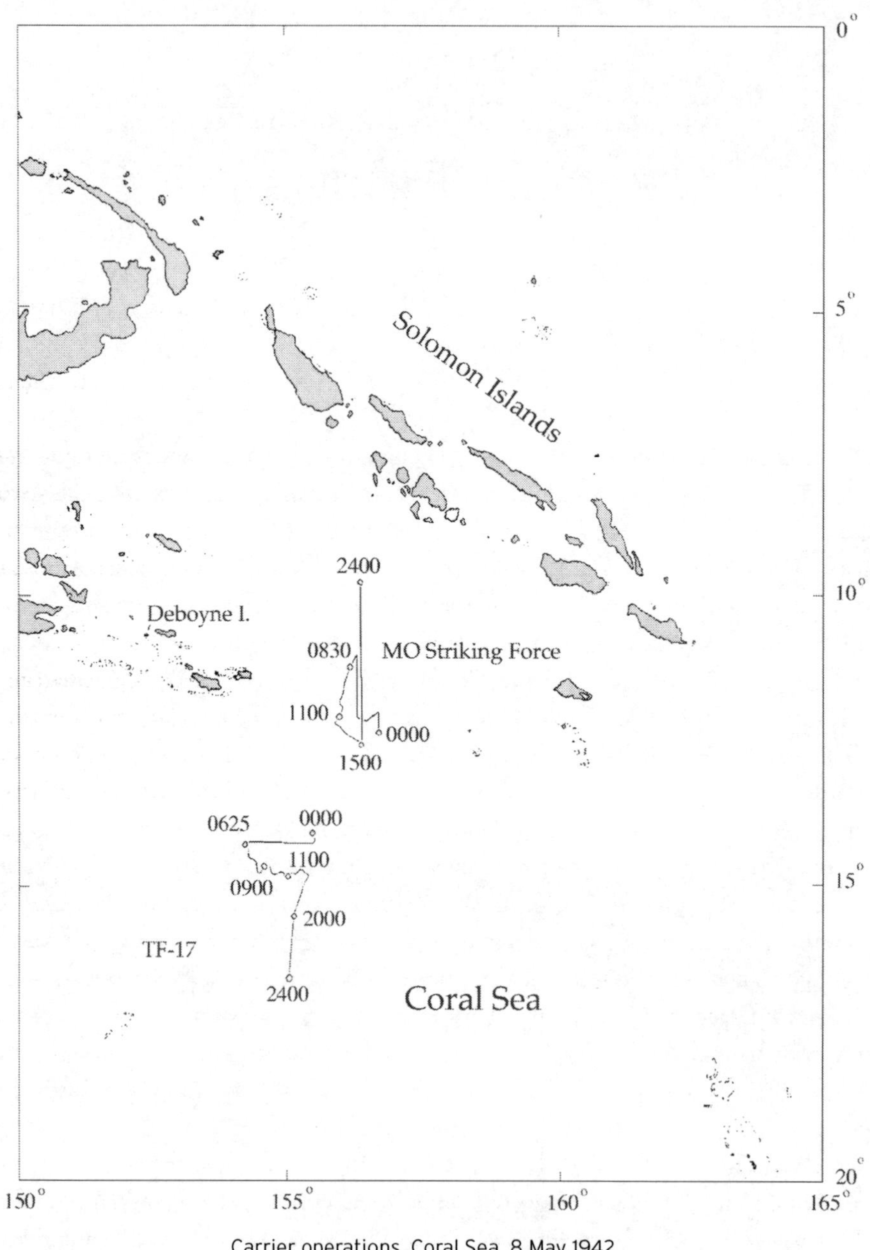

Carrier operations, Coral Sea, 8 May 1942

At 0657, four minutes after sunrise, Fletcher steadied on the Point Option course of 125 degrees at fifteen knots. TF-17 would not be blanketed this day by the overcast along the frontal zone. The cold front was only "quasi-stationary." Overnight it shifted northeast and east, while TF-17 broke out to the west. Now there was light haze, only a few cumulus clouds, and visibility to seventeen miles. The edge of the frontal zone rested thirty to fifty miles north and northeast. Given the nature of weather forecasts Fletcher did not know that in advance. There is no evidence that either he or Fitch contemplated taking shelter in the bad weather, as attractive as that prospect later appeared. They recognized the value of the "weather gauge," but under the tactical circumstances, with the Japanese carriers possibly quite close, they could not take advantage of it. Fitch directed the *Yorktown* to launch her own combat air patrol of four F4Fs and the eight SBDs for the anti-torpedo-plane patrol, but after a half hour when he saw no sign of imminent takeoffs, he queried Buckmaster. Finally at 0724, the first *Yorktown* planes took to the air. Buckmaster apologized. He had spotted the attack group for immediate launch and had to shift aircraft around to clear the deck for the anti-torpedo-plane patrol to take off. Now TF-17 could only wait to see what the search turned up and fondly hope it could attack before the enemy's own strike appeared.[3]

The first hint of trouble came at 0802, when the *Yorktown*'s radar picked up a bogey eighteen miles northwest. Lieutenant Gill, the *Lex*'s fighter director, unleashed combat air patrol fighters only to have the intruder disappear off the radar screen at 0816. Even so, it was obvious an enemy plane "got a good look" at TF-17. Biard emerged from his green-curtained radio room to whisper to Fletcher that a Japanese snooper transmitted "English, English, English" and busily tattled about TF-17 to its base. Fullinwider in the *Lexington* likewise informed Fitch the enemy had found them. Sherman dryly predicted that the Japanese strike group would show up around 1100, and that a "simultaneous onslaught" could destroy the carriers from both sides. That was precisely Fletcher's reasoning when he detached Crace's Support Group the previous day.[4]

If the TF-17 search did not succeed in finding the enemy almost immediately, there could be no "simultaneous onslaught." Fortunately at 0820 Lt. (jg) Joseph G. Smith from VS-2 had the good luck of spotting MO Striking Force in the midst of thick clouds and squalls. He reported by voice radio the position of two carriers, four heavy cruisers, and three destroyers, but interference prevented the *Lexington* from copying the whole message. Ens. Everleigh D. Willems and Commander Dixon, the two VS-2 pilots in adjacent sectors, alertly relayed Smith's entire transmission to TF-17. "Contact 2 carriers 4 cruisers many destroyers bearing 006 dist 120 speed 15 at 0820." Smith's radioman also repeated the radio message by key. Not immediately receiving an acknowledgment, Smith started back to base as briefed. Ostensibly Smith placed the Japanese force only 120 miles due north of TF-17, almost spitting distance. Even more thrilling, Fletcher followed at 0837: "Believe we have been sighted by enemy carrier plane." Fitch barked the only possible response: "Launch striking group." A minute later he told the *Lexington* and *Yorktown* to omit the torpedo planes. It occurred to Sherman that the *Yorktown* might not understand why the TBDs could not go, although the target certainly appeared well within their range. He asked Buckmaster whether the *Yorktown* had the *Lex*'s "Point Zed," a separate reference point used by the search to prevent eavesdropping Japanese from deducing the actual bearing and distance back to TF-17. However, Sherman himself was unsure whether his pilot actually used Zed or not. After a few anxious minutes both Fletcher and Fitch were satisfied Smith meant Zed. That placed the target bearing 028 degrees, 175 miles from TF-17. As yet Smith had not provided its course, a crucial factor. If the MO Striking Force headed away, it would be at or beyond the absolute limit of the TBDs and F4Fs. Nevertheless, at 0847 Fitch ordered the whole strike group to go. Aware it was a real gamble, Fletcher told Fitch to recommend a Point Option course that would decrease their return flight. Fitch replied that once the morning search was recovered (expected by 1000), TF-17 should steam toward the enemy. At 0857

Fletcher confirmed his original warning: "Enemy received contact report on us at 0822." Three minutes later the first of thirty-nine *Yorktown* strike planes (six fighters, twenty-four dive bombers, and nine torpedo planes spotted as one deck load) rolled down her flight deck. The *Lexington* started launching her thirty-six planes (nine fighters, fifteen dive bombers, and twelve torpedo planes) at 0907. By 0925 the two air groups, widely separated as usual according to doctrine, had departed for the target.[5]

At 0908 while the TF-17 strike groups took off, the *Yorktown* transmitted by flag hoist orders from Fletcher to Fitch to "assume tactical command of the fleet." Fletcher later explained that he did so "to reduce signalling between carriers and to allow [Fitch] complete freedom of action for his carriers and air groups." It was a logical decision. Fletcher had employed his main weapon, and the Support Group watched the back door to Moresby. The immediate problems of attack and defense were best left to his subordinates, while he concentrated on the big picture. Hoping MacArthur's aircraft could intervene (any attack would help), Fletcher relayed Smith's contact report to Comsowespacfor, along with his own position. In the meantime Cincpac advised no fuel was available in the area other than previously noted, although he assumed that in an emergency (as this was) Leary would furnish the *Bishopdale* and *Kurumba*. The *Tangier* advised, and Leary confirmed, the *Bishopdale* was actually at Nouméa, not Efate. The *Tippecanoe* with a strong destroyer escort was due at Nouméa on 10 May to restock from the *Bishopdale*. Until then Fletcher was on his own.[6]

Fitch himself was surprised to receive tactical command at that juncture, but welcomed the opportunity. P. D. Stroop, the fiery flag secretary, thought a non-aviator admiral like Fletcher had no business commanding a carrier task force. Attending to necessary matters, the two carriers launched fighters and recovered the first combat air patrol and ten *Lex* SBDs. The rest of the search was expected back shortly, but one SBD deliberately remained far from base. On his own initiative, Dixon followed up Smith's contact and discovered the enemy was more distant than the first reports indicated. At 0934 he radioed that two carriers and a battleship were located 140 miles due north of Zed, which worked out to 191 miles northeast of TF-17. He also provided course, 180 degrees, and speed, twenty-five knots, but that vital information did not come through. Dodging Zeros and storms Dixon stayed on station for more than an hour, one of the very few instances in 1942 when a U.S. plane actually shadowed a contact. The increased distance to the enemy gave Fitch pause. He must soon change course northeast to cut down the distance his own strike groups had to fly. However, he was committed to the southeast Point Option course at least until 1000, when the rest of the dawn search SBDs should be back.[7]

Tension this morning gripped not only TF-17 but also the various components of the MO Operation. Given Inoue's order to reschedule the Port Moresby landing to 12 May, Gotō sought to reunite the widely scattered elements of the MO Attack Force north of the Louisiades. He directed the convoy, its escorts, and two cruisers of the 6th Cruiser Division to rendezvous that afternoon forty miles east of Woodlark. They would resume the advance once the way was cleared. Well to the southeast, Takagi's MO Striking Force approached the battle in a grimmer, chastened attitude. Hara now had ninety-six flyable planes (thirty-eight fighters, thirty-three carrier bombers, and twenty-five carrier attack planes) on the *Shōkaku* and *Zuikaku*, down from 109 the previous day. The eight elite carrier attack crews lost the previous evening lessened his combat potential far more than simple numbers indicated. Also if anything, the Japanese aviators were even more exhausted than their U.S. counterparts. Rough seas extinguished Takagi's hope of using cruiser float planes for search to free up carrier attack planes for the strike, though by moving north during the night away from TF-17, he needed just seven to cover a southerly arc to 250 miles. They departed at 0615. At that time MO Striking Force was in the midst of the band of bad weather about 220 miles northeast of TF-17. Takagi continued north to meet the *Kinugasa* and *Furutaka* from the 6th Cruiser Division but would hasten south to rapidly decrease the range once the U.S. carriers were found. Four land attack planes from Rabaul and three flying boats from Tulagi searched beyond the Louisiades. Bombers waited at Rabaul, but soggy runways threatened to keep them on the ground. The battle soon shifted out of range of Deboyne's float planes patrolling the waters south of the Louisiades.[8]

One of Takagi's search planes, commanded by PO1C Kanno Kenzō, indeed discovered TF-17 at 0822. Kanno gave its bearing and range from MO Striking Force as 205 degrees and 235 miles. The actual distance at that time was about 225 miles, so Kanno's report was much more accurate than Smith's. The *Shōkaku* and *Zuikaku* immediately spotted a strike of sixty-nine planes (eighteen fighters, thirty-three carrier bombers, and eighteen torpedo-armed carrier attack planes) under Commander Takahashi. After they departed at 0930, Takagi worked up to thirty knots to follow them into battle. Ironically only his decision to steam south at high speed would allow the shorter-ranged TF-17 strike groups to attack MO Striking Force.[9]

"NO VITAL DAMAGE OUR FORCE"

The *Yorktown*'s radar picked up an unidentified aircraft thirty-nine miles northeast. A few minutes later that shadower or another was detected twenty-five miles northwest. The *Lexington* refueled newly landed search Dauntlesses and spotted them for immediate launch to reinforce the anti-torpedo-plane patrol. By about 1000 Fitch feared imminent attack. A returning scout reported twelve aircraft forty-five miles northwest of TF-17. While the ten SBDs scrambled aloft, combat air patrol fighters chased several suspicious radar contacts. Two *Yorktown* fighters destroyed a hapless Type 97 flying boat that Americans later concluded was the sole shadower. The smoke that marked its demise was clearly visible northeast of the ships. No one ever spotted Kanno's torpedo plane or realized that enemy carrier-based aircraft searched that day. Like Dixon, Kanno remained within sight of the opposing task force for more than an hour and radioed vital information, including homing signals, to guide the approaching strike group. Radio intelligence kept Fletcher and Fitch informed of Kanno's transmissions. Unfortunately unlike the previous day, the Japanese strictly enciphered their aircraft radio transmissions, so little of the actual messages could be read. At 1029 the *Lexington* landed five tardy SBDs from the morning search (which left three still out), and also a strike TBD with engine trouble.

Fitch finally turned northeast toward the enemy striking force. At 1043 he drew TF-17 into the "Victor" defensive formation specified in Fletcher's operations order and based on Sherman's ideas. The two carriers deployed abreast on the fifteen-hundred-yard circle (which placed them three thousand yards apart), with the five cruisers on the three-thousand-yard circle and the seven destroyers at four thousand yards and outboard of the gaps between the cruisers. The function of the screen was to deliver strong antiaircraft fire to protect the carriers against air attack. One Japanese aviator who bombed TF-11 in February described the "ring formation, which the United States Navy boasted to the world."[10] The IJN's philosophy with regard to carrier defense was diametrically different. Under air attack, the screening ships backed off to give the carriers more room to maneuver freely. The U.S. Navy practice was a compromise, because the carrier captains still considered radical maneuvers key to evading bombs and torpedoes. It was up to the screening ships to keep out of their way but stay close enough to offer antiaircraft support.

The U.S. Navy's task force antiaircraft doctrine was about to get its first test at the hands of excellent opponents. Up to this point the ships had either been overwhelmed at Pearl Harbor or merely weathered skirmishes with level bombers. In neither case did the antiaircraft perform well. The ships wielded two types of antiaircraft weapons: heavy for long-range fire and light for close-in defense. Using shells with time fuses, the heavy antiaircraft guns—dual purpose 5-inch/38s in the *Yorktown* and most of the destroyers, and the older, less powerful 5-inch/25 antiaircraft in the *Lexington* and the cruisers—had a maximum effective slant range of about ten thousand yards and normally did not open fire beyond that distance. The fire control radar that a few of the ships mounted was not yet much of a factor. The 5-inch guns either used (ideally) director or local control to fire at individual targets ("continuously pointed fire" or "shoot to hit") or laid barrages through which the enemy planes must pass to deliver their payloads. The light automatic weapons, 1.1-inch cannons in quadruple mounts and single 20-mm cannons and .50-caliber heavy machine guns, operated solely under local control using tracers. Usually only the ship being attacked had much of a chance to employ them to good effect. Because light antiaircraft enjoyed an effective range of one to two thousand yards at most—out near to where enemy planes released their bombs and torpedoes—most of their kills were of "revenge" variety after the attackers did their job.[11]

A gunnery expert, Fletcher held no illusions about the likely effectiveness of antiaircraft. He knew the principal means of destroying enemy aircraft were the seventeen combat air patrol fighters and twenty-three dive bombers on anti-torpedo-plane patrol, but they must be deployed correctly. Four fighters from each carrier were already aloft, along with eighteen SBDs (ten *Lexington*, eight *Yorktown*), but the F4Fs were low on fuel. The *Lexington* ranged five fighters and five SBDs and the *Yorktown* four fighters on deck, ready for launch. At 1051 it looked as if they were going to be needed. The *Yorktown* announced on TBS: "Warning. Have many aircraft bearing 020 distance 68 miles." Two minutes later Gill gave the old carnival barker's call, "Hey, Rube," which recalled the combat air patrol fighters overhead. The TF-17 strike groups were silent until 1057, when suddenly the *Yorktown* heard Joe Taylor, commanding officer of VT-5, tell Burch, leader of the *Yorktown* dive bombers: "OK Bill, I'm starting in." That answered the *Yorktown*'s prayers that their strike leaders had sighted the enemy carriers and, as instructed, coordinated their attacks.[12]

At 1101 both carriers scrambled their reserve aircraft. Gill dispatched the nine fighters to intercept the incoming Japanese, now some twenty miles northeast. Three of the Wildcats clawed for altitude looking for dive bombers; the other six stayed low to hunt torpedo planes. Eight *Yorktown* and three *Lexington* dive bombers likewise sought torpedo planes to the northeast, but a dozen *Lex* SBDs remained on station in their assigned sectors two thousand yards out from the ships. Gill kept the eight original combat air patrol fighters eight thousand feet overhead. At 1111 Fitch swung TF-17 right to 125 degrees, nearly directly into the wind, and ordered flank speed, twenty-five knots. Takahashi's strike group had TF-17 in sight at 1105. The thirty-three carrier bombers advanced at fourteen thousand feet, while the eighteen carrier attack planes, lugging torpedoes, and all eighteen Zero escorts executed a fast, shallow dive from ten thousand feet. Gill's split deployment of the combat air patrol miscarried. Clouds shielded the torpedo planes from the six Wildcats prowling low, while the three F4Fs that climbed after dive bombers ended up well below them. The SBD anti-torpedo-plane patrol bore the brunt of the attack and suffered heavily. Only one carrier attack plane fell before the strike actually approached TF-17, but Zeros blasted four *Yorktown* SBDs out of the sky. Having penetrated the outer layer of the air defense virtually intact, the strike group prepared to take on the two carriers.[13]

Wearing an old doughboy-style helmet, Fletcher stood outside with Lewis and several staff officers on the flag bridge, binoculars trained northeast. Snatches of dialogue between FDO and pilots brayed over the radio speaker in flag plot, but as yet the action was too distant to see from ships and besides was far too fast to follow. Having given Fitch tactical command, Fletcher could do no more under the immediate circumstances. Stroop put it well: "Oh, at this point in time—as far as the senior people were concerned—you were completely helpless. You were depending on the training that had been given to the fighter pilots in the air, and you were dependent on the training and practice [of] the gunners." At 1113 the port side 5-inch guns on the *Lexington* and the cruisers on that flank opened fire. The black blossoms of their exploding shells pointed the way to Japanese planes six or seven thousand yards out. Ens. Ralph V. Wilhelm, a *Portland* SOC pilot aloft during the battle, marveled that the "sky was just a solid blanket of antiaircraft bursts all between 1000 and 3000 feet altitude." Yeoman Tom Newsome, the TBS combat talker standing just inside the doorway in the *Yorktown* flag plot, heard Fletcher tell Lewis, "They're going to bop us."[14]

Thirteen torpedo planes swarmed around the *Lexington* in an arc that extended from her port beam and across both bows in the dreaded "anvil" attack. "As they came over the screen against the *Lexington*," Captain Early in the *Phelps* wrote, "all hell broke loose with everyone from 5-inch, 1.1 [inch] and 20-mms." Sherman ordered right full rudder to turn away from lead torpedo planes off his port bow, but the massive *Lex* took thirty to forty seconds to start swinging to starboard. At the same time four *Zuikaku* carrier attack planes charged in from the *Yorktown*'s port beam. Her 5-inchers pounded away at the specks of incoming torpedo planes about seven thousand yards off. Thirty seconds later every automatic weapon that could bear cut loose. To Buckmaster there appeared to be nine attackers, but they included some Zero fighters. Antiaircraft fire downed one torpedo plane, but the others roared in. At 1118 he called for emergency flank speed and swerved away hard to starboard as soon as the lead torpedo planes dropped their fish. The nimble *Yorktown* swiftly swiveled southwest and worked up to thirty knots. The torpedoes passed harmlessly to port, and another carrier

Capt. Elliott Buckmaster, 1941.
Courtesy of U.S. Navy, via Robert J. Cressman

attack plane succumbed to antiaircraft fire before it could get clear. TF-17 broke up as the carriers maneuvered independently to avoid torpedoes. Kinkaid with the *Minneapolis*, *New Orleans*, and destroyers *Dewey*, *Morris*, *Anderson*, and *Phelps* tried to stay close to the *Lexington* with varying degrees of success, while Poco Smith's *Astoria*, *Portland*, and *Chester* and destroyers *Aylwin*, *Russell*, and *Hammann* slipped neatly around the *Yorktown*.[15]

The *Yorktown* weathered the torpedo attack without damage, but Fletcher did not yet know whether such good fortune attended the *Lexington*, now moving away while under assault by dive bombers. The *Yorktown*'s turn came at 1124, when a long string of dive bombers materialized high over the port beam. There began a deadly duel of wits between Buckmaster and fourteen pilots of the *Zuikaku* Carrier Bomber Squadron. Attacking one at a time in close succession, each plane appeared to aim for the island. Buckmaster waited until the pilot was committed in his dive, then swung the rudder hard over sharply toward the attacker to present only a narrow cross-deck target. Nearly every Japanese swooped to fifteen hundred feet or below before unleashing his bomb, which was easily visible as it plummeted toward the *Yorktown*. At the last second the personnel on the navigating and flag bridges hit the deck. By the time one bomber pulled out low over the water, Buckmaster already started jockeying to thwart the next assailant in line. In between the furious antiaircraft barrages, his shouts for course changes rang out to the flag bridge one deck below. An admiring Newsome watched the twisting *Yorktown* "making snakes in the water" with her wake. A dozen near misses smothered the carrier. Six bombs cleared the island by only a few feet. Their blasts heaved huge geysers close on the starboard side between the bow and the bridge and scattered bomb fragments all over the island. Lewis later joked, "Frank Jack and I could almost reach out and catch them. Right then I was resigned to the thought that I, from Lewis' Switch, Texas, was destined not to survive this war." Several close misses wildly rocked the ship and raised the stern clear out of the water. One to port caved in a seam under the armored deck and opened fuel tanks to the sea, leaving a long trail of oil. The *Yorktown* sustained only one hit. At 1127 a 250-kilogram semi–armor-piercing bomb sliced steeply through the flight deck amidships only fifteen feet out from the island and detonated just above the fourth deck deep inside the ship. The blast wiped out a repair party (sixty-six sailors killed or seriously wounded), caused considerable structural damage, and knocked out the air search radar. Thick black smoke billowed from the hole in the flight deck, but the fires were swiftly extinguished. Shrapnel venting the boiler intakes forced the engineers to secure three fire rooms, which reduced speed to twenty-five knots. No *Zuikaku* dive bombers succumbed to antiaircraft fire or fighters, but a VF-2 Wildcat knocked down one of two *Shōkaku* Type 99s that shifted over from the *Lexington* to dive against the *Yorktown*.[16]

The actual air attack subsided about 1131, although battles between defenders and retiring Japanese planes raged for several more minutes. The *Yorktown* and *Lexington* ended up about six miles apart, the *Lex* to the north. Fletcher tried raising Fitch, but the *Lexington* was not transmitting on TBS or the fighter director circuit. For anxious minutes the *Yorktown*'s radar was not working, and the *Chester*'s radar kept vigil. Pederson told the fighters: "Protect the force." It was obvious the *Lexington* was damaged, but as yet no one knew precisely how much. "At times the *Lex* was almost invisible due to bombs and torpedoes around her. They got shorts, splinters, and duds everywhere." Kinkaid's report offered an even more dramatic description: "Great clouds of smoke were pouring from her funnels and she was listing to port. Her speed was reduced only momentarily, the list was corrected promptly and she continued on at 25 knots and seemed to be under control. Great pools of fuel oil covered the surface of the water in her wake, and the air was filled with the sweetish odor of it mixed with the acrid fumes of gun powder." Nine torpedo planes scored two hits on the *Lexington*'s port side, although some thought there were as many as five. The first fish exploded underneath the forward gun gallery, jammed the one usable flight deck elevator in the up position and buckled the port aviation gasoline tanks, causing numerous leaks. The second torpedo caused more apparent damage by flooding several compartments that opened a list of 6 to 7 degrees to port. Water leaking into a trio of fire rooms forced three boilers to be shut down, reducing speed to 24.5 knots. Seventeen dive bombers attacked the *Lex*. One 242-kilogram high explosive "land" bomb, striking the corner of the flight deck forward, wiped out a 5-inch gun crew and ignited a tenacious fire in flag quarters. A second bomb, exploding high on the port side of the massive smoke stack, caused little damage. As with the *Yorktown*, near misses by bombs opened seams underwater. No other ship in TF-17 was damaged, although the *Minneapolis* evaded two torpedo planes that originally lunged at the *Lexington*.

To Fletcher the distant *Lexington* looked in good shape, and he knew the *Yorktown* could still steam and fight. As Poco Smith later wrote: "All in all, we seemed to have come out of this skirmish very well." With great relief Fletcher radioed Nimitz and Leary: "First enemy attack completed[,] no vital damage our force." He did not know whether the enemy carrier commander could say the same.[17]

THE LULL

The carriers attended to damage control and landed shot-up planes and those low on gasoline. Among those coming on board the *Lexington* was Dixon, just back from the vicinity of the Japanese carriers. Only gradually did the carriers account for all their defending planes. Twenty fighters (including three from the VF-2 strike escort that had to turn back early) and twenty-three SBDs fought for TF-17. Three F4Fs (two VF-2, one VF-42) and five SBDs (four *Yorktown*, one *Lexington*) failed to return. An SBD with a wounded pilot crashed into the water while trying to land on the *Lexington*. Numerous other planes were bullet-damaged, some beyond repair. Claims by U.S. aircraft numbered thirty-two planes, and antiaircraft gunners tallied another twenty-eight. The latest estimate is that defending aircraft accounted for perhaps ten (four carrier bombers and six carrier attack planes), whereas antiaircraft probably downed two carrier attack planes and a carrier bomber. Final Japanese losses were far higher because of ditched and jettisoned aircraft.[18]

Back on the air at 1151, Fitch ordered, "All ships close *Lexington* and rejoin formation." He desperately wanted to shorten the return leg of his strike planes. Busy conducting flight operations, the *Yorktown* could not approach the *Lex* for another hour. At 1204 Burch, leading the returning *Yorktown* strike SBDs, piped up that enemy fighters were attacking. "We need help!" Without a working radar the *Yorktown* had no idea where he was and whether fighters could even get to him. The erstwhile pursuers turned out to be escort F4Fs, and Burch soon had TF-17 in sight. Several encounters between returning strike planes turned out poorly for the Japanese. VF-42 escort fighters downed the gallant Kanno's search plane and finished off the carrier bomber flown by Takahashi, the strike leader. At 1210 Sherman tried raising his own attack leader, Cdr. Bill Ault, to ask for a strike report, but there was no answer. A few minutes later the *Lexington*'s radar detected incoming aircraft fifteen to twenty-five miles north. They proved to be the reappearing U.S. attack group. At 1220 Fitch gave Fletcher the first damage estimate for the *Lexington*. "Maximum speed 24; 2 torpedo hits possibly more port side; Number 4 fireroom flooded; Number 2 and 6 leaking but under control; all fires out; many casualties in both; flight deck elevators jammed up." The *Lex* appeared to be "steaming easily and having no apparent trouble." Buckmaster replied at 1221 with news on the *Yorktown*. "Maximum speed reduced to 25 knots due to damage of 3 boilers. One bomb hit." At 1222 he happily announced her radar was now working. Soon his engineers advised all boilers would shortly be on line. Commander Fitz-Gerald aptly described the mood of the moment in his diary: "Don't know how long this lull will last. It all depends upon how much damage our planes have done to the enemy carriers."[19]

The *Yorktown* dispatched a relief combat air patrol of three fighters and started recovering planes from the strike congregating overhead. The squadron commanders, as well as Schindler, the roving staff gunnery officer who fought with VS-5, hustled up to flag plot to brief Fletcher. On the way to the target the *Yorktown* torpedo planes encountered Joe Smith's search SBD returning to base. Smith (who had radio trouble) pointed the correct heading to the target. Around 1039 in the midst of a deep overcast, the *Yorktown* group found two carriers, six cruisers, and three destroyers moving south across an open space. One carrier, the smaller of the two, soon disappeared from view. The *Yorktown* leaders thought they hit the trailer hard with at least two 1,000-pound bombs and two torpedoes, leaving her afire forward and amidships. The bad news was that as far as they knew, no one attacked the lead carrier, because they never saw any *Lexington* strike planes. Both the strike pilots and those who flew in defense of TF-17 remarked on the numerous Zero fighters and their fierce tenacity. Many SBDs came back with their wings riddled and self-sealing fuel tanks punctured. Fletcher informed MacArthur of the hurt enemy carrier and requested his bombers attack. The message failed to include its position. A more comprehensive summary he sent to Nimitz, MacArthur, and King also provided no location for the enemy carriers, illustrating how distracted the TF-17 staff had to be. Advised by MacArthur of the oversight, Fletcher replied at 1344 with the estimated enemy position as of 1100. By then it was a very cold contact.[20]

By 1300 the *Yorktown* recovered thirty-five planes (five F4Fs, twenty-one SBDs, and nine TBDs) from her strike group, while one VF-42 F4F landed on the *Lexington*. Two SBDs failed to return and one ditched near the task force. Another shot-up Dauntless plowed spectacularly into the *Yorktown*'s stack. Arnold made preparations to re-arm the strike, but it took considerable time to check out the many bullet-damaged SBDs. At 1300 Fletcher closed the *Lexington* group a few miles northeast. In the meantime at 1243, still with no sign of her strike group, the *Lex* started clearing her flight deck by launching a relief combat air patrol of five F4Fs and Dixon with nine SBDs for anti-torpedo-plane patrol. During that takeoff a serious explosion forward and deep inside the ship thundered up through the bomb elevator. Outside the *Lexington* no one was aware of it, but the mishap spelled the beginning of the end of the gallant ship.

NO SECOND STRIKE

Fletcher continued to defer to Fitch, whom he placed in tactical command, but he thought long and hard about the overall situation. A message from Comsowespacfor received during the attack on TF-17 greatly added to his worries by signaling the renewed Japanese advance against Port Moresby. Thirteen large transports, escorted by a light cruiser and three destroyers, were seen at 1030 about forty miles southwest of Jomard Passage and headed southwest. Fletcher understood that if Crace adhered to the plan he broadcast the previous afternoon, the Support Group at dawn should have been about 160 miles from the convoy's reported position. Presumably Crace would attack. However, he must have help, particularly if carriers intervened. In fact Leary relayed the wrong position and omitted word that all Japanese ships, except for the Moresby striking force, were now thought to be well *north* of the Louisiades.[21] From the scanty information at hand it seemed to Fletcher that only one of two carriers of the Moresby striking force might be out of action. Since 1230, TF-17 monitored numerous enemy radio transmissions from the northeast that heralded the return of the Japanese first attack wave to its carriers. At 1252 Biard advised Fletcher that it appeared that one carrier was working the planes of the other carrier that was not transmitting, even though her own aircraft tried repeatedly to raise her.[22]

Fletcher deliberated whether to linger to launch a second attack that risked a second air assault. Otherwise he could withdraw southwest, regroup, and take on the carriers and the convoy the next dawn. The immediate situation with regard to the *Yorktown* Air Group was not promising. Less than a dozen SBDs and eight TBDs were operational, and for the latter only seven aerial torpedoes remained. Just seven VF-42 F4Fs were flyable (another was aloft on combat air patrol). Because of the strong Japanese fighter defense, a strike should go escorted, but that looked to be impossible. Defense of TF-17 must come first. Fighters and SBDs had to be ready to relieve those aloft that were low on fuel. Also the poor weather in the vicinity of the enemy carriers might make it difficult to find them again. Fletcher knew little of the *Lexington*'s situation, whether her strike ever attacked anything and when it might return. Besides, a ship that already suffered two torpedo hits was especially vulnerable. After the loss of the *Neosho*, fuel became another serious consideration. Thus Fletcher decided rather quickly against sticking around to launch a second strike. Poco Smith put it well: "Fletcher was forced to clear the area, get well south, fuel his units, ascertain damage, and lick wounds." At 1315 Fletcher queried Fitch. "In view enemy fighter plane superiority and undamaged carrier I propose retiring. What do you think?" Nine minutes later after talking it over with his staff, Fitch replied, "Affirmative."[23]

Part of the long-awaited *Lexington* strike group finally showed up. From 1322 to 1328 the *Lex* landed eleven VB-2 SBDs, Ens. Marvin M. Haschke's VS-2 SBD from Ault's command section, and a VF-2 F4F flown by Lt. Noel A. M. Gayler, who led the torpedo escort. There was no trace of the eleven VT-2 TBDs, the shortest-ranged of all the planes, three SBDs (including Ault's), and five VF-2 F4Fs. Commander Hamilton, commanding officer of VB-2, regretfully told Fitch and Sherman that he never found a target in the deep overcast and dumped his bombs to get back. Haschke could not add much other than the group command section split up while bombing what looked like an unhurt carrier. Well after the action, Gayler saw one undamaged carrier about fifteen miles west of the one that was burning. Fitch considered whether the *Lex* and *Yorktown* planes attacked the same carrier, or if more than two enemy carriers were present. Watching the *Lex* strike planes land, Fletcher advised Fitch: "Tomorrow may re-arm this ship with your planes and renew attack." He added at 1334: "As soon as all planes are recovered or hope given up head south-southwest at best practicable speed." That would position TF-17 on the flank of the invasion convoy and offered the advantage of drawing nearer to Crace and the Allied air bases. Fitch, though, was not ready to give up on VT-2, although Sherman feared the worst. Fitch advised Fletcher at 1341 that he was heading north to "close our returning planes." Fletcher wondered if there were any returning planes to find. "*Yorktown* reports all planes returned or hope given up." Growing impatient, he added: "When do you propose to head to the southward?" Fitch responded: "As soon as aircraft recovered." Fletcher trusted the judgment of his good friend, and so for the time being kept TF-17 in the area. He radioed Nimitz and Leary at 1352: "*Yorktown* can now make 30 knots. I propose retire tonight to fill *Yorktown* complement planes as far as possible from *Lexington* and send that ship to Pearl." In fact, that opportunity was gone forever.[24]

"SUSPEND ATTACK AND HEAD NORTH"

After the lead element of the *Yorktown* strike group sighted MO Striking Force in an open space between squalls, the two carriers separated while launching and recovering fighters.

Hara's flagship *Zuikaku*, screened by the two cruisers of Takagi's 5th Cruiser Division and three destroyers, drew nine thousand meters ahead of the *Shōkaku*, whose two escorting cruisers trailed eight thousand meters astern. At 1100 the *Zuikaku* group disappeared into a squall and escaped attack except by one strafing fighter, but twenty-four *Yorktown* SBDs set the *Shōkaku* afire with two 1,000-pound bombs at the cost of two SBDs shot down. Ably protecting VT-5, four VF-42 fighters shot down two defending Zeros without loss, but all nine TBDs fired their torpedoes from too great a range against the speedy *Shōkaku*. Emerging from the rainstorm Hara groaned when he saw her "burning furiously." His gloom was dispelled at 1125, when MO Striking Force got word from Takahashi that the "*Saratoga*" had sunk. At 1145 two *Lex* SBDs led by Ault put another 1,000-pound bomb into the *Shōkaku*'s tender topside, although she handily evaded all eleven torpedoes from Commander Brett's VT-2 TBDs. The other two SBDs found and attacked the *Zuikaku* but achieved only a near miss. The storms scattered the *Lexington* attackers, who lost three F4Fs and one SBD. Two other SBDs, including Ault's, and an F4F became disoriented in bad weather. Sixteen Zeros fought in the two air battles and claimed thirty-nine U.S. planes shot down for the loss of the two. It appears they actually accounted for two SBDs and three F4Fs from both strike groups.[25]

After the third bomb hit, the *Shōkaku*'s Captain Jōjima urgently requested permission to retire. A carrier that could not handle aircraft was of no use in battle except as a target. At 1210 the *Shōkaku* departed northeast at thirty knots, along with two heavy cruisers and two destroyers. After seeing the stricken flattop clear of the immediate area, all except one destroyer turned back. In the meantime the *Shōkaku* strike planes were told to land on the *Zuikaku*, but not all of them got the word. At 1240 Takagi ordered Hara to "reorganize combat strength, course approximately north," but MO Striking Force could not withdraw any time soon. The *Zuikaku* remained committed to heading southeast into the wind to recover the strike. Between 1310 and 1410 she landed forty-six aircraft from both carriers, but delays in striking aircraft below into the hangar (Japanese carriers did not park planes on their flight decks) forced deck crew to push a dozen shot-up planes over the side. Seven other planes ditched. At 1430 Hara counted just nine carrier bombers and carrier attack planes available for a second strike. Only two heavy cruisers and one destroyer actually screened the *Zuikaku*. The two prior aborted fueling efforts left Takagi deeply worried about oil. His two cruisers were at 50 percent, but some of the destroyers dipped as low as 20 percent. On the positive side, returning strike crews insisted that they sank the *Saratoga*-class carrier, and that more than three bombs struck the *Yorktown*-class carrier, "Enough to practically assure sinking." In addition they claimed torpedoing a battleship and damaging a light cruiser. Takagi reported to Inoue at 1430 there were "no prospects for a second attack today," but he also probably thought a second strike was not necessary. Thirty minutes later he turned MO Striking Force north.[26]

South Seas Force radioed orders at 1545 to "suspend attack and head north," thus ratifying Takagi's decision to retire. All morning Inoue had been nervous about advancing until his forces ended the threat the U.S. carrier force poised south of the Louisiades. At 1030 he instructed all forces not immediately involved in the carrier battle to withdraw northeast. Shortly afterward he learned that a Rabaul-based search plane discovered an enemy battleship, two cruisers, and four destroyers prowling southwest between the Louisiades and Port Moresby. That was Crace's Support Group, again magnified by an over-anxious search crew. Because the U.S. carriers were out of range, the 5th Air Attack Force intended to send bombers against the battleship group, but heavy rains pinned them to the ground at Rabaul. Once Inoue heard of the *Shōkaku*'s pounding, the severe plane losses, and that Takagi canceled a second strike, he decided to break off the battle, even though he sank two enemy carriers or at least knocked them out of action. Without direct air cover, the slow invasion convoy was especially vulnerable to his great bugbear land-based air, and he worried the supposed battleship group spotted southwest of the Louisiades might also include an undamaged carrier. Inoue's staff still had not sorted out the Allied deployment after all the confusion of the previous day. At 1620 he formally postponed the invasion of Port Moresby and directed the seaplane base at Deboyne be evacuated. Port Moresby would fall another day. The forces assigned to the RY Operation, which included MO Striking Force and part of Shima's old Tulagi Invasion Force, were to reassemble northeast of the Solomons to support the capture of Ocean and Nauru islands on 15 May. That part of the original plan, at least, would go ahead. Fletcher did not know it yet, but he had won the Battle of the Coral Sea.[27]

"THIS SHIP NEEDS HELP"

At 1355, while Fletcher waited for the rest of the *Lexington* strike group to show up or for Fitch to relent and withdraw, the *Lex* signaled ominously "fires are not out." Before Fletcher could get further details, a formation of unidentified torpedo planes approached from the north without the proper recognition maneuvers. The *Yorktown* briefly opened antiaircraft fire before it was realized the intruders were the long awaited VT-2 TBDs running on fumes. Everyone was elated to see them. Sherman, for one, thought the whole squadron might have gone in the water. While they shuffled into the landing circle, the *Lex* passed fighter direction to the *Yorktown* because she could no longer train her radar. By 1413 the *Lexington* landed ten TBDs and one F4F. Another VT-2 TBD ditched twenty miles northwest. Fitch dispatched the *Dewey* in an unsuccessful attempt to find its crew. In the meantime he changed course southwest at twenty-five knots. It was time to go. Up in flag plot Stroop plotted the direct course to Brisbane, the closest refuge for the failing carrier.[28]

At 1422 Fitch dropped a bombshell. "Strong indications additional enemy carrier has joined up." He later explained that his information came from Fullinwider's radio intelligence team. Biard in the *Yorktown* made no such finding, but Fletcher could not afford to take any chances. Besides, Fitch had reason other than Fullinwider to think more Japanese carriers might be present. The newly returned VT-2 pilots claimed five torpedo hits on a carrier they swore was previously untouched. That corroborated Gayler's report. Moreover, Lt. Edwin W. Hurst, the VT-2 executive officer, told Fitch that he saw yet another undamaged carrier twenty miles south of the one VT-2 attacked. At 1432 Fletcher relayed that discouraging word to Nimitz and Leary. The *Yorktown* pilots insisted the carrier they plastered was the *Kaga*, so perhaps she showed up after all. Another candidate was the auxiliary carrier *Kasuga Maru* that Cincpac listed as a possible participant. She was thought to have reached at least the northern Solomons. Not formidable in her own right, the *Kasuga*

Maru could still recover planes that otherwise might have been lost. Fullinwider and the *Lexington* aviators were wrong. The Japanese in truth enjoyed no carrier reinforcements. At least photos taken by the *Yorktown* strike crews decisively demonstrated the carrier they attacked was badly damaged. Fletcher radioed Nimitz and MacArthur a reassessment of four or probably more torpedo and three 1,000-pound bomb hits that left one carrier "burning badly." As yet he did not know the *Lex*'s possible score.[29]

At 1434 the *Lexington* ominously advised that her coding room was "temporarily out of commission" and requested the *Yorktown* relay important radio messages. That turned out to be her last TBS transmission. Fires raging forward under the hangar deck threatened the ship, though no word of this peril was vouchsafed to Fletcher. He pondered another possible way to get at the enemy massing to the north. A second air strike still seemed out of the question for all the reasons noted previously. That left a possible night surface attack by the cruisers and destroyers in Kinkaid's Attack Group. The delay in withdrawing TF-17 meant the enemy carriers, perhaps 135 miles north, might still be in reach of a surface force if it had enough fuel for high-speed steaming. At 1442 Fletcher queried his destroyer squadron commanders, Early in the *Phelps* and Hoover in the *Morris*. "Am considering night surface attack. Will your fuel situation permit? Assume that high speed will be required most of tomorrow and fuel from cruisers the day after." Before Fletcher heard back, the worsening situation on the *Lexington* finally became manifest. At 1442 black smoke billowed underneath the flight deck as result of a second big explosion. It was now evident the great warship faced mortal jeopardy. Sherman briefly hoisted the breakdown flag and signaled at 1450: "Fire amidships is not under control." Five minutes later, after great clouds of smoke streamed from aft and out of the stack, Sherman changed the flag hoist to: "This ship needs help." Fletcher inquired, "What assistance is practicable?" Observing the F4Fs, SBDs, and TBDs parked aft on the *Lexington*'s flight deck, he also asked how many fighters she could launch, if indeed she could still handle planes. Things, though, had gone too far for that. Fletcher warned MacArthur: "*Lexington* condition much worse" and requested "all possible air coverage." He gave his position, course, and speed of twenty knots, but cautioned "may have to slow."[30]

At 1510 Fletcher resumed tactical command from Fitch and ordered three destroyers to assist the *Lexington*. The *Phelps*, *Morris*, and *Anderson* approached the stricken carrier. After Sherman requested ships on hand pick up personnel if necessary, Kinkaid also stayed close with the *Minneapolis* and *New Orleans*. At 1512 *Yorktown* deployed a relief combat air patrol of four F4Fs and ten SBDs for anti-torpedo-plane patrol, then landed planes, including five F4Fs and nine SBDs from the *Lexington*. Lt. Cdr. Charles R. Fenton, commanding officer of VF-42, took a section of fighters out fifteen miles to check if the *Yorktown*'s YE homing signal was working properly—a vital consideration if the *Yorktown* had to launch a strike group. Another huge blast inside the *Lexington* blew out hull plating near the fire rooms and damaged the boiler uptakes. Water pressure in the hangar deck fire curtains failed and released a great surge of flames. Sherman no longer could control the rudder. He tried to steer with the engines to place the wind at right angles and blow the smoke away from the ship.[31]

Not knowing how long the *Lexington* could keep up, Fletcher divided TF-17 to retain part of the force ready for combat. The *Astoria* (Smith's flagship), *Chester*, and *Portland* remained with the *Yorktown*. Reorganizing the destroyers took more time. Early and Hoover agreed that Hoover would support the *Lexington* with the *Morris*, *Hammann*, and *Anderson*, while the *Phelps* stood by should Fletcher need her for "tonight's work." Early thought the *Phelps* and the two *Farragut*-class destroyers, *Aylwin* and the temporarily absent *Dewey*, had "plenty of fuel" for a night sortie.[32] Because of the failing *Lex*, Fletcher shelved plans for a surface attack. She careened wildly through the formation, forcing escorts out of her way. At 1600 after another massive blast, the *Lexington* blew off steam, slowed, and finally drifted broadside in the gentle swell. Fletcher pulled off with his three cruisers and three destroyers to maneuver in the vicinity, while Kinkaid with the other two cruisers and three destroyers kept close contact with the *Lex*. "Utilize as necessary," he told Kinkaid, "if *Lexington* must be abandoned." Lines snaked down her side, and the evacuation of wounded and non-essential personnel began. Through Hoover in the *Morris*, Fitch advised Fletcher that the fire was out of control, and the crew was coming up on deck. Hoses and pumps no longer had power, and fire-fighting assistance from destroyers alongside was insufficient to stem the conflagration consuming the *Lex*. Her loss was now only a matter of time. At 1700 the *Yorktown* suddenly became apprehensive of imminent air attack, either from radar or Biard's radio intercepts. Seven F4Fs raced skyward to augment the four F4Fs and ten SBDs already aloft. Biard reported to Fletcher at 1702 that one enemy carrier announced: "There is a chance. There is a chance. There is a chance." Fletcher in turn warned TF-17: "Prepare to repel air attack." Nothing came of the sudden alert, but it could be seen that the *Lexington*'s crew was abandoning ship.[33]

At least the situation vis-à-vis the Port Moresby invasion convoy had been resolved. Fletcher heard first from an AAF search plane, later confirmed by MacArthur, that the transports actually lurked that afternoon up near Kiriwina, 180 miles north of Jomard Passage, and were retiring northwest under bombing attacks from Moresby-based planes. That removed the immediate threat to Port Moresby and the need for TF-17 to rush west to help Crace fight off an invasion. Fletcher could afford to take his time and hopefully enhance the combat readiness of the *Yorktown* and her planes. For his own part Crace spent the day steaming south wondering what was happening to Fletcher. He hoped to fuel if the situation remained quiet, but repeated aircraft contacts kept TG-17.3 on edge. That afternoon he learned from radio traffic that the TF-17 aviators hit one carrier hard, but that a third carrier might have reinforced the Japanese. Meanwhile the *Hobart* and the three destroyers faced a "very bad" fuel situation, but Crace did not yet feel secure enough to provide them oil. To add to his troubles the *Walke* stripped the reduction gear in her starboard engine. Finally that evening with the definite evidence the invasion convoy had withdrawn, Crace authorized the *Hobart* to fuel the *Perkins*, then escort the stricken *Walke* to Townsville. He hoped in the next day or two to fuel the *Australia*, *Chicago*, and *Perkins* from the *Kurumba* at Cid Harbor about 130 miles north of Townsville.[34]

A SAD SIGHT

If for Crace the final phase of the Battle of the Coral Sea was anticlimactic, the rest of TF-17 faced one more ordeal. Once Fletcher realized that Fitch was abandoning the *Lexington*, he ordered Kinkaid to "take charge and expedite getting personnel off." The nearly three thousand crew would need considerable time to abandon ship and reach the rescue ships. Once the sun set in an hour, the flaming carrier would be a beacon for the enemy. After another massive explosion at 1737, Fletcher detached Early and two more destroyers to the *Lex*, leaving him just the *Russell*. In case the rescue group got separated during the night, he set a rendezvous well southward for 0700 the next morning. It was sickening to witness the death throes of the giant warship. Poco Smith recalled how the fire gradually overtook the planes parked aft. They "turned a reddish brown, and 'popped' one after another, like cockroaches on a hot griddle." Circling overhead on combat air patrol, Lieutenant Leonard of VF-42 was amazed how "fires, explosions large and small, debris blowing over the side made her look like hell afloat." Fortunately the crew left in timely and remarkably orderly fashion. Aided by a gentle sea, they stayed afloat long enough for small boats to transfer nearly all to the nearby screening ships.[35]

The sun set at 1818, and the *Yorktown* landed the last aircraft. The biggest explosion yet ripped the *Lexington*'s topside. "The whole flight deck seemed to heave into the air—burning planes, girders, and debris rained down." The stern was a mass of flames, and the hull glowed cherry red in spots. Sherman and his senior officers were still on board conducting their final inspection. Fletcher directed Kinkaid to sink the *Lexington* with torpedoes, then rejoin the main body to southward when he could. It had to be one of the hardest orders Fletcher ever gave. Certain no living crewman was left on board, Sherman finally left the *Lex* at 1830 and joined Kinkaid and Fitch in the *Minneapolis*. After carefully checking the sea for survivors, the rescue ships sheered off to rejoin the main body. They brought 2,770 men, 92 percent of the *Lexington*'s complement. The completeness of the rescue brought grim pride in what otherwise was a tragedy for the navy and the nation. The *Phelps* received the task of sinking the *Lex*. At 1915 Early fired five torpedoes into the flaming mass, which refused to sink. Finally at 1952 the *Lexington* rolled over and slipped beneath the sea. A tremendous underwater explosion caused Early to think the *Phelps*'s stern had been blown off. The concussion reverberated as far as twenty miles, where it was felt by the rest of TF-17. By 2027 all but the *Phelps* had caught up. Fletcher headed south at twenty knots, while the *Portland* and *Morris* followed more slowly, while transferring survivors.[36]

THE VIEW FROM ON HIGH

That evening after leaving Kinkaid to his dreary duty, a somber Fletcher was composing the message to inform Cincpac of the sinking of the *Lexington*, when he received one from Nimitz. "Congratulations on your glorious accomplishments of the last two days. Your aggressive actions have the admiration of the entire Pacific Fleet. Well done to you and your officers and men. You have filled our hearts with pride and have maintained the highest traditions of the Navy." Although warmly appreciated, Cincpac's praise rang hollow with the loss of the *Lex*. The message Fletcher sent at 1938 to Nimitz and Leary explained that after an internal explosion, "cause unknown," the *Lexington* burned and sank. "Believe majority of personnel rescued." TF-17 retired southward. The *Yorktown* had thirty-five operational planes (fifteen fighters, twelve dive bombers, and eight torpedo planes), with a dozen more SBDs usable after repairs. Although the *Yorktown* also suffered underwater damage, it was "probably unimportant." Finally Fletcher cautioned: "It is necessary to refrain from offensive action for two or three days to make necessary minor repairs." As will be shown, perhaps as many as thirty-six hours elapsed before Nimitz actually knew of the loss of the *Lexington*.[37]

Seven May at Pearl, 8 May in the Coral Sea, was an important day for Cincpac, not only for the battle it seemed his forces were winning, but also because he formally assumed command of the Pacific Ocean Areas. That evening he summarized for King, Leary, and Halsey the progress of the battle from the information at hand. A Japanese carrier went down the previous day. That day one enemy carrier was surely crippled, the *Yorktown* and *Lexington* damaged, the *Lex* severely. Fletcher's fuel situation was "critical." TF-17 might confront two carriers the next day with only the *Yorktown* in shape to fight. "Halsey's position indeterminate but estimate can't reach Coral Sea before 11th Washington date at earliest." Nimitz urged King to furnish the necessary carrier aircraft "to make good heavy plane losses and to provide a proper reserve for the actions which we know will follow." In turn McCormick's War Plans Section chalked up a "red letter day." Despite the damaged *Lexington*, the two-to-one odds facing the *Yorktown*, and the delay before Halsey's arrival in the Coral Sea, the situation was "generally favorable."[38]

Although Nimitz was unwittingly ignorant of the final phase of the Battle of the Coral Sea, his counterpart Yamamoto certainly was not. On the evening of 8 May as MO Striking Force withdrew north to refuel, Hara transmitted a lengthy summary of the battle. Takagi noted the lack of planes in the *Zuikaku*. "The situation indicated above does not allow any prospects for carrying out attacks on 9 May." Inoue announced to Combined Fleet that he postponed the MO Operation, because of the loss of the *Shōhō* and damage to the *Shōkaku*, and requested Yamamoto's approval. The RY Operation against Ocean and Nauru would proceed as planned. Inoue's tale of woe fell like a ton of bricks on the Combined Fleet staff, who believed his forces sank one U.S. carrier, probably finished off another carrier, and routed the remnants. Inoue must renew the battle and seize Port Moresby. At 2200 Yamamoto ordered Inoue: "On this occasion you are requested to destroy the enemy to the fullest extent of your power." This "request" caused consternation at South Seas Force headquarters. Inoue issued new orders. Marumo's Support Force was to suspend the evacuation of the advance seaplane base at Deboyne and use its float planes to find and attack enemy ships. The MO Striking Force would fuel, then search on the morning of 9 May for enemy forces. Gotō was to take two heavy cruisers of the 6th Cruiser Division and most of the 6th Destroyer Squadron to cooperate with MO Striking Force and destroy the enemy. Inoue did not indicate just when he might resume the advance on Port Moresby, and Yamamoto would discover simply ordering something was not the same as accomplishing it. Port Moresby was out of reach, and there was nothing the Japanese could immediately do about it.[39]

A CRITIQUE

In his private diary rewritten after the loss of the *Lexington*, Ted Sherman described the action on 8 May as "well fought" and "couldn't have been done differently." By the time his book *Combat Command* appeared in 1950, though, he discovered many reasons to castigate Fletcher's handling of TF-17 on 8 May. That afternoon, while the *Lexington* fought her losing battle against the fires, the *Yorktown* enjoyed a "practically intact" air group further reinforced by the *Lexington* planes still aloft. "In spite of this no further search was made for the enemy carriers nor were any additional attacks sent off." Sherman brushed off any question of retaining aircraft for defense. "No Japanese aircraft came near us during the afternoon." Forrest Biard's memoir described Fletcher's inaction on 8 May in much the same acerbic terms as 7 May. The admiral need only have followed his advice to score a great victory. Biard averred that beginning around 1230 he told Fletcher the *Zuikaku* was busy recovering *Shōkaku* planes as well as her own, meaning the *Shōkaku* had to be at least temporarily disabled. "After presenting the evidence for this I argued for another strike, a strike that should be able to get both carriers." The opportunity for surprise was especially favorable after 1315, when he intercepted a report from the *Zuikaku* that one U.S. carrier was sunk and another badly damaged. "I felt confident that we should be able to give the Nips a truly smashing surprise." However, Fletcher balked at "making a difficult decision" and "did nothing." Soon the *Lexington*'s deteriorating condition compelled him to deal with her, rather than attacking the enemy as he should have done. The criticism of National Security Agency historian Frederick Parker was more general. "Fletcher and Inouye were apparently unable to assimilate and evaluate the unique and voluminous reports both undoubtedly received from COMINT and other sources about plane losses and carrier damage sustained by their enemy counterpart. Accordingly, each chose similar courses of action late in the afternoon of 8 May: each broke contact with the enemy and retired from the scene." Parker even insinuated that Fletcher invented the third carrier on 8 May as an excuse to cut and run. "Sensing that his intentions to retire might be misunderstood, Fletcher also advised Nimitz and MacArthur that 'another enemy carrier has joined enemy force.'" Parker did not elaborate, so the logical inference is that third carrier had to be the product of Fletcher's imagination. Of course, Fitch actually advised Fletcher of the suspected presence of an additional carrier.[40]

So what were the prospects for TF-17 staying to fight on the afternoon of 8 May? Sherman and Biard ignored the practical aspects of their recommended course of action. The *Yorktown* Air Group was far from "practically intact." Many fighters and dive bombers were temporarily out of commission from battle damage. An immediate search-attack mission would have counted less than a dozen SBDs and seven vulnerable TBDs, but no F4Fs to escort them into the teeth of fierce fighter opposition that already filled the *Yorktown*'s hangar with shot-up SBDs and F4Fs. The weather in the vicinity of the Japanese carriers was poor, and the fact that they were homing their airplanes meant that their aviators, too, had trouble finding their way back. Fletcher had no idea what damage the *Lexington* strike group inflicted on 8 May, except later from a radio message from the missing Commander Ault who reported one bomb hit on a carrier. Also at least for the time being, Fletcher deferred to Fitch. Biard, who asserted the change in tactical command took place the day before, recalled Fletcher responding on the afternoon of 7 May to his recommendation then for a second strike: "No, that is not for me to decide. My friend and classmate, Admiral Fitch, has been given tactical command. I trust his judgment completely." That statement fitted much better the circumstances on 8 May.[41]

Once the *Lexington* faltered and the presence of a fresh Japanese carrier was suspected, there could be no second air strike. Besides it was late in the day for search-attack missions into bad weather. Fletcher's only offensive option at that point was a night surface attack by Kinkaid's cruisers and destroyers, but if the enemy possessed one or even two undamaged carriers that option was highly dubious. Their location was only known in general terms, so the Attack Group would have to search for them. That risked being spotted before evening and subjected to carrier attack, not to mention losing the vital factor of surprise. The Moresby striking force could simply avoid combat if it chose. Besides, given the condition of the *Lexington* after 1442, it did not seem wise to detach any ships from TF-17. With justification Fletcher explained: "It is believed that the decision not to renew the attack on the eighth, although probably based on incorrect information, resulted in saving the lives of 92 percent of *Lexington*'s personnel, a large portion of which would have been lost if the Attack Group had not been present when the ship sank."[42]

Parker's claim that on the afternoon of 8 May Fletcher received "unique and voluminous reports" from comint and other intelligence sources regarding the condition of the Japanese carriers is not borne out by the documents. At 1210 Belconnen radioed the text of an urgent plain language transmission, rebroadcast by a Tokyo station, in which a Japanese plane, call sign *Kame Kame* 1 ("believed to be VT," but actually Commander Takahashi's carrier bomber), reported the *Saratoga* was sunk. Biard and very likely Fullinwider heard this Japanese transmission as well. Beginning at 1240 ships in TF-17 used radio direction finding to deduce that an enemy ship was transmitting from bearing 010 degrees. Biard heard from Japanese radio messages that at least one plane was ditching near the enemy task force. Shortly thereafter one carrier, which he believed to be the *Zuikaku*, worked the planes of the other carrier, thought to be the *Shōkaku*. At 1315 Tokyo relayed a plain language message from the Commander, Striking Force (call sign Moo1), to the 5th Air Attack Corps, Gunboat Division 8, Comcrudiv Six (the first mention of the 6th Cruiser Division being present), and Commander in Chief Fourth Fleet, which stated: "In addition to sinking one carrier we're sure there were 3 hits on one other. 0920 position 14-40, 155-50, approximate speed 16. 1100 [1300 Z–11]." At 1335 the daily Cincpac intelligence bulletin noted that the striking force south of the Solomons included the 5th Carrier Divisions and the 5th, 6th, and 18th Cruiser Divisions. The carrier *Ryukaku* was also perhaps in the New Britain area, and the converted carrier *Kasuga Maru* had arrived at Buka north of Bougainville. It appeared that Ocean and Nauru were targeted for early invasion. At 1536 Biard reported to Fletcher that the *Zuikaku* evidently stopped trying to home missing planes, and at 1600 the *Shōkaku* requested the *Zuikaku* to relay her messages. He called the *Shōkaku*'s transmitter "definitely an emergency rig." The "sending" was "slow and unsteady." That only confirmed what Fletcher knew before, that one carrier was hard-hit.[43]

The above messages constituted *all* of the comint furnished to Fletcher on the afternoon and evening of 8 May. Not even the analysts at Pearl and Melbourne secured much more that day. Only late that evening did Hypo provide Belconnen and the Copek addressees the partial text of a message that Hara sent summarizing the 7 May action. Not until the next morning (9 May in the Coral Sea, 8 May at Pearl) did Hypo start relaying on the Copek network decrypts derived from messages sent by Takagi and Hara the night before. Those messages offered the first detailed summaries for the 8 May action: claims, damaged incurred, plane strengths, and losses. Very little of this was ever provided to Fletcher, and it never played a role in his decision on 8 May to withdraw.[44]

As Morison stated, the Battle of the Coral Sea, the very first carrier-versus-carrier battle in history, was "a tactical victory for the Japanese but a strategic victory for the United States." He should have added "and the Allies," because the Australians certainly played an important, if underappreciated, role. Had the invasion troops got through to Port Moresby, they would have almost certainly overwhelmed the smaller, poorly trained Australian garrison. The cost of Fletcher's victory was severe: the *Lexington* and destroyer *Sims* sunk, oiler *Neosho* fatally damaged, and seventy carrier aircraft lost. The *Yorktown* suffered a bomb blast deep in her vitals, and additional hull damage left a long trail of oil in her wake. The loss of the *Lex* was due to a material defect, not any leadership failing. Fumes from leaking aviation gasoline tanks penetrated a compartment where electric generators were left running. The resulting explosion doomed the great carrier. Sherman described it as "a losing battle from the beginning, but we did not know it then. We fully expected to save the carrier." In some respects the prebattle expectations of the U.S. Navy were exaggerated, as Commander Fitz-Gerald on the *New Orleans* aptly chided in his diary: "We cannot expect to engage superior enemy forces and get away without some losses." Tactical defeat or no, Fletcher certainly accomplished his mission to prevent the invasion of Port Moresby. The Battle of the Coral Sea represented the first major Japanese strategic reverse of the war. For its part the South Seas Force lost the light carrier *Shōhō* on 7 May and on 8 May suffered heavy damage to the big carrier *Shōkaku* that put her in the repair yard for nearly three months. Both carriers were scheduled to participate in the Midway offensive in early June. So was the *Zuikaku*. Although undamaged, she suffered heavy plane losses that would keep her out of the next battle. Thus not only did the MO Operation miscarry, but Japan also lost the services, at least temporarily, of all three carriers to one for the Americans. That alone reverses the common judgment of Fletcher's so-called tactical defeat. Less than four weeks later the gallant *Yorktown* would help win another desperate battle that only crowned the Allied victory in the Coral Sea.[45]

CHAPTER 15

From the Coral Sea to Pearl Harbor

"WE ARE ALL SHORT OF OIL, RUNNING LIKE HELL"

Grateful for the cover of darkness, Fletcher's battered TF-17 withdrew late on 8 May south into the Coral Sea. Because Port Moresby was spared assault, the Battle of Coral Sea was an Allied victory. Leary confirmed early on 9 May that the invasion convoy remained in retreat. Whether the same was true for the Moresby striking force, no one could say. Fletcher knew *Yorktown* planes pounded one carrier on 8 May but heard nothing of what the *Lex* strike might have accomplished other than Commander Ault's radio report of a bomb hit on an unidentified carrier. There were strong indications of the presence of a third Japanese carrier. Given the shaky condition of TF-17, Fletcher had no desire to renew battle immediately. The 2,770 *Lexington* survivors crowding the screening ships seriously affected their ability to fight. Halsey's TF-16 (*Enterprise* and *Hornet*) neared the New Hebrides from the northeast but needed three days or more to intervene in the Coral Sea. Fletcher sought to clear any pursuit, redistribute survivors, and fuel thirsty destroyers from the cruisers.

At dawn on 9 May the *Yorktown* sent a dozen SBDs northward seeking pursuers. After her radar failed, Fletcher relied on the *Chester*'s CXAM radar. However, he took the unusual precaution of deploying a destroyer as radar picket, stationing the *Russell* twenty miles astern. Captain Early noted how the "situation is very wearing on the nerves." The *Portland*, *Morris*, and *Phelps*, detached the previous evening in connection with the loss of the *Lex*, rejoined without incident. Around 0900 Lt. (jg) Frederic L. Faulkner of VS-5 spotted a carrier force bearing 310 degrees and 175 miles from TF-17 and on course 110 degrees, speed twenty-five knots. His radio cut out in the midst of the transmission, leading listeners in the *Yorktown* to speculate whether he was shot down. His wingman, Ens. Laurence G. Traynor, completed the message.[1]

With enemy carriers in hot pursuit, Fletcher rang up twenty-five knots, formed the ships into the Victor disposition, and called the senior aviators to flag plot. The *Yorktown* had sixteen SBDs and seven TBDs available to attack. The vital need to defend TF-17 precluded a fighter escort. According to Joe Taylor, Fletcher declared: "In spite of what we've been through, it looks as though we're not going to get away with it. But by God, we'll go down like Americans." The tactical situation, with TF-17 steaming away at nearly top speed, would compel an extremely long strike mission. The SBDs might get back "if we yet are still afloat," but Taylor's TBDs had no chance. They would have to try to get as close as they could to the coast of Australia before ditching. Thus Fletcher reserved the option of counterattack only if the enemy was about to attack. Commander Dixon volunteered to lead a preemptive search-strike mission of four SBDs to pinpoint the enemy carriers. Fletcher agreed. He detached the destroyer *Aylwin* to fall back twenty miles on the port quarter to join the radar watch and help to guide returning planes. Ens. Harry Frederickson of VB-5 wrote in his diary: "We fully expected to be attacked and everyone was very down hearted and scared." At 0936 while the strike was being organized the *Chester* warned of bogeys on radar. Fletcher increased speed to twenty-eight knots, "As high as he dared," Kinkaid later wrote, with destroyer fuel so "desperately low." Fletcher ordered them to report their fuel every four hours instead of once a day. Under routine circumstances the cruisers could have provided oil, but not with the enemy breathing down on them. Commander Fitz-Gerald wrote in his diary, "We are all short of oil, running like hell."[2] Smith declared only Fletcher's careful attention to fueling permitted that high-speed run on the ninth. Armed with 1,000-pound bombs, Dixon and three other very courageous VS-2 orphans departed around 1000. Soon after, Fletcher learned with relief that Biard's radio intelligence unit never intercepted any search reports. At 1042 he advised Fitch and Kinkaid in the *Minneapolis* that it was "very doubtful whether we were spotted."[3]

Aided by the broad oil slick that trailed the *Yorktown* for fifty miles, Faulkner and Traynor found TF-17 around 1130. Faulkner quickly briefed Fletcher and his staff. Determined to get air support from Australia but unwilling to break radio silence, Fletcher told Commander Schindler, his much-traveled staff gunnery officer: "I want you to go to Australia. Your plane will leave in ten minutes." He told him to fly to the air base at Rockhampton about 350 miles southwest, contact MacArthur or Leary, and request an immediate strike by AAF bombers at Townsville. Schindler's ride turned out to be a bullet-holed SBD flown by another patched-up veteran, Lt. (jg) Hugh W. Nicholson, slightly wounded the previous day. Cdr. Dixie Kiefer, the *Yorktown*'s beloved executive officer, and several VS-5 pilots accosted Schindler while he grabbed his flight gear; they pinned aviator wings on his chest as a token of their respect for his five combat flights. Schindler and Nicholson departed about 1240. Fletcher told them not to try to return to the ship that day, but to make their way back the best they could.[4]

That afternoon Fletcher received Cincpac orders to withdraw "old" TF-17 (*Yorktown, Astoria, Portland, Chester*, and four destroyers), plus the *Lexington*, to the West Coast "if practicable," otherwise to Pearl. Fuel would be available at Tongatabu. Kinkaid's two cruisers and the Desron One destroyers from former TF-11 were to join Halsey for round two. Obviously Nimitz never received Fletcher's message reporting the loss of the *Lexington*. Fletcher could not again break radio silence to correct him; nor was he yet sure whether he would get TF-17 out of the Coral Sea intact. During the tension-filled afternoon, the two picket destroyers *Russell* and *Aylwin* failed to appear. That was understandable. As far as they knew, TF-17 was only going to advance at eighteen knots on 140 degrees. Fletcher detached the *New Orleans* to act as shepherd. She found both destroyers huddled together and led them home.[5]

Dixon's strike returned after a long search having sighted nothing but a "mesa type reef," where white water resembled ship wakes. Fletcher still could not be sure that was what Faulkner actually saw. He posed two alternatives to Kinkaid and Fitch. If he could assume the carriers had given up, he would fuel the destroyers by moonlight while proceeding east to Nouméa. But if there was reason to believe the Japanese pressed on, he would release the destroyers to Brisbane for fuel and run south with the heavy ships for Sydney. Meanwhile, he finally learned from Fitch that the *Lexington* strike the previous day claimed hits on the *Shōkaku* by two 1,000-pound bombs and at least five torpedoes. "Carrier was on fire and still circling when last seen but believed to be sunk." Fitch also explained that "intercepted traffic by *Lex* RI Unit further indicates this and that another carrier from north joined remaining *Zuikaku* yesterday afternoon." In turn Fitch and Kinkaid recommended making for Nouméa, "Unless information definitely indicates carriers are heading this way." Fletcher concurred. He reduced speed to twenty knots to conserve fuel. Having steamed southeast all day, TF-17 was now six hundred miles west of Nouméa. At 1655 a message from Leary confirmed that Schindler came through. "Will send all available planes to attack." Fourteen bombers checked the waters east of Townsville without success until dark. Fletcher finally accepted that Faulkner spotted Lihou Reef, mistaking "rocks for ships and breakers for wakes." He asked Faulkner if he could have been mistaken. Faulkner decided that he was. Relieved, Fletcher replied: "That's all I wanted to know." That evening TF-17 monitored what sounded like radio signals from a nearby carrier. Although that jangled nerves again, nothing further developed. The 9 May scare might have been an "amusing incident" as Morison called it, but only well after the fact. Dixon's valiant flight never received the credit it deserved. That night Kiefer handed out "grog" to the exhausted pilots, "which made everyone happy."[6]

Fletcher planned to fuel the destroyers on 10 May and redistribute the *Lexington* survivors to Smith's cruisers. Kinkaid would then proceed to Nouméa to join Halsey, while TF-17 stopped at Tongatabu for fuel before continuing north. The Support Group was also to report to Leary. Fletcher prepared dispatches advising Nimitz, Leary, and Crace and arranged for two SOCs from the *New Orleans* to fly them to Nouméa the following morning. The message to Crace offered his apology. "Sorry to leave you in precarious position and congratulate you on your victory over bombers. Thank you for your unselfish and efficient cooperation." On 10 May more false alarms kept TF-17 on edge for several hours and prevented fueling of destroyers. Radar detected bogeys, later identified as B-17s, crossing the Coral Sea from New Caledonia to Australia. Commander Fitz-Gerald in the *New Orleans* mused, "From the way things have been going for the past 48 hours we all have begun to think that Fletcher has cracked up." Sherman complained that Fletcher continued to "run from our shadows." Even under the threat of attack, he did not exactly "run." He dropped to fifteen knots to save fuel. Low on fuel and therefore lacking stability, at least two destroyers took on water ballast.[7]

At Yamamoto's express order, Takagi's MO Striking Force, with Hara's flagship *Zuikaku* as its main fighting component, sought to reopen the battle on 10 May. Takagi spent 9 May fueling west of Tulagi. Thinking all U.S. carriers were sunk, Inoue ordered him to find and attack, "to the fullest extent of strength," any battleships and cruisers that foolishly remained behind. That evening as the Port Moresby invasion convoy dropped anchor at Rabaul, MO Striking Force moved south into the Coral Sea. By that time the *Zuikaku*'s operational plane strength grew to forty-five planes (twenty-four fighters, thirteen carrier bombers, and eight carrier attack planes). Before dawn on 10 May, from 340 miles southwest of Tulagi, she launched eight fighters to search 250 miles to southward. At that time TF-17 was more than 450 miles farther south. The search sighted only forlorn *Neosho*, decks awash and drifting without power. Previous errors by the *Neosho* in reporting her position led the *Monaghan* astray and delayed the rescue. Takagi judged the oiler a waste of bombs, thus sparing the *Neosho* until the destroyer *Henley* appeared the next day, recovered her crew and sank her. At 1230 Takagi changed course northeast to cut back around San Cristóbal on 11 May, close Rabaul from the southeast, and finally complete delivery of the Zero fighter reinforcements that so bedeviled the timing of the MO Operation. On the afternoon of 10 May Combined Fleet formally postponed the invasion of Port Moresby to July. Inoue's South Seas Force concentrated on the capture of Ocean and Nauru northeast of the Solomons, now set for 17 May. The MO Striking Force was to cover Admiral Shima's Invasion Force as it proceeded northeast from Bougainville. Things already went wrong for the RY Operation. On 10 May near Buka the *S-42* torpedoed Shima's flagship, the agile minelayer *Okinoshima*. She capsized the next day.[8]

By late afternoon on 10 May with TF-17 southwest of New Caledonia, Fletcher finally felt clear of pursuit. He transferred the *Lexington* survivors to the *Portland* and *Chester* and recommended to Nimitz that transports meet him at Tongatabu. Nimitz was way ahead of him. The transports were already there and should be ready to sail on 17 May. The oiler *Kanawha* would provide TF-17 the necessary fuel for the return voyage. On 11 May, Kinkaid left for Nouméa with the *Minneapolis*, *New Orleans*, *Phelps*, and *Dewey*, along with Smith and the *Astoria* and *Anderson*, which would rejoin TF-17 at Tongatabu. Fletcher offered Kinkaid a heartfelt farewell, praising his "efficient and loyal cooperation," especially for the rescue of the *Lexington* personnel. "Good luck and good hunting to you and the officers and men with you." Kinkaid replied, "Departing ships are proud to have served under you during recent actions and hope to have that honor again soon." That would occur much sooner than anyone could have realized. On the morning of 15 May Fletcher completed an uneventful passage around New Caledonia and dropped anchor in the familiar harbor of Tongatabu. By that time Nimitz's entire Pacific strategy had changed, and Fletcher would play a vital part in its implementation.[9]

"ELIMINATE WEST COAST DESTINATION"

Nimitz found it difficult to follow the battle at long range with only fragmentary information. As of the night of 7 May, Hawaiian time (8 May in the Coral Sea), he assessed the general situation as favorable. The next morning decrypts revealed that the Japanese had postponed the invasion of Port Moresby, but the *Shōkaku* sustained only "slight damage." Some of her planes had reinforced the intact *Zuikaku*, still a potent threat, and the auxiliary carrier *Kasuga Maru* was also believed in the Solomons. Therefore that afternoon Nimitz gave Fletcher the order to pull out and to detach Kinkaid's group to Halsey's TF-16. Unaware as yet of the loss of the *Lexington,* he explained to King that damage to both U.S. carriers and heavy plane losses "reduced their effectiveness to the point where combat with undamaged carriers and shore based aircraft would result in almost certain loss [of] both carriers." They could not be of any immediate assistance to Halsey. Moreover, Pearl was not the place to conduct "extensive repairs." The carriers and also the rest of "old" TF-17, which likewise required upkeep after their arduous cruise, should go straight to Bremerton. That day Nimitz also informed the Puget Sound Navy Yard that the *Saratoga*'s repairs must be completed in late May on schedule, because she was "urgently required."[10]

Eight May at Pearl proved unsettling, as new decrypts challenged fundamental beliefs that Nimitz held about Japanese strategy. The previous day Layton's "scorecard" had laid out the whole familiar panoply of a far-ranging enemy South Pacific offensive. The *Kaga* and *Soryū* were thought en route to Truk, the invasion of Ocean and Nauru was imminent, and it was "probable" that carriers would raid either Fiji or New Caledonia. Layton also presented new evidence of some sort of operation against Oahu possibly scheduled after 15–17 May, with indication of joint action between aircraft and submarines. On 8 May, though, Rochefort put a real damper on the long anticipated Japanese onslaught in the South Pacific. "Efforts to locate any additional fleet units to reinforce Jap fleet [in the Coral Sea] have failed to disclose any major units headed that way." Instead, there were "signs of renewed activity in other areas" that might involve a "striking force" to be formed from at least two or three of the four elite carriers of the 1st and 2nd Carrier Divisions, two fast battleships, and two heavy cruisers. These powerful forces might depart homeland waters and "commence operations 21 May." Their exact "objective or mission" was "not indicated," but it was hard not to think of Midway and Oahu.[11]

It is not known precisely when Nimitz learned of the loss of the *Lexington.* Most likely it occurred early on 9 May (Hawaiian time), perhaps from a routine retransmission of Fletcher's original message. Layton was there when he got the bad news. "Subdued and a little shocked," Nimitz responded: "They should have saved the *Lexington.*" Then his aggressive nature took hold. "Remember this. We don't know all about the enemy. We don't know how badly he's hurt. You can bet your boots he's hurt, too. Remember this—the enemy has to be hurt. His situation is not all a bed of roses." Layton admired Nimitz's spirit, which rarely betrayed doubt. With possible Japanese mischief in the central Pacific, Nimitz changed his mind about sending TF-17 to the West Coast. The *Yorktown* might be patched up for a fierce battle from which Nimitz would not shrink, despite the loss of the *Lexington.* Thus early that same morning he told Fletcher, "Eliminate West Coast destination." Nimitz's subsequent action was equally characteristic. That afternoon he radioed Cominch: "I recommend Rear Admiral Frank Jack Fletcher be designated as task force commander with rank of Vice Admiral and awarded Distinguished Service Medal for distinguished service in line of his profession involving highest qualities [of] seamanship endurance and tenacity in conduct of operations during a cruise of approximately 11 weeks in February March April and May 1942 and for successful action of May 4 6 and 7th during which he inflicted heavy losses on the enemy." Nimitz worked tirelessly to build and sustain morale. He thought such a gesture was warranted despite the loss of the *Lexington.* Not one to nitpick or second-guess his commanders (at least not yet), he appreciated what Fletcher actually accomplished, rather than the what-ifs of the critics. King was not as tolerant, replying on 11 May: "Approval of recommendations your 092219 must await further details as to dispositions and operations."[12]

On 9 May radio intelligence based on an increasingly rich haul of decrypts offered further details regarding Japanese plans for Ocean and Nauru. Nimitz advised Halsey and Fletcher that the Moresby striking force, built around the *Zuikaku* and the 5th Cruiser Division, was to fuel off Bougainville, then cover the Ocean-Nauru invasion ships apparently coming south from Jaluit. Other forces, including two heavy cruisers from the 6th Cruiser Division, might also support. Radio intelligence disclosed that flying boats searched daily in the Makin-Ellice-Solomons triangle seven hundred miles out from Makin. Nimitz met with McCormick's war planners to consider whether the *Yorktown* should remain south for one more operation, instead of returning immediately to Pearl. Halsey would get another carrier, "apparently not badly damaged," with about two-thirds of the normal plane complement. In the end Cincpac held to the original plan to withdraw TF-17. The Japanese carriers had land-based air support, and the *Yorktown* would be at a "grave disadvantage" in a fight because she was not 100 percent effective. In this case, "Inflicting damage on your opponent is not compensation for being sunk yourself." The *Yorktown* desperately needed time in the yard, not only to repair bomb damage, but also for normal upkeep. Nimitz wisely recognized the "need to husband present carrier strength for future operations, some of which must now be in areas now completely uncovered," notably the central Pacific. The *Yorktown*'s swift return to Pearl in late May would pay dividends that no one then foresaw.[13]

A REVERSAL OF STRATEGY

After leaving Pearl on 30 April, Halsey's TF-16 (*Enterprise* and *Hornet*) steered southwest at fifteen knots. While Fletcher and Takagi exchanged blows, Halsey was more than sixteen hundred miles northeast. He increased speed to draw in range of Efate on 11 May to check the state of the airfield for his cargo of marine fighters but ended up sending them to Tontouta field on New Caledonia. The immediate crisis having passed, he maneuvered in the vicinity of Efate while fueling from the *Sabine* and *Cimarron*. Kinkaid was to join him as soon as possible. With word of the impending assault on Ocean and Nauru, Halsey's attention shifted northward. He wanted nothing better than to sink the *Zuikaku*, thought to be part of the covering force along with four heavy cruisers. On 12 May he learned from Nimitz that the invasion would likely take place on 17 May, but also that the *Zuikaku* might already have left for home. On 13 May Kinkaid sailed from Nouméa with the *Minneapolis*, *New Orleans*, and two destroyers to meet TF-16 in the Santa Cruz Islands east of the Solomons. That same day Halsey started northwest from Efate hoping to tangle with the Ocean-Nauru Invasion Force a few days later.[14]

The loss of the *Lexington*, once King's proudest command, hit him hard. Now his entire opening strategy in the Pacific seemed in jeopardy. By 1 June Japan could strike anywhere along the Alaska-Hawaii-Australia line. Most of this vast area was only weakly defended. On 9 May, as soon as King learned of the loss of the *Lex*, he informed the Admiralty that he would withdraw the carrier *Wasp* from the Atlantic, leaving only the *Ranger*.

The *Saratoga* would also soon rejoin Nimitz. Yet until mid June he would have only two intact carriers. Consequently on 12 May King informed Nimitz and General Marshall that he considered it "inadvisable" to allow TF-16 to advance into "forward areas beyond own shore based air cover and within range enemy shore based air," until "necessity requires" Sopac be defended or "unless especially favorable results are to be expected." Allied land-based air still comprised only a few bombers and flying boats, useful mainly for searches. King definitely changed his mind since late March and early April, when he criticized Fletcher for not risking his lone carrier to counter Japanese moves in the upper Solomons. At that time the loss of the *Yorktown* would have left that door wide open. Cominch's new cautious policy provided a dramatic vindication of Fletcher's stratagem of not allowing the enemy to sight TF-17 unnecessarily.[15]

King followed with an even more startling proposal. "In order to preserve our carriers during such attack it may be better to operate one or more carrier groups from shore" and to reinforce these planes with land-based bombers and flying boats rushed in from Hawaii and Australia. He urged Marshall to expand the air bases on New Caledonia, Efate, Fiji, and Tongatabu, but Nimitz must do his share as well. Starting immediately with those *Lexington* and *Yorktown* planes and service personnel "that can be spared," Cincpac was to establish aircraft service units to support one carrier air group each at New Caledonia and Fiji. King despaired of obtaining adequate land-based air strength to defend the islands he deemed absolutely vital to his Sopac strategy. Consequently he resorted to the dubious expediency of displacing aviators and aircraft uniquely adapted for mobility on carrier decks. Although King actually mentioned only the two air groups rendered supernumerary by loss of or damage to their flight decks, he implied the *Enterprise* and *Hornet* air groups might be so employed to "preserve" their carriers. The next day King reiterated his desire that carrier planes and personnel be committed ashore. The navy was to "afford every possible assistance" to build up air bases at New Caledonia and Fiji, "including aid by ground crews and relief pilots from *Lexington* and *Yorktown* as available." He wanted the air units in position by 25 May if possible.[16]

By 13 May (14 May across the date line) it looked to Nimitz that of all the possible Japanese threats, the one against Midway-Oahu was by far the most dangerous. The last thing he wanted in that instance was to have his carriers bereft of planes and crews that Cominch had tied up in a static defense of the South Pacific. Nimitz mounted definite steps to ensure such a calamity did not occur. That evening he relayed to Halsey Cominch's concern over not exposing TF-16 beyond the range of friendly land-based air support and within range of enemy shore-based aircraft. However, he added his own interpretation that enemy "shore-based air" referred to fighters, dive bombers, and torpedo planes and, by implication, not the ubiquitous flying boats used on long-range search. The fifty-plus Wildcats on Halsey's two carriers comprised a far better defense for the flattops than any available land-based air cover. "Have full confidence in your discretion," Nimitz informed Halsey. That applied even more to his next communication, sent a few minutes later as an "eyes only" message for Halsey. He told Halsey to ensure that the enemy located TF-16 the next day, then withdraw south and not expose his carriers to any form of counterattack. Nimitz calculated the mere presence of TF-16 would compel the much-weaker Ocean-Nauru Invasion Force to retire and clear the way for Halsey's speedy recall to Pearl. Halsey understandably never logged the second message, and it is doubtful King ever knew of it. Having hoped to surprise the Ocean-Nauru Invasion Force, Halsey simply noted that Cominch's caution "greatly restricts the operations of this force at present." He turned TF-16 northwest directly toward Tulagi, so its far-stepping flying boats would be certain find him first thing the next morning.[17]

Having already secretly contrived Halsey's sighting as an excuse to pull him out, Nimitz laid out his case to King in the strongest fashion. The Japanese carrier striking force, "loaded with attack gas," would strike some populous area, "probably Oahu, possibly West Coast." Nimitz deemed it vital to "maintain our striking forces in a state of maximum mobility to act against advancing enemy forces or to conduct offensive operations as opportunity presents." This was not the right time to deploy carrier planes ashore, even those from the *Lexington* and *Yorktown*, which together did not even make up one full group. "I intend return *Yorktown* to Pearl and use these planes with *Yorktown* air personnel for bringing *Yorktown* Air Group up to strength. This group will be useful pending *Yorktown* repairs for assisting still inadequate defense of Oahu and will be available for *Yorktown* as soon as her repairs are finished." Nimitz blandly noted if Halsey advanced north from the New Hebrides, "It appears improbable he can keep out of range of long range sea planes." That exposure would "reduce but perhaps not prevent" him from taking on the forces threatening Ocean and Nauru. "Halsey has ample latitude," which, unknown to King, he was exercising. Nimitz, though, did not have the same freedom of action due to Cominch's directive of 27 April to keep two carriers in the South Pacific. He asked King to reconsider, so TF-16 "may be retained or moved in accordance with information received." Moreover, King's "reference to conserving carriers is interpreted to mean that they should not be risked against superior forces in defense of bases which can defend themselves. In this I concur." Of course no South Pacific island bases could yet "defend themselves," but Nimitz did not mention that. Instead he requested guidance on how the Pacific Fleet should deal with the "next and almost certain attack" on Port Moresby. "If enemy drive to southeast is not indicated," he asked King to "give consideration to moving Halsey to Central Pacific, second move *Saratoga* to this area as soon as practicable. Time and distances involved require a definite decision in the near future."[18]

Tulagi did its part on the morning of 15 May (14 May at Pearl) to bring about the decision Nimitz desired. One flying boat spotted Halsey's two carriers 445 miles east and warily shadowed it for several hours. The effect on Inoue was all that Nimitz could have hoped. He immediately canceled the invasion of Ocean and Nauru, reinforced the air contingent at Rabaul, and concentrated his cruisers and destroyers three hundred miles north of Rabaul to prepare for a night battle if the Americans should raid there. For his own part Halsey remained in the area until his radio intelligence unit confirmed that he had been spotted, then scooted off to the east to meet Kinkaid at a new rendezvous and start back toward the New Hebrides.[19]

The next day King countered Nimitz's proposal to return the carriers to Pearl. The possible landing attack on Midway that so worried Cincpac was only a diversion to lure U.S. forces out of the South Pacific, with the secondary goal to eliminate Midway as a sub refueling base. The real offensive would kick off from Truk around 15–20 June, with five to seven carriers, four battleships, and strong land-based air. "It seems probable that not only Moresby but either NE Australia or New Caledonia and Fijis may be objectives." The threat to the island bases "seems so serious that I regret you prefer not to employ *Yorktown* and *Lexington* personnel ashore." King also regretted the advance of TF-16 had "led to its discovery by enemy." Yet despite all his differences with Nimitz over the strategic situation, Cominch showed his own great strength of character and willingness to accept Nimitz's judgment by lifting, at least "temporarily," his dictum for two carriers to be in the South Pacific at all times.[20]

That evening Nimitz seized his temporary discretion to order TF-16 to return to Pearl. He explained to King, Halsey, and Leary that Japan evidently planned "three separate and possibly simultaneous enemy offensives." The first would target the Aleutians with a few carriers and cruisers, the second was to be another try for Port Moresby, and the third, the big push with most of the carriers, threatened the "Midway-Oahu line." He was unsure as to the timing, "but believe sighting Halsey in south yesterday caused postponement Ocean and Nauru operations and will expedite northern and central operations." Cincpac lacked the strength to oppose all three offensives, but he must fight for Midway. "Shall endeavor to move out battleships and *Saratoga* support as soon as light forces for escort can be made available." On the strength of his belief in his radio intelligence and his willingness to meet the Japanese carriers head-on, Nimitz defied Cominch and redeployed his fleet to fight, even to the extent of repairing the *Yorktown* at Pearl so she could participate as well. Now Cincpac must win.[21]

TONGATABU INTERLUDE

When Fletcher reached Tongatabu on 15 May, Nukualofa harbor was crowded with ships from a stateside troop convoy. He expected to stay a few days to fuel and release the *Lexington* survivors to a transport. At the same time he provided Cincpac a detailed assessment of the *Yorktown*'s damage. Poco Smith arrived that evening with Fitch and Sherman. Cincpac gave Fletcher the *Barnett*, one of the empty transports, and desired her to sail to San Francisco along with the *Chester*, due for refit. Fitch was to ride the *Chester* and later reform TF-11 around the *Saratoga*. After escorting Fitch clear of the area, TF-17 was to return to Pearl. Fletcher loaded another transport as well and requested permission to change Fitch's destination to San Diego. Nimitz concurred. As part of the Cominch plan to strengthen the South Pacific air bases, Fletcher transferred the personnel of the *Lex*'s Torpedo Squadron Two for eventual transport to Suva and Nouméa. Had King insisted, the rest of the *Lexington* and *Yorktown* air groups would have stayed behind, with incalculable effect on the upcoming Battle of Midway. The transports were ready to sail on the sixteenth, but not Fletcher. The oiler *Kanawha* never arrived, and no one was sure where she was. Told to expect fuel at Tongatabu, Fletcher had run TF-17 nearly dry. The *Yorktown* came into port on her small load of auxiliary diesel fuel. The cruisers were not much better off. But no U.S. ships at Tongatabu had oil to spare. On 16 May the armed merchant cruiser HMAS *Kanimbla* arrived with a convoy from Brisbane. When Capt. William L. G. Adams, RN, paid his arrival call, Fletcher asked whether he could provide any fuel. Adams brought the *Kanimbla*

Admiral Fletcher and Admiral Fitch, USS *Yorktown*, 15 May 1942.
This is the only known photo of Fletcher on board the *Yorktown*.
Courtesy of John C. Fitch

alongside. The *Yorktown* engineers grumbled at the quality of the oil ("The stuff was lousy, loaded with sulfur or something"), but they were glad to get it.[22]

On 17 May Fletcher returned Adams's call. Learning that he would soon report to Crace in Australia, Fletcher asked him to relay a personal message. In fact Crace and Adams never did meet. Instead Adams wrote a letter on 29 May to Crace, noting that Fletcher "was very anxious for me to convey to you his very great appreciation of your co-operation with you in all the operations in which you have been acting in company; in particular did he stress your ready accedence to any of his wishes in regard to the use of such cruisers as you could spare to assist him and also his pleasure at your waiving all questions of seniority between you." Regarding Crace's mission and the 7 May air attack, Adams explained that Fletcher "particularly wanted you to know that it was his intention to follow you & give you air support that day, but that due, I understand, to the circumstances surrounding the sinking of the larger carrier by the Americans themselves, of necessity, he was unable to carry out his original intentions. He felt that he left you badly in the lurch and as I said, was very anxious that you should understand his position." Grateful for the message, Crace accepted Fletcher's explanation. He reserved his ire for the tardy land-based air sighting reports and the "friendly" planes who bombed him.[23]

CORAL SEA LESSONS

While TF-17 rested at Tongatabu the Coral Sea battle remained very much on Fletcher's mind. Fitch's staff worked with Sherman and Buckmaster to compile the detailed action reports, not only narratives, but also numerous comments on lessons learned in the very first carrier-versus-carrier engagement. Realizing this was a lengthy process, Buckmaster provided Kinkaid a short list of recommendations to deliver to Halsey. The principal commanders hashed over the most important aspects of the battle, particularly the proper use of land-based air. Fletcher opened the discussion on 11 May, telling Nimitz, Halsey, and Leary although the "quality of our personnel [is] greatly superior to enemy and our material generally superior," there was need for improvement. "Due to no repeat no fault of personnel the full value of shore based planes and forces afloat is not being obtained under our present organization." The Japanese were "better organized" in that regard. He thought they accomplished all of the long-range searches from shore and reserved all the carrier planes for the strike. He also urged more fighters for the carriers. Fitch agreed with Fletcher, except that he believed enemy carrier aircraft also searched. The Japanese had achieved "higher coordination" between their land- and carrier-based air, "in contrast to our present situation." Fitch warned (incorrectly) that enemy carriers and shore-based planes were radar-equipped. Based on pilot reports he thought German Messerschmitt 109 fighters also flew from the Japanese carriers. That was wrong, but in any event enemy fighters and torpedo planes "greatly outperformed our present carrier types." Antiaircraft fire was not all that good, but still better than Japanese. Fitch also proposed the combat air patrol at twenty thousand feet to ensure altitude superiority.[24]

Given the dire threat to the South Pacific, the criticisms of Fletcher and Fitch regarding land-based air resonated in Washington. On 13 May King asked Nimitz about the plans made prior to the battle to coordinate land-based air and the carriers. Nimitz in turn requested Fletcher's comments, "In order to assist [and] determine potentialities in cooperative use of air forces" in the South Pacific. Diplomatic as ever, Fletcher noted that in the past three months Leary "kept me fully informed of the results of his shore based air searches and on the few occasions when radio silence has permitted a request for shore based air cooperation it has been extended expeditiously and fully." However, the restrictions of radio silence prevented him from keeping Leary apprized of his changing location, fuel situation, and future moves. Perhaps under certain circumstances it would be "more logical" for the officer in charge of the land-based air to call all the shots, or at least advise the task force commander afloat where to move, fuel, and attack to best advantage. Presumably the man ashore would have more up-to-date information on enemy movements than the carrier task force commander and could coordinate land-based air and carrier forces. Otherwise except for previously scheduled attacks on shore bases, there could be no real coordination of the available air power. Fitch and Smith "generally concur," Fletcher noted, but that subject was too complicated for a single dispatch.[25]

MacArthur submitted a detailed summary of Sowespac air operations and declared: "Coordination with task force was attained." Leary described the present arrangement for coordinating land-based air and fleet operations as "the best possible," given the existing conditions. It could be improved only if the carrier task force commander somehow kept the shore-based commanders aware of his intentions, perhaps by air or shuttling destroyers. "Closest liaison [is] maintained here with headquarters shore based air by using common operations room, and all information is retransmitted to interested commands at once." That was not exactly truthful, given long delays in forwarding vital information to Fletcher. Sowespac did not solve that problem, as Fletcher would discover in August. Leary's message crossed one from Nimitz, another diplomat, who noted there would soon be a plan in place for air coordination in the South Pacific. "From present knowledge believe Fletcher's operations were remarkably well timed and executed at the location where the enemy was most vulnerable and he little subject to attack by enemy shore based air." That stands as an accurate statement of Fletcher's achievement in the Coral Sea. MacArthur seconded Nimitz's assessment. "Consider your forces in recent action were handled with marked skill and fought with admirable courage and tenacity." MacArthur, too, was "most anxious to perfect air-naval cooperation."[26]

On 19 May Nimitz summed up the question of coordinating land and carrier based air. He declared that land-based air had indeed helped Fletcher in his "highly successful" attack on Tulagi and in the subsequent carrier battle. There was, however, a notable lack of success by high-altitude level bombing. Nimitz concurred that MacArthur needed dive bombers and torpedo planes (which in fact MacArthur's own AAF experts did not appreciate or desire) and praised the Japanese advantage of having their long-range planes manned by naval aviators to permit the closest coordination with forces afloat. The carrier task force commander had the responsibility of keeping his land-based counterpart aware of "all possible preliminary info as to his intentions." At the same time shore commanders should devise "attack missions designed to render the greatest possible assistance to the fleet TF when it is engaged." However, that deficiency would persist.[27]

On another front, King questioned Nimitz and Fletcher on 11 May: "While not familiar with all of the circumstances attending operations last week I feel that I must express my feeling that Dog Dogs might have been used in night attacks on enemy especially since junction of Task Forces Eleven and Seventeen made a large number of destroyers available." The Cincpac War Plans diary noted that "fragmentary reports led one to agree," but that entry is crossed out (by Nimitz?). Yet again Cominch's message went to Fletcher in a cipher he did not hold, so he was unaware King questioned his conduct of the battle. Nimitz referred to the Cominch message when telling Fletcher to submit a short narrative of the battle. Fletcher requested and got a retransmission. Sensitive to the criticism of Fletcher implied in the Cominch message, Nimitz kept it under wraps ("copies not distributed") and handled it as "sealed secret," then the highest level of classification. On 17 May Fletcher detailed the organization of the two surface attack groups of cruisers and destroyers, Crace's mission on the seventh, and the reasons (previously elaborated elsewhere) why no further surface attacks were attempted. "Acting on my best judgment on the spot no opportunity could be found to use destroyers in night attacks on the enemy except the attack by the Support Group which I ordered." King never responded, but Fletcher would soon have to explain his actions personally to Nimitz.[28]

"EXPEDITE ARRIVAL"

On the morning of 18 May the *Kanawha* finally turned up at Tongatabu, and Fletcher started fueling. The navy's first oiler (AO-1), she carried half the capacity of the new fast fleet oilers and only filled TF-17 to 75 percent. Unless Cincpac set another fueling rendezvous, Fletcher lacked the option of extended high-speed runs on the return voyage. The summons from Nimitz came that afternoon. "Expedite arrival Taskfor 17 at Pearl." After releasing Fitch to San Diego earlier than anticipated, Fletcher was to return to Pearl by the direct route. By dawn on 19 May the *Kanawha* fueled the *Portland* to less than full capacity and gave the last of her oil to the *Astoria* and *Yorktown*. Fletcher informed Nimitz that he expected to depart Tongatabu at 1300 that day and reach Pearl at 1630 on 27 May. Later that morning the *Kaskaskia* stood in at Tongatabu. Fletcher had her top off the *Portland* and left with the rest of TF-17 at 1500. The *Portland* was to catch up by dark. The *Yorktown*'s crew envisioned merely a stopover at Pearl, then a few glorious months stateside while the carrier mended her wounds. Instead, she was about to face her sternest trial. Nimitz prodded Halsey with a sharp, "Expedite return to Hawaiian area." TF-16 was not to raid any bases on the way back or let the enemy sight it. Having refueled off Efate, Halsey started northeast at seventeen knots to bring him back to Pearl on 26 May.[29]

Nimitz stressed to King the importance of retrieving the carriers from the South Pacific. The information he received on the *Yorktown*'s damage showed that the Pearl Harbor Navy Yard could repair her in a "reasonably short time." Regarding the flood of radio intelligence being furnished by all three code-breaking teams, he acknowledged "considerable difference in estimates based probably on the same data." The latest decrypts at Pearl did not sustain the supposition that the enemy was concentrating his fleet at Truk in order to threaten the South Pacific. "Believe he may well try to capture vital Hawaiian Area at this time before reinforcements afforded our war production can be received. Will watch situation closely and return Halsey to southwest if imminent concentration that direction is indicated." King relented on 17 May. "I have somewhat revised my estimate and now generally agree with you except I believe enemy attempt to capture Midway and Unalaska will occur about May 30th" or "shortly thereafter. The enemy South Pacific offensive will be started middle or latter part of June and will be strong attempt to capture Moresby plus northeast Australia or New Caledonia and Fiji." Regarding the last estimate King was indeed correct. His analysts had detected and focused on the Japanese preparations to assemble much of the Combined Fleet at Truk *following* their inevitable success off Midway. A concentration at Truk would constitute a grave threat to King's whole South Pacific strategy. At the same time Nimitz and his planners had worried since the Pearl Harbor debacle that the Japanese might return to the central Pacific with overwhelming strength. Each commander naturally emphasized the evidence that pointed toward what he personally considered the worst scenario.[30]

King's own estimate of the enemy's Midway offensive likewise was most daunting. The Midway attack force might include the four carriers of the 1st and 2nd Carrier Divisions and possibly the *Zuikaku*, along with four fast battleships, two cruiser divisions, at least two squadrons of destroyers, and a landing force. There were indications the First Fleet battleships "may take up a supporting position to westward of Midway," a forecast everyone promptly forgot. King thought the enemy might lead with a carrier raid on Oahu and then attempt to "trap and destroy a substantial portion of the Pacific Fleet." The "appropriate strategy," he advised, "is to make strong concentration Hawaiian area." However, in light of the Japanese intention to force a battle with their greatly superior forces, he judged it best "chiefly to employ strong attrition tactics and not repeat not allow our forces to accept such decisive action as would be likely to incur heavy losses in our carriers and cruisers." Even so, King grew concerned the now fiercely aggressive Nimitz might take the bit in his teeth and directly confront the Japanese carriers. One way to keep him cautious was to see if he might part with the damaged *Yorktown.* On 18 May he asked Nimitz to consider sending her directly to the Puget Sound Navy Yard, "In order to avoid exposure to attack, to save shipment of material to Pearl, to refresh personnel and possibly [save] overall time to prepare [her] for service." If the *Yorktown* could soon be made ready to fight, Nimitz definitely wanted her. Seizing on Fletcher's report that TF-17 fuel was low, he replied on 20 May that he must first bring the *Yorktown* to Pearl for fuel. "If operations feasible contemplate using *Yorktown* as support for Halsey. If not feasible contemplate sending to Puget." On the twenty-first he instructed both Halsey and Fletcher to maintain strict radio silence and not routinely advise when they were seven hundred miles out from Pearl. "Search plane will contact you and report on its return." Cincpac took no chances in keeping secret his carrier redeployment to the central Pacific. He employed a neat bit of radio deception suggested by MacArthur. Beginning 28 May the *Tangier* was to mimic the radio calls of a carrier task force operating in the South Pacific. That night her PBYs also attacked Tulagi, and the puzzled Japanese thought they were carrier planes.[31]

Departing Tongatabu, Fletcher set off northeast at fourteen knots. On 21 May he detached Fitch's three ships while east of Samoa. Isolated from the incredible activity Cincpac initiated to prepare for the Japanese Midway offensive, the return voyage of TF-17 proceeded uneventfully and in good spirits despite the never-ending paperwork. On 26 May, one day out from Pearl, Fletcher expressed his appreciation to TF-17 for a most remarkable cruise. "On this the one hundredth day since our departure from Pearl, I wish to congratulate all hands upon the successful operations, the splendid seamanship, the remarkable engineering performance and the fine spirit which has marked each of these hundred days."[32]

CHAPTER 16

Time Is Everything

THE MI OPERATION

Admiral Yamamoto permitted no deviation from his plan to destroy the Pacific Fleet in one huge battle.[1] Deep embarrassment over the Doolittle raid only hardened his resolve. That insult also brought the army on board, not only for the MI and AL (Aleutian) operations, but also for the eventual invasion of Hawaii. From 28 April to 4 May chart maneuvers and critiques laid out the strategy for the Second Operational Phase. The MO Operation would terminate on 10 May with the capture of Port Moresby. Midway and the western Aleutians would fall in early June, followed in July by Fiji and Samoa (FS Operation). Assaults against the Hawaiian Islands could start perhaps in October. "As a result of the smooth progress of the first-phase operations," Yamamoto explained, "we have established an invincible strategic position" that "cannot be maintained if we go on the defensive." Instead, "in order to secure it tenaciously, we must keep on striking offensively at the enemy's weak points one after another." Now was the perfect time to draw out what was left of the enemy's battleships, carriers, and cruisers and finish them off before numerous warships under construction could intervene. Imperial General Headquarters formally approved the MI Operation on 5 May.[2]

To the concurrent MI and AL operations the Combined Fleet committed more than two hundred ships (including ten carriers) and air units with an authorized strength of more than eight hundred aircraft. At their head was, as Walter Lord quipped, "A dazzling army of twenty admirals." The Northern Force (Vice Adm. Hosogaya Boshirō, Fifth Fleet commander) was to invade Adak, Kiska, and Attu in the Aleutians. Rear Adm. Kakuta Kakuji's 2nd *Kidō Butai* (2nd Striking Force) would provide carrier support with sixty-three planes of light carriers *Ryūjō* and the new *Junyō*. To capture Midway itself, Vice Adm. Kondō Nobutake's Attack Force, built around his Second Fleet, received two fast battleships, eight heavy cruisers, light carrier *Shōhō* (twenty planes), a seaplane carrier, a converted seaplane tender, and two destroyer squadrons, as well as numerous transports and auxiliary ships. Admiral Nagumo's elite First Air Fleet (1st *Kidō Butai*) included carriers *Akagi*, *Kaga*, *Sōryū*, *Hiryū*, *Shōkaku*, and *Zuikaku*, screened by two fast battleships, two heavy cruisers, and a destroyer squadron. Its authorized strength of 387 carrier planes would overwhelm Midway's air strength, reduce its ground defenses, and open the way for the invasion. In line with his quest for victory through decisive battle, Yamamoto for the first time committed his entire battle line.

The Main Force comprised the seven First Fleet battleships (including the *Yamato*), two destroyer squadrons, light carrier *Hōshō* (fifteen planes), and two fast seaplane carriers crammed with midget submarines and torpedo boats. The Main Body under Yamamoto would back up the attack on Midway, while the Guard Force, led by Vice Adm. Takasu Shirō (Commander, First Fleet), initially covered the Aleutians operation. Vice Adm. Tsukahara Nishizō's Base Air Force (Eleventh Air Fleet) would furnish shore-based aircraft.[3]

On 8 May Combined Fleet planners made the changes necessary due to losses suffered in the Coral Sea and announced the timetable of events for the MI and AL Operations.[4] Fletcher's victory cost the MI Operation the *Shōhō* and *Shōkaku*. Light carrier *Zuihō* (twenty-four planes) would replace her sister *Shōhō* in Kondō's Attack Force. Midway was to be invaded early on N-Day, 7 June (Tokyo time; 6 June Midway local time), the last significant moonlight for nearly a month. Inspired by Fletcher's surprise 4 May carrier strike on Tulagi, the opening gambit now included a reprise of Operation K, the night reconnaissance and bombing of Pearl Harbor by flying boats in March. The object of the Second Operation K was to determine if Pearl Harbor contained the U.S. carriers and battleships. If they were not present, Combined Fleet could operate under heightened alert ready for any ambushes. A refueling rendezvous between the two flying boats and submarines was to take place the evening of 30 May (Hawaii local time) at French Frigate Shoals, northwest of the Hawaiian Islands. The flight could be rescheduled up to 2 June if necessary.[5] Other subs from the Advance Force would scout ahead of the attack forces. On N–5 (2 June, Tokyo time; 1 June, Midway local time), a dozen subs were to assemble along two deployment lines positioned five hundred miles northwest and west of Oahu to watch for and attack U.S. heavy ships expected to hasten north from Pearl Harbor after the offensive began.

The 8 May Combined Fleet message also specified *simultaneous* carrier strikes at dawn on N–3 (4 June/3 June) by Kakuta against Dutch Harbor in the Aleutians and Nagumo against Midway. That would awaken the clueless Pacific Fleet to its danger and provoke the desired response. Nagumo's prime objective was to surprise Midway's aircraft on the ground. Later on N–3 Day, the lead element of the Midway assault force, coming east from Saipan, would penetrate Midway's air search range from the southwest. Nagumo was to press his attacks the next two days until he destroyed Midway's air force and softened up the island for invasion. On N–1 Day (6 June/5 June) Kondō would set up a seaplane base on tiny Kure Island fifty-five miles west of Midway, while Hosogaya landed troops on Adak and Kiska in the Aleutians. The Adak foray was merely a raid in force. The men were to withdraw and occupy Attu on N+5 (12 June/11 June). Before dawn on N–Day (7 June/6 June) five thousand elite naval and army troops would storm Midway. If things went as planned, special pioneer troops would restore the airstrip to operation yet that day for the first of thirty-six Zero fighters being transported on the carriers, and nine land attack planes staging in from Wake. Six flying boats would also deploy there.

With the fall of Midway, the "decisive fleet battle" phase (the vital aspect of the MI Operation) would commence. The huge train of oilers could support the Combined Fleet for one additional week in the eastern Pacific. Japanese forces would regroup to deal with the U.S. Fleet that would only just be flushed out of Pearl. The decisive battle force was to deploy in a giant rectangle. Yamamoto's Main Body (the three most powerful battleships) would take station six hundred miles northwest of Midway, with Nagumo's six carriers three hundred miles east. Scurrying down from the Aleutians to form the northern corners of the box, Takasu's four Guard Force battleships were to move five hundred miles north of Yamamoto, while Kakuta's 2nd *Kidō Butai* (reinforced by the *Zuihō* from Kondō) took the corresponding slot five hundred miles north of Nagumo. The balance of Kondō's Attack Force would cover Midway and serve as bait. The staff drew up specific responses depending on exactly where the U.S. ships showed up, either to the south, north, or east. If as hoped, the Pacific Fleet drew up in full array off Midway, Kakuta was to race south to join Nagumo and attack, while Takasu linked up with Yamamoto. After subs and carrier aircraft wore down the Americans, Yamamoto's big guns would finish them off.

Following the inevitable annihilation of the Pacific Fleet, Yamamoto's battleship force would return to Japan. Planning would start in earnest for the invasion of Hawaii, possibly late that year. Meanwhile, the isolation of Australia through the conquest of the South Pacific would be complete. On 15–20 June Kondō's Attack Force and Nagumo's five 1st *Kidō Butai* carriers were to assemble at Truk to regroup for the invasions of Fiji and Samoa, set for July by the troops of the newly activated 17th Army. Inoue and the 17th Army would also seize New Caledonia and Port Moresby. In the northern Pacific, Hosogaya would hold onto Midway, the gateway to Hawaii and also the Aleutians. To foil more desperate lunges against the homeland, the Northern Force would wield the four fast *Kongō*-class battleships, eight heavy cruisers, carriers *Ryūjō*, *Junyō*, *Zuihō*, and later the repaired *Shōkaku*.[6]

On 14 May Hara's summary of air group casualties in the Coral Sea demonstrated not even the *Zuikaku*, undamaged but minus 40 percent of her aviators, could participate in the MI Operation. She required time to work up a new, properly trained air group. The absence of supernumerary carrier squadrons left Nagumo no other alternative. Even the sight of torn-up *Shōkaku* when she limped in on 17 May did not alter Yamamoto's supreme confidence, although chief of staff Ugaki thought her "very lucky to have got off lightly with such damage." Repairs would take three months. The *Zuikaku* showed up on the twenty-first. Hara was to bring her out in mid June after the victory to join the forces concentrating at Truk for the FS Operation. The absence of the 5th Carrier Division reduced Nagumo to four carriers and 250 planes, including twenty-one Zeros meant for Midway. Yamamoto judged them more than sufficient. Japanese intelligence believed both the *Yorktown* and *Saratoga* succumbed in the Coral Sea; the *Lexington* had either gone down in the January sub attack or was still under repair. Thus the Pacific Fleet could defend Midway with at most two or three big carriers (*Enterprise*, *Hornet*, and possibly *Wasp*), two or three converted carriers, two battleships, four or five heavy cruisers, seven or eight light cruisers, thirty destroyers and twenty-five subs. To Yamamoto the big challenge was to coax these meager forces out to fight. The two U.S. carriers sighted on 15 May off Tulagi had ample time to return to Hawaiian waters. Yet the *Tangier*'s adroit radio deception and the 28 May Tulagi raid by her PBYs, which Inoue misinterpreted as a carrier strike, led to doubts on that score.[7]

At the final Midway planning conference on 25 May, Nagumo unexpectedly informed Yamamoto that he could not sail on the twenty-sixth as planned. The carriers desperately needed another day to complete necessary preparations for battle. Therefore the 1st *Kidō*

Butai must postpone the initial Midway strike from N–3 Day (4 June/3 June) to N–2 Day (5 June/4 June). Yamamoto reluctantly approved. He refused at that late date to reschedule N–Day (7 June/6 June), delay the Aleutians attack, or otherwise alter the timetable. He took the calculated risk that on N–3 Day, Midway's air search would not patrol west far enough to sight the lead elements of Kondō's Attack Force scheduled to close within six hundred miles of Midway that afternoon. That last-minute change fostered the mistaken impression that the AL Operation was always intended to serve as a diversion for Midway. On 26 May Kakuta's 2nd *Kidō Butai* left Ominato in northern Japan bound for the foggy Aleutians. Nagumo's 1st *Kidō Butai* departed the Inland Sea on 27 May, the anniversary of the glorious 1905 Battle of Tsushima and Japan's Navy Day, to the cheers of Yamamoto's Main Force and the big ships of Kondō's Attack Force. The Midway invasion convoy sailed from Saipan on 28 May, and Yamamoto and Kondō left Japan on 29 May.

By 30 May, however, two more components of Yamamoto's plan unraveled. Nearly all the Advance Force submarines failed to sail on time from Kwajalein and consequently reached their picket lines between Midway and Oahu up to two days late. Moreover, the sub detailed to refuel the flying boats in the Second Operation K found U.S. ships guarding French Frigate Shoals. That forced the cancellation of the Pearl Harbor reconnaissance flight. Had the flying boats gone forth on the night of 30–31 May as planned, they would have found no heavy ships at Pearl. That might have given Yamamoto pause to reflect. Unusually heavy radio activity intercepted from Hawaii disclosed the Pacific Fleet might be on alert. Ugaki mused that the premature exposure of the offensive could hasten the decisive encounter with the enemy heavy forces, "Which is welcome," but he feared a concentration of U.S. subs. Aware of some of these suspicions, Nagumo steadily progressed toward his fateful confrontation at Midway.[8]

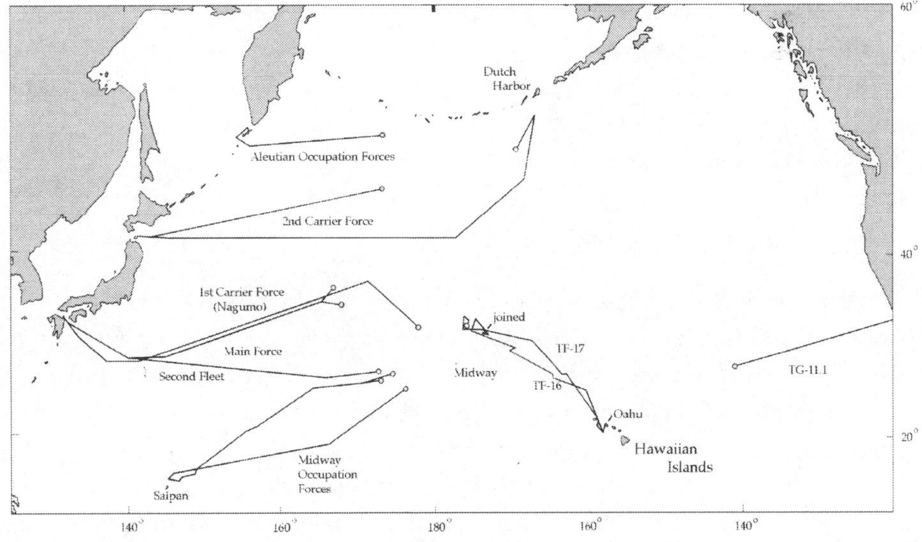

Midway campaign, movements to 0000, 4 June 1942

Many aspects of Yamamoto's plan provoke comment. The Aleutians offensive contributed nothing beneficial that remotely offset the dangerous dispersal of valuable resources. A Japanese victory at Midway would crack open the North Pacific as readily as the South Pacific. Yet the Aleutians venture fit in with Yamamoto's concept of keeping his main forces hidden well north of Midway, where U.S. air searches could not penetrate, and of using Kondō's Attack Force to entice the U.S. Fleet out to fight. He hoped to conceal his true strength (in his mind the Main Force battleships), until it was too late for the few American carriers and battleships to evade and run. Therefore Yamamoto, who brilliantly planned the Pearl Harbor attack around the unprecedented power of his carriers, employed them at Midway mainly to clear the way for the battlewagons, cruisers, destroyers, and midget subs. Perceptions of the Coral Sea battle only reinforced the fragility of the flattops. Hara reported on board the *Yamato* on 24 May to lament missed opportunities. Normally ebullient, he confessed that on 7 May he was so frustrated he wanted to resign his commission. On the eighth his carriers took such a pounding that he was glad to withdraw. Takagi briefed the Combined Fleet staff on 25 May. Both received sympathetic hearings with rueful commiseration of their personal misfortunes, but no one regarded the Coral Sea setback as serious given the destruction of two U.S. carriers. The staff blamed Inoue's lack of fortitude for the failure to pursue the retreating Americans. Capt. Kuroshima Kameto, the senior staff officer, opined to Ugaki, "We must not depend upon the air force too much; the surface force must be prepared to sacrifice itself in its place when necessary." Good old-fashioned naval guns and ship-launched torpedoes might be best after all. Noting the vulnerability of carriers, Ugaki remarked, "A good use of the air arm was to seek victory by hitting the enemy's weak point." Yamamoto's heavily scripted overall plan depended far too much on surprise. Its initial stages rendered his dispersed forces vulnerable to reverse ambush and defeat in detail. Apparently no one other than perhaps Kondō took note that in the Coral Sea, the U.S. carriers appeared much earlier than expected and frustrated the entire enterprise. In one of the great ironies of history, the Combined Fleet's MI plan became the mirror image of its brilliant attack on Pearl Harbor six months before, except in this case Yamamoto, not Kimmel, deeply underestimated the quality of his foe, and acted as if he knew their intentions rather than carefully assessing their capabilities.[9]

A QUESTION OF COMMAND

On the afternoon of 27 May, after a cruise of 101 days, two raids, and a battle, Fletcher's TF-17 gathered at the narrow entrance of Pearl Harbor right on schedule. Its arrival was a surprise, because Cincpac had reckoned fuel shortage would delay its return until the twenty-eighth. The *Yorktown* still trailed oil from seams opened on 8 May. On the way in, her sailors noted the encouraging absence of the beached battleship *Nevada*, since refloated and dispatched to the West Coast, which was where they thought they, too, would shortly be. Off Ford Island loomed the *Enterprise* and *Hornet*. Nimitz happened to be on the *Big E* awarding decorations. He would have a great deal to say to Fletcher later that day. The *Yorktown* executed a clockwise turn around Ford Island. If the removal of the *Nevada* was a positive sign, the forlorn bow of the capsized *Utah*, the *Arizona*'s skeletal mainmast, and the vast flat bottom of the *Oklahoma* reminded all of the 7 December outrage. The *Yorktown* moved alongside Pier B-16 in the navy yard's repair basin, opposite the channel from the *Enterprise*.[10]

Coming into Pearl, Fletcher felt an unsettling premonition about the *Yorktown*'s ultimate fate, but had no clear idea how that might occur. If a trip to Bremerton was not in the cards, she needed a couple of weeks to get patched up. A staff officer strode on board to tell Fletcher that Nimitz wished to see him. Already prepared for the usual arrival call to Cincpac, Fletcher thought he amply earned the right to a quick drink first and strolled ashore to get one. Then he collected Poco Smith, reported to headquarters at the submarine base, and found Nimitz and Draemel awaiting him. To Fletcher's surprise, Nimitz, "Normally the calmest of people," appeared "exceptionally disturbed." Asked how he felt after such a long, hard cruise, Fletcher replied, "Pretty tired." Smith wondered, "How long the old poops and even the young officers can stand the strain." Nimitz explained that under normal circumstances Fletcher and the *Yorktown* deserved a rest, but things were far from normal. "We have to fix you up right away and send you out to Midway." The mention of Midway took Fletcher aback. The intelligence he saw in the last several weeks contained no hint of danger there. Nimitz explained that Midway would be invaded in the next several days and added sarcastically the Japanese were so confident of victory, they already appointed the officer who was to take command there in August. He never explicitly stated this amazing intelligence was derived from breaking the enemy code. Fletcher already knew that was the case. Smith did not, but as one of the navy's early cryptographers, he quickly figured it out.[11]

Nimitz followed the bombshell about the enemy's Midway offensive with shocking news that Bill Halsey was hospitalized after arriving the previous afternoon. Halsey's haggard features shook even Nimitz's legendary calm. Ever since February he suffered from unbearable itching all over his body due to "general dermatitis." The tremendous stress exacerbated an underlying allergic skin reaction and prevented him from getting rest. On the recent cruise to the South Pacific the fierce tropical sun forced Halsey to remain in his flag quarters, "Which irked him to no end." Capt. Miles Browning, chief of staff, and Cdr. William H. Buracker, operations officer, actually ran TF-16, with Halsey's "advice and concurrence." That could not continue. Now gaunt, shrunken, and exhausted, Halsey clearly was in no shape to fight. Missing Midway was to be "the most grievous disappointment" in his career.[12]

Halsey's sudden illness threw Nimitz into a terrible quandary. He had counted on his most aggressive and experienced warrior to lead the carriers in their toughest battle, one that could decide the war in the Pacific. The obvious candidate to replace Halsey was Rear Adm. Leigh Noyes, a personable Vermonter and classmate of Fletcher and Fitch, who once seemed destined for great things. Short, stocky, "mild and meticulous," said by King to be "physically unable to talk without using his hands," Noyes earned his wings in 1937 as a fifty-one-year-old captain and became a "capable pilot." That year his *Lexington* conducted the extensive search for Amelia Earhart. In 1938 he became chief of staff in King's Aircraft, Battle Force. Promoted rear admiral in July 1939, Noyes served as director of naval communications. There his career took a wrong turn, partly due to the controversy over whether radio intelligence was properly handled before the Pearl Harbor attack. Noyes came out to Pearl in March 1942 under ambiguous circumstances without a billet, the unkind rumor being his superiors simply wanted to get rid of him. In April he took Fitch's place as Halsey's shore administrator. Some questioned his tenacity and judgment. A renowned naval aviator, who served under Noyes both in the light cruiser *Richmond* in 1934 and the *Lexington*, recalled, "The whole tenor and tone of those ships changed for the worse." King, who knew Noyes well (and bullied him unmercifully), said, "Everyone knew he had trouble making decisions." On 3 June Poco Smith privately described Noyes as "a washout."[13]

Such judgments were too harsh. In need of additional carrier task force commanders because of King's demand for single-carrier task forces, Nimitz was more than willing to give his friend Noyes a second chance. Noyes was to get the *Saratoga* task force, once she completed repairs in June, but instead, Fitch would reform TF-11 with the *Saratoga*. Nimitz then earmarked Noyes for the *Hornet* task force (TF-18) directly under Halsey, CTF-16 in the *Enterprise*. At the same time Fletcher was to remain CTF-17 in the *Yorktown* and later direct Fitch's TF-11 as well. Nimitz sought Capt. Ted Sherman for the *Wasp* task force expected in San Diego about mid June. Like classmate Pete Mitscher in the *Hornet*, Sherman was already selected for rear admiral. Mitscher himself would very much have liked his own carrier task force, but he was in line for Patrol Wing Two to ease the burden of Rear Adm. Pat Bellinger. In May when John McCain left for the South Pacific, Bellinger took over Pacific Fleet's patrol wings. Indeed Bellinger, another pioneer aviator, was another potential CTF-16, but Nimitz needed him where he was.[14]

To Nimitz's surprise Halsey fervently recommended Rear Adm. Raymond Spruance (Comcrudiv Five), his cruiser task group commander, to succeed him as CTF-16. Indeed he declared Spruance was the only admiral to whom he would willingly entrust the two carriers. Halsey laid the foundation with a 25 May letter to Fletcher, who as Comcrupac was Spruance's superior. Halsey praised Spruance's "outstanding ability, excellent judgment, quiet courage" and declared he was "fully and supremely qualified to take command of a force comprising mixed types." On 26 May Halsey proposed Spruance retain the whole elite Carriers, Pacific Fleet (Carpac) staff, exchanging only flag lieutenants. Nimitz barely knew him but he was aware of Spruance's sterling reputation as a naval strategist. That would soon change, for Spruance was slated to relieve Draemel as Cincpac chief of staff. Earlier in May Nimitz wrote privately to King requesting the change, because Draemel, his principal planner, disagreed with his fundamental strategy. At the same time Wilson Brown's precarious health meant Draemel could relieve him as Pacific Fleet's amphibious commander. Spruance was a logical candidate for chief of staff. Like Draemel he had a strong background of study and teaching at the Naval War College and thoroughly understood the operational art. He also brought the benefit of recent combat experience. Trusting Halsey's judgment, Nimitz acceded, primarily, it appears, to ensure continuity of command within TF-16, rather than, as is so often stated in hindsight, from an underlying belief that Spruance might actually do better than Halsey at Midway. In 1965 Nimitz could say, "It was a great day for the Navy when Bill Halsey had to enter the hospital." He certainly did not think so at the time. He procrastinated until the evening of 27 May before informing King that Halsey was incapacitated by an "obscure allergy," and he had already named a successor to lead TF-16. A strong case can be made that Halsey's presence was sorely missed at Midway.[15]

On the twenty-sixth Spruance repaired to the *Enterprise* to make his call on Halsey and found flag country unusually still. He learned Halsey had been admitted to the hospital and that Nimitz wanted to see him. Then Nimitz floored him by placing him in command of TF-16 for the defense of Midway. Afterward he would come ashore to run the Cincpac staff. Unlike Fletcher, Spruance already knew from high-level messages shared by Halsey that a battle for Midway was in the offing, but he was astonished at becoming CTF-16 in his boss's place. "Since I was not an aviator, and there were aviators senior to me at Pearl Harbor, I thought one of them would take over from Halsey." A 1907 Annapolis graduate, Spruance cut his teeth in destroyers and taught five years at the Naval War College, where he became renowned as a naval strategist. Promoted to rear admiral in 1940, he organized the Tenth Naval District in the Caribbean before taking Crudiv Five in September 1941. Age fifty-five, medium height and slender, with a quiet and contemplative disposition and an addiction to long walks, he was a brilliant thinker, an excellent seaman, and a "cold fish." Lt. Cdr. Victor D. Long, Crudiv Five flag secretary, described his boss as "essentially . . . a machine," who "had no emotions or didn't show them." Others, however, noted the twinkling eyes and the dry sense of humor. Spruance worshipped logic and order. He and Halsey were very close, although they were fire and ice.[16]

Suddenly placing Spruance in charge of TF-16 forced Nimitz to change his plans regarding Noyes, who was senior both to Fletcher and Spruance. Noyes must remain ashore for the time being. Nimitz would not willingly entrust the carrier striking force to someone devoid of battle experience or, for that matter, even recent sea duty. Like Kimmel and Pye, Nimitz did not regard being a naval aviator with carrier experience the indispensable credential for a carrier task force commander. He explained to King on 29 May that he was going to wait until after the upcoming battle to reorganize the carriers. "At this time it is essential that our organization be stabilized as much as possible." Thus he held up scheduled reliefs of Mitscher by Capt. Charles P. Mason and Buckmaster by Capt. Arthur Davis, the valued Cincpac aviation staff officer.[17]

Therefore if, as it seemed likely, the *Yorktown* could fight, Fletcher would lead all the carriers at Midway. After explaining the TF-16 command situation to Fletcher and Smith, Nimitz discussed the *Yorktown*'s condition. Fletcher's arrival a day earlier than expected proved crucial. On 26 May War Plans hoped she might be ready to go in four days; otherwise an immediate trip to Bremerton was in order. Now from talking with Fletcher, Nimitz estimated the carrier should be ready in forty-eight to sixty hours. He directed she be brought into dry dock the next morning with the special (and risky) dispensation of not removing aviation gasoline beforehand. The navy yard was to complete hull repairs by 0630 on 29 May and refloat her to refuel. Thus Nimitz counted on Fletcher to depart on 30 May. Reestablishing her watertight integrity would be difficult in such a short time. The loading of ammunition, provisions, and supplies was to begin as soon as possible. The other ships would also require working day and night. Nimitz authorized liberty for the long-suffering TF-17 sailors. For Fletcher other news was not so good. Former *Saratoga* squadrons were replacing nearly all his trusted *Yorktown* aviators.[18]

Draemel and Smith withdrew, leaving Fletcher alone with Nimitz. To Fletcher's astonishment, Nimitz brought up King's damning charges that TF-17 had not promptly raided Bougainville and Rabaul in March and April. He also reiterated the criticism over the failure to execute night surface attacks in the Coral Sea battle. "As the reason for this probing gradually dawned on Fletcher, both he and his interrogator became increasingly embarrassed. Frank Jack, never fluent of speech, found himself virtually tongue-tied. He muttered something about wanting to consult his records, and Nimitz agreed that was a reasonable request." In addition to a personal explanation, Nimitz wanted something in writing to submit to King. Thus he deferred the matter to the next day. The awkward interlude ended when Spruance dropped by to ask about the *Yorktown*. He was greatly relieved to hear, "She'll be joining you." The three admirals discussed the coordination of both carrier task forces before and during the battle, a vital consultation that would have been impossible had TF-17 returned on 28 May after Spruance sailed.[19]

THE MIDWAY PLAN

At dinner Nimitz reconvened the conference that now included Fletcher, Spruance, Noyes, Draemel, and Smith, along with important staff. Having briefed senior army and navy commanders that morning, Nimitz again elucidated his ideas regarding the offensive against Midway and the Aleutians. He was superb in these prebattle conferences. Fletcher thought Nimitz was "rather shocked by the enormity of it all, but still he remained calm and imperturbable. These were his best characteristics." Spruance admired Nimitz's "intelligence, open-mindedness, approachability for anyone who had different ideas, and above all, his utter fearlessness and his courage in pushing the war." To Spruance "an offensive fighting spirit is of the utmost importance in the top commanders." Nimitz encouraged his subordinates through quiet confidence laced with humor not cheerleading histrionics or the coercion of a taskmaster.[20]

Nimitz distributed Cincpac Operation Plan 29-42 that McCormick's War Plans Section just compiled. Against the Midway-Hawaii line, Japan could employ four or five big carriers, two to four fast battleships, and seven to nine cruisers with commensurate numbers of destroyers, up to two dozen submarines, and a powerful landing force. (Actual strength was even greater because of the participation of the First Fleet's battleships, hints of which the code breakers detected but which, for unexplained reasons, the analysts discounted.) Smaller but powerful forces, including carriers, threatened the Aleutians. The two offensives would commence shortly. Subs would first reconnoiter U.S. fleet dispositions and form blocking lines to catch ships that sortied to succor Midway. There might even be another night bombing of Pearl Harbor by flying boats, as in March. The carriers would close swiftly to overwhelm Midway's defense and open the way for invasion. King believed that "N-Day," when the Midway and Aleutian landings would take place, was 3 June, but Nimitz leaned toward 5 June (one day prior to the real N-Day). The initial carrier air attacks could begin on 3 or 4 June, likely from northwest of Midway, while heavy ships pounded the defenses at night. The landings themselves might occur at night. Should Midway fall, the Japanese would immediately rush in aircraft and base defenses to consolidate their hold. As for the Aleutians, Nimitz elected only to reinforce its shore-based aircraft and form TF-8 under Admiral Theobald, with two heavy cruisers, three light cruisers, and four destroyers. Nimitz made Midway his personal battle. Exercising "general tactical command" from Pearl, he positioned all of the forces and approved the search patterns.[21]

What was available for Midway? Nimitz wisely ruled out the seven old, slow battleships of Pye's TF-1 based at San Francisco. They still lacked the vital air support and screening ships essential when battling forces supported by carriers. As usual King hoped to use the battleships, but Nimitz declared on 24 May that he would hold them on the West Coast "until objectives for their striking power are more definite." He thought in the back of his mind they could pummel Midway should he have to retake it. Eventually he hoped to use converted auxiliary carriers to protect the battleships, but now he had only the *Long Island*, the first U.S. auxiliary carrier. The *Saratoga* was far more valuable with the carrier striking force than shepherding old battleships. Such a passive role did not sit well with a restive Pye, who thought he should take an active role in the defense of Midway or at least the Hawaiian Islands.[22]

Having dispensed with the battleships, Nimitz reckoned on four basic assets. Spruance's TF-16 (*Enterprise* and *Hornet*) would be in position off Midway by 1 June; TF-17 (*Yorktown*) would join the next day. Fletcher received tactical command of both task forces, which totaled 230 planes. Fitch's TF-11 (*Saratoga*) should depart San Diego on 5 June, too late to fight at Midway unless the Japanese were considerably delayed. Bellinger (CTF-9, shore-based aircraft) was to deploy as many navy, marine, and army aircraft onto Midway as the small atoll could comfortably hold. That ultimately numbered 125 planes under Capt. Cyril T. Simard, the island commander. Long-range searches by PBYs from Midway and Johnston would locate suitable targets, both for the carriers and land-based bombers that included B-17s shuttling in from Hawaii. Simard's marine fighters must defend the air base against certain fierce and unremitting air attack. A proud wearer of the submariner's dolphin insignia, Nimitz anticipated a stellar performance from Rear Adm. Robert H. English's Pacific Fleet subs (TF-7). A dozen boats would form a scouting line west of Midway, patrol their sectors until contact was made, then swarm in. All available subs would reinforce them. Finally, more than two thousand resolute, well-armed marines would defend Midway itself.

Weaker than his opponents in most categories, Nimitz could no longer simply meet them head-on. McCormick put it well. "Not only the directive from [Cominch] but also common sense dictates that we cannot now afford to slug it out with the probably superior approaching Japanese forces." Instead, "We must endeavor to reduce his forces by attrition—submarine attacks, air bombing, attacks on isolated units." Thus, "If attrition is successful the enemy must accept the failure of his venture or risk battle on disadvantageous terms for him." McCormick took notice of King's all-too-accurate fear that the Japanese intended to trap the surface forces but thought the extensive air reconnaissance should forestall that calamity. It was vital to get the maximum effect out of Midway's air, "Without exposing our carriers to danger of destruction out of proportion to the damage they can inflict. We must calculate the risk and must accept the danger when our prospects of frustrating or destroying the enemy carriers are sufficiently good."[23]

Nimitz looked carefully into the deployment of his carriers, the key to success at Midway. As excellent as radio intelligence was in predicting Japanese strategic intentions, he had relatively little actual information, other than his own common sense, as to how the enemy might go about reducing Midway. An important clue from a decrypt appeared in Layton's scorecard on 21 May. "Staff member 1st Air Fleet request [*sic*] weather data from 3 hrs. prior to take off on 'N'-2 day. Asked to be informed of any BLUE activity that area. Planes will be launched 50 miles N.W. of Midway attacking from N–2 days until N-day." Thus Nimitz deduced that for two days prior to the invasion the whole carrier force would strike Midway "from short range, say 50 to 100 miles," to pulverize its air defenses. Midway's own planes "must try to inflict prompt early damage to Jap carrier flight decks if recurring attacks are to be stopped." Nimitz tasked Davis, his fleet aviation officer, to "visualize as closely as possible [the Japanese] method of operation and OUR best counter tactics." He wanted Davis to keep in mind, "Where does Halsey best fit into this picture, remembering we can ill afford loss of carriers." It was vital to determine the best initial position for the U.S. carriers. Nimitz had previously directed Bellinger to fashion a search pattern that would find the enemy carriers before they could close Midway. Bellinger explained, "Each day's search must cover enemy movements to such a distance that the next day's search will reach the enemy carrier's probable launching radius before he can reach it." Thus he proposed a dawn search by the PBYs to seven hundred miles.[24]

Replying on 26 May, Davis warned Nimitz that "unless early, and preferably advance, serious damage is done to enemy CVs," Midway's aircraft would have little effect. Bellinger's suggested long-range search offered "the best chance for us to get in the first effective blows, not only with Midway planes but also with both our carrier planes and our submarines." The proposed pattern of searches from Midway and Johnston "will leave an excellent flanking area northeast of Midway for our carriers. With prompt action by both carriers and submarines, these forces should best be able to do their stuff." Davis stressed it was "particularly important that the carriers be able to take action at the earliest possible moment." Bellinger's search plan "should make it practicable for our carriers to be reasonably close to Midway and thus in position for early action when opportunity arises." Therefore, "Our supporting CVs should be close in for best chance of success, and the full VP [flying boat] search will justify this."[25]

Nimitz agreed that the sector northeast of Midway was the best initial location for his carrier striking force. From there the carriers could "seize opportunity to obtain initial advantage against carriers which are employing their air groups against Midway." The goal was to "inflict maximum damage on enemy by employing strong attrition tactics," but "not accept such decisive action as would be likely to incur heavy losses in our carriers and cruisers." Cincpac's separate letter of instruction to Fletcher and Spruance directed them to "be governed by the principle of calculated risk which you shall interpret to mean the avoidance of exposure of your forces to attack by superior enemy forces without good prospect of inflicting, as a result of such exposure, greater damage to the enemy. This applies to a landing phase as well as during preliminary air attacks." Spruance's flag lieutenant, Robert J. Oliver, recalled that Nimitz told Spruance no matter what not to lose his carriers. If things got too rough, he was to withdraw and let Midway fall. Any enemy foothold so far east could be recaptured later. Fletcher doubtless received the same instructions.[26]

The defense of Midway posed a daunting task. The Japanese "have amply demonstrated their ability to use their carrier air with great ability," and "we can no longer underestimate their naval air efficiency." That is a rather surprising admission that showed that prior to the loss of the *Lexington*, Japanese prowess was not recognized. Nimitz's decision to fight at Midway was all the more courageous. Japan held the initiative. The Combined Fleet outnumbered the Pacific Fleet in all classes of combat ships. Its carrier aircraft enjoyed longer range and the fighters possibly superior performance. Its amphibious forces were experienced and highly efficient. The weaker Pacific Fleet must resort to attrition tactics rather than direct confrontation. Yet Nimitz had strong reason for optimism at Midway. The situation certainly warranted taking a "calculated risk." His men were "just as brave, and those who have been properly trained are believed to be better than their opposite Jap number." The remarkable radio intelligence gave him sufficient warning to gather his forces in secret. Japan must expose its precious carriers to counterattack vastly abetted by the element of surprise. The enemy would confront a "fairly strong" land-based air force beyond supporting range of his own shore-based aviation. "Our submarines have demonstrated considerable superiority." The assault on Midway would prove costly to the attackers. The battle was far from the desperate gamble that is often portrayed. Although the odds still favored Japan, Nimitz had devised a careful plan where victory would pay enormous dividends.[27]

"FLETCHER DID A FINE JOB"

On the evening of 27 May Fletcher returned to the *Yorktown* with a great deal on his mind, not the least to correct Cincpac's impression of his previous conduct. The next morning he delivered a lengthy letter that summarized his operations in the Coral Sea. Not having time to recast the narrative, he apologized for including long excerpts from the Coral Sea action report submitted separately to headquarters. Endeavoring to explain his command decisions and clear up any misunderstandings, Fletcher emphasized, "Trying to operate under these conditions and maintain radio silence is very exasperating, also the condition of fuel weighs heavily on the mind of the Task Force Commander." His letter and a follow-up interview removed the last of Nimitz's concerns. On 29 May Nimitz wrote privately to King that he had investigated "what appeared to be a lack of aggressive tactics" on Fletcher's part and the absence of night surface attacks in the Coral Sea. "Both of these matters have been cleared up to my entire satisfaction and, I hope, will be to yours." The "long delay and lack of aggressive tactics" Nimitz attributed to the "lack of sufficiently reliable combat intelligence upon which to base operations, to the necessity for replenishment of fuel and provisions, and to the replacement of defective leak proof tanks in the fighter planes." He concluded: "I hope, and believe that after reading the enclosed letter, you will agree with me that Fletcher did a fine job and exercised superior judgement in his recent cruise to the Coral Sea. He is an excellent, seagoing, fighting naval officer and I wish to retain him as a task force commander for the future. I will be greatly pleased if you can approve my recommendation of award of distinguished service medal to Fletcher and his designation as a task force commander with the rank of Vice Admiral as previously recommended by despatch."[28]

Certainly emerging with a lighter heart on 28 May after meeting Nimitz, Fletcher continued preparing for the swift sortie of TF-17. That morning the *Yorktown* eased into dry dock number one, which was quickly pumped out so the hull could be mended. More than a thousand shipfitters swarmed on board to shore up interior damage and restore watertight integrity. At the same time, the ship was provisioned and supplied. Before the dock was fully dry, Nimitz, Fletcher, and Buckmaster sloshed through the water inspecting her hull and encouraging the yard workers, who "got into the spirit of the thing and really turned to." Relieved the exterior damage appeared "minor," Nimitz issued orders that afternoon for TF-17 to sail at 0900, 30 May. Still, the task "was a large order, and everyone connected with the job sensed there was something big about to happen."[29]

In the meantime, Spruance's TF-16 got under way: first the eleven destroyers, five heavy cruisers, and one light antiaircraft cruiser, two fleet oilers, and finally, toward noon, the *Enterprise* and *Hornet*. That was almost the exact same time, 29 May in Japan, that Yamamoto's own Main Body put to sea. With Spruance now CTF-16, Kinkaid took over the cruiser task group (TG-16.2). In a surprise move Spruance named the *Enterprise*'s Capt. George D. Murray (USNA 1911, wings 1915, aviator number 22) as Commander, Air (CTG-16.5), even though Mitscher in the *Hornet* was not only senior, but also soon to step up to rear admiral. Spruance obviously preferred to concentrate the carrier command in the *Big E*, but Mitscher could not have been very pleased. They would not get along particularly well at Midway.[30]

Another rocky relationship, that of Fletcher and his radio intelligence officer, Lt. Forrest Biard, finally broke up on 28 May. Bags packed, Biard approached Fletcher and Lewis the day before, asking to be released back to Hypo. He explained that because he had been away from base so long, he was certain someone else attuned to the latest developments would be more useful. In truth, the deeply embittered Biard simply wanted off the *Yorktown* and away from Fletcher. He interpreted his profound disagreements with Fletcher over the evaluation of radio intelligence in battle, admittedly an arcane art, as direct personal attacks on his competency. To his extreme surprise, especially as he felt certain Fletcher "ended up hating," as well as distrusting him, Fletcher proved very unwilling to part with him but wanted him to stay for the fight at Midway. That reluctance is particularly notable, for Fletcher already had at hand a more congenial replacement, an old shipmate, Commander Fullinwider, the former TF-11 radio intelligence officer who rode the *Yorktown* back from Tongatabu. Yet instead of immediately casting off a truculent subordinate, Fletcher demonstrated mature leadership and loyalty in valuing the able but difficult Biard, despite their sharp differences. Only after dogging Fletcher, who truly had many other things on his mind, Biard finally received permission to leave, after Fletcher himself went to Nimitz and secured Fullinwider in his place. Biard had intended to remain a few days to brief his successor. Learning he was to be Fullinwider, Biard departed immediately. His memoir severely criticized Fullinwider ("a terrible handicap to me"), although Fitch praised his advice at Coral Sea. Fullinwider certainly made mistakes, but he did intercept key search reports on the morning of 7 May that Biard missed.[31]

Fletcher was understandably apprehensive over losing most of his highly valued veteran aviators. On the afternoon of 27 May the Carpac administrative office ordered Burch's Scouting Five, Taylor's Torpedo Five, and Fenton's Fighting Forty-two detached from the *Yorktown* Air Group. They were to draw replacement pilots and planes and embark in the *Saratoga* in the next ten days. The only remaining original *Yorktown* squadron was Lieutenant Short's Bombing Five. Joining the group were the three *Saratoga* squadrons stranded at Pearl since February. Only Lt. Cdr. Maxwell F. Leslie's Bombing Three had recent carrier time, having gone with the *Enterprise* on the Tokyo raid. Lt. Cdr. Lance E. Massey's Torpedo Three was green. Lt. Cdr. John S. Thach's Fighting Three brought twenty-seven new Grumman F4F-4s, the latest version of the Wildcat. It featured folding wings and six .50-caliber machine guns, instead of four, but only half the ammunition per gun. Fletcher welcomed the increased number of fighters. Pederson, the group commander, thought he was responsible for the shake-up. Earlier in May, not knowing Midway was in the offing, he recommended to Comcarpac that the *Yorktown* squadrons receive a well-earned break. "I told [Noyes] if we were going out to battle I wanted my old air group—that even tho tired and needing a rest they were experienced and used to working together." Noyes refused to relent. Pederson recalled that when Fletcher found out about the new air group, he "was very upset and furious with me for not letting him know of the change. I was really caught in the middle of that one! However, he didn't stay angry too long." As Fletcher told Walter Lord, "It wasn't a question of quality—none could be better—but these new men just weren't used to the ship." Nimitz stuck with the original orders. Events proved that Fletcher and the *Yorktown* would have no cause to complain of their ex-*Saratoga* brethren, far from it.[32]

Ironically the much-improved model of torpedo bomber that all the squadrons long craved finally reached Pearl on 29 May in a convoy from Alameda with the Torpedo Eight Detachment (whose parent unit sailed in the *Hornet*) and twenty-one brand new Grumman TBF-1 Avengers. Much faster than the TBDs, the TBFs were also far bigger and heavier. Remarkable for such a big plane (wingspan fifty-four feet, weight 15,905 pounds fully loaded), the Avenger proved an excellent carrier aircraft, long ranged and rugged. As yet only the *Hornet* and the *Saratoga* possessed arresting gear strong enough to take them. Noyes sent six TBFs to Midway in time to fight in the battle. The same stateside convoy also delivered two fresh fighting squadrons, VF-5 (an original *Yorktown* unit) and VF-72, but too late to fight at Midway.[33]

In the brief interval before sailing, Fletcher's staff grappled with a thousand necessary details. Cdr. Hal Guthrie, the combat intelligence and damage control officer, first learned the details of the Midway operation on the morning of 29 May, when he and Cdr. Gerry Galpin, the operations officer, accompanied Fletcher to headquarters. Guthrie followed with obvious interest the progress of the repairs on the *Yorktown*, as her watertight integrity had been compromised, and had serious doubts whether she would survive the next battle. Buckmaster was more sanguine. "The seams were re-riveted, and the bulkheads, doors, and hatches were repaired as best they could in the time they had. My understanding was that it was a patch job, but good enough for us to go to sea, to get into whatever was to happen."[34]

Fletcher and the staff enjoyed a warm reunion with Cdr. Butch Schindler, the peripatetic gunnery officer last seen on 9 May prior to his hurried flight to Australia. After accomplishing his mission, Schindler flew to Sydney where he visited the *Chicago*, then stopped off in New Zealand before hitching a ride to Pearl in a large flying boat. The staff also welcomed Cdr. Michael B. Laing, RN, the new British naval liaison officer. A non-aviator, he had been executive officer in 1940–41 of venerable HMS *Furious* in raids against Kirkenes in Norway and Petsamo, Finland, and also the western Mediterranean. Laing's hope for action would not be disappointed. Schindler later described him as a "grand shipmate, a real seaman [who] possessed a typical British sense of humor."[35]

On the morning of 29 May the *Yorktown* left dry dock number one and returned to Pier 16 to resume loading supplies. Work on her innards continued unabated. Nimitz wrote King that she "will be in all respects ready to give a good account of herself." His particularly appropriate postscript evoked the attitude of the entire Pacific Fleet toward fighting at Midway: "We are actively preparing to greet our expected visitors with the kind of reception they deserve, and we will do the best we can with what we have." Bright and early on 30 May Nimitz came on board the *Yorktown* to bid farewell to Fletcher and Buckmaster. He wanted Buckmaster to tell the crew that after the present assignment they were going back to Bremerton for repairs and to enjoy a long leave. For now, however, their task was to help win the biggest battle yet in the Pacific War.[36]

POINT LUCK

Preceded by Hoover's destroyers *Morris*, *Anderson*, *Hammann*, *Russell*, and *Hughes* and Smith's heavy cruisers *Astoria* and *Portland*, the *Yorktown* nosed out to sea shortly after Cincpac's visit. The brief but busy sojourn at Pearl left the *Yorktown* crew in an excellent mood. Buckmaster relayed over the loudspeaker to a cheering ship's company Nimitz's promise of stateside leave following the next battle. "And not just for any two weeks, either!" Smith could not resist teasing Fletcher, signaling: "May 18 issue of *Time* contains slanderous statement about you." Wary of his friend's wicked sense of humor, Fletcher simply asked Smith to include the magazine in the first guard mail delivery via destroyer. The offending article proved to be an overview of the Pacific Fleet's early raids that in a brief mention described Fletcher as "scholarly," probably because his official naval biography disclosed that he had attended both the navy and army war colleges. A letter from a mutual friend that accompanied the magazine noted how an amused J. O. Richardson suggested the "slander suit," and that Fletcher's wife Martha had concurred.[37]

A terrible accident instantly sobered the high spirits in the *Yorktown*. That afternoon the air group appeared overhead after flying out from Kaneohe. Thach's VF-3 landed first, which challenged the flight deck crew to fold properly the unfamiliar wings of the new F4F-4s. The fourth fighter bounced high on touchdown and floated over the barrier directly onto the back of another Wildcat. Its propeller sliced through the cockpit. Despite the danger of whirling props and fire, the flight deck crew, joined by executive officer Dixie Kiefer, tore through the crushed Wildcat to save its pilot, but Lt. Cdr. Donald A. Lovelace had been killed instantly. The quality of some of the subsequent landings likewise validated Fletcher's concern that the air group included numerous rookies. By sundown TF-17 shaped course northwest at twenty knots toward Midway. The *Yorktown*'s operable air strength was seventy-one planes (twenty-five F4Fs, thirty-four SBDs, and twelve TBDs).[38]

By the time Fletcher sailed, Nimitz had decided on a specific initial position (latitude 32° north, longitude 173° west) 325 miles northeast of Midway to station the carriers while awaiting the enemy approach. He dubbed it "Point Luck." Prior to enemy contact Fletcher was to operate north and east of Luck, Spruance north and west. Toward noon, they were to approach Luck, and, if necessary, communicate by aircraft message drop. Cincpac's dispatch to Spruance called the arrangement "not mandatory" and "intended only to assist initial coordination." The version in Appendix 2 of Op-Plan 29-42 stated that it was "not intended to restrict the operation of either force in any manner but to avoid having embarrassing or premature contact made with own forces." As will be seen, by deliberately not uniting the two task forces Nimitz profoundly shaped how the battle was fought.[39]

On 29 May Cominch provided Nimitz, Fletcher, and Theobald a new estimate of enemy strength and intentions. He now agreed with Nimitz that N-Day, the actual day of the landing, was very likely 5 June. The Midway occupation force apparently left Saipan on 28 May (local time), whereas the Midway Striking Force of the *Akagi*, *Kaga*, *Hiryū*, and *Sōryū* (Cardivs One and Two), four fast battleships, and six heavy cruisers departed Japan the day before. The air attacks on Midway would commence early on 3 June, Midway time. "Believe *Zuikaku* will either form part of the Striking Force or will join convoy as escort on 1 June." King was less certain about the scope and timing of the Aleutians venture with perhaps two small carriers (Cardiv Three), a converted carrier or seaplane tender, and five heavy cruisers, plus screen. The enemy could reach Kiska on 31 May or 1 June, "Which seems badly timed as effort at diversion." Instead, the carriers might strike Unalaska beginning 31 May and 3 June, with an invasion later. "Purpose of attack on date earlier than Midway might be effort at diversion." In fact, as has been seen, the Japanese never intended the AL Operation as a diversion.[40]

On 30 May after TF-17 sailed, Cincpac radioed the task force commanders his latest and most detailed take on the composition of the enemy forces. The Midway Striking Force comprised the familiar four formidable carriers (fortunately not also *Zuikaku*), but its screen numbered only two fast battleships, two heavy cruisers, and a dozen destroyers—a correct estimate. The Midway occupation force should have two or three heavy cruisers, two seaplane carriers, two to four seaplane tenders, twelve to eighteen transports and cargo ships, and a close cover force of one carrier or converted carrier, two fast battleships, five heavy cruisers, and ten destroyers. About sixteen subs preceded the other forces to scout the Hawaii-Midway area. Nimitz's estimate, like King's, failed to include Yamamoto and the battleships of the First Fleet. He also reiterated his belief that the landing at Midway was set for 5 June, a day earlier than the actual Japanese plan. Thus like King, Nimitz estimated the preliminary carrier air attacks could begin the night of 2–3 June. A decrypt revealed a possible rendezvous 685 miles west of Midway, near the extreme strike radius of the B-17s. Given the surmised schedule, that meeting might take place on 31 May or 1 June. Although King speculated that might be where the *Zuikaku* would join the Midway Striking Force, Nimitz labeled it a refueling point. He directed Midway to have B-17s there those two afternoons. They found nothing. No Japanese ships had yet come that far east. Nagumo planned to swing well north before turning southeast toward Midway. The rendezvous itself referred to a later event involving one of Kondō's auxiliaries. Nimitz did not reveal to Fletcher and Spruance that the source of detailed radio intelligence was drying up. The IJN finally implemented the long overdue change with a new cipher codebook and additive table, although some commands used the old system a short while. Thus Hypo and its colleagues in Washington and Melbourne could only analyze radio traffic and break recent messages sent in the old cipher.[41]

On Sunday, 31 May, the oddly appropriate anniversary of the Battle of Jutland, two TF-1 battleships and two destroyers (another joined on 1 June) under Admiral Anderson left San Francisco to patrol six hundred miles northwest. That sortie resulted from a bout of nerves by Pye, who was disappointed not to fight in defense of Midway or at least deploy to Hawaii. On 28 May he announced to TF-1 that intelligence "indicates probability" of an air raid on Alaska or California during the "coming week." He put TF-1 on alert, with antiaircraft guns manned, and canceled shore leave. Even so, he directed the action be kept "confidential," to not "unduly alarm" civilians. It is understandable that someone surprised at Pearl Harbor would never risk anything like that again, but Cincpac was aghast at the prospect of the massive security leak that might warn Japan that something was up. McCormick called Pye's order "very dangerous" and "wholly unnecessary." Fearing a sort of Doolittle raid in reverse by a couple of auxiliary carriers, Pye then informed Nimitz that evening of his intention to send Anderson to sea. "Exposure of Batdiv 4 is believed justifiable on view unavailability vessels more suitable for task to be assigned." The next day Nimitz approved. It was important to maintain morale in TF-1 and facilitate training, but from that point Pye's days as CTF-1 were numbered. Nimitz ordered the *Long Island* to proceed immediately from San Diego to join TF-1 at San Francisco and asked Pye to evaluate her use in covering the battleships. Perhaps that would keep Pye busy until the battle for Midway was over.[42]

On 31 May TF-17 steamed uneventfully northwest toward its fueling rendezvous the next afternoon. Overnight it traversed the waters destined for part of the northern Japanese submarine picket line. Even if those subs had arrived on schedule (1 June, west longitude date), they were too late to detect TF-17. Spruance's TF-16, of course, already lurked far to the northwest. On the morning of 1 June Fletcher's cruisers fueled the destroyers. That day the *Yorktown*'s crew handed out battle gear. To prevent confusion between the two bombing squadrons, Buckmaster temporarily changed Bombing Five's designation to Scouting Five. The weather closed in that afternoon. Twenty minutes after the destroyers finished their drink, the Fueling Group hove into sight. Each cruiser latched onto an oiler. At sundown Fletcher released the *Cimarron* and destroyer *Monssen* to a holding area six to seven hundred miles east of Midway and tucked the *Platte* and *Dewey* astern of TF-17 as it continued west. At dawn on 2 June, as TF-17 closed Point Luck from the southeast, the *Yorktown* took her turn alongside the *Platte*. The skies were overcast, with intermittent patches of misty rain and fog. After the *Yorktown* completed fueling, Fletcher dispatched the oilers to safer waters and headed west toward Point Luck ninety miles off. Although TF-17 sheltered behind Midway's wide-ranging patrol planes, the *Yorktown* mounted a precautionary SBD search. A special flight of two SBDs discovered TF-16 in the midst of clouds sixty miles west of Point Luck and dropped a message to Spruance setting the rendezvous at Luck that afternoon. TF-16 experienced an uneventful trip out. Spruance topped off his ships on 31 May, and from 1 June marked time northeast of Midway, awaiting either Fletcher or the enemy, whoever came first.

That afternoon Fletcher gained a better idea when additional reinforcements might reach him. Nimitz radioed that Fitch's TF-11 (*Saratoga*, *Chester*, light antiaircraft cruiser *San Diego*, and four destroyers) would depart Pearl about 6 June. "Desire this force join TF17." Cincpac would provide the route and set the tentative rendezvous. In fact, the estimate was too optimistic. Nimitz had originally intended for Fitch to assemble TF-11 at San Diego by the afternoon of 4 June, but on 30 May he told Capt. Dewitt C. Ramsey, the new commanding officer of the *Saratoga*, not to wait, but sail at the "earliest practicable time." Ramsey's TG-11.1 departed San Diego on 1 June with the *Sara*, *San Diego*, and four destroyers. Fitch in the *Chester* and two transports filled with *Lexington* survivors only reached San Diego on the second. He could not refuel and clear the harbor before the afternoon of 4 June. To his great regret that would be far too late to fight in the Battle of Midway.[43]

Nimitz also suggested Fletcher consider moving his initial area of operation north rather than northeast of Midway, "To insure being within early striking distances of objectives." Nothing new had changed in his "estimate of enemy plans which included a northwesterly approach for striking force." Nimitz did offer new details on the invasion plans of Midway. Two special pioneer battalions were to restore the airfield as soon as possible to take planes being ferried on the carriers and seaplane tenders, while bombers and flying boats waited at Wake to stage to Midway. The landing force itself comprised Japanese "marines" and a special army unit. "They are even bringing guns captured on Wake." Nimitz was confident his commanders "have the stuff to smear their plays. Watch for razzle dazzle."[44]

CARRIER TACTICS

On the afternoon of 2 June TF-16 hove into view fifteen miles southwest of TF-17. Unlike the previous month at the Coral Sea, Fletcher did not unite the two task forces, but directed TF-16 to take position ten miles to the south and remain within visual signaling distance. The task forces were to keep five to ten miles apart, with TF-16 holding station to the southwest. Fletcher reluctantly followed Nimitz's direct orders, based on the preference of the top naval aviators for separated carrier task forces. Every reference by Cincpac referred to the task forces as distinct entities. Even the two TF-16 carriers were to maneuver independently under air attack. Fletcher himself much preferred an integrated striking force. In 1947 he told Morison he "automatically assumed command" of the carrier striking force at the rendezvous. "However, due to the lack of time for conferences, drill, preparation of plans and organization," the "clumsy and illogical method was adopted of leaving Spruance in command of his two [carriers], while I retained command of the *Yorktown* Task Force and overall tactical command of the combined force." The two task forces "operated in close vicinity, but not as a tactical unit." Unaware of Cincpac's dictum, critics questioned why Fletcher did not immediately join TF-16 and TF-17, particularly in light of the integral multi-carrier task forces so successful later. Bates incorrectly described Cincpac having organized the carriers "into a single striking force," but did not know why Fletcher failed to incorporate them into the same formation. In truth unlike the Japanese, the U.S. Navy had not yet worked three carriers together, except as George Murray emphasized in November 1942, only "to a very limited extent" and then "*only* for simple, peacetime operations."[45]

Nimitz, however, had his own reasons for not joining the three carriers that went well beyond the worry of employing experimental tactics in battle. He had resolved the contradiction between the Ultra decrypt hinting that carriers would repeatedly strike Midway from very close and the considered belief of his trusted advisor Davis that the carriers would stand well off and refrain from shuttle attacks until they had neutralized

Midway's air force. Nimitz now believed the Japanese carriers would do both. The enemy would most likely operate his carriers again in two separate, mutually supporting groups, as it was thought they had repeatedly done before. Separating the carrier groups by at least double the limit of visibility (say fifty miles) prevented a single snooper from spotting both groups. That was the cherished dispersion tactic of the top U.S. naval aviators, but not of Capt. Ted Sherman and Fletcher.[46]

Thus Cincpac Op-Plan 29-42 opined, "One or more carriers may take up close-in daylight positions" to the northwest for up to two days to knock out Midway's air force, while "additional carrier groups and fast battleships" covered these "attacking carriers against our surface forces." Nimitz clearly believed such an initial separation of enemy carriers greatly enhanced his chances for a devastating counterattack, particularly if it came as a complete surprise. The key was to take advantage of surprise to eliminate one enemy carrier group at the outset. The group attacking Midway was likeliest to be spotted first. There was the added benefit of possibly catching its planes on deck being rearmed for further strikes against the island. The primary weapon for this attack was to be Spruance's TF-16 (*Enterprise* and *Hornet*), kept "cocked and primed" as a single unit, while other forces handled searches. Once one Japanese carrier group appeared within range, Fletcher, wielding tactical command, would instantly release Spruance to hurl his full striking power of 120 planes, capable of destroying at least two carriers at once. Browning's staff was to ensure this supremely vital attack went off without a hitch. In the meantime, Fletcher would decide whether TF-17 (*Yorktown*) engaged the second enemy group—the most desirable course of action—or followed up Spruance's attack. Fletcher retained the flexibility to launch searches and fill in with attacks against one group or the other as necessary. Should events go the way Nimitz, Fletcher, and Spruance hoped, the second phase would see three U.S. carriers finish off the two remaining flattops. In truth, Nagumo never divided his four carriers. That misunderstanding on the part of Nimitz and others would cause grave repercussions in the subsequent battle.[47]

At the rendezvous Fletcher and Spruance exchanged op orders and combat air patrol schedules. Lt. Cdr. Leonard J. "Ham" Dow, the TF-16 staff communications officer, would direct all fighters when the two task forces were in close proximity. Fletcher also reset the clocks in the carrier task forces to Zone plus 10, two hours ahead of the local Midway time (Z+12), as a sort of daylight savings time. Thus for the carriers morning twilight at Point Luck started at 0540 rather than the local time of 0340, and sunrise was 0627 rather than 0427. That time difference would bedevil certain future historians, who forgot to convert times properly and thus contributed to the battle's persistent myths. From here, unless otherwise specifically noted, all times will be Z+12, used by Midway itself and in nearly all secondary sources on the battle.

On the afternoon of 2 June Fletcher followed Cincpac's suggestion to move north of Midway, rather than keep to the northeast. The two task forces headed west at fourteen knots during the night to gain proper position, should, as expected, the Japanese carriers show up at dawn on 3 June northwest of Midway. If the enemy was delayed, Fletcher planned to work northward during most of the day and then retire southward toward Midway to avoid running afoul of a possible surface force approaching in the darkness. Anticipation in both task forces ran high. "Morale was excellent."[48]

CHAPTER 17

The Battle of Midway I
"Give Them the Works"

A DAY OF WAITING

Overnight on 2–3 June Fletcher shifted the carrier striking force west to the new operating area 175 miles west of Point Luck and 260 miles north of Midway. Nimitz predicted that 3 June would see simultaneous carrier strikes on Midway and the Aleutians. That would have occurred had Japan kept the original plan.[1] On board the *Yorktown*, anticipation was high, and "scuttlebutt was thick." The "sensible and confident" demeanor of the veteran carrier impressed Commander Laing. Tasked by Nimitz only to search northeast of Midway, Fletcher did not rely on the island's seven-hundred-mile search to cover the front door, especially because the weather northwest remained worrisome. Before sunrise the *Yorktown* dispatched twenty SBDs to scan a two-hundred-mile semicircle oriented southwest to northeast (240–060 degrees) and to ensure that neither of the two suspected carrier groups (Midway attack force and its covering force) was within range. Ten miles southwest of TF-17, Spruance's TF-16 was poised with attack aircraft crammed onto the *Enterprise* and *Hornet* flight decks. Having completed flight operations, Fletcher turned north at twelve knots. Dawn revealed a low overcast with occasional breaks and moderate southeast winds. The search pilots who flew northwest struggled in squalls that greatly reduced visibility in that crucial direction.[2]

Around 0445 both carrier task forces monitored an urgent Cincpac message relaying a flash report that Dutch Harbor in the Aleutians was under attack. Nineteen planes from Admiral Kakuta's 2nd *Kidō Butai* (*Ryūjō* and *Junyō*) bombed Dutch Harbor at 0345 Midway time. Nimitz flashed one of his "dazzling" smiles. "Well," he told Layton, "this ought to make your heart warm." His own relief must have been tremendous, for he risked American fortunes in the Pacific on the accuracy of radio intelligence. To Fletcher and Spruance word of the Japanese strike reinforced the expectation Midway might soon be attacked. At 0650, almost on cue, the *Yorktown*'s radar picked up a suspicious contact twenty-one miles northeast. Fletcher directed four fighters to intercept, warned TF-16 by TBS radio, and concentrated his own ships in defensive formation. Spruance ordered his duty carrier, the *Hornet*, to turn into the wind to launch the combat air patrol. Radar, however, tracked the bogey passing off to the east. He quickly canceled the fighter scramble, which would have entailed a massive respot of the *Hornet*'s deck to retrieve them. The contact was a Midway search plane.[3]

At 0904 a Midway PBY (Ens. James P. O. Lyle of Patrol Squadron Fifty-one) radioed the sighting of two cargo ships 470 miles southwest (bearing 247 degrees) from base. Twenty minutes later Ens. Jewell H. Reid of VP-44, in the sector north of Lyle, flashed the words, "Main body," which was seven hundred miles southwest (bearing 261 degrees) of Midway. Two cargo ships were only a nuisance, but if the so-called main body included the carriers, Cincpac's own carrier deployment was in serious error. With TF-16 and TF-17 at least 850 miles northwest, there could be no battle that day. It dawned on Nimitz that "main body" might not be the appropriate term. At 1007 he advised that he believed the group just reported was the "attack and occupation force," and that he "expected" the "striking force" to be "separated."[4]

Nimitz's surmise was correct. Persistent nasty weather effectively cloaked Admiral Nagumo's four carriers, now six hundred miles northwest of Midway and 550 miles distant from Fletcher. Yamamoto's battleship force, located six hundred miles northwest of Nagumo, also plowed through fog. The Midway search discovered part of Admiral Kondō's Attack Force closing from the west and southwest in four groups. Reid's "main body" was the Invasion Force and associated Seaplane Carrier Force, escorted by a destroyer squadron. His navigation was good. When first sighted, the transports bore 260 degrees and 675 miles from Midway. Kondō's own main force of two fast battleships, four heavy cruisers, and light carrier *Zuihō* gained on them from astern, as did the Close Support Force (four heavy cruisers and two destroyers) from the southwest. These powerful formations remained beyond sight of Midway-based planes. Nonetheless, encountering U.S. flying boats so far from base brought unwelcome surprise. The Japanese expected Midway's air searches to extend no more than six hundred miles, a line Kondō would have crossed only that afternoon after the morning search already turned for home. The two cargo ships at 470 miles were small minesweepers coming from Saipan via Wake Island. Although close as to their actual distance of 460 miles, Lyle in fact located them too far south. Instead of southeast of the transport force, they were two hundred miles northeast and in fact the unwitting vanguard of the whole force. In flagship *Yamato* Admiral Ugaki was appalled to find minesweepers out in the lead and decried the Invasion Force's "premature exposure." He wished Nagumo could have hit Midway that dawn.[5]

Midway coaxed more details from Reid on the "main body," eventually described as eleven ships steering due east at nineteen knots. Fletcher kept to his own plan of heading north and later reversing course to stay in the same area north of Midway. Just to make certain the enemy was not closing in, the *Yorktown*'s afternoon search of nineteen SBDs covered the same southwest-northeast arc to two hundred miles. Fletcher's caution proved justified after Midway PBYs again faced "zero visibility" beyond 450 miles northwest. At 1445 Nimitz summarized the day's developments. "Believe striking force has not yet been located." Those ships, "probably combatant," first sighted seven hundred miles west of Midway, "may be escort group heading toward a rendezvous with the occupation vessels sighted closer in." Nine B-17s left Midway to attack "the supposed escort group." As yet "there is not enough yet in the picture at either place to confirm or deny my previous estimates or to warrant change in initial developments."[6]

After sundown Fletcher swung southwest intending to be two hundred miles north of Midway at dawn on 4 June, and again ready to fight according to plan. Midway struck its first blow. That evening Cincpac relayed reports that nine B-17s bombed the transport main body 575 miles west of Midway. The target was a mixed force of eleven ships, including two or three battleships, one carrier, two or three cruisers, destroyers, and transports. The bombers claimed hits on the two largest warships and also a transport left burning. In fact the transport force, whose mightiest ship was a light cruiser, suffered no damage. Four radar-equipped PBYs sortied from Midway for a moonlight torpedo attack. "The situation is developing as expected," Nimitz advised. The carriers, "our most important objective," will soon turn up. "Tomorrow may be the day you can give them the works." That night he slept on a cot in his office.[7]

The foggy night of 3–4 June proved especially tense for the task forces that were, in Fletcher's words, "biting their nails" wondering why the enemy carriers had not yet appeared. Hopefully in the morning the search would find them promptly. "We couldn't afford to wait," he later recalled. "We had to strike first, strike swiftly and strike in great force." Before dawn he learned about the night torpedo attack that took place about 0230 against the main body five hundred miles southwest of Midway. Cincpac claimed a hit on a large transport, and in fact the PBYs had torpedoed the big oiler *Akebono Maru* with minor damage. One PBY crew reported encountering an enemy plane near the target area, so a carrier might also be nearby.[8]

"ENEMY CARRIERS"

Starting at 0415 Midway dispatched twenty-two PBYs to sweep the western semicircle from 200 to 020 degrees. Given predictions of two enemy carrier groups operating independently, the searchers had orders to cover their individual sectors to seven hundred miles, or until *all four* carriers were reported. Only then were they to take refuge in the Laysan and Lisianski atolls southeast beyond Midway. At the same time sixteen B-17s (two later aborted) under Lt. Col. Walter C. Sweeney thundered aloft to bomb the transport force. Midway would redirect them if carriers were discovered within range. The single biggest concentration yet of heavy bombers in the Pacific gave Sweeney a splendid opportunity to see what they could do against maneuvering ships. Any damage they inflicted only made the job of the U.S. carriers that much easier. Captain Simard prepared additional striking forces if carriers approached within two hundred miles. Six new Grumman TBFs and four army B-26 medium bombers lugged torpedoes, whereas twenty-seven marine SBD and SB2U scout bombers carried 500-pound bombs. Midway's fighter defense comprised twenty-eight marine F2A-3 Buffaloes and F4F-3 Wildcats, backed by efficient radar and strong antiaircraft.[9]

Early on 4 June Fletcher steered TF-17 and TF-16 (225 operational planes) southwest at 13.5 knots to be two hundred miles north of Midway at dawn. He again depended on the Midway search to find opposing carriers believed closing from the northwest, but he took precautions in case one carrier group flanked him to the north. As the enemy should already be close, he committed only ten *Yorktown* SBDs to a dawn "security" search of the northern semicircle to one hundred miles. At 0420 as the eastern sky glowed red, the

Yorktown launched six combat air patrol F4Fs and the ten SBDs, then spotted the first deck load of eight F4Fs, seventeen SBDs, and twelve TBDs. This time Schindler did not fly. In the event of a surface action, Fletcher needed his special talents to coordinate gunnery by different ships. Some ten to fifteen miles south, Spruance had 120 planes, the full striking force of the *Enterprise* and *Hornet*, ready to go on Fletcher's order when the first enemy carriers turned up. Fifty-one F4Fs from the three carriers were allocated for combat air patrol under Commander Dow, the *Enterprise* fighter director. No TF-16 combat air patrol had yet deployed, due to the necessity to break the deck spot if the strike was not launched before those fighters had to land. Once the *Yorktown* completed flight operations, Fletcher brought both task forces around to the east at fifteen knots.[10]

At 0500 (0730 Pearl local time), Layton predicted to Nimitz that in precisely an hour a Midway-based search plane would discover enemy carriers 175 miles northwest (bearing 325 degrees) from Midway. From there, he thought, the Midway carrier group would open its attack to crush the island's air force.[11] Fletcher lacked such an exact forecast, but he knew something must break shortly. Nimitz's intelligence was on the mark. At 0430 Nagumo's 1st *Kidō Butai*, the most powerful task force in the Pacific, glided southeast in the growing light 240 miles northwest of Midway and only a little over two hundred miles west of Fletcher's carriers. It was now the vanguard upon which the fury of the Pacific Fleet was about to descend. Operating together, unlike Cincpac's prediction, the four elite carriers (247 operational planes, including twenty-one fighters for Midway) comprised Nagumo's own 1st Carrier Division (*Akagi* and *Kaga*) and 2nd Carrier Division (*Hiryū* and *Sōryū*), under Rear Adm. Yamaguchi Tamon. The formidable screen, under Rear Adm. Abe Hiroaki (commanding officer, 8th Cruiser Division), contained fast battleships *Haruna* and *Kirishima*, Abe's own heavy cruisers *Tone* and *Chikuma*, and Rear Adm. Kimura Susumu's 10th Destroyer Squadron (light cruiser *Nagara* and eleven destroyers).[12]

Like Fletcher and Spruance, Vice Adm. Nagumo Chūichi, age fifty-five, was no naval aviator, but a surface warrior known as a particularly sharp and aggressive torpedo expert. Promoted to rear admiral in 1935, he led light cruisers in the opening stage of the China Incident, and in 1939 he rose to vice admiral in charge of the four *Kongō*-class fast battleships. Afterward, he served as president of the Naval Staff College. In April 1941 the IJN entrusted Nagumo, who had no previous aviation experience, with the First Air Fleet of carriers. Late that year he formed the *Kidō Butai*, the operational command of six elite carriers that constituted the greatest concentration of naval aviation yet achieved. Nagumo won great success attacking Pearl Harbor, supporting the invasion of the Dutch East Indies, and in the Indian Ocean. By necessity like Fletcher and Spruance, he relied on the advice of his carrier experts. Unlike his U.S. Navy counterparts, Nagumo appears to have shown little interest in the actual mechanics of carrier air operations. It became increasingly apparent by Midway that he was out of his depth, worn down by the responsibility of commanding a force whose technical intricacies he had not mastered. Such passivity resulted from a system where top commanders almost invariably (Yamamoto a rare exception) decided in favor of staff recommendations, once the staff officers themselves reached consensus. Cdr. Genda Minoru, the brilliant air staff officer who largely planned the air portion of the attack on Pearl Harbor, and senior strike leader Cdr. Fuchida Mitsuo, who executed that plan in flawless fashion, exerted an overconfident influence on Nagumo. The chief of staff was Rear Adm. Kusaka Ryūnosuke, a non-aviator who nevertheless captained two carriers. He refereed the debates and served as conciliator. At Midway illness slowed Genda, and Fuchida did not fly because of a recent appendectomy. Their incapacity contributed to a lack of decisiveness by Nagumo in the top level of command.[13]

Nagumo's first order of business on 4 June was to mount his Midway strike and dawn search. Thirty-six *Akagi* and *Kaga* Type 99 carrier bombers, thirty-six bomb-armed Type 97 carrier attack planes from the *Sōryū* and *Hiryū*, and thirty-six Zero fighters from all four carriers assembled with an ease that again demonstrated the marvelous coordination between carrier divisions and air groups that was far superior to the U.S. Navy's. Because each carrier only launched a portion of her strength as a single deck load, takeoff and assembly went quickly. Yet the downside of such cooperation in the face of opposition was that all four carriers were committed to the eventual recovery of the Midway strike. By 0445 the 108 planes formed in a single strike group and set off southeast toward Midway. The distance at launch, 240 miles, was far beyond what the U.S. carriers could accomplish. The favorable southeasterly wind permitted Nagumo to close the target even while conducting air operations. The dawn search did not go as well. One carrier attack plane each from the *Akagi* and *Kaga* and four Type 0 reconnaissance seaplanes from the *Tone* and *Chikuma* handled nearly the entire eastern semicircle to three hundred miles, except a short-ranged *Haruna* Type 95 seaplane flew the northernmost sector to 150 miles. The two carrier attack planes left for their assigned sectors west and southwest of Midway along with the strike, but the cruiser planes scheduled for north of Midway were tardy. Because of a slipup, the *Tone* Number Four aircraft departed at 0500. Even worse, Nagumo's staff committed the key blunder of assigning too few planes to such a wide expanse of ocean. Bates judged the search as insufficiently "dense." Beyond 150 miles the planes were too far apart to cover their sectors adequately. Nagumo ignored that the Midway strike was going in a day late and that the Americans were already aware of the approach of at least part of the Invasion Force.[14]

Such slackness reflected Nagumo's strong confidence that he had surprised Midway. Even so, he tucked a card up his sleeve, actually in the hangar decks of the four carriers. In the unlikely event the search discovered U.S. ships, he readied a second wave of 101 aircraft (thirty-four *Sōryū* and *Hiryū* carrier bombers, forty-three *Akagi* and *Kaga* torpedo-equipped carrier attack planes, and twenty-four escort Zeros) that could surely handle anything that might turn up. This contingency rose from Combined Fleet orders as a precaution should U.S. carriers already be off Midway. No one in the 1st *Kidō Butai* seriously believed that would happen. Nagumo allotted only twelve Zero fighters for defense, but the reserve escort and the Zeros being transported for Midway could fight if necessary. Once the Midway strike returned, its strong escort could swell the combat air patrol. To Nagumo the MI Operation shaped up as a repeat of the April frolic in the Indian Ocean.[15]

Contacts from the Midway PBYs came in fast and furious, to Simard if not as yet to Nimitz, Fletcher, or Spruance.[16] At 0523 Lt. (jg) Howard P. Ady of VP-23, handling the sector 312–320 degrees, radioed in code: "Aircraft sighted." He quickly identified a single-engine seaplane. At 0530 he followed with: "Enemy carriers." The *Enterprise* (and possibly the *Yorktown*) logged that electrifying message at 0534, but never heard his amplifying report placing those carriers bearing 320 degrees and 180 miles from Midway.

Wary of Zeros, Ady's lumbering PBY edged in at low altitude. He only ever saw two carriers amidst the widely dispersed screen and, as instructed, continued on his search. At 0552 the U.S. carriers did copy a plain language message from the PBY in the sector immediately south of Ady. Lt. (jg) William E. Chase of VP-23 trumpeted: "Many planes heading Midway, bearing 310 distance 150." That had to be the Japanese strike group, showing again the Midway operation was unfolding as predicted. The PBY crews rebroadcast their sighting reports to ensure they were received. Pearl picked up one of Ady's repeats at 0555 (0825 Hawaii time), causing Nimitz to remark to Layton: "Well you were off only five minutes, five degrees and five miles." With respect to Layton, both the timing and Ady's navigation were slightly off. When first sighted about 0530, Nagumo's carriers were forty miles northwest of where Ady put them.[17]

Fletcher learned of Ady's critical sighting from a Midway plain language broadcast at 0603 for Sweeney's B-17s. "Two carriers and battleships bearing 320 distance 180 course 135 speed 25." He naturally assumed that position referred to 0600, putting the two carriers two hundred miles southwest of TF-17. In fact Nagumo's four carriers were nearer to 220 miles away. For Spruance's TF-16, the distances were 180 miles (supposed) and two hundred miles (actual). Given Nimitz's plan, the mention of only two carriers certainly did not surprise Fletcher and Spruance or, as will be shown, the *Hornet*'s Pete Mitscher. It was logical to assume the PBY disclosed the carrier group that was attacking Midway. Those two carriers should continue closing Midway to recover their planes and rearm them for another go. Should enemy search planes discover either TF-17 or TF-16, that second strike, as well as the thunderbolt from the covering force, would pummel them instead. For the time being the *Yorktown* was committed to its easterly course to retrieve the morning search. No matter, for the plan called for Spruance to move TF-16 into range and swiftly strike in hopes of taking out the entire Midway carrier group in one blow. Fletcher anticipated that Midway's search would soon also pinpoint the covering force of two carriers. Then the *Yorktown* could destroy one of those flattops or at least keep them occupied until Spruance could recover his strike and attack again. Fletcher's other alternative was to commit the *Yorktown*'s planes in support of Spruance's assault.

Fletcher did not hesitate. At 0607 he ordered Spruance by TBS: "Proceed southwesterly and attack enemy carriers as soon as definitely located. I will follow as soon as planes recovered." Spruance had come around at 0600 northwest (330 degrees) to keep station southwest of TF-17. Now at 0611 after receiving Fletcher's order, he swung TF-16 southwest to 240 degrees at twenty-five knots. Spruance did not acknowledge the order, leaving Fletcher to wonder whether TF-16, too, monitored the 0603 message or simply followed orders to steam southwest. At 0622 he called by TBS to the rapidly diverging Spruance: "Have you received report 2 CV and BB bearing 320 distance 180 miles from Midway course 135 speed 25? This on 4265 [Midway plane frequency]." The incomplete communication logs do not record a reply, but at 0623 both carrier task forces received the Cincpac rebroadcast on the Fox Schedule of the original sighting report.[18]

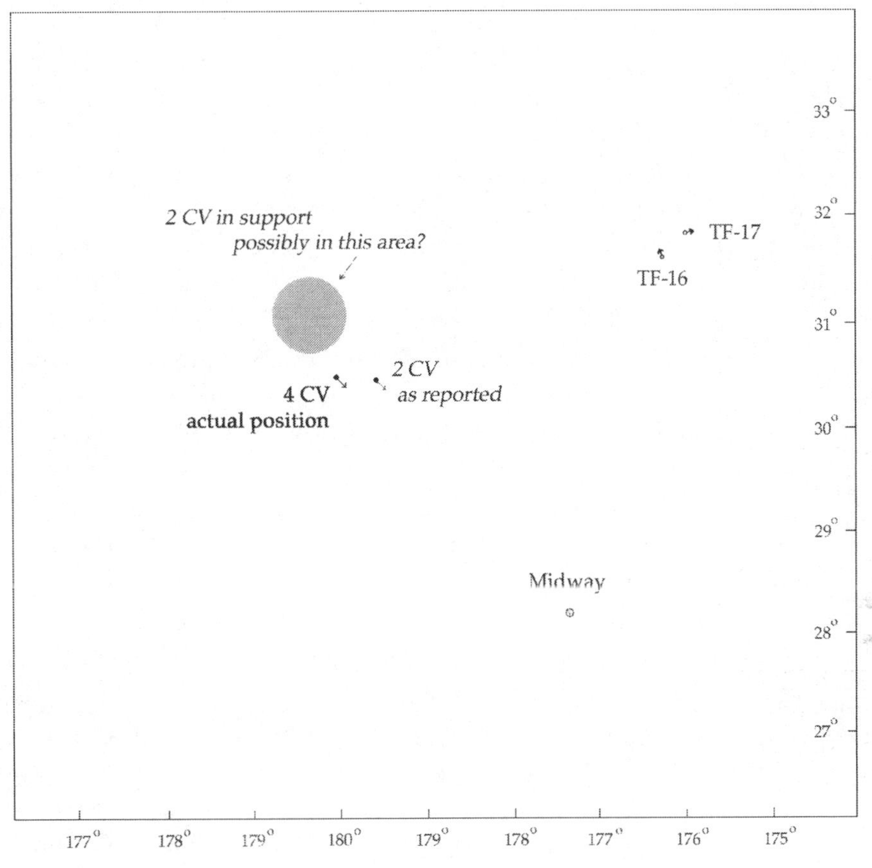

Estimate of the situation, 0600, 4 June 1942

Fletcher's first major decision of the Battle of Midway, to divide his force and direct Spruance to attack the two carriers, completely conformed to Nimitz's plan. However, some have asserted that from the very beginning Spruance enjoyed virtual independence. Commander Buracker, TF-16 operations officer, and Lieutenant Oliver, Spruance's flag lieutenant, declared that Nimitz intended from the start to give Spruance a free hand. Bates thought Spruance already left Fletcher's control when he started to come around to the west at 0600, while Fletcher continued east. Following their lead, Cdr. Thomas B. Buell's authoritative biography *The Quiet Warrior* likewise had Spruance deciding early on 4 June on his own when and where and even *if* to strike, without any reference to a mutually agreed plan. To Buell, Fletcher's attack order was "superfluous," because "Spruance was already on his way." In fact Spruance changed course at 0600 simply to maintain relative position on TF-17. He did not turn toward the enemy until he received Fletcher's order. Unlike his overprotective champions (and, later, Nimitz), Spruance always acknowledged that Fletcher indeed controlled both carrier task forces at Midway.[19]

MOUNTING THE TF-16 STRIKE

Spruance's role in the initial phase of the battle was carefully circumscribed, with little discretion on his part. When he thought TF-16 was within range of one of the enemy carrier groups he was to dispatch every *Enterprise* and *Hornet* strike plane (seventy-one dive bombers and twenty-nine torpedo planes, plus twenty escort fighters) in a coordinated surprise assault. In truth he could do little else, given his flight decks were configured not only with attack aircraft but also combat air patrol fighters. The limiting factor for range was the maximum accepted radius of 175 miles for the TBDs and escort fighters, the new F4F-4 Wildcats. In contrast, the SBD dive bombers could go well beyond two hundred miles. Spruance's task appeared straightforward. However, few aspects of the Battle of Midway are less understood than the circumstances behind the launch of the U.S. strike groups.[20]

At 0615 Spruance reckoned the target, if correctly reported (a big "if," which was why Fletcher added "as soon as definitely located"), to be about 175 miles away. Should he launch immediately? Mitscher thought so. He directed the *Hornet* aircrews, less group and squadron commanders, to man planes, but stood down when the *Enterprise* did not turn into the wind. In truth the relative position of the opposing forces, the wind direction and velocity, and tactical considerations made the decision of when and how to launch the strikes much more complex than it might first appear. TF-16 opened the battle poised on the enemy's left flank, an admirable tactical position, but one that meant the track of the enemy carriers crossed ahead at nearly a right angle to the incoming U.S. strike planes. Finding them was no sure thing. There must be some margin for error if the target did not appear at the expected intercept point and the strike must search for it. However, an immediate launch at 0615 actually translated to an outbound leg of well over 175 miles, too much under the chancy circumstances for TBDs and F4Fs. That was because the breeze blew from the southeast at a modest six knots, so little that the carriers had to steam above twenty-five knots to generate enough wind velocity over the deck for flight operations. Diverging southeast would take them on a tangent away from the target and substantially increase the distance their planes must fly to get there. If the launch, as expected, lasted forty-five minutes, the target would be twenty miles farther away, closer to two hundred miles, when the groups could actually depart. Fletcher's TF-17 faced different circumstances in the Battle of the Coral Sea, when on both days the Japanese obligingly steamed toward the U.S. carriers. When Fitch launched at two hundred miles he counted on the target being thirty miles closer when his planes arrived. Spruance had no such assurance. Browning suggested the launch begin at 0700, when the enemy should be 155 miles away. When the strike planes actually departed, that distance should have increased to 175 miles. Eager to attack as soon as good judgment would permit, Spruance readily agreed. At 0638 he ordered the *Enterprise* and *Hornet* to commence launching at 0700.[21]

Bates later laid out the advantages of an immediate launch at 0615: the greater opportunity for surprise and lessened chance of being caught in turn with one's own planes still on deck. Yet he offered effusive praise for Spruance for taking the "calculated risk" of delaying his launch for about an hour. "This was a courageous decision, and one that paid off handsomely. It was an excellent demonstration of the will of the Commander;

that quality which, in conjunction with the mental ability to understand what is required, enables the Commander to ensure for his command every possible advantage which can be obtained." Actually Spruance had very compelling reasons for following Browning's advice to wait. Bates did not realize that immediate launch meant either sending the dive bombers out alone, which ruled out a coordinated group attack, or imperiling the shorter-ranged TBDs and F4Fs. Ironically while Bates lauded Spruance for holding off the launch, Morison asserted that he actually intended to wait nearly three hours, from 0607 until 0900, before launching, only to be talked out of it by the astute Browning. This particular myth seemed plausible given Browning's enhanced reputation after the battle. The citation for his DSM read in part: "By his expert planning and brilliant execution he was largely responsible for the rout of the enemy in the Battle of Midway." Morison's claim, however, for such a delay arose from his error in reading an entry in the TF-16 war diary. He failed to realize that because the carriers went by Z+10 time, the 0900 (Z+10) in that document equated to 0700 (Z+12) in Midway local time used in most historical accounts of the battle. Spruance certainly never desired a disastrous three-hour delay. He just wanted to attack as soon as he could do so effectively.[22]

Unfamiliar with carrier procedures, Spruance understandably left all details strictly in the hands of his staff experts Browning and Buracker and captains Mitscher and George Murray. While in his cruiser flagship, Spruance had closely involved himself in planning. That day in the *Enterprise*, however, he preferred to "stand in the background while the staff went about its business," and "reserved himself only to those major decisions which had a direct bearing on the objective." Unfortunately Spruance's trust was misplaced. Browning had CTF-16 order "deferred departure," that is, each strike group was to circle until all of its squadrons had taken off, then maintain tactical contact all the way to the target. Because U.S. carrier plane types differed significantly in range, cruising speed, and optimum cruising altitude (in strong contrast to the Japanese), getting all of them to the target at the same time posed a real challenge. Yet coordination was vital to divide the combat air patrol fighters and antiaircraft, especially given the strong defenses encountered in the Coral Sea. The dive bombers and torpedo planes should attack in concert, or at least the SBDs should dive in just ahead of the TBDs. Mitscher and Murray already made special provision for that form of attack. Assuming the direction to the enemy force was obvious, Browning did not designate the outbound course for the strike. However, he instructed Mitscher and Murray to employ "search-attack" procedure, used "when the location of the objective is indefinite to such a degree as to necessitate preliminary search." That meant part of each group (usually the scouting squadron) was to form a scouting line en route to the target. Browning also emphasized that each group make certain it attacked a different carrier. It is interesting that he did not implement existing (if little used) provisions for "wing tactics," in which the senior air group leader, in this case the *Hornet*'s Cdr. Stanhope C. Ring, coordinated the attacks of the two groups in succession. That day, however, each group was to attack simultaneously.[23]

At 0700 the *Enterprise* and *Hornet* turned south on slightly different courses into the feeble wind and bent on twenty-eight knots. The screen split to cover each carrier. The target was thought to bear 239–240 degrees at 155 miles, but Nagumo was actually 175 miles away, bearing 245 degrees. Once the carriers completed flight operations, Spruance planned to decrease the return leg by closing to one hundred miles of the target. That entailed advancing southwest at twenty-five knots for three hours after the groups departed. The flag provided no formal Point Option—the course and speed TF-16 would steer after the launch—but the *Hornet* understood that "in lieu thereof closing of the enemy was indicated." On the face of it, mounting a strike of this magnitude did not seem a particularly tough problem. In peacetime a U.S. carrier customarily crowded her entire air group of seventy-three planes on the flight deck in the order fighters, dive bombers, and torpedo planes, then launched them "in one continuous operation." The "book" decreed that such mass takeoffs normally required twenty minutes, somewhat less with "skilled pilots and trained flight deck crews." However, it was always understood such a full group launch was an artificial situation unlikely to occur during wartime, when aircraft would be needed for other duties. Indeed to this point, only the huge *Lexington* ever spotted as many as fifty planes at one time for a combat mission. And circumstances changed. Planes now equipped with armor and self-sealing fuel tanks were heavier, requiring longer takeoff runs and hence more deck room. The carriers could no longer accommodate all their strike planes in one deck load, making it difficult for each group to ensure its squadrons simultaneously reached the target. Browning followed doctrine and gave both captains latitude to organize their strikes as they saw fit. Neither did particularly well, but one solution proved much worse than the other.[24]

In the *Hornet*, Mitscher, although well seasoned in carriers, had no actual wartime combat experience and lost valuable additional training time due to the Tokyo raid. He simply followed the old group launch doctrine, spotting well forward the twenty assigned VF-8 fighters—eight combat air patrol, ten escort, and two standby F4Fs—then all thirty-four operational SBDs. Half the dive bombers, including Ring's, carried single 500-pound bombs; the balance 1,000-pound bombs. Room remained aft on the flight deck for six TBDs from Torpedo Eight. The other nine Devastators would come up the aft elevator once the deck was clear and take off last of all. Although the fighter escorts had the same short strike radius as the TBDs, Mitscher would launch them first. Evidently he counted on getting the second small deck load aloft before the rest of the strike wasted too much fuel waiting for it to form up and depart. On the basis of initial combat reports from the Coral Sea, he decided dive bombers needed protection more than torpedo planes. He gave all ten F4F escorts to the SBDs for the gas-consuming climb to twenty thousand feet, while the slower torpedo planes followed at low altitude. He expected Ring to maintain tactical cohesion all the way to the target.[25]

Murray in the *Enterprise* adopted the same arrangement he employed on the 24 February raid against Wake, reserving the short-ranged strike components for a second deck load. Thus his initial spot comprised eight combat air patrol fighters and all thirty-seven SBDs, armed variously with single 500-pound bombs, a mixed bag of one 500-pound and two 100-pound bombs, and, the last eighteen, one 1,000-pound bomb each. Murray worried the fully fueled SBDs, particularly those burdened with 1,000-pounders, needed as much deck space as possible for takeoff. That was even more true this day because of the slight wind. The second deck load, waiting in the hangar, comprised the escort of ten VF-6 F4Fs and fourteen TBDs from VT-6. Like Mitscher, Murray directed his escort F4Fs to cover the

SBDs at high altitude, while the TBDs stayed down low. However, the group and squadron leaders worked out a contingency plan for the escorts to dive to the aid of the torpedo planes if they encountered strong fighter opposition.[26]

The TF-16 launches began shortly after 0700 but proceeded slowly as plane after plane rumbled aloft and circled overhead. By 0742 the *Hornet* cleared her deck of the first fifty-eight planes and started spotting the remaining nine TBDs. The takeoff of the *Big E*'s forty-five aircraft lagged after four Dauntlesses suffered mechanical failure. They had either to be struck below or run out on outriggers to clear the deck. Only after the last SBD lifted off could deck crews start bringing the escort F4Fs and TBDs up from the hangar. Observing from the *Enterprise*'s flag shelter, Spruance grew increasingly impatient over the obvious holdup. The launch unfortunately seemed a repeat of the 24 February affair, where because of delays in getting the SBDs off, the whole group was thirty minutes late. In this connection Murray recalled what his old boss Adm. Joseph Reeves had said: "*Time*, gentleman, remember *Time*," because "time is a terribly important thing" with regard to launches. "If they can be done without the complication of planes failing to start on deck; if the engines will start and warm up properly, and they'll all take off—the thing goes beautifully." If not, like this day, there was trouble.[27]

Time was up as far as Spruance was concerned. At 0740 Lieutenant Slonim, the radio intelligence officer, alerted him of a possible enemy sighting of TF-16.[28] Anxious to get something going as soon as possible, Spruance abruptly dispensed with the coordinated attack. Browning concurred, because he, too, worried about the tardy takeoffs. At 0745 via flashing light the flag signalers told Lt. Cdr. Clarence Wade McClusky, the group leader circling at the head of thirty-three *Enterprise* SBDs, to "proceed on mission assigned." He departed southwest minus the VF-6 escort fighters, about to be launched, while the spotting of the VT-6 TBDs had barely begun. At the same time Ring obsessively arrayed the thirty-four *Hornet* SBDs in group parade formation, as if preening for an air show, while they and the ten ill-starred VF-8 escort F4Fs slowly climbed toward high altitude. The *Hornet* completed launch of the last nine TBDs at 0755. While the VT-8 TBDs formed up low over the water, Ring signaled his departure. The VF-6 escort fighters, climbing high, had of course missed McClusky's SBDs, but Lt. James S. Gray, their leader, tagged onto the *Hornet* TBDs mistaking them for the *Enterprise* torpedo planes. Finally at 0806 the last TBD of Lt. Cdr. Eugene E. Lindsey's VT-6 lifted off the *Enterprise* long after every other squadron had cleared out.[29]

At 0806 Spruance resumed the base course of 240 degrees at twenty-five knots. In the past half hour wary listeners in TF-16 monitored radio transmissions from an apparent shadower. Finally at 0815 lookouts in the *Northampton* sighted a twin-float seaplane lurking thirty miles south. Ham Dow, the *Enterprise* fighter director, broke radio silence on the medium-range high-frequency fighter circuit to direct combat air patrol fighters after the intruder. By that time TF-16 itself had separated into two ad hoc task groups under Murray and Mitscher that would cruise independently until sunset. Heavy cruisers *Northampton*, *Vincennes*, and *Pensacola* and five destroyers accompanied the *Enterprise*; the *Minneapolis* (Kinkaid's flagship), *New Orleans*, light cruiser *Atlanta*, and four destroyers joined the *Hornet*. Kinkaid informed Mitscher, his junior, that he would conform to his movements.[30]

Unknown to Spruance, a potential catastrophe was in the making. His air strike already fractured into three elements, each going in a different direction. Out in the lead, McClusky figured the enemy carriers would continue to make twenty-five knots while advancing toward Midway to recover their planes. He worked out an intercept course that allowed for their maximum advance. Thus his thirty-three SBDs headed out on 226 degrees, well south of the course of 240 degrees that Spruance announced the carriers would take while closing the enemy. McClusky anticipated finding the target at about 142 miles. Lindsey, leaving fifteen minutes later, chose 240 degrees for his fourteen VT-6 TBDs. Ring led the thirty-four *Hornet* SBDs, ten F4Fs, fifteen TBDs, and, unwittingly, the ten VF-6 escort F4Fs *west* on course 265 degrees, taking them far to the northwest of Spruance's designated target. Ring also evidently intended to go out to 225 miles if necessary. It appears that Mitscher, worried by Ady's PBY report of only two carriers, took it upon himself to search for and strike the supposed second group of enemy carriers thought to be behind the lead group. Not all of these widely diverging flights could possibly find Nagumo.[31]

THE *YORKTOWN*'S ATTACK

Once Spruance received the order to attack, he threw in everything he had. Fletcher had other matters to consider. At 0622 the *Yorktown* sent aloft a relief combat air patrol of six F4Fs and prepared to recover the search SBDs and the first combat air patrol. During that process the radio boomed forth in plain language: "Air Raid, Midway." By 0645 after the landings, Buckmaster respotted the strike group for takeoff. At that time the two enemy carriers were thought to be more than two hundred miles southwest, well out of range. Fletcher faced all of the constraints of wind direction and relative positions already imposed on TF-16. Nagumo was actually more than 225 miles away. In the absence of word of additional enemy carriers, Fletcher resolved to close within strike range of the original contact to retain the option of following up Spruance's attack. He pointed TF-17 southwest (225 degrees) at twenty-five knots and estimated he could start launching his strike about 0830, when the distance to the original target should have shrunk to 160 miles. In the interval, he waited to see whether the Midway search could turn up the second enemy carrier group. Then he could judge whether to hit it or keep after the first target. Thus at 0648 he advised Spruance and Smith: "Shall follow TF-16 to southwestward and launch attack when within range. Two carriers unaccounted for."[32]

Critics charged that Fletcher dithered, whereas Spruance acted decisively. Although Bates lauded Spruance for postponing his attack until TF-16 moved closer and enhanced its chances for success, he chided Fletcher for opting to "withhold launching," instead of immediately joining the TF-16 onslaught. No "courageous" decision here, or an "excellent demonstration of the will of the Commander" showing "the mental ability to understand what is required." Instead, Bates castigated Fletcher for violating the truism, "It is generally best to throw all of your available strength . . . in a coordinated attack rather than launch them piecemeal in uncoordinated attacks." He conceded Fletcher might have had the unlocated carriers on his mind, but condescendingly presumed, "His actions were somewhat colored by his experiences in the Battle of the Coral Sea wherein the Japanese nearly surprised him."

The plain facts are that the *Yorktown* was out of effective range of Nagumo until after 0830, and that Fletcher attacked as soon as he reasonably could. His decision to hold off the *Yorktown*'s launch exactly mirrored the one for which Bates so highly praised Spruance, who, not so coincidentally, happened then to be president of the Naval War College and Bates's direct superior. Morison likewise noted Fletcher "delayed launching, however, for over two hours," but later conceded that he might have done so "properly."[33]

Like the *Enterprise* (if not the *Hornet*), the *Yorktown* reckoned the extreme attack radius of the F4F-4s at 175 miles, the same as the TBDs. Commander Thach, commanding officer of VF-3, said he would go that far, which Commander Leslie, commanding officer of VB-3, thought was "really giving a lot." Coping with the same disadvantages as TF-16, Fletcher, cued by his aviation advisors Arnold (air officer) and Pederson (air group commander), handled them much more astutely. "We were frantic for additional information," Arnold recalled, "but we had to launch our planes just on the one contact report." He plotted the course and speed of the two enemy carriers to be almost directly downwind from Midway and assumed, like McClusky, they would continue southeast into the wind to shorten the range and recover their strike. By the time the *Yorktown* planes could reach that enemy force, it might be only ninety miles from Midway, but Arnold did not think Japanese carriers would approach Midway that close so early in the battle. He calculated they would stay at least 120 miles distant. That translated to approximately 150 miles, bearing 230 degrees from the *Yorktown*'s anticipated launch position. Therefore if the strike did not find the enemy at the intercept point, it could count on the target being to the right, the northwest. Arnold told the strike leaders not to proceed southwest beyond the line of bearing between the assumed Japanese position and Midway. If the enemy was not there, they were to turn right and fly northwest along the reciprocal of the Japanese course. "They all agreed that this made good sense and all of them carried out this plan exactly."[34]

To ensure the strike had enough fuel for extended search and still delivered a coordinated attack, Pederson worked out another running rendezvous like the *Yorktown* found so effective earlier. The first deck load comprised Leslie's seventeen VB-3 SBDs (with 1,000-pound bombs) and Commander Massey's dozen VT-3 TBDs with torpedoes. Leslie's SBDs were to circle the *Yorktown* for fifteen minutes, while the slow Devastators took off and departed at once. Then the flight deck crews were to bring up from the hangar Lieutenant Short's seventeen VS-5 SBDs, all warmed up and ready to go. They should get aloft in time to follow Leslie's SBDs on their way out. The SBDs were to climb to fifteen thousand feet en route to the target. Going last of all, but with the fastest cruise (139 knots as opposed to 110–20 knots for the others), Thach's eight F4Fs were to take off just after the SBDs and remain at low level to cover VT-3. If everything went according to plan, Thach should pass underneath Short and Leslie and catch up to Massey after about forty-five minutes, so the group could maintain vertical integrity long enough to reach the target.[35]

Fletcher stated in his report that TF-16 commenced launching at 0710 with a Point Option course of 240 degrees at twenty-five knots. As he had no other way of knowing that, Spruance must have furnished him that useful information by TBS radio (to "follow" TF-16 Fletcher had to know where it was going). Arnold certainly learned of the TF-16 Point Option course and speed (he recalled twenty-four knots) soon after Fletcher. Expecting to dispatch the *Yorktown* strike group against the same carriers, Arnold thought TF-16 could never maintain its stated rate of advance and end up anywhere near where its pilots could expect to find it on their return. TF-16 had committed a "terrible blunder," that he certainly did not want TF-17 to emulate. Believing erroneously that Spruance, blessed with Halsey's prestigious air staff, exercised tactical command over both task forces, Arnold worried Fletcher would simply comply with that Point Option course and speed. He never understood that Spruance was indeed subordinate to Fletcher, and that Spruance never issued any orders to TF-17. After Arnold expressed "violent protest" over the TF-16 Point Option, Buckmaster sent him down to the flag bridge. Arnold "explained to Fletcher who partially understood and asked me what Pt. Option speed should be." To that he replied, "It was not an exact science but a matter of judgement and that I thought it should be 10–12 knots and *not* 24 [*sic*]." To Fletcher's retort, "But we must close the Japs," Arnold responded, "With the wind as it is we simply could not close at anything like 24 knots." Frequent diversions off the base course for air operations would prevent that. Fletcher gave Arnold "official permission" to alter the *Yorktown*'s Point Option estimate of advance to eighteen knots. Arnold was greatly surprised he had not referred it "back to T.F. 16 for concurrence." Fletcher, in tactical command, needed not consult TF-16, but simply let Spruance handle the details of his own strike. In turn Arnold relayed the eighteen-knot Point Option speed to the squadron commanders, but privately told them to figure on twelve knots for Point Option. His "only excuse" for not following orders was that "*something had to be done.*"[36]

While TF-16 completed its laborious launch—its planes briefly appeared "on the horizon like a swarm of bees"—TF-17 endured an uneasy hour and a half with armed and fueled planes perched on the *Yorktown*'s flight deck. Fletcher learned from Cincpac that Midway took its lumps, but its airfield was still operational. He did not know that Midway's aircraft had begun their gallant but unsuccessful forays against Nagumo's powerful fighter defense. At 0810 Fletcher warned TF-17 the *Hughes* had sighted a strange aircraft to the south. Six minutes later the *Enterprise* could be heard directing fighters after a shadower much farther south. At 0821 the *Astoria*'s lookouts spotted another twin-float seaplane thirty miles south. To this juncture Fletcher did not think the enemy knew his exact whereabouts, so Fullinwider's radio team in the *Yorktown* failed to pick up the same Japanese radio transmissions monitored by the *Enterprise* and Hypo at Pearl.[37]

Still concerned after all this time that the Midway search never discovered the second enemy carrier group, Fletcher reluctantly determined about 0825 not to commit his entire strike to the first attack. Instead he directed the seventeen SBDs of Short's VS-5 remain in reserve and also reduced Thach's fighter escort from eight to six Wildcats. Short's SBDs could either search or attack at the appropriate time with a six-plane division of F4Fs as escort. Thach was livid at the change. His experimental defensive tactics (later dubbed the "Thach Weave") required multiples of four planes, although Fletcher and Buckmaster knew nothing of that. Racing up to air plot, Thach was all set to argue with Arnold, until he learned the orders came from above and would not be changed. Again Arnold was not party to Fletcher's deliberations. Set to take off first, Leslie was not even aware that VS-5, still in the hangar, would not be following him. Fletcher's decision violated standard doctrine for carriers to strike hard and swiftly, not only for the biggest attack, but also because of the risk of being caught with armed and fueled planes. However, in light of his uncertainty as to the location of all four enemy carriers, and his role in Nimitz's overall plan, he desired a force in hand to commit when necessary. Fletcher trusted his radar to give warning in the event of an incoming strike, so VS-5 could rapidly clear the deck. Circumstances would demonstrate the vast wisdom of an action that on its face appeared overly cautious.[38]

At 0838 Fletcher changed course southeast into the wind at twenty-eight knots to launch aircraft. The distance at that time to the northwest-southeast track of the enemy carriers was reckoned about 160 miles. Leslie's seventeen VB-3 SBDs circled as directed, while Massey's dozen Devastators departed at 0850. Thinking VS-5 would be trailing, Leslie himself left at 0902. Thach's six F4Fs took off five minutes later and headed out at once. Six other fighters relieved the second combat air patrol. At 0914 Fletcher informed Spruance by TBS: "Launched three-fourths of group at attack same carriers." After completing flight operations, he took the Point Option course of 225 degrees at twenty-five knots. The *Yorktown* spotted the flight deck with the dozen remaining fighters (including the refueled second combat air patrol) and the seventeen VS-5 SBDs ready for instant launch.[39]

By 0920 Fletcher had to feel that so far things were going well. The Japanese did not prevent the U.S. carriers from getting in the first blow of 151 planes intended to reduce the opposition to a more manageable two carriers. It was a powerful opening move, indeed the winning stroke if everything followed the plan and the attackers could return to intact carriers. The next two hours, while the three U.S. carriers confidently raced southwest at twenty-five knots, would see if Nimitz's bold stratagem worked, or whether the Japanese could counterattack first.

THE "GRAND SCALE AIR ATTACK"

In the meantime Fletcher's counterpart Nagumo experienced a morning full of twists and turns. At 0620 his strike of 107 planes (one carrier attack plane aborted) tore through the two dozen marine fighters defending Midway and shot down sixteen F2As and F4Fs with little loss. Thereafter dive and level bombers enthusiastically pummeled military installations and tried to put the airfield temporarily out of commission. Seven planes fell or ditched near the target, with numerous others damaged. Greatly impressed by the fierce antiaircraft fire and fighter defense, strike leader Lt. Tomonaga Jōichi advised base at 0700: "There is need for a second attack wave." American flying boats peeking out of the clouds alerted Nagumo at 0542 that his own position was pinpointed. If the Midway strike planes were as efficient, he could expect the counterattack shortly. The carriers reinforced their combat air patrol with Zero fighters drawn from the second strike wave held in reserve for possible ship targets. At 0705 the swiftest land-based attackers, six TBF Avengers from the VT-8 detachment and four army B-26 Marauder medium bombers, all armed with torpedoes, encountered the carriers 170 miles northwest of Midway. Their furious assault against the *Akagi*, although unsuccessful and costly (five TBFs and two B-26s), enormously magnified their numbers to the Japanese. Nagumo anticipated only two squadrons of flying boats, a squadron of "Army bombers," and a fighter squadron at Midway, although those numbers could be "doubled in an emergency." That certainly appeared to be the case.[40]

To Nagumo it was obvious Midway required further attention. The reserve of seventy-seven dive bombers and torpedo planes packed in the hangar decks of the four carriers could deliver an even more powerful blow. However, that would be contrary to Yamamoto's orders. The forty-three carrier attack planes had to be reequipped with bombs for land targets in place of torpedoes (the thirty-four carrier bombers were not yet armed). Before Nagumo took that drastic step he must be completely confident no U.S. carriers skulked nearby. As yet nothing from the dawn search contradicted his strong impression that no enemy ships, let alone carriers, were in the area. By 0700 the search planes were supposed to start their doglegs three hundred miles out, although, of course, some were late, one in particular. The cruiser float plane flying the north-northeast sector already turned back because of bad weather. At 0715, notwithstanding the still incomplete search, Nagumo directed the carriers to rearm the carrier attack planes. Crewmen swarmed to replace the torpedoes hanging from the seventeen *Akagi* and twenty-six *Kaga* carrier attack planes with 800-kilogram high explosive land bombs for horizontal bombing. The arduous, time-consuming process of switching such heavy, cumbersome ordnance was only actually attempted once before, as a test in the *Hiryū*. The thirty-four carrier bombers on the *Hiryū* and *Sōryū* would be armed with 242-kilogram land bombs once actually spotted on decks. Before that, fighters could also be landed to restore the strength of the escort.[41]

Nagumo could not expect to launch his second Midway attack for more than two hours. Rearming should take ninety minutes, with forty minutes more to spot the second wave on the flight deck and warm up engines. That cut things very closely. The returning first Midway strike would be very low on fuel and must be recovered immediately thereafter. Nagumo made the decision, because he still believed the MI Operation was a strategic surprise, even though the Americans had one day's warning. He acted with the concurrence of his advisors and most likely at their urging. Kusaka later condemned "intolerable" second-guessing by Combined Fleet that declared Nagumo should have kept half of his strength in reserve "indefinitely" against ships that "might not be in the area at all." Even though exchanging torpedoes for bombs was unusual, it could hardly have come as a complete surprise. It is difficult to believe Nagumo actually contemplated only one strike against Midway on 4 June, whether or not Combined Fleet would have approved.[42]

Thus it was a terrific jolt at 0740, when the *Tone* Number Four plane searching the 100-degree line belatedly reported "ten surface ships" bearing 010 degrees and 240 miles from Midway. That contact was two hundred miles northeast (bearing 052 degrees) of the 1st *Kidō Butai*. The enemy headed southeast (150 degrees) at twenty knots. That was the sighting report that Slonim in the *Enterprise* intercepted for Spruance. Hypo at Pearl had it as well, but no code breaker could read its enciphered message. The search plane commander was PO1c Amari Yōji. One Japanese author wrote it was "fool's luck" that Amari was the one to find the enemy, though Nagumo could count himself fortunate that anyone from his perfunctory effort ever did. That Amari got away late due to the balky catapult was not his fault, but the position he gave for the enemy was well north of his assigned search sector, and in fact fifty-three miles north of Spruance's actual location. TF-16 was only about 175 miles northeast (bearing 067 degrees) from the Japanese carriers. The *Chikuma* Number

One plane flying the search sector 077 degrees had passed to the north within twenty miles of TF-16 and TF-17 but missed them due to cloud cover.[43]

Nagumo responded immediately to the new potential threat. At 0745 he directed his carriers, "Prepare to carry out attacks on enemy fleet units." Those *Akagi* and *Kaga* carrier attack planes that still had torpedoes were to keep them. The *Hiryū* and *Sōryū* carrier bombers also had yet to be spotted on deck and warmed up, although that was a relatively swift process. At 0747 Nagumo told Amari, "Ascertain ship types and maintain contact." There ensued over the next two hours one of the strangest colloquies in the history of naval warfare. Nagumo and Abe (the senior cruiser admiral) tried without success to elicit clear and unambiguous reports from Amari, who proved remarkably cautious and tentative.[44] Even though Nagumo told his force, "Prepare to carry out attacks on enemy fleet units," there appears to have been no firm staff consensus whether the U.S. force included a carrier. Amari, the man on the spot, had yet to answer that question. Unspoken was the puzzle of why else would U.S. ships even be there other than with a carrier. Apparently none of Nagumo's staff noticed the enemy's reported course also pointed into the wind, suggesting a carrier conducting flight operations.[45]

Soon after Amari's ominous sighting report, the 1st *Kidō Butai* fell under attack by a new wave of land-based planes, and even submarine *Nautilus*, that kept the ships scurrying the next half hour. Diverted from the transports, Sweeney's fourteen B-17s sighted the far distant Japanese force around 0730 and slowly closed at high altitude. The Fortresses deployed into several small formations for level attacks against individual carriers that maneuvered in tight circles to avoid bombs. Sweeney first noted damage only to one carrier, but after collating accounts the army crews claimed at least five bomb hits that left three carriers in flames. Those exaggerations fueled subsequent stories that the AAF had turned the tide of the battle. The B-17s harmed no Japanese ships. Simultaneously the lead element of VMSB-241, sixteen SBD-2s, braved heavy fighter opposition to attack the *Hiryū* and lost half their number. The survivors claimed two hits, but the carrier was unhurt. Defending Zeros likewise forced the eleven SB2U Vindicators of VMSB-241 to settle for an unsuccessful foray against the battleship *Haruna* that cost four dive bombers. The Japanese admired the bravery of their opponents, but thought little of their skill.[46]

Amari radioed Nagumo at 0758 that the enemy ships changed course east (080 degrees). At 0809 he described the enemy as five cruisers and five destroyers. That seemed a fairly definite statement, but Kusaka finally became suspicious why such ships would even be present without a carrier. The staff considered whether after dealing with the amateurish land-based air attacks to go ahead with the second Midway strike and for the time being ignore the U.S. surface ships. Yamaguchi, apparently alarmed because carrier-type planes (the single-engine marine dive bombers) swarmed over his flagship *Hiryū*, violently disagreed. "Consider it advisable to launch attack force immediately," he signaled Nagumo. A rising star, Yamaguchi would certainly have agreed with Vice Adm. Frederick J. Horne, who warned in 1937 after Fleet Problem XVIII: "Once an enemy carrier is within striking distance of our fleet no security remains until it—its squadrons—or both, are destroyed." Yamaguchi did not hide his dissatisfaction with Nagumo's indecisive leadership. Around 0820 he apparently directed the *Sōryū* and *Hiryū* to start spotting their thirty-four carrier bombers on deck to go after the enemy ships. Beginning at 0825 the *Akagi*, *Kaga*, and *Hiryū* launched ten Zeros as relief combat air patrol and the *Sōryū* her high-speed Type 2 reconnaissance plane. Only about eleven fighters remained on board the four carriers. At the same time one hundred Midway strike planes, all low on fuel and some shot up besides, neared the force or already loitered overhead.[47]

At 0830, however, the picture altered much for the worse, when Amari belatedly advised, equivocally as usual, "Enemy force [is] accompanied by what appears to be a carrier." Again that should not have come as a total surprise, with carrier-type planes already identified among those assailing the 1st *Kidō Butai*. Yet confirmed carrier opposition caught Nagumo in a dilemma. At that point he would need time, because of the need to spot and warm up planes, even to mount a partial strike. Yamaguchi had no doubt what Nagumo should do and had not hesitated to tell him. Valid reasons existed for Nagumo to follow his advice, not the least of which was to get in a carrier strike as soon as possible. Prospects for a fighter escort, though, were sparse. Kusaka and Genda vehemently disagreed, and they swiftly swayed Nagumo into postponing any second attack. The carrier bombers that Yamaguchi was spotting up on deck had yet to be armed and warmed up before launch. That process might take a half hour. In the interval some or even many Midway attackers might ditch before flight decks were again open to receive them. Thus Nagumo resolved to land the Midway strike as soon as possible, then recycle the combat air patrol, regroup his task force, and complete the rearming. His "grand scale air attack" of seventy-seven strike aircraft (seventeen *Akagi* and twenty-six *Kaga* carrier attack planes with torpedoes and thirty-four *Sōryū* and *Hiryū* carrier bombers) and fighter escorts should be ready to depart in about two hours. Nagumo and the staff must have judged that any real danger to the carriers in the meantime was minimal.[48]

The risk of losing many of the Midway first attackers to the sea evidently was the overriding factor in the decision to delay the second strike. Kusaka later declared, and Genda and Fuchida concurred, that they also worried that the precipitous strike Yamaguchi recommended could only have a few escort Zeros. A strong fighter defense could overwhelm a small escort and shred the bombers just the way their own combat air patrol ground up the enemy. This particular excuse almost certainly arose from hindsight to justify the decision that ultimately decided the course of the battle. In fact the staff assigned only a dozen fighters (three from each carrier) to accompany the reorganized "grand scale air attack." That hardly squares with their supposed concern over defending U.S. fighters. Instead, Nagumo and his advisors perceived the situation as sufficiently favorable not to force them to commit an unbalanced attack. The second strike could wait until everything was ready to go. The methodical Kusaka distrusted precipitate actions, preferring "a concentrated single stroke after sufficient study and minute planning." He and ex–fighter pilot Genda felt fully confident their own superb Zeros, rapidly reinforced by the former Midway escort, would annihilate whatever the bumbling Americans might throw against them. Fuchida reflected their optimism. "It was our general conclusion that we had little to fear from the enemy's offensive tactics." Even Hara's green 5th Carrier Division performed well in the Coral Sea Battle by sinking two carriers. Nagumo's decision to stand temporarily on defense and accept attack resembled the one that Spruance himself would make two years later on 19 June 1944 in the Battle of the Philippine Sea.[49]

At 0830 Nagumo directed Yamaguchi to "prepare for second attack" by arming his carrier bombers with 250-kilogram semi–armor-piercing bombs. With the air attacks from Midway tailing off, he reassembled his task force and turned into the slight wind to recover the fuel-starved Midway attackers. At 0837 the *Akagi* and *Kaga* began landing aircraft. The *Hiryū* and *Sōryū* followed suit after arming their carrier bombers and striking them below in the upper hangar decks. Three carrier attack planes ditched, and destroyers swiftly rescued the crews. At 0917 with most of the first wave snugly on board, Nagumo changed course northeast (070 degrees) at thirty knots. That would match the enemy's previous turn to the east and keep the carriers pointed toward the fickle wind, which had shifted to 050 degrees at six knots. By blinking light he transmitted his plan "to contact and destroy the enemy task force." When Nagumo turned away, the 1st *Kidō Butai* had approached within about 135 miles of Midway, close to Arnold's estimate.[50]

Nagumo radioed Yamamoto and Kondō at 0855 to report the enemy force of one carrier, five cruisers, and five destroyers discovered 240 miles north of Midway. "We are heading for it." With Amari's reliability in serious doubt, Nagumo had, as previously noted, augmented the search with the *Sōryū*'s high-speed reconnaissance plane and dispatched a seaplane to relieve Amari. Uncertainty over the accuracy of Amari's navigation might have been another consideration for delaying the 0830 attack. By 0900 Nagumo anticipated unleashing his great air strike in ninety minutes. Moreover, Yamaguchi advised that the *Sōryū* and *Hiryū* could each dispatch nine carrier attack planes (back from the Midway) between 1030 and 1100. Presumably the *Akagi* and *Kaga* carrier bombers would also be available at that time. That third wave could mop up any big ships left after Nagumo's hammer blow finished off the U.S. carrier. In the meantime Amari radioed that he was homeward bound, but then, about 0840, unexpectedly placed two additional cruisers northwest of the main body. Abe ordered him to stay on station. At 0901 Amari replied that he would comply, and that incidentally, at 0855 he had spotted ten enemy torpedo planes "heading toward you." During his brief withdrawal Amari stumbled across TF-17 while the *Yorktown* launched her strike. True to form he only noticed two ships from the screen besides the dozen VT-3 TBDs heading out. One wonders if under the circumstances Nagumo was particularly worried about yet another small wave of enemy planes. Repeatedly urged by Abe, Amari conscientiously stayed on station despite dwindling fuel until after 0940, but in the interval he gave his superiors no additional information.[51]

In retrospect Amari's failures to develop his contacts deeply harmed the Japanese cause. Had he come through promptly and clearly with word of U.S. carriers (which certainly were nearby), Nagumo might have attacked them using whatever planes were at hand. The Midway-based planes that raided the 1st *Kidō Butai* between 0800 and 0830 would have slowed the process of spotting and launching the strike, but at least a part of the Japanese strike planes should have got aloft before the Midway attackers would have to ditch. That blow might not have won the battle for Nagumo, but it certainly could have increased the cost to the Pacific Fleet.

SWEATING OUT THE STRIKE

Fletcher's wait after 0920 in the *Yorktown*'s flag plot recalled two recent interludes of intense inaction. He could do little else than sit on the transom, pace the flag bridge, or lean over the chart table to ponder yet again the meager enemy data entered on the plot. All ears were attuned to the bulkhead speaker for additional sighting reports and to the phone circuits for alerts from the radar shack (Fletcher's great advantage over Nagumo) and ship lookouts. Hovering unobtrusively, Commander Laing, the British naval liaison officer, jotted in his little black notebook. He disapproved of the physical layout of the flag bridge and the procedures the fleet used to keep track of contacts. The first was "inadequate," the other "rudimentary." Later at Pearl he stressed the need for a grid system to facilitate secure reporting of positions and recommended the British lettered coordinate system. He swiftly acquired a copy via the attaché in Washington and presented it to Nimitz, who was very grateful and soon had the Pacific Fleet adopt the grid concept. Laing would have been far more appalled had he seen Nagumo and his staff simply huddled in a corner of the *Akagi*'s cramped navigation bridge.[52]

The only new land-based air sightings referred to the invasion forces now three to four hundred miles west of Midway. At 0857 Sweeney informed base that his B-17s damaged one carrier, but he gave no position. His was the first word from the Midway strike. Dubious about the effectiveness of the Flying Forts against ships (and the accuracy of AAF damage assessments), Fletcher could only hope that was correct. For a time the TF-16 combat air patrol could be seen circling south of TF-17. Dow directed *Enterprise* fighters after various bogeys that were friendly cruiser float planes flying inner air patrol against subs. At 0949 he tapped one of the distant VF-3 sections for a similar mission with the same result. This problem would persist until all aircraft were equipped with identification, friend or foe (IFF) gear. It is not known whether the Japanese heard any of these FDO transmissions, but they certainly did in other 1942 carrier battles.[53]

The TF-16 planners thought their strike would reach the target around 0920, but no contact reports came through at that time. The minutes weighed more heavily on Spruance than Fletcher. His planes had been aloft for up to two hours longer and were low on fuel. The first indication the two admirals received that any of their planes contacted the enemy occurred at 0956, via the fighter net, the combat air patrol frequency the strike planes shared. Someone identifying himself as "Grey" stated he was flying over eight destroyers, two battleships, and two carriers. Four minutes later "Grey" advised that after having flown over the enemy force for a half hour, he was "returning to the ship due to the lack of gas." He said the Japanese did not have a combat air patrol, repeated the composition of the enemy force, and gave its course "about north." Listeners in the *Yorktown* were uncertain of "Grey's" identity, but surmised one TF-16 squadron attacked the carrier group without meeting fighter opposition. The *Enterprise* indeed had a "Grey" on the mission, Lieutenant Gray, commanding officer of VF-6, who led the fighter escort. In the heat of the moment Browning failed to make the connection. Both he and Spruance thought that McClusky, the group commander, transmitted those messages. They deplored that instead of attacking, "McClusky" was requesting permission to return for fuel. Fuming, Browning grabbed the microphone in the *Enterprise*'s flag shelter and exclaimed at 1008: "McClusky attack, attack immediately!" A minute later he repeated the message, but remembered to preface it with the voice code names for the *Enterprise* and *Enterprise* Air Group commander. Browning then inquired whether the target was in sight but never heard an acknowledgment. The failure to indoctrinate U.S. carrier pilots to make contact reports once they sighted the enemy proved a serious flaw.[54]

At 1014 Spruance relayed to Fletcher the gist of the "Grey" messages he wrongly attributed to the *Enterprise* group commander, and added: "My course 285." Since relieving the combat air patrol at 0955, Spruance turned west to 260 degrees at twenty-five knots. At 1005 he swung northwest (285 degrees) at twenty-seven knots to "close enemy now on northerly course." That ended any pretense of TF-16 holding to the Point Option solution and ever going where its pilots expected on their return. The staff's over-optimistic rate of advance to the southwest for Point Option proved disastrous when TF-16 had to match the movements of the enemy carriers. At 1020 in response to Spruance's new course, Fletcher brought TF-17 around to 290 degrees. Thanks to Arnold's understanding of the Point Option issue, the *Yorktown* strike pilots enjoyed a far better idea of where TF-17 was likely to be. Between 1015 and 1030 snippets of radio conversations hinted at least part of the strike assailed enemy carriers. Leaders were heard assigning targets, and one exhorted, "Don't let this carrier escape," a sentiment fervently shared by the eavesdroppers in TF-16 and TF-17. So little came over the radio, though, that Fletcher and Spruance had no idea whether their attacks were successful. They worried about the many new radar contacts that developed after 1000 to westward, but no one positively identified enemy planes. With the two task forces widely separated, Pederson took control of the *Yorktown* combat air patrol fighters at 1102 to check out a bogey discovered thirty-five miles north of TF-17. Dow likewise kept the *Enterprise* fighters busy chasing contacts to the west. All unidentified aircraft were friendly.[55]

By 1100 Fletcher, highly frustrated over not having received additional contact reports, sat on the seventeen VS-5 SBDs for nearly two hours. As far as he knew Midway's planes and the carrier strikes found only the same two carriers, not the second group. The wait grew intolerable. In the next forty-five minutes the *Yorktown* must break the spot to land combat air patrol fighters and the strike group that should return shortly. At 1104 he radioed Spruance: "When your planes return give me enemy position course speed. I have one squadron [of] bombers ready." Fletcher proposed to search the northwest quadrant and asked Spruance's opinion. At 1110 Spruance gave latitude 30° 38′ north, longitude 178° 30′ west, as the estimated position of the enemy force at 1015, when it was seen circling at twenty-five knots. The unmentioned source of that information was Gray, leading the first strike planes to return to the *Enterprise*. Having never dived, his ten F4Fs retained the altitude to pick up the *Enterprise*'s YE homing signal and flew directly back to base. They landed around 1050. The position Gray gave was forty miles northeast of the actual Japanese location. About 1115 Fletcher received a message from Cincpac relaying Simard's assessment of his attacks against the group of two carriers and eight to ten other ships located northwest (bearing 320 degrees) of Midway. The Midway strike ran into fierce fighter opposition ten miles from the target. No one saw any torpedoes strike home, but the marine dive bombers claimed two hits on one carrier, "resulting in extremely heavy column of smoke."[56]

Fletcher finally got word of his own carrier strike. By 1120 the seventeen SBDs of Leslie's Bombing Three reappeared overhead little worse for the wear. They came directly from the target, aided by the accurate Point Option estimate that the *Yorktown*'s YE homing signal only confirmed. A flashing light relayed tremendous news that VB-3 sank one carrier. Fletcher passed the word to TF-17 by flag hoist and alerted TF-16 by TBS: "One enemy aircraft carrier sunk. *Yorktown* received the credit." Leslie's SBDs could wait until Massey's short-legged TBDs and Thach's F4Fs could land, but there was no sign of them.[57]

"THE MOST GOD-AWFUL LUCKIEST COORDINATED ATTACK"

Six days elapsed before Fletcher learned more details of the high drama, sacrifice, and glory of the past two hours, when U.S. carrier aviators fatally damaged three carriers and won the Battle of Midway. The actual sequence of events was stranger than anyone could have imagined; as Arnold wrote in 1965, it was "the most god-awful luckiest coordinated attack." Two powerful formations of SBDs, one launched ninety minutes before the other, converged simultaneously to catch the 1st *Kidō Butai* at a highly vulnerable moment. That vulnerability arose after other squadrons, both from Midway and the carriers, gallantly pressed their attacks at enormous cost in the teeth of fierce fighter opposition.[58]

The first U.S. carrier planes found the target because of a highly unusual personal decision. During the first half hour after the departure of the *Hornet* strike group, Lt. Cdr. John C. Waldron, commanding officer of VT-8, grew more frustrated and angry after Ring, the group commander, set the westerly course for his fifty-nine planes (thirty-four SBDs, ten F4Fs, and fifteen TBDs). To Waldron that was a serious blunder. He preferred attacking the two carriers already located southwest of TF-16, rather than seek others thought to be somewhere to the west. After a vehement exchange with Ring, who demanded that Waldron just follow him, Waldron swung VT-8 left at about 0825 to head southwest. Gray's ten VF-6 escorts, cruising twenty thousand feet above, stayed with Waldron. Ring's strong force moved westward completely out of the picture and eventually disintegrated. First the VF-8 escort fighters broke off for lack of fuel, and all ten ditched in a vain effort to find TF-16. Then VB-8 with half the SBDs turned southeast, vainly seeking the enemy along the reported Japanese track. Most ended up at Midway, but three returned to the *Hornet*. Meanwhile, Ring with the VS-8 SBDs proceeded all the way to 225 miles, found nothing, then reversed course straight to the *Hornet*. Mitscher's great gamble to find the second enemy carrier group ended in disaster.[59]

Waldron's instincts proved uncannily accurate, as he aimed directly toward Nagumo's force. At 0910 the VF-6 F4Fs from their lofty height sighted distant ships almost dead ahead beyond a low cloud bank. Near the water, Waldron noticed smoke on the horizon. The 1st *Kidō Butai* first espied the low-level intruders at 0918, just after turning northeast. As the ships evaded at high speed, thirty Zeros tore into the new wave of attackers. Waldron bravely bored straight toward the nearest carrier, the *Sōryū*, but by 0936 all fifteen lumbering TBDs, likened by one VT-8 pilot to "flying freight cars bearing the white star," fell to fighters. Only Ens. George H. Gay survived. The few torpedoes that VT-8 managed to fire missed their targets. Perched high over the eastern edge of the carrier force, Gray never saw the

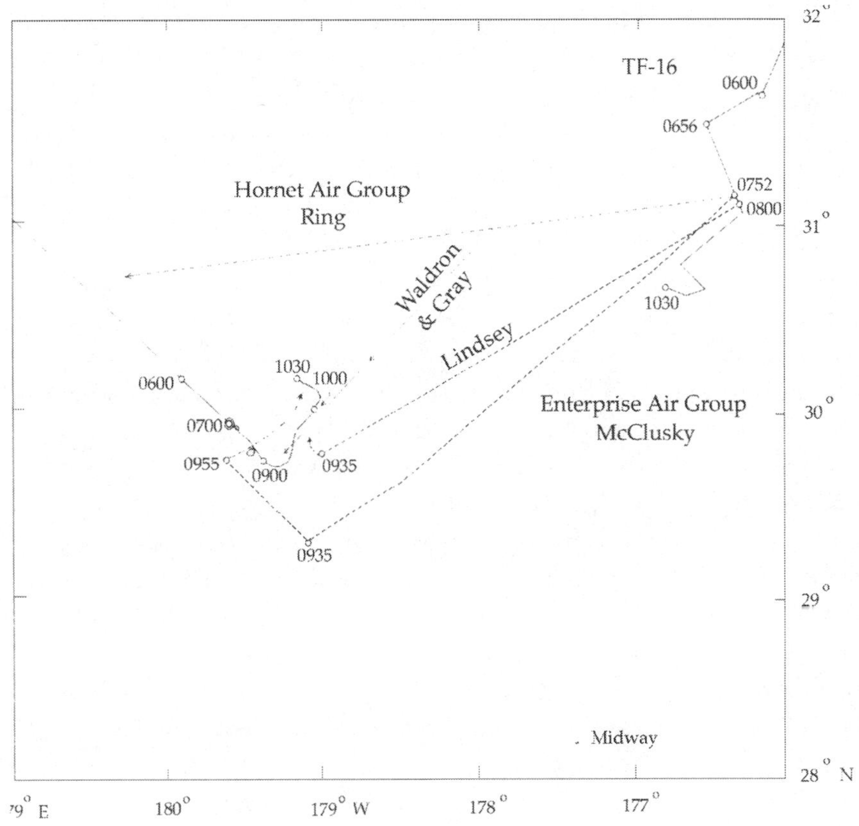

The *Hornet* and *Enterprise* attacks, 4 June 1942

actual torpedo attack through the clouds. Although the *Enterprise* SBDs were his primary responsibility, he previously arranged with Lindsey's VT-6 to descend if they radioed they were in trouble from enemy fighters. Gray heard no such call for assistance (Waldron never knew to ask) and patiently awaited McClusky's SBDs.[60]

At 0938 Nagumo's lookouts sighted more enemy planes coming in low over the water. Lindsey's fourteen VT-6 TBDs went down alone on the 240-degree track and nearly missed the 1st *Kidō Butai* to the north. At 0930 he sighted smoke thirty miles northwest. Steaming northeast at high speed, the Japanese carriers forced VT-6 to close from astern, a poor angle for the slow TBDs. Zeros swarmed the prolonged approach. Far above, Gray did not know VT-6, too, fought and died nearby. Worried about fuel, he made the "Grey" transmissions that so irritated Browning, and at 1010 left for home without firing a shot. Valiant VT-6 split to try to catch one of the carriers in an anvil attack. Around 1000 one element drew near enough to the *Kaga* to fire torpedoes but missed the swiftly moving flattop. The other element chased the *Hiryū* but never got close enough to score. Only five TBDs escaped the vicinity of the 1st *Kidō Butai*, and one soon ditched.

Even as VT-6 completed its gallant attack, the *Yorktown* aviators shed their blood in the pending Japanese disaster. Only the *Yorktown* strike established group integrity. The running rendezvous went well, and by 0945 Thach's six VF-3 F4Fs eased into covering position over the twelve TBDs of Massey's VT-3 cruising at fifteen hundred feet. Flying at fifteen thousand feet, Leslie's VB-3 sighted the TBDs far below. Due to an electrical glitch four SBDs (including Leslie's) inadvertently jettisoned their 1,000-pound bombs but stayed in formation. Bomb or no, Leslie was leading his attack. So accurate was the estimate of Arnold and Pederson, the *Yorktown*ers did not even have to fly to the end of their navigational leg before finding the enemy. At 1003 VT-3 discerned smoke to the northwest and discovered ships twenty to twenty-five miles off. Thach and Leslie followed Massey's turn. Japanese lookouts spotted the torpedo planes easily enough but missed the dive bombers above. While Massey assaulted the *Hiryū*, the combat air patrol grew to forty-one fighters. The Zeros chasing the remnants of VT-6 ran straight into Massey and Thach. Like a reluctant pied piper, VT-3 enticed Zeros down to the wave tops. The relentless interceptors prevented the escort F4Fs from protecting the TBDs. Torpedo Three's sacrifice (ten of twelve shot down) opened the skies over the carriers at exactly the right instant. Closing from the southeast, Leslie discerned two carriers relatively close together, with possibly a third to the west. Unaware VS-5 had not made the mission, he radioed Short at 1015: "How about you taking the one to the left [evidently the *Hiryū*] and I'll take the one on the right [*Sōryū*]? I'm going to make an attack." Somewhat puzzled at not receiving a reply, he stalked the *Sōryū*, northernmost of the three carriers, and still hoped to attack in concert with VT-3. Leslie thought it a great shame no one else was around to take on the other juicy targets.[61]

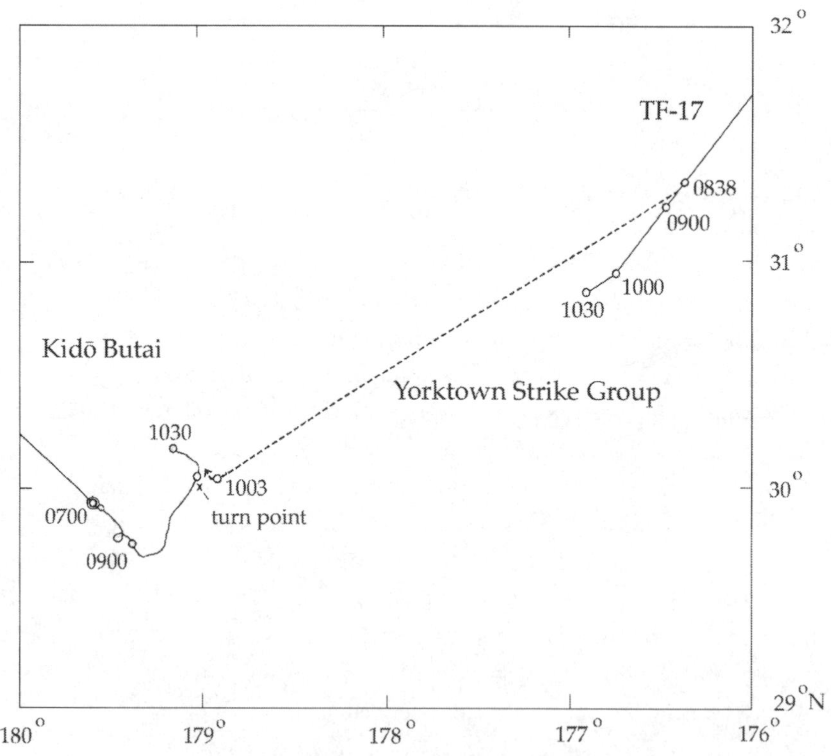

The *Yorktown* attack, 4 June 1942

Unknown to Leslie, other dive bombers already drew a bead on the flotilla of flattops. McClusky's *Enterprise* SBDs undertook quite an odyssey since their hasty departure at 0745. He anticipated contact at 0920 about 142 miles out. Nothing was there, so he flew southwest for fifteen more minutes, then pivoted northwest on the reciprocal bearing of the original Japanese course toward Midway. He planned to hold that heading until 1000 and venture northeast for a short time, before finally turning east for home. Fuel became a real problem. Finally at 0955 he reaped the lucky break his careful reasoning deserved. Below, the long white wake of a destroyer beckoned northeastward. McClusky believed she must be rejoining the main body. In fact the *Arashi* had remained behind to keep the *Nautilus* down while Nagumo cleared the area. Paralleling her track, McClusky was supremely gratified at 1002 to sight the carrier force far to the northeast. If he sent a contact report, Spruance and Fletcher never monitored it.

Nagumo's time was up. The torpedo attacks that consumed the last hour (and still continued) disrupted preparations for the "grand scale air attack" originally scheduled to launch at 1030. Busy handling fighters, no carrier yet spotted any carrier bombers or torpedo planes. The combat air patrol Zeros either circled at low altitude low on gas and ammunition, chased VT-3 while it desperately closed the *Hiryū*, or tangled with VF-3 Wildcats. The 1st *Kidō Butai* was momentarily defenseless against a surprise dive bombing attack. At 1022 McClusky, closing from the west, confronted two carriers. An ex–fighter pilot unfamiliar with dive bombing procedure, he erred by pushing over against the *Kaga*, the nearer carrier. Instead, he should have taken the lead squadron to the more distant target and allowed the trailing SBD squadron to attack the first carrier. Some twenty-eight SBDs, nearly the entire force, followed McClusky down and soon smothered the *Kaga* with perhaps ten hits. Realizing the neighboring carrier was not being attacked, Lt. Richard H. Best, commanding officer of VB-6, tried to round up his men, radioing: "1st div., 2nd div., stay with me and come on over. Don't let this carrier escape." In the end only he and his two wingmen broke off after the *Akagi*. In perhaps the most splendid single performance of the battle, they secured two 1,000-pound bomb hits and a damaging near miss. At the same time, Leslie led VB-3 against the *Sōryū* off to the north. Nine pilots plastered her with three 1,000-pound bombs. Seeing that carrier was doomed, the other four attacked screening ships.[62]

Seven decisive minutes (1022–1028) saw Nagumo lose three-quarters of his carrier strength, and with it the Battle of Midway. On all three stricken flattops, heavy bombs shattered flight decks and penetrated into the hangars. Fierce flames torched fueled and armed aircraft, as well as ordnance left lying around after the hasty rearming. Fire-fighting systems were either destroyed by the blast or incapable of dealing with the intense flames. Reminiscent of the fiery destruction of the *Lexington* less than a month before, it was only a matter of time before the inferno reached aviation gasoline tanks and magazines and finished off the three proud warships. Nagumo himself was dazed by one of the most stunning reversals in history. One moment he was poised to seize victory by destroying the U.S. carrier and reducing Midway, the next he had to take cover. Only twenty minutes after the *Akagi* was hit, he crawled out of a bridge window after flames isolated the island and descended by rope to the flight deck. Nagumo made his way down to the relatively secure anchor deck to meet a boat from the light cruiser *Nagara*. Of the once mighty 1st *Kidō Butai* carriers only the *Hiryū* remained untouched.[63]

Yamamoto followed the distant battle as best he could from flagship *Yamato* six hundred miles northwest. The fragmentary radio traffic indicated everything was going well. The premature discovery of a U.S. carrier off Midway only sweetened the pot, because Nagumo should have had planes ready to deal with her. Then "optimism" turned to "deepest gloom," as Yamamoto again learned far more quickly than his counterpart at Pearl Harbor that the battle took a calamitous turn for Japan. The ruin of Yamamoto's strategy of widely separated advances was the inability of his task forces to support each other. Kondō's Attack Force was 350 miles southwest of Nagumo. Despite its considerable surface strength he had just the light carrier *Zuihō*. Only the 2nd *Kidō Butai* (*Ryūjō* and *Junyō*) could provide substantial carrier air support, but Kakuta would require three days just to reach the Midway area. In the meantime Yamamoto could only hope his battleships, cruisers, and destroyers could draw close enough to the American carriers to overwhelm them with high-caliber shells and torpedoes. If things looked grim for the Japanese, they still had the *Hiryū* led by Yamaguchi, an aggressive and resourceful commander. The *Yorktown* would soon feel her sting. Fletcher, too, would evacuate his flagship by means of a rope and seek refuge on a cruiser while still unsure whether his side was winning the battle.[64]

CHAPTER 18

The Battle of Midway II
Counterattacks

THE SECOND SEARCH

On the heels of VB-3's proud announcement of sinking a carrier, Fletcher finally learned that the enemy had pinpointed TF-17. At 1120 he signaled by flag hoist: "We have been sighted." Fullinwider's team missed the numerous exchanges between Amari and his irritated superiors, while the *Chikuma* Number Five plane (PO1c Takehashi Masataka), sent to relieve Amari's *Tone* Number Four plane, first sighted TF-17 at 1045. Takehashi was much more aggressive than the enigmatic Amari. A more formidable snooper prowled nearby. At 1000 WO Kondō Isamu's special *Sōryū* Type 2 reconnaissance plane reached the enemy position provided by Amari but found nothing. Sweeping southward, he discovered TF-17 an hour later, then located and properly identified all three U.S. carriers. After his radio malfunctioned, he raced home to deliver his news.[1]

The need to land the *Yorktown* strike group assembling overhead, coupled with certain knowledge the enemy found TF-17, demanded Fletcher swiftly deploy the seventeen VS-5 SBDs held in reserve the past three hours. As far as he knew, the search and the several land- and carrier-based attack waves only found two of the four enemy carriers. From all indications they were already crippled, if not destroyed outright. VS-5 could do no immediate good there. It was crucial to ferret out the second carrier group, now believed north or northwest of the lead pair. Fletcher detailed ten SBDs to search northwest and north (280–020 degrees) two hundred miles from TF-17. The other seven, armed, were to be struck below to clear the flight deck. They could join the second strike once the first wave was recovered. Preparations were already under way for rearming the SBDs and TBDs expected to land shortly. The six F4Fs earmarked for a possible VS-5 strike would instead reinforce the half-dozen fighters waiting to relieve the current combat air patrol.[2]

At 1135 a radar contact twenty-five miles northwest added to the sense of urgency. The *Yorktown* started launching the twenty-two aircraft at 1139. Spruance suggested to Fletcher the *Yorktown* "locate [and] track carriers already attacked," as well as "search northwest quadrant for possible third carrier." He obviously believed his planes attacked only two carriers. TF-16 will "strike again," but must first recover and rearm its first wave. Once the *Yorktown*'s flight deck was clear, two stray shot-up *Enterprise* strike SBDs thumped down at 1150, followed by six combat air patrol F4Fs and Thach's four escort F4Fs (of the rest, one was shot down, the other landed on the *Hornet*). The last Wildcat flipped over on deck, suspending recovery until crews could clear the wreck and re-rig the barriers. Leslie's VB-3 waited patiently in the landing circle, but no VT-3 TBDs showed up. In the meantime Fletcher broke radio silence to ask Cincpac to tell Midway that TF-17 attacked the two carriers previously reported but that he had "no indication of location additional carriers which have sighted this force." Ironically some newly returned aviators could have told him about all four carriers and affirmed three were knocked out of action. Events quickly became so hectic on the *Yorktown* that no one had the opportunity to brief Fletcher.[3]

THE *HIRYŪ* RETALIATES

At 1152, as the *Yorktown* started landing planes, her radar detected a strong contact thirty-two miles southwest (255 degrees) that quickly materialized into a "large group of bandits." Climbing furiously, the twelve newly launched combat air patrol F4Fs hastened westward in pairs. Buckmaster ceased fueling the fighters on deck and buttoned up the ship, including the new precaution of purging the lines in the aviation gasoline fuel system and filling the voided spaces around the stowage tanks with carbon dioxide gas. Fletcher increased speed to 30.5 knots. The screen deployed two to three thousand yards from the *Yorktown*, one heavy cruiser on each bow and the five destroyers filling in the rest of the circle. The nearest element of Spruance's TF-16 creased the southeast horizon fifteen miles distant from TF-17. Busy recovering planes, the *Enterprise* and *Hornet* themselves were ten miles apart. Dow had nineteen F4Fs aloft on combat air patrol. Another twenty-five Wildcats sat on board the two carriers, but with both flight decks spotted for landing they were not available. Just as Fletcher feared, dividing the carriers divided the defense. Dow did what he could to help TF-17. He dispatched eight *Hornet* fighters to intercept incoming planes thirty miles northwest, but only four pilots answered the call. At the same time he deployed the VF-6 patrol as a blocking force to protect TF-16. Four of seven F4Fs stretched their orders and hurried toward TF-17. Thus twenty scattered fighters defended TF-17, too few to stop a determined assault.[4]

The devastating attack left only Yamaguchi's *Hiryū* to carry on the fight. At 1050 while Nagumo shifted his flag to the *Nagara*, Abe assumed temporary command of the first *Kidō Butai*. He divided the force to support the burning carriers and to escort the *Hiryū*, pulling off rapidly northeast. Only thirty-seven operational planes remained on board the *Hiryū*: ten Zero fighters (including three intended for Midway), eighteen Type 99 carrier bombers, and nine Type 97 carrier attack planes. Twenty-seven Zeros from all four carriers and an *Akagi* carrier attack plane from the morning search circled overhead. At 1050 eighteen carrier bombers and six Zeros under Lt. Kobayashi Michio started taking off. Still being rearmed, the carrier attack planes would not be ready for at least another hour. The *Hiryū* first wave was only a fraction of what Nagumo could have hurled at the U.S. carriers had he only been left alone and not fiddled with rearming. From Takehashi's shadowing of TF-17, Yamaguchi gained a much better idea where the U.S. carriers were. At 1100 TF-17 was ninety-five miles and TF-16 just ninety-one miles northeast of the *Hiryū*. Kobayashi proceeded out at low altitude and only later climbed. That was why the *Yorktown*'s radar did not detect him farther out. His escorts rashly tangled with several stray

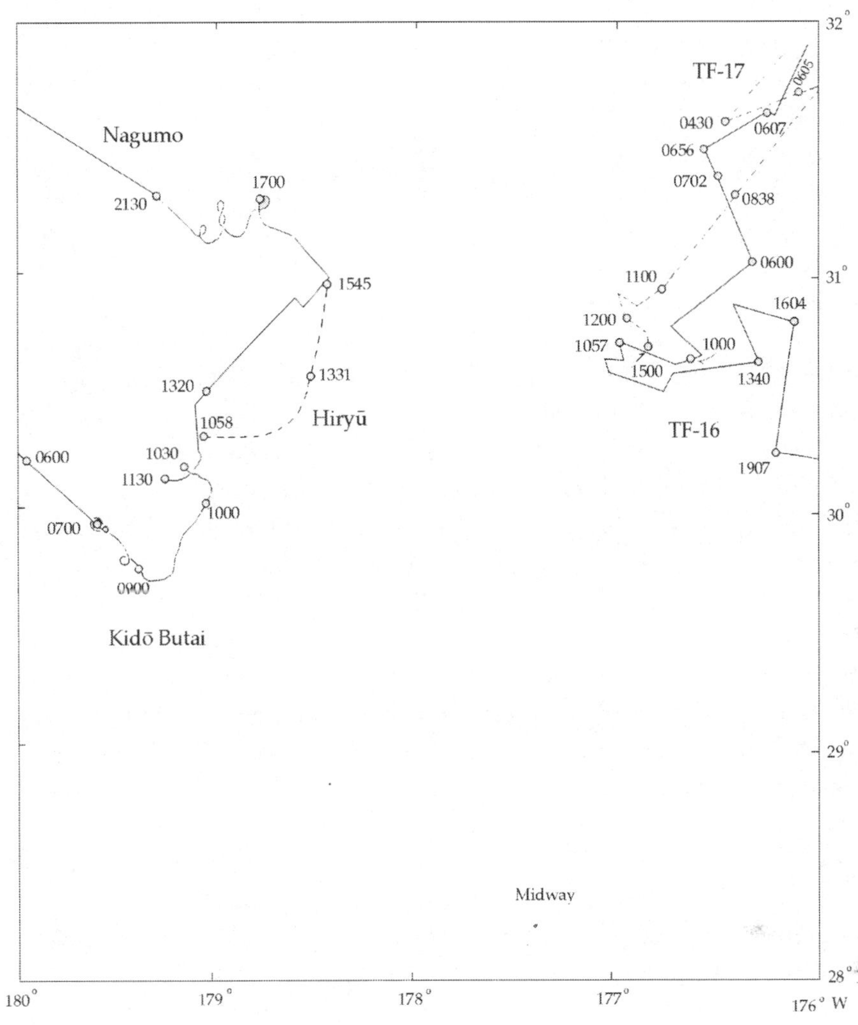

Carrier operations, 4 June 1942

Enterprise SBDs. Two shot-up Zeros turned back; the other four never resumed proper position before Kobayashi sighted TF-17 at 1155.[5]

At 1201 a combat air patrol pilot radioed eighteen Japanese planes were "heading for the ship." Using the *Yorktown*'s code name, Pederson exhorted: "Come on you Scarlet boys, get them!" Fletcher was bending over the chart table in flag plot, when one of the staff advised: "The attack is coming in, sir." Lifting both arms to his head, he replied, "Well, I've got on my tin hat. I can't do anything else now." Out to the west seven VF-3 F4Fs shredded Kobayashi's formation. About eight carrier bombers went down, while the others lunged at TF-17 in small flights from different directions. Fletcher swung southeast away from the incoming aircraft. At 1206 screening cruisers and destroyers cut loose with five-inch guns against widely scattered targets. Their black shell bursts were visible to TF-16, even though the ships themselves were below the horizon. Fletcher, Lewis, and most of the staff moved outside on the flag bridge to observe the attack. Standing alongside Schindler, Mike Laing, the brash British naval liaison officer, busily scribbled notes. They were all about to receive a lesson in dive bombing like the one Nagumo experienced that morning. Many Japanese considered the *Hiryū* Air Group their best, and this battle demonstrated the accuracy of that assessment.[6]

It was fortunate only seven carrier bombers actually broke through the fighters to assail the *Yorktown*. At 1211 the first *Hiryū* plane screamed in steeply from astern. Buckmaster tried more of his maneuvering magic to evade bombs, but this pilot would have none of it. He pressed his dive to the limit. At about one thousand feet fierce fire from 1.1-inch and 20-mm cannons chopped the plane into three parts, but its 242-kilogram high explosive land bomb tumbled free and blew a hole a dozen feet across in the flight deck aft of the center elevator. The blast inflicted horrific casualties to the two 1.1-inch gun mounts abaft the island and penetrated the hangar. Only quickly opening the sprinklers, and water curtains quenched three SBD fires that could have been disastrous. The next three bombs all fell just astern of the twisting *Yorktown*. Number five made up for them. That 250-kilogram ordinary bomb pierced the flight deck ten feet inboard from the island, burrowed deeply into the vitals, and detonated in the stack uptakes just below the second deck. The resulting fire was only a minor distraction. The explosion ruptured the uptakes for six boilers, knocked two out of commission, and extinguished the fires in all but one other. Thick smoke from the fire and exhaust gasses that could not be vented choked the fire rooms and other parts of the ship. The *Yorktown* rapidly lost speed. The sixth bomb sliced through the forward elevator platform and penetrated to the third deck before detonating. The resulting blaze, quickly contained, was a sparkler compared to the bonfires that consumed the three Japanese carriers. A nearby magazine was flooded, and the forward aviation gasoline tanks were not in danger. The seventh bomb missed close to starboard. The attack cost the *Hiryū* thirteen carrier bombers (including Kobayashi) and three Zero fighters. It appears F4Fs shot down eleven Type 99s and three Zeros, while TF-17 antiaircraft bagged two Type 99s and tragically a VF-8 F4F.

Dense smoke poured into the island, including flag plot, whose occupants had no choice but to join the admiral and the rest of the staff outside. Smoke also filled Radio I, located one deck below the flag bridge, and blocked the interior passageway. After first stripping the ECM of its special flag cipher rotors, Charles Brooks's team followed the *Yorktown* communicators up through an escape hatch into the clear. Radios elsewhere on board remained operational. Fletcher and the staff descended to the flight deck and beheld the carnage around 1.1-inch mounts. For the time being Fullinwider's radio intelligence team waited in the small flag radio compartment aft of flag plot. Fortunately the thick smoke did not enter there. They had not handled much trade that day, and Fullinwider was not with them when the attack came in. He returned and brought them out.[7]

With thick, black smoke streaming from the stack, the island, and forward hangar deck, the *Yorktown* glided to a stop. Fletcher dashed off a radio message to Nimitz and Spruance: "Have been attacked by air 150 miles north of Midway." He then took a turn around the flight deck and in the hangar to see the damage for himself. In the meantime Buckmaster hoisted the breakdown flag and conferred with his department heads. Lt. (jg) John E. Greenbacker, the ship's secretary, recalled: "We all waited with that helpless feeling knowing we were a sitting target." Dixie Kiefer described the situation as "quite grim." Repair parties patched the large hole in the flight deck, while the engineers tried to clear the fire rooms and get most of the boilers back on line. The radar was not functioning, and most communication systems were disrupted.[8]

Buckmaster requested the *Portland* take radar guard and directed the *Yorktown* planes aloft go to the other carriers. The only two surviving VT-3 TBDs ditched near the task forces. The VF-3 combat air patrol Wildcats split between the *Enterprise* and *Hornet*, but fifteen VB-3 SBDs (all but Leslie and his wingman who later ditched) opted for the *Enterprise*. The *Yorktown* planes were welcome after the TF-16 air groups suffered terrible losses in the morning strike. The *Hornet* recovered only twenty of thirty-four SBDs, but even worse saw no sign of the fifteen VT-8 TBDs and ten VF-8 escort fighters. Midway later advised that eleven VB-8 SBDs took refuge there. The other planes were gone forever. Only four of fourteen TBDs and fifteen of thirty-three SBDs reached the *Enterprise*. Perhaps seven SBDs ditched because they could not find TF-16. Due to Browning's gross overestimation of the Point Option rate of advance, the *Enterprise* ended up forty miles northeast of where the strike expected to find her. McClusky was very bitter the ship never updated his pilots.[9]

A distant spectator to the attack on TF-17, Spruance did not know precisely what happened. From the heavy smoke he assumed the *Yorktown* was hard hit. To Kinkaid with the *Hornet* group, one far-off ship appeared to be "exploding—high columns of black smoke shooting into the air." The constant air operations entailed in landing the strike and recycling the combat air patrol compelled Spruance to continue steaming southeast at high speed into the feeble breeze, instead of going northwest to aid TF-17. Therefore he detached heavy cruisers *Vincennes* and *Pensacola* and destroyers *Balch* (with Capt. Edward P. Sauer, Comdesron Six) and *Benham* from the *Enterprise*'s screen and replaced them with the *New Orleans* from the *Hornet* group. The *Vincennes*'s Capt. Frederick L. Riefkohl led the four ships northwest at thirty knots. They and some fighters were all Spruance could spare for the time being for TF-17.[10]

TRANSFERRING THE FLAG

Fletcher faced a hard decision. Extensive damage rendered the *Yorktown* immobile, possibly for a considerable time. Her radar was out, communications still uncertain, and flag plot most definitely "untenable." Fletcher intended for Spruance's TF-16 to carry the fight for the time being, while he concentrated on saving the *Yorktown*. That meant towing if Buckmaster could not get her going again. Under the circumstances Fletcher thought it best to shift to Smith's flagship *Astoria* instead of over to the *Hornet*. At 1238 he summoned a boat from the *Astoria* to fetch him, his staff, three communication watch officers, Fullinwider's radio intelligence team, and selected men from the enlisted flag allowance. Commander Laing would remain behind. After observing Fletcher and Lewis carefully during the battle, he later characterized both as "quite unflappable."[11]

Once the boat arrived, the staff officers clambered down a line to get on board. Fullinwider remarked that after the *Lexington*, he was getting to be an old hand at this.

When Fletcher's turn came, he tried the rope but was not up to it. "I'm too damn old for this sort of thing," he said. "Better lower me." The boatswains looped a bowline beneath his arms and eased him into the boat. By 1323 its passengers clambered on board the *Astoria*. Correspondent Foster Hailey quipped the "smoke-begrimed" men looked "like refugees from a chain gang." While the boat made a second trip to get the rest of the men, Fletcher joined Poco Smith in the familiar confines of the cruiser's flag plot on the signal platform.[12]

Fletcher's first order from the *Astoria* was to Capt. Laurance T. DuBose's *Portland* to take the *Yorktown* in tow. Shortly thereafter Riefkohl's four welcome reinforcements positioned themselves among the screen ships circling the *Yorktown*. Riefkohl had feared the *Yorktown* might be abandoned and was pleasantly surprised to find her on an even keel. Because her CXAM radar was superior to the SC sets on the other cruisers, the *Pensacola* took over radar guard. By TBS Fletcher told Spruance, who had gone out of sight to eastward, "As soon as possible join this unit." He composed an explanatory dispatch for Cincpac that he directed the *Astoria* fly to Midway for transmission, so as not to alert enemy radio direction finders to the stationary TF-17. The message noted the *Yorktown*'s three bomb hits left her dead in the water, but "apparently seaworthy." "Unless otherwise directed TF-17 will protect and salvage *Yorktown*," while Spruance continued to "engage enemy." As far as Fletcher knew, two enemy carriers remained intact, a surmise confirmed at 1345, when Nimitz relayed Simard's declaration that the Midway planes only ever saw two carriers. At 1408 the *Astoria* catapulted Commander McLean with two SOCs to deliver the message to Midway. By the time he reached there, the battle took yet another unusual turn.[13]

At 1355 while the *Portland* prepared to pass tow lines, to everyone's amazement the *Yorktown* started moving under her own power. "Suddenly, there was a great burst of steam from our stack, then another, and amid cheers from all hands we got underway." Loud cheers also rang out from the screen. With tremendous effort the *Yorktown* engineers mended the uptakes sufficiently to get three boilers on line, which would soon give Buckmaster twenty knots. He replaced the breakdown flag with a signal announcing, "My speed five," and broke out a huge new battle ensign. Fletcher gratefully canceled orders for the tow, reformed the screen, and headed southeast to clear the area. The *Yorktown* was far from out of danger. Radar discovered a bogey out to the west. Suspicious, Fletcher hoisted the signal: "Prepare to repel air attack." To the east a snooper could be seen tumbling in flames, thanks to the TF-16 combat air patrol. The victim was Takehashi's *Chikuma* Number Five plane that bravely shadowed the two task forces for more than three hours.[14]

When Fletcher changed course due east, the *Yorktown*'s crew exulted: "Bremerton, here we come." By 1420 the *Yorktown* worked up to fifteen knots, but the light winds were insufficient to land safely the ten search SBDs, scheduled to return at 1500. Buckmaster radioed that he was redirecting them to Midway. The search reported no sightings up to this point. Fletcher prudently formed the Victor formation, spacing the screen close around the carrier on a two-thousand-yard radius. He stationed one cruiser on each bow and quarter (the *Astoria* off the starboard bow) and spread the seven destroyers in between. These precautions were necessary. At 1427 the *Pensacola*'s radar discovered bogeys forty-five miles northwest, evidently a rapidly closing attack group.[15]

STRIKE TWO

The hard-driving Yamaguchi and the *Hiryū* were at it again, this time with ten torpedo-armed carrier attack planes and six Zero fighters under Lieutenant Tomonaga, who led the dawn strike against Midway. They played their part in Yamamoto's effort to regain the initiative. He postponed the Midway landings, directing the transports to sidestep north and take station five hundred miles west, while he concentrated all his forces northwest of Midway for decisive battle on 5 June. Kondō was to unleash the four fast heavy cruisers of Rear Adm. Kurita Takeo's 7th Cruiser Division to bombard Midway before dawn and neutralize that source of enemy air power. The *Sōryū* reconnaissance plane that landed on the *Hiryū* confirmed the presence of the *Yorktown*, *Enterprise*, and *Hornet*, first learned from the interrogation of a captured U.S. Navy pilot. That bitter news dashed Nagumo's hopes for daylight surface revenge. Carrier air power of that magnitude could smash his ships before they got close enough to shoot. The few surviving *Hiryū* carrier bombers reported attacking one carrier and five cruisers ninety miles east and leaving the flattop in flames. One down, two to go. The *Hiryū* could still destroy or cripple all the U.S. carriers and open the way for the overwhelming surface strength to prevail. Tomonaga's strike departed at 1331. At that time TF-17 was merely eighty-three miles southeast, TF-16 112 miles. Tomonaga sighted a U.S. task force at 1430 about thirty-five miles off. Its carrier steamed normally at twenty-four knots, with no evidence of fire, so the *Hiryū* aviators assumed she must be different than the one the first wave pounded.[16]

Pederson, the *Yorktown* FDO, had only six F4Fs provided by TF-16 to defend against the new wave of attackers. They headed out to intercept. Thach's eight VF-3 F4Fs were spotted aft on the flight deck ready to go. Once again Buckmaster suspended refueling and purged the aviation gasoline system with CO_2. Six of the Wildcats had only the fuel saved from the morning combat air patrol. Spruance's two carriers, twenty and thirty-five miles southeast of TF-17, could offer no immediate assistance. Dow kept seven F4Fs to protect TF-16 and hustled the other eight northwest, but they would not make it in time to forestall another attack on the *Yorktown*. There were thirty-four Wildcats on board the *Enterprise* and *Hornet*, but with their flight decks spotted for recovery, they could not launch for twenty minutes. The lead division of four F4Fs missed the strike descending through the clouds and had to double back, but at 1438 the rear pair of F4Fs intercepted fourteen miles northwest of TF-17. They destroyed one carrier attack plane, but the alert Zero escort swiftly shot down both Wildcats. Lookouts saw all three planes fall in flames ten miles out.[17]

At 1440 Buckmaster turned the *Yorktown* to starboard directly into the wind to launch the eight F4Fs. The *Pensacola*, on her port quarter, caught sight of rapidly moving torpedo planes six miles out and blasted away with her 8-inch main battery and 5-inch guns. The other ships on that side followed suit, and as the enemy drew within range they added their array of light antiaircraft. Standing alongside Smith on the wing of the *Astoria*'s signal platform, Fletcher saw a torrent of fire erupt beyond the *Yorktown*. In peril both of Zeros and friendly antiaircraft, Thach's Wildcats hammered away at the attackers, but the surviving *Hiryū* pilots—skilled, determined, and flying fast aircraft—caught the *Yorktown* in a split attack. They dropped their torpedoes closer in than at the Coral Sea. With only twenty knots, Buckmaster lacked the speed to evade, and the approaching fish were too close to dodge. From 1443 to 1444 two torpedoes struck the *Yorktown* close together amidships on the port side. From off the opposite side Fletcher could see the geysers of brown smoke and water abreast of her island, as the carrier heeled sharply to port. The air battle raged a few minutes, before the Japanese drew off to the west. Five VF-6 F4Fs from TF-16 engaged the departing attackers, as did the mixed division of four that missed the initial interception. The *Hiryū* lost five carrier attack planes (including Tomonaga's) and two Zeros—far fewer than TF-17 thought. Four VF-3 F4Fs were shot down.

The jubilant Japanese aviators reported they disabled a second carrier. To the dismayed Americans it was painfully obvious that the *Yorktown* sustained multiple torpedo hits and was very badly damaged. With white smoke issuing from the stack, she rapidly lost way and took on an alarming list to port that exceeded 20 degrees. As the flight deck canted steeply, Capt. Francis W. Scanland in the *Astoria* whispered: "My God, she's going to capsize." Others who watched the *Yorktown*'s distress shared that fear, not to mention those on board to whom catastrophe loomed. At 1455 Fletcher directed the *Balch*, *Benham*, *Russell*, and *Anderson* to stand by the *Yorktown*, while the rest of the screen circled protectively. The next move was Buckmaster's. He alone knew the condition of his own ship and whether she could be saved. Just prior to the *Yorktown* being hit, he informed Fletcher by visual message that one of the late morning search planes just discovered a previously undiscovered Japanese carrier. Events intervened before he could add its composition and position. Presumably (or at least hopefully) Spruance received the full report, for he must deal with it. Fletcher radioed Cincpac that "after second heavy attack," the "*Yorktown* apparently sinking." Although two enemy carriers had been destroyed so far, he bitterly complained: "Have no idea location carriers attacking Task Force 17."[18]

THE "FOURTH CARRIER"—MYTH AND FACT

If Fletcher was not particularly surprised another carrier strike rocked the *Yorktown*, very likely fatally, Spruance and Browning in the *Enterprise* were truly shocked. They had convinced themselves no enemy carriers were still in fighting shape, and so the carrier portion of the Battle of Midway was already won. That startling assessment is reflected in a message that Spruance sent at 1404 to Nimitz and Fletcher forty minutes before the second attack on TF-17. It noted that from 0930 to 1100 the TF-16 and TF-17 air groups had attacked a force that comprised "probably" four carriers, two battleships, four heavy cruisers, and six destroyers. "All four CV [are] believed badly damaged," along with one or two heavy ships. Spruance made that assessment despite reports of participants like Dick Best of VB-6, who insisted that they personally saw only three carriers set afire. Equally inexplicably, Spruance repeated the old position that fighter pilot Gray gave as of 1015, which was thirty-eight miles northeast of where the attack actually took place. Spruance's SBD pilots could have easily told him where the enemy carriers were. TF-16 plane losses were "heavy." Spruance did not discuss his plans, but simply requested "positions of enemy units and tracking data as practicable." He showed no great sense of urgency.[19]

When it came to appraising the damage inflicted on the Japanese carriers in the morning strikes, Spruance and Browning somehow added three ones and got four. Perhaps the staff simply credited the one carrier that Midway planes claimed to set afire. Planes that took off from their carriers before they were damaged at 1030 could have executed the first attack on the *Yorktown*. Understandably the action reports, written once the accepted sequence of the battle was established, neglected to mention this exaggerated damage assessment and saved Spruance from being accused of inertia. Another enduring myth of the Battle of Midway is the anxiety over the so-called fourth carrier. According to entrenched belief, Fletcher and Spruance both learned rather quickly that the morning attack knocked out only three carriers, while number four slipped off somewhere to cause trouble. Embellishing this tale is an episode where Browning supposedly urged Spruance to rearm the surviving SBDs for an immediate search-strike mission against the fourth carrier. Spruance is said to have refused in order to preserve his dwindled striking force intact, waiting until someone else found the last carrier so he could finish her off. This legend serves to explain the three hours of inaction by TF-16 between landing the morning strike and when, simultaneously, Spruance learned the *Yorktown* was being attacked the second time and that another enemy carrier was spotted. After 1200, in truth, only Fletcher actually worried about intact Japanese carriers, to him numbers three and four.[20]

Spruance had cause other than overestimating the damage to the enemy for not following through on his pledge to Fletcher at 1145 to "strike again" immediately. Plane losses were terrible. So was the sudden realization of what the staff's Point Option fiasco contributed to the carnage. Only about ten *Enterprise* SBDs could fly a second strike, and no one wanted to send the three flyable TBDs out again. At 1300, though, the fifteen VB-3 SBDs mostly restored the *Enterprise*'s dive bomber strength. The *Hornet*'s losses were even worse: all fifteen torpedo planes, ten fighters, and fourteen SBDs (though later it was learned eleven SBDs landed at Midway). Nonetheless, Mitscher, not one to mope around, advised Spruance at 1310 that the *Hornet* had twenty SBDs ready to go again. They and the ten *Enterprise* SBDs comprised a powerful force available almost immediately for a second strike. It is interesting that Spruance did not send them to finish off all the crippled carriers, which, if they were as badly damaged as he thought, should not have limped far from the site of the original attack.[21]

Instead, Spruance and his staff retained the happy image of all four enemy carriers sunk or crippled that morning. TF-16 could afford to lick its wounds and wait until after the fearsome Zero combat air patrol fighters ditched before attacking again. Plane strength needed to be conserved to deal with the Midway invasion if the Japanese pressed on. In truth, inertia prevailed in the *Enterprise* flag shelter on the afternoon of 4 June, and Spruance has received a pass from the critics. Dick Best, for one, certainly wondered at the time why more was not being done to hit the remaining Japanese ships he, at least, knew included an undamaged carrier. The staff likewise allowed the combat air patrol situation to deteriorate as F4Fs were brought in for fuel. From 1330 to 1430 combat air patrol numbers dropped from twenty-five to twenty-one, including only six fighters guarding TF-17, with no readily available reinforcements. At 1340 Fletcher had ordered Spruance to approach TF-17 "as soon as possible," yet by 1430 the distance between the *Enterprise* and *Yorktown* had not lessened. Light winds forced Spruance to steam eastward at high speed for flight operations.

After one more combat air patrol launch and recovery cycle, he finally turned northwest at 1400. He later apologized to Fletcher: "We tried our best to close you after the first attack, but it seemed that every mile we made toward you in between air operations was more than lost when we had to launch or recover." At the same time, though, Mitscher did contrive to move the *Hornet* task group a little closer to TF-17.[22]

Messages deploying fighters to protect TF-17 refuted any remaining illusions in the *Enterprise* flag shelter that the Japanese carriers were done for. At 1444 Spruance's budding reputation as a nearly infallible combat leader hung in the balance. Distant antiaircraft bursts appeared on the western horizon, and Fletcher radioed Cincpac in plain language: "Am being heavily attacked by air." It was tremendously fortunate for Spruance that when he learned there was truly an intact and aggressive enemy carrier, an instant solution appeared. At 1445 Spruance intercepted the same plain language voice message from a VS-5 search pilot that Buckmaster had passed Fletcher. It placed one carrier, two battleships, three heavy cruisers, and four destroyers at latitude 31° 16′ north, longitude 179° 05′ west, and steaming due north at fifteen knots.[23]

Students of the battle rightly praised Fletcher's decision to send a second search using planes he had the "foresight" to reserve for the unexpected. However, things were far from that simple. If all of VS-5 had strictly followed orders, the *Hiryū* might still not have been found. Their designated search area was in fact too far north. The decision paid off as Fletcher hoped only because another pilot displayed the kind of brilliant personal initiative of a Waldron or McClusky that meant the difference between victory and defeat. Lt. Samuel Adams and wingman Lt. Harlan R. Dickson found nothing in their own sector (300–320 degrees). Nor were any other VS-5 crews more successful. Instead of heading directly back to the *Yorktown*, Adams took it upon himself to swing well south to check whether the enemy carriers ever advanced as far north as anticipated. The extent of that detour is apparent when one realizes that at 1430, he placed the *Hiryū* force more than 150 miles from the base where he himself was supposed to land a half hour later. The two SBDs fought off a Zero before starting for home.[24]

Although Fletcher erred in his estimate of the enemy's location, his decision to search rather than strike nevertheless was logical given the circumstances. The navy's reconnaissance doctrine and training, already inadequate in the Battle of the Coral Sea, had not improved at Midway. No effective tracking of targets was accomplished at all. Had Fletcher known at the outset that all four (or even three) Japanese carriers were together, he might have sent all the *Yorktown* strike planes out together and perhaps bagged the *Hiryū* along with the rest. If someone at the scene had only radioed later that morning that three carriers were afire, he could have used all of VS-5 to hunt the fourth. Either move could conceivably have saved the *Yorktown*. Of course the same was true for Nagumo, who suffered with Amari as his point man. The search for and tracking of targets would remain a Pacific Fleet weakness throughout 1942. Finally, one wonders whether Spruance could have even attacked had Adams not so fortuitously reported the *Hiryū*. There was little time before sunset for Spruance to conduct a separate search and follow-up strike.

Adams placed the new target more than 160 miles northwest of the *Enterprise*, and that distance was increasing. Given all the same drawbacks of wind direction and limited range, Spruance could not escort the SBDs, even though the enemy's air defense might be quite strong. In fact Adams perhaps erred in locating the *Hiryū* as far as thirty-eight miles too far west, so the distance from TF-16 might have been closer to 125 miles. At 1510 Spruance alerted the *Hornet*: "Prepare to launch attack group immediately[,] information later." He followed at 1518 with the target's composition, location, and course. By 1542 the *Enterprise* lofted twenty-five SBDs, including fourteen from VB-3, but he did not actually order Mitscher to launch his strike group, less escort, until 1539.[25]

Mitscher had not monitored Adams's report and did not know at first another carrier was sighted. Twenty *Hornet* SBDs were ready to go, but at 1510 he was preoccupied with recovering the other eleven VB-8 SBDs just back from Midway. Simard had refueled and rearmed them and sent them to find and attack the enemy carriers to the northwest. Afterward they were to proceed to the *Hornet*, or return to Midway if she could not be found. The eleven SBDs never in fact even searched for the enemy, but simply followed the carrier's homing signal directly back to TF-16 on a short flight. Mitscher strangely observed in his action report, "Had [they] located the enemy and made their attack prior to their return, they probably would not have been ready to send on the next flight." At 1604 the *Hornet*'s first deck load of sixteen SBDs began taking off. At 1613, after they got away, Mitscher used the open flight deck to recover three fighters and two strike SBDs that just developed mechanical trouble. Then at 1616 he committed a colossal error by prematurely turning the task group westward. That abruptly concluded the launch before the *Hornet* could spot the second deck load of fifteen SBDs warming up in the hangar. Marooned on board were group commander Ring, both squadron commanding officers, their executive officers, and flight officers, in fact the entire leadership. Seven minutes later, evidently informed of his blunder, Mitscher swung back around southeast into the wind to resume the launch. Then he decided it would take too much time. At 1624 after scrambling to determine who was senior among the fourteen SBDs of the first deck load patiently circling overhead, he signaled Lt. Edgar E. Stebbins, the engineer officer of VS-8, "Take charge [and] proceed on this attack." Stebbins headed out against the target assumed to bear 278 degrees, distance 162 miles. Therefore thirty-eight SBDs (three others aborted) sortied westward to gain revenge for the savaging of the *Yorktown*. Buell blamed Browning and TF-16 staff, who "bungled every aspect of the planning and execution of the second launch." Browning and company certainly had their problems on 4 June, but the second strike was definitely not one of them. Mitscher deprived his strike of all its leaders and half its strength. The egregious handling of the *Hornet* was solely his responsibility.[26]

THE *YORKTOWN* ABANDONS SHIP

Only fifteen minutes after the second attack, Buckmaster regretfully signaled: "I am abandoning ship." The two aerial torpedoes inflicted terrible harm. Initially it was thought they struck about fifty feet apart and opened separate holes each estimated at twenty feet high and twenty to thirty feet long, although that damage seemed "unusually extensive for an aerial torpedo." Not only did the three port-side fire rooms flood, but the concussion itself also extinguished all boiler fires, with an immediate loss of steam pressure. At the same time all electrical power failed despite the diesel auxiliary engines, rendering the ship completely dark. The rudder was jammed 15 degrees to the left. The latest research, based on observation of the sunken *Yorktown*, revealed the torpedoes hit immediately adjacent to each other in the "most vulnerable section of the ship." They blasted one huge hole roughly sixty by thirty feet that caused "more internal damage than previously thought." Very swiftly the alarming list to port exceeded 25 degrees, angling the flight deck steeply toward the sea. Lacking power Buckmaster could not counter flood to right the ship or even use emergency lighting below deck. Without working phones and bullhorn there was no way to coordinate the damage control by a crew coping in the dark on the canted decks. Buckmaster worried that the old gal would simply continue to roll over and capsize with twenty-three hundred men still on board. He must get them off as quickly as possible.[27]

As the screen circled two thousand yards out, observers in the *Astoria* estimated the *Yorktown*'s list neared 30 degrees when Buckmaster's doleful signal fluttered aloft. Fletcher recalled: "I was biting my nails thinking that Captain Buckmaster made his decision to abandon ship too late." In his endorsement of Buckmaster's "Report on Loss of Ship," he was "firmly convinced" that Buckmaster "used good judgement in reaching his decision to abandon ship when he did." From "the appearance of the *Yorktown* at the time the order was issued, any other decision would have been extremely unsound." Buckmaster deeply appreciated Fletcher's unswerving support, particularly later when criticisms mounted that he had prematurely abandoned ship. Michael Laing, who stood on the canted deck with Buckmaster when he ordered the crew off the *Yorktown*, considered he did so "too early in my opinion." He "supposed the best thing Buckmaster could have done was to get rid of the useless mouths and keep damage control parties, gun crews, engineers etc to fight and if possible save the ship." Laing did not explain how Buckmaster could have gone about sorting out the necessary personnel given how dire he perceived the condition of the ship. No U.S. naval ship yet provided for an emergency salvage crew to remain on board in the event it became necessary for the others to abandon ship. On Fletcher's recommendation, Cincpac directed immediately after Midway that every ship organize such a force, but Buckmaster lacked that resource on 4 June. Nor did the U.S. Navy realize just how tough its modern construction would be. Nimitz, for one, accepted that when Buckmaster decided to abandon ship, "the situation appeared very critical." Historians condemned the decision because the *Yorktown* was still afloat the next day without help. Morison first claimed that after the emergency repairs at Pearl the *Yorktown*'s watertight integrity was better than before and that Buckmaster should have taken it into account in his precipitous decision to leave her. Later, though, he acknowledged the "hasty" nature of the repairs and fears "she would turn turtle," but still condemned Buckmaster for abandoning "unnecessarily." The team of analysts who recently examined the photos of the sunken *Yorktown* likewise thought she "may have been prematurely abandoned," commenting that after a list exceeded 15 degrees, "self preservation is an overriding consideration."[28]

The *Yorktown*'s crew threw rafts overboard and snaked lines down the side. The *Balch*, *Benham*, *Russell*, and *Anderson* lowered boats and moved in closer to pick up swimmers. Soon "the oil-covered sea was alive with bobbing heads, small rafts and 5-inch shell casings." Rafts gathered men so they could be towed by motor boats to cargo nets slung alongside the waiting destroyers. John Greenbacker recalled how Buckmaster had "hated to give the order to abandon ship" and indeed "disliked to practice it," regarding the abandon ship drills to be "destructive of morale and confidence." Thus the *Yorktown* had not run such a drill since the war began. It was quite fortunate that the ocean "was almost as smooth as a rug," although "had the sea kicked up or had the carrier been ablaze when abandoned, there would have been heavy loss of life." One hundred miles to the west the Japanese would have affirmed the second condition, as they struggled to save the remnants of three crews whose carriers, once the pride of the IJN, were transformed into huge blowtorches.[29]

Fletcher had much on his mind as he contemplated his uncertain air protection, the carrier's imminent loss, and the rescue of her huge crew. Several bogeys tracked by the *Pensacola*'s radar impelled him at 1504 to signal: "Standby to repel air attack," as if any task force could be in less condition to receive one. Things looked more serious at 1509 when enemy aircraft were reported thirty-six miles southeast. Fletcher directed the screen to form the Victor formation after aircraft were detected bearing 280 degrees, distance eighteen miles. He radioed TF-16 and Midway requesting air cover during the rescue. The *Balch* and *Anderson* backed clear, but the *Russell* and *Benham*, surrounded by men in the water, remained where they were and continued recovering survivors. No attack developed. At least one intruder was an old friend, the *Tone* Number Four plane, which at 1515 radioed the sighting of a large U.S. force (TF-16) bearing 102 degrees and 120 miles from its point of origin. Amari added, tentatively as usual, that there "appears" to be a carrier twenty miles ahead of the first group. That was the *Yorktown*.[30]

The rescue proceeded in an orderly fashion without panic. As each destroyer filled with oil-soaked survivors, she eased away from the carrier and returned to the screen. "Filled" was the right word. The *Benham*, *Balch*, and *Russell* together rescued more than seventeen hundred men. The 725 in the *Benham* alone brought "standing room only," according to her commanding officer, Lt. Cdr. Joseph M. Worthington. The presence of so many men on board the tin cans not only brought overcrowding, but also serious stability problems. The *Morris* and *Anderson* recovered about 450 men. Last in, the *Hammann* and *Hughes* together saved more than one hundred sailors. After 1600, when nearly all the crew had left the *Yorktown*, Buckmaster made his final inspection. "It was necessary to move hand over hand to keep from falling," because in places the decks were "covered with oil, very slippery." As he proceeded through the darkness he could hear, even over the roar of the aft auxiliary diesel engine, that deeper in, "Great bubbles of air [were] being replaced at intervals by water." He thought the *Yorktown* might capsize at any moment. After returning topside to check if everyone was off (actually, it was learned later, two injured men were left behind), he strode the length of the hangar deck and left the forlorn ship via the stern. A boat brought him to the *Hammann*. By 1646 the rescue was completed, having recovered 2,280 men.[31]

To everyone's surprise the *Yorktown*, the port edge of her hangar deck dipped near the water, did not simply roll over and sink. Instead she "rocked on swells," and at times seemed to "regain some of her trim then leaned over again as though tired of the struggle." To Fletcher and Smith it became apparent the *Yorktown* "had ceased settling and had become, at least temporarily, stabilized." Smith remarked: "I believe she will hang there and not sink." Fletcher agreed. At 1615 he radioed Cincpac: "*Yorktown* badly listed and abandoning. She does not appear to be settling now. Suggest you send tugs in attempt to salvage. Survivors cannot be distributed to Task Forces 16 and 17 without seriously impairing military efficiency by over manning." The "over manning" was an important consideration. So many survivors rendered most of his destroyers "almost helpless." Fletcher considered whether to try once again to have a cruiser tow the *Yorktown*. So did others. In 1947 one cruiser captain, most likely Riefkohl, questioned "why we left the *Yorktown* the first night without picking her up and towing her away." In the end Fletcher decided against it. Establishing the tow meant the risk of getting personnel back on board and hoping the enemy did not attack in the meantime. The Japanese obviously had the *Yorktown*'s exact location. At 1627 the TF-16 combat air patrol finished off a snooper within easy sight of TF-17. That and yet another shadower caused another alert of possible air attack. Unaware of the final outcome of the carrier battle, Fletcher worried the enemy could still deliver another air attack before dark (1842) or send a night surface attack group to finish off the crippled carrier. Those same drawbacks militated against having a destroyer go alongside the *Yorktown* to provide electrical power for a salvage effort. Under the circumstances in the midst of a fierce battle, Fletcher could have justifiably torpedoed and sunk the *Yorktown* then and there. Instead he planned to withdraw eastward that night, separate out a salvage party, put the other survivors in the *Portland* and two destroyers, then return with the *Astoria* group.[32]

At 1715 Fletcher set course due east at fifteen knots toward where he last saw TF-16. A few minutes later the *Astoria* slowed to let the *Hammann* come alongside to deliver Buckmaster. A sympathetic Max Leslie, rescued by the *Astoria* after ditching that afternoon, recalled, "It was a sober, impressive, sorrowful and yet rewarding scene to see this gallant officer quietly plod his way up the gangway where he could gain a brief respite before further action." Tall Buckmaster was "hatless, coatless, shirt unbuttoned at the neck, no neck tie, wringing wet from perspiration and salt water and with absolutely nothing in his possession except an indomitable spirit to continue the battle God willing." After briefing Fletcher, Buckmaster laid out the salvage effort and compiled a list of essential personnel scattered among the destroyers. Before going too far from the *Yorktown* Fletcher attended to another vital matter. At 1800 after learning which destroyer had the fewest survivors (and thus was most combat-ready), he directed Captain Hoover (Comdesron Two) to have the *Hughes* (with only twenty-three passengers) "stand by *Yorktown*." Lt. Cdr. Donald J. Ramsey, her skipper, received orders not to permit anyone to board the *Yorktown* and was authorized to "sink her if necessary to prevent capture or if serious fire develops." Ramsey thus faced the daunting task of keeping company with the derelict until one of three events occurred: she sank, the enemy showed up, or the salvagers returned. At 1830 when the *Hughes* reversed course, the *Yorktown* was about twelve miles off, hidden in the setting sun. Fletcher never saw his noble flagship again.[33]

CUTTING SPRUANCE LOOSE

At 1811 Spruance advised Fletcher via TBS that the *Enterprise* and *Hornet* were attacking the fourth carrier, the one the *Yorktown* search plane discovered that afternoon. It is interesting that he now used the term "fourth carrier," for that differed from what he believed just a few hours before. His new perception arose from the reports of a Midway PBY (Ens. Theodore S. Thueson), which while on its return leg from the dawn search prowled the scene of the morning attack. At 1600 Thueson spotted three burning ships and soon identified them as carriers, confirming what Best and others told the TF-16 staff all along. Spruance advised Fletcher that the *Hornet* was about thirty miles east of him and that he planned to steam west until he recovered his strike groups. "Have you any instructions for further operations?" Fletcher replied: "Negative. Will conform to your movements." Thus he gracefully conceded to Spruance the freedom to fight the battle without further reference to him. After the *Yorktown* was hit, he had the right to shift his flag to the *Hornet* and continue in tactical command of the carrier striking force. But so far as he knew, Spruance and the elite aviation staff were doing a good job handling TF-16. Transferring command to the *Hornet* might cause confusion at a crucial juncture of the battle. Fletcher never brandished the ego of one who must run the whole show no matter what, or who hated to share the credit. In fact he was criticized in official circles for "voluntary relinquishment of tactical command to a junior." Gordon Prange correctly called the change of command an "act of selfless integrity and patriotism in action." However, Fletcher's creditable action opened the door for others to minimize his true role in the Midway victory.[34]

The release of TF-16 from Fletcher's command at that exact time meant a great deal to Spruance. "He was my senior, and I did not know what he wanted to do himself or what he wanted me to do. His reply was a message I have always appreciated." That was especially true, because Spruance mulled what would subsequently be one of the most controversial decisions of the Battle of Midway. He resolved, once he recovered his second strike, to clear the area to the east. He still had no clear idea of Japanese dispositions, losses, and intentions—despite the growing belief that most if not all the carriers were knocked out—and especially feared a night surface engagement, where his superior carrier air strength would avail him nothing. Heavy guns and torpedoes could quickly even the score. Radio intelligence revealed that several snoopers very likely reported his general location and probably his strength. Powerful surface forces, fast battleships, cruisers, and destroyers were not distant. About sunset Fletcher sighted first the *Enterprise* and then the *Hornet* group steaming southeast while busy recovering aircraft. He turned TF-17 in their direction and politely declined a request from Spruance for help. Fletcher knew as well as Spruance the Japanese could join the party at almost any time. He returned the *Vincennes* and *Pensacola* to TF-16, but kept the two destroyers loaded with survivors. By 1915 Spruance reassembled his scattered task force into one disposition and steadied on 090 degrees. Fletcher kept station fifteen miles to the north. Spruance intended to withdraw east until midnight in order to avoid any lunging warships, then come back around to the west and by dawn position himself within air support range of Midway.[35]

A "GLORIOUS PAGE"

Thirteen hundred miles southeast, Nimitz spent a stressful 4 June trying to get some normal work done between frequent checks of the operations plot for the latest information. Following at long distance what could be the decisive naval battle of his career proved especially frustrating. Only Midway maintained close contact by virtue of the underwater cable. Thus Nimitz had a fair idea of how the battle was progressing from the viewpoint of the island. Because of radio silence he knew very little about how his own carriers fared. Early that afternoon came distressing news from Fletcher that the *Yorktown* was crippled. That was overtaken by Spruance's grand announcement that his planes not only found all four Japanese carriers, but also badly damaged them. Next he learned the *Yorktown* was hit hard again, making it painfully obvious at least one enemy flight deck was still intact. Almost immediately, in yet another timely reverse of momentum, a search plane discovered the *Yorktown*'s assailant or perhaps another carrier altogether. Hopefully TF-16 could destroy the rest of the carriers before dark. A Midway PBY (Thueson) offered highly encouraging word that three enemy carriers were burning. Also gladdening the heart of a former submariner, Nimitz heard the *Nautilus* had torpedoed a previously damaged *Sōryū*-class carrier. All was not rosy. The PBY that snooped the three burning carriers also warned of Zero fighters that should not have been aloft since the morning attack. Cincpac warned at 1847, "May indicate Jap carrier still on loose." At 1907 he advised Fletcher and Spruance that as of 1829 the Japanese were "believed homing planes," another indication enemy air power was not crushed. Thueson in fact encountered only one orphaned Zero and saw it ditch.[36]

Nothing came from Spruance regarding the fourth carrier located several hours before. The accumulated tension coupled with the dearth of up-to-date information finally cracked even Nimitz's renowned calm. That evening he appeared "frantic," according to Layton, "As frantic as I've ever seen him," as he badgered his communications officer for fresh reports. Near to midnight, though, Nimitz reflected on the extraordinary events of 4 June, and he did not yet know the half of it. With the battle still much in doubt, he responded with one of the inspiring gestures that was so typical of the man. A message to all commands announced: "You who participated in the Battle of Midway today have written a glorious page in our history. I am proud to be associated with you. I estimate that another day of all out effort on your part will complete the defeat of the enemy." Just after midnight 5 June Midway local time, Nimitz advised: "Reports are incomplete at present but believe enemy will if he can muster sufficient air continue duel with our 2 remaining carriers in order to proceed with landing attack on Midway," and, "It is certain that he has at least one carrier able to operate aircraft." Probably more for King's benefit than from any actual information, he added: "We are executing night attack with appropriate types." Finally the *Saratoga*, scheduled to reach Pearl early on 6 June, "will be despatched as soon as fueled."[37]

The evening of 4 June after his second strike returned, Spruance prepared a summary, but it is not certain when he radioed it. The message proclaimed the heartening results of the TF-16 afternoon strike. From 1700 to 1800 the *Enterprise* and *Hornet* bombed a force of one carrier, two battleships, two or more heavy cruisers, and several destroyers; they left the carrier "burning fiercely" and a battleship also on fire. The enemy withdrew west at fifteen knots. Destroyers were noted approaching that force from the southeast, and off in that direction three ships, "Believed CV's previously attacked," were seen on fire. Spruance asked to be kept informed of likely targets that shore-based search might find on 5 June and advised that as of 0400 5 June he would be 170 miles northeast of Midway. That wonderful report, evidently received by Cincpac after midnight Midway local time, elicited another "dazzling smile." Now the tide of battle had definitely turned. At 0145 Nimitz described the second attack as "superb."[38]

It was all of that. At 1700, twenty-four *Enterprise* and *Yorktown* SBDs ambushed the *Hiryū*, the sole undamaged carrier, just before Yamaguchi could mount his third strike of six carrier bombers and nine fighters. Four bombs struck forward and threw the forward elevator up against the island. Uncontrollable fires gutted the hangar and doomed the *Hiryū* and any realistic hope for Yamamoto to grasp victory out of what was now Japan's most demoralizing defeat. Before dark the *Hiryū* and her disconsolate consorts weathered attacks by fourteen *Hornet* SBDs and twelve B-17s without further harm. Nagumo witnessed the devastation of his sole operational carrier. He still hoped for a night surface battle and even pulled destroyers away from the other stricken carriers but relented when he received search reports that the U.S. ships withdrew eastward out of reach. Even more disillusioning, he learned at 1830 that the *Chikuma* Number Two plane discovered no fewer than four U.S. carriers in addition to one seen burning and listing. That formidable force was steaming westward. The unintentional exaggeration of American strength (the additional flattops were thought to be auxiliary carriers) landed the final blow. Nagumo rounded up his force and hauled out to the northwest. Shortly after 1900 both the *Sōryū* and *Kaga* sank, the latter after burning nearly to the waterline. The *Akagi*, already abandoned, lasted until just before dawn. In the meantime Nagumo left the failing *Hiryū* behind with two destroyers.[39]

On the night of 4 June help was on the way in the form of Kondō's Main Force roaring up from the southwest eager to overtake the American carrier force and annihilate it. He had two fast battleships, four heavy cruisers, one light cruiser, seven destroyers, and light carrier *Zuihō*. From the south, one light cruiser and eight destroyers, part of the escort of the transport force, hastened to join him. Kondō also counted on Nagumo's two fast battleships, two heavy cruisers, one light cruiser, and four available destroyers. These forces converged on a point 175 miles northwest of Midway and one hundred miles west of the *Yorktown*. At the same time Kurita's bombardment group of four heavy cruisers rapidly closed Midway. Finally around midnight Yamamoto, 450 miles northwest of Midway, resignedly concluded the MI Operation was a complete failure. He canceled the night battle and ordered Kondō, Nagumo, and Kurita to meet him 350 miles northwest of Midway. He later directed the transports to withdraw westward and arranged for the other ships to refuel on 6 June, seven hundred miles northwest of Midway. The great eastern Pacific offensive was over, and the Japanese sought only a clean getaway. Only the *I-168* loosed a few shells against Midway early that morning. That was merely a nuisance, but soon the lone submarine would accomplish more in the Battle of Midway than all the rest of the Combined Fleet.[40]

TO SAVE THE *YORKTOWN*

Although composed several hours apart under different circumstances, the two messages that Fletcher sent on the afternoon of 4 June to Nimitz regarding the condition of the *Yorktown* actually reached him within fifteen minutes. Unfortunately he received the later one first. Written after the carrier was torpedoed at 1444, it described her "badly listed and abandoning." The earlier message, the one McLean delivered to Midway, noted that three bomb hits left the *Yorktown* "dead in the water," but still "apparently seaworthy," which certainly she no longer was. The earlier message also affirmed, "Unless otherwise directed Task Force 17 will protect and salvage *Yorktown*," although by the time Nimitz read it, Fletcher was retiring eastward to regroup. Nimitz gladly replied, "Affirmative." For a brief time, at least, Cincpac believed the *Yorktown* was better off than she was, and if he could provide help there was a good chance to save her. He mustered his resources. The nearest ocean tug was the *Vireo*, an old former minesweeper waiting out the attack near Pearl and Hermes Reef 120 miles east of Midway. Nimitz ordered her to proceed to the *Yorktown* some 160 miles northwest and take her under tow. However, with a top speed of ten knots, the *Vireo* could not arrive before midday on the fifth. Next Nimitz redirected the destroyer *Gwin* (with Cdr. Henry R. Holcomb, Comdesdiv 22), which had left Pearl on 3 June to reinforce TF-16. She could now join the salvage effort on the afternoon of the fifth. Other potential salvage ships were much farther away. On the morning of 4 June, almost as an afterthought, Nimitz instructed the modern ocean tug *Navajo* to load salvage and rescue gear at Pearl, then sail for French Frigate Shoals southeast of Midway. She could not reach the *Yorktown* until the afternoon of 7 June. To relieve TF-17 of the burden of the survivors, the fast new submarine tender *Fulton* sailed from Pearl that night with two old four-piper destroyers from the offshore patrol as escort. The *Fulton* received a specific course to steam toward Midway, while Fletcher was to have the ships carrying the *Yorktown* survivors take the reciprocal bearing and intercept her around noon on 6 June southeast of Midway. The ocean tug *Seminole* would follow the *Fulton*.[41]

Thus Nimitz informed Fletcher: "Tugs enroute to tow *Yorktown* with constructor and salvage officers." In the meantime, Fletcher was to "retain enough men on board *Yorktown* who know ship and furnish DD escort to assist salvage party." Only it was already too late. No able-bodied crew remained in the *Yorktown*. Cincpac's order crossed a message Fletcher sent at 1845 describing in sobering detail the actual situation. "*Yorktown* received 3 bomb hits first attack; 2 or more torpedo hits on second attack. All boilers out of commission. Ship listed 30 degrees and abandoned when apparently about to capsize. Still afloat no appreciable change in trim down by the head. Will not attempt to tow her by cruiser. Destroyer standing by." By then Fletcher, of course, retired eastward to clear the area that night in case the Japanese warships showed up.[42]

Fletcher's decision to leave the *Yorktown* on the night of 4 June without attempting salvage drew bitter criticism. The February 1943 Cominch Secret Information Bulletin No. 1 declared that the *Yorktown* "might have been saved if she had not been completely abandoned during the night but salvage work carried on." The same bulletin also categorically disapproved of Spruance's decision to withdraw that night. "Task Force 16 would have done better if it had headed westward and not eastward after attacking the *Hiryū* in order to follow up the successes of 4 June." Late in 1942, however, Japanese messages found on Guadalcanal sketched the menace of superior surface forces to TF-16 had it continued westward. When told of them, Spruance felt, "The weight of a score of years has been lifted from my shoulders." By 1948 Bates and also Morison completely agreed with the wisdom of Spruance's actions, pointing out that Kondō and Nagumo could possibly have engaged him in night combat had TF-16 gone west or even stayed in the same area. If one accepted the logic of Spruance's decision, how could Fletcher, with only four cruisers and whose destroyers were far less combat ready, be criticized for leaving the stricken, stationary *Yorktown*? She was even closer to the enemy than TF-16, and moreover Fletcher was aware the Japanese knew her position. If they were hell-bent on a night surface battle north of Midway, they would have hardly neglected to finish off the crippled carrier and deal with the ships left behind to protect her.[43]

In light of his hindsight, Bates thought it would have been "wiser" for Fletcher to have left two destroyers with "a limited number of key salvage personnel" to try to improve the condition of the ship. The destroyers could keep a radar watch. If enemy ships did appear they would have enough notice to sink the *Yorktown* and hopefully recover the salvagers. Of course by the time Fletcher realized the *Yorktown* was not going to sink immediately, all the men were off, and night approached. The problem of how to organize those "key salvage personnel" still remained. According to Poco Smith, "The unfortunate aspect of the situation was that the crew of *Yorktown* had been pulled at random, not by selection, from the sea." Under the circumstances that pertained on the night of 4 June, he thought TF-17 "could not hover on the scene while sorting them out and selecting those whose experience best qualified them for the salvage job in hand." No one considered what a small salvage party might have actually accomplished at night in a steeply listing ship without power, and the destroyers ready to bug out if the enemy showed up. Saving the *Yorktown* required a far better organized and equipped effort. The question became whether it would be in time.[44]

CHAPTER 19

The Battle of Midway III
Finale

A FRUSTRATING FIFTH

On the night of 4 June following a naval victory seldom equaled, Fletcher's TF-17 (minus stricken *Yorktown* and guardian *Hughes*) and Spruance's TF-16 (*Enterprise* and *Hornet*) withdrew east. After releasing Spruance from his command, Fletcher looked to facilitate the salvage of the *Yorktown* and secure the proper disposition of her survivors. He left the next phase of the fighting solely to Spruance, who reckoned that night that although four carriers had been disabled or sunk, the battle was far from over. One damaged carrier might still be operating, or a fresh flattop reached the area. He would avoid a night battle with surface ships that could devastate his force, then determine where best to commit the fragile air power of the *Enterprise* and *Hornet*, now some sixty-five flyable SBDs, fifty-four F4F fighters, and three TBDs. Spruance desired by first light on 5 June to be 175 miles northeast of Midway, from where he could either engage surviving carriers if any remained in range, pursue retreating forces, or protect Midway in the remote event the invasion was still on.[1]

Early that morning Midway reported a brief shelling believed from a sub, actually the *I-168*. Cincpac's 0300 bulletin set off alarm bells. The *Tambor* (Lt. Cdr. John W. Murphy), one of eleven subs taking up the northeast-southwest arc one hundred miles from the island, warned that as of 0217 "many unidentified surface ships" lurked only ninety miles west of Midway. Spruance awoke to word that Midway was about to be invaded. At 0420 he raced southwest toward Midway. TF-16 must break through the covering force and disrupt the landing. At the same time Captain Simard warily continued the scheduled air operations. At 0415 ten PBYs taxied out for the dawn search, reduced this day to 250–020 degrees to only 250 miles. A few minutes later eight B-17s sought the ships located by the *Tambor* just to the west. First light revealed "foggy haze," with scattered squalls and low visibility. The *Tambor*'s intruders were actually Kurita's bombardment force of four heavy cruisers. After penetrating the U.S. sub line unseen, Kurita drew within fifty miles of his objective, when at 0045, in response to Yamamoto's orders, he retired northwest to the great fleet rendezvous. At 0218 his lookouts discerned the surfaced *Tambor* at almost the same instant her watchers spotted ships. While evading, the *Mikuma* swung into the path of the *Mogami*, which struck her amidships on the port side above the waterline. The collision bent the *Mogami*'s slender bow all the way back to the forward turret. It later had to be cut off. Kurita left the less-damaged *Mikuma* behind to escort the stricken *Mogami* to the west, while he took the two intact cruisers to join Yamamoto.[2]

Murphy trailed the cripples until sunrise when, following his original orders, he submerged. At 0600 he radioed his only amplifying report that placed two "*Moyagi* (*sic*)" cruisers, one damaged, 115 miles west of Midway and headed west at seventeen knots. Nimitz had the message in hand by 0630, Midway local time, but it failed to ease his deep concern. The "many" ships could have pressed on to Midway. Only Simard could clarify the situation. After consulting Cincpac, Admiral English, the Pacific Fleet sub commander, alerted his skippers at 0647: "Believe enemy will attempt landing Midway today." All eleven subs were to surface, run at top speed to within five miles of the island, and "develop all contacts." At 0707 Nimitz forwarded the initial PBY contacts made at 0630. The first placed two battleships 125 miles west of Midway and westbound at fifteen knots, and the second noted two destroyers on nearly the same bearing but closer in at one hundred miles. He told King, Fletcher, Spruance, and Simard of "strong indications" Japan "will attempt assault and occupation Midway regardless past losses." At the time, though, only the two imperiled heavy cruisers were anywhere near Midway.[3]

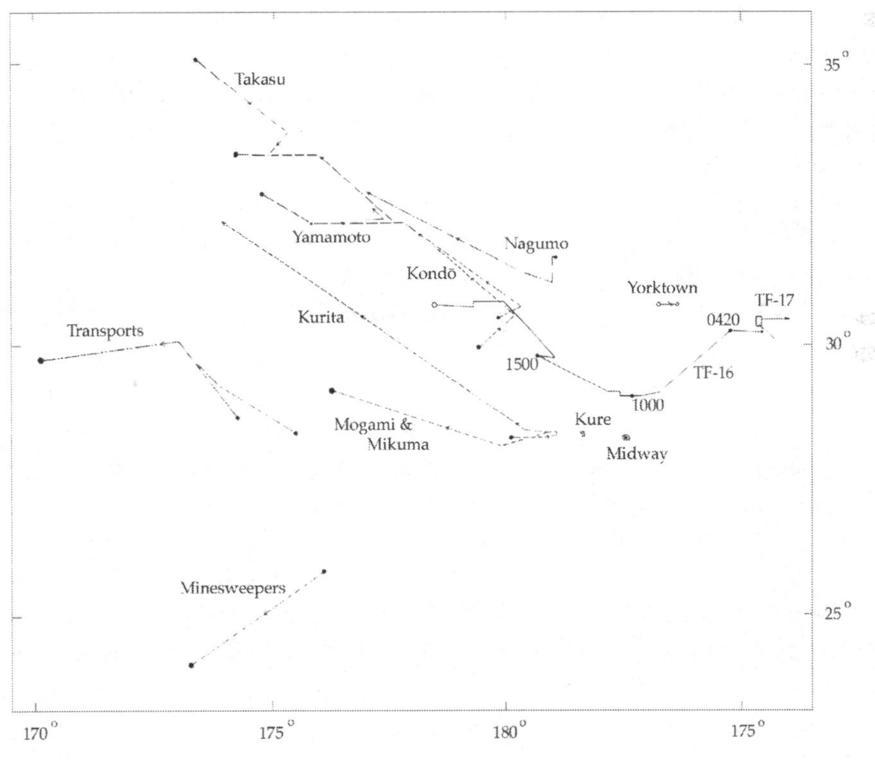

Carrier operations, 5 June 1942

Closing Midway rapidly from the northeast, Spruance awaited fresh intelligence to help him decide how best to counter an invasion. The skies cleared sufficiently by 0830 for the carriers to deploy a combat air patrol. They also prepared strike groups of SBDs. Spruance advised Cincpac he might cross English's sub line "in pursuit of Jap units." Sixty miles was as close as he cared to approach Midway. He turned west. The supposed battleship-cruiser targets were then some 150–180 miles southwest, just within strike range. Apparently Browning recommended attacking, but Spruance wanted to see what else was happening, particularly whether any carriers were sighted. That soon occurred. Around 0900 Cincpac detailed two sightings 240 and 250 miles northwest of Midway and about forty-five miles apart. At 0800 Lt. Donald G. Gumz of VP-44 sighted a burning carrier, two battleships, and three or four cruisers bearing 324 degrees, 240 miles from Midway. They retired northwest at twelve knots. Twenty minutes later Ens. David Silver of VP-24 reported a carrier 335 degrees and 250 miles from Midway, course 245 degrees. B-17s would take on the first (Gumz's) contact once they dealt with the ships to the west. The two "battleships" west of Midway grew to three, now 130 miles out. About two hundred miles northwest (325 degrees) of Midway were ten more ships, including five destroyers, said to be hastening northwest at twenty-five knots.[4]

Silver's single carrier was 220 miles northwest of TF-16, but because Cincpac and Simard soon dismissed it, Spruance did too. At 240 miles Gumz's damaged carrier was well out of strike range, given the same contrary, light southeasterly winds as the previous day. To attack a target that was downwind, Spruance would have to steam at high speed almost directly away during launch, and thus considerably increase the outbound leg of the mission. Concerned about the possible assault on Midway, he resolved for the time being not to pursue the crippled carrier to the northwest. If the invasion was actually under way, the putative "fifth" carrier could well be within attack range of Midway. During the next two hours TF-16, heading west, passed north of Midway while retaining the option of pursuing either the ships to the west or northwest. Because of the *Monaghan*'s critically low fuel, Spruance detached her to rescue a downed PBY crew and then join the *Yorktown* salvage force. His other six destroyers were not markedly better off.[5]

Deciding by 1120 there was no longer a direct threat to Midway, Spruance chased the burning carrier, reckoned then about 225 miles ahead. Unfortunately that contact was "rather cold." With only one chance before dark to hit one part of the widely scattered Japanese forces, he held off as long as he dared in case an undamaged carrier popped up within range. Buell questioned whether Spruance should have searched, but considering how close he was to Midway, that would have unnecessarily duplicated the shore-based effort. At 1223 he learned that Midway's radio direction finder detected enemy signals bearing 315 degrees, at least confirming the general direction. Midway advised the battleship force previously located 130 miles to the west was actually three *Mogami* or *Tone* class cruisers, two of which were damaged. They were said to be trailing a cavalcade of six transports and two light cruisers, a very misleading report because the transport force was actually nearly four hundred miles farther west.[6]

If the hurt carrier maintained reported course and speed, Spruance could count on gaining about ten miles every hour. It appears he intended to unleash the *Enterprise* and *Hornet* SBDs at 1500, with the target about 190 miles ahead. Running southeast into the wind during launch would increase the outbound leg to 225 miles, a very long haul for SBDs lugging 1,000-pound bombs, but doable if TF-16 resumed closing the target at high speed.

At 1420, however, Spruance belatedly learned from Cincpac that the target, now greatly enhanced, might actually be thirty-five miles farther northwest. When Gumz returned to Midway, he gave a new position for the "burning carrier" as of 0930 and added a nearby second carrier, "not burning," two battleships, three heavy cruisers, and five to ten destroyers. Nimitz declared, "This force particularly carriers is your best target." Unfortunately Cincpac erred by attributing the updated position to 0800 rather than 0930 and failed to forward the message in a timely fashion. Now with the carrier force substantially farther from TF-16, some 230 miles as opposed to 195 miles, Browning urged all SBDs take off immediately. The need to turn away while launching would raise the outbound navigational leg toward 270 miles, but he relied on the usual over-optimistic Point Option advance of twenty-five knots to shorten the return flight sufficiently for them to make it back.[7]

Trusting the judgment of his top aviation advisor, Spruance naturally concurred. The new attack plan triggered an eruption in the *Enterprise*. The orphaned squadron leaders Lieutenant Short (VS-5) and Lt. Dewitt W. Shumway (VB-3) could hardly believe the strike orders. Hoping the air staff was "approachable" (certainly the case in Fletcher's *Yorktown*), they sought help from above to get the orders modified. Murray and the wounded McClusky were appalled. The four officers stormed into the flag shelter to protest personally to Browning. McClusky flatly stated SBDs could not go 270 miles with a 1,000-pound bomb and have a prayer of coming back. He urgently requested they be rearmed with 500-pound bombs and the launch be delayed at least an hour to gain a few more precious miles relative to the target. Browning adamantly refused. The discussion became so heated that Spruance strolled over and asked what was the matter. After hearing both sides of the argument, he overruled his imperious chief of staff for the first time. "I'll do whatever the pilots want." His pride grievously injured, Browning stomped down to his stateroom and fumed until another staff officer cajoled him into returning topside. The revised plan substituted 500-pound bombs for the SBDs equipped with the bigger payload (probably half the total), but the strike was to leave on schedule. It appears the TF-16 staff simply instructed the *Hornet* to rearm with 500-pound bombs and set Point Option on 315 degrees at twenty-five knots. In yet another episode of incredible negligence, no one in the *Enterprise* thought to inform Mitscher that the enemy was actually somewhere else than previously reported. They blithely assumed that Mitscher had all the information they did and could figure out on his own how to get his planes there. Mitscher, naturally thinking the enemy must still be within range of SBDs with 1,000-pound bombs, did not bother rearming his Dauntlesses that carried them.[8]

At 1500 Spruance reversed TF-16 southeast into the wind, and within forty-five minutes sixty-five SBDs scurried northwest in three groups. The *Hornet*, reckoning the target as a damaged carrier bearing 315 degrees and 212 miles, sent two deck load strikes. Commander Ring led the first wave of twelve SBDs armed with 500-pound bombs. The second wave of twenty-one SBDs, some with 1,000-pound bombs, left a half hour later. The one flight of thirty-two *Enterprise* SBDs expected to find two carriers bearing 324 degrees, 265 miles. All suffered disappointment. Ring searched one hundred miles beyond the expected intercept point but found only a lone light cruiser or destroyer 278 miles out. Near to sundown his pilots scored no hits on the agile warship. The *Enterprise* SBDs attacked the same opponent with the same poor results but tragically lost Lt. Sam Adams of VS-5, one of the great heroes of the battle. The second *Hornet* flight never sighted anything and turned back with its bombs. The object of everyone's attention was the doughty destroyer *Tanikaze*, which also evaded a blizzard of bombs from B-17s and winged one bomber that later splashed.[9]

The *Tanikaze*'s stellar defense was Japan's only high point on an otherwise dismal 5 June. Her presence stemmed from confusion resulting from the haste in abandoning the burning *Hiryū*. At dawn two destroyers supposedly provided the coup de grâce with a salvo of torpedoes and took off. Yet at 0630 a search plane from light carrier *Hōshō* with Yamamoto's Main Force sighted the wrecked *Hiryū* adrift. Yamamoto inquired of Nagumo whether she had indeed sunk. Nagumo sent the *Tanikaze* back to find out. Ensign Silver showed up about forty minutes before the valiant carrier slipped beneath the waves. In turn Gumz discovered Kondō's Main Force, including two fast battleships and light carrier *Zuihō*, bound for the fleet rendezvous. The impression of a ship "burning" probably arose from the dense smoke Japanese ships showed when they were moving fast. Unfortunately Gumz drastically underestimated their speed, twenty-four knots instead of twelve. Spruance never had a chance to attack them. It is not known what led Gumz to believe a second carrier was present. The elderly *Hōshō* was nowhere nearby.[10]

After dispatching his dive bombers Spruance hastened northwest at twenty-five knots to close the enemy. At that time Nimitz belatedly advised: "Believe enemy through lack of air support probably considers he is unable to carry out landing and is retiring." The second carrier, said previously not to be burning, was now "smoking badly and proceeding at slow speed." That optimism expired when Spruance heard "disquieting information" from the lead group of B-17s that turned up only a single cruiser (the *Tanikaze*). After dark the SBDs had not returned. Despite the risk of subs, Spruance courageously illuminated the carriers with the deck side lights and shone searchlights overhead to guide the flyers home. These measures were extremely successful. Many pilots made their first night carrier landing without a hitch. Only one *Hornet* SBD ditched from lack of fuel (the crew was rescued). The others landed safely, though not all on their own carriers. Spruance decided his planes hit two separate light cruisers or destroyers. He was irritated that two *Hornet* SBDs that set down on the *Enterprise* carried 1,000-pound bombs despite his express order to rearm with 500-pounders. It only reinforced his increasing distrust of Mitscher, who certainly could counter with his own case against the TF-16 staff.[11]

After recovering his planes, Spruance slowed to fifteen knots to conserve oil, now at a critical state in his destroyers. Almost as if reading his mind, Nimitz directed the *Cimarron* to break off her circuit seven hundred miles east and rendezvous with Spruance on 8 June 175 miles north of Midway. The oiler would follow a designated latitude west so Spruance could meet her earlier if necessary. It is interesting Nimitz took this task upon himself, instead of waiting for Spruance to set his own fueling rendezvous. Keeping an eye on the Aleutians, he needed TF-16 ready should he wish to send it north. With the northwest no longer productive, Spruance sought to cut across a possible line of retreat of the forces west of Midway. Once again he proceeded cautiously at night lest he run afoul of battleships. He would see what his own search might turn up the next morning, when TF-16 would be so far from Midway the PBYs would require three hours just to reach its location.[12]

Nimitz radioed a summary of the situation on the evening of 5 June. He believed (correctly) he could verify the sinking of two carriers on 4 June. Given the "enemy is without air," he suggested his commanders consider surface attacks by light forces, but he did so mostly for King's benefit. Later that night he again encouraged his weary forces, whose "efforts and sacrifices," that were "crowned with glorious success," had "already changed the course of the war in the Pacific in our favor." The "enemy is attempting to withdraw his wounded ships." Thus "if you follow up your success vigorously he will be so crushed that his total defeat will be inevitable." In truth Nimitz was deeply disappointed that his main forces had not achieved more on 5 June. Later he was irate that when the *Tambor* made her 0215 contact, the enemy ships were seen heading west away from Midway. Her inaccurate reporting squandered Spruance's pursuit.[13]

ON THE PERIPHERY

Well away from the main action, Fletcher also endured a frustrating 5 June. The previous night he approved the plan to salvage the *Yorktown*. The essential personnel were to assemble in the *Astoria*, then shift to the *Hammann*. At the same time the *Hammann*, *Balch*, and *Benham* were to transfer their other passengers to the *Portland*. Buckmaster would then lead those three destroyers back to the *Yorktown* and undertake the salvage. The *Anderson* would also hand over her load of *Yorktown* personnel to the *Portland* and escort Fletcher's *Astoria* to the *Saratoga* group. Captain DuBose would take the *Portland*, *Morris*, and *Russell* southeast to meet the *Fulton* pounding up from Pearl and off-load the survivors. Thereafter TF-17 would reassemble around the *Saratoga*. The plan sounded simple, but its execution took longer than anyone foresaw.[14]

Just after sunrise on 5 June, when about 175 miles southeast of the *Yorktown* and 250 miles northeast of Midway, Fletcher started west at ten knots, as slow as he cared to go and still retain some protection against subs. Fortunately the sea was relatively calm, with light southeasterly winds. At 0600 the *Balch* moved alongside the *Portland* to off-load survivors by means of trolley lines rigged to use mail bags as breeches buoys. At the same time the *Benham* came abreast of the *Astoria* to deliver her designated salvage personnel. So many *Yorktown*ers were eager to volunteer, they had to be prevented from coming across. Then the *Benham* took her turn alongside the *Portland* for the really big transfer of nearly seven hundred men. With the destroyers down to 50 percent fuel and no certainty of the next refueling opportunity, the *Portland* provided oil in return for the *Yorktown* men. The *Benham* remained alongside for four hours. One of the *Portland*'s officers, amazed at how many men were coming over, called out: "You must think this ship is the Grand Hotel!" While the *Benham* was busy with the *Portland*, Buckmaster took the 180 men of the salvage crew over to the *Hammann*. Yeoman Frank Boo was one, having implored Fletcher to allow him to go back and retrieve an unfinished Coral Sea action report from the flag office. At the same time Fletcher sent his trusted emissary Schindler to the *Portland*. He would ride the *Fulton* to Pearl and brief Cincpac. At 1230 Fletcher turned southeast into the wind to ease conditions and expedite the transfers and fueling. Cincpac set the rendezvous with the *Fulton* on 6 June 650 miles northwest of Oahu. The *Saratoga*, *San Diego*, and four destroyers were to depart Pearl that afternoon and meet Fletcher before dark on 7 June 475 miles northwest of Pearl.[15]

Confident the tide of the battle turned, Nimitz radioed Fletcher at 1317: "Will make every effort to save *Yorktown*. Take no steps for her destruction without referring decision to me." That was certainly Fletcher's intention. The *Anderson* took her turn alongside the *Portland* to relinquish her load of survivors and draw fuel. The *Portland* accommodated the *Hammann* and likewise fueled the *Balch*, which already off-loaded personnel. Near sundown Fletcher released Buckmaster (CTG-17.5) with the *Hammann*, *Balch*, and *Benham* to rejoin the *Yorktown* and *Hughes* 150 miles northwest. He himself headed southeast at twenty-five knots with the *Astoria*, *Portland*, *Morris*, *Anderson*, and *Russell* toward the *Fulton*. Fletcher also asked Cincpac to direct the oiler *Platte* to meet him on the afternoon of 6 June to fuel before he joined the *Saratoga* group.[16]

In the meantime Commander Ramsey's *Hughes* faithfully stood guard alone over the disabled carrier. The jittery night brought only one brief radar contact. After dawn, however, her SC radar detected an enemy aircraft circling twenty miles northwest. Indeed the *Chikuma* Number Four seaplane radioed the sighting of a *Yorktown*-class carrier listing and adrift north of Midway. Yamamoto ordered the *I-168* to locate and destroy her. That morning the *Hughes* sent a party on board the *Yorktown* and found the two wounded men, but also unsecured cipher materials. The Naval War College analysts cited that as evidence of "unnecessary haste" when the *Yorktown* was first abandoned. Little *Vireo* took the *Yorktown* under tow early that afternoon and inched eastward with the carrier (her rudder jammed hard over) "yawing quite badly." Later that afternoon Commander Holcomb in the *Gwin* joined the *Hughes* and took charge. The *Monaghan*, detached from TF-16, soon appeared on the scene. The destroyers furnished small salvage parties that despite their enthusiasm did not accomplish much before being recalled at dark. Any serious effort to save the *Yorktown* required Buckmaster's professionals.[17]

On the morning of 5 June Pye swept out of San Francisco with the other five TF-1 battleships, the *Long Island*, and five destroyers to join Anderson's battleship group on patrol. The previous morning he informed Nimitz of his intention, "Unless otherwise directed," to proceed to a "support position" one thousand miles west of California. His battleships would form a last line of defense should the Japanese get past the carriers and make for Hawaii. When Nimitz failed to respond immediately, Pye sent a second message only a few hours before sailing. He no longer talked about assuming a "support position," but simply stated he would advance one thousand miles and await orders. If none were received, he would return to the West Coast on 19 June. Nimitz replied with a grudging "affirmative" several hours after TF-1 went to sea. McCormick pointed out that Cincpac had nothing to do with initiating this apparently useless cruise that only served to raise morale among the battleship sailors.[18]

SETTLING FOR THE *MIKUMA*

At dawn on 6 June with TF-16 about 340 miles northwest of Midway, the *Enterprise* dispatched eighteen SBDs (including five from the *Hornet*) to search the western semicircle to two hundred miles. At the same time the *Hornet* prepared a strike. At 0645 Ens. William D. Carter placed one carrier and five destroyers just 128 miles southwest (233 degrees) of TF-16 and crawling west at ten knots. The southwesterly wind now allowed Spruance to close the target while conducting flight operations. He advised he was charging the enemy at twenty-five knots and told any destroyer badly short of fuel to break off for the *Cimarron*. Having finally taken the measure of Browning and the Carpac staff, Spruance directed Kinkaid to have cruiser float planes search southwest to 150 miles and track any ships located. With the enemy so close and winds favorable, the SOCs could undertake the "tactical scouting" so lacking the previous two days and also reserve the SBDs for strikes.[19]

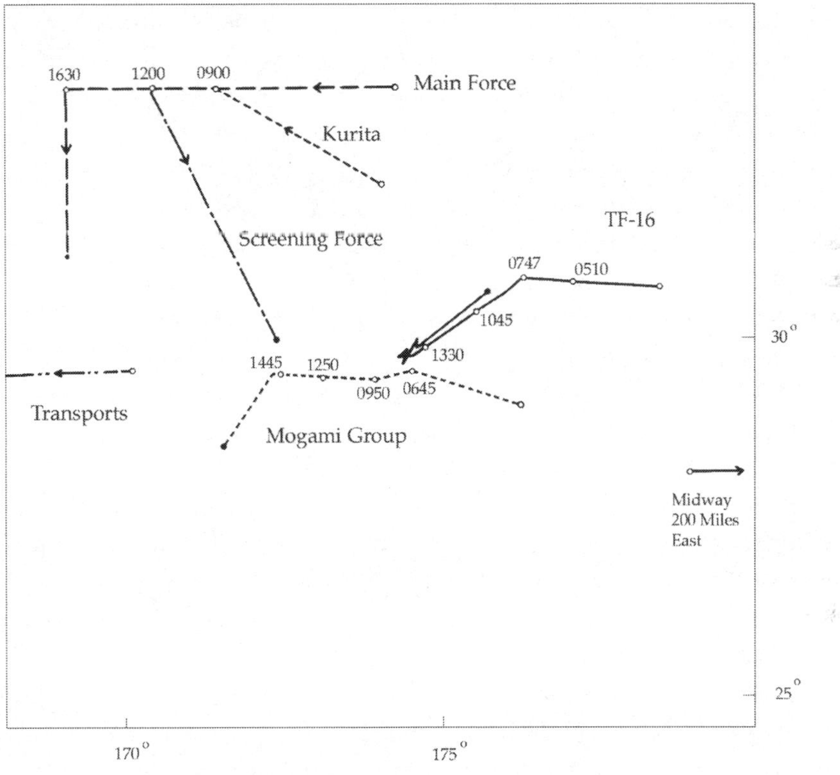

Carrier operations, 6 June 1942

At 0730, another *Hornet* search pilot, Ens. Roy P. Gee, dropped a message on the *Enterprise*'s deck. At 0645 he sighted two enemy cruisers and two destroyers 133 miles southwest (209 degrees) of TF-16 and headed southwest at fifteen knots. Thus the "cruiser" force was fifty miles southeast of the "carrier" force. Gee's ship identification was much better than Carter's, but not his navigation. Only the *Mikuma* and *Mogami* and destroyers *Arashio* and *Asashio* were present near Carter's location. They plodded west at twelve knots, the battered *Mogami*'s best speed. The confusion engendered by the two initial reports persisted until after the war. Spruance naturally desired the "carrier" first. At 0757 twenty-six SBDs and eight F4Fs started taking off from the *Hornet*. At the same time the *Enterprise* respotted her flight deck to recover the search SBDs. Spruance noted in his war diary because the

Enterprise had "but few planes exclusive of search planes in the air," he held the balance of her group "in reserve for additional attack as required." In fact the *Enterprise* had eighteen flyable SBDs in addition to those on search, more than a "few." Spruance obviously adopted Fletcher's earlier tactic of wait-and-see with part of his striking force. About that time King transmitted a message in the clear addressed to Nimitz but obviously meant for the Japanese. Cominch praised the forces fighting at Midway who, he predicted, "Will continue to make the enemy realize that war is hell." That day the *Mikuma-Mogami* force joined the ranks of those introduced to Gen. William Sherman's timeless dictum.[20]

At 0838 after five search SBDs landed on board the *Hornet*, Mitscher hastily changed Carter's original sighting report of a carrier to a battleship. Like John Nielsen the previous month, Carter was surprised when asked about the carrier he supposedly discovered. Spruance personally checked the text of the message drop that Carter made on the *Enterprise*. It, like the radio message, gave "1 CV." Evidently Carter's radioman misunderstood him to say "1 CV" when he meant "1 BB." This was yet another example of how the task force commanders were at the mercy of the sighting reports. At 0850 Browning advised the *Hornet* group, "Target BB instead of CV." Mitscher also learned from Carter and Gee that they had not searched their sectors after sighting enemy ships. He cautioned Spruance, "This leaves an area from ahead and to port beam of enemy BB not searched where carrier may be." Spruance's foresight in using the cruiser SOCs paid off, because they already covered the area in question.[21]

The *Hornet*'s strike found the cruisers at 0950. The bowless *Mogami* looked so different than her sister *Mikuma*, now thought to be the fabled battleship. The more agile *Mikuma* evaded all bombs (although the *Hornet* flyers claimed three hits), but the hurt *Mogami* suffered two 1,000-pound hits. Antiaircraft accounted for one SBD. Slonim's radio intelligence unit in the *Enterprise* interpreted anxious calls for help as coming from no less than the commander of the Second Fleet (Kondō). At 0950 Spruance informed the task force, "We believe he is in the battleship being bombed." That is another example of the casual dissemination of radio intelligence that later would not be tolerated. With such a tempting target at hand, the *Enterprise* launched thirty-one SBDs with 1,000-pound bombs and twelve fighters. At the last minute Spruance added the three flyable VT-6 TBDs in hopes of torpedoing the battlewagon, but he told the senior surviving TBD pilot not to go in if he saw any accurate antiaircraft fire at all. The TBDs never attacked. At least five bombs tore up the *Mikuma* topside and started fires that eventually cooked off the torpedo stowage. The *Arashio* moved in to take off the crew. Despite two more hits, the mutilated *Mogami* lurched westward.[22]

Circumstances militated against continuing the pursuit, but for the time being the aggressive Spruance kept his ships pointed southwest. At 1242 he released the *Maury* (14 percent fuel) and *Worden* (22 percent) to retire to the *Cimarron*. The four remaining destroyers were only marginally better off.[23] Cautioned by Slonim's radio team, Spruance alerted TF-16 of "possible attack by long range bombers from Wake Island." Despite all, he lingered for one more try to finish off the tenacious cripples. At 1420 after the second *Hornet* strike of twenty-four SBDs and eight F4Fs departed, Spruance reversed course to stay beyond seven hundred miles of Wake, the accepted radius of enemy land-based bombers.

With the target only ninety miles off, he need not close farther. Nimitz advised that the *Saratoga* would provide replacements for TF-16. "I will arrange for transfer of planes to you on completion of your fueling," with "deployment thereafter" to "depend on the situation." Spruance did well to look to the stormy North Pacific, for Cincpac warned, "Interception of enemy forces returning from Aleutians may be attempted."[24]

In the meantime the *Hornet* flyers put another 1,000-pound bomb into the *Mogami* (the "CA"), while the "BB" (*Mikuma*) crew abandoned ship. Because of the initial confusion, the TF-16 staff still did not know the exact composition of the force they pounded for the last five hours. Spruance authorized a photo mission by two *Enterprise* SBDs. By the time they returned at 1900, he decided that he "pushed our luck to the westward far enough" and turned northeast. The four remaining destroyers were critically low on fuel, and his aviators were exhausted. The excellent photos taken by the last *Enterprise* flight proved the hapless *Mikuma* was indeed a cruiser. Before these photos could be evaluated, Spruance advised Cincpac that the "battleship" was left "gutted and abandoned," one destroyer was sunk, and two heavy cruisers, including possibly the flagship of the Second Fleet, suffered 1,000-pound bomb hits. Nimitz eventually concluded TF-16 attacked the *Mogami* and *Mikuma* and three or four destroyers and finished off the *Mikuma*. As late as 1943 Cominch disagreed, asserting there were two groups all along, one of which might have included a battleship, and that all the ships had been damaged and one heavy cruiser sunk. That three full carrier strikes put down only one already damaged heavy cruiser and let another cripple escape vastly reinforced the extraordinary nature of the circumstances of 4 June, when the SBDs caught all four carriers with fueled and armed planes in their hangar decks.[25]

By the evening of 6 June the code breakers confirmed to Cincpac that the leader of the First Air Fleet (Nagumo) had shifted from the *Akagi* to light cruiser *Nagara*. Thus the *Akagi* either sank or was severely damaged. It certainly did look if at least one crippled carrier sank on 5 June, although no one knew how many, if any, got away. Spruance radioed that all four carriers were destroyed, but Nimitz did not accept that glorious assessment for another week. As yet he saw no evidence the carriers in the Aleutian waters were being shifted south toward Midway. Instead they might be ordered back to Japan. Even so, he warned his commanders that the enemy retirement "may be temporary." A search plane again sighted Japanese carriers south of the Aleutians. "All forces must be alert and prepared for enemy action." Nimitz informed King of the *Saratoga*'s imminent departure from Pearl. She would deliver plane reinforcements to TF-16 and then "act as circumstances indicate." Spruance's carriers would go to the Aleutians "if situation continues favorable in Midway area."[26]

THE "ONE BLOT"

Returning to the *Yorktown* at 0220 on 6 June, Buckmaster found her condition essentially unchanged, except a bit more down by the bow. From then on he acted vigorously in a way even Morison praised. The salvage party climbed on board at 0330. Buckmaster personally inspected all accessible compartments. After dawn while the *Vireo* continued her slow tow, the *Hammann* moved snugly alongside the *Yorktown*'s high (starboard) side and provided power for pumps and also water to extinguish the one small fire that smoldered forward.

The other five destroyers circled two thousand yards out on antisubmarine patrol. By early afternoon counter flooding and weight jettisoned topside had reduced the *Yorktown*'s list by 2 degrees. Things were looking up. Buckmaster anticipated bringing the engines back on line once he could pump dry the necessary spaces and returning the *Yorktown* to Pearl under her own power. All he needed were the two salvage tugs that were en route. Suddenly at 1336 shocked lookouts spotted a spread of four torpedoes churning directly for the starboard side of the linked *Hammann* and *Yorktown*. One fish from Lt. Cdr. Tanabe Yahachi's *I-168* struck the destroyer, and two others, running close together, passed underneath and blew a huge hole amidships near the bottom of the *Yorktown*'s hull. The shattered *Hammann* sank by the bow in three minutes. Her depth charges exploded under the surface, killed many of her crew, and inflicted severe shock damage to the carrier. Extensive flooding took 5 degrees off the *Yorktown*'s list as she settled deeper into the water. Buckmaster hoped he could still save his ship. "With help will bring her in." He spoke more from emotion than calculation, as all damage control failed. By dark the salvage crew abandoned ship. First light on 7 June revealed the *Yorktown* listing sharply to port, with the edge of her flight deck almost awash. At 0444 she started to turn over on her port side and at 0501 capsized and sank by the stern, not to be seen again for fifty-six years.[27]

The initial reaction to the loss of the *Yorktown* under such circumstances was surprise that a sub penetrated a screen of five destroyers and picked her off. Critics later speculated whether Fletcher unnecessarily delayed her salvage and thus rendered her an easy target. Morison described Fletcher and Buckmaster undertaking nothing constructive until noon, 5 June, when finally they "decided to do what they should have done the previous evening, to send a proper salvage party on board the carrier and attempt to bring her to port." That lassitude supposedly prevailed even after a dawn message that Ramsey, commanding officer of the *Hughes*, was said to have radioed Cincpac (and presumably Fletcher), advising the *Yorktown* could be saved. Robert Barde likewise blamed Fletcher's "indecision," in that "had prompt salvage efforts been instituted on 5 June, the ill fortune of the *Yorktown* on the following day might have been avoided." He agreed that Fletcher had to be goaded into action by Ramsey's message. In July 1942 Nimitz remarked in his endorsement of Buckmaster's Loss of Ship Report that, "in general," he "approved" Fletcher's actions. Later he changed his mind. He and Potter declared in *The Great Sea War*, "Prompter and more determined damage control might have saved the *Yorktown*." The charge that Fletcher and Buckmaster sat on their hands until noon on 5 June can be dismissed out of hand. From the evening of 4 June the two men busily organized the salvage effort. Equally telling, there was no Ramsey message. His report did not mention sending one, and the Cincpac message file has no record of it. If one cannot fault the will of both Fletcher and Buckmaster to save the *Yorktown*, their judgment can certainly be questioned. The transfer process took longer than they anticipated. Smith regretted, "We had lost thirty-six important hours in the attempted salvage of *Yorktown*." Instead, as noted, the key was to have the last ditch salvage parties already organized. Fletcher suggested that to Nimitz on his return to Pearl. Nimitz issued a letter of instruction to that effect, and King directed that if possible one or two salvage tugs be made available to the task forces whenever action was pending.[28]

In retrospect it appears the *Yorktown*'s sudden complete loss of power, her dire condition, and the nearness of the enemy combined to delay effective salvage. Had any one of these factors not been present, Fletcher and Buckmaster would have had an easier time saving her. In hindsight probably the only way to have avoided the *I-168* was if a cruiser commenced towing her either the night of 4/5 June or early the next morning. That did not appear feasible under the circumstances prevailing at the time. Morison called the "abandonment and subsequent loss" of the *Yorktown* "the one blot on an otherwise golden scroll of victory" at Midway. It certainly harmed the reputations of both Fletcher and Buckmaster. Perhaps all of that was not too high a cost for such a tremendous triumph. On 8 June Spruance wrote Fletcher, "It was tough luck that the *Yorktown* had to stand those two attacks," and, "If it had not been for what you did and took with the *Yorktown*, I am firmly convinced that we would have been badly defeated and the Japs would be holding Midway today."[29]

NEW FLAGSHIP, NEW MISSION

Early on 6 June Fletcher detached DuBose's group (*Portland, Morris,* and *Russell*) crammed with *Yorktown* survivors to meet the oncoming *Fulton*. He himself pressed eastward with the *Astoria* and *Anderson* to fuel from the *Platte*. That afternoon Nimitz had to delay the departure of the *Saratoga* group (TG-11.1) until the next morning (it had only arrived on 6 June) and postponed the rendezvous until 8 June two hundred miles closer to Pearl. Fletcher had time to fuel, reunite his force, and be there on schedule. Late that afternoon came the sad news of the torpedoing of the *Yorktown*. Fletcher could only hope Buckmaster's optimism of saving her was warranted. Near to sundown he completed fueling. Not until well after dark did the last of the nearly twenty-two hundred survivors cross over to the *Fulton* and her two escorts. DuBose returned as expected early on 7 June and took his turn alongside the *Platte*. Later that morning Fletcher released the oiler to Pearl, while TF-17 shaped course southeast to meet the *Saratoga* task group the next day. Even the terrible word of the sinking of the *Yorktown* could not erase the great relief on the U.S. ships as the staggering scope of the Midway victory became apparent.[30]

Inasmuch as overall enemy intentions remained unclear despite the debacle off Midway, the top brass reassessed their options. King speculated whether the second enemy carrier group had already left the Aleutians. "Consider strong possibility that part or all of this force departed that area night of 4/5 June for rendezvous to the southwest with retreating Midway forces and possibly with the remainder of the Combined Fleet." The Alaskan command begged to differ. Rear Adm. Charles S. Freeman (Commander, Northwest Sea Frontier) warned that the situation there was "rapidly deteriorating." The enemy's puzzling "cat and mouse tactics" were "wearing us down preliminary to delivering all out attack." Now that Midway was secure, Freeman recommended "quick reinforcement" of Alaska, where the "need approaches desperation." King swiftly changed his mind. Citing Freeman's message with its "indications of continued presence of Orange force in the Aleutians," he told Nimitz to consider sending the *Saratoga* there with a strong force and offered land-based air reinforcements as well.[31]

Nimitz already inclined in that direction and chose Spruance to go north. That afternoon he set the rendezvous for the morning of 10 June 650 miles northeast of Midway. Fletcher would provide the planes and personnel to restore the *Enterprise* and *Hornet* to "best practicable strength," and return to Pearl. TF-16 was to voyage north to the aptly named Point Blow, only 425 miles southwest of Dutch Harbor. There on the afternoon of 12 June he would come under the command of CTF-8, his classmate "Fuzzy" Theobald, whose mission was to "destroy or drive out enemy forces in the Aleutian-Alaskan area." Nimitz explained to King why he did not commit Fletcher and the *Saratoga* instead. Not only did the job properly require two carriers, but also the ragtag *Saratoga* Air Group itself was not ready for combat.[32]

On the afternoon of 8 June Fletcher transferred his flag and incorporated the *Saratoga* group into TF-17. The giant old carrier was in excellent shape, much enhanced after the repair of the torpedo damage and a major refit. Capt. Dewitt Clinton "Duke" Ramsey, who took command in May, was a 1912 Annapolis graduate from New York who qualified as naval aviator number forty-five in 1917. Sharp-witted, level headed, and personable, he prospered in a wide variety of operational and staff posts as well as at the Naval War College. In 1937–38 he served as the fleet aviation officer for Cincus, then as executive officer of the *Sara*, before reporting in 1939 to Buaer. As Jack Towers's protégé, he rose to assistant chief in 1941. The *Saratoga* improved dramatically under Ramsey's firm hand. Fletcher found him a highly capable and congenial shipmate. Ramsey only reached Pearl on 6 June and immediately refueled. The *Saratoga* now carried 107 planes (forty-seven fighters, forty-five dive bombers, and fifteen torpedo planes, including ten new TBFs) from all or parts of seven squadrons, most of which never served together. Ramsey sailed the next morning with the *Saratoga*, *San Diego*, oiler *Kaskaskia*, and five destroyers. Fitch, disappointed to miss Midway, reached Pearl in the *Chester* on 8 June.[33]

Fletcher's reconstituted TF-17 set off at fifteen knots to meet TF-16 some seven hundred miles northwest. Likewise that day Spruance reassembled his force and saw to its logistical needs. At dawn he met the *Cimarron* 235 miles north of Midway and fueled his destroyers, all of which were nearly out of oil. The *Balch* and *Monaghan*, accompanied by the orphaned *Hughes*, rejoined after their grim sojourn with the *Yorktown*. Later that day the oiler *Guadalupe* arrived from Midway with a welcome load of aviation gasoline and more black oil. Spruance fueled during the day, ran northeast at night, and resumed fueling on the ninth. Another overnight dash at twenty knots saw him to the rendezvous with Fletcher. Then it was the stormy Aleutians and perhaps another carrier battle.[34]

Early on 9 June occurred the last gasp of the MI Operation. Cincpac intercepted plain language messages, complete with position, course, and speed, purportedly from a disabled enemy fleet unit fumbling about northeast of Wake. Nimitz, who knew Spruance was in no position to intercept anyway, correctly warned him, "This may be deception." Yamamoto detailed Admiral Takagi's 5th Cruiser Division to simulate the calls of a battleship in distress and hopefully draw overconfident pursuers into a trap. He had no takers. Equally symbolic of the vast reversal of fortune, the *Nagara* drew alongside flagship *Yamato* that day and delivered chief of staff Kusaka, air staff officer Genda, and a few others (but not Nagumo) to report to Yamamoto. Kusaka prefaced his statement: "I don't know what to say except to offer utmost apologies."[35]

During 9 June the odds of Spruance having to sail north dramatically lessened. Theobald's searchers found no trace of the Japanese in the Aleutians. Consequently King reinstated his assessment that the Midway and Aleutian attack forces, now three carriers including the *Zuikaku*, gathered somewhere in the northwest Pacific and predicted they would race down to the South or southwest Pacific before the United States could react. Therefore deploying Spruance to the Aleutians was "questionable." Nimitz replied that if nothing major turned up in the Aleutians that day or the next, he would return Spruance to Pearl Harbor. The enemy might have landed troops somewhere in the Aleutians, but he had no proof. In fact the Japanese occupied both Kiska and Attu in the western Aleutians on 7 June without resistance.[36]

By dawn on 10 June a thick overcast shrouded the two carrier task forces. Scheduled to reach far-off Point Blow on 12 June, Spruance was in a bind, because no aircraft could fly. After 0800 he received a welcome reprieve. Nimitz told him not to start north until he received new orders. Meanwhile, he told Fletcher to arrive at Pearl during forenoon on 13 June. Nimitz explained to King that TF-16 would stay where it was until he knew more of what transpired in the Aleutians. Having located each other by radar, the two task forces moved south in hopes the weather might cooperate later that afternoon. In less than an hour heavy fog closed in. By dawn on 11 June, about two hundred miles south of the original rendezvous, the weather cleared sufficiently for flight operations. The *Saratoga* promptly ferried ten SBDs and five TBDs to the *Enterprise* and nine SBDs and ten TBFs to the *Hornet*. Immediately thereafter Fletcher set course for Pearl eight hundred miles southeast, while TF-16 started north toward Point Blow, now twelve hundred miles away.[37]

Spruance did not get far. Shortly after 0900 Nimitz ordered TF-16 to return to Pearl. The previous day he learned of enemy troops on Kiska and Attu and conceded a "strong screening force" would contest any U.S. reaction to the loss of the two islands. Instead, he proposed to recall TF-16 and the "fleet units" of Theobald's TF-8 to Pearl and later commit them against a "greater threat to our interests," namely Port Moresby and the South Pacific bases. King approved, "Especially as regards preparation TF 16 for future operations." He did suggest the TF-8 cruisers and destroyers join Pye's TF-1 battleships, "For operations and training approximately on line Dutch Harbor [to] Pearl pending further developments." Nimitz previously directed TF-1 to a position 1,650 miles northeast of Midway (Pye reached there on the tenth), and had Pye maneuver the next four days, primarily to see how the *Long Island* worked with the battleships. He briefly contemplated joining TF-1, TF-8, and the *Kaskaskia* at Point Strike, eleven hundred miles north of Oahu, but soon regained his senses. King would only commit the old battleships to action without proper air support. Nimitz cut short Pye's cruise and told him to take TF-1 to San Pedro. Only the fleet oiler *Kaskaskia* went north.[38]

As Fletcher drew closer to Pearl, he learned that he would not have the *Saratoga*, or indeed TF-17, for long. Nimitz stated on 12 June that Fitch was to reorganize TF-11 around the *Sara* immediately upon her return to Pearl, then run out to Midway around 18 June with a load of replacement aircraft. In the meantime the cruisers of old TF-17 needed upkeep in the Pearl Harbor Navy Yard. Fletcher had no idea where he personally would end up in the next few days.[39]

WELCOME HOME

The victory at Midway sublimely vindicated Nimitz's aggressive but perilous strategy of confronting the Japanese carriers while they were exposed assaulting an important base. He asserted that the battle had "frustrated the enemy's powerful move against Midway that was undoubtedly the keystone of larger plans," and certainly did not exaggerate. Yamamoto's "larger plans" sought no less than the destruction of the Pacific Fleet. By late June, from more recent information derived from radio intelligence and the interrogation of prisoners, Nimitz concluded that four large carriers and a heavy cruiser went down, plus possibly another heavy cruiser and a destroyer. The cost of victory was high: the *Yorktown, Hammann*, 144 aircraft, and 362 dead sailors, marines, and airmen, including 104 carrier pilots and aircrew. Actual Japanese losses comprised the *Akagi*, *Kaga*, *Sōryū* and *Hiryū*, the *Mikuma*, more than 250 aircraft, and more than 3,057 dead. Contrary to legend, Japanese casualties did not include the majority of their carrier aviators. Instead only 110 pilots and aircrew, mainly from the valiant *Hiryū* Air Group, were lost.[40]

Immensely relieved by the scope of the victory, Nimitz was humble in the face of the effusive praise. "All participating personnel, without exception, displayed unhesitating devotion to duty, loyalty and courage." The what-ifs would come soon enough. Not content with congratulatory messages, Nimitz made a point of greeting every group returning to Pearl, beginning the evening of 8 June with the *Fulton* loaded with *Yorktown* survivors. Cheerful and sincere, Cincpac shook hands with numerous men, commiserated with their loss, and told them how proud he was of what they did. Schindler briefed him on Fletcher's perception of the battle and the crippling of the *Yorktown*. On the ninth when the *Gwin* and *Benham* reached port, Nimitz likewise sounded out Buckmaster for details as to her loss. What he learned dispelled his concern that errors by Fletcher might have cost a second carrier within a month.[41]

On the evening of 12 June with the arrival of the Fueling Group directly from TF-16, Nimitz received the clearest statement yet of what transpired. Spruance wrote a letter on the eighth when it looked as if a side trip to the Aleutians might substantially delay his return. His straightforward description of his decisions and actions cemented his reputation as one of the navy's finest leaders. Spruance expressed his "admiration for the part that Fletcher in the *Yorktown* played in this campaign." There was "a fine and smoothly working co-ordination between the two Task Forces before the fighting commenced." During the battle "the *Yorktown*'s attack and the information her planes furnished were of vital importance to our success, which for some time," Spruance noted with characteristic understatement, "was hanging in the balance." Because the *Yorktown* happened to be between TF-16 and "the enemy's fourth and still functioning carrier," she "took his blows." Another personal letter Spruance wrote on 8 June thanked Fletcher. "You were certainly fine to me all during the time the two task forces were operating together under your command, and I can't tell you how much I appreciate it." Fletcher reciprocated the good feeling, describing Spruance as "a splendid officer and a wonderful person," whose "two outstanding qualities were excellent judgment and courage."[42]

The biggest welcome took place on 13 June, when both carrier task forces entered Pearl to cheers and triumphal celebrations. A reception of a different sort occurred eight hours later when Nagumo reported to Yamamoto in Hiroshima bay. He had to answer for why the heart of Japan's magnificent carrier force now lay on the bottom of the Pacific. That day Fletcher shifted his flag to his administrative office ashore. There to his surprise he found Yeoman Boo, last seen departing with the ill-fated *Yorktown* salvage party. "Spence, I see a ghost," Fletcher remarked to Lewis. Boo told of crawling back on board early on 6 June onto the dark, deserted warship, with its eerie silence and slippery canted decks, as he accompanied Buckmaster on his predawn inspection. Unfortunately for history, Boo was pressed into the salvage efforts and could not retrieve the final TF-17 Coral Sea report from the locked flag office, where it rests still. Paperwork kept Fletcher busy for the next few days, but he had the satisfaction of knowing from Nimitz that his days as a carrier task force commander were far from over.[43]

Nimitz was generous with praise for his two task force commanders. On 13 June he included in a letter to King: "Inasmuch as Fletcher was the Senior Task Force Commander in the Battle of Midway and did an excellent job, despite the fact that the *Yorktown* was lost, I desire to reiterate the recommendation which I recently made by despatch and amplified to you in a personal letter, that Fletcher be designated a Task Force Commander with the rank of Vice Admiral and that he be awarded the Distinguished Service Medal." The next day Nimitz recommended to King that Spruance also receive the DSM "for exceptionally meritorious service involving highest qualities seamanship endurance and tenacity in handling of his task force [in the] Midway engagement which resulted in defeat and heavy losses to enemy fleet." King let the matter of Fletcher's promotion rest, then on 19 June asked Nimitz whether "upon review of handling of Task Force 17 during Midway operations," his views had changed. Nimitz replied: "During Midway operations Fletcher was senior task force commander in area and responsible for activities Task Forces 16 and 17. For his services Midway and prior services Coral Sea I reiterate with added emphasis my recommendations in my 092219 of May that Fletcher be designated Task Force Commander with rank Vice Admiral and awarded Distinguished Service Medal." He again urged Spruance be decorated "for distinguished service as Commander Task Force 16 in Battle of Midway." King gracefully acceded. "All being done as recommended."[44]

HARSH LESSONS

Spruance commented in his 8 June letter to Nimitz that carrier "operations during this period have been most interesting and instructive." They were all that and more, because they revealed serious flaws in U.S. aviation doctrine. In the two decades since the commissioning of the *Langley*, many pioneer aviators seethed over what they perceived rank injustice that prevented them from leading the carrier task forces and, for that matter, the whole navy. That non-aviators Fletcher and Spruance led the carriers at the climactic Battle of Midway especially galled them. Yet the pioneers decisively shaped the nature of the weapon that fate placed into the hands of those they considered incompetent to wield it. At Midway several of their number held key positions in Spruance's TF-16. Marc Mitscher and George Murray were the captains of the *Hornet* and *Enterprise*, Miles Browning the TF-16 chief of staff and Spruance's principal advisor. As previously noted, the citation for Browning's DSM portrayed him "largely responsible" for bringing about the destruction of the enemy carriers at Midway. Historian Clark Reynolds fully concurred, stating that on the morning of 4 June Browning made "one of the shrewdest calculations in naval history." Thus it could seem, despite the regrettable presence of the gun-club admirals, that the old line aviators indeed made the difference at Midway.[45]

The U.S. carrier attacks on the morning of 4 June certainly exceeded expectation. Three of four Japanese carriers sustained mortal damage before they could respond in kind. Even the trade of the *Yorktown* for the fourth carrier did not affect the outcome of the battle. Midway truly was an "incredible victory," but (with apologies to Walter Lord) not so much, as commonly thought, in terms of the overall disparity of odds. Instead "incredible" better described the chances of such a poorly framed U.S. attack succeeding so brilliantly. The U.S. carriers were extremely fortunate to defeat a foe who, with a few telling exceptions, handled his aircraft far better than they did. The Achilles' heel of Japan's carrier force was defense, primarily from the lack of radar and adequate shipboard antiaircraft guns. The American weakness was teamwork above the squadron level. Given the mission of full-out assault by TF-16, it fell to Browning to coordinate the strike with Murray and Mitscher. Other than ordering "deferred departure," meaning each air group was to go out as a unit in hopes of executing a concerted attack, he allowed each captain latitude to organize his strike and proceed as he saw fit. The CTF-16 staff offered no further guidance other than to point in the direction of the enemy carriers. They all did a terrible job. Fletcher and Spruance had the right to expect, once having maneuvered their task forces within striking range, that the carriers could accomplish their prime mission of delivering an effective attack and afterward retrieve their aircraft. Yet only the highly innovative *Yorktown*, best of all the 1942 carriers, had contrived to get all her strike planes simultaneously to the target. The TF-16 effort, upon which so much depended, proved very nearly a shambles. Most of the *Hornet* planes never even laid eyes on the enemy, and at the outset the *Enterprise* group fragmented into three widely separated elements. In addition the *Enterprise*'s failure to advance to Point Option, where her pilots expected to find her, lost numerous planes that otherwise survived the strike. Glorious success resulted not from any careful forethought or planning by the top brass of TF-16 but from individual initiative on the part of a few splendid leaders, the heroic sacrifice of the torpedo planes, and the dazzling skill of some of the dive bomber pilots.

Why did things go so badly with TF-16? Perhaps Bill Halsey, who kept a tight rein on his staff and his captains, was sorely missed after all. Out of necessity Spruance gave Browning a free hand to run the aviation part of the show. Browning in turn tried his best to keep his inexperienced new boss completely isolated from the process. That was in marked contrast to Fletcher, who over several months developed a close relationship with Buckmaster and several trusted mid-level *Yorktown* aviators. Only on the afternoon of 5 June, when Murray and other *Enterprise* aviation leaders vehemently protested Browning's recommendation to send the SBDs beyond maximum range, did Spruance intervene with regard to air operations.

By repute a "knowledgeable and brilliant" aviation tactician, Browning's saturnine, sarcastic personality led to serious doubts as to his judgment and mental stability. It was said he needed the right kind of boss "to sort out good and bad ideas," and that "Halsey had the facility of taking the best advice of Browning and overruling him when his own judgement came into conflict." One *Enterprise* observer concluded that Spruance, lacking an aviation background, was definitely "handicapped in having an aviator of Browning's type as chief of staff to advise him on air operations." Had Halsey been at Midway, he could have been expected to know what to ask and when precisely to step in. The mounting of the great TF-16 strike might not have become the fiasco it was, the neglect of Point Option could have been averted, and the aggressive Halsey might have prevented the lethargy that followed recovery of the morning attack.[46]

Despite a few farsighted individuals, the question of carrier air coordination remained largely unrecognized even after the fiasco at Midway. When Fletcher returned to Pearl he found an urgent request from Nimitz seeking his personal views on carrier tactics "in light of the Coral Sea and Midway actions." No one could claim more carrier battle experience. Following the lead of Ted Sherman (considered a pushy JCL outsider by the pioneer aviators), Fletcher fervently advocated the carriers be concentrated at least as pairs in the same task force and within the same screen. Nearly everyone else, starting with King, stuck with the old concept of single-carrier task forces and some degree of separation, although after Midway Browning also remarked to the "great advantage" of a two-carrier task force. Fletcher argued that only multi-carrier task forces provided the air strength required for effective attack and defense, as well as for the searches that circumstances often compelled the carriers themselves to make. Alone among the top carrier commanders, he stressed the necessity for coordinated strikes by air groups from different carriers, instead of the doctrinaire "wave attacks" that Fitch and Sherman employed in the Coral Sea. Fletcher desired to "present the maximum number of planes (particularly VF) to the enemy at one time" to "thin out enemy VF opposition" and "not give him the opportunity of attacking our incoming planes in piece-meal fashion." He did not understand that Japan had already effectively integrated air groups from different carriers—no one on the U.S. side did—but he certainly saw the possibilities. In that, Fletcher was far ahead of his time on the U.S. Navy side. As will be seen, his assessment remarkably foreshadowed the multi-carrier tactics that the U.S. Navy would finally adopt in mid 1943 only after considerable debate. Prior to that, King constrained the carriers, each with its own modest screen, to operate singly and keep at least five to ten miles apart. The senior CTF in tactical command was to provide a sort of loose coordination. Nothing as yet was being done to achieve tactical integration of air groups from different carriers, although as will be seen there was growing concern about coordinating squadrons within the same air group.[47]

The Midway action reports featured many general comments and recommendations regarding carrier warfare. No one could dispute the principal lesson: strike the first blow to catch your opponent with his planes still on deck. Equally indisputable, both land-based and carrier air must do a better job finding and tracking enemy carriers. Aside from the initial sighting reports, Fletcher and Spruance received almost no updates on the movements of the *Kidō Butai*. Nonetheless, Nimitz declared they and Simard on Midway "showed sound judgement and decision in correctly interpreting the many confused situations that came up during the action." The carriers preferred not to use their aircraft to search unless absolutely necessary, so they could reserve them for strikes. Fletcher noted that even when near Midway, the *Yorktown* had to launch an afternoon search to locate the additional carriers. That was "regrettable," but necessary until shore-based air improved. Nimitz concurred. Unfortunately the U.S. Navy cruisers never possessed long-range float planes of the quality of their Japanese counterparts.[48]

The key lesson for the offense, earned at the expense of the brave TBD crews, was to ensure that dive bombers and torpedo planes executed coordinated attacks to mass their firepower and divide the defense. Browning correctly described the TBD airplane as "fatally inadequate," hampered even more with Mark XIII aerial torpedoes that were "too slow" and lacked "punch." Vast improvement in torpedo aircraft, at least, was at hand in the Grumman TBF-1 Avengers. The TBFs offered, as Murray later noted, the "happy coincidence" of an economical cruising speed and endurance about the same as SBDs and F4Fs (when equipped with belly tanks), that made for a "fairly homogenous group." Another aspect of the attack that proved inadequate was fighter escort. To Fletcher the folding wing F4F-4s represented no improvement over the fixed-wing F4F-3s, except more F4F-4s could be carried. He echoed the call of Halsey and others of the "urgent necessity" for detachable fuel tanks to increase their effective attack radius beyond 175 miles. Spruance and Browning rated the Grumman Wildcat "greatly inferior" in comparison with the nimble Japanese Zero. On 20 June Nimitz relayed their fears to King, noting the "extreme and apparently increased superiority performance of 0 fighters" was mitigated only by the vulnerability of Japanese planes and the superior tactics of the U.S. Navy fighter pilots. "Overall results have been bad and will be serious and potentially decisive with improvement that must be expected in enemy tactics." Remarkably, he called for army Curtiss P-40F Warhawk fighters to replace navy F4F Wildcats and Brewster F2A Buffaloes in all marine fighting squadrons defending forward bases and even asked that the P-40F "or comparable type" be tested for carrier suitability. In the meantime the F4F-4s must be lightened, and their ammunition supply increased even should that require reverting to four guns in place of six. The swift introduction of the Vought F4U-1 Corsair fighter was an "absolute priority." Thus after Midway the top fleet commanders experienced a serious crisis of confidence over the effectiveness of the basic U.S. carrier fighter, a worry that would soon influence Fletcher's most controversial command decision.[49]

Happily it appeared that fighter direction at Midway had improved considerably over Coral Sea. Ship antiaircraft fire also seemed much better. It was thought many more attacking planes were shot down before they could get within range to deliver their payloads. The fleet awaited the introduction of the powerful quad 40-mm heavy automatic guns that would greatly increase firepower beyond the range of the lighter 1.1-inch and 20-mm cannons. Because the torpedo plane was the enemy's "most effective aircraft weapon," Nimitz relayed Fletcher's recommendation for a closer screen around the carrier, the destroyers on a fifteen-hundred-yard radius, the cruisers at two thousand yards. If the disposition broke up because of evasive maneuvers, the screen was to fill the gaps without the necessity of a signal from the task force commander.[50]

On 15 June King again badgered Nimitz over the failure of the task forces to execute night surface attacks with cruisers and destroyers. Nimitz queried Fletcher, Spruance, and Fitch, then responded with what he hoped was the definitive reply. The "advent of carrier borne aircraft in fast moving carrier task forces has greatly curtailed such opportunities and has made such attacks prohibitive unless destroyers are present in numbers considerably in excess of defensive screen requirements." Not only were destroyers too scarce, but their "fuel situation" also tended to be "precarious even without high speed [steaming] at night." Nimitz assured King, "The question you raise is constantly in my mind and also in the minds of my task force commanders who can be counted upon to exploit favorable opportunities."[51]

A fascinating postscript to the Battle of Midway is the persistent and largely successful effort to deny that Spruance ever served under Fletcher's command or, if so, only briefly and tangentially, and to downplay Fletcher's role in the battle.[52] Popular historian Fletcher Pratt's influential early treatment of Midway, widely endorsed by the navy, set the tone by inexplicably failing even to acknowledge Fletcher's presence, much less that he was in command.[53] After the war the much more powerful Bates and Morison stepped forward on Spruance's behalf. They were inspired by his superb performance as leader of the amphibious offensives that won the Pacific War and his obvious wisdom and modesty. It is therefore ironic that Spruance himself always emphasized his own subordinate status and sought to highlight his old commander's part in the victory, as if trying to make amends for the growing Midway legend. In 1947 he shot down Morison's proposed statement that declared, although Fletcher "automatically" assumed tactical command when the two task forces met, he had "wisely" designated Spruance "Officer in Charge of Air Operations," meaning Spruance "was the actual commander on the spot during the carrier actions of June and the ensuing days."[54] Morison finally acknowledged that Fletcher held tactical command after the rendezvous of TF-16 and 17 on 2 June, but as Fletcher "possessed no aviation staff and Spruance had Halsey's, it was probably fortunate that Spruance exercised practically an independent command during the crucial actions of 4–6 June." One can now judge which task force staff was the more effective. In 1959 Spruance made it a point to copy by hand for Potter a report, "Primarily to let you see what I said about Frank Jack Fletcher on the last page. He did a splendid job." So, of course, did Spruance, and to embellish the story on his behalf is truly gilding the lily. Fletcher, for his own part, stayed clear of the Midway command controversy. However, he could not refuse his old friend Poco Smith who posed the question in 1964 for his own book on Midway. Fletcher responded: "I invite your attention to the remark which was supposed to have been made by [Marshal Joseph] Joffre. Something like this: 'I cannot say who won the battle of the Marne, but there is no doubt who would have lost it.'"[55]

CHAPTER 20

A Brief Intermission

REORGANIZING THE CARRIERS

In the two weeks from just before to after the Battle of Midway, Nimitz changed his mind with amazing frequency as to who would run his carrier task forces. On 28 May he sought King's approval for the scenario devised after Halsey (Comcarpac) suddenly became ill. Spruance was only to have the *Enterprise* for Midway, then relieve Draemel as chief of staff. Fletcher would relinquish the *Yorktown* for repairs but apparently was earmarked for the *Enterprise* until Halsey's return. Fitch was already set for the *Saratoga* and Noyes the *Hornet*. Ted Sherman would receive the *Wasp* group when it reached San Diego. Rear Adm. Charles A. Pownall (another JCL) was to relieve Noyes as shore administrator for the absent Halsey. On 30 May the Bureau of Naval Personnel (Bupers) issued the necessary orders to Noyes and Sherman. King, though, refused to release Pownall, whom he wanted to run the patrol plane replacement squadrons being set up on the West Coast. Nimitz could only tap Capt. James M. Shoemaker, commanding officer of NAS Pearl Harbor, for the Carpac administrative chores. King threw another monkey wrench into Nimitz's plans on 1 June when he tabbed Sherman as deputy Cominch chief of staff for operations. Certainly evaluating the captain who lost the beloved *Lexington* also crossed his mind. Eagerly anticipating a carrier task force, Sherman learned the daunting news of "permanent duty" in Washington. Nimitz could only console, "Better luck next time."[1]

On 5 June, in the midst of the battle, Nimitz offset Sherman's unavailability by nominating Mitscher for the *Hornet* task force and giving Noyes the *Wasp*. Still in need of an aviator of flag rank to substitute for Mitscher as Commander, Patrol Wing (Compatwing) Two, he again asked King for "Baldy" Pownall. On 8 June, the day after the *Yorktown* sank, Nimitz informed King that Fitch would get the *Saratoga* as originally planned, but Fletcher "will be given a rest and probably take *Wasp* group." Nimitz gave no indication where Noyes was to go, but the *Enterprise* task force would be open when Spruance came ashore. The "probably" in reference to Fletcher indicated Nimitz's unease whether he blundered in losing the *Yorktown*. By 12 June Nimitz returned Fletcher to his good graces by reinstating plans for Noyes to the *Wasp*. The next day he requested permission to promote Fitch to vice admiral and name him Comcarpac if Halsey could not return.[2]

The Pacific Fleet staff changed again, as Nimitz turned "from those I found to those I choose." On 14 June Draemel relinquished his post as chief of staff to relieve Wilson Brown in the Amphibious Force. Although very disappointed to leave, Draemel was exhausted from the strain of the first six months of the war. Nimitz gave Spruance a few days rest before assuming his new duties as chief of staff. Some insiders believed it was a great shame that Spruance had to give up his task force and very likely lose a well-merited promotion to vice admiral. For him personally, it was the best thing that could have happened. Spruance stayed clear of the Solomons vortex that consumed so many careers, and Nimitz came so to value him that he became Cincpac's closest associate in the Pacific campaign. Spruance would return to combat to lead the central Pacific offensive when the fleet's margin of superiority was not only already decisive, but also constantly growing.[3]

On 15 June Nimitz formally reorganized the carrier striking force along the lines dictated by King at the April conference. Each task force was centered on a single carrier, the antithesis of Japanese practice. Fitch took over TF-11 in the *Saratoga*, with Kinkaid in charge of cruisers *Minneapolis*, *New Orleans*, and *Astoria*. Fletcher received TF-16 and the *Enterprise*, with Smith leading cruisers *Louisville*, *Portland*, *Chester*, and *Atlanta*. Admiral Mitscher became CTF-17 in the *Hornet*, screened by cruisers *Northampton*, *Salt Lake City*, *Pensacola,* and *San Diego* under newly promoted Rear Adm. Howard H. Good (former captain of the *New Orleans*). Noyes was slated for TF-18 and the *Wasp* (due at San Diego on the ninteenth); Rear Adm. Norman Scott would lead its cruisers *Quincy*, *Vincennes*, *San Francisco*, and *San Juan*.[4]

Although Fletcher, senior among the active carrier task force commanders, broke his flag in the *Enterprise* as CTF-16, he did not inherit, as one might expect, Halsey's vaunted aviation experts. Instead they went to the *Hornet* to join Mitscher. Browning himself departed on 18 June to the States, and former operations officer Commander Buracker went to NAS Pensacola. Buracker's reassignment was long in the works, but Nimitz temporarily detached Browning, evidently because no one but Halsey could manage him. Spruance appears not to have criticized Browning's performance, having written on 8 June with characteristic tact, "Halsey's splendid staff have made my job easy." Thirty years later Spruance's former flag lieutenant, Capt. Robert Oliver, revealed the full truth about Browning's misadventures on 4–5 June. As noted, the citation for Browning's DSM included fulsome praise for his decisive contribution to the Midway victory, but it is vital to note the recommendation did not come from Spruance, but Halsey after he and Browning returned in September to Pearl. If Spruance differed with that description of Browning's role at Midway, he did not hurt his close friend Halsey by contesting it.[5]

The evidence is strong that Spruance did confide to Nimitz his bitter dissatisfaction for Mitscher and the *Hornet*. One suspects Spruance learned more of reasons behind the *Hornet* Air Group's misadventures on 4 June than have ever been revealed. Except for Waldron's VT-8, it failed to go to the designated target. On 5 June Nimitz had slated Mitscher to get TF-17 permanently, but after 13 June that prospect faded. Nimitz advised King that Mitscher would only be CTF-17 for one cruise, then follow his original orders. Instead he again asked King to part with Ted Sherman, this time to relieve Mitscher as CTF-17. In case King declined, Nimitz eyed another possible successor. The loss of the *Yorktown* deprived Capt. Arthur Davis of a billet. The carriers other than the *Enterprise* all had new captains. Thus Nimitz asked King whether Davis could relieve George Murray, "when or if" Murray was promoted to flag rank, which Nimitz urged be soon. Ironically on 7 December Murray faced summary relief after the *Enterprise* nearly collided with the battleship *Oklahoma* in November, but his star rose swiftly due to his excellent war performance. At the same time Elliott Buckmaster's fortunes waned, despite the *Yorktown*'s solid claim as the best wartime carrier to date. Unlike Ted Sherman, the loss of his ship permanently tainted him. Selected for rear admiral, Buckmaster left Pearl on 18 June to run NAS Norfolk. After two years in the training command, he finally returned to the Pacific in charge of the western Carolines and later naval forces in South China.[6]

Award ceremony on board the Enterprise, 17 June 1942. Front row (left to right): Vice Adm. William L. Calhoun, Admiral Fletcher, Rear Adm. Thomas C. Kinkaid, Rear Adm. William Ward Smith, Rear Adm. Marc A. Mitscher, Rear Adm. Robert H. English. *Courtesy of U.S. Navy, via Col. W. W. Smith Jr.*

On 17 June Nimitz placed TF-16 and TF-17 on forty-eight-hour notice for "rest, reorganization and training." Although the carriers were available for an emergency, "This period of readjustment is very seriously needed and every day of training for the next ten days and not to exceed two weeks will pay great dividends later." Noyes concurred with regard to his new flagship *Wasp*, in San Diego reequipping with more modern aircraft. He advised Nimitz that he could sail on 25 June, but stressed even two more days of training would make a great difference. Nimitz approved. He also ordered alterations to the *Enterprise*'s arresting gear to allow her to operate the big TBF torpedo bombers. That would take about two weeks. The *Hornet* likewise would get the CXAM radar that formerly belonged to the battleship *California*. In the meantime, on 22 June Fitch took the *Saratoga* force out to Midway to deliver army fighters and marine dive bombers to beef up that much depleted air garrison.[7]

The ink was barely dry on the latest carrier task organization before Nimitz scrambled it again. On 21 June he proposed to King that Mitscher immediately take Patrol Wing (Patwing) Two. With Ted Sherman still off limits, he desired Fitch as CTF-17 in the *Hornet* after his Midway ferry trip. At the same time he gave Fletcher the *Saratoga* as CTF-11, while Kinkaid, erstwhile TF-11 cruiser commander, warmed Halsey's chair in the *Enterprise* as CTF-16. Rear Adm. Mahlon S. Tisdale (USNA 1912) would take the TF-16 cruisers. Nimitz tabbed Poco Smith to command Fuzzy Theobald's surface forces in the Aleutians. Cominch approved all the changes and detailed Carleton H. Wright to the TF-11 cruisers. Another newly frocked rear admiral from the class of 1912, "Boscoe" Wright was an ordnance specialist who was captain of the *Augusta*, King's Atlantic Fleet flagship. On 24 June Nimitz announced the latest carrier reorganization, effective 30 June after the *Sara*'s return from Midway. With the *Saratoga* the most combat-ready carrier, Fletcher moved to the head of the pack. At the same time Davis relieved Murray in the *Enterprise*, which freed Murray for promotion. Nimitz brought him onto his staff for temporary duty while reserving him for future carrier command. Mitscher's fate was in Nimitz's hands after King advised on 25 June, "Recent orders to Murray intended to enable you to make such assignment of Mitscher as you may see fit." Nimitz saw fit to put Mitscher ashore. Fortunately his banishment from the carriers did not last forever. Stricken by grief over the loss of his aviators, Mitscher thought his career was over, but in the next eighteen months he patiently worked his way back into Nimitz's trust (if not Spruance's) to lead the fast carrier task forces to victory in the Pacific War. Mitscher's performance at Midway surely played a part in Spruance's decisions in June 1944 during the Battle of the Philippine Sea.[8]

To go ahead of the narrative, it is useful here to note that Nimitz tasked Murray to look into revising the cumbersome organization of naval air in Hawaii and San Diego, with its bifurcated carrier and patrol wing commands. Halsey's inconvenient absence proved especially detrimental. His acting administrative surrogate lacked the rank and authority of a true type commander. On 11 July Nimitz named Fitch acting Comcarpac, which numbered his days as CTF-17. Again Fitch, so valued as an aviation administrator, could not escape being Halsey's understudy ashore. Three days later Nimitz formally recommended to King that the carriers and patrol wings be merged into a single entity under a vice admiral designated "Commander, Air, Pacific Fleet." It is interesting that at this juncture Nimitz envisioned this officer (Halsey if healthy, otherwise Fitch or possibly Bellinger) strictly as an administrator. In the meantime Bellinger left for Washington as Cincpac's emissary to detail the proposed reorganization to Cominch. While there a physical exam showed a mild heart condition. On 16 July to his disgust Bupers recommended he be relieved. Nimitz designated Mitscher temporary Commander, Patrol Wings, Pacific Fleet, in Bellinger's place. Yet desiring to "withhold recommendation for [Bellinger's] relief," he queried Washington as to when Halsey could resume his duties as Comcarpac. Bupers responded that Halsey could not return to work until after 15 September. At the same time King co-opted Bellinger as deputy chief of staff, not exactly an assignment that boded much rest. That reduced yet again the number of aviator admirals available to Nimitz. Therefore in the absence of both Halsey and Bellinger, he recommended to King that Fitch be promoted to vice admiral and take over Patrol Wings Pacific, as well as Carriers Pacific. Without waiting for a reply he had Fitch relieve Mitscher and Murray replace Fitch as CTF-17 in the *Hornet*. Thus by the end of July the Pacific Fleet's carrier task force commanders comprised two non-aviators (Fletcher and Kinkaid), one JCL (Noyes), and one authentic pioneer aviator (Murray), the first to rise that high.[9]

REBUILDING THE AIR GROUPS

The fatigue of a long campaign and devastating losses compelled reorganization of the carrier air groups as well. Both Fletcher and Spruance stressed the need to replace exhausted personnel and to continue training. The long-term solution was to create a replacement command on the West Coast to hasten formation of carrier replacement air groups and ensure their swift readiness for combat. Nimitz reassigned seventy-four carrier pilots who fought in the early raids, at Coral Sea or Midway. That was a much more comprehensive program of pilot replacement than in Japan, where most of the former Nagumo force carrier aircrews bolstered the air groups on the remaining carriers. Nimitz's policy would eventually pay huge dividends in enhanced combat effectiveness as U.S. carrier aviation vastly expanded. Even so, he retained a leaven of combat veterans. On 16 June he advised King that the available rested pilots would rebuild depleted squadrons on the active carriers. Browning, on the West Coast, would "assist expediting all necessary action connection [with the] formation and training [of] replacement carrier air groups" until Halsey could return to Pearl.[10]

Restoring the carrier groups in Hawaii to full combat effectiveness proved difficult. At Midway three torpedo squadrons suffered virtual annihilation. Only VT-8 easily reformed around an existing nucleus. At the same time a surfeit of VF pilots filled out the VT squadrons. The two *Enterprise* dive bombing squadrons also sustained terrible losses. By contrast VB-3 and the two *Hornet* dive bombing squadrons came through tolerably well. From Fletcher's old team in the *Yorktown* only VS-5 remained. Priority went to venerable *Saratoga*, whose air group under highly respected Cdr. Harry Donald "Don" Felt (USNA 1923) comprised perhaps the best-trained squadrons remaining in the fleet. Two were old-line *Saratoga* outfits: VB-3 of proud *Yorktown* veterans who sank the *Sōryū* and helped finish the *Hiryū*, and VS-3, which trained at San Diego since February. The largest of the new fighter units, VF-5, joined the *Saratoga*, along with rebuilt VT-8. The *Enterprise* Air Group changed greatly after Midway. Lt. Cdr. Wade McClusky went home for a rest, replaced by Lt. Cdr. Max Leslie, former VB-3 skipper and another hero of the battle. The two dive bombing squadrons were VB-6 and the original VS-5 from the *Yorktown*. VT-3 coalesced around a few experienced pilots, while VF-6 returned with new faces but many seasoned pilots. The *Hornet* kept her two dive bombing squadrons but received VF-72 in place of hapless VF-8, and a restored VT-6. Cdr. Walter F. Rodee (ex–VS-8 commanding officer) replaced Commander Ring who went ashore with Mitscher.

Although considerably smaller than the *Yorktown*-class carriers, the *Wasp* wielded an air group nearly as large. Her design featured an innovative folding deck edge number one elevator located port side forward in contrast to center line lifts on all the other carriers. Since commissioning in 1940, the *Wasp* spent all of her time in the Atlantic. In spring 1942 she twice delivered British Spitfires to besieged Malta but encountered no Axis aircraft or submarines in the Mediterranean. Winston Churchill quipped on 11 May: "Who said a

Wasp could not sting twice?" Lt. Cdr. Wallace M. Beakley, former commanding officer of VF-5, led the *Wasp* Air Group. Capt. Forrest Sherman's first task at San Diego was to reequip his two scouting squadrons with SBDs and a recently formed VT-7 with TBFs. He also initiated what one of the squadrons described as "a high pressure training schedule which crowded a month's training into a week's time."[11]

An interim solution to the carrier fighter woes was to increase their strength yet again from twenty-seven to thirty-six F4F-4 Wildcats, nearly double the number just two months before in the Coral Sea. Comcarpac expanded the *Saratoga*'s VF-5 by stripping pilots from VF-3 and VF-8 training ashore and soon beefed up the *Enterprise* and *Hornet* VF squadrons as well, but the smaller *Wasp* could only handle thirty F4Fs. Authorized strength for the groups in the *Saratoga*, *Enterprise*, and *Hornet* grew to eighty-eight planes (thirty-six fighters, thirty-six dive bombers, and sixteen torpedo bombers); the *Wasp* seventy planes (thirty fighters, thirty dive bombers, and ten torpedo bombers). The additional airplanes hurriedly crammed on board these flattops proved a mixed blessing. They imposed severe limitations, particularly for the elderly *Saratoga* with one slow operating elevator and smaller enclosed hangar. All the carriers now required more time to conduct air operations, because of the increased numbers of planes, especially those with folding wings, and the longer takeoff runs necessary for the heavier aircraft. The massive TBFs especially proved a handful.[12]

By early July Fletcher and three carriers received a mission of great strategic importance. Left behind at Pearl, the *Hornet* continued experimenting. Still stung by the *Enterprise*'s poor performance in the first 4 June launch, Murray amalgamated the two *Hornet* dive bombing squadrons into one flying twenty-four SBDs and similarly restricted the fighting squadron to thirty-two F4Fs and the VT squadron to twelve TBFs. The other aircraft were spares. Including the group commander's TBF, that made for a much more easily handled operating strength of sixty-nine planes. Murray and the *Hornet*'s Capt. Charles Mason devised a series of deck load strike scenarios. The fighters customarily deployed in eight-plane flights to be used in the following manner: the first for combat air patrol, the second with the first wave deck load strike (SBDs and TBFs) spotted on the flight deck, the third waiting in the hangar with the second strike wave, and the fourth as reserve combat air patrol. These reforms went a long way to increase flexibility and reduce launch times, but they did not address the failure to coordinate attacks by air groups from different carriers as the Japanese already did. Thus they risked reducing offensive action to a series of small, unsupported strikes that might not be decisive in battle. The U.S. Navy would not rectify that deficiency until long after Fletcher relinquished his carrier command.[13]

CHAPTER 21

Watchtower

WHERE NEXT AFTER MIDWAY?

Following the great victory as TF-17 steered northeast of Midway, Fletcher startled Lt. (jg) George E. Clapp, one of his communication watch officers in the *Saratoga*, by asking his opinion where next they should fight. The gloomy Aleutians beckoned. No one knew how deeply the Pacific Fleet might become mired in a northern campaign. Clapp declared they should go back to the South Pacific and stop the enemy there. Fletcher told his staff to heed the young officer's advice. The Aleutians were a sideshow. The central Pacific could take care of itself until the United States could advance to the Mandates in strength. The same was not true in the South Pacific Area, where Ghormley was about to assume command, or for MacArthur's Southwest Pacific Area where Port Moresby remained in danger.[1]

Fletcher had no idea a South Pacific offensive was already in the works and that he would play a central role. The destruction of four carriers at Midway dramatically evened the balance of power. On 8 June MacArthur offered to sweep Japan out of Rabaul and back to Truk, and thereby gain "manifold strategic advantages." Just give him two of Nimitz's carriers and one marine division. In fact MacArthur's bold design was simply a ploy for additional strength. He had no specific plan. Besides winning the victories that enabled MacArthur even to consider such an ambitious undertaking, Nimitz himself started the ball rolling in late May. Up to that point King proffered no timetable for his cherished advance through the New Hebrides and the Solomons to Rabaul. He merely remarked to Ghormley in April that it might begin that fall. Everything depended on how quickly Sopac could create the necessary support bases. Nimitz did not want to remain passive that whole time. On 27 May, even as he made ready to defend Midway, he offered MacArthur a marine raider battalion to rough up the seaplane base at Tulagi. MacArthur declined, deeming the raiders too few for the job. King himself favored strong raids to neutralize or destroy advance bases, "especially Tulagi," but he, too, judged one battalion insufficient for that task. The "permanent occupation of Tulagi [is] not contemplated or approved at this time." On 1 June Nimitz retorted that he never intended the raiders to hold Tulagi but simply "nullify" its base facilities to prevent the enemy from consolidating his hold.[2]

MacArthur's Rabaul proposition resonated with army planners, who were so miserly in the Pacific in favor of Europe, but King already intrigued to redirect MacArthur toward the

Netherlands East Indies. The British Eastern Fleet should join MacArthur to seize Timor, or perhaps capture bases in the Andaman and Nicobar Islands in the eastern Indian Ocean. Such actions, King informed Stark and Nimitz on 9 June, "Should serve to divert much of remaining enemy sea forces from strong action in New Guinea area which is now his likely next move." That would "enable us not only to deal with such a thrust but to mount an operation designed to weaken his hold on Solomons and Bismarcks." By "us," King meant himself, Nimitz, and Ghormley, not MacArthur. "Such a correlated effort might well develop into getting pincers on [the enemy] applied in the areas west and east of New Guinea." King's proposals were as unrealistic as MacArthur's Rabaul adventure. New Guinea meant too much to MacArthur ever to leave it to Nimitz. Meanwhile, the organization of the vast South Pacific Area proceeded steadily. On 11 June King inquired when Sopac could attack ships and bases, to which Ghormley replied he anticipated moving through the unoccupied New Hebrides, Santa Cruz, and the Ellice islands, "As soon as prospect of reinforcement is more favorable." Ghormley did not actually answer the question. He saw no reason to hurry until he had adequate forces and could supply them.[3]

In the aftermath of the Midway victory, Nimitz considered where next to deploy his carriers. The *Wasp* was due in Pearl in early July to restore the number of available flattops to four. As usual Japan's strongest opposition would come from its carriers, about which Midway prisoner interrogations and Ultra decrypts revealed much. The first-line carriers were the *Shōkaku* (completing repairs), *Zuikaku*, *Zuihō*, *Ryūjō*, and the new *Junyō* and *Hiyō*, in addition to the old *Hōshō* and converted carrier *Kasuga Maru*. Nimitz could counter with the *Saratoga*, *Enterprise*, *Wasp*, and *Hornet*. Aside from the *Ranger* in the Atlantic and several auxiliary carriers either in service or soon to be commissioned, they were all the flattops the U.S. Navy would have until summer 1943, when the first of the new *Essex*-class carriers might reach the Pacific.[4]

To comply with King's April order, never rescinded, to keep two carriers in the South Pacific until further notice, Nimitz planned for Fletcher to return to the Coral Sea about 15 July. He could thwart any modest advances and also support limited amphibious attacks, such as the recapture of Tulagi. Two carriers would relieve the first pair later in August, but around 20–24 August they could all briefly operate together. On 22 June Nimitz radioed Ghormley (but not King) a brief outline of his plans. "Desire [to] exhaust possibilities of employing striking power [of] these forces particularly during overlap to eject enemy from such of Solomon–New Guinea–New Britain bases as may be practicable."[5]

COMINCH UPS THE ANTE

On 23 June after a brief inspection of Palmyra, Nimitz returned to find a dispatch from Cominch prefaced: "Handle this with the greatest of secrecy." King finally felt constrained to lay out his own offensive scenario. With British carrier support, MacArthur was to capture Timor "or other suitable place" northwest of Australia. Simultaneously Ghormley, with two of Nimitz's carriers, would invade Tulagi. "British have been given target date August first." Thus King struck first with a solid concept. Marshall explained to MacArthur on 24 June that King insisted Tulagi must come before Rabaul, otherwise land-based air posed too great a risk to its ships. That day King detailed the principal invasion forces for "Tulagi and adjacent islands." Cincpac was to supply at least two carriers and suitable screen, plus two marine fighter and two dive bomber squadrons, in addition to the fighter-equipped marine observation squadron already en route to the South Pacific. Nimitz must arrange for carriers or aircraft transports to deliver these aircraft to the combat area. King suggested the *Wasp* remain at San Diego to continue carrier-qualifying pilots and later take one marine squadron south. Army planes waiting in Hawaii to reinforce MacArthur would supplement Sopac's shore-based air contingent. MacArthur's own air strength in northeast Australia and at Port Moresby would also participate, along with the Australian Squadron (TF-44) and subs. Once the marines took the objectives, King also expected a generous MacArthur to furnish the garrisons to hold them. McCormick's War Plans Section questioned the availability of the marine squadrons needed for key forward airfields once captured or constructed. Their pilots were not yet carrier qualified and could not land back on board a flattop if necessary. Otherwise the carriers themselves might have to remain in place to provide air cover, not a desirable course of action. Thus, "Because of air difficulty it may not be possible to meet the August 1st date." However, no airfield existed near enough to Tulagi even to permit marine aviation to join the initial stage of the offensive. That misled Nimitz into thinking their services might not be required immediately.[6]

As of 24 June only Fletcher's TF-16 (*Enterprise*) and Mitscher's TF-17 (*Hornet*) were available. The *Enterprise*'s arresting gear was being strengthened to handle TBFs and the *Hornet* fitted with CXAM radar. Because Nimitz was to meet King in San Francisco about 1 July, he asked permission to postpone their departure. The delay was vital, because Nimitz hoped to exchange the *Saratoga* (in Fitch's TF-11 off Midway) and *Wasp* (in Noyes's TF-18 at San Diego) for the *Enterprise* and *Hornet*. By that time Fletcher would have TF-11 in place of Fitch. King concurred. On 26 June Nimitz replied that TF-18 would escort the Second Marine Regiment, also at San Diego, to the South Pacific to join the proposed operation. TF-11 would remain at Pearl awaiting developments. King approved these arrangements, but lacking Marshall's concurrence he had as yet no joint directive. Nimitz was to go ahead with preparations anyway.[7]

Nimitz advised that Ghormley would exercise overall command of the Tulagi operation, while Fletcher ran the "surface forces made available from fleet," that is, the carriers, cruisers, and destroyer screens. Yet there was ambiguity regarding the question of command. McCormick wrote on 29 June that Fletcher "will be in tactical command," but did not say whether just of these forces or the whole operation. Nimitz ordered Noyes to depart San Diego on 1 July. The marine squadrons would remain in Hawaii until their pilots were carrier-trained. "Their employment must await completion of air fields in objective area." Nimitz understood the "quickest possible construction" of airfields must follow the initial landings, but believed that would need time. Retaining the marine squadrons would have serious consequences, for a suitable airfield did open up during the actual invasion. Fletcher came into the picture on 29 June. Cincpac Op-Ord 34-42 directed TF-11 (*Saratoga*, three heavy cruisers, six destroyers, and two fleet oilers) to depart Pearl on 5 July for the South Pacific Area to support amphibious operations. Fletcher was to meet Noyes's TF-18 (*Wasp*, one heavy cruiser, one light cruiser, seven destroyers, four transports, and one cargo ship) on 10 July on the equator near Christmas Island and assume tactical command. At the same time Fletcher would pass to the "direct operational control" of Ghormley. More detailed instructions would follow after Nimitz returned from seeing King on the West Coast.[8]

THE SECOND SAN FRANCISCO CONFERENCE

On 29 June Nimitz and McCormick flew out from Pearl. The conference could not begin before 3 July, and Nimitz anticipated an opportunity to relax with his wife. The next morning while setting down at NAS Alameda, the massive four-engine Sikorsky XPBS-1 flying boat struck a floating log, flipped over, and sank. The copilot died, and most of the passengers were injured, some severely. To the nation's great good fortune Nimitz sustained only bad bruises and cuts, but McCormick cracked two vertebrae. The implications of having Nimitz killed or incapacitated at that particular moment are staggering. The only likely candidates to replace him at the helm of the Pacific Fleet were Royal Ingersoll, in charge of the Atlantic Fleet, and Ghormley, who was on hand and more familiar with the theater. The Guadalcanal campaign might have ended much differently.[9]

Nimitz got back to business on 2 July, seeing Rear Adm. Richmond Kelly Turner, who had been Cominch assistant chief of staff (plans). King offered his services to Nimitz, suggesting, "Since [Turner] has been intimately involved with developments planned for amphibious operations in South Pacific he might well be employed in that connection." Nimitz, who did not know Turner well, took the hint and gave him the South Pacific Amphibious Force. A 1908 Annapolis graduate, Turner fell under the spell of naval aviation, earned his wings in 1927 as a JCL commander, and served in several aviation billets. In 1936 while teaching at the Naval War College, he renounced the aviation career path as too restrictive (not "well rounded"), and thus less likely to secure him flag rank. He requested a battleship and in 1938 received the *Astoria* in Crudiv Six. A tough, bright, even brilliant officer, "Terrible Turner" was also arrogant, abrasive, irascible, and domineering, grasping for power where he had no business. Only strong-willed commanders kept him in check. Fletcher greatly respected Turner, praising him in a 1940 fitness report as "one of the most intelligent and forceful men in the service," but Turner never dominated their relationship. In October 1940 upon Turner's departure from the *Astoria*, Fletcher was overheard while shaking hands to say: "Well, Kelly, we never got along, but you always gave me a good ship." In 1963 Fletcher told Turner's biographer George Dyer, "Any Captain who relieved Kelly Turner was in luck. All he would have to do is back off on the thumb screws a bit to have the perfect ship."[10]

Turner's feat of mounting the Sopac amphibious offensive on incredibly short notice set him on course to be among the half-dozen U.S. naval officers most responsible for victory in the Pacific. But Turner—like everyone else—made occasional errors in judgment. According to the distinguished historian Richard B. Frank: "As is often the case with Turner, immediately after a large credit entry in our ledger on his performance, we must add a black mark." Although admiring Turner's "bold aggressive leadership," Gen. Merrill B. Twining recognized his "colossal ego," in that he "insists he will accept full responsibility for any mistakes he may have made—and then vehemently insists he never made the slightest error."

Rear Adm. Richmond Kelly Turner, circa 1943.
Courtesy of U.S. Navy

Such was the case with Turner's post hoc comments that he knew Pearl Harbor was in danger prior to 7 December 1941. His obsession with projecting an aura of infallibility drove him relentlessly to shade or even misrepresent past events to vindicate his actions and shift blame to others, notably Fletcher.[11]

On 2 July Turner filled in Nimitz on Cominch's plan for the "limited amphibious offensive," about which, as King noted, he knew more than anyone else. The goal was to seize islands that could provide mutually supporting airfields for land planes and suitable seaplane bases. Turner selected unoccupied Ndeni in the Santa Cruz Islands as the initial objective. It lay 250 miles north of Espíritu Santo in the New Hebrides and 350 miles southeast of Tulagi, the nearest enemy base in the southern Solomons. He particularly valued Ndeni as a forward air base to cover the eastern flank of the Solomons but was unaware of its highly inappropriate terrain. Next would come Tulagi, along with adjacent Florida Island, and, also, eighteen miles south, Lunga Point, located on the part of the coastal plain of north central Guadalcanal best suited for an airfield. Turner also recommended heavily reinforcing Espíritu Santo, the gateway to the Solomons, and occupying Funafuti in the Ellice Islands, eight hundred miles east of Ndeni, to guard the right flank. He was the first to pinpoint Guadalcanal as the major objective. Tiny Tulagi and nearby Florida Island possessed no flat land that could readily be turned into an airfield. Unknown to him, intelligence revealed that the Japanese already started clearing the grassy plain at Lunga Point for a possible "land plane runway." The development of Guadalcanal as a major air base would seriously endanger hopes for a swift Allied offensive and even threaten Efate and New Caledonia. Once Turner's part in the Cominch-Cincpac conference ended, he and his staff would stop off at Pearl for briefings before proceeding to Auckland to join Ghormley. On 3 July, learning the conference would not begin until the next day, Nimitz had Spruance delay Fletcher's departure from Pearl until Turner could reach Pearl. The rendezvous of TF-11 and TF-18 could take place farther south off Tongatabu.[12]

King and his entourage swept into San Francisco later on 3 July after hammering out a tough compromise with Marshall for the Solomons offensive. Dated 2 July, the "Joint Directive for Offensive Operations in the Southwest Pacific Area" called for the capture of the New Britain, New Ireland, and New Guinea area in three stages. Task One was the seizure of Santa Cruz (Ndeni), Tulagi, and "adjacent positions" about 1 August. Cincpac would designate the commander of Task One, presumably Ghormley. In that connection the boundary between Sopac and the Southwest Pacific Area (SWPA) in the Solomons was to be shifted sixty miles west to longitude 159° east, just west of Guadalcanal. MacArthur's role in Task One was to interdict "enemy air and naval activities westward of operating area" that is, tie up forces at Rabaul. In turn he would exercise direct command of Task Two (securing the rest of the Solomons and retake Lae and Salamaua on the northeast coast of New Guinea) and Task Three (the capture of Rabaul and surrounding positions). The Joint Chiefs would assign the forces for all three tasks, set the schedule, and determine when overall command would pass from Nimitz to MacArthur. They could also order the withdrawal of naval forces "upon completion of any phase," should the operation "unduly jeopardize aircraft carriers." Also the naval task force commander was to retain immediate tactical control of the Amphibious Force during all three tasks. The Joint Chiefs directed Ghormley to visit MacArthur in Melbourne to coordinate planning.[13]

King led off on 4 July by explaining the Joint Chiefs' directive. Wary of MacArthur, he emphasized the line of demarcation between SWPA and Sopac was, in his words, no "Chinese Wall," where naval forces crossing into SWPA automatically came under MacArthur's control. Nimitz recommended that TF-16 (*Enterprise*) reinforce TF-11 (*Saratoga*) and TF-18 (*Wasp*) in the South Pacific, leaving only TF-17 (*Hornet*) above the equator. King cautiously agreed. Rear Adm. Randall Jacobs, the chief of Bupers, advised that Fletcher's promotion to vice admiral was in the works. If necessary he would secure presidential authority for the three stars in advance of the formal notification. Turner summarized plans for the Task One offensive and stressed that the anticipated airfield in the Tulagi area must be operational within one week of the landing. He then took the overnight flight to Pearl.[14]

Subsequent discussions concerned mainly administrative matters. King released the newly arrived *North Carolina* from Pye's TF-1 to TF-16. The first U.S. battleship since the World War I era, the "Show Boat" displaced 44,800 tons at full load with a top speed of twenty-seven knots, wielded nine 16-inch guns, a secondary armament of ten twin mounts of 5-inch dual-purpose guns, and a formidable close-in antiaircraft complement. Set to follow in August were her sister *Washington* and the *South Dakota*, first of another class of modern battleships. The gun-club admirals long dreamed of pitting the new battleships against their enemy counterparts, but now it was their speed and antiaircraft that was particularly valued. Envying Yamamoto the fast battleships that often screened his big carriers, Nimitz wanted to see how one of his own could protect his flattops. King again directed him to look into stationing a division of old battleships in the South Pacific. It was another curious example of the surface officer–aviator (King) wanting to fight the old battleships, while the surface officer–submariner (Nimitz) excluded them for the time being. Nimitz believed the old battleships, with their "concentrated powers of destruction," could still play a vital combat role, but he balked at committing them until their antisubmarine screen was stronger and they possessed adequate air cover against land-based bombers that threatened even carriers.[15]

Departing San Francisco the evening of 5 July, Nimitz reached Pearl the next morning. In his absence, his own commanders were busy planning the Solomons offensive.

THE PLANNING AT PEARL

Spruance and Fletcher also read the Joint Chiefs' directive on 2 July. To the War Plans Section, now temporarily under Captain Steele, the upcoming amphibious assault on Tulagi posed the same risks that Japan faced in June. "As was amply demonstrated at Midway, an attacker who has not neutralized shore-based air in advance is at a great disadvantage." Should surprise not be achieved, enemy carriers might also counterattack. All the initial objectives lay within the reach of airfields at Rabaul, whose vigorous air search rendered surprise unlikely, as Brown, Fletcher, and Halsey could all attest. Early detection offered the alternative either of "wading on in" with the "hope of getting local air superiority" before being "sunk," or withdrawing. Much depended on whether MacArthur's heavy bombers could pummel Rabaul at the right time. Steele opined if that effort were successful, "The task is a cinch." Otherwise, "We may lose a carrier."[16]

On the afternoon of 5 July Turner joined Spruance, Fletcher, Fitch, and Kinkaid at Cincpac headquarters, where he laid out the proposals he previously presented to Nimitz. The airfield on Espíritu Santo must be functioning by 28 July, even if that required borrowing construction gear intended for Guadalcanal. There should be two landing exercises in Fiji beginning about 23 July to rehearse the plan. The Second Marines were to occupy Ndeni about D–2 Day (30 July), after a destroyer reconnoitered the site. MacArthur's air offensive was to commence on D–2, while Sopac deployed seaplane tenders and PBYs to Ndeni and to Malaita, east of Tulagi, for the essential long-range searches. The main assault would capture Tulagi, Florida Island, and Lunga Point on Guadalcanal. Turner preferred the marines to land after naval gunfire and carrier strikes softened up the beaches. On 5 July in summarizing his plans, the Cincpac Greybook noted, "CVs close in will provide fighter coverage (about three days) and will dive bomb defended positions before the landing." Turner's views prevailed. On 6 July Nimitz submitted his outline to Ghormley, tactfully describing it as merely a suggested course of action reached after consultation with Fletcher and the Cincpac staff. TF-16 (*Enterprise*) would proceed south in addition to the *Wasp* and *Saratoga*. Even TF-17 (*Hornet*) might eventually participate. The overall operation the Cincpac staff charmingly dubbed "Pestilence." Task One was "Watchtower," the rehearsal "Dovetail," and the occupation of Ndeni, "Huddle." Tulagi was "Ringbolt" and Guadalcanal, immortally, "Cactus." Nimitz ordered Fletcher's TF-11 (plus the *Vincennes*) to depart Pearl at 0800 on 7 July, two days later than originally intended. On the way he was to conduct a full-scale air and shore bombardment exercise on the island of Hawaii. Transport Division Twelve (four APDs) would accompany TF-11, then proceed directly to Nouméa to embark

Admiral Fletcher receiving the DSM from Admiral Nimitz, 6 July 1942.
Courtesy of American Heritage Center, University of Wyoming–Laramie

the First Marine Raider Battalion. Nimitz rescheduled the rendezvous with Noyes to 19 July three hundred miles west of Tongatabu. Ghormley would take direct control of both task forces on 10 July as previously planned.[17]

Turner later claimed Fletcher was "very much opposed in Pearl Harbor to undertaking the attempt against Guadalcanal, as he felt sure that it would be a failure." If indeed Fletcher was so vehemently pessimistic as Turner subsequently alleged, one wonders why Nimitz did not simply replace him. Fletcher was not one to dissemble. Nimitz certainly knew what he thought about the prospects of success in the Solomons. Thus Fletcher may not have been as gloomy as Turner later charged. "Nimitz gave me the impression," Fletcher wrote in 1947, "that the landing force would be ashore in two days and could dig in and accept air attack." He could certainly accept that scenario. He recalled in 1963 that Nimitz again invoked the restrictions placed on the carriers for the Battle of Midway that demanded they were not to be risked in situations where they could not inflict comparable damage to the enemy.[18]

During the afternoon of 6 July Nimitz took Fletcher aside and surprised him by producing a U.S. Navy DSM and citation that read: "For exceptionally meritorious service as Task Force Commander, United States Pacific Fleet. In that position of great responsibility he exercised command of his Task Force with marked skill and resourcefulness, as a result of which heavy losses were inflicted on the enemy in the Coral Sea in May, 1942, and again, off Midway Island in June, 1942." Nimitz had hoped to decorate the two Midway commanders at the same time, with a formal parade in dress whites and all the flourishes, but Spruance's award had not arrived. If Fletcher was going to get his decoration before he left for battle, it had to be then. Unfortunately that private ceremony in Cincpac's office marked all the official acclaim Fletcher ever received for Coral Sea and Midway. He knew his promotion to vice admiral was in the works, but Nimitz could not say when. Dinner that evening included, in addition to Nimitz and Fletcher, Fletcher's good friend and classmate Vice Adm. William L. Calhoun (Commander, Service Force, Pacific Fleet, or Comserforpac), Spruance, Turner, Murray, and Col. Melvin J. Maas, fresh from Washington. After a pleasant time Fletcher returned to the *Saratoga* and made ready to sail next morning for the Solomons.[19]

SETTLING IN THE *SARA*

Although Fletcher was CTF-16 for two weeks, the *Enterprise*, in dock the whole time, was just a mailing address. On 1 July the Comcrupac staff and flag complement filed back on board the *Saratoga* to run TF-11. Cdr. Butch Schindler, the staff gunnery officer, now ranked next after Capt. Spence Lewis, following the departure of Cdr. Gerry Galpin, the operations officer. In late June Galpin exchanged billets with Cdr. Charles O. Humphreys, the *Minneapolis* executive officer. A genial, stocky Marylander, Owen Humphreys (USNA 1922) was a noted athlete who qualified in submarines. A senior staff member called him "very able, positive; [with] unusual ability; aggressive." Galpin, like Lewis and Buckmaster, later received the DSM for the victories of Coral Sea and Midway, and Schindler was awarded the Navy Cross for his Coral Sea combat missions. Cdr. Sam Latimer, Lt. Cdr. Alexander Thorington, Lt. Cdr. Harry Smith, and Lt. Cdr. Charles Brooks retained their jobs of flag secretary, assistant operations officer, flag lieutenant, and radio officer respectively. After Midway

Fletcher brought Lt. Cdr. Oscar Pederson (USNA 1926), the former *Yorktown* Air Group leader, on his staff as air operations officer. That formalized the arrangement for aviation expertise that he forged on board the *Yorktown*. A new radio intelligence team led by Lt. Gilven Slonim (USNA 1936) reported as well. Slonim served ably in the *Enterprise* with Halsey and with Spruance at Midway. There were now five communication watch officers, and CSM Demps Gordy handled visual communications. The enlisted flag complement and marine detachment remained largely intact.[20]

The most unusual addition to the TF-11 staff was another aviator, forty-four-year-old Col. Melvin J. Maas, Marine Corps Reserve, who happened to be a serving Republican congressman from Minneapolis. A World War I veteran first elected to the House in 1926, Mel Maas received a Carnegie Medal for talking a crazed gunman in the Capitol into giving up his weapon. As ranking minority member on the House Naval Affairs Committee, he worked closely with Carl Vinson, the powerful Democratic chairman from Georgia, to pass the bills that brought about the two-ocean navy. A strong proponent of naval rearmament, particularly aviation, Maas fostered the expansion of the Marine Corps Reserve. He led a marine reserve aviation squadron in the 1930s and spent part of the summer of 1941 with Halsey in the *Enterprise* and at Midway analyzing patrol plane operations. In May 1942 Maas secured a leave of absence from Congress. Lt. Gen. Thomas Holcomb, the commandant of the Marine Corps, requested Maas be attached to the Cincpac staff. Nimitz responded he would be "delighted." An eager if not particularly skillful pilot, the burly, rotund, cigar-smoking raconteur was not only a well-connected politician, but he was also much liked. Maas's official title on Fletcher's staff was simply, "Marine Officer." He proved a sharp observer, keen opponent at darts, and ultimately an unusual ally. His contemporary notes, hitherto unknown to historians, are invaluable for understanding the background of the Guadalcanal campaign.[21]

The *Sara*'s flag quarters were situated port side forward on the main deck, one deck below the flight deck. There Fletcher had the usual commodious stateroom and pantry, along with a guest cabin and six cabins for his senior staff officers. Capt. Duke Ramsey's suite was located to starboard, opposite the flag quarters. After the *Sara* sailed he relinquished these lavish in-port quarters to a grateful Maas and stayed in his sea cabin on the navigating bridge in the remodeled island. The *Saratoga*'s flag bridge was one level up from the navigating bridge, where a screened platform neatly surrounded flag plot and adjacent admiral's sea cabin. The open sky forward position perched on the roof of the flag bridge in place of the large fighting top cut away during the recent refit. Lookouts shared that space with the big Mark 37 gunnery director and FD fire control radar array. The denizens of sky forward soon discovered if they leaned over the rail, they could misuse their powerful binoculars to look over Fletcher's shoulder as he sat outside in his swivel chair reading his dispatches. They enjoyed their unique access to inside information until the gunnery officer, Lt. Cdr. Fremont B. Eggers, happened, while snooping, to drop his helmet onto the admiral. Embarrassed to have to go down to the flag bridge to retrieve his tin pot, Eggers categorically ordered sky forward cease the eavesdropping. That was unfortunate because they were participating in one of the pivotal actions of the Pacific War.[22]

THE VOYAGE SOUTH

The morning of 7 July Fletcher's TF-11 snaked through the confined channel from Pearl Harbor to the open sea. Six destroyers of Desron One fanned out on alert for lurking I-boats. Capt. Samuel B. Brewer now ran Desron One and TG-11.4. He knew Fletcher well, having served with him in 1918 in the old *Benham*. Cdr. Hugh W. Hadley's Transport Division Twelve joined the screen. Traveling empty, his four APDs, former four-piper destroyers, hitched a ride south. Rear Adm. Carleton Wright's TG-11.2 emerged next. Flagship *Minneapolis*, *New Orleans*, and *Astoria* were Crudiv Six stalwarts, while the *Vincennes* came out in March 1942 with the *Hornet* task force. Flamboyant *Saratoga*, sole unit of Captain Ramsey's TG-11.5, was the star of the show, but the ponderous afterguard of fleet oilers *Platte* and *Cimarron* (Capt. Ralph H. Henkle's TG-11.6) disclosed to sharp observers that this task force had an ocean to cross and might not return soon. Indeed these seventeen ships were the first to set out from Hawaii for the six months of hell of the Guadalcanal campaign. Five remained in the Solomons forever; three, ripped open by torpedoes, eventually limped back for repairs. On 8 July during air and gunnery exercises, aerial bombs and heavy shells thudded into unoffending Cape Kahae near the southeast tip of Hawaii. That afternoon Fletcher headed southwest at fifteen knots to rendezvous on 19 July with Noyes west of Tongatabu.[23]

The night of 8 July Fletcher copied the radio summary of Nimitz's directive designating Ghormley task force commander for Task One. Ghormley was to "seize and occupy Santa Cruz Islands Tulagi and adjacent positions" about 1 August. Nimitz provided TF-11 under Vice Admiral Fletcher (the first time his impending promotion was noted), TF-16 (Rear Admiral Kinkaid), TF-18 (Rear Admiral Noyes), additional marine forces, including aviation, and several support ships. TF-44 (now under Rear Adm. Victor A. C. Crutchley, RN, who relieved Rear Adm. John Crace in June) was to come east from Australia. Nimitz also arranged logistical support. In addition to the *Platte* and *Cimarron* with TF-11, the *Kaskaskia* would leave Pearl about 20 July. The old oiler *Kanawha*, already in the South Pacific, was to fuel TF-18, then advance to Nouméa. To keep the fleet oilers filled, the chartered tankers *Mobilube* and *W. C. Yeager* would haul 225,000 barrels from San Pedro to Nouméa around 22 July. Two others (the *Esso Little Rock* and *E. J. Henry*) were to reach Nouméa on 2 August with a similar load. Nimitz reserved the option to divert those chartered tankers to Samoa, Tongatabu, Fiji, or New Zealand as necessary. Thereafter he expected to make three such deliveries per month and offered aviation gasoline and other needed stores for the Pacific Fleet task forces as requested. Nimitz also advised that he "may from time to time issue further instructions in connection this operation." He affirmed his "full confidence" in Ghormley's "ability to carry this operation to successful conclusion."[24]

The two TF-11 oilers replenished the destroyers and APDs on 12 July on the equator between Christmas and Canton islands. Nimitz advised Ghormley, Fletcher, and Noyes that Kinkaid's TF-16 would sail from Pearl on 15 July with the *Enterprise*, battleship *North Carolina*, heavy cruiser *Portland*, light cruiser *Atlanta*, and seven destroyers. TF-16 was to reach Tongatabu on the twenty-fourth, where fuel would be waiting courtesy of the *Kanawha* and *Mobilube*, which Nimitz redirected there in place of Nouméa. Unfortunately it soon looked as if only two carriers might actually be available for Watchtower after all. On the evening of 13 July as TF-11 approached Samoa, Fletcher learned that the *Wasp* suffered a serious mechanical casualty to her starboard high-pressure turbine, "Evidenced by loud scraping noise even at lowest speeds." The *Wasp* could make fifteen knots on her port engine. If it became necessary to lift the rotor to effect repairs, Noyes recommended taking her into Tongatabu, some twelve hundred miles southeast. Repairs should take about four days, with the help of the destroyer tender *Whitney*. Nimitz worried he might have to replace TF-18 with TF-17 (*Hornet*), which he planned to keep near Pearl. The lack of defending aircraft rendered even Hawaii vulnerable to a sudden carrier strike.[25]

On 15 July Ghormley postponed Dog-Day from 1 August tentatively to 7 August and set the Fiji rehearsals (Dovetail) for 27 July. He later cited the tardy arrival of the transports at Wellington and problems in handling their cargo due to bad weather. The delay was probably inevitable given the rushed preparations but risky if the enemy swiftly committed additional forces to the Solomons. On 16 July Fletcher released Transport Division (Transdiv) Twelve southwest to Nouméa. He awaited the rest of his force west of Tongatabu before commencing the offensive in the Solomons. Confirmation came of his promotion to vice admiral. Impatient with the delay in Washington, Nimitz again requested King and Jacobs allow Fletcher to assume that rank "at once." King confirmed Fletcher's promotion, to rank from 26 June. Thus Fletcher got his three stars as the navy's seventeenth vice admiral. That promotion cleared up any question of his seniority, particularly over Noyes.[26]

COMMANDING THE EXPEDITIONARY FORCE

The radio summary of Ghormley's Sopac Op-Plan 1-42 that Fletcher received the evening of 16 July both pleased and puzzled him. In addition to TF-18, he received tactical command of TF-16, but unexpectedly also of nearly everything else in Watchtower. Ghormley divided the South Pacific Force into two task forces: Fletcher's TF-61, the Expeditionary Force, and Rear Adm. John McCain's TF-63, Shore Based Air. TF-61 comprised the three carrier task forces (11, 16, and 18), Turner's whole Amphibious Force (TF-62), and Crutchley's TF-44. In turn McCain's aircraft, supported by a few seaplane tenders, would conduct long-range searches and limited air strikes. The operations plan tasked MacArthur's Southwest Pacific air force to "interdict" Japanese forces to westward of Tulagi and Guadalcanal and reconnoiter the Solomons "as arranged" by McCain. U.S. subs from Australia and Pearl would, it was hoped, intercept ships off Rabaul and Truk. Fletcher was to supervise the Watchtower rehearsals in Fiji about 27 July, seizure of the Tulagi area "and adjoining portion Guadalcanal" on D-Day (7 August) and construction of an airfield, the occupation of Ndeni soon afterward, and finally the defense of the lodgment "until relieved." In addition to conducting normal searches, McCain was to "cover approach and operations in Tulagi area by scouting," execute air strikes, "render aircraft support on call," and "initiate patrol plane scouting from Ndeni by D–2 Day and from Malaita on Dog Day."[27]

Ghormley desired the "interested commanders" to confer regarding the coordination of "air activities." About D–5 day he expected to move Sopac headquarters to Nouméa and break his flag in the old fleet auxiliary *Argonne* coming south from Pearl. The written version of the Sopac operations plan, copies of which would be dropped off at Tongatabu for Fletcher, Noyes, and Kinkaid, would treat logistics, communications, and intelligence, but it offered no additional insights into how Ghormley expected to accomplish the mission. He simply placed "the senior officer present of the naval forces which were made available to me" in "tactical command of the operation." It was a just a matter of telling Fletcher and McCain "what to do, not how to do it," which was what Nimitz did to him. Surprised to be handed virtually the whole show in the Solomons, Fletcher explained on 27 July to Rear Adm. Daniel J. Callaghan, Sopac chief of staff, that he was pleased with the additional responsibility, but he had thought Ghormley was going to exercise personal command.[28]

Vice Adm. Robert L. Ghormley, 1942.
Courtesy of National Archives (80-G-12864)

Ghormley's hands-off attitude toward Watchtower has yet to be explained. He did not participate in the preliminary planning either in Washington or Pearl. Nimitz did describe the outline he presented merely as a suggestion, implying Ghormley could alter the plan if he desired. The tight time schedule could justify Ghormley's reluctance to make major changes, but his diffidence perhaps originated from the earlier controversy over the nature of the Pacific command. In early April Nimitz urged that for the time being Cincpac retain direct control over carrier task forces in the South Pacific Area, instead of turning them over to Comsopac. King concurred but made it clear during the first San Francisco conference that when the South Pacific offensive finally came to pass, Ghormley would be subject only to broad policy directives from above. Clearly by the end of June Nimitz understood Ghormley must come into his own in Sopac. So apparently did Ghormley, who later explained: "I appreciated I had no naval forces whatever under my direct command, except such forces from the Pacific Fleet that might be sent into the area from time to time." Yet, "During the time these fleet units were in the South Pacific Area they were to be under my *tactical command*" (Ghormley's emphasis). However, Nimitz's 8 July letter of instructions for Task One (Watchtower) directed Ghormley, "Exercise strategic command in person in the operating area which is interpreted initially to be the New Caledonia–New Hebrides area." If, as it seems, Nimitz had not meant to discourage Ghormley from taking an active role in executing Watchtower, he erred badly by using the words "strategic command in person." There is every reason to believe the Nimitz desired Ghormley to have tactical as well as strategic command in Sopac. He couched all recent orders turning over the Pacific Fleet task forces to Sopac in terms that preserved Ghormley's prerogatives. Ghormley could have requested clarification from Nimitz regarding that apparent oxymoron and thereby confirmed his greater personal control.[29]

Perhaps another factor behind Ghormley's reluctance concerned his feelings toward the Watchtower plan. When he first heard of it on 26 June, his "immediate mental estimate of the situation was that we were far from ready to start any offensive." An observer described him as "flabbergasted," as indeed was everyone. On 8 July Ghormley and MacArthur jointly offered King and Nimitz their opinion of the offensive. Available ground troops were "adequate" for all three tasks, if not the shipping needed to transport and supply them. The real problem was aviation, both the land and carrier-based. Task One required the Amphibious Force and supporting carriers to linger in the target area from thirty-six hours to four days, "Where they will be outside the range of any supporting air and exposed to continued hostile air surface and submarine attacks." Yet MacArthur's air strength was insufficient to deter Japan from massing air and naval strength against Tulagi. The carriers "will be themselves exposed to attack by land based air while unprotected by our land based aviation," making it "extremely doubtful that they will be able to furnish fighters escort to the transport area, especially should hostile naval forces approach." Surprise was "improbable" due to "the depth of the existing hostile reconnaissance."[30]

Having reached their conclusions "independently" and "confirmed" them in person at Melbourne, MacArthur and Ghormley recommended that Task One be postponed. To go ahead "without a reasonable assurance of adequate air coverage during each phase" meant "the gravest risk." The recent enemy defeat at Coral Sea and Midway perfectly demonstrated what could befall an amphibious offensive that lacked proper preparation. Unless the Allies could assault Rabaul almost at the outset—and they lacked the strength for such an audacious move—Japan could rush planes and ships to the Solomons in such numbers to "expose the initial attacking elements to the danger of destruction by overwhelming force." Therefore Task One should be "deferred pending the further development of force" to enable all three tasks to take place "in one continuous movement." In the meantime Ghormley would strengthen the New Hebrides and occupy the Santa Cruz Islands, while MacArthur accelerated airfield construction in eastern New Guinea. Some details regarding the offensive plan might change after input from the Amphibious Force and carrier force commanders, "who have not yet arrived," but not the overall gloomy assessment. At that juncture Ghormley indicated no desire to give the "carrier force commander" tactical command of the entire landing operation.

King brooked no delay of Task One. Now was not the time for such extreme caution. King himself exuded confidence all three tasks would proceed quickly and smoothly. Armed with the approval of the Joint Chiefs, he emphasized to Ghormley, MacArthur, and Nimitz that Watchtower must proceed as planned before the enemy could consolidate his hold on the Solomons. Nimitz was providing a third carrier and thirty-five B-17s from Pearl, and the flow of replacement planes would be accelerated. Ghormley realized any unjustified delay meant summary relief. "Considering recent known disposition hostile forces," he declared on 12 July, "I consider means now prospectively available [to] Sopac sufficient for accomplishment [of] Task One." However, the caveat was MacArthur must have "sufficient means for interdiction hostile aircraft activities based on New Britain–New Guinea–Northern Solomons Area." The "basic problem of this operation is the protection of surface ships against land-based aircraft during the approach, the landing and the unloading." Much later Ghormley stoutly defended his original proposal to postpone the offensive. Thus when he turned over tactical command of most of Watchtower to Fletcher, he certainly had strong misgivings about the general plan. Someone unsympathetic might conclude Ghormley, in essence, said to King and Nimitz: If you do not agree with my estimate of the situation, then your man can run the show. Yet it is also important to note why Ghormley was so concerned: the threat of land-based aviation. In that light it seems logical he might want to accord the carrier commander the flexibility to meet the threat, or to withdraw if things got too hot for the flattops.[31]

On 2 August Ghormley explained to Nimitz, "[In] an operation such as we are undertaking, the strategic control has to be where communications are as perfect as possible. The modern Commander under such conditions can not be on a ship at sea where radio silence prevails and where his forces are so scattered that his vision is entirely dependent upon communications." Thus Ghormley's reluctance to exercise direct command perhaps resulted from his concern his communications were indeed far from "perfect." The need for radio silence meant he often would only have "his operation order and some guessing" on which to base his picture of "tactical dispositions." However, he failed to fathom that those precise conditions also applied to Fletcher, except that Fletcher was even more handicapped than his boss, in that he could not even freely transmit messages of his own without the risk of giving away his position.[32]

In truth Ghormley placed Fletcher in a difficult situation. Normally the officer in tactical command was in ready touch with all major elements. After the Battle of the Coral Sea, Fletcher and others proposed the top operational commander coordinate things from ashore, where he would likely be better informed of the overall picture than in a carrier. He could issue orders at will without worrying about disclosing his presence. However if Fletcher stayed in the *Saratoga*, the requirement of radio silence would make it nearly impossible to manage his suddenly enhanced command. At the same time his physical separation isolated him from the planning process. The Naval War College analysis of the Battle of Savo Island, written by Commodore Bates and Cdr. Walter D. Innis, noted how later wartime experience favored the "Supreme Tactical Commander" riding a heavy cruiser, from where he could operate with the Amphibious Force during the landings or join the covering force should enemy forces appear. Yet they approved the decision to give the whole Expeditionary Force to Fletcher, even though he was "the only combat trained carrier task force commander within the command." Instead, "it was felt that it was more important to retain him within the carriers than to give him the freedom of action to go where he desired," that is, with the Amphibious Force, the real "scene of action." That was pure hindsight. Both Ghormley and Fletcher fully anticipated attacks on the carriers, with plenty of "action." No one dreamed the Japanese would fail to find the carriers not only before, but also during the landings.[33]

Bates and Innis revealed their complete misunderstanding of the role of Fletcher's carriers. Pederson, the TF-61 air staff officer, explained in a 1944 lecture, "The overall mission of the carriers was twofold: first, to furnish air support for the assault, and second, and subsequently, to prevent any large scale attempt by the Japanese to retake Guadalcanal." Fletcher certainly expected a big carrier battle either during or soon after the landing phase. He remained with the carriers not simply by choice, but from necessity. Perhaps had Nimitz known and approved of Ghormley's command structure, he would have sent Fletcher south along with Turner to oversee the detailed planning. In that case he would have had to name another flag officer as CTF-11 and entrust the striking force to the inexperienced Noyes. That he was reluctant to do.[34]

COPING WITH CATASTROPHE

In the halcyon days of late May, the Naval General Staff looked forward, after the certain decisive victory at Midway, to shifting the focus to the Southeast Area. A four-pronged offensive in early July would start in New Caledonia to enable land-based air to seal off the northern Coral Sea. Soon afterward, Port Moresby would fall to another seaborne assault. Finally, the fall of Fiji and Samoa (the FS Operation) would complete the isolation of Australia. Later that year Combined Fleet could start carving up the Hawaiian Islands. Midway dealt a terrible blow to those grandiose ambitions. Not only did losing the four elite carriers substantially reduce the carrier fleet, but the destruction of so many planes also caused a chronic shortage for the entire IJN that Japan's low aircraft production scarcely alleviated. The situation was only a little less gloomy with regard to trained naval aircrews, of whom the air command likewise produced insufficient numbers to man fully all the existing units, not to mention future expansion.

The Midway fiasco forced a complete reevaluation of strategy. On 11 June Imperial General Headquarters postponed the FS Operation for two months. In the meantime Seventeenth Army was to assault Port Moresby by land via the north coast of Papua (the RI Operation). Base Air Force would serve as the "mainspring" of a gradual advance toward Samoa. Concentrated air power at Tulagi and Guadalcanal would first support the capture of Efate, then leapfrog to New Caledonia and Fiji, and finally Samoa. On 17 June the high command instituted the SN Operation ("Solomons–New Guinea"). Lunga Point on Guadalcanal was to be ready by mid August for twenty-seven fighters and twenty-seven medium bombers, and within a month forty-five fighters and sixty medium bombers. The first substantial force reached Guadalcanal on 1 July. In turn, the main SN convoy left Truk on 29 June, but false fears of U.S. intervention delayed its arrival until 6 July. Its nearly twenty-six hundred naval pioneers, guarded by about 250 troops, erected an elaborate camp at Lunga and laid out the nearby airfield and an associated dummy airstrip to confuse Allied bombers.[35]

On 11 July Imperial General Headquarters formally canceled the FS Operation. For the time being the Indian Ocean, rather than the Pacific, looked more promising in an expanded raiding effort against British commerce by cruisers and destroyers based out of Burma. On 14 July the IJN underwent major reorganization. Vice Adm. Tsukahara Nishizō, commanding Base Air Force, took over the South Seas Area, now divided into an Inner South Seas Force (Inoue's Fourth Fleet) and Outer South Seas Force (Eighth Fleet) under Vice Adm. Mikawa Gunichi. That gave Mikawa direct control of naval operations in New Guinea, New Britain, and the Solomons. His surface force comprised the heavy cruiser *Chōkai* and the familiar 6th and 18th Cruiser Divisions. In August the fighters, medium bombers, and flying boats of the 6th Air Attack Force (26th Air Flotilla) were to shift from the homeland to the Solomons, while the 5th Air Attack Force concentrated on New Guinea. Seventeenth Army headed to Rabaul to organize the land assault on Port Moresby. Its first phase involved the establishment of a supply base and airfield at Buna on the north coast of Papua. Troops would push south from Buna through the forbidding Owen Stanley mountains and threaten Port Moresby from the north. When the navy finally controlled the northern Coral Sea, Mikawa would also execute another amphibious attack on Port Moresby. The lead convoy reached Buna on 21 July. Ships filtered additional men and supplies to Buna, while troops marched rapidly south to Kokoda in the midst of the mountains.[36]

The Pestilence offensive against the Solomons, New Guinea, and New Britain, of which the Watchtower assault on Tulagi and Guadalcanal was only the first phase, arose because MacArthur, King, and Nimitz believed the way was open to seize the stronghold of Rabaul. Watchtower would initiate the grand Allied counteroffensive to win the Pacific War. However in July, while Ghormley assembled his far flung forces, Japanese fortunes rebounded to the extent that they would soon consolidate their defense of the Solomons. Radio intelligence and air reconnaissance picked up numerous hints presaging an enemy advance in New Guinea and outward from the Solomons. On 13 July MacArthur cautioned that a "major advanced air operating base" on Guadalcanal would threaten Efate and northwestern New Caledonia. On the ninteenth the Cincpac War Plans Section told Nimitz: "It is now a race to see whether or not we can kick [Japan] out in time, and with present forces." MacArthur did not seem as concerned about New Guinea, where the building of an airfield at Buna in mid August was to inaugurate Task Two of Pestilence. The sudden Japanese occupation of Buna proved a particularly unpleasant surprise. Little did MacArthur grasp he now faced a bitter campaign in rugged mountains and deep jungles where the enemy would drive within twenty miles of Port Moresby. Nimitz demonstrated more prescience. On 17 July he warned King, "It is unsafe to assume that the enemy will not exert every effort to recover the positions we may take from him." If Washington did not strongly support the offensive by "a steady flow of replacements" of troops and aircraft from the United States, "Not only will we be unable to proceed with Tasks Two and Three," but also, "we may be unable even to hold what we have taken."[37]

CHAPTER 22

The 27 July Conference

ASSEMBLING THE FORCES

On 18 July Ghormley directed Fletcher to loiter west of Tongatabu until Noyes and Kinkaid appeared, then form the carrier striking force. Later, Turner's amphibious ships and Crutchley's cruiser force would join him. For the next week, therefore, Fletcher could do little beyond plan in isolation. On 21 July the *Platte* transferred her remaining oil to the *Cimarron*, then left for Nouméa with a destroyer to fetch more fuel from the *W. C. Yeager* and return in late July. With TF-61 gathering three hundred miles west of Tongatabu, the group with the farthest to go was Turner's at Wellington. Informed Turner could reach the assembly area on 26 July, Fletcher set the grand rendezvous for that afternoon, after which the combined force would conduct rehearsals in Fiji to the northwest.[1]

Noyes's TF-18 with the ailing *Wasp* and Transdiv Two dropped anchor at Tongatabu on 18 July. The *Wasp* engineers brilliantly accomplished the brutal work of lifting the rotor and replacing the blading in her starboard high-pressure turbine. On 21 July she attained twenty-five knots. Cincpac certainly dodged a bullet. Even so, the reliability of the *Wasp*'s power plant over the long term was in question. It might not hold up if light winds compelled long runs more than twenty-five knots to launch fully loaded planes. Noyes recommended she return to Pearl, "At first available opportunity after employment now started." On 23 July TF-18, less the transports, contacted TF-11. The next day Fletcher transferred the *Vincennes* to Noyes and detached the destroyer *Hull* to Suva to fetch important visitors.[2]

Having left Pearl on 15 July Kinkaid anticipated a routine run to Tongatabu. En route the *North Carolina* and *Portland* fueled destroyers "with usual efficiency," according to an admiring Commander Laing, the RN liaison officer. Prevailing light winds forced Kinkaid to increase speed for flight operations and burn more fuel than he liked. On 23 July he was shocked to learn that local time at Tongatabu was Z–12, although the Tonga Islands were east of the 180th meridian. The date line snaked eastward to include them. Thus TF-16 was a day late. "We kept very quiet about it," Kinkaid later wrote, and doubted "Nimitz or Fletcher know it to this day." On 25 July he found Tongatabu's harbor filled with auxiliaries and began refueling his depleted ships from the *Kanawha*, *Mobilube*, *Whitney*, and the store ship *Aldebaran*. The *North Carolina* only fueled to 60 percent. To make the scheduled rendezvous, TF-16 cleared the anchorage before sunset due to the difficulty of getting large ships through the harbor channel in darkness. Kinkaid gratefully sighted the other forces on

26 July, released the auxiliaries to Turner's TF-62, and took position eight miles to starboard of TF-11. He later blamed the fog at Tongatabu for his delay but recalled, "Fletcher looked at me skeptically and said: 'We don't have fog in the tropics.'"[3]

After a long flight from Pearl detouring around storms, Turner belatedly reported to Ghormley at Auckland on 15 July. Two days later in Wellington he broke his flag in the *McCawley*, one of eight transports and four cargo ships of Transdivs Eight and Ten that hastily re-embarked the personnel, equipment, and supplies of the recently arrived First Marine Division. Its able commander, Maj. Gen. Alexander Archer "Archie" Vandegrift, was also known as "Sunny Jim" due to his cheerful disposition. Lt. Col. Merrill "Bill" Twining, the assistant operations officer, contrasted the gentlemanly Vandegrift with their new amphibious admiral, "A loud, strident, arrogant person who enjoyed settling all matters by simply raising his voice and roaring like a bull captain in the old navy." Twining thought Turner's "peers understood this and valued him for what he was, a good and determined leader with a fine mind—when he chose to use it." Vandegrift's staff already began detailed planning for the Tulagi-Guadalcanal operation. They were skeptical of Turner's Ndeni scheme because it diverted vital troops from the main effort. Their scheme of maneuver sent most of the division against Lunga to capture the all-important airfield, but not by frontal assault. Instead, the landing would take place at Red Beach, five miles east. Now the two staffs, amphibious force and marine division, had to create an operational plan. They did not have much time. Unlike some of the Washington brass, Vandegrift was fully aware how difficult the task was going to be at the sharp end. He distrusted the navy's will to support him. Events at Guadalcanal would only enlarge the omnipresent chip on marine shoulders.[4]

On 22 July Turner led the twenty-six ships of TF-62 and TF-44 out of Wellington. Crutchley's mixed Australian-American TF-44 comprised heavy cruisers *Australia*, *Canberra*, *Chicago*, and *Salt Lake City*, light cruiser *Hobart*, and the nine destroyers. Promoted rear admiral in February 1942, Victor Alexander Charles Crutchley, forty-eight, was a distinguished Royal Navy officer who received the Victoria Cross for great gallantry and brilliant seamanship in May 1918 during the failed attempt to block Ostend. In 1940 he commanded the famous old battleship *Warspite* and took her into battle at Narvik. Tall and big-framed, Crutchley wore a full beard and mustache to hide wound scars. His intelligence, careful demeanor, and meticulous approach to planning and operations deeply impressed his American colleagues.[5]

On the afternoon of 26 July all of Fletcher's task forces met on schedule at the rendezvous west of Tongatabu and 350 miles south of Fiji. The sight of seventy-one ships offered an impressive demonstration of sea power. Transdivs Two and Twelve and Mine Squadron Two reported for duty to Turner, who released the *Salt Lake City* to TF-18. The forces maneuvered in general contact while their leaders decided exactly what they were going to do with all this naval might.

GATHERING THE BRASS

On 21 July Ghormley in distant Auckland directed the "staff representatives" of Fletcher, Turner, and McCain to confer prior to the campaign. A destroyer was to embark McCain "and/or staff members" at Suva on 26 July and deliver them to TF-61 the following morning. Ghormley's own "staff representatives" would accompany McCain's party, "If practicable." Ghormley himself did not intend to go and perhaps not even furnish any senior staff. To Fletcher that was unacceptable. He swiftly replied that he would hold the conference in his flagship "at earliest opportunity after rendezvous." It was "highly important to confer with McCain and your representative [at the] earliest practicable date." Fletcher, Noyes, and McCain comprised a mini reunion of the class of 1906, but, incredibly, their classmate Ghormley would not take time from his administrative duties to meet his top commanders prior to the most important event in his career. Instead, probably only in response to Fletcher's insistence, he released his chief of staff, Rear Adm. Daniel Callaghan, to fly up from Auckland.[6]

This photo of the USS *Saratoga* (CV-3) was taken 17 September 1942; she was Admiral Fletcher's flagship from July to October 1942.
Courtesy of Naval War College, Capt. Archibald H. Douglas Collection

On the morning of 27 July the attendees assembled in the *Saratoga*. Noyes came from the *Wasp* and Kinkaid from the *Enterprise*. Turner, Vandegrift, Callaghan, and staff accompanied McCain in the *Hull*. The *Sara* did not behave herself during the transfers. When she rolled, McCain ended up "waist deep in the ocean." Fletcher welcomed his guests with a few general remarks, then dismissed all but the top officers and their chiefs of staff to the captain's quarters, where Colonel Maas had a buffet lunch waiting. Afterward the juniors attended separate meetings for intelligence, communications, and related topics. Twining tried to "play dumb" and stay with the brass, but Fletcher addressed him by name and "politely suggested" he get himself some refreshments. In the captain's quarters Twining discovered his boss, Lt. Col. Gerald C. Thomas, "deep in conversation" with Maas, who "was interested in what we had to say."[7]

The senior officers conferred in private for nearly four hours. The only contemporary record appears in the notes Callaghan submitted to Ghormley. Participants who later discussed the conference did so, of course, in full knowledge of the unexpected disaster two weeks later at Savo. Vandegrift's 1964 memoir described Fletcher, whom he had not previously met, as "distinguished looking," but "nervous and tired." He professed surprise Fletcher "appeared to lack knowledge of or interest in the forthcoming operation." Even worse, Fletcher "quickly let us know he did not think it would succeed." To his "arbitrary objections, expressed forcefully, we replied as best we could but obviously failed to make much impression." In 1945 Turner charged that Fletcher "made many remarks against the execution of the plan," blaming him for "initiating the whole thing." Turner "merely" replied they were following King's orders. He told his biographer Dyer he was deeply disappointed with Fletcher but could not appeal given Ghormley's disinterest. "Whom to, and who was I to do so? Fletcher was my old boss, and at that moment the most battle experienced commander in our Navy. It was his judgment and my job to live with it." Perhaps Turner did "live with it," but he never ceased his carping. Capt. Thomas G. Peyton, his chief of staff, characterized the conference to Dyer as "one long bitter argument." He was "amazed and disturbed by the way these two admirals talked to each other" and "never heard anything like it." Questioning "the whole upcoming operation," Fletcher "kept implying that it was largely Turner's brainchild, and mentioning those who planned it had no real fighting experience." Thus he "seemed to be doubting the competence of its parent." Moreover, Fletcher complained the operation was "too hurriedly and therefore not thoroughly planned, the Task Force not trained together; and the logistic support inadequate." Turner just "kept saying 'the decision has been made. It's up to us to make it a success.'"[8]

Two other participants gave very different recollections as to the tone of the conference. Characterized by Dyer as "more used to the sharp give and take during the councils of the naval great" than Peyton, Kinkaid offered a "much calmer view" of a meeting that was "animated rather than stormy." Turner "asked for a lot of things, much of which he didn't get, because they were not in the realm of the possible." At the close of the conference Kinkaid happened to hear Turner ask Vandegrift, "How did I do?" to which Vandegrift replied, "All right." That was Kinkaid's "personal assessment." For his own part Fletcher asserted in 1947 to Hanson W. Baldwin, "At no time was there any friction between Turner and myself." He told Dyer in 1963, "Kelly was no shrinking violet and always spoke his piece in conferences. But there was no bitterness in the discussion. Plenty of opinions [were] vigorously expressed as to what or could be done." Fletcher naively underestimated Turner's rancor and deviousness.[9]

Kinkaid noted the gathering was "somewhat unusual" for a "final conference." The plans were "hurriedly made" and "many details remained to be worked out." Given the scope of the operation, the first U.S. amphibious offensive since 1898, that was a profound understatement. "Some of us were until then," Kinkaid noted, "unaware of the procedure to be worked out." They included Fletcher, whose "lack" of "knowledge" of operational details is perfectly understandable, given he was far away when Turner and Vandegrift did their planning. His supposed disinterest is belied by the searching questions he directed to his new subordinates. Indeed, Fletcher was very interested. Unlike earlier at Pearl, he found himself responsible for a great deal more than the carriers, but being tied to those carriers severely limited his ability to control the rest. Unfortunately Turner, Vandegrift, and Peyton took his queries as personal affronts. Fletcher hurt their tender feelings—hence their laments about "arbitrary objections," the "many remarks against the execution of the plan" and the apparent questioning of the "whole upcoming operation." He exercised his one chance to conduct a thorough and not always polite critique of their plan.[10]

Taking Callaghan aside, Fletcher expressed his pleasure for having "tactical command of the operation." However, he had expected Ghormley "to exercise that function." Comsopac should "not hesitate to change tactical disposition if he thought it necessary," for he "might be in much better position to see the whole picture." Callaghan, though, "Hoped that need for such action would not arise." Fletcher should fly messages ashore to keep Ghormley informed and "promised to do this at every opportunity." Callaghan also told his boss, "We are shy of many of Turner's annexes to his operation order and of Admiral Fletcher's orders." However, they "promised to land all these at Suva on 31 July" for McCain to forward by air to Nouméa.[11]

As Callaghan's notes demonstrate, a great deal was discussed. It is useful here to deal in turn with the five topics most directly related to Fletcher and the carriers and offer the necessary background to understand the decisions that were reached.

DEFINING THE MISSION OF THE CARRIERS

Easily the most contentious of the many issues, at least according to subsequent accounts, was carrier air support for the Amphibious Force. Over the years Turner and the marines condemned Fletcher's statements about the carriers and his later actions off Guadalcanal. To assess the validity of their charges, it is crucial to understand what Fletcher believed at the time, bearing in mind that he claimed Nimitz invoked the same provision regarding carrier employment as at Midway. "You will be governed by the principle of calculated risk which you shall interpret to mean the avoidance of exposure of your forces to attack by superior enemy forces without good prospect of inflicting, as a result of such exposure, greater damage to the enemy." Furthermore, a fundamental transformation in naval power had just taken place. Carriers usurped the prime strategic role of battleships in that their principal opponents were their enemy counterparts, and they should only to be committed to battle in the proper circumstances. Yet the few existing big carriers also had to lead the way to provide air support for an amphibious offensive. That albeit necessary dual role boded great peril, as Japan discovered at Midway, and greatly complicated how the carriers could and should be used in combat.[12]

In a memo prepared for Fletcher on 15 July, Maas appreciated that a swift assault before Japan solidified its hold in the southern Solomons could achieve strategic surprise. Yet success hinged on whether supporting air, both carrier- and land-based, could neutralize "all initial opposition" and enable the Amphibious Force to execute its mission "quickly and neatly." Failure could mean the loss of key assets, carriers and elite marines, and imperil the whole South Pacific. Because the Allies should enjoy a vast initial superiority of strength, Maas judged that surprise, although "very important," was "not absolutely essential" if the enemy gained only a few days warning. "Far more important," he stressed, "in fact probably all-important, is the necessity that *we* not be surprised. Every precaution must be taken against our own force being surprised or trapped." Given Coral Sea and Midway, where Fletcher did the surprising, he comprehended that a "responsible commander" must be prepared should enemy carriers suddenly appear in the Solomons. He later explained, "We all expected they would show up shortly after the landing." Fletcher was one of the few top leaders who anticipated the Japanese would throw in everything they could once they realized the Allies had come back to the Solomons to stay.[13]

Fletcher contemplated two alternatives for employing the carriers. In the first scenario the carriers would pound the target area starting on D-6 or D-5 days and bombard shore positions on D-2 or D-1. That would give sufficient warning for Japan to respond in strength. The second option was to hope for surprise, trusting to shore-based air to reduce the enemy's search capability and darkness to hide the final approach to the target. Carrier air attacks and ship bombardments would start only at dawn on D-Day. "This will involve a much greater risk of loss in both planes and attacking troops," Maas noted, "but will minimize the danger of successful counter-attack by enemy reinforcements before our mission has been accomplished." Fletcher preferred the second alternative. Because of restricted waters between Tulagi and Guadalcanal, carriers could only support the landings from the east off Malaita or southward in the Coral Sea beyond Guadalcanal. Recommending the latter station, Maas considered whether to deploy TF-11 (*Saratoga*) and Noyes's TF-18 (*Wasp*) in concert seventy-five miles south of Tulagi. They would strike ground targets and provide fighter cover for themselves and the distant invasion force. At the same time Kinkaid's TF-16 (*Enterprise*), operating fifty miles east of the other two carriers, would search the northern semicircle and strike should enemy carriers be discovered. In place of three cruisers detached for shore bombardment, Maas recommended reinforcing the main body with the *North Carolina* and two destroyers from TF-16. Also curious if the new battleship could truly enhance a carrier task force, Fletcher consulted the *Saratoga*'s executive officer, Cdr. Cato Glover, an old friend fresh from the Cominch staff, who urged: "Take her. She can be a great help close in with her tremendous AA power." Later on D-Day, if searches and other intelligence proved negative, TF-16 could join attacks against shore targets and hasten the reduction of enemy positions.[14]

Commander Pederson, Fletcher's air staff officer, tackled the organizational and tactical details necessary for the carriers to carry out their assigned tasks. He compiled his preliminary air plan before he knew for certain the *Enterprise* would also participate. Thus he gave much thought to how the *Saratoga* and *Wasp* alone could handle the concurrent missions of air support for the landings, fighter cover for the carriers and invasion forces, searches, and still retain a force in hand if enemy carriers materialized. The limited endurance of U.S. aircraft, particularly fighters, dictated the carriers must remain within eighty miles of the landing beaches during daylight. That would entail a vast shuttling back and forth, working the carriers harder from dawn to dusk than ever before. For D-Day only, Pederson proposed operating all the fighters from the *Wasp* and the dive bombers and torpedo planes from the *Sara*. That redeployment was to take place once the carriers launched their initial D-Day flights and last until late afternoon. If the *Wasp* happened to be sunk or disabled that day, he reckoned most of the fighters should still be aloft. Such radical combinations of carrier air complements had been tried before, but Fletcher wanted to know what Noyes thought before ruling on Pederson's idea.[15]

On 20 July, a week before the conference, Turner submitted his TF-62 task organization and requirements for air support. He created two transport groups: X-Ray (ten transports, six cargo ships) for Guadalcanal, and Yoke (three transports, four high-speed transports) for Tulagi. Fletcher was to supply three heavy cruisers and four destroyers for the X-Ray Group and one light cruiser and two destroyers to Yoke. A group of five DMS high-speed minesweepers and a screening group with three heavy cruisers and eight destroyers would also protect the invasion force. Turner desired one VF squadron and three VSB squadrons for close air support, "With one additional squadron each type [on the] first two hours of D-Day." The transport combat air patrol was to comprise two VF squadrons. "Approximately half of available aircraft" were to be aloft "continuously during daylight." Fletcher replied on 21 July via radio from Tongatabu that "in general" he approved of the plan. He assigned the *Astoria*, *Quincy*, and *Vincennes* and four destroyers to the X-Ray fire support group and the *San Juan* (with Admiral Scott) and two destroyers to Yoke. Crutchley's TF-44 (less the *Salt Lake City*) would comprise the Screening Group. Fletcher would announce during the upcoming planning conference how many planes he would provide. Turner's use of the term "squadrons," rather than the required numbers of planes or sorties, was confusing. The air planners needed more concrete information.[16]

On 21 July, a day that cost the *Saratoga* five F4Fs in crashes, Pederson hitched a ride on the TBF flying dispatches to Tongatabu to brief Noyes and obtain the full version of Sopac Op-Ord 1-42. Via a letter Pederson brought back that afternoon, Noyes responded he knew nothing about the impending operation other than what was in the dispatches and wanted until the twenty-second "to study the set up." In the meantime Pederson updated his draft air plan to include the *Enterprise*. He now recommended keeping all three carriers together and starting at dawn on D-Day farther west than in his previous plan, that is, off the southwest coast of Guadalcanal and about seventy-five miles southwest of Tulagi. From there the carriers could work into the prevailing southeasterly wind and maintain the interval of seventy-five to eighty miles from the target areas. Pederson proposed a carrier formation of TF-11 (*Saratoga*) in the center, with TF-18 (*Wasp*) and TF-16 (*Enterprise*) deployed four to six miles off each quarter. Initially forty-two *Wasp* planes would strike Lunga on Guadalcanal, while thirty-nine *Enterprise* aircraft hit Tulagi. Twenty-two *Saratoga* F4Fs would fly combat air patrol for the carriers and transports, while eight TBFs searched the northern semicircle. An hour after dawn, a second wave of thirty-seven *Sara* planes would attack Guadalcanal, where her air group commander was to coordinate air strikes. At the same time the *Enterprise* would reprise her first Tulagi mission with thirty-one planes and detail her CAG to handle the Yoke attacks. The *Wasp* was to land the *Sara*'s fighters as well as her own, while her SBDs and TBFs flew from the *Saratoga* only for the rest of D-Day. Both carriers would support Lunga and fly combat air patrols, leaving Tulagi to the *Enterprise*. Maas and Schindler rode the 22 July shuttle flight to Tongatabu and delivered the draft air plan to Noyes.[17]

On 24 July Noyes flew out to the *Saratoga* and met with Fletcher for five hours, interrupted only by lunch and the inevitable dart game. Fletcher formally designated him Commander, Air, to take tactical command of the three carrier task groups "when directed." As Noyes explained, he was to run the carriers, "Usually during air operations and the movements preceding and subsequent thereto." Fletcher was self-conscious about his dearth of personal aviation experience. He felt he must take advantage of the presence of an aviator flag officer to handle routine operations while reserving the big decisions for himself. Unfortunately that divided command, as Kinkaid complained, contributed to a "built in" delay for the dissemination of plans. Fletcher's lack of intimate knowledge of aviation was his Achilles' heel as a carrier striking force commander.[18]

A JCL, Noyes had little real aviation experience himself and relied on his own flag captain, Forrest P. Sherman of the *Wasp*. A New Englander like Noyes, Sherman, age forty-six, was intelligent (second in the class of 1918), renowned for his practical and esoteric talents, and also extremely ambitious. Obvious ability put him on the fast track to command. A naval aviator since 1922, from 1937 to 1941 Sherman served as aviation officer for Combatfor and Cincus and in the CNO's War Plans Division, and after December 1941 on the Cominch staff. He took command of the *Wasp* on 31 May at Norfolk. Noyes regarded Forrest Sherman as his de facto chief of staff. Cdr. Bradford E. Grow, the able TF-18 operations officer, acknowledged Noyes "probably received advice from Capt. Sherman more than me." Lt. (jg) Thomas R. Weschler, a *Wasp* junior officer of the deck, remarked that Sherman, once he felt confident the *Wasp* was in good hands, spent half his time as TF-18 chief of staff, a responsibility he took "very seriously." To Weschler, Noyes seemed tentative and unsure of himself. "I thought Admiral Leigh Noyes did not have the big picture, and that Captain Sherman was really the one who was carrying him." Grow commented that although Noyes "delegated authority," he "knew at all times what was going on." Noyes's own small staff worked out the details of decisions he reached with Sherman. Grow recalled: "I never heard Adm. Noyes criticize anyone. It was a pleasure to work for him."[19]

Fletcher and Noyes examined Pederson's idea of temporarily switching the *Sara*'s fighters to the *Wasp* and the *Wasp*'s SBDs and TBFs to the *Sara*. Fletcher even considered putting all one hundred fighters on one carrier and splitting the dive bombers and torpedo planes between the other two flattops. The resulting fighter wing offered the advantage of swift deployment on combat air patrol. He finally rejected the radical concept, "Due to lack of time to test and perfect such an organization." Noyes took the draft plan back to the *Wasp*, where Sherman and Grow reworked the scheme and removed the references to shuffling planes between carriers. The resulting Carrier Aircraft Op-Plan 1-42 provided a "very tight" schedule, specifying the composition and payloads of all flights, as well as exact launch and recovery times. At any given time one carrier was to be ready to launch planes. To Pederson the operations plan resembled a "railroad time schedule." He admired its intricacy, which required hitherto unprecedented carrier cooperation. Forty F4Fs and thirty-three SBDs would open the D-Day attacks against Lunga and Tulagi, while forty-five SBDs in three waves executed follow-up attacks on Tulagi, where initially the marines might face the toughest opposition. The *Enterprise* was to search two hundred miles northward with eight bomb-armed TBFs, while the three carriers retained an "air reserve" of twenty-nine TBFs to attack enemy carriers or reinforce shore strikes as needed. Sherman and Grow labored to complete the draft plan so Noyes could present it on 27 July.[20]

Rear Adm. Leigh Noyes *(left)* and Capt. Forrest P. Sherman, USS Wasp, August 1942. *Courtesy of National Archives (80-G-12786)*

At the conference Turner and his staff got their first look at what the carriers proposed to do for them during the landings. Callaghan observed "some confusion re: details—argument re: air support from CV Task Forces on D day." Although "everyone deplored lack of time to plan carefully and thoroughly," they "saw no out but to whip plans into shape as rapidly as possible." Fletcher recalled in 1947, "Most of the conference was taken up in planning how to arrange our fighter protection over both the landing and the carriers. I believe we modified our plans and I distinctly remember Turner and his staff were very pleased." That must have been the case. Turner never commented adversely about the quantity and quality of the carrier air support on 7–8 August, just that he did not get any on the ninth.[21]

HOW LONG SHOULD THE CARRIERS SUPPORT THE AMPHIBIOUS FORCE?

The length of carrier support for landings was an old bone of contention. In 1934–35 during planning for offensive operations against the Mandates, the marines desired the carriers to stay until their land-based air became established ashore, but naval planners rejected that proposal due to the "risk of immobility." The 5 July Cincpac War Plans summary of Turner's plan stated the planning session at Pearl envisioned carrier air coverage for "about three days," the inference being D-Day, D+1, and D+2. Fletcher certainly thought that was the case. On 15 July Maas urged the landings be completed "as quickly as possible," on "D+1 if at all possible," to permit "early withdrawal" of the three carriers. If not on D+1, the carriers should depart Guadalcanal "no later than the end of D+2." The goal was to "strike suddenly and hard, and as soon as the seizure is accomplished and the landing force firmly established, withdraw task forces from the area." In that regard it is important to cite at length what Fletcher replied to Baldwin in 1947:

> At the time of the conference with Turner and Callahan [*sic*] before the action I do not believe that the length of time the carriers would remain off Guadalcanal was brought up, except perhaps casually. That subject had been covered at some length in a conference between Nimitz, Kelley [*sic*] Turner and me at Pearl. I pointed out to Nimitz that the stay of the carriers to provide the umbrella would be very limited. Nimitz gave me the impression that the landing force would be ashore in two days and could dig in and accept air attacks. At the time of the conference to which you refer I expected to remain off Guadalcanal for three days or perhaps four if the landing was delayed.

Callaghan wrote in the conference minutes: "Task Force must withdraw to South from objective area (i.e. general advanced position) within two days after D-Day! [Callaghan's emphasis]" That he meant three days is confirmed in a message from Ghormley to Fletcher on 2 August: "Am informed you plan to withdraw carrier support from Tulagi prior to Dog plus 3 Day."[22]

Three days of carrier support would have been sufficient had events followed the sequence established at Pearl, where War Plans exuberantly imagined unloading the transports and withdrawing them the same day. Turner's own plans were almost as optimistic. He originally intended to use the Second Marines to occupy Ndeni on D–2 Day but soon proposed postponing the Ndeni phase until late on D+1. The Expeditionary Force would remain together and preserve the chance of achieving surprise during its approach. Turner boldly suggested a "Deceptive and roundabout route so as to arrive at Guadalcanal at the western end of the Island." Having the Santa Cruz Occupation Force (one heavy cruiser, four destroyers, four transports, and one cargo ship) accompany the rest of the Amphibious Force would permit Vandegrift to augment the assault with one battalion to seize sites peripheral to Tulagi harbor. On the evening of D-Day, after retrieving that battalion, the Santa Cruz force would depart for Ndeni. Turner anticipated landing all other troops by the night of D+1 and withdrawing their transports. "If things go well," he explained in a 25 July letter to Fletcher, "it seems likely we may be able to send Transport Division Two [with the Second Marines] to the rear [that is, Ndeni] on the night of D-Day, and probably the rest of the transports out on the night of D plus one Day." Along with the main body of transports would go "about all the Pacific Fleet combatant ships." That did not include Crutchley's TF-44. The plan to release the Ndeni force the first night evidently caught Callaghan by surprise. "This sounds too sanguine," he wrote in his notes, but conceded, "They believe it can be done."[23]

Although Turner thought the seventeen transports and APDs and escorts should not need to stay beyond D+1, his 25 July letter posed a hitherto unrecognized problem that doubtless arose from a dose of Vandegrift reality. "The great difficulty is going to be with the five cargo vessels [the sixth was to go to Ndeni] that might take from three to six days to unload [from early as the end of D+2 to the end of D+5]." Nonetheless, "We will need air protection during this entire period." However, Fletcher "can rest assured that we will get this done as soon as possible." Two days later at the conference Turner proposed the five cargo ships "be anchored as close as possible to beach" while they off-loaded supplies and gear, and that Crutchley's TF-44 (and apparently also the minesweepers) remain behind and screen them. He reduced his estimate of their unloading to four days (D+3) but did not specify the basis behind this new optimism.[24]

Thus Turner expected to withdraw most of the Amphibious Force—the transports and Pacific Fleet cruisers and destroyers—by the evening of the second day, D+1. The smaller component of five cargo ships and Crutchley's TF-44 would remain at least until D+3, but possibly to D+4 or D+5, that is, three to five days later. Turner insisted they have air cover the whole time. The true question was whether Fletcher should (or even could) park the three carriers off Guadalcanal for an uncertain interval until the five cargo ships unloaded and got clear. He responded to Turner, Vandegrift, and Callaghan that the carriers were only going to remain until the end of D+2, that is, three days. Callaghan recorded that fact in his notes, but the length of time Fletcher committed to keeping the carriers off Guadalcanal quickly became misunderstood. Apparently several participants just recalled the "two" in D+2 and erred in thinking that meant two days instead of three.

It is highly significant that Turner's post-battle complaints simply lumped all the troop transports in with the cargo ships and cleverly concealed the fact that he once planned to withdraw them separately. He claimed that from the beginning he made it clear to Fletcher and Callaghan that the whole Amphibious Force, not just one portion of it, must stay off Guadalcanal for four or five days, but Fletcher only offered air protection for two days. That particular charge, of course, constituted the heart of the case against Fletcher's conduct at Guadalcanal. In 1943 Turner informed Adm. Arthur J. Hepburn, who investigated the Savo debacle, how Fletcher "warned" that he "proposed to remain in the area south of Guadalcanal no more than two days." That was despite Turner's urgent plea "to remain as long as possible, as I was certain the transports could not unload in two days." Of course the record shows that up until the afternoon of 8 August (D+1), Turner confidently believed he *could* unload all the transports in two days. Instead he only worried about the cargo ships. In 1945 he claimed in his Amphibious Force administrative history that at the *Saratoga* conference Fletcher asked "how many days it would take to land troops," to which he responded "about five days." Yet Fletcher "stated that he would leave the vicinity of the Solomons after two days because of danger of air attacks against the carriers, and because of the fuel situation." If Turner's account is to be believed, Fletcher showed remarkable prescience by realizing ten days early that several subsequent unforeseen delays in bringing up oil would render the carrier task force short of fuel on 8 August. In fact, Turner all along liberally salted his own recollections with self-serving hindsight. Furthermore, he remarked in his administrative history that Fletcher had vowed, "If the troops could not be landed in two days then they should not be landed," but "in any case, he would depart at that time." No one else charged such cowardly callousness. In 1946 Turner complained to Baldwin, "Fletcher announced that he could not or would not stay there any longer than about forty-eight hours after the landing," but that Turner had "protested and finally said that he more or less had to stay there for at least four days for the ships simply could not be unloaded within forty-eight hours." Again Turner deliberately failed to differentiate between transport ships and cargo ships. It was said after the war that Rear Adm. Donald Ramsey (former commanding officer of the *Hughes* and Hepburn's assistant in the Savo investigation) had claimed that on 27 July Turner privately upbraided Fletcher: "You S.O.B. if you do that [withdraw the carriers] you're yellow." Supposedly Callaghan never heard the comment, so Turner himself had to be its ultimate source. Whether Turner ever actually said any such thing to Fletcher is another matter entirely.[25]

Vandegrift also described Fletcher only agreeing to stay two days. He recalled to Brig. Gen. Samuel B. Griffith that he attempted in vain to get Fletcher to understand that the "permanent lodgment in strength" required "air cover for a minimum of four days" to get the men, their arms, equipment, and supplies "ashore and established." According to Vandegrift's memoir:

> Suddenly Fletcher interrupted Turner to ask him how long he would take to land my troops on Guadalcanal. Turner told him about five days. Fletcher said he was going to leave the area in two days because he refused to risk air attack against his carriers for a longer period. My Dutch blood was beginning to boil, but I forced myself to remain calm while explaining to Fletcher that the days "of landing a small force and leaving" were over. . . . Although Turner heatedly backed me, Fletcher curtly announced that he would stay until the third day [i.e., through D+1]. With that he dismissed the conference.

Twining, who saw Vandegrift immediately after the conference, described him as "deeply disturbed," because Fletcher relegated the amphibious offensive to the status of a "raid" that was unlikely to be successful. Hence Fletcher "would not agree to expose his force for more than forty-eight hours" despite, according to Twining, being "pressed sharply and stoutly by Turner." Fletcher supposedly dismissed Vandegrift's "concerns about the fate of our amphibious forces, especially the fate of the landing force left ashore." Again it can be charged there was a healthy measure of hindsight in these recollections.[26]

A proposed two-day carrier stay, however, appeared in accounts by other carrier leaders. Kinkaid's memoir stated, "Discussion, for the most part, centered around the air support to be provided by the carriers and around the control of air support in the combat area." Turner requested air cover for several days until the troops could be established ashore, but, "Fletcher decided that two days of exposure of CVs was all that calculated risk warranted." Kinkaid had refreshed his memory with Morison and the Naval War College analysis, both of which asserted Fletcher stated the carriers would stay only two days. In 1949, Forrest Sherman recalled that after the *Saratoga* conference: "I am sure that [Noyes] returned with the understanding that carrier air support would be required only two days. That this was unrealistic is now quite apparent, but we had never conducted such an operation before and had much to learn." Noyes commented in 1950 that Fletcher "stated that Admirals King and Nimitz had both told him that they did not wish the carriers kept in the vicinity of Guadalcanal longer than two or three days at the most."[27]

The most influential historical treatments of Guadalcanal reflect the lack of consensus as to what Fletcher actually said regarding his intended stay off Guadalcanal. According to

Morison, Fletcher informed Turner, "He had been ordered not to hold his carrier force within supporting distance of Guadalcanal for more than two days." He cited no source for such an "order." Jeter A. Isely and Philip A. Crowl asserted in 1951 that Fletcher proposed staying four days (to D+3, 10 August) but, "Without warning to either Turner or Vandegrift, he began considering an even earlier withdrawal from the zone of conflict." According to Dyer, Fletcher said he would not "support the Guadalcanal landings for more than two days, that is no later than the morning of Sunday, 9 August 1942," but again offered no documentary support. A careful historian, Richard Frank postulated that Fletcher at first would only stay two days, but "relented" and promised three days after Turner and Vandegrift expressed their indignation. These historians did not have the benefit of the key documents in the Maas and Pederson papers. Nor did they analyze Turner's stated intention to withdraw, by the night of D+1, all but the five cargo ships and Crutchley's TF-44 and assess what effect that declaration might have had on Fletcher's own thinking.[28]

FIGHTERS FOR LUNGA

Another contentious issue for the conference concerned when fighters could be expected to operate from Lunga airfield and whether the carriers would supply them. Marine doctrine declared "every effort should be made" to have marine aircraft participate in the initial landings, ideally from a carrier devoted "solely for their use." On 15 July Maas anticipated that Turner would get the local airfields operational as soon as possible for the marine squadrons that Nimitz was furnishing from Hawaii. "Marines thereby may provide their own air protection for the occupying forces." Two marine squadrons were already in Sopac: VMF-212 (eighteen F4F-3A Wildcats) at Efate and VMO-251 (a marine observation squadron with sixteen F4F-3P Wildcats) at New Caledonia. Cominch also assigned newly formed Marine Air Group (MAG) Twenty-three (thirty-six F4F-4s in VMF-223 and VMF-224 and twenty-four SBD-3 dive bombers in VMSB-231 and VMSB-232). As noted, Nimitz resolved in late June to retain MAG-23 at Pearl until all squadrons were fully equipped and qualified for carrier landings. He assumed he had plenty of time because no airfield in the immediate combat area could be ready to receive planes until at least a week after the landings. By early July, though, it became evident the Lunga airfield neared completion. Had Cincpac felt a sense of urgency, the *Enterprise* could have embarked the better trained of the two VMF squadrons (and its ground crews) and solved a great dilemma.[29]

The auxiliary carrier *Long Island* offered another means of delivering at least part of MAG-23 ready to fly. Again Cincpac saw no reason to hurry. Only on 28 July did he return the *Long Island* to Pearl after delivering planes to Palmyra. Ghormley assumed the *Wasp* carried some MAG-23 planes, but on 11 July Nimitz informed him they were still in Hawaii. Instead, "about" 1 August, the *Long Island* and aircraft transport *Hammondsport* would start south with MAG-23. On 22 July, though, Nimitz temporized. Now just the *Long Island* with one VMF squadron and one VMSB squadron would leave Pearl about 1 August, with the rest of MAG-23 to follow two weeks later. However, no marine ground crews could accompany the planes if they flew directly to Guadalcanal from the *Long Island*, and Sopac had no surplus maintenance personnel.[30]

Concerned by 21 July the Lunga airfield might be ready even sooner than expected, Turner urged McCain to arrange for VMO-251 and VMF-212 to fly to Guadalcanal as soon as possible after the invasion. "Ammunition, fuel and oil will be furnished by this force." Two small merchant ships were to deliver aviation supplies to Lunga on D+1 while PBYs ferried in key members of the ground crew. The two MAG-23 VMF squadrons would replace them in their former bases. Turner failed to take note that without belly tanks, neither squadron could fly the 550 miles to Lunga from Espíritu Santo, the nearest airfield. McCain suggested to Fletcher on 27 July that the carriers furnish belly tanks to enable the marine fighters to reach Lunga. Otherwise they all must all await the *Long Island.* On 28 July Nimitz set 2 August for the *Long Island*'s departure from Pearl with VMF-223 and VMSB-232. Gear and ground personnel would leave a few days later in the slow transport *William Ward Burrows.* At 1100 on 13 August (D+6) the *Long Island* was to be 350 miles east of Guadalcanal and at some later time launch planes to Cactus.[31]

In light of Fletcher's stated intention to withdraw prior to D+3 (10 August), McCain proposed a contingency plan. Assuming the Lunga airfield could receive planes within forty-eight hours, Fletcher was to leave one or two VF squadrons, a move McCain conceded was "undesirable from carrier's point of view." On D+4 on their way out, the carriers could also deliver belly tanks to Maj. Harold W. Bauer's VMF-212 Wildcats on Efate. Bauer could take his fighters to Lunga on D+6 and with the *Long Island* contingent relieve the navy fighters. Ghormley in turn was reluctant to impose restrictive conditions on Fletcher after he and MacArthur specifically warned of the danger to the carriers if they lingered too long off Guadalcanal. On 2 August he radioed Fletcher the essentials of McCain's proposal. If the Lunga field was ready, Fletcher should consider dropping off two fighting squadrons to stay until D+6, when the belly-tank-equipped Efate fighters could join them. At some point, Ghormley did not specify when, the *Long Island* was to fly her fighters to Lunga and then "receive carrier planes for subsequent return to carriers." It must be noted that happy event could not occur on D+6, for the *Long Island* was too slow to get into ferry range that day. If enemy carriers did show up, Fletcher would not even get his fighters right away, for Ghormley added: "Only on contingency no hostile carriers be detected subsequent to landing your fighters these fighters would be immediately released to you." Of course it would be when enemy carriers did show that the carriers would really need those Wildcats.[32]

Dyer dismissed Ghormley's plan as a carrier "strip-tease." Even so, Fletcher did check it out. On 3 August when TF-61 passed through the New Hebrides, four F4Fs delivered belly tanks to Efate to see if they could be installed on Bauer's Wildcats. Maas also dropped in flying a *Saratoga* SBD. Cincpac reported the *Long Island*'s capability for handling aircraft. She could land twelve planes in one cycle, but if the first dozen planes were fighters, another twelve planes could also come on board after the first batch was stowed in the hangar. The figure of twenty-four fighters is significant. According to Pederson, Fletcher was "prepared to send 24 VF to base at Guadalcanal if the field was usable." Major Bauer explained to McCain that installing the belly tanks on the marine F4F-3As would be a ten-day job, even if all fittings were available, which they were not. Instead he hoped the carriers could deliver some F4F-4s for VMF-212 to "fly to the Solomons and use up there until permanent replacements come." McCain wrote a request to Fletcher that after the invasion he dispatch fourteen carrier F4F-4s with belly tanks to Efate. He could either retrieve their pilots with his own SBDs or let them fly Bauer's old marine F4F-3As back to the carriers. Maas had already left for the *Saratoga*, so McCain gave the dispatch to an *Enterprise* pilot. Somehow its delivery was delayed. Only late on 4 August did Kinkaid learn of it via Captain Davis and forward it to Fletcher. Davis himself advised against trading for the non-folding-wing marine F4F-3As, which Bauer confessed were in "awful shape." Due to the "number of operating planes aboard now we would definitely not want any more *non*-folding wing types."[33]

Early on 5 August McCain informed Ghormley, Fletcher, and Turner that belly tanks could not be installed on Bauer's Wildcats. Instead Fletcher should not only leave fighters at Guadalcanal but also fly fourteen more F4F-4s with belly tanks to Efate to allow VMF-212 to reinforce the navy fighters already at Guadalcanal. McCain preferred to retain his marine F4F-3As at Efate and fit them for belly tanks as well. When the *Long Island* finally did send her load of MAG-23 planes to Lunga, she could recover the navy fighters and ultimately return them to the carriers. Dawn on 5 August found TF-61 already nearly three hundred miles west of Efate and steaming directly away. That was too far to ferry the belly tanks to Efate unless Fletcher scrapped the invasion timetable. That was where the fighter issue rested when the landings began. Fletcher would have to see whether indeed the field at Lunga could actually receive fighters, and if the tactical situation might allow him to leave some there.[34]

The Watchtower offensive is accurately described as proceeding on a shoestring. Nothing is truer in that respect than Nimitz's failure to have land-based planes ready to operate from Guadalcanal. Had the *Enterprise* brought VMF-223, already equipped for belly tanks or even just its F4Fs for others to fly, and left it at Efate or Espíritu Santo, the carriers would not have worried about remaining off Guadalcanal to protect that part of the invasion force that could not swiftly unload and depart. Nor would McCain have had to offer harebrained plans to make up for their lack. Yet the successful deployment of VMF-223 (or other fighters) depended on when the marines actually captured the Lunga airfield, readied it for planes, and furnished the necessary fuel, ammunition, and ground crews.

LAND-BASED AIR SEARCH AND ATTACK

The conferees discussed the available shore-based air in MacArthur's Allied Air Forces, Southwest Pacific Area, and McCain's TF-63 with Sopac. MacArthur's airmen were to interdict Rabaul and probe north and northeast of New Guinea toward New Britain, the upper Solomons, and east across the Coral Sea and strike naval forces before they could threaten the Expeditionary Force. The new field at Milne Bay, on the east tip of New Guinea, allowed RAAF medium bombers to overfly the Solomons from Buka southeast to New Georgia. B-17 heavy bombers could strike Rabaul. The navy's original plan depended on preinvasion bomber raids against Rabaul and the auxiliary airfield at Buka, but a strong effort was far beyond the capability of MacArthur's hard-pressed flyers. Now he agreed only to attack Rabaul from D-Day to D+3 and bomb enemy naval forces if detected within 550 miles of Port Moresby. Ghormley warned Nimitz on 29 July, "U.S. forces under MacArthur are not as strong as I expected," and charged that Washington did not recognize that weakness.[35]

Sopac could do nothing about MacArthur's contribution, vital as it was. McCain's TF-63 was another matter. His assets, scattered at New Caledonia, Efate, Fiji, and the soon-to-be completed field at Espíritu Santo, comprised three seaplane tenders with thirty PBY flying boats and an equal number of B-17 bombers. The fast, well-armed B-17s hunted eight hundred miles but required long runways. The lumbering PBYs, flying from sheltered inlets, could go out seven hundred miles. Their principal task was to warn of ships advancing southeast from Rabaul, south from Truk, or southwest out of the Marshalls. Most of McCain's air bases were distant from Guadalcanal, greatly restricting how far his planes could roam beyond the invasion area. Thus he would leapfrog some of his forces to forward positions. Beginning on D–1, PBYs from the tender *McFarland* at Ndeni would search northeast of the Solomons. On D+1 the *Mackinac*'s PBYs would move into Malaita, only eighty miles east of Lunga. McCain presented his operations plan to Fletcher and Turner on 27 July. Turner told Hepburn in 1943 that Fletcher had promised in the event McCain did not complete his searches, the carriers would "fill in for short-range scouting, both morning and late afternoon, to protect against the approach of surface forces." He wrote in 1945 that Fletcher had "agreed to send late in the afternoon of each day [that] the Expeditionary Force was in Guadalcanal[,] scouting planes from the carriers up through the Solomons as far as they could go and return safely before dark." The conference notes do not reflect this, but it makes perfect sense. Fletcher certainly did not want to be surprised. On 29 July he warned McCain of a possible hole in the search plan northeast of the Solomons. By dawn of D-Day an enemy carrier could slip undetected to within strike range of the invasion forces. Fletcher suggested possible remedies that McCain promised to implement if possible. On 31 July McCain's amended operations plan stated, "As soon as practicable[,] daily search tenders and bases will report coverage of assigned sector in percentage including delineation of those parts not searched." That notification was vital if Fletcher must supplement any searches, but as will be seen McCain's reports would not be timely.[36]

At the conference McCain promised thirty B-17s, specially fitted for long-range missions, would pummel the invasion areas on 31 July. He would repeat the raids daily until D–1 with up to nine B-17s, but he soon discovered his air offensive was in jeopardy. In truth only nine B-17s actually had the necessary additional fuel tanks. On the twenty-ninth he cautioned Ghormley that he could only attack on the thirty-first, "With as many of these planes now so equipped." Only rapid progress on the Espíritu Santo airfield, where a B-17 landed successfully on 29 July, got McCain out of a real jam. Beginning on 31 July TF-63 opened a series of modest air strikes against Tulagi and Guadalcanal that kept the equally modest Japanese forces there off balance.[37]

LOGISTICAL WORRIES

In 1963 Fletcher explained to Dyer, "[Turner] and I spent most of our time picking on Dan Callaghan because of the poor logistics situation," especially fuel oil. Ghormley wrote Nimitz on 29 July that of Sopac's many problems, "The big one right now is fuel," and on 2 August, "It is nip and tuck on oil." It is worthwhile examining the state of Sopac's fuel supply, which became such a contentious issue in the early withdrawal of the carriers from Guadalcanal.

On 27 July the *Cimarron* gave some oil to the *North Carolina*, which had hurried out of Tongatabu before fully fueling. Fletcher also intended the *Cimarron* to fuel TF-11 on 28 July and the next day tender the last of her oil to the rest of TF-16. He counted on the *Platte* to refuel TF-18 on 29 July after she returned from Nouméa with oil from the chartered tanker *W. C. Yeager*. Three more tankers were thought to be nearing the area. The *Kaskaskia* was due at Suva on 31 July with a convoy from Pearl, which included the *San Francisco* and destroyer *Laffey* for Noyes and the transport *Zeilin* and cargo ship *Betelgeuse* urgently required by Turner. Likewise the second installment of West Coast chartered tankers, the *Esso Little Rock* and *E. J. Henry*, was to reach Nouméa on 2 August.[38]

Because TF-61 and TF-62 would no longer pass near Nouméa on their approach to the Solomons, the oil coming in from the West Coast was needed instead at Fiji and Efate. On 27 July Fletcher recommended to Callaghan that one incoming chartered tanker be diverted to Fiji to refill fleet oilers and the other proceed directly to Efate to fuel destroyers. Once the *Cimarron* was empty, he sent her to Nouméa to secure the balance of the *W. C. Yeager's* oil and that of the RAN auxiliary oiler *Bishopdale* (total ninety thousand barrels) and rejoin TF-61 off Efate. He also asked that the *Kanawha* and the ammunition ship *Rainier* advance from Tongatabu to meet TF-62 on 30 July in the Fiji group. Turner likewise requested the *Kaskaskia*, *Zeilin*, and *Betelgeuse* from the Pearl convoy join him there that same day instead of continuing to Suva. Ghormley concurred and issued the necessary orders on 28 July. They rerouted the *E. J. Henry* to arrive 1 August at Suva and the *Esso Little Rock* at Efate on the second. By that time the *Cimarron*, with the last of Nouméa's oil, should already have found TF-61 at Efate, and the refilled *Platte* and *Kaskaskia* "presumably" would have left for Nouméa, where they would wait until summoned.[39]

Callaghan had queried Fletcher and Turner whether in light of the enemy buildup D-Day might be advanced. Both "strongly and earnestly" said no, citing "fueling difficulties" and the need to conduct rehearsals in Fiji. "Much argument" ensued "at this point," Callaghan wrote Ghormley, "but [they] reiterated [their] recommendation." That was especially telling, for Ghormley had reason to believe Japan "will commence some operations on 29 July from New Britain area." He questioned whether Fletcher could dispense with phase one, the rehearsal, and start the invasions early. Fletcher responded on 28 July, via a message flown to Suva, that "irrespective of value exercise of phase one this force will be short estimated more than fifty thousand barrels after emptying *Platte* and *Cimarron* on 31 July." It was "imperative that ships depart [Fiji] area fully fueled and that they be topped off enroute from *Kaskaskia* and *Cimarron*." Clearly Fletcher (and Turner) now expected the *Kaskaskia* to join the task force off Fiji instead of continuing to Nouméa. As will be shown that did not occur. For his own part Turner agreed D-Day could not be advanced. "This force urgently requires full preparation period. State of readiness of force lower than expected. Strongly advise no change in plan."[40]

On 28–30 July Fletcher's three carriers marked time south of Fiji while Turner conducted three days of landing rehearsals. The carriers only participated on the last day to test the draft air plan, flying simulated strikes against the training area forty to fifty miles north. In the meantime Fletcher attended to logistics and refined his plans. TF-11 spent much of the twenty-eighth drawing oil from the *Cimarron*. The next day was Kinkaid's turn, but there was not enough oil for the *North Carolina*. The *Cimarron* and a destroyer then left to secure the rest of Nouméa's supply and catch up with TF-61 at Efate during the run to the Solomons. The *Platte* likewise reappeared on 29 July with her load of Nouméa fuel and tended to Noyes's TF-18. She reserved the last of her oil for TF-62, which also got some fuel from the *Kanawha*. Turner certainly counted on the *Kaskaskia* for more oil on the way to the objective, but on 29 July Ghormley cautioned that her convoy was now twenty-five hours behind schedule. He directed Turner to set a new rendezvous for 31 July. That delay was still acceptable, because Turner did not intend to leave Koro until late that day. On 30 July Comsopac told him to release the *Kanawha* to Suva to refill from the *E. J. Henry* but to hold the *Platte* and *Rainier* and forward both with escort to Nouméa. Advancing the empty *Platte* to where oil was no longer available did not make much sense, but Fletcher and Turner could accept that action if the *Kaskaskia* appeared by 1 August and the chartered tanker *Esso Little Rock* reached Efate the next day as planned. They would be sorely disappointed on both scores.[41]

King stressed to Ghormley the "utmost importance" of not postponing D-Day beyond 7 August. He even hoped "this date may be anticipated, if possible, in order that enemy not be given time to perfect installations now under construction in objective areas for use against us." Ghormley assured him on 30 July, "Every effort has been and is being made to comply for reasons you have indicated." Early on 2 August he told Fletcher that on 3 August he would announce the seventh as Dog-Day, "Unless you previously inform me impossible to meet that date." Receiving no objection, Ghormley did so. The time for preparation rapidly neared its end. The fight to reclaim the Solomons was about to begin.[42]

CHAPTER 23

From Fiji to Guadalcanal

TASK FORCE PLANS

On 30 July Fletcher activated TF-61 Op-Ord 1-42 dated 28 July 1942. Following the task organization Ghormley specified in Sopac Op-Plan 1-42, he divided TF-61 into two huge task groups: TG-61.1 (Air Support Force) under Noyes and Turner's TG-61.2 (Amphibious Force). However, the old task force numbers continued to be used interchangeably. In turn Noyes's Air Support Force comprised three task units:

- TU-61.1.1 (Fletcher): *Saratoga*; heavy cruisers *Minneapolis*, *New Orleans*; destroyers *Phelps*, *Farragut*, *Worden*, *Macdonough*, *Dale*
- TU-61.1.2 (Kinkaid): *Enterprise*; battleship *North Carolina*; heavy cruiser *Portland*; light cruiser *Atlanta*; destroyers *Balch*, *Maury*, *Gwin*, *Benham*, *Grayson*
- TU-61.1.3 (Noyes): *Wasp*; heavy cruisers *San Francisco*, *Salt Lake City*; destroyers *Lang*, *Sterett*, *Aaron Ward*, *Stack*, *Laffey*, *Farenholt*

The operations order accounted for all the destroyers that might join prior to the invasion, but not all did.[1]

Fletcher's operations order described the mission of TF-61 in the broadest terms: seize, occupy, and defend Tulagi and adjacent positions, as well as the Santa Cruz Islands. The role of Noyes's Air Support Force was tactical support to the Amphibious Force en route to the Tulagi area, air support "on D Day and subsequently," defense of the carriers, and "air searches as seems advisable or as ordered." Fletcher directed the Amphibious Force to depart the Fijis on the evening of 1 August, advance northwest at twelve knots through the southern New Hebrides to a point 420 miles south of the southwestern tip of Guadalcanal, and turn north to the invasion area. "On departure of carriers" after conclusion of the landings, Turner was to call on McCain's TF-63 for "special aircraft missions." All ships were to fuel to capacity before leaving Fiji and later top off the short-legged destroyers, high-speed minesweepers, and high-speed transports. The *Enterprise* and *Wasp* would furnish aircraft director teams to Turner in the transport *McCawley* (X-Ray Squadron) at Guadalcanal and *Neville* (Yoke Squadron) at Tulagi, and the *Saratoga* would provide an FDO for the *Chicago* in the Screening Group. On 30 July Maas delivered Ghormley's copy of the TF-61 operations order to Suva for McCain to forward, but Ghormley did not receive it until September and blamed Fletcher.[2]

Turner's TF-62 Operation Plan A3-42 (30 July 1942) laid out the procedures and timetable for the invasions and treated in great detail ship formations and movements, debarkation schedules, gun and bombing targets, and communications. Subsequently Admiral Crutchley, commander of the Screening Group, devised deployment plans for his cruisers and destroyers to protect the landing force. Turner's "Attack Force Retirement Plan" reflected his desire to detach the Santa Cruz Occupation Force (heavy cruiser *Quincy*, four destroyers, four transports, and one cargo ship) on D-Day. He "tentatively planned" beginning the night of D+1 to withdraw Admiral Scott's "AP Group" (one light cruiser, two destroyers, five high-speed minesweepers, and nine transports) to Nouméa. Crutchley's "AK Group" of five cargo ships and old TF-44 (heavy cruisers *Australia*, *Canberra*, and *Chicago*, one light cruiser, and nine destroyers) was to pull out "about D plus 4 days." It is interesting that Turner omitted heavy cruisers *Astoria* and *Vincennes*. Crutchley, for one, assumed they would go out with Scott. The four APDs of Transdiv Twelve were also not listed as departing. Instead, they were to fuel on D-Day from the big transports, then re-embark the First Marine Raider Battalion (on 7 August if possible) and be ready to conduct as yet unspecified raids "as required" in the Solomons. Turner likewise signaled his intention to land his Amphibforsopac headquarters at Guadalcanal at some future date, ostensibly to oversee building the naval base, but he hankered to run those raids and lead troops in battle. Of course Turner's retirement schedule depended on events proceeding fairly close to plan, but it also meant that if Fletcher indeed thought things were going well, he could reasonably expect Turner to adhere to it.[3]

If the affairs of the Amphibious Force seemed settled by 1 August, fervent discussion still raged as to how the carriers should be employed. Kinkaid in particular objected to the plan. In line with the tactical thought favored by most senior carrier aviators, his flag captain Davis in the *Enterprise* deeply distrusted concentrating the carriers, even as individual task units deployed five miles apart, let alone the multi-carrier formation Fletcher personally advocated. Kinkaid recommended each carrier be separated by at least fifty miles. The initial carrier attack against Tulagi and Guadalcanal should be doubled in size to knock out the opposition as quickly as possible and free the aircraft for other tasks. Each carrier task unit should operate independently, even choose its own ground support targets "instead of objectives requested by Comamphib [Commander, Amphibious Force] and control by him in AP area." Each carrier would also direct her own combat air patrol. Kinkaid and Davis worried that enemy carriers, in combination with strong air opposition from Rabaul and Buka, might intervene in the landings. They sought greater flexibility for each carrier group to conduct its own defense and counterattack. Noyes bristled that Kinkaid's suggestions were "either not practical in my opinion or contrary to agreements made at conference of force commanders and approved by [Fletcher]." Had Turner known Kinkaid hoped to limit his control over air support missions, he would have been livid. Noyes set a meeting for the "air representatives of carrier captains and TF commanders" the following morning in the *Wasp*.[4]

Rear Adm. Thomas C. Kinkaid, front row, second from left, and TF-16 staff, July 1942.
Courtesy of U.S. Navy, via Col. W. W. Smith Jr.

Meanwhile, Kinkaid did not relent. On 2 August before the meeting he wrote Noyes (copy to Fletcher) to propose more radical changes in plan. All three carriers should not approach Guadalcanal from the southwest. "I believe this force will be sighted prior to D–2 day (if it has not already) by either subs or aircraft and that we should have an alternate plan that provides for one CV operating to the N.E. [of the] Solomon Islands." That carrier should deploy "about 100 miles north of Tulagi to eastward of Santa Isabel Island, keeping far from the other carriers but the same distance from Tulagi." That offered "certain advantages that are worthy of careful consideration." The lone carrier's search would augment reconnaissance north of the Solomons, her planes could knock out seaplane bases on Malaita and Santa Isabel, and her fighters intercept inbound bombers. Equally important to Kinkaid, such a separation "provides for dispersion of our CV's which is considered most desirable in view of probable contact with enemy search planes as early as Dog minus 3 day." In that event "we may expect enemy CV to disrupt our schedule." The northern carrier force "could intercept enemy aircraft carriers which might otherwise approach Tulagi area undetected." Kinkaid also voiced concern should the carriers adhere to the original plan. Because searchers could appear as early as 4 August, he must know if the *Enterprise* had the authority as the sole fighter director carrier to break radio silence and intercept bogeys "at any time from D–3 day on." There should be additional strikes on D-Day between dawn and when the troops actually started landing. "We have a strong force and can deliver a heavy first blow." Kinkaid explained in his postscript that he was "trying to make constructive suggestions *before* [his emphasis] the final plan is made. When the plan is decided upon I am all for it regardless."[5]

Instead of meeting in the *Wasp*, Noyes flew over to the *Saratoga* on 3 August to confer with Fletcher. Unfortunately the available sources are silent as to what they discussed, but their main objection to Kinkaid's revisions can be surmised. Two carriers could not support a third 150 miles away. Worse, that separation would be in the direction the Japanese carriers would likely appear. The detached carrier might merely serve to give warning before she was sunk. Fletcher and Noyes justly refused to disperse their carriers. On 4 August Noyes issued Air Operation Plan 2-42 that would be in force on D-Day. All three carriers would operate together southwest of Guadalcanal. Noyes added nine dive bombers to the opening strikes to increase the total to 127 planes and doubled the SBDs attacking Lunga to thirty-six. Acknowledging increasing fears the carriers might be spotted on the way in, he raised the total combat air patrol over the carriers to twenty-four F4Fs at the expense of the transports. To compensate, he reinforced the number of SBDs assigned to support the Amphibious Force. Throughout D-Day each sector was to have nine dive bombers and four fighters continuously available for ground support. Except for one flight of eight *Saratoga* TBFs earmarked for an attack mission, he held the other thirty TBFs for "scouting or attack as dictated by last minute developments." The revised plan also improved readiness for emergency launchings and made it easier for the carriers to keep close together. Including the combat air patrol over the carriers and transport areas, at least thirty to thirty-six fighters and twenty-seven to thirty bombers would be aloft at any one time. Pederson commented, "Each carrier knew exactly what was required and the plan worked very smoothly during the actual operation."[6]

THE APPROACH

On 31 July the two task groups loitered south of Fiji tying up loose ends. Ghormley himself was in the process of switching his headquarters from Auckland to the *Argonne* at Nouméa. Turner evaluated the rehearsals as "rather unsatisfactory," but judged them useful. Vandegrift called the exercises "a bust." Pederson's candid opinion was "in so far as the carrier air force was concerned they were a waste of time." TF-62 spent that day and the morning of 1 August draining the *Kanawha* and *Platte* and rearming from the *Rainier*. Ghormley changed his mind about sending the *Platte* to Nouméa and told Turner to dispatch her to Suva along with the *Rainier* and *Kanawha* to replenish when the *E. J. Henry* arrived. However, he neglected to forward the filled *Kaskaskia* to Turner. By then TF-62 left the vicinity of Koro minus the three vital ships from the Pearl convoy. The *Kaskaskia*'s absence prevented Turner from refueling his destroyers. He radioed Ghormley she "is now required," and that it was "most urgent" the *Zeilin* and *Betelgeuse* also report to TF-62. "Otherwise Dog Day should be deferred." On the evening of 1 August Fletcher and Turner started westward from one hundred miles south of Fiji. Fletcher took the Air Support Force out ahead, intending to fuel the *Saratoga*, the destroyers, and if possible the cruisers on 3 August while Turner caught up.[7]

The convoy that included the *Kaskaskia*, *Zeilin*, *Betelgeuse*, *San Francisco*, and *Laffey* finally reached Suva on the afternoon of 1 August. That night the *Zeilin* and *Betelgeuse*, escorted by two of Turner's destroyers, left for TF-62, but without the *Kaskaskia*. The *San Francisco* departed Suva the next day after fueling and joined TF-18 on 4 August, but the

Laffey ran aground and had to return to Pearl for repairs. Inexplicably Ghormley had not advanced the *Kaskaskia* to Turner along with the others, but kept her at Suva. That was despite McCain's explicit warning that the *W. C. Yeager* and *Bishopdale* at Nouméa had in fact only sixty-five thousand barrels for the *Cimarron*, instead of the ninety thousand Fletcher expected. The logistical plan unraveled further when the *E. J. Henry*, the chartered tanker Ghormley diverted to Suva, did not show up on 1 August as directed. Thus the *Platte* could not replenish her cargo. With the *Kaskaskia* unavailable during the approach, Turner's only source for additional oil was the *Esso Little Rock*, due on the second at her new destination of Efate. Therefore he sent sixteen short-legged ships ahead to fuel there beginning the morning of 3 August. That dawn he was gratified when the *Zeilin* and *Betelgeuse* finally caught up, but he learned soon after that the *Esso Little Rock* never appeared. No one knew where she was. The thirsty ships had no choice but to rejoin TF-62.[8]

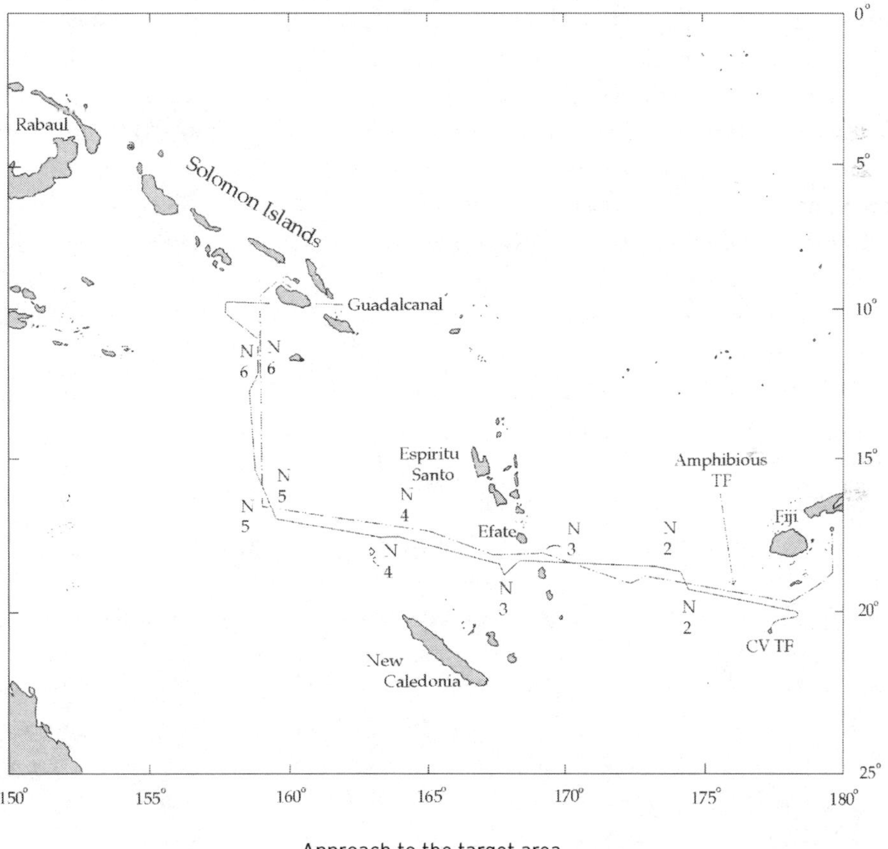

Approach to the target area

On 3 August, as the carriers passed forty miles south of Efate, Fletcher gladly sighted the *Cimarron* on schedule and started fueling, first the greedy *Saratoga* to 70 percent, then the destroyers. Because the *Cimarron* brought much less fuel than anticipated, he could not top off his destroyers—a deficiency that loomed large in the next several days. For example, the *Grayson* refueled only to 85 percent, the *Gwin* 82 percent. Because Fletcher could not fill his ships, oil became his "main consideration during the run from the Fijis to the Solomons." Kinkaid reckoned on 4 August his heavy ships had fuel for three days at fifteen knots, plus four days at twenty-five knots, but that the destroyers had only three days at fifteen knots, plus two days at twenty-five knots. It would take nearly three days at fifteen knots just to get to the target area. As will be seen Kinkaid's fuel estimates were too pessimistic, but they were what he provided Fletcher. Turner stressed to Dyer, "Enroute from Koro to the Solomons my big worry was OIL, OIL, OIL [Dyer's emphasis]." To get him off the hook, Fletcher flew a message to Efate recommending Ghormley send the oilers at Suva to Efate or Nouméa "immediately." If Turner could not get fuel at Efate, his "top off situation may be serious."[9]

On 4 August, still with no word of the *Esso Little Rock*, Turner gave nearly all of his destroyers, high-speed minesweepers, and high-speed transports some oil from his own transports and cargo ships. Fletcher helped by sparing the last of the *Cimarron*'s load for the RAN light cruiser *Hobart* and two of Turner's destroyers. On the evening of 4 August Fletcher released the empty *Cimarron* and destroyer *Aaron Ward* to return to Nouméa, where the *Esso Little Rock* might have gone if she followed her original orders. The fuel situation grew even more complex that day. The Australian fleet oiler *Bishopdale* hit a friendly mine while leaving Nouméa to secure more oil in Brisbane. Although she did not suffer severe damage, she was no longer available. After dropping the ball, Ghormley belatedly looked into sending the *Kaskaskia* directly out to fuel Turner, but by that time no escort was at hand. The valuable fleet oiler had to wait at Suva until 5 August when the destroyer *Perkins* arrived. Then she would accompany the *Platte*, *Rainier*, and *Perkins* to Nouméa. The *E. J. Henry* finally began transferring oil to the *Platte* only at noon on 4 August, three days later than anticipated.[10]

The third installment of chartered tankers intended for Nouméa all cleared San Pedro by 18 July, with anticipated arrivals on 12–15 August. On 1 August, citing Fletcher's warning of fuel shortages, Nimitz directed Calhoun (Comserforpac) to dispatch at the "earliest practicable date" two "big, fast" chartered tankers from San Pedro to Nouméa to supplement already scheduled deliveries. They were to reach Nouméa by 25 August, about a week before the fourth regular group of chartered tankers. Moreover, fleet oiler *Sabine* should be in Samoa by the thirteenth. Even so, Ghormley, with ample reason to doubt the timely arrival of chartered tankers, perceived another shortage of oil looming for Sopac in mid month. On 4 August he secured diversion of a Wellington-bound tanker to Nouméa on 14 August.[11]

Fourth August, when TF-61 passed north of New Caledonia into the Coral Sea, was the first day the enemy search might make contact. Fletcher timed his penetration of the Tulagi air umbrella after its searchers should have started home. The *Saratoga* deployed combat air patrol fighters thirty miles north in the danger zone. Several suspicious radar contacts turned out to be B-17s. Slonim's monitoring of radio messages gave Fletcher no reason to believe he was detected. At sunset the task force was 530 miles southeast of Tulagi. Ironically that day the Japanese missed a huge opportunity to uncover the whole invasion force. Two experimental Kawanishi Type 2 flying boats staged through Tulagi for long-range reconnaissance. One flying boat scouted Fiji. The second flew along the New Hebrides chain toward Efate, then south to New Caledonia, up along its coast, and back north to Tulagi. Only bad weather and very bad luck prevented the premature discovery of TF-61.[12]

If being sighted on 4 August was a remote possibility, the failure on 5 August to detect TF-61 less than five hundred miles from Tulagi greatly surprised Fletcher and his cohorts. The weather started clear, with scattered clouds that thickened during the afternoon. That morning Turner stopped his huge convoy to allow the *Zeilin* to transfer seventeen newly graduated ensigns to other ships in TF-62. He risked the maneuver despite the threat of subs, which Crutchley certainly took seriously. Also worried about subs, Fletcher ordered Turner, "Get underway immediately." He recalled to Dyer: "I just figured that Kelly was punch drunk, and my short despatch would snap him out of it. When I next saw him . . . we laughed together about the incident, and he admitted he might not have been very bright. But he still said there were no Jap submarines anywhere around." By 1100 Turner got his mass of ships pointed northward. At noon the carriers followed. By sunset Tulagi was less than four hundred miles away. That night Fletcher started staying on the *Sara*'s flag bridge twenty-four hours a day.[13]

On the morning of 5 August the *Esso Little Rock* finally showed up at Suva after a baleful miscue. She reached Efate early on the morning of 4 August, two days late, but one of Turner's destroyers, the *Wilson*, quite incorrectly told her to clear off. The *Esso Little Rock* steered east to Suva in Fiji. There she contributed some of her cargo to the *Platte*. The *Perkins* came into Suva the afternoon of the fifth and left the same evening for Nouméa with her little convoy. The empty *Cimarron* and *Aaron Ward* also headed to Nouméa after having fueled TF-61 off Efate. Because the *Esso Little Rock* turned up at Suva, they would find no oil at Nouméa. Thus all the careful plans for the logistical support of TF-61 miscarried due to Ghormley's failure to advance the *Kaskaskia* to TF-62, the tardy appearance of the two chartered tankers, and the paucity of escorting destroyers in Sopac. Nimitz took note of the "fuel trouble" in Sopac and shrewdly observed, "The trouble seems in distribution rather than a lack of fuel." Fletcher would lack ready access to fuel when he really needed it, with portentous results.[14]

Thursday, 6 August, was the crucial day of the approach, as the two huge task groups, a dozen miles apart, steadily advanced north toward Guadalcanal. The sprawling Expeditionary Force could hardly avoid enemy searchers, but dawn providentially brought heavy overcast with frequent squalls and haze. Fletcher was greatly relieved. He had fully expected to fight his way through air strikes to reach the objective—something often forgotten when historians considered the initial Allied surprise. Noyes assumed tactical command of the Air Support Force and specified the maneuvers to bring the carriers to the predetermined launch position seventy-five miles southwest of Tulagi an hour prior to dawn on 7 August, D-Day. McCain worried a small enemy detachment believed on Malaita might interfere with the *Mackinac* when she advanced there on D-Day to service PBYs. Therefore Noyes directed the eight *Saratoga* TBFs already reserved for a D-Day strike to attack Malaita and a point on southeast Florida Island. To increase the impact of the opening strikes, he assigned seventeen more TBFs to bomb Lunga and Tulagi an hour after sunrise. At the same time eight *Enterprise* TBFs were to search west to northeast two hundred miles to cover the Solomons up past New Georgia, Santa Isabel, and beyond. Six other *Enterprise* TBFs waited with torpedoes to attack whatever the search might turn up.[15]

At Fletcher's express order, TG-61.1 took the calculated risk of flying no searches on 6 August so as not to alert the Japanese to the presence of carrier planes. Noyes later called that "one of the most important factors in the surprise." Two flights of ten fighters patrolled forty miles ahead to watch for snoopers. During the late morning, radar detected a bogey passing twenty-five miles east, but cloud cover was such that Turner's convoy was not sighted. That afternoon the combat air patrol tried unsuccessfully to find four other contacts discovered on radar. One, thought perhaps a search plane on its return leg to Tulagi, closed to ten miles when visibility barely exceeded one mile. Slonim's team heard no frantic squawks on known enemy radio frequencies. TF-61 remained undiscovered. That fortunate happenstance offered the Allies an unforeseen but tremendous advantage at the outset of the campaign. At dawn three flying boats left Tulagi to cover the southern sector. The center aircraft passed very close to TF-61 about 0800 but missed it in the overcast. The western aircraft relented after only 370 miles because of poor visibility. Had weather permitted it to fly the mission as briefed, it could hardly have missed the spread-out TF-61. Afternoon radar contacts must have been U.S. shore-based search planes. Turner reconfigured TF-62 into X-Ray and Yoke squadrons. By sunset Guadalcanal loomed only eighty-five miles northeast, with Tulagi fifty miles beyond. After dark the three carriers altered course northwest at twenty-two knots, then at 2230 turned north to the initial point. They wielded 234 operational aircraft (ninety-eight fighters, ninety-six dive bombers, and forty torpedo bombers). At 2250 light cruiser *San Juan*, the lead ship of the Yoke Group, swung northeast to clear the western tip of Guadalcanal before turning eastward toward Tulagi. Fifteen minutes later the X-Ray Group, bound for Lunga on Guadalcanal, executed the same maneuver. TF-61 was ready to begin the first Allied counteroffensive of the Pacific War. Ghormley exhorted Fletcher, Turner, and McCain, "Electrify the world with news of a real offensive," and "Sock 'em in the Solomons."[16]

THE INTELLIGENCE PICTURE AT THE OUTSET

During the Expeditionary Force's approach, Fletcher kept a close eye on the intelligence estimates of enemy strength and likely intentions furnished by Nimitz, Ghormley, and MacArthur. It is useful to compare the portrait painted by intelligence just prior to the attack with the true Japanese situation.

Turner and Vandegrift judged the First Marine Division (Reinforced) of nineteen thousand men easily strong enough for the job. On 26 July Comsopac intelligence placed some three thousand Japanese troops on Guadalcanal, of whom one thousand were construction workers. Turner's 30 July operations plan raised the Lunga total to 5,275, including a reinforced regiment, along with 1,850 men defending Tulagi. That gave Vandegrift pause and certainly validated his decision to flank rather than storm Lunga. The defenders actually numbered twenty-eight hundred men, but only 250 were combat troops. Nine hundred sailors, including many service personnel, were deployed on or around Tulagi.[17]

The effectiveness of Japanese shore-based aviation rested on its strength, utilization of forward air bases on Buka, Bougainville, and Guadalcanal, and its ability to absorb the fury of MacArthur's interdiction. Startling new intelligence on 29 July put six land-based Zero fighters at Lunga. McCain's modest strikes against Tulagi and Lunga, however, encountered only a few Zero-type float fighters. By 6 August it was evident that no land planes yet advanced there, to the great relief of TF-61. MacArthur's final estimate was 139 planes (fifty-six fighters, thirty-eight bombers, twenty-four flying boats, and twenty-one float planes) on New Britain and in the Solomons, and thirty more aircraft in New Guinea. That estimate was close to the mark. On 7 August the 5th Air Attack Force numbered 129 operational planes, including thirty-one delivered the previous day by the auxiliary carrier *Yawata Maru*. Rabaul had thirty-nine fighters (plus twenty being assembled), thirty-two land attack planes, sixteen carrier bombers, two land reconnaissance planes, and four flying boats. Seven flying boats and nine float fighters were at Tulagi, but actually there were no planes on New Guinea. The first flight of nine new medium bombers was already on its way from Tinian to Rabaul.[18]

Ever since the Battle of the Coral Sea, Allied intelligence placed the 6th Cruiser Division (four heavy cruisers), the 18th Cruiser Division (two old light cruisers), and the 6th Destroyer Squadron (one old light cruiser and a dozen aging destroyers) around Rabaul, along with about eight subs and two seaplane tenders. That was correct, except after 14 July the destroyers operated as separate divisions. By the end of July radio intelligence revealed the commander of the new Eighth Fleet had come south. By 5 August Ghormley listed the naval force at Rabaul as three or four heavy cruisers and four light cruisers of the 6th and 18th Cruisers Divisions, along with four to six divisions of destroyers and five sub divisions, including some operating northeast of Australia. In fact Admiral Mikawa, the Eighth Fleet commander, reached Rabaul on 30 July. He concentrated on reinforcing the Buna lodgment with his five heavy cruisers (the *Chōkai* plus the 6th Cruiser Division), three old light cruisers, destroyers, and subchasers. On 6 August one light cruiser and two destroyers left with a Buna convoy, while all five heavy cruisers prepared to sail on 7 August from Kavieng on New Ireland northwest of Rabaul. Three would support the Buna convoy, and two would join the two light cruisers and a destroyer at Rabaul. Four submarines patrolled off Port Moresby and northeast Australia, while five I-boats returned to Truk after prowling the same area.[19]

Of far more immediate importance to Fletcher than any surface strength at Rabaul was the location of the carriers. Intelligence placed them in homeland waters, either in port or training at sea, although the *Zuikaku* might have started south to Singapore. On 24 July Ghormley averred there was "no evidence of carrier support" in the Rabaul area. A week later Cincpac intelligence had Japanese carriers "conducting exercises." Ghormley sounded a cautionary note. The carriers, although "believed in home waters," had "adopted same communication practices" encountered prior to the attack on Pearl Harbor and the battles of Coral Sea and Midway. On 5 August Cincpac still placed the Japanese carriers "in home waters probably in port." Ghormley concurred, but again observed, "Some indications of pending operations." On the evening of 6 August Sowespac reported its air search planes sighted a seaplane tender and three destroyers northwest of Rabaul. Shortly after midnight on 7 August MacArthur declared that photos showed the supposed tender was actually a converted carrier. Cincpac correctly concluded it was an auxiliary carrier transporting planes to Rabaul but did not bother to tell Fletcher. In fact she was the *Yawata Maru*. Fletcher was not unduly concerned but kept in mind the presence of a small carrier in the Rabaul area.

He would learn in the next three weeks that radio intelligence was far from infallible. Common sense compelled him not just to rely completely on the vagaries of radio intelligence but take necessary steps to prevent enemy carriers from surprising him in the Solomons.[20]

Japanese naval intelligence proved a nonfactor in predicting future Allied moves. Aware of sporadic air attacks on Guadalcanal and Tulagi, Mikawa queried Inoue on 23 July whether the United States might invade the Solomons prior to mid August, when the first Zero fighters were to deploy at Lunga. "Absolutely not!" Inoue responded. The high command, Yamamoto included, blithely discounted any major Allied counteroffensive before the autumn of 1943. Thus Tokyo was not perturbed on 1 August when air searches in the Bay of Bengal revealed the extent of Eastern Fleet diversionary demonstrations against the Andaman and Nicobar Islands. Aware at least one large convoy left the West Coast in early July, Japanese intelligence postulated it merely reinforced Australia. Even the Eighth Fleet staff agreed the Allies bombed the Solomons and Tulagi merely to hinder airfield construction. Consequently Mikawa bent his efforts toward securing the supply route to Buna and supporting the assault on Port Moresby. The discovery on 3 August of the new Allied airfield at Rabi on Milne Bay at the eastern tip of New Guinea elicited planning for a massive bombing mission, set for 7 August by the 5th Air Attack Force. Mikawa assumed this powerful strike would go a long way in neutralizing the troublesome airstrip. In fact the attack never went forward because of much more urgent business in the supposedly somnolent Solomons.[21]

CHAPTER 24

The Watchtower Landings

THE OPENING MOVE

An hour before dawn on 7 August, Dog Day, Fletcher's three TF-61 carriers (with Noyes, CTG-61.1, in tactical command) closed Point Victor, thirty miles west of Guadalcanal. The main Watchtower objectives, Lunga on the big island's central coast and Tulagi eighteen miles north, were sixty to seventy-five miles northeast of the carriers. The waning moon shone feebly in the clear skies, but a dark wall of clouds barred the way to the target. In fact the door was wide open, and the key components of the invasion force had already come in. After rounding the west tip of Guadalcanal, the two parts of Turner's invasion force (TG-61.2) had passed on opposite sides of the mountainous mass of Savo. Scott's Yoke Group aimed for Tulagi nestled within the south coast of Florida Island, while Turner's own X-Ray Group cut directly across the large coastal bight bound for Lunga Point.[1]

Fletcher's own TU-61.1.1 (*Saratoga*) constituted the point of the arrowhead, with Kinkaid's 61.1.2 (*Enterprise*) five miles off its port quarter and Noyes's 61.1.3 (*Wasp*) in the corresponding slot to starboard. "Blue flashes from engine exhausts flickered and burned—first only here and there, but all at once as if at the flip of a massive switch they covered two-thirds of each flight deck." More than one hundred aircraft noisily warmed up on deck. Promptly at 0530 the carriers swung southeast into the eighteen-knot wind. The air operations plan called for simultaneous dawn attacks by ninety-three aircraft (forty-four fighters, forty-eight dive bombers, and one torpedo plane). The *Enterprise*'s initial deck load included eight fighters for screen combat air patrol over the distant cruisers and transports. Inevitably in the darkness given inexperienced aviators and three carriers in close proximity, the rendezvous miscarried. Flight leaders gathered whom they could and headed out to their assigned targets. Once the first deck load got away, the carriers spotted planes for follow-up attacks, combat air patrol, ground support, searches, and inner air patrol on lookout for subs. Growing daylight revealed the "inspiring sight" of "three carriers steaming at high speed in line abreast at intervals only great enough to prevent mutual interference of their destroyer screens."[2]

Purple Base on board the transport *Neville* controlled air support flights in the Yoke sector. To southward, Orange Base in Turner's flagship *McCawley* directed flights against Lunga. Fighters assumed two combat air patrol stations: the carrier combat air patrol above the carriers and the screen combat air patrol between Tulagi and Guadalcanal. Controlled by Lt. Henry A. Rowe's Red Base in the *Enterprise*, the carrier combat air patrol comprised sixteen to twenty-four F4Fs in two-hour patrols. The fighters checked out suspicious radar contacts but spotted no enemy planes. The screen combat air patrol comprised eight to sixteen F4Fs directed by Lt. Robert M. Bruning, Black Base FDO in the *Chicago* in Crutchley's TG-62.6. In between flight operations Noyes repeatedly reversed course in a rough fifteen-mile square to maintain relative position in relation to the targets while keeping twenty-five to thirty miles from Guadalcanal's west coast. Strike planes and fighters shuttled back and forth from the invasion areas and combat air patrol stations as the carriers tried to hold to Noyes's intricate timetable.

Turner, seeing what he took to be seaplanes rising off Lunga, announced at 0611, "Enemy planes now taking off." No further word reached the carriers until 0647, when they were told incorrectly that U.S. planes landed at Lunga after destroying enemy fighters. No enemy aircraft were present. Kinkaid later explained the difficulty in piecing together the situation based only on radio transmissions, returning pilots, message drops, and visual signals. Boscoe Wright, Fletcher's cruiser leader, called communications "terrible." The carriers "knew nothing of what went on at Guadalcanal, though occasionally they picked up scraps of TBS." Even worse for Fletcher personally, "The *Saratoga* couldn't get anything on her radio or TBS" and "had to depend on the *Minneapolis*." Turner's communications were erratic at best and not all that informative.[3]

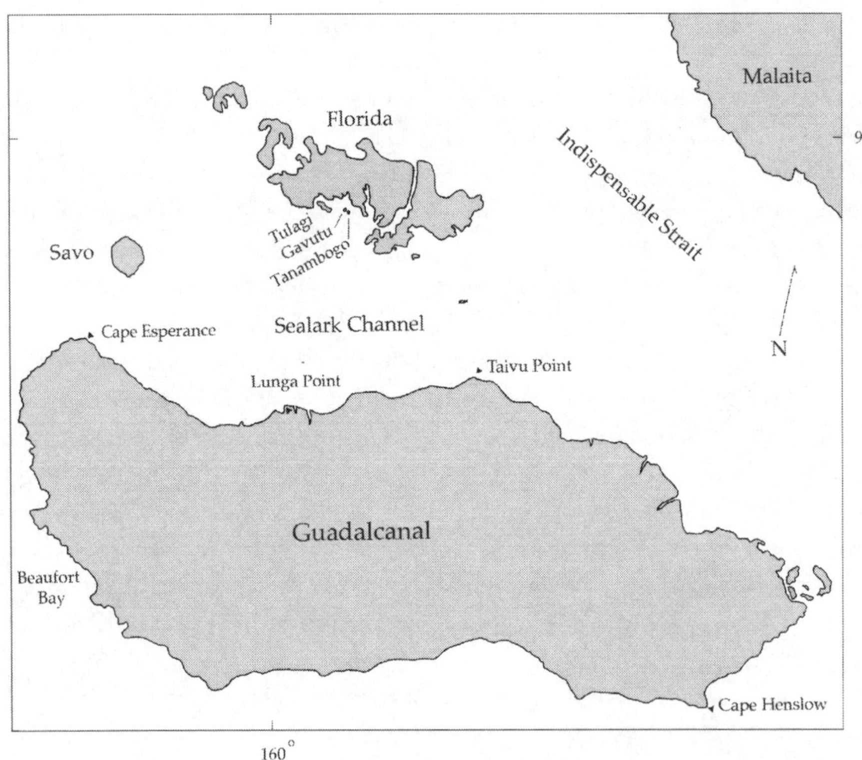

Guadalcanal and vicinity

The invasion seemed to be proceeding well. A report at 0759 told of an unopposed landing at Tulagi, where *Wasp* planes claimed (and got) thirteen planes torched on the water. *Saratoga* pilots newly back from Lunga spoke of little return fire. At 0824 Turner confirmed the Tulagi landings took place on time with "no beach opposition." The marines landed first on Florida, then Tulagi, where initial opposition grew heavy, and late that morning on tiny Gavutu, also against fierce resistance. A causeway linked Gavutu to Tanambogo, another stronghold. By 0913 when the First Marine Division splashed ashore at Red Beach on Guadalcanal, bombardment and air strikes scattered the defenders almost beyond redemption. Unfortunately Vandegrift did not understand he could seize the airfield immediately. At 0953 Turner reported that the landing on Red Beach was unopposed and that ships' gunfire silenced Gavutu island. The dawn search northwest beyond Santa Isabel turned up just a small tanker east of New Georgia. Fresh from coordinating strikes over Lunga, Felt landed on board the *Sara* at 1058 and told Fletcher he had trouble finding any resistance at Guadalcanal at all.[4]

THE EMPIRE STRIKES BACK

Although the morning went quite well despite heavy fighting at Tulagi and Gavutu, the question remained when Japanese aircraft would counterattack. MacArthur offered no clue how his crucial interdiction fared against the Rabaul airfields. Perhaps not well, for at 1025 Cincpac cautioned Ghormley and Fletcher that Rabaul unleashed eighteen bombers and seventeen fighters against the invasion. Nine minutes later Pearl advised, "Enemy subs are on move to attack Blue Occupation Force at Tulagi." Sophisticated radio intelligence informed Cincpac of these distant events, but simple eyesight proved vital, too. About the same time as the Cincpac warnings, a plain-language message transmitted on a special frequency advised: "24 bombers headed yours." The call sign identified the sender as PO Paul E. Mason, an Australian coast watcher hiding near Buin in southern Bougainville, three hundred miles northwest of Lunga.[5]

Rabaul and Tokyo awoke to grave peril in the Southeast Area at 0630, when the Tulagi garrison radioed: "Under intense enemy bombing." In the short run only Admiral Mikawa's Eighth Fleet and Rear Adm. Yamada Sadayoshi's 5th Air Attack Force could respond. Within two hours they knew the worst. A huge amphibious force with at least one carrier and a battleship assaulted Tulagi and Lunga. Mikawa gathered his heavy ships to sortie that afternoon, directed subs to Tulagi, and arranged for naval troops to leave for Guadalcanal in the next few days. Most of Yamada's twin-engine land-attack planes were preparing to strike the worrisome airfield at Milne Bay on the tip of New Guinea, but the Solomons must come first. His aviators favored aerial torpedoes against ships, but high explosive "land" bombs already crammed the bombers perched at Rabaul. Yamada feared to delay to rearm his planes with torpedoes lest they be caught on the ground, just as the U.S. Navy planners hoped MacArthur would do. Three land-attack planes left to examine the waters around Tulagi and Guadalcanal. Yamada needed to know where the U.S. carrier was in relation to the target area. He missed a great opportunity. For three hours a lookout station on the southwest coast of Guadalcanal watched two carriers and a battleship cavort to westward, but it could not establish radio communication with headquarters. At 0950 twenty-seven Type 1 land-attack planes under Lt. Egawa Renpei and eighteen Zero fighters started taking off from Rabaul to hunt U.S. carriers. Nine Type 99 carrier bombers of the newly arrived 2nd Air Group were to comprise a second wave to bomb transports and U.S. troops already ashore. Sending them was a quixotic gesture. Armed with just two small 60-kilogram bombs each, the carrier bombers lacked the range to fly to Guadalcanal and return. They were to ditch at Shortland south of Bougainville. Thus Yamada would expend all nine dive bombers but hopefully not their crews.[6]

Foreknowledge of the incoming aerial attack did not necessarily mean Noyes's TG-61.1 could mount an adequate defense. The two threatened locales, carriers and invasion force, were more than sixty miles apart. Fletcher rightfully accorded the three precious carriers top priority, but even they spread across twenty miles while individually handling flights. At 1130 the carrier combat air patrol numbered twenty-four F4Fs, with twenty-four being readied to relieve them. The situation over the transports was not as good. The screen combat air patrol stood at fourteen F4Fs, but by 1300 all must depart for lack of fuel. Only eight F4Fs were to replace them. Given the tricky mechanics of carrier operations, the flattops simply could not launch or recover aircraft on demand, as Nagumo learned to his vast dismay at Midway. Bombers flying ground support missions could tie up flight decks and delay the launch of combat air patrol reinforcements. The screen combat air patrol needed thirty minutes to reach station, and dwindling fuel often forced it to leave early. TG-61.1 started advancing southeast roughly parallel to the Guadalcanal coast and twenty to thirty miles distant to keep sixty to seventy-five miles from Lunga and Tulagi. The wind unfortunately abated, forcing sprints above twenty-eight knots to conduct flight operations. That was hard on the *Wasp*'s uncertain turbines and enormously costly in fuel. The *Saratoga*'s next fighter launch, set for noon, comprised eight F4Fs for carrier combat air patrol and four Wildcats on screen combat air patrol. Noyes authorized four more F4Fs to depart seventy-five minutes early to reinforce the screen combat air patrol. The sixteen F4Fs took off at 1203. Four fighters headed out from the *Enterprise* on screen combat air patrol, along with a pair to relieve the section escorting the strike coordinator over Lunga. Four F4Fs flying ground support received no targets (neither did the previous batch) and circled as a sort of low-altitude combat air patrol. Noyes suspended fighter ground support flights and added them to the carrier combat air patrol.[7]

High mountains blocked the *Chicago*'s radar. The parade of planes only partly equipped with IFF radio transmitters likewise hampered Bruning's efforts. Nevertheless he directed the four *Enterprise* F4Fs northwest after a large bogey. It is doubtful the *Enterprise* radar ever picked up the same contact, but Rowe, the carrier FDO, overruled Bruning. He diverted the same four fighters south still well short of Savo. Rowe also hastened northward four carrier combat air patrol F4Fs under Lt. (jg) Theodore S. Gay. The trap miscarried. The four F4Fs previously on screen combat air patrol ended up back at the carriers, their place to be taken by Gay. At 1311 the *Enterprise*, following the flight schedule, lofted Lt. (jg) Gordon E. Firebaugh's four VF-6 F4Fs for screen combat air patrol, and another two for the Lunga strike coordinator. Fourteen VT-3 TBFs followed to patrol ahead for lurking subs. Their departure also freed up the flight deck for rapid combat air patrol recovery.

Lacking carrier contacts and the freedom to seek them on his own, Egawa simply kept his bombers pointed southeast toward the ships known to be off Lunga. In fact he caught another bad break when Rowe's quarry, the land-attack plane searching south of Guadalcanal, ran into thick clouds after 1230. It unwittingly discontinued its mission only a few miles short of the carriers, but scouting eastward, it discovered twenty-seven escorted transports off Lunga. For the time being only the eight VF-5 F4Fs patrolling at twelve thousand feet defended the Amphibious Force. At 1315, near Savo, Lt. James J. Southerland suddenly encountered Egawa's bombers descending through the clouds. His four F4Fs and the four led by Lt. Herbert S. Brown tore into the intruders in a fierce air battle that cost five Wildcats.[8]

At 1315 the carrier combat air patrol stood at twenty-four F4Fs and the screen combat air patrol eighteen, including ten VF-6 fighters under Gay and Firebaugh en route. Fletcher ordered TF-61 to prepare to repel air attack. Soon after, he heard a report that twenty-five enemy aircraft bombed the transports. Sixteen *Wasp* F4Fs raised the carrier combat air patrol to forty fighters. The ratio changed in the next half hour to forty-four Wildcats on carrier combat air patrol and twenty-nine on screen combat air patrol. Finally realizing no bogeys threatened the carriers, Rowe rushed eight F4Fs north to Tulagi, but they arrived too late to fight. Gay and Firebaugh bravely harassed the withdrawing Japanese planes far up the Solomons, but lost four of their number. For the time being Fletcher and Noyes only knew of a ruckus over the invasion area and continued the air support flights on schedule. The three battered survivors of the VF-5 combat air patrol, including one badly wounded pilot, returned to the *Saratoga*. After taking down their statements, the VF-5 yeoman hastened to flag plot to read them to Fletcher, where he enjoyed "a cup of coffee with the Old Boy & everything." The VF-5 pilots estimated thirty-six to fifty twin-engine medium bombers, strongly escorted, sliced through defending F4Fs and bombed the transport force anchored off Lunga. Perhaps three bombers and two Zeros went down. One ship was on fire. About twenty-five bombers wheeled eastward over Florida Island and disappeared north. Nothing was known of the Gay and Firebaugh flights until later, when six surviving F4Fs landed.[9]

As many as fifty medium bombers assailing Guadalcanal and Tulagi meant, as Maas wrote that night, "MacArthur (Dug-Out Doug) did *not* neutralize Rabaul." Japanese air responded to the invasion in strength, if not as yet effectively. The land-attack planes claimed one destroyer sunk and a hit on a transport. Actually they bombed Crutchley's screen off Lunga without damage. Perceiving land-based Zeros were possibly superior in performance even to those on the carriers, the U.S. Navy long wondered how its carrier planes would fare against them. The truth proved demoralizing. Seventeen Zero escorts engaged thirty-four U.S. aircraft (eighteen F4F-4s, sixteen SBD-3s). U.S. Navy credits were seven twin-engine bombers destroyed (plus five probable) and two fighters. Nine F4Fs and one dive bomber went down. Despite fierce opposition, Japanese losses proved surprisingly light. Four land-attack planes fell to fighters, one ditched off Buka, and another crashed back at Rabaul. VF-6 destroyed two escort Zeros. The ten Zeros that returned to Rabaul (five more stopped at Buka) completed an extraordinary eight-hour mission hitherto unprecedented for single-engine fighters. The land-attack crews claimed fifteen Grumman fighters, and the Zero pilots no less than thirty-six (including seven unconfirmed), plus seven

U.S. carrier bombers. The few U.S. aircraft actually brought into battle greatly impressed their opponents, who reckoned upward of ninety intercepting Grummans. Even the Japanese official history declared its strike battled sixty-two U.S. Navy fighters.[10]

"POSSIBILITY ENEMY CV THIS VICINITY"

At 1400 Turner warned Fletcher of enemy dive bombers as well. Another partially garbled message reported about twenty-five planes withdrawing southeast at three thousand feet. As yet Fletcher and Noyes could not confirm the presence of the dive bombers. Jumpy ship lookouts might have mistaken SBDs as hostile planes. Inasmuch as dive bombers could not normally fly the nearly twelve-hundred-mile round trip between Rabaul and Guadalcanal, perhaps they came from a carrier. That would have meant that radio intelligence, God forbid, completely missed a sortie of first-line flattops from home waters. Unwilling to go to that extreme, Fletcher wondered whether the culprit might be the auxiliary carrier Sowespac located the previous day north of Rabaul. At 1455 he suggested to Noyes and Kinkaid there be a search the next morning "toward Rabaul in view enemy CV reported there."[11]

Radio transmissions copied at 1455 described a dive bomb attack on Guadalcanal, this time battled by the twenty-four F4Fs on screen combat air patrol. The nine carrier bombers flew south along the northern boundary of the island chain, and, shielded by mountains from the Screening Group's land-blocked radars, they achieved complete surprise. A 60-kilogram bomb killed twenty-one men in the destroyer *Mugford.* Fifteen VF-5 and VF-6 F4Fs claimed fourteen dive bombers, five more than were there, and did bag five. The four survivors reported a light cruiser on fire. Yamada's one-way mission actually damaged one destroyer, but did pay off another way. The appearance of carrier-type aircraft so far from home multiplied the confusion on the U.S. side. Kinkaid commented to Noyes that the "presence [of] dive bombers indicates possibility enemy CV this vicinity" and suggested a search. Concerned only three *Enterprise* F4Fs could scramble, he asked the *Saratoga* and *Wasp* to reinforce the combat air patrol. Only one example of the many appalling lapses in communications, Fletcher received these 1514 and 1527 TBS messages at 1555 and 1558 respectively, possibly via the *Minneapolis.* Fletcher certainly shared Kinkaid's fears of possible carrier opposition. That evening Maas mused: "If [enemy] carrier got to rear (CV Dive-Bombers) then search and interdiction by MacArthur very poor (failure) and same by McCain not very good." Fletcher noted the dive bombers were last seen retiring west instead of northwest directly to Rabaul. That only heightened suspicion of a carrier. He anticipated an all-out air attack the next day. By moving farther away from Rabaul, he might reduce the vulnerability of his own carriers to a double punch from land and carrier-based planes. At 1600 he told Noyes to shift the predawn launch point one hundred miles southeast from the one that day. Noyes chose Point Roger, thirty-two miles southwest of Cape Henslow (seventy miles from Lunga, eighty-five miles from Tulagi), and devised the maneuvers to bring the carriers there at 0600 on 8 August.[12]

Fletcher's 1600 message also directed Noyes to "make early search," by which he meant prior to sunset at 1818. At the same time he had the *Saratoga* reallocate a dozen SBDs from a scheduled ground mission to a brief sweep for a "suspected carrier" fifty to ninety miles northwest. Calls for air support waned, and some planes already returned without being allocated targets. In the meantime Noyes suggested to Fletcher at 1627 that the dive bombers were "probably land based from Rabaul via Buka or Kieta." That was correct in the sense Rabaul was actually the point of origin, but no one on the U.S. side appreciated that Yamada simply expended his carrier bombers. However by informing Fletcher that Kinkaid "has already been told to search," Noyes demonstrated he, too, hedged his bets. Kinkaid switched to northward eight of fourteen *Enterprise* TBFs patrolling ahead for subs. None of the dusk searches found enemy ships or planes because none were there.[13]

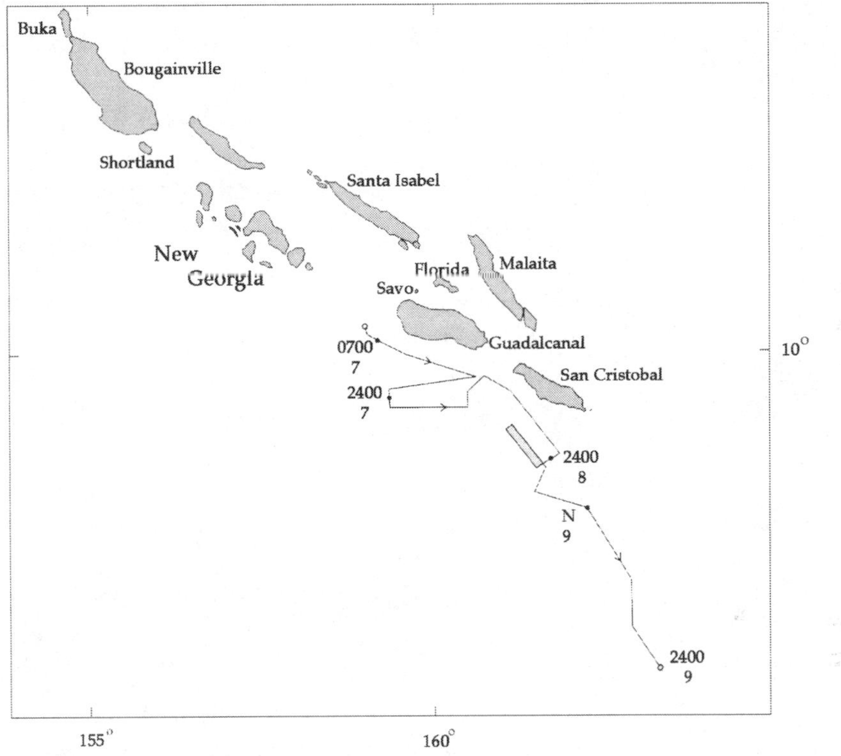

Task Group 61.1 track chart, 7-9 August 1942

Still concerned over possible carrier opposition, Noyes also modified the normal rotation of carrier duties on 8 August. The *Wasp* was to search northwest in the direction of Rabaul "primarily for reported Cast Victor" and handle standby combat air patrol, while the *Enterprise* took primary responsibility for the carrier and screen combat air patrols, and additional ground support missions "if requested." In contrast, Ramsey was to keep the *Saratoga* in strict reserve, spotting fighters and an attack group for immediate launch should a carrier be discovered or radar detect an inbound bombing attack. At noon on 8 August the carriers would exchange roles, the *Enterprise* handling the afternoon search, *Sara* assuming the main combat air patrol and ground support load and the *Wasp* going into reserve. Thus Noyes anticipated the *Saratoga*'s flight deck being locked up tight from dawn to noon on 8 August, but there would be unforeseen complications.[14]

THE END OF A LONG DAY

By sunset on 7 August TG-61.1, cruising twenty miles south of Guadalcanal, had come nearly as far east as Cape Henslow, near where flight operations were to resume the next dawn. The afternoon passed without further enemy contact, but three fighters could not find their way back from the invasion area and ditched. That day the three flattops conducted an amazing 703 takeoffs and 687 landings, the most ever in one day up to that point. Nine F4Fs and one SBD fell to enemy action, and operational accidents cost five F4Fs and one SBD. Another Wildcat had to be jettisoned because of crash damage, and five were badly shot up. The exhausted carrier aviators had the satisfaction of knowing "Terrible Turner" praised "all air squadrons for their excellent work." Deeply surprised the carriers were not attacked, Fletcher, Noyes, and Kinkaid all sensed they got away with something so far. Maas wrote in his diary, "Expected attack on our carriers did not materialize tho we were fully expecting one. Tense all day." Later that evening Fletcher learned that as of 1600, radio direction finders at shore bases placed Japanese subs just to eastward between Malaita and San Cristóbal. Thus TG-61.1 was wise to undertake a seventy-mile dogleg southwest during the night to clear the area.[15]

Kinkaid's TU-61.1.2 went its own way southward. That afternoon he had been "very much annoyed" to discover one of his destroyers, the *Gwin*, was "dangerously low on fuel." He later complained she was never topped off while on detached duty from 30 July and 3 August with Fletcher's TU-61.1.1. On 3 August before being returned, the *Gwin* had in fact fueled along with all the TG-61.1 destroyers and was at 82 percent capacity. Her log for 6 August showed 52 percent. The *Gwin* was not the only one of Kinkaid's destroyers low on fuel. The *Grayson* was down to 55 percent fuel on 6 August (42 percent on 7 August); the others had little more. Kinkaid cautioned Fletcher on the seventh that most of his destroyers had oil for two days at fifteen knots, but the *Gwin* only enough for somewhat over a day at that speed. It appears in this instance Kinkaid greatly overstated the deficiency in that he erred in using fifteen knots instead of twenty-five knots. He later explained that if he had been "well out to sea," one of his heavy ships would have immediately fueled the *Gwin*, but "that was not advisable" because of possible air and sub attacks. Therefore he secured permission from Fletcher to go off alone, fuel the *Gwin*, and rejoin the other carriers at Point Roger just prior to dawn. The *North Carolina* commenced fueling the destroyer in the "pitch black night" without showing any lights. After "efficiently" executing the "slow and delicate operation," the *Gwin* by midnight had drawn 56,642 gallons of fuel oil, which restored her to 79 percent of capacity.[16]

Lacking detailed summaries from Turner, Fletcher still knew very little of what actually occurred in the landings. The X-Ray Group at Guadalcanal seemed to fare well, with few calls for ground support. Fresh from duty as the Yoke strike coordinator, Felt described the fighting still raging on Tulagi and tiny Tanambogo. Confirming the serious nature of the situation there, the carriers monitored a message that evening from Scott to Turner advising that neither Tulagi nor Tanambogo were taken. "Unloading not yet commenced; estimated time complete unknown." Felt told Ramsey that Turner himself requested a bombing mission against Tanambogo at dawn on 8 August, and that he promised to do it. However, Kinkaid's overnight absence greatly complicated the situation. The *Enterprise* was to be duty carrier and should handle that attack, but Fletcher rightly refused to break radio silence (TF-16 was already too distant for TBS) to alert Kinkaid and transmit the lengthy details regarding times and targets. Instead at Ramsey's urging, he authorized the *Saratoga* to furnish the flight, even though Noyes directed she remain in reserve. The *Saratoga* prepared a strike of eighteen SBDs and eight bomb-armed VT-8 TBFs to depart just after 0600.[17]

That evening Maas critiqued air operations based on what he learned from Felt and others. It was obvious that dividing shore-based air between MacArthur and McCain was not working. "Army air-operating over water *must be* under Navy (or Marine) command." Likewise Maas faulted the arrangements for air support in the target area. "Air operations in support of Marine landing operations *should be* headed up by Marine aviation." He deplored that Turner at Guadalcanal insisted also on running the air show over distant Tulagi, instead of letting Purple Base do its job. "Air missions broke down because Turner (Adm.) gave our planes no mission when they reported on station over Tulagi. When the Air Group Comdr. [Felt] in the air over area gave them missions (targets) in the absence of orders from Director Control on *McCawley*, he was reprimanded by Turner, who couldn't even see what was going on."[18]

MacArthur's much-anticipated interdiction of Rabaul air power amounted to little. Fletcher learned that evening that eight B-17s reportedly "put all bombs" on the airfield that morning, but with no estimate of damage. Maj. Gen. George C. Kenney, the new commander of the SWPA Allied Air Force, had hoped to employ twenty Fortresses in the AAF's greatest concentration yet in the southwest Pacific. In truth it was only on the afternoon of 7 August that thirteen B-17s bravely bombed Vunakanau Field just west of Rabaul and lost one bomber to an estimated twenty-six fighters. The great hope vested in MacArthur's heavy bombers proved sadly misplaced. The raid cost Yamada no planes either aloft or on the ground, and the runways were repaired before the Guadalcanal strike returned. Late that afternoon nine land-attack planes arrived from Tinian, with eighteen more set to follow the next day. In a message later deciphered by Allied intelligence, Yamada listed thirty land-attack planes available for the eighth after starting with thirty-two the day before. When Kenney read the intercept he boasted to MacArthur that on 7 August his B-17s destroyed or damaged the other hundred or so bombers he believed had been there. His self-serving postwar memoir crowed that his planes blew up seventy-five of 150 bombers parked wingtip to wingtip on Vunakanau Field and forestalled further air attacks against Guadalcanal. In truth 7 August 1942 was no replay in reverse of the 8 December 1941 debacle at Clark Field, because no land-attack planes even remained at Vunakanau to be bombed. It was a ridiculous claim, a disservice to the gallant AAF flyers who flew the perilous long-range mission to Rabaul.[19]

The Sowespac update on the night of 7 August also revealed that the B-17s had seen six large and fourteen smaller ships in Rabaul harbor. In nearby St. George's Channel, six more ships steamed southeast toward the Solomons, while northwest of Rabaul, one cruiser, three light cruisers, and a destroyer headed west at twenty knots. Other air searches that day proved negative. Thus as of midnight on 7–8 August there seemed to be no immediate surface threat to the invasion area. In fact Mikawa sortied that afternoon from Rabaul with five heavy cruisers, two light cruisers, and a destroyer. If unmolested during daylight on 8 August, he could deliver a night surface attack at Tulagi around midnight on 8–9 August.[20]

AIR SUPPORT ON DOG PLUS ONE

Before dawn on 8 August the *Saratoga* and *Wasp* task units approached Point Roger from the southwest. The *Enterprise* force, back from its fueling errand, closed from the southeast. Alerted to Kinkaid's presence by radar, Fletcher maneuvered to let him pass ahead and take his place on the port side of the formation. Sliding into proper position, Kinkaid felt "very much pleased" with his navigation. By jockeying for position, though, the *Saratoga* was a dozen miles short of Point Roger at 0600, when Fletcher turned TG-61.1 northeast into a gentle breeze for flight operations. With the marine success, the need for ground support flights lessened, but the transport force, located seventy-five to ninety miles northwest of the carriers, still needed protection. Twelve *Wasp* SBDs fanned out to the west, north, and northeast (280–040 degrees) to 220 miles to check an area that included Santa Isabel and the whole New Georgia group. The *Enterprise* deployed four F4Fs as screen combat air patrol and four SBDs against subs. By far the busiest carrier in the first launch cycle was the *Saratoga*, which by rights was not supposed to fly any aircraft except in an emergency. Before daybreak she dispatched Felt with nineteen SBDs and eight bomb-armed TBFs to handle Turner's urgent request the previous evening to strike Tanambogo at dawn. Fletcher and Ramsey would be ill served by this act of kindness. When the time came, Turner's Orange Base, micromanaging the Tulagi sector from distant *McCawley*, failed to provide a target and wasted much of the *Sara*'s effort. The SBDs eventually left still lugging their bombs, but Orange Base finally released the VT-8 TBFs against Tanambogo.[21]

About the time the first wave left the *Saratoga*, Ramsey reminded Fletcher of the loss of five VF-5 pilots the previous day, one of whom SBDs sighted on a beach on northwest Guadalcanal. He requested Turner check out that area, while planes from the other carriers kept a sharp lookout. Fletcher relayed the message to Turner, who on his own detailed two high-speed minesweepers to that task. Ramsey sent four F4Fs north on an unscheduled screen combat air patrol to overfly the area where their fellow pilots went down. He also deployed four F4Fs on carrier combat air patrol, the first from any carrier that morning. As evidence of a more relaxed atmosphere the whole staff, less Fletcher and the duty officer, joined Maas at 0715 for breakfast in the captain's mess. The *Enterprise* also took advantage of the lull for a special search of six SBDs between Guadalcanal and San Cristóbal looking for two fighter pilots lost the previous evening. Unfortunately all the mercy missions found no one.[22]

By 0800 sixteen F4Fs circled the carriers, and the same number manned the screen combat air patrol. Rowe ran short of fighters. Limited fuel capacity forced frequent combat air patrol rotations, and the inability of the *Saratoga* fighters to participate greatly hampered matters. Thus at 0758 Kinkaid requested permission from Noyes to add eight VF-5 F4Fs to the 0830 and 1030 carrier combat air patrol cycles. Noyes swiftly disapproved, reminding Kinkaid, "*Saratoga* must be ready to launch for or in case of attack." By 0925 Noyes finally discovered *Sara* aircraft aloft. He bristled the *Saratoga* "does not appear to be complying with my orders for today's operations which require her until noon to maintain fighters and attack group ready for launching at all times in case of bombing attack or locating of enemy CV." In future, Noyes told Ramsey, "Please refer conflicting request to me." This message crossed one from Ramsey at 0946 stating, "Red Base again requests 8 VF for Combat Patrol from me. Advise." Obviously expecting Noyes's approval, Ramsey lofted eight F4Fs for carrier combat air patrol at 0952, before the *Wasp* could reply. Wisely he told them to stay close and watch for new orders. Ramsey then respotted the *Sara*'s deck forward and started recovering eight F4Fs and the eighteen SBDs back from their fruitless mission over Yoke Group. Felt's SBD and the eight VT-8 TBFs had yet to return from the Tanambogo strike. At 1015 an exasperated Noyes directly challenged Fletcher, who in this case acted as a subordinate task unit commander. "Your 072246 negative. Invite your attention to present situation if enemy CV should be located and I ordered your attack group launched. Your fighters should also be ready for launching for actual bombing attack until noon." Certainly the *Saratoga* had not complied with his orders. Ramsey used visual signals to recall the eight F4Fs at 1023. The VT-8 landings, however, did not go well. One Avenger that was unable to attack Tanambogo could neither drop its tail hook nor bomb load. Finally at 1045 after some ten to fifteen minutes of fruitless attempts, the errant TBF set down, followed by Felt three minutes later.[23]

Thus by 1049 all *Sara*'s planes were back on board, but it was already too late. Watching from the flag bridge alongside Fletcher, Maas fumed at the failure to respot the huge deck to launch fighters. As it turned out, there was very good reason to be irritated. At 1038 the *Saratoga* monitored a coast-watcher message from northern Bougainville stating that forty large twin-engine planes passed overhead at 0942 headed southeast. FDO Bruning in the *Chicago* repeated that warning at 1044. He estimated they could reach Tulagi as early as 1115, an error in judgment as will be shown. Fletcher directed TF-61 to "prepare to repel air attack," but the main fighter reserve of twenty-six F4Fs sat immobilized until plane handlers could reshuffle the *Sara*'s jammed flight deck. It is interesting that Dyer, Turner's biographer, blamed Fletcher's supposed anxiety over the possible presence of an enemy carrier for the delay in providing fighter defense for the invasion force. The exact opposite is true. Convinced no carriers prowled the Solomons, Ramsey declined to tie up his air strength so needlessly. His persuasiveness and reputation as a pioneer aviator swayed Fletcher, always conscious of his own lack of aviation experience, to permit the *Saratoga* to defy Noyes's orders. He gambled that she could furnish Turner's vital ground support mission and still respond to a threat. Ramsey's estimate of the enemy carrier situation proved justified, when the *Wasp*'s morning search turned out negative. However, his affirmation that the *Saratoga* could quickly provide F4Fs to defend the task force was sadly in error.[24]

THE COMBAT AIR PATROL FIASCO

Conscious of lost opportunities, Yamada determined to strike hard and fast. From the many carrier aircraft his aviators encountered the previous day, he concluded two or possibly three carriers lurked east or northeast of Tulagi. Following a comprehensive search of the whole southern Solomons, all available land-attack planes, armed properly with torpedoes, would attack. Yamada concentrated his search of three bombers and two flying boats mostly northeast and east of Tulagi. Lt. Kotani Shigeru led twenty-six land-attack planes (three soon aborted) and fifteen Zero fighters southeast at low altitude along the northern fringe of the Solomons chain. He listened for search reports to learn where the enemy carriers were located. If found in range he would attack them, or otherwise hit the invasion force. TF-61 again enjoyed vital warning. The low-flying bombers rattled the jungle hilltop hideout of Lt. W. J. Read, guarding Buka Passage off northern Bougainville, four hundred miles northwest of Lunga. He radioed the sighting report that TF-61 received at 1038. Turner got TF-62 under way. Each transport squadron and its screen aimed for the center of the channel for freedom of maneuver to evade air attacks. So far, so good. However, Bruning's estimate that these enemy planes could threaten Tulagi by 1115 actually required an average speed for the more than the four hundred miles of an impossible 270 knots. It appears he confused Read at Buka in north Bougainville with Mason, located one hundred miles closer in southern Bougainville. Unfortunately Rowe, the TF-61 FDO, was not thinking more clearly. At 1050 he estimated that bombers could reach Tulagi between 1100 and 1200, a time interval that was for the most part still far too sanguine.[25]

At 1050 ten F4Fs flew screen combat air patrol, with eight other Wildcats en route. Eight more F4Fs circled TG-61.1, which was twenty-five miles south of Cape Henslow and thus seventy-five miles from Lunga, ninety miles from Tulagi. Fifty F4Fs (nine *Wasp*, fifteen *Enterprise*, and twenty-six *Saratoga*) perched on board the three flattops. Unaware of the *Saratoga*'s current unavailable condition, Rowe suggested she rush all her fighters to Tulagi, there to be joined by half the *Wasp* fighters. That would leave the *Enterprise* F4Fs and the rest of the *Wasp* fighters to defend the carriers. At 1101 the *Enterprise* scrambled thirteen F4Fs for carrier combat air patrol. Before Ramsey could follow suit, Noyes must free the *Saratoga* from the obligation to remain in reserve until noon. Fletcher also had his say in the matter. Sent by Ramsey to the flag bridge to explain the combat air patrol options, Felt outlined the threat to the Amphibious Force. He strongly recommended the *Saratoga* comply with Rowe's call for most of the fighters to defend Turner's ships, rather than the carriers. Fletcher retorted the Japanese "won't attack the transports. They're going after us and get us." Pointing out that Turner's ships were between the oncoming strike and TF-61, Felt counseled: "Let's get our fighters off and protect those fellows." Fletcher "gave in and said all right." Noyes concurred. At 1105, finally convinced the morning search discovered nothing, he released all twenty-six *Sara* F4Fs for Tulagi. Due to incredibly poor fleet communications characteristic of the whole operation, the *Saratoga* did not log his approval until 1135.[26]

Even had Noyes's authorization arrived at 1105, the *Saratoga* could launch no fighters at once and later only a few at a time—a crucial setback for Rowe's plan to defend the transports. It was necessary to respot the SBDs and TBFs to free up the F4Fs for takeoff, and other problems arose as well. Maas deplored the "confusion and delay," due to "continual and last-minute changes in number of planes to be launched and resultant changes in frequency set up because of different missions installed using different frequencies." The radios in fighters originally assigned as strike escorts had to be reset from attack to combat air patrol frequencies but required three or four changes to get the proper settings. The pilots were even uncertain which planes to man and complained that deck crews removed belly tanks from some F4Fs. Those tanks could only be replaced on the hangar deck, and no one had time for that. Only at 1141 did just eight of twenty-six fighters get away, one of which lost a shoddily installed belly tank while taking to the air. The preceding hour had not offered an edifying demonstration of carrier skill to Fletcher, who certainly could contrast the *Sara*'s dismal performance with the crack *Yorktown*.[27]

Although Bruning did not have the incoming raid on radar, he expected it shortly. Therefore he deployed the eighteen screen combat air patrol F4Fs at seventeen thousand feet to ensure altitude superiority, but the enemy did not appear. At 1130 Noyes, conscious his own fighters did not have belly tanks, recalled the fifteen *Wasp* F4Fs on screen combat air patrol for fuel. Inexplicably he included the eight that just took off at 1043 and which still had plenty of gasoline. At 1140 the *Wasp* scrambled nine F4Fs to relieve them, as well as thirteen SBDs for anti-torpedo-plane patrol, and cleared her deck for rapid recovery. Rowe hurried the first eight VF-5 F4Fs northward along with the nine VF-71 F4Fs, but they would need nearly thirty minutes to reach Tulagi. Six *Saratoga* F4Fs followed at 1150. Until these reinforcements could arrive, only three VF-6 Wildcats under Mach. Donald E. Runyon protected the entire invasion force, a shocking lapse of fighter defense. At 1202 Rowe implored the *Saratoga* to rush all remaining fighters to Tulagi. True to form it took eight minutes to get an affirmative back from Noyes. By that time the air battle had ended.[28]

Turner's two separate squadrons cruised in Sealark Channel. At 1155 lookouts suddenly spied to eastward a gaggle of medium bombers cutting around the east tip of Florida Island. Because the search never turned up the U.S. carriers, Kotani continued southeast to Tulagi. Fletcher received a huge break. About 1000 the Kawanishi Type 2 flying boat on the 130-degree line from Rabaul passed within a few miles of the carriers but never saw them. By keeping north of the Solomons and flying at low level (and hoping until the last moment to pinpoint enemy carriers northeast of Tulagi), Kotani completely avoided radar detection. The Yoke Squadron cut loose with heavy antiaircraft at twin-engine torpedo bombers skimming the waves. To the southwest, Turner's flagship *McCawley* led the X-Ray Squadron into two 30-degree turns away from the oncoming Japanese. His four divisional columns steaming abreast resembled a school of minnows, but they possessed a strong bite. "The fire of all these ships was so extensive and of such volume that the Japanese pilots showed utter confusion and state of mind and reacted accordingly." Kotani swung the whole strike south away from the Yoke ships to take on the X-Ray Squadron, which presented him only their sterns. Fierce gunfire dropped one bomber after another. Some foolhardy Japanese actually flew among and hopped over the ships or maintained highly vulnerable parallel courses. Few ever released torpedoes, and many were seen to crash in flames. A bomber plowed into the boat deck abaft the stack of the transport *George F. Elliott* and set her afire. Only the hapless destroyer *Jarvis* absorbed a fish. Fortunately Turner's stout defense repulsed the strike with only a little help from the few U.S. Navy planes in the area. One SBD shot down a Zero south of Yoke Group. Runyon's three F4Fs circled seventeen thousand feet over the X-Ray Squadron until the radio revealed torpedo planes at low level. Diving in, the Wildcats engaged bombers retiring westward and splashed four land-attack planes and one Zero without loss.[29]

The entire attack lasted only ten minutes, and the scattered raiders fled west at high speed. Yamada was shocked how few land-attack planes turned up at Rabaul. Of the twenty-three, no fewer than seventeen succumbed, mostly to Turner's remarkably effective antiaircraft fire. All surviving bombers were badly shot up, and one later crashed. Those who returned bore tales of incredible success: four large cruisers, three light cruisers, two destroyers, and three transports sunk, and severe damage to a large cruiser, a destroyer, and six transports. Yamada himself reduced this hysterical tally to one heavy cruiser, one destroyer, and nine transports sunk, plus three light cruisers and two unknown ships badly damaged—still incredibly wide of the mark. In truth the toll was heavy damage to one transport (which later sank) and one destroyer.[30]

At 1203 the carriers monitored a voice report of forty twin-engine bombers attacking the transports with bombs and torpedoes. Turner warned Fletcher of forty torpedo planes, and for once the message actually got through. Twenty-three F4Fs from the *Saratoga* and *Wasp* arrived too late to engage the enemy. At 1215 the *Saratoga* finally managed to loft her last eleven F4Fs and hasten them north. At the same time Noyes reinforced the carrier combat air patrol to thirty-four F4Fs. Exuberant VF-6 pilots could be heard assuring each other all enemy planes were shot down. Likewise at 1219 Fletcher was gratified to learn from Turner that the raid caused "very little damage." It could have been much worse, given the confusion in calculating the time of the attack and the failure to muster fighters to meet it.[31]

WINDING DOWN

The combat air patrol simply could not maintain its vast strength of nearly seventy fighters. By 1315 it looked to Fletcher and Noyes as if the carriers might not be attacked after all. It was also high time for the carriers to shift roles in accordance with Noyes's operating schedule. The *Saratoga* was to replace the *Enterprise* as the main duty carrier, the *Enterprise* go on standby and search, and the *Wasp* take the *Sara*'s place in reserve. Thus Rowe suggested to Noyes the *Wasp* recall all her F4Fs. The other two carriers should deploy six F4Fs on carrier combat air patrol and six on screen combat air patrol and recover the rest for refueling. In the next hour the *Wasp* landed all twenty-four F4Fs and also eleven SBDs back from an air support mission to Tulagi. Only the thirteen SBDs on anti-torpedo-plane patrol remained aloft. After more arduous respotting of cumbersome SBDs and TBFs, the *Sara* took on board eleven fighters at 1328. At 1345 nine *Enterprise* SBDs sortied for Tulagi on one last air support mission, and fourteen TBFs departed on a comprehensive afternoon search. Its western sectors actually originated at the northwest tip of Guadalcanal (ninety miles northwest of the carriers) and extended two hundred miles to the midpoint of Choiseul and well into the Coral Sea. The other half of the search commenced from the east tip of Guadalcanal and covered Indispensable Strait and northeastern Malaita.[32]

Suddenly a coast watcher warned of inbound enemy planes. At 1356 Fletcher cautioned the task force, "Standby for air attack within next half hour." The threat arose at a particularly bad moment when all three carriers were busy recovering Wildcats. The carrier combat air patrol still numbered forty fighters, but twenty-two were about to land. At the same time the screen combat air patrol comprised sixteen F4Fs, all of which must soon leave because of fuel. Turner likewise raised the alarm and got the transports moving again, to the great detriment of his plans to finish unloading that day. At 1410 Fletcher ordered TF-61, "Prepare to repel air attack." He finally had his fill of the *Saratoga*'s chronic congestion. Thirty-one SBDs lumbered into the sky for no other reason than to free deck space to handle fighters. Five TBFs also departed to watch for subs. The scare was a false alarm, and by 1440 Rowe implemented his combat air patrol plan. All that time the carriers maintained a constant relative position with regard to Lunga (seventy-five miles) and Tulagi (eighty-five miles), while maneuvering in the strait between Guadalcanal and San Cristóbal. That refuted charges, to be examined below, that Fletcher already started withdrawing the carriers at noon on 8 August.[33]

Toward sundown the carrier portion, at least, of the Watchtower landings was winding down. Total takeoffs and landings on 8 August, although numerous, were half the previous day. Only one F4F ditched, pilot recovered. Just three F4Fs and four SBDs actually engaged enemy planes, with claims of four bombers and two fighters. The marines had, so far as Fletcher knew, captured all of the initial objectives. The last air support mission that afternoon received no targets from Orange Base. On both days the carriers provided remarkably effective ground support, considering the rudimentary state of the art, but combat air patrol protection was dismal. Turner's invasion force weathered three fierce air assaults with relatively little help. The biggest surprise so far was that the carriers themselves had not been attacked, particularly as the enemy demonstrated he could strike hard at long distance. Kinkaid recalled, "We could not reasonably hope that Japanese search planes would fail to locate us during the period of our operations south of Guadalcanal—it seemed obvious we were there—but that is just what happened. Nor were we molested during this period by Japanese submarines." Fletcher could not count upon such good fortune lasting very long, and other serious matters demanded his immediate attention. It was high time to reevaluate the situation, and that is precisely what he did.[34]

CHAPTER 25

The Recommendation to Withdraw the Carriers

THE MESSAGE

Around 1807 on 8 August, eleven minutes before sunset, the *Saratoga* broke radio silence (as opposed to TBS short range traffic) to transmit a dispatch from Fletcher to Ghormley, information Turner, McCain, and Noyes. "Total fighter strength reduced from 99 to 78. In view of large number of enemy torpedo and bomber planes in area recommend immediate withdrawal of carriers. Request you send tankers immediately to rendezvous decided by you as fuel running low." That message resulted from discussion in flag plot and brief consultation via TBS with Noyes, in temporary tactical command of the carrier group. Colonel Maas, the marine aviator on the TF-61 staff, participated in the deliberation and knew all the factors that influenced the decision. Two hours later he wrote a private analysis of the situation that declared (his emphasis): "*Withdrawal of carriers at end of second day not ordered*, but should have been. Fletcher proposed it on his initiative." Maas believed Fletcher should "be commended for his judgment, courage, and tactical farsightedness."[1]

To Fletcher's legion of critics message 080707 of August 1942 defined his naval career. In 1943 Turner bitterly complained to Morison that Fletcher left him "bare-arse." In 1945 he officially characterized the action as nothing less than "desertion," undertaken for reasons "known only" to Fletcher. Vandegrift described Fletcher, "Running away twelve hours earlier than he had already threatened during our unpleasant meeting." Official judgments were equally unsparing. On 23 August 1942 Nimitz condemned the withdrawal as "most unfortunate," a comment he repeated in *The Great Sea War*. In December Admiral Pye, president of the Naval War College, called the pullout "certainly regrettable," which risked "the whole operation." In 1943 Admiral Hepburn's final Savo report labeled Fletcher's action a "contributory cause of the disproportionate damage" incurred in that battle. The Cominch Secret Information Bulletin No. 2 gave short shrift to the reasons attributed to Fletcher's decision, including needless worry about "bombing and torpedo planes." The 1950 Naval War College analysis of Savo expanded on Pye's original points and concluded, "Such a precipitous departure" would "seriously jeopardize the success of the entire operation" and "prevent the inauguration of Task Two."[2]

Historians accepted the official judgments without question. Morison wrote, "It must have seemed to [Turner] then, as it seems to us now, that Fletcher's reasons for withdrawal were flimsy." The carriers "could have remained in the area with no more severe consequences than sunburn." Marine Brigadier General Griffith, historian as well as participant, completely concurred. He conceded, "Fletcher did have a point. We just couldn't lose our carriers, but damn it, how the Marines suffered!" Vice Admiral Dyer did present Fletcher's side, but his sympathies lay with Turner. The situation did not justify the carrier withdrawal. That was also the carefully considered judgment of Richard Frank, who concluded Fletcher, rightly or wrongly, placed the preservation of his carriers ahead of everything else. All other accounts derive from these key analyses.[3]

However, the supposedly airtight case against Fletcher is deeply flawed. Turner obscured the fact that he always intended to pull out the Amphibious Force incrementally. A key message from Turner boding some change in plan never reached Fletcher in time. The depiction of the fuel state of some ships is shockingly inaccurate and highly prejudicial to Fletcher. The fairest and most proper basis for analyzing Fletcher's recommendation is to recreate, as best as can be done at this late date, the situation as he and others actually understood it at the time. There are three crucial factors: (1) necessity—what Fletcher knew of the situation at Guadalcanal and whether he believed it was vital to keep the carriers there after 8 August, (2) security—if he thought the carriers would be safe in light of what he deemed was their prime mission, and (3) supply—his estimation of the fuel in TG-61.1 and whether it was a valid reason to consider in withdrawing.

Was It Necessary to Stay?

Turner predicated the invasion plans on most of the Amphibious Force leaving by sundown on D+1, 8 August, if the situation permitted. Considerable debate on 27 July centered on how long Fletcher should keep the carriers in hostile waters in support of the *portion* of the invasion force that must stay behind, possibly for several more days. Fletcher's intent, whether clearly understood by others or not, was to remain until sundown 9 August (D+2). Of course, no partial withdrawal of the Amphibious Force ever took place. Excepting the hurt destroyer *Jarvis*, Turner held all his ships on station until the evening of 9 August. Thus the first important issue concerns Turner's actual intentions on 8 August, as opposed to his later representations. Did Turner change his plans? Did he keep his superiors properly advised of his situation?

Maas's personal situation estimate on the evening of 8 August alleged Turner "did not keep Fletcher informed." A few days later he called communications "very bad" and wrote that "most of the time" Fletcher "got no information" or "very inadequate dope, and mostly very late,—too late to be useful." Turner, though, stoutly maintained in a 16 August 1942 report on communications, "A reasonably complete history of the essential features of the operations was promptly transmitted." That is highly debatable, especially in light of his claim that he took it upon himself to provide "operational bulletins to the superior command echelons," particularly as Fletcher "could not break radio silence to report progress." It is vital to note Turner suffered no similar restraint. As evidence, he gave Ghormley the text of the radio messages the *McCawley* sent out on 7–9 August to CTF-61 on the task unit commander's frequency (2122 kilocycles). He asserted "all were received" and assumed Comsopac copied these messages as well.[4] He erred on both counts. Ghormley's endorsement disclosed that he could not receive messages on 2122 kilocycles and contended, correctly, "It is doubtful" Fletcher "could hear more than fragments of the blind transmissions on that frequency." In truth Fletcher received very few of Turner's messages on 2122. Ghormley blamed the failure of Turner's "higher echelon communications" on the selected frequencies (drawn from standard Pacific Fleet procedure), "plus a lack of equipment in the transports."[5] However, Turner did not originate all his messages from the *McCawley*. His report mentioned, but did not identify, eight messages delivered on the morning of 8 August by boat to the *Astoria* for immediate transmission on a different frequency. With one exception noted below, all were highly routine. Ironically all of the Turner messages that the *Astoria* transmitted on 8 August went through without any difficulty and certainly contributed to the impression all fared well at Guadalcanal.[6]

Early on 8 August, Ghormley prodded Turner: "Report situation." Not until mid-morning did he and Fletcher copy a long message from CTF-62 that related events as of 2100 on 7 August. Message 071030 of August 1942 (2130, 7 August local time) does not appear in Turner's list of the above-mentioned "despatch reports" transmitted from the *McCawley* and thus was one of the *Astoria* messages received straightaway on the eighth. Prefaced "Situation summary Watchtower," Turner's only detailed update for 7 August is worth quoting in full:

> Approach a complete surprise 18 enemy seaplanes destroyed on water one small anchorage. No enemy ships present. In both areas opened shore bombardment 1910 GCT 6th [0610, 7th, Z–11] with ships and planes light gun opposition soon silenced. Landings began Florida area 2040 [0740] initial opposition light Guadalcanal 2210 [0910] no opposition.
>
> At 0220 GCT 7th [1320] about 25 enemy Type 97 bombers passed overhead dropped several bombs no damage proceeded toward carriers 2 shot down 2 damaged. About 10 enemy Type 99 dive bombers made 1 250 pound hit on *Mugford* 0400 [1500] considerable damage after deck house 2 guns 2 engines 15 missing 5 dead 9 seriously injured. 2 enemy planes shot down.
>
> Situation at 0900 [2100, 7th] Guadalcanal all troops ashore estimated occupy west line Tenare [*sic*] River and on east security line about Longitude 160-06 in neither places in contact with enemy. On Florida side Halavo occupied no opposition. Tulagi occupied except east and fight continues Gavutu captured heavy casualties Tanambogo still in hands of enemy attack underway.
>
> Tomorrow request maximum fighter cover 2 VSB squadrons continuously in area. Request scouting against approach enemy surface force from westward.
>
> Early morning 8th expect to send out Santa Cruz Occupation Force less *Pres Jackson*, *Wilson*, plus *McCawley*, *Fuller*, *Heywood*, *Trever*, *Mugford*, some other APs later in day. Tonight 2 DMS searching for fighters shot down near Russell Island. One *Wasp* dive bomber shot down by Zero according to pilot wounded gunner lost.[7]

The salient point is that Vandegrift was safely ashore with the whole Lunga force, eleven thousand men, holding a three-mile front without opposition, but still a mile short of the great prize, the airfield. It would be reasonable to assume that by dark on 7 August, the X-Ray Squadron transports (as opposed to the cargo ships) were empty or nearly so. The marines still cleaned out the Tulagi area. Turner desired "heavy air support" and "maximum fighter cover" on the eighth. One task was accomplished easily, the second a disaster. The carriers twice searched north and west on the eighth. The message demonstrated Turner's desire to hold to the plan of withdrawing a significant portion of the invasion force on 8 August. The units mentioned were heavy cruiser *Quincy*, three destroyers, a reduced Ndeni force of three transports and one cargo ship, two other X-Ray transports (including the *McCawley*), one Yoke transport, one high-speed minesweeper, and damaged *Mugford*. That left four X-Ray and three Yoke transports, most of which at least should also depart that day. Turner's original plan called for the four APDs of Transdiv Twelve to re-embark the First Raider Battalion once it finished with Tulagi. The five cargo ships were to anchor close to the Lunga shore for as long as it took them to unload. Nothing in Turner's message indicated he had changed any of these arrangements.

Other than flash reports of the noon attack and a short summary at 1430 of the damage, Fletcher received no additional information from Turner prior to his recommendation. That afternoon Fletcher summarized for TF-11 the situation based on the radio messages and observations by his aviators. Lunga, Gavutu, and Tulagi were occupied, leaving only Tanambogo. There was "no serious damage our forces from air attacks either yesterday or today." So far the offensive cost the enemy nearly forty planes, but, "Our plane losses [are] light in comparison." Subsequently *Saratoga* fighter pilots advised Fletcher that one transport was on fire a mile north of Red Beach, and nearby a destroyer, "apparently in trouble," moved close to shore. Turner's 1430 summary of the attack (which got through to Fletcher) identified the *George F. Elliott* and *Jarvis* as the stricken ships. The VF-5 pilots also reported that when they left, the X-Ray transports, deployed three abreast in column, maneuvered off the north coast of Guadalcanal, while to the north the Yoke transports could be seen "apparently engaged in developing into formation." These were further hints of a possible imminent departure by Turner's force. The last air support flight returned without attacking, another indication the fighting was nearly over. Maas's situation estimate demonstrates Fletcher believed that afternoon the "transports [were] unloaded,—all troops were ashore," and that only the cargo ships had to continue unloading. Fletcher heard the previous evening that the transports at Tulagi had not yet started unloading, but nothing from Turner or anyone else pointed to further difficulties there. Thus as far as Fletcher knew, most of the invasion force should have no reason to linger. Wright commented in 1952, "We in the *Minneapolis* were manning the same circuits that Fletcher did and about all we knew about happenings in the Guadalcanal-Tulagi area was that the shore operations had been completed successfully." That was clearly how Nimitz judged the situation based largely on the same few messages. The War Plans Section commented, "Evidently the operation is proceeding satisfactorily."[8]

Such sanguine appreciations of Watchtower's progress were dead wrong. Although Turner had composed his 7 August situation report by 2130 the same evening, he did not actually have the *Astoria* transmit it until a dozen hours later. In the meantime circumstances changed radically. Late on the seventh after learning of heavy casualties sustained at Tulagi, Vandegrift asked Turner for one of the two battalions of the Second Marines held in reserve afloat. Already earmarked for Ndeni, the whole regiment was supposed to sail to Santa Cruz on 7 August after collecting its First Battalion. Turner had already postponed the Ndeni departure to the eighth, and by omitting the transport *President Jackson*, he conceded the First Battalion would not re-embark that day. Now at 0150 on 8 August, he pleasantly surprised Vandegrift by committing both reserve battalions to Tulagi, thereby putting all the Second Regiment's riflemen ashore after sunrise. At 0217 the *McCawley* radioed Ghormley and Fletcher to note, ambiguously: "Owing to reinforcements Florida area [,] will not commence retirement as planned." Typically, neither addressee received the message prior to a routine rebroadcast sometime late on 9 August. Questions remain as to Turner's precise intentions, and what he meant by "will not commence retirement as planned." Ostensibly that delay only applied to the four transports, one cargo ship, one heavy cruiser, and four destroyers of the Ndeni force that were to have gone out the evening of 7 August, and not to the rest of the transports that should soon be unloaded if they were not already. Although Turner abandoned the immediate execution of the Ndeni landing, his own pet project, he did not bother to advise his superiors. Possibly his unexpected generosity sought to provide enough riflemen to finish off Tulagi quickly to release the whole Second Marines for Ndeni.[9]

Turner left strong indications that later in the morning of 8 August he fully envisioned releasing the *McCawley* but aimed to remain himself. The *Astoria* found out, presumably when the *McCawley*'s boat brought the messages to be transmitted, that Turner and his staff would transfer on board later that morning. At breakfast the *Astoria*'s executive officer alerted correspondent Joe James Custer, who slept in the unoccupied flag sea cabin, that he must relinquish it because Turner would soon be on board. Later that day Custer heard that Turner postponed his arrival. As noted, Turner never explained what he intended to do with the *Astoria* and *Vincennes* after the landings, but it is likely he planned use them to support the marine raiders and Transdiv Twelve to "conduct raid operations as required."[10]

The tardy unloading of all the transports and cargo ships disastrously affected Turner's plans. The extended fighting in and around Tulagi tied up landing beaches and prevented the delivery of supplies. The transports there sat idle—hence Scott's warning on the evening of the seventh. In contrast, the X-Ray Squadron at Lunga did not budge even during the air attack, and its troops certainly faced no opposition ashore. Yet by the evening of 7 August Turner already noticed "excessive delays occurring at Red Beach" in the unloading of supplies. He blamed the absence of marine pioneers to empty the boats. Even after they appeared, the "situation did not materially improve." Heaps of crates were not being shifted inland fast enough. Finally at 0130 on 8 August, Turner suspended unloading because "the beaches were so congested." Only after 0700 did the transfer of supplies resume at Red Beach. Word at 1037 of incoming planes caused Turner to get under way to meet the attack, which he did in sterling fashion. After the false alarm at 1355, things really fell apart. The ships required more than three hours to regain position and did not resume unloading until nearly sundown. Turner followed Vandegrift's suggestion to relocate further unloading west to the beach situated east of the mouth of the Lunga River and north of the airfield, where the marines secured the shoreline. The new beach soon became clogged as well. The sailors and marines bickered over what should be done and who was at fault.[11]

By late afternoon on 8 August it must have galled Turner he was not going to get any of the invasion force out that day, despite all of his optimistic predictions at Pearl and at the 27 July conference. That applied especially to the X-Ray transports, all of which had disembarked their troops and nearly all the gear and supplies. Given this was the first Allied amphibious offensive in the Pacific, delays arising from inexperience could not fairly be held against anyone. But Turner did not candidly inform his superiors that something he directly supervised went even temporarily amiss. Perhaps he rationalized the laconic warning sent early on 8 August, that the "retirement would not commence as planned," offered sufficient explanation. Yet if he had honestly reported the delays, Fletcher would have had powerful reason to risk staying. Turner did not imagine his one cautionary message did not reach his superiors in time, and his eagerness to shift blame led him to dissemble about many facts. Afterward he never admitted there was ever any reason to think most of the Amphibious Force might retire on the second day. Therefore he could depict Fletcher's next act as outright "desertion." Nor did Bates and Innis take note, despite being aware of Turner's 071030 of August 1942. Instead they faulted Fletcher, when he made his recommendation, for having "failed to inform [Ghormley] fully of the delicate nature of the situation at Tulagi-Guadalcanal." In truth, Turner failed to notify Fletcher of the "delicate nature of the situation." Bates and Innis (and Morison) are effectively rebutted in the memoirs of Rear Adm. Geoffrey G. O. Gatacre, RAN, who was Crutchley's staff officer for operations and intelligence in the *Australia*. In 1982 Gatacre wrote regarding Fletcher's recommendation to withdraw the carriers, "The original plan called for a majority of the transports to leave the combat area by the night of 8th/9th August, and Admiral Fletcher may have been unaware that unloading was greatly behind schedule." The evidence shows that Gatacre was entirely correct.[12]

Were the Carriers Secure Off Guadalcanal?

Having charged without any basis in fact that Fletcher knew of Turner's unloading woes but nevertheless abandoned him, critics postulated that his principal reason was unwarranted fear for the safety of his carriers. This insecurity arose from Fletcher having lost one carrier in each of his two recent battles and a disinclination to make it three for three, no matter how much that might compromise the overall mission. The critics ignore the possibility Fletcher might actually have learned something at Coral Sea and Midway, especially as he now found himself in the reverse role of his erstwhile opponents in supporting an amphibious thrust deep into enemy-controlled waters. Perhaps he really saw compelling reason to get the carriers clear of the invasion area and prepare for action. Just as he thought that with the marines ashore Turner's immediate task neared its end, he understood the job of the carriers had only begun. In the short term they were the only shield against powerful naval and ground forces intent on destroying the marine lodgment. A large counter-landing would require strong carrier support to sweep away naval opposition before the actual landing force drew within range. Fletcher envisioned another grim carrier battle soon. He must be ready for enemy carriers at any time, despite rosy intelligence estimates from Pearl—the most recent on the afternoon of 8 August—placing the carriers in home waters. Intelligence could be wrong, and the resulting surprise quite deadly, as the Japanese at Coral Sea and Midway could attest, not to mention Kimmel at Pearl Harbor. Hindsight has obliterated the validity of Fletcher's prudence.[13]

The tactical necessity of protecting a fixed point put heavy demands on the defensive capabilities of Fletcher's carriers. They were accustomed to strike swiftly and draw clear of retaliation. Now they were exposed not only to the threat of opposing carriers, but also subs (messages reported several en route) and the more vigorous than anticipated land-based air. So far as Fletcher knew on 8 August, only eight B-17s struck the main Rabaul airfield the previous afternoon, while its bombers were busy attacking Turner. MacArthur announced no follow-up attack, except after dark on 8 August by a handful of RAAF Catalina flying boats. Moreover, encountering land-based Zero fighters so far from base proved a disheartening surprise. Only the Zero fighter's incredible endurance permitted that mission and all the subsequent ones against Guadalcanal. Even worse, the awesome prowess of the land-based escort pilots only reinforced the negative comments voiced after Midway about the Grumman F4F-4 Wildcat fighter. Also distressing, despite coast-watcher warnings, the carriers failed to mount an adequate defense of the invasion force. The poor performance of radar, inexperience, bad luck, and bad decisions bungled the ever-difficult fighter direction. Turner's ships were fortunate to escape as lightly as they did. As if all that was not enough, the unforeseen presence on 8 August of medium bombers wielding torpedoes so far from base boded ill for the carriers. As the Maas papers and other sources show, Fletcher considered all these factors as he mulled whether to propose the early withdrawal of the carriers.

Grumman Wildcat fighters, of course, constituted Fletcher's principal defense against air attack. Just in two days, nine F4Fs were shot down, six ditched or crashed, and six others returned badly shot up and required lengthy repairs. Those twenty-one F4Fs comprised 20 percent of Fletcher's fighter strength. The critics dismissed or minimized the significance of those losses, pointing out that the three carriers at Midway started with seventy-nine Wildcats, only one more than the seventy-eight F4Fs Fletcher currently had operational. What they ignored is that the whole Midway battle cost the carriers only nineteen F4Fs (six shot down and thirteen ditched or crashed), plus three that went down on the *Yorktown*. At Coral Sea a dozen F4Fs (eight shot down, four ditched) were destroyed, with nine more on the sunken *Lexington*. Thus by 1530 on 8 August, Fletcher had lost more F4Fs off Guadalcanal than in each of his previous battles. Yet he could only reckon the air fighting on D-Day and D+1 as preliminary skirmishes in a very long campaign, with no source short of Pearl for fighter replacements. The big brawls were yet to come. On 24 September Fletcher explained the need for carrier replacement air groups at convenient places like Suva, Nouméa, and Tongatabu. "In two days of supporting the landing against air attack, the carriers lost approximately 20% of their fighter strength. Yet they also had to be prepared to repel an expected attack by enemy carriers at some later date with no prospects of replacing their current losses." Pederson stressed in his 1944 lecture, "The carriers could not afford to engage in a war of attrition over a period of time with land based planes" and still accomplish their mission of stopping a big counteroffensive against Guadalcanal. "If the carriers had remained to suffer further losses they would have been in no condition to do so."[14]

The heavy fighter losses again elicited grave doubt over the combat effectiveness of the Grumman F4F-4 Wildcat. The 50 percent casualties suffered by the first F4Fs to engage land-based fighters carried significance beyond its stark number. It was a truism that sleek land-based aircraft outperformed heavier carrier planes, but such a difference between two nominal carrier fighters, the Zero and Wildcat, was deeply disturbing. In 1963 Fletcher remarked: "Nobody mentions the matter, for fear of bringing down the wrath of the aviators upon them, the Japanese Zero's all wore Seven League Boots [and] our aviators gave them a lot of god damned respect." Kinkaid also was "much interested in what returning pilots had to say about the situation in the landing area and, even more so, in their attitude regarding the Japanese air performance." He recalled the "loss of fighter planes during [7 August] gave us pause," and that "at first our pilots were greatly discouraged." The truth of that is reflected in a routine message regarding machine guns and ammunition that Lt. Louis H. Bauer, commanding officer of VF-6 in the *Enterprise*, sent on 13 August to Pearl. Although pleased at the ruggedness and overall protection of the F4F-4, he dramatically concluded: "Pilots are anxiously awaiting faster and better fighters. Repeat pilots are anxiously awaiting faster and better fighters." The Battle of the Eastern Solomons on 24 August and the brilliant success of the marine fighter pilots at Guadalcanal at least partially restored the fleet's confidence in the Wildcat. Yet on 8 August, the evident failings of the F4F-4s when finally matched against Zeros flown from land bases weighed heavily on Fletcher's mind.[15]

The badly flawed placement of fighters also severely compromised the air defense on 7–8 August. Analysis showed that inferior altitude, dispersal of assets, and remarkably effective fighter opposition devastated the screen combat air patrol on 7 August. The commanding officer of VF-5 likened the piecemeal commitment of his F4Fs to scraps tossed into a "Japanese meatgrinder." Inadequate numbers of fighters over the Amphibious Force on 8 August, despite the early warning, stemmed primarily from the *Saratoga*'s inability to launch F4Fs on demand. Maas unfairly blamed Noyes, but Fletcher and Ramsey were at fault for furnishing the dawn Tanambogo strike that Turner requested. According to Ramsey, "In a large complement of mixed types such as was embarked in the *Saratoga*, flexibility in the use of fighters is seriously compromised." Bruning, the FDO in the *Chicago*, bore the brunt of the criticism for fighter direction, largely unwarranted given that high terrain blocked his radar. He never detected the second strike on 7 August or the one on the eighth. The carriers fared no better, because they operated in the shadow of Guadalcanal's high mountains. Kinkaid had recommended they move farther out to sea for unfettered radar coverage, but that would have curtailed fighter support for Tulagi and Lunga.[16]

If handling the combat air patrol was not problem enough, Fletcher learned on the afternoon of 8 August that the enemy cleverly employed a mixed assault force to divide the defense, very much as on 7 May against Crace. The returning combat air patrol pilots and Turner's 1430 summary described a coordinated assault by eight horizontal bombers to draw off defending fighters ("Fooled us," according to Maas), which opened the way for a low-level sneak approach by forty twin-engine torpedo planes. That assessment was wrong. There were no horizontal bombers, and the torpedo attack by twenty-three land-attack planes proved both inept and very costly, but Fletcher did not know that yet. The sudden appearance of numerous medium bombers toting torpedoes, land-based air's most effective antiship weapon, provided another strong reason for concern, especially given the combat air patrol's questionable performance. Fletcher had not expected torpedo planes, certainly not ones augmented by fierce Zero escorts, could even reach him off distant Guadalcanal. He queried Noyes whether the noon attackers "were actually carrying torpedoes," and was assured they did. Maas wrote that night, "The use by Japs of long-range torpedo planes makes our present position untenable, dangerous, and foolhardy." That was particularly true if the carriers could legitimately get clear without harming the overall mission.[17]

The basic role of the carriers in the Watchtower landings was, of course, to provide air support, in particular fighter cover. The week before the invasion Ghormley and McCain had, as noted, suggested Fletcher leave fighters behind at Lunga when the carriers withdrew. Fletcher considered detaching twenty-four F4Fs temporarily to Lunga, but that was not possible. First and foremost he had no place to send them. As far as he knew, the airstrip was still in enemy hands. Maas noted on the evening of 8 August, "Vandegrift failed to make Lunga Airfield first objective and prepare it for fighters. We could have left fighters and got out of area." Kinkaid's memoir confirmed that harsh assessment. Not until the evening of 10 August did Fletcher learn Vandegrift had overrun the Lunga airstrip on 8 August. Indeed, the Lunga field was never a feasible option, because it remained unfinished. But the Japanese thoughtfully left construction equipment so the marines could smooth it out by 11 August. However, even if conditions had allowed the carrier F4Fs to come into Lunga on 7 or 8 August, they had no aviation supplies and trained ground personnel on hand to service the planes. Regarding fighter support, it was Fletcher's carriers or nothing.[18]

Fletcher strongly advised in his 24 September analysis of carrier operations that bases for land-based aircraft should be established, "Within the shortest possible distance of the objective prior to any invasion effort." Land planes should stage into the objective as soon as the airfield was ready to take over air defense and release the carriers to withdraw. On 9 October Admiral Halsey went further. "However the danger exists that the more important and more fundamental fact may be lost sight of that the land plane bases and the operating units thereon should be available in supporting positions *before* [Halsey's emphasis] the operation is undertaken at all. It is only by this provision in advance that the risking of carriers in restricted covering positions can be avoided." Thus the question of protecting the carriers off Guadalcanal was much more complex than one might infer from Fletcher's critics.[19]

Was the Carrier Group Short of Fuel?

Fletcher's controversial message to Ghormley concluded with his request to send oilers "immediately to rendezvous decided by you as fuel running low." Oil certainly was an important consideration in his mind. In 1947 he told Hanson Baldwin he had actually "recommended the withdrawal because of shortage of fuel." Sixteen years later, he contradicted himself, explaining to Dyer that fuel was not the primary reason, that his "despatch didn't say anything about needing to withdraw to fuel." Instead if Ghormley approved, he "wanted to fuel as soon as tankers could reach me, as my staff had told me fuel was running low on some of the short-legged destroyers, and Task Force Sixty One had never been belly full since its formation." Fletcher's critics debated whether security or low fuel played the greater role in his perceived desire to bug out. They opted for the former but were prepared to denigrate him for both reasons. "It is idle to pretend that there was any urgent fuel shortage in this force," Morison declared. Thus it is vital to determine precisely the fuel state of Fletcher's ships on 8 August, its effect on the tactical situation, and whether he was justified in citing fuel as a factor influencing his operations, if not a critical reason to warrant withdrawal.[20]

Maas wrote on 8 August that the "task forces need fuel." Fletcher recalled to Baldwin, "We were surprised to find the destroyers running short almost at once and some of the carriers and cruisers used much more fuel than we expected." He blamed the excess consumption on the high-speed bursts necessary to gain enough wind velocity in the light breezes that prevailed for much of 7 August and the next day. The carrier task units certainly observed a sharp drop in fuel in their routine noon reports. Kinkaid's war diary noted that as of noon on 8 August, "Fuel situation this force is becoming critical." He "estimated the destroyers have fuel for about three days at 15 knots and the heavy ships have little more." Noyes advised that his destroyers had only enough fuel for thirty-one hours at twenty-five knots. The destroyers of Fletcher's own task unit were only a little better off, with oil for thirty-five hours at twenty-five knots.[21]

Rear Adm. Worrall Reed Carter's official history of fleet logistics in the Pacific noted that Fletcher fueled his ships on 3–4 August, but a serious lack of foresight caused a shortage of oil at a critical juncture on the eighth. "Why Fletcher could not have refueled on 4 and 5 August and held on a day longer is not clear." The reason is perfectly clear. Fletcher would have been delighted to top off his ships on 5–6 August, but because the *Kaskaskia* and *Esso Little Rock* had not come forward, no additional oil was available. Its absence proved crucial on 8–9 August.[22]

At least Admiral Carter conceded Fletcher might have been low on fuel, although wrongly assessed it to be his own fault. Other critics, however, assailed the notion TG-61.1 ever experienced a fuel shortage on 8 August, or at least one that could curb operations. Pye's Savo analysis noted, "The *Wasp* and *Saratoga* in their reports indicated no concern about shortage of fuel." Ship action reports, though, rarely mentioned fuel; that was the responsibility of the task force commander. Maj. John L. Zimmerman's official Marine Corps monograph on Guadalcanal first cited the deck logs of Fletcher's ships to prove fuel should not have been behind his haste to retire the carriers. Computing each ship's "average daily consumption" from 1 to 8 August, Zimmerman gauged how long it could steam just with the fuel on hand on the eighth. All ships could have operated for "at least four days." The carriers had enough oil for seventeen days, the battleship *North Carolina* eight days, the cruisers eleven days, and the destroyers "about 7 days," except for the *Benham* (three days) and *Grayson* (two days). His methodology is grossly flawed. From 1 to 6 August the carrier task group did no high-speed steaming. Only on D-Day itself did the carriers consistently step up beyond twenty knots. Further, the figures listed for 8 August were the noon fuel reports only, before the additional large expenditure that afternoon.[23]

More formidable was the tag team of Naval War College analysts and Morison, who collaborated in their research. Griffith claimed their work "categorically refutes Fletcher's statement that his ships were short of fuel." Bates and Innis contended the *Cimarron* "topped off" a dozen of Fletcher's destroyers on 3–4 August, and thereafter they "were refueled as necessary from the heavy ships of the various task groups." A "check of the logs" revealed that on 8 August the destroyers of Fletcher's own TU-61.1.1 (*Saratoga*) "averaged about seventy-five percent capacity," whereas those of Kinkaid's TU-61.1.2 (*Enterprise*) had only 42 percent and Noyes's TU-61.1.3 (*Wasp*) 44 percent. Cruiser fuel in all three task units was 50 percent or more. Of the carriers, only the *Enterprise* "was running low and had fuel for three more days of operation." Accordingly, "Although the fuel in the command was diminishing daily it was not at this time so critically low as to force retirement from the area." Moreover, Fletcher's intention to stay one more day, if Ghormley refused to give permission, demonstrated, "He was fully prepared to operate with the fuel on hand." Morison concurred. "It can now be ascertained from ships' logs that at noon 8 August the destroyers still had enough fuel for several days' operations, and they could have been refueled from the cruisers and carriers, as well as from fleet oilers." As in his discussion of the Wake relief, Morison provided a footnote that listed the fuel on 8 August for most of the ships in Kinkaid's and Noyes's task units (but just the *Saratoga* herself in Fletcher's own task unit). Instead, regarding the *Saratoga* group, he wrote, "[The destroyer] *Dale* had just been topped off and was 97 percent full, the other five destroyers averaged three quarters full." Morison noted, "The destroyers' daily expenditures varied from 12,000 to 24,000 [gallons]," and fuel capacity ranged from 127,000 to 184,000 gallons. "The cruisers (capacity 618,000 to 839,000 gallons) were half full or better." Thus according to Morison, the carrier group experienced no "urgent fuel shortage."[24]

The only other historian to examine the oil situation of TG-61.1 in detail, Dyer listed fuel figures for 7–9 August for all of the ships he believed were present. He did not list capacities or assess actual fuel percentages. An author of a book on naval logistics, Dyer stressed the baleful influence of excess worry by naval commanders over what he called AFFAG (Ammunition, Fuel oil, Food, and Aviation Gasoline) to the detriment of completing the mission. On 8 August both Fletcher and Kinkaid suffered from the "virulent" form of AFFAG disease, and only the destroyer *Grayson* in Kinkaid's task unit merited a "critical" grade for fuel shortage.[25]

In truth the Naval War College analysts, Morison and to a lesser extent Dyer, committed surprising errors in describing the fuel state of Fletcher's ships on 8 August. Bates and Innis emphasized the destroyers were "topped off" on 3–4 August. Actually none were filled to full capacity, because there was not enough oil to go around. They also averred the destroyers of Fletcher's TU-61.1.1 averaged about 75 percent of capacity on 8 August. Morison not only accepted their figures for five of the destroyers he thought were present (ignoring that the *Hull* and *Dewey* were detailed to TF-62), but he also commented the *Dale* had just fueled to 97 percent. Because no fleet oilers were with the force, that fuel would have come from a heavy ship. So, if the *Dale* could refuel, why not the other destroyers? In fact the war diaries and deck logs show that on 8 August only destroyers *Phelps*, *Farragut*, *Worden*, and *Macdonough* were actually with Fletcher's own TU-61.1.1. Their logged fuel figures average just 46.8 percent of capacity, *not* "about seventy-five percent." The absent *Dale* indeed fueled to 97 percent, but it was on 6–7 August from the merchantman *Oliver Wendell Holmes* while both ships lay at anchor at Espíritu Santo. Subsequently the *Dale* escorted two ships to Efate, arriving at noon on the eighth. Why Bates and Innis gave the average fuel state for the TU-61.1.1 destroyers as 75 percent remains a mystery. Yet their figures for the destroyers of

Kinkaid's TU-61.1.2 (42 percent) and Noyes's TU-61.1.3 (44 percent) compare well to the 44.2 percent and 45 percent respectively derived capacities given in the authoritative 1945 U.S. Fleet Tactical Publication FTP-218, "War Service Fuel Consumption of U.S. Naval Surface Vessels." In addition to placing the *Dale* in TU-61.1.1, Bates and Innis, Morison, and Dyer all inflated TU-61.1.3 by adding the *Laffey* (on her way to Pearl for repairs) and the *Aaron Ward* busy chaperoning the *Cimarron*. This error originated in the sloppy assumption that because these destroyers appeared in the TF-61 Op-Ord 1-42 (28 July 1942), they all had to be present on 8 August. As with Morison's discussion of the Wake relief, the fuel consumption figure for destroyers (twelve to twenty-four thousand gallons per day) he gave with the 8 August fuel listing is misleading. Their vast expenditure in battle might easily consume half again as much oil as his larger amount.[26]

With an overall average of 45.3 percent of fuel capacity on 8 August, it can no longer be doubted *all* thirteen of Fletcher's destroyers were low on fuel.[27] The six cruisers averaged 52 percent fuel. It is clear when reckoning available fuel that Fletcher, Noyes, and Kinkaid used the standard practice of going by the lowest ship in each category. The basis for their estimates of steaming endurance was less reliable than those derived from empirical data unavailable in 1942. Even so, Fletcher and Noyes came close to the mark regarding destroyer fuel. Fletcher's low destroyer, the *Macdonough*, had fuel for about thirty-six hours (1.5 days) at twenty-five knots, whereas he calculated thirty-five hours. Likewise Noyes reported his destroyers could steam thirty-one hours (1.3 days) at twenty-five knots, while the *Sterett* had enough oil for about thirty-six hours at twenty-five knots. By citing fifty hours (2.1 days) at twenty-five knots Fletcher erred with the cruisers. The actual figure was sixty-five hours (2.7 days) for the *Minneapolis*, ostensibly the low ship. Perhaps, though, he based his estimate on figures that Kinkaid provided for TU-61.1.2. Kinkaid's fuel reports represented his ships having less fuel than later calculations could support. Dyer called his 7 August dispatch regarding destroyer fuel (two days at fifteen knots) "misleading," if Fletcher quoted it properly in his 9 September 1942 report. Moreover, Kinkaid's war diary for 8 August had complained, "Fuel situation [in] this force is becoming critical," and that he "estimated the destroyers have fuel for about three days at 15 knots and the heavy ships have little more." With the oil on hand the *Grayson*, by far his lowest destroyer, could only steam 3.6 days at fifteen knots, but the TF-16 war diary badly erred in stating the heavy ships had "little more." So Kinkaid's fuel reports to Fletcher may have been much too pessimistic, but Fletcher himself never had the luxury of personally counting every barrel in every ship. He had to take the word of his subordinates.[28]

Thus with the possible exception of the *Grayson*, the ships of TG-61.1 would not have run dry if they faced a third day of heavy steaming and combat off Guadalcanal. However, their fuel situation was certainly much more worrisome than generally perceived, and certain to have deteriorated rapidly. By noon of 9 August, after running mostly at fifteen knots after sundown on the eighth, average destroyer fuel decreased to 35.2 percent. That would have been considerably less had Fletcher stayed off Guadalcanal again conducting extensive air operations or dodging air attacks. Moreover, just parking the carriers within air support range for another day or two was not all there was to it, something all the critics ignored. Fletcher had to be ready to execute the second half of his mission, which entailed the prospect of fighting another carrier battle to prevent a landing force from retaking Tulagi and Lunga. One must therefore examine his options with regard to fuel to help assess its role in his desire to withdraw the carriers.

The Naval War College analysts and Morison assumed that Fletcher could simply refuel his destroyers from his heavy ships at will, such as Morison wrongly wrote of the *Dale*. Ordinarily such fueling was routine but required good weather and freedom from imminent air or sub attack. In September 1942, however, Fletcher informed Ghormley that fueling the destroyers from the cruisers "was not practicable." They, too, were low on oil. He did tell Baldwin in 1947 he could "possibly" have "stayed one more day" if he had "fueled destroyers at night," but that would have depended on whether he accepted the real risks of remaining on station. Such reduced fuel in the task group would have severely limited his ability to maneuver in a highly uncertain tactical situation. In January 1943 Rear Adm. George Murray independently confirmed Fletcher's assessment. According to Murray, "The carrier task force problem, so far as refueling is concerned, hinges on destroyer consumption," an "interesting sidelight [that] should be kept constantly in mind." While "in an advanced area a task force cannot afford to approximate the low limit of fuel for the simple reason that it then is virtually immobilized for offensive operations involving 48 hours of high speed steaming." That "low limit" pertained when the fuel in the heavy ships fell to "40/50% of their capacity," without the offsetting advantage of having the destroyers at 90 to 100 percent of fuel. "With the heavy ships fueled to 40/50%, the destroyers to 90%, it is possible to carry out any offensive operations such as a raid involving a 2,000 mile operation." By noon on 8 August, Fletcher's TF-61 had already dropped below Murray's minimum requirements with regard to the destroyers and the *Enterprise* (and was close with the gluttonous *Saratoga*), while cruiser fuel neared the lower limit. Also by the time Murray's TF-17 reached Sopac at the end of August, the worst of the fuel supply problems had eased, and he could afford to be more sanguine with regard to steaming limitations. Fletcher faced a much more uncertain logistical situation in early August.[29]

What about the fleet oilers the critics thought just waited in the wings ready to be called forward? Turner told Baldwin in 1946 that Fletcher "did not want to risk bringing the tankers within range of Jap planes off Guadalcanal, so he planned to retire to the South in vicinity of the New Hebrides in order to refuel." Thus Fletcher supposedly fretted his oilers could suffer a fate similar to the *Neosho* in May and deliberately kept them away. Turner managed to ignore his own real fuel worries during the approach and landing phase of Watchtower. In truth Fletcher never had the option on 8 August of summoning the oilers to Guadalcanal, because none were within a thousand miles. After fueling TF-61 on 3–4 August near Efate, the empty *Cimarron* and the destroyer *Aaron Ward* ventured south to Nouméa in the vain hope of finding the *Esso Little Rock*, which in the meantime turned up at Suva. The *Cimarron* group left Nouméa at dawn on the seventh bound for Suva to refill and come back out to Espíritu Santo. That whole trip of about fifteen hundred miles would require six days, counting time in harbor. In turn the *Platte* and *Kaskaskia*, both nearly full, departed Suva on the evening of 5 August, along with the *Rainier* and the destroyer *Perkins*, and were due at Nouméa on the afternoon of 8 August. Ghormley had thought to direct the destroyer *Cummings* (escorting a transport at Efate) to intercept the convoy on

6 August and release the *Kaskaskia* and *Perkins* to split off to Efate. The *Cummings*, however, could not join in time. The whole convoy continued to Nouméa, one thousand miles by sea from Fletcher's current location close under southeast Guadalcanal. Thus even if one or both oilers cleared Nouméa by midnight on 8–9 August, Fletcher could not count on fuel reaching TG-61.1 before the evening of 11 August, unless he went south to get it. If he did stay off Guadalcanal, his fuel would soon be critically low, greatly restricting his mobility. The massive refueling necessary to fill the whole force would require at least two full days, immobilizing the carriers until 14 August.[30]

Should Fletcher have split the force and pulled out only part to fuel? Nimitz's 23 August endorsement (the one in which he called the carrier withdrawal "most unfortunate") speculated whether it was "practicable to fuel one carrier task force at a time, leaving two available for support of the operations." The 1943 Cominch Secret Information Bulletin No. 2 similarly posed that possibility. In the meantime Fletcher addressed that issue. "Due to fact that all TFs were equally short of fuel," his 9 September 1942 report to Ghormley explained, "it would not have been possible to retire one TF at a time." Despite the assertions to the contrary, Fletcher was indeed correct. It is also doubtful, no matter how he rationalized later, that given his strong concern over the security of his carriers, he would have divided his ships and kept a weaker force off Guadalcanal. Nimitz, though, disregarded Fletcher's reasoning. His *The Great Sea War* again proposed fueling the task groups one at a time.[31]

Fletcher also had to worry he might not even get all the fuel he needed no matter what he did. Not counting the old, slow, and small *Kanawha* busy fueling ships passing through Fiji, the *Platte*, *Kaskaskia*, and *Cimarron* (once she refilled) contained virtually all of the readily available oil in the entire Sopac area. If one should be sunk or incapacitated, her cargo could not be replaced until the arrival of the next batch of chartered tankers not expected at Nouméa before 12 August. Subs posed a real peril. On 26 July while escorting the *Platte* back to TF-61, the *Worden* picked up survivors from an army transport torpedoed seventy-five miles southeast of Nouméa. On 6 August Comsopac relayed a report from the *Cimarron* warning of three or four subs encountered twice within eighty miles of Nouméa. On both occasions the *Aaron Ward* dropped depth charges and claimed sinking two subs. The *Cummings* thought she bagged a sub near Efate. The presence of subs and too few escorting destroyers made any passage north by the oilers a risky prospect.[32]

In the absence of a perceived emergency that might have compelled Fletcher to keep the carriers on station despite the danger, it can be argued that inadequate fuel was another powerful reason, or at least a strong reinforcing reason, to withdraw TF-61.

ASSEMBLING ALL THE PIECES

At 1525 on 8 August Fletcher announced to Noyes, "In view of possibility of torpedo plane attack and reduction in our fighter strength I intend to recommend immediate withdrawal of carriers." In the event Ghormley disapproved (the message just said "in case we continue present operation"), Fletcher thought they should return to the same waters as on the eighth, the strait between Guadalcanal and San Cristóbal. Noyes responded at 1615 "affirmative to both questions" and suggested if the carriers did stay, they should adopt the same operating plan as on 8 August. It is inconceivable Noyes did not discuss the situation with Capt. Forrest Sherman, his closest advisor, who evidently concurred with his answers to Fletcher. In 1949 Sherman wrote Morison: "On the afternoon of the eighth I felt that the Japanese response had been strong, but had no reason to be apprehensive over a temporary withdrawal. It was not until after the night action that the situation became critical." That certainly implies that Sherman thought, as did Fletcher, that Crutchley's Screening Group could take care of itself in the temporary absence of the carriers.[33]

Brig. Gen. Melvin J. Maas, U.S. Marine Corps Reserve, circa 1950.
Courtesy of Minnesota Historical Society

Written the evening of 8 August 1942, Maas's invaluable explication of the reasons behind the recommendation to retire the carriers coincides closely with Fletcher's recollections years later to Baldwin and Dyer. As quoted at the beginning of this chapter, Maas strongly supported Fletcher's action by laying out all of the relevant factors of necessity, security, and supply: "To stay meant fighter protection for landing force and for finishing unloading cargo ships. Daily bombing attacks from Rabaul. To leave meant leaving Marines without air protection. To stay means endangering the carriers. We have too few to risk them at this time. The task forces need fuel. Attrition is rapidly reducing fighter strength of carriers. In addition to increasing danger from shore-based air attack, every hour increases danger from Jap subs, now gathering and heading for us." Fletcher recalled to Dyer that he was fully aware he led most of the surviving U.S. carriers, and that there would be no replacements until mid 1943. Not only could Japan mass superior carrier strength in the Solomons, but it was also the most likely course of action. Fletcher's greatest concern was risking the carriers in situations where they could not inflict greater or even comparable damage to the enemy.

They must be preserved in the face of land-based air and sub opposition to deal with the enemy carriers certain to appear very soon. Nimitz had reimposed the restrictions that applied at Midway, and Fletcher "felt he had no choice but to obey his instructions."[34]

Maas understood the "Marines cannot be dislodged by bombers. They will take a drubbing, and their losses will be greater without carriers." However, the best chance Japan had of destroying the landing force was "by an expedition similar to ours." He outlined Fletcher's plan of action. "To be able to intercept [and] defeat such an effort, our carrier task forces must be fueled and away so as not to be trapped here." Likewise Fletcher recalled to Baldwin in 1947 if he had stayed and fueled destroyers at night, "We would have to proceed quite slowly to our [fueling] rendezvous and would be caught in a very bad position if enemy carriers appeared on the ninth. I think we all expected they would show up shortly after the landing." Maas explained on 8 August: "By withdrawing to, say, Noumea, or Tongatabu, we can be in a position to intercept and pull a second Midway on their carriers. If, however, we stay on here and then, getting very low on fuel, withdraw to meet our tankers, *and* if *they* should be torpedoed, our whole fleet would be caught helpless and would be cold meat for the Japs, with the resultant loss of our fleet, 2/3 of our carriers, and we would lose Tulagi as well, with *all* the Marines there and perhaps all the transports." Maas then placed the withdrawal of the carriers in a wider context: "It is true, Marines will take a pounding until their own air gets established (about 10 days or so), but they can dig in, hole up, and wait. Extra losses are a *localized* operation. This is balanced against a potential *National* tragedy. Loss of our fleet or one or more of these carriers is a real, worldwide tragedy." To put it bluntly, was the risk of having one or more carriers possibly crippled or sunk worth staying to protect five cargo ships that Fletcher thought would remain off Lunga? Maas thought no. A proud marine, he could hardly be accused of being unsympathetic to the Corps. Pederson in his 1944 lecture completely agreed with his colleague. "The correctness of the decision to withdraw the carriers is one that is still in dispute. When viewed from the viewpoint of the marines ashore it was questionable. But when looked at the broader strategic picture it has proved correct."[35]

CHAPTER 26

The Savo Disaster

QUIET NIGHT

Mel Maas spent the afternoon of 8 August with Fletcher, as frantic alerts alternated with dead calm. He joined the deliberations that led to the recommendation to withdraw the carriers one day early. At 1745, a half hour before sunset, Maas went below to eat. The three carriers cruised thirty miles southeast of Cape Henslow (that is, eighty-five miles southeast of Lunga) and had not already pulled out, as commonly asserted. Noyes, in tactical command, prescribed the customary nighttime dogleg to clear the immediate area, in this case southwest of San Cristóbal, from where TG-61.1 could retire, if Ghormley approved, or return north and again at dawn on 9 August support whatever part of Turner's Amphibious Force lingered in the invasion area.[1]

By leaving Maas missed an important event. Ens. Robert B. Stahl, one of the notorious eavesdroppers in the *Sara*'s sky forward, recalled that during the afternoon he heard someone say on the flag bridge below: "Cruisers?" Fletcher and the staff hurriedly conferred, but to Stahl's dismay they shifted out of earshot into flag plot.[2] The commotion arose from an 1837 message transmitted from Canberra that placed, at 1025, three cruisers, three destroyers, and two seaplane tenders or gunboats off the southeast coast of Bougainville, some 320 miles northwest of Lunga.[3] The enemy held course 120 degrees, speed fifteen knots, and therefore could have come a good long way. The position and composition corresponded well with information Fletcher received about 0630 from reports of the submarine *S-38* observing St. George's Channel sixty miles south of Rabaul.[4] Years later Yeoman Tom Newsome, Fletcher's combat talker, vividly remembered the evening conference in flag plot. Fletcher wanted to attack immediately, if feasible. Ramsey assured him that the carriers could not search and conduct night strikes, except in bright moonlight, which was not the case that night. Otherwise the risk of losing the planes was too great, especially with a big carrier battle in the offing. Fletcher released the strike crews. He explained in 1947 to Baldwin, "Of course the carriers would have been of no value in a night action." A longtime surface warrior who had yet to fight a surface battle, Fletcher naturally was "confident that the cruisers could look out for themselves in that kind of action." His trust proved sadly misplaced.[5]

Fletcher later commented, "At the time my decision to withdraw was made it was not known that enemy forces were approaching," a fact confirmed from the Maas papers. Yet the Savo debacle spawned a persistent myth that the carriers knew by mid afternoon in plenty of time to strike the cruiser force, but, inexplicably, Fletcher chose not to attack. It appears that when the 1025 message was actually received about 1845, the *Saratoga* alerted Torpedo Eight for possible launch. One TBF pilot told correspondent Clark Lee about a few cruisers and destroyers detected to the north. "Get your life jacket and helmet. Maybe we'll be taking off soon to hit those babies." However, VT-8 stood down. Lee subsequently placed this exchange in the afternoon. On 10 August a VF-5 pilot repeated a rumor in his diary: "To cap matters off, on the 8th, we knew from scout planes' reports that Jap surface forces were coming into our area. At one point they were only 150 miles away, with no plane protection at all. But no dive bombers or torpedo planes were sent out, nothing was done." After sundown on 8 August when Fletcher actually learned of the existence of the force, no one knew where it was. At no time during daylight on 8 August was it within 150 miles of the carriers. In 1943 Captain Riefkohl (*Vincennes*) and Capt. William G. Greenman (*Astoria*) stated to Admiral Hepburn that they heard warnings of the cruiser force sometime that afternoon, but the *Astoria*'s communications officer declared that was not so. Crucial in the creation of this myth was the lengthy delay in forwarding the late morning contact report. It seemed incredible it did not reach the carriers much earlier than it did. Exhaustive investigation by Hepburn, as well as postwar analyses by Admiral Dyer and Commo. Bruce Loxton, RAN, confirmed the first inkling of the enemy cruiser force reached the Amphibious Force and the carriers only after sundown—far too late for Fletcher, at least, to do anything about it.[6]

Thus on the evening of 8 August Fletcher, while awaiting Ghormley's response, held to the plan of shifting the carriers south but retained the option of returning to Guadalcanal. At 1857 in the fading light the carrier task units formed a column and swung southeast at fifteen knots. Newsome recalled no dissension regarding the withdrawal or anxiety over the Screening Group, especially against what was thought a much weaker surface force. Even with the expected imminent departure of the Santa Cruz landing force and the escorted transports, Crutchley should have five heavy cruisers (including the *Astoria* and *Vincennes*), a light cruiser, and nine destroyers, all equipped with radar. Illustrating the lack of concern that evening in the *Saratoga*, Maas dined and played darts with some of the staff until 2000, then he repaired to his cabin to write his situation estimate. He did not learn until the next day of the sighting report of cruisers logged on the evening of the eighth.[7]

Such information Fletcher personally received the balance of that night did nothing to dispel the initial impression that an immediate surface threat to the Screening Group was unlikely. The latest intelligence still rated naval strength in the Rabaul region at just three or four heavy cruisers and four light cruisers, plus a destroyer squadron. Air searches seemingly accounted for most of them. At 2047 Leary advised that at 1101 another aircraft placed two heavy cruisers, one light cruiser, and a smaller ship only seven miles from 1025 search contact. Very likely both planes spied the same force. The other aircraft sightings that morning and early afternoon (but that Comsowespac only reported that evening) amounted to a few ships strung out from Buka to Shortland. That certainly fitted Leary's notion, radioed after 2230, that the enemy was occupying Buka and Bougainville in strength. McCain's negative search summary finally arrived about midnight. Turner's evening 7 August situation report (only received, as previously noted, by Ghormley and Fletcher late on the morning of the eighth) had requested special scouting against an approach of forces from westward. The *Enterprise*'s afternoon search, extending 260 miles west and 220 miles north from western Guadalcanal, certainly helped fill that lack. At 2155, in one of the few *McCawley* messages to reach its addressees straightaway, Turner predicted the so-called seaplane tenders mentioned in the earlier aircraft sighting report were bound for Rekata Bay on Santa Isabel, 130 miles northwest of Lunga, where they could use "torpedo planes" to menace the Amphibious Force. The soundness of that assessment will be discussed below. Turner desired McCain to bomb Rekata the next morning. Fletcher knew the *Enterprise* afternoon search sighted no activity at Rekata or nothing at all for that matter, but if the supposed seaplane group kept advancing at fifteen knots, it would not have yet come far enough to be sighted. McCain replied at 0254 on 9 August that his planes would check out Rekata as early as possible. B-17s would bomb about noon, and PBYs would be on call for a night torpedo strike.[8]

At 2330, 8 August, after passing beyond southern San Cristóbal, the three carrier groups angled southwest for ninety minutes, then at 0100 wheeled northwest toward Guadalcanal about 115 miles distant. At 0330 Fletcher finally received the message Comsopac composed nearly five hours before. "Recommended withdrawal [of the] carriers [is] approved." Ghormley differed with the critics who argued, "Fletcher could have stayed longer." He called it "a question of judgment," where "hindsight is better than fore sight." Obviously, "The enemy could arrive in force and catch our Task Force short of fuel," so Fletcher's request "had to be considered very seriously." Ghormley accorded "the man on the spot" the benefit of the doubt, because he "knew the situation in detail; I did not." Ironically, Fletcher told Callaghan on 27 July that his boss would probably enjoy a superior appreciation of the overall situation and thought Comsopac could better assess the impact of withdrawing the carriers a day early.[9]

Ghormley's dispatch also resolved the deteriorating fuel situation. The *Kaskaskia* and *Platte*, escorted by the *Clark* and hopefully the *Perkins*, were to depart Nouméa at dawn on 9 August, cut east around New Caledonia, and head northwest toward Espíritu Santo at fifteen knots. They should join TG-61.1 during daylight on 10 August as it came south to meet them. Comsopac's earlier plan called just for the *Platte* and *Clark* to start north on the forenoon of the ninth. The *Perkins* dinged a propeller coming into Nouméa on the eighth, and if Fletcher also needed the *Kaskaskia*, he would have to provide the escort. Now with TG-61.1 low on oil, both fueling groups would go north and keep at least six miles apart, so the same sub could not target both oilers. Should the *Perkins* not participate, as was likely, the two oilers were to draw near the *Clark* for "maximum protection." Although pleased to have both oilers because he needed that additional fuel, Fletcher worried that they might have to be entrusted to only one destroyer.[10]

At 0400 as TG-61.1 drew within seventy-five miles of Guadalcanal and 135 miles of Tulagi, Fletcher led the carrier column around to the northeast, then at 0430 swung them southeast into echelon to make for the fueling rendezvous. Because the formation would loosen considerably, he provided a position for reassembly after dawn. Having seen the carriers safely onto their new heading, he retired to his sea cabin on the flag bridge. The stress of the last several days also took its toll on him. Again it must be emphasized that nothing Fletcher learned that night altered his belief that Turner had pulled out most, if not all, of the transports according to plan, leaving just TF-44 and the cargo ships, and that the first stage of Watchtower was ending on a high note.

FRANTIC NIGHT

Late on the afternoon of 8 August Turner received welcome news that the marines finally overran much of Lunga, including the all-important airfield. Also it seemed he finally got a handle on the unloading of supplies and gear. He recalled in 1950 that he alerted TF-62 "to *prepare* to depart early on the 9th, as the hourly unloading reports from the X-Ray Group led me to believe that the supply situation on shore would then be reasonably good." Turner did not elaborate whether he meant the whole force of transports and cargo ships or just the transports, but after the morning of 8 August he never admitted he ever envisioned withdrawing any of them separately. After sunset he copied Fletcher's message to Ghormley proposing to pull out the carriers. Within the hour came the tardy Comsowespac sighting report of three cruisers, three destroyers, and two seaplane tenders or gunboats discovered off central Bougainville more than eight hours before. In Turner's retrospective account these two messages ignited incandescent anger in the *McCawley*, but whether that occurred immediately or actually a little afterward remains unclear. Ostensibly if the supply situation was as favorable as Turner thought or hoped it was, carrier air support during daylight on 9 August might not be necessary, for most of the Amphibious Force would have already cleared the area. In that event it also would not matter what the mixed group of ships found near Bougainville might do. They did not seem to Turner (as they did not to others) to be a surface force intent on sweeping through the invasion area that night. What really appears to have ruined Turner's evening was word that Yoke Group's unloading at Tulagi "was lagging," meaning he might not get all his landing force out "early on the 9th" after all. Suddenly the message from Fletcher and the belated sighting report took on highly sinister implications.[11]

The venomous account Turner wrote for his administrative history called Fletcher's recommendation to pull out the carriers "almost unbelievable," because it "changed considerably the plans which had been arranged." Obviously that circumstance would only have pertained if Turner had anticipated having the carriers remain on 9 August, which was, of course, what Fletcher said he would do on 27 July. Therefore Turner had every right to be perturbed when Fletcher proposed to leave early. But as detailed before, Turner's assertions of such a betrayal collide head-on with his equally vehement insistence that Fletcher declared the carriers would not stay beyond two days. If Fletcher indeed warned he would withdraw after only two days, Turner could scarcely profess astonishment when it came to pass. Indeed, Turner succeeded in getting it both ways. He propagated the contradiction concerning Fletcher's preinvasion pledges and the fable that he himself had always anticipated keeping the entire Amphibious Force in the invasion area for four to five days, because transports as well as cargo ships needed that long to unload. It also usefully soft-pedaled criticism of the extended delays in unloading.[12]

Thus with contradiction and myth, Turner tainted Fletcher's action as "desertion" in the face of the new peril revealed by the 1025 sighting report. He deduced the enemy tenders would use the sheltered waters of Rekata Bay to employ float torpedo planes and professed to fear such strikes more than the massive land-based air attacks already weathered on 7–8 August. Although accepted without question, Turner's assessment that the seaplane tenders themselves could execute torpedo attacks is highly suspect. Intelligence available to him amply demonstrated that Japanese seaplane tenders, unlike those in the U.S. Navy, handled only single-engine float planes that were far too light to wield torpedoes. Only by servicing flying boats could these tenders even contribute to a torpedo threat. Even so, the limited number of available flying boats would pose far less threat than the fast twin-engine land planes that already assailed the Amphibious Force. Instead a far likelier explanation for the suspected presence of seaplane tenders was to reestablish the reconnaissance capability lost with the fall of Tulagi. Yet Turner, working from an obsolete premise based on his earlier aviation experience, conveniently seized on the supposed torpedo threat from seaplane tenders to go ahead and execute his previously mentioned "prepare to depart" order and withdraw the entire Amphibious Force before sunrise on 9 August. He certainly intended to return sometime later to complete the unloading.[13]

Turner drew up a report as of 2000, 8 August, which, like the previous night, he inexplicably did not transmit for eighteen hours, whereas a prompt airing of his concerns might have given Fletcher a reason to stay.[14] CTF-62 message 090230 (1330, 9 August) is also worth quoting in full:

> Progress retarded today by beach congestion stubborn enemy resistance north side one enemy air attack and one false alarm. Desire express appreciation for warnings by coast watcher Bougainville.
>
> *Elliotts* fire caused by torpedo plane diving on board fire out of control removed personnel and had ship torpedoed but she grounded on shoal and is still burning *Jarvis* anchored not taking water engines and boilers okeh hull bottom open from frame 30 to 55 deck damaged can make 4 to 7 knots own power will try to get her to Roses [Efate] starting tonight 14 enlisted missing 7 wounded.
>
> Continuing discharge of cargo tonight plan temporary retirement from area tomorrow see separate dispatch [CTF-62 message 081405, noted below].
>
> Shore Guadalcanal Kukoom and airfield occupied. Enemy troops and construction workers scattered considerable stores equipment captured. No advance yet to east. Condition airfields reported separately.
>
> Florida area Marines hold Tulagi Gavutu and Tanambogo except for occasional snipers. Assault on Makambo planned for 2300 GCT on 9th [1000 on the tenth]. Severe enemy resistance after initial landing required use all 3 battalions of 2nd Regiment. This will delay Apricot [Ndeni] operation. Recommend use there of 7th Regiment [then in Samoa]. In view further operations CTF 62 remains on *McCawley*.

Thus Turner completely abandoned the idea of pulling out just the empty or near-empty transports and their escorts and leaving Crutchley's TF-44 to protect the five partially unloaded cargo ships anchored close off Lunga. He never explained that radical departure from the original plan.

At 2045 Turner summoned Vandegrift and Crutchley to the *McCawley* to confer in person as soon as possible. That action would cause serious consequences, later laid at Fletcher's door. Turner stated in 1950 he needed to see Vandegrift, "Largely for the purpose of asking him to go to Tulagi to find out and report the exact situation as to the amount of cargo that had been landed." That was a curious errand for a division commander. One wonders why he did not send a staff officer or simply direct the commander of the Yoke Group transports, Capt. George B. Ashe in the *Neville*, or the local marine commander, Brig. Gen. William H. Rupertus, or both, to report. Perhaps the supply situation at Tulagi seemed such a mess that Turner thought only Vandegrift's clout could straighten it out. His "chief purpose" for seeing Crutchley was "to consult him as to his views on the tactical situation, including reports of enemy ship movements and as modified by Fletcher's departure."[15]

Vandegrift could get to the *McCawley* simply by taking a boat to the X-Ray transports off Lunga. Crutchley, though, was in his flagship *Australia* twenty miles away near Savo. Warning he might not return that night, he turned over temporary command of his own patrol group to Captain Bode of the *Chicago* and took the *Australia* to Lunga. He boarded the *McCawley* at 2235, where he found Turner "disturbed over the question of keeping in the area, a large number of ships" and that he "intended to withdraw the surface forces [that is, everything] the next day." Crutchley agreed the surface force spotted that morning did not look strong enough to challenge him. The absence of additional sighting reports of ships closing Guadalcanal, as well as the Comsowespacfor dispatch regarding reinforcements for Buka and Shortland, certainly reinforced that reasonable impression. Turner explained what appears now to be the less credible threat from "torpedo carrying float planes" possibly operating from Rekata Bay.[16]

Vandegrift finally reached the *McCawley* about 2315. Himself exhausted, he thought Turner and Crutchley looked "ready to pass out." The conference lasted forty minutes. Vandegrift stated that he did not have an accurate tally of supplies landed on Guadalcanal but confirmed Turner's belief "we are all right" there. He could not say the same for Tulagi. Given the concern over torpedo planes at Rekata, Vandegrift conceded all transports and cargo ships should depart before dawn, but he specified certain items that must be landed yet that night. He understood the withdrawal was to take place, "Provided the military situation and logistics in the Tulagi area justified," and that Turner would soon return with the rest of the goods. The two commanders left the *McCawley* just before midnight. Saying, "Your mission is much more urgent than mine," Crutchley courteously took Vandegrift in his barge directly to the DMS *Southard* for the trip to Tulagi. As they parted he remarked: "Vandegrift, I don't know that I can blame Turner for what he's doing," a comment that Lt. Col. Jerry Thomas, who was present, "judged to be less than commendatory."[17]

Turner informed TF-62 at 0118 that all ships would retire east at 0630 and compiled a dispatch for Ghormley, Fletcher, and McCain describing his plans to pull out the Amphibious Force:

> Air attacks today resulting in loss of *Elliott* severe damage *Jarvis* probably increasing tomorrow and absence air support require me to withdraw all ships temporarily from this area to avoid unwarranted loss. Separate situation summary [090230 noted above]. This to obtain cooperative measures. Stores and ammunition landed estimated adequate for troops for thirty days replenishment must be accomplished in that time.
>
> Will pass out through Lengo Channel beginning nineteen hours Zed ninth [0600 on the tenth, *sic*, mistake for "eighth"?] speed 13 then course 117 past San Cristobal and toward Button [Espíritu Santo]. Request fighter and antisubmarine air cover.

The message lacked the assurances given Vandegrift that the situation at Tulagi would determine if the withdrawal occurred. The *McCawley* finally radioed it about 0405, and, true to form, no one received it. In the interval, dire events befell the Screening Group that, oddly enough, tarnished Fletcher's reputation much more than those directly responsible for its defense.[18]

DEADLY NIGHT

The Japanese task force that the RAAF aircraft misidentified at 1025 as three cruisers, three destroyers, and two seaplane tenders or gunboats was, of course, Admiral Mikawa's formidable array of five heavy cruisers, two old light cruisers, and one destroyer. He aimed to strike the Allied fleet between Tulagi and Lunga after midnight on 9 August. When discovered, he loitered east of Bougainville, awaiting the return of his dawn search. Knowing he was sighted and fearing air attack yet that afternoon, Mikawa tried to confuse the watcher by reversing course. Free of shadowers after 1200, he resumed his southward advance at twenty-four knots. Passing unscathed through the upper Solomons, he was by sundown just 130 miles from Lunga and two hundred miles from Fletcher's carriers. At 2313 he launched two reconnaissance seaplanes to scout the anchorage and drop flares when the assault force drew near. At 0025 on 9 August one float plane pinpointed a group of cruisers lurking south of Savo where he wanted to penetrate the sound. Mikawa targeted them first. The moonless sky and bad weather proved ideal.[19]

At night Crutchley relied on two destroyers as roving radar pickets for early warning should enemy ships pass north or south of Savo. He deployed the two cruiser-destroyer groups to block the Japanese no matter which approach they tried. Northeast of Savo, Riefkohl's group comprised his *Vincennes*, the *Astoria*, *Quincy*, and two destroyers, while Crutchley's own group with the *Australia*, *Canberra*, *Chicago*, and two destroyers patrolled to the southeast. Covering the back door, Scott's group of two light cruisers and two destroyers shuttled north and south between the Yoke and X-Ray transport areas. Five destroyers, four APDs, and four DMSs screened the transports. Aground off Florida, the stricken transport

George F. Elliott burned, while the hurt *Jarvis*, contrary to orders, limped west to retire via western Guadalcanal. As noted, Turner's summons caused Crutchley to relinquish command of his group to Bode in the *Chicago*. For some reason Bode let the *Canberra* lead his formation. At 2345 as the *McCawley* conference broke up, the *Ralph Talbot*, the picket destroyer northeast of Savo, warned on TBS of a plane headed east over Savo. Neither Turner nor Crutchley copied this message. After delivering Vandegrift to the *Southard*, Crutchley regained the *Australia* about 0115. Given the late hour, the difficulty of effecting a night rendezvous near Savo, the planned predawn withdrawal, and the fact that he, like Turner (and Fletcher), perceived no immediate threat, Crutchley patrolled just west of the X-Ray transport area until first light.

Mikawa's force cut between Savo utterly undetected by the westerly picket destroyer, the *Blue*. Keen eyesight augmented by excellent optics decisively trumped Allied radar. Discerning the unsuspecting *Chicago* group, Mikawa launched torpedoes about 0138 and opened fire five minutes later. Right on cue the float plane circling over Lunga dumped green flares south and east beyond the X-Ray area, effectively silhouetting the Allied ships. Bode's two cruisers responded with utter confusion as Mikawa battered the *Canberra* and torpedoed the *Chicago*'s bow. Swinging counterclockwise around Savo, Mikawa raked Riefkohl's *Vincennes* group from two sides and annihilated it. All three U.S. heavy cruisers sustained fatal damage, but the Japanese were barely scratched. Gatacre, the Screening Group operations officer, later wrote that in accordance with the plan for the split deployment, "An enemy force had encountered one cruiser group and had been deflected into the maw of the other." Only he and Crutchley never dreamt "the maw would be closed!"[20]

After sweeping around Savo, Mikawa's entire force by 0220 tore away northwest at thirty knots. He reasoned he could not reach the Allied transports until nearly first light, when he could expect a beating from carrier planes. In addition to preserving his own limited strength, a speedy retirement might draw pursuing carriers into easy range of bombers based at Rabaul. If he could reach Vella Lavella, two hundred miles northwest of the battle area, he thought he would be safe. Final reports tallied seven heavy cruisers, a light cruiser, and six destroyers either sunk or fatally damaged. Given the highly exaggerated air claims on 8 August, it is no wonder some in the Japanese high command concluded on 10 August that the Americans had evacuated Guadalcanal. Criticism of Mikawa's failure to take out the transports mounted only after that happy event failed to come to pass.

Mikawa came and went before Turner and Crutchley knew anything of the battle other than gun flashes and flickering light from burning ships. Squalls rendered visibility toward Savo quite poor, and lightning continued to mimic gunfire. When the flares appeared, the X-Ray transports and cargo ships ceased unloading, and without orders headed east. At 0156 Turner barked to Crutchley, "Form up your force to repel enemy attack," and twenty minutes later radioed Fletcher to alert him, "Surface forces attacking near Savo apparently on our outpost vessels." Crutchley summoned the X-Ray destroyers into a blocking force northwest of Lunga, but they misunderstood and raced toward a designated point five miles from Savo. For an appreciable time Bode said little over TBS, and the *Vincennes* group kept silent. Not until 0245 did Scott hear any kind of contact report from the *Chicago* group. At 0307 Bode finally revealed that the *Chicago* had been torpedoed and was "slightly down by the bow," and the *Canberra*, attended by two destroyers, was afire five miles southeast of Savo. He also warned of enemy ships "firing to seaward," although Mikawa was long gone. A few minutes later Crutchley could provide Turner only the obvious fact of a "surface action," and that the "situation" remained "undetermined." Because heavy rain obscured the battle area, he knew little more as he interposed the *Australia* between Savo and the X-Ray transports. Turner was appalled to learn at 0330 that Comsopac approved the carrier withdrawal, and at 0345 again tried to awake Fletcher to the danger at Savo. "Surface attack on the screen coordinated with use of aircraft flares. *Chicago* hit torpedo. *Canberra* on fire." Aware the carriers could do nothing before dawn, Turner still hoped to get the Amphibious Force moving out by then. At 0435 he cautioned TF-62, "It is urgent for this force to depart this area at 0630," and, "If *Canberra* cannot join retirement in time she should be destroyed."[21]

Bewilderment plagued the ships off Savo. At 0515 the *Ralph Talbot* reported she was badly damaged by gunfire, but unwittingly gave the impression her misfortune just happened rather than nearly three hours before. At 0525 the destroyer *Patterson* radioed the *Canberra* had abandoned ship and that she rescued her crew. About that time the *Patterson* briefly exchanged fire with the *Chicago*. By first light at 0547 Crutchley possessed only scant news from Bode and none from Riefkohl. "Situation obscure," he alerted TF-62, "be prepared to give battle at dawn in the vicinity of the transport groups." Not until well after sunrise did he learn from the destroyer *Selfridge* that the *Astoria* was burning and that four destroyers recovered her crew. As late as 0819 Crutchley told Turner he had nothing on the *Vincennes* or *Quincy*. In fact the *Quincy* sank at 0238 and the *Vincennes* a dozen minutes later, both with great loss of life.[22]

As Turner tried to fathom the extent of the whipping inflicted on the Screening Group, he heard from Vandegrift in the *Neville* that Tulagi, Gavutu, and Tanambogo were taken, and the last defended position, tiny Makambo Island, would be assaulted after dawn. The bad news was "practically no ammunition, rations, water or AA had been landed except that carried by troops." Ashe only began the unloading at Tulagi at 2340, 8 August, and kept going all night despite the nearby battle and heavy rains. To Turner's great credit he decided to remain despite the threat from aircraft, subs, and surface ships. At 0624 he told his commanders to "cancel departure," and at 0641 had the *McCawley*'s jinxed radio transmit to Fletcher that he was "unable [to] depart as planned because insufficient supplies have been landed. Request [air] cover for attack on enemy surface force this area." Neither Fletcher nor Ghormley received that message. To free up the escort, Turner authorized the *Selfridge* to sink the crippled *Canberra*, which expired at 0800. The *Astoria* still fought for her life out near Savo. Now Turner would see what mayhem the Japanese could cause before he got clear of Guadalcanal.[23]

WHAT SHOULD FLETCHER HAVE DONE?

At 0930 Mikawa exhaled a sigh of relief as he safely passed Vella Lavella. The absence of instant retaliation intensified the sting of Savo. To Fletcher's many critics, that compounded his unnecessary and blatant error of pulling out the carriers too early. Nimitz commented on 23 August, "Absence of all the carrier task forces on the morning of the 9th permitted the enemy to make a clean getaway." Hepburn described the enemy commander at Savo hastening away, "To avoid, if possible, the air attack to be expected from our forces at dawn," and mordantly observed, "The only part of our force capable of making such an attack were [*sic*] at the same time retiring in the opposite direction because of the same apprehension." Pye's analysis challenged Fletcher's failure, given the battle was only 150 miles distant, to have "planes over the Japanese ships—some of which were probably damaged—shortly after daylight." Subsequent critics even accused Fletcher of intentionally abandoning the Amphibious Force. These charges rest on the presumption Fletcher possessed knowledge of the Battle of Savo Island he did not actually have.[24]

Analysis of Turner's communications reveals the pattern of missed messages lasted through 9 August and beyond. The carriers (and Comsopac) failed to intercept nearly all the dispatches the *McCawley* transmitted that night. Around 0300, though, Kinkaid in the *Enterprise* monitored Crutchley's message to Turner regarding a surface action but heard absolutely nothing else from that quarter the rest of the night. At that early hour, while Fletcher awaited Ghormley's decision whether he could withdraw, the three carrier task units, deployed in a widely spaced column, steered toward the south coast of Guadalcanal. Kinkaid, the most junior carrier admiral, deplored the lack of "timely and accurate information of the surface actions" that might have enabled the carriers to strike at dawn. Turner and Crutchley, of course, knew little more of what transpired at Savo, but they were in a much better position to find out than the carriers. Given the paucity of information and the absence of any directive from Fletcher or Noyes, Kinkaid neither acted on his own nor broke radio silence to consult them. Comsopac's approval reached Fletcher and the others at 0330, and without further ado he brought the carriers around to the southeast.[25]

Kinkaid did not think he understood the situation off Guadalcanal sufficiently well to attack. However by 0400, after hearing more snatches of radio traffic from Crutchley and perhaps Turner, Forrest Sherman in the *Wasp* decided it was absolutely essential to attack at Lunga only 120 miles distant. The *Wasp* still had an armed strike spotted on the flight deck. Her air group, "fresh, highly trained, qualified for night operations and eager for combat," could make all the difference up north. Sherman beseeched Noyes to seek Fletcher's permission for the *Wasp* task unit to close Guadalcanal "at maximum speed" and attack. In 1949 he related to Morison that he made "three separate but unsuccessful recommendations [to Noyes] for action along that line," and that a staff officer made "a similar recommendation." To Noyes, though, it was obvious that by turning away from Guadalcanal, Fletcher already made up his mind. He told Sherman that Fletcher "had all the information [they had] and that he would order us to attack if he thought best to do so," but "meanwhile we would keep the [post-dawn] rendezvous."[26] Sherman was crestfallen, and word certainly got around the *Wasp* of the failure to attack. The situation strongly resembled the night of 24–25 October 1944 in the Battle of Leyte Gulf, when Vice Adm. Marc Mitscher declined to challenge Admiral Halsey's run to the north to engage Japanese carriers off Cape Engaño. A successful strike against Mikawa initiated up to an hour before dawn was possible, but only if everything went perfectly. Noyes regretted Fletcher did nothing to help Guadalcanal. Sherman later agreed with historian Fletcher Pratt that exhaustion, "Not with the local tiredness of seventy-two hours on duty, like the crews of the cruisers, but with the accumulated fatigue of many months of the most arduous command of the war," contributed to Fletcher's supposed lassitude, though he was never in a position to make such a personal judgment. Sherman never actually saw Fletcher during the Guadalcanal campaign and did not know the whole situation that morning.[27]

Like Noyes, Sherman, and Kinkaid, the critics believed Fletcher indeed possessed "all the information" regarding the surprise assault at Savo, but nevertheless chose to run away. Bates indignantly informed Morison that the TF-16 war diary demonstrated Fletcher knew of the Savo action as early as 0300 but dawdled until he secured Ghormley's approval a half hour later, then "acted at once to get out of the area without waiting clarification of the surface action report." Fully in accord, Morison discussed Sherman's doomed proposal for the *Wasp* to close Guadalcanal "at high speed" and attack. He could not resist adding the phrase, "With a few well-fueled destroyers," a distinction Sherman never made and which certainly did not exist on 9 August. Instead, Fletcher "hightailed out of the area" and betrayed Turner.[28]

The critics ranked that inglorious retreat the worst of Fletcher's numerous wartime sins. Yet there is no evidence the *Saratoga* or TF-11 even knew until after sunrise of a fight at Savo, much less terrible defeat. Wright told Morison in 1943, "Frank Jack certainly wouldn't have pulled out had he known what happened." In 1952 he declared: "Neither Ghormley or Fletcher knew at this time that a major surface action had taken place near Savo." In 1963 Harry Smith, the former flag lieutenant, explained to Dyer, "For some reason the *Saratoga* did not or could not copy [Turner's] blind [not receipted] despatches sent that night, and it wasn't until other ships sent us the news by blinker or infrared that we started to get the word about the Battle of Savo." Fletcher's 1947 letter to Baldwin avowed it was "shortly after daylight of the ninth we began to intercept garbled radio messages indicative of action of some kind." Dyer quoted Fletcher's 9 September 1942 report to the effect that news of the night battle reached "the force" at 0400 [actually at 0300], but that Fletcher told him, "It wasn't until much later that I was awakened and given the first indication of Savo." Fletcher recalled that he first knew between 0500 and 0600. However, George Clapp, the communication watch officer on duty, confirmed that Fletcher's original statement to Baldwin was correct. Clapp recalled it was definitely after sunrise (0634), when he personally brought a message describing the loss of a cruiser up to flag plot. Only the duty officer was present. According to Maas's diary, the rest of the staff was below having breakfast with him, another strong indication the *Saratoga* was unaware of trouble up north. Rousing the skivvy-clad admiral in his sea cabin constituted one of Clapp's most vivid memories of the war. Fletcher reacted with profound surprise. Asked by Dyer how he might actually have responded had he truly known of Savo as early as 0300, Fletcher said, "Since we were on a northerly course, I might well have continued on it."[29]

What were Fletcher's options at about 0645 when he belatedly learned of the surface fight up north? The first consideration is the status of the carriers. The *Enterprise*, which Noyes's schedule placed in strict reserve, was to have combat air patrol and a strike group ready to launch, while the *Wasp* handled combat air patrol and the *Saratoga* searched and kept F4Fs on standby. At 0600 and a half-hour before sunrise, the *Sara* had launched eight SBDs to sweep 175 miles northwest and routinely examine the waters west of Guadalcanal.

The easternmost sector crossed just west of Lunga. Kinkaid took it upon himself at 0615, in defiance of Noyes's orders, to dispatch two SBDs to Lunga to drop aerial photos to Vandegrift and see what transpired there. About sunrise the carrier task units, steaming southeast at fifteen knots while fifteen to twenty miles apart, established visual contact and maneuvered to resume the task group cruising formation. At that time Cape Henslow was roughly one hundred miles north, and Savo seventy-five miles beyond.[30]

Fletcher's initial knowledge of the previous night's disaster was very sketchy. As yet he did not realize the whole Amphibious Force remained behind. Nor did he know the extent of the tremendous harm inflicted on Crutchley's Screening Group. In 1963 when Dyer asked whether anyone urged him to attack, Fletcher replied, "One or two of my staff recommended that we go back." He declined, because if he were the enemy commander he "would have planned on all our carriers coming back and would hit them with all my land based air." However, he admitted, "If I had it to do all over again that morning and knew about our losses, I would leave one carrier group behind to fuel, and would move two carrier groups up to attack and to continue to provide air support to Kelly Turner." He added, though, "This did not occur to me at the time as being sound," a conclusion fully sustained by the evidence. Obviously the pounding Fletcher endured over the years from the critics took its toll. After the war Kinkaid declared on the basis of hindsight that the carriers should have turned around and chased the retreating cruisers. It is doubtful he would have thought so at the time, when he was more pessimistic than Fletcher or Noyes about the critical fuel situation and the risk of air counterattack.[31]

Closest to when Fletcher actually decided to continue withdrawing, his 9 September report to Ghormley more reliably indicated his thoughts at that time. He conjectured therein that if the carriers had been closer to Guadalcanal, "In the position they would have been, had they remained in the area" (that is, twenty-five miles instead of more than one hundred miles south), it was "barely possible that with definite information" a morning search might have found the enemy force. However, he would have required "sufficient fuel available to operate indefinitely at high speed," which TG-61.1 did not possess. The first thing that evenhanded hindsight demonstrates is that Fletcher needed that "definite information" well before sunrise for any chance to catch the triumphant Mikawa. If first undertaken at 0730—about the earliest any planes could have departed after Fletcher *actually* became aware of Savo—an attack mission of 275 miles could have only reached the lower New Georgia group. Even that would have required the carriers to make a twenty-five-knot sprint (at a ruinous price in oil) to shorten the return flight by seventy-five miles and also exposed them "much further to the northwest." By 0645 Mikawa was nearly three hundred miles northwest of TG-61.1. When this hypothetical strike could have first reached southern New Georgia, he would have been 115 miles beyond. Fletcher's report warned that carriers could not "normally" strike ships that attacked at Guadalcanal at night and "retired at high speed four hours or more before daylight." By 9 September beleaguered Cactus discovered that central truth on its own. Mikawa's great gamble paid off.[32]

In the absence of a clear call for help, which TG-61.1 certainly never received, Fletcher believed the fight off Savo had been a night action and was already concluded. In that event his planes could do nothing. To have the carriers loiter off Guadalcanal would delay his fueling, which he must complete to be ready to battle enemy carriers, and also lengthen his exposure to air attack. Moreover the *Sara*'s search could be expected to report promptly if a sea battle raged off Guadalcanal. Fletcher broke radio silence to raise Turner, but without success. Perhaps the one fair criticism is that before going farther from Guadalcanal, Fletcher did not try harder to learn more what had occurred there. In this context it is again useful to recall what Sherman told Morison in 1949: "It was not until after the night action that the situation became critical."[33]

UNCOVERING A TRAGEDY

Having decided he must press on to the fueling rendezvous, Fletcher waited six hours before the carriers finally drew out of reach of land-based bombers. At 0838 Belconnen relayed a warning from coast watcher Read in northern Bougainville that a formation of aircraft passed overhead at 0807 going southeast. At 0839 Noyes forwarded a message the *Wasp* intercepted between the *McCawley* and a *Saratoga* search SBD: "Appreciate knowing Admiral Fletcher's plan by message drop." Fletcher kept trying unsuccessfully to get into direct radio communication with Turner. The *Saratoga* search returned at 0930 with negative contacts except for the damaged destroyer *Jarvis* limping southwest of Guadalcanal. At 1009 Noyes provided Fletcher the opening paragraph (the rest was not recovered) of Turner's 0105 order to retire (first transmitted at 0405): "Air attacks today resulted in loss *Elliott* severe damage *Jarvis* probably increasing tomorrow and absence air support require me to withdraw all ships temporarily from this area to avoid unwarranted loss." Maas reported to the *Sara*'s flag bridge about the same time Fletcher received confirmation from Mason at Buin of at least ten bombers headed southeast. Thus he might expect the strike by noon. Rabaul loosed seventeen torpedo-armed land-attack planes and fifteen Zeros. Only if carriers and battleships could not be found were they to hit transports. A search plane radioed at 1000 that amphibious ships remained at Tulagi, but snoopers never came closer than sixty miles to the carriers.[34]

Fletcher, however, did not know he had not been sighted. Still ten miles apart, the carriers continued to prepare their air defense. The pair of *Enterprise* SBDs that flew to Guadalcanal saw no enemy ships or evidence of a surface action. At 1114 Fletcher resumed tactical command of TG-61.1 and ordered Noyes, "Double combat air patrol and standby for air attack." It is possible Slonim's radio intelligence team in the *Saratoga* intercepted traffic between Rabaul and its searchers that indicated something was up. At 1155 radars discovered a large bogey, perhaps "many aircraft," fifty miles northwest and closing. Twenty F4Fs hastened to intercept but advised at 1215 the bogey was a B-17. After the search failed to turn up carriers, the Japanese strike pounced on what was first thought to be a hurt battleship leaking oil southwest of Guadalcanal. Ship identification had not improved since Coral Sea, for the quarry was luckless *Jarvis*, which splashed two planes before going down with all hands. The disappointed Japanese thought they sank a British *Achilles*-class light cruiser and regretted not finding anything bigger.[35]

It was only while Fletcher awaited the reported strike that he finally accumulated enough bits and pieces of rebroadcast messages to grasp the appalling defeat of the Screening Group.

At 1150 he radioed Ghormley: "Am receiving dispatches from Turner describing heavy losses in cruisers in engagement which continues to westward. Are you receiving them?" Once the air threat ended at the eight-hundred-mile mark from Rabaul, the entire staff, less Fletcher and the duty officer, assembled in the flag quarters for a somber lunch. That afternoon Maas recorded in his diary, "Things going quite badly at Tulagi. Japs attacked & sank or damaged four cruisers etc." No one could fathom how a few cruisers and destroyers wrought such havoc against a superior number of radar-equipped warships. At 1345 Comsopac warned of a "considerable force sighted east of Bougainville heading southeast." Maas deplored that "latest report [of] Jap troops assaulting Guadalcanal." The marines were "now without air support." By that time the carriers were 250 miles southeast of Lunga. The best way they could help Vandegrift was to expedite refueling.[36]

That afternoon Ghormley complained to Fletcher, McCain, and Nimitz that he had received no situation summary from Turner, except the one for 7 August, and asked them to forward any pertinent information. At 1415 Fletcher relayed everything he had. It did not make pleasant reading:

> Following summary of messages delivered from Turner, quote: At 081645 [0345 on the ninth] surface attack on screen coordinated with use aircraft flares *Chicago* hit torpedo *Canberra* on fire. At 2100Z [0800] heavy actions continue to westward. More of our ships in trouble. Submarines in area. At 2152Z [0852] *Quincy* sunk by torpedoes and gunfire. Air attack enroute. At 2325Z [1025] *Vincennes* sunk by gunfire and torpedoes 0245 [1325] casualties heavy. At 2350 [1050] *Astoria* has fire in wardroom destroyer ordered to pump and [cargo ship] *Alchiba* to tow through Lunga channel to Roses [Efate] as chance to save her. Movements require protection which I am unable to provide. Unquote.

Fletcher concluded by asking Ghormley to "direct Turner to make reports direct to you info to me." This message is perhaps the most telling contemporaneous evidence that Fletcher had no inkling of the existence, much less the scope, of the Savo disaster until long after sunrise on 9 August.[37]

Bates and Innis deplored that Fletcher showed "little concern" for Turner's plight and so ruthlessly abdicated his command responsibility for the Expeditionary Force. Their accusation is valid to the extent that Fletcher weighed priorities and determined his best course of action was to swiftly restore full mobility to the carrier task force by refueling. However, they also found it "surprising" neither Ghormley nor Fletcher advised Turner that Fletcher departed with the carriers, as if Noyes might be expected to drop him off somewhere. They also charged Turner was "not advised of his succession to command or of his superior's plans." Again it must be noted the confusion in the minds of the critics about the nature of Fletcher's command. They failed to grasp that he was tied to the carriers despite having the whole Expeditionary Force. That was an error Nimitz did not repeat. In July 1943 after reading the Hepburn report, Capt. George L. Russell, King's flag secretary, commented, "When Rear Admiral Noyes [*sic*] decided to retire, it may or may not have been with the concurrence of Vice Admiral Fletcher, but whether it was or not, he took

Vice Admiral Fletcher with him." Furthermore, "I don't know what Vice Admiral Fletcher contributed to the operation." It is unfortunate—or incredible—that neither Fletcher's superiors nor Hepburn ever officially asked him to describe his command relationships and decisions during the Guadalcanal landings. Suffice it here to note that by the morning of 9 August Fletcher believed he had no choice but to move the carriers south for fuel to prepare for the big carrier action that must be in the offing. As noted, the noon fuel state of the destroyers averaged 35 percent. The heavy ships were also getting low. It was high time to begin the lengthy refueling process.[38]

Fletcher's message to Ghormley crossed one from Nimitz to Ghormley again offering well meant but unwittingly ill-timed praise. "Your shipmates in Pacific Ocean Areas are watching your progress with great admiration." Soon afterward a shocked Nimitz passed Fletcher's dire news to Cominch. The dispatch reached Washington after midnight on 9 August. Russell violated King's injunction against interrupting his sleep by bringing the word that burst the bubble of excessive optimism regarding the prospects for Watchtower's easy success. King recalled it as the "blackest day of the whole war."[39]

At 1415 MacArthur placed four enemy cruisers northeast of Bougainville and headed northwest. They looked like the culprits that struck Savo the previous night. However, Ghormley cautioned, "Indications enemy landing forces [are] proceeding against Cactus." Radio intelligence hinted of Mikawa's plans to send a small convoy with naval infantry to the west tip of Guadalcanal. Once Mikawa realized the strength of naval forces in the area, he had recalled the convoy, but the *S-38* picked off one of the transports in St. George's Channel. Another venerable, valiant southwest Pacific S-boat won the only immediate revenge for Savo. On the morning of 10 August, in an action reminiscent of the *I-168* at Midway, the *S-44* sank the heavy cruiser *Kako* as she was about to enter Kavieng harbor on New Ireland. No one on the Allied side knew that good news for two weeks.

Late on the afternoon of 9 August Ghormley queried Fletcher about the radio frequency of Turner's messages. Fletcher replied 2122 kilocycles, but "reception [is] very poor; am missing most of his transmissions." At 1850 Ghormley ordered Turner to withdraw all naval forces to Nouméa. Unsure whether the Second Marines ever landed at Ndeni, he gave Turner three options. If the regiment was still at Guadalcanal it was to remain there. If it was already at Ndeni, it was to stay there. Otherwise he should drop off the Second Marines at Espíritu Santo. McCain was to withdraw the *Mackinac* and her PBYs from Malaita, although she had been supposed to stay until relieved by the *Ballard* on 13 August. Likewise Ghormley directed the *McFarland* and her PBYs pull out of Ndeni if the Second Marines were not there. Thus McCain's long-range search suffered crippling blows. Ghormley told Fletcher, "Cover movement as practicable without interference with fueling."[40]

Indeed Turner was already in the midst of pulling out his forces after a rough day cleaning up after the loss of the cruisers. The appearance of only a few SBDs demonstrated that Fletcher's carriers had gone. After the first coast-watcher warning Turner suspended unloading at 0840 and herded the transports and cargo ships into defensive formation. Air attack seemed imminent, and he was painfully aware he lacked fighter support. By 1100 when no strike turned up, he recalled his ships. Vandegrift told him that vital equipment and supplies for Tulagi remained in three Yoke transports, and one in the X-Ray Group held similar necessary cargo for Lunga. Turner directed those ships to resume unloading, but the others were to retrieve their landing boats and prepare to depart. He detailed the barely unloaded cargo ship *Alchiba* to take the *Astoria* in tow, but at 1215, before that could occur, the cruiser sank. Turner ordered all survivors placed in transports. Early that afternoon he notified the X-Ray Group (six transports and five cargo ships, the damaged *Chicago*, three destroyers, and the five high-speed minesweepers) to get under way at 1500 and withdraw. In the meantime he took the *McCawley* over to Tulagi and personally led the Yoke Group (six transports, one cargo ship, and four APDs, the *Australia*, *San Juan*, *Hobart*, and nine destroyers) eastward at 1700. That afternoon only a "small quantity" of additional matériel was landed at Lunga, although Tulagi did get ten days' worth of supplies, that only just, according to Ashe, averted "catastrophe." Sunset on 9 August found Vandegrift's marines totally on their own, minus much of their equipment and supplies (cargo ships *Betelgeuse* and *Alchiba* left with 50 and 75 percent respectively of their cargoes), not to mention fourteen hundred men (mostly Second Marines) still in transports. Vandegrift certainly did "stand alone" at Guadalcanal.[41]

THE GOAT

On 12 August as TF-62 neared Nouméa, Turner transmitted the first detailed summary of Savo. He outlined the split deployment of the Screening Group that intercepted "enemy CAs DDs or torpedo boats probably subs," with "heavy running actions" continuing about forty minutes. He knew of "no knowledge of damage to enemy except one sub probably sunk." Late on the night of 11–12 August copies went to King and the White House. On the thirteenth King explained to Roosevelt that battleships *South Dakota* and *Washington* and light cruiser *Juneau* would more than compensate for the sunken heavy cruisers. In 1949 Morison opined the loss of the four cruisers at Savo "delayed the completion of Operation 'Watchtower' for several months," a judgment Turner called an "exaggeration." Savo inflicted its greatest blow to the navy's pride. Initially it was thought only the misreported handful of cruisers and destroyers first sighted on 8 August off Bougainville sprang the colossal surprise. Not until October did prisoners of war reveal there were five heavy cruisers, two light cruisers, and one destroyer.[42]

The main causes of the Savo disaster were inadequate night battle training, inexperience, insufficient number of destroyers, over-reliance on radar, and a lack of readiness by very tired captains and crews, greatly abetted by the belief of the top commanders that no surface threat existed that night. Other factors certainly applied, but in truth the Screening Group failed. Crutchley honestly told Turner: "The fact must be faced that we had adequate force placed with the very purpose of repelling surface attack and when that surface attack was made, it destroyed our force." On 8 September the third Cominch-Cincpac conference discussed Savo at length and singled out Crutchley's night disposition for criticism. The long delay by Comsowespac in forwarding the cruiser sighting report on 8 August "made no difference," because it was still "received in time to be acted upon." Ghormley bore "overall responsibility," although the "immediate responsibility" was Turner's. "Final judgment" must await "receipt of completed reports." On 8 October Nimitz queried

Ghormley for his "opinion as to the responsibility for the dispositions and actions" at Savo. "Such a blow cannot be lightly passed over, and we owe it to the country to do our best to fix the responsibility for that disaster, and to take the action necessary to prevent a recurrence." The "final reports" proved unavailing. In December King assigned Hepburn the task of investigating Savo and assessing fault.[43]

Turner was adamant he would accept no blame for the disaster. Nothing he did—nor any action of Crutchley's that he previously approved—contributed in any way to the debacle. Marine Gen. Bill Twining put it well. "In [Dyer's biography of Turner] there is a particularly illuminating passage of intemperate denials wherein [Turner] places blame for the disaster on just about everyone in the world except himself and Mother Teresa." Turner deflected complaints concerning the inadequate radar picket and the divided deployment of the Screening Group (important factors in the defeat) onto the faulty search that misidentified the Japanese ships. He also castigated the precipitate withdrawal of the carriers that forced him to convene the conference, pull Crutchley and the *Australia* off line, and fatally weaken the western cruiser group. Ultimately, though, it was all Fletcher's fault. "It was expected that the covering force would prevent the arrival of superior enemy forces in the vicinity of Savo Island, but that expectation was not well founded." Moreover, "When seven enemy cruisers and seven [*sic*] destroyers arrived to combat the five cruisers and six destroyers on outpost duty, no help was given by other naval forces either to support our attack or to destroy the enemy naval forces during their retirement." Thus Turner cast aspersions not only on Fletcher, but also Rear Adm. Norman Scott, who led the nearby group of two light cruisers and two destroyers. Scott, who died a hero's death at Guadalcanal in November 1942, could not answer such a challenge. Turner's shifting of the blame worked brilliantly. Morison's *Two Ocean War* condescendingly decreed the "worst of all blunders that night," above any failure by the Screening Group, was "'Frank Jack'" pulling out the carriers. This interpretation is an astonishing tribute to Turner's ability to mask his own culpability.[44]

Critics roundly condemned the search effort by carriers and shore-based air alike.[45] Divided between Sowespac, Aircraft, South Pacific Force (Airsopac), and TG-61.1, the search was badly coordinated, with poor ship identification and tardy reporting of results. Yet the area was huge and remote from the few friendly air bases with only a handful of search planes. At the same time the stronger than expected response of enemy air power constrained Fletcher to shift the carriers south of Guadalcanal and unfortunately reduced that part of the central Solomons his planes could examine. None of this should have surprised anyone. Nevertheless, no enemy force reached Guadalcanal totally undetected. The search network, feeble as it was, did sight Mikawa on 8 August. Regretfully the word got to Fletcher too late to strike Mikawa that day, while Turner perceived no immediate surface threat. Turner recalled in his 1945 history that Fletcher promised if land-based air could not cover any sectors, the carriers would "fill in for short-range scouting, both morning and late afternoon, to protect against the approach of surface forces." Yet "so far as is known," Fletcher "never sent his scouting planes in any direction, but this fact was learned only considerably later." Where Turner "learned" that "fact"is not known, because it is demonstrably false. Obviously, though, it was just one instance of how he blackened Fletcher's reputation.

The following year he told Baldwin the carriers *never* scouted the Slot on 8 August. In fact Fletcher's comprehensive afternoon search only missed Mikawa by thirty miles.[46]

Hepburn indicted Fletcher for contributing to the "disproportionate damage" sustained by the ships at Savo. "The withdrawal of the carrier groups on the evening before the battle" was "responsible for Admiral Turner's conference, which in turn was responsible for the absence of the *Australia* from the action," and that Turner's "need to confer with his senior commanders cannot be questioned." However, it is strongly debatable whether that particular conference was really justified. It is vital to stress once again if Turner truly believed that Fletcher said all along the carriers would only remain two days, he should have planned accordingly and not been surprised. Instead, he insisted on an immediate face-to-face meeting with his two top subordinates. Vandegrift's presence might have been necessary for Turner to gain a better idea of conditions ashore, but Crutchley personally led one of two groups of cruisers and destroyers that guarded Savo. Although Crutchley had queried Turner that morning for a summary of the plan—logical in that he was second in command of the Amphibious Force and standing orders existed for a major withdrawal that night—he did not necessarily require or desire to meet directly with his boss. Turner claimed to Hepburn he never intended to pull the *Australia* off her patrol station but did not explain how Crutchley would otherwise reach the conference. Then he amended his statement to the effect that he thought things would be quiet at least until midnight, because no surface force should arrive before Crutchley and the *Australia* could resume guard duty. Of course, neither Turner nor Crutchley thought anything was going to happen that night, so much that Crutchley felt justified not returning on station.[47]

Bates and Innis concurred with Hepburn. Turner's decision to confer with his subordinates was "sound" and of "extreme importance." They based their conclusion on the false premise that Turner had intended all along to keep the transports and the cargo ships off Guadalcanal for a full five days. Hence the prospect of being forced to withdraw "two days ahead of time," with "serious implications for the marines ashore," mandated that Turner summon Crutchley and Vandegrift to coordinate the revised plan. Although in general agreement concerning Vandegrift's attendance, Morison still wondered why Crutchley, too, had to be present. In contrast, Twining called the conference a "tragic folly" and decried efforts to whitewash Turner's actions, particularly with regard to Crutchley. Turner could have just sent a message or even detailed staff officers to brief his two subordinates. "Nothing could have been accomplished at such a meeting, and nothing was accomplished," although Twining conceded, "Turner was left uncovered by Fletcher's flight and had to pull out through no fault of his own."[48]

The more realistic explanation, however, is that by 2000 on 8 August, Turner already decided to abandon incremental withdrawals and instead pull out the entire force by the next dawn, despite not having landed all the men and supplies even from the transports. He desired his two top commanders ratify what was certain to be viewed as a controversial move. In keeping with Turner's bullheaded reputation as someone not disposed to "consult" anyone, the meeting by all indications constituted more a lecture than any actual "consultation." Vandegrift hated to see all the ships depart but acquiesced mainly because he thought the supply situation at Guadalcanal was "all right," although he could not say the same for Tulagi. Because Turner steadfastly supported Crutchley's night combat dispositions, it is understandable Crutchley never complained about the odd circumstances that kept him out of the most important battle of his career. In turn his staff officer Gatacre did not "deny" that Turner was "right" in summoning his boss, but strongly deplored the resulting absence of flagship *Australia*, considered the most battle-ready ship in the Screening Group. He believed her presence might have made all the difference.[49]

The leaders of the Amphibious Force and the First Marine Division all closed ranks to condemn Fletcher. It was in their interest to do so. However, there remained the question of whom to blame for the unloading woes and the consequent failure to leave adequate supplies, despite having kept the transports and cargo ships off Guadalcanal through most of 9 August. All that could not be laid solely at Fletcher's door. Maas and Pye independently questioned why Turner withdrew without completing the unloading. Bates and Innis admitted the marines had only half their sixty-day allotment of supplies and four instead of ten units of fire. Yet they excused the poor performance of the Amphibious Force on 9 August by stating that Turner, upon "realizing the difficulty of getting supplies ashore" and that "practically no supplies had been landed all day," decided "nothing was to be gained by remaining." That begs the question why Turner did not do more to organize and expedite the unloading, although in truth much of the chaos arose from everyone's gross inexperience. It is interesting that Turner told Hepburn in 1943 that he felt "certain the transports could not be unloaded in two days," but on 20 August 1942 he directed the Seventh Marines and Fifth Defense Battalion at Samoa to embark "in such manner as will ensure AP's unloading in 48 hours AK's [cargo ships] in 72 hours unloading day and night." That schedule accorded with his pre-7 August prognostications that the feat could be done, but once confronted with the responsibility for the breakdown at Tulagi and Guadalcanal, Turner averred such speed in unloading the transports was never possible.[50]

Anticipating criticism for the bungled Watchtower supply situation, Turner attempted to shift the responsibility to Vandegrift. He blamed the marine pioneers at Red Beach for not unloading the boats and shifting supplies inland and explained to the commander of the Seventh Marines, "There were two primary reasons for failure to completely unload: first the vast amount of unnecessary impediments taken, and second a failure on the part of the 1st Division to provide adequate and well organized unloading details at the beach." The marines did not quietly abide Turner's self-exoneration. Citing the division supply officer, Twining charged, "Very little unloading was accomplished after the enemy torpedo plane attack on the afternoon of 8 August." Moreover, on 9 August the "disorder" in the Amphibious Force again became manifest when some transports never even retrieved all their landing boats before hauling out. Vandegrift deplored the intransigence of Captain Ashe, the Yoke Group transport commander, as a major cause for the unloading fiasco at Tulagi, while Twining laid the responsibility for the mess at Guadalcanal on Capt. Lawrence F. Reifsnider, Ashe's X-Ray Group counterpart. Twining also thought Turner should have landed all the marines still on board the transports. In what stands as a fair assessment given all the circumstances, Dyer stated the Amphibious Force did a "commendable job" unloading despite inexperience and highly adverse circumstances.[51]

Any risk that Turner would suffer relief or even rebuke over Savo swiftly faded. He was too valuable to the war effort and enjoyed a strong ally in Spruance, who knew him well from the Naval War College. On 8 September Nimitz even told King that should Ghormley's health fail, he preferred Turner as Comsopac. By early 1943 when Hepburn actually began his inquiry, the Guadalcanal campaign was won, and Turner played a pivotal role. Hepburn granted him and Crutchley full opportunity to describe the situation at Savo and explain their actions. As usual, Turner proved a persuasive advocate on his own behalf and received the benefit of every doubt. Indeed Russell explained to King in July 1943 that Turner emerged from Hepburn's Savo investigation with "pretty much a clean bill of health." That verdict was not merely expedient but just. As one of Nimitz's inner circle, Turner led the amphibious forces during some of the toughest invasions in the Pacific and contributed significantly to the defeat of Japan. But that does not erase the fact that Turner, to salvage his reputation and career, relentlessly misrepresented events to malign Fletcher and others.[52]

"It does not necessarily follow that because we took a beating," Russell sagely suggested, "somebody must be the goat." Turner and Crutchley were exonerated; Bode and Riefkohl were censured; and Ghormley, Fletcher, and Noyes were found wanting. However, Hepburn never accorded Fletcher or Noyes the same thorough hearing as Turner and Crutchley before condemning their actions, indeed never even extended them the courtesy of consulting them. In March 1943 as his investigation neared its end, Hepburn passed through San Francisco. Fletcher was nearby in Seattle, and Noyes in San Diego. Nor did Turner or the marines ever acknowledge their obligation to Fletcher to seize their objectives swiftly and expedite unloading to clear out as quickly as possible and reduce the risk to the carriers of being caught in a static covering position. Fletcher explained to Dyer, "A defensive decision was in order on 8 August, although perhaps not exactly the one I made at the time." He, unlike Turner, was prepared to consider that his decisions may have erred—even when those actions, at least until after he actually learned of the defeat at Savo, were not only fully defendable but, as Maas stressed on 8 August, also sound.[53]

On 13 August Crutchley's action report offered perhaps the best perspective of events at that moment. "The success or failure of this operation cannot yet be judged as it depends on our ability to hold what we have taken and to make use of it for further offensive operations."[54]

CHAPTER 27

Covering Cactus

DEFENSIVE DECISIONS

Assessing the Guadalcanal campaign years afterward, Turner deplored two unnecessary "defensive decisions" at the outset that "helped bring on months of hard and costly defensive and offensive fighting." The first was Fletcher's precipitate carrier withdrawal that prevented the Amphibious Force from completely unloading. It also caused the debacle at Savo by forcing Turner to summon Crutchley away from his cruiser group. The second was Vandegrift's sudden resolve to form a defensive perimeter around Lunga, instead of eradicating the "nucleus" of opposition on Guadalcanal. Turner judged the First Marine Division, if properly deployed (that is, dispersed) around the huge island, fully capable of repulsing any attempt to secure a lodgment. In truth, both Fletcher and Vandegrift predicated their decisions on the belief the Japanese would soon reappear in great strength. Vandegrift most feared a massive counter-landing over the Lunga beaches to seize the airfield, and Fletcher understood only his flattops stood in the way of hostile carriers that had to support such an enormous undertaking.[1]

Vandegrift prefaced the 11 August message announcing his perimeter defense by stating the "position here [is] secure but feel that considerations not previously apparent should be presented." He had a point. Ghormley and MacArthur had not looked much beyond the initial landing phase, but Nimitz, Fletcher, and Vandegrift independently recognized Japan would respond viciously. King and Turner seem to have assumed the seizure of Guadalcanal would open the way for Task Two, the advance to Rabaul's periphery. Vandegrift's decision to circle the wagons until Japan could be defeated at sea was so logical given circumstances at the time and so completely vindicated by subsequent events, only Turner ever questioned it. On the other hand, judgments of Fletcher's handling of the carriers in the two weeks after the landing were harsh. He clearly failed to meet the expectations of some of his superiors (Ghormley the possible exception), who thought just having TF-61 in Sopac meant it could always dominate the waters surrounding Guadalcanal. Instead, "considerations not previously apparent" also applied to the carriers after Savo. Therefore it is vital to analyze Fletcher's orders and understand the special conditions that pertained.[2]

On 10 August Ghormley repeated his warning of a "landing attack" against Cactus. Nimitz emphasized the "successful accomplishment" of Task One now hinged on preventing a landing assault on Guadalcanal. Ghormley was to "use carrier task forces as practicable in opposition." MacArthur's search planes must "detect and report movement in time and that when our carriers are in range of enemy aircraft their bases be bombed in such a manner as to effect maximum damage during such period." In truth, MacArthur had too few resources to accomplish such formidable tasks. Comsopac issued a new directive on 11 August that dissolved the Expeditionary Force. TF-61 was to protect the Espíritu Santo–Nouméa line, support the Guadalcanal garrison by destroying the "hostile attack force," and "cover movement of our aviation ground crews ground equipment and aviation supplies into Cactus area." Ghormley hoped to give Fletcher "about 24 hours warning of hostile landing attack force moving against Cactus."[3]

Ghormley well understood Fletcher faced no easy task. To Nimitz, he articulated his views on "island warfare," a "tough nut." Cactus required regular deliveries of supplies, equipment, and reinforcements, but Espíritu Santo, the nearest support base, remained only weakly developed and defended. Sopac must run supply ships through "very restricted waters" menaced by land-based air, subs, and surface raiding forces. Given adverse conditions in the initial landings, "We are lucky to have gotten out as much as we did." Holding Guadalcanal in proximity of Rabaul was like having the "bull by the tail," and the "bull doesn't like it." One solution was to get aircraft to Guadalcanal to protect the vast logistical effort necessary to sustain Cactus. On 10 August in the absence of firm word from Turner that the Lunga airfield was ready, Ghormley redirected the *Long Island* to Suva. "At any moment" an amphibious threat might appear, "and remembering Midway, we know that such an expedition will be heavily covered by air except this time it will be shore based air instead of carrier based air, leaving their carriers free to operate against ours." The Japanese might hold off landing on Guadalcanal until their carriers came south. Ghormley deemed it vital to "exercise the greatest care in using [the U.S.] carriers to operate against surface forces protected by shore based aviation when the enemy might work a squeeze play and strike them with his carriers."[4]

Callaghan did well relaying the concerns Fletcher raised on 27 July, for Ghormley's assessment closely reflected Fletcher's own thinking. Enemy carriers remained foremost in Fletcher's mind, as he prepared to wage the big battle he must win to retain control of imperiled Cactus. No one realized Japan would begin by reinforcing Guadalcanal in a manner very difficult for carrier and land-based air alike to stop. Providing close air cover for transporting supplies and men to Cactus would prove most difficult. Fletcher could not simply station his few flattops off Guadalcanal indefinitely to make up for the absence of shore-based air. Pederson observed in 1944, "Carriers cannot be expected to do more than support the assault phase of an amphibious operation," whereas the "lack of air facilities at Guadalcanal required the carriers to be in position to furnish support." He recalled Fletcher fully realized the "defensive task of patrolling a given area was dangerous but the role was forced upon us by the urgency of the situation that then existed." The Allies learned that lesson. In November during the Torch invasion of North Africa, a dedicated land-based air contingent swiftly deployed ashore.[5]

The withdrawal of the PBYs from Ndeni compounded the risk of exposing the carriers in advanced positions. McCain's long-range searches now originated far to the rear, which drastically "shortened the margin of warning [TF-61] could receive of any impending attack." Long delays persisted in forwarding search results. McCain's 9 August summary ("all sectors negative") did not go out until 0114 on the tenth. As soon as Fletcher could circumvent radio silence by flying messages ashore, he requested McCain to send "as soon as possible after completion searches," the "negative and positive information and percentage of coverage." In turn Ghormley explained to Leary and MacArthur, "[The]retired position [of] our carriers while awaiting enemy attack with relation distance Rabaul to enemy objectives makes necessary they receive information [of] enemy naval surface movements [at the] earliest moment." The failure to coordinate carrier and land-based air constituted one of the gravest Allied weaknesses in the Solomons campaign.[6]

TF-61 REFUELS

Before Fletcher could do anything for Cactus, he must refuel. On the afternoon of 10 August he was relieved to find the *Platte* and *Kaskaskia*, screened only by the *Clark*, five hundred miles from Guadalcanal and 150 miles southwest of Espíritu Santo. Kinkaid's TF-16 fueled first, to the joy of the *Grayson*'s Lt. Cdr. Frederick J. Bell, who noted, "We were rapidly reaching the bottom of our fuel tanks." Some destroyers had only 12–15 percent of capacity. The carrier aviators welcomed the rest. Constant flight operations on 7–9 August caused near exhaustion. Fletcher flew a message to Efate advising Ghormley that he anticipated completing fueling on the afternoon of 12 August and would remain southwest of Espíritu Santo "awaiting orders." He requested the return of the destroyers lent to Turner and asked whether Efate still needed the fighter belly tanks. After the *Kaskaskia* and *Platte* left for Nouméa to refill from chartered tankers, he desired the *Cimarron*, which left Suva on the tenth after restocking, to meet him on the thirteenth to top off destroyers. Fletcher could take nothing for granted in the rickety Sopac logistical setup.[7]

At sunrise on 12 August while TF-11 fueled, two SBDs discovered a surfaced sub twenty-six miles south. Strangely, the I-boat at first stayed and fought but submerged after sustaining heavy damage. Fletcher detached the *Grayson* and *Sterett* to keep the sub down until dark to permit TF-61 to get clear. There were no further sightings that day. The interloper was the *I-175* hunting transports withdrawing from Guadalcanal. Coming off second best, she limped to Rabaul. Allied intelligence read at least part of a situation report the *I-175* subsequently radioed and deduced that a sub might have sighted the U.S. carriers. Fletcher received a Cincpac warning to that effect on 14 August.[8]

By 12 August TF-61 drained the *Platte* and *Kaskaskia* of 176, 212 barrels that brought most ships toward full capacity. Fletcher added the *Gwin* to escort the oilers safely clear. After detaching the Fueling Group, he proceeded southeast to meet the *Cimarron* the next noon 150 miles west of Efate. Because TF-61 required so much oil merely following a week of "almost normal cruising," its regular resupply must be ensured. In a message delivered on 14 August, Fletcher requested the two oilers, after replenishing, be sent to another rendezvous with TF-61. In the meantime he would retain the *Cimarron* nearby. Fletcher's status report, which Ghormley forwarded to Nimitz, raised new concern at Pearl over the Sopac oil situation. On 10 August Ghormley, incredibly, declined Cincpac's offer of an additional oil shipment from the West Coast. Nimitz queried again whether more oil was necessary. He had to know immediately, "owing to long distance and time involved." The latest figures of supply and consumption finally persuaded Ghormley he could experience another "serious fuel shortage" by mid September.[9]

Fletcher, marking time, did not expect to move the carriers very far. Nimitz chafed at this perceived inactivity, especially as intelligence continued to show the Japanese carriers remained at home. On 11 August (12 August in Sopac) McCormick remarked that TF-61 "still" occupied "a retired position presumably awaiting necessity for covering reinforcements to the Tulagi area." Although Japan assembled "a strong striking force," Nimitz told Ghormley it might not come south for seven to ten days, owing to the "need for logistics arrangements plus necessity assemble destroyer screen." In that interval Ghormley was to employ "every means available" to "strengthen our position" at Guadalcanal "prior to arrival above force in area." Carrier aircraft must furnish air cover "as long as necessary" while shore-based air afforded "maximum protection."[10]

Perhaps distrusting Cincpac's estimate, Ghormley never told Fletcher the carriers might not appear for at least seven days. Little seemed to be happening to organize the move of supplies and aircraft to Cactus. Ghormley's diversion of the *Long Island* to Suva delayed the arrival of marine aircraft at Cactus for several days, but Vandegrift was not yet ready for them. Late on 10 August Turner finally declared the airfield could take fighters the next day. Ammunition and gasoline was available, but no aviation ground personnel. On the twelfth Vandegrift, eager for air support, reported, "Improved fueling facilities can be made available for fighters." Declaring "imperative" the "early establishment of air" at Cactus, Ghormley ordered McCain to load all available high-speed transports with aviation supplies and personnel and rush them to Guadalcanal. The *Long Island* would then transport the planes to Cactus. She was to be at Espíritu Santo on 16 August and run the ferry mission soon afterward. McCain offered the good news that a PBY-5A amphibian actually touched down briefly at the Lunga airstrip.[11]

The *Cimarron* hove into view of TF-61 on 13 August, accompanied by six destroyers, the result of a fortuitous encounter the previous dawn with TF-62 southeast of Espíritu Santo. In turn Fletcher returned them to their former task forces and retained the *Wilson* and *Aaron Ward* to protect the *Cimarron*.[12] Late that afternoon Efate, about 150 miles northwest, reported being shelled. Fletcher steered northwest to cut off the retreat of whatever force menaced the island. Just before sundown he learned actually Tulagi, 650 miles northwest, was attacked. He increased speed to twenty knots and directed the slower *Cimarron* group to meet him later roughly halfway to Guadalcanal. Overnight as TF-61 pounded northwest, no new information came from Tulagi or Guadalcanal. The daily Cincpac intelligence bulletin still opined all first-line carriers remained in Japan, but Fletcher took no chances. Departing before dawn on 14 August, SBDs searched two hundred miles west and north with negative results. Later that morning word finally came that the attack on Tulagi the previous evening was only a brief raid. Fletcher dropped to fifteen knots but continued northwest until he confirmed Tulagi was safe. Subs caused the ruckus. The *I-123* bombarded Lunga on the morning of 13 August, and the *I-122* assailed Tulagi that evening.[13]

Fletcher informed his task group commanders that should they run into enemy warships, TF-61 would divide into Wright's Surface Attack Group (one battleship, five heavy cruisers, one light cruiser, and four destroyers) and Noyes's Air Attack Group with the three carriers and eleven destroyers. Wright's chief mission was "defense of carriers against surface attack," presumably at night, but he might be employed on "special" missions if required. Fletcher, however, could ill-afford such ventures. The carriers needed those ships for protection. Sopac suffered from the lack of a dedicated surface force to react to small or medium scale efforts to land troops and supplies at Guadalcanal, but it was impractical for TF-61 to furnish it.[14]

Near sundown on 14 August, with no further alarms, Fletcher broke off to rejoin the *Cimarron* 325 miles southeast of Guadalcanal. In the absence of a direct threat to Cactus, he seized the opportunity to fuel in case the next batch of chartered tankers was also tardy. The *Chester Sun* reached Nouméa on 11 August, a day ahead of schedule, but two more tankers supposed to arrive on the thirteenth failed to show. The *Platte* drew oil from the *Chester Sun* on 14 August, but TF-62 and TF-44 took their share, while empty *Kaskaskia* awaited another tanker "due today or tomorrow." Lacking destroyers, Ghormley retained the *Gwin* and *Clark* to escort the Fueling Group. Light cruiser *San Juan* with Rear Adm. Norman Scott (senior cruiser flag officer with TF-61) awaited the opportunity to return to the carriers. At sunrise on 15 August Fletcher encountered the *Cimarron* group and directed all destroyers to top off. In 11.5 hours the oiler serviced no fewer than seventeen cans. Cdr. Russell M. Ihrig, her captain, proudly reported to Comserforpac the "very great improvement" made "in the technique of fueling at sea and in the reduction of the time involved." When the *Cimarron* came out to the Pacific in April 1942, "The average time between completing pumping to one destroyer and commencing pumping to another was approximately 45 minutes." Now that interval averaged twenty minutes. The *Cimarron* routinely fueled two ships at a time despite "fairly radical course changes." Because "the pumping rate is fairly constant," Ihrig judged any further gain "can be made only by reducing the time of approach and connecting up." Destroyer skippers rapidly increased their skill. "Cruiser time is still too great," although "roughly halved as experience has been gained." Underway refueling progressed enormously since the dark days of December 1941. Morison misunderstood, because he only witnessed the process following that marked improvement.[15]

OFFENSIVE PATROL

After sundown on 15 August Fletcher detached the *Cimarron*, with more than half her oil, and a destroyer to Efate to stand by for Comsopac orders. He cruised toward the center of the Coral Sea, just as in March and April, and passed about three hundred miles south of Guadalcanal. TF-61 would keep within twelve hours of strike range (two hundred miles) of Cactus, except when actually fueling. The *Cimarron* delivered a message to Comsopac advising Fletcher's intention to linger in the vicinity of familiar Point Corn, 325 miles south of Guadalcanal, "awaiting developments and your orders." Some ships ran low on food. "Will transfer provisions if necessary so should be able to remain in area not over 3 weeks." The full force must refuel about 19 August, a process that must occur every six to seven days to ensure TF-61 never was so low in oil as on 10 August. Fortunately the oil deficit at Nouméa greatly eased. The tanker Ghormley diverted from New Zealand appeared on the fourteenth and replenished the *Kaskaskia*, while the two tardy tankers hove in the next day to top off the *Platte*. At the same time the fleet oiler *Sabine* neared Suva.[16]

On the evening of 15 August four APDs slipped into Lunga with supplies and aviation support personnel in the form of 120 untrained but willing sailors from CUB-1. The slow *William Ward Burrows*, carrying the actual marine ground crews, would only reach Efate on 17 August. With rations in great shortage and the marines living largely on captured food, Turner desired the *Alhena* and *Fomalhaut* go in "as soon as possible," followed by the *Fuller* and *Zeilin* with additional base defense troops. Subs and aircraft hit Tulagi and Guadalcanal "without any apparent hindrance," while "surface vessels may be expected at any time for the purpose of blockading the port and bombarding the positions ashore." Turner wanted McCain to institute daily antisubmarine PBY patrols around Cactus beginning 16 August and conduct "offensive sweeps" with B-17s up the Solomons to deter surface raids. Fletcher was to maintain a squadron of carrier fighters over Lunga for six hours every day. Each large ship going into Cactus should have two escort destroyers. It is unclear whether Turner actually expected Fletcher to park the carriers off Guadalcanal and provide this escort on demand. Ghormley admitted that "hostile subs and aircraft" cavorted "quite freely" off Guadalcanal and tasked McCain to fly the antisubmarine patrols and bomber sweeps. However, he said nothing to Fletcher about fighter patrols or destroyers he knew the carriers could not supply. Vandegrift's own marine squadrons would partially mitigate that grave situation, but their deployment might be further delayed. On 13 August the *Long Island*'s captain rated his marine fighter pilots too inexperienced to go into Cactus. Ghormley reacted in fury. "I need fighter planes at Cactus now and have counted on those in *Long Island* as available." Nimitz, who bore much of the responsibility for not having planes ready for Cactus, replied the pilots were carrier-qualified. McCain offered to provide a leavening of pilots drawn from VMF-212 at Efate. Fletcher and McCain were to furnish air cover when the *Long Island*, light cruiser *Helena*, and two destroyers left for ferry mission to Lunga.[17]

By sunrise on 16 August TF-61 neared the end of the westward leg of its patrol southwest of Guadalcanal. Fletcher heard nothing to indicate the APD unloading at Cactus suffered any harm. After the *Saratoga* launched a routine search, he headed southwest to keep beyond seven hundred miles of Rabaul and avoid being sighted. Strong air patrols kept watch for subs. All carrier searches were negative. The only word of enemy contact came at 1300. McCain placed a tender and destroyer off southeast New Georgia, 375 miles north of TF-61. The Airsopac flyers actually sighted the small Gizo Invasion Force setting up a base in New Georgia for four float planes. That afternoon Ghormley advised Fletcher that Scott would bring out the *Platte* and *Kaskaskia*, screened by the *San Juan*, *Clark*, and *Gwin*, to meet him the morning of 18 August seventy-five miles southwest of Espíritu Santo. The *Long Island* task group was to depart Efate on 17 August, "or as soon thereafter as possible," bound for a launch point sixty miles southeast of San Cristóbal and 220 miles from Lunga. Fletcher anticipated refueling, then covering the *Long Island*'s reinforcement mission. Overnight he retraced his route three hundred miles south of Guadalcanal. At the same time the destroyer *Oite*, racing out of Rabaul, brought the first reinforcements to Guadalcanal. No one from the Allied side ever saw her deliver 113 sailors of the Yokosuka 5th Special Landing Force to Tassafaronga west of Lunga and depart. Late on the morning of 17 August, with no hint of enemy contacts, Fletcher swung southeast to meet Scott near Espíritu Santo.[18]

That evening the *Long Island* advised she would attain the fly-off position at 1500 on 20 August. The next two supply runs to Cactus were to comprise the *McFarland* with aviation supplies on the afternoon of 21 August, and the *Alhena* and *Fomalhaut* the next day with food and ammunition. Running the blockade to Cactus, Ghormley explained to King, Nimitz, and MacArthur, risked "excessive loss of shipping," unless supply ships had strong escorts and close carrier air support. That, however, risked carrier fighters and destroyers that Fletcher would need in "next few days." Between 19 and 21 August Japan could unleash a major amphibious attack, supported by four carriers and four battleships. Ghormley minced no words. "A determined enemy carrier attack against our carriers while planes of latter are protecting ships in Cactus area might spell disaster," for Fletcher's carriers constituted "the principal defense of this area and of our lines of communication from U.S. to Australia and New Zealand."[19]

DEFINING THE THREAT

Profoundly shocked the United States actually seized the initiative, Yamamoto nonetheless realized the real opportunity to turn the table and avenge Midway. Like Nimitz in April, he recognized by seizing and holding such an advanced position, the enemy must expose himself. His means would be the Advance Force (Second Fleet) under Kondō and Nagumo's diminished carrier striking force (*Kidō Butai*). On 8 August Yamamoto combined the two fleets under Kondō into the Support Force, to "support" the "cleaning out" of the Solomons. In turn Kondō coordinated planning with Tsukahara, in charge of the Southeast Area as well as Base Air Force, and Mikawa's Eighth Fleet (Outer South Seas Force). Yamamoto canceled the Indian Ocean commerce raiding expedition assembling in Burma and redeployed its two heavy cruisers, one light cruiser, and seventeen destroyers to distant Truk. Once these "decisive battle forces" prevailed in the Solomons, Port Moresby came next. Combined Fleet headquarters would shift to Truk, the better to exercise overall control. Although confident, Yamamoto at least took the new threat seriously. Fretting about delays to the New Guinea offensive already under way, Imperial General Headquarters dismissed the Solomons invasion as a nuisance because of the exaggerated air claims on 8 August and the only too true Savo victory. Consequently Tokyo assigned a token nine thousand troops to reconquer Tulagi and Guadalcanal. The army provided the elite Ichiki Detachment (twenty-four hundred) under Col. Ichiki Kiyonao and Maj. Gen. Kawaguchi Kiyotake's 35th Brigade (six thousand). Ichiki's troops were being shifted from Saipan to Truk, while the Kawaguchi Detachment waited on Mindanao. The navy furnished the Yokosuka 5th Special Landing Force (six hundred). Optimists wondered whether the Solomons even required all these men, who might better be used for the Port Moresby assault.[20]

Kondō was ready to go, but Nagumo's carrier fleet roiled after the loss of five carriers and three hundred aircraft that spring. Many surviving aviators had been fighting since Pearl Harbor and desperately needed rest, but circumstances compelled most to remain and season the many rookie pilots. On 14 July in a major fleet restructuring, the First Air Fleet became the Third Fleet. Each carrier division now contained two big carriers and a small one with mostly fighters. Nagumo's own 1st Carrier Division comprised the *Shōkaku*, *Zuikaku*, and *Zuihō*; Admiral Kakuta's 2nd Carrier Division comprised the *Junyō*, *Hiyō* (a converted liner like the *Junyō*), and *Ryūjō*. With greater emphasis on defense, the air complement of the six carriers rose to three hundred planes (141 fighters, ninety carrier bombers, and sixty-nine carrier attack planes). As an integral surface component, the Third Fleet counted two fast battleships, four heavy cruisers, and a destroyer squadron. Yamamoto recognized the failure to detect approaching enemy aircraft was largely responsible for the defeat at Midway. In early August Nagumo's flagship *Shōkaku* received Type 2 air search radar, as installed in the battleship *Ise* just before Midway. History might have been quite different had the *Akagi* been so equipped on 4 June. Only the *Shōkaku*, *Zuikaku*, and *Ryūjō* were ready to go. Even to bring them to full strength of 177 planes (seventy-eight fighters, fifty-four carrier bombers, and forty-five carrier attack planes) required stripping the other carriers.[21]

On 11 August Kondō's Advance Force departed Kure with four heavy cruisers, the old, formidable twenty-five-knot battleship *Mutsu* (in place of two older, fast battleships in refit), one light cruiser, and five destroyers. The sleek seaplane carrier *Chitose* and five destroyers came south separately. Renewed U.S. activity in the northern Pacific caused jitters should there be a reprise of the Doolittle raid. Poco Smith's Aleutian cruiser force bombarded Kiska on 8 August, while the light cruiser *Boise* raided the picket line east of Japan. On 12 August searchers discovered one *Boise* float plane adrift only 450 miles east of Honshu. Suspecting an air attack, Yamamoto swiftly redeployed Kondō east of the Bonin Islands and mobilized aircraft and subs for defense. Kakuta's 2nd Carrier Division rushed its remaining planes to bases in eastern Japan. Worries of a carrier raid soon subsided. Kondō resumed his voyage, arriving at Truk on 17 August, the same day as the *Chitose* force. Nagumo sailed on 16 August to Truk with the *Shōkaku*, *Zuikaku*, and *Ryūjō*, two fast battleships, two heavy cruisers, one light cruiser, nine destroyers, and four fast fleet oilers. To be in on the kill, Yamamoto followed the next day with his Main Force of battleship *Yamato*, converted carrier *Kasuga Maru*, and three destroyers. The odds tilted more in his favor after 15 August, when the IJN finally instituted major revisions in Naval Codebook D. The change just prior to Midway had not frozen out Allied code breakers very long, but this one nearly shut the door at a very significant point of the Pacific War.[22]

On 11 August Nimitz offered King, Ghormley, and MacArthur details of the enemy striking force about to be unleashed in the "near future." Careful analysis discerned the "close association" between the Second and First Air (Carrier) Fleets and fleet commanders in the Bismarcks-Solomons area. Intelligence deduced the carrier force now comprised the *Shōkaku*, *Zuikaku*, *Ryūjō*, and *Hōshō*, along with two battleships and four heavy cruisers. The Second Fleet included two fast battleships, four heavy cruisers, a converted seaplane tender, and two destroyer divisions. This estimate was remarkably accurate, differing mainly in the substitution of the *Mutsu* for the battleships *Haruna* and *Kongō* and the absence of venerable *Hōshō*, relegated to training. However, U.S. intelligence did not detect the substitution of Third Fleet for the First Air Fleet until November 1942.[23]

Nimitz had deployed three carriers and one fast battleship to the South Pacific. Taking into account the *Wasp*'s unreliable turbines, he informed King, Ghormley, and Fletcher on 6 August of his intention to send Murray's TF-17 (*Hornet*) south in about ten days to relieve Noyes's TF-18 "on station." Fletcher would briefly command all four carriers at once, an unprecedented concentration of U.S. naval air power. After waiting five days (and absorbing the news of Savo), King demurred. This plan "seems to me to unduly expose Hawaiian area because relief on station will involve absence of carrier group for some 12 to 15 days." He asked Nimitz to look into rotating carriers, "So that at all times at least one such group will be within say 1200 miles of Pearl except when extraordinary circumstances warrant otherwise." King did not consider Watchtower an "extraordinary circumstance." His reluctance to commit TF-17 was yet another example of holding something back, of not going all-out even in operations he himself initiated. Inevitably he urged that, "In view [of] Japanese concentrations that appear to be directed toward Rabaul," Nimitz consider shifting three to five old battleships to Tongatabu. McCormick wryly noted, "Cincpac will probably not desire to do that." Nimitz explained the South Pacific kept Japan too busy to launch a major attack even against Midway. A simple carrier raid was more possible, but highly unlikely. Even so, retaining one carrier group to counter a Midway strike risked having this carrier sunk "without compensating damage to enemy." Nimitz lacked the necessary logistical framework to supply the old battleships in the South Pacific. "Doubt BB usefulness unless we can operate them in close support [in the] Cactus area," which he certainly would not do. The carriers and fast battleships, in concert with shore-based air, must do the job. "While developments next few days may change my opinion I believe that maximum carrier strength will be needed in South and that this can be obtained best by an overlapping relief of carrier task forces on that station." Nimitz compromised by summoning to Pearl TF-1, then at sea exercising with TF-17, "For possible use against landing attack this area." No slow battleships would go south "unless so directed by you."[24]

Nimitz was delighted when comint revealed the high level of alert in Japan over the *Boise*'s foray. That clever feint seemingly caused the whole 2nd Carrier Division to remain on homeland defense and delayed deployment of the other carriers to Truk. On 14 August (15 August in Japan), Layton opined all the flattops stayed in homeland waters, and "no movement of carriers to other areas will take place within the next week." That day Nimitz was gratified when King approved sending TF-17 south. On 17 August Murray sailed with the *Hornet*, two heavy cruisers, a light cruiser, six destroyers, and a fleet oiler. Likewise fast battleships *South Dakota* and *Washington* should be in Sopac by mid September. Understandably Ghormley made the pitch to keep all four carriers for the foreseeable future, but Nimitz disapproved. The *Wasp* must return at the "earliest date consistent with military situation existing on arrival [of] TF 17," but her air group could remain as replacements. That was already necessary. Fletcher reported on 17 August the *Saratoga* and *Enterprise* alone required thirty-six planes to regain authorized strength.[25]

The Cincpac intelligence bulletin Fletcher read on 16 August placed the *Hiyo*, *Junyō*, and *Zuihō* one thousand miles east of Tokyo (hence the slight concern of a Midway raid), but the other carriers were "still in Japan." The commander in chief of the Second Fleet might be near Saipan, with "slight indications" he was going south. That pleasing scenario sketched apparent hesitation in committing carriers to the South Pacific, where the Pacific Fleet was concentrating all its main battle assets. The change in the Japanese navy cipher sounded the one cautionary note. The Greybook groaned. "Our hopes of reading their important traffic in the near future is remote." In fact Nagumo's *Kidō Butai* left southern

Japan at the same time that particular Cincpac intelligence bulletin circulated. The *Hiyō* and *Junyō* actually trained in the Inland Sea, and the *Zuihō* was in port. Only their aircraft staged to eastern Japan. Kondō (commander in chief, Second Fleet) already neared Truk. Unlike at Coral Sea and Midway, Allied radio intelligence now stayed one or two steps behind the Japanese, making the defense of Guadalcanal all that much harder. However, its shortcomings paled to insignificance when compared to the incredible intelligence failure Japan experienced over Guadalcanal.[26]

THE RACE TO REINFORCE GUADALCANAL

By mid August Tokyo chafed to begin its Solomons counteroffensive. Only the Ichiki Detachment reached Truk, with the Kawaguchi Detachment due on 23 August. Equally disturbing, the Ichiki Detachment rode two old army transports capable of just nine knots that would need five days to cross the eleven hundred miles to Guadalcanal. That delay might waste the best opportunity to finish off the invaders once and for all, for the U.S. attack teetered on disaster. Most of the invasion troops had apparently withdrawn. The remnant at Lunga had not yet got the all-important airfield up and running. Japan must act decisively before the Allies could rebound. Truk enjoyed an abundance of destroyers, giving Mikawa the idea of dispatching the Ichiki Detachment in two echelons (the KI Operation). On 15 August he directed Rear Adm. Tanaka Raizō, commanding the 2nd Destroyer Squadron, to deliver these troops to Guadalcanal. Six destroyers (the "Volunteer Force") were to embark Ichiki and nine hundred lightly equipped men, depart Truk the morning of 16 August, and land them the night of 18 August at Taivu Point twenty miles east of Lunga. Ichiki would strike overland for the airfield. Ichiki's Second Echelon (fifteen hundred men with artillery) would leave Truk on 16 August in the two army tubs, escorted by light cruiser *Jintsu* and two patrol boats, and disembark at Taivu Point on the evening of 22 August. Mikawa designed the route to keep the convoy well clear of search planes ranging northeast from the troublesome Allied air base at Rabi on Milne Bay. He believed Rabi was the nearest Allied airfield to Guadalcanal. Ignorant of the air base on Espíritu Santo, he thought searches from that direction only flew out of distant Efate. Three destroyers from the *Chitose* force would beef up the convoy escort on 18 August. The rest of the Second Echelon convoy, transport *Kinryū Maru* with five hundred landing force sailors and two patrol boats, would catch up on 19 August. Closing from the west, Mikawa's flagship *Chōkai*, Gotō's 6th Cruiser Division (three heavy cruisers), and two destroyers covered Tanaka's right flank. The 5th Air Attack Force pounded Lunga and stepped up searches in the southern Solomons. Should U.S. carriers be discovered, Tanaka was to pull back and wait until Combined Fleet destroyed them.[27]

The counteroffensive proper (KA Operation) was to commence on 24 August, when two battalions of the Kawaguchi Detachment left Truk. By then Kondō's Support Force would be poised north and east of Guadalcanal. After Ichiki seized the airfield, Zero fighters would advance there on 27 August, the day before Kawaguchi landed. After mopping up Guadalcanal, Kawaguchi would retake Tulagi by amphibious assault. Other troops were to seize Port Moresby. Japanese optimism grew unbounded. On 16 August Mikawa's staff estimated the U.S. force at Lunga numbered just two thousand dispirited troops who might flee to Tulagi at any time. The next day they speculated Lunga might only require the Ichiki First Echelon and the Guadalcanal garrison acting in concert, freeing the naval landing sailors for New Guinea. A rude surprise waited at Guadalcanal, where Vandegrift's eleven thousand crack marines were dug in with artillery and tanks.[28]

Late on 17 August, en route to his next fueling rendezvous off Espíritu Santo, Fletcher received the first definite warning of "enemy forces indicated assembling." Citing the daily Cincpac intelligence bulletin that the *Shōkaku*, *Zuikaku*, and *Ryūjō* might "shortly" venture south, Ghormley added the Second Fleet of perhaps two battleships, four heavy cruisers, and numerous destroyers could be in the Bismarcks-Solomons region by 21–22 August. A convoy "shortly" to depart Truk was to meet another force on 21 August, with Guadalcanal the "probable final destination." He told Fletcher to expedite refueling. A more detailed Cincpac assessment the morning of 18 August revealed crucial elements of Japanese plans to reoccupy Guadalcanal but missed other equally important aspects. Three heavy cruisers and screening destroyers, thought to have left Kavieng on 16 August, would reprise the Savo night attack. The actual Invasion Force evidently sortied from Truk in two echelons, possibly to unite on 18 August 425 miles southeast of Truk and seven hundred miles northwest of Guadalcanal. The lead element comprised perhaps three transports carrying "Jap marines." The second convoy, loaded with "Army shock troops," departed Truk the morning of 17 August. Cincpac suspected there was a covering force of three or four heavy cruisers, plus destroyers. The assault on Guadalcanal could occur as "early as 20 August, but actual date is not indicated." Despite tremendous success in uncovering plans for the KI Operation, Pearl never discovered the Volunteer Force destroyers crammed with Ichiki's First Echelon that neared Guadalcanal. Conspicuously absent was any mention of carriers that were already at sea.[29]

Patiently waiting for the enemy offensive to develop, Fletcher attended to immediate concerns. On 18 August he effected rendezvous with Scott and the Fueling Group seventy-five miles southwest of Espíritu Santo. The *San Juan* resumed her place in the screen of TF-18, and Scott superseded Wright in command of the Surface Attack Group. Fletcher hoped to complete fueling all three task forces on 18 August, but strong winds and rough seas did not permit. By sunset TF-11 and TF-16 had finished, except for the *North Carolina*, which had oil to spare and indeed fueled one destroyer. The carriers stood out northwest of Espíritu Santo to cover the *Long Island* task group coming from Efate. Near midnight, unseen and unsuspected, the six Volunteer Force destroyers successfully deposited Ichiki's advance force at Taivu.[30]

That day Fletcher also bid farewell to Col. Mel Maas, who transferred to the *Platte* for passage to Efate. Following the Savo battle, Maas ailed from a throat infection and bronchitis. When he felt better, he judged it high time to "be moving on," because it looked like TF-61 faced "a long indefinite patrol job." He was eager to undertake an inspection tour in the South and southwest Pacific and resume his duties in Congress. It is worthwhile to quote Maas's impressions of Fletcher written at the close of his tour of duty in the *Saratoga*: "*Vice Admiral Frank Jack Fletcher*. The tops. Finest type Admiral. Experience, brains, exceptional ability. Human, an American in the finest sense. Knows fundamentals of naval tactics and employment. Better than a genius. A man of intelligence. Marked for a 4-star Admiral. 4.0."

This remarkable evaluation, by an independent observer, a marine aviator present during all the crucial TF-61 command decisions, offers powerful rebuttal to the critics who claimed Fletcher manifested timidity and incompetence during the Guadalcanal landings.[31]

Unaware Japanese reinforcements already slipped into Cactus, Ghormley promulgated Sopac Op-Ord 2-42. TF-61 received TF-44 to join "soonest possible." Fletcher's primary task remained the destruction of "hostile vessels prior to their arrival in and while in the Cactus-Ringbolt Area." Turner's TF-62 was to "defend seized area" with the marines and "expedite movement food and ammunition into Cactus-Ringbolt area." Aside from supporting the defense, McCain's TF-63 was to get the marine aircraft to Cactus as soon as possible and "extend scouting to northwest and north" by moving PBYs back up to Ndeni. Ghormley could offer "no positive info as to presence of carriers with hostile force," but "such presence," he cautioned, is "considered highly probable." Cincpac intelligence was not yet ready to agree. Early on 19 August Crutchley with the *Australia*, *Hobart*, and destroyers *Selfridge*, *Bagley*, and *Patterson* departed Nouméa to the west to meet TF-61 the next day south of Guadalcanal. Given that Ghormley knew TF-61 fueled northeast off Espíritu Santo prior to seeing *Long Island* task group safely well *southeast* of Guadalcanal, he should have routed Crutchley east of New Caledonia and north past Espíritu Santo. On the morning of the nineteenth Fletcher dispatched two SBDs to Espíritu Santo to deliver a message explaining where he was and what he would be doing.[32]

At 0815 on 19 August while the *Platte* and *Kaskaskia* fueled TF-18, a plain language message squawked, "Hostile vessels bombarding Tulagi." One of McCain's B-17s identified the intruders as three destroyers and a sub. Three destroyers from the Volunteer Force tarried in Cactus waters to prevent "the escape of enemy troops." The *Hagikaze* and *Kagerō* intermittently shelled Tulagi while the *Arashi* traded shots with coastal guns at Lunga. Enemy warships brazenly maneuvering in daylight off Cactus struck another bitter blow to the U.S. Navy's pride. When they appeared off Guadalcanal without prior warning, Fletcher was 450 miles southeast covering the *Long Island*, too far away to intervene. Many not understanding the situation (and some who did) held it against him. At noon two B-17s broke up the party, blasted the *Hagikaze*, and jammed her rudder. To the delight of the marines, the stricken destroyer limped out of the area accompanied by the *Arashi*.[33]

That afternoon TF-18 finished fueling and released the *Platte* and *Kaskaskia* and two destroyers to Efate. While moving northeast to contact the *Long Island* task group, Fletcher had twenty-eight SBDs sweep southwest to northeast to 250 miles, nearly to San Cristóbal. Kinkaid considered this "extensive" search "well founded," for the bombardment of Tulagi "well might" presage "an attempt at reoccupation." Later that day the boxy profile of the *Long Island*, crowded with marine planes, materialized four hundred miles southeast of Lunga. The entire force turned northwest at fifteen knots, bound for the fly-off point the following afternoon. Other than raiders gamboling between Tulagi and Guadalcanal, sighting reports that afternoon revealed a seaplane tender at Rekata Bay on Santa Isabel, and two cruisers, two destroyers, and a small craft anchored off Shortland. The Cincpac daily intelligence bulletin placed the 2nd Destroyer Squadron in the Rabaul area (Tanaka's Second Echelon convoy actually steamed southeast from Truk); a heavy cruiser, seaplane carrier *Chiyoda*, and four or five destroyers in the Truk area (Kondō was already there with a much stronger force); and part of an air group at Gasmata in New Britain (its flying boats actually flew from Rabaul and Shortland). The *Hiyō*, *Zuihō*, and *Junyō* supposedly remained in home waters, "But may move soon." However, Cincpac found "no concrete indications" the *Shōkaku*, *Zuikaku*, and *Ryūjō* had left Japan, but "possibility [of an] undetected move to south exists." Of course Nagumo sailed three days before. That afternoon Turner shared with Vandegrift daunting news that "strong enemy shock troops and naval support may be enroute to arrive within next 3 days," but he promised support with "our maximum strength." Vandegrift responded that evening with the clearest report yet of what actually transpired. All enemy ships were destroyers, one set afire by a B-17. He was unaware Ichiki confidently tramped westward to storm Lunga.[34]

At dawn on 20 August the *Enterprise* furnished a dozen TBFs and six SBDs to search northwest to two hundred miles. Six Avengers extended their sectors to 260 miles to cross Guadalcanal, Tulagi, Florida, and eastern Santa Isabel. The *Mackinac* and light minelayer *Breese* reached Ndeni to resume the vital PBY search missions 650 miles northwest. At 0759 a B-17 placed an "enemy force" twenty miles southeast of Savo, that is, between Lunga and Tulagi. At that time TF-61 was 250 miles southeast and could hustle into strike range if necessary. No additional reports reached Fletcher until 1020, when Ghormley advised the enemy cruiser spotted southeast of Savo now retired northwest at twenty-five knots. Only then did the *Enterprise* relay the results of her morning search. One aircraft surprised a surfaced sub fifty miles north, but it alertly dived before the plane could attack. The contact was a unit of the 13th Submarine Division (*I-121*, *I-122*, and *I-123*) patrolling east of San Cristóbal. North of Savo another *Enterprise* plane came across a "*Kako*-class" heavy cruiser retiring at twenty knots, obviously the same warship the B-17 reported. Another B-17 confirmed a "cruiser" passed north through Indispensable Strait between Santa Isabel and Malaita. The thrice-sighted warship was the *Kagerō*. After shelling Tulagi around sunrise, she loosed a few rounds into the Lunga perimeter and, harassed by search planes, pulled out.[35]

At 1300, an hour short of the fly-off point near San Cristóbal, TF-61 encountered a suspicious radar contact twenty-five miles south. No attack eventuated, but one *Wasp* SBD chased a flying boat north beyond San Cristóbal. It is not known if Slonim's radio intelligence team picked up enemy aircraft transmissions (there certainly were some). Fletcher remained vigilant. The *Big E*'s afternoon search, two hundred miles northwest, sought enemy activity off Tulagi and Guadalcanal and surface forces that might close for a surprise night attack. Soon the thirty-one marine aircraft from the *Long Island* winged northwest to the Cactus airstrip. With no enemy ships present off Guadalcanal, Fletcher turned southeast to cover the *Long Island*'s retirement. The only sighting that day other than the "cruiser" retiring from Savo was five ships at Shortland.[36]

Later that evening with the *Long Island* safely clear, Fletcher maneuvered southward toward a new rendezvous with TF-44 the following noon 250 miles southeast of Lunga. McCain arranged for six APDs to join the tender *McFarland* set to run supplies into Tulagi and Guadalcanal that day. At dawn on 22 August a slower convoy of the *Alhena* and *Fomalhaut* and three destroyers was to come in and clear out by sunrise on 23 August. Declaring this mission "essential repeat essential to continuation of defense," Turner requested "all possible protection" when his ships approached and remained at Cactus. Fletcher or McCain could "turn this unit back temporarily if essential to safety but every effort should be exerted to get this shipment through." Thus Fletcher anticipated operating close to Guadalcanal the next few days. On the afternoon of the twentieth, Ghormley cautioned a powerful assault against Cactus could begin anytime up to 23 August. Yet the Cincpac daily bulletin again listed no change "in estimated CV locations," placing all carriers in or near home waters. That afternoon Nimitz forecast a huge increase in the number of destroyers thought in or en route to the Bismarcks-Solomons area. They "may be employed for quick transport and infiltration [of] troops." Therefore, "Carrier aircraft must be employed to prevent landings particularly if attempted prior to arrival enemy carriers." Of course, Nimitz, Ghormley, and Fletcher all remained unaware the Japanese already accomplished such "quick transport and infiltration" of men to Guadalcanal. Vandegrift first became suspicious on 20 August after learning one of his patrols ambushed a small force of Japanese soldiers east toward Taivu Point. Hitherto the marines only encountered naval troops.[37]

Twenty August, when Sopac won the first heat in the frantic race to reinforce Cactus, shone in the long calendar of the Guadalcanal campaign. The planes from the *Long Island* roared low over Lunga and to the cheers and tears of their fellow marines set down on Henderson Field, christened in honor of Maj. Lofton R. Henderson, a marine squadron commander killed at Midway. The next installment of Japanese reinforcements, coming by slow boat, would have to run the gauntlet of Fletcher's carriers, McCain's Airsopac, and Vandegrift's newly arrived Cactus Air Force. Nonetheless, a substantial portion of the Combined Fleet ("a force only slightly less powerful than that at Midway") had come south to ensure the safe passage of the Second Echelon convoy. The resulting carrier battle could decide the campaign.[38]

RETHINKING THE KI OPERATION

Shortland-based flying boats, ranging nearly as far as Espíritu Santo, scouted ahead of Tanaka's Second Echelon convoy creeping southeast from Truk. On the morning of 20 August, with the convoy 425 miles and two days out of Guadalcanal, one Shortland searcher made a chilling discovery. First, a cruiser and two destroyers appeared sixty miles east of San Cristóbal, then twenty miles beyond, a carrier, a cruiser, and two destroyers. A U.S. carrier force located within six hundred miles of the Second Echelon convoy caused uproar at Rabaul and Truk, particularly as the Americans supposedly gave up on Guadalcanal. With the high command already in a tizzy, a second U.S. carrier materialized nearby. The flying boat covering the adjacent sector found one carrier, four cruisers, and nine destroyers 240 miles southeast of Tulagi. The two contacts were seventy miles apart, and the carriers did not resemble each other. Indeed, the *Long Island* group was the object of the morning sighting, when the *Wasp* SBD chased away the intruder. That afternoon the second search crew glimpsed one of Fletcher's carriers. These powerful forces lay just beyond land-based air strike range. With no friendly ships within three hundred miles, Tanaka felt particularly exposed. Gotō's three heavy cruisers and a destroyer advanced to Rekata Bay 130 miles northwest of Lunga, while Mikawa's flagship *Chōkai* and a destroyer cruised east of Buka. However, Kondō's Advance Force had come only as far as Truk, seven hundred miles northwest of

Tanaka. Nagumo's incoming *Kidō Butai* was two hundred miles beyond Kondō. Invoking orders to withdraw in the event a U.S. carrier turned up, Tanaka turned north that night.[39]

The unanticipated arrival of two enemy carriers boded ill for Combined Fleet's plans. Yamamoto at first thought they set their sights on the Second Echelon convoy and ordered Kondō to concentrate his Support Force and hurry south to protect Tanaka. Kondō canceled Nagumo's scheduled fueling stopover and set a new rendezvous the next morning 120 miles east. Having come east all the way from Burma via Borneo, the 7th Cruiser Division (*Kumano* and *Suzuya*) likewise skipped Truk to join the *Kidō Butai* at sea, but its six accompanying destroyers had to go there for fuel. That evening Kondō sailed from Truk with five heavy cruisers, one light cruiser, the *Chitose*, and two destroyers. He left the battleship *Mutsu* behind until the six destroyers could screen her. Insufficient fuel was available at Truk, which severely dislocated the fleet's logistical plans. Late on 20 August, after learning from the Guadalcanal garrison that twenty carrier-type aircraft landed at Lunga, Yamamoto changed his mind. Now it seemed the U.S. carriers simply ferried those planes and entertained no designs against the Second Echelon convoy, which evidently remained undiscovered. His paramount goal was to deny the enemy effective use of Guadalcanal's airfield until he could retake it. That night he ordered all commands to destroy the Lunga air base through air attack and ship bombardments. Hopefully the Ichiki would finish the job before the Second Echelon convoy drew within strike range. The arrival of the marine planes and Yamamoto's reaction set the course of the rest of the Guadalcanal campaign. Base Air Force orchestrated another comprehensive search for 21 August to ferret out carriers should they linger. To give the Support Force time to assume covering position, Tsukahara also postponed Tanaka's arrival at Taivu Point two days to 24 August, after which any opposition at sea should be gone.[40]

21 AUGUST

On 21 August Fletcher looked to a major assault against Cactus commencing possibly that day. McCain's lead element of six APDs and the *McFarland* was to arrive that evening and Turner's group the next day. At 0522 the *Saratoga* intercepted a message from Vandegrift announcing a "strong raid by enemy east [over the] Tenaru River." At least two warships were in support. With TF-61 some 375 miles southeast, only McCain's B-17s could help Guadalcanal. (As it turned out, the weather prevented them from finding targets there.) TF-61 closed Guadalcanal at twenty knots. On the way Fletcher would collect Crutchley's TF-44 at 1230 when 270 miles from Lunga. Vandegrift explained the situation. Beginning 0330 Japanese troops, strength "uncertain," assailed the perimeter from the east across the Tenaru (actually Ilu) river, while enemy ships ("type uncertain") withdrew before dawn. Hugely outnumbered, Ichiki's nine hundred men impaled themselves on strong defenses. Vandegrift did not doubt he could defeat the present assault but deeply worried about future efforts. "If not prevented by surface craft enemy can continue night landings beyond our range of action and build up large force. Request every means available be used to prevent this."[41]

A tragic attack by two jumpy *Wasp* search SBDs against the *Mackinac*, 140 miles north at Ndeni, elicited Ghormley's rebuke to Fletcher: "Insure all units your command informed location own units in operating area." At 0852 Fletcher advised if enemy ships remained off Tulagi and Guadalcanal, he would strike at 1330 from 250 miles southeast of Lunga. Action that day looked distinctly possible should the Japanese reinforce their attack. At 1034 Fletcher rang up twenty-four knots. An hour later he learned from Cactus that Tulagi had not been threatened and that enemy troops at Lunga "fled eastward." Marines, supported by tanks, swept across the Ilu river and killed nearly eight hundred Japanese, including Ichiki. Gladly acknowledging much more favorable circumstances at Cactus, Fletcher reduced speed at noon to fifteen knots. Crutchley's TF-44 hove into view right on time. Fletcher forwarded the *Selfridge* to Noyes, incorporated the two Australian cruisers and the *Bagley* and *Patterson* into his own TG-61.1 (TF-11), and gave Crutchley the TF-11 cruisers in place of Wright. However, he retained Scott, slightly junior to Crutchley, in charge of the whole Surface Attack Group. Doubtless he was concerned over differences in doctrine between the two navies and wondered whether that might have played a role at Savo.[42]

That afternoon Fletcher learned that a PBY late in the morning came across four cruisers and one destroyer 225 miles east of Buka and within three hundred miles of Cactus. The shadower later advised the enemy steamed north at eighteen knots. Should those Japanese be playing possum and later reverse course, they could storm Tulagi harbor after midnight. Meanwhile, a *Wasp* SBD shot down a flying boat fifteen miles ahead of TF-61. The Kawanishi had warned base at 1045 of U.S. ships, types unknown, distant 530 miles and headed southwest at twenty knots. Its last transmission, at 1116, was simply: "We are engaged in aerial combat." Slonim's radio intelligence team probably monitored its messages, indicating the enemy knew Fletcher's location.[43]

Laying out his battle plans, Fletcher considered whether to rush cruisers and destroyers to defend Lunga and Tulagi that night, as Vandegrift and others wanted. At twenty-five knots, a surface group could reach Savo a few hours after midnight. However, such sketchy details as Fletcher gained of the Battle of Savo offered little confidence in the present night fighting capability of his force, given the acute lack of training and possible faulty doctrine. Narrow waters, where surrounding high mountains could block radar, were no place to be at night with the current scratch team, especially with Japan's demonstrated high ability in night fighting. Fletcher cautioned his captains that because of the "extremely poor performance" of their 5-inch night illumination "star shells," they must "rely on search light illumination." Cincpac also noted the "sizeable increase [of the enemy's] previous Dog Dog strength," now thirty to thirty-five destroyers, and pointedly reminded Sopac of the enemy's boast of "quote superior night torpedo technique unquote," that soon "may be up for test." Thus Fletcher felt disinclined under the present circumstances to take such a surface night fighting exam, where his air strength could not come into play. "Unless we obtain further information from Cactus," he would search at dawn from south of Guadalcanal's southeast tip and seek enemy ships near Lunga. The *Saratoga* would search, the *Wasp* have a strike group ready, and the *Enterprise* would assist in the combat air patrol and contribute strike planes "whenever operations permit."[44]

In any event, Fletcher did not want to run smack into a surface force waiting in ambush. With commendable caution, he gave Boscoe Wright an ad hoc group of four heavy cruisers and six destroyers to advance twenty miles ahead after sunset and "prevent night attack [against] this force."[45] Wright was to rejoin at dawn southeast of Cape Henslow. During the late afternoon of 21 August, no additional sighting reports reached Fletcher. According to the Cincpac daily intelligence bulletin, six heavy cruisers and associated destroyers (led by commander in chief, Second Fleet) and two submarine divisions either had reinforced fleet forces in the Bismarcks or were en route. The *Zuihō*, *Hiyō*, and *Junyō* trained off Honshu, whereas Pearl still had "no indication other CV's have departed Japan." Based on sightings on the twentieth, MacArthur estimated naval forces between Bougainville and Guadalcanal numbered three heavy cruisers, one light cruiser, five destroyers, one converted seaplane tender, and other auxiliary ships. Evidently the great offensive against Cactus had not yet materialized. Vandegrift definitely thought so, eagerly informing the six inbound APDs and the *McFarland* that all hostile ships departed before sunrise and that his search planes found none within seventy miles. "Conditions warrant entering" for "speedy unloading," particularly as the marines were down to one day's "baker ration." Ghormley concurred. He ordered the *Alhena* and *Fomalhaut* to proceed ahead with two destroyers. Fletcher and McCain were to "provide maximum practicable air coverage," while the two cargo ships unloaded stores on 22 August and the following day when they cleared out. Such support, Ghormley conceded, should be "consistent with your assigned tasks," which for Fletcher, of course, was to be ready to meet the major effort against Cactus. Soon afterward Vandegrift asked, because of the ongoing battle at Lunga, that the *Fomalhaut*'s entry be delayed. Turner obliged by having her peel off southeast of San Cristóbal, while the *Alhena* and *Helm* trailed two destroyers to Tulagi.[46]

While TF-61 closed Guadalcanal, visibility decreased. The combat air patrol investigated several suspicious contacts. Near sundown, Fletcher set course 295 degrees at sixteen knots. Wright's screening group raced ahead into the deepening gloom. Once twenty-two miles beyond the main body, the six destroyers formed a line spaced three miles apart; the cruisers deployed in pairs five miles astern. That evening Ghormley complained to Fletcher of "enemy landing forces last night [in] Cactus area" and pointedly reminded him both Cincpac's 20 August message and his Op-Ord 2-42 decreed carrier aircraft must prevent such actions. Later that night he described the attack on Vandegrift's perimeter on the night of 20–21 August as an amphibious assault by a well-equipped force from two ships, type unknown, and again implied Fletcher let them skip through. Simultaneous with Ghormley's second message, Vandegrift radioed a summary of the destruction of the Ichiki Detachment. Prisoners revealed they left Truk on 16 August in six destroyers and came ashore three days later thirty kilometers east of Lunga. No more troops in fact reached Guadalcanal after that day, but several thousand more were on the way.[47]

Yamamoto and his commanders endured a highly frustrating 21 August. A strong force of twenty-six torpedo-armed land-attack planes and thirteen Zeros unsuccessfully hunted the waters around and south of Guadalcanal. From messages sent by its missing flying boat, Base Air Force concluded U.S. carriers patrolled the southern Solomons, but beyond strike range. Kondō's Advance Force joined briefly with Nagumo's *Kidō Butai* southeast of Truk, then separated while Nagumo fueled from his oilers. Nagumo advised that as of sunset on 23 August, he would be three hundred miles northeast of Lunga. He presumed his three carriers would remain undetected, for the flying boats he thought searched out of Efate should already have turned home. Kondō planned for the whole Support Force to cover Tanaka's landing on the twenty-fourth with the standard panoply of the Japanese naval battle: separate task forces of surface ships preceded by subs fanning out ahead in scouting lines to spot the enemy and catch him unaware. Plowing southward from Japan, seven I-boats from the 1st Submarine Squadron aimed for the 160-mile-long "A" deployment line that veered northeast from 130 miles east of Guadalcanal into the waters east of Malaita and northeast of San Cristóbal. Two subs from the 3rd Submarine Squadron coming from Rabaul, and a third boat from Truk, were to assume the "B" deployment line, a sixty-mile line running east to west from 160 miles southwest of Guadalcanal. They could intercept forces approaching from the Coral Sea. At the present time, though, only the old *I-121*, *I-122*, and *I-123* scouted east of San Cristóbal. Once the other subs moved into position, they were to switch northwest to the waters adjacent to Guadalcanal. Mikawa therefore reimposed Tsukahara's orders for the Second Echelon convoy to reach Guadalcanal the evening of 24 August. Tanaka nosed back around into the same northerly approach as before. A Japanese unit reported two U.S. transports and a light cruiser 130 miles southeast of Guadalcanal. In night combat off Lunga the *Kawakaze* fired torpedoes at the two destroyers but did not bother the six APDs and seaplane tender already at Lunga and Tulagi. Her stern blown off, the *Blue* still floated. Thought by the Americans to be a motor torpedo boat rather than a warship, the intrepid *Kawakaze* never revealed a definite radar contact—another example of the U.S. Navy's unreadiness to fight a night surface action.[48]

22 AUGUST

Preceded by Wright's Screening Group, Fletcher cautiously advanced northwest through the darkness toward the waters south of Guadalcanal. The weather on 22 August was raw, with rough seas, occasional squalls, and gusty southeast winds. Fourteen *Saratoga* SBDs searched from west to northeast two hundred miles to see what transpired. By dawn TF-61 drew within seventy-five miles of Cape Henslow and 120 miles from Lunga, from where the carriers could strike anything found at Tulagi and Guadalcanal or environs. The *Saratoga* also launched Don Felt to fly directly to Henderson Field and check out the runway. Fletcher carefully considered the advantage of a convenient base where his aircraft could take temporary refuge if they could not easily return to the carriers. That would considerably extend their strike range. Felt's personal judgment of the situation at Cactus was crucial. He also took along for transmission a message to bring Ghormley up to date. Noting the 20 August sub sighting and recent encounters with patrol planes, Fletcher declared his belief that TF-61 was "sighted from time to time" and asked if Comsopac could confirm it. Yet again he complained "communications [are] most unsatisfactory," with sighting reports "received very late." The *Saratoga*'s radio facilities had definitely not improved. Fletcher acknowledged Vandegrift's request for close support at night to prevent the enemy from landing troops, but "consider it inadvisable to send cruisers and destroyers into Cactus nightly." Lastly he cautioned that TF-61 "must retire on 24th for fuel and redistribution of provisions." To retain his readiness to steam at high speed and fight, he intended to keep to his schedule of refueling about every six days.[49]

At sunrise the Screening Group fell back to the TF-61 main body. With his disposition reformed, Fletcher turned southeast after having approached within ninety-five miles of Lunga. Geography and wind direction dictated his carriers should keep to the east, with more freedom to maneuver, instead of passing south of Guadalcanal. Initial search contacts revealed only one enemy ship anywhere near Guadalcanal. Two *Saratoga* SBDs overtook the *Kawakaze* tearing northwest beyond Malaita and strafed. Felt returned with the news Fletcher hoped to hear. Henderson Field could shelter and service a carrier strike group if necessary. Felt promised the marines the *Sara* would deliver necessary communication supplies the next day. In the meantime Turner hustled the *Alhena* and *Helm* to Tulagi, with the *Fomalhaut* to come in the next day. Again the lack of ship contacts signaled the much feared counteroffensive was probably at least another day off. Fletcher signaled Noyes and Kinkaid that TF-61 would hold the current southeasterly course until 1130, then swing east. By dawn on 23 August he wanted to be east of Malaita and 120 miles northeast of Lunga to flank a southward thrust from Truk. Later that morning radar discovered a bogey fifty-five miles northwest and closing. A skillful intercept by the combat air patrol destroyed a Kawanishi flying boat in the midst of heavy squalls twenty-six miles southwest of TF-61. Fletcher assumed the enemy once more knew his location. That afternoon twenty *Saratoga* SBDs searched the sector northwest-east to two hundred miles. Scott used the relatively tranquil interlude to detail the tactical organization of his Surface Attack Group of one battleship, six heavy cruisers, three light cruisers, and eight destroyers.[50]

At 1630 after clearing San Cristóbal, Fletcher turned north toward his planned operating area east of Malaita. The Cincpac daily intelligence bulletin again proffered "no positive indications to show change in carrier locations," but noted an "undetected departure recently" of the "inactive" *Zuikaku*, *Shōkaku*, and *Ryūjō* "subsequent to 16 August should not be disregarded." That was not particularly helpful. Actual contacts that afternoon were again remarkably sparse. The only worrisome sighting was a cruiser two hundred miles northwest of Guadalcanal, though its reported course and speed of twenty-four knots aimed directly for the Santa Cruz Islands, the *Mackinac*'s roost. Even though the enemy cruiser was nearly five hundred miles away, McCain ordered the *Mackinac* and *Breese* to clear out that evening after refueling the PBYs but return to Ndeni the next day to continue servicing the all-important search. At 1710, fifty miles southeast of San Cristóbal, the feathery white streak of a torpedo wake bubbled between the *Enterprise* and *Portland* in Kinkaid's TF-16, then the fish broached the surface. Lookouts in TF-18 on the port side of the task force likewise sighted a torpedo wake, thought possibly from another sub. The elderly *I-121* escaped after an audacious if unsuccessful attack. After dark Fletcher took precaution against surprise attack of the surface variety by stationing Crutchley with the *Australia* and several destroyers west of TF-61. He also prepared another situation summary to Ghormley and McCain for the *Saratoga* to fly to Cactus the next morning. It advised the TF-61 searches conducted from south of Guadalcanal yielded only the one destroyer north of Malaita that speedily withdrew. The carriers downed another flying boat and encountered a sub southeast of San Cristóbal, more proof Fletcher's location had to be well known to the enemy. With hostile carriers probably en route, he recommended Ghormley arrange for TF-61 to refuel on 25 August "with 3 tankers if possible." The whole business should require less than a day.[51]

That night in response to the message Felt delivered that morning to Cactus, Ghormley laid out for Fletcher the latest estimates that "point strongly to enemy attack in force on Cactus area 23–26 August." One or two battleships, ten heavy cruisers, five light cruisers, ten or eleven destroyer divisions, and a great number of subs skulked within six hundred miles of Rabaul. Sixty fighters and sixty to one hundred bombers operated from airfields in the New Britain area, with more on the way. The enemy had enough troops available to overwhelm Vandegrift's marines. The "presence of carriers possible but not confirmed," whereas the "only evidence sighting you" was the Cincpac message of 14 August noting a possible sub contact. Ghormley conceded radio communications were "not satisfactory," but "making every effort to improve." Acknowledging it was "important" to refuel TF-61, he desired it be done "soonest possible and if practicable [with] one carrier task force at a time retiring for that purpose." To that end the *Platte*, *Cimarron*, and two destroyers would, by the morning of 24 August, be loitering 125 miles northwest of Espíritu Santo and 350 miles southeast of Lunga. They would again keep at least ten miles apart to prevent one sub from targeting both. The *Kaskaskia* was unavailable, but the *Sabine* and a destroyer had reached Espíritu Santo on the twenty-second. Two oilers were ample, though, if Fletcher refueled his task forces one at a time. Of course the enemy must cooperate and allow him to do so.[52]

The Guadalcanal garrison radioed Rabaul late on 21 August that the Ichiki First Echelon was "practically annihilated" in a futile assault against Lunga. Such grim news required confirmation, but the counteroffensive continued to evolve. Because of severe storms, Tsukahara reluctantly canceled the planned bombing raid on 22 August against Lunga. He concluded his missing flying boat fell to a carrier southeast of Guadalcanal. By noon Tanaka's Second Echelon convoy, zigzagging southeast at nine knots, drew within four hundred miles of its objective. Mikawa's inability to refuel at sea forced him to take two heavy cruisers and a destroyer to fuel at Shortland, while Gotō with the other two heavy cruisers and two destroyers took his place west of the convoy. Some three hundred miles north of Tanaka, Kondō's entire Support Force pushed southward into the prevailing trade winds and would close within two hundred miles of Tanaka before the next dawn. The 7th Cruiser Division finally caught up with Nagumo, while the *Mutsu* and six destroyers left Truk in hopes of joining Kondō's Advance Force in time to fight. In view of the weather and the manifest danger of the Lunga-based planes, Tsukahara proposed that Nagumo's carriers knock out the airfield on 23 August and then deliver close air support to Tanaka on the twenty-fourth during his final approach to Taivu Point. Fully aware of his vulnerability, Tanaka vigorously seconded the request. Yamamoto preferred not to risk the *Kidō Butai*'s premature exposure, but he did authorize Nagumo to strike Lunga on the twenty-fourth if other air and surface forces failed to neutralize the air base. Now only one day remained before the grand offensive to retake the Solomons truly commenced.[53]

RECKLESSNESS OR INACTION?

Fletcher's performance from 10 to 22 August elicited sharp criticism. "Since the initial landing," McCormick complained on 19 August, "not much of anything has been done by our Task Forces." He certainly reflected Nimitz's own acrid opinion. Cincpac's report of 24 October 1942 averred that from 9 to 23 August, cruisers and destroyers "bombarded Guadalcanal and Tulagi almost nightly with impunity." Fletcher left the door open because of his misguided efforts to "conceal the carriers," by keeping "well to the south out of contact range of hostile aircraft." Hence, "None of the many small groups of Japanese ships that operated in the close waters between Tulagi and Guadalcanal was attacked by either carrier air groups or by our surface ships." Moreover, the Japanese took advantage of the respite to mass "powerful forces," while "simultaneously restricting the flow of supplies and armament" to Cactus. "*Every chance should be taken to strike and destroy separated units of the Japanese Fleet.* There were opportunities up to 24 August to strike small Japanese forces. Had these been grasped, the main effort by the Japanese on 24 August might have been delayed or have been made with a smaller force." Stung by the message describing two large destroyers shelling Lunga on 19 August, Rear Adm. Ted Sherman, on the Cominch staff, wondered how the enemy even got through to Cactus. "I can't understand what our CV's are doing to let that happen. I think our CV task forces are being very poorly handled." Historians likewise disapproved of what they perceived as Fletcher's strange inertia and disinclination to fight. Richard Frank described how the "record of Fletcher from Savo Island to the Eastern Solomons shows he drifted from prudence to paralysis."[54]

Fletcher's superiors manifestly preferred bold action to disrupt the enemy buildup, which, however, actually took place at distant Truk. Prior to the approach of the Second Echelon convoy, only a few destroyers and subs roamed the lower Solomons. Nimitz erred in describing almost nightly bombardments by cruisers and destroyers, and "many small groups" of enemy ships off Tulagi and Guadalcanal.[55] Sporadic shelling by a few elusive destroyers and subs frustrated the U.S. Navy and bruised its ego but hardly constituted a decisive threat to marines. From 9 to 23 August, Japan only managed, using swift destroyers and stealth, to land one thousand lightly equipped infantrymen, whom Vandegrift's dug-in marines outnumbered ten to one.[56] A few destroyer-loads of infantry could not overrun the First Marine Division. That required artillery and other heavy weapons, plus many more men and supplies that only transports could bring. First, the Japanese must destroy or neutralize Fletcher's carriers.

Fletcher's only actual "bold" course of action between the landings and the approach of the enemy carriers would have been to raid Rabaul or Truk. No other targets of consequence existed nearby, certainly nothing that could have delayed the counteroffensive or whittled it down ahead of time. To go after Rabaul or Truk meant relinquishing shore-based air support and confronting the effective air search network certain to detect TF-61 long before it could strike. North of the Solomons, Fletcher was blind beyond his own limited air search and vulnerable to a trap sprung by his fiercest foes, the undiscovered enemy carriers. Any or all of these alternatives posed grave danger, without the corresponding opportunity to inflict comparable loss to the enemy. It risked seriously weakening TF-61 prior to the appearance of Nagumo's *Kidō Butai*. A severe defeat at that juncture would have cost Guadalcanal.

In the two weeks following the Savo action, only two options existed: recklessness or a perceived inactivity. Fletcher properly preserved his force and prepared for battle, while at the same time offering Cactus limited support. Committing cruisers and destroyers from TF-61 to some sort of static defensive patrol off Tulagi and Lunga simply was not wise.

Nor could the carriers linger off Guadalcanal providing fighter cover. Former marine staff officer and historian Herbert Christian Merillat, certainly no admirer of Fletcher, recognized in his postlanding strategy the "classic role of a 'fleet in being.'" The U.S. carriers kept "their enemy counterpart at a cautious distance from the embattled island until one side or the other should find an occasion propitious for forcing the other into a 'decisive battle.'" Although "few marines were aware of it," Merillat thought, "they had reason to be grateful to the American carriers' distant prowling." Those flattops, "so long as they lasted," provided "distant cover for the movement of supplies and reinforcements to Cactus."[57] At that point in the Guadalcanal campaign, Fletcher's ostensible "inaction" served the Allied cause far better than the alternative.

CHAPTER 28

The Battle of the Eastern Solomons I
In the Land of the Blind

LYING IN WAIT

Twilight on Sunday morning, 23 August, the seventeenth day after the invasion, faintly registered in the rainy skies fifty miles east of Malaita.[1] Lacking the raw strength to meet the Japanese fleet head-on, Fletcher's TF-61 (three carriers, 216 planes) resumed the role, familiar from Coral Sea and Midway, of defending an exposed position against a strongly supported amphibious attack. Overnight he deployed to 130 miles east of Lunga, within supporting distance, yet beyond the reach of float planes in the central Solomons. Starting 670 miles southeast of Rabaul and just within its powerful search and strike network, Fletcher intended to work southeast into the wind and remain alert, while Ndeni PBYs combed the crucial sectors north and northwest of Guadalcanal.[2]

Despite repeated forecasts from Ghormley (if not Nimitz), the enemy had not returned in strength after the devastating raid against Savo. Should this day prove as quiet as the last few, Fletcher must start detaching his task forces one by one, as Ghormley directed, to refuel from the *Platte* and *Cimarron* northwest of Espíritu Santo. Fifteen *Enterprise* dive bombers and nine torpedo planes left to examine the northern semicircle to 180 miles, as far west as Santa Isabel and north of Guadalcanal and Malaita. Two *Saratoga* TBFs departed at 0615 for Cactus carrying Schindler with the previously noted 22 August Comsopac message, radio matériel, and ten pounds of frozen strawberries from the flag mess. The *Saratoga* spotted a strike group on deck, and Schindler alerted Vandegrift that it might drop in at Henderson Field, possibly even that day. Sunrise brought stronger winds, thirty-two knots and gusts, accompanied by fierce squalls. At breakfast Fletcher read a special Cincpac Ultra message advising that the "Orange striking force" of two *Shōkaku*-class carriers, two fast battleships, and four heavy cruisers was now "indicated" to be "in or near Truk area," and thus not nearer to Cactus than one thousand miles. "In Truk-Rabaul area" was "Cinc Second Fleet" with "possibly" two fast battleships and "definitely" four heavy cruisers. This valuable intelligence, however, failed to answer the prime question of when the assault on Guadalcanal might come. With the Japanese carriers so distant, such a move now seemed unlikely for several days.[3]

The *Enterprise* search encountered only two distant subs running south. One slithered beneath the waves one hundred miles north of the task force; the other, 150 miles northeast, first submerged, only to surface and be forced to dive again. The first boat was *I-11* en route to the B deployment line southwest of Guadalcanal; the second, *I-17* bound for the A deployment line east of Malaita. Neither suffered much damage. The *Enterprise* planes slotted in the westerly sectors, including southern Santa Isabel Island and northwest of Malaita, returned early because of foul weather. Fletcher could not rule out the enemy's presence in that crucial quadrant, but he knew shore-based planes should cover at least part of the affected area.

First word from a Ndeni flying boat reached the *Saratoga* at 0942. Lt. (jg) Francis C. Riley of VP-23 placed eight ships roughly 250 miles north of Cactus and 350 miles northwest of TF-61.[4] He gave no description, course, or speed. At 1013 the PBY in the adjacent sector to the east ran across two-float seaplanes seventy-five miles southeast of Riley's contact and 275 miles northwest of TF-61. Either they were Rekata float planes patrolling ahead of the approaching force, or they came from cruisers. At 1135 when nothing more came of the supposed eight ships, Fletcher signaled Noyes and Kinkaid his intent to continue southeast at fifteen knots until sunset. That would cut by half the run to the fueling rendezvous, then 175 miles southeast. He already gave Noyes tentative orders to refuel at dawn on the twenty-fourth. The skies cleared, but rough seas persisted along with the brisk wind. At 1154 the *Saratoga* monitored Riley's amplifying report identifying two cruisers, three destroyers, and four transports closing Guadalcanal from the northwest at seventeen knots. Finally with definite word, Fletcher swung TF-61 swung around to 310 degrees at fifteen knots. Felt summoned all dive bomber and torpedo pilots to the *Saratoga*'s cavernous wardroom to await attack orders when the carriers moved within range. That, too, became a lengthy process. TF-61 had to turn sharply away from the base course to launch or recover planes. The delay did allow shore-based air more time to seek carriers that must come before any other objective.[5]

At 1250 Ghormley granted Fletcher's request, radioed that morning from Cactus, for three oilers. On the mornings of 24 and 25 August, the *Platte* and *Cimarron* were to be within fifty miles of the designated rendezvous northwest of Espíritu Santo. The *Sabine* would join them on the twenty-fifth. According to the noon fuel report, the TF-61 destroyers averaged 57 percent, although the heavy ships had plenty. Oil was not critical, but TF-61 required timely refueling to retain the freedom to maneuver at high speed should a fight break out. Battle was not the time to rely on heavy ships for fuel. Fletcher must soon get on with his refueling.[6]

Additional search contacts secured that afternoon from Ndeni-based PBYs solely concerned three subs located 180 miles and 150 miles northwest and 240 miles northeast of TF-61. Two were possibly the same boats the SBDs roughed up that morning. If heavy ships, including carriers, supported Riley's convoy (as it seemed some must), they proved remarkably elusive. Clearly frustrated Fletcher did not storm into attack range as quickly as possible, Kinkaid suggested TF-16 dash northwest at twenty-five knots, then at 1500, when the convoy should be 250 miles away, unleash an *Enterprise* strike. After hitting the target about 1645, her planes would return after sundown. Kinkaid echoed his call on 2 August for TF-16 to operate well north of the other two carriers, securing the dispersion the pioneer aviators desired when confronting enemy carriers. Fletcher simply directed the *Enterprise*,

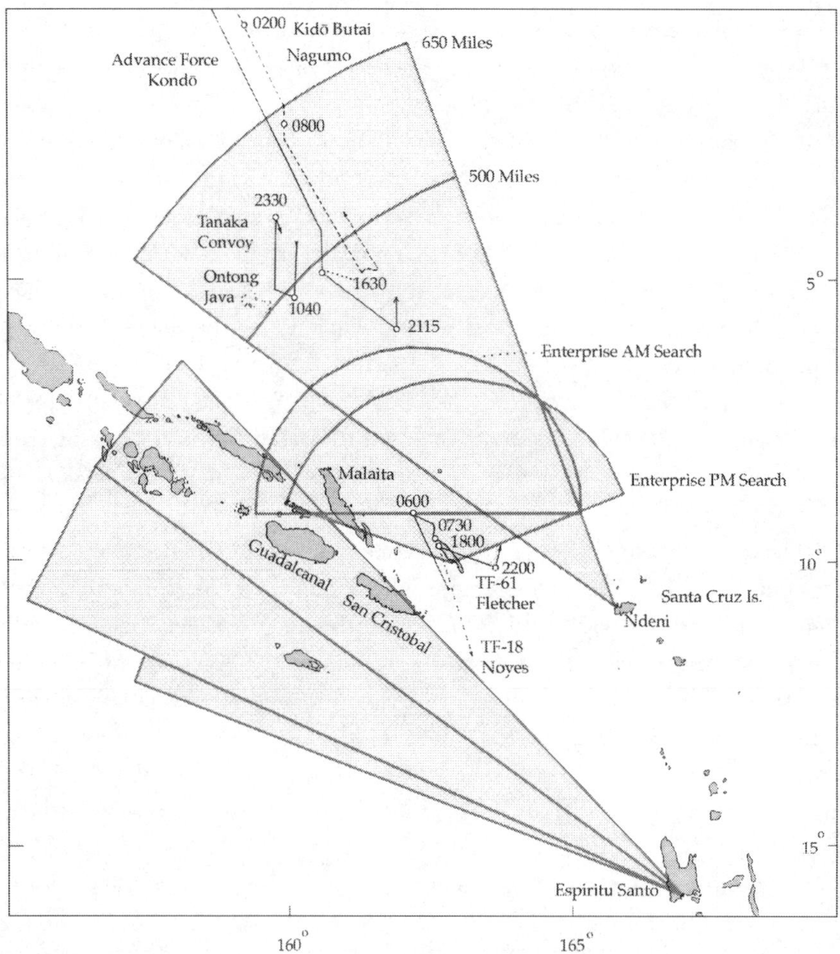

Task force operations, 23 August 1942

the duty carrier, to execute a vital precautionary search of the northern semicircle to two hundred miles. Kinkaid resignedly complied, launching twenty *Enterprise* SBDs at 1425.[7]

Fletcher resolved to attack that afternoon if possible but resisted the impulse to hit the convoy at maximum range. He hoped instead to locate enemy carriers. His preferred weapon was the *Saratoga*'s strike group, with all thirty-one SBDs and six of thirteen TBFs ready to go. If the convoy held the reported course and speed, it should, by 1430, be 275 miles northwest (and 170 miles north of Lunga). No advocate of carrier dispersion, Fletcher did not relish splitting TF-16 off to attack on its own. Even Kinkaid's plan to launch from a slightly lesser distance required the planes to return after dark, with the worry of night carrier landings by inexperienced pilots and danger from subs caused by illuminating the carriers. Fletcher's hole card was Henderson Field. Should nothing better than the convoy turn up by 1415, he intended to play it. After an "interminable" two hours, Felt set down the telephone with a "satisfied grin" and joyfully announced: "Let's go, boys! No carriers have been found. We will attack the cruisers." Fletcher ordered him to strike the convoy, then stage south to Henderson

Field, landing by sunset if possible, and return to the *Sara* at 0730 the next morning east of Malaita. No escort fighters would go; the flight was too long. At 1440 the thirty-seven planes departed northwest. Watching from the *North Carolina*, Michael Laing wondered if Fletcher acted from additional information of which he was unaware. Otherwise, "This seems like a long shot." Truly, Fletcher took a grave risk similar to the Japanese search-strike mission on 7 May that caused Admiral Takagi and Admiral Hara so much grief in the Coral Sea. Much rode on Felt's shoulders. Fletcher could hardly afford to lose his force. He judged the strike capable of defeating the surface force thought approaching Guadalcanal and relied on the marines to protect his planes while on the ground.[8]

Anxiously watching from Nouméa, Ghormley made certain Fletcher knew of the convoy. In turn McCain demanded the *Mackinac* (returning to Ndeni) maintain "contact with enemy force reported by [Riley]." At 1409 Leary placed two destroyers and two cargo ships near Shortland as of 1140. "Request you hit them now," Ghormley shot back. Nearly five hours later, MacArthur explained his flyers needed "a minimum of seven hours for execution [of] missions against targets given by you as it is impossible due to dangers involved to use Moresby or Milne Bay except as topping off fields." He avowed the B-17 strike on Rabaul the previous day had "telling effect." Ghormley cautioned Vandegrift, "Sightings indicate two groups enemy ships converging Guadalcanal." They could arrive "tonight." Vandegrift fully understood the threat. At 1615 he dispatched nine marine SBDs, thirteen F4Fs, and the *Saratoga* TBF against the convoy now believed well within two hundred miles of Lunga. McCain hurriedly organized a night strike by five PBYs from Espíritu Santo, with B-17s to go in the next dawn. He again demanded the *Mackinac* update her sighting reports. For his own part Turner ordered the *Fomalhaut* out that evening with the disabled *Blue*. The cargo ship cleared out as directed, but the destroyer had to be scuttled. In the past three days two cargo ships, six APDs, and one seaplane tender had deposited either all or a big portion of their cargoes at Lunga and Tulagi, relieving in part the severe shortage of supplies.[9]

Ninety minutes after Felt's strike group left, Ghormley warned Fletcher of the imminent danger to Cactus and alerted him to "be prepared send surface detachment to destroy enemy forces Cactus area tonight." At that time TF-61 was 170 miles distant by sea from Lunga—seven hours at twenty-five knots. Fletcher could have a surface force there before midnight or by 0200 at a more economical twenty knots. To comply, though, it must leave almost immediately, but that was up to Ghormley. Fletcher certainly would not take his whole task force there. He already dealt strongly with the convoy to the north. Cargo ships starting out from Shortland could not possibly reach Guadalcanal before late the next morning. A sighting report that Leary relayed at 1701 confirmed that they had not even left Shortland.[10]

GROPING IN THE DARK

Fletcher experienced the familiar gut-wrenching wait for strike results that was, as one Japanese carrier captain described, a "thousand seconds" passing "like as many years."[11] Felt should have reached the target around 1630. Nothing was forthcoming from other commands, notably McCain's Airsopac. Fletcher pondered the latest hot intelligence from Pearl. The Cincpac daily bulletin unequivocally placed the *Shōkaku* and *Zuikaku* "enroute Japan to Truk," while a heavy cruiser and "possibly" two fast battleships were in the Truk "area" or "vicinity." Thus Cincpac amended his earlier announcement that morning of two *Shōkaku*-class carriers "in or near Truk." The term "in or near" is not the same as "enroute to," although Nimitz seemed not to have noticed the difference. Even so, Fletcher now had good reason to believe the nearest carriers were still north of Truk, itself more than eleven hundred miles distant from his present position. In fact, Nagumo cruised only three hundred miles northwest of TF-61, and Kondō's Advance Force drew even closer. The reason for this colossal failure by the same radio intelligence network that forecast the Coral Sea and Midway battles will be examined later. Its immediate effect was to delude Fletcher into believing it was safe to detach his task forces one at a time to fuel.[12]

After 1700 Kinkaid heard from the *Enterprise* pilots back from the afternoon search of a "slightly damaged" sub one hundred miles northwest of TF-61, and possibly a cargo ship and light cruiser or destroyer anchored off northern Malaita. The search again encountered bad weather to the northwest, this time about 145 miles out. Oddly Kinkaid did not think these contacts sufficiently important to forward to Fletcher until the next morning. At 1800, eleven minutes prior to sundown, Fletcher reversed course to the southeast. No planes to westward appeared on the *Sara*'s radar. Whether or not Felt's raiders found the convoy, they must have gone to Guadalcanal as instructed. Twenty minutes later, "There being no enemy carriers in immediate vicinity," Fletcher directed Noyes to proceed to the fueling rendezvous 210 miles south. The departure of the *Wasp* (sixty-three planes) left Fletcher 150 operational aircraft in the *Saratoga* and *Enterprise*, including the thirty-eight at Cactus.[13]

With Noyes's TF-18, Richard Frank wrote, disappeared "the best chance in 1942 for the United States Navy to have potentially decisive quantitative superiority in a carrier action." Morison considered detaching the *Wasp* at that juncture yet another example of Fletcher's lamentable predilection for unnecessary fueling at critical times. "Once more, the destroyers' logs prove that this anxiety was unwarranted." Of course Morison, aware unlike Fletcher of enemy carriers in the neighborhood, applied his usual omniscient hindsight. Fletcher's evaluation of the situation was a "bad guess." He should somehow have divined the presence of carriers nearby. Frank faulted Fletcher for not finding "as much significance in the presence of a convoy and in the submarine sightings as did some of his subordinates." Yet the only subordinate on record is Davis in the *Enterprise*, who wrote afterward that the discovery of three subs rushing south "pointed strongly to the possibility of a considerable enemy movement to the southward along the track of the advancing submarine screen." Again, Davis showed wisdom after the fact. His boss Kinkaid did not even think it vital to advise Fletcher immediately of the last sub sighting on the twenty-third.[14]

The critics discounted the importance of Cincpac's radio intelligence. That night's summary by McCormick's War Plans Section bespoke the favorable interpretation at Pearl, based largely on the same intelligence and sightings, that completely justified Fletcher's action. Despite the "comparatively large number of enemy cruisers, destroyers, transports, and freighters" that turned up "recently in the Rabaul area," McCormick judged they would offer "a fine target for Fletcher if they ever come within his reach." In turn, "Enemy striking forces previously mentioned heading toward the Southwest Pacific" were "now indicated" to be "in the Truk area." This "being the case, they cannot arrive in the Tulagi area before the 27th or 28th, local date." Fletcher could also read a chart. He took advantage of that supposed window of opportunity to refuel his three task forces in succession. To wait risked all three carrier groups being caught short of oil when the Japanese carriers finally did show up.[15]

That evening Ghormley declined to order TF-61 cruisers and destroyers to proceed to Cactus, but time and distance had already negated that option. MacArthur relayed another coast-watcher report that five ships, "Including one very large," were still at Shortland as of 1330. That again reduced any chance of the second pincer showing up at Guadalcanal. Later Leary detailed a concentration of ships off southern Bougainville that again argued any coordinated amphibious assault against Cactus had to be more than a day away.[16]

Fletcher maneuvered to approach his intended dawn position from the east. He would start ninety miles east of Malaita and 170 miles northeast of Lunga, and thus was forty miles farther east than on the twenty-third. Late that evening Vandegrift radioed that his own strike returned without finding the convoy in poor visibility, but he did not mention the *Saratoga* planes. Only well after midnight on 24 August did two messages clarify the situation for Fletcher. The first, received at 0124, elicited much anger in the *Saratoga*. The *Mackinac*, back at Ndeni since 1430, finally advised that the convoy of three transports, one light cruiser, and two destroyers had "radically" changed course at noon. Riley did not in fact shadow it but searched as much of the balance of his sector as the weather allowed. He reacquired the contact; when last seen at 1230 the convoy was retiring northwest. Thus the Japanese scooted out of range well before the launch of the *Saratoga* strike. Why it took thirteen hours to advise Fletcher of that crucial event no one ever explained. Nor did anyone bother to tell Fletcher that thick clouds forced the PBYs to curtail their search of certain vital sectors at five hundred miles instead of 650 miles. Even that reduced area received only 70 percent coverage. Schindler, waiting at Lunga, provided the best news. Although Felt never found the convoy, all the planes reached Cactus and were prepared to "hit enemy on arrival." Due to "delay in gassing," Schindler requested they return to *Saratoga* at 1030 instead of at 0730. Fletcher felt tremendous relief the *Sara*'s flyers were safe. Now he needed to retrieve them as quickly as possible and see what transpired on 24 August.[17]

THE OTHER SIDE

The dawn of 23 August, the penultimate day of the KI Operation, saw Tanaka's Second Echelon convoy plodding straight in from three hundred miles north of Guadalcanal. Angling southeast, Nagumo's *Kidō Butai* and Kondō's Advance Force crossed Tanaka's track about two hundred miles north. Nagumo planned to continue southeast, but keep north beyond the reach of flying boats he thought were based no closer than Efate. By dawn on the twenty-fourth he would be roughly halfway between Malaita and Ndeni and 250 miles northeast of Lunga. From there he could destroy the U.S. carriers that patrolled south of San Cristóbal. Kondō, reinforced by three destroyers, was to shift from southwest of the *Kidō Butai* to sixty miles northeast and guard Nagumo's left flank with seaplane searches three hundred miles to eastward. Only if Tsukahara's Base Air Force failed to pound the Lunga airfield on 23 August would plans change. In that event Nagumo was to spin off a carrier detachment to raid Guadalcanal on the twenty-fourth and also give Tanaka close air cover. Frozen out of carrier command, Rear Admiral Hara now led the 8th Cruiser Division in the

Kidō Butai. Should a carrier strike against Lunga be necessary, he would form a mini support force with flagship *Tone*, *Ryūjō*, and two destroyers. With only nine Type 97 carrier attack planes the *Ryūjō* offered little real offensive firepower, but her twenty-four Zero fighters could protect the convoy.[18]

Fully aware of his vulnerability to any form of attack, Tanaka noted the baleful appearance of Riley's flying boat 275 miles north of Guadalcanal. To make matters worse, the *I-11*, one of two subs encountered that morning by *Enterprise* SBDs, radioed the sighting of carrier-type planes only 180 miles southeast of the convoy. Worried American carriers might have moved up more quickly than anyone realized, Mikawa once again told Tanaka to pull away until the situation cleared. Wearily complying at 1040, Tanaka apprehensively awaited results of searches by Base Air Force and Kondō's whole force. Tanaka's nearest source of support remained Mikawa's Outer South Seas Force shuttling back and forth to refuel at Shortland.

Also alerted by the *I-11* to an enemy carrier much farther north than previously thought, Kondō and Nagumo supplemented the shore-based search effort. It seemed so many aircraft crisscrossing the eastern Solomons could not fail to ferret out the opposition, but that happy result did not occur. Tsukahara learned nothing from his own search, except the land-attack plane on the 115-degree line did not return. Perhaps it succumbed to poor weather; no one on the Allied side claimed it. At 1400 Nagumo executed his own precautionary scout 250 miles ahead, but at that time TF-61 was 375 miles southeast. Like Fletcher, Nagumo played hide-and-seek until he could locate the opposing carriers. He strongly suspected the Allies had not sighted his ships and sought to preserve that advantage by not closing prematurely within reach of the short-range planes at Lunga and the flying boats from distant Efate. At 1740 he radioed that unless otherwise instructed, he would retire north all night (150 miles), then at 0700 turn back southeast. Kondō's afternoon search likewise yielded nothing. The Advance Force kept pace with the *Kidō Butai* until late afternoon, then forged ahead southeast before also turning north at 2115. Kondō never realized TF-61 was only 275 miles beyond. He planned to start the next morning as scheduled sixty miles east of Nagumo. Kondō cautioned Yamamoto the whole Support Force must soon refuel and set a convenient rendezvous for 26 August north of the Solomons.[19]

Overseeing the offensive as the *Yamato* fueled 180 miles southeast of Truk, Yamamoto learned that storms again prevented Tsukahara's land-attack planes from taking out the Lunga airfield. He therefore ordered Nagumo to strike Guadalcanal on the afternoon of 24 August "with appropriate force." He stipulated the attack take place only if in the meantime no U.S. carriers turned up. Consequently Nagumo directed Hara's Support Force to depart south at 0400 on 24 August and hit Lunga that afternoon, while the rest of the *Kidō Butai* again sallied southeast. Tsukahara reluctantly permitted Mikawa and Tanaka to postpone the landing to the twenty-fifth and canceled the bombardment of Lunga scheduled for that night. The *Kagerō* did not get the word and briefly shelled the perimeter after midnight on the twenty-fourth. Evidently a flash report of the light bombardment of Lunga reached Fletcher, but he judged correctly it was not a serious attack.[20]

Had the clouds cooperated on 23 August, all six carriers would have fought. The Airsopac flying boats, of course, flew out of Ndeni rather than Efate 450 miles farther south. All things being equal they should have pinpointed Kondō and Nagumo as well as Tanaka. One of Kondō's cruisers even glimpsed a PBY fly past in the overcast. Fletcher greatly benefited from the chaotic weather that disrupted searches by the Rabaul land-attack planes and Shortland-based flying boats that should have seen TF-61. The stage was set for the naval action that would come to be known to the Allies first as the Battle of the Stewart Islands (islets near TF-61) and ultimately the Battle of the Eastern Solomons.

CHANGING ILLUSIONS

Early on the morning of 24 August Fletcher's reduced TF-61 continued toward the planned dawn position ninety miles east of Malaita. The *Saratoga* and *Enterprise* counted fifty-five fighters, thirty-three dive bombers, twenty-two torpedo bombers, and two photo reconnaissance planes, plus the *Sara*'s thirty-one dive bombers and seven torpedo bombers expected back at 1030 from Cactus. The *Enterprise* again scheduled routine forenoon and afternoon searches, while the *Saratoga* handled combat air patrol. Fletcher intended to work closer to Malaita into the same area as the previous afternoon. The Point Option course for the morning search was to be 280 degrees. Given the need to run into the brisk twenty-four-knot southeast wind for periodic flight operations, the actual westerly rate of advance might only be six knots. Fletcher did not anticipate significant action that day, but as usual he was wary.[21]

Twenty minutes before sunrise, the *Saratoga* lofted eight combat air patrol F4Fs, and the *Enterprise* twenty SBDs, to search the northern semicircle to two hundred miles. Three additional SBDs from the Enterprise were assigned to inner air patrol. The overcast skies offered hints of clearing. The *Enterprise* finally blinkered to Fletcher the results of her previous afternoon search, namely the sub attack and enemy ships possibly anchored off Malaita. Fletcher queried why Kinkaid had not reported sooner and if the *Enterprise* sent bombers to investigate. Kinkaid responded he did not do so the previous evening "because of doubt due difference of opinion [of] observers," and his disinclination to "use [blinking] lights after dark this area to make report of doubtful accuracy." Nevertheless he arranged for the dawn search to check that site. The morning proceeded uneventfully. Fletcher directed the *Enterprise*, once she recovered her forenoon search, to take flight duty for the rest of the day, while the *Sara* rearmed and refueled the planes from Cactus and held them in reserve to strike.[22]

Like the previous day, the hardworking PBYs tended by the *Mackinac* at Ndeni sought Japanese forces north of the Solomons. Six VP-23 Catalinas covered an arc bearing 306–348 degrees to 650 miles, taking them east and northeast of Bougainville. Also like the previous day, that vast area encompassed all the task forces threatening Guadalcanal, but now visibility was better. All six PBYs contacted the enemy.

Their reports, at least those actually received, strongly influenced the course of the battle. The correlation of call signs (based on plane numbers) and the arrangement of search sectors (clockwise from west to east) were purely coincidental. Fletcher could not determine from its call sign what sector an aircraft actually searched, a fault Airsopac did not remedy until November.[23]

Call Sign	Sector (Degrees)	Plane No.	Patrol Plane Commander
1V37	306-313	23-P-1	Ens. Theodore S. Thueson
3V37	313-320	23-P-3	Lt. Joseph M. Kellam
5V37	320-327	23-P-5	Ens. Gale C. Burkey
7V37	327-334	23-P-7	Ens. James A. Spraggins
8V37	334-341	23-P-8	Lt. (jg) Robert E. Slater
9V37	341-348	23-P-9	Lt. Leo B. Riester

Table 28.1 The Ndeni Search

Yamamoto's plan for 24 August set forth the extensive air search of the Solomons and the waters east and south to find the U.S. carriers that posed the greatest peril to Tanaka's Second Echelon convoy slowly closing Guadalcanal. Edging southeast during the day, Kondō's Advance Force (five heavy cruisers, one seaplane carrier, one light cruiser, five destroyers) and Nagumo's *Kidō Butai* (two carriers with 142 planes, two battleships, three heavy cruisers, one light cruiser, eight destroyers) would do all in their power to destroy them. At the same time, Tsukahara's Base Air Force was to blast the Lunga airfield and finally open the way for the landing the next day. Operating separately from Nagumo, Hara's Support Force (one light carrier with thirty-three planes, one heavy cruiser, two destroyers) would dash past Tanaka's convoy to draw into strike range of Guadalcanal. Should no U.S. carriers be detected by noon, *Ryūjō* aircraft were to surprise the Lunga-based planes on the ground. Yamamoto gave Hara the option of waiting to recover his strike planes or routing them northwest to Buka, while he headed north to refuel.[24]

At 0600 after recycling northward all night, Japanese forces assumed their former relative positions. Farthest east, Kondō's Advance Force cruised southeast at sixteen knots while watching the *Kidō Butai*'s left flank. According to plan he was to keep station sixty miles east of the carriers. Nagumo, however, had diverged northwest instead of going north the previous night (and not told anyone), so Kondō was actually 120 miles southeast of him. The Advance Force itself was five hundred miles northwest of Ndeni and 360 miles north of TF-61. Out on the west flank, the Second Echelon convoy (one light cruiser, two destroyers, three transports, and four patrol boats) again inched southward from 275 miles northwest of Guadalcanal. Separating from Nagumo at 0400, Hara sped south at twenty-six knots on a course roughly parallel to Tanaka's. Two hours later he was seventy miles northeast of the convoy. Two pairs of Mikawa's heavy cruisers with a few destroyers converged on Tanaka from the west. The centerpiece of the array, Nagumo's *Kidō Butai* (*Shōkaku* and *Zuikaku*), started southeast before dawn at fifteen knots from 140 miles northeast of the convoy, 415 miles north of Lunga, 450 miles northwest of TF-61, and six hundred miles northwest of

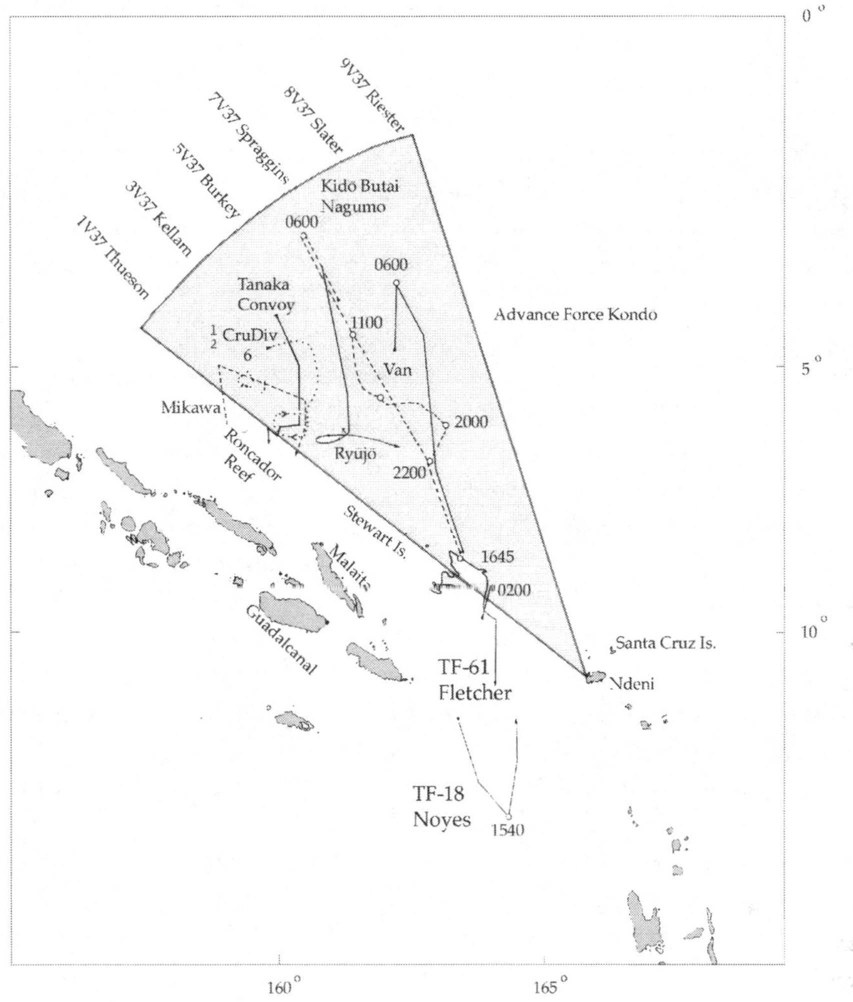

Task force operations, 24 August 1942

Ndeni. In case U.S. carriers had worked around to the east, Nagumo dispatched nineteen carrier attack planes to cover the eastern semicircle to 250 miles.[25]

The first actual sighting by the Ndeni PBYs occurred at 0900 in one of the two central sectors. Ens. James Spraggins's 7V37 happened on a light cruiser headed south. Neither Fletcher nor Kinkaid monitored his 0905 contact report, which was 310 miles north of TF-61. Spraggins glimpsed one of Hara's two destroyers but placed it sixty miles east of its actual location. Continuing northwest, he unwittingly slipped between Hara's Support Force and its parent, Nagumo's *Kidō Butai*, off to the northeast. Spraggins made no other contacts during the mission. Thus the Ndeni search missed its first vital opportunity to pinpoint Nagumo promptly that morning. At 0935 the *Enterprise* copied a message from Ens. Gale Burkey's 5V37, in the other center sector, of one carrier, two light cruisers, and one destroyer, headed south. Burkey nailed Hara's Support Force 275 miles northwest of

TF-61. Kinkaid thought Fletcher also knew of the contact, especially after he relayed that vital information by TBS at 0945 to the *Saratoga* and received an acknowledgment. The *Saratoga*'s air plot recorded that transmission (or at least part of it) but missed the call sign "5V37," noting the "source of *Enterprise* information was unknown." Even so, air plot did not bother to check with flag plot to see if Fletcher also had the message, which he did not. Other searchers working northwest of Guadalcanal likewise located and promptly reported nearly all the ships in their respective sectors. Sweeping west of Burkey, Lt. Joseph Kellam's 3V37 found Tanaka's convoy at 0953 situated 260 miles north of Guadalcanal and three hundred miles northwest of TF-61. Not surprisingly, Fletcher and Kinkaid never copied his contact report. Kellam continued searching his sector. About the same time, southwest of Santa Isabel, a B-17 from Espíritu Santo found a cruiser 125 miles west of Lunga and 250 miles west of TF-61. At 1003 Ens. Theodore Thueson's PBY 1V37, covering the westernmost sector, discovered two light cruisers and a destroyer near Ontong Java atoll, 220 miles northwest of Lunga and more than three hundred miles from TF-61. Fletcher heard both of those reports immediately. The B-17 came across the destroyer *Kagerō* retiring up the Slot, while Thueson encountered Mikawa's main body southwest of Tanaka's convoy.[26]

Thus McCain's searchers successfully charted enemy deployment north and northwest of Guadalcanal and quickly acquired the *Ryūjō*, the most important target, although Fletcher did not know it. He deduced the ships found by the B-17 and Thueson's 1V37 had pulled out after shelling Cactus the previous night. He saw no evidence of the feared two-pronged attack on Cactus. Nevertheless at 1012 he alerted Kinkaid to ready a strike group "as soon as possible." At that moment after the launch of eight SBDs and six TBFs to counter the serious sub threat, only two SBDs and nine TBFs remained on board the *Enterprise*. The morning search and first inner air patrol, however, waited to come on board, though they, too, must be serviced before a strike.[27]

At 1016 Fletcher monitored a report from PBY 9V37 of two cruisers and two destroyers "distance 450 bearing 337." Lacking further information, he assumed the PBY's point of origin was Ndeni, which, if correct, positioned those enemy ships 330 miles north of TF-61 and in excess of 250 miles northeast of the cruiser group discovered near Ontong Java. Now the Japanese appeared to be operating across a broad front. Very quickly Fletcher received evidence that a carrier might be involved, an alarming situation indeed. At 1030 9V37 radioed it was being attacked by three aircraft, type not given, while 5V37, a different PBY, reported: "Attacking [*sic*] by aircraft fighting plane type Zero. I am returning to base." Due to the specific mention of Zero fighters, as opposed to seaplanes, Fletcher later described the 5V37 message as the "first indication that enemy carriers might be in the vicinity." However, he had no idea where 5V37 was (having *not* received Burkey's earlier report of a carrier) and, for that matter, only supposition as to the location of 9V37. It did not appear out of the realm of possibility that 5V37 ran afoul of Zeros based out of Buka. More ominous, at 1050 yet another PBY, 8V37, claimed hostile interceptors, but this time supplied a definite position that translated to 330 miles north of TF-61 and sixty miles southwest of where 9V37 *might* be. Now to Fletcher it seemed the enemy main force might be more concentrated. The reports of 9V37 and 8V37 provided even "stronger indications of an enemy carrier."[28]

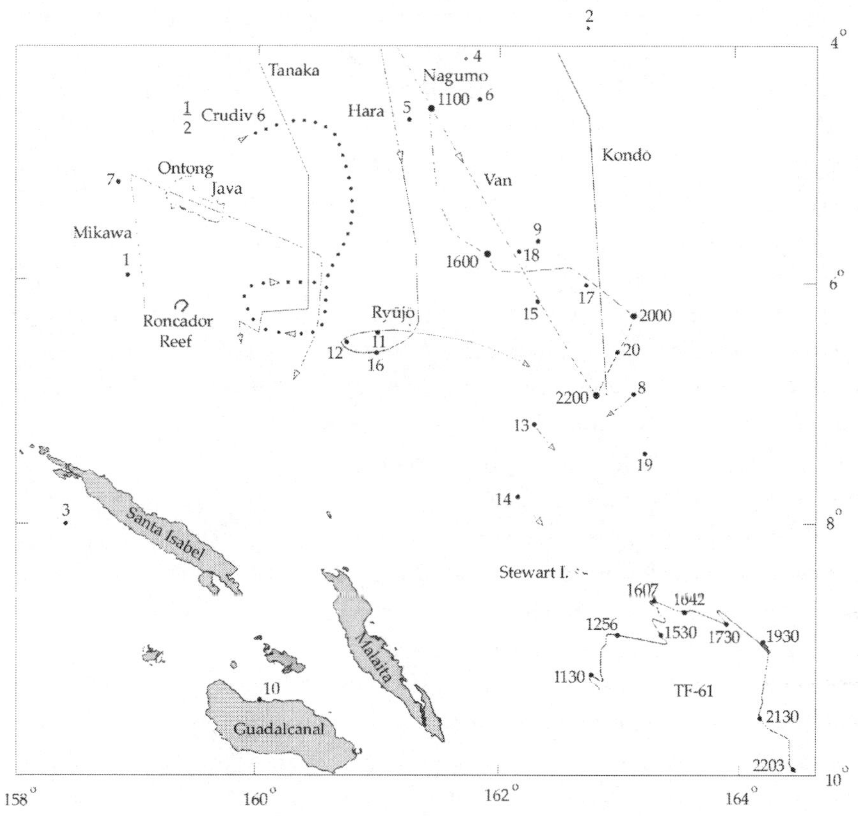

Principal sighting reports received by CTF-61, 24 August 1942

Key:

1. 1003 PBY 1V37 Thueson; 2 light cruisers, 1 destroyer
2. 1016 PBY 9V37; 2 cruisers, 2 destroyers
3. 1016 B-17 22V40; 1 cruiser
4. 1050 PBY 8V37; attacked by aircraft
5. 1110 PBY 5V37 Burkey; 1 aircraft carrier, 2 cruisers, 1 destroyer, originally sent 0935
6. 1117 PBY 8V37; 1 light cruiser
7. 1242 PBY 1V37 Thueson; 2 cruisers, 1 destroyer
8. 1320 *Saratoga* radar contact, bearing 350 degrees, 112 miles, course 220 degrees
9. 1405 PBY 3V37 Kellam; 1 small aircraft carrier, 2 cruisers, 1 destroyer
10. 1440 Air raid reported by Cactus
11. 1523 TBF 1V395 Jett; 1 aircraft carrier, 1 heavy cruiser, 1 light cruiser, 3 destroyers
12. 1550 *Saratoga's* first strike attacked 1 aircraft carrier
13. 1607 *Saratoga* radar contact, many bogeys bearing 320 degrees, 103 miles
14. 1700 Returning *Saratoga* strike planes sighted Japanese strike group
15. 1735 *Saratoga's* second strike attacked 1 battleship, 4 heavy cruisers, 6 light cruisers, 6–8 destroyers
16. 1815 B-17s Manierre attacked 1 aircraft carrier
17. 1815 B-17s Sewart attacked 1 small aircraft carrier, 3 heavy cruisers, 2 destroyers
18. 2000 SBD Davis sighted 2 aircraft carriers, 4 heavy cruisers, 6 light cruisers, 8 destroyers, originally sent 1500
19. 2130 PBY 14V37 Corbett; 5 vessels
20. 2133 PBY 13V37 Brady; unidentified vessels

Lt. Leo Riester's 9V37, flying the easternmost sector from Ndeni, had in fact reported the two cruisers and two destroyers at 1016. He snooped Kondō's Advance Force, and his navigation was off by only a few miles to the east. The seaplane carrier *Chitose* scrambled three nimble Type 0 observation seaplanes (code-named Pete) that hounded the PBY for more than an hour. The distant *Mackinac* mistakenly assumed Riester's assailants to be Zero fighters and broadcast word to that effect. At 1144 when Riester turned his damaged plane back toward base, he correctly identified his foes as three "cruiser seaplanes," but Fletcher did not copy that message. The 5V37 warning, of course, originated from Burkey, whose lumbering PBY evaded two *Ryūjō* Zeros for more than an hour before escaping. PBY 8V37 was Lt. (jg) Robert Slater, handling the sector between Spraggins (7V37) and Riester (9V37) to the east. Slater sent no messages at that time, so any reference to 8V37 was a garble. Passing near enough to Nagumo's *Kidō Butai* to be seen by its lookouts, Slater never noticed the carrier force in the haze. That was the final missed opportunity for the Ndeni search to have found Fletcher's most dangerous opponent.[29]

While contemplating the prospects for battle, Fletcher was gratified to see Felt's raiders appear overhead fresh from the muck of Guadalcanal. At 1035 the *Saratoga* launched a dozen combat air patrol F4Fs and landed eight combat air patrol F4Fs, twenty-nine SBDs, and seven TBFs. The additional TBF was Schindler's. The past evening after the harrowing long-range search/strike through intermittent squalls ("Some just terrible pile of weather," Felt recalled), Felt got the strike down safely at Henderson Field, greatly helped by flares set alongside the runway. The ground crews refueled the planes, a laborious process given the primitive means available. Later that night while marine SBDs patrolled adjacent waters on the lookout for approaching enemy ships, the *Saratoga* crews waited alongside their planes ready to hasten aloft and attack. The only opposition was a brief shelling by what was thought a sub, actually the *Kagerō*. After dawn with both skies and coast clear, Felt had the SBDs toggle their defused 1,000-pound bombs into the mud for their grateful marine hosts, then took off for the rendezvous east of Malaita. Two SBDs turned back due to engine trouble, but the other *Saratoga* flyers uneventfully reached TF-61 after spotting the ships from a long way off. Correspondent Clark Lee, who flew the mission, described the vicinity of home plate: "Long swells were running but the air was clear and unclouded, with an after-the-storm freshness." Of course the brilliant skies offered no hindrance to others seeking TF-61.[30]

"WITH ONE BOOT OFF"

Lee noticed "an atmosphere of quiet excitement" on board the *Saratoga*. "This was the day." At 1103 as the last of Felt's planes touched down, Fletcher alerted all ships that he required full boiler power in thirty minutes. At the same time Kinkaid advised that "Art's boys" were "ready now," meaning the *Enterprise* strike group (twenty-five SBDs and nine TBFs, plus fighter escort) could take off at any time. "Quiet excitement" pervaded the *Saratoga*, but the *Enterprise* seethed. Kinkaid knew of Burkey's 5V37 carrier contact for ninety minutes and waited for Fletcher to charge north so his "boys" could attack. Inaction seemed inexplicable. At 1116, in exasperation, Kinkaid queried Fletcher by TBS: "Are you guarding for contact reports?" Fletcher replied, "Many reports are garbled. Do you have any definite reports of enemy?" Kinkaid certainly did. All proved familiar to Fletcher except the startling "5V37: 1 CV 2 CL [light cruiser] 1 DD Lat 04-40 Long 161-15 course 180." He responded that he had all except that one and asked Kinkaid to repeat the longitude. That of course was the original contact of the *Ryūjō* force that Burkey radioed at 0935. Fletcher's failure to copy the 0935 message *and* the repeat Kinkaid relayed by TBS at 0945 exemplified the terrible communications that plagued the U.S. Navy in the South Pacific. Naturally assuming Burkey's sighting had just taken place, Fletcher charted the enemy carrier force bearing 343 degrees, distance 281 miles. Kinkaid, who knew the contact was nearly two hours old, reckoned its current position at 245 miles northwest, bearing 336 degrees.[31]

Fletcher now understood the enemy "had commenced his full scale attempt to retake Guadalcanal." The contact reports that he actually received revealed a concentration of ships 275 to three hundred miles northwest of TF-61 and advancing across a front of forty to sixty miles. That impression was reinforced after 1117, when someone rebroadcast the original 7V37 (Spraggins) 0905 contact report of a light cruiser but wrongly attributed it to PBY 8V37, which previously warned of being attacked by enemy planes. That light cruiser (actually one of Hara's destroyers) was forty miles east of Burkey's carrier contact. Fletcher now must fight his battle without the *Wasp*, a situation resembling that of Confederate Lt. Gen. James Longstreet on the second day at Gettysburg. Lacking one of his three divisions, Longstreet complained to Maj. Gen. John B. Hood that he did not care "to go into battle with one boot off." Fletcher would have agreed. Cincpac intelligence obviously erred badly by placing all the Japanese carriers north of Truk. Now the discovery of one carrier almost certainly meant two or three others were stashed nearby. "We did not believe [Japan] would attempt this attack without at least 3 carriers," recalled Pederson. The "invasion force which had turned back the previous day was somewhere to the northward of the striking force, ready to move in when the way was clear." Again Nagumo held the weather gauge. The southeasterly winds allowed him to conduct flight operations while continuing to close his enemy.[32]

Word of the carrier sighting filtered down to Felt, newly back from Cactus, along with orders to go again right away. Given the long distance to the target, he commented, "That's beyond our range." His tired pilots needed some rest. "Let's just take it easy," he added. "You keep getting intelligence and when those things are within our range, we'll go." Fletcher concurred. At 1127 he turned north and ordered the refueling and rearming of the *Saratoga* planes be expedited "for an attack mission pending the closing of the enemy and further information from reconnaissance planes." The situation again resembled 7 May at Coral Sea, where Fletcher loosed ninety-three planes against what he thought were two big carriers, only to net the small carrier *Shōhō* while the *Shōkaku* and *Zuikaku* remained hidden. The following day the dangerous pair inflicted fatal damage to the *Lexington*. Now this day they, plus perhaps some friends, lurked somewhere north of TF-61, possibly within strike range. Above all Fletcher must know whether that were so. "In order to verify these [search] reports and guard against a repetition of the attack made under similar circumstances on the 23rd which never found its objective, I reluctantly ordered Commander Task Force Sixteen to immediately launch a search."[33]

Kinkaid advised Fletcher the *Enterprise* had twenty F4Fs, twenty-five SBDs (with 1,000-pound bombs), eight TBFs (two 500-pound bombs each), and the group commander's TBF ready to go. From this pool of planes he proposed to employ twelve SBDs and eight TBFs for the afternoon search. Fletcher told him at 1137 to dispatch that planned search "as soon as possible" along the suggested arc of 290–090 degrees to 250 miles. TF-61 would steer a Point Option course due north and average ten knots. Fletcher's "reluctance" stemmed from having to waste so many dive and torpedo bombers for a follow-up search. Had the Airsopac searchers discovered all the carriers, those planes could have joined the attack. He held back the fifty *Saratoga* strike planes (twelve F4Fs, thirty SBDs, and eight TBFs) for the time being to see if the *Enterprise* or the shore-based search could find the other carriers. With the *Sara*'s flight deck spotted for takeoff, he directed the *Enterprise* to maintain the combat air patrol and inner air patrol and also recover and service the *Saratoga*'s fighters. Rooted in Pederson's preinvasion planning, that unprecedented example of enhanced coordination between carriers greatly improved combat air patrol flexibility. Once the *Saratoga*'s strike departed, the role of the two carriers would switch. The *Enterprise* was to form a second strike group from her remaining SBDs and TBFs; the *Sara* would refuel fighters from both carriers and arm her own few TBFs (those that could not accompany the first strike) with torpedoes so they could join the second wave.[34]

Fletcher constantly worried about having to absorb a carrier attack without knowing its point of origin. The likelihood of that calamity increased after 1150, when radar detected a bogey. Four F4Fs encountered a sleek, fast, huge flying boat thirty miles southwest and shot it down in flames at 1213 after a long chase away from the task force. Given the distant intercept, Fletcher doubted this snooper ever sighted TF-61. Nor did Slonim's radio intelligence team hear any radio transmissions. Fletcher knew he could not count on such good luck all afternoon. The victim was a Type 2 flying boat. Shortland indeed copied no messages from the missing plane. That proved terribly bad luck for Hara's *Ryūjō* force.[35]

Given the wide area to be covered, Kinkaid increased his search to sixteen SBDs and seven TBFs and delayed departure until the SBDs, to augment their range, switched to single 500-pound bombs. The *Big E* also prepared sixteen F4Fs for combat air patrol and six SBDs to relieve the antisubmarine patrol. While waiting for the launch, Kinkaid informed Fletcher that the *Enterprise*'s earlier search had only eyeballed another sub to the east. Poor visibility prevented the check for possible ships off northern Malaita, but the afternoon search would not proceed far enough south to do so. He also advised that the intermediate air patrol had bombed yet another sub twenty-five miles southeast of the task force.

Fletcher laid out his plans to Kinkaid at 1216. The *Saratoga* had ready a strike group to go once searchers established fresh contact with one or more carriers. The *Enterprise* was to service the dozen *Saratoga* combat air patrol fighters sent aloft at 1040. Fletcher queried Kinkaid how many planes he would have after the *Enterprise* search departed and what would be left for a second strike. TF-61 turned southeast at 1229 for the *Enterprise* to launch the forty-five planes on deck. After the next launch and recovery cycle, around 1330, Kinkaid advised he would have an attack group of twenty-three SBDs (*sic*, actually thirteen) armed with 1,000-pound bombs, six TBFs with torpedoes, the command TBF, and twenty escort F4Fs. Hoping Fletcher would relent and release him to attack immediately, he again emphasized, "Enemy sighted by plane consists of 1 CV 2 cruisers 1 DD bearing 340 distance 250 miles." Fletcher, though, waited a little longer to see if the new search turned up something more substantial before committing the *Saratoga* group. "Will hold your attack group in reserve for possible second carrier," he replied at 1242. "Do not launch attack group until I direct you." Nothing more regarding the enemy's carriers was immediately forthcoming. At 1242 Thueson's PBY 1V37 radioed that the force previously reported near Ontong Java included heavy cruisers and was retiring north at twenty knots. At 325 miles from TF-61, this group was not only far out of strike range but also lacked carriers.[36]

After the search took off, the *Enterprise* recovered eight combat air patrol F4Fs, six TBFs, and eight SBDs from antisubmarine patrols and the twelve *Saratoga* combat air patrol F4Fs, who had just ambushed a low-flying twin-engine bomber. The Japanese plane splashed only seven miles short of TF-11, after having veered directly toward the *Sara*. It was thought to have carried a torpedo. The crew never raised headquarters by radio, and Slonim's team heard no suspicious messages. Yet it seemed certain to Fletcher: "The presence of these planes clearly indicated that our position must be known to the enemy." Ironically he actually knew much more about Japanese dispositions than they did of his, plus he enjoyed the fleeting advantage of understanding a battle was in the offing. Yamamoto's admirals strongly suspected, but could not prove, the presence of U.S. carriers within strike range. Neither plane downed by the TF-61 combat air patrol in fact got the word out before being lost. The odds, though, would shift decisively in favor of whoever found his opponent's main body first.[37]

Startled by U.S. flying boats farther north than expected, Nagumo fretted they already spotted him. Thus he belatedly implemented a tactical plan, the rationale behind the concept of the Third Fleet, devised following the Midway debacle. A vanguard of battleships, cruisers, and destroyers was to form a scouting line one hundred to 150 miles ahead of the carriers, conduct its own search, warn the main body of enemy scouts, and finish off the enemy task force once carrier air crippled it. The vanguard would also absorb air attacks that might otherwise hit the carriers. The rapid deployment south afforded the *Kidō Butai* no opportunity to test the new tactic. This day Rear Adm. Abe Hiroaki took the vanguard of two battleships, four cruisers, and two destroyers only ten miles ahead of the main body and spread them along a twenty-mile front—a belated separation, although far less than doctrine, that would still pay great dividends. So did a last-minute decision that modified the previously scheduled search southeast by battleship and cruiser float planes. Concerned at the last minute that the waters nearest to Guadalcanal lacked adequate coverage, the Third Fleet staff fortuitously added a plane to fly the 165-degree line to three hundred miles.[38]

At noon, hearing no word of U.S. carriers, Hara proceeded with the Lunga airfield strike. Six *Ryūjō* carrier attack planes (each with six 60-kg land bombs) and nine strafing Zeros hoped to surprise the enemy planes on the ground. Six other Zeros served as escort. By 1250 the twenty-one planes departed south for Lunga two hundred miles distant. Hara could have had the strike stage to Buka while he withdrew his ships safely north to refuel. Thinking he was safe, he lingered to await the return of his planes in four hours. Hara's overconfidence doomed the *Ryūjō*.[39]

At 1320 while Fletcher awaited possible fresh search contacts before committing the *Saratoga* strike, her new SG radar registered "many" bogies bearing 350 degrees, distance 112 miles. Instead of closing, the contact headed away southwest (220 degrees) on a tangent directly toward Lunga 235 miles distant. Only a carrier could have furnished such a strike, if indeed that was what it was. Given it was thought Japanese planes did not attack beyond 250 miles, the supposed flattop might lurk only 120 miles north of TF-61. In that case *Enterprise* searchers should have readily sighted her, but they remained silent. Fletcher ordered the *Sara*'s strike to launch immediately. The Japanese could attack at any time and possibly catch her planes on deck, a catastrophe to be avoided at all cost. Moreover, considerations of time and distance dictated his strike must depart very soon or risk returning after sundown.[40]

Lacking additional intelligence, Fletcher's only viable target remained Burkey's lone carrier actually reported at 0935, but which he thought was only found about 1100. Still reckoning a wrong position that was too far north, Pederson, allowing for the enemy's maximum southward advance, specified the outbound strike leg as 320 degrees to 216 miles. If the target did not turn up there, Felt could count on it being off to the north. Such a long mission again precluded fighter escort, so Fletcher released the dozen *Sara* F4Fs to augment the combat air patrol. At 1340 TF-11 bent on twenty-five knots southeast into the brisk wind and lofted the fifty planes. Fletcher launched the attack "on the most meager information which was three hours old and had never been confirmed." Such were the charming quirks of carrier warfare. For the time being he ignored the source of the supposed Guadalcanal strike, the possible carrier not far to the north. That was wise, for that flattop never existed. The radar contact was a phantom due to atmospheric interference. Hara's Support Force was in excess of 150 miles northwest of the putative point of origin of that "strike." No other ships were closer than one hundred miles.[41]

WHERE THE ONE-EYED MAN IS KING

At 1338 while Fletcher unleashed the *Sara*'s strike group against the cold carrier contact, the *Enterprise* mustered eight F4Fs against a new bogey. The wily twin-float seaplane finally succumbed at 1401 near the Stewart Islands, thirty miles northwest of TF-61. Fletcher failed to realize the significance of one more snooper, but it meant the world to Nagumo. In this game of high stakes he, unlike Fletcher, did not juggle confusing and conflicting sighting reports. Nagumo had only one. Special Duty Ens. Fukuyama Kazutoshi's *Chikuma* Number Two aircraft flew the special 165-degree line that was the last-minute addition to the late morning search. His all-important farewell was: "Spotted large enemy force. Being pursued by enemy fighters, 1200 [Z–9, local time 1400]." Nagumo did not receive that report until 1425 after the *Chikuma* blinkered it up the line. The message gave no position, but from the flight plan and elapsed time, Nagumo's staff estimated with uncanny accuracy the target bore 153 degrees, distance 260 miles. The bearing was almost dead on and the actual distance to TF-61 only ten miles farther. The force catapulted float shadowers to amplify the contact.[42]

Nagumo now could attack. The *Shōkaku* and *Zuikaku* counted fifty-one Zero fighters, fifty-four Type 99 carrier bombers, thirty-six Type 97 carrier attack planes, and one Type 2 carrier reconnaissance plane. Nine Zeros flew combat air patrol. Swearing never again to be caught with armed planes on board, the Third Fleet staff devised three strike waves, each a small, handy deck load in size. Reckoning carrier bombers could more easily breach strong fighter defenses than torpedo planes, the first two waves would comprise all fifty-four carrier bombers, escorted by twenty-four Zeros. Their mixed loads of high explosive and semi–armor-piercing bombs would blast flight decks and antiaircraft guns and penetrate vitals to knock out propulsion. Only then would the third wave of thirty-six carrier attack planes and twelve fighters finish off the target with torpedoes. That tactic arose from the heavy loss of torpedo planes at Coral Sea and Midway. The sequence also offered the advantage of not having armed planes stacked in the hangars until the enemy's offensive threat was neutralized.[43]

Unaware the die was cast, the *Saratoga* recovered three SBDs—the two orphans from Cactus and one strike abort. At the same time the *Enterprise* sent up eight combat air patrol F4Fs and prepared a strike "ready for possible second enemy carrier in area." The remaining few *Saratoga* TBFs would join them "if ordered." Fletcher stood northwest at fifteen knots to close the returning *Enterprise* afternoon search. News of a second enemy carrier reached him, even as the daily Cincpac intelligence bulletin falsely soothed the *Shōkaku* and *Zuikaku* had only come as far south as the "Truk area," with "all other carriers [except the auxiliary *Kasuga Maru*] believed home waters."[44]

At 1357 Kellam's 3V37 warned of "suspicious vessels" and eight minutes later described them as one small carrier, two cruisers, and one destroyer headed southeast. The position attributed to Kellam's contact converted to 345 degrees, two hundred miles from TF-61. That was "far from the position in which the first carrier was expected to be." The *Saratoga* strike group, if it sighted nothing on its outbound leg (a distinct possibility because the original search contact was hours old), could end up nearly one hundred miles southwest of this new second carrier. Therefore at 1435 Fletcher radioed Felt to tell him that at "course 350 T[rue,] distance 150 from your present position 1 CV 2 CL 1 DD." Fletcher had no idea whether Felt ever heard the message. The reported longitude of the 3V37 contact was actually 2 degrees of longitude farther west, for Kellam indeed spotted the already discovered *Ryūjō* force. This misstated position only added to the confusion. While Fletcher considered the grim implications should his main blow go astray, Kinkaid queried whether he, too, knew of the second carrier. Impatient to launch the *Enterprise*'s strike of eleven SBDs, eight TBFs, and eight F4Fs, Kinkaid also worried TF-61 would not advance far enough by 1630 to be where his returning afternoon searchers could find it. "We must make good course 335 speed 20 to intercept Point Option." Fletcher at once complied and asked Kinkaid whether he had "heard anything of your [search] boys that went out about two hours ago?" Kinkaid replied, "Negative."[45]

Fletcher still had only bits of the puzzle. At 1440 Cactus radioed it was under attack by twin-engine bombers, fighters, and carrier-type bombers, seemingly confirming the *Sara*'s radar contact of planes launched from a carrier not far north of TF-61. Yet the *Enterprise* searchers, who fully covered that area, never reported a carrier. Actually it was only the twenty-one *Ryūjō* planes that struck Lunga. Bad weather forestalled an earlier attack by the Rabaul-based land-attack planes. The *Mackinac* relayed the opinion of an unidentified PBY pilot (evidently Burkey) that the "carrier previously reported" was the distinctive, island-less

Ryūjō. Fletcher could only hope Felt's *Saratoga* flyers would see that for themselves.[46] At 1500 the *Saratoga* landed twenty F4Fs (including sixteen *Enterprise*) and took over combat air patrol support. Kinkaid asked Fletcher whether he also copied a message from *Enterprise* scout 1V395, inevitably to be told no. He informed Fletcher that 1V395 sighted one carrier, one heavy cruiser, one light cruiser, and three destroyers bearing 320 degrees and 210 miles from TF-11. That was just about where Fletcher could expect the original 5V37 carrier contact to be by that time. It was, of course, once again Hara's *Ryūjō* force that Burkey found nearly six hours before.

Soon after receiving word his planes bombed Lunga, Hara was snooped almost simultaneously by three separate *Enterprise* search sections: Lt. Cdr. Charles M. Jett's two VT-3 TBFs (1V395 in the 320–330 sector), Lt. Stockton Birney Strong's two VS-5 SBDs in the next sector north, and Ens. John H. Jorgenson's mismatched pair of VS-5 SBD and VT-3 TBF closing from the southwest. Yet a fourth search section, two VT-3 TBFs led by Lt. John N. Myers, showed up a few minutes later. After transmitting its contact report, Jett's section executed a horizontal bombing run from twelve thousand feet and missed the *Ryūjō*'s stern by only 150 meters. Zeros broke up Myers's attempt at a similar attack and shot down his wingman, Mach. Harry Corl, a Midway TBD survivor. Unless Felt turned north against the second (Kellam's 3V37) carrier contact, he aimed directly for Jett's carrier, but Fletcher was unsure where Felt was going. He mulled whether to launch the second strike group (mostly *Enterprise* planes) against Jett's target, but those planes must return in the dark. Making things much worse, Fletcher heard a different *Enterprise* searcher (9V395) advise at 1525 that he bombed, but missed, one of a pair of carriers. Maddeningly, the position of this vastly significant encounter did not come through, and Fletcher did not know the particular sector 9V395 handled. Kinkaid did but seems never to have provided Fletcher an estimate based on that knowledge. To bemused CTF-61, the enemy force now appeared to number four carriers: one pair, location regretfully unknown, and the two already reported, widely separated singletons.[47]

The adventures of the search planes covering the skies over Kondō and Nagumo exceeded even the swarm around the *Ryūjō*, but only snippets leaked to those who most needed to know. On its return leg Slater's 8V37 PBY ran across the Advance Force, fought through the pugnacious *Chitose* seaplanes, and at 1346 transmitted a contact report of one heavy cruiser and four unidentified ships on course 140 degrees and 475 miles northwest of base. Not surprisingly, neither Fletcher nor Kinkaid received that particular message that would have reemphasized the peril north of TF-61. By 1430 the first representatives of the far-ranging *Enterprise* afternoon search also latched onto Kondō. Lt. John T. Lowe's two VB-6 SBDs counted three heavy cruisers, several destroyers, and other ships on course 180 degrees, speed twenty knots. He tapped out a contact report and at 1447 shook up the Advance Force with near misses against the heavy cruiser *Maya*. The *Enterprise* immediately copied Lowe's report of three heavy cruisers and three destroyers, course 180 degrees, speed twenty knots, and located them 240 miles NNW of TF-61 and just north of the false carrier contact attributed to Kellam. At 1449 Kinkaid forwarded the contact by TBS to Fletcher, who invariably did not receive it. Both admirals relied overmuch on TBS and should have used visual signals to confirm the receipt of key messages.[48]

A more spectacular discovery occurred at the same time Lowe attacked Kondō. Flying the adjacent sector to westward, VB-6 skipper Lt. Ray Davis (9V395) discerned Abe's vanguard in the haze. While maneuvering to bomb one of the cruisers, he sighted farther north a very large carrier loaded with planes. She was Nagumo's flagship *Shōkaku* in the process of launching her first wave of eighteen carrier bombers and nine Zeros. Several miles astern the *Zuikaku* followed suit with nine carrier bombers and six Zeros. Lt. Cdr. Seki Mamoru quickly formed up his attack group and started southeast. Eager to bag one flattop, Davis and wingman Ens. Robert C. Shaw swung upwind while climbing to fourteen thousand feet. They adroitly evaded combat air patrol Zeros but not the *Shōkaku*'s radar. Word of incoming enemy planes, the first to be detected by Japanese shipborne radar, failed to reach the *Shōkaku*'s bridge in timely fashion. No one warned the nine Zeros on combat air patrol of nearby intruders, although five of the nine *Shōkaku* escort Zeros broke away in a futile bid to catch the two SBDs. Only at the last instant did *Shōkaku* lookouts discern the danger. The carrier executed a sharp evasive turn just in time to evade one 500-pound bomb ten meters to starboard. The second bomb landed ten meters beyond. Then a terrible snafu bedeviled the American side. Davis's carefully composed report ("2 CV's with decks full," with position and course) had, as noted, only reached the *Enterprise* and *Saratoga* in garbled form. Thus exceptionally poor radio reception prevented Fletcher and Kinkaid from hurling the second strike directly against Nagumo. The SBDs certainly shook up the *Kidō Butai*. Nagumo scrambled fifteen Zeros, raising the combat air patrol to twenty-nine, including the five escorts whose absence reduced Seki's fighter protection to ten. The spotting and arming of Lt. Takahashi Sadamu's second strike wave of twenty-seven carrier bombers and nine Zeros proceeded at a frenzied pace before more surprises dropped out of the sky.[49]

Ignorant of the position of Nagumo's two carriers to the north, Kinkaid notified Fletcher at 1530 that Jett's report of one carrier to the northwest was "good." Fletcher replied: "If you consider contact good send your boys in." Kinkaid confirmed at 1536 he would "launch when ready unless otherwise directed." Four minutes later Fletcher advised he would turn southeast at 1800 to retire at twelve knots. Kinkaid must work in that course change when planning the second strike.[50] Dwindling destroyer fuel was certainly at the back of Fletcher's mind. The noon fuel reports revealed the TF-11 destroyers averaged 45 percent and the TF-16 destroyers 44 percent. Since then TF-61 steamed at high speed, with prospects for more sprints. The heavy ships still had plenty of oil, but they could not readily fuel destroyers in the midst of a battle.[51]

Kellam's PBY 3V37 came across TF-16 while on its return leg to Ndeni. Unsure whether base ever copied his original contact reports, Kellam flashed by blinking light to the *Enterprise*: "small enemy carrier bearing 320 True distance 195 miles." Along with the correct position (as opposed to the earlier error in transmission), Kellam gave its course and speed and mentioned he saw a separate group of three light cruisers, two destroyers, and three transports fifty miles beyond. Kinkaid forwarded Kellam's carrier contact to the *Saratoga* at 1543 but oddly omitted the convoy. The position Kellam gave for the carrier proved almost identical to what Jett provided. Fletcher replied, "[It] appears to be same one as from your aircraft." A few minutes later he overheard welcome radio traffic from *Saratoga* flyers pounding an enemy carrier. Which of the two solitary flattops was still unclear, but Fletcher was greatly relieved his strike found one of them. Kinkaid, though, balked at dispatching the second strike unless Fletcher assured him TF-61 would continue northwest until they could be recovered. Otherwise he judged the mission as too long. Fletcher responded at 1558 that he would not hold Kinkaid's proposed northwesterly Point Option course, "Due to possibility of night torpedo attack." Again like Spruance at Midway, he feared bumping into a surface force after dark, a unappealing prospect especially when the hidden main body included battleships and heavy cruisers in addition to a swarm of torpedo-wielding destroyers.[52]

At 1602 with the second TF-61 strike still under deliberation, both carrier radars registered a large group of bogeys one hundred miles northwest. Seki's first strike of thirty-seven planes was coming straight in. At that same moment, 225 miles NNW of TF-61, the *Shōkaku* and *Zuikaku* dispatched Takahashi's nearly identical second wave. Abe's vanguard force surged ahead to finish off the U.S. carrier force in night surface combat. Time indeed expired for Fletcher, for TF-61 was about to suffer the feared air attack from an unlocated force. Even so, the gremlins that interfered all day with the American search effort finally afflicted the Japanese. The *Hiei* seaplane in the sector adjacent to the dead Fukuyama reestablished contact with the U.S. striking force. However, its contact report placed Fletcher's carriers fifty miles farther south than their actual position and also had them moving away southeast at twenty knots. Evidently it must have sighted TF-61 during one of its brief stints in the wind for air operations in between lunges to the northwest. Thus ill advised as to the enemy's position and course, Takahashi started southeast expecting to find the target around 1800, close to sundown. Nagumo's carriers turned east to await the results of the two strikes.[53]

A "BAD PREDICAMENT"

When the incoming attack first appeared on radar, TF-61, heading northwest at twenty knots, was 140 miles east of Malaita and thirty miles southeast of the Stewart Islands. Fletcher's own TF-11 (*Saratoga*) was in the lead, Kinkaid's TF-16 (*Enterprise*) holding station ten miles off its port quarter. Fletcher brought TF-61 all the way around southeast into the wind to deploy additional combat air patrol fighters and unleash his hoarded second strike. Working up to twenty-five knots, the two task forces burrowed through "long heavy swells," with destroyers "bouncing almost out of the water." Fletcher told Kinkaid to "close me immediately" and ordered him to dispatch his strike. "To say the least we were in a bad predicament," Pederson recalled. "All of our attack planes were committed on missions with the main enemy force still unlocated and his planes coming in to attack us. The best we could do was to get ready for an air attack and hope for the best."[54]

TF-61 finally had an adequate number of defending fighters. Twenty-four F4Fs circled overhead, with another twenty-two Wildcats poised on the *Saratoga*. Rowe, the *Enterprise* FDO, requested the *Sara* immediately scramble all sixteen *Enterprise* Wildcats and hustle them northwest for distant intercept. The *Saratoga* then cleared her deck of all remaining planes: a half-dozen VF-5 Wildcats to reinforce the combat air patrol and the five torpedo-equipped VT-8 TBFs and two VB-3 SBDs armed with 1,000-pound bombs. At 1620 the

Saratoga told VT-8 skipper Lt. Harold H. Larsen and Lt. (jg) Robert M. Elder, leading the VB-3 section, to join the *Enterprise* strike group about to be launched. The *Saratoga* then landed four fighters, whose pilots jumped out to help the plane handlers push the planes aft so they could refuel and get away as quickly as possible. Spurred by reports of enemy aircraft at twenty-seven miles and closing, Kinkaid released the *Enterprise* to launch seven F4Fs, eleven SBDs, and eight TBFs. Aware of a firm position only for Burkey's original single-carrier contact (amplified by Jett and Kellam), he reluctantly directed Max Leslie, the group commander, to attack that target even though the first *Saratoga* group may already have done the job. The distance to the objective, 260 miles, precluded fighter escort. Kinkaid reassigned the seven F4Fs to the combat air patrol. He also authorized Leslie to take refuge at Cactus should he find it too hard to return to TF-61.[55]

Eleven combat air patrol F4Fs hunted forty miles northwest. Sixteen more hastened out in support. Twenty-six fighters, including the four about to take off from the *Saratoga*, remained near the ships in reserve. That raised the total to fifty-three Wildcats. At 1629 the fighter circuit radio receiver in the *Sara*'s flag plot sounded warning from Gunner Charles E. Brewer of VF-6: "At 1 o'clock above this is Red 2, tally ho! There are about 1 or 2 . . . 9 bogeys unidentified about 12,000 feet, 300. . . . Many ahead of those. . . . Bogey bears 350 [degrees], 20 [miles], Angels 12 [altitude twelve thousand feet]. They're dive bombers." The fighter circuit became so overloaded, no one could figure out exactly what was going on. Fletcher continued relaying the bearing and distance to the enemy planes and hoped "for the best." Garbed in blue "anti-flash" suits to help prevent burns, he and his staff moved outside to the flag bridge for a ringside view. One level above, Clark Lee stood alongside Schindler and the lookouts ranged around sky forward. Beyond the port quarter, nearly ten miles off and in direct line of approaching enemy planes, TF-16 presented a brave sight. Eight screening ships in tight Victor formation deployed in a two-thousand-yard radius around the *Enterprise*, with the massive *North Carolina* five hundred yards farther astern. Kinkaid bent on twenty-seven knots (top speed for the battlewagon) and readied for more, while TF-11 made twenty-eight knots. The last plane, Leslie's TBF, lumbered down the *Enterprise*'s flight deck at 1639. Greatly relieved to get away prior to the actual attack, he sought his flock of SBDs and TBFs forming up for the strike. Low on gas, three antisubmarine SBDs and at least half the twenty *Enterprise* search SBDs and TBFs circled hoping to keep out of trouble.[56]

At 1640, as Brewer radioed, "OK, let's go give them hell," watchers in the *Saratoga* noticed "a puff of smoke" materialize northwest beyond TF-16. A Zero downed by the combat air patrol fell with a "long plume of smoke trailing into the sea." Instantly, "Another Jap plane plunged in flames, until the air was full of those long trailers of smoke." The *Enterprise* and her screen "burst into flame." The "sky blossomed with the black and yellow bursts of their exploding shells." Overhead, planes "flashed through the smoke, the sunlight glinting on their wings." The *North Carolina* looked like she was burning, "So concentrated and intense was her AA fire." Kinkaid maneuvered evasively, while Fletcher turned TF-11 northeast out of the wind to force dive bombers to attack crosswind. At first the *Enterprise* weathered the assault with only splashes from near misses, but at 1644, after a bomb struck aft on the flight deck, a "long streamer of smoke trailed out to the rear of the still speeding ship." Onlookers in TF-11 also noted at least one other hit, but the *Enterprise* did not appear badly damaged. They also perceived a "deliberate attack" against the *North Carolina*.[57]

Observers in the *Sara* also wondered when the numerous attackers would hit TF-11. Next to Lee a lookout "tensed suddenly" and screamed, "Dive bombers overhead coming down out of sun!" Then, "Torpedo planes coming in from port quarter!" The *Enterprise* likewise reported torpedo planes, but none flew the strike. The cause of the *Sara*'s alarm proved to be a hurt F4F seeking to land. At 1655 Fletcher turned into the wind to accommodate the cripple, which flipped over and ensnared itself in the wire barrier. TF-16 ceased fire at 1656. To Lee it seemed the Japanese came and went with "incredible speed." Fletcher radioed Ghormley and McCain: "First attack completed; *Enterprise* hurt; another attack coming in." Surprised neither the fifty-odd dive bombers nor deadly torpedo planes ever pounced on TF-11, he did not know only Seki's twenty-seven dive bombers and ten Zeros executed the strike. Eighteen *Shōkaku* carrier bombers went after the *Enterprise*, and nine from the *Zuikaku* stalked the *Saratoga*. Intense antiaircraft caused three *Shōkaku* carrier bombers to switch to the *North Carolina*, while F4Fs turned away the *Zuikaku* planes short of TF-11. Three joined the assault on the *Enterprise*, and four took on the *North Carolina*. Now all depended on whether the second Japanese strike could follow up this attack.[58]

CHAPTER 29

The Battle of the Eastern Solomons II
Anticlimax

RECOVERY PHASE

Once the attack ceased, Fletcher's top priority was to recycle fighters to reestablish a fresh combat air patrol before a second strike turned up. Radar detected unidentified planes to the northwest and even tracked a large southbound bogey passing fifty miles to westward. The *Saratoga* landed fighters from both carriers and hoped to recover her first strike before sunset, barely an hour off. The *Enterprise*, no longer billowing smoke, appeared to be doing fine. Asked if he could handle planes, Kinkaid replied: "Negative now," but "possible later." Knowing his strike faced a tough time getting back, Kinkaid detached the *Grayson* to stand forty miles north, "Pick up pilots who may be short on gas," and rejoin TF-16 at noon 250 miles southward. Again Kinkaid's judgment was questionable regarding fuel. The hard-luck *Grayson*, at 28 percent earlier that day, had the least oil of his destroyers. She was evidently picked because she wore the pennant of Commander Holcomb, Comdesdiv 22.[1]

At 1730 after the *Saratoga* recovered twenty-seven F4Fs, Fletcher reversed course northwest at twenty-five knots to close lagging TF-16. The *Sara* frantically respotted fighters for launch, even while Fletcher and Kinkaid warily tracked the suspected enemy group circling to the southwest. Kinkaid described the damage to the *Enterprise*: "Two bomb hits aft. Damage apparently light. Fires under control. Some underwater damage not yet located." Oddly he did not mention the third bomb that exploded just abaft the island. At 1749 the *Enterprise* commenced landing fighters and patient SBDs and TBFs from the afternoon search and antisubmarine patrol. The *Saratoga* dispatched fifteen F4Fs to restore the combat air patrol. By 1805, when she started bringing in her first strike, the sun dipped to the horizon. The *Sara* began bringing in fuel-starved SBDs and TBFs "so quickly and skillfully," the flight deck "quickly crowded with planes," with many more "circling in the air." Likewise by 1810, the *Enterprise* had with equal efficiency recovered thirty-three aircraft (twenty SBDs, four TBFs, and nine F4Fs). Davis called a brief halt and respotted the deck to enable five Wildcats to take off on combat air patrol.[2]

At 1813 the *Enterprise*'s steering motors shorted out. She lurched to starboard, nearly collided with the *Balch*, and circled at ten knots while Davis tried fruitlessly to steer with engines. The *Big E* was in a terrible fix. Fortunately at 1827, just as twilight waned, the supposed enemy strike prowling seventy miles west abruptly turned away and disappeared northwest off radar. Pilots from the first *Saratoga* strike group informed Fletcher that at 1700 they saw at least eighteen dive bombers, nine torpedo planes, and three fighters 110 miles northwest of TF-61. Radar had tracked this group that could have finished off the *Big E.* Fletcher radioed Ghormley to request a tug to take her under tow. The nearest, the *Navajo*, was at Nouméa. Davis fortuitously regained control and gingerly pointed his hurt carrier southeast. Two SBDs and one TBF ditched from lack of fuel.[3]

Capt. Arthur C. Davis, USS *Enterprise* (CV-6), 22 July 1942.
Courtesy of National Archives (80-G-13038)

By 1915 as Kinkaid gratefully regained twenty-five knots, he saw TF-11 seven miles east. The *Saratoga* had recovered all planes overhead, twenty-eight SBDs, eight TBFs, and thirty-one F4Fs, that jammed her flight deck. During the landings, Ramsey, to make more room, even risked striking aircraft below via the one slowly cycling amidships elevator. Inevitably one F4F hurtled the barrier, flipped over, and pitched into the open elevator well. Only the snagging of its wings on the edge of the flight deck prevented the Wildcat from plunging into the hangar and catastrophically disabling the elevator in the down position. Despite gridlock, the *Sara* opened enough space to bring in three TBFs and two SBDs from her second strike. At 1930 the *Sara* closed up shop. Her air losses were surprisingly light: three F4Fs, one SBD, and two TBFs. With the *Enterprise* strike expected to stage to Guadalcanal, Fletcher did not think anyone else would come back that night.[4]

REEVALUATING THE SITUATION

Following the attack, Fletcher received new information on the Japanese forces, but it did not clarify much. At 1815 a B-17 strike leader (Maj. Ernest R. Manierre) reported bombing a "large" carrier near the target assigned to the *Saratoga*'s first strike but gave no damage estimate. Felt described to Fletcher how he plastered a carrier at 1600 within twenty miles of the one Manierre's B-17s later attacked. He never copied Fletcher's 1435 message redirecting him north toward what was in fact a false contact, but flew the mission as briefed. At 1536 he had sighted one small carrier, one heavy cruiser, and two destroyers and deployed twenty-two SBDs and five VT-8 TBFs against the flattop, six SBDs and two TBFs after the cruiser. Appalled no bombs hit the swiftly turning flattop, Felt dived in, followed by the six SBDs that fortuitously shifted over from the cruiser. Several 1,000-pound bombs and at least one torpedo were seen to strike the carrier, and one torpedo supposedly hit the cruiser. No *Saratoga* planes fell. Felt stayed until 1620, watching in fascination as the flattop ran "in circles to the right pouring forth black smoke which would die down and belch forth in great volume again." The attackers vowed they had sunk the distinctive *Ryūjō*. Slonim recalled "quite an argument" whether the carrier succumbed, but no one in the *Saratoga* could say for certain one way or the other.[5]

In turn Larsen's tiny second *Saratoga* strike brought news of ships discovered north, rather than northwest, of TF-61. The five TBFs and Elder's two SBDs flew northwest after the false 3V37 contact at 1405 of a single carrier and escorts, actually the *Ryūjō* force ninety miles to the west. At 1755 after searching through heavy clouds, Larsen and Elder attacked a formidable force of one *Mutsu*-class battleship, four heavy cruisers, and a dozen or more destroyers steaming southeast at fifteen to twenty knots. Elder claimed setting the battleship on fire, and Larsen one torpedo hit on a cruiser. Two TBFs failed to rejoin. Larsen and Elder never saw a carrier, but Fletcher soon learned that at 1815 a different B-17 strike group (Maj. J. Allan Sewart) bombed a small carrier, three heavy cruisers, and two destroyers about thirty miles east of where Larsen and Elder attacked.[6]

Fletcher deduced the carrier and land-based strikes must have hit the two light carriers (the *Ryūjō* to the west, another in the east) that evidently flanked the enemy main force. Nothing else was forthcoming from the two large carriers that *Enterprise* searcher 9V395 (Lieutenant Davis) spotted nearly five hours before. Kinkaid's search summary at 2013 finally did identify two big carriers, four heavy cruisers, six light cruisers, and eight destroyers that, as of 1500, were only two hundred miles northwest of TF-61 (and surprisingly close to the erroneous Kellam contact). Fletcher figured Larsen had encountered part of its screen, reckoned at 1740 about 185 miles north of TF-61. Had the main force continued southeast at twenty knots, it could, by 1930, be within 160 miles of TF-61. If Fletcher then turned northwest at twenty to twenty-five knots, he might bring about a night surface battle in four or five hours. The staff debated that audacious course of action, but Fletcher soon resolved to withdraw south at fifteen knots in the wake of wounded TF-16. Slonim described him "collapsing into a chair," joking: "Boys, I'm going to get two dispatches tonight, one from Admiral Nimitz telling me what a wonderful job we did, and one from King saying 'Why in hell didn't you use your destroyers and make torpedo attacks?' and by God, they'll both be right."[7]

Retiring TF-11 on the evening of 24 August became Fletcher's most controversial decision of the battle. He never explained why he rejected night battle, but one can note some factors that very likely influenced him at that time. Comparing his available surface strength (three heavy cruisers, a light cruiser, and seven destroyers) with the ships reported to the north demonstrated the enemy's distinct advantage in numbers, not to mention superior night fighting tactics. Extracting the *North Carolina* from TF-16, even if Fletcher wanted to risk the inexperienced battleship in such uncertain circumstances, would cost valuable time. Rapidly decreasing destroyer fuel also limited his options for high-speed steaming. The *Saratoga*'s overcrowded flight deck perhaps also figured in his decision not to seek a night battle. He also had no real idea of the losses the big strike sustained in the attack on TF-16, but good reason to believe only one enemy carrier suffered any significant damage in return.

At 2214 Fletcher advised Ghormley that TF-11 and TF-16 headed south "toward the fueling rendezvous." The *Enterprise* sustained "some underwater damage," but with steering restored, she no longer needed the tug. Fletcher regretted not learning of the two large carriers "in time" to attack, but reported *Saratoga* planes smashed the *Ryūjō*, "Left burning badly," and roughed up cruisers and a battleship in a separate force. He could not say what damage the *Enterprise* attack group might have caused but stated those planes were to remain at Cactus "until further orders." TF-11 and 16 "must fuel tomorrow," but Noyes's "Task Force 18 is fueled today [and] will stand toward Cactus to support that place in accordance operation order." At least Fletcher assumed that was where Noyes would go, but Noyes would do much more.[8]

Kinkaid provided Fletcher more sobering news. The *Enterprise* suffered seventy-four killed and one hundred wounded, the center elevator was inoperable, and an unspecified number of "after compartments" had flooded. Twenty-six aircraft were "missing," but presumably included planes on the *Saratoga* and at Cactus. At 2040 the *Sara*'s radar showed approaching "friendly planes," *Enterprise* aircraft that did not go to Guadalcanal. In the light of the nearly full moon, six TBFs appeared above TF-16. Kinkaid courageously illuminated his ships for landing. The second TBF plowed spectacularly into the crane abaft the *Enterprise*'s island and fouled the deck, forcing Davis to ask the *Saratoga* at 2134 whether she could take four more planes. Ramsey replied, "Affirmative, in about 15 minutes." Fletcher also authorized lights to be shown. Following another furious respot, the *Saratoga* recovered the four lucky TBFs by 2205. Thus Fletcher learned the *Enterprise* strike never rendezvoused. In rapidly worsening weather the TBFs sighted ship wakes in the dwindling twilight about 275 miles out, only to recognize Roncador Reef north of Santa Isabel. Unaware of the option to fly to Henderson Field, the Avengers dumped their fish and fortuitously found home plate. Late that evening Vandegrift radioed that the eleven *Enterprise* SBDs set down safely without contacting the enemy. A half hour after the last TBF landed on the *Saratoga*, Davis entreated Ramsey to take another orphan on board. "Affirmative," Ramsey gamely replied, "but it will be a tight fit." At 2303 Leslie's TBF thumped down on the *Sara* after a 6.5 hour flight. He explained to Fletcher he, too, never sighted Japanese ships. It was fortunate, given the *Sara*'s crammed flight deck, the eleven SBDs never showed. She had ninety-three aircraft (forty-three F4F-4s, one F4F-7, thirty-two SBDs, and seventeen TBFs) from both groups. Things got so bad that plane handlers even tipped some F4Fs onto their noses to stack them close together and open more room forward. The air department performed magnificently in compensating for the *Sara*'s real drawbacks in battle.[9]

Following TF-16 by an hour, Fletcher monitored some, but not all, the contacts transmitted by two radar-equipped PBY night searchers from Ndeni. At 2133 Lt. (jg) Norman K. Brady encountered "unidentified vessels in rain" about two hundred miles north of TF-61, roughly at the location of the light carrier group that flanked the main body to eastward. A half hour later Ens. William C. Corbett warned of five ships only 145 miles northwest of TF-11 and closing at twenty knots. The Japanese were pushing hard in pursuit. McCain directed the *Mackinac* to get her PBYs up an hour before first light on 25 August and clear out. Ghormley agreed with Fletcher that as many as four carriers chased TF-61 from "northward Malaita," and only one had sustained damage. He pointedly reminded Fletcher of Cincpac's 20 August message warning of increased numbers of enemy destroyers and the "Jap boast of [night] torpedo technique," hardly a ringing endorsement for a night surface fight. Ghormley also imparted to Vandegrift cheery news of "enemy carriers heading toward northern Malaita," that "may hit your positions at day light." He told the *Hornet* task force, staging south from Pearl, to refuel "as soon as possible" and be ready for "offensive operations" to westward of the rendezvous with TF-61. TF-17 still only neared Fiji and was one thousand miles from the battle area. Much could happen in the three days it required to get there.[10]

A BRIEF PURSUIT

If the situation on the evening of 24 August confused the U.S. commanders, their Japanese counterparts smugly contemplated their glorious victory. Kondō's own Advance Force (five heavy cruisers, one light cruiser, five destroyers, and seaplane carrier *Chitose*) and Nagumo's *Kidō Butai* (*Shōkaku*, *Zuikaku*, two battleships, three heavy cruisers, one light cruiser, and eight destroyers) weathered disconcerting attacks by a few dive bombers, but took their revenge by hurling seventy-three aircraft against the U.S. carriers. Soon joined by Abe's vanguard, Kondō raced south to destroy the cripples. The top commanders were unaware of the sinking of the *Ryūjō* in Hara's Support Force. Cornered that afternoon by the *Saratoga*'s first strike, the *Ryūjō* absorbed one torpedo, which knocked out steering and propulsion, and severe blast damage from near misses by 1,000-pound bombs. Hara detailed the destroyers to sink the burning carrier while he left in the *Tone* in accordance with Nagumo's orders. Following an unsuccessful attack by Manierre's three B-17s, the *Ryūjō* went down after dark.[11]

Nagumo knew his first wave found the U.S. carriers. At 1650 a fresh shadower, the *Chikuma* Number Five seaplane, corrected the erroneous position report of the *Hiei* searcher. Yet Takahashi, leading the second wave, copied neither that vital message nor Nagumo's rebroadcast telling him the U.S. carriers were east of where he was headed. Some second wave aircrews heard both messages but wrongly assumed Takahashi did, too. Nor did the second wave notice the returning *Saratoga* first strike cut southeast across its flight path. Consequently Takahashi fetched up too far west and south to sight Fletcher's carriers. At 1730 Takahashi again missed another golden opportunity from Seki's post strike report, also rebroadcast by the *Shōkaku*, that others in his group did copy. At 1743 he reached where he expected to find enemy carriers, but saw only open water. The second strike was eighty-three miles southwest of TF-16. Takahashi searched westward in vain until sunset and reluctantly turned for home. His failure to find TF-61 and finish off the stricken *Enterprise* became the crucial Japanese mistake of the battle.[12]

About the same time Takahashi finally gave up, Sewart's four high-flying B-17s encountered Abe's vanguard thirty miles ahead of Nagumo's main body. Sewart claimed multiple bomb hits on a nonexistent carrier but actually missed the destroyer *Maikaze*. Later his Fortresses skirmished with Nagumo's combat air patrol but failed in the setting sun to discern nearby *Shōkaku* and *Zuikaku*. Neither Army Air Force navigation nor its ship identification was on the mark. Sewart's 1810 report of another small carrier, three heavy cruisers and two destroyers was what led Fletcher to believe there was a carrier thirty miles east of the force Larsen struck.[13]

For his own part Kondō kept east of Nagumo's carriers as both task forces aimed for the gap between Malaita and the Santa Cruz Islands. The *Chitose* (Elder's "battleship"), while stopped to recover aircraft, noticed Larsen's tiny strike at 1740. Near misses from the two SBDs inflicted severe damage. The five VT-8 TBFs scored no hits against Kondō's four swift heavy cruisers. Two Avengers ditched (their crews were rescued) after encountering far-ranging combat air patrol Zeros. That evening Kondō also sought the U.S. carriers to the south and absorbed Abe's vanguard. Special night search float planes fanned out looking for targets. From Truk, Vice Adm. Komatsu Teruhisa, leading the submarine fleet, roused his ten I-boats in pursuit.[14]

Only at 1900 did just twelve of Seki's original thirty-seven planes reach home. Nagumo announced at 1928 after debriefing Seki the first strike scored more than three bomb hits on an *Enterprise*-class carrier. A *Zuikaku* report claimed two bomb hits on a different carrier. The enemy remnant was fleeing at twenty-five knots. Nagumo decided to head north to refuel after recovering his second wave. He got an argument from his flag Capt. Arima Masafumi, who advised vigorous pursuit, but Nagumo declared the battle was already won. His final assessment, transmitted at 2040, chalked up six bomb hits on a "new-type" carrier (the *Essex*) and another carrier and battleship set afire. Kondō independently reached the same optimistic conclusion, radioing at 2005 that he would pursue only until midnight to the last known enemy position to finish off disabled carriers.[15]

Retrieving the second wave proved exceptionally difficult. Starting at 2015 the carriers recovered twenty-eight of thirty-six planes. Takahashi learned to his great regret of the bungled opportunities to finish off the U.S. carriers. Seven carrier bombers went missing, and another ditched. Nagumo turned on searchlights and broadcast radio homing messages until all hope was lost. Incredibly two hours later, three errant carrier bombers turned up flying on fumes. Slonim's radio intelligence team in the *Saratoga* eavesdropped the homing efforts Fletcher correctly attributed to the strike group that never found TF-61. "These planes were later heard in the evening trying to home on their carrier but received no answer," Pederson recalled. As will be shown, Hypo analysts listening in at Pearl wrongly decided many enemy aircraft splashed that night vainly seeking their own carriers. The *Shōkaku* and *Zuikaku* in fact lost nine fighters and twenty-four dive bombers, leaving one hundred aircraft (forty-one fighters, twenty-five dive bombers, and thirty-four torpedo planes) available the next day.[16]

Kondō's lookouts made no contacts before the stipulated time. His night air search overtook only a lone "light cruiser" (the *Grayson*) running away. The bloodied U.S. carriers obviously fled beyond reach. Kondō called off the pursuit at 2330 and led the surface force north at twenty-four knots to refuel. At the same time Yamamoto's Combined Fleet Main Force (one battleship, one converted carrier, and three destroyers) approached the battle area from the northwest. He exulted the "Second Solomons Sea Battle" (Savo was the first) left two U.S. carriers in flames and sent the whole enemy force packing. It is fascinating to consider, especially in contrast to his vehemence after the Coral Sea battle, that Yamamoto endorsed the decision of his top commanders not to harass the beaten enemy. Kondō broke off the battle when it was "appropriate under the circumstances," but Nagumo was to be ready to attack any "damaged ships" that turned up the next morning. Learning of the loss of the *Ryūjō*, Yamamoto theorized that carriers skulking southeast of Guadalcanal had hoped to ambush the Second Echelon convoy, only to encounter the unlucky Hara and suffer a devastating surprise assault. Ugaki called the *Ryūjō* a splendid, if unwitting, "decoy" (as did historians) and strongly regretted not actually finishing off the hurt U.S. carriers. Their temporary escape made no difference in the short run, because the Allied defense of Guadalcanal was doomed. To the top brass only severe communication failures and poorly framed contact reports prevented an even more decisive Japanese victory.[17]

Now that his forces swept away all significant naval and air opposition, Yamamoto directed the KI Operation to proceed and deposit the Ichiki Second Echelon at Guadalcanal on the evening of the twenty-fifth. Near to midnight on 24 August, when 190 miles north of Guadalcanal, Tanaka received orders once more to go in. Having seen smoke from the burning *Ryūjō*, he understandably entertained "grave doubts about this slow convoy's chances of reaching its goal." Yamamoto rejected the vehement recommendation of Tanaka's superior Tsukahara for Nagumo's carriers to bomb the Guadalcanal airfield. Evidently Yamamoto thought the *Ryūjō*, before expiring, destroyed Lunga's planes on the ground. Three destroyers rushing down from Shortland would finish the job that night. Yamamoto and his two fleet commanders exhibited an astonishing level of wishful thinking and were in for sore disappointment.[18]

CACTUS SOLVES ITS OWN PROBLEM

By following Kinkaid's TF-16 south, Fletcher ensured TF-11 would not fight on 25 August unless the Japanese advanced within range of the *Saratoga*'s planes. Thus he passed the torch to Noyes's TF-18 with the *Wasp* (sixty-two planes). Noyes started north late on the afternoon of 24 August after rapidly refueling. TF-18 worked up to twenty knots, as fast as he dared push the *Wasp*'s tender propulsion plant. He soon intercepted radio messages that portrayed a full-blown carrier battle in which the *Enterprise* was hit and Fletcher also withdrawing. Rather than simply close Cactus 350 miles northwest, he resolutely reinforced Fletcher and Kinkaid east of Malaita. In the early hours of 25 August TF-18 swept past TF-16, TF-11, and finally the *Grayson* moving hell-bent in the opposite direction. Now only the Japanese carrier fleet loomed ahead of Noyes, with every expectation of renewing battle at dawn.[19]

Committed to refueling, Fletcher followed the action by radio, but it is uncertain what messages the *Saratoga* succeeded in copying. Thus it is not known whether he (or Noyes, for that matter) ever received Vandegrift's warning of warships bombarding Lunga after midnight. The second message stated that seven attacking destroyers now drew off to the northeast. In fact three destroyers breezed into the anchorage off Lunga Point looking in vain for U.S. ships and loosed a few rounds toward the airfield for ten minutes before turning north to swell Tanaka's antisubmarine escort. The shelling inflicted little damage (the leader of the destroyers thought as much), and only served to stir up Vandegrift and his flyers. Six marine and navy SBDs harassed the retreating destroyers. Vandegrift certainly counted on Fletcher's close support, but Ghormley knew better. He urged MacArthur to commit his subs against the ships assailing Guadalcanal, because there were "no friendly vessels [in] that area."[20]

That night the two Airsopac PBYs probed the dark waters north of Malaita and Guadalcanal, trusting their radar to locate targets and the bright moonlight to identify what turned up. At 0149 McCain relayed an "unauthenticated aircraft contact report," first transmitted at 2105, of an "enemy carrier group" discovered only 120 miles north of Lunga and speeding south at twenty-five knots. Fortunately at 0225 Ensign Corbett, who made that contact, corrected its position to 180 miles north of Guadalcanal and reduced its speed to fifteen knots. Around 0340 five float planes from Mikawa's cruisers bombed Lunga, again without noticeable result. Vandegrift went all out against the carriers north of Malaita. Well before sunrise he sent a strike of eight marine and navy SBDs and ten F4Fs. Shortly thereafter a wary Noyes launched the *Wasp* dawn search from east of Malaita and 250 miles from Lunga. Likewise Fletcher, then 120 miles south of Noyes, wrung out ten *Saratoga* SBDs to sweep two hundred miles north.[21]

Lt. (jg) Charles P. Muckenthaler, the first PBY from the dawn search to make contact, squawked of attacks by aircraft. His reported position was 170 miles north of TF-18 and three hundred miles north of TF-11. Those Japanese planes, if carrier-based, had to originate from a different group than the one bearing down on Cactus from the north. Nimitz read an ominous estimate that "from all appearances an aerial attack will be carried out against our holdings in Tulagi-Guadalcanal at daybreak followed by an attempted landing." To Ghormley, Fletcher, and McCain he stressed, "Situation [is] still critical," but the "exchange of damage to date seems to be in our favor. Let's finish off those carriers." In the next several hours carriers from both sides failed to materialize, while Lunga-based planes blasted the invasion convoy. Beginning at 0930 messages from Cactus and various Airsopac searchers mentioned at least one transport seen afire. Finally at 1055 Lt. James Murphy's PBY confirmed, after carefully checking the area, that the convoy of seven destroyers and two cruisers (but no carriers) had left a burning transport behind and slunk away. Later, PBYs encountered scattered groups of battleships, cruisers, and destroyers likewise retiring northward, the nearest more than three hundred miles northeast of Lunga and three hundred miles north of TF-18.[22]

The immediate threat to Guadalcanal had passed. The ships Corbett first sighted that night (and mistakenly identified as a carrier force) were Tanaka's Second Echelon convoy, the only force actually steaming toward Guadalcanal. Two of the three destroyers that shelled Lunga joined after dawn, giving Tanaka one light cruiser, seven destroyers, and four patrol boats escorting three slow transports. By 0800 he was within 150 miles of Guadalcanal, as close as he would get. After seeking the nonexistent carrier group, the Cactus SBDs settled for the convoy so conveniently served up without air cover. They bombed the big transport

Kinryū Maru (which burned), hit another transport, and roughed up Tanaka's flagship *Jintsu*. At 1015 three B-17s sank the destroyer *Mutsuki*, which had stopped to rescue survivors. Totally isolated, a dazed Tanaka ordered a retreat. By preventing Japanese reinforcements from reaching Guadalcanal, the valiant Cactus flyers transformed an indecisive clash of carriers into an Allied strategic success.[23]

Fletcher's morning search was negative, as was Noyes's, but *Wasp* SBDs destroyed three ship-based float planes. With no other targets reported within reach, Noyes angled northwest toward the invasion convoy being assailed north of Lunga. At 1326, when about 275 miles distant, he loosed twenty-four SBDs and ten TBFs—every available attack plane—at extreme range and continued northwest to shorten their return flight. The *Wasp* strike carefully searched the designated area and shot down a flying boat that trailed them from the vicinity of TF-18 but sighted no ships. On the way back they checked out Rekata Bay, the suspected float plane lair on the north coast of Santa Isabel, but found nothing. The disappointed strike crews turned southeast for home. Just before sundown the *Wasp* landed them and shaped course southeast toward TF-11. Noyes did everything he could under the circumstances to harm the enemy and support Fletcher, but Nimitz and King never accorded him any credit.[24]

TF-11 REGROUPS

Fletcher's TF-11 followed Kinkaid's TF-16 with the hurt *Enterprise* toward the oiler rendezvous between San Cristóbal and Espíritu Santo. When air searches showed no sign of pursuit, the chief concern became subs. At 0910 Ens. George G. Estes, flying intermediate air patrol from the *Enterprise*, caught two big subs on the surface only fifteen miles ahead of TF-11. Certain he destroyed one, he dropped a message onto the *Saratoga*'s deck describing the encounter. On his way back south to TF-16, he discovered a surfaced sub in the same location as the previous attack, strafed, then returned to the *Sara* to land. Lookouts sighted yet another I-boat to the southwest. Fletcher detached three destroyers to attack and keep it down. At 1330 a cluster of ships emerged ahead. TF-16 guzzled oil from the three oilers. Kinkaid revised his damage estimate of the *Enterprise* to three "medium" bombs and three damaging near misses. Sprung hull plating flooded one large aft compartment, which "prevents maneuvering at high speed." Fortunately her propulsion system was untouched. The *Enterprise* had thirty-one flyable planes (six F4Fs, twenty SBDs, and five TBFs) and could operate fifty if necessary. Kinkaid recommended proceeding to Nouméa "when practicable" to "effect temporary repairs," but obviously the *Enterprise* required extended time in a proper ship repair facility.[25]

With oilers in abundance, Fletcher filled TF-11 to near capacity. From TF-16 he drew the *North Carolina*, light cruiser *Atlanta*, and destroyers *Grayson* and *Monssen*, giving the *Saratoga* a screen of one battleship, three heavy cruisers, two light cruisers, and nine destroyers. Kinkaid retained heavy cruiser *Portland* and three destroyers. Another destroyer would join him after transferring personnel and matériel. Victory claims by U.S. aircraft totaled fifty-seven planes, and antiaircraft chalked up twenty-four more victims. The two carriers sorted their air groups. Plane losses on 24 August came to only sixteen aircraft: five

F4Fs and four TBFs shot down or missing, one F4F, two SBDs and one TBF ditched, and two F4Fs and one TBF jettisoned. The *Saratoga* absorbed seventeen *Enterprise* F4Fs and six TBFs, raising her air complement to eighty-nine planes (forty fighters, thirty-one dive bombers, seventeen torpedo planes, and one reconnaissance aircraft). The *Enterprise* retained eight fighters, twenty-two dive bombers, five torpedo planes, and one reconnaissance plane but was to leave most of them behind prior to departing Sopac. The *Saratoga* took her turn with the *Sabine* that evening. Only numerous sub contacts interrupted a quiet day.[26]

Contact reports that Fletcher copied revealed all enemy ships, including the battered invasion convoy, had retired north beyond air search range. The daily Cincpac intelligence bulletin belatedly acknowledged the *Zuikaku*, *Shōkaku*, and *Ryūjō* in the Solomons area, while the *Zuihō*, *Junyō*, and *Hiyō* "have all earmarks of departing Japan," perhaps "within last 48 hours." If so, they could reach the Solomons in the next week. The converted carrier *Kasuga Maru* was thought to be near Truk but bound for Rabaul. Among other fleet units in the New Britain area or headed there were four cruiser divisions and two destroyers squadrons. "Cinc Combined Fleet" flagship had left home waters for Truk. The proximity of such powerful enemy forces to Sopac hardly came as news to Ghormley and Fletcher, but at least there was welcome respite from battle.[27]

Fletcher intended to send Kinkaid south to between Efate and New Caledonia to await further orders that would likely mean a return to Pearl. He also provided a message for Ghormley that the *Enterprise* was to fly to Efate on 26 August as TF-16 passed by. It outlined the current situation and explained that TF-11 expected to complete fueling the night of 25 August and rejoin Noyes's TF-18 east of Malaita. Fletcher recommended the fragile *Wasp* remain "until situation clears," and desired TF-17 (*Hornet*) to join him "as soon as practicable." In any event TF-11 and TF-18 must provision in ten days. That entailed visiting an island base, because big ships could not easily draw large amounts of food stores at sea. Well aware Ghormley might require a separate surface force, Fletcher offered Crutchley's TF-44 (*Australia*, *Hobart*, and three destroyers), plus the *Salt Lake City*. TF-44 should come under direct Comsopac control, "As radio silence precludes proper command by me." That night Fletcher released Kinkaid's TF-16 to southward. After the fast, highly efficient refueling session, augmented TF-11 turned north toward San Cristóbal to find TF-18. The empty *Platte* and *Cimarron* left for Nouméa, while the *Sabine*, which retained some oil, started for Espíritu Santo.[28]

"WE MUST BE ON ALERT"

The morning of 25 August brought bitter disillusionment for a hitherto ebullient Japanese high command. By 1100 when Yamamoto's Main Force met the *Kidō Butai* 350 miles northwest of Guadalcanal, he knew the mauling of the Second Echelon convoy prevented any troops from landing. He called off the KI Operation and directed the *Zuikaku* to cover Tanaka's retreat. Even worse, he soon understood the U.S. carriers survived their ordeal surprisingly well. Around midnight while redeploying southward, the *I-17* and *I-15*, operating independently 125 miles east of San Cristóbal, had simultaneously sighted carrier forces retiring at twenty knots. Neither sub could maneuver into attack position.

Komatsu ordered all boats in pursuit. After sunrise several subs piped up with fresh contacts of task forces 130–150 miles from the sightings reported the previous night. At 0800 the *I-9* reported a battleship 330 miles southeast of Lunga, actually Fletcher's TF-11. After running afoul of an enemy plane and some destroyers, the *I-9* limped to Truk. The *I-15* encountered a southbound force at 0915 that comprised a battleship, an *Enterprise*-class carrier, two cruisers, five destroyers, and two oilers supposedly forty miles northeast of the *I-9* contact. That obviously was TF-16, but the *I-15* placed it too far north. The rest of daylight brought no new contacts by subs, although they eagerly sought carriers. That evening Komatsu ordered all of them back to their previous picket lines. During the day Yamamoto took his Main Body to 330 miles of Guadalcanal, before relenting and rejoining Kondō and Nagumo to the north. "We must be on alert," Ugaki decreed. Apparently one U.S. carrier and a battleship had refueled southeast of San Cristóbal and kept watch by "sending out search planes, some of which our search planes met" to their detriment between Malaita and Ndeni. The report by the missing flying boat that afternoon of a carrier five hundred miles southeast of Shortland led Ugaki to believe it located "yesterday's damaged carrier." Actually the flying boat had, as noted above, sighted TF-18 with the fully battle-ready *Wasp*.[29]

With U.S. air power in the region, carrier and land-based, manifestly active and quite dangerous, Yamamoto revised his plans. The battle for the Solomons would be "a prolonged one." The recapture of Guadalcanal must now precede the destruction of the U.S. fleet, but Lunga's air force had to disappear before the transports could be risked again. Destroyers would resume infiltrating troops into Guadalcanal. In Rabaul Tsukahara reiterated his call for Nagumo's carriers to strike Lunga, but Ugaki urged careful deliberation before undertaking that extreme measure. Combined Fleet needed to regroup and bring in more land-based aircraft. Beginning 26 August, Kondō and Nagumo were to refuel at sea. Lacking oil, two fast battleships had to retire to Truk to await the arrival of another tanker from Japan. Nagumo did not consider the slower but more powerful *Mutsu* an adequate stand-in. The remainder of Kondō's Support Force should be ready to fight in a few days. In early September light carrier *Zuihō* and two more fast battleships were to come south from Japan, followed by the *Hiyō* and *Junyō* in early October as soon as their air groups were ready.[30]

TACTICAL LESSONS

The Eastern Solomons became the most intensively studied carrier action yet. The single overriding complaint concerned communications: poorly functioning radios, delayed contact reports, and other shortcomings in passing vital information. Captain Davis described communications as "weak to the point of danger," and Kinkaid stated, "Communication failures are the primary cause of many tactical errors." Fletcher submitted an entire report on the failure of communications. The problem did not admit to a quick fix and dogged the U.S. Navy for the rest of the year.[31]

Several commentators described a visible deterioration of enemy pilot skills, a premature assessment that the next carrier battle would show. Fletcher called fighter direction "not entirely satisfactory although much better than previously experienced." The intercept of lone shadowers continued to excel, but the carriers still seemed at a loss concentrating combat air patrol fighters to defeat strike groups. Yet ship antiaircraft improved considerably, and the fast battleship had proven invaluable. At the same time fighter escorts remained weak, particularly for the vulnerable torpedo planes. Some leaders, notably Davis, recommended limiting torpedo planes to moonlight strikes and finishing off cripples, or using them as horizontal bombers. Fletcher strongly disagreed. The aerial torpedo was the most powerful antiship weapon in the air arsenal. His fears for the misuse of torpedo planes soon came true.[32]

The carriers appeared more satisfied with the Grumman F4F-4 Wildcat, although acknowledging its inferiority to the Zero. As noted previously, the only immediate action in the absence of better fighters was to have more Wildcats. Fletcher even desired a dedicated "fighter carrier," if enough other carriers were available to accomplish the offensive mission. Kinkaid concurred. Up to this point the carriers depended chiefly on surprise to compensate for numerical or matériel inferiority, but now, in the face of extensive shore-based air, that no longer pertained. Kinkaid rated fighter strength according to the anticipated opposition. For "normal operations" the carriers should each have forty F4Fs instead of the current thirty-six, but against tougher defenses there should be sixty. To conduct amphibious offensives, such as Watchtower, where the carriers themselves must support ground operations, one carrier should have one hundred or more fighters. Increasing fighter strength, however, correspondingly reduced offensive power in the form of dive bombers and torpedo planes. The whole issue needed careful consideration.[33]

Fletcher continued to oppose the single carrier task forces he was ordered to use on 24 August. His 24 September letter on carrier tactics called for carrier task forces assigned to the same mission to remain together for "mutual support and protection" and not separate "unless there is some strong tactical reason." In this he followed the iconoclastic Rear Adm. Ted Sherman. Fletcher elaborated these views in his 25 September endorsement of the *Enterprise* Eastern Solomons report. Davis urged the individual carrier task forces draw at least fifteen miles apart in the event of air attack. Fletcher strongly disagreed. "To an attacking air group, it makes little difference whether the carriers are separated by 5 or 20 miles but to the defenders it makes a great deal. By keeping the carriers separated 15–20 miles there is always the danger that the full fighter force may not be brought to bear decisively against the enemy as happened at Midway." Davis opined, "The joint operation of more than two carrier forces is too unwieldy." Fletcher countered that according to "our recent experiences" a task force commander could handle three carrier task forces "almost as easily as two." Even four could operate together "without too much difficulty." The "advantages to be gained from such a concentration of air power would more than offset any disadvantages." He prophesied the "tendency will be to operate more and more carriers together as our offensive gains momentum."[34]

MAKING SENSE OF THE EASTERN SOLOMONS

Despite intensive analysis, the battle as a whole remained a mystery. The exceptionally poor communications and numerous failures by the search to report correctly the enemy's strength and position rendered Fletcher, as Slonim explained to Morison, "Thoroughly confused throughout the action." Fletcher thought there were at least two and very possibly three separate enemy carrier task forces with four flattops. Due though to the "incompleteness of last contact reports," he could not "fix with any degree of accuracy" their positions. Fletcher's 6 September 1942 preliminary report designated "Task Force A" the group of ships he thought included the light carrier *Ryūjō*, which the *Saratoga*'s aviators claimed to have sunk. He speculated the *Ryūjō* launched the evening strike that fortuitously missed TF-61. East of Task Force A was "Task Force B" with the big carriers *Shōkaku* and *Zuikaku*, which likely dispatched the huge strike of eighty aircraft that hit TF-16. Larsen's mini-strike very likely targeted B's screen, possibly damaging a battleship and two cruisers. Fletcher supposed another light carrier force, "Task Force C," operated southeast of Task Force B and was the source of the Cactus-bound strike detected early that afternoon on radar. The confusion persisted long after the battle. The *Ryūjō* remained in the Cincpac intelligence bulletins for a week. Ghormley told Nimitz on 3 September it was likely Fletcher's and McCain's bombers hit different carriers and that the *Ryūjō* was just badly damaged. Pederson remarked in late 1943, "[The] consensus of those of us who were there is that there were 4 Jap carriers." Of course, only three Japanese carriers fought in the Eastern Solomons. The phantom Task Force C resulted from misidentification and incorrect navigation by search planes and Sewart's B-17s. Even nailing down the loss of the *Ryūjō* proved difficult. The cryptanalysts were not certain until January 1943, when they deciphered a naval message that deleted her from the navy list.[35]

The other fundamental question raised by the battle was how the Japanese carriers could reach the Solomons without radio intelligence predicting and confirming their movements. Fletcher discussed the intelligence failure with Nimitz when they next met. He brought up the Cincpac daily intelligence bulletin, received on 23 August, placing all Japanese carriers north of Truk, where instead as many as four flattops had secretly closed within a few hundred miles of TF-61. According to Layton, Fletcher "cussed so loudly about the intelligence being bad," but he was not the only one deeply concerned. Even while the battle raged, Captain Steele's daily summary of radio intelligence had noted: "It now seems probable that Jap CVs are about to enter Truk. If this is so they can hardly arrive in the Solomons before August 27th, local date." The day after the battle Rochefort's Hypo analysts admitted their bafflement. "Success of a large task force including carriers in reaching the Solomons without detection by R.I. indicates that radio security practices of the Japs are effective insofar as concealing actual movements is concerned." The experts finally deduced the initial inclusion of the carrier forces in the local communication net really meant they were already present instead of just en route. Layton later decided the reason the expected carrier arrival report at Truk had not been intercepted was that, unknown to the Allies, the striking force bypassed Truk and kept going south. In the end, "You can't always be right," and "that's what RI is all about."[36]

Despite an at least temporary strategic victory in the Battle of the Eastern Solomons, many thought Fletcher should have done much better. He should have taken advantage of what they perceived was a highly advantageous tactical position on the evening of 24 August. The extremely exaggerated claims of aircraft destroyed in the attack on TF-16 (at least eighty-four planes shot down by combat air patrol and antiaircraft), as well as tantalizing hints from radio intelligence of additional heavy plane losses, had mesmerized Nimitz. His preliminary report postulated that 24 August cost the enemy "the best part of three or four carrier groups destroyed in action," or "most of the Japanese aerial striking force available that day." The eighty planes that were annihilated assailing TF-16 represented "at least one large and one small carrier group." Moreover, "The second attack group that missed locating Task Force 61 late in the afternoon could have been the other large carrier air group," whose "planes were later in the evening heard trying to home their carrier." Thus, Nimitz speculated, "Some or all of the group were lost." Given confusing reports of twin-engine bombers attacking Cactus on 24 August, he was uncertain whether carrier planes also struck Henderson Field, whose defenders claimed eleven single and twin-engine bombers and seven fighters. "If so, the Japanese lost the best part of three carrier groups in the action of 24 August, and perhaps much of a fourth if a carrier group joined in the attack on Guadalcanal." Consequently, "Not only was the enemy landing expedition turned back, but we had definitely won control of the air." At the same time Fletcher's own air losses (sixteen planes) were extraordinarily low. Despite damage to the *Enterprise*, "We still had intact practically two full carrier air groups." At the same time, the "*Wasp* Task Force was fueled and proceeding North to join TF-61 as it retired southward. The *Hornet* Task Force was nearby enroute." Therefore Nimitz strongly regretted that Fletcher withdrew the *Saratoga* group and wasted all 25 August refueling. At the same time Noyes's TF-18 merely "took position in the general area southeast of Guadalcanal prepared to repel further Japanese attack."[37]

In his ignorance of actual events, Nimitz was extremely unfair. The final Cincpac battle report, dated 24 October 1942, not only repeated the earlier comments regarding heavy enemy air losses, but also strongly questioned Fletcher's actions: "*The withdrawal of the Saratoga Task Force on the night of 24 August broke off the engagement.* At this time the enemy carrier air forces were depleted. Based on hindsight it appears that had the *Saratoga* group remained in the vicinity occupied on the 24th, they might have been able to strike the enemy with air and probably surface forces, since the Japanese heavy units continued to close during the night and did not reverse course until the forenoon (afternoon for some groups) of 25 August." Cincpac described Japanese vulnerability on 25 August not only to carrier air attacks, but also surface combat from Fletcher's task groups. "We must use our surface ships more boldly as opportunity warrants." However, "The distances involved, the problem of coordinating widely scattered forces, along with inadequate communication facilities and training, together prevented the victory from being as decisive as it should have been had planes and surface forces come to grips with the enemy after his air forces were largely destroyed on the 24th of August." The Cominch 1943 Battle Experience Bulletin echoed Nimitz's opinion of poor leadership at Eastern Solomons. "Task forces must anticipate repeated attacks and be prepared to repel them and not be in an unprepared and disorganized condition," referring to TF-11 on the evening of 24 August. "Our task force took the defensive more than the offensive," whereas "effort should be made to follow up initial successes in order to completely annihilate the enemy whether it is daylight or dark." On 25 August, however, the "attitude was too defensive," especially because "an offensive by Task Force 18 might have resulted in complete destruction of the enemy."[38]

Of course, the tactical situation Fletcher actually faced on the evening of 24 August was far less sanguine than Nimitz and King ever appreciated.[39] They considered the supposedly decimated Japanese easy pickings for the *Saratoga* and *Wasp* flyers had Fletcher only mustered the courage to stay and fight. In fact, Cincpac vastly overestimated Japanese carrier plane losses. The actions on 24 August cost the *Shōkaku* and *Zuikaku* just thirty-three aircraft. Far from having his air groups "largely destroyed," Nagumo enjoyed his full aerial torpedo capability of thirty-four carrier attack planes and retained half his dive bombers, as well as forty Zero fighters. The battleships, cruisers, and destroyers led by Kondō and Abe were too formidable for Fletcher to take on alone in surface combat. As so often, the operative word is "hindsight." Just a spectator to the attack on TF-16, all Fletcher had to go on that evening, while he deliberated whether or not to withdraw TF-11, were the initial impressions of tired fighter pilots who landed on the *Saratoga*. That night it looked as if three of four enemy carriers remained untouched, and that powerful surface forces closed fast. He did not gain a fuller picture of the defense of TF-16 until after contacting Kinkaid the next afternoon. The compilation of victory claims only came after collating the action reports. Criticism of Noyes as merely standing toward Guadalcanal instead of seeking to engage carriers to the north was extremely unjustified. Noyes went where he thought the enemy's main body would be. He did not find it, because the Japanese themselves pulled out. Nimitz's mention of the *Hornet* task force being nearby was especially misleading. During the battle TF-17 was fully one thousand miles away and could not possibly have intervened for several days.

The negative impression persisted of Fletcher's failure to pursue.[40] Morison partially heeded Slonim's explication that the battle "exemplified the difficulties in the exercise of command at the point of contact." Thus "by playing up these difficulties," Slonim thought Morison could mitigate "some of the criticism of Admiral Fletcher which seems to be somewhat harsh." Of his old commander, Slonim condescendingly stated: "We all know Mr. Fletcher was not the greatest of war leaders, but I think his problems were sufficiently great to justify some of the errors." In truth Fletcher's problems were far more profound than Slonim ever understood. Enjoying better, but by no means comprehensive, access to Japanese records than wartime analysts, Morison conceded when Fletcher "decided to call it quits for the day," he was "amply justified" in escaping the charge of Kondō's "sea-going cavalry force." Morison favorably compared Fletcher's decision to the wisdom Spruance demonstrated on the night of 4 June in backing out of harm's way at Midway. "It was not known whether the Japanese had had enough, but it was clear that their available gunfire power was much greater than Fletcher's, and night was no time to test the truth of this estimate." Yet Morison condemned what he, too, perceived a lack of an aggressive spirit combined with Fletcher's characteristic obsession with fuel. "How badly did his destroyers need that drink of fuel oil for which he took *Saratoga* completely out of the battle scene on the 25th?" Instead, "As long as the issue was in doubt, every available carrier aircraft should have been used to protect our tenuous lease on Guadalcanal. That is what they were there for. Fletcher won the battle to be sure; but only because the Japanese were more timid than he."[41]

Fletcher's decision to withdraw was tactically wise; he did need to fuel his destroyers and the rest of TF-11, for that matter, to permit the extended high-speed operations that renewed battle would demand. Vandegrift already had as many or more carrier planes as

Cactus could handle. Fletcher always had to keep in mind that only the intervention of the Japanese heavy fleet forces would ensure in the end whether or not the marines held Cactus. Their carriers were his primary objective. Kondō and Nagumo in truth withdrew their fleets not from timidity, but overconfidence. They would be back, and Sopac ready to meet them, in part due to Fletcher's well-measured responses during the Battle of the Eastern Solomons. Morison's final verdict, "American movements too were unaggressive, largely from want of intelligence about the enemy," is a fair assessment. So, however, is Nimitz's considered judgment that despite all Fletcher's perceived failures to take advantage of the situation, the Battle of the Eastern Solomons was "a victory that turned back the first major assault of the Japanese to regain Guadalcanal-Tulagi and gave us several weeks of valuable time to consolidate positions there."[42]

CHAPTER 30

The Right of the Line

NEW THREATS

The indecisive carrier clash on 24 August in the Eastern Solomons brought Fletcher no real relief, for heavy units of the Combined Fleet remained poised north of the Solomons. On the night of 25 August after bidding farewell to Kinkaid's TF-16 (*Enterprise*), he started north with TF-11 (*Saratoga*) to rejoin Noyes's TF-18 (*Wasp*) guarding the gap east of Malaita. Fletcher could hardly wait to restore TF-61 to three flattops with Murray's TF-17 (*Hornet*), due in the next several days. All three task forces should have no oil worries for the next week, but TF-11 and TF-18 dug deeply into their food and could only fully restock in port.[1]

The lack of pursuit certainly perplexed Ghormley. The only perceived enemy advance on 25 August occurred well beyond Sopac's left flank. Search planes discovered nine ships passing five hundred miles west of Guadalcanal toward the airfield at Milne Bay (Rabi) on the east tip of New Guinea. Its fall would imperil MacArthur's Sowespac, already rocked by the fierce assault through the mountains toward Port Moresby. Ghormley also apprehended danger developing all the way across on his right flank, with as many as three undamaged carriers cutting his line of communication from Hawaii. On the evening of 25 August he cautioned that these carriers "may approach Solomons–New Hebrides area from a longitude to the eastward of Ndeni" and told Murray to "be prepared for such possibility."[2]

If Ghormley's worry could be dismissed as a bout of nerves, Cominch landed a bomb shell. He professed his "growing conviction that force enemy is now massing for counterattack may repeat may be directed against [Fiji] or [Samoa], then [Guadalcanal-Tulagi]." The Japanese might crush the right flank before taking Guadalcanal head on. Ghormley wasted no time informing his commanders the enemy forces not sighted on 25 August "may attack" Fiji or Samoa. Neither island group possessed adequate air defense or even search capability. For his own part, Nimitz deemed raids on Fiji or Samoa "improbable." Fletcher's own carriers menaced the enemy's right flank, while logistical problems like those that convulsed Sopac would cripple an enemy advance so far southeast. "No enemy tankers have been sighted in area of operations or to eastward." Cincpac did endorse Ghormley's fervent request for powerful air reinforcements in light of the "critical" situation. "Lets not let this offensive die on the vine." Washington must kick in the necessary strength if phase one of Watchtower was to succeed. Nimitz did not initiate the offensive into the Solomons but would do all in his power to ensure its triumph. On 27 August he told Ghormley, Fletcher, McCain, Turner, Noyes, and Vandegrift they were all "doing grand jobs" and to "keep hitting hard at every opportunity."[3]

HOLDING PATTERN

On 26 August Fletcher contacted Noyes one hundred miles southeast of San Cristóbal. The day was generally quiet with regard to sightings, confirming the general Japanese withdrawal. Nimitz resolved to repair the *Enterprise* at Pearl rather than distant Bremerton. He canceled, "for the time being," orders for Noyes's TF-18 to proceed to Pearl and authorized Fletcher to draw upon the *Enterprise* planes as needed. Cincpac's message crossed one from Ghormley advising that one of Fletcher's three carrier groups must go to Tongatabu, "As soon as situation warrants for provisioning and short upkeep period." That would also buttress his tender eastern flank. That evening Efate transmitted a dispatch flown in by Kinkaid advising that the *Enterprise*, *Portland*, and three destroyers had "sufficient fuel and provisions to reach Pearl if not delayed." The next morning Ghormley told Kinkaid to make for Tongatabu, passing south of Fiji, but cautioned him to be alert for hostile forces. On 27 August the *Enterprise* flew fourteen SBDs and three TBFs to Efate and retained eight F4Fs and eight SBDs for defense. TF-16 reached Tongatabu on 30 August. The planes the *Enterprise* left behind proved vital for the defense of Cactus.[4]

Ghormley told Murray on 26 August to approach the waters halfway between San Cristóbal and Espíritu Santo and await orders to join TF-61. Once there TF-17 was, during nighttime hours, to keep east of the direct line between Guadalcanal and Espíritu Santo "on account scheduled ship movements on that line." Turner was preparing to send the *William Ward Burrows* and six smaller ships to deliver more badly needed supplies. They were to reach Cactus at dawn on 29 August, take about two days to unload, and return by the same route. Ghormley expected Fletcher to cover the transit of that vital convoy.[5]

After sunrise on 27 August Fletcher closed San Cristóbal to within 235 miles southeast of Lunga. He resumed the pattern of cruising southward during daylight and north at night. As before, he did not care to go closer to Lunga than 225 miles. That was the extreme limit (eight hundred miles) of bomber strikes from Rabaul. Long-range flying boats already patrolled fifty miles east of that line. Subs were always a big concern, particularly as the mission so restricted the TF-61 operating area. Duke Ramsey recalled it was "Fletcher's policy to change our general location from day to day within the area assigned as one means of affording protection against the ever present submarine threat." TF-61 relied on strong antisubmarine air patrols and zigzagged at thirteen knots during daylight, following the best advice of the destroyer squadron commanders that slower speed maximized the performance of their sound gear to detect subs. That tactic would soon be sorely tested.[6]

It was obvious by early 27 August that Comsopac never received the messages Fletcher gave Kinkaid to deliver to Efate. Therefore the *Saratoga* flew copies to the *Mackinac* at Ndeni, 125 miles east. TF-61 would operate east and south of San Cristóbal until TF-17 joined. Ghormley issued orders to Murray to meet TF-61 on the morning of 28 August 140 miles southeast of San Cristóbal and 220 miles northwest of Espíritu Santo. The light cruiser

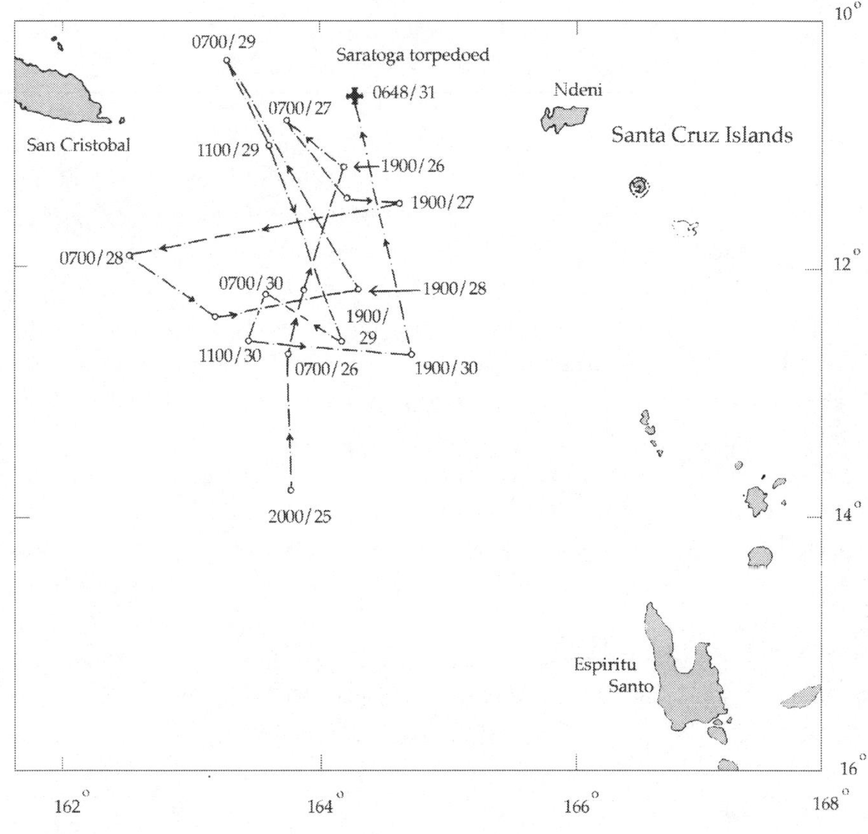

TF-61 track chart, 26–31 August 1942

Phoenix was to join as well, in exchange for the *San Juan*, which was to accompany Kinkaid to Pearl. Ghormley did not know exactly where Murray was and whether TF-17 could even make that rendezvous on time.[7]

That morning Fletcher's aircraft sighted one I-boat fifty miles east, while another submarine turned up 125 miles northwest of the carriers. Later when nearly three hundred miles southeast of Lunga, *Wasp* combat air patrol fighters destroyed a flying boat that edged within twenty miles of TF-11 and briefly tracked the U.S. carriers. Fletcher transferred four *Saratoga* F4Fs to Noyes, giving the *Wasp* sixty-six flyable planes (thirty fighters, twenty-five dive bombers, and eleven torpedo planes), while the *Sara* operated eighty-five aircraft (thirty-six fighters, thirty-one dive bombers, seventeen torpedo planes, and one photo reconnaissance plane). By early afternoon McCain's PBYs located more warships withdrawing 450 miles north of Lunga and more than five hundred miles northwest of TF-61. By sundown after steaming 125 miles southeast, Fletcher turned southwest to make for the rendezvous with TF-17 and cover the passage of the next Guadalcanal supply mission. In another failure on Airsopac's part, only that evening did the *Mackinac* advise that a PBY had sighted four cruisers at 0935 only 250 miles northwest of Lunga and closing at twenty knots.[8]

Ghormley issued a revised "concept of operations." Given that "hostile strength and intentions" remained undetermined, Sopac "must employ to the utmost limits our land based aircraft strength, while improving the Cactus-Ringbolt position." He did not desire Fletcher's carriers operating beyond or even anywhere near the extreme limit of McCain's air support. Therefore TF-61 "should for the present" keep south of latitude 10° south, roughly level with Guadalcanal, "Unless a promising target is located within striking distance." Meanwhile, Fletcher was to cover "the movements of supplies and reinforcements into the Cactus area," and McCain "continue an extended and intensive search as operating limitations permit." Ghormley later explained he believed the enemy would "come again," very likely "from a position further eastward." The Japanese were "feeling out to the eastward" and might raid Samoa or Fiji, or strike Espíritu Santo, which they "doubtless knew was our base for supplies." Consequently the carriers must "remain as far to the eastward as possible, and still be in position to support Cactus in case of necessity." He worried the Japanese might try an "end run" and come in from behind. Thus Fletcher was doing exactly what Ghormley wished. If he was not to go north of latitude 10° south, he should not linger too far south either.[9]

Fletcher initiated his usual southeast run at dawn on 28 August from fifty miles off San Cristóbal and 210 miles southeast of Lunga. Neither TF-17 nor the *Phoenix* showed up, so he kept moving south. Intelligence continued to place enemy ships far north of Guadalcanal. Cincpac estimated the *Zuihō* and a battleship division ("including new *Yamato*") about to depart Kure but did not speculate what the elusive *Zuikaku*, *Shōkaku*, and *Ryūjō* might be up to. Pearl also warned of an invasion of Ocean Island, although that would not be confirmed for several days. The little *William Ward Burrows* convoy passed ten miles south of TF-61 bound for Guadalcanal. One of the *Saratoga*'s afternoon search sighted TF-17 120 miles to the east. In anticipation, Fletcher had prepared a message for that SBD to drop to Murray. It set a new rendezvous for sunrise, 29 August, east of San Cristóbal near latitude 10° south and 210 miles southeast of Lunga. Fletcher preferred to cover the arrival of the *Burrows* convoy from there to intercept any forces coming from the direction of Malaita. More good news was that nineteen F4F-4s with belly tanks and twelve SBD-3s would soon fly from Espíritu Santo to Cactus. After Admiral Scott shifted his flag to the *San Francisco*, Fletcher dispatched the *San Juan* to Tongatabu. After dark TF-61 turned northwest for the dawn meeting with TF-17.[10]

Ghormley's daily situation report mentioned no sightings on the twenty-eighth, but that night Vandegrift dealt the enemy a stinging setback. The Japanese were up to their old tricks. Having failed to secure the seas around Guadalcanal for slow transports, they resumed the tactic, dubbed the "Rat" Operation, of using destroyers to sneak lightly equipped troops into Guadalcanal. Nearly five thousand men were to come over five successive nights beginning 28–29 August. To augment Base Air Force's bombing assault on Lunga, the *Shōkaku* and *Zuikaku* temporarily transferred thirty of forty-one Zero fighters to Buka to serve as escorts. Without them Nagumo's carriers could not be expected to fight. Now eleven Cactus SBDs tore into four destroyers discovered that evening seventy miles north of Lunga, blew up one, and ran the others off. That so discouraged the leader of three other destroyers coming in separately, he turned back just short of Guadalcanal. So far the Cactus Air Force lived up to its promise, but the Japanese would return in greater strength.[11]

During the night Fletcher crowded latitude 10° south, ready to intervene if the convoy needed help at Guadalcanal, and then started southeast. In a gesture Crutchley's Commonwealth sailors appreciated, TF-61 half-masted colors in mourning for the Duke of Kent, the brother of King George VI recently killed in an air crash. Soon Admiral Murray's TF-17 hove into sight with the *Hornet*, Admiral Good's heavy cruisers *Northampton* and *Pensacola* and light cruiser *San Diego*, and Captain Hoover's five Desron Two destroyers. The *Hornet* operated its streamlined air group of seventy aircraft (thirty-two fighters, twenty-four dive bombers, thirteen torpedo planes, and one photo reconnaissance plane) with sixteen spares (five fighters, eight dive bombers, and three torpedo planes). Murray also brought twenty F4Fs for the carrier fighting squadrons, but the ex-*Enterprise* fighters had already provided enough replacements. Following his usual policy, Fletcher kept southeast toward Espíritu Santo. No significant ship sightings came in during the day. Although Cincpac intelligence could not locate the *Shōkaku*, *Zuikaku*, and *Ryūjō*, it linked their planes with the base at Buka and offered the old refrain of the *Hiyō*, *Junyō*, and *Zuihō* about to depart homeland waters "shortly." Fletcher flew more dispatches to Ndeni for transmission to inform Ghormley TF-17 had joined, but the food situation in TF-11 and TF-18 was "becoming acute." He proposed to provision and fuel them "successively." Another message told the errant *Phoenix* to meet TF-61 the next morning in the original rendezvous 135 miles southeast of San Cristóbal. After dark, following a 150-mile run southeast, Fletcher marked time before gathering the *Phoenix* in the morning.[12]

Only well after dark on 29 August did Leary relay a coast-watcher alert that five cruisers or large destroyers had departed Shortland at 1245. They were five destroyers in the second Rat installment. Turner ordered the *William Ward Burrows* to flee Cactus temporarily, but she ran aground off Tulagi and resisted all attempts to free her. That night the five destroyers landed one thousand men and artillery at Taivu Point east of Lunga. They were the first reinforcements to reach Guadalcanal since the Ichiki First Echelon eleven days before. Worried about SBDs circling overhead in the darkness, the destroyer leader disobeyed orders to attack the grounded transport off Tulagi. Nonetheless, the inability of both the Airsopac search and daily Cactus air patrols to detect those incoming destroyers boded ill for the future.[13]

After dawn on 30 August the *Phoenix* finally appeared 125 miles southeast of San Cristóbal. Working southeast during the day, Fletcher reorganized TF-61 as follows:

- TG-61.1 (Fletcher): *Saratoga;* battleship *North Carolina;* heavy cruisers *Minneapolis, New Orleans;* light cruiser *Atlanta;* seven destroyers
- TG-61.2 (Murray): *Hornet;* heavy cruisers *Northampton, Pensacola;* light cruisers *San Diego, Phoenix;* seven destroyers
- TG-61.3 (Noyes): *Wasp;* heavy cruisers *San Francisco, Salt Lake City,* HMAS *Australia;* light cruiser HMAS *Hobart;* seven destroyers

For surface combat, Fletcher detailed Scott's TG-61.6 (Surface Attack Group) of one battleship, seven heavy cruisers, four light cruisers, and nine destroyers to fight, while the three carriers and twelve destroyers operated separately as TG-61.5 (Air Attack Force) under Noyes.[14]

Others coveted Fletcher's powerful force. Alarmed at the battle raging at Milne Bay, especially when Japan reinforced the beachhead, MacArthur warned the Solomons might only be a diversion for another major assault on New Guinea. Lacking his own naval support, he wanted Comsopac assigned to the "added mission of covering Milne Bay area." Predictably Ghormley declared just having his carriers "in being on the flank of any hostile attack on Australia" constituted "a greater contribution to MacArthur's assistance than any sacrifice given at this time of carriers in the Milne Bay area." Instead TF-61 must be "centrally located" and "prepared to operate anywhere on the front Samoa-Milne Bay." Such flexible deployment was necessary "until the strength of the hostile main effort is determined and it has been committed to a definite line of action." For the present, Cactus and Milne Bay must bear "hostile infiltration tactics and the initial shock of a hostile main effort." Nimitz fully concurred. "Consider while enemy holds airfields on east coast New Guinea that operation our carriers Milne area would seriously endanger their availability for tasks for which they are more suitable and are urgently needed." Ghormley did not offer to return Crutchley's TF-44 to MacArthur, but King suggested to Nimitz he do so.[15]

Ironically the Australians on their own drove the Japanese out of Milne Bay, while Ghormley dealt with his own urgent matters. Soon he must retire his carrier task forces in succession to provision. "Other naval strength [is] vital to cover transport of supplies and personnel to Cactus." On 30 August he directed Fletcher to release one carrier task group to reach Nouméa on 2 September and started two fleet oilers north with fuel and interim food for the two carriers remaining on station. Fearing Japanese carriers that could swoop in at any time, he was reluctant to withdraw all three carriers at the same time and mandated Fletcher continue to shield the steady stream of supply ships going into Cactus. In Turner's pipeline were a destroyer and three little YPs (district patrol craft) on 31 August, cargo ship *Betelgeuse* and a destroyer on 1 September, and cargo ship *Fomalhaut* and three APDs on the third. The prognosis for Sopac's long-range fuel situation looked good. In September three brand-new fleet oilers were to join the *Cimarron*, *Sabine*, and *Guadalupe* and permit release of the hard-used *Platte* and *Kaskaskia* for refit.[16]

After dark Fletcher reversed course for the customary turnaround near latitude 10° south between San Cristóbal and Ndeni. Cactus reports were encouraging and discouraging. In a skillful ambush marine fighters claimed eighteen land Zeros, and in truth bagged nine carrier Zeros operating from Buka, a severe blow for Nagumo. That afternoon, though, a second strike sank the high-speed transport *Colhoun* but did not molest the stricken *William Ward Burrows*. Neither McCain nor Cactus could counter enemy ships shuttling up and down the Slot. Two SBDs on moonlight patrol missed what was believed at least two cruisers and two destroyers discharging troops and cargo at Taivu Point, while ten dive bombers only secured a near miss on a cruiser. Actually a destroyer and four patrol boats dropped off five hundred men and four artillery pieces without loss. The nightly Guadalcanal troops runs became all too easy. "At this distance," King declared, "it is difficult to understand how enemy operations such as [the 30 August landings noted above] and the destroyer bombardment [the night of 24–25 August] can approach [Lunga] and proceed relatively unmolested." He did not appreciate that swift warships leaving Shortland about noon could draw into strike range of Cactus only after dark, deliver their loads, and scoot out of air attack range by dawn.

Only by repeated carrier raids against Shortland, parking a carrier task force southwest of Guadalcanal, or the permanent stationing of a surface strike force at Lunga could effect the complete interdiction King desired. Whether any of that was feasible or even possible was another matter entirely.[17]

THE *SARA* SMACKED

Just before midnight on 30 August, Noyes left with TF-18 (*Wasp*) for Nouméa. Fletcher's other two carriers were to patrol east of San Cristóbal the next two days, then meet the two oilers north of Espíritu Santo. The balance of the night as TF-61 drew near latitude 10° south was quiet except for a curious incident. At 0210 the *Saratoga*'s radar picked up a surface contact nine miles west. Fletcher detailed the *Farragut* to investigate the contact, which meanwhile closed to eleven thousand yards. The *Farragut* soon reported four ships proceeding due north. Fletcher told her to challenge and executed an emergency turn to starboard. Receiving no reply, the *Farragut* closed, only to recognize and report a carrier. "Are you sure you're not following this force?" Fletcher retorted. The *Farragut* sheepishly responded. "It is possible we are." The destroyer had mixed up the bearings provided by TBS. Fletcher resumed base course of 340 degrees. At first light, TF-61 drew within twenty-five miles of latitude 10° south and was about seventy-five miles east of San Cristóbal. Fletcher turned southeast and zigzagged at the customary thirteen knots. Seven destroyers screened TF-11. Operating several miles off the port quarter, the *Hornet* provided routine combat air patrol, search, and antisubmarine patrols.[18]

At 0641 while zigzagging, TF-11 turned to 180 degrees, its destroyers scrambling to attain proper position. Six minutes later the TBS blared: "Torpedo headed for carrier on course 050 True!" The *Macdonough*, patrolling thirty-five hundred yards off the *Sara*'s starboard bow, registered a sonar contact four hundred yards dead ahead. A few seconds later, a periscope popped up only ten yards off her bow, followed by a scraping sound on her hull. The destroyer rolled two depth charges, but unfortunately failed to arm them. At the same time a torpedo broached the surface close aboard her port quarter. Cdr. Yokota Minoru of the *I-26* fired a spread of six torpedoes from a 120-degree angle off the huge carrier's bow. The *Macdonough* indeed brushed his hull. Ramsey ordered right full rudder and full speed to swing the *Saratoga* to starboard and comb torpedo wakes. He nearly succeeded. Overestimating target speed, Yokota aimed most of his fish well ahead. Even so, at 0648 a deep running torpedo sliced inside the *Sara*'s turn and grazed the new starboard blister just aft of the island. Murray in the distant *Hornet* saw a geyser of water rise higher than the *Saratoga*'s mast and instantly turned TF-17 away. The effect of that blast at close hand was quite dramatic. The *Sara* "went into a fit and fairly lifted itself out of the water and then shook itself good," like a "house in a severe earthquake." High up on the flag bridge Fletcher "banged his head against something," that "cut his forehead" and caused blood to run "all over his face." Bending over the plot, he found dripping blood a nuisance and summoned a pharmacist's mate to slap on a bandage so he could get on with business. The medical department duly entered Fletcher's name on the casualty list that miraculously numbered only a dozen, with no fatalities. Months later to his intense surprise and embarrassment, he received the Purple Heart for what he deemed a trifling wound. Yet the circumstances completely conformed to the criteria set for the decoration. Fletcher was the top U.S. naval officer awarded the Purple Heart in World War II. He never reported the injury to his superiors, so the wound had nothing to do with his subsequent relief.[19]

Listing to starboard, the *Saratoga* reached sixteen knots, but at 0653 her engines stopped. "Within a few minutes the giant ship was dead in the water under a leaden, but clearing sky." Fletcher ordered the destroyers to circle the carrier and released the *North Carolina* to take refuge in TF-17. At 0705 he broke radio silence to inform Ghormley, McCain, and Noyes that the *Saratoga* had been torpedoed one hundred miles east of San Cristóbal and 220 miles southeast of Lunga. TF-61 was at the edge of strike range of bombers based at Rabaul. Fletcher alerted Wright to prepare the *Minneapolis* and *New Orleans* to handle the tow. Captain Brewer (Comdesron One) cautioned the sub "can get through this circle" and requested more air cover. The *Minneapolis* furnished SOCs for inner air patrol. Now it was up to Ramsey's experts to mitigate the effects of the *Sara*'s impairment and restore mobility. They found themselves in a fix worse than the *Saratoga* faced on 11 January. At that time despite a torpedo hit on the port side amidships that flooded three fire rooms, the *Sara* maintained sixteen knots. Now in unwitting symmetry, the *I-26*'s torpedo struck almost exactly opposite on the starboard side. Though only one fire room out of sixteen flooded, the whole propulsion system failed. Instead of conventional steam-driven turbines, the *Saratoga* utilized an innovative turboelectric drive. Shock damage, though, tripped the circuit breakers and knocked out the whole system. On his way to report to Fletcher and Ramsey, Cdr. Vincent W. Grady, the engineer officer, remarked to Clark Lee: "Doesn't look so good." Although there was trouble with the electrical boards in main control, he "hoped to get one shaft going soon."[20]

The *Saratoga*'s list increased to 6 degrees. Scuttlebutt later recounted that when the "cans [were] running all around dropping depth charges, and the ship was listing more," Fletcher supposedly yelled down to Ramsey just below on the navigating bridge: "Duke, when are you going to counter flood? I think you ought to counter flood." Ramsey is said to have replied, "Okay, Admiral, just wait a while." When Fletcher asked again, Ramsey "leaned back and looked up and said: 'Goddammit, Admiral, I'm the captain of this ship, and I'm not going to counter flood until I think it's right.'" Fletcher then replied, "Yeah, I guess you are." It was said Fletcher relented because "Ramsey was such a quiet man that if he spoke up like that" Fletcher "really knew that he'd pushed him to the end right there." If this incident indeed occurred as recounted much later, Fletcher in the heat of the moment must have had in mind the excessive list the *Yorktown* rapidly assumed at Midway. On 11 January the *Saratoga* counter flooded to right the ship, but Ramsey no longer had that option, ironically because of the elaborate starboard buoyancy blister installed that spring while repairing torpedo damage from the first hit. In this case the experts adroitly transferred oil from starboard to eight small voids on the port side and dumped two large oil tanks in the starboard blister. However, little margin remained for more underwater damage.[21]

On his next trip to the bridge Grady called out to Lee: "Maybe we can get her going after all!" He soon had the list under control and the number four propeller shaft turning over. The *Sara* swung gingerly to port and moved at five knots. The destroyers reformed the screen. In the past half hour they twice depth-charged the sub, but without success. Fletcher detailed the *Monssen* to hold it down until dark, while Murray provided the *Bagley* to take her place in the *Sara*'s screen. Fletcher's goal after clearing the immediate area was to see the *Saratoga* Air Group, her prime battle asset, safely ashore. He and others were acutely conscious they were still within range of Rabaul's bombers. At 0900 the *North Carolina*, now with TF-17, reported many bogeys bearing 120 degrees, distance twenty-three miles, and thought to be planes hunting the crippled carrier. Much later Cato Glover explained, "It was somewhat of a miracle that we were spared, due to the fact that our destroyers sank the sub and the Jap planes never located us." In fact the *I-26* survived, and no planes were coming, but the impression of imminent danger existed all the same.[22]

The *Saratoga* maneuvered slowly into the wind to launch aircraft, but her turboelectric drive shorted out again. Fletcher told the *Minneapolis* to take her in tow. Destroyers resumed circling, and the *Bagley* fired depth charges at a contact that failed to develop into a sub. By 1104 when the cruiser sent across the first line, Grady's men succeeded in bringing the *Sara* back to even keel. The *Minneapolis* started ahead slowly at 1136, dragging her mammoth tow southeast into the wind. The *Sara* greatly assisted by gradually working up to seven knots. That, along with the fifteen-knot wind, provided the "fortuitous circumstances" that permitted flight operations. Cincpac justly praised the "unique performance" of a carrier launching planes while being towed. At 1230 twenty SBDs and nine TBFs started taking off for Espíritu Santo 275 miles southeast. That was too far for F4F Wildcats with internal fuel only, but the wind was too light for a fighter loaded with a belly tank to take off. Schindler accompanied the flight, carrying a dispatch to Ghormley with the bare details of the attack and Fletcher's intention to "make best speed" southeast. Schindler was also to inquire where Ghormley wanted the other *Saratoga* planes sent. At 1547 the *Saratoga* gratefully cast off the tow and attained twelve knots on her own. Fletcher proffered a heartfelt "well done" to both the *Saratoga* and *Minneapolis*. A half hour later he returned the *Bagley* to TF-17. If the *Sara*'s unpredictable propulsion system behaved, TF-11 would soon get clear of possible pursuit.[23]

GETTING HELP

With the shocking news of the torpedoing of the *Saratoga*, Ghormley recast his plans. At 0830 he directed Fletcher to "report condition *Saratoga* as soon as possible" and promised to have the ocean tug *Navajo* and a destroyer meet TF-11 off Espíritu Santo in two days. When the *Saratoga* was hit, Noyes was two hundred miles southeast. He turned toward Fletcher and after receiving Ghormley's orders, shaped course northeast to intercept TF-11 by dawn. He also released Crutchley with the *Australia*, *Hobart*, and *Selfridge* to proceed to Brisbane and rejoin MacArthur. Ghormley impatiently awaited additional word from Fletcher. In its absence he redirected the two oilers to a new rendezvous northeast of Espíritu Santo with Murray's TF-17 on 2 September. During the day Murray maneuvered at fifteen knots to keep within visual distance of the *Saratoga* and released the *Phoenix*, *Patterson*, and *Bagley* to catch up to Crutchley. Fletcher detached Murray at sunset to proceed independently to the revised fueling rendezvous. At 2050 Ghormley radioed McCain to ask whether any of his planes had seen the *Saratoga* since 0700 and if he "heard anything from Fletcher." Airsopac PBYs indeed covered TF-11 most of the day, and McCain's dozing communicators finally acknowledged that *Saratoga* planes had landed at Espíritu Santo six hours before. McCain suggested Fletcher fly to Efate all remaining planes not required to protect TF-11, "particularly as many fighters as can be spared," while a destroyer brought spare parts and maintenance personnel. A well-trained air group might make all the difference in holding Guadalcanal. In another message McCain very astutely forecast, "Cactus can be a sinkhole for enemy air power and can be consolidated expanded and exploited to enemy's mortal hurt."[24]

Early on 1 September Noyes left for Nouméa unsure he had fuel to get all his destroyers there. He did, just barely. Murray closed San Cristóbal while watching for trouble at Cactus. The *Saratoga* made fourteen knots, but the partially disabled turboelectric drive required "thorough examination and test prior departure Sopac area." Fletcher told Ghormley he did not, "at present," need the *Navajo* but wanted her to stand by just in case. Twenty *Saratoga* SBDs and twelve TBFs had deployed to Espíritu Santo, leaving thirty-six fighters on board. "Will await your instructions on where and how many to fly off." TF-11 had provisions at reduced rations to last to 10 September. Fletcher judged two cruisers and four destroyers enough to screen the *Saratoga*. Ghormley sent the *Guadalupe* to fuel TF-11 and the *Cimarron* to TF-17.[25]

Fletcher's caution regarding the *Sara*'s propulsion proved justified when she had to slow to ten knots that morning. Nothing untoward occurred as TF-11 limped east of Espíritu Santo. Ghormley left to Fletcher's discretion the number of planes needed for the voyage to Pearl and told him to fly the rest to Efate the next day. Fletcher was to draw the minimum necessary provisions at Tongatabu and utilize the repair ship *Vestal* and tug *Seminole* to help effect temporary repairs. On the morning of 2 September Fletcher sent three TBFs to Espíritu Santo with his plans. The *Saratoga* still hobbled along at ten knots, but he could not say whether she could even make Tongatabu on her own. Therefore he retained the *Navajo* and requested the *Seminole* help get the huge carrier safely up the channel into Tongatabu harbor. He expected to reach there on 6 September. On 4 September the *Saratoga* engineers completed temporary repairs. "Only then," one historian stressed, "could the engineering plant report anything resembling normal capability, despite the fact that the total direct damage caused by the torpedo amounted to the flooding of one boiler room and the partial flooding of another." TF-11 arrived at Tongatabu on 6 September without further incident. Once the *Saratoga* was patched and her escort refueled and provisioned, she could start north for Pearl.[26]

Twenty-eight Saratoga fighters flew to Efate to join the twenty-two SBDs and thirteen TBFs there. All fought at Guadalcanal. Fletcher kept eight F4Fs, eight SBDs, and four TBFs. Nimitz notified King, "All aircraft that can be spared from *Enterprise Saratoga* being transferred Comsopac for use present campaign." The deployment of carrier aircraft and pilots to fight from shore bases was "necessary because of lack of suitable Army type planes for Guadalcanal fighting," but "most uneconomical" given "our present shortage trained carrier air groups." The army must live up to its commitment to the Watchtower offensive by supplying the necessary air reinforcements that Sopac required to fight and win in the Solomons. "Lets give Cactus the wherewithall [*sic*] to live up to its name. Something for the Japs to remember forever."[27]

ACCOUNTING FOR THE DISASTER

The torpedoing of the *Saratoga* on 31 August, which sidelined that carrier for three months, caused Fletcher criticism, both for being in sub-imperiled waters and for not taking proper precautions. Commander Laing, the British naval liaison officer riding the *North Carolina*, commented it was "rather remarkable that the Japanese had not been able to torpedo a ship sooner than they did, observing the length of time U.S. forces had been operating in the area and the slow speeds usually employed." The Royal Navy already had their fill of enemy submarine successes, having lost three carriers and a battleship to U-boats in the open sea. Nimitz's report of 31 October 1942 emphasized that during much of August, Fletcher crisscrossed the same waters east and south of the Solomons. In particular, from 26 to 31 August TF-61 had, while covering the route from Espíritu Santo to Cactus, loitered within a rectangle only 150 miles long by sixty miles wide, despite evidence subs concentrated there. The "mission did not require that the Task Force be restricted to this area." Ghormley took issue, giving credence, unlike Nimitz, to the threat from northeast of Espíritu Santo. As noted, he endeavored to deploy his carriers "as far to the eastward as possible," while still protecting the crucial Espíritu Santo–Cactus line. In January 1943 Noyes, too, asserted, "The general directives for the support of the Cactus area required Task Force 61 to operate in that general area." Fletcher emphasized the danger subs and land-based air posed to largely static patrolling. "If the carrier remains there, it is only a question of time until she is hit by a torpedo or bomb." Instead, carriers should be "risked in areas where enemy forces are likely to be encountered only when our forces are ready to attack." Then they should "strike hard by continuous air attacks until objective is achieved" and depart. Circumstances, though, never gave Fletcher that option.[28]

Ghormley, Fletcher, and Noyes became discredited from blunders attributed to them in the Solomons campaign. One who remained untainted was Rear Adm. Dewitt Ramsey. When interviewed in February 1943 in connection with the loss of the *Wasp*, Ramsey testified that in "covering the Guadalcanal–Espiritu Santo line," it was "necessary for the *Saratoga* to be projected in the areas in which she was cruising." Furthermore, "It apparently was the belief of the responsible officers with whom the general subject was discussed that the continuance of our operations in a relatively small area, well knowing that we were sighted almost daily by the enemy, would result in a large concentration of Japanese submarines in that area and the eventual torpedoing of some of our units in spite of all precautions that we could take." To the question how it was possible to cover the Espíritu Santo–Guadalcanal line "without projecting carriers into an area in which submarines were known to be active," Ramsey affirmed, "It was necessary risk which had to be taken at that time." He spoke as a close confidant of Fletcher and certainly reflected his old boss's thinking.[29]

Fletcher's affinity for daylight steaming at thirteen knots was also controversial. Boscoe Wright later attributed it to his "concern for conserving his fuel supply," which "led him to take what I believe to be unwarranted risks." Nimitz's 31 October 1942 report condemned speeds that "were too slow for waters known to contain submarines." By then it seemed obvious, "If the fuel situation made it necessary to run at such speeds as 13 knots, then the Task Force should have been removed to a locality of fewer submarine contacts."

However, Fletcher did not keep to thirteen knots simply due to fuel worries or natural torpidity. Instead he followed the destroyer antisubmarine doctrine current at the time. When asked in January 1943 whether a cruising speed of sixteen knots was "adequate under the circumstances," George Murray noted the effectiveness of the destroyer underwater detection gear deteriorated significantly at fifteen knots and above. "While it is generally held by large numbers of destroyer captains that they can provide an effective sound screen and detect the presence of submarines in an area when steaming at fifteen knots or below, the experience of carrier task forces definitely indicates that high speeds with less effective sound gear affords better protection for the heavy ships." Capt. Forrest Sherman likewise stated in January 1943, "The effectiveness of listening gear as now installed in our destroyers drops off rapidly at speeds above 15–16 knots." Thus Fletcher steamed at thirteen knots to enhance sonar reception. Of course, it became manifest on 31 August and in the succeeding fortnight that U.S. destroyer sound gear and training were not up to the task. Only on 7 October, after subs picked off the *Saratoga*, *Wasp*, and *North Carolina*, did Cincpac direct, "In probable submarine waters speeds of 15 knots or better will be maintained and particular care will be given to A/S Screening disposition."[30]

Critics also disputed Fletcher's reaction to the strange encounter that occurred four hours before the *Saratoga* was torpedoed thirty miles north. Ghormley chided him for not taking full precautions in the event the radar contact was a sub. Cincpac concurred. The Cominch Secret Battle Experiences Bulletin No. 2 observed that a "well organized and conducted search" at the time of first contact "might have been worth while." Morison referred to the "acrimonious debate" this incident is said to have engendered, but if so, the acrimony was all on the side of the critics. Phantom radar contacts at night were not particularly unusual. Fletcher did send the *Farragut* to check out the contact, even if her response turned into a fiasco. He did not know at the time that ships other than the *Saratoga* also had that contact on radar.[31]

Central to the question of how the *Saratoga* came to be torpedoed is the number of available destroyers given King's vehement insistence each carrier must always operate singly within her own task force. On 31 August TF-11 and TF-17 each had seven destroyers in their separate screens. Had Fletcher combined the two carriers in the same disposition, as he repeatedly advocated, there would have been one screen of fourteen destroyers. Murray certainly perceived the lack and asked Ghormley on 2 September for more destroyers "in view present increased submarine threat this area." He recommended at least two destroyers per heavy ship. In January 1943 Murray proposed a dozen destroyers ideal for a carrier task force. Nimitz certainly recognized the paucity of destroyers was key to the sub troubles in the South Pacific. The "greatest improvement" in antisubmarine protection would occur "when there are sufficient destroyers to provide a solid sound front in a complete circular screen."[32]

Nimitz likewise decreed on 31 October, "Carrier task forces are not to remain in submarine waters for long periods, should shift operating areas frequently and radically, must maintain higher speed, and must in other ways improve their tactics against submarine attack." Conceding that carriers were vital for holding Guadalcanal, he recognized they must "venture into submarine waters only when necessary, and while there . . . operate in a suitable manner to reduce the submarine hazard." Such laudable goals were not feasible given the conditions Fletcher actually faced in August 1942. Ramsey recalled in February 1943, "No provision had been made for accommodating a large aircraft carrier in any port adjacent to the waters of the Coral Sea." Thus, "It was necessary, in the interest of meeting the requirements of our mission, to remain underway in the areas previously stated and to fuel underway with comparative frequency." In January 1943 Forrest Sherman explained, "The operations off the Solomons, during the time that I was there, involved keeping carriers at sea for such long periods that fuel consumption and endurance between refuelings were always matters of concern." The carriers should move in "when required, and when their work is done retire from those positions, at the highest speed permitted by the endurance of their escorting ships." Fletcher concurred.[33]

PACKED OFF TO PEARL

The crippling of Fletcher's flagship caused an awkward command situation, in that he wore two hats, CTF-61 in overall command and CTF-11 in charge of the *Saratoga* group. Ordinarily once a flagship sustained damage, the admiral simply shifted to another ship in his force. In this case, with mandated single carrier task forces, Fletcher would need to displace Noyes or Murray, but Nimitz and Ghormley offered no guidance. On 2 September Ghormley told Fletcher to designate one heavy cruiser and three destroyers to escort the *Saratoga* to Pearl, along with the *Atlanta* and two destroyers. While Fletcher estimated his "own readiness to depart for Pearl," the remaining ships were to draw provisions at Tongatabu and "await orders to join other task force." That implied Fletcher was to leave as well, but Ghormley was unsure where Nimitz stood in the matter. On 5 September he informed Fletcher that "in view of contemplated operations," Admiral Wright was to have the one TF-11 heavy cruiser to remain in Sopac. That eventuated from a conversation between Ghormley and Noyes on 3 September in Nouméa. Ghormley made it clear he wanted Noyes to serve as CTF-61 in Fletcher's place. In turn Noyes asked for the cruisers and destroyers of old TF-11 "to break up enemy night raids by cruisers and destroyers to Cactus." Ghormley agreed "in principle" and formed TF-64, but "wished to keep it under his own hand for the present." Fletcher had suggested Crutchley's TF-44 for a separate Sopac surface force, but Ghormley did not follow through.[34]

On 6 September Fletcher advised Nimitz and Ghormley of temporary repairs that should permit the *Saratoga* to depart for Pearl in three or four days. Wright's *Minneapolis* and four destroyers had enough fuel to reach Nouméa. The rest of TF-11 required more oil for the run to Pearl, but none was available at Tongatabu. The time had come for Ghormley to know whether he could dispense with Fletcher, but he was reluctant to go ahead and relieve him. He radioed Nimitz (information to Fletcher): "I assume you want Fletcher return Pearl with *Saratoga*. I am preparing make Noyes Comtaskfor Sixty One." Nimitz replied, "Affirmative." The next day Ghormley created TF-64 under Wright with the *Minneapolis*, light cruisers *Boise* and *Leander*, and four destroyers and assigned it "temporarily" to Turner. Sopac Op-Plan 3-42, issued on 9 September, formally named Noyes CTF-61.[35]

Fletcher in the meantime readied truncated TF-11 for the voyage north. With the help of the *Vestal*'s experts, the *Saratoga*'s engineers heeled the ship sharply to port and patched the torpedo hole. The *Sara* was not the only behemoth at Tongatabu hankering for a distant dry dock. On 3 September TG-2.9 under Rear Adm. Willis Augustus "Ching" Lee (Commander, Battleship Division Six) turned up with the new fast battleship *South Dakota*, light cruiser *Juneau*, and three destroyers. Lee was to clear the harbor at dawn, 6 September, before TF-11 arrived, and join Noyes's TF-18 two days later northeast of New Caledonia. On the way out the battleship scraped an uncharted rock pinnacle and tore a hole in her bottom. Lee predicted (he called it a "tobacco juice estimate") that repairs would require two weeks in dock. Ghormley substituted the *South Dakota* for the *Atlanta* in TF-11. Lee was to await the battleship *Washington* expected at Tongatabu in a few weeks. Wright left for Espíritu Santo on 10 September, the day the new fleet oiler *Kankakee* stood into Tongatabu. Fletcher advised he would sail on 12 September to reach Pearl on the twenty-first. Ghormley offered TF-11 a gracious farewell. "We will all miss you. You are leaving us much of your hard hitting striking force and your example as fearless fighters and a skilled persevering team as demonstrated by *Saratoga* engineers. Hurry back we will need you. Well done." Hurrying back to the South Pacific in the restored *Saratoga* was precisely Fletcher's own intention, but others had a different idea.[36]

IN FLETCHER'S ABSENCE

While Fletcher slogged north with his two maimed giants, *Saratoga* and *South Dakota*, momentous events rocked Sopac, as terrible misfortune befell his classmate and successor Leigh Noyes.[37]

While the *Wasp* replenished at Nouméa, Murray's TF-17 patrolled southeast of Guadalcanal. On 3 September Ghormley further restricted the carriers to south of latitude 12° south (120 miles farther south than the 27 August order) and east of the Ndeni–Espíritu Santo line unless, as always, "promising targets" appeared. That ended any chance of swift carrier intervention at Cactus. Ignoring that direct order, Murray crossed the Ndeni–Espíritu Santo line and cruised the southern Solomons as far west as Rennell island, south of Guadalcanal. After he started back east, the *I-11* very nearly torpedoed the *Hornet* on 7 September. Only the great good luck of a plane dropping a depth charge, which touched off warheads of two incoming fish, prevented catastrophe. The next afternoon Murray advised Ghormley of the circumstances and his belief the enemy detected him. He requested permission to operate within three hundred miles of Lunga as necessary. "Astounded" Murray deliberately contravened his orders, Ghormley "invited" his attention to the revised directive and icily counseled him to hasten "at good speed" east of longitude 166° east. Murray nonetheless ventured northeast toward the Santa Cruz Islands through waters previously teeming with subs and only at sundown on 8 September again crossed the boundary. Others beside Ghormley noticed Murray's impulsive actions.[38]

On 8 September Noyes nosed TF-18 (*Wasp*) out of Nouméa in temporary company with Turner's flagship *McCawley*. Planning to transport the Seventh Marines to Lunga, Turner requested two additional land-based fighter squadrons and two SBD squadrons to beef up the Cactus Air Force. If McCain could not furnish them, "Presumably the carriers will help." He also desired Noyes to run a constant daylight antisubmarine air patrol between San Cristóbal,

Malaita, and Guadalcanal and be prepared to strike any threatening forces "within a few hours." Noyes responded he could not release any carrier planes or keep the flattops in one restricted area for antisubmarine patrols. Up to his old tricks in making unfeasible demands, Turner's acrid reply left no doubt his opinion of Noyes differed little from his pungent feelings toward Fletcher. Perplexed, Noyes summarized the exchange so Ghormley would not "misunderstand" his position. "I am sure you realize I want to be of every assistance possible in this operation but the point about being tied down to operating within a fixed distance of Guadalcanal is one I feel sure you agree with me about. I had not thought that anyone even considered it wise to land any aircraft from these remaining carriers."[39]

Ghormley reiterated TF-61 must remain south of latitude 12° south and east of the Ndeni–Espíritu Santo line except for extraordinary circumstances. He wanted the carriers close to the line of communication between the main island groups. Noyes proposed to swing TF-61 north and east of the Santa Cruz Islands, seeking "tactical advantage" by flanking the next offensive from the east. "This would involve withdrawing the close support that we had previously given to Cactus [meaning the ships proceeding from Espíritu Santo to Guadalcanal], but Admiral Ghormley felt that with our carriers reduced to two this must be accepted." That plan also avoided the nest of subs between San Cristóbal and Espíritu Santo. On 11 September Noyes met Murray east of Espíritu Santo and reformed TF-61 with the *Wasp* and *Hornet* (154 planes). In the meantime General Kawaguchi consolidated his forces at Taivu Point and marched west to seize Lunga. Kondō left Truk on 9 September with the entire Support Force, including Nagumo's *Kidō Butai*. The arrival of the *Zuihō* restored Nagumo to three carriers, but with only 129 planes. Continuing to underestimate U.S. strength, Yamamoto expected Kawaguchi to eliminate the air base at Guadalcanal while Kondō destroyed U.S. carriers attempting to relieve the beleaguered garrison.[40]

Ghormley released twenty-four VF-5 fighters from Efate to Cactus. Murray delivered eighteen spare Wildcats to Espíritu Santo, but they lacked belly tanks and could not reach Lunga on their own. McCain asked Noyes to deliver the eighteen F4Fs to Guadalcanal. He responded with alacrity, retrieved them, and crossed Comsopac's northwest limit to draw within ferry range of Cactus by dawn on the thirteenth. Presented with a fait accompli, Ghormley approved. Kawaguchi's night assault ran into ferocious opposition on "Bloody Ridge." At dawn Noyes's carriers dispatched the fighters from 290 miles southeast of Guadalcanal. Wary of enemy carriers and a powerful surface force believed patrolling north of the Solomons, Noyes withdrew southeast toward Santa Cruz to resume the original flanking position. With Ghormley's blessing, McCain committed as many stranded carrier planes as Cactus could handle. That evening a dozen SBDs and six TBFs from the beached *Saratoga* group also flew to Guadalcanal. They and the forty-two Wildcats received in the last two days courtesy of the carriers helped turn the tide in the face of fierce air attacks. That night the marines won the Battle of the Ridge and thus round two in the fight for Guadalcanal.

On 14 September Turner's TF-65 convoy sailed from Espíritu Santo, covered by Wright's TF-64 (three cruisers and six destroyers). Noyes sallied west through the Santa Cruz Islands to guard Turner's advance from one hundred miles northeast. Late that morning a PBY warned of four battleships and seven carriers 325 miles northwest of TF-61 and closing. Noyes resolutely turned toward them and rang up twenty-three knots despite the *Wasp*'s suspect turbines. He realized the report was likely an exaggeration but possibly represented a superior force. The PBY corrected its report to three battleships, four cruisers, four destroyers, and one transport, while another Catalina located one carrier, three cruisers, and four destroyers two hundred miles north of the original contact. McCain's searchers found Kondō's Advance Force, with Nagumo's *Kidō Butai* ranged behind it. Noyes dispatched a tactical scouting group of fourteen *Wasp* SBDs to 275 miles, followed by thirty-nine *Hornet* strike planes. He expected an air counterattack at any time. So did McCain, who ordered all but the seaplane tenders *Curtiss*, *Mackinac*, and *McFarland* to flee Espíritu Santo. Two hours passed before Noyes heard from McCain that the enemy ships were seen withdrawing north. After his own search turned up no U.S. carriers, Yamamoto had ordered the whole Support Force to break off for fuel. In turn the *Wasp* SBDs missed Kondō by only fifty miles. The day was one of blunted expectations, one of the great "almosts" of the Guadalcanal campaign. A carrier strike against Kondō would have touched off a donnybrook on the fifteenth.

Believing the grave danger to TF-65 persisted, Noyes regained his covering position to the north. Himself moving warily west, Turner worried that shadowers could call in air strikes and powerful surface forces to intercept at night. However, unlike the previous day, the Airsopac searches on the fifteenth proved surprisingly quiet. The enemy in fact passed north out of range, but flying boats sighted both TF-61 and TF-65. Turner's detection triggered an air strike from Rabaul that never found him. The snooper contacting the carriers did not survive long enough to report back. Noyes stressed to Murray the vital need for all possible support for Turner. While the transports proceeded into Lunga the next day, Noyes intended to range ahead out beyond Rennell island, south of Guadalcanal. On the afternoon of 15 September when TF-61, cruising at sixteen knots, was 150 miles southeast of San Cristóbal (and one hundred miles south of where the *Saratoga* was torpedoed), Noyes completed routine flight operations and turned to resume the westerly base course. TF-61 had unwittingly penetrated the center of another sub deployment line, and the *I-19* unleashed the single most devastating salvo of the war. Two torpedoes struck the *Wasp*, igniting vast fires and huge explosions fed by the aviation gasoline tanks, munitions, and armed and fueled planes parked in the hangar. Flaming like a torch, the doomed carrier took an 11-degree list. "Shirt, hair, and ears burned in the flash," Noyes was lucky to survive a fiery blast that swept over the bridge. The *Wasp* was "pretty well shattered from number two elevator well down and forward at least to the splinter deck." Only thirty-five minutes after the attack, Sherman consulted with Noyes and ordered abandon ship. The *I-19* salvo not only finished the *Wasp*, but also plowed through Murray's TF-17 six miles northeast. Damage from one fish later caused the destroyer *O'Brien* to sink. Another torpedo ripped a huge hole in the *North Carolina*'s port bow and flooded the forward magazines. She quickly corrected a 5.5-degree list and held twenty-five knots. Murray cleared out to eastward, while Scott rescued the *Wasp*'s crew. She sank that evening with forty-six planes, while twenty-five aircraft reached the *Hornet*. Because the Japanese fleet had retired, the sinking of the *Wasp* did not compromise Turner's vital mission.[41]

While Turner's TF-65 reinforced Guadalcanal, Murray's TF-17 with the *Hornet*, the fleet's sole remaining intact carrier, stayed in the rear off Espíritu Santo. On 20 September Ghormley directed Murray to operate "in general" between latitudes 13° and 20° south and longitudes 165° to 177° east, while avoiding the direct routes between New Caledonia–Espíritu Santo and New Caledonia–Fiji. Recognizing such a vast operating region was essentially meaningless, Nimitz suggested Ghormley consider withdrawing his heavy ships to Nouméa "or other protected anchorages except when employed for specific tasks." That would "decrease hazard from subs, conserve fuel, save wear and tear and give air groups better chance to train." King opined, "It is obvious that protracted operations of our task forces on a strategically static basis in submarine infested waters is proving increasingly hazardous." That precisely reflected the departed Fletcher's fervent belief. With the enemy carrier force at least temporarily inactive, Ghormley released Murray to Nouméa for the long awaited opportunity to reprovision and rest.[42]

Rear Adm. Leigh Noyes.
Courtesy of National Archives (80-G-302350)

Leigh Noyes's tenure as CTF-61 lasted less than a week. He faced bitter recriminations for losing the *Wasp*. Ghormley charged TF-61 should not have even been there. "It was urgent and vitally necessary that this convoy get to Guadalcanal safely, but I did not expect that it would be necessary to augment the air coverage given by our land-based aircraft from [Espíritu Santo] and from Guadalcanal." Thus the carriers should not have gone "into the area which was infested by submarines in order to provide air cover to these transports unless such became an urgent necessity." Ghormley did admit his orders gave Noyes the "freedom of action if the situation demanded that close air coverage be given," and to "do it unhesitatingly." Yet Ghormley preferred the carriers to deploy forward only "if the enemy carriers came into the picture as a threat to our task forces." He also criticized Noyes for taking insufficient precautions against subs by repeatedly crossing his previous track in waters where they lurked. Noyes and Sherman vigorously defended their movements, responding that the *Wasp* succumbed where TF-61 had to be in order to protect Turner's convoy from hostile forces to the north. Noyes also pointed out the attack on the *Wasp* occurred "150 miles from nearest point of crossing an old track, and in an area which had not been entered or approached previously."[43]

The paucity of destroyers and King's stubborn insistence (ratified by Nimitz) that carriers cruise singly in separate screens at all times strongly contributed to the loss of the *Wasp* as well as the crippling of the *Saratoga*. The 1943 Cominch Secret Battle Experience Bulletin did acknowledge that Noyes had "too few destroyers," but rebuked him for not employing them "to best advantage." Sherman, however, declared that a screen on a four-thousand-yard circle was "in accordance with standard practice" and "based to a considerable extent on the maximum utilization of sound gear." The lack of destroyers was especially acute when changing course, when they had to rush to regain relative position ahead while their increased speed reduced the effectiveness of sound detection. Capt. Robert Tobin, Comdesron Twelve with TF-18, explained in February 1943, "The screen should be disposed completely around the carrier with the destroyers maintaining true positions at all times" to offer adequate protection no matter how the carrier maneuvered. "Ten to twelve destroyers would be required, depending upon sound conditions," to cover a four-thousand-yard radius. King's analysts allowed that the "determination of escort requirements as demonstrated by tactical experience, particularly for carrier operations, has an important bearing on other operations in prospect and on the distribution of destroyers." However, King never accepted his responsibility in the torpedoing of the carriers in 1942 in the South Pacific. Thin screens of four to seven destroyers per task group remained the norm throughout 1943 even in multi-carrier formations, but beginning in January 1944 each carrier task group savored the protection of fourteen to sixteen tin cans.[44]

Admiral Halsey trenchantly observed on 9 October that employing the carriers in the Solomons "for a protracted period as a covering force for an operation in a fixed geographical location" violated a "most important principle" of war. It was "of the utmost importance that all responsible commanders recognize the fact that defensive employment of carriers which ties them down to restricted areas or fixed geographical points invites disaster." Although necessary under the circumstances, Halsey judged, "We were extremely lucky not to have suffered heavier damage and loss in these operations." Others entertained a different notion of the importance of the carriers in the Guadalcanal campaign. The Marine Corps official aviation history commented, "The loss or temporary inactivation of the Navy's carriers had one salutary effect: Navy planes and pilots who otherwise would have been unemployed were pouring into Henderson Field." Quipped Lt. Gen. Ross E. Rowell, Commander, Marine Air Wings, Pacific, "What saved Guadalcanal was the loss of so many carriers." Therefore the planes deployed on the carriers were actually "unemployed." That, of course, denigrated the strategic covering mission of the carriers and the bitter fighting they endured. Rowell and his marine compatriots would not have found it so amusing if the U.S. carriers had gone down in such a way that their planes were also lost, and consequently the Combined Fleet spearheaded the recapture of Guadalcanal.[45]

CHAPTER 31

The Clean Sweep

"A REST WILL DO HIM GOOD"

On 21 September Fletcher's flagship *Saratoga* eased into her mooring at Pearl. Across the channel the *Enterprise* occupied a repair berth, while dry dock number 2 beckoned the wounded *Sara*. Fletcher explained to Nimitz the misfortunes that occurred on his watch as CTF-61: maiming of one carrier in a puzzling battle and a second torpedoed by a sub, plus the little he knew of the Savo debacle. The debriefing took place in Cincpac's new headquarters perched on Makalapa Hill north of the harbor. The bright, breezy office reflected Nimitz's cheerful personality, a welcome tonic that boosted Fletcher's spirits. So did word that while the *Saratoga* was being repaired at Pearl he would go home for two weeks, then spend two weeks of temporary duty in Washington with Cominch. In early September, King and Nimitz had discussed possible temporary jobs for Fletcher in Washington. Nimitz ordered Fletcher to be back at Pearl by early November to take TF-11 with the restored *Saratoga* down to the South Pacific. Fletcher told Nimitz, "He felt fine and was ready for further operations." Nimitz accepted him at his word. Fletcher must have spoken persuasively. A photo taken at that time shows he lost weight and appeared tired, if not haggard, due to the incredible strain he endured not only at Guadalcanal, but also the preceding eight months.[1]

Contrary to general belief, Fletcher's return to Pearl did not spell the end of his carrier command. He remained Commander, Cruisers, Pacific Fleet, and CTF-11. Other widespread changes in command did occur in his absence. The big amalgamation of the carriers and patrol wings finally came to pass on 1 September, when Fitch became Commander, Air Force, Pacific Fleet. He was only a fill-in for Halsey, who reported for duty in Washington on 29 August after extended medical leave. The San Francisco conference derailed that succession. King looked to jettison prickly Rear Adm. John Towers as chief of Buaer. His solution was to pack Towers off to Nimitz as Commander, Aircraft, Pacific Fleet (Comairpac) in the rank of vice admiral, while McCain relieved Towers at Buaer. McCain in turn was to hand off Aircraft, South Pacific Force, to Fitch, an equally tough fighter but a better administrator. Nimitz now desired Halsey, whom he found well rested and fit, to resume his post as senior Pacific Fleet task force commander. Halsey would spell Fitch as Comairpac until Towers could arrive in mid October, then take TF-16 with the repaired *Enterprise* to Sopac. That arrangement put Kinkaid out of a job, but Nimitz, who thought well of him, already had another billet in

Vice Adm. Frank Jack Fletcher, 17 September 1942. "He did appear to be in good shape except for a slightly strained expression about the eyes, which you have become so accustomed to seeing in the eyes of others returning from active operations" (Admiral McCain describing Fletcher to Admiral Nimitz, 30 September 1942).

Courtesy of Cdr. Samuel E. Latimer Jr.

mind. On 15 September Nimitz used the occasion of an award ceremony on the deck of the *Big E* to announce Halsey's return to the fleet. Spruance received his DSM for Midway and Kinkaid a DSM for leading the TF-11 cruisers in the Battle of the Coral Sea.[2]

Nimitz departed Pearl on 24 September to consult Ghormley and other key commanders and personally unravel just what befell Sopac. While laying over at Palmyra, he encountered McCain and Fletcher's old associate Col. Mel Maas winging north. When asked about Noyes, McCain replied he was "all right, just suffering a little from the blast." Nimitz then remarked of Fletcher: "We are going to give him a 'blow' (rest) on the mainland." McCain responded: "I was going to write to you about him, but I didn't. Two or three of these fights are enough for any one man. A rest will do him good." Maas opined Fletcher was very tired and needed time to recover. Nimitz asked McCain to sound out Fletcher as to how he felt and to report back to him.[3]

Unaware his fate was being discussed, Fletcher closed up shop on 27 September and released the Comcrupac staff and flag complement on leave.[4] That afternoon he and Spence Lewis joined McCain on the overnight flight to NAS Alameda. From there Fletcher and Lewis were fly commercial air to Washington, while McCain stopped off in San Diego before resuming his trip to the same destination. The long hop from Oahu to the West Coast gave "Slew" McCain ample opportunity to converse at length with his old classmate and friend. On 30 September as promised McCain wrote Nimitz from San Diego:

> I talked with Fletcher. He said he was very concerned and very apprehensive as to the location and character of service of his task group, both before the hit and until arrival at Pearl, also very tired. He added that he was in good shape and rested now and after a little leave would be ready to go again. He did appear to be in good shape except for a slightly strained expression about the eyes, which you have become so accustomed to seeing in the eyes of others returning from active operations. I told him that he should not ask to go on another detail until he felt at his best; that he owed that both to himself and to the job. He thought this over for awhile and said, "You are right, I will take as long a leave as I can get, and if I feel my best will ask to go again and I am sure I will." I feel he should be taken at his word.

From this Nimitz finally grasped that Fletcher merited the same sensitive consideration afforded Halsey in his long recovery, for the very good reason that Fletcher bore the same intense pressure much longer. Nimitz understood the vital need to rest senior commanders as well as junior officers and planned a "recuperation center for flag officers" on Oahu. His own efforts to relieve stress, such as comfortable quarters and congenial housemates, pistol shooting range and horseshoe pitch, paid dividends by increasing his own stamina.[5]

Nimitz returned to Pearl on 5 October after a long and exciting trip to the South Pacific. It included an inspiring overnight stay on Guadalcanal with Vandegrift—something for which Ghormley never found the time. He came back imbued with the belief Guadalcanal could be held if everyone showed sufficient fortitude. One shining example of that cardinal virtue was Bill Halsey, whose presence in Sopac was vital. Nimitz decided to send him south ahead of TF-16. He wrote Ghormley on 8 October that Halsey and Spruance would reach Nouméa around 16 October, the same day TF-16 (*Enterprise*) left Pearl under Kinkaid's temporary command. Nimitz assured Ghormley, "Halsey will report to you for duty and be subject to your operational control for so long as he is in your area." He could "confer face to face with Halsey on the many problems that will confront the two of you in the weeks ahead," an opportunity never accorded Fletcher. Once TF-16 arrived, Halsey would shift to the *Enterprise* as "senior Pacific Fleet task force commander afloat." Kinkaid, "who is now an experienced carrier task force commander," would, when relieved as CTF-16, take over TF-17 in the *Hornet* in Murray's place. The *Enterprise* and *Hornet* were slated for new captains, but Arthur Davis and Charles Mason (both selected for rear admiral) would not be detached until "the newcomers are sufficiently familiar with the situation." The *Saratoga* would also have another skipper, but Duke Ramsey (likewise awaiting two stars) would remain "until his relief is ready." Nimitz further explained, "Fletcher is expected back in time to take T.F.11 down to your area, probably in early November. If, by any chance, Fletcher does not return, [Rear Admiral Frederick] Sherman is expected to be available for this task force." Ted Sherman, former captain of the *Lexington*, served as a deputy Cominch chief of staff since early June, but Nimitz just discovered he was now available for a carrier command. The rest of the 8 October letter contained surprisingly trenchant criticism (for Nimitz) of Comsopac's recent decisions to retain TF-17 at sea instead of safely in harbor and not bring the battleship *Washington* forward from Tongatabu. Nimitz's patience neared its end. "In closing let me again urge you to take such calculated risks as may be warranted in order to continue the attrition which we are now inflicting on the enemy's sea and air forces."[6]

On 12 October Nimitz informed King that he knew of Sherman's prospective orders to report to Cincpac for duty and of King's intention for him to relieve Murray as CTF-17. The ax was about to fall for George Murray, after both King and Nimitz independently decided on his removal. Nimitz advised he already earmarked Kinkaid to replace Murray after Halsey took over TF-16. "Inasmuch as Sherman's movements could not conveniently be speeded up in time to relieve Murray before Kinkaid could relieve him, I propose to adhere to my previous plan to have Kinkaid relieve Murray. After Sherman reports I will employ him as commander of the first available Task Force." That might be Fletcher's TF-11, for Nimitz explained:

> When Fletcher returned to Pearl from the south, he stated that he felt fine and was ready for further operations. Subsequently Colonel Maas informed me at Palmyra that Fletcher had indicated he was tired and needed a rest. I asked McCain to talk to Fletcher on this subject on their way to the Mainland. McCain has informed me that he believed Fletcher will be ready for service again at sea after his present rest. If he is in all respects ready to return to sea duty when the *Saratoga* is ready in early November, I will be glad to have him. If you feel that Fletcher needs a longer period of rest, I suggest that he be retained ashore in some capacity, in which case I propose to use Sherman as task force commander of the *Saratoga* task force.

Nimitz said nothing about Fletcher's permanent removal from the carriers. Instead he wanted Fletcher back when fully fit and trusted King to follow through as they personally agreed the month before in San Francisco.[7]

The same was not true for the unlucky Leigh Noyes, a pariah after the fiery loss of the *Wasp*. In the 12 October letter to King, Nimitz described Noyes as a "spare flag officer," who was to step in as Comairpac in the brief interval (ultimately only one day) between Halsey's departure for Sopac and the arrival of Towers from Washington. Afterward Noyes was to report to Towers for duty. However, "If Noyes can be employed advantageously elsewhere," King should do so, "because I will have Ramsay [sic] and Mason as spare flag officers when they are relieved of their commands." Obviously Nimitz had no thought of returning Noyes to carrier command, but Cominch's idea of "advantageous employment" turned out to be the Pacific Coast Section of the Board of Inspection and Survey. Nimitz wrote home on 27 October that Noyes "will probably hate me for it but I didn't pick the job." In 1949 King observed that Noyes "had a very good chance" in the South Pacific, "but missed it." However, the 1943 investigation of the loss of the *Wasp* exonerated Noyes and Forrest Sherman, leading Nimitz to declare that Noyes's decisions were "justified" and that no one was to incur blame. Nevertheless Noyes spent the balance of the war in the Board of Inspection and Survey, succeeding as president in March 1945. He retired in 1946 as a rear admiral, with no recognition for his combat service. Forrest Sherman, a rising star, thought that was unjust. In 1950 when he was chief of naval operations, he arranged for his old boss to be advanced to vice admiral on the retired list. A grateful Noyes replied: "Thanks so much for your efforts in my behalf, without which I am sure it would never had gotten through."[8]

On 15 October Nimitz read the message that effectively terminated Ghormley's tenure as Comsopac. Warning of "all out enemy effort against Cactus," Ghormley declared his resources were "totally inadequate to meet situation" and demanded reinforcements. He appeared to have lost all hope. Nimitz conferred with Captain McCormick, who concurred, "The critical situation there requires a more aggressive Commander." Nimitz informed King of his desire to replace Ghormley with Halsey. King approved, and on 16 October Nimitz issued the necessary orders. Writing home the next day, he described his "sore mental struggle," the "hours of anguished consideration" that concluded his friend Ghormley was "too immersed in detail and not sufficiently bold and aggressive at the right time." Kinkaid kept TF-16, which granted Murray a reprieve as CTF-17, and Halsey soon named Kinkaid CTF-61 in charge of all Sopac carrier task forces.[9]

FLETCHER IS OUT

On 22 October in full anticipation of Fletcher's imminent return, of which he heard nothing to the contrary in the past three weeks, Nimitz instructed Admiral Wright to return from Sopac to Pearl by 5 November. Wright was to resume his post as Commander, Cruisers, TF-11, because Fletcher would be taking the *Saratoga* task force south around 10 November. On 23 October, though, Nimitz received a terse message from Bupers: "Officer Signal Number 64 [Vice Adm. Frank Jack Fletcher] being detached present duties proceeding direct from Washington to duty Com 13 and Comnorwestseafron. Request nomination Comcrupac."

Com 13 referred to commandant of the Thirteenth Naval District (Pacific Northwest), and the Northwest Sea Frontier comprised the coastal waters of those states and the Alaskan sector. Nimitz proposed Kinkaid for Fletcher's replacement as Commander, Cruisers, Pacific Fleet. King agreed. Fletcher would not return to Pearl Harbor even for the customary change of command, so that particular relief took place on 29 October in absentia, with Fletcher in Washington, D.C., and Kinkaid in the South Pacific.[10]

King had a perfect right to relieve Fletcher or anyone else under his command. He was responsible for fighting the naval war and entitled to choose his own leaders. Whether the relief was justified is another matter. It may have seemed after the departure of Ghormley and Noyes that Fletcher's ouster was just part of the clean sweep of the discredited Sopac leadership. In truth, though, Fletcher never had a fig of a chance with King despite Nimitz's demonstrably strong support. Fletcher reported on 30 September to "Main Navy," so familiar from his days with the old Bureau of Navigation, but a far different place under King's steely grip. He found himself frozen out like an unwanted orphan and did not know his fate was already decided. Although King and Nimitz discussed a number of temporary jobs for Fletcher in Washington, none materialized. Cominch and his minions barely gave him the time of day. Secretary Knox (who only returned from Brazil about two weeks after Fletcher's arrival) "was the only person that would listen to me." Amazingly no one in Cominch headquarters bothered to debrief the most battle-experienced task force commander in the U.S. Navy. Absorbed in the planning for the Torch Operation (the invasion of North Africa) set for early November, not to mention crises that raged from the Solomons to Stalingrad, King's staff had no time for an admiral whom the boss obviously already discarded.[11]

Once Ernie King got down on someone, he never changed his mind. Only first impressions counted. From far-off Washington Fletcher had appeared hesitant and timid that spring in the South Pacific, lost the *Lexington* and *Yorktown*, failed to sweep away the opposition before Savo, and suffered damage to the *Enterprise* and *Saratoga*. King rarely went beyond his initial, perhaps erroneous, perceptions to determine what really happened. In 1949 he described Fletcher (whom he called "Edward J. Fletcher") as someone with "not very much in the way of brains," and who had "ideas but did not know how to work them out." King recalled that he "frequently had to press Admiral Nimitz to take proper and drastic action about officers whose accomplishment was not up to standard." Here King himself took the "proper and drastic action" by seizing the fortuitous opportunity of an open vice admiral's billet. Its present incumbent, Charles Freeman, would turn sixty-four, ordinarily the mandatory retirement age, on 19 November. In a few instances newly promoted rear admirals commanded naval districts and sea frontiers while awaiting operational postings, but for senior admirals the districts were the elephant's graveyard. King probably thought Fletcher should feel grateful just to keep the three stars. Pye and Brown, for example, reverted to rear admiral when they were relieved. Yet King begrudged those vice admirals he could not for some reason demote, remarking to Nimitz in December that he "is frequently embarrassed by officers who are Vice Admirals for the duration." At the same time someone from Washington evidently hinted to Nimitz that Fletcher himself had asked or implied he wanted to go ashore. Nimitz wondered to Kinkaid whether that were so, and Kinkaid personally broached the subject to his old friend Fletcher.

In January 1943 Fletcher firmly contradicted that particular Washington calumny, writing Nimitz, "Kinkaid surprised me very much by saying that you had asked him if I had applied for or desired shore duty. I can assure you nothing was further from my mind, and my orders came as a complete surprise and as a considerable shock." That Nimitz perceived duplicity on the part of Cominch insiders is suggested by the remarks in 1983 of Admiral Layton, the former Cincpac intelligence officer. Ordinarily highly critical of Fletcher, Layton stated that although King judged Fletcher incompetent, Nimitz did not concur. "But then Nimitz was a loyal commander, loyal to his subordinates. King was, well, I think there were people on King's staff who were jealous of Fletcher."[12]

Ironically in Ted Sherman, Nimitz had a suitable replacement for Fletcher readily available. For survival if nothing else, Sherman while in Washington assiduously presented his actions in the Coral Sea (where he lost King's beloved *Lexington*) in the best possible light at the expense of Fletcher, Buckmaster, and the *Yorktown*. He resembled Turner in never admitting a mistake. While in the States, Sherman reaped the public plaudits for the Coral Sea victory, including meeting Winston Churchill. His quest for carrier command bore fruit on 29 September, when he heard King was considering him for sea duty. King wanted another naval aviator as a carrier task force commander, and Sherman "was the only one available with sufficient rank and experience, without going down to very junior people." On 3 October King himself told Sherman that although he was "very much pleased" with his work in Washington, Sherman "was needed out at sea." The next day in a vivid demonstration of how indeed Sherman basked in official favor due to his Coral Sea reputation, he engaged in an "off the record" talk with President Roosevelt "about carriers" and received FDR's personal congratulations. Oddly Fletcher, who led the victorious Allied forces in that same engagement (as well as Midway and the Eastern Solomons), was readily at hand but never invited to the White House—a particularly reprehensible example of official ingratitude. The Navy Department kept him away from the press even though it had already announced the loss of the *Yorktown*. It is interesting that Roosevelt raised with Sherman the problem of "strain" that task force commanders faced "night and day," and thought "they should be periodically pulled out for a rest." One wonders if he spoke of Halsey or whether King already laid the groundwork for Fletcher's relief when he and Under Secretary of the Navy James V. Forrestal visited the White House on 2 October. Otherwise Roosevelt, who followed naval affairs closely, might have questioned Fletcher's sudden exile.[13]

Informing Cincpac he was coming, Sherman left Washington on 12 October for California for a brief leave and to assemble his staff of mostly former *Lexington* officers. He was to be in Pearl before the end of the month. Now the way seemed open for King's protégé to take the reins of TF-11 in the *Saratoga*. That was very likely what King desired once he heard from Nimitz that Kinkaid, not Sherman, would relieve Murray as CTF-17. Nimitz was already on record with Cominch and Comsopac preferring Sherman if Fletcher proved temporarily unavailable. Sherman flew into Oahu early on 27 October to the good news that Fletcher was no longer in the picture. However instead of becoming CTF-11 in his place, Sherman only received the use of a house on Ford Island in which to await another command. That very day, after Capt. Dewitt Ramsey was relieved as commanding officer of the *Saratoga*, Nimitz, to everyone's surprise, instantly frocked him rear admiral and gave him TF-11, effective 30 October. Sherman confided to his diary he was "a little disappointed" not to get the *Saratoga* task force, "But feel I will be promptly employed and nothing to worry about." Such "disappointment," though, was particularly bitter for a man with Sherman's ego, because Ramsey was considerably junior to him.[14]

Nimitz hinted prior to 27 October he would not follow King's script and anoint Sherman as CTF-11. On the twenty-fourth, the day after he learned of Fletcher's relief, he requested Bupers not to reassign the Comcrupac staff but keep it intact for TF-11. The only exceptions were Captain Lewis, who was "available for such duty as Bupers may desire," and Commander Pederson, already ordered as the *Enterprise*'s navigator. Lewis (USNA 1910) was too senior for a task force chief of staff either for his classmate Sherman or Ramsey (USNA 1912). Besides, Lewis had been at sea for nearly three years and merited a new assignment. Significantly, several officers whom Nimitz wished to retain in the TF-11 staff did the same duty as those whom he knew Sherman already selected for his own carrier staff.[15]

Rear Adm. Dewitt C. Ramsey, 1943.
Courtesy of U.S. Navy

To promote a captain and have him immediately hoist his flag in his former ship was unusual, but not unheard of. In June Rear Adm. Marc Mitscher briefly remained in the *Hornet* as CTF-17 and would have stayed had not Midway tarnished his reputation with Nimitz. Yet now in the case of TF-11, Nimitz selected a junior flag officer over a more senior admiral who was not only on hand but also slated for that slot. Why did Nimitz completely change his mind regarding Sherman? He came to esteem Ramsey, in particular for how well he handled the *Saratoga*, but he had been equally strong on Sherman since May and June when hoping to snare Sherman for the *Wasp* and then the *Hornet* task forces. Since then Sherman himself did nothing to forfeit the trust either of King or Nimitz, except perhaps Nimitz now recognized him intriguing with the Washington brass. Nor was Sherman anything but rock solid with Halsey, the new Comsopac. Granted a new factor at Pearl was Comairpac Towers, for whom Ramsey was a valued associate. Also Towers was no fan of Ted Sherman, whom he disliked for his "overbearing style of leadership," an interesting criticism from someone who enjoyed much the same reputation. No evidence appears that Towers played any role in Nimitz's decision, or that he was even consulted. For lack of sources one can only speculate why Nimitz spurned Sherman. A reasonable explanation is he used Ramsey's appointment as CTF-11 to protest the high-handed way King dealt with Fletcher in violation of their understanding in September.[16]

Fletcher relieved Freeman on 21 November in a ceremony in Seattle. It was a bittersweet occasion for the admiral who was retired and the other who was relegated. A reporter interviewed the new Com 13, who puffed on a corncob pipe: "Admiral Fletcher's eyes snap when he speaks of his recent duty, but he holds himself back from too much reminiscing. 'I don't want to get kicked in the pants by the Navy Department,' he confided. 'I'm having my first press conference today and I've got to be careful.'" Fletcher did allow himself to observe: "I feel like all Navy men. I would rather be at sea. But I'll say that if I have to be on land, I'd rather be here than anywhere else, under the circumstances. It is a highly important job." He reiterated that sentiment to Nimitz in January 1943. "The fortunes of any one man of are no consequence in this war, and if I have to have shore duty, this is about the best assignment there is." Platitudes, though, could not remove the pain of his removal from combat. Captain Lewis accompanied his boss into exile as assistant commandant of the Thirteenth Naval District. Fletcher tried his best to help get Lewis promoted, but his influence now meant little. Lewis did not get his two stars, at least not yet.[17]

While Fletcher spoke with the Seattle reporters, he did not know that in the faraway South Pacific his good friend Tom Kinkaid was experiencing his last full day as CTF-16. The contrast between the fates of Fletcher and Kinkaid, though, was profound. In Kinkaid's case, Nimitz could react before losing another of his trusted commanders.

RELIEF AND REVIVAL

To understand how differently Kinkaid was treated from Fletcher, one must examine how the carriers performed in October and November 1942 in the South Pacific.[18]

George Murray's TF-17 (*Hornet*, two heavy cruisers, two light cruisers, and six destroyers) spent a month doing what it could to help cover Cactus, but one lone carrier could accomplish little except at great risk. On 5 October the *Hornet* raided Shortland to help stem the "Tokyo Express" that delivered men, weapons, and supplies to Guadalcanal, but the weather and a paucity of targets ruined a bold effort. Norman Scott's cruisers and destroyers won the Battle of Cape Esperance on the night of 11–12 October, but the effect was only temporary. On 13–14 October heavy ships pummeled Lunga and nearly destroyed the Cactus Air Force on the ground. A day later Imperial transports brazenly discharged their loads in broad daylight. The grave danger to Cactus panicked Ghormley and led to his relief. The next day *Hornet* aircraft again tried to derail the Express but found only slim pickings. Murray headed east to rendezvous on 24 October with Kinkaid's TF-16 (*Enterprise*, battleship *South Dakota*, one heavy cruiser, one light cruiser, and six destroyers) 250 miles northeast of Espíritu Santo.

Halsey started aggressively as Comsopac, just as King and Nimitz desired. He hurled Kinkaid's TF-61 against a powerful carrier force coming down against Cactus. The resulting Battle of Santa Cruz on 26 October pitted four Japanese carriers (*Shōkaku*, *Zuikaku*, *Zuihō*, and *Junyō* with 194 planes) against two U.S. carriers (175 planes). Only a mechanical failure prevented the *Hiyō* from participating. Kinkaid fought from a position of disadvantage. Instead of holding his carriers southeast of Guadalcanal, Halsey rashly committed them northeast of the Solomons out near the limit of friendly land-based air support. The exchange of blows left the *Hornet* fatally damaged and the *Enterprise*'s innards torn by bombs, in return for knocking out but not sinking the *Shōkaku* and *Zuihō*. The customary deployment of the two U.S. carriers into separate task forces ten miles apart once more split the defense, as Fletcher feared. Every Japanese strike found its target, whereas most of the U.S. planes, sent out in three small, isolated flights, never sighted any enemy carriers. Kinkaid swiftly withdrew the injured *Enterprise*, which recovered nearly all the aircraft aloft in epic fashion (like the *Saratoga*'s less celebrated performance on 24 August) and pulled clear of pursuit. The Japanese overhauled the burning hulk of the *Hornet* early the next morning and avenged the Doolittle raid.

The Battle of Santa Cruz, dubbed the "South Pacific Naval Battle" by the jubilant, if battered Japanese, ended in a tactical defeat for the United States. Yamamoto believed he destroyed the entire U.S. carrier force and opened the way to Guadalcanal. Regrettably the 17th Army failed to capture the Lunga airfield. Now he need only regroup, beat down the aircraft remaining at Lunga, and transport overwhelming numbers of troops and matériel to Guadalcanal to root out the garrison. Santa Cruz cost Japan ninety-nine carrier planes and many irreplaceable veteran aircrews. The South Pacific Naval Battle was in fact an Allied strategic victory. The *Enterprise* survived with ninety-five planes (and most of the aviators from the eighty planes that were lost), while the marines held Henderson Field. Halsey was very lucky to escape total disaster had the *Enterprise* and all the carrier aircraft accompanied the *Hornet* to the bottom of the sea.

A disgusted Towers raged that non-aviators lost yet another carrier. Murray passed through Pearl on his way to command NAS Pensacola and related a tale of woe of how Kinkaid mishandled TF-61. Towers urged Nimitz to relieve Kinkaid immediately with Mitscher and end the travesty of black shoes in carriers. Nimitz did not buy that, nor was he willing yet to remove Mitscher from the doghouse. Instead he sent Ted Sherman south to Sopac to form a task force around two or three auxiliary carriers. Everyone agreed the small carriers must serve together in one formation within the same screen. Sherman, the greatest proponent of multi-carrier task forces, got no argument on that score. By the time Sherman reached Nouméa on 16 November, Halsey fought and won his most decisive engagement. To Sherman's surprise Halsey gave him TF-16 in the *Enterprise*.[19]

On 10 November after Halsey learned of another imminent major push against Cactus, Kinkaid's TF-16 (partially repaired *Enterprise*, two battleships, one heavy cruiser, one light cruiser, and eight destroyers) hastened north from Nouméa. Former Sopac chief of staff Rear Adm. Dan Callaghan, who was covering a convoy to Cactus, released one heavy cruiser and two destroyers to join Kinkaid on the twelfth. On the night of 12–13 November, before TF-16 could get within range of Guadalcanal, Callaghan and Scott valiantly pitted five cruisers and eight destroyers against a bombardment force that included two fast battleships. They saved Cactus at the cost of their lives. On 13 November, to Halsey's intense displeasure, Kinkaid was still not in position to use his aircraft or Ching Lee's two fast battleships to prevent another night bombardment of Lunga ahead of a large force of transports coming down the Slot. The next day Kinkaid flew off nearly all his planes in searches and strikes with orders to fly to Henderson Field, while he cleared out with the *Enterprise*. Relentless air attacks by the Cactus Air Force and *Enterprise*'s Air Group Ten almost wiped out the convoy, but only Lee's great surface victory on the night of 14–15 November prevented another huge bombardment that again could have pulverized the U.S. planes on the ground. Thus the last Japanese attempt to reconquer Guadalcanal ended in complete failure. The epic victory earned Halsey his fourth star.

Kinkaid felt deep satisfaction over the employment of the *Enterprise* and Air Group Ten in the Naval Battle of Guadalcanal. He kept the wounded carrier to the rear behind the shield of land-based air support and awaited the enemy to come calling. The *Big E* then shuttled her planes to a land base and pulled out in timely fashion before absorbing any counterattack. "This time," Kinkaid boasted, "the air group on the carrier was utilized more effectively than ever before." He offered the November operation as a model for carriers in constricted waters within the enemy's air search network. Halsey chose not to contest Kinkaid's evaluation or publically criticize him, but his subsequent actions reflected his strong disapproval of Kinkaid's performance both at Santa Cruz and in the Naval Battle of Guadalcanal. Halsey also perceived the solution was at hand. On 16 November he informed Sherman that he would relieve Kinkaid as CTF-16 in the *Enterprise* and act as senior carrier task force commander when Ramsey brought down TF-11 (*Saratoga*) late that month. Although Kinkaid was "an excellent man," Halsey told Sherman, the relief "had to be done." The next day Halsey informed Nimitz he would retain only the two light antiaircraft cruisers and destroyers in the TF-16 screen and form the heavy cruisers and the *Brooklyn*-class light cruisers into surface striking groups to be split among Kinkaid, Admiral Tisdale (TF-16 cruiser commander), and Boscoe Wright, the TF-11 cruiser commander. "This is absolutely no reflection on Tom Kinkaid," Halsey emphasized, "as I consider he has done a fine job," but "I am merely placing my tools where I believe they would be most useful." Halsey felt it would be "inexcusable to have a man of Sherman's Air experience not utilized in the *Enterprise* when he is available." As for Kinkaid, Halsey explained, "As soon as I can get some flag officers I would like to send Tom back to the States for a rest. He has done a noble job and has been at it a long long time." To take Sherman's place in the auxiliary carriers, Halsey requested either Murray or Charles Mason. Nimitz selected Mason.[20]

Kinkaid reacted to his sudden relief with disbelief and anger. He truly liked carrier command. Sherman told him on 18 November he had not "instigated" the change in command. Kinkaid replied he "knew that but he was disappointed to be relieved just as he knew how to handle aircraft." Kinkaid then shocked Sherman by saying "he had decided he needed a rest and instead of going to command cruisers felt he wanted to go back to Pearl Harbor." Sherman heard that Kinkaid could not get in to see Halsey later that day. Instead, chief of staff Miles Browning relayed Kinkaid's desire to be sent back to Pearl immediately for a rest. That, Sherman judged, did not make "a very good impression." On 20 November he traveled to Espíritu Santo to see his old boss Jake Fitch, who to his surprise "was quite free with his criticism of Kinkaid's handling the task force." Fitch told Sherman that Kinkaid should have immediately attacked on 26 October after receiving a predawn PBY report of enemy carriers and then criticized Kinkaid's failure to support Murray once the *Hornet* became disabled. Likewise with regard to the Naval Battle of Guadalcanal, Fitch disagreed with Kinkaid's decision to release the *Enterprise*'s planes to Cactus, "which was jammed and couldn't effectively handle them." Cincpac, too, did not altogether condone Kinkaid's conservative withdrawal of the *Enterprise* on the afternoon 14 November. In the general report of 18 February 1943, Spruance suggested Kinkaid might have remained closer to Guadalcanal and retrieved at least a portion of the *Enterprise* Air Group, then, with the support of the *Washington* and his own heavy cruisers, finished off the enemy cripples and stragglers.[21]

The Sopac reorganization took place on 23 November. In place of TF-16, Kinkaid received TF-67 (three heavy cruisers, two light cruisers, and six destroyers), with Tisdale as second-in-command. Halsey's orders reassigning Kinkaid to TF-67 contained what Sherman called an "unusual first paragraph telling what fine work he had done, but in view of tactical situation it was necessary to assign him elsewhere." Sherman considered it "a very flowery paragraph to save his feelings." The next day Kinkaid left Nouméa for Espíritu Santo to join TF-67, but confided to Sherman that he was "going home for a rest when R.Adm. Wright gets down here." Unlike the common perception, Kinkaid's departure from Sopac had nothing to do with any orders from Washington or Pearl but was due strictly to his reluctance to return to cruisers. He left in a huff because Halsey would not keep him in carriers. Wright formally relieved Kinkaid on 28 November, and two nights later fought the disastrous Battle of Tassafaronga according to Kinkaid's tactical plan because he lacked the time to work out one of his own.[22]

It is evident the bad feelings that erupted between Kinkaid and Halsey after the October 1944 Battle of Leyte Gulf actually originated in November 1942. Yet the delicacy with which Halsey handled Kinkaid's relief and hasty departure, sans billet, preserved Kinkaid's reputation both within the navy and subsequently among historians. Fletcher never received the same consideration. Arriving on 2 December at Pearl, Kinkaid found a surprisingly sympathetic Cincpac, who advised he was seeking approval for Kinkaid to relieve Admiral Theobald as commander of the North Pacific Area and CTF-8. To sweeten the pot because Kinkaid was not particularly eager to go to the Aleutians, Nimitz recommended (and Kinkaid subsequently received) a gold star in lieu of a second DSM for his actions in the Battle of the Eastern Solomons. The citation praised Kinkaid's "keen leadership, determined action and outstanding resourcefulness in driving off and destroying a large attacking force." Fletcher, though, never received any official recognition either for his overall command in that battle or sinking the *Ryūjō*. Later in December Kinkaid accompanied Nimitz to the third Cominch-Cincpac conference in San Francisco, where King confirmed the new assignment in the Aleutians. King, too, had tired of Fuzzy Theobald's lack of initiative and constant wrangling with the army. After spending

Christmas with the Fletchers in Seattle, Kinkaid relieved Theobald on 4 January 1943 and prepared to retake Attu and Kiska in the western Aleutians.[23]

Nimitz certainly stepped in to save Kinkaid's career and retain him in a combat assignment, and there is every indication he would have done the same for Fletcher if he had just been given the opportunity. Two letters reflect Cincpac's attitude toward his two erstwhile black shoe carrier admirals. In March 1943 when Ted Sherman and Duke Ramsey still led the only two fast carriers in the Pacific Fleet, McCain requested Ramsey resume the post of assistant chief of Buaer. Nimitz demurred. The "proposal you make concerning Ramsey is a very difficult one for me," and "only after long reflection" had Nimitz reached a decision. "As you well know, our competent carrier task force commanders have been passing through their commands so rapidly that we have suffered somewhat from stability and lack of permanency. Ramsey is undoubtedly as good a carrier task force commander as we will ever get, and with the present limited number of carriers, I think it would be a mistake to take him out. The Japanese do not use amateurs or Makee-learns in similar jobs; and we should have the best people available in our limited number of carriers." The only carrier task force commanders whose exits Nimitz had not personally arranged or condoned were Fletcher and Kinkaid, presumably the "competent carrier task force commanders" to whom he referred. Nimitz had stated his position on black shoe carrier admirals to Halsey on 18 December 1942. Halsey had placed Admiral Mason in charge of TF-65 over the more senior (but non-aviator) Rear Adm. Harry W. Hill simply because the task force included two auxiliary carriers as well as Hill's two old battleships. Nimitz did not care for it. "I am sure you agree with me," he wrote Halsey, "that there are many line officers thoroughly capable of taking command of a task force which has in it aircraft carriers, and that nothing would be more harmful to the morale of our senior officers than to create the impression that only aviators may command task forces which have carriers included." Nimitz spoke not only for Hill but also for the departed Fletcher and Kinkaid. Whether Halsey agreed became moot because, strictly speaking, there were no more black shoe carrier admirals.[24]

CHAPTER 32

War on the Periphery

COM 13

A brief review of Fletcher's naval career after November 1942 is useful especially to illustrate his status with his superiors and peers. From headquarters in Seattle, Fletcher supervised the many activities of the Thirteenth Naval District, covering the states of the Pacific Northwest and the territory of Alaska. He also ran the Northwest Sea Frontier that protected shipping in coastal waters in cooperation with Canadian authorities and aided in the effort to transport huge amounts of lend-lease matériel from the West Coast to Vladivostok in the USSR's Maritime Province. His top priority in early 1943 was to build up bases and resources in Alaska to sustain the offensive of Admiral Kinkaid's North Pacific Force against Attu and Kiska, the two Japanese footholds in the Aleutians. In May Attu fell to Kinkaid, cutting off Kiska, which Japan secretly evacuated in July prior to the Allied invasion in August.[1]

Fletcher watched enviously from long distance as the major Pacific offensives began to unfold. After the Japanese evacuated Guadalcanal in February 1943, Admiral Halsey's Third Fleet ground its way up the central Solomons to gain position from which to strike the great fortress of Rabaul. To westward, Vice Adm. Arthur S. Carpender's Seventh Fleet ran the amphibious operations of the Southwest Pacific Area. General MacArthur regrouped his forces following the capture in January of the stronghold at Buna and prepared to assault Lae and Salamaua farther up the New Guinea coast. If Bill Halsey was the navy's favorite warhorse, Vice Adm. Raymond Spruance, the Pacific Fleet chief of staff, emerged as one of its brightest leaders and Nimitz's closest associate. On 5 August Spruance took command of the Central Pacific Force and the task of seizing the Gilbert Islands (Operation Galvanic), the first stop in the direct thrust toward Japan. He retrieved his old friend Rear Adm. Kelly Turner from the South Pacific to handle amphibious operations.

To someone who craved action as much as Fletcher, shore duty in the States was purgatory. Morison declared that after being relieved of his carrier task force in the fall of 1942 Fletcher "received commands more commensurate with his abilities." Whether or not one agrees with Morison's low assessment of those "abilities," the question remains what else Fletcher might have done. Even had he taken TF-11 (*Saratoga*) back to the South Pacific in November 1942, his time in the carriers would have been short, certainly not beyond the spring of 1943. Not being a naval aviator told decisively against him. So did his age and exalted rank of vice admiral. Younger aviator rear admirals lined up to lead the carriers being constructed in stateside yards. Their boss in the Pacific Fleet was never going to be Fletcher. As he realistically told Colonel Maas in August 1942, he "does not believe he is the man to run an air show," although he did a remarkably good job as a stand-in for the aviation leaders, who were either busy elsewhere or too junior for such a carrier command.[2]

What possible billets were available for Fletcher? On 1 July 1943 the U.S. Navy had eighteen vice admirals. One was a bureau chief, four served on staffs, five (including Ghormley and Fletcher) commanded sea frontiers, three held administrative commands (service force, air force) within fleets, two ran amphibious fleets, two were area commanders, and one led the air force within an area. In August 1943, well aware of the limited number of jobs for vice admirals, Fletcher requested demotion to rear admiral if it could mean a combat command at sea. Nimitz gently replied that he "appreciated the spirit" in which Fletcher made his offer but had nothing for him in the Pacific Fleet for the next six to eight months, "Unless we have some unfortunate casualties." He suggested Fletcher relay to King and Admiral Jacobs (chief of Bupers) "the same thought that you expressed in your letter to me, on the chance that casualties will occur in my area." That did not sound too promising.[3]

CARRIER TACTICS RESOLVED

On 24 September 1942 Fletcher compiled for Nimitz his conception of carrier tactics, premised on "the past nine months" of "operating with from one to three carrier task forces against Japanese Naval and Air forces." In that time, "Many lessons and new ideas have been gained." Certainly no one else accrued more experience leading carriers in battle. Nimitz, eager to standardize carrier tactics, passed Fletcher's analysis to Halsey for comment. Responding on 9 October, Halsey concurred with most of Fletcher's positions, in particular that the high command repeatedly placed the carriers in jeopardy by employing them defensively off Guadalcanal. On 9 December Nimitz forwarded Fletcher's letter, Halsey's response, and extracts from action reports of the 26 October Santa Cruz battle to all Pacific Fleet aviation type commanders, task force commanders, carrier captains, and others, including Noyes, Mitscher, and Buckmaster, who led carriers in battle. The "enclosures present comment and opinion on many features of carrier employment, together with recommendations covering material, based on the latest experience of Carrier Task Forces." The "lessons learned must be given earliest application to future operations of this nature, and steps must be taken to improve material conditions so far as possible." The "current lull in carrier activity occasioned by our losses" made it "an appropriate time to crystalize service thought" regarding carrier tactics.[4]

Comairpac Towers summarized the many responses for Cincpac in April 1943. Easily the most contentious issue remained multi-carrier task forces. Fletcher recommended, as often noted, that carrier task forces must stay together for "mutual support and protection." Ahead of most aviation professionals, he recognized that radar and increased numbers of fighters rendered invalid the old fear of massing carriers. Halsey, on the other hand, held to the old theory that concentrating the carriers was "fraught with grave danger" and ran counter to prewar doctrine. In spring 1942 he compromised to the extent of organizing TF-16 into what he later called the "ideal carrier task force" of "two carriers tactically concentrated until air attack is actually approaching and tactically re-concentrated immediately the attack has withdrawn." Halsey cautioned, "More than one carrier *task force* [i.e., two carriers] should *not* normally be operated in close proximity; the general thumb rule being that at least twice the visibility separate the forces at all times." No clear consensus emerged, with opinion almost equally divided between concentration and dispersion.[5]

Rear Adm. Frederick "Ted" Sherman, the greatest advocate of incorporating more than one carrier in the same screen, argued that as many as four carriers could thus be accommodated. "Dispersion at sea permits the enemy to concentrate his attack on single units and defeat us in detail." As Halsey's senior carrier task force commander, Sherman profited from the "lull" in early 1943 to experiment with running carriers in the same screen. Capt. H. S. Duckworth, Sherman's chief of staff, explained that his boss "convinced Admiral Halsey the multi carrier idea was correct & he allowed us to demonstrate combined simultaneous air operations on signal from the flagship." The key problem was coordinating simultaneous flight operations from different carriers, but Sherman and Duckworth discovered that individual flattops did not have to point directly into the wind when launching and recovering aircraft. "It was sufficient to have the carrier face in the general direction of the wind and that a variance of 30° over the bow could be tolerated." Aided by Cdr. Robert Dixon, the air operations officer, they also worked out rendezvous procedures so that the air groups did not interfere with each other. Sherman urged the creation of "more or less permanent" task forces of two or three carriers that trained together. "It is not enough to throw two single-carrier task forces together on the eve of battle. Their combat efficiency *as a team* will be much higher if they have trained and practiced together until team work becomes automatic." His goal was to create a standardized doctrine so that different carriers could swiftly integrate into a powerful task force.[6]

In May 1943 Sherman brought the *Enterprise* to Pearl Harbor, where he "continued to develop the necessary formations and tactics for multi-carrier groups." That was timely because the new *Essex* soon arrived, followed by sisters *Yorktown* (CV-10) and *Lexington* (CV-16). Their air groups comprised thirty-six Grumman F6F-3 Hellcat fighters, thirty-six SBD-5 Dauntless dive bombers, and eighteen TBF-1 Avenger torpedo bombers. During the same interval the *Independence*, *Belleau Wood*, and *Princeton*—three new *Independence*-class light carriers converted from light cruiser hulls—also reached Pearl. After some adjustments, their air groups numbered twenty-four F6F-3s and nine TBF-1s. Sherman fully demonstrated the validity of his tactical concepts, which justified Fletcher's faith in multi-carrier task forces. Issued on 10 June 1943, the Current Tactical Orders and Doctrine U.S. Pacific Fleet (PAC-10) decreed task groups must incorporate their carriers in the same screen and criticized the old concept of single-carrier task forces.[7]

Ted Sherman won the tactical war, but lost his personal battle. When it came time in late July 1943 to organize multi-carrier task forces, he reluctantly returned to the South Pacific to relieve Admiral Ramsey in charge of the *Saratoga* task force. Duckworth with part of the staff remained at Pearl to serve Rear Adm. Charles "Baldy" Pownall and Rear Adm. Alfred E. Montgomery, the prospective carrier task force commanders. Duckworth recalled, "All Ted Sherman wanted was a little recognition but he gritted his teeth & stuck to his job in spite of the oversights because he knew his tactics were right & would eventually would be recognized. I, by very odd circumstances, was the one to demonstrate them to the Navy." As Pownall's chief of staff, Duckworth planned the successful 31 August raid on Marcus, the first combat for the new carriers. The *Essex*, *Yorktown*, and *Independence* formed in the same screen, along with a fast battleship, two light cruisers, and ten destroyers, for "more effective air defense with fewer fighters per carrier than when the carriers operated independently and a greater concentration of antiaircraft fire when under attack." Pownall then hit the Gilberts with the *Lexington*, *Princeton*, and *Belleau Wood*.[8]

Having personally tested the multi-carrier concept at Marcus, Duckworth likewise planned Montgomery's massive 5–6 October raid against Wake Island, employing three big carriers and three light carriers, three heavy cruisers, four light cruisers, twenty-four destroyers, and two fleet oilers. Their 372 aircraft were the biggest concentration of U.S. carrier air power to date. Montgomery exercised the carriers in different combinations: a single group of six, two groups of three, and three groups of two. During the actual attack, the *Independence* and *Belleau Wood* operated in a separate task group covering the bombardment force. According to Duckworth, the "tactical lessons were demonstrated in [1942] & all we did was apply them in the summer & fall of 1943." Regarding Marcus and Wake, "The formation & tactics used on these raids were practically unchanged when I returned to sea 18 months later." The new Pacific Fleet fast carrier task force comprised four and more independent carrier task groups (ideally of two big carriers and one light carrier) that operated separately as necessary to accomplish the mission. That arrangement satisfied the need for concentrating enough air strength in one disposition to matter, yet offered the tactical flexibility desired by those who favored dispersion.[9]

In early November 1943 Sherman led the *Saratoga* and *Princeton* on two successive forays against Rabaul in support of Halsey's invasion of Bougainville. The second raid included Montgomery's task group (*Essex*, *Bunker Hill*, and *Independence*) approaching from a different direction. Sherman and Montgomery reached the central Pacific in time for Galvanic, the invasions of Tarawa and Makin in the Gilberts, set for 20 November. The handling of the carriers during Galvanic, the greatest commitment of carriers to date, is very instructive when compared with the August 1942 Watchtower offensive against Guadalcanal. Divided into four task groups, Pownall's TF-50 of six large carriers and five light carriers (684 planes) "constituted the first use of the fast carrier task force as it continued through the rest of the war." In addition, eight escort carriers with 218 planes (including forty-four F6F Hellcats ready to base at Tarawa) provided close air support for the Galvanic invasion forces. In 1942 Fletcher could scarcely have dreamt of nineteen carriers and nine hundred carrier planes for the Guadalcanal-Tulagi landings. The aircraft on the jeep carriers alone nearly equaled the air strength (234) of the *Saratoga*, *Enterprise*, and *Wasp* on 7 August 1942.[10]

In November 1943 U.S. naval intelligence estimated Japan might have two hundred land-based planes in the Marshalls and Gilberts and at Wake. (Actually there were about ninety.) The closest enemy air bases in the Marshalls were only 200–225 miles distant from Makin, the northerly of the two objectives. Truk, where it was thought the Combined Fleet lurked in strength, was thirteen hundred miles west of Makin. That potential threat deeply troubled Spruance and Turner, the Galvanic amphibious commander. On 29 October

Spruance advised, "If a major portion of the Jap Fleet were to attempt to interfere with Galvanic, it is obvious that the defeat of the enemy fleet would at once become paramount." A dearth of cruisers and destroyers forced him to assign five new fast battleships to screen the two northern carrier groups, Pownall's own TG-50.1 (*Yorktown*, *Lexington*, and *Cowpens*) and Rear Adm. Arthur W. Radford's TG-50.2 (*Enterprise*, *Belleau Wood*, and *Monterey*). Montgomery was to have TG-50.3 (*Essex*, *Bunker Hill*, and *Independence*) off Tarawa, while Sherman's TG-50.4 (*Saratoga* and *Princeton*) would not arrive until later, after raiding Nauru to the southwest. Should the Japanese fleet sortie against the Gilberts, Spruance expected a surface action, for which he must have those battlewagons. The "possibility of an enemy attack in force on the Makin Area with little or no warning necessitates that on and after D-Day, the carrier task groups operating there with the new battleships in their screens must remain in as close tactical supporting distance of the Northern Attack Force as the nature of their air operations and fuel situation permits." In that way Pownall's and Radford's carriers would also "provide very effective fighter protection against enemy air attacks coming from the Marshalls against our ships at Makin," but, of course, at their own considerable risk if the planes went after them instead. Turner "insisted," as he had in August 1942 off Guadalcanal, "that all the carriers be tied down off the target beaches" to protect the unloading of his transports. For his own part Fletcher had to take into account a possible sudden appearance by the Combined Fleet during the Guadalcanal landings, but he certainly lacked the awesome air power available to Spruance.[11]

Towers and his aviators were irate at what they considered a terrible misuse of carrier air power. Instead of retaining the freedom to smash all air bases within the Marshalls, TF-50 had to deploy in limited defensive sectors near the invasion forces. Deploring Spruance's intransigence, Clark Reynolds explained: "Defensive sectors, the aviators knew very well, would attract Japanese land-based planes by the score, something any South Pacific veteran would have never allowed. Certainly Halsey would not have, after his troubles holding onto Guadalcanal the year before. Mobility was the only defense when carriers lay within range of enemy air bases and long range bombers." "Unable to exploit their carriers' maneuverability," Pownall and Radford were "little more than sitting ducks for the enemy's planes, submarines, and now fleet." Fletcher was in even a worse fix in August 1942 while staked out south of Guadalcanal well within range of Rabaul's planes. He could never imagine neutralizing their air bases prior to or during the landings, for he had only the three carriers that were also the sole source of close air support for the landing force.[12]

Towers and his carrier admirals strongly protested Spruance's plans to Nimitz, who compromised to the extent of allowing Pownall to strike the nearest bases in the Marshalls prior to the landings. Thereafter TF-50 must take up the "defensive cruising sectors." Because of land-based air attacks, one of which torpedoed the *Independence* off Tarawa, "Towers' worst fears had been realized the very first day of the invasion." Moreover, "What lay in store for the carriers over the following days could only be surmised." Thus, "Livid with Spruance for his tactics of immobilizing the carriers offshore," Towers urged that Spruance "modify existing orders which restrict operations of all three carrier task groups to very limited areas between Tarawa and Mili." He should unleash them "against the air bases in the Marshalls instead of maintaining a defensive position with the extreme likelihood of great damage from submarine and aircraft attack, particularly aircraft torpedo attacks around dusk." On 21 November Nimitz directed Spruance to give Pownall's carriers "greater freedom of movement consistent with their mission." In the first six days of Galvanic the Japanese managed only three air strikes of consequence. The Combined Fleet never did show up. From 19 November to 8 December (including the post-Galvanic strikes against the Marshalls), the fast carriers lost thirty-six aircraft (5.2 percent) to all causes. On 7–8 August 1942 alone, Fletcher's losses approached 10 percent (including 20 percent of his fighters), with no immediate prospect of replacements. On 24 November 1943 (D+4) a submarine sank the escort carrier *Liscome Bay* off Makin with great loss of life. Although actually on schedule, the army troops on Makin were blamed for not prosecuting their offensive swiftly enough and thus prolonging Turner's stay. In 1942, however, no one other than Colonel Maas criticized Vandegrift for his hesitant advance against Lunga. Nor were Turner's demands in 1942 for continuous carrier support to D+4 and beyond similarly questioned. Fletcher escaped successful sub attack during the landings, but within five weeks I-boats crippled one U.S. carrier and sank another.[13]

If Towers was justified for all his strident criticisms of Spruance's and Turner's restrictive policy for the fast carriers in Galvanic, Fletcher deserved enlightened consideration of his infinitely weaker carrier strength when similarly hamstrung supporting Turner's August 1942 landings at Guadalcanal. Yet Towers and others showed scant understanding that Fletcher faced the same dangers but with far fewer resources. Instead, he sneered Fletcher just "ran away." Towers and his aviator admirals, who enjoyed such terrific numerical, qualitative, and matériel superiority over the Japanese during the Pacific offensives of 1943–45, never realized what it was like for the pioneers of 1942 who fought and repeatedly won against the odds.[14]

"BY THE BACK DOOR"

Fletcher's break came unexpectedly in late September 1943, after MacArthur expressed dissatisfaction over Carpender's handling of the Seventh Fleet. Admiral Kinkaid came to mind as an experienced (and available) amphibious commander who got along well with the army. Thus Nimitz proposed to Washington that Fletcher take over the North Pacific Area and North Pacific Force and retain the Northwest Sea Frontier as well. King acquiesced, and consequently on 11 October Fletcher relieved Kinkaid, while Rear Adm. Sherwoode A. Taffinder took his place as Com 13. Fletcher moved his headquarters to Adak in the Aleutians. His principal offensive assets were the "Strategic Air Force," made up of the Eleventh Air Force and Fleet Air Wing Four, and a "covering force" of a few old cruisers and destroyers. Having regained the Aleutians, the North Pacific Area's prime missions were to safeguard the region through which the majority of lend-lease shipments reached the Soviet Union and to prepare for offensive operations, possibly in the spring of 1945, against Paramushiro in the northern Kurile Islands. Continued pressure from the northeast troubled Japan, which feared invasion from that quarter, and would bolster the Soviet Union's position should it come into the Pacific War. Fletcher knew precisely who was responsible for his resurrection. On 4 December he wrote Nimitz that he "was very pleased to be brought back into the Fleet, even by the back door."

Given that Halsey, Spruance, and Kinkaid were firmly locked in the top Pacific Fleet combat slots, the North Pacific Area was the best operational billet Fletcher could possibly have expected.[15]

Fletcher did not have much with which to fight in the dreary Aleutians, but he did what he could, mostly with aircraft whose brave crews regularly flew perilous long-distance raids against Paramushiro and the rest of the northern Kuriles. On 7 January 1944 Nimitz directed that strikes against the Kuriles continue and advised Fletcher of the possibility, once suitable bases were constructed, that Boeing B-29 Superfortress very heavy bombers might join the North Pacific (Norpac) Area's effort against Japan. On 4 February Rear Adm. Wilder D. Baker's TG-94.6 (two old light cruisers and seven destroyers) conducted the first ship bombardment of Japanese home territory by shelling Paramushiro—an action Morison described "very creditable." At the same time Spruance rampaged through the Marshalls, seizing Kwajalein atoll among others and bypassing several strong points. Nimitz encouraged Fletcher to keep up the pressure. Current strategic policy dictated only feints against the Kuriles, but that could change quickly and Norpac must be ready. Fletcher did everything he could to follow Nimitz's directive to take the fight to the enemy and keep morale high. In April 1944, the same month Fletcher formed the Alaskan Sea Frontier, Cdr. Harold Hopkins, RN, who was Michael Laing's successor as British naval liaison officer with the Pacific Fleet, visited the Aleutians. He was impressed the U.S. Navy had assigned "one of its most distinguished flag officers" as Commander, North Pacific Area and Force (Comnorpac), a truth one wonders ever registered with the Japanese. Hopkins praised Fletcher's "forceful and energetic leadership" that "imbued the officers and men of his command with an offensive spirit that was outstanding in a locality where ninety per cent of the time, the climate was vile and life could be monotonous and dreary in the extreme." Far from assuming they were in a backwater, the American sailors and airmen whom Hopkins met in the Aleutians "imagined [as did Fletcher] that they were blazing the trail for a northern offensive that would end in Japan." A month later Fletcher learned of Operation Keelblocks, a plan by the Joint Chiefs to seize the northern Kuriles and ensure clear access to the Soviet Far East ports in the event the Russians entered the Pacific War.[16]

In June 1944 while Admiral Spruance's Fifth Fleet invaded the Marianas, Fletcher launched several diversionary raids with his striking force of two heavy cruisers, two light cruisers, and nine destroyers against the Kuriles. On 22 June Nimitz wrote Fletcher that the "offensive use of the forces at your disposal, both air and surface, has kept the enemy worried and confused." He reiterated "our strategic concept still includes the possibility of a northern assault in 1945." After the grand strategic conference at Pearl with Nimitz and MacArthur, President Roosevelt visited Adak on 3–4 August 1944 in a trip that certainly emphasized, at least temporarily, the importance of the northern area. Cincpac's draft plan for Keelblocks called for Fletcher to protect Kamchatka and the Komandorskiye Islands. Fletcher countered by recommending assaults against the central and southern Kuriles first, the better to confront Japan directly. Nimitz's deputy chief of staff, Rear Adm. Forrest Sherman, agreed with Fletcher's assessment.[17]

In June Admiral Mitscher's TF-58 (the designation of the fast carriers while in the Fifth Fleet) easily won the Battle of the Philippine Sea, the first carrier battle since October 1942, while Turner captured Saipan (a defeat that brought down Premier Tōjō Hideki's government), Tinian, and Guam. Flat Tinian was rapidly converted into a vast air base to enable the B-29s to begin pounding the Japanese home islands late that fall. In September Spruance transferred his mobile forces to Halsey's Third Fleet and began charting the invasions of Iwo Jima and Okinawa. Freed of direct amphibious responsibilities after most of his amphibious ships were loaned to Admiral Kinkaid's Seventh Fleet with MacArthur, Halsey essentially ran the fast carriers (CTF-38 Mitscher merely became his deputy) tearing up the western Pacific. In October Halsey supported MacArthur's invasion of Leyte in the central Philippines. The great naval battle of Leyte Gulf resulted in a decisive U.S. victory, but the decoying of Halsey away from San Bernardino Strait to chase nearly empty carriers left a bitter legacy when powerful surface forces attacked Kinkaid's escort carriers. Afterward Japan resorted increasingly to kamikaze suicide air attacks that harassed TF-38, now under McCain.

Meeting 8 December 1944 at Pearl Harbor. *Left to right*: Admiral Nimitz, Lt. Gen. Delos C. Emmons, Admiral Fletcher, Admiral Spruance, Lt. Gen. Simon B. Buckner. *Courtesy of National Archives (80-G-290984)*

The poor autumn weather in the North Pacific further restricted Fletcher's opportunities for harming the Kuriles, and Nimitz correspondingly reduced his strength. In contrast to the vast armadas of Spruance, Halsey, and Kinkaid, Fletcher could count on the fingers of one hand every one of his warships larger than a destroyer. Understandably on 5 October he told Rear Adm. John L. McCrea, his new surface strike commander, if during a bombardment mission "conditions arise which will unduly expose our forces to enemy concentration of air power without protection of our fighters or low visibility, retire at discretion, giving due consideration to the calculated risk." Fletcher just wanted McCrea to "go out and shoot up the Kuriles. Make your own plans. Just keep me informed as to what you propose to do, and if I don't like what you are doing, I'll tell you so." McCrea recalled: "I don't know whether I could have, if I had been in his spot, trusted somebody that I didn't know at all to that extent, but that's what he did. He never stopped me or anything." Like Nimitz, Fletcher did not micromanage his subordinates. McCrea got to know Fletcher well during the long winter in Adak, and they became "close friends." Aware of his boss's controversial record in the Guadalcanal campaign, McCrea nevertheless declared Fletcher "a good officer."[18]

On 1 December 1944 Nimitz acknowledged Fletcher's September recommendation to invade the central and southern Kuriles, telling him to draw up plans to seize Matsuwa and Etoforu islands. In response to renewed interest by the Joint Chiefs in Keelblocks, Fletcher attended planning sessions at Pearl on 3–8 December with Nimitz, Spruance, and the top Alaskan army generals. With the defeat of Germany imminent, the USSR might be expected to declare war on Japan in the spring of 1945. The planners at Pearl believed the Soviets might need help defending the Kamchatka peninsula and roughed out Keelblocks II, a two-phase operation that would see U.S. forces help secure Kamchatka, build airfields, then assault Paramushiro. Although "sufficient naval forces are potentially available," the required troops and shipping, though, could scarcely be spared from the other planned Pacific offensives. It would be necessary to wait and see just when or if the USSR entered the Pacific War and determine then what might be available.[19]

After what Fletcher characterized as Nimitz's "perfect hospitality," he returned in good spirits to Adak only to discover that his job as Comnorpac was in jeopardy. Somehow he learned that Taffinder, Rear Adm. Alan G. Kirk (the senior U.S. amphibious leader in the Normandy D-Day assault), and "possibly others" had been offered his command. Fletcher felt sufficiently perturbed to contact Jacobs at Bupers, who explained, "No definite decision had been made but that my detachment had been under consideration and my assignment to the General Board was a possibility." Jacobs asked Fletcher what he wanted, only to be told he would take that up personally with Cincpac. Fletcher did so in a blunt missive to Nimitz on 16 December:

> Since I have been invited by the Chief of Personnel to express my wishes, I will do so categorically:
>
> 1) I am perfectly willing to remain here as long as you would like my services, subject to provisions noted below.
> 2) If I am to be superseded before any important operations start in this area I wish it to be done well in advance. To arrive just after Kinkaid

cleaned up Attu and depart just before some other started another show would be too much for my vanity.

3) If I am to be retained here more or less indefinitely I would like to have a month's leave. I can pick my time when this would be entirely feasible.
4) Regardless of all other considerations I, like all the officers in the Navy, will be delighted to serve under you whenever and wherever and under any conditions you desire.

No doubt surprised Fletcher knew of the behind-the-scenes effort to replace him, Nimitz responded in a conciliatory manner. No direct reply to the 16 December letter survives in either man's papers, but the fact is Fletcher remained and Nimitz certainly attempted to smooth things over.[20]

King's agenda for the Cominch-Cincpac conference held on 24–26 November 1944 at San Francisco indeed included the question of whether it is "agreeable to Cincpac to have Vice Admiral Fletcher relieved as Comnorpacfor." Just why King considered replacing Fletcher is not known, but it probably involved renewed hopes for a much greater effort in the North Pacific. In addition, Secretary of the Navy James Forrestal strongly desired to revitalize the General Board. Once combining senior-admiral "elder statesmen" and rising young stars, the Board previously served as the navy's prime advisory and policy-setting body, but by the early 1930s it had lost much of its powers to the chief of naval operations. During his tenure as Cominch-CNO, King further trimmed its responsibilities. By the fall of 1944 the General Board comprised only elderly retired admirals, not "young combat-experienced flag officers." That is understandable. No active admirals preferred such tame Washington duty when there was fighting to be done and careers to be advanced. King neither got along with Forrestal nor truly wished to resuscitate the General Board, but nevertheless at the conference he stated, "Very capable Flag Officers must be placed on the General Board as soon as possible." Fletcher, due to his war record, probably seemed an ideal candidate whom King felt could be spared from the fighting front. Furthermore, he was no intriguer likely to cause Cominch any trouble.[21]

King, also at Forrestal's order, proposed that Admiral Towers (deputy Cincpac and Nimitz's logistics czar) replace Vice Adm. William Calhoun, longtime commander of the Pacific Fleet's Service Force. Calhoun's job was in doubt because he had not adequately developed the forward bases. King and Nimitz decided that Towers would stay where he was, but Rear Adm. William "Poco" Smith would eventually relieve Calhoun. Nimitz in turn recommended that Calhoun either receive "a fighting job" or relieve Fletcher as Comnorpac. Admiral Fitch (deputy chief of naval operations for air) boldly countered on his friend Fletcher's behalf to ask whether Calhoun "would be satisfactory on the General Board." The minutes recorded that none of Nimitz's "proposals were approved." Later in the meeting King inquired directly of Nimitz what he thought now about removing Fletcher, but the minutes noted without explanation, "It was decided *not* to relieve Admiral Fletcher" (emphasis in original). Thus Fletcher stayed where he was, while in March 1945 Calhoun took over the much-shriveled South Pacific Area from Vice Adm. John Newton. By not getting dumped Fletcher must have been perceived by all as doing a satisfactory job. So Nimitz stuck with him, but their relationship suffered. Perhaps the corrosive presence of Kelly Turner (Commander, Amphibious Force, Pacific Fleet) in Nimitz's inner circle had a deleterious effect, for he never ceased reviling Fletcher for "abandoning" him at Guadalcanal.[22]

END GAME

In early 1945 Fletcher kept the heat on the Kuriles with sporadic bombardments in addition to constant small-scale air attacks. That January King revealed to him plans for "Project Hula," which involved transfer, between April and December 1945, of 250 frigates, patrol craft, minesweepers, landing craft, and similar small ships from the U.S. Navy to the USSR. These ships would give the Soviets the capability to undertake their own limited amphibious operations against Japan. Delivery would take place at an Aleutian base, so it would be necessary to bring Soviet sailors there and train them before turning over the ships. Fletcher suggested locating that base at Cold Bay and provided the necessary facilities. At Yalta in February 1945 the Allies secured Soviet agreement to enter the war with Japan following the victory over Germany, after a minimum of three months to transfer troops east and stockpile supplies in Siberia.[23]

In February–March 1945 after one of the fiercest battles of the war, Spruance's Fifth Fleet took Iwo Jima only 650 miles from Tokyo. The invasion of Okinawa in the Ryukyu Islands followed in April, and during the bloody three-month ground campaign the "Fleet that Came to Stay" fended off a blizzard of kamikaze air attacks that inflicted grievous losses in ships and personnel. The end of the war in Europe in May 1945 forecast Soviet entry into the Pacific War later that summer. The current iteration of Keelblocks recognized the Russians could take care of the Kuriles and assault Hokkaidō themselves, with American forces only needed to secure the line of communication from the United States to the Maritime Provinces. Fletcher asked for four escort carriers and stronger surface forces to screen convoys and an additional heavy bomber group to deal with air bases in the Kuriles. Nimitz suggested to King that seven escort carriers, three heavy cruisers, and twenty-six destroyers be sent. A grateful Fletcher said that would "result in the early neutralization of the entire Kurile area."[24]

These reinforcements were still in the process of moving into the Aleutians when the body blows of two atomic bombs, the Soviet declaration of war, and the USSR's speedy conquest of Manchuria caused Japan on 15 August to agree to surrender. Fletcher received orders to patrol the Japanese coast north of latitude 40° north and to clear mines in the Tsugaru Strait in anticipation of landing on Hokkaidō and in northern Honshū. The Soviets retook southern Sakhalin island and assaulted the Kuriles, with Norpac only an interested spectator. The formal Japanese surrender took place on 2 September in Tokyo Bay, presided over by General of the Army MacArthur, Fleet Admiral Nimitz, and Admiral Halsey on board the battleship *Missouri*. In the meantime Fletcher broke his flag in the amphibious command ship *Panamint*, formed his task force, and departed Adak for Japan. Traversing Tsugaru Strait on 8 September, he entered Mutsu Bay in northern Honshū, and the next day received the surrender of Japanese forces in northern Japan. Thus Fletcher, one of the few remaining old timers of 1941–42, treasured the satisfaction of directly participating in the final victory over Japan. That fall he relinquished command of the North Pacific Area and Alaskan Sea Frontier and left to join the General Board in Washington.[25]

Admiral Fletcher's tenure as Comnorpac brought recognition from the War Department and the Canadians, if not the U.S. Navy. General of the Army Hap Arnold presented the Army DSM to Fletcher, the first naval officer whom he personally decorated. The citation praised Fletcher for displaying "broad vision, tireless energy, and an unusually complete grasp of Army Air Forces tactics and capabilities in expertly solving the many problems involved in combined Army-Navy air operations." In requesting the British government to name Fletcher a Companion of the Order of the Bath (Military Division), the Royal Canadian Air Force cited him for having "worked closely and in the utmost harmony with Air Officer Commanding, Western Air Command," where Fletcher "always provided assistance when required and in mutual coast defence and shipping problems has co-operated to the fullest extent." It is interesting that Australia never showed any interest in decorating Fletcher for fighting and winning the Battle of the Coral Sea, the anniversary of which is enthusiastically celebrated as a national holiday.[26]

In December 1945 Nimitz returned to Washington to relieve Fleet Admiral King as chief of naval operations, and the post of commander in chief, U.S. Fleet, was abolished. At the same time Halsey received promotion to fleet admiral. The arguably more deserving Admiral Spruance briefly replaced Nimitz as Cincpac before becoming president of the Naval War College. Fletcher himself reported as a senior member of a General Board that was in trouble. During the war the Board mainly analyzed ship design, but in 1945 the CNO created the Ship Characteristics Board that performed the same basic task. That meant the General Board was itself a relic in a navy striving to restructure to confront the nuclear age. On 1 May 1946 Fletcher rose to chairman of the General Board, but the debate over its redundancy and mission did not concern him much longer. The navy lowered the mandatory retirement age to sixty-two, which he would attain on 29 April 1947. That March, at the behest of Secretary of the Navy Forrestal, Towers relieved Fletcher as General Board chairman. With Towers's eager concurrence, Forrestal planned to use the reorganized board to trump Nimitz, whose appointment as CNO Forrestal vigorously opposed. Glad to leave internecine navy politics behind, Fletcher retired on 1 May 1947, the same day he was advanced to four stars.[27]

Frank Jack and Martha Fletcher greatly enjoyed their life on their beloved colonial farm Araby near La Plata, in rural southeastern Maryland. However, the postwar assault on his professional reputation and wartime performance certainly saddened them. Adm. Frank Jack Fletcher died on 25 April 1973 at the age of eighty-seven and rests in Arlington National Cemetery alongside Martha, who passed away the next year.

CONCLUSION

"An Excellent, Sea-Going, Fighting Naval Officer"[1]

THE EVOLUTION OF AN IMAGE

The common perception of an historical figure is far more influential than reality itself. A sad example of that paradigm is Frank Jack Fletcher, an obscure rear admiral at the start of World War II who remained little known during that conflict despite his part in three vital victories in 1942. That year Admiral King restricted publicity of top naval tactical commanders for security reasons. The only exception was Admiral Halsey, dubbed "Bull" by exuberant reporters. The curtain of anonymity started to lift in 1943, and soon national magazines regularly featured articles on celebrated admirals, notably not Fletcher. His most prominent coverage in the wartime press came that year in a piece on the Battle of the Coral Sea written by Fletcher Pratt, a breezy popular historian well connected to Secnav's Office of Public Relations. Pratt quaintly described Fletcher, whom he evidently never met, as "an old sea dog out of Admiral Benbow's time," hardly a ringing endorsement in a modern technological war. More ominously, both Pratt and reporter Gilbert Cant completely omitted Fletcher in their 1943 accounts of Midway, but designated Raymond Spruance as the sole U.S. carrier commander in that battle. (Pratt likewise substituted Thomas Kinkaid for Fletcher in his brief treatment of the Battle of the Eastern Solomons.) In 1944 Pratt incorporated his articles, sans corrections regarding Fletcher, into the book *The Navy's War*, whose credibility Secretary Knox's handsome foreword further enhanced. Thus certain powers in Washington grudgingly allowed Fletcher public credit for Coral Sea (they could not plausibly give it to anyone else) but denied him any role in the ultimate triumph at Midway. In this regard it is useful to recall what Rear Adm. Edwin Layton said in 1983: "People on King's staff who were jealous of Fletcher." Fletcher did write the brief essay on Midway (Aubrey Fitch handled the one on Coral Sea) for the unofficial 1946 photographic history *Battle Stations! Your Navy in Action*, and Capt. Walter Karig's 1947 *Battle Report Pacific War: Middle Phase* presented Fletcher in a favorable light. That represented the pinnacle of his popular reputation. Thus Fletcher, unlike Halsey and to a lesser extent Spruance, emerged from World War II with virtually no public persona. However, three independent but closely cooperating groups sharpened their knives and determined to fill that lack with unflattering portrayals of their own.[2]

The Marine Corps never forgave Fletcher for what it considered despicable behavior in not saving Wake Island and later abandoning Guadalcanal. He came to epitomize the resentment the Corps felt toward the dominant partner, the U.S. Navy. Brig. Gen. Samuel Griffith, former marine raider and an historian, reflected their general attitude. "Haul Ass' Fletcher, that's what we used to call him. Why, that was his best maneuver. He could break all records getting away from something he didn't like." In 1943 staff officers of the First Marine Division created the unofficial "George Medal" ("Let George Do It") that symbolized their frustration over the navy's perceived failure to support them at Guadalcanal. The obverse depicted an admiral's hand dropping a hot potato to a marine. "In the original design," wrote marine historian Henry I. Shaw, "the sleeve bore the stripes of a vice admiral intended to be either" Ghormley or Fletcher, "but the final medal diplomatically omitted this identification." Even so, the intent remained completely clear. Eventually even Ghormley was rehabilitated. If not agreeing with his decisions, Griffith's 1963 Guadalcanal book showed remarkable sympathy for Comsopac, and Samuel Eliot Morison already asserted in 1949, "Admiral Ghormley did as well as anyone could have done," and that "he was the victim of circumstances." That left Fletcher the only unredeemable naval villain of Guadalcanal.[3]

Given such outright animosity, it is understandable that Marine Corps historians would not show much objectivity toward Fletcher, though to their delight, they did not have to spearhead this particular assault. Responding to complaints by Rear Adm. Milo Draemel over criticisms of Fletcher in the 1947 Marine Corps monograph *The Defense of Wake*, its author, Lt. Col. Robert Heinl, wrote his boss Brig. Gen. William E. Riley: "Morison's third volume (which has just been cleared for publication by the Secretary of the Navy) contains a devastatingly critical treatment of the Wake relief attempt, in which neither Admiral Fletcher nor Admiral Pye is spared. Considering that the Marines on Wake were the ultimately aggrieved parties of these admirals' actions, we have been sparing and meticulous almost to the point of gentleness." Morison's subsequent attack on Fletcher at Guadalcanal was equally "devastating," leading Griffith to chortle: "There wasn't much left of old 'Haul Ass' when Sam Morison got through with him."[4]

In 1942 President Roosevelt himself chose Professor Morison of Harvard University to write a "contemporaneous" *History of United States Naval Operations in World War II*. Probably no other nautical-minded historian of the era combined outstanding excellence in research with a sparkling, eminently readable style. Commissioned into the Naval Reserve, Morison received virtual carte blanche, "not to be censored" except in the "necessity of safeguarding information which might endanger national security," nor forbidden from exercising "free criticism of officers." In 1947 Secretary of the Navy James Forrestal proclaimed in his foreword to Morison's volume 1 that it "is in no sense an official history," and Morison himself was solely responsible for its contents. By default if nothing else, Morison became the U.S. Navy's voice interpreting World War II. His work constituted, according to Rear Adm. Richard Bates, the "official un-official history."[5]

Morison made the most of his unparalleled opportunity by traveling extensively to battle fronts to collect documents and interview participants. He saw combat on several occasions. Yet he did not get out to the Pacific theater until 1943, when the Allies irrevocably took the offensive. It was much more difficult for him to collect sources from the earlier period and really appreciate what it was like in 1941–42. For reasons never made clear, Morison took a strong dislike to Fletcher, whom he never met during the war itself. Heinl correctly described Morison's tone toward Fletcher in volume 3, published in 1948, as unusually harsh. Whether it was also just is addressed in chapters 2 and 3 of the present work. In 1951 Opnav solicited an official review of volume 3 from Vice Adm. Vincent Murphy, one of the Cincpac War Plans officers directly responsible for planning the relief of Wake. Murphy averred Morison's treatment did "grave injustice to Admiral Fletcher," and "some of it, both in language and in what is represented as fact, appears to be an almost studied attempt to discredit and smear this officer." Resonating within Opnav, Murphy's reproach forced Morison to moderate his tone somewhat in future printings of volume 3 and address a few minor errors. The effect was more cosmetic than substantive, but the damage to Fletcher was already done. Morison never did acknowledge, despite Murphy's authoritative testimony, that he (and Heinl) in fact misrepresented the actual circumstances behind the attempted relief of Wake. Nor did Morison ever rethink his overall sarcastic opinion of Fletcher that reached its crescendo in his discussion of the Guadalcanal landings and Savo.[6]

While Morison compiled his early volumes, Bates, the third major Fletcher critic, entered the lists. Tasked in 1946 by the CNO, Fleet Admiral Nimitz, to "study and evaluate" the naval battles of World War II, Admiral Spruance, the new president of the Naval War College, personally chose "Rafe" Bates, a conscientious researcher and naval intellectual, to run the project. Proud of his "outspoken attitude toward command failures," Bates explained that these battles revealed "many, many errors in command on both sides, and I am pointing them out as I see them, without any malice of any kind." His purpose was "solely to improve the professional judgment of the Navy." Bates never intended to write objective history, but a "critical analysis," because "without criticism the studies would have no value." Yet he often went much too far. Vice Adm. David C. Richardson, formerly one of his assistants in the Analysis Section, recalled in 1992 that his old boss "was inclined to be critical anyway; it was an ego thing. If he could find a little bit of criticism, and in almost anything that anybody does there's room for some criticism, then he would condemn." As noted, Bates's 1947 treatment of the Battle of the Coral Sea enthusiastically employed hindsight to second-guess and nitpick virtually every decision Fletcher made, though without the comprehensive U.S. and Japanese sources required for such a conclusive assessment. Much of what Bates postulated was simply wrong. Morison relied greatly on Bates's findings. They became good friends and compared notes.[7]

In compiling a "critical analysis" of the Battle of Midway, Bates faced a real conflict of interest. Spruance, his direct superior at the Naval War College, was also one of the principal Midway commanders. In the years since Pratt and Cant excluded all mention of Fletcher in that battle, a virtual cult grew around Spruance, whose superb leadership of the amphibious offensives that won the war in the Pacific ranked him arguably the finest U.S. naval combat commander of World War II. Spruance's splendid personal qualities of high intelligence, wisdom, and modesty engendered great admiration and loyalty, none more than from Bates and Morison. It seemed to them, and to many others, that the brilliance Spruance showed in the many difficult campaigns of 1943–45 must have likewise brought about the stunning success at Midway. Pratt's 1946 book *Fleet Against Japan* (foreword by Nimitz) decisively dubbed Spruance the "victor of Midway," an encomium Spruance personally refused to accept. Bates's own Midway analysis, completed in 1948, rendered Fletcher just lukewarm endorsement but accorded Spruance only copious praise. The same was true for Morison's volume 4 (1949), which relied heavily on Bates. Indeed, Bates's penultimate version was even more laudatory of Spruance. Richardson recalled how Bates "was being very critical of all sorts of actions by people in command other than Spruance—unwarranted criticisms." To the disgust of his assistants Bates reworked their draft "to extol Spruance all the more." Bates took his rewrite for final approval to Spruance, who, according to Richardson, "wouldn't have any part of Bates's glorification of him" and directed that he revise it. Given how flattering even the final product was, Spruance must have rejected a virtual hagiography of himself.[8]

Bates and Cdr. Walter Innis next tackled the disaster at Savo. The end piece of the Watchtower invasions of Guadalcanal and Tulagi proved especially fertile ground for Bates's form of critical analysis. Not surprisingly Fletcher, because he supposedly withdrew the carriers prematurely with no justification and thereby jeopardized the whole operation, emerged as Bates's chief, but by no means only, blunderer. At the same time Morison's volume 5 (1949) concurred in judging Fletcher's behavior as craven prior to Savo and sharply criticized his role in the Battle of the Eastern Solomons. The appearance of Bates's classified Savo study in 1950 hard on the heels of Morison's volumes 3, 4, and 5, along with the official Marine Corps monographs on Wake Island (1947) and Guadalcanal (1949), completed the derogatory image of Fletcher from which virtually every substantial criticism is derived. Completing their projects with such amazing speed precluded not only extensive interviews of essential participants, but also prevented the necessary distance for reflection and a measured analysis of indispensable voluminous sources such as the dispatch files. Without even a hint of an open mind, the triad of critics had already prejudged Fletcher, and by wielding hindsight with the delicacy of a battle-ax they fashioned their histories to fit a foregone conclusion.

Fletcher for his own part cooperated with Bates and Morison in the initial stages of their work. In early 1947 Spruance provided drafts of the Naval War College's Coral Sea analysis to Fletcher and Fitch for comment. Bates waited uneasily for their responses, acknowledging Fitch "should not have much to say, as he does not come in for much comment either way, but Admiral Fletcher may have some feelings." Fitch evidently never responded, but Fletcher begged off, explaining to Spruance that he had "neither time nor proper facilities" to conduct a careful review. "While not entirely agreeing in all conclusions of the War College pamphlet particularly where they have described my motives and other mental processes," he considered "it generally correct as to effects and logical as to conclusions." Contacted by Morison regarding his Midway research, Fletcher replied in December 1947: "I dislike to attempt to reconstruct these actions from memory years afterward, with no records at hand and no time for proper study and preparation of a statement." Nevertheless he was "glad to assist you in any way and am happy to say that the principal points you found confusing, if not the details, are quite clear in my mind." All Fletcher had was memory, because he tragically retained *no* papers from his 1941–42 carrier commands. Everything prior to Midway, indeed all of his personal files from September 1939, went down in the *Yorktown*. His Guadalcanal papers later disappeared because of the unusual nature of his relief as Comcrupac and CTF-11, when King did not permit him to return to Pearl for the usual change of command, but had him report directly to Seattle. In the press of wartime events Fletcher never retrieved his papers. They were simply destroyed as successive commanders cleaned out the files. It was a terrible blow to the defense of his reputation. In 1950 in reply to a proposal from Opnav for a detailed critique of Morison's volume 4, Fletcher called it, "An undertaking entirely beyond my capabilities at the present time." Such a project "would require my entire attention over a long period of time as well as my access to all records of correspondence, logs, communications, and so forth." Instead of a bitter crusade to reclaim his reputation, Fletcher preferred quiet retirement at his Maryland farm Araby. In 1964 he told his friend Vice Adm. William "Poco" Smith, "For years I have refused to commit myself to prospective authors about WWII," because "I had no notes or data and my memory is so bad that I was afraid I would give false information." Even so, the misrepresentation of his war record was painful. Admiral Dyer recalled Fletcher "was a bit disturbed by what Morison and others had said about his actions or inactions and thought that they were uninformed of the instructions under which he was operating. He would say 'They're just damn ignorant.' "[9]

Unfortunately the "ignorant" ultimately included Fletcher's once indispensable champion, Fleet Admiral Nimitz, whose opinion of Fletcher eroded dramatically by late 1944 when he tried unsuccessfully to replace him as Comnorpac. In 1946 Nimitz changed his mind regarding the carrier command at Midway, stating officially that Fletcher had only "local command" (whatever that meant), whereas Spruance exercised "local tactical command" of both TF-16 and TF-17 and thus masterminded the victory. Of course, that completely contradicted what Nimitz declared to King on 20 June 1942: "Fletcher was senior task force commander in area and responsible for activities Task Forces 16 and 17." Moreover, Spruance himself never gave any orders to TF-17. One wonders whether Nimitz's new perception of Fletcher resulted from his profound respect and affection for Spruance and his close association and friendship with Kelly Turner, who was Fletcher's chief vilifier. As shown in his work with historian E. B. Potter, Nimitz also came fully to accept the case made by the Fletcher critics. In 1963 he commented on Griffith's history of Guadalcanal: "I am sorry that so many of the Navy participants are dead—and cannot read *The Battle for Guadalcanal.* I am sure that Halsey, Turner, Ghormley, and many others would heap high praise and would not want to change one word." Significantly Nimitz did not mention Fletcher, who was very much alive. Griffith, of course, was one of Fletcher's severest critics and flayed him in his book.[10]

Only one of Fletcher's peers stood up for him publicly against the tidal wave of castigation. In 1964 Poco Smith rather reluctantly decided to write his book *Midway: Turning Point of the Pacific* primarily because he felt strongly that Morison did not do Fletcher "credit at either Midway or Coral Sea." However, Smith was no uncritical admirer of his friend Fletcher, explaining to Vice Adm. Elliott Buckmaster in 1966: "Now, Fletcher was not the smartest Task Force Commander of the war. I admit that I found him selfish at times. But he carried the full responsibility both at Coral Sea and Midway—until he turned over to Spruance after shifting to my Flagship. . . . When Fletcher turned over to Spruance, the battle was won, but we did not know it." Another of Fletcher's few defenders within the navy was Capt. Marvin E. Butcher, who in 1987 wrote the article "Admiral Frank Jack Fletcher, Pioneer Warrior or Gross Sinner?" for the *Naval War College Review*. Butcher came down strongly on the side of "pioneer warrior," emphasizing how Fletcher had to adapt to a "new technology" of naval warfare. Butcher cautioned his fellow officers that they should "hope" to "perform as well" as Fletcher, "Should we be so tested at the onset of a war for national survival." A few historians such as Robert Cressman and myself also wrote books and articles that strongly supported Fletcher, as did a biography by Stephen D. Regan. In 1999 Fletcher was inducted into the Carrier Aviation Hall of Fame on board the USS *Yorktown* (CV-10). Yet as demonstrated by the most recent judgments quoted in the introduction to this book, little real progress has been made toward his restoration.[11]

The dilemma for those who perceived the unfair treatment of Fletcher was that even they accepted the basic accuracy of Morison, Bates, and the marine historians, despite the manifest lack of objectivity. Therefore one could seemingly only make excuses for Fletcher. However, he no longer requires apologists. Newly discovered primary sources and reinterpretation of previously known documents not only question the basic assessments of the critics, but also elucidate key factual errors in their work. What they wrote is mirrored in a comment in 1869 by former Confederate Maj. Campbell Brown, stepson of Lt. Gen. Richard S. Ewell and a member of his staff. To the postwar accusations that Ewell's failure to attack Cemetery Ridge on the evening of 1 July 1863 cost the victory at Gettysburg, Brown responded: "The discovery that this lost us the battle is one of those frequently-recurring but tardy strokes of military genius of which one hears long after the minute circumstances that rendered them at the time impracticable, are forgotten." In the postwar criticisms of Fletcher's operations, it is amazing how so many crucial "minute circumstances" came to be "forgotten" or ignored.[12]

AN EVALUATION

The attack on Pearl Harbor transformed the aircraft carrier into the most powerful weapon afloat, the principal arbiter of success or failure in the naval war. Carriers led offensives, particularly in the absence of supporting land-based air, and were the principal means of defense against enemy carriers. For the very first time in naval history, fleets fought at great distances without the opposing ships ever coming within sight of one another. A task force had to be prepared, often with little or no warning, to deliver or absorb furious carrier air attacks, "pulses of firepower" according to one historian of naval tactics.[13] The battle, and effectively the whole naval campaign, could literally be lost in a span of minutes. Neither Imperial Japan nor the United States opened the war with many carriers, and the admirals who led them wielded precious assets not readily replaced. The desperate campaigns of the first year expended the carriers and aviators of both sides at a fearsome rate. Up to November 1942 the Japanese lost six of a dozen first-line carriers and light carriers, while four of six big U.S. carriers were sunk. Such carnage largely neutralized carrier participation in the naval war until the late summer of 1943, when the U.S. Navy began adding many new flattops. The next actual carrier battle did not occur until June 1944, by which time the hugely superior American naval forces were literally unstoppable.

In December 1941 Japan went to war with the preponderance of carrier and naval strength in general and swept across a vast amount of territory. However, once the U.S. carriers were committed to battle in May 1942 (as opposed to hit-and-run raids), the IJN won no more strategic victories. By November 1942, Japan's naval spearhead was blunted and the empire irretrievably committed to the defense in the Pacific. During nearly that whole period, Fletcher was the principal American carrier commander in action, leading the task forces in three of the first four carrier battles, during which six Japanese carriers were sunk for the loss of two U.S. carriers. That was when U.S. equipment was sometimes inferior, its aviators inexperienced, and the IJN never more skilled or dangerous. Expected to surmount steep odds if necessary to thwart the enemy, Fletcher was also strictly enjoined to preserve his force, for the nation could not afford to lose it. Just surviving a close engagement with Japanese carriers was a signal achievement, let alone the seizing of and retaining the strategic advantage in every battle. Wise in hindsight and severely discounting the friction of warfare, Fletcher's detractors held unreasonably high expectations of just what could be achieved under those circumstances. They believed that except for his incompetence, excessive caution, and obsession with refueling, the U.S. carriers would simply have overwhelmed the enemy, just as in 1944–45 when American naval superiority was decisive. "But," as U. S. Grant wrote in his memoirs, "my later experience has taught me two lessons: first, that things seem plainer after the events have occurred; second, that the most confident critics are generally those who know the least about the matter criticised."[14]

Displaying flexibility and nerve, Fletcher performed at Coral Sea, Midway, and even at Guadalcanal better than anyone could have reasonably anticipated. In light of the latest interpretation, Captain Butcher's label of "pioneer warrior" is certainly the most appropriate. Like other commanders forced by a superior enemy onto the defensive in the opening campaigns of a war, Fletcher had to carefully feel his way while he rapidly assimilated a new operational art. To adopt, as the critics demanded, a full-out, aggressive approach at that time and with such limited resources would have required a commander as talented as Nelson for just a chance of victory. Otherwise, total disaster was far more likely. In retrospect it appears Fletcher's well-measured style of command was actually the most appropriate for that particular time of peril, when the Pacific Fleet was outnumbered and operating on the tactical defensive even during its Guadalcanal counteroffensive. Cautious when necessary, Fletcher proved decisive when the situation called for it. As Admiral Murphy observed in 1951, "Whatever [Fletcher's] failures may have been, a reluctance to fight was not one of them." In fact, Fletcher came to epitomize the observation of Sun Tzu that the commander who knows when to fight and not to fight will be victorious.[15]

It is fascinating to consider why Fletcher, a well-seasoned naval officer but carrier neophyte lacking a technical background in naval aviation, developed or at least recognized such advanced concepts for carrier employment. He also fostered the creativity that led, in particular, to the *Yorktown*'s remarkably effective performance. The fundamental reason is that Fletcher did not already think he knew it all. Thus he was particularly receptive to advice from the younger aviator leaders, who offered fresh, cutting-edge opinions based on the latest operational flying experience. That certainly was not always the case with many senior aviators, pioneers and JCLs alike, who proved reluctant to discard years of hard-earned but obsolete aviation lore in favor of innovative new ideas. That drawback was especially evident in the climactic Battle of Midway. With much that still is mysterious, Marc Mitscher's dramatic failure with the *Hornet* remains incomprehensible in contrast to his later splendid performance in 1944–45 at the head of the Fast Carrier Task Force. Yet even with regard to 1944 one close observer, Adm. John S. Thach, recalled that Mitscher was "an old-time aviator" who "figured that he had the experience within himself and he never took to new ideas or wasn't able to recognize them as well as [Vice Adm. John] McCain." Mitscher "had his own convictions and he didn't see the need to hear from anybody else much." Likewise Miles Browning, who bungled the planning of the great TF-16 strike on 4 June, epitomized the know-it-all attitude to the extent of actively discouraging direct exchanges between Spruance and the *Enterprise* group and squadron commanders.[16]

In the chaotic first year of the Pacific War, when basic carrier doctrine was only being hammered out, perhaps the common sense of a prudent and pragmatic non-aviator like Fletcher trumped purely technical expertise. Of course, the ideal commander should possess both attributes, but in 1942 such paragons were not available while Fletcher and those like him held the line in the Pacific. The advent of the younger aviator admirals who were far more qualified in carriers meant that Fletcher's time leading carrier task forces would be brief. Those who found fault with Fletcher perceived in him a lack of offensive spirit—an impression carefully nurtured by King, Turner, Frederick Sherman, Morison, and Bates. As historian Martin Stephens said of the Royal Navy in *The Fighting Admirals*, much was forgiven a commander if it was thought he was aggressive. With Fletcher, truly a fighting admiral who never lost a battle, nothing was forgiven and very little applauded.[17]

Task Organizations

1) 17 December 1941: Task Force 14, Rear Adm. Frank Jack Fletcher

TG-14.1—Escort—Rear Adm. Aubrey W. Fitch
TU-14.1.1—Rear Admiral Fitch
Saratoga (CV-3)
TU-14.1.2—Rear Admiral Fletcher
Astoria (CA-34), *Minneapolis* (CA-36), *San Francisco* (CA-38)
TU-14.1.3—Desron Four—Capt. Cornelius W. Flynn
Selfridge (DD-357), *Henley* (DD-391), *Blue* (DD-387), *Bagley* (DD-386), *Helm* (DD-388), *Ralph Talbot* (DD-390), *Mugford* (DD-389), *Jarvis* (DD-393), *Patterson* (DD-392)
TG-14.2—Train—Cdr. Clifton A. F. Sprague
TU-14.2.1—Commander Sprague
Tangier (AV-8)
TU-14.2.2—Cdr. William B. Fletcher Jr.
Neches (AO-5)

2) 6 January 1942: Task Force 17, Rear Adm. Frank Jack Fletcher

TG-17.1—Escort—Rear Admiral Fletcher
TU-17.1.1—Cruisers—Capt. Elliott B. Nixon
Louisville (CA-28), *St. Louis* (CL-49)
TU-17.1.2—Carrier—Capt. Elliott Buckmaster
Yorktown (CV-5)
TU-17.1.3—Destroyers—Capt. Frank G. Fahrion
Hughes (DD-410), *Sims* (DD-409), *Walke* (DD-416), *Russell* (DD-414)
TG-17.2—Train (Convoy 1005)—Capt. Schuyler Mills
Lassen (AE-3), *Kaskaskia* (AO-27), SS *Lurline*, SS *Monterey*, SS *Matsonia*, SS *Jupiter*
TG-17.3—Troops—Brig. Gen. Henry L. Larsen, USMC

3) 1 February 1942: Task Force 17, Rear Adm. Frank Jack Fletcher

TG-17.1—Striking Group—Rear Admiral Fletcher
TU-17.1.1—Cruisers—Capt. Elliott B. Nixon
Louisville (CA-28), *St. Louis* (CL-49)
TU-17.1.2—Carrier—Capt. Elliott Buckmaster
Yorktown (CV-5)
TG-17.2—Support Group—Capt. Frank G. Fahrion
Hughes (DD-410), *Sims* (DD-409), *Russell* (DD-414), *Walke* (DD-416)

TG-17.3—Fueling Group—Cdr. Houston L. Maples
Sabine (AO-25), *Mahan* (DD-364)

4) 16 February 1942: Task Force 17, Rear Adm. Frank Jack Fletcher

TG-17.2—Cruisers—Rear Adm. William Ward Smith
Astoria (CA-34), *Louisville* (CA-28)
TG-17.4—Destroyers—Capt. Charles P. Cecil
Anderson (DD-411), *Hammann* (DD-412), *Sims* (DD-409), *Hughes* (DD-410), *Walke* (DD-416)
TG-17.5—Carrier—Capt. Elliott Buckmaster
Yorktown (CV-5)
TG-17.6—Fueling Group—Cdr. Harry R. Thurber
Guadalupe (AO-32), *Russell* (DD-414)

5) 10 March 1942: Task Force 11, Vice Adm. Wilson Brown

TG-11.1—Rear Adm. Frank Jack Fletcher
TG-11.2—Rear Adm. Thomas C. Kinkaid
Minneapolis (CA-36), *San Francisco* (CA-38), *Indianapolis* (CA-35), *Pensacola* (CA-24)
TG-11.4—Capt. Alexander R. Early
Phelps (DD-360), *Dewey* (DD-349), *Dale* (DD-353), *Macdonough* (DD-351), *Hull* (DD-350), *Clark* (DD-361), *Bagley* (DD-386), *Walke* (DD-416)
TG-11.5—Capt. Frederick C. Sherman
Lexington (CV-2), *Yorktown* (CV-5)
TG-11.7—Rear Adm. John G. Crace, RN
TU-11.7.1—Rear Admiral Crace
HMAS *Australia*, *Chicago* (CA-29), *Astoria* (CA-34), *Louisville* (CA-28)
TU-11.7.2—Capt. Charles P. Cecil
Anderson (DD-411), *Sims* (DD-409), *Hammann* (DD-412), *Hughes* (DD-410)

6) 2 April 1942: Task Force 17, Rear Adm. Frank Jack Fletcher

TG-17.2—Rear Adm. William Ward Smith
TU-17.2.1—Rear Admiral Smith
Astoria (CA-34), *Portland* (CA-33), *Pensacola* (CA-24), *Chester* (CA-27)
TU-17.2.2—Capt. Charles P. Cecil
Anderson (DD-411), *Hammann* (DD-412), *Hughes* (DD-410),
TG-17.3—Rear Adm. John G. Crace, RN
TU-17.3.1—Rear Admiral Crace
HMAS *Australia*, *Chicago* (CA-29)
TU-17.3.4—Cdr. Francis X. McInerney
Perkins (DD-377), *Lamson* (DD-367)

TG-17.5—Capt. Elliott Buckmaster
TU-17.5.1—Captain Buckmaster
Yorktown (CV-5)
TU-17.5.2—Capt. Gilbert C. Hoover
Morris (DD417), *Sims* (DD-409), *Russell* (DD-414)
TG-17.6—Capt. Ralph H. Henkle
Platte (AO-24), *Walke* (DD-416)

7) 6 May 1942: Task Force 17, Rear Adm. Frank Jack Fletcher

TG-17.2—Attack Group—Rear Adm. Thomas C. Kinkaid
TU-17.2.1—Rear Adm. Kinkaid
Minneapolis (CA-36), *New Orleans* (CA-32)
TU-17.2.2—Rear Adm. William W. Smith
Astoria (CA-34), *Chester* (CA-27), *Portland* (CA-33)
TU-17.2.4—Capt. Alexander R. Early
Phelps (DD-360), *Dewey* (DD-349), *Farragut* (DD-348), *Aylwin* (DD-355), *Monaghan* (DD-354)
TG-17.3—Support Group—Rear Adm. John G. Crace, RN
TU-17.3.1—Rear Admiral Crace
HMAS *Australia*, *Chicago* (CA-29), HMAS *Hobart*
TU-17.3.4—Cdr. Francis X. McInerney
Perkins (DD-377), *Walke* (DD-416)
TG-17.5—Air Group—Rear Adm. Aubrey W. Fitch
TU-17.5.1—Rear Admiral Fitch
Yorktown (CV-5), *Lexington* (CV-2)
TU-17.5.4—Capt. Gilbert C. Hoover
Morris (DD-417), *Anderson* (DD-411), *Hammann* (DD-412), *Hughes* (DD-410)
TG-17.6—Fueling Group—Capt. John S. Phillips
Neosho (AO-23), *Tippecanoe* (AO-21), *Sims* (DD-409), *Worden* (DD-352)
TG-17.9—Search Group—Cdr. George H. DeBaun
Tangier (AV-8)

8) 19 May 1942: Task Force 17, Rear Adm. Frank Jack Fletcher

TG-17.2—Rear Adm. William Ward Smith
Astoria (CA-34), *Portland* (CA-33)
TG-17.4—Capt. Gilbert C. Hoover
Morris (DD-417), *Anderson* (DD-411), *Hammann* (DD-412), *Russell* (DD-414), *Aylwin* (DD-355)
TG 17.5—Capt. Elliott Buckmaster
Yorktown (CV-5)
TG 17.6—Rear Adm. Aubrey W. Fitch
Chester (CA-27), *Barnett* (AP-11), *George F. Elliott* (AP-13)

9) 2 June 1942: Carrier Striking Forces, Rear Adm. Frank Jack Fletcher

Task Force 16, Rear Adm. Raymond A. Spruance
TG-16.2—Cruisers—Rear Adm. Thomas C. Kinkaid
TU-16.2.1—Capt. William D. Chandler
Northampton (CA-26), *Pensacola* (CA-24), *Atlanta* (CL-51)
TU-16.2.2—Rear Admiral Kinkaid
Minneapolis (CA-36), *New Orleans* (CA-32), *Vincennes* (CA-44)
TG-16.4—Destroyers—Capt. Alexander R. Early
Desron One—Captain Early
Phelps (DD-360), *Dewey* (DD-349), *Worden* (DD-352), *Aylwin* (DD-355), *Monaghan* (DD-354)
Desron Six—Capt. Edward P. Sauer
Balch (DD-363), *Conyngham* (DD-371), *Maury* (DD-401), *Benham* (DD-397), *Ellet* (DD-398), *Monssen* (DD-436)
TG-16.5—Air—Capt. George D. Murray
Enterprise (CV-6), *Hornet* (CV-8)
TG-16.6—Tankers—Capt. Ralph H. Henkle
Platte (AO-24), *Cimarron* (AO-22)
Task Force 17, Rear Admiral Fletcher
TG-17.2—Cruisers—Rear Adm. William W. Smith
Astoria (CA-34), *Portland* (CA-33)
TG-17.4—Destroyers—Capt. Gilbert C. Hoover
Morris (DD-417), *Anderson* (DD-411), *Hammann* (DD-412), *Russell* (DD-414), *Hughes* (DD-410)
TG-17.5—Air—Capt. Elliott Buckmaster
Yorktown (CV-5)

10) 7 August 1942: Task Force 61 (Expeditionary Force), Vice Adm. Frank Jack Fletcher

TG-61.1—Air Support Force—Rear Adm. Leigh Noyes
TU-61.1.1 (TF-11)—Vice Admiral Fletcher
Cruisers—Rear Adm. Carleton H. Wright
Minneapolis (CA-36), *New Orleans* (CA-32)
Destroyers—Capt. Samuel B. Brewer
Phelps (DD-360), *Macdonough* (DD-351), *Worden* (DD-352), *Farragut* (DD348)
Air—Capt. Dewitt C. Ramsey
Saratoga (CV-3)
TU-61.1.2 (TF-16)—Rear Adm. Thomas C. Kinkaid
Cruisers—Rear Adm. Mahlon S. Tisdale
Portland (CA-33), *North Carolina* (BB-55), *Atlanta* (CL-51)

Destroyers—Capt. Edward P. Sauer
Balch (DD-363), *Maury* (DD-401), *Gwin* (DD-433), *Benham* (DD-387), *Grayson* (DD-435)
Air—Capt. Arthur C. Davis
Enterprise (CV-6)
TU-61.1.3 (TF-18)—Rear Adm. Leigh Noyes
Cruisers—Capt. Charles H. McMorris
San Francisco (CA-38), *Salt Lake City* (CA-25)
Destroyers—Capt. Robert G. Tobin (Comdesron Twelve)
Farenholt (DD-491), *Lang* (DD-399), *Sterett* (DD-407), *Stack* (DD-406)
Air—Capt. Forrest P. Sherman
Wasp (CV-7)
TG-61.2 (TF-62)—Amphibious Force—Rear Adm. Richmond Kelly Turner
Transport Group X-Ray (62.1)—Capt. Lawrence F. Reifsnider
Transdiv Afirm (62.1.1)—Capt. Paul S. Theiss
Fuller (AP-14), *American Legion* (AP-35), *Bellatrix* (AK-20)
Transdiv Baker (62.1.2)—Capt. Charlie P. McFeaters
McCawley (AP-10), *Barnett* (AP-11), *George F. Elliott* (AP-13), *Libra* (AK-53)
Transdiv Cast (62.1.3)—Captain Reifsnider
Hunter Liggett (AP-27), *Alchiba* (AK-23), *Fomalhaut* (AK-22), *Betelgeuse* (AK-28)
Transdiv Dog (62.1.4)—Capt. Ingolf N. Kiland
Crescent City (AP-40), *President Hayes* (AP-39), *President Adams* (AP-38), *Alhena* (AK-26)
Transport Group Yoke (62.2)—Capt. George B. Ashe
Transdiv Easy (62.2.1)—Captain Ashe
Neville (AP-16), *Zeilin* (AP-9), *Heywood* (AP-12), *President Jackson* (AP-37)
Transdiv Twelve (62.2.2)—Cdr. Hugh W. Hadley
Colhoun (APD-2), *Gregory* (APD-3), *Little* (APD-4), *McKean* (APD-5)
Fire Support Group Love (62.3)—Capt. Frederick L. Riefkohl
Quincy (CA-39), *Vincennes* (CA-44), *Astoria* (CA-34), *Hull* (DD-350), *Dewey* (DD-349), *Ellet* (DD-398), *Wilson* (DD-408)
Fire Support Group Mike (62.4)—Rear Adm. Norman Scott
San Juan (CL-54), *Monssen* (DD-436), *Buchanan* (DD-484)
Minesweeper Group (62.5)—Cdr. William H. Hartt Jr.
Hopkins (DMS-13), *Trever* (DMS-16), *Zane* (DMS-14), *Southard* (DMS-10), *Hovey* (DMS-11)

Screening Group (62.6)—Rear Adm. Victor A. C. Crutchley, RN
HMAS *Australia*, HMAS *Canberra*, HMAS *Hobart*, *Chicago* (CA-29)
Desron Four—Capt. Cornelius W. Flynn
Selfridge (DD-357), *Patterson* (DD-392), *Ralph Talbot* (DD-390), *Mugford* (DD-389), *Jarvis* (DD-393), *Blue* (DD-387), *Helm* (DD-388), *Henley* (DD-391), *Bagley* (DD-386)
Landing Force (62.8)—Maj. Gen. Alexander A. Vandegrift
Guadalcanal Group (62.8.1)—Major General Vandegrift
Tulagi Group (62.8.2)—Brig. Gen. William H. Rupertus

11) 24 August 1942: Task Force 61, Vice Adm. Frank Jack Fletcher

TG-61.1 (TF-11)—Vice Admiral Fletcher
TF-44—Cruisers—Rear Adm. Victor A. C. Crutchley, RN
HMAS *Australia*, HMAS *Hobart*
TG-11.2—Heavy Cruisers—Rear Adm. Carleton H. Wright
Minneapolis (CA-36), *New Orleans* (CA-32)
TG-11.4—Destroyers—Capt. Samuel B. Brewer
Phelps (DD-360), *Macdonough* (DD-351), *Dewey* (DD-349), *Worden* (DD-352), *Farragut* (DD-348), *Patterson* (DD-392), *Bagley* (DD-386)
TG-11.5—Air—Capt. Dewitt C. Ramsey
Saratoga (CV-3)
TG-61.2 (TF-16)—Rear Adm. Thomas C. Kinkaid
TG-16.2—Cruisers—Rear Adm. Mahlon S. Tisdale
Portland (CA-33), *North Carolina* (BB-55), *Atlanta* (CL-51)
TG-16.4—Destroyers—Capt. Edward P. Sauer
Balch (DD-363), *Maury* (DD-401), *Benham* (DD-397), *Ellet* (DD-398), *Grayson* (DD-435), *Monssen* (DD-436)
TG-16.5—Air—Capt. Arthur C. Davis
Enterprise (CV-6)
TG-61.3 (TF-18)—Rear Adm. Leigh Noyes
TF-18—Cruisers—Rear Adm. Norman Scott
San Juan (CL-54), *San Francisco* (CA-38), *Salt Lake City* (CA-25), *Selfridge* (DD-357)
Screen—Capt. Robert G. Tobin
Farenholt (DD-491), *Aaron Ward* (DD-483), *Buchanan* (DD-484), *Lang* (DD-399), *Sterett* (DD-407), *Stack* (DD-406)
Carrier—Capt. Forrest P. Sherman
Wasp (CV-7)—Captain Sherman

12) 30 August 1942: Task Force 61, Vice Adm. Frank Jack Fletcher

TG-61.1 (TF-11)—Vice Admiral Fletcher

TG-11.2—Cruisers—Rear Adm. Carleton H. Wright

Minneapolis (CA-36), *New Orleans* (CA-32), *North Carolina* (BB-55), *Atlanta* (CL-51)

TG-11.4—Destroyers—Capt. Samuel B. Brewer

Phelps (DD-360), *Dewey* (DD-349), *Farragut* (DD-348), *Macdonough* (DD-351), *Worden* (DD-352), *Monssen* (DD-436), *Grayson* (DD-435)

TG-11.5—Air—Capt. Dewitt C. Ramsey

Saratoga (CV-3)

TG-61.2 (TF-17)—Rear Adm. George D. Murray

TG-17.2—Cruisers—Rear Adm. Howard H. Good

Northampton (CA-26), *Pensacola* (CA-24), *Salt Lake City* (CA-25), *San Diego* (CL-53)

TG-17.4—Destroyers—Cdr. Arnold E. True

Morris (DD-417), *Russell* (DD-414), *Anderson* (DD-411), *Mustin* (DD-413), *O'Brien* (DD-415), *Patterson* (DD-392), *Bagley* (DD-386)

TG-17.5—Air—Capt. Charles P. Mason

Hornet (CV-8)

TG-61.3 (TF-18)—Rear Adm. Leigh Noyes

Cruisers—Rear Adm. Norman Scott

San Francisco (CA-38)

TF-44—Rear Adm. Victor A. C. Crutchley, RN

HMAS *Australia*, HMAS *Hobart*, *Phoenix* (CL-46), *Selfridge* (DD-357)

Screen—Capt. Robert G. Tobin

Farenholt (DD-491), *Aaron Ward* (DD-483), *Buchanan* (DD-484), *Lang* (DD-399), *Sterett* (DD-407), *Stack* (DD-406)

Carrier—Capt. Forrest P. Sherman

Wasp (CV-7)

Notes

INTRODUCTION

1. Nathan Miller, *War At Sea*, 211; Kennedy, *Freedom from Fear*, 549; Beach, *Salt and Steel*, 126; Murray and Millett, *A War to be Won*, 210. The accusations that Fletcher was known as a "traitor" and that he was tried and convicted of "cowardice" appear in Schom's *The Eagle and the Rising Sun*, 324, 335–36, 339, 362.

2. Morison, *History of United States Naval Operations in World War II*, 1:ix.

3. Letter Rear Adm. Oscar Pederson, USN (Ret.), to Lundstrom (13 October 1974).

4. Interview of Adm. Frank Jack Fletcher by Walter Lord (17 February 1966), courtesy of the late Walter Lord.

CHAPTER 1. THE WORLD TURNED UPSIDE DOWN

1. Deck logs *Minneapolis* (CA-36) and *Astoria* (CA-34) 4–13 December 1941, National Archives, Record Group 24 (RG-24). Morison, *United States Naval Operations* 3:212, erred in keeping Fletcher in the *Minneapolis* on 7 December, whereas he switched to the *Astoria* on 4 December. Fletcher corrected Morison on 9 October 1948 (in Adm. Frank Jack Fletcher Papers), but Morison never amended his text. Description of Pearl Harbor on 13 December 1941 from Abercrombie and Pratt, *My Life to the Destroyers*, 9–10. For an early assessment of the Pearl Harbor attack, see message 081015 December 1941 Cincpac to Opnav, in Cincpac Secret and Confidential Message File (hereafter CSCMF), RG-38, microfilm roll 521.

2. Interview of Adm. Frank Jack Fletcher by Dr. Gordon Prange (17 September 1966), courtesy of Robert J. Cressman. Letter Commander, Battle Force, Pacific Fleet (Combatfor), to Cincpac, Appointment of temporary vice admirals (30 July 1941), in RG-313, Cincpac Secret Correspondence, box 4498, noted, "Commander Battleships has under his command the major fighting power of the U.S. Fleet."

3. For the development of the Japanese carrier force, see Peattie, *Sunburst*, chapters 3 and 6. For Japanese naval strategy, Evans and Peattie, *Kaigun*, chapters 8 and 13. Both are superb.

4. The principal source for Cincpac's strategic views and decisions is: War Plans, Cincpac Files, Captain Steele's "Running Estimate and Summary," also known as the "Cincpac Greybook" (hereafter Greybook), in the Operational Archives, Naval Historical Center (hereafter NHC), microfilm NRS-1971-58. McMorris quote from Briefed Estimate of the Situation as of 10 December, in Greybook, 8.

5. For the life and family of Frank Jack Fletcher, see first of all his papers at the American Heritage Center, University of Wyoming–Laramie. Regan's *In Bitter Tempest* is based largely on these papers. The Fletcher Papers are reasonably comprehensive until 1939. Also useful are the available extracts from his service record (6132 Fletcher, F. J.) furnished under a freedom of information request by the National Personnel Records Center. For Fletcher's first fifteen years in the navy he officially signed his name "Frank J. Fletcher." The first known document signed "Frank Jack Fletcher" is an application dated 8 February 1917 requesting leave to get married. Thereafter he used all three names. "Jack" was the maiden name of Fletcher's grandmother Nancy Jack Fletcher, and Fletcher's father's name was Thomas Jack Fletcher. For Frank Friday Fletcher see Reynolds, *Famous American Admirals*, 122–23. For general information on the movements and promotions of naval officers, U.S. Navy, Bureau of Navigation, *Navy Directory of the U.S. Navy and U.S. Marine Corps Officers* (1920–1942) and U.S. Navy, Bureau of Navigation/Bureau of Naval Personnel, *Register of Commissioned and Warrant Officers of the U.S. Navy and Marine Corps* (1906–1947).

6. National Archives, RG-24, deck log *Dale* (DD-4); letters Secretary of the Navy to Ens. F. L. (*sic*) Fletcher, "Gunnery Trophy awarded for Spring Battle Practice 1911" (17 July 1911) and Frank Friday Fletcher to Thomas Jack Fletcher (12 October 1911), in Fletcher Papers. On the Veracruz expedition, see Sweetman, *The Landing at Veracruz*, and Fletcher Papers.

7. On the *Maggie*, Medical Officer, USS *Margaret*, to Squadron Commander, Patrol Force, Sanitary Inspection of Vessel and Personnel (10 December 1917); CO [Commanding Officer], USS *Margaret*, to Secretary of the Navy (Secnav), Report of Material Readiness of Ship for War (20 December 1918), both in Fletcher Papers. Buranelli, *Maggie of the Suicide Fleet*, quote, 18. For the *Benham* (DD-49), see her deck log in RG-24, and in RG-45, Subject File, box 1037, USS *Benham*, which includes her war diary, combat reports, and Judge Advocate General, Court of Inquiry to inquire into the Collision of the USS *Benham* and the USS *Jarvis*, July 26, 1918 (28 August 1918). Fletcher's Navy Cross citation was the boilerplate version given to wartime skippers who had not sunk any U-boats.

8. Text of the *New Mexico*'s commendations in Fletcher Papers. Duncan, *Rickover*, 61–62. Capt. Frederick A. Edwards, oral history, 219–22; and Rear Adm. Charles E. Loughlin, oral history, 34, 36–37 (quote).

9. Sweetman, 164. Trimble, *Admiral William A. Moffett*, 47–48.

10. Richardson and Dyer, *On the Treadmill to Pearl Harbor*, 125–26.

11. Nineteen members of the class of 1906 made flag rank before 7 December 1941 and three more during the war. For Fleet Problem XXI see RG-313, Records Relating to the U.S. Navy Fleet Problems I to XXII, 1923–1941, National Archives, microfilm M964. Fletcher's quote is from roll 36. Richardson and Dyer, 223.

12. For the general activities of Crudiv Six, see Cincus to Secnav, Annual Report for the period 1 July 1940–30 June 1941 (15 August 1941) in U.S. Congress, *Pearl Harbor Attack* (hereafter PHA), part 33, 1243–78; and Commander, Scouting Force, Annual Report 1 July 1940–30 June 1941, in NHC, microfilm NRS-403. Letter Wilson Brown to Chester Nimitz (14 November 1941), in Vice Adm. Wilson Brown Papers; message 272107 November 1941 Bunav to Cincpac, CSCMF, roll 508.

13. Messages 272337 November 1941 Opnav to Cincpac and Commander in Chief, Asiatic Fleet (Cincaf), PHA, part 33, 1176; 280447 Cincpac to CTF-2 and Commander, Fourteenth Naval District (Com 14), 280627 Cincpac to Opnav, 282153 CTF-8 to Cincpac, 282200 Cincpac to CTF-8, 290348 Cincpac to CTF-8, all November 1941, in CSCMF, roll 521.

14. Messages 040237 Cincpac to CTF-3, 020750 Cincaf to Opnav (info Cincpac), 031850 Opnav to Cincpac, all December 1941, in CSCMF, roll 521. For Halsey's trip to Wake, see Comairbatfor war diary, and for TF-12, Comcruscofor war diary, both in RG-38, war diaries.

15. *Seattle Times* (22 November 1942); Vice Adm. George C. Dyer, oral history, 182; letter Dyer to Lundstrom (19 January 1977).

16. Letter William Ward Smith to Elliott Buckmaster (23 April 1966), in Rear Adm. Oscar Pederson Papers; Prange, *Miracle at Midway*, 97; William Ward Smith, *Midway*, 61.

17. For the development of naval aviation: Turnbull and Lord, *History of United States Naval Aviation*; Van Deurs, *Wings for the Fleet*; and Reynolds, *Admiral John H. Towers*.

18. Richard K. Smith, *First Across!*, 128, 136–37, 158, 183.

19. Wilson, *Slipstream*, 138. On the Morrow Board, Turnbull and Lord, 249–58.

20. Cdr. Thomas G. W. Settle's memo to captain, Naval Air Station (NAS) Lakehurst (31 May 1939), in Robinson and Keller, *"Up Ship!"*, 200–202. The outspoken Settle (USNA 1919) qualified as a lighter-than-air naval aviator in 1927 and retired a vice admiral. Letter Vice Adm. H. S. Duckworth to Lundstrom (13 May 1972). On JCLs, Reynolds, *Towers*, 223; also King and Whitehill, *Fleet Admiral King*, 187–93.

21. For the early development of carrier tactics, Wildenberg, *All the Factors of Victory*.

22. Chief, Bureau of Medicine and Surgery, to Chief, Bunav, Physical Examination for flying of F. J. Fletcher, Commander, USN (12 March 1928), noted "defective visual acuity" and "depth perception" (Fletcher Papers). Reynolds, *Towers*, 284.

23. For the evolution of U.S. carrier aviation from the 1920s up to 7 December 1941: Hone, Friedman, and Mandeles, *American and British Aircraft Carrier Development 1919–1941*; Grossnick, *U.S. Naval Aviation 1910–1995*; Larkins, *U.S. Naval Aircraft 1921–1941*; Lundstrom, *The First Team*; MacDonald, *Evolution of*

the Aircraft Carrier; Reynolds, *Towers*; and Wildenberg, *Destined For Glory*. See also Hone, "The Evolution of Fleet Tactical Doctrine in the U.S. Navy, 1922–1941." The carrier tactical documents in force on 7 December 1941 were: Commander, Aircraft, Battle Force, Pacific Fleet: Current Tactical Orders and Doctrine, U.S. Fleet, Aircraft Volume One—Carrier Aircraft—USF-74 (Revised) and Current Tactical Orders, Aircraft Carriers, U.S. Fleet, USF-77 (Revised), both issued in March 1941, in Operational Archives, NHC.

24. Halsey and Bryan, *Admiral Halsey's Story*; and Potter, *Bull Halsey*.

25. Richardson and Dyer, 220–22. Cincpac to Secnav, Annual Report for 1 July 1940–30 June 1941 (15 August 1941), PHA, part 33, 1243–78, including 1245, 1257, the establishment of permanent task forces. The later reorganization and establishment of the task forces is covered in Pacific Fleet Conf. Letter 14CL-41 (31 October 1941), in PHA, part 33, 1291–94.

26. Morison, *United States Naval Operations*, 3:236–37. For Fitch's movements, see Commander, Carrier Division One, war diary, 7–15 December 1941.

27. Vice Adm. Vincent R. Murphy, USN (Ret.), a Cincpac war planner in 1941, wrote an official review of Morison's volume 3 (7 September 1951) in a letter to Rear Adm. Charles C. Hartman, DCNO (Administration), in the Office Files of the Director of Naval History, box 20. Murphy stated that Kimmel's choice of Fletcher was "not perfunctory by any means" and that "this whole account is a travesty of history and should not go unchallenged." Prodded here as in other instances by Murphy's comments, Morison added in later editions of volume 3 that "today, with the record before us, it is evident that the failure to relieve Wake resulted from Admiral Pye's decision not to risk the loss of any of his three precious carriers and not from any lack of aviation knowledge." Letter Kimmel to Stark (15 December 1941), Adm. Harold R. Stark Papers. Kinkaid, *Four Years of War in the Pacific: A Personal Narrative*, 30–31, an uncompleted memoir in the Adm. Thomas C. Kinkaid Papers.

CHAPTER 2. "TO RETRIEVE OUR INITIAL DISASTER"

1. Greybook, 4, 19, 28, 30; message 091812 December 1941 Opnav to Cincpac, CSCMF, roll 522. Briefed Estimate of the Situation as of 10 December, Greybook, 8.

2. Edward S. Miller, *War Plan Orange*, 238–46; Cressman, *A Magnificent Fight*, chapters 1–2. Quotes from the text of Cincpac to CNO, Wake Island—Policy in regard to construction and protection of (18 April 1941), courtesy of Robert J. Cressman. Cincpac to Opnav, Survey of Conditions in Pacific Fleet (26 May 1941), in PHA, part 33, 1208–14.

3. For the heavy bomber mystique and the Philippines, see Harrington, "A Careless Hope," quote from Henry Stimson, 223; memo, Marshall to Stark (12 September 1941), in PHA, part 33, 1170; and Bartsch's exhaustive study *December 8, 1941*.

4. Message 171458 October 1941 Opnav to Cincpac, CSCMF, roll 521. Cincpac to Comairbatfor, Commander, Patrol Wing (Compatwing) Two, Preparations to base aircraft at Wake (10 November 1941), in RG-313, Cincpac Operation Orders, box 19. Kimmel testimony, in PHA, part 22, 397.

5. For Wake Island operations, see especially Cressman, *Magnificent Fight*; quote from Edward Miller, 289; McMorris testimony, in PHA, part 22, 530.

6. *William Ward Burrows* (AP-6) deck log. Messages 080142 Com 14 to *William Ward Burrows*, 100915 *William Ward Burrows* to Com 14, 101425 Com 14 to *William Ward Burrows*, all December 1941, CSCMF, roll 522. CO, *William Ward Burrows* AP-6, Enemy Action against Johnston Island, December 15, 1941, Report of, in Ships History, NHC. On the radar transported in the *William Ward Burrows*, letter Commandant, Fourteenth Naval District, to Cincpac, Radar Installation on Wake (27 November 1941), in RG-313, Cincpac Secret Correspondence, box 4853.

7. For the operations of TF-12, see the war diaries of Comcruscofor, Commander, Scouting Force, Pacific Fleet (Comscofor), and the *Lexington* (CV-2); for TF-8 see the Comairbatfor war diary.

8. Draft operations order in Greybook, 41–44, also memo on page 75.

9. Comscofor war diary, 11 December 1941. Abercrombie and Pratt, 8. Messages 110453, 112125, 121707, 130823, and 140106 December 1941 Cincpac to CTF-12, CSCMF, roll 521; 111900 and 112244 December 1941 CTF-12 to Cincpac, 121657 December 1941 CTF-12 to CTF-9, all CSCMF, roll 522; 130039 December 1941 CTF-12 to Cincpac, CSCMF, roll 523.

10. Beatty, "The Background of the Secret Report." Kinkaid memoir, 29. Message 130707 December 1941 Cincpac to NAS Wake, CSCMF, roll 521.

11. Greybook, 45. USS *Tangier* (AV-8) deck log. For the *Tangier*, see Wukovits, *Devotion to Duty*, 64–70. "Mixed bag," from letter Rear Adm. Berton A. Robbins to Dr. Lloyd J. Graybar (11 November 1976); also Rear Adm. George H. DeBaun, USN (Ret.), to Graybar (1 August 1976), both in Dr. Lloyd J. Graybar Papers. Heinl, "We're Headed for Wake," is useful but unreliable as to chronology and must be used with caution. For the diversion of the *William Ward Burrows*, see her deck log, which cites message 132230 December 1941 from Com 14.

12. McMorris testimony, PHA, part 22, 530; Kimmel testimony, PHA, part 22, 396. Cunningham with Sims, *Wake Island Command*, 104–5. Letter Com 14 to NAS Wake, Evacuation of personnel and unloading (17 December 1941), in RG-313, Cincpac Secret Correspondence, box 4499.

13. Greybook, 13 December 1941.

14. Greybook, 13 December 1941; McMorris testimony, PHA, part 22, 530–32; Murphy letter to Hartman (7 September 1951).

15. Rochefort testimony, in PHA, part 23, 680–83. On 11 December Washington had estimated ten Japanese carriers were in the Pacific, of which six in several groups were reported east of the longitude of Wake. Counting these carriers, there were in home waters or "in position for offensive operations," about seven battleships, twelve cruisers, and twenty to forty destroyers. Opnav warned that the "Mandates bases also may be serving strong striking groups including [those] carriers which operate Eastern Pacific." Message 120040 December 1941 Opnav to Cincpac, CSCMF, roll 522.

16. Brown, *From Sail to Carrier Task Force*, chapter "The Battle of Salamau-Lae," 6, an unpublished memoir; also Brown's review of Morison's volume 3, *Rising Sun in the Pacific*, 5, both in Brown Papers. Cincpac Op-Ord 40-41 (2000, 13 December 1941) in RG-313, Op-Ords. According to an intelligence memo submitted on 14 December 1941 to Brown, B-17 bombers might be moved up (presumably to Midway) to bomb the Marshalls to "divert attention when we move in to attack," Brown Papers. Basic source for the Jaluit diversion is CTF-11 (Comscofor) to Cincpac, Operations of Task Force Eleven December 14–27, 1941 (26 December 1941), in RG-313, Action Reports.

17. On Brown's appearance while superintendent of the Naval Academy, see letter Bennett to Graybar (17 August 1976), Graybar Papers. Bennett (USNA 1941) described how Brown's "head jerked from some kind of malady. It wasn't reassuring." Brown memoir, 6, Brown Papers. Appreciation of orders received from the commander in chief, U.S. Pacific Fleet, on December 14, estimate of the situation and preliminary conclusions (15 December 1941), appendix to CTF-11 action report (26 December 1941). Vice Admiral Pye, Discussion of decision to retire task forces 14 and 11 (22 December 1941), PHA, part 23, 1062.

18. Ugaki, *Fading Victory*, 47–48, 54; Goldstein and Dillon, *Pearl Harbor Papers*, 164–65, 227, 230.

19. McMorris, PHA, part 22, 531. For the oilers, see Wildenberg's *Gray Steel and Black Oil.*

20. Comcardiv One war diary. On the *Saratoga*'s condition, see interview of Cdr. Alfred M. Pride (former executive officer, *Saratoga*) by Buaer (16 June 1942), NHC, 4; Vice Adm. Paul D. Stroop, oral history, 69–70; Stroop letter to Graybar (19 January 1977), and Capt. Corben C. Shute, USN (Ret.), to Graybar (27 July 1976), both in Graybar Papers. The *Saratoga*'s total fuel capacity prior to her 1942 refit was about 2,365,000 gallons (56,300 barrels), roughly 360,000 gallons (8,700 barrels) of which were required for stability and not used since commissioning. When she entered Pearl on 15 December, she had about 400,000 gallons still on board, but could not draw upon them because of the layout of the fuel tanks, the fear of losing suction, and the salt water in the tanks. For an excellent analysis of the *Saratoga* as a carrier, see Stern, *The Lexington Class Carriers.*

21. *Astoria* deck log, 4 December 1941.

22. Cincpac Op-Ord 39-41 (15 December 1941). Primary sources for TF-14 in the Wake relief are: CTF-14 to Cincpac, Report of Operations 16–29 December 1941 (28 December 1941); Comcardiv One war diary, 16–29 December 1941; deck logs of the ships; the messages in CSCMF; and the remarkable collection of letters from TF-14 veterans and others written in 1976–77 to Dr. Lloyd J. Graybar of Eastern Kentucky University for his excellent article, "American Pacific Strategy after Pearl Harbor." Messages 152325, 160029 Cincpac to Comdesron 5, 160355 Cincpac to CTF-11, all December 1941, CSCMF, roll 521. Cincpac Op-Ord 41-41 (15 December 1941) to USS *Drayton.*

23. Kimmel testimony, in PHA, part 22, 456.

24. McMorris testimony, PHA, part 22, 531. Japan, *Senshi Sōsho*, 38:102, 196–97, 298. Messages 142231 December 1941 Com 14 to Cincaf, CSCMF, roll 523; 150555 December 1941 Cincpac to CTF-11, CSCMF, roll 521.

25. Op-Ord 39-41, Greybook, 47. Vice Admiral Murphy recalled in 1951 that it was "his impression" Fletcher was "given a definite day to fuel so that all ships would be full for the run in and, possibly, for the run out," letter to Hartman (7 September 1951). Likewise Vice Adm. W. W. Smith thought Fletcher's fueling was geared to the operations plan (Op-Plan), (c. 1950) review of Morison's volume 3 (Office Files of the Director of Naval History, box 20). Review by Rear Adm. John D. Hayes, USN (Ret.), of W. Scott Cunningham's *Wake Island* in *Shipmate* (September–October 1961). The fuel capacity of the *New Orleans*–class cruisers was only about 14,900 barrels as opposed to 20,000 for the other heavy cruisers. Admiral Hayes once told Frank Uhlig Jr. that nobody really knew the extreme range of any ship (Frank Uhlig, personal communication with Lundstrom). Pacific Fleet Confidential Letter 18CL-41, 16 December 1941, "Excessive Fuel Consumption," in PHA, part 24, 1493. Because peacetime steaming efficiency was grossly overestimated, Kimmel became deeply concerned over his depleted fuel stocks. On 16 December he informed Stark that the fleet had used more than four hundred thousand barrels of oil in just one week. That exhausted his issue stock and compelled him to dip into his reserve. He urgently requested four more *Cimarron*-class oilers in December and another four in January just to transport fuel from the West Coast to Pearl, not to mention what was required to fuel task forces at sea. That comprised all of the modern oilers then in service in the U.S. Navy. Message 162137 December 1941 Cincpac to Opnav, CSCMF, roll 521.

26. Text of CTF-14 Op-Ord 1-41 (19 December 1941) illustrated in Wukovits, *Devotion to Duty*. See also the letters Capt. John F. Miller, USN (Ret.), to Dr. Lloyd Graybar (23 July 1976 and 27 September 1976), Graybar Papers, that also include a copy. Message 180336 December 1941 Cincpac to NAS Wake, CSCMF, roll 521; Cincpac Op-Ord 42-41 to CTF-8 (18 December 1941).

27. *Saratoga* deck log; letter V. R. Murphy to Hartman (7 September 1951). When dealing with naval ships, "full capacity" is always considered 95 percent of the actual volume of the fuel tanks. The *Saratoga* left San Diego on 8 December fueled to about 73 percent of full capacity (68 percent of her radius oil) and virtually ran out of fuel eight days later after several days of high-speed runs.

28. Letter Rear Adm. Ralph E. Mills, USN (Ret.), to Dr. Lloyd Graybar (12 September 1977), Graybar Papers.

CHAPTER 3. THE WAKE "FIASCO"

1. Messages 152149 Opnav to Cincpac, 152301 Cincpac to Opnav, 160050 Opnav to Cincpac, all December 1941, in Greybook, 50–51. Messages 162105 Secnav to Cincpac and 170057 Cincpac to Secnav, both December 1941, in CNO Top Secret "Blue" File microfilm (hereafter CNO TS Blue File). Messages 171307 Bunav to Cincpac and 171358 Secnav to Combatfor, both December 1941, in CSCMF, roll 523. Message 171307 relayed Admiral Nimitz's desire to retain the Cincpac staff in their present assignments. The message was seen and initialed by every staff department.

2. Message 180328 December 1941 Cincpac to Pacific Fleet, CSCMF, roll 521. Quote on Pye from Vice Adm. William W. Smith, USN (Ret.), original draft of Midway book, 62, in Vice Adm. William Ward Smith

Papers. Kimmel described Pye on 26 May 1941 as "able, vigorous, and loyal," PHA, part 33, 1210. Quote from King in Whitehill memo, 31 July 1949, in Fleet Adm. Ernest J. King Papers, box 7, Naval War College (hereafter NWC). On Pye bringing in his own staff, message 180407 December 1941 Cincpac to Opnav and Bunav, CSCMF, roll 521. That move was not popular as witnessed by the file copy that bears the notation "Horse Sh!" Letter Rear Adm. M. F. Draemel to Gen. W. E. Riley, USMC (28 January 1948), in S. E. Morison Office Files, box 18, Operational Archives, NHC.

3. Rochefort testimony, PHA, part 23, 680–83. Secret Message 161615 December 1941 Opnav to Cincpac, CSCMF, roll 523. The estimate gave Japanese carrier plane strengths as *Akagi*, *Kaga*, *Shōkaku*, *Zuikaku* sixty planes each, *Sōryū* and *Hiryū* forty-two planes each, and *Hōshō* and *Ryūjō* thirty planes each. Messages 172133 and 172301 December 1941 Cincpac to CTF-11 and CTF-14, in CSCMF, roll 521.

4. Messages from the 5th Carrier Division and 1st Destroyer Squadron war diaries in Goldstein and Dillon, 228–30, 248–49; Rear Adm. Kusaka Ryūnosuke, Nagumo's chief of staff, expressed his regrets for having broken radio silence, 166.

5. Comairbatfor (CTF-8) war diary. Message 191850 December 1941 Cincpac to CTF-11 and CTF-14, CSCMF, roll 521. Cincpac Op-Ord 43-41 (18 December 1941) sending TF-17 to Midway and Op-Ord 45-41 (22 December 1941) for TF-13 to go to Johnston and Palmyra.

6. CTF-11 action report (26 December 1941) and appendix "Appreciation of orders received . . ." (15 December 1941). Message 182146 December 1941 Cincpac to CTF-11 and CTF-14, in CSCMF, roll 521. Adm. Harry D. Felt, oral history, 104.

7. *Saratoga* deck log, 18 December 1941; Pride interview by Buaer (16 June 1942); Comairbatfor, Current Tactical Orders Aircraft Carriers U.S. Fleet, USF-77 (Revised), March 1941. Messages 182146 and 200339 December 1941 Cincpac to CTF-11 and CTF-14, in CSCMF, roll 521. CTF-14 action report (28 December 1941).

8. Message 202300 December 1941 Wake to Com 14 and Cincpac, CSCMF, roll 523. *Saratoga* deck log, 20/21 December 1941.

9. Estimate by Admiral Pye on 20 December, Greybook, 76; Pye's Discussion of decision to retire task forces 14 and 11 (22 December 1941), in PHA, part 23, 1062–63; Letter Draemel to Riley (28 January 1948), in Morison Office Files, box 18. Messages 202337 and 21057 December 1941 Cincpac to CTF-8, CTF-11, and CTF-14; 210147 December 1941 Cincpac to Opnav; all in CSCMF, roll 521.

10. Message 210157 December 1941 Cincpac to CTF-8, CTF-11, and CTF-14. Sprague's comments appear on his copy of CTF Op-Ord 1-41 (19 December 1941) in Wukovits. Letter DeBaun to Graybar (1 August 1976), Graybar Papers.

11. CTF-11 report (26 December 1941). Vice Adm. George Dyer's account in Stillwell, *Air Raid Pearl Harbor!*, 4546. Dyer was executive officer of the *Indianapolis*. Vice Adm. Wilson Brown, memo to Chief of Staff [Capt. M. C. Robertson] (21 December 1941), in Brown Papers. Also Brown testimony, in PHA, part 23, 763.

12. Cressman, *Magnificent Fight*, 176–77; Japan, *Senshi Sōsho*, 38:175, 191. Letter Rear Adm. Edwin T. Layton to Graybar (29 August 1976), Graybar Papers.

13. McMorris, PHA, part 22, 531. Morison, *United States Naval Operations*, 3:243–44. For Fletcher's response, see his letter of 19 October 1948 to Morison, in Fletcher Papers. Lt. Col. Robert D. Heinl, author of *The Defense of Wake*, the official Marine Corps account, wrote (11 February 1948) that on 22 December 1941 the TF-14 destroyers had "adequate fuel." According to their "average daily consumption" in the previous week the destroyers "had from 11 to 12 days' fuel on hand" and could be fueled from the oiler and the cruisers. Of course Heinl did not take into account that the destroyers would burn much more fuel if compelled to steam at high speed for extended periods. Morison wrote that a destroyer "could easily surpass 15,000 gallons *per diem* in a running fight," but even he vastly understated fuel expenditure under such conditions. Admiral Murphy commented in his official review of Morison's volume 3, "The footnote figures on fuel are misleading." At twenty-five to thirty knots, "The fuel consumption might well be three times the figures given," letter to Hartman (7 September 1951).

14. Fuel figures from deck logs on the individual ships. Fuel expenditure data from the invaluable U.S. Fleet, War Service Fuel Consumption of U.S. Naval Surface Vessels, FTP-218 (1 September 1945), NHC, microfilm NRS-275.

15. Letter Vice Adm. Ralph Earle Jr., USN (Ret.) to Graybar (1 August 1976), Graybar Papers. Of the seven former TF-14 destroyer officers (including Earle) whom Graybar contacted in 1976, all but one agreed with Fletcher fueling the destroyers on 22–23 December 1941 before approaching Wake.

16. FTP-218, 1.

17. CTF-14 report (28 December 1941). Letter Capt. Richard D. Shepard, USN (Ret.), to Graybar (29 July 1976), in Graybar Papers. Fueling on 22 December went as follows (amounts in gallons):

	Fuel on hand	% of full	Time Z-11	Delivered*
Bagley	80,639	53	0604–0816	52,459
Ralph Talbot	96,939	64	1005–1059	34,860
Henley	103,018	68	1223–1338	39,938
Jarvis	90,918	60	1421–1601	55,650

*For the *Ralph Talbot* and *Jarvis*, the amount of fuel delivered tallies with the entry in the *Neches* deck log. The *Henley*'s log notes the receipt of 39,938 gallons, whereas the *Neches* shows 30,060 gallons, possibly a misprint. The *Bagley*'s log shows 52,459 gallons delivered, but the figure for fuel on hand required interpolation because of errors in arithmetic.

18. Wildenberg, *Gray Steel*, 171; Pye quote, PHA, part 22, 549. For fueling deficiencies see documents in File S55 in RG-313, Cincpac Secret Correspondence, box 4853, and in RG-19, Bureau of Ships, box 699. Letter Shepard to Graybar (29 July 1976) and Capt. Joel C. Ford, USN (Ret.), to Graybar (2 August 1976), in Graybar Papers. On 10 February 1942 the Pacific Fleet issued its first general instructions for fueling at sea in its Tactical Bulletin 2-42.

19. Messages 220901 and 220917 December 1941 Cincpac to CTF-8, CTF-11, and CTF-14, CSCMF, roll 521.

20. In condemning Fletcher for not taking direct action to prevent Wake's fall, Morison, *United States Naval Operations*, 3:251, cited four "conflicting" orders Pye supposedly sent on 22 December. The first called for him to push the *Saratoga* ahead to within two hundred miles of Wake and attack any ships located there, but Pye soon canceled that move. Pye is said then to have directed Fletcher to send the *Tangier* completely *unescorted* to evacuate Wake, but again countermanded the order. Morison even declared such obvious "irresolution" at Pearl all the "more reason why Fletcher should have pressed forward to meet the enemy"! These four dispatches never existed, but arose from Morison's faulty interpretation of recollections of Pye's 20 December (21 December, east longitude) orders that merely canceled Brown's Jaluit attack and forbade Fletcher from providing air cover to the *Tangier*. Nothing was said about sending Sprague ahead without escorting destroyers or having him evacuate Wake. The Cincpac Message File shows that Pye actually issued no other orders to TF-14 until late on 21 December (22 December, Wake time).

21. For Ensign Murphy's flight, Cressman, *Magnificent Fight*, 168–70, 174–76. Cunningham's 20 December 1941 report that Murphy delivered is in PHA, part 24, 1467–78. Pye's Discussion of decision to retire task forces 14 and 11 (22 December 1941), PHA, part 23, 1063.

22. Message 221035 December 1941 Cincpac to CTF-8, CTF-11, and CTF-14, CSCMF, roll 521.

23. CTF-14 report (28 December 1941).

24. Messages 221621 and 221649 December 1941 Cincus to CTF-14, in CSCMF, roll 521. For the invasion of Wake, Cressman, *Magnificent Fight*, chapter 8. Morison, *United States Naval Operations*, 3:247, wrongly assumed that Gotō's 6th Cruiser Division cruised on its own 150–200 miles east of Wake, "as if tempting Admiral Fletcher to come in." Actually those cruisers operated close to the island.

25. Message 221801 December 1941 CTF-11 to CTF-14, CSCMF, roll 523; CTF-11 report (26 December 1941).

26. Message 221941 December 1941 Cincpac to CTF-8, CTF-11, and CTF-14, in CSCMF, roll 521.

27. Message 221706 December 1941 Opnav to Cincpac, Greybook, 72.

28. Sources on the deliberation of recalling the Wake relief expedition: (1) Estimate by Admiral Pye regarding enemy investing Wake—0700—December 22, 1941, Greybook, 77–78; (2) Decision by Admiral Draemel as to action regarding enemy investing Wake—0700—22 December 1941, Greybook, 82; Pye's Discussion of decision to retire task forces 14 and 11 (22 December 1941), PHA, part 23, 1062–64.

29. Message 221800 December 1941 Wake to Cincpac and Com 14, CSCMF, roll 523. Estimate of Captain McMorris as to action regarding enemy investing Wake (0800 December 22), Greybook, 79–81.

30. William Ward Smith, 13–14, whose account is based on information from Vice Adm. Vincent Murphy. Message 222256 December 1941 Cincpac to Opnav, Greybook, 72, noted: "Wake is a liability. In view present extensive operations I am forced to conclude that risk of one task force to attack enemy vicinity of Wake is not justifiable." Smith recalled he was "astounded" that morning to learn of the recall. Kimmel told Smith, "You and I are not in on this one. Keep out of it." Kimmel wrote Smith that he had only restrained himself with "difficulty." "I kept my mouth shut. I am sorry now that I did so." Smith, 14; letter Kimmel to Smith (2 November 1964), Smith Papers. Message 221952 December 1941 Wake to Cincpac and Com 14, in CSCMF, roll 523. For the surrender of Wake, see Cressman, *Magnificent Fight*, chapter 9.

31. Letter Capt. Jack E. Gibson, USN (Ret.), to Graybar (10 August 1976), Graybar Papers. Interview of Rear Adm. Harry Smith, USN (Ret.), by Dr. Stephen D. Regan (13 July 1986), furnished by Dr. Regan. Morison, *United States Naval Operations*, 3:254. Letter Fletcher to W. W. Smith (7 December 1964), Smith Papers, and also Smith's undated (c. 1950) review of Morison's volume 3 in Office Files of the Director of Naval History, box 20. Kinkaid memoir, 48. Hoyt's *How They Won the War in the Pacific*, 33, pointed out that Lord Horatio Nelson had the luxury of having his enemy in sight, and had Fletcher failed to win a "clear-cut victory," he would have "undoubtedly been court-martialed." Morison also cited Adm. Joseph M. Reeves, a former commander in chief of the U.S. Fleet and carrier expert who served on the Roberts Commission. Reeves derided the relief as a "disgrace to the United States Navy" and exclaimed, "By Gad! I used to say a man had to be both a fighter and know how to fight. Now all I want is a man who fights." Kinkaid lashed back in his unpublished memoir by describing the Nelson quote as "beyond publishable comment" and that Reeves "should have known better." Vice Admiral Murphy likewise decried such histrionics. "Responsible and competent officers are not paid to play to the galleries—the stakes are too high," Murphy letter to Hartman (7 September 1951).

32. Lt. Col. R. D. Heinl, USMC, Notes on an interview with Adm. Aubrey W. Fitch, USN (Ret.) (13 June 1947), USMC Historical Section, via Cressman. On Douglas, see letter Fletcher to W. W. Smith (7 December 1964), Smith Papers. Letter Vice Adm. P. D. Stroop to Graybar (19 January 1977), Graybar Papers.

33. *Saratoga* deck log. Here is the schedule of fueling on 23 December (amount in gallons):

	Fuel on hand	% full	Time Z-11	Delivered
Selfridge	125,799	67	0545–0811	60,060
Mugford	94,188	62	0839–1037	44,982
Patterson	89,923	59	1107–1236	44,520
Helm	108,620	71	1302–1418	40,530
Blue	96,421	63	1432–1618	55,398

The amount of fuel delivered is from the *Neches* deck log. Message 230839 December 1941 Cincpac to CTF-14, CSCMF, roll 521. For the reinforcement of Midway, see *Tangier* deck log.

34. Morison, *United States Naval Operations*, 3:243–44.

35. Lundstrom, *First Team*, 35.

36. Japan, *Senshi Sōsho*, 38:202. Yokohama Air Group *Kōdōchōsho* (Combat Log), 22 December 1941, Japan, War History Office, via Dr. Izawa Yasuho.

37. Sherman, *Combat Command*, 74.

38. Greybook, 81.

39. Letter Murphy to Hartman (7 September 1951).

40. Kinkaid memoir, 43–44. Stroop to Graybar (19 January and 17 June 1977), in Graybar Papers.

41. Pye's Discussion of decision to retire task forces 14 and 11 (22 December 1941), PHA, part 23, 1063. Commander, Scouting Force (Brown) war diary, 22 December 1941; Commander, Aircraft, Battle Force (Halsey), war diary, 22 December 1941. Morison, *United States Naval Operations*, map, 3:238–39, wrongly placed TF-11 bearing 125 degrees, 744 miles from Wake. This was on Wake's side of the date line, which Brown actually never crossed, and is in fact more than 230 miles west of Brown's actual position. Fitch interview by Heinl (13 June 1947).

42. Chitose Air Group *Kōdōchōsho*, 23 December 1941, via Dr. Izawa Yasuho.

43. Letter Nimitz to W. W. Smith (27 December 1964), letter Rear Adm. Harold C. Train, USN (Ret.), to W. W. Smith (30 December 1964), both in Smith Papers; also Smith's undated (c. 1950) review of Morison's volume 3. On Nimitz's arrival, see also Rear Adm. Harold C. Train, oral history, Columbia University, 267–68. Admiral Stroop came to believe that the recall was "wise," commentating that a desperate carrier battle at that time would likely have proven disastrous for the U.S. Navy. Letter Stroop to Dr. Lloyd Graybar (17 June 1977), Graybar Papers. Kinkaid memoir, 49.

44. Memo FDR to Capt. J. R. Beardall (16 December 1941), Franklin D. Roosevelt, Papers as President, Map Room File, box 36. Letter Vice Adm. Frank E. Beatty, USN (Ret.), to Harry Elmer Barnes (21 December 1966), Dr. Harry Elmer Barnes Papers. Churchill, *The Second World War*, 667. Messages 271810 December 1941 Opnav to Cincpac, and 280147 December 1941 Cincpac to Opnav, both Greybook, 120. Pye testimony, PHA, part 23, 1062–70. Whitehill memo (31 July 1949), King Papers, box 7, NWC.

45. The exceptions are Graybar, "American Pacific Strategy after Pearl Harbor"; Cressman, *Magnificent Fight*; and Urwin's *Facing Fearful Odds*, which have brief but favorable treatments of Fletcher.

46. In Washington, Rear Adm. John Towers had as early as 16 December recognized the need for more than one carrier to be committed to the relief of Wake (Reynolds, *Towers*, 370).

47. Heinl, *Defense of Wake*, 37, averred that Fletcher was to be at Wake on "23 December, east longitude date," but he never acknowledged that Kimmel had postponed D-Day for twenty-four hours. However, Heinl's bibliography, 64, cited Cincpac Op-Ord 39-41, which clearly called for Fletcher's arrival on 24 December, east longitude date. Morison knew the actual D-Day as well as Heinl. It appears in his papers at the NHC. Yet he chose not to discuss it at all in volume 3, *The Rising Sun in the Pacific*, and indeed adduced no evidence of any kind of relief plan other than simply a mad rush to Wake. Morison also declared (*United States Naval Operations*, 3:237) that Brown's Jaluit diversion was to take place "on or before 22 December," but that phrase appeared nowhere in Brown's orders and the day itself was wrong. In fact according to Cincpac Op-Ord 40-41, Brown was to attack "as near to local daylight D minus one day as practicable." When Kimmel postponed D-Day by twenty-four hours, D–1 Day became 23 December east longitude date (22 December, Hawaiian time), so Morison, like Heinl, cited the wrong date. Brown enjoyed discretion to switch targets or call off the attack altogether, but not to change the day. In the first edition (1948) of volume 3, 237, Morison judged the "failure to relieve Wake" resulted from "poor seamanship and a want of decisive action, both on Fletcher's part and on Pye's." The charge of "poor seamanship" arose from his caustic perception of Fletcher's fueling delays, very unfair because the whole fleet suffered such woes in December 1941. Subsequent editions omitted that reference, but Fletcher's reputation was already harmed. Because of Vice Admiral Murphy's criticisms, Morison attempted to backpedal by singling out Pye's caution as the reason why TF-14 did not fight for Wake and asserting, wrongly, that Fletcher was "ordered by dispatch to fuel when and where he did because it was hoped to have Admiral Brown's task force join him." The timing of the refueling arose from planning prior to Fletcher's departure and not to any subsequent Cincpac "dispatch." In 1963 in the popular condensation *Two-Ocean War*, 138, Morison changed his mind, even largely exonerating Pye. "This fiasco, however, was more the fault of Admiral Fletcher, who wasted time on unnecessary refueling, when he should have pressed on to relieve Wake."

48. Letter Kimmel to W. W. Smith (2 November 1964), Smith Papers.

49. Layton, *And I Was There*, 334, 340–41. Layton, the former Cincpac intelligence officer, died early in the process of writing his memoir, which coauthors Capt. Roger Pineau, USNR (Ret.), and John Costello completed. The Rear Adm. Edwin T. Layton Papers at the NWC show that he personally wrote very little of *And I Was There*. He spoke of the Wake relief on 11 May 1983 to his coauthors, but simply stated that he did not wish to delve into the matter of Fletcher and Wake, "Because I am not first hand with that." However after Layton's death, Pineau and Costello drew upon the sentiments Layton expressed in his 1970 oral history that upbraided Pye as a "Nervous Nellie," who recalled the Wake relief "the minute he had an excuse" and "deprived the Navy of the chance to catch the enemy unawares in much the same circumstances as we were able to do at Midway six months later." Their discussion of the relief completely confused the original concept, which certainly sought no "decisive" battle, with the "bait" role Wake was to assume *after* it was reinforced. Layton was actually ambivalent over the prospects of success by the Wake relief. By the mid 1970s after reading extensively in Japanese sources, he had certainly changed his mind about a December 1941 battle between U.S. and Japanese carriers and offered unequivocal opinions about Japanese carrier superiority at that time. He wrote often of the value of the early 1942 raids in preparing the U.S. carriers for the eventual crucial battles to regain the initiative in the Pacific. For an example of Layton's revised thinking on Wake, see Layton to Graybar (29 August 1976), Graybar Papers, in which he stated "the decision to abandon Wake was the wiser decision." Yet in 1983 Layton told his coauthors that Pye should have gone ahead to "recover some national morale" and intimated that Fletcher "had a yellow streak down his back."

50. Beach, 65–67.

51. Manchester, *Goodbye, Darkness*, 169.

52. Letter Murphy to Hartman (7 September 1951).

CHAPTER 4. TO SAMOA WITH A CARRIER

1. Message 292229 December 1941 Cincpac to All Ships Present in Hawaiian area, CSCMF, roll 524.

2. For Nimitz, see above all Potter, *Nimitz*. A short biographical sketch, this author's, is in Bradford, *Quarterdeck and Bridge*, 327–44. On Knox's January offer to Nimitz, Potter, *Nimitz*, 3–5. For Stark's comment to King, King, 357. Copies of the lamentably few surviving letters from Nimitz to his wife Catherine are in the Fleet Adm. Chester W. Nimitz Papers.

3. The principal biography of King is Thomas B. Buell, *Master of Sea Power*. See also the chapter by Love in his edited collection, *The Chiefs of Naval Operations*, 137–79. For King becoming Cominch, Furer, *Administration of the Navy Department in World War II*, 126. King's comment on "fixers" is from the Muir memorandum (31 July 1949), in King Papers, NWC.

4. On Samoa, Coletta, *United States Navy and Marine Corps Bases, Overseas*, 332–40. Greybook, 50; message 142346 December 1941 Opnav to Cincpac, CSCMF, roll 523.

5. Greybook, 53–67, 73, 121. Messages 220301, 281631, 300035 Cincpac to Opnav, 261908 and 291431 Opnav to Cincpac, all December 1941, in CSCMF, roll 524.

6. Message 301740 December 1941 Cincus to Cincpac, in Greybook, 121.

7. Messages 310123 and 310515 Cincpac to Opnav, 300501 Cincpac to Bunav, all December 1941, CSCMF, roll 524; 040131 January 1942 Cincpac to Opnav, CSCMF, roll 1.

8. Messages 302005 Cincpac to CTF-11, 310315 and 310703 Cincpac to Comcruscofor, all December 1941, in CSCMF, roll 524. Comcruscofor war diary. Potter, *Nimitz*, 19–21.

9. Officer Bio File, NHC. USS *Yorktown* (CV-5), deck log.

10. Frank and Harrington, *Rendezvous at Midway*, and Cressman, *That Gallant Ship*.

11. Conversation with Rear Adm. William N. Leonard, USN (Ret.), 30 August 1996. Bill Leonard fought as a fighter pilot in the *Yorktown* and was assistant operations officer of TF-38 in 1944–45 and later a carrier captain and a carrier division commander. Officer Bio File, NHC. Clark with Reynolds, *Carrier Admiral*, 77–78, 82–83.

12. Letter Rear Adm. William N. Leonard to Lundstrom (27 August 1996); conversations 30 August 1996 and 25 September 1997. He described Clark as a "congenital nose-out-of-joint guy." Clark, 77–78, complained that Buckmaster was "too easygoing" and put "too much faith in his heads of departments." Rear Adm. Hubert E. Strange, the *Yorktown*'s aerologist, wrote in *A Full Life*, 58–59, that Clark "tried to run the ship with the chief master-at-arms" and Buckmaster "kept the peace and avoided confrontation." Smiley comment in a questionnaire to Robert Cressman.

13. Cincpac Op-Ord 48-41 to CTF-17 (31 December 1941), in RG-313, Cincpac Op-Ord File. Letter CTF-17 to Cincpac (5 January 1942) and enclosed TF-17 Op-Ord 1-42 (5 January 1942), in RG-313, Op-Ord File, Crudiv Four.

14. Conversation in 1997 with Capt. Vane M. Bennett, USN (Ret.).

15. Cincpac Op-Ord 48-41; CTF-17 5 January 1942 letter. Messages 042049 Cincpac to Cominch, 090625 Cincpac to CTF-17, both January 1942, in CSCMF, roll 1.

16. Messages 062046 Comcruscofor to Cincpac and 090625 Cincpac to CTF-17, January 1942, in CSCMF, roll 1. TF-17 (Comcruscofor) war diary. CTF-17 to Cincpac, Reinforcement of Samoa (5 February 1942), in Op-Ord File, Crudiv Four.

17. Messages 021748 Cominch to Cincpac, 022235 Cincpac to Cominch, both January 1942, in Greybook, 122.

18. Greybook, 123–35, 143–53. Message 140411 January 1942 Cincpac to Cominch, Greybook, 153.

19. Message 090445 January 1942 Cincpac to Cominch, Greybook, 142. Halsey and Bryan, 85. Comairbatfor (CTF-8) war diary. Cincpac Op-Ord 3-42 (9 January 1942) and Cincpac Op-Plan 4-42

(9 January 1942). Messages 090445 January 1942 Cincpac to Cominch, Greybook, 142; 110735 January 1942 Cincpac to CTF-8 and CTF-17, CSCMF, roll 1.

20. Ugaki, 61–62.

21. Message 111520 January 1942 Navsta [Naval Station] Tutuila to Opnav and Cincpac, CSCMF, roll 1. Comcrubatfor (CTF-14) war diary. Greybook, 156. Messages 170121 Cincpac to Navsta Samoa and 170529 Cincpac to Cominch, both January 1942, in CSCMF, roll 2. Japan, *Senshi Sōsho*, 38:306, 49:39. Ugaki, 73–74.

22. TF-17 war diary. CTF-17 report (5 February 1942). For the refueling incident, see CTF-17 (Comcruscofor) to Cincpac, Damage sustained by USS *Yorktown* while fueling from USS *Kaskaskia* (22 January 1942) in RG-313, Cincpac Flag Files; and CO USS *Kaskaskia*, Fueling at sea operations conducted by this vessel with USS *Yorktown* on January 17, 1942 (30 March 1942), in RG-313, Cincpac Secret Correspondence, S55, box 4840. Fletcher was surprised to learn the *Kaskaskia*'s commanding officer, Cdr. Walter L. Taylor, supposedly gave the helmsman responsibility for maintaining position rather than conning the ship himself. Later Taylor vehemently denied that was the case, explaining that he "regretted" that Fletcher "apparently inferred such" from his "somewhat hastily prepared despatch." He blamed the placement of hose connections on the *Yorktown*.

CHAPTER 5. THE FIRST COUNTERATTACK

1. CTF-8 to CTF-17, Letter of Instructions (17 January 1942), in Op-Ord File, CTF-8. Message 221825 January 1942 CTF-8 to Cincpac, CSCMF, roll 2. Halsey flew this message, a summary of his plans, to be radioed from Samoa.

2. CTF-8 Letter of Instructions (17 January 1942), in Op-Ord File, CTF-8. TF-17 Op-Ord 2-42 (25 January 1942), in Op-Ord File, Crudiv Four.

3. Messages 172135 Com 14 to Cominch, Cincpac, and all CTFs; 202145 Cincpac to all CTFs; both January 1942 in CSCMF, roll 2. Messages 202150 Cominch to Cincpac, and 212217 Cincpac to CTF-11, both January 1942, in Greybook, 179–80. Messages 220055 Cincpac to all CTFs, and 242000 *San Francisco* to Cincpac, both January 1942, in CSCMF, roll 2.

4. Clark, 83–84.

5. Messages 230941 CTF-17 to CTF-8, 232115 CTF-8 to CTF-17, 241135 CTF-17 to Cincpac and CTF-8, and 242257 CTF-17 to Cincpac, January 1942, in CSCMF, roll 2.

6. Layton, "24 *Sentai*—Japan's Commerce Raiders," 53–61.

7. Comscofor (CTF-11) war diary. Greybook, 183. Messages 252227 Cincpac to all CTFs; 270143 Com 14 to Cominch, Cincpac, and all CTFs; both January 1942, in CSCMF, roll 2. Messages 271945 Cominch to Cincpac and 280311 Cincpac to CTFs, both January 1942, Greybook, 193. Letter Nimitz to Catherine Nimitz (29 January 1942), in Nimitz Papers.

8. Interview of Cdr. Leonard J. Dow by Buaer (29 September 1942), Operational Archives, NHC. Fleet Adm. William F. Halsey Jr., Life of W. F. Halsey Jr.—Memoir, 333, in Virginia Historical Society; also Halsey and Bryan, 89. TF-8 Op-Ord 1-42 (28 January 1942), Op-Ord File, CTF-8.

9. CTF-8 to CTF-17, Letter of Instructions No. 2 (28 January 1942), in Op-Ord File, CTF-8.

10. CTF-17 to TF-17, Modification of Attack Plan (29 January 1942), in Op-Ord File, Crudiv Four. CO USS *Yorktown* to Cincpac, Attack of *Yorktown* Air Group on Jaluit, Mili, and Makin in Marshall and Gilbert Islands—Report of (5 February 1942), in Action Report File.

11. CTF-17 to Cincpac, Report of Engagement January 31, 1942 (9 February 1942), Action Report File. Message 220137 January 1942 Cincpac to all CTFs, CSCMF, roll 2. CTF-17 Modification of Attack Plan (29 January 1942).

12. Japan, *Senshi Sōsho*, 38:368, 370–71, 384, 405.

13. Comairbatfor (CTF-8) war diary. For convenience despite crossing the date line Fletcher kept TF-17 on west longitude time unlike Halsey's TF-8, which skipped ahead a day to east longitude time. Here to avoid confusion, the dates for TF-17 will be converted to east longitude time. Message 302000 January 1942 CTF-8 to Cincpac, Greybook, 203. TF-17 war diary.

14. Greybook, 194. Message 310138 January 1942 Cincpac to CTFs, CSCMF, roll 3.

15. TF-17 war diary. Halsey and Bryan, 89–90.

16. The title for this section comes from the *Enterprise* Plan of the Day, 1 February 1942. Basic source on TF-8 raids, CTF-8 to Cincpac, Action in the Marshall Islands, 1 February 1942 (9 February 1942); also Lundstrom, *First Team*, 63–77. For TF-17: CTF-17 to Cincpac (9 February 1942); CO USS *Yorktown* to Cincpac (5 February 1942), which includes the Report of the Air Group Commander and of the pilots who participated in the Jaluit, Makin, and Mili raids; CO USS *Louisville* to Cincpac, Engagement Report (6 February 1942); CO USS *St. Louis* to CTF-17, Report of Operations January 6 to February 6, 1942 (6 February 1942); Comdesdiv Three to CTF-17, Report of Action (7 February 1942); CO USS *Hughes* to Cincpac, Action Report (6 February 1942); CO USS *Sims* to Cincpac, Action off Mili, Marshall Islands, report of (5 February 1942); CO USS *Walke* to Comdesdiv Three, Report of Action 31 January 1942 (5 February 1942); CO USS *Russell* to Cincpac, Action in Gilbert and Marshall Islands, participation in (5 February 1942); TF-17 war diary; *Yorktown* deck log; also Lundstrom, *First Team*, 77–80. Strange, 60; Leonard letter to Lundstrom (6 June 1997); *Yorktown* report (5 February 1942).

17. *Yorktown* report (5 February 1942). Japan, *Senshi Sōsho*, 38:392–93.

18. *Yorktown* report (5 February 1942), TF-17 war diary, Comdesdiv Three report (7 February 1942).

19. TF-17 war diary, CTF-17 report (9 February 1942), *Yorktown* report (5 February 1942), Comdesdiv Three report (7 February 1942). Clark, 85.

20. *Yorktown* report (5 February 1942); Japan, *Senshi Sōsho*, 38:392.

21. Comdesdiv Three report (7 February 1942); *Hughes* report (6 February 1942); *Russell* report (5 February 1942); *Sims* report (5 February 1942); Japan, *Senshi Sōsho*, 38:400–401; Clark, 85.

22. CTF-17 report (9 February 1942); message 010040 February 1942 CTF-17 to CTF-8, CSCMF, roll 3; *Louisville* report (6 February 1942).

23. *Yorktown* report (5 February 1942), *Yorktown* deck log; Frank and Harrington, 61; message 010133 February 1942 CTF-17 to CTF-8, CSCMF, roll 3; Japan, *Senshi Sōsho*, 38:401.

24. CTF-17 report (9 February 1942); messages 010221 CTF-8 to CTF-17 and 010736 CTF-8 to Cincpac (info CTF-17), February 1942, in CSCMF, roll 3. Potter, *Halsey*, 47. To the cry, "Haul ass with Halsey," the *Yorktown*ers later retorted, "But fight with Fletch!" Frank and Harrington, 65.

25. Messages 010626 CTF-8 to CTF-11, 010901 Cincpac to CTF-8, 011941 Cincpac to all CTFs, and 012231 Cincpac to all CTFs, February 1942, CSCMF, roll 3. Halsey and Bryan, 96. Fletcher interview by Prange (17 September 1966).

26. CTF-8 report (9 February 1942); Japan, *Senshi Sōsho*, 38:438; Greybook, 209; message 070453 February 1942 Cincpac to Cominch, CSCMF, roll 3. In the first edition of volume 3, Morison referred to the "more cautious" Fletcher, a comment he later removed after criticism by Vice Adm. Poco Smith and Vice Adm. Vincent Murphy (who called it "again a dirty dig at Admiral Fletcher") in their reviews in Office Files of the Director of Naval History, box 20; Potter, *Nimitz*, 40; Halsey and Bryan, 96.

27. Cincpac to Secnav, Report of Action, Marshall–Gilbert Island raids, by Task Forces Eight and Seventeen (10 February 1942); message 082219 February 1942 Cincpac to Secnav, CSCMF, roll 3. Navy Dept. Communiques No. 39 (12 February 1942, released 13 February 1942) and No. 40 (13 February 1942); Potter, *Halsey*, 51. On the Japanese pursuit, Japan, *Senshi Sōsho*, 38:405–6; and reaction: Ugaki, 81, 84; and Layton, "Flea Bites Dog," 5, an undated paper on the early carrier raids furnished to the author by Rear Adm. Edwin T. Layton, USN (Ret.).

28. CTF-8 report (9 February 1942), message 060833 February 1942 CTF-8 to CTF-11, CSCMF, roll 3.

CHAPTER 6. TO THE SOUTHWEST PACIFIC

1. Lundstrom, *The First South Pacific Campaign*, chapter 4.

2. Hayes, *The History of the Joint Chiefs of Staff in World War II*, 55–59; messages 070015 January 1942 Cominch to Cincpac, Greybook, 141; 191815 January 1942 Cominch to Cincpac, CSCMF, roll 2; 241740 January 1942 Cominch to Cincpac, Greybook, 185; 292110 January 1942 Cominch to Cincpac, Greybook, 203; and 292200 January 1942 Cominch to Cincpac, in CSCMF, roll 2. Coulthard-Clark, *Action Stations Coral Sea*, a groundbreaking study based on Adm. John G. Crace Papers (including a superb diary) in the Imperial War Museum.

3. Greybook, 184. Messages all January 1942: 241740 Cominch to Cincpac, Greybook, 185; 261721 Cominch to Cincpac, 270103 Cincpac to Cominch, Greybook, 192; 272333 Cominch to Cincpac, 282117 Cincpac to Cominch, Greybook, 197; 301707 Secnav to Comcrubatfor, CSCMF, roll 3. On Leary, see interview of Rear Adm. Edwin T. Layton by Capt. Roger Pineau and John Costello (11 May 1983), in Layton Papers, 109.

4. Greybook, 209–10. Messages 020126 February 1942 Com 14 to Opnav, CSCMF, roll 3; 051555 February 1942 Cominch to Cincpac, CNO TS Blue File; 080245 January 1942 Cincpac to Combatships (Commander, Battleships, Battle Force), CSCMF, roll 1. Greybook, 227–39, with text of Briefed Estimate of Situation, 5 February 1942.

5. Message 061513 February 1942 Cominch to Cincpac, Greybook, 220; 062352 February 1942 Cominch to Cincpac and Comanzac, Greybook, 221; 050401 February 1942 Cincpac to Cominch, CSCMF, roll 3. Comscofor (TF-11) war diary and CTF-11 to Cincpac, Cruise of Task Force Eleven, from January 31 to March 26, 1942 (23 March 1942), copy in Brown Papers.

6. Greybook, 210–12. Messages February 1942: 080139 Cincpac to Cominch, CSCMF, roll 3; 080239 Cincpac to Cominch and 092245 Cominch to Cincpac, CNO TS Blue File. Frank Uhlig personal communication with Lundstrom. Fuquea's "Task Force One," strongly differed with Nimitz's decision not to commit the battleships to action, but his reluctance to use the old battleships was wise given strategic, tactical, and logistic considerations.

7. Greybook, 212–13. Message 120459 February 1942 Cincpac to Cominch, CNO TS Blue File.

8. Greybook, 214. Halsey and Bryan, 96–97. Cincpac Op-Ord 15-42 to CTF-16 (11 February 1942).

9. TF-16 Op-Ord 2-42 (12 February 1942), TG-16.2 Op-Ord 1-42 (14 February 1942), in Op-Ord File. Messages 130405 Cincpac to Cominch, 140007 Cincpac to Comairbatfor and Comcruscofor, February 1942, CSCMF, roll 4. Greybook, 214.

10. Messages 122200 Cominch to Comanzac, 141835 Cominch to Cincpac and Comanzac, both February 1942, in CNO TS Blue File. Message 140022 February 1942 CTF-11 to Comanzac, CSCMF, roll 4. Messages 140336 Comanzac to Cominch, 150244 Comanzac to CTF-11, both February 1942, in Greybook, 223–26. Coulthard-Clark, 48.

11. Greybook, 216. Messages 151830 Cominch to Cincpac and 152225 CTF-11 to Cincpac, both February 1942, in CNO TS Blue File. Message 160135 February 1942 Cincpac to CTF-16, in CSCMF, roll 4. For the Wake raid, Lundstrom, *First Team*, 111–17.

12. W. W. Smith, 15–16, also letter Col. W. W. Smith Jr., U.S. Army, to Lundstrom (28 October 1999). Messages 292200 January 1942 Cominch to Cincpac, CSCMF, roll 2; and 070055 February 1942 Cincpac to *St. Louis* and *Astoria*, CSCMF, roll 3.

13. Messages 032107 Bunav to Cincpac, 050221 Cincpac to Bunav, and 070117 Cincpac to Com 11, all January 1942, in CSCMF, roll 1. Messages 072235 Comcruscofor to Bunav, 072357 Com 11 to Cincpac, and 091820 Combasefor (Commander, Base Force) to Cincpac, all February 1942, in CSCMF, roll 3. Officer Bio Files. *Yorktown* deck log.

14. CTF-14 report (28 December 1941). Biard, "The Pacific War Through the Eyes of Forrest R. 'Tex' Biard"; also numerous personal communications from Biard. Biard's memoir is scathingly critical of Fletcher, asserting he was totally incompetent and indecisive, lacking any appreciation of the value of radio intelligence that he, Biard, was supplying. He also charged that Fletcher was personally abusive when he refused a direct order to discuss radio intelligence in front of the staff and the enlisted flag complement, and that Fletcher complained about him to Nimitz. Every effort is made in the present work to address Biard's criticisms point by point to determine if they are sustained by other documentation. For Radio Intelligence Unit assigned to the *Yorktown*, see also P. E. Seaward, RM1c, USNR, and W. W. Eaton, RM2c, USN, Final Report of the R.I. Unit of the USS *Yorktown* covers period 16 February 1942 to 22 May 1942 (23 May 1942), RG-457, SRH-313, Pacific Fleet Mobile Intelligence Unit Reports.

15. U.S. Naval Administration in World War II, Commander in Chief, U.S. Pacific Fleet and Pacific Ocean Areas, Administrative History, 15–17. Message 052303 January 1942 Cincpac to Comscofor, CSCMF, roll 1; 030323 February 1942 Cincpac to Cominch, CSCMF, roll 3. Greybook, 244.

16. Clark, 86–87. Messages 122108 *Yorktown* to Cincpac, 122247 Cincpac to *Yorktown*, February 1942, in CSCMF, roll 4. Officer Bio Files. On Kiefer, see Cressman, *Gallant Ship*, 153; on Arnold, Leonard letter to Lundstrom (6 June 1997).

17. Messages 160135 Cincpac to CTF-16 (info CTF-17), 160301 Cincpac to CTG-16.2, and 160331 Cincpac to Comanzac and CTF-11, all February 1942, in CSCMF, roll 4. TF-17 war diary.

18. Messages 200237 CTF-11 to Cincpac, 200753 CTF-11 to *Chicago* and Cincpac, both February 1942, CSCMF, roll 4; and 232146 February 1942 CTF-11 to Cincpac and Comanzac, CSCMF, roll 5. For the 20 February action, see CTF-11 to Cincpac, Report of Action of Task Force Eleven with Japanese Aircraft on February 20, 1942 (24 February 1942) and Lundstrom, *First Team*, 85–109.

19. Brown report (23 March 1942); Greybook, 242, 244. Messages 232214 CTF-11 to Cincpac and 251209 Cincpac to Cominch, February 1942, in CNO TS Blue File; 250100 February 1942 Comanzac to Cincpac, Greybook, 254; and 260450 February 1942 CTF-11 to Cincpac, in CSCMF, roll 5.

20. Greybook, 246. Message 261630 February 1942 Cominch to CTF-17, CTF-11, and Comanzac, Greybook, 255–56.

21. TF-17 war diary. Message 250249 February 1942 Cincpac to all CTFs, CNO TS Blue File. Message 271939 February 1942 Cincpac to all CTFs, CSCMF, roll 5. The messages Fletcher could not break were 272045 Cominch to Cincpac, CTF-11, CTF-17, and Comanzac; and 280255 Cincpac to *Neosho* (info CTF-11 and CTF-17); both February 1942, in CSCMF, roll 5.

22. Greybook, 246. Message 280417 February 1942 Cincpac to CTFs, CSCMF, roll 5; 280559 Cincpac to Cominch and 270542 CTF-11 to Cincpac, February 1942, in Greybook, 256–57. Brown later reflected on the trouble he would have faced had the *Lexington* sailed from Pearl with only the regulation month of provisions instead of the second month her supply department had squirreled away in defiance of fleet orders, review of Morison's volume 3, Brown Papers.

23. Task Force 17 war diary. Message 272045 February 1942 Cominch to Cincpac, CTF-11, CTF-17, and Comanzac, in CSCMF, roll 5. The second message, 280255 February 1942 Cincpac to *Neosho* (info CTF-11 and CTF-17), CSCMF, roll 5, proved trivial—Cincpac arranging for army passengers to go south on the oiler *Neosho*'s return trip. Pearl rebroadcast it on 9 March.

24. Letter Leonard to Lundstrom (27 August 1996). Leonard stressed the isolation of admiral and flag captain should not be overstated, because "sweet reason says it would be normal and worthwhile for these experienced gents to get their heads together freely & frequently & in my experience they *did*." Interview of Raymond W. Kerr, one of the marines in the TF-17 flag complement, by Lundstrom (12 July 1999).

25. Correspondence and conversations with Frank W. Boo and Thomas I. Newsome, former CTF-17 flag yeomen. USS *Yorktown* Roster of Officers, May 1942, and deck log. Commander, Cruisers, Pacific Fleet (Comcrupac) Flag Allowance Muster Roll, July–September 1942. Letter Vice Adm. W. G. Schindler, USN

(Ret.), to Lundstrom (4 June 1972). Letter Vice Adm. E. Buckmaster, USN (Ret.), to Vice Adm. W. W. Smith, USN (Ret.) (22 August 1964), in Smith Papers.

26. Conversations with Thomas Newsome and Norman W. Ulmer, a former TF-17 signalman. Newsome conversations. Biard, "The Pacific War," 5, likewise described the layout of the *Yorktown*'s flag bridge. Boo letter to Lundstrom (17 February 1996). In Hailey's *Pacific Battle Line*, 150, and from anecdotal accounts Fletcher was also called "Whiskey Jack," but neither Tom Newsome nor Norman Ulmer (e-mails to Lundstrom, 7 February 2000) ever recalled hearing that epithet. In March and April 1942 in the Coral Sea Fletcher did designate some of his rendezvous as Points Rye, Gin, Scotch, Bourbon, etc. (William Ward Smith, 19–20). Perhaps that is where that particular name might have got started.

27. Interviews and correspondence with Hollis C. Hollis and Norman Ulmer, both former TF-17 signalmen, and George E. Clapp, one of the four TF-17 communication watch officers. Interview of Lt. Cdr. Clarence C. Ray, Communication Officer, USS *Yorktown*, by Buaer (15 July 1942), Operational Archives, NHC.

28. Letter Newsome to Lundstrom (7 August 1996), conversation (11 December 1997). Boo letter to Lundstrom (17 February 1996), relating that he had retired as a chief warrant officer after twenty years of service. Norman Ulmer conversation (10 December 1997). Raymond Kerr conversation (12 July 1999).

CHAPTER 7. "THE BEST DAY'S WORK WE HAVE HAD"

1. Message 021615 March 1942 Cominch to CTF-11 and Comanzac, in National Archives, RG-38, Cominch 00 File; 030100 March 1942 Comanzac to CTF-11 and CTF-17, CSCMF, roll 5.

2. Letter CTF-11 to CTF-17 (5 March 1942), in Cincpac Flag Files. Comscofor (CTF-11) war diary, CTF-11 report (23 March 1942). CTF-11 (Comscofor) to Cincpac, Report of Attack on Enemy Forces in Salamaua-Lae Area, March 10, 1942 (25 March 1942).

3. CTF-11 Op-Ord 5-42 (6 March 1942), attached to CTF-11 report (25 March 1942).

4. CTF-11 Op-Ord 5-42 (6 March 1942); letter CTF-11 to CTF-17 (5 March 1942), in Cincpac Flag Files. Reynolds, *The Fast Carriers*, 25.

5. Comscofor (TF-11) war diary; CTF-11 report (23 March 1942); *Yorktown* deck log; memo CTF-17 to CTF-11 (6 March 1942), in Brown Papers. F. C. Sherman's personal diary, reconstructed beginning 19 May 1942, typescript copy in Adm. Frederick C. Sherman Biographical File, Officer Bio Files, NHC. I am indebted to Jeffrey Barlow for providing me a copy of this invaluable document. CTG-11.5 Air Op-Ord 2-42 (7 March 1942), enclosed in CTG-11.5 (CO USS *Lexington*) to CTF-11, Report of Bombing attack on enemy shipping and shore establishments in Salamaua-Lae area, March 10, 1942 (15 March 1942).

6. Letter Fletcher to Brown ("My dear Wilson") (11 March 1942), in Brown Papers. W. W. Smith, 18; also undated (c. 1950) review of Morison's volume 3. Diary of Rear Adm. J. G. Crace, RN, in Crace Papers (hereafter Crace diary). Crace wrote in his diary on 6 March that he had a "horrid feeling" the Anzac Squadron might end up with the carriers instead of forming part of an attack force. "That will be too awful." Notes of Crace's meeting with Brown 7 March in Crace diary (7 March 1942). Coulthard-Clark, 52. CTF-11 report (23 March 1942).

7. Crace diary; HMAS *Australia* war diary, AWM 124 [4/216] in Australian War Memorial.

8. Messages 060355, 060518, and 060805 Comanzac to CTF-11 and CTF-17, all March 1942, in CSCMF, roll 5; 062015 March 1942 Com 14 to Cincpac and all CTFs, CSCMF, roll 5.

9. Japan, *Senshi Sōsho*, 49:28–31, 104–7.

10. Japan, *Senshi Sōsho*, 49:107–13, 117–18.

11. Comscofor (CTF-11) war diary; CTF-11 report (23 March 1942); message 070115 March 1942 CTF-17 to CTF-11, in Brown Papers. Messages 070506 March 1942 Comanzac to CTF-11 and CTF-17, 071026 March 1942 Comanzac to CTF-11 and CTF-17, CSCMF, roll 5. Brown memoir, 22, Brown Papers. CTF-11 report (25 March 1942).

12. It is interesting that the detailed TF-11 war diary did not record the changes of course and speed at 0200 on 8 March, but it appears in the *Yorktown*'s deck log and the *Australia*'s war diary. Crace diary (8 March 1942); Sherman diary (19 May 1942).

13. Japan, *Senshi Sōsho*, 49:118–20, 130. Message 072040 March 1942 Comanzac to CTF-11 and CTF-17, CSCMF, roll 5. Annex B to CTF-11 Op-Ord 5-42 (6 March 1942); Comscofor (CTF-11) war diary, Sherman diary (19 May 1942).

14. CTF-11 report (25 March 1942), visual message 080555 March 1942 CTF-11 to TF-11. Crace diary (8 March 1942); Lt. (jg) Floyd. E. Moan (VB-5, *Yorktown*) diary (11 March 1942), from Capt. Floyd E. Moan, USN (Ret.), via James C. Sawruk.

15. CTF-11 report (25 March 1942); messages 090315 and 091300 March 1942 Comanzac to CTF-11 and CTF-17, CSCMF, roll 6. CTG-11.5 Air Op-Ord 3-42 (9 March 1942), attached to CTG-11.5 report (15 March 1942).

16. CTF-11 Op-Ord 6-42 (9 March 1942). Crace diary (9 March 1942).

17. CTG-11.5 report (15 March 1942); CO USS *Yorktown* to Cincpac, Attack made by Yorktown Air Group against Enemy Forces at Salamaua and at Lae, New Guinea (12 March 1942); and CO USS *Yorktown* to Cincpac, The Attack made by the USS *Yorktown* Air Group, March 10, 1942 (15 March 1942). Ludlum, 30–34. Cressman, *Gallant Ship*, 67–69. Lundstrom, *First Team*, 126–32. The *Lexington* had long since immobilized the tiny aft elevator, letter Duckworth to Lundstrom (9 March 1972). Message 212115 February 1942 *Lexington* to Comairbatfor, CSCMF, roll 4, had urged that the after elevators in the *Lexington*-class carriers be modernized, "In order to facilitate deck spotting of fighter planes and offensive plane operations."

18. CTF-11 report (25 March 1942); Biard, "The Pacific War," 7; Japan, *Senshi Sōsho*, 49:123–26.

19. CTG-11.5 report (15 March 1942); CTF-11 report (25 March 1942). Ludlum, 34; Moan diary, 11 March 1942; message 100216 March 1942 *Yorktown* to CTG-11.5 (info CTF-11), Brown Papers; Brown's review of Morison's volume 3, 10, Brown Papers.

20. CTG-11.5 report (15 March 1942), CTF-11 report (25 March 1942). Japan, *Senshi Sōsho*, 49:124–25.

21. Japan, *Senshi Sōsho*, 49:126.

22. Letters Fletcher to Brown (11 March 1942) and Brown to Fletcher (12 March 1942), visual message 122342 March 1942 CTG-11.1 to CTF-11, all in Brown Papers. Smith undated review of Morison's volume 3.

23. Brown memoir, 25–26; Greybook, 267, 271; messages 151520 and 151525 March 1942 CTF-11 to Cominch, Greybook, 289, 292. Japan, *Senshi Sōsho*, 49:163–65. Kimball, *Churchill & Roosevelt*, 1:415–16. Also text in Brown Papers. Message 031855 April 1942 Cominch to Cincpac, CSCMF, roll 8. Ted Sherman gloated in his diary (19 May 1942) that King did not even mention TF-17, although in retrospect King does not seem to have deliberately insulted Fletcher.

24. Messages 120335 March 1942 Cincpac to CTF-11 and CTF-17, CSCMF, roll 6; 071820 March 1942 Cominch to Cincpac (info CTF-11), in Cominch 00 File. Buell, *Master*, 174–75.

25. Crace diary (12–13 March 1942); W. W. Smith 20–21, and undated review of Morison's volume 3; *Astoria* deck log; Coulthard-Clark, 58–59.

26. Comscofor (TF-11) war diary; TF-17 war diary. Message 130025 March 1942 Comanzac to CTF-17 and *Chicago*, CSCMF, roll 6.

27. Messages 201940 February 1942 Cominch to Cincpac, CSCMF, roll 4; 011847 March 1942 Cincpac to Cominch, CSCMF, roll 5; 070315 April 1942 Cincpac to Pacific Fleet, CSCMF, roll 8. Whitehill memo (14 August 1949), in King Papers, NWC. For Brown's subsequent service, see Brown, "Aide to Four Presidents." The oft-repeated story that King directed Nimitz to relieve Brown as CTF-11 has no basis in fact but appears to have arisen from an error in Hoyt, 72, where Brown is confused for Fletcher as the target of King's 31 March 1942 rebuke. Potter, *Nimitz*, 44, then built upon Hoyt's mistake by stating that King "insisted that Brown was not aggressive enough to lead combat forces." In fact Brown lacked the stamina and agility for

a wartime sea command. The *Lexington*'s flag bridge, high up in the island over the navigation bridge, had no emergency sea cabin for the admiral because that space now housed the YE aircraft homing transmitter and receiver. Brown suffered from having to climb a half dozen decks every time he was called from his flag quarters up to the flag bridge. Brown memoir, 9, 14; letter Duckworth to Lundstrom (9 March 1972). When the *Lex* went into the navy yard in April, the flag emergency sea cabin was restored (message 240423 March 1942 Navy Yard [NY] Pearl Harbor to NY Puget Sound, CSCMF, roll 7).

CHAPTER 8. ALONE IN THE CORAL SEA

1. Message 131535 March 1942 Cominch to CTF-17, Greybook, 288.

2. Messages 130025 March 1942 Comanzac to CTF-17, Greybook, 287; 130339 March 1942 Cincpac to CTF-17, Greybook, 288.

3. Message 160821 March 1942 CTF-11 to Cominch, CNO TS Blue File. Fletcher explained his strategy for March and April in his 28 May 1942 letter to Nimitz, in Nimitz Papers.

4. Messages 161635 February 1942 Cominch to Cincpac, Greybook, 226; and 222200 February 1942 Cominch to Cincpac, Greybook, 243. Lundstrom, *First South Pacific Campaign*, 48–56.

5. CTF-11 report (23 March 1942); message 131433 March 1942 CTF-17 to Cincpac, CSCMF, roll 6; Crace diary, 21 March 1942.

6. Messages 130307 March 1942 Cincpac to CTF-11 and CTF-17, Greybook, 287; 132145 Cincpac to Comdesron 2 and *Platte*, 132235 CTF-17 to Comanzac and Cincpac, 142236 CTF-17 to *Tippecanoe*, 142355 CTF-17 to Comdesron 2 and *Platte*, all March 1942, in CSCMF, roll 6.

7. Greybook, 271. Messages 130339 March 1942 Cincpac to CTF-17, Greybook, 288; 132141 March 1942 CTF-17 to Comanzac, Greybook, 271; 160217 March 1942 CTF-17 to Comanzac, Greybook, 292. Messages 150159 Cincpac to TF-13, 182330 CTF-17 to Cincpac, 192301 Cincpac to CTF-19, 172211 Cincpac to CTF-17, 182300 CTF-17 to *Tippecanoe*, and 190625 *Tippecanoe* to CTF-17, all March 1942, in CSCMF, roll 6.

8. TF-17 war diary. Messages 190015 March 1942 Comanzac to CTF-17, CSCMF, roll 6; 210833 March 1942 CTF-17 to Comanzac, etc., Greybook, 313; 200733 March 1942 Comanzac to CTF-17, CSCMF, roll 7; 191400 March 1942 Cominch to Cincpac, Greybook, 311–12; 210535 March 1942 Cincpac to CTF-13, Greybook, 314; 220520 March 1942 Comanzac to Flag Officer Commanding Australian Squadron, CSCMF, roll 7. Crace diary, 22 March 1942.

9. TF-17 war diary; *Astoria* deck log; Ralph V. Wilhelm personal diary, 22 March 1942, courtesy of Ralph Wilhelm, who was a lieutenant junior grade and SOC pilot in the *Portland*.

10. Message 201830 February 1942 Cominch to Commander in Chief, Atlantic Fleet (Cinclant), and Cincpac, CSCMF, roll 4. For Mitscher, see: Taylor, *The Magnificent Mitscher*, and Coletta, *Admiral Marc A. Mitscher and U.S. Naval Aviation*. On McCain: Reynolds, *Admirals*, 206–7; and the portrait in his grandson John McCain's *Faith of My Fathers*, 3–46. On McCain becoming CTF-18, message 122059 March 1942 Cincpac to Cominch, CSCMF, roll 6.

11. Greybook, 270; messages 122059 Cincpac to Cominch, 131430 Cominch to Cincpac, 142155 Cincpac to Cominch, all March 1942, in CSCMF, roll 6; 162043 March 1942 Cominch to Cincpac, Greybook, 293.

12. Admiral Duncan's account is in Mason, *The Pacific War Remembered*, 63–69. Halsey and Bryan, 101. Potter, *Nimitz*, 67; Hoyt, 71–72; Mason, 68; message 220119 March 1942 Cincpac to Cominch, CSCMF, roll 6. Duncan recalled the message as, "Tell Jimmy to get on his horse."

13. Messages 191905 Cominch to Cincpac, 161238 Admiralty to Opnav, 171820 Cominch to Admiralty, all March 1942, in CNO TS Blue File.

14. Greybook, 297–99; message 222157 March 1942 Cincpac to Cominch, CSCMF, roll 7; 131955 and 150451 Cominch to Cincpac, both March 1942, CSCMF, roll 6; 232130 March 1942 Cincpac to Cominch,

CNO TS Blue File. Floyd Beaver, a former signalman in the TF-11 enlisted complement, recalled in his fine memoir how Fitch, "an unusually short man for a Naval officer," had a "a brisk, no-nonsense manner and an impressive nose," soon "fitted into the *Lexington* in a way Brown never had" (Floyd Beaver, *Chief*, 168).

15. Potter, *Nimitz*, 47. Memorandum Frank Knox for the President (9 March 1942), Safe Files, Franklin D. Roosevelt Presidential Library and Museum, Hyde Park, brought to my attention by Jeffrey Barlow. The nine selectors were Stark and King, Joseph Reeves (former Cincus), Claude Bloch (former Cincus and also Commander, Fourteenth Naval District), James O. Richardson (former Cincus), Harry Yarnell (former commander in chief of the Asiatic Fleet), Edward C. Kalbfus (former Combatfor), Rear Adm. Randall Jacobs (Nimitz's successor at Bunav), and Rear Adm. Richard S. Edwards (Cominch deputy chief of staff).

16. Message 272000 March 1942 Cominch to Cincpac, Cominch 00 File.

17. TF-17 war diary. Greybook, 295; messages 250035 Comanzac to CTF-17, 220211 Cincpac to Commander, Service Force, Pacific Fleet (Comserforpac), 250033 Cincpac to CTF-17, all March 1942, CSCMF, roll 7.

18. Message 270604 March 1942 Comanzac to CTF-17, CSCMF, roll 7; TF-17 war diary; W. W. Smith, 21–22; *Astoria* deck log; messages 280119 Cincpac Intelligence Bulletin (hereafter Cincpac Intel. Bull.) and 280715 *Tangier* to Cincpac, both March 1942, CSCMF, roll 7.

19. Greybook, 304; messages 281322 Comanzac to CTF-17 and 281635 Cominch to Comanzac, both March 1942, in CSCMF, roll 7.

20. Letter Fletcher to Nimitz (28 May 1942), in Nimitz Papers; Fletcher Memorandum to Cincpac, Operations of Task Force Seventeen in the Coral Sea Area—March 16 to April 20 (23 June 1942), in action report file; W. W. Smith, 22; TF-17 war diary; messages 282151 Cincpac to Comanzac, 290109 Comanzac to CTF-17, 290512 Comanzac to Cincpac, 290635 Comanzac to CTF-17, 290158 Comanzac to CTF-17, and 290119 Comanzac to CTF-17, all March 1942, CSCMF, roll 7.

21. Letter Fletcher to Nimitz (28 May 1942), in Nimitz Papers; Greybook, 304–5; messages 291325 Comanzac to CTF-17, 292346 CTF-17 to Comanzac, 300233 Comanzac to CTF-17, 300435 Comanzac to CTF-17, 300855 Comanzac to CTF-17, all March 1942, in CSCMF, roll 7.

22. Japan, *Senshi Sōsho*, 49:130–35.

23. Messages 301400 and 301715 March 1942 Comanzac to CTF-17, in CSCMF, roll 7.

24. Message 301930 March 1942 Cominch to CTF-17, in Greybook (322), CSCMF (roll 7), and original with King's notation in Cominch 00 File. Messages 302359 Comanzac to CTF-17, 310106 Comanzac to Cominch, and 310230 Comanzac to CTF-17, all March 1942, in CSCMF, roll 7.

25. W. W. Smith, 61–62; letter Fletcher to Nimitz (28 May 1942), in Nimitz Papers; TF-17 war diary; messages 310245 CTF-17 to Cominch and 311455 Cominch to CTF-17, March 1942 in CSCMF, roll 7; letter Fletcher to W. W. Smith (1 September 1964), in Smith Papers.

26. Messages 310315 CTF-17 to Cincpac and 312051 CTG-17.2 to Comanzac, March 1942, in CSCMF, roll 7; TF-17 war diary; Desron Two war diary; Commander, Cruisers (Comcru) TF-17 war diary; Greybook, 306.

27. Crace diary, 31 March 1942.

28. Message 311455 March 1942 Cominch to CTF-17, Greybook, 324; message 010323 April 1942 Cincpac to Navsta Samoa, CSCMF, roll 8; Crace diary, 1 April 1942; messages 012327 CTF-17 to CTF-19, 012328 CTF-17 to *Bridge*, 012348 CTF-17 to Tutuila, all April 1942, CSCMF, roll 8; 011040 April 1942 *Sumner* to Cincpac, Greybook, 326.

29. Message 020250 April 1942 CTF-17 to Comanzac, Cominch 00 File; TF-17 war diary; *Yorktown* deck log.

30. Greybook, 307; messages 012228 Comanzac to CTF-17, 021227 Comanzac to CTF-17, 030427 Cincpac Intel. Bull., 031800 Cominch to CTF-17, all April 1942, in CSCMF, roll 8.

31. TF-17 war diary; Comcru TF-17 war diary; Greybook, 333; message 040145 April 1942 Comanzac to CTF-17, CSCMF, roll 8; 040650 April 1942 CTF-17 to Comanzac, Greybook, 347.

32. TF-17 war diary, Comcru TF-17 war diary, *Astoria* deck log, Crace diary, 8–10 April 1942.

33. Messages 100100 CTF-17 to unknown (retransmitted as Comanzac to Cincpac), 100320 CTF-17 to Comanzac, and 100348 CTF-17 to Comanzac, all April 1942, CSCMF, roll 8.

34. Cincpac Administrative History, 17–18, with Cincpac's 23 March 1942 letter in Appendix II-1, NHC. Messages 311830 March 1942 Secnav to All Navy (Alnav), Greybook, 325; 091307 April 1942 Bunav to Cincpac, CSCMF, roll 8; 100505 April 1942 Cincpac to Pacific Fleet (Pacflt), Greybook, 347.

35. Fletcher speech of 27 October 1946, Fletcher Papers; Frank and Harrington, 73–74; Linzey, *God Was at Midway*, 56–58.

36. Crace diary, 11–14 April 1942; messages 110641, 111056, 111155, 120700, and 121453 Comanzac to CTF-17, 090107 Cincpac Intel. Bull., all April 1942, in CSCMF, roll 8; Coulthard-Clark, 61–68.

37. Letter Fletcher to Nimitz (28 May 1942), in Nimitz Papers; messages 130725 April 1942 *Yorktown* to Commander, Carriers, Pacific Fleet (Comcarpac) Material Officer, Pearl, CSCMF, roll 8; 140147 April 1942 CTF-17 to Cominch and Cincpac, CSCMF, roll 9; 120145 Comanzac to *Tippecanoe*, 112027 Cincpac to Comanzac, both April 1942, CSCMF, roll 8; *Yorktown* deck log.

38. Message 142027 April 1942 Cincpac to CTF-17, Greybook, 346. TF-17 war diary.

39. Greybook, 344; letter Fletcher to Nimitz (28 May 1942), memo Fletcher to Nimitz (23 June 1942), letter Nimitz to King (29 May 1942), all in Nimitz Papers.

CHAPTER 9. NIMITZ TAKES CHARGE

1. Messages 042048 April 1942 Combatfor to Cincpac, CSCMF, roll 8; 270247 Cincpac to Cominch, 280049 Cincpac to Cominch, 310415 Cincpac to Opnav, all March 1942, in CSCMF, roll 7.

2. Great Britain, *War With Japan*, 2:120–31; Macintyre, *Fighting Admiral*, chapter 13.

3. Messages 051400 and 081315 Cominch to Special Naval Observer London, both April 1942, in CNO TS Blue File; Kimball, 1:442–43; Greybook, 308; messages 082307 Cincpac to Cominch and 091825 Cominch to Cincpac, April 1942, in CNO TS Blue File; messages 110335 and 110351 April 1942 Cincpac to CTF-1 and CTF-11, in Cominch 00 File.

4. Message 091750 April 1942 Cominch to Cincpac, CSCMF, roll 8.

5. Hayes, 96–98; messages 041725 Cominch to Cincpac and Comanzac, 070451 Cincpac to Cominch, March 1942, CSCMF, roll 5.

6. Hayes, 98–100; messages 171640 March 1942 Cominch to Comanzac and Comsowespac, CSCMF, roll 6; 041300 April 1942 Cominch to Comsowespac and Comanzac, Greybook, 330.

7. Message 031905 series April 1942 Cominch to Cincpac, Greybook, 328–30; Greybook, 332, 341; 041850 Cominch to Cincpac and 051849 Cincpac to Cominch, April 1942, Greybook, 331.

8. On Stark's resignation, see: Simpson, *Admiral Harold R. Stark*, 126–32; Brodhurst, *Churchill's Anchor*, 216–17; and for a different version, Richardson and Dyer, 441–42, which is much less flattering to Roosevelt. Whitehill memo (31 July 1949), King Papers, NWC.

9. Greybook, 341–42; message 110535 April 1942 Cincpac to Cominch, in Cominch 00 File; 141416 April 1942 Cominch to Cincpac, CSCMF, roll 9.

10. For code breaking in the Pacific, see: Parker, *A Priceless Advantage*; Benson, *A History of U.S. Communications Intelligence during World War II*; Layton, "America Deciphered Our Code"; Holmes, *Double-Edged Secrets*; Layton, *And I Was There*; Budiansky, *Battle of Wits*; Prados, *Combined Fleet Decoded*; and Michael Smith, *The Emperor's Codes*. It is useful to list here the relevant versions of Naval Codebook D designated by the Allies as "JN" for Japanese naval code and when they were instituted: JN-25A, June 1939; JN-25B, 1 December 1940; JN-25C, 27 May 1942; and JN-25D, 14 August 1942. An excellent analysis of the early JN-25 versions appears in Budiansky, "Too Late for Pearl Harbor."

11. Layton and Rochefort most often communicated by secure telephone (interview of Rear Adm. Donald M. Showers, USN, by Lundstrom [14 May 2002]). Layton noted in a letter (10 January 1974) to Lundstrom: "My advantage was that I talked each day, many times a day with those *directly* responsible for traffic analysis, for the sketchy & incomplete descriptions, and could follow up, or cause to be followed up the incomplete pieces, the questioned areas." Parker, 21; letter Layton to Lundstrom (7 April 1975).

12. Japan, *Senshi Sōsho*, 49:164–65; Fuchida and Okumiya, *Midway*, 48–54.

13. Japan, *Senshi Sōsho*, 49:165–66; Fuchida and Okumiya, 54–62; Japan, *Senshi Sōsho*, 43:96.

14. Japan, *Senshi Sōsho*, 49:166–67, with extract of Combined Fleet Secret No. 694, Second Operational Phase, First Stage Strength Allotment (10 April–end May 1942).

15. Message 212235 June 1942 Cincpac to Cominch, CSCMF, roll 16, reported that prisoners taken in the Battle of Midway identified the carrier sunk at Coral Sea as the converted carrier *Shōhō* and stated the *Ryūkaku* did not exist. Greybook, 341; message 110641 April 1942 Comanzac to Comsowespac and Cincpac, CSCMF, roll 8.

16. Japan, *Senshi Sōsho*, 49:167–68; message 152049 April 1942 Opnav to Cincpac, CSCMF, roll 9.

17. Greybook, 352; message 170626 April 1942 Comanzac to Cincpac, CNO TS Blue File; 172015 April 1942 Cincpac to Comanzac, Cominch 00 File; Greybook, 364; Potter, *Nimitz*, 67; message 172035 April 1942 Cincpac to Cominch, in Cominch 00 File.

18. Biard, "The Pacific War," 10; letter Halsey to Doolittle (24 April 1942), copy in King Papers, NHC.

19. Ugaki, 111–12; Greybook, 365; memo Capt. F. C. Dickey to Commo. R. W. Bates, NWC (14 October 1946), relaying Dickey's conversation with Fletcher, in Bates Papers, series II, box 12.

20. Message 182032 April 1942 Cominch to Cincpac, in Cominch 00 File; Greybook, 365; messages 190457 Cominch to Cincpac, 190535 Cincpac to CTF-1 and CTF-11, 192109 Cincpac to CTF-11, 220345 Cincpac to CTF-11 and CTF-17, and 220541 Cincpac to CTF-17, all April 1942, in Cominch 00 File.

21. Interview of Adm. Arthur Davis by Dr. Gordon Prange, 30 January 1963, via Robert J. Cressman; Bath, *Tracking the Axis Enemy*, 171, citing Lt. Cdr. F. M. Beasley, RN, who visited Nimitz on 22 January 1942. On Draemel: Hoyt, 91.

22. Layton interview by Pineau and Costello (11 May 1983), 90; Cincpac Enemy Activities File in April–May 1942, in RG-457, SRH-272; Rear Adm. Edwin T. Layton, oral history, 17, 28; Potter, *Nimitz*, 80; Pacific Fleet Administrative History, NHC, 144–45.

23. Greybook, 366; text of the 22 April 1942 Estimate of the Situation in Greybook, 371–407.

24. Greybook, 375; message 230051 April 1942 Cincpac to Cominch, CNO TS Blue File.

25. Gwyer and Butler, *Grand Strategy*, vol. 3, part 2, 503. Clark G. Reynolds has presented the case that King deliberately adopted a "fleet-in-being" strategy with his carriers to avoid decisive battle and harass the enemy with raids until the time was right to concentrate the fleet and engage the enemy under advantageous strategic conditions. See his "U.S. Carriers and the Fleet-in-Being Strategy of 1942." It is questionable, though, that King indeed was following a coherent fleet-in-being strategy. Nimitz, not he, initiated the necessary concentration of the fleet for battle, first in the South Pacific and then at Midway. Instead King seems to have preferred keeping his carriers dispersed and not risk heavy battle. He simply adopted a raiding strategy of nonconfrontation and delay until his South Pacific bases were fully capable of defending themselves. After the Battle of the Coral Sea, King sought to limit the direct involvement of the carriers themselves in the defense of key South Pacific bases, preferring to employ their aircraft ashore. Before Midway he recommended sending the *Yorktown* directly to the West Coast to reduce the participation of the U.S. carriers. During the early stages of the Guadalcanal campaign he restricted the number of carriers committed to battle to three, and Nimitz had to press him to commit the *Hornet* and retain the *Wasp*. The impetus to battle, rather than strategic advances, came from Nimitz not King.

26. Minutes of Conversations between Cominch and Cincpac, Saturday, April 25 (26 April 1942), in Pacific Conferences, King/Nimitz, 1942–1945, in NHC microfilm NRS-1972-22.

27. Minutes of Conversations between Cominch and Cincpac, Sunday, April 26, 1942 (27 April 1942), NRS-1972-22. King's declaration regarding MacArthur was wishful thinking. He was unaware of MacArthur's backdoor wheedling of Marshall for carriers of his own by complaining that without them his Sowespac naval force was "unbalanced," message 24 April 1942, MacArthur to Marshall, in General of the Army Douglas MacArthur Papers, roll 593.

28. Minutes of Conversations April 26, 1942, NRS-1972-22.

29. Minutes of Conversations between Cominch and Cincpac, Monday, April 27 (27 April 1942), in NRS-1972-22. Message 272058 April 1942 Cominch to Cincpac, CNO TS Blue File; 282047 April 1942 Cincpac to Cominch, in Cominch 00 File; Greybook, 416; 291530 April 1942 Cominch to Cincpac, CNO TS Blue File.

30. Cincpac Op-Plan 23-42 (29 April 1942), in Op-Ord File; letter Cincpac to CTF-16, Carrier Task Forces, Future Employment (29 April 1942), in NA, RG-38, Headquarters Cominch Records, box 258; message 020641 May 1942 Cincpac to Comsowespac, Greybook, 453.

31. Message 011108 May 1942 Com 14 to Opnav, Belconnen, Com 16, and "written up for Cincpac info," CSCMF, roll 10. Message 011108 May 1942 Com 14 to Opnav, etc. The history of radio intelligence has been affected by selective editing. The wartime SRH-012 *The Role of Radio Intelligence in the American-Japanese Naval War (August, 1941–June, 1942)*, 239–40, in RG-457, offered an edited version of the Com14 011108 message that conveniently omitted the text of this estimate of raids against Samoa and Fiji. Comint historians have neglected this extremely important message showing that as of 30 April Midway was not yet believed to be an imminent Japanese target. For a recent iteration of the Midway myth, see Beach, 107–10. For Layton's view at that time, see SRH-272, Cincpac Enemy Activities File, 27 April, 30 April, and 2 May 1942.

32. Message 021430 May 1942 Cominch to Cincpac and Comsowespac, Greybook, 453.

CHAPTER 10. CLEARING FOR ACTION

1. TF-17 war diary; *Yorktown* deck log; messages 162023 Cincpac to CTF-17, 192147 Cincpac to CTF-17, 211016 CTF-17 to Cincpac, 240128 CTF-17 to Navobs (Naval Observer) Suva, and 250240 Comcarpac Admin to CTF-17, all April 1942, CSCMF, roll 9. Strange, 60–61; W. W. Smith, original draft of Midway book, 129–30, in Smith Papers.

2. Messages 192109 April 1942 Cincpac to CTF-11 and CTF-17, in CNO TS Blue File; 210207 and 220109 April 1942 Cincpac Intel. Bull., CSCMF, roll 9; 220345 Cincpac to CTF-11 and CTF-17, and 220541 Cincpac to CTF-17, both April 1942, in Cominch 00 File.

3. Morison, *United States Naval Operations*, 4:16.

4. Messages 200915 April 1942 Comsowespacfor to Anzacfor (Anzac Force), CSCMF, roll 9; 220410 April 1942 Comsowespac to Cominch, in CNO TS Blue File; 250357 April 1942 Cincpac to CTF-17, Greybook, 412; 270653 April 1942 Comsowespacfor to CTF-17, Greybook, 414; 262000 April 1942 CTF-17 to Comsowespacfor, CSCMF, roll 10.

5. Message 150411 April 1942 Cincpac to Cominch, Greybook, 350; 162220 April 1942 Cominch to Comsowespacfor, Greybook, 358; 180135 April 1942 Comanzac to Cominch, CSCMF, roll 9; Crace diary, 19 April 1942; 262205 April 1942 Cincpac to all CTFs, CSCMF, roll 10.

6. The basic source on Brett's air operations is Air Commo. Francis W. F. Lukis, OBE, Air Officer Commanding North East Area, Report on Coral Sea Engagement (29 May 1942), in Australian Archives, series AA1969/10/0/119, item 273/25A. For organization, see Ashworth, *How Not To Run An Air Force!*; and Assistant Chief of Air Staff, Intelligence, Historical Division, Army Air Forces Historical Studies: No. 9, The AAF in Australia to the Summer of 1942 (July 1944). Messages 222158 CTF-17 to Comsowespacfor and 250418 Cincpac to Comsowespacfor, both April 1942, CSCMF, roll 9.

7. Message 250357 April 1942 Cincpac to CTF-17, CSCMF, roll 9; 262010 April 1942 CTF-17 to *Tangier*, CSCMF, roll 10; *Tangier* war diary; U.S. Naval War College (Capt. Richard W. Bates), *The Battle of the Coral Sea May 1 to May 11 Inclusive, 1942 Strategical and Tactical Analysis*, 24–27 (hereafter Bates, *Coral Sea*).

8. War Plans 22 April 1942 Estimate of the Situation, Annex on fuel situation, TF-16, 17, 18, 11 in Southwest Pacific, Greybook, 395–99; messages 250100 CTF-17 to Cincpac, 251921 Cincpac to CTF-17, and 250229 Comsowespac to Cincpac, April 1942, CSCMF, roll 9.

9. Messages 260251 Cincpac to Comsowespacfor, 260327 Cincpac to CTF-17, and 260329 Cincpac to *Tippecanoe*, April 1942, CSCMF, roll 10.

10. Messages 242215 Comdesron 2 to Commander, Destroyers, Pacific Fleet (Comdespac), 250100 CTF-17 to Cincpac, 280041 Cincpac to CTF-17, April 1942, CSCMF, roll 10.

11. Letter Leonard to Lundstrom (26 August 1996) and conversation (25 September 1997). Letter Rear Adm. Murr Arnold, USN (Ret.), to Lundstrom (9 April 1972). Arnold replied to W. W. Smith (7 March 1965): "First of all I would like to clarify any possible doubt that you might have concerning my opinion of Adm. Fletcher. I liked him, and I liked working for and under him." Letter Rear Adm. Oscar Pederson, USN (Ret.), to Joseph Harrington (21 July 1964), Pederson Papers.

12. CTF-17 Op-Ord No. 2-42 (1 May 1942), in Commander Task Force Seventeen to Commander in Chief, U.S. Fleet, The Battle of the Coral Sea, May 4–8, 1942 (27 May 1942).

13. CTF-17 Op-Ord 2-42 (1 May 1942). Fletcher considered shifting his flag either to the *Indianapolis*, which left San Francisco for Australia on 15 April, or the *Chester* (message 310307 March 1942 Cincpac to *Indianapolis*, CSCMF, roll 7). Letter Fletcher to Nimitz (28 May 1942), in Nimitz Papers; message 280925 April 1942 CTF-17 to Cincpac, Greybook, 414; Cominch to Cincpac, etc., Commander Task Force 17 (Commander Cruisers, Pacific Fleet) Report of Action, The Battle of the Coral Sea, May 4–8, 1942, Comments on, (18 November 1942), Forwards comments of Rear Adm. Edward C. Kalbfus, president of the Naval War College.

14. Base Air Force operational strength as of 1 May (after the arrival of the Genzan Air Group) amounted to twenty-three Zero fighters, forty-two land attack planes, and thirteen flying boats, a total of seventy-eight planes (Japan, *Senshi Sōsho*, 49:205).

15. Message 181915 April 1942 Cincpac to all CTFs, in Greybook, 362, gives the estimated numbers of aircraft on Japanese carriers. The *Ryūkaku* was thought to be another *Shōkaku*-class carrier. The attribution of forty-two dive bombers is apparently a typographical error for twenty-one. A converted submarine tender, the light carrier *Shōhō* had twenty aircraft (ten Zero fighters, four Type 96 fighters, and six Type 97 carrier attack planes).

16. Messages 290309 Cincpac Intel. Bull., 300426 Comsowespac to CTF-11 and CTF-17, April 1942, in CSCMF, roll 10.

17. Japan, *Senshi Sōsho*, 49:169–76, summarizes Japanese planning for the MO Operation. The text of South Seas Force Order 13 (23 April 1942), is in pp. 176–85, and the orders of the MO Attack Force in 194–98.

18. For Inoue, see Evans and Peattie, 482–86, and Peattie, 159–61.

19. Planning for Support Force and the Tulagi Attack Force is in Japan, *Senshi Sōsho*, 49:200–202.

20. See Japan, *Senshi Sōsho*, 49:189–91, for the formation of the MO *Kidō Butai*, including text of Order No. 1 (28 April 1942). The *Tōhō Maru* was an excellent requisitioned ten-thousand-ton tanker built in 1936 with a capacity of ninety-three thousand barrels of oil and a top speed of twenty knots.

21. Japan, *Senshi Sōsho*, 49:176–85, 194–98, 214–19, 221–25.

22. Morison, *United States Naval Operations*, 4:12–13.

23. For career details on the Japanese admirals, I am indebted to Jean-François Masson, who is translating the wartime issues of the IJN's Register of Officers on the Active List, and also to Andrew Obluski; for Hara see also Prange, *At Dawn We Slept*, 200–201.

24. Japan, *Senshi Sōsho*, 49:186–87, with text of Combined Fleet Secret Radio No. 907 of 29 April 1942, and p. 192 for the text of 5th *Sentai* Secret Radio 838 of 30 April 1942. See also Lundstrom, "A Failure of Radio Intelligence."

CHAPTER 11. THE BATTLE OF THE CORAL SEA I

1. Principal documentary sources on the Battle of the Coral Sea include: CTF-17 to Cominch, The Battle of the Coral Sea, May 4–8, 1942 (27 May 1942), with reports of group, unit, and ship commanding officers (in RG-38, Action Reports, and also in NHC microfilm NRS-459); Comcrudiv Six (CTG-17.2) to Comcrupac (CTF-17), Engagement with Japanese Force 7–8 May, 1942 in Coral Sea (28 May 1942); H.M. Australian Squadron, Operations in the North Coral Sea—5th to 11th May, 1942, copy in Crace diary and in AWM [393/1] HMA Sqdrn Reports of Proceedings; war diaries, including Comcardiv One (Fitch), Comcru TF-17 (Smith), Crudiv Six (Kinkaid), Desron One (Early), and Desron Two (Hoover); Air Commo. Francis W. F. Lukis, OBE, Air Officer Commanding North East Area, To HQ, Allied Air Forces, Victoria Barracks, Melbourne, Report on Coral Sea Engagement (29 May 1942), in Australian Archives, series AA1969/10/0/119, item 273/25A; and message #AG 719, May 13, 1942, Melbourne to Chief of Staff, summary of air ops 2–12 May 1942, in RG-165, OPD Exec File 2, Item I1. Official analyses include: U.S. Fleet, Headquarters of the Commander In Chief, Secret Information Bulletin No. 1, Battle Experience from Pearl Harbor to Midway December 1941 to June 1942 including Makin Island Raid 17–18 August (15 February 1943); U.S. Navy, Office of Naval Intelligence, Publication Section, Combat Intelligence Branch, Combat Narratives, *The Battle of the Coral Sea: Consisting of the actions at Tulagi, May 4th; off Misima, May 7th; and in the Coral Sea on May 8th, 1942*; Bates, *Coral Sea*; and Admiralty Naval Staff, Historical Section, Battle Summary No. 45, *Battle of Coral Sea 4–8 May 1942*. Serious studies of Coral Sea include: Morison, *United States Naval Operations*, vol. 4, chapters 2–4; Gill, *Royal Australian Navy*, vol. 2, *1942–1945*, chapter 2; Lundstrom, *First South Pacific Campaign*, chapter 11; Willmott, *The Barrier and the Javelin*, chapters 5–8; Lundstrom, *First Team*, chapters 10–12; Coulthard-Clark, chapters 6–8; and the indispensable Japanese source, Japan, *Senshi Sōsho*, vol. 49, chapter 5.

2. Message 300907 April 1942 Cincpac to CTF-17 and CTF-11, in CSCMF, roll 10; in fact the *Shōei Maru* was one of the ships assigned to build the Deboyne base. Message 010830 May 1942 Comsowespacfor to CTF-17, in CSCMF, roll 10, informed Fletcher that the Saipan Base Force was thought to include nine transports and cargo ships, about eight "Marus," eight converted patrol craft, two converted minesweepers, and other auxiliaries.

3. *Neosho* deck log; W. W. Smith, 26. Cominch Secret Information Bulletin No. 1 criticized Fletcher for fueling at all in possible sub-endangered waters.

4. Messages 020044 and 020335 May 1942 Comsowespacfor to CTF-17, in CSCMF, roll 10.

5. CTF-17 report (27 May 1942).

6. Bates, *Coral Sea*, 31.

7. Air Officer Commanding North East Area, Report on Coral Sea Engagement (29 May 1942); Gillison, *Royal Australian Air Force 1939–1942*, 516–17; Japan, *Senshi Sōsho*, 49: 227–29.

8. CTF-17 report (27 May 1942); CO USS *Yorktown* to Cominch, U.S. Aircraft Action with Enemy, Report of (26 May 1942); Ludlum, 39–40; Biard, "The Pacific War," 11; Japan, *Senshi Sōsho*, 49:235.

9. Messages 020745, 021037, and 021525 May 1942 Comsowespacfor to CTF-17, CSCMF, roll 10; TF-17 report (27 May 1942); statement Fletcher to Bates (September 1946), in Bates, *Coral Sea*, 28. Rear Adm. Edward C. Kalbfus, president of the Naval War College, declared that Fletcher here "demonstrated" the "extreme importance" of topping off destroyers whenever possible.

10. Message 030213 May 1942 Cincpac Intel. Bull., CSCMF, roll 10; Japan, *Senshi Sōsho*, 49:228–30.

11. Message 030230 May 1942 Comsowespac to CTF-17, CSCMF, roll 10; CTF-17 report (27 May 1942); memo Dickey to Bates (14 October 1946). Gill, 2:44. Feldt, *The Coast Watchers*, 109, noted that Donald G. Kennedy on Santa Isabel sighted and reported two ships at Thousand Ships Bay.

12. Bates, *Coral Sea*, 31, 33, and 16, where he referred to the plan as a Japanese "Cannae"; message 030300 May 1942 Comsowespacfor to CTF-17, CSCMF, roll 10. The message Fletcher could not break was 030241 May 1942 Cincpac to CTF-16 and CTF-17, CSCMF, roll 10.

13. W. W. Smith, 26. Aerology Section, Office of the Chief of Naval Operations, The Battle of the Coral Sea (April 1944). The principal source for the Tulagi strike is CO USS *Yorktown* to Cincpac, Attack made by *Yorktown* Air Group on Enemy Forces in Tulagi and Gavutu Harbors (11 May 1942). Strike reports are in *Yorktown* report (26 May 1942). Schindler's Memorandum to Cincpac, Notes on the Coral Sea Action May 4–8, 1942 (22 May 1942); for his pleading to go, conversation (6 August 1996) with TF-17 flag yeoman Thomas Newsome.

14. Interview of Lt. Cdr. William O. Burch by Buaer (3 September 1942), Operational Archives, NHC; see also pilot accounts in Ludlum, 40–46.

15. Japan, *Senshi Sōsho*, 49:230–34.

16. Messages between Fletcher and Smith in Comcru TF-17 war diary; also W. W. Smith, 28–29; Moan diary, 9 May 1942. Bates asserted (*Coral Sea*, 41), based on the recollections of Capt. Thomas M. Shock of the *Chester*, that not until twilight did Fletcher first mention the idea of a cruiser foray against Tulagi, but this is corrected by the messages in Smith's war diary noted above.

17. Lundstrom, *First Team*, 174–78; Ludlum, 43–65; Morison, *United States Naval Operations*, 4:28.

18. Ens. Harry A. Frederickson (VB-5) diary (4 May 1942), via James C. Sawruk. Message 180200 May 1942 Comsowespacfor to Cincpac, CSCMF, roll 12, noted "further confirmation" of nine ships sunk on 4 May in the vicinity of Tulagi. The source was Leif Schroeder, a planter who became a petty officer in the Royal Australian Navy, Feldt, 109. Coast watchers on Guadalcanal also watched the distant attack; see Clemens, *Alone on Guadalcanal*, 106–7. For actual damage, Japan, *Senshi Sōsho*, 49:233.

19. Cincpac to Cominch, Naval Action in Coral Sea Area 4–8 May 1942, First Endorsement (17 June 1942); Schindler memo (22 May 1942).

20. Messages 040145 Cincpac Intel. Bull.; 040236 Comsowespacfor to CTF-17; 040950, 041102, and 041402 Comsowespacfor to CTF-17, all May 1942, CSCMF, roll 10. Japan, *Senshi Sōsho*, 49:239.

21. Crace diary, 4 May 1942; Bates, *Coral Sea*, 33, 39.

22. Crace diary, 5 May 1942. Messages 030241 Cincpac to CTF-16 and CTF-17, 042002 CTF-17 to Cincpac, and 042135 Cincpac to CTF-16 and CTF-17, May 1942, in CSCMF, roll 10. For the importance of the unbroken message 030241 first transmitted on 3 May, see below.

23. Japan, *Senshi Sōsho*, 49:235.

24. Messages 042226 CTF-17 to Cincpac, 050321 Cincpac to CTF-17, 050042 Comsowespacfor to CTF-17, 050241 Comsowespacfor to CTF-17, 050245 Comsowespac to CTF-17, and 050121 Cincpac Intel. Bull., all May 1942, in CSCMF, roll 10.

25. Ludlum, 66; messages 182348 CTF-11 to Bunav, 222008 Bunav to CTF-11, April 1942, in CSCMF, roll 9.

26. Ted Sherman claimed in a review of Morison's volume 4 (letter Sherman to Rear Adm. Charles Wellborn, 16 August 1950, DNC, Office Files, box 20) that he never saw CTF-17 Op-Ord 2-42 and "had no idea of the plans, orders and directions under which we were operating in the Coral Sea." According to Sherman, Fitch informed him after visiting the *Yorktown* on 5 May that "there was no operation order, that the only information he received from Fletcher was that it was to be a 'day to day affair.'" Sherman further stated that "although Fitch was designated Commander, Air, in the Task Force organization, this lack of information as to the OTC's plans and mission handicapped us severely during the entire battle." No one else ever mentioned this specific criticism (not even Sherman in his private diary in May 1942). It is inconceivable that Fitch did not received a copy of Op-Ord 2-42, particularly as on 6 May he took over as CTG-17.5 (Commander, Air) when Fletcher amalgamated the three task forces. Also it is hard to understand given the fluid situation how Fletcher could have done anything other than a "day to day affair." CTF-17 report (27 May 1942); Biard, "The Pacific War," 11; Japan, *Senshi Sōsho*, 49:235.

27. Messages 050528 Comsowespacfor to CTF-17 and 050249 Comsowespac to Cincpac, May 1942, in CSCMF, roll 10; Greybook, 435; SRH-272 Cincpac Enemy Activities File 4–5 May 1942. Japan, *Senshi Sōsho*, 49:233–34.

28. Messages 030241 Cincpac to CTF-16 and CTF-17, rebroadcast as 050355, and the original decrypt in 020344 series Com 14 to addressees Copek messages, all May 1942, in CSCMF, roll 10; Lundstrom, "A Failure," 103–6; Greybook, 432.

29. Message 050345 May 1942 Cincpac to CTF-16 and CTF-17, in CSCMF, roll 10; Greybook, 435. Japan, *Senshi Sōsho*, 49:230.

30. Message 050329 May 1942 Cincpac to CTF-16 and CTF-17, CSCMF, roll 10; Lundstrom, "A Failure," 107–10, 111–12; Japan, *Senshi Sōsho*, 49:233.

31. Message 050823 May 1942 Comsowespacfor to CTF-17, CSCMF, roll 10.

32. CTF-17 report (27 May 1942).

33. Comcru TF-17 war diary, 6 May 1942.

34. Messages 060145 Comsowespacfor to CTF-17, 060211 Cincpac to CTF-16 and CTF-17, 060025 and 060107 Comsowespac to CTF-17, May 1942, in CSCMF, roll 10; Japan, *Senshi Sōsho*, 49:239–40.

35. Japan, *Senshi Sōsho*, 49:241–43. Morison, *United States Naval Operations*, 4:31, wrongly stated Takagi never learned Fletcher was to the south and that his subsequent movement toward TF-17 was only a coincidence. Also Fletcher did not enjoy "bright sunlight," but instead operated under a thick overcast.

36. Messages 060246 and 060744 Comsowespac to CTF-17, 060925 Comsowespacfor to CTF-17, May 1942, CSCMF, roll 10; Crace diary, 6 May 1942; messages 060145 and 060330 May 1942 Comsowespacfor to CTF-17, in CSCMF, roll 10.

37. Fuel data for all TF-17 ships either has not survived (*Lexington* and *Yorktown*) or is not available (HMAS *Australia* and *Hobart*). From their deck logs, the cruisers *Minneapolis* and *New Orleans* had about 85% fuel; the *Astoria*, *Chester*, and *Portland* more than 95 percent; and the *Chicago* 72 percent. The destroyers of Early's Desron One had between 70 and 80 percent, except for the *Phelps* at 89 percent, whereas Hoover's newer but shorter-ranged Desron Two destroyers had more than 92 percent fuel.

38. CTF-17 report (27 May 1942); CTG-17.5 report (18 May 1942).

39. CTG-17.5 report (18 May 1942); Crace diary 6 May 1942.

40. Japan, *Senshi Sōsho*, 49:243–45; Lundstrom, "A Failure," 112–13.

41. In his official National Security Agency monograph *A Priceless Advantage*, Frederick Parker took issue with my earlier iteration of the 6 May 1942 comint blunder discussed in my April 1983 article in *Cryptologia*: "A Failure of Radio Intelligence." Parker saw no conflict between the picture created by comint and air searches and the actual Japanese dispositions. He described (28) that at dawn on 7 May, Fletcher knew of one carrier sighted west of Bougainville and that the invasion convoy and "protective covering forces were also loitering in the Solomons Sea west of Bougainville." Fletcher supposedly directed his air search "east of the Louisiades where COMINT had foretold, and aerial reconnaissance had already located, Japanese transports, a carrier, and other warships that represented a threat to Crace." Of course this completely ignored the presence of MO Striking Force northeast of TF-17.

Parker did not address the perilous situation that actually faced TF-17 on 6 May brought about by erroneous interpretations by the code breakers of incomplete Japanese messages. As noted, he asserted "there is no indication that erroneous decisions were made on partial message texts." Instead for 6 May, he claimed (32), "It is difficult to imagine what more the combat intelligence centers might have contributed concerning the Japanese forces prior to the engagement." Parker then noted my ignorance in 1983 of Capt. Forrest Biard's memoir, which in truth is not even germane to the situation on 5–6 May, and concluded (32): "In the context of the total intelligence picture available to Admiral Fletcher, there may never be another situation in which a single source of information proves more supportive. Moreover, it is equally difficult to imagine a situation in which the two intelligence sources proved more complementary than COMINT and aerial reconnaissance were on 5 and 6 May 1942." The interpretation of the events of 6 May here differs fundamentally with Parker, who did not have the benefit of studying the crucial Japanese documents on the Battle of the Coral Sea that provide the essential background for the decrypts. The true measure of the contribution of code breaking requires comparison of its findings with Japanese sources and an in-depth analysis of the circumstance that commanders actually faced. Parker did not discuss the key discrepancies between code breaker prognostications and the actual tactical situations and rarely mentioned any mistakes on the part of the code breakers. Instead he believed that errors were most often the result of commanders not properly using the intelligence information that was provided them. The brilliance of the technical achievement of breaking the Japanese code should not obscure the dangerous failures of interpretation by the code breakers and intelligence analysts that on occasion imperiled the forces in action.

CHAPTER 12. THE BATTLE OF THE CORAL SEA II (OFFENSE)

1. Japan, *Senshi Sōsho*, 49:271–74.

2. Air Officer Commanding North East Area, Report on Coral Sea Engagement (29 May 1942).

3. Visual message 060600 May 1942 CTG-17.5 to *Lexington* and *Yorktown*, in Coral Sea, Battle of, Dispatches, Task Force 17 and Task Group 17.5, RG-38, Cincpac Flag Files, hereafter *Lexington* dispatches. Fitch saved these messages while abandoning the *Lexington* on 8 May and they are vital for reconstructing the events of 7 May.

4. Letters Arnold to Lundstrom (9 April and 24 April 1972); letter Arnold to W. W. Smith (7 March 1965), in Smith Papers.

5. Messages 060754 and 060925 Comsowespacfor to CTF-17, 061226 and 061335 Comsowespac to CTF-17, May 1942, in CSCMF, roll 10.

6. W. W. Smith, 22.

7. Message 061655 May 1942 CTF-17 to CTG-17.3 (info CTG-17.2 and CTG-17.5), copy in Crace's diary. Fletcher also told Crace to monitor NPM 128 and NPM 122 for radio messages on the Cincpac Fox Schedule, but apparently Crace had trouble doing so. See his report Operations in the North Coral Sea—5th to 11th May, 1942.

8. Bates, *Coral Sea*, 54; Morison, *United States Naval Operations*, 4:37, 39; Gill, 2:49; Willmott, 233–34. The most unusual criticism of "Crace's Chase" appeared long afterward in the bitter memoir of TF-17 radio intelligence officer Forrest Biard, "The Pacific War," 12. He claimed that on the morning of 7 May Spence Lewis (the "dovish" chief of staff) inexplicably confided that Fletcher detached Crace solely because he did not want to share the glory. Fletcher parked the Anzac Squadron "well south of Jomard Passage" and "out of the area in which we will in all probability meet the Japs" simply to deny "medals" to "Britishers and Australians." Biard then professed suitable indignation to Lewis, not only at Fletcher's crass ("almost criminal") behavior, but also because he himself already divined the danger of air attack to Crace. "Here I knew finally," Biard declared, "that all the serious misgivings I had gathered about our professionally almost senile task force commander were valid." Far from keeping Crace out of the action, Fletcher placed the Support Group precisely where he thought the Japanese must go to assault Port Moresby. There would have been medals aplenty for Crace's force had things gone according to plan. Biard obviously did not understand the reasons behind the Jomard stratagem. His manifest disdain for Fletcher led him, as always, to think the worst of everything. Perhaps Lewis, renowned for his sense of humor, simply pulled the overly serious lieutenant's leg.

9. Letter Adm. Sir John Crace to Maj. C. S. Goldingham (17 November 1957), copy in Crace diary. Coulthard-Clark, 145. Letter Schindler to Lundstrom (28 June 1972). The *Chicago* had the weakest antiaircraft armament of the U.S. cruisers present: eight 5-inch/25 antiaircraft guns, four 1.1-inch quad mounts, and eight .50-caliber machine guns, whereas the other cruisers had a dozen 20-mm cannons in place of the .50-calibers. The *Australia* wielded eight 4-inch antiaircraft guns in twin mounts, two 2-pounder (40-mm) quad mounts and eight .50-cal. machine guns; the *Hobart* carried eight 4-inch antiaircraft guns in twin-

mounts, two 2-pounder quad mounts, and twelve .50-caliber machine guns. The *Farragut* had five 5-inch/38 dual purpose guns and eight 20-mm cannons; the *Perkins* and *Walke* each had four 5-inch/38 and four 20-mm each (Bureau of Ordnance, Armament Summary, December 1941).

10. Point Option is the spot where pilots could expect to find the carriers on their return. It is always expressed as a course and speed. Point Option moves constantly (as do ships).

11. Message 060050 (*sic*, the logged time of receipt was 2058 GCT or 0758, 7 May, Z–11) May 1942 CTF-17 to CTG-17.2 and CTG-17.5, in *Lexington* dispatches.

12. Ludlum, 67–68.

13. According to the Biard memoir ("The Pacific War"), 12, Fletcher then turned over tactical command of TF-17 to Fitch, but the evidence does not support this assertion. Fitch never acknowledged receiving tactical command on 7 May. Nor did he issue any orders beyond those to the *Lexington* and *Yorktown* to execute his air operations order No. 1. No ships in TF-17 noted a change of command on 7 May. It could perhaps be construed from Biard's account that Fletcher might have *thought* he turned over tactical command but inexplicably Fitch never got the word. However, Fletcher never ceased issuing orders to TF-17, including all course changes, nor did he reassume tactical command later. It could be argued Fitch might have anticipated receiving tactical command. Sherman noted in his diary on 20 May 1942 there was a "confusion of command" on the afternoon of 7 May. However, it appears from what he subsequently wrote in *Combat Command*, 100, that he actually meant unwarranted delay in reaching a decision. Sherman never stated that Fletcher had or ever considered relinquishing tactical command on 7 May. Fitch was surprised on 8 May when Fletcher did suddenly turn over tactical command to him. According to Poco Smith, 22, during the evening of 7 May Fletcher gave tactical control to Fitch, who ordered all combat air patrol fighters into the air. Later after the skirmish over TF-17, Smith stated that Fletcher resumed command and declined to make a night surface attack. No evidence exists for that either. It appears that Biard confused 8 May with 7 May. As will be seen certain of his recollections better fit the circumstances on the eighth.

14. Lt. Frank F. Gill, The Battle of the Coral Sea, Report of Action 7–8 May, 1942, by Fighter Director, in "*Lexington* Papers," RG-38, Action Reports.

15. Comcru TF-17 war diary, 7 May 1942, also *Minneapolis* war diary, 7 May 1942. Fullinwider's radio log has not survived, nor has the complete TF-17 message file for 7 May 1942, so it is not possible to state precisely his findings. However, Hypo's daily intelligence report (Combat Intelligence, Fourteenth Naval District, Communication Intelligence Summary, May 7, 1942, in RG-457, SRMN-012, p. 256) does give readings undoubtedly based on some of the same transmissions possibly intercepted by Fullinwider. Hypo, at least, was aware that at 0840 a Japanese search plane radioed that enemy ships bore 170 degrees and eighty-two miles from Rossel. Another report at that time identified one battleship, two cruisers, seven destroyers, and "what appears to be a carrier" on course 030 degrees, speed twenty knots. If Fullinwider indeed read these transmissions, he was certainly justified in warning that TF-17 had been located. At 1121 Nimitz radioed Halsey and Fletcher: "Enemy radio broadcast received Hawaii 0710 Item Quote Enemy one battleship 2 cruisers 7 destroyers and one probable carrier sighted course 030 speed 20" (message 070021 May 1942 Cincpac to CTF-16, 17, CSCMF, roll 10). It is not certain from Biard's memoir, which includes excerpts from his personal radio log, how much of this radio traffic his team actually intercepted. Significantly, he never did acknowledge that the Japanese in fact sighted TF-17 that morning. Indeed he based much of his charge of Fletcher's incompetence by asserting the Japanese had not done so. Biard's account of his radio intercepts and advice to Fletcher will be analyzed in a separate note.

16. CO USS *Neosho* to Cincpac, Engagement of USS *Neosho* with Japanese Aircraft on May 7, 1942, Subsequent Loss of USS *Neosho*, Search for Survivors (25 May 1942). The actual distance between the two forces was 285 miles not 325, and the difference was due to poor navigation on the part of the *Neosho*. CTF-17 report (27 May 1942); Bates, *Coral Sea*, 56. Willmott, 243, wrongly stated that Fletcher knew at this time that the *Neosho* and *Sims* were under heavy attack.

17. Visual message sent at 1031 from CTF-17 to CTG-17.5 and CTG-17.2, in *Lexington* dispatches. There is some confusion as to what exactly Nielsen thought he saw. The *Yorktown* action report (16 May 1942) stated that he had actually meant to send four heavy cruisers (CA) and two destroyers, but that error occurred with the wrong encoding of two aircraft carriers (CV) instead of two destroyers. The *Lexington* report (15 May 1942) gave the amended total as two cruisers and two destroyers. Nielsen himself later related that he saw two cruisers and four destroyers (Ludlum, 69). Biard, "The Pacific War," 13; Cressman, *Gallant Ship*, 96; Newsome conversation, 6 August 1996.

18. Subsequently it was thought the carriers lurked in the sector McDowell had not completely searched. MO Striking Force was too far south to be found by the *Yorktown*'s morning search.

19. Nimitz called this decision "courageous" (Potter and Nimitz, *The Great Sea War*, 216).

20. CTF-17 report (27 May 1942); message 062345 May 1942 CTF-17 to CTG-17.5, *Lexington* dispatches.

21. Japan, *Senshi Sōsho*, 49:276–77.

22. Japan, *Senshi Sōsho*, 49:273–74. I am most indebted to James C. Sawruk for identifying Captain Horgan's flight as responsible for this vital report.

23. Morison, *United States Naval Operations*, 4:20, stated the contact that Nielsen made was Marumo's Support Force that included two old light cruisers. In fact, the position of Nielsen's contact, northeast of Misima, and its southeasterly course conformed exactly to MO Main Force. Having fled Deboyne for safer waters, Marumo was about forty miles southwest of Gotō and withdrawing *northwest* toward the Trobriand Islands. Nielsen missed the Port Moresby convoy because it had already gone on past to the southwest. Japan, *Senshi Sōsho*, 49:280–81, 287.

24. Japan, *Senshi Sōsho*, 49:280–81.

25. Bates, *Coral Sea*, 56, stated that at 0930 (Z–11) the *Neosho* reported "many planes" in latitude 16° 05′ south, longitude 159° 08′ east. The source of this citation is a summary of events in the *Minneapolis* war diary. The timing is odd, because according to the *Neosho* action report (25 May 1942) and war diary, the enemy planes were not even sighted until 0935 (1005 Z–11.5). Also the position is the same that was included in the message sent at 1021 (1051 Z–11.5). The supposed 0930 message does not appear in another, much more detailed summary notes compiled on 7 May by the *Minneapolis* and also included in the war diary. No other ship in TF-17 recorded the 0930 message, nor is it in the Cincpac Secret and Confidential Message File. There is no indication it actually existed. Had Biard known of it, he would certainly have cited it because it would have bolstered his case that the 5th Carrier Division was attacking the Fueling Group.

26. *Neosho* report (25 May 1942); Commander, Destroyers, Pacific Fleet, to Secretary of the Navy, Sinking of the USS *Sims* (DD-409) by Japanese Bombers in the Coral Sea on May 7, 1942 (8 July 1942).

27. Japan, *Senshi Sōsho*, 49:278–79; *Neosho* report (25 May 1942), *Sims* report (8 July 1942).

28. Message 062369 May 1942 Comsowespacfor to CTF-17, CSCMF, roll 10: "Our aircraft bombed with damage not observed enemy force consisting 10 AP [transport ship] 1 CV 16 warships posit 10-34 South 152-36 East course 285 at 2048 GCT 6th [0748/7]. Also sighted 3 AP 4 DD posit 10-41 South 152-30 East course 285 at 2100 GCT 6th [0800/7]. Another report 11 enemy vessels including 5 AP position 10-43 South 152-13 at 2055 GCT 6th [0755/7th]."

29. Captain Biard's account of 7 May 1942 in his *Cryptolog* article ("The Pacific War"), 12–14, is presented in the form of an annotated chronology drawn from his contemporary notes, memory, and Morison's account. TF-17 used Zone–11.5 time until 1700, which the NWC Analysis and Morison converted to Zone–11 by subtracting thirty minutes. It is not always clear whether Biard referred to Z–11.5 or Z–11 time. (All times noted herein are Z–11.)

Biard asserted that quite early that day he deduced from radio intercepts that certain Japanese units, which he soon identified as the 5th Carrier Division, threatened the *Neosho* and *Sims* well to the southeast of TF-17. Therefore the *Shōkaku* and *Zuikaku* had to be east of TF-17 and not northeast, north, or northwest. Biard stated that he furnished this evidence, which he deemed incontrovertible, to Fletcher and Lewis, who chose to disregard it. It is not possible without consulting the original log of intercepts kept by Biard's radio operators to determine exactly what Japanese messages he read and when he did so. That log, if it still exists, has not been found. Other than Biard, the only other sources of direct information on the 7 May 1942 radio intercepts are the "Final Report of the R.I. Unit of the USS *Yorktown*" (23 May 1942) (hereafter "Final Report"), submitted by the two radio operators, P. E. Seaward, Radioman first Class, and W. W. Eaton, Radioman second Class, in RG-457, SRH-313, Pacific Ocean Mobile Radio Intelligence Unit Reports 1942, and an incomplete list of messages and translations included in the Hypo daily summary (SRMN-012).

The problem with Biard's account is that he included information and deductions that were, in fact, not made until later, in some cases much later. His 0903 entry described a Japanese surface unit "soon to be identified as an aircraft carrier and later established to be the large aircraft carrier *Zuikaku*" that was in touch with search aircraft. Significantly Biard did not say *when* these identifications were made, but structured his account as if such already occurred on the morning of the seventh. Similarly, Biard mentioned the carrier *Shōkaku* as originator of several messages that morning, but it was not until either very late on 7 May or early 8 May that the *Shōkaku* and *Zuikaku* were tentatively linked to specific call signs. Hypo advised Halsey (and also apparently Fletcher) at 0552 on 8 May (message 071852 May 1942 Com 14 to CTF-16, CSCMF, roll 10) that the radio frequency 7035 was "used by carrier believed *Shokaku* also 6630 by carrier and planes giving homing info 0900 GCT [2000 7 May]." That message still referred to the enemy carriers by their call signs "Siso" and "Suso" instead of conclusively identifying them by ship names.

Another example of where Biard might have wrongly ascribed a definite identification is the entry for 0916, which gave an important message from a search plane to an addressee "later identified tentatively (and correctly)" as commander of the 5th Carrier Division. Biard also attributed several subsequent messages to that officer. However, Hypo did not note the 5th Carrier Division as an originator or addressee among the aircraft messages intercepted on the morning of the seventh, so again it is not known when that particular identification was first made.

To justify his conclusion that enemy carriers were to the east, Biard stated: "We had received reports from other Allied search units in the prior two days that enemy forces were headed our way from the east of us. The chances were very good that the planes which discovered *Neosho* and *Sims* were from carriers now to the east of us." No such reports placing Japanese forces in that direction can now be found.

Biard did acknowledge intercepting messages from a source different from the one he believed was shadowing the *Neosho* and *Sims*. One message received at 0957 mentioned one battleship and two cruisers. He related that he told Fletcher that this message referred to a sighting of Crace's detached force, and that intercepts revealed that the 5th Carrier Division was sending a strike group against the *Neosho* and *Sims*. Again there is considerable doubt whether these identifications had actually yet been made at that time or presented in that way. According to Biard, Fletcher then asked him whether he should "recall" the Fueling Group and have it "join us," but Biard argued against the move, noting it was too far away. Biard advised keeping radio silence because: "So far no one had found us." He added: "This time the Admiral took my advice. I think I can say it was the only time he did so during the entire Battle of the Coral Sea. Perhaps it was the only time that our radio intercept work influenced him in his decision making." Of course the record shows that Fletcher *already* knew, not only from radio intelligence but also from actual radar contacts, that the Japanese had sighted *him*, not just Crace or the Fueling Group. Biard never acknowledged that enemy search planes found and shadowed TF-17 on the morning of 7 May. Further it is highly unlikely that Fletcher would have ever considered "recalling" the distant *Neosho* and *Sims*, which would have meant bringing them closer to the enemy.

Biard cited another flagrant instance that morning when Fletcher stubbornly refused to accept that the two Japanese carriers were east of TF-17. At 1043 he recorded that Comcardiv 5 advised at 1040 that he would change course to 280 degrees, speed twenty knots, the order to be executed at 1045. In essence the Japanese commander was providing his strike group a new Point Option course. Biard was correct. That was Takagi announcing the change of course to MO Striking Force to head west toward the Louisiades. However, there then occurred, in Biard's words, a "calamitous misfortune." Fullinwider in the *Lexington* reported the gist of that message as an enemy search plane giving course and speed of TF-17 as 280 degrees at twenty knots. According to Biard, Fletcher then asked why the two radio intelligence teams did not agree, to which Biard replied that a contact report would not include an execute order set for five minutes hence. He recalled that he also asked Fletcher to come to the chart with him to see that TF-17 was only going about ten knots (and, Biard stressed, no carrier search pilot would *ever* mistake a ten-knot wake for a twenty-knot wake). "At no time recently had we been on any course approximately 280 degrees." To Biard, "Even a cretin would have been convinced of the correctness of my arguments, but not Fletcher."

Again Biard, although later shown to be correct in his basic assumption, greatly overstated in his memoir any case that he could possibly have made to Fletcher. The "Final Report" acknowledged Biard's reading of the change of course and execute signal, but noted that the message "looked very much like it was a report of our course and speed." Indeed unlike Biard's assertion, TF-17 *was*, at that exact instant, steering a course and speed almost identical to what the enemy had seemingly reported. Since 1024 TF-17 steamed on 290 degrees, and at 1041, just before this discussion supposedly occurred, Fletcher increased speed from twenty-three to twenty-five knots. How could Biard have told the admiral any differently? Biard also did not mention that Fullinwider could be excused for misreading the message, because it was known Japanese search planes had certainly sighted TF-17.

Given such obvious contradictions with the contemporary record, it is impossible to say precisely what Biard actually did tell Fletcher on the morning of 7 May 1942 as opposed to what he might have added later because of hindsight. For an example of how an uncritical acceptance of Biard's memoir has led historians astray, see Prados, who referred to him as "Baird." Prados asserted, 309, that on the morning of 7 May Fletcher was "scared silly to learn from the *Neosho* attack that the Imperial Navy strike forces were behind him as well as in front." In truth, though, Fletcher did not perceive a threat to the east at that time and did not learn until late afternoon that air attacks had badly damaged the *Neosho*. Prados chided Fletcher for throwing away Biard's "priceless gift" of vital radio intelligence on the location of the enemy carriers solely because of his "animosity toward his radio intelligence officer." According to Prados, Biard also undertook radio direction finding (actually a function of the *Yorktown* communicators) and was "plotting the coordinates of the *Zuikaku*'s broadcasts until her planes landed about 2:00 PM." Supposedly that precious intelligence "went completely to waste" by Fletcher's inaction. The record supports none of Prados's suppositions.

30. Comcru TF-17 war diary, *Minneapolis* war diary, Crace diary. Unlike the famous quote in Stanley Johnston, *Queen of the Flat-Tops*, 181, Dixon did not use "Dixon to carrier." Aside from advising the results of the strike, he wanted to warn the *Lexington* that the strike had expended its ordnance and that preparations to rearm aircraft should begin. Unlike the more modern *Yorktown*, the *Lex* lacked adequate bomb elevators and ammunition hoists, greatly slowing down the process. Letter Duckworth to Lundstrom (9 March 1972).

31. Ludlum, 73–74; message 070318 May 1942 CTF-17 to CTG-17.5, in *Lexington* dispatches.

32. Japan, *Senshi Sōsho*, 49:282–84.

33. In addition to the relevant action reports, see Lundstrom, *First Team*, 197–205. Since writing that book, I spoke with Ishikawa Shirō, who flew one of the *Shōhō*'s Type 96 carrier fighters in the battle. He provided additional evidence that demonstrates that eight fighters defended the *Shōhō*, not six as is commonly accepted even in Japan.

34. Japan, *Senshi Sōsho*, 49:285–86.

CHAPTER 13. THE BATTLE OF THE CORAL SEA II (DEFENSE)

1. Visual message 070306 May 1942 CTG-17.5 to CTF-17, in *Lexington* dispatches. The latest summary by Comsowespac of sightings in the Louisiades area was sent at 1240 (070140 May 1942 Comsowespac to CTF-17, CSCMF, roll 10). Sherman diary, 20 May 1942; Sherman, 100. In his review of Morison's volume 4, Sherman wrote that Fitch "desired to launch a second attack at targets in the vicinity of the sunken *Shōhō* but this was disapproved by Fletcher," letter Sherman to Wellborn (16 August 1950, DNC, Office Files, box 20).

Given Fitch's 070306 message to Fletcher cited above stating that "target prospects are poor" there, it appears that Sherman overstated Fitch's enthusiasm for that course of action. Burch interview by Buaer (3 September 1942); CTF-17 report (27 May 1942); Japan, *Senshi Sōsho*, 49:287.

2. Sherman diary, 22 May 1942. Biard, "The Pacific War," 13–14, described a fervent thirty-minute discussion in flag plot down on one knee brandishing radio intercepts to Fletcher seated on the transom. Biard claimed that Fletcher sat inert, making no effort to consult with Fitch, supposedly in tactical command. Fletcher then declared: "Young man, you do not understand. *I* am going to attack *them* tomorrow," to which Biard replied, "But Admiral, they are going to attack you *today*" (Biard's emphasis). If Fletcher had turned over tactical command, as Biard asserted, that would have been Fitch's decision. "The picture being painted by our radio intercepts just could not permit this inertia, this indecision, this divided command." Biard never forgave Fletcher for not taking his advice, and the incident is the centerpiece of his anti-Fletcher philippic. Former Yeoman Thomas Newsome, who was Fletcher's combat talker, vividly remembered the conversation. He recalled that Biard, "A bantam rooster," differed with the admiral and repeatedly punctuated his rejoinders by a sharp, "With respect, sir!" To Newsome it appeared neither man gave an inch. Newsome conversation, 6 August 1996. Again it is vital to stress that Fletcher had *not* turned over tactical command but exercised full control of TF-17. Far from ignoring Fitch or leaving everything to him, he sent at least two messages requesting possible options while the strike planes were landing. Rather patiently given the circumstances, he gave the fiery Biard the chance to state his case, but chose not to accept his counsel. Biard consistently ignored other factors that might have contributed to Fletcher's decisions and failed to acknowledge that Fletcher constantly consulted with others.

3. Messages 070329 CTF-17 to CTG-17.5, 070350 CTG-17.5 to CTF-17, May 1942, both in *Lexington* dispatches. Sherman diary (22 May 1942); Sherman letter to Wellborn (16 August 1950, DNC, Office Files, box 20); *Lexington* action report (15 May 1942). In *Combat Command*, 100, Sherman opined that because there was no second strike to Deboyne, the carriers must search again, but Fletcher hesitated too long making his decision and wasted the opportunity to do anything more that afternoon. The timing of the signals between Fletcher and Fitch, however, do not bear out Sherman's charge that Fletcher dawdled. Kinkaid memoir, 96; Bates, *Coral Sea*, 60; Morison, *United States Naval Operations*, 4:43.

4. Lt. Frank F. Gill, The Battle of the Coral Sea, Report of Action 7–8 May, 1942, by Fighter Director, *Lexington* Papers. Japan, *Senshi Sōsho*, 49:288–89; *Kōdōchōsho* (combat logs) of the Fourth, Tainan and Genzan air groups. Messages 070220 Comsowespacfor to CTF-17 and 070426 CTF-44 to Comsowespacfor, May 1942, in CSCMF, roll 10; Biard, "The Pacific War," 14.

5. For the activities of the Support Group on 7 May, see Crace diary; his report Operations in the North Coral Sea—5th to 11th May, 1942; and CTF-44 to Secretary, Naval Board, Attack by Torpedo Bomber and High Level Bomber Aircraft—7th May, 1942 (21 May 1942), copy forwarded by Comsowespacfor to Cominch (26 May 1942); CO USS *Chicago* to Cincpac, Action Against enemy aircraft, May 7, 1942—Report of (11 May 1942); also Coulthard-Clark, 90–107.

6. Ens. John W. Rowley from VB-5 attacked the *Shōhō* but became disoriented after chasing an enemy plane. Fortunate not to have run afoul of the Zeros, he later ditched off the New Guinea coast and was rescued along with his radioman. Frank and Harrington, 101.

7. CTF-44 report (21 May 1942); Japan, *Senshi Sōsho*, 49:288; personal diary and information from Lt. Col. Wallace Fields, USAF (Ret.), a copilot in one of the B-17s. Morison, *United States Naval Operations*, 4:39, rightly praised the Support Group's efforts, but went too far in stating, "Japanese attack was of the same type and strength as the one that sank the H.M.S. *Prince of Wales* and *Repulse*" on 10 December 1941. In that case the Japanese employed fifty twin-engine torpedo bombers and sixteen level bombers, whereas Crace faced twelve torpedo planes and twenty-two level bombers, counting the three B-17s. Also the skill of the Japanese on 7 May was much diminished compared to 10 December.

8. Message 070440 May 1942 Comsowespac to CTF-17, CSCMF, roll 10; Crace diary.

9. Lundstrom, *First Team*, 210. Messages 070449 CTF-17 to CTG-17.5, 070505 CTG-17.5 to *Yorktown* and *Lexington*, and 070615 *Lexington* to *Yorktown*, all May 1942, *Lexington* dispatches. Letter Arnold to Lundstrom (9 April 1972).

10. Messages 070418 *Neosho* to [All U.S. Naval Vessels], 070545 Cincpac to *Tippecanoe*, 070618 *Neosho* to Radio Wahiwa, 070405 Naval Observer Suva to Opnav, and 070605 Comsowespacfor to CTF-17, all May 1942, CSCMF, roll 10. Message 080755 May 1942 Cincpac to Cominch, Cominch 00 Files, noted that it was in the "late afternoon" the *Neosho* and *Sims* were "heavily bombed" and the "*Sims* sunk." Message 070621 May 1942 CTF-17 to CTG-17.5, *Lexington* dispatches.

11. Crace diary; Operations in the North Coral Sea—5th to 11th May, 1942.

12. Japan, *Senshi Sōsho*, 49:289–90.

13. Japan, *Senshi Sōsho*, 49:290–91. The message announcing the change in course of the U.S. carrier force to 120 degrees was attributed to an *Aoba* float plane temporarily operating out of Deboyne. It is not clear whether this report referred to Crace or Fletcher. Certainly the Support Group never changed course to 120 degrees, but the carriers occasionally did when conducting air operations.

14. *Yorktown* report (16 May 1942); Japan, *Senshi Sōsho*, 49:302.

15. Fitz-Gerald was gunnery officer of the *New Orleans* and an astute observer of events. Flatley comment in "Fury in Air over Coral Sea Win Glory for Fliers Here," *Kansas City Star* (18 March 1951). Lundstrom, *First Team*, 209–15.

16. Japan, *Senshi Sōsho*, 49:292–93.

17. Lundstrom, *First Team*, 214–16. Comdesron One (CTU-17.2.4) to Cominch, Engagement with Japanese Force 7–8 May 1942 in Coral Sea (22 May 1942); Capt. A. R. Early, Memorandum for Admiral Theobald, U.S. Navy, USS *Dixie* (11 May 1942), RG-313, Comscofor General Correspondence, box 59; Lt. Frank F. Gill, The Battle of the Coral Sea, Report of Action 7–8 May, 1942, by Fighter Director, *Lexington* Papers.

18. Messages 070131 Cincpac Intel. Bull., 070828 Comsowespac to all CTFs, May 1942, in CSCMF, roll 10.

19. Lundstrom, *First Team*, 216–17; letter Rear Adm. Oscar Pederson to Joseph Harrington (21 July 1964), in Pederson Papers.

20. The Biard memoir, "The Pacific War," 14, included the text of many intercepted transmissions from the Japanese strike group. In numerous instances he specifically identified the senders and addressees, that is, ComCardiv 5, *Shōkaku*, *Zuikaku*. Again there is a strong question whether these detailed identifications only occurred after the fact. The Hypo summary for 7 May simply referred to the individual carriers by their call signs Siso and Suso, which is very likely all that Biard knew at that exact time. Stroop, oral history, 97–98; Ray interview by Buaer (15 July 1942); messages 071031 and 071253 May 1942 Cincpac to CTF-16 and CTF-17, CSCMF, roll 10.

21. Japan, *Senshi Sōsho*, 49:292–94.

22. Message 071051 May 1942 CTG-17.5 to CTF-17, *Lexington* dispatches. Stroop, oral history, 97; letter Sherman to Wellborn (16 August 1950, DNC, Office Files, box 20). Sherman wrote in *Combat Command*, 102, "We reported [Japanese carriers only thirty miles east] to Fletcher, but he was inclined to discredit it. It was confirmed after the war that the Japanese carriers were very close to us. It might have been an excellent opportunity for a night torpedo attack by our destroyers or by the *Lexington* torpedo plane squadron, which was trained in night landings. But, instead, Fletcher decided to head south to avoid a chance encounter with the enemy during the hours of darkness." Sherman chose not to mention in his book the long delay in informing Fletcher and that the Japanese carriers were never in fact nearer to TF-17 than about one hundred miles, which was hardly "very close."

23. CTF-17 report (27 May 1942); message 160200 May 1942 CTF-17 to Cincpac, Greybook, 468–69; Kinkaid memoir, 99; Cincpac First Endorsement (17 June 1942); Biard, "The Pacific War," 15.

24. Ludlum, 77; letter Vice Adm. Turner Caldwell to R. J. Cressman (20 April 1984), courtesy of Robert Cressman; letter Caldwell to J. C. Sawruk (18 January 1987), courtesy of James Sawruk.

25. Japan, *Senshi Sōsho*, 49:295–300.

26. Messages 071245 CTG-17.5 to CTF-17 and 071339 CTF-17 to CTG-17.5, May 1942, in USS *Yorktown*, List of Dispatches and Signals sent, received, and intercepted in May 8, 1942, enclosure to CO USS *Yorktown* to Cincpac, Report of Action of *Yorktown* and *Yorktown* Air Group on May 8, 1942 (25 May 1942), hereafter *Yorktown* dispatches.

27. Messages 071245 CTF-17 to Comsowespacfor, 071024 CTF-17 to Cincpac, and 071219 Comsowespacfor to all CTFs, all May 1942, in CSCMF, roll 10. The *Bishopdale* was a large (17,357 tons), modern (1937) fleet oiler with a top speed of only 11.5 knots. Built in 1916, the *Kurumba*, an "oil supply vessel," displaced only 7,930 tons, with a top speed of ten knots. Neither ship had trained for underway refueling (Straczek, *Royal Australian Navy*).

28. Crace diary; message CTF-17 to CTG-17.3, no date and time group, is included in *Lexington* dispatches. The fact that Fitch had it meant that it must have at least been sent over by the *Yorktown*.

29. Ugaki, 122; Japan, *Senshi Sōsho*, 49:300–303; Potter and Nimitz, 216; letter Duckworth to Lundstrom (29 October 1972).

CHAPTER 14. THE BATTLE OF THE CORAL SEA III

1. CTF-17 report (27 May 1942); letter Duckworth to Lundstrom (29 October 1972).

2. Morison, *United States Naval Operations*, 4:46; message 071835 May 1942 Comsowespac to all CTFs, CSCMF, roll 10. Principal documents for 8 May operations include CTF-17 report (27 May 1942); CTG-17.5 report (18 May 1942); CO USS *Lexington* to Cincpac, Report of Action—The Battle of the Coral Sea, 7 and 8 May 1942 (15 May 1942); *Lexington* Papers (including reports of VF-2, VB-2, VS-2, and VT-2); *Yorktown* report (25 May 1942); Commander Cruiser Division Six (Commander Task Group 17.2) to Commander Cruisers, Pacific Fleet (Commander Task Force Seventeen, Engagement with Japanese Force 7–8 May, 1942 in Coral Sea (28 May 1942). CTU-17.2.2 to Cincpac, Action Report (17 May 1942); Comdesron One (CTU-17.2.4) to Cominch, Engagement with Japanese Force 7–8 May 1942 in Coral Sea (22 May 1942); and CTG-17.5.4 (Comdesron Two) to Cominch, Action in Coral Sea Area on May 8, 1942, report of (18 May 1942); Crace diary, 8 May 1942; and H.M. Australian Squadron, Operations in the North Coral Sea—5th to 11th May, 1942. For a detailed account of air operations, see Lundstrom, *First Team*, chapter 12.

3. Aerology Section, Office of the Chief of Naval Operations, The Battle of the Coral Sea (April 1944).

4. Lt. Frank F. Gill, The Battle of the Coral Sea, Report of Action 7–8 May, 1942, by Fighter Director, *Lexington* Papers; Biard, "The Pacific War," 16; Sherman diary, 20 May 1942; Sherman, *Combat Command*, 103.

5. Messages in *Yorktown* dispatches.

6. *Yorktown* dispatches; CTF-17 report (27 May 1942); messages 072209 Cincpac to CTF-17, 072030 *Tangier* to Comsowespacfor, and 072332 Comsowespacfor to Cincpac, May 1942, CSCMF, roll 10.

7. Stroop, oral history, 115–16; CO Scouting Squadron Two Report for May 7, 1942 and May 8, 1942, in *Lexington* Papers.

8. Japan, *Senshi Sōsho*, 49:303–6.

9. Japan, *Senshi Sōsho*, 49:306–7.

10. *Japan Times & Advertiser* (14 March 1942).

11. The *Lexington* had twelve 5-inch/25 guns, twelve 1.1-inch quad mounts, thirty-two 20-mm cannons and twenty-eight .50-caliber machine guns; the *Yorktown* had eight 5-inch/38s, four 1.1-inch quads, twenty-four 20-mm and eighteen .50-cal. machine guns. The heavy cruisers each had eight 5-inch/25s, four 1.1-inch quads, and twelve 20-mm guns. The destroyer leader *Phelps* had two 1.1-inch quads and four 20-mm guns (her eight 5-inch/38s were single-purpose only); the *Dewey* and *Aylwin* had five 5-inch/38s and four 20-mm cannons,

and the four Desron Two destroyers (*Anderson*, *Hammann*, *Russell*, and *Morris*) each had four 5-inch/38s and four 20-mm cannons. Some ships had additional machine guns beyond the official authorization listed here (Bureau of Ordnance, Armament Summary, December 1941, and supplements). For a description of the guns, see Campbell, *Naval Weapons of World War Two*. For how they were employed at Coral Sea: USS *Yorktown* Air Defense Doctrine, enclosure to *Yorktown* report (25 May 1942), and Comcrupac to Ships Operating in my Command, Antiaircraft Defense of Task Forces (15 June 1942), in RG-38, Cincpac Flag Files.

12. *Yorktown* dispatches.

13. Lundstrom, *First Team*, 245–46. Sherman took the criticism of Gill's fighter direction as a personal affront: "As I was Commanding Officer of the *Lexington* at the time and the fighter direction was under my supervision. I considered I was in a better position to judge than the Captain of the *Yorktown*" (letter Sherman to Wellborn, 16 August 1950, DNC, Office Files, box 20).

14. Stroop, oral history, 103; Ralph Wilhelm diary, 8 May 1942, courtesy of Ralph Wilhelm; conversation with Thomas Newsome (6 August 1996).

15. Early memo for Theobald (11 May 1942), RG-313, Comscofor General Correspondence, box 59.

16. Newsome conversation (15 July 1999); W. W. Smith, 42, and Smith unedited Midway manuscript, 154.

17. W. W. Smith, 46. Message 072356 May 1942 CTF-17 to Cincpac, CSCMF, roll 10. The date and time group for this message is 072356, that is, 1056 on 8 May, Z–11 time, but that was before the attack, so the message was actually composed and sent later.

18. Lundstrom, *First Team*, 269–70.

19. *Yorktown* dispatches; Lt. Cdr. Phillip F. Fitz-Gerald diary, 8 May 1942, via Kenneth Crawford.

20. *Yorktown* report (25 May 1942); Schindler memorandum (22 May 1942); messages 080137 CTF-17 to Comsowespac, 080204 CTF-17 to Cincpac, 080215 Comsowespac to CTF-17, and 080244 CTF-17 to Comsowespac, May 1942, in CSCMF, roll 11.

21. Message 080101 May 1942 Comsowespacfor to CTF-17, CSCMF, roll 11. The position for the convoy Leary gave was latitude 11° 44′ south, longitude 151° 35′ east on course 210 degrees, whereas the original sighting report made by a B-25 was latitude 7° 44′ south, longitude 151° 35′ east, course 310 degrees (see Air Officer Commanding North East Area, To HQ, Allied Air Forces, Report on Coral Sea Engagement [29 May 1942]).

22. In Biard's memoir, "The Pacific War," 16–17, the *Zuikaku* and *Shōkaku* are again specifically identified, but it is still not certain whether he knew at the time. The Final Report of the R.I. Unit of the USS *Yorktown* (23 May 1942) simply noted that it was believed the carrier using the call sign Siso was the one hit, because "*Suso* started taking *Siso*'s planes aboard."

23. W. W. Smith, 46; *Yorktown* dispatches.

24. *Yorktown* dispatches; message 080252 May 1942 CTF-17 to Cincpac, CSCMF, roll 11.

25. Japan, *Senshi Sōsho*, 49:313–15; Hara quote from U.S. Strategic Bombing Survey "Truk Report," Supplemental Report, Truk Naval and Naval Air Team No. 3. U.S. intelligence also heard the rebroadcast of Takahashi's signal (see below). At 1217 Takahashi, who stayed behind to assess damage, advised: "Cancel *Saratoga* sinking report, wait." Later returning VF-42 escort fighters shot down the brave strike leader, whose warning would be ignored. Lundstrom, *First Team*, 271. The latest research on Coral Sea by James C. Sawruk and this author has revealed the hitherto unsuspected attacks on the *Zuikaku* by Lt. (jg) William S. Woollen of VF-42 and Ens. Marvin M. Haschke and Ens. John D. Wingfield of VS-2.

26. Japan, *Senshi Sōsho*, 49:317–18.

27. Japan, *Senshi Sōsho*, 49:323–24.

28. They were the last of the *Lexington* strike planes to land. Still aloft were two or three SBDs of the command escort, including Commander Ault who was wounded, and also probably a VF-2 F4F from the torpedo escort. Only Ens. Harry Wood's SBD crew survived. Stroop, oral history, 105.

29. *Yorktown* dispatches; message 090355 May 1942 CTG-17.5 to CTF-17, *Lexington* dispatches; messages 080332 CTF-17 to Cincpac, 080348 CTF-17 to CTG-17.3, 080235 Cincpac Intel. Bull., and 080344 CTF-17 to Cincpac, May 1942, CSCMF, roll 11.

30. *Yorktown* dispatches. Some questioned whether Sherman should have got some planes over to the *Yorktown.* In his diary on 9 May Commander Fitz-Gerald related how he spoke with several *Lexington* aviators who said they wanted to fly over to the *Yorktown* "but were not allowed to." Thus "Sherman's refusal to fly those planes off the *Lex* just because he thought he could control the fires, was sheer bull headed stubborn stupidity." Lt. Noel Gayler of VF-2 stated in his Buaer interview (17 June 1942) that he and several other fighter pilots wanted to try to fly over to the *Yorktown,* even though some F4Fs were so low on gasoline they might not make it. It is unfortunate that Fitch had not instructed the *Lex* strike planes to land on the *Yorktown,* but neither he nor Sherman realized the grave danger the fires forward posed to the *Lexington.* It seems in retrospect the *Lex* might have got a half dozen more F4Fs and eleven VB-2 SBDs to the *Yorktown* before her steering failed, but that is strictly hindsight.

31. *Yorktown* dispatches.

32. Early memo for Theobald (11 May 1942), RG-313, Comscofor General Correspondence, box 59; at noon the *Phelps* was at 63 percent and the *Aylwin* 57 percent, but the *Dewey* only 43 percent. A day's hard steaming reduced them on the ninth to 47 percent, 45 percent, and 23 percent respectively.

33. *Yorktown* dispatches; Biard, "The Pacific War," 17.

34. Message 080532 May 1942 Comsowespac to CTF-17, CSCMF, roll 11; Crace diary.

35. W. W. Smith, 47; Lundstrom, *First Team*, 282.

36. *Lexington* report (15 May 1942); Commander Cruiser Division Six (Commander Task Group 17.2) to Commander Cruisers, Pacific Fleet (Commander Task Force Seventeen), Engagement with Japanese Force 7–8 May, 1942 in Coral Sea (28 May 1942); Comdesron One to CTG-17.2, Sinking of USS *Lexington* (14 May 1942); Early memo for Theobald (11 May 1942), RG-313, Comscofor General Correspondence, box 59.

37. Message 080713 May 1942 Cincpac to CTF-17, CSCMF, roll 11; 080838 May 1942 CTF-17 to Cincpac, in Cominch 00 File.

38. Message 080935 May 1942 Cincpac to Commanding General (CG) Bobcat etc., CSCMF, roll 11 ("Bobcat" is the code name for Bora-Bora); 080755 May 1942 Cincpac to Cominch, Cominch 00 File; Greybook, 443. The next day Cominch ordered VF-5, VF-72, and the VT-8 Detachment equipped with new Grumman TBF-1 torpedo bombers to proceed from Norfolk to Alameda, message 081900 May 1942 Cominch to Cinclant, CSCMF, roll 11.

39. Japan, *Senshi Sōsho*, 49:326–27. On 9 May the *Zuikaku* had available twenty-four fighters, nine carrier bombers, and six carrier attack planes, with another fighter, eight carrier bombers, and eight carrier attack planes expected to be ready in a couple of days.

40. Sherman diary (22 May 1942); Sherman, 116; Biard, "The Pacific War," 16–17; Parker, 30.

41. *Yorktown* report (25 May 1942); message 090355 May 1942 CTG-17.5 to CTF-17, *Lexington* dispatches. The *Lexington* and the *Yorktown* tried to guide the wounded Ault back to TF-17 but never had him on radar. At 1454 Ault gave his farewell: "OK, So long people. We got a 1000 lb. hit on the flat top." He and his radioman were never found. *Yorktown* dispatches. Biard, "The Pacific War," 14.

42. CTF-17 report (27 May 1942).

43. Parker, 30. Message 080110 May 1942 Belconnen to Combined Addressees, CSCMF, roll 11; *Yorktown* dispatches; Biard, "The Pacific War," 16. The quoted text of the Tokyo message relayed at 1315 (Z–11) is Hypo's version from SRH-278, 262–63. Message 080235 May 1942 Cincpac Intel. Bull., CSCMF, roll 11. Biard, "The Pacific War," 16.

44. Messages 080856, 080912, 082028, and 082156 Com 14 to Combined Addressees; 082301 Opnav to Combined Addressees, all May 1942, in CSCMF, roll 11.

45. Morison, *United States Naval Operations*, 4:63; Sherman, 63; Fitz-Gerald diary (9 May 1942). Prados, 290, proposed a dramatic new interpretation. "Though it is not clear from available sources," Combined Fleet never intended to employ the *Shōkaku* and *Zuikaku* in the Midway Operation. He cited Professor Michael Barnhart as his authority. There is no documentation supporting Prados's assertion. The 5th Carrier Division appeared in the Midway planning documents cited in *Senshi Sōsho*, volume 43. On page 96 of that volume is Combined Fleet Secret Radio 29 of 8 May 1942, which provided the first timetable for the MI Operation. In it the damaged *Shōkaku* is *removed* from Nagumo's 1st *Kidō Butai*. Furthermore, Professor Barnhart in an e-mail to Lundstrom (8 September 2000) did not confirm the statement Prados had attributed to him.

CHAPTER 15. FROM THE CORAL SEA TO PEARL HARBOR

1. *Russell* war diary; Early memo for Theobald (11 May 1942), RG-313, Comscofor General Correspondence, box 59. Conversations of Capt. Frederic L. Faulkner, USN (Ret.), and Capt. Laurence C. Traynor, USN (Ret.), with James C. Sawruk.

2. Fitz-Gerald diary, 9 May 1942.

3. Ludlum, 92–93; Capt. Joseph G. Smith, USN (Ret.), phone conversation with Lundstrom, 23 November 1984. The four VS-2 pilots who flew the mission were Dixon, Smith, Lt. Hoyt D. Mann, and Ens. John A. Leppla. Frederickson diary, 9 May 1942. Kinkaid memoir, 115; W. W. Smith undated (c. 1950) review of Morison's volume 3. Comcru TF-17 war diary.

4. Vice Adm. W. G. Schindler, USN (Ret.), "The Finale of the Battle of the Coral Sea," enclosed in his 4 June 1972 letter to Lundstrom.

5. Message 090117 May 1942 Cincpac to CTF-17, Greybook, 452. In 1947 Fletcher told Capt. Fred C. Dickey at the Naval War College that he recalled receiving orders on 8 May from Cincpac to withdraw from the Coral Sea, but he was mistaken as to the day; Bates, *Coral Sea*, 103.

6. Messages 090301 CTF-17 to CTG-17.2, 090347 CTF-17 to CTG-17.2 and CTG-17.5, 090355 CTG-17.5 to CTF-17, and 090445 CTG-17.5 to CTF-17, all May 1942, in *Lexington* dispatches. Message 090355 May 1942 Comsowespacfor to CTF-17, Greybook, 447. Morison, *United States Naval Operations*, 4:60–61. Ludlum, 93; Frederickson diary, 9 May 1942.

7. Messages 091116 CTF-17 to CTF-44 and 092102 CTF-17 to Cincpac, May 1942, in Cominch 00 File; Fitz-Gerald diary, 10 May 1942; Sherman diary, 22 May 1942. *Anderson* and *Dewey* logs.

8. Japan, *Senshi Sōsho*, 49:328–30, 250–54.

9. Messages 100303 CTF-17 to CTG-17.2, 100835 Cincpac to CTF-17, 110450 CTF-17 to CTG-17.2, and 110525 CTG-17.2 to CTF-17, May 1942, in *Lexington* dispatches; 100830 CTF-17 to Cincpac and 100845 Cincpac to CTF-17 and CTG-17.5, May 1942, in Cominch 00 File; Smith, 48–49.

10. SRH-272, 7–8 May 1942; messages 090117 Cincpac to CTF-17 and 090207 Cincpac to Cominch, May 1942, Greybook, 452; 090031 May 1942 Cincpac to NY Puget Sound, CSCMF, roll 11.

11. SRH-272, 7–9 May 1942; message 090054 May 1942 Com 14 to Combined Addressees, CSCMF, roll 11.

12. The Greybook entry, 472, for 8 May 1942 noted "distressing news from the Coral Sea," but this must have been written early on the ninth, otherwise the timing is inexplicable. Layton, oral history, 28; message 091507 May 1942 Cincpac to CTF-17, Cominch 00 File; 092219 May 1942 Cincpac to Cominch, CSCMF, roll 11; 111325 May 1942 Cominch to Cincpac, Cominch 00 File.

13. Message 100045 May 1942 Cincpac to CTF-16 and CTF-17, CSCMF, roll 11; Greybook, 473.

14. TF-16 war diary. Messages 120041 Cincpac to CTF-16 and CTF-17, 120429 Cincpac Intel. Bull., May 1942, CSCMF, roll 11.

15. Buell, *Master*, 200; Brodhurst, 224–25, with the text of King's communications with the Admiralty; message 121945 May 1942 Cominch to Cincpac, CSCMF, roll 11.

16. Messages 121950 and 132140 Cominch to Cincpac, May 1942, Greybook, 464, 467.

17. Greybook, 479; message 140319 May 1942 Cincpac to CTF-16, CSCMF, roll 11; letter Layton to Lundstrom (12 June 1974); Layton interview by Pineau and Costello (11 May 1983). Lundstrom, *First South Pacific Campaign*, 144–49, 154–55.

18. Message 140639 series May 1942 Cincpac to Cominch, Greybook, 465–67; Greybook, 481.

19. Japan, *Senshi Sōsho*, 49:255–58; TF-16 war diary; message 150445 May 1942 CTF-16 to CTG-17.2, CSCMF, roll 11.

20. Message 152130 May 1942 Cominch to Cincpac, Greybook, 468.

21. Greybook, 482; messages 160307 May 1942 Cincpac to CTF-16, Greybook, 469; 160325 May 1942 Cincpac to Cominch, Greybook, 471; 170025 May 1942 Cincpac to Cominch, CSCMF, roll 12.

22. Messages 132043 May 1942 Cincpac to CTF-17, Greybook, 458; 122113 Cincpac to CTF-17, 140439 Cincpac to CTF-17, 142330 CTF-17 to Cincpac, 142348 CTF-17 to Cincpac, 152358 CTF-17 to Cincpac, 160105 Cincpac to CTF-17, 160905 Cincpac to CTF-17, all May 1942, CSCMF, roll 11; 170320 May 1942 Fletcher to Cincpac, CSCMF, roll 12. Frank and Harrington, 136.

23. Letter Adams to Crace (29 May 1942) in Crace diary, 4 June 1942.

24. Message 110439 May 1942 CTF-17 to CTG-17.2, *Lexington* dispatches; 110216 May 1942 CTF-17 to Cincpac, Cominch 00 File; 112100 May 1942 CTF-11 to Cincpac, Greybook, 463.

25. Messages 131412 Cominch to Cincpac, 140125 Cincpac to CTF-17, May 1942, CSCMF, roll 11; 152126 May 1942 CTF-17 to Cincpac, Greybook, 471.

26. Messages May 1942: 142100 series Cominch to Cincpac, Greybook, 460–61; 170508 Comsowespacfor to Cincpac, Greybook, 470; 170537 Cincpac to Comsowespacfor, Greybook, 469–70; 190345 Comsowespac to Cincpac, Greybook, 493.

27. Message 200359 May 1942 Cincpac to Cominch, Greybook, 486–87.

28. Message 111245 May 1942 Cominch to Cincpac, Greybook, 468; Greybook, 475; 141826 May 1942 CTF-17 to Cincpac, CSCMF, roll 11; 150825 Cincpac to CTF-17, 160200 CTF-17 to Cincpac, May 1942, Greybook, 468–69.

29. Message 180357 Cincpac to CTF-17, 182322 CTF-17 to Cincpac, and 180403 Cincpac to CTF-16, May 1942, CSCMF, roll 12; 171927 May 1942 Cincpac to CTF-16, Greybook, 491.

30. Greybook, 483; message 170407 May 1942 Cincpac to Cominch, Greybook, 490; 172220 May 1942 Cominch to Cincpac, Greybook, 489–90.

31. Messages 172220 May 1942 Cominch to Cincpac, Greybook, 489–90; 182030 May 1942 Cominch to Cincpac, Greybook, 492; 210137 May 1942 Cincpac to Cominch, Greybook, 488; 220135 Cincpac to CTF-16 and CTF-17, and 240543 Comsowespac to Cincpac, May 1942, CSCMF, roll 12.

32. Comcru TF-17 war diary, 26 May 1942.

CHAPTER 16. TIME IS EVERYTHING

1. The basic U.S. documentary sources for the Battle of Midway are: Cincpac to Cominch, Battle of Midway (28 June 1942) with the enclosures CTF-17 to Cincpac, Battle of Midway—Forwarding of Reports (26 June 1942); CTF-16 to Cincpac, Battle of Midway; forwarding of reports (16 June 1942); Comcru TF-17 to Cincpac, Report of Action (12 June 1942); and CO NAS Midway to Cincpac, Report of Engagement with Enemy, Battle of Midway, 30 May to 7 June 1942 (18 June 1942). Cincpac to Cominch, Battle of Midway, Second Supplementary Report (8 August 1942) covers submarine operations. See also CO USS *Yorktown* to Secnav, Loss of Ship—Report on (17 June 1942). In 1947 the Office of Naval Operations published *The Japanese Story of the Battle of Midway*, which is a translation of the battle report of Vice Adm. Nagumo

Chūichi's First Air Fleet (1st *Kidō Butai*), hereafter Nagumo report. The original text is in NHC microfilm JD1 along with the Midway battle reports of the *Akagi*, *Kaga*, *Sōryū*, and *Hiryū*, translated excerpts of which are in WDC Document 160985B.

Official studies include: U.S. Fleet, Headquarters of the Commander In Chief, Secret Information Bulletin No. 1, Battle Experience from Pearl Harbor to Midway December 1941 to June 1942 including Makin Island Raid 17–18 August (15 February 1943); U.S. Navy, Office of Naval Intelligence, Publication Section, Combat Intelligence Branch, Combat Narratives, *The Battle of Midway* (Washington, 1943); U.S. Naval War College (Commo. Richard W. Bates), *The Battle of Midway including the Aleutian Phase June 3 to June 14, 1942* (hereafter Bates, *Midway*); and U.S. Army, Headquarters Far East Command: Japanese Monograph No. 88: *Aleutian Naval Operation March 1942–February 1943* and Japanese Monograph No. 93: *Midway Operations May–June 1942.*

The literature on the Battle of Midway is vast. Serious analyses include: Morison, *United States Naval Operations*, vol. 4; Fuchida and Okumiya; Tuleja, *Climax at Midway*; W. W. Smith; Lord, *Incredible Victory*; Japan, *Senshi Sōsho*, vol. 43; Barde, *The Battle of Midway*; Prange, *Miracle*; Willmott; Lundstrom, *The First Team*; Cressman et al., *"A Glorious Page in Our History"*; and Parker. Cressman et al., *Glorious Page*, offers the most accurate chronological narrative of the entire battle from the U.S. side, and *Senshi Sōsho*, vol. 43, the most comprehensive Japanese account. Unfortunately the classic Fuchida and Okumiya must be used with caution.

2. Fuchida and Okumiya, 95–97, 99; Japan, *Senshi Sōsho*, 43:92–94.

3. Lord, 15; Japan, *Senshi Sōsho*, 43:71–77.

4. Combined Fleet Secret Radio 29 of 8 May 1942, text in Japan, *Senshi Sōsho*, 43:96–97.

5. Fragmentary decrypts relating to the Second Operation K, the so-called #2 King Campaign, caused considerable consternation among U.S. code breakers and planners, some of whom thought it portended a major assault on Oahu. See RG-457, SRMN-005, Op-20-G Files of Memoranda and Reports relative to the Battle of Midway, and also Rear Adm. Edwin T. Layton's unpublished paper, "2nd Operation K," copy furnished by Admiral Layton.

6. Combined Fleet Operation-Order 14 (12 May 1942), cited in Japan, *Senshi Sōsho*, 43:106–14; Fuchida and Okumiya, 86–87; Prange, *Miracle*, 70; Japanese Monograph No. 88, 25–29.

7. Japan, *Senshi Sōsho*, 43:114; Prange, *Miracle*, 47–48; Ugaki, 127; Fuchida and Okumiya, 105–9.

8. Japan, *Senshi Sōsho*, 43:119–21; Ugaki, 128; Layton, "2nd Operation K"; Ugaki, 131.

9. Ugaki, 128, 142.

10. *Enterprise* deck log.

11. Fletcher interview by Prange, 17 September 1966; W. W. Smith, 55; Fletcher interview by Lord, 17 February 1966; letter W. W. Smith to "Mark" (3–9 June 1942) in Smith Papers. Captain Biard, the former language officer with the TF-17 radio intelligence unit, claimed in his memoir, "The Pacific War," 17, that even before TF-17 returned to Tongatabu, Fletcher was receiving voluminous reports regarding the upcoming Midway offensive. That led him to consult Biard, who explained all about Hypo and assured him "the information could be trusted." There is no evidence at all that any of this ever occurred. Nimitz told Layton not to mention Midway in the daily intelligence bulletins: "Don't even hint about it," and "Hold this one real close" (Layton interview by Pineau and Costello, 11 May 1983). Only the high-level messages between King and Nimitz, occasionally also with MacArthur and Halsey, discussed the impending Midway offensive. Fletcher lacked the ciphers to read them. None were ever addressed to him. The message files demonstrate that Fletcher indeed knew nothing about the threat to Midway before he entered Nimitz's office on 27 May.

12. Halsey and Bryan, 106; W. W. Smith, 55; letter Rear Adm. William H. Buracker, USN (Ret.), to Walter Lord (10 March 1966), copy in Adm. Raymond A. Spruance Papers, coll. 37, box 2; letter Rear Adm. William H. Ashford Jr., USN (Ret.), to Cdr. Thomas B. Buell (24 November 1971), Rear Adm. William H. Ashford Papers.

13. NHC, Officer Biographical File; Buell, *Master*, 116; quotes from King in Whitehill memo, 14 August 1949, in King Papers, NWC, box 7; personal communication from Lt. Cdr. Richard H. Best, USN (Ret.); letter W. W. Smith to "Mark" (3/9 June 1942) in Smith Papers.

14. Messages all May 1942: 070155 Cincpac to Bunav, CSCMF, roll 10; 082359 Cincpac to Bunav, 150105 Cincpac to Bunav, 162221 Bupers (Bureau of Naval Personnel) to Cincpac, CSCMF, roll 11; and 281929 Cincpac to Cominch, CSCMF, roll 13. Coletta, *Patrick N. L. Bellinger and U.S. Naval Aviation*, 297, 302.

15. Letter Ashford to Buell (24 November 1971); letter Comcarpac to Comcrupac (25 May 1942), Spruance Papers, coll. 37, box 1. The specific recommendation for Draemel's relief does not appear in either the King or Nimitz papers. The only relevant dispatch is 261525 of May 1942, "Connav" [Chief of the Bureau of Navigation?] to Cincpac, CSCMF, roll 12. It was sent in reply to a query by Nimitz on 24 May whether action was taken on his serial 01354 of 7 May 1942. Unclear as to what he meant, King replied in message 261525 if the query "relates to officers Nos. 28 [Brown], 65 [Draemel] and 74 [Spruance], necessary approval obtained & appropriate orders issued in each case." In fact Nimitz's letter (in NHC, Nimitz Papers) referred to the problem of the large population of Japanese aliens residing in Hawaii. E. B Potter, Nimitz's close associate and biographer, alleged in *Nimitz*, 84, that Spruance's sterling qualities were already so obvious that Nimitz "must have suspected" that switching him for Halsey "was not altogether for the worse," because "Halsey's impulsive boldness might have invited disaster." That is hindsight at its worst. Prange, *Miracle*, 81; message 280339 May 1942 Cincpac to Cominch, CSCMF, roll 13.

16. Thomas B. Buell, *The Quiet Warrior*, 133–34; Forrestel, *Admiral Raymond A. Spruance, USN*, 35. Letter Vice Adm. Victor D. Long to Cdr. Thomas B. Buell (7 November 1971), Spruance Papers, coll. 37, box 2; W. W. Smith, 62.

17. Letter Nimitz to King (29 May 1942), Nimitz Papers.

18. Message 280233 May 1942 Cincpac to NY Pearl Harbor, CSCMF, roll 13; Greybook, 512; letter W. W. Smith to "Mark" (3/9 June 1942).

19. Potter, *Nimitz*, 86.

20. Fletcher interview by Prange (17 September 1966); letter Spruance to Potter (1 December 1964) in Potter Papers.

21. Cincpac Op-Plan 29-42 (27 May 1942), in RG-38, Op-Ord File; messages 211930 and 251735 May 1942 Cominch to Cincpac, CNO TS Blue File; Commander in Chief, U.S. Pacific Fleet and Pacific Ocean Areas, Command History (1946), Naval Administrative Histories, 74.

22. Message 250215 May 1942 Cincpac to Cominch, Greybook, 528.

23. Text of the 26 May situation estimate in Greybook, 506–21; letter Nimitz to Draemel (23 May 1942), text appended as D1 in Unit History, NAS Midway (14 September 1945).

24. Cincpac Enemy Activities File, 21 May 1942, SRH-272. Letter Nimitz to Davis (undated, but 24–25 May 1942) and Compatwing Two (Rear Admiral Bellinger) memorandum (23 May 1942), text appended as D3 and D4 in Unit History, NAS Midway (14 September 1945). On 18 May a decrypt (181900 May 1942 Com 14 to Combined Addressees, CSCMF, roll 12) revealed that a staff officer of the First Air Fleet was requesting that weather reports be made three hours prior to takeoff from N–2 Days to N-Day, "As we plan to make attacks roughly from the (northwest?)," and that "on the day of the attack we will endeavor to blank at a point 50 miles northwest of Afirm Fox [AF] and move pilots off as quickly as possible." Nimitz took that warning seriously and immediately (182145 May 1942 Cincpac to Midway, Greybook, 496) changed the submarine *Cachalot*'s orders to "patrol that area until further orders." The Japanese message originated prior to the change in Nagumo's plan that delayed the first carrier strike on Midway from N–3 to N–2 day.

25. Letter Davis to Nimitz (26 May 1942), text appended as D2 in Unit History, NAS Midway (14 September 1945).

26. Op-Plan 29-42 (27 May 1942); Cincpac Letter of Instruction delivered 28 May 1942 by War Plans to CTF-16 and CTF-17; Buell, *Quiet Warrior*, 134.

27. Greybook, 508, 516.

28. Letters Fletcher to Nimitz (28 May 1942), Nimitz to King (29 May 1942), Nimitz Papers.

29. Message 290205 May 1942 Cincpac to TF-17, CSCMF, roll 13; letter Buckmaster to W. W. Smith (22 August 1964), Smith Papers.

30. TF-16 war diary; *Enterprise* war diary. Indeed on 31 May after receiving an authorizing dispatch from Bupers, Mitscher took the oath and accepted the appointment as temporary rear admiral to date from 4 December 1941 (*Hornet* deck log). However, he remained in a captain's billet and continued to be regarded as such. CO USS *Hornet* to Cincpac, Report of Action—4–6 June 1942 (13 June 1942).

31. Biard, "The Pacific War," 15, 17; Capt. Forrest R. Biard, oral history 98. Fullinwider's new radio operators were W. H. "Tack" Walvoord, M. G. Albertson, and Raymond A. Rundle, radiomen, first class. See RG-457, SRH-313, Memo for Cdr. P. P. Leigh, USNR, Task Force Sixteen (USS *Enterprise*—Flag (Midway Battle, 3–6 June 1942) (11 September 1945); and also Raymond A. Rundle, oral history, Naval Security Group (September 1983), RG-457.

Captain Biard never ceased to revile Fletcher, whom he repeatedly accused of gross incompetence and of trying to harm his career. However, his unremitting portrait of an hysterical, profane, and inept Fletcher is nowhere evident in any of the other available primary sources and completely contradicted by surviving members of the staff and flag complements. For example, Rear Adm. Murr Arnold, USN (Ret.), former *Yorktown* air officer, wrote W. W. Smith (13 September 1965), "Fletcher was *all right* [Arnold's emphasis] in my book and didn't deserve any criticism from Morison" (Smith Papers). Nor do Biard's charges stand after a detailed analysis of all the events. Discussing the unpublished memoir that Biard furnished him, Rear Admiral Layton told coauthors Roger Pineau and John Costello: "I wouldn't want to quote any of this." Layton added: "That's Biard's problem. I think he's pretty inclined to think that he is always right. I may suffer from the same disease" (11 May 1983 interview transcript, 96, Layton Papers). Perhaps Vice Adm. Walter Schindler from the TF-17 staff made the fairest evaluation: "We had a Japanese language officer (I'm not sure of his name) on our staff with four [*sic*] Japanese language radio operators. They did an excellent job in intercepting enemy radio traffic. However, this traffic was not always timely or correctly translated or interpreted. Thus this intelligence was sometimes most useful and at others, confusing" (letter Schindler to Lundstrom, 4 June 1972).

32. Letter Pederson to Joseph Harrington (21 July 1964), Pederson Papers; letter Pederson to Lundstrom (16 September 1974); Fletcher interview by Lord (17 February 1966).

33. Lundstrom, *First Team*, 318, and *The First Team and the Guadalcanal Campaign*, 7, 10, 13.

34. Rear Adm. Harry A. Guthrie questionnaire (c. 1966) to Walter Lord, courtesy of Walter Lord; letter Buckmaster to W. W. Smith (22 August 1964), W. W. Smith Papers.

35. Letter Capt. M. B. Laing, RN, to Col. Robert E. Barde, USMC (6 December 1966), via Mark Horan; details of Laing's career from Commo. Bruce Loxton, RAN (Ret.); Vice Adm. W. G. Schindler questionnaire (c. 1966) to Walter Lord.

36. Letter Nimitz to King (29 May 1942), Nimitz Papers.

37. Frank and Harrington, 147; letter W. W. Smith to "Mark" (3/9 June 1942), "Mark" to W. W. Smith (23 May 1942), Smith Papers; *Time* (18 May 1942), 18.

38. Lundstrom, *First Team*, 319; Lt. Joseph P. Pollard, oral history.

39. Messages 300227 and 300231 May 1942 Cincpac to CTF-16, CSCMF, roll 13; Cincpac Op-Plan 29-42.

40. Messages 300050 and 301745 May 1942 Cominch to Cincpac, Cominch 00 File.

41. Message 310221 May 1942 Cincpac to all CTFs, CSCMF, roll 13. The substance of this secret dispatch appeared on the front page of the 7 June *Chicago Tribune* in the celebrated security leak involving reporter

Stanley Johnston. Message 310357 May 1942 Cincpac to NAS Midway, Greybook, 533; 280428 May 1942 Belconnen to Combined Addressees, Greybook, 545.

42. Message 282150 May 1942 CTF-1 to TF-1, CSCMF, roll 13; Greybook, 564; messages 290408 May 1942 CTF-1 to Cincpac, 292010 May 1942 Cincpac to CTF-1, 012341 June 1942 Cincpac to Comcarpac Admin, and 022053 June 1942 Cincpac to CTF-1, all in CSCMF, roll 13.

43. Messages 022039 June 1942 Cincpac to CTF-16 and CTF-17; 302055 May 1942 Cincpac to *Saratoga*; 011733 CTG-11.1 to Cincpac, 030141 Fitch to Cincpac, both June 1942, CSCMF, roll 13.

44. Messages 022205 June 1942 Cincpac to CTF-17, Cominch 00 File; and 022319 June 1942 Cincpac to CTF-4, CTF-9, CTF-17, CTF-16, and Midway, CSCMF, roll 13.

45. Letter Fletcher to Morison (1 December 1947), Fletcher Papers; Bates, *Midway*, 62–63; Interview of Rear Adm. George D. Murray by Buaer (25 November 1942), NHC. Murr Arnold wrote: "The bald truth is that we simply didn't know how to maneuver 2 or 3 carriers in one formation" (letter to W. W. Smith, 18 February 1965, Smith Papers). Adm. John Thach remained highly critical of the decision to operate the carriers in two separate task forces (Thach, oral history, 273–75).

46. Letter Davis to Nimitz (26 May 1942), NAS Midway history.

47. Cincpac Op-Plan 29-42 (27 May 1942). "Cocked and primed" from M. R. Browning Memorandum for Admiral Spruance (13 June 1942), in RG-38, Cincpac Flag Files.

48. Pollard, oral history.

CHAPTER 17. THE BATTLE OF MIDWAY I

1. Message 310357 May 1942 Cincpac to CTF-4, CTF-9, CTF-16, CTF-17, and NAS Midway, Greybook, 533; SRMN-012 with the daily fleet intelligence summaries noted on 31 May (p. 458), "It is still believed that initial attack by the striking force will be on Midway and the Aleutians on 3 June (local)," and on 3 June (p. 485), "It had been expected that this attack [on Dutch Harbor] would take place simultaneously with the attack on Midway."

2. Pollard, oral history; letter Laing to Barde (6 December 1966).

3. Message 031637 June 1942 Cincpac to all CTFs, CSCMF, roll 13; Layton, oral history, 48.

4. Midway contact reports in CO NAS Midway to Cincpac, Report of Engagement with Enemy, Battle of Midway, 30 May to 7 June 1942 (18 June 1942). See also Pertinent Extracts from Communications Logs Relative to Midway Attack, in Franklin D. Roosevelt Papers as President, Map Room File, box 36. This undated communication log (hereafter TF-16 communication log) is absolutely invaluable in providing radio messages recorded nowhere else. Messages 032513 and 032207 June 1942 Cincpac to all CTFs, CSCMF, roll 13.

5. Ugaki, 137.

6. Messages 040017 Cincpac to all CTFs and 040245 Cincpac to Cominch, June 1942, in CSCMF, roll 14.

7. Messages 040711, 040811, 041035, and 041203, June 1942, Cincpac to all CTFs, CSCMF, roll 14.

8. Fletcher interview by Prange (17 September 1966); TF-16 communication log; messages 041505 and 041617 Cincpac to all CTFs, June 1942, CSCMF, roll 14.

9. VP-44 Op-Ord No. 13-44 (4 June 1942), courtesy of James Sawruk; message 041803 June 1942 Cincpac to all CTFs, CSCMF, roll 14.

10. Comcrupac to Cincpac, Battle of Midway (14 June 1942), RG-38.

11. Layton, oral history, 30. It has been reported that Layton made his celebrated prediction as early as 27 May (see Potter, *Nimitz*, 83, and Prange, *Miracle*, 102). Prange, 408, even discounted Layton's direct testimony that the remark occurred on the morning of 4 June only an hour before he and Nimitz learned of the sighting

of Nagumo's carriers. Unfortunately the description of the incident in Layton's posthumously published *And I Was There*, 430, 438, compounds the error of Potter and Prange. Likewise Parker, 53, was misled.

12. The principal sources for the 1st *Kidō Butai* include: the Nagumo report; the four carrier reports in WDC Document 160985B; Japanese Monograph No. 93; Japan, *Senshi Sōsho*, vol. 43; Fuchida and Okumiya; and Prange, *Miracle*.

13. Prange, *Dawn*, 107–9; Evans and Peattie, 529; Fuchida and Okumiya, 112. Capt. Hara Tameichi in *Japanese Destroyer Captain*, 34–35, described Nagumo, under whom he served in the early 1930s, as a "brilliant and aggressive naval officer and a most kind-hearted man." For a comparison of U.S. and Japanese command styles, see Layton, oral history.

14. Bates, *Midway*, 86.

15. Japan, *Senshi Sōsho*, 43:297; Ugaki, 141; Prange, *Miracle*, 214–15. Vital new research on Nagumo has recently appeared in the *Naval War College Review*: Isom, "The Battle of Midway," and Parshall, Dickson, and Tully, "Doctrine Matters." The forthcoming book *Shattered Sword* by Parshall and Tully will revolutionize interpretations of the Battle of Midway and refute many currently held myths. Isom is also writing a book on Midway.

16. CO NAS Midway to Cincpac, Report of Engagement with Enemy, Battle of Midway, 30 May to 7 June 1942 (18 June 1942).

17. TF-16 communication log; Layton, oral history.

18. TF-16 communication log; message 041823 June 1942 Cincpac to all CTFs, CSCMF, roll 14.

19. Letter Buracker to Lord (10 March 1966) in Spruance Papers, coll. 37, box 2; interview of Lt. Robert J. Oliver by Thomas B. Buell (5 October 1971), in Spruance Papers, coll. 37, box 3. Bates, *Midway*, 122; Buell, *Quiet Warrior*, 144–46.

20. Letter Spruance to Forrestel (14 December 1962), Spruance Papers, coll. 37, box 7: "I wanted to hit the Japanese carriers as early as possible with all the air strength available for this purpose."

21. Mears, *Carrier Combat*, 52–53; Buell, *Quiet Warrior*, 146. TF-16 war diary.

22. Bates, *Midway*, 122–23. Morison, *United States Naval Operations*, 4:113; Citation File, NHC. See my introduction to the 1987 reprint of Buell's *Quiet Warrior*, x–xv.

23. Letter Oliver to Buell (5 August 1971), in Spruance Papers, coll. 37, box 3; TF-16 war diary and communication. Basic procedures and definitions were set down in Comairbatfor, Current Tactical Orders and Doctrine, U.S. Fleet Aircraft, Vol. One, Carrier Aircraft, USF-74 (Revised) of March 1941, and in Comairbatfor, Current Tactical Orders, Aircraft Carriers, U.S. Fleet, USF-77 (Revised) of March 1941.

24. Air Operations Officer to CO USS *Hornet*, Defects Observed During the Action Off Midway on June 4, 1942 (12 June 1942); letter Arnold to W. W. Smith (18 February 1965), Smith Papers; letter Henry Salomon Jr., to S. E. Morison (13 August 1947), in Morison Office Files, box 23; USF-77 (Revised); Murray interview by Buaer (25 November 1942); CTF-16 [Rear Adm. Thomas C. Kinkaid] to Cincpac, Recent Operations of Task Force Sixteen (10 September 1942), in RG-38, Action Reports.

25. CO USS *Hornet* to Cincpac, Report of Action—4–6 June 1942 (13 June 1942); Lundstrom, *First Team*, 333; Gay, *Sole Survivor*, 115. Photos exist of the *Hornet* planes arrayed on deck, National Museum of Naval Aviation Museum, NAS Pensacola.

26. CO USS *Enterprise* to Cincpac, Battle of Midway Island, June 4–6, 1942—Report of (8 June 1942) and CO USS *Enterprise* to Cincpac, Air Battle of the Pacific, June 4–6, 1942—Report of (13 June 1942). For the procedures used at Wake, see CO USS *Enterprise* to Cincpac, Report of Action on February 24, 1942 (Zone Minus Twelve) Against Wake Island (8 March 1942). For details of the *Enterprise* launch, Mark Horan has graciously shared his unparalleled knowledge of the *Enterprise* Air Group in the Battle of Midway.

27. On 24 February the launches were slowed by poor visibility when halos of water droplets stirred up by propellers encircled each SBD as it ran up the deck. One SBD pilot crashed due to the disorientation. Murray interview by Buaer (25 November 1942).

28. This was the sighting report transmitted by the *Tone* Number Four search plane at 0740, although the message was timed 0728. Ugaki, 149, confirmed Yamamoto monitored that message at 0740. Slonim's "A Flagship View of Command Decisions," 85, stated this message was "a plain language contact report" that gave "our position and the composition of our force." Potter, *Nimitz*, 94, asserted that Hypo at Pearl deciphered it. However, Hypo's Running Log of Midway Operations, 4 June 1942, in SRMN-012, 500, related that at 0740 an enemy plane (call sign Meku 4) "sends on 7110 to Mari a 4 kana nigori despatch, his number 3." Hypo did intercept a plain language from Mari at 0747.

29. Letter Rear Adm. M. R. Browning to S. E. Morison (8 October 1947), Morison Office Files, box 23; Buell, *Quiet Warrior*, 147. Bates wrote Morison (31 August 1948) claiming the *Enterprise* was "not too slow in launching VT" because torpedo planes always had to be brought up from the hangar. Thus this "delay was purely carrier operation and not mismanagement." Bates also erred that the "*Enterprise* completed her launch about the same time as the *Hornet*." The *Hornet* finished eleven minutes ahead. Bates Papers, series I, box 2.

30. Comcrudiv Six to CTF-16, Report of Action, June 4, 1942 (11 June 1942).

31. Lundstrom, *First Team*, 335–36; letter Capt. C. W. McClusky to S. E. Morison (c. 1947), Morison Office Files, box 23.

32. Comcrupac to Cincpac, Battle of Midway (14 June 1942); CO USS *Yorktown* to Cincpac, Report of Action for June 4, 1942, and June 6, 1942 (18 June 1942); CTF-17 to Cincpac, Battle of Midway—Forwarding of Reports (26 June 1942); Comcru TF-17 war diary.

33. Bates, *Midway*, 125; Morison, *United States Naval Operations*, 4:114; Morison, *Two-Ocean War*, 154.

34. Lord, 154; letter Arnold to W. W. Smith (18 February 1965), Smith Papers; letter Capt. O. Pederson to S. E. Morison (5 December 1947), Pederson Papers.

35. Letter Rear Adm. Oscar Pederson to Lundstrom (13 October 1974), where he noted the *Yorktown* was "mildly criticized" for taking that risk; Lundstrom, *First Team*, 340.

36. Comcrupac report (14 June 1942); Arnold letter to W. W. Smith (18 February 1965). Letter Arnold to Morison (30 October 1947), in Morison Office Files, box 23.

37. Pollard, oral history.

38. Letter Rear Adm. Oscar Pederson to Lundstrom (16 September 1974); Thach, oral history, 273; letter Rear Adm. M. F. Leslie to W. W. Smith (15 December 1964), Smith Papers.

39. Basic air reports include: CO USS *Yorktown* report (18 June 1942), Commander Bombing Squadron Three [Lt. Cdr. M. F. Leslie] to Commander *Yorktown* Air Group, Attack Conducted June 4, 1942, on Japanese Carriers Located 156 miles NW Midway Island—Narrative Concerning (7 June 1942); Commander Bombing Squadron Three [Lt. D. W. Shumway] to CO USS *Enterprise*, Report of Action—period 4 June 1942 to 6 June 1942, inclusive (10 June 1942); CO, Fighting Squadron Three, to CO USS *Yorktown*, The Battle of Midway—Combat Report (12 June 1942). For VT-3: Report by Wilhelm George Esders, Combat Air Patrol, U.S. Navy (6 June 1942); and Statement by H. L. Corl, Mach., USN (15 June 1942), copies in Pederson Papers. TF-16 communications log.

40. Nagumo report, 14, 2; Cressman et al., *Glorious Page*, 69–73.

41. Nagumo report, 14; Japan, *Senshi Sōsho*, 43:313–14. The articles by Isom and Parshall, Dickson, and Tully provide invaluable new information and insights for the discussion of Japanese carrier rearming techniques and their impact on Nagumo's decisions.

42. Prange, *Miracle*, 214–15. Tomonaga's message did not actually use the words, "There is need for a second attack wave," but "Kawa Kawa Kawa," SRMN-012, 500. That appears to have been a predetermined code recommending a second attack and adds to the impression that Nagumo had considered this contingency all along.

43. Nagumo report, 15; Japan, *Senshi Sōsho*, 43:304–12; Agawa, *The Reluctant Admiral*, 314 (Agawa read Amari's given name as "Hiroshi"); Gakken Pacific War series, *Shōkaku-kei Kūbō*, 155. Amari later converted

to night fighters and died on 13 May 1945 over Okinawa (Hata and Izawa, *Japanese Naval Aces and Fighter Units in World War II*, 402).

44. Comparing the message log in the Nagumo report and Hypo's running log in SRMN-012 shows that Nagumo's call sign was "Mari," Abe's "Seso," and Amari's "Meku 4." Isom's stirring defense of Amari's actions is not warranted given the facts. Also his assertion, based on statements in the Nagumo report (7, 42), that Nagumo himself only received word of the sighting "about" 0800, is contradicted by the message Nagumo indeed sent Amari at 0747: "Ascertain ship types and maintain contact." That time is independently confirmed by Hypo, which logged it at 0747 as "Mari comes back to Meku 4 with plain text: 'Retain contact,'" SRMN-012, 500.

45. Nagumo report, 15; Willmott, 388.

46. Cressman et al., *Glorious Page*, 75–82.

47. Nagumo report, 15; Fuchida, 169–70; Prange, *Miracle*, 232; DCNO (Air), Administrative Histories, Vol. XVI, *Aviation in the Fleet Exercises, 1911–1939*, 163.

48. Nagumo report, 7; Prange, *Miracle*, 232–33.

49. Prange, *Miracle*, 225, 231–33; Ugaki, 161; Fuchida and Okumiya, 163.

50. Nagumo report, 16–17.

51. Nagumo report, 17.

52. Letter Laing to Barde (6 December 1966). Jon Parshall personal communication.

53. NAS Midway report (18 June 1942); Cincpac rebroadcast the message at 1007 (042151 June 1942 Cincpac to all CTFs, CSCMF, roll 14).

54. TF-16 communication log; TF-16 war diary; Lundstrom, *First Team*, 343–44. Morison, *United States Naval Operations*, 4:122, quoted McClusky's retort: "Wilco, as soon as I find the bastards," but that is apocryphal. McClusky sighted distant Japanese ships at 1002, CO USS *Enterprise* report (13 June 1942).

55. TF-16 communication log, TF-16 war diary.

56. TF-16 communication log; message 042301 June 1942 Cincpac to all CTFs, CSCMF, roll 14.

57. Comcru TF-17 war diary.

58. Letter R. A. Spruance to C. W. Nimitz (8 June 1942), in RG-38, Action Reports. Spruance included a copy in his 8 June 1942 letter to Fletcher, Spruance Papers, coll. 12, series 1, box 2. Mark Horan, coauthor of "*A Glorious Page in our History*," brought this important letter to my attention. Letter Arnold to W. W. Smith (18 February 1965), Smith Papers. Lundstrom, *First Team*, 341–64, and Cressman et al., *Glorious Page*, 91–110.

59. Lundstrom, *First Team*, 344–48.

60. Mears, 68.

61. TF-16 communication log; the original of Leslie's report (10 June 1942) in Pederson Papers; letter Leslie to W. W. Smith (15 December 1964), Smith Papers.

62. Fuchida and Okumiya, 177, stated the *Akagi* had her full strike on deck and that in five minutes would have launched them all. That is false, as research by Parshall and Tully has established. The Japanese Official History noted that aside from a few fighters no carriers had any planes on deck. Lt. Cdr. Richard Best, the first to dive on the *Akagi*, recalled to this author seeing only six or seven Zeros spotted far aft. One combat air patrol Zero took off during his dive. Also Leslie's report (7 June 1942) stated that he did not see any planes on the deck of the carrier [*Sōryū*] that VB-3 attacked. TF-16 communication log.

63. Research by Parshall and Tully shows that instead of having drawn off to the north prior to the SBD attack, the *Hiryū* was actually positioned in the middle of the other three carriers.

64. Ugaki, 149.

CHAPTER 18. THE BATTLE OF MIDWAY II

1. Comcru TF-17 war diary; *Sōryū* battle report, WDC 160985B; Nagumo report, 21.

2. Comcrupac reports (14 June 1942 and 26 June 1942); CO USS *Yorktown* report (18 June 1942); Commander, Bombing Squadron Five (temporarily designated as VS-5) to CO USS *Enterprise*, Report of action 4–6 June 1942 (7 June 1942), in RG-38, Action Reports.

3. TF-16 communication log. Message 050001 June 1942 CTF-17 to Cincpac, CSCMF, roll 14. Morison, *United States Naval Operations*, 4:131, asserted that Thach provided Fletcher "the first visual evidence that three Japanese carriers were burning and exploding," and that Fletcher then sent out the VS-5 search specifically to find the fourth carrier. Of course, VS-5 left before Thach landed, and Thach never met with Fletcher before Fletcher left the *Yorktown*. Thach corrected Morison (letter 11 April 1949, in Morison Office Files, box 23), explaining he was speaking with Arnold and that they were about to go to flag plot when the attack came in. Nor did anyone else from the strike brief Fletcher. His subsequent messages that afternoon clearly demonstrate he did not know three carriers had been hit.

4. For the first attack on the *Yorktown*, see Lundstrom, *First Team*, 374–87. After witnessing the inferno on the *Lexington*, Machinist Oscar W. Myers devised an "ingenious CO_2 purging system" for the fuel lines above the gasoline stowage tanks and arranged to fill the voids around the stowage tanks with carbon dioxide. It was a tremendous achievement that other carriers adopted but unfortunately not in time to save the *Wasp*. CO USS *Yorktown* to Chief, Buaer, Comments on Air Department Material and Equipment (18 June 1942) and citation in CO USS *Yorktown* to Cincpac, Recommendation for Awards (18 June 1942), copies in Smith Papers.

5. *Hiryū* battle report WDC 160985B; Lundstrom, *First Team*, 369–72.

6. Dialogue in Fighter Director School, NY Pearl Harbor, Battle of Midway Island (3 April 1943); Foster Hailey, "Valor at Midway," *New York Times* (23 June 1942); Newsome conversation (6 August 1996); Schindler questionnaire to Walter Lord.

7. George Clapp conversation (10 February 2000); Rundle, oral history. In Fletcher interview by Walter Lord (17 February 1966), Fletcher recalled suffering a slight head wound while dropping for cover in flag plot during the dive bombing attack. The cut was bandaged; he remained there working on the charts and was surprised later to receive a Purple Heart. Fletcher confused the attack on 4 June with the torpedoing of the *Saratoga* on 31 August 1942.

8. Message 050035 June 1942 CTF-17 to Cincpac and CTF-16, CSCMF, roll 14; letter Fletcher to Cdr. Joseph Bryan, III, USNR (13 September 1948), in Fletcher Papers; Capt. John E. Greenbacker account of the Battle of Midway (c. 1966) from Captain Greenbacker.

9. CO USS *Portland* to Cincpac, Action Report (11 June 1942); Bates, *Midway*, 136–37; letter Salomon to Morison (13 August 1947).

10. Comcrudiv Six report (11 June 1942); CO USS *Vincennes* to Cincpac, Action Report—4 June 1942 (9 June 1942); *Vincennes* deck log; CTG-17.4 (Comdesron Six) to CTF-17, Japanese Torpedo Plane Attack on USS *Yorktown* During Battle of Midway, June 4, 1942—Report of (12 June 1942).

11. Letter Rear Adm. W. G. Schindler to Dr. Thaddeus Tuleja (24 September 1958), furnished by Dr. Tuleja; *Astoria* deck log; Rundle, oral history; letter Laing to Barde (6 December 1966).

12. Tuleja, 158–59; W. W. Smith, 116; Hailey, 173–74.

13. CO USS *Portland* report (11 June 1942); CO USS *Pensacola* Report of Engagement with Enemy Aircraft on June 4, 1942 (8 June 1942); messages 050140 CTF-17 to CTF-16, 050430 Midway to Cincpac, 050145 Cincpac to all CTFs, and 050557 Cincpac to all CTFs, June 1942, CSCMF, roll 14; *Astoria* deck log.

14. Pollard, oral history; W. W. Smith, 118; Comcru TF-17 war diary; Lundstrom, *First Team*, 367, 395; Sawachi, *Middowē Kaisen*, 499.

15. Message 050235 June 1942 *Yorktown* to Cincpac, CSCMF, roll 14.

16. Nagumo report, 23–25, 41; Ugaki, 145.

17. For details of the air actions involved in the second attack on the *Yorktown*, see Lundstrom, *First Team*, 391–411.

18. CO USS *Yorktown* report (18 June 1942); Hailey, 177; message 050315 June 1942 CTF-17 to Cincpac, CSCMF, roll 14.

19. Message 050204 June 1942 CTF-16 to Cincpac (info CTF-17), CSCMF, roll 14.

20. Buell, *Quiet Warrior*, 151–52; Barde, 301–2; Prange, *Miracle*, 283. There is no documentation for the assertion that Browning wanted to launch an immediate second strike but that Spruance refused.

21. Message 050147 June 1942 Cincpac to CTF-17, CSCMF, roll 14. CO NAS Midway report (18 June 1942); TF-16 communication log.

22. It is fascinating to compare the situation facing Spruance at 1300 with TF-17 on the afternoon of 8 May at Coral Sea, where Fletcher is lambasted for not unleashing an immediate second strike against MO Striking Force. After reading a draft of this chapter, Commander Best wrote the author, "Can't imagine the grounds for that msg [Spruance's 050204 reporting all four carriers badly damaged] in view of the fact that two hours earlier I reported in Spruance's hearing that three Japanese carriers would not operate any aircraft that day but that a fourth to the north of the three was untouched. At no time after I left the flag bridge did anyone ask if I had any info on the position of the fourth carrier." Best believed no one who came back from the mission was asked either. "The staff had the same arrogance about the aviators' knowledge as the fliers had for the flying savvy of senior aviators (commanders and above)," letter Best to Lundstrom (15 May 2000). Letter Spruance to Fletcher (8 June 1942).

23. TF-16 communication log; message 050247 June 1942 CTF-17 to Cincpac, CSCMF, roll 14.

24. W. W. Smith, 95; Willmott, 406, 450. CO, Bombing Squadron Five report (7 June 1942). Cdr. W. C. Short, in Morison Office Files, box 22, questioned the Japanese estimate of the *Hiryū*'s position. Short called Adams's contact report "by far the clearest, most accurate, and deliberate contact report made by any carrier-based aircraft in the entire war." Bates, *Midway*, 140, erred in stating that the VS-5 SBD that found the *Hiryū* was in the extreme left sector. Adams actually flew the next sector to the north.

25. TF-16 communication log; *Hornet* Air Operations Officer report (12 June 1942).

26. CO USS *Hornet* report (13 June 1942); Comcrudiv Six report (11 June 1942); and valuable insight from Mark Horan. Buell, *Quiet Warrior*, 153.

27. CO USS *Yorktown* report (18 June 1942); Bureau of Ships, USS *Yorktown* Loss in Action Midway June 4–7, 1942, War Damage Report No. 25 (9 March 1943). Dulin et al., *The Loss of the USS Yorktown (CV-5)*, 31. Letter Buckmaster to W. W. Smith (22 August 1964).

28. CO USS *Yorktown* to Secnav, Loss of Ship—Report on (17 June 1942), First Endorsement CTF-17 to Secnav (23 June 1942), Second Endorsement Cincpac to Secnav (7 July 1942). Fletcher interview by Prange (17 September 1966); Buckmaster letter to W. W. Smith (22 August 1964) stating, "Admiral Fletcher is one of the finest, and so was Spence Lewis." Letter Laing to Barde (6 December 1966). Apparently Laing's report to the Admiralty was so critical of how U.S. Navy fought at Midway it remains classified in Britain today. Morison, *United States Naval Operations*, 4:135; Morison, *Two-Ocean War*, 157; Dulin et al., 32.

29. CTG-17.4 (Comdesron Two) to Cominch, Report of Action, June 4, 1942 (4 June 1942). CTG-17.4 (Comdesron Six) to CTF-17, Japanese Torpedo Plane Attack on USS *Yorktown* During Battle of Midway, June 4, 1942—Report of (12 June 1942); Hailey, 177; Greenbacker account of the Battle of Midway; W. W. Smith, 123.

30. Comcru TF-17 war diary; Nagumo report, 26–27.

31. CO USS *Balch* to Cincpac, Report on Japanese air action against Yorktown, June 4, 1942, USS *Balch* (12 June 1942); CO USS *Benham* to Cincpac, Action Report—Battle of Midway (10 June 1942); CO USS *Russell* to Cincpac, Action Report (10 June 1942); CO USS *Anderson* to Cincpac, Report required by U.S. Navy Regulations, Art. 712, concerning engagement with Japanese carrier based planes, near Midway Island,

on June 4, 1942 (5 June 1942); CO USS *Hughes* to Cincpac, Report of Battle with Japanese Aircraft on June 4, 1942 (11 June 1942); CO USS *Morris* to Cominch, Midway Island Action of June 4, 1942—report on (13 June 1942); CO USS *Hammann* to Cincpac, Action Report, 4–6 June 1942 (16 June 1942); letter Buckmaster to W. W. Smith (22 August 1964).

32. Hailey, 177; W. W. Smith, 131; message 050415 June 1942 CTF-17 to Cincpac, CSCMF, roll 14; letter S. E. Morison to Fletcher (10 December 1947), Fletcher Papers; Dorris et al., *A Log of the Vincennes*, 218; letter Fletcher to Morison (15 December 1947), Fletcher Papers.

33. Letter Leslie to W. W. Smith (15 December 1964); Comcru TF-17 war diary; CO USS *Hughes* to Cincpac, Operations in Connection with USS *Yorktown* from time of abandonment about 0301, GCT, June 5, 1942, until sinking at 1659, GCT, June 7, 1942 (11 June 1942).

34. Comcru TF-17 war diary; TF-16 war diary; letter Fletcher to Morison (1 December 1947); Prange, *Miracle*, 386. In a memo to Bates (copy in Morison Office Files, box 23), Capt. Ralph C. Parker commented: "So while I am no great 'Fletcher fan,' I think he was absolutely right in what he did. In modern armies the commander who thinks that he and only he can do his job is too full of self-deception to be wholly trustworthy; while the one who consciously sacrifices what is best for the cause to his own pride and ambition is a scoundrel who ought to be shot!"

35. Letter Spruance to Forrestel (14 December 1962); Buell, *Quiet Warrior*, 154–55; CTF-16 war diary; Comcru TF-17 war diary. Morison in his usual attempt to deny that Fletcher exercised true tactical command of the carrier striking force stated that with this message Fletcher simply "confirmed" Spruance's "freedom of movement," Morison, *United States Naval Operations*, 4:141.

36. Messages 050540 Midway to Cincpac (relayed by Cincpac to all CTFs), 050510 CTU-7.1.6 (*Nautilus*) to Comsubpacflt (Commander, Submarines, Pacific Fleet), 050621 Midway to Cincpac, 050647 Cincpac to all CTFs, and 050707 Cincpac to all CTFs, June 1942, CSCMF, roll 14. Information of Thueson's contact from James Sawruk.

37. Layton, oral history, 34; Potter, *Nimitz*, 95; messages 050913 Cincpac to all CTFs, 051225 Cincpac to Cominch and all CTFs, June 1942, CSCMF, roll 14.

38. Messages 050912 CTF-16 to Cincpac, 051135 Cincpac to Midway, 051345 Cincpac to Cominch, June 1942, CSCMF, roll 14.

39. Cressman et al., *Glorious Page*, 137–39; Nagumo report, 8–11.

40. Ugaki, 145–52; Fuchida and Okumiya, 212–20.

41. Messages 050415 CTF-17 to Cincpac, 050430 Midway to Cincpac, 050500 Cincpac to CTF-17, 050515 Cincpac to *Vireo*, 050529 Cincpac to *Gwin*, 042045 Cincpac to Comserforpac, 050621 Cincpac to *Fulton*, and 050644 Cincpac to Comserforpac, June 1942, CSCMF, roll 14.

42. Messages 050721 Cincpac to CTF-17 and 050645 CTF-17 to Cincpac, June 1942, CSCMF, roll 14.

43. Cominch Secret Information Bulletin No. 1, Battle Experience from Pearl Harbor to Midway (February 1943); Cdr. J. J. Rochefort, Combat Intelligence, Fourteenth Naval District, Memorandum for Fleet Intelligence Officer, Battle of Midway, Enemy dispatches regarding (15 October 1942), in RG-457, SRMN-005; Buell, *Quiet Warrior*, 174–75. Bates, *Midway*, 143; Morison, *United States Naval Operations*, 4:142.

44. Bates, *Midway*, 142; W. W. Smith, 151.

CHAPTER 19. THE BATTLE OF MIDWAY III

1. CTF-16 report (16 June 1942), letter Spruance to Nimitz (8 June 1942), CTF-16 war diary.

2. Messages 051433 Cincpac to all CTFs, 051500 CTU-7.1.3 [*Tambor*] to Cincpac, relayed 051559 Cincpac to all CTFs, June 1942, CSCMF, roll 14. Comsubpacflt to Cincpac, Battle of Midway—Submarines report of (31 July 1942). CO NAS Midway report (18 June 1942). Ugaki, 151–52; Lacroix and Wells, *Japanese Cruisers of the Pacific War*, 477–78.

3. Messages 051800 CTU-7.1.3 [*Tambor*] to Cincpac 051847 CTF-7 to CTG-7.1, 051800 CTF-7 to TF-7 (info Cincpac), and 051907 and 051915 Cincpac to CTF-16 and CTF-17, June 1942, CSCMF, roll 14.

4. Messages 052036 CTF-16 to Cincpac, 052053 and 052055 Cincpac to all CTFs, 052129 Cincpac to CTF-16, June 1942, CSCMF, roll 14. CO NAS Midway report (18 June 1942); copy of Gumz's report via James Sawruk.

5. TF-16 war diary.

6. Letter Spruance to Nimitz (8 June 1942); Buell, *Quiet Warrior*, 156; messages 060023 Cincpac to CTF-16 and 060105 Cincpac to all CTFs, June 1942, CSCMF, roll 14.

7. Messages 052130 Midway to Cincpac, 060123 Cincpac to CTF-16, June 1942, CSCMF, roll 14. At noon (1430 Hawaii time) Midway cabled its update of Gumz's sighting report that clearly stated the new position as of 0930 (060000 June 1942 Midway to Cincpac, CSCMF, roll 14). It then took Cincpac headquarters nearly two hours to get the message out to the task force commanders. Barde, 353; Buell, *Quiet Warrior*, 157–58.

8. Barde, 353–55; Buell, *Quiet Warrior*, 157–58; Mark Horan personal communication; TF-16 war diary; TF-16 communication log; CTF-16 report (16 June 1942); CO USS *Hornet* report (13 June 1942); CO USS *Enterprise* reports (8 June 1942 and 13 June 1942).

9. Details of attacks in carrier action reports and Cressman et al., *Glorious Page*, 149–50.

10. Ugaki, 153–54; Fuchida and Okumiya, 199–200, 224–25. Messages 230632 and 230747 June 1942 Midway to Cincpac, CSCMF, roll 16. Silver's sighting helps to resolve a controversy as to the likely location of the *Hiryū*'s sinking. Nagumo's report, 10, 54, gives identical positions that differ only by west or east longitude, namely: latitude 31° 27.5′ north, longitude 179° 23.5′. The Japanese official history (Japan, *Senshi Sōsho*, 43:381) favored the east longitude position, but the location of Silver's contact argues strongly that west longitude is correct.

11. Messages 060237 Cincpac to all CTFs, 060315 Cincpac to CTF-16, June 1942, CSCMF, roll 14; letter Spruance to Nimitz (8 June 1942); letter Spruance to Forrestel (9 February 1963), in Spruance Papers, coll. 37, box 7; Buell, *Quiet Warrior*, 158–59.

12. Messages 060717 Cincpac to *Cimarron*, 060741 Cincpac to all CTFs, June 1942, CSCMF, roll 14; TF-16 communication log.

13. Messages 060625 Cincpac to CTF-16 and 060801 Cincpac to all CTFs, June 1942, CSCMF, roll 14. Cincpac to Cominch, Battle of Midway, Second Supplementary Report (8 August 1942), Nimitz's endorsement of English's report, concluded: "Our forces should have destroyed many enemy ships on 5 June. A foremost cause for their not doing so was *Tambor*'s faulty reporting of contact along with her overcautious maneuvers for the four hours she was in sight of Japanese vessels west of Midway beginning 0215 5 June (Plus 12)."

14. Comcrupac report (14 June 1942); Comcru TF-17 war diary.

15. Comcru TF-17 war diary; W. W. Smith, 139–40; *Portland* and *Astoria* war diaries; Worthington, "A Destroyer at Midway," 6; message 052121 June 1942 Cincpac to CTF-17, CSCMF, roll 14; Boo account to Walter Lord, enclosed in letter to Lundstrom (17 February 1996); letter Schindler to Tuleja (24 September 1958).

16. Messages 060117 Cincpac to CTF-17, 061115 CTF-17 to Cincpac, 061331 Cincpac to *Platte*, June 1942, CSCMF, roll 14.

17. CO *Hughes* report (11 June 1942); Nagumo report, 38. Bates, *Midway*, 101. CO USS *Yorktown* to Secnav (17 June 1942), Second Endorsement Cincpac to Secnav (7 July 1942). George Clapp, one of the flag communication watch officers, is adamant none of the flag ciphers were compromised because they were secured prior to the shifting of the flag to the *Astoria*. Radioman W. H. Walvoord did the same for Fullinwider's RI group (from Rundle, oral history).

18. Messages 050430 CTF-1 to TF-1, 051719 CTF-1 to Cincpac, 060050 Cincpac to CTF-1, June 1942, CSCMF, roll 14; Greybook, 571. See also CTF-1 to Cincpac, Report on Cruise 5–19 June 1942 (7 July

1942), RG-313, Cincpac Secret Red 106, box 4563. Pye noted Cincpac's visit in early July "clarified the situation" and gave "proper direction" to the efforts of TF-1.

19. For the 6 June operations, see TF-16 war diary; TF-16 communication log; CTF-16 report (16 June 1942); CO USS *Hornet* report (13 June 1942); CO USS *Enterprise* reports (8 June 1942 and 13 June 1942); and Cressman et al., *Glorious Page*, 153–56, 162–63.

20. TF-16 war diary; message 062000 June 1942 Cominch to Cincpac, CSCMF, roll 14.

21. TF-16 communication log.

22. TF-16 communication log; message 070756 June 1942 CTF-16 to Cincpac, CSCMF, roll 14. One notation in the communication log described the enemy commander as "C-in-C Orange Fleet," which meant Yamamoto, but Orange is probably an error for Second.

23. *Phelps* 27 percent, *Aylwin* 24 percent, *Conyngham* 29 percent, and *Ellet* 29 percent; figures from their deck logs and fuel capacities given in FTF-218, War Service Fuel Consumption of U.S. Naval Surface Vessels (1 September 1945).

24. Messages 070015 Midway to Cincpac, 070121 Cincpac to CTF-16, June 1942, CSCMF, roll 14.

25. Buell, *Quiet Warrior*, 162; message 070756 June 1942 CTF-16 to Cincpac, CSCMF, roll 14; Cominch Secret Information Bulletin No. 1, Battle Experience from Pearl Harbor to Midway (February 1943).

26. Messages 070224 Com 14 to Combined Addressees; 070629 Belconnen to Combined Addressees; 070705 Cincpac to CTF-11, CTF-16, and CTF-17; 070803 Cincpac to Cominch; 070829 Cincpac to Cominch; all June 1942, CSCMF, roll 14.

27. Morison, *United States Naval Operations*, 4:155. CO USS *Yorktown* to Secnav (17 June 1942), with First (23 June 1942) and Second Endorsements (7 July 1942); Comdesron Six to CTF-17, Report of Japanese Submarine Attack on USS *Yorktown* June 6, 1942, and the sinking of the *Yorktown* June 7, 1942 (14 June 1942); Tanabe, "I Sank the *Yorktown*"; messages 070305 Benham to Cincpac and CTF-17, 070336 CTG-17.5 to Cincpac and CTF-17, CSCMF, roll 14; Cressman, *Gallant Ship*, 174–79.

28. Layton, oral history, 55; Morison, *United States Naval Operations*, 4:154–55; Barde, 347; CO USS *Yorktown* to Secnav (17 June 1942), with First (23 June 1942) and Second Endorsements (7 July 1942); Potter and Nimitz, 246; W. W. Smith, 151–52; Pacific Fleet Secret Letter 25L-42 (30 June 1942); message 081935 June 1942 Cominch to Cincpac, Greybook, 559.

29. Morison, *United States Naval Operations*, 4:153; letter Spruance to Fletcher (8 June 1942).

30. Comcru TF-17 war diary; *Astoria* and *Portland* war diaries; messages 070051 Cincpac to CTF-17 and CTG-11.1, 071915 CTG-17.5 to Cincpac, June 1942, CSCMF, roll 14; 080511 June 1942 Cincpac to Cominch and all CTFs, CSCMF, roll 15.

31. Messages 071530 Cominch to Cincpac, 071611 Comnorwestseafron (Commander, Northwest Sea Frontier) to Cincpac, 071954 Cominch to Cincpac, June 1942, CSCMF, roll 14.

32. Messages 080351 Cincpac to Cominch; 080429 Cincpac to CTF-8, CTF-16, and CTF-17; 081910 CTF-8 to Cincpac; 082029 Cominch to Cincpac; all June 1942, CSCMF, roll 15.

33. *Saratoga* war diary; Lundstrom, *First Team*, 429–30; Reynolds, *Famous American Admirals*, 271–72.

34. *Saratoga* war diary, TF-16 war diary.

35. Message 091803 June 1942 Cincpac to CTF-16, CSCMF, roll 15; Ugaki, 158, 160.

36. Messages 100045 June 1942 Cominch to Cincpac, Cominch 00 File; 101957 June 1942 Cincpac to Cominch, CNO TS Blue File; 110411 June 1942 Cincpac to Cominch, CSCMF, roll 15.

37. TF-16 war diary; *Saratoga* war diary; message 101931 June 1942 Cincpac to CTF-16, and CTF-17, CSCMF, roll 15.

38. Messages 111841 Cincpac to CTF-16, 110929 Cincpac to Cominch, June 1942, CSCMF, roll 15; 111645 June 1942 Cominch to Cincpac, CNO TS Blue File; 082135, 122030, 142303 June 1942 Cincpac to CTF-1, CSCMF, roll 15.

39. Message 130329 June 1942 Cincpac to CTF-11, CSCMF, roll 15.

40. Cincpac report (28 June 1942); detailed casualty list for both sides in Sawachi; analysis of Japanese aircrew losses from James Sawruk.

41. Cincpac report (28 June 1942); Cressman et al., *Glorious Page*, 167–68; Norman W. Shaw, *Screened Her Going Down*, 351–53; letter Schindler to Tuleja (24 September 1958).

42. Letters Spruance to Nimitz (8 June 1942), Spruance to Fletcher (8 June 1942); Fletcher interview by Prange (17 September 1966).

43. Message 140112 June 1942 Comcrupac to Cincpac, CSCMF, roll 15; Boo account to Walter Lord, enclosed in letter to Lundstrom (17 February 1996).

44. Letter Nimitz to King (13 June 1942), Nimitz Papers; message 150117 June 1942 Cincpac to Cominch, CSCMF, roll 15; messages 191920 Cominch to Cincpac, 202013 Cincpac to Cominch, 211515 Cominch to Cincpac, June 1942, CSCMF, roll 16.

45. Letter Spruance to Nimitz (8 June 1942); Reynolds, *Fast Carriers*, 28; Citation File, NHC.

46. Letter Ashford to Buell (24 November 1971); letter Vice Adm. W. Frederick Boone to Cdr. T. B. Buell (20 November 1971), in Spruance Papers, coll. 37, box 1. On Browning, see also the appendix by Clark Reynolds in Cressman et al., *Glorious Page*, 214–16, and Dr. Harold L. Buell, "Death of a Captain."

47. Cincpac Memorandum to Rear Adm. A. W. Fitch and Rear Adm. F. J. Fletcher, Aircraft Carrier Task Force Tactics (9 June 1942), and the replies: CTF-11 to Cincpac, Aircraft Carrier Task Force Tactics (undated) and Fletcher Memorandum to Cincpac, Aircraft Carrier Task Force Tactics (15 June 1942); M. R. Browning Memorandum for Rear Admiral Spruance (13 June 1942); R. A. Spruance Memorandum to Cincpac (13 June 1942); all available in RG-38, Cincpac Flag Files.

48. Cincpac report (28 June 1942); Fletcher memorandum (15 June 1942).

49. Browning memorandum (13 June 1942); Murray interview by Buaer (25 November 1942). Spruance memorandum (13 June 1942), Browning memorandum (13 June 1942); Lundstrom, *First Team*, 441–47; message 210317 June 1942 Cincpac to Cominch, CSCMF, roll 16.

50. Message 102151 June 1942 Cincpac to all CTFs, CSCMF, roll 15.

51. Messages 151310 Cominch to Cincpac and 172033 Cincpac to Cominch, June 1942, CSCMF, roll 15. Fitch wrote in his undated memo on carrier tactics that carrier task force commanders could only risk detaching light forces for night attacks when there was a "high probability" of success. Fletcher in his memo to Cincpac (15 June 1942) acknowledged the desirability of following up air attacks with surface forces, but only if the enemy carriers had been knocked out.

52. For example, a recent entry on Spruance in a respected military encyclopedia stated: "When his friend Halsey was temporarily ill, Spruance took command of the American carrier force that fought and won the most crucial and decisive naval engagement of World War II" (Chambers, *The Oxford Companion to American Military History*, 673). Beach's *Salt and Steel*, 113–14, acknowledged that Spruance was "subordinate to Fletcher" but took Fletcher out of the battle so early, "It fell thus to Spruance to make the crucial decisions when to attack (he selected exactly the right time) and when to run away from Yamamoto's surface forces."

53. Pratt's articles describing Spruance as the sole carrier commander at Midway first appeared in *Harper's Magazine* ("The Mysteries of Midway," 133–45; "The Knockout at Midway," 246–53). In the fall of 1943 the Bureau of Naval Personnel reprinted the articles. On 6 December 1943 Cdr. Charles G. Moore Jr., an old shipmate of Fletcher, wrote Adm. Randall Jacobs, chief of Bupers, "It is an odd type of reporting of a battle which fails to mention the name of the senior officer or that he was even present." Moore commented that Pratt, "Having done so handsomely by Admiral Fletcher in the Coral Sea story, no doubt found it advisable to select another hero for Midway. This is journalistically understandable, although it is a bit like saying that since Nelson had achieved so greatly in the Battle of the Nile it would be more appropriate to give somebody else the credit for Trafalgar" (memo in Fletcher Papers). The next year Pratt incorporated his Midway piece without revisions in the book *The Navy's War*, foreword by Secretary of the Navy Frank Knox. Likewise Gilbert Cant's 1943 *America's Navy in World War II*, also

written with Navy Department help, failed to mention Fletcher even being at Midway. In 1946 Pratt's *Fleet Against Japan*, foreword by Fleet Admiral Nimitz, 53, described Spruance as the "victor of Midway."

54. Fletcher to Morison (1 December 1947), Morison statement, both in Fletcher Papers.

55. Morison, *United States Naval Operations*, 4:84–85. Spruance to Potter (24 December 1959), Spruance Papers, coll. 37, series I, box 7. Fletcher to Smith (12 August 1964), Smith Papers.

CHAPTER 20. A BRIEF INTERMISSION

1. Messages 281929 May 1942 Cincpac to Cominch, 301615 May 1942 Bupers to Cincpac, 011445 June 1942 Cominch to Cincpac, and 031430 June 1942 Cominch to Cincpac, CSCMF, roll 13; 100235 June 1942 Cincpac to Com 11, CSCMF, roll 15.

2. Messages 060045 June 1942 Cincpac to Cominch, CSCMF, roll 14; 082029 Cominch to Cincpac, 122253 Cincpac to CTF-18, June 1942, CSCMF, roll 15; letter Nimitz to King (13 June 1942), in Nimitz Papers.

3. On 1 July Draemel relieved Brown as Commander, Amphibious Force, Pacific Fleet (Comamphibforpac) and left Phibpac (Amphibious Force, Pacific Fleet) on 10 August to command the Fourth Naval District in Philadelphia. His tenure as Cincpac chief of staff during that very rough period earned him the DSM. He retired in 1946 as a rear admiral (NHC Officer Biographical File).

4. Message 160131 June 1942 Cincpac to Pacflt, CSCMF, roll 15.

5. Letter Spruance to Nimitz (8 June 1942); Citation File, NHC; Buell, *Quiet Warrior*, 164.

6. Buell, *Quiet Warrior*, 164–65. Spruance's otherwise blandly written action report (16 June 1942) cautioned, "Where discrepancies exist between the *Enterprise* and *Hornet* reports, the *Enterprise* report should be taken as the more accurate," a strong hint that Mitscher and the *Hornet* performed poorly at Midway. Message 142359 June 1942 Cincpac to Cominch, CSCMF, roll 15. Letter Nimitz to King (13 June 1942); letter Buckmaster to W. W. Smith (22 August 1964). On the close call between the *Enterprise* and *Oklahoma*, see *Enterprise* deck log and CO USS *Enterprise* to Comairbatfor, Near Collision *Oklahoma-Enterprise*, November 10, 1941 (12 November 1941), from RG-313, Comairbatfor General Correspondence, via James Rindt. Murray's career teetered prior to the attack on Pearl Harbor. Halsey requested on 18 November that he be detached, an action Kimmel evidently endorsed. On 8 December Halsey advised Cincpac, "In view excellent work of subject officer during current operations recommend my Serial 0979 of 18 November 1941 be canceled." Kimmel concurred. On 13 February 1942 Halsey reiterated his request to Bunav that all reference to the 10 November 1941 incident be expunged from Murray's personnel file. Since then his "conduct and shiphandling have been superb." Messages 052145 Opnav to Cincpac, 081756 CTF-8 to Cincpac, 091733 Cincpac to Opnav, December 1941, in CSCMF, roll 508; Comairbatfor to Chief, Bunav, "Captain George D. Murray, U.S. Navy." (13 February 1942), in RG-38, Cincpac Flag Files.

7. Messages 180121 June 1942 Cincpac to CTF-16 and CTF-17, CSCMF, roll 15; 192356 CTF-18 to Cincpac, 210140 NY Pearl Harbor to Buships (Bureau of Ships), June 1942, CSCMF, roll 16; 192303 Cincpac to Cominch, 192301 Cincpac to CTF-11, June 1942, in CNO TS Blue File.

8. Messages 220055 Cincpac to Cominch, 231442 Cominch to Cincpac, 242347 Cincpac to Pacflt, June 1942, CSCMF, roll 16; letter Nimitz to King (24 June 1942), in Nimitz Papers; message 251440 June 1942 Cominch to Cincpac, CNO TS Blue File.

9. Coletta, *Bellinger*, 314–18; Cincpac to Cominch, Pacific Fleet, Air Arm, Upper Echelon, Command of (14 July 1942), RG-313, Comairpac (Commander, Aircraft, Pacific Fleet) General Correspondence; messages 162248 Bupers to Cincpac, 180051 Cincpac to Compatwing Two, July 1942, CSCMF, roll 18; 220523 Cincpac to Bupers, 212300 (*sic*, actually 26 July) Bupers to Cincpac, 262305 Cincpac to Cominch, 272059 Cincpac to CTF-17, 291925 Cominch to Cincpac, July 1942, CSCMF, roll 19.

10. Messages 151300 Cominch to Cincpac; 152201, 170331, 170425 Cincpac to Cominch, June 1942, CSCMF, roll 15.

11. For the air group reorganizations, see Lundstrom, *First Team Guadalcanal*, 8–16.

12. On *Saratoga*'s use of one elevator, Stern, 111–12.

13. CTF-17 to Cincpac, Report of Air Raid on Buin-Faisi-Tonolei (14 October 1942); Murray interview by Buaer (25 November 1942).

CHAPTER 21. WATCHTOWER

1. Conversation with George Clapp, 4 June 2001.

2. Message 080731 June 1942 Comsowespac to Cincpac, CSCMF, roll 14; narrative by Vice Adm. Robert L. Ghormley, South Pacific Command April 1942 through October 1942 (22 January 1943), 2; Jeffrey G. Barlow, "Taking the Offensive: Admiral Ernest J. King and the Decision To Seize Guadalcanal," (1999) unpublished paper, 15–16, courtesy Jeffrey Barlow. Messages 280351 May 1942 Cincpac to Comsowespacfor and letter MacArthur to Cincpac, 29 May 1942, in MacArthur Papers. Messages 010100 Cominch to Cincpac, 020455 Cincpac to Comsowespacfor, June 1942, CNO TS Blue File. Frank's *Guadalcanal* offers the best overall account of the planning and events of the Guadalcanal campaign.

3. Hayes, 142; messages 100046 June 1942 Cominch to Comnaveu (Commander, U.S. Naval Forces, Europe) (info Cincpac), CNO TS Blue File; 111530 Cominch to Comsopac, 140616 Ghormley to Cominch, June 1942, Comsopac war diary; Greybook, 581.

4. Message 210245 June 1942 Cincpac to Cominch, CSCMF, roll 16; Greybook, 598. For the Japanese carriers, messages 222341 June 1942 Opnav to Cincpac, 012131 July 1942 Cominch to Cincpac, CSCMF, roll 17; and 222230 July 1942 Opnav to Cincpac, CSCMF, roll 19. The first estimates properly gave the names *Junyō* and *Hiyō*, but the 22 July message "corrected" their readings to "*Hayataka*" and "*Hitaka*," an error that persisted throughout the war.

5. Greybook, 599; message 230017 June 1942 Cincpac to Comsopac, CSCMF, roll 16.

6. Messages 231255 June 1942 Cominch to Comsowespacfor, Greybook, 601; Chief of Staff to MacArthur 24 June 1942, MacArthur Papers; 231415 and 242306 June 1942 Cominch to Cincpac, Greybook, 602–3; Greybook, 669.

7. Messages, all June 1942: 241943 Cincpac to Cominch and 262041 Cincpac to Cominch, CSCMF, roll 16; 251840 Cominch to Cincpac, Greybook, 603; Greybook, 670; 271415 Cominch to Cincpac, CNO TS Blue File.

8. Messages 272251 June 1942 Cincpac to Cominch, CNO TS Blue File; 272301 Cincpac to CTF-18 and 300015 Cincpac to CTF-11, CTF-18, and CTF-3, June 1942, Cominch 00 File; Greybook, 672.

9. Potter, *Nimitz*, 109–11; messages 302155 Comairtransron (Commander, Air Transport Squadron) 2 to Opnav, 031941 Cincpac to Com 12, June 1942, CSCMF, roll 17.

10. Message 011445 June 1942 Cominch to Cincpac, CSCMF, roll 13; on Turner, see Dyer, *The Amphibians Came to Conquer*, 1:130, 150.

11. Frank, 433; Twining, *No Bended Knee*, 70–71. In December 1945 Turner testified that just prior to 7 December 1941 he had believed only part of the Japanese fleet would conduct the invasions in the Far East. The rest, "including the battleships and carriers," would confront the Pacific Fleet, either by opening the war with a "heavy" raid against Hawaii (he gave the odds of that at better than 50–50) or by deploying into the Mandates or the Carolines to prevent Kimmel from advancing westward. Asked during the hearings why he did not send a categorical warning to Kimmel that Pearl Harbor would likely be attacked, Turner replied he did not consider that necessary, for the 27 November 1941 "war warning message" ordered Kimmel to "execute an appropriate defensive deployment." No contemporary documentation exists for Turner's claims, which if true meant he committed gross dereliction of duty for not warning his superiors of circumstances so diametrically opposed to the basic assumptions behind the navy's war plans. Turner testimony, PHA, part 4, 1962–63.

12. Dyer, 1:272, citing Turner's 3 July 1942 memo to Cincpac, but in box 16 of the Adm. Richmond Kelly Turner Papers, the memo is dated 5 July 1942. Message 210556 June 1942 Comsowespacfor to Cincpac, CSCMF, roll 16. Message 040057 July 1942 Cincpac to CTF-18, CNO TS Blue File.

13. Message 022100 July 1942 Cominch to Cincpac, Greybook, 605–6.

14. Conversation between Cominch and Cincpac, 4 July (5 July 1942).

15. Conversation between Cominch and Cincpac, 5 July (5 July 1942); letter Nimitz to Melville V. Grosvenor (28 June 1942), in Adm. John S. McCain Papers.

16. Greybook, 704. Estimate—An Offensive for the Capture and Occupation of Tulagi and Vicinity (6 July 1942), in Greybook, 709–43. Chagrined by the poor accuracy of the high-flying B-17s at Midway, the War Plans Section actually proposed that the heavy bombers attack from an altitude of seventy-five to one hundred feet.

17. Kinkaid memoir, 189–90; Greybook, 707. Messages 070125 July 1942 Cincpac to Comsopac, Comsopac war diary; 070231 and 062229 Cincpac to Comsopac, July 1942, CSCMF, roll 17.

18. Comamphibforpac Administrative History, 46. Turner's own recollections, written in October 1945, of the planning and execution of Guadalcanal landings appear on pages 43–50. Letter Fletcher to Hanson W. Baldwin (8 July 1947), in Fletcher Papers.

19. Text of Fletcher's DSM citation and date of award in Citation File, NHC. Col. Melvin J. Maas diary, in Congressman Melvin J. Maas Papers.

20. Staff roster and Pederson's orders in Pederson Papers; biographies in Officer Biographical Files, NHC; quote on Humphreys in Col. M. J. Maas undated memorandum (c. August 1942); for the Radio Intelligence Unit, see Kenneth E. Carmichael, oral history, Naval Security Group (September 1983), RG-457.

21. Maas Papers; Zehnpfennig, *Melvin J. Maas*, sketches Maas's life but is far less useful than the Maas Papers themselves in covering his time with Fletcher in the *Saratoga*. Message 132129 June 1942 Cincpac to Commandant, Marine Corps, CSCMF, roll 15.

22. Stern, 65, 70; Stahl, "Back to Savo Island," 19–20.

23. General sources on movements and composition of TF-11 include the war diaries of TF-11, Comcru TF-11, Desron One, and the fleet oilers.

24. Message 090633 July 1942 Cincpac to Comsopac, CNO TS Blue File and Comsopac war diary. The actual letter of instruction was Cincpac to Comsopacfor (9 July 1942). The chartered tankers are identified in message 012122 July 1942 Comserforpac to Port Director San Pedro, CSCMF, roll 17.

25. Messages 122359 Cincpac to CTF-16, 112241 CTF-18 to Cincpac, 122341 Cincpac to Comserforpac, 140510 CTF-18 to Cincpac, 141135 Cincpac to CTF-11, July 1942, CSCMF, roll 18; Greybook, 619, 770, 772; *Wasp* war diary.

26. Messages, all July 1942: 160612 Comsopac to Cincpac, Greybook, 620; 141927 Cincpac to Cominch, 151500 Cominch to Cincpac, 152343 Cominch to Cincpac, and 170827 Cincpac to CTF-11, CSCMF, roll 18.

27. Message 170602 July 1942 Comsopac to CTF-11 etc., RG-313, Comsopac, Comsopac Message File.

28. Message 172250 July 1942 Comsopac to CTF-18, Comsopac Message File. Comsopac Op-Plan 1-42 (16 July 1942) in RG-38, Op-Ord File. Ghormley, "The Tide Turns," 59, an unpublished memoir available in NHC; Ghormley narrative, 12. For the 27 July conference, see Comsopac File, Callaghan's Report of the Conference (28 July 1942), copies in Morison Office Files, box 24, and in Ghormley's "Tide Turns," 65–69.

29. Letter Cincpac to Vice Adm. Robert L. Ghormley, USN, Prospective Commander South Pacific Area and South Pacific Force (12 May 1942), copy in Op-Ord File. Ghormley, "Tide Turns," 24; message 090633 July 1942 Cincpac to Comsopac, CNO TS Blue File. Adm. Henry A. Wiley, a former Cincus, denigrated "strategical command" in his memoir *An Admiral from Texas*, 287: "Except for a concentration of the fleet

once a year, the commander in chief was expected to exercise what was called 'strategical command,' whatever that means, but not tactical command."

30. Ghormley, "Tide Turns," 40; Gerald C. Thomas unpublished manuscript, "Of Coconuts & Their Prelude," 7, Thomas Papers. Messages 081012 series July 1942 MacArthur-Ghormley to Cominch, Cincpac, and Chief of Staff, CNO TS Blue File.

31. Hayes, 148–53. Jeffrey G. Barlow personal communication. He is the most knowledgeable historian concerning U.S. Navy strategy in the Pacific War. Messages July 1942: 102100 Cominch to Comsopac, Comsopac war diary; 112000 Comsopac to Cominch, Comsopac Message File.

32. Letter Ghormley to Nimitz (2 August 1942), Nimitz Papers; Callaghan conference notes (28 July 1942).

33. U.S. Naval War College (Commo. Richard W. Bates and Cdr. Walter D. Innis), *The Battle of Savo Island August 9, 1942 Strategical and Tactical Analysis*, 18 (hereafter Bates and Innis).

34. Cdr. Oscar Pederson, "Air Operations," Lecture Army & Navy Staff College (13 January 1944), in Pederson Papers. Morison, *United States Naval Operations*, 4:268–69, described Turner enjoying "complete autonomy from the moment of sailing," because Fletcher "limited his command in practice to the three carrier groups." Under the circumstances Fletcher had no real option but to stay with the carriers. Turner did not exercise "complete autonomy," because he followed a plan that Fletcher approved.

35. Japan, *Senshi Sōsho*, 49:364–69, 377–89.

36. Japan, *Senshi Sōsho*, 49:367–68, 389–407.

37. Message 131147 July 1942 Comsowespac to Comsopac, CSCMF, roll 18. Greybook, 776; text of 17 July 1942 letter in Greybook, 774–75.

CHAPTER 22. THE 27 JULY CONFERENCE

1. Message 180558 July 1942 Comsopac to CTF-11, Comsopac Message File; *Platte* and *Cimarron* war diaries.

2. *Wasp* war diary. Messages July 1942: 182230 CTF-18 to Comsopac, Greybook, 622; 210802 CTF-18 to Comsopac, Greybook, 626; 211106 CTF-18 to Comsopac, Comsopac Message File.

3. TF-16 war diary; Kinkaid memoir, 191–95; [Royal Navy] Fleet Intelligence Bulletin No. 8, Fleet Operations, Mid and S.W. Pacific—[Report of Cdr. M. B. Laing on USS *North Carolina*], in Australian Archives, MP 1857 Dept. of Defence (Navy Office, Historical Records Files), File 108A, courtesy of Commo. Bruce Loxton, RAN (Ret.), hereafter Laing report.

4. For Turner's general activities, see the Commander, Amphibious Force, South Pacific Area (Comamphibforsopac) (TF-62) war diary. Twining, 43.

5. Loxton with Coulthard-Clark, *The Shame of Savo*, 28–30.

6. Messages July 1942: 210630 Comsopac to CTF-61, CTF-62, and CTF-63, Comsopac Message File; 210820 CTF-11 to Comsopac, Greybook, 626. Morison, *United States Naval Operations*, 4:280, stated Ghormley was busy "flying up to Nouméa to his flagship *Argonne*." Ghormley did not leave until 1 August, after Callaghan had already rejoined him. Message 310537 July 1942 Comsopac to Comsopacfor, CNO TS Blue File. Ghormley stated in "Tide Turns," 64, "I was desirous of attending this conference, but I found that it was impossible for me to give the time necessary for travel with possible attendant delays."

7. *Saratoga* and *Hull* deck logs; Twining, 45. Lt. (jg) Frank O. Green, USNR, diary (27 July 1942), via Frank O. Green. He was a VF-5 pilot who witnessed the "excitement" of McCain's dunking.

8. Callaghan conference notes (28 July 1942); Vandegrift, *Once a Marine*, 120; Comamphibforpac Administrative History, 46; Dyer, 1:301–2.

9. Dyer, 1:301–2; letter Fletcher to Baldwin (8 July 1947).

10. Kinkaid memoir, 207.

11. Callaghan conference notes. In Dyer, 1:302, Fletcher had expected Ghormley to join him in *Saratoga*, but that makes no sense in light of what Fletcher told Callaghan at the conference.

12. Cincpac Letter of Instruction (28 May 1942). Correspondent Clark Lee wrote of a conversation with one of Fletcher's younger staff officers, whom he chided for the failure to relieve Wake. "How about this present mission. . . . Are we going to risk this carrier?" The officer responded: "Not if we can help it." Lee, *They Call It Pacific*, 323–24.

13. Colonel Maas, Estimate of the Situation (15 July 1942), Maas Papers; letter Fletcher to Baldwin (8 July 1947).

14. Maas estimate (15 July 1942). Glover, *Command Performance With Guts*, 37.

15. Undated (c. early July 1942), handwritten first draft air operation plan in Pederson Papers, marked "Excellent" by either Fletcher or Lewis.

16. Messages 200135 Comamphibforsopac to CTF-11 and 210948 CTF-11 to CTF-62, July 1942, Comsopac Message File.

17. Letter Noyes to Fletcher (21 July 1942), undated (c. 22 July 1942) handwritten second draft air operation plan, both in Pederson Papers; Maas diary, Maas Papers.

18. Maas diary; letter Rear Adm. Leigh Noyes to Cominch, Cominch Report of Operations, Request of Corrections thereto (undated, c. 1944), copy in Fletcher Papers.

19. On Sherman, Reynolds, *Famous American Admirals*, 306–8; letters Rear Adm. Bradford E. Grow, USN (Ret.), to Lundstrom (28 August 1996, 7 September 1996); Vice Adm. Thomas R. Weschler, USN (Ret.), oral history, 81, 88–89. Weschler did admit, 92, his knowledge of Noyes was not firsthand. "Really the only time I ever saw" him was when he would "walk up and down the quarterdeck, in greens, wearing his aviation pigskin gloves." Weschler "always had the impression of him as being sort of a mannequin, rather than really being a flesh-and-blood naval officer who was in the thick of decisions and ready to take over and set the course."

20. CTF-11 to Cincpac, First Endorsement of *Saratoga*'s Report of Action Against Enemy (Japanese) Forces in Solomon Islands Area on August 24, 1942 (24 September 1942); Pederson lecture (13 January 1944); Carrier Aircraft, USS *Wasp*, Operation Plan 1-42 (27 July 1942), in Op-Ord File.

21. Callaghan conference notes; letter Fletcher to Baldwin (8 July 1947).

22. Edward Miller, 197–99. Greybook, 707; letter Fletcher to Baldwin (8 July 1947); Callaghan conference notes; message 020240 August 1942 Comsopac to CTF-61, Greybook, 631; memo Rear Adm. John S. McCain, Air Support subsequent to Occupation (undated, c. 1 August 1942), noted the carriers would leave D+2½ days, McCain Papers.

23. Comamphibforpac Administrative History, 44; letter Turner to Fletcher (25 July 1942) in Turner Papers, box 1, and Dyer, 1:307–8; Callaghan conference notes.

24. Letter Turner to Fletcher (25 July 1942), Callaghan conference notes.

25. Turner's Memorandum for Admiral Hepburn (1943), in Adm. Arthur J. Hepburn, USN (Ret.), to Cincpac, Report of informal inquiry into the circumstances attending the loss of the USS *Vincennes*, USS *Quincy*, USS *Astoria*, and HMAS *Canberra*, on August 9, 1942, in the vicinity of Savo Island (13 May 1943), 267–81. Comamphibforpac Administrative History, 46. Notes from interview of Vice Adm. R. K. Turner by Hanson Baldwin (10 October 1946), in Morison Office Files, box 26. In box 26 is a memo of a conversation by a Morison staffer with "Ramsay," presumably Rear Adm. Donald Ramsey, stating Callaghan did not know of Turner's supposed "S.O.B." remark. The memo was later altered to state that Callaghan *did* know of the comment. Callaghan died on 13 November 1942, so that emendation did not come from him.

26. Griffith, *The Battle for Guadalcanal*, 35; Vandegrift, 120; Twining, 45.

27. Kinkaid memoir, 207–8, 230. Letter Vice Adm. Forrest P. Sherman to S. E. Morison (14 February 1949), Morison Office Files, box 26. Letter Noyes to Rear Adm. Charles Wellborn (12 August 1950), in DNC, Office Files, box 20.

28. Morison, *United States Naval Operations*, 4: 281; Isely and Crowl, *The U.S. Marines and Amphibious War*, 116; Dyer 1:300; Frank, 54.

29. Isely and Crowl, 41; Maas estimate (15 July 1942).

30. Messages July 1942: 100616 Comsopac to Cincpac, Comsopac Message File; 100941 Cincpac to Comsopac and 192129 Cincpac to *Long Island*, CSCMF, roll 18; 222211 Cincpac to Comsopac, CSCMF, roll 19.

31. Messages July 1942: 210335 Comamphibforsopac to Comsopac, Comsopac war diary; 290513 Cincpac to Comsopac, CSCMF, roll 19, modified by 022115 August 1942 Cincpac to TG-2.6, CSCMF, roll 20.

32. McCain memo, Air Support Subsequent to Occupation, McCain Papers; message 020240 August 1942 Comsopac to CTF-61, Greybook, 631.

33. Dyer, 1:300–301; message 022357 August 1942 Cincpac to Comsopac, CSCMF, roll 20; Pederson lecture (13 January 1944); Maj. Harold W. Bauer, USMC, diary, 3 August 1942, via Nimitz Museum; A. C. Davis Memo for Admiral Kinkaid (4 August 1942), Pederson Papers.

34. Message 041436 August 1942 Commander, Aircraft, South Pacific Force (Comairsopac) to Comsopac, Comsopac war diary.

35. Message 191034 July 1942 Comsowespac to Comsopac, Greybook, 622–23; letter Ghormley to Nimitz (29 July 1942), Nimitz Papers.

36. Comairsopac war diary; Turner 1943 memo to Hepburn, 268; Comamphibforpac Administrative History, 47. Messages July 1942: 290857 CTF-61 to CTF-63, 300820 CTF-63 to CTF-61, Greybook, 628; 310811 Comairsopac to Comsopac, Comsopac war diary.

37. Message 290041 July 1942 Comairsopac to Comsopac, Comsopac war diary; Comairsopac war diary.

38. Dyer, 1:301; TF-11 war diary. Messages July 1942: 160345 and 190235 Cincpac to Comsopac, CNO TS Blue File; 012122 Comserforpac to Port Director San Pedro, CSCMF, roll 17.

39. Callaghan conference notes; messages 271930 Chief of Staff Comsopac to Comsopac, 280950 Comsopac to Port Director Roses, Suva, and Nouméa, 281030 Comsopac to CTG-2.3, and 282007 Cincpac to Comsopac, July 1942, CSCMF, roll 19.

40. Callaghan conference notes. Messages July 1942: 272211 Comsopac to CTF-61 and 280201 CTF-61 to Comsopac, Comsopac war diary; 281500 CTF-62 to Cincpac, CSCMF, roll 19. Dyer, 1:437, erred calling phase one the invasion and phase two the occupation of Ndeni, when in fact the invasion was phase two and Ndeni simply a part of it.

41. TF-11, Comamphibforsopac, and *Platte* war diaries. Messages July 1942: 290330 Comsopac to CTF-62, Comsopac war diary; 300246 Comsopac to CTF-62, 300331 Comsopac to Comairsopac, CSCMF, roll 20.

42. Messages 281830 July 1942 Cominch to Comsopac, Comsopac war diary; 292325 July 1942 Comsopac to Cominch, CNO TS Blue File; 011205 August 1942 Ghormley to Fletcher, CNO TS Blue File.

CHAPTER 23. FROM FIJI TO GUADALCANAL

1. TF-61 Operation Order 1-42 (28 July 1942), in RG-38, Op-Ord File. As will be shown the *Dale*, *Aaron Ward*, and *Laffey* were not present with the carriers on 7–9 August, although the ONI Combat Narrative *Landing in the Solomons 7–8 August 1942* (1943, NHC), Bates and Innis, Morison, and Dyer all erred in placing them there.

2. TF-61 Op-Ord 1-42; Ghormley, "Tide Turns," 64; Maas diary (30 July 1942) for Suva flight.

3. TF-62 Operation Plan A3-42 (30 July 1942), in Op-Ord File.

4. Message 011200 August 1942 CTF-18 to CTF-61 (info *Saratoga*, *Enterprise*, CTF-16), in Pederson Papers.

5. Letter Kinkaid to Noyes (2 August 1942), info CTF-61, Pederson Papers.

6. Air Support Force, USS *Wasp*, Flagship, Operation Plan 2-42 (4 August 1942), in Op-Ord File.

7. Comamphibforpac Administrative History, 44; Vandegrift, 121; Pederson lecture (13 January 1944); Bartsch, "Operation Dovetail." Message 312000 July 1942 CTF-62 to Comsopac, CSCMF, roll 20.

8. Messages 011125 *San Francisco* to Comsopac, 011330 Comsopac to CTG-2.3, 010111 Comairsopac to Comsopac Admin, 011210 Comsopac to Comsowespac (noting urgent need for fuel in the New Caledonia area), 022030 Comdesron Four to CTF-61 and CTF-62, August 1942, CSCMF, roll 20. Dyer, 1:309–10, asserted the *Kaskaskia* did not sail because she did not "get the word" due to a faulty cipher machine. However, Ghormley never included the *Kaskaskia* in sailing orders issued to the other ships.

9. TF-11, TF-16, *Saratoga, Cimarron,* and *Grayson* war diaries; *Saratoga, Grayson,* and *Gwin* deck logs; Dyer, 1:397; message 030150 August 1942 CTF-61 to Comsopac, CSCMF, roll 20.

10. *Cimarron, Platte* war diaries; messages 042335 Comsopac to Cominch, 042337 Cincpac to Comsopac, 042357 Comsopac to Cincpac, 041350 Comsopac to *Kaskaskia*, 042137 *Rainier* to Comsopac, 042348 Comsopac to *Rainier*, August 1942, CSCMF, roll 20.

11. Messages 012229 Cincpac to Comserforpac, 042044 Comserforpac Sub Com to Comserforpac, 041030 Comsopac to Commander, Service Squadron, South Pacific (Comseronsopac), 050110 Comseronsopac to Comsopac, August 1942, CSCMF, roll 20. The third installment comprised the *Chester Sun* and *Eastern Sun* (each eighty-five thousand barrels) and old *Deroche* (fifty-five thousand barrels); the fourth installment the *Pacific Sun, Western Sun,* and *Flagship Sinco.* The chartered tankers that Calhoun rerouted were the *J. W. Van Dyke* (105,000 barrels) and *Sinclair Rubilene* (sixty-five thousand barrels). Regarding U.S. merchant tankers, "fast" was a misnomer because until the late 1930s top speeds were commonly no greater than 13.5 knots.

12. *Saratoga* war diary; Japan, *Senshi Sōsho*, 49:415; additional information on the flights to Fiji and New Caledonia from Hyakutake Nobushige, via James Sawruk.

13. Dyer, 1:314; Maas diary.

14. Standard Oil Company, *Ships of the Esso Fleet in World War II*, 247–48; message 050317 August 1942 *Rainier* to Comsopac, CSCMF, roll 20; Greybook, 817. Noyes in his 15 August 1950 review of Morison's volume 4 called attention to the failure of the oilers to appear at Efate.

15. Messages 050341 August 1942 CTF-18 to CTF-61, 060403 August 1942 CTF-18 to CTF-61, cited in CO, Torpedo Squadron Eight, to CO, USS *Saratoga*, Report of Operations—Tulagi, Guadalcanal, and Malaita Area, on 7 and 8 August 1942 (12 August 1942).

16. TF-11, TF-16, Comamphibforsopac war diaries; letter Noyes to Wellborn (12 August 1950). Japan, *Senshi Sōsho*, 49:429–30; message 061040 Comsopac to CTF-61, CTF-62, and CTF-63, Comsopac war diary.

17. Message 260530 July 1942 Comsopac to Comamphibforsopac, CSCMF, roll 19; Japan, *Senshi Sōsho*, 49:384.

18. Messages 211200 July 1942 Comsopac Intel. Bull., 290530 July 1942 Comsopac Intel. Bull., CSCMF, roll 20; 310059 July 1942 Cincpac Intel. Bull., 060255 August 1942 Comsowespac to all CTFs, CSCMF, roll 20; Japan, *Senshi Sōsho*, 49:410–15, 430.

19. Messages 191310 July 1942 Comsopac Intel. Bull., CSCMF, roll 19; 310346 July 1942 Comsopac Intel. Bull., 020610 August 1942 Comsopac Intel. Bull., 040455 August 1942 Cincpac Intel. Bull., 050330 August 1942 Comsopac Intel. Bull., CSCMF, roll 20; TF-62 Operation Plan A3-42 (30 July 1942); Japan, *Senshi Sōsho*, 49:409–10, 430.

20. Messages 240742 July 1942 Comsopac Intel. Bull., CSCMF, roll 19; 310059 July 1942 Cincpac Intel. Bull., 310346 July 1942 Comsopac Intel. Bull., 050313 August 1942 Cincpac Intel. Bull., CSCMF, roll 20. On the Japanese carriers after Midway, Japan, *Senshi Sōsho*, 49:431–32. Messages 060700 Comsowespacfor to all CTFs and 061349 Comsowespac to all CTFs, August 1942, CSCMF, roll 20. Dyer, 1:386, wrongly denied the presence of a carrier and declared the contact just a couple of destroyers.

21. Japan, *Senshi Sōsho*, 49:403–4, 415–16, 427–28, 446–47.

CHAPTER 24. THE WATCHTOWER LANDINGS

1. Message 062045 August 1942 Cincpac to Cominch, CNO TS Blue File. Principal documentary sources relating to the Guadalcanal landings include: Commander, Amphibious Force, South Pacific to Cincpac, Solomon Islands Operation, August 7, 8, and 9, 1942 (22 February 1943); CO USS *Saratoga* to Commander in Chief, U.S. Pacific Fleet, Report of Action Tulagi-Guadalcanal Offensive 7–8 August 1942 (19 August 1942); CO USS *Enterprise* to Commander in Chief, U.S. Pacific Fleet, Operations in Support of Occupation of Tulagi-Guadalcanal August 7–8, 1942, Report of (24 August 1942); CO USS *Wasp* to Commander in Chief, U.S. Pacific Fleet, Capture of Tulagi-Guadalcanal Area 7–8 August 1942 (14 August 1942); Adm. Arthur J. Hepburn, USN (Ret.), to Cincpac, Report of Informal Inquiry into Circumstances Attending the Loss of USS *Vincennes* etc. on August 9, 1942, in Vicinity of Savo Island (13 May 1943, hereafter Hepburn report). Official sources include ONI Combat Narrative, *The Landing in the Solomons 7–8 August 1942* (1943) and Bates and Innis. The secondary literature on the Guadalcanal campaign is extensive. The best single source is Frank's *Guadalcanal.* Also insightful is Herbert C. Merillat, *Guadalcanal Remembered.* For naval operations, see Japan, *Senshi Sōsho*, volume 49, and Morison, *United States Naval Operations*, volumes 4 and 5. For the Marine Corps: Zimmerman, *The Guadalcanal Campaign*; and Hough, Ludwig, and Shaw, *History of U.S. Marine Corps Operations in World War II*, volume 1. The U.S. Army's official history, John Miller Jr., *Guadalcanal*, is useful beyond its immediate subject. For air operations, see: Thomas G. Miller Jr., *The Cactus Air Force*, and Lundstrom, *First Team Guadalcanal.* The war diaries of TF-11, TF-16, Comamphibforsopac, and the *Saratoga* are useful for the basic operational chronology. For a detailed account of the carriers on 7–9 August 1942, see Lundstrom, *First Team Guadalcanal*, chapters 3 and 4.

2. Calhoun, *Tin Can Sailor*, 52; Kinkaid memoir, 222.

3. Messages transmitted during the Guadalcanal landings appear scattered in action reports and war diaries. One of the most important sources is the *Saratoga* war diary. Kinkaid memoir, 220. Conversation with Rear Admiral "Bosco" (*sic*) Wright (12 November 1943), in Morison Office Files, box 27.

4. *Saratoga* war diary; Commander, *Saratoga* Air Group to CO USS *Saratoga*, Report of Action During Tulagi-Guadalcanal Offensive 7 and 8 August 1942 (12 August 1942).

5. Messages 062325 and 062336 August 1942 Cincpac to Comsopac, CNO TS Blue File.

6. Japan, *Senshi Sōsho*, 49:439–44, 457. Lundstrom, *First Team Guadalcanal*, 41–46.

7. Lundstrom, *First Team Guadalcanal*, 46–47.

8. Lundstrom, *First Team Guadalcanal*, 48–55.

9. Lundstrom, *First Team Guadalcanal*, 56–62. Ens. F. J. Blair diary, via Foster Blair's family.

10. Maas memorandum (7 August 1942), Maas Papers; Lundstrom, *First Team Guadalcanal*, 62–63. Japan, *Senshi Sōsho*, 49:452, 455.

11. *Saratoga* war diary.

12. Lundstrom, *First Team Guadalcanal*, 64–68; *Saratoga* war diary; Maas memo (7 August 1942).

13. *Saratoga* war diary.

14. *Saratoga* war diary.

15. *Saratoga* war diary; Maas diary; message 071142 August 1942 Comsopac to CTF-61 and CTF-62, CSCMF, roll 20.

16. Kinkaid memoir, 227–28; *Gwin* deck log and war diary; *Grayson* deck log; TF-16 war diary.

17. CO USS *Saratoga* to Cincpac, Report of Action Tulagi-Guadalcanal Offensive 7–8 August 1942 (19 August 1942); Commander, Saratoga Air Group report (12 August 1942); message 070843 August 1942 CTG-62.2 to CTF-62, CSCMF, roll 20.

18. Maas memo (7 August 1942).

19. Message 071219 August 1942 Comsowespac to Cincpac, CSCMF, roll 20; Japan, *Senshi Sōsho*, 49:455; Lundstrom, *First Team Guadalcanal*, 71–72; Kenney, *General Kenney Reports*, 61.

20. Message 071219 August 1942 Comsowespac to Cincpac, CSCMF, roll 20. Evans, *The Japanese Navy in World War II*, 226–28.

21. Kinkaid memoir, 228; CO *Saratoga* report (19 August 1942).

22. *Saratoga* war diary; Maas diary.

23. *Saratoga* war diary; CO *Saratoga* report (12 August 1942); Maas memorandum *Watch-Tower*, Maas Papers.

24. *Saratoga* war diary; CO *Saratoga* report (12 August 1942); Maas memo *Watch-Tower*; Dyer, 1:387.

25. Japan, *Senshi Sōsho*, 49:455–57; Lundstrom, *First Team Guadalcanal*, 74–75; *Saratoga* war diary. MacArthur advised Ghormley (message 061402 August 1942, CSCMF, roll 20) that Read (call sign JER) was located "on north Bougainville," whereas Mason (call sign STO) was near Buin in southern Bougainville. He repeated the message late on 7 August (070927 Comsowespac to Comsopac, CSCMF, roll 20, relayed by Comsopac to all U.S. Navy ships).

26. *Saratoga* war diary; Felt, oral history, 107–8.

27. Maas memorandum Tulagi: *Employment of Aircraft Deficiencies*, Maas Papers; Ens. John P. Altemus diary, via John P. Altemus; Green diary; Lundstrom, *First Team Guadalcanal*, 75–76.

28. Lundstrom, *First Team Guadalcanal*, 75–76.

29. Lundstrom, *First Team Guadalcanal*, 76–79.

30. Japan, *Senshi Sōsho*, 49:458–59.

31. *Saratoga* war diary.

32. *Saratoga* and TF-16 war diaries; CO USS *Enterprise* to Cincpac, Operations in Support of Occupation of Tulagi-Guadalcanal August 7–8, 1942, Report of (24 August 1942).

33. *Saratoga* and Desron One war diaries; CO *Saratoga* report (12 August 1942).

34. Kinkaid memoir, 220.

CHAPTER 25. THE RECOMMENDATION TO WITHDRAW THE CARRIERS

1. Message 080707 August 1942 CTF-61 to Comsopac (info CTF-62, 63, CTG-61.1), CSCMF, roll 20. Maas memorandum AB *Watchtower* (8 P.M. 8 August 1942), Maas Papers.

2. S. E. Morison Pacific Notebook VI, conversation with Turner (14 May 1943), in Morison Office Files, box 27; Morison, *United States Naval Operations*, 5:28; Vandegrift, 128–29; Cincpac to Cominch, 1st Endorsement, Comsopac Preliminary Report—Solomon Islands Operation (23 August 1942); Potter and Nimitz, 254; President, Naval War College, to Cominch etc., Comments on Action Reports concerning activities in the Solomon Islands, August 7, 8, and 9, 1942 (8 December 1942); Hepburn report (13 May 1943), 53; Bates and Innis, 94.

3. Morison, *United States Naval Operations*, 5:27–28; Berry, *Semper Fi, Mac*, 58–59; Frank, 94.

4. CTF-62 to Comsopac, Despatch reports of operations during occupation of Tulagi and Guadalcanal (16 August 1942), copy in Hepburn report, 645–53. Eager to rebut criticism even before it was voiced, Turner cited a message (121620 August 1942 Cominch to Cincpac [info Comsopac, CTF-8, Cinclant], CSCMF, roll 21) ordering the top commanders to keep him informed of "pertinent information as to state of affairs."

5. Comsopac to Cominch, First Endorsement, Commander Task Force 62 Communications During the Occupation of Tulagi and Guadalcanal (6 September 1942), copy in Hepburn report, 644.

6. CTF-62 report (16 August 1942). The eight *Astoria* messages, all August 1942 in CSCMF, roll 20, are: 062010 CTF-62 to Cincpac; 062020 CTF-62 to Comsopac; 062235, 062240, and 062246 Comamphibforsopac to Comsopac; 070205 CTF-62 to Comsopac; 070145 Comamphibforsopac to

Comsopac, Comairsopac, and CTF-61; and 071030 CTG-61.2 to Comsopac and CTF-61, and info addressees. They included a lengthy outline of suggested troop deployments for Task Two, instructions on approaching the Lunga airfield after it was operational, notes regarding mine clearing, and a dispatch from a United Press correspondent.

7. Messages August 1942: 071330 Comsopac to CTF-62, CSCMF, roll 20, and 071030 CTG-61.2 to Comsopac and CTF-61, Greybook, 639.

8. Messages August 1942: 080150 CTF-61 to TF-11, in Desron One war diary; 080330 CTG-61.2 to Comsopac and CTF-61, 070843 CTG-62.2 to CTF-62, CSCMF, roll 20. USS *Saratoga*, Fighting Squadron Five Combatant Flight Operations Report, Guadalcanal and Tulagi Areas (8 August 1942), copy in Altemus diary. Maas memo AB Watchtower. Letter Rear Adm. Carleton H. Wright to Rear Adm. Charles Wellborn (9 February 1952) in DNC, Office Files, box 20. Greybook, 820.

9. Comamphibforsopac war diary; Thomas unpublished manuscript, 21; Comamphibforsopac staff log, in Turner Papers, box 36. Message 071517 August 1942 CTF-62 to Comsopac and CTF-61, which appears in Turner's communication report (16 August 1942) in Hepburn report, 645. The Maas Papers show Fletcher did not have the 071517 message on 8 or 9 August; Ghormley had it later on 9 August (Ghormley's staff log, Vice Adm. Robert L. Ghormley Papers, via Jeffrey Barlow). Cincpac did not log it until 11 August, CSCMF, roll 20. Bates and Innis, who had access to 071517 in the Hepburn report (660, 671) never used it, particularly, 83, where they analyzed Turner's decisions on 8 August.

10. Custer, *Through the Perilous Night*, 118–19.

11. Comamphibforsopac staff log; Thomas unpublished manuscript, 21; Commander, *Enterprise* Air Group to CO, USS *Enterprise*, Narrative and Comments concerning the Tulagi-Guadalcanal Air Action and Landing Force Operations of 7–8 August 1942 (10 August 1942).

12. Bates and Innis, 64, 95; Gatacre, *Reports of Proceedings*, 169.

13. Message 080141 August 1942 Cincpac Intel. Bull., CSCMF, roll 20.

14. Morison, *United States Naval Operations*, 5:27–28; Bates and Innis, 93. Comcrupac to Cincpac, Carrier-Task Forces, some lessons learned in operating of (24 September 1942), RG-38, Cincpac Flag Files; Pederson lecture (13 January 1944).

15. Dyer, 1:391; CO *Saratoga* report (12 August 1942); Kinkaid memoir, 225; message 122231 August 1942 *Enterprise* to Cincpac, CSCMF, roll 21. In 1949 Capt. Leroy C. Simpler, former commanding officer of VF-5 in the *Saratoga*, recalled that after his last flight on 8 August he spoke with the "Skipper," who asked him if he had seen any action. Simpler replied that he had not but that some of the others did fight. The "Skipper" commented, "He was lucky in not having been engaged and that it was just as well." Simpler later complained: "What kind of a way was that for a C.O. to talk? It was tough enough for me to get Leroy [that is, himself] to get into a plane and go out after the Nips, and an attitude like that on the part of the Skipper made it double tough to have to send my boys up to fight." Some believed Simpler referred to Fletcher, because he certainly bore Fletcher ill-will, but by using "skipper" and "C.O." rather than "admiral" Simpler meant Captain Ramsey (letter Roger Pineau to Morison, 19 February 1949, in Morison Office Files, box 27).

16. Interview of Lt. Cdr. L. C. Simpler by Buaer (26 February 1943), NHC; Maas memo AB *Watchtower*; CO *Saratoga* report (12 August 1942).

17. Maas memo AB *Watchtower*. The 7 May fight occurred 420 miles from Lae, 450 miles from Rabaul.

18. Maas memo AB *Watchtower*; Kinkaid memoir, 232. On 8 August the *Enterprise* solicited eight VF-6 volunteers to fly ashore to Lunga, according to the diary of Ens. Francis R. Register (8 August 1942), via Brandon Wood. Message 101220 August 1942 CTF-62 to CTF-61 and Comsopac, CSCMF, roll 21. Turner's Op-Plan A3-42 had called for two small steamers to land aviation gasoline and bombs on D+1 Day. On 6 August, Ghormley delayed their deployment and on 8 August directed them to off-load their cargoes at Espíritu Santo (messages 061000 Comsopac to Port Director Efate and 080012 Comsopac to *Dale* and Comgen (Commanding General) Roses, August 1942, CSCMF, roll 20). Vandegrift brought some aviation gasoline and ammunition, but no lube oil.

19. Comcrupac, Carrier Task Forces (24 September 1942); Commander, Air Force, Pacific Fleet (Vice Adm. W. F. Halsey) to Cincpac, Carrier Task Forces, some lessons learned in operating of (9 October 1942), in RG-38, Cincpac Flag Files.

20. Message 080707 August 1942 CTF-61 to Comsopac (info CTF-62, CTF-63, and CTG-61.1), CSCMF, roll 20. Letter Fletcher to Baldwin (8 July 1947); Dyer, 1:392; Morison, *United States Naval Operations*, 5:28.

21. Letter Fletcher to Baldwin (8 July 1947). Bates and Innis, 93, reasoned, "Two days of flight operations in the vicinity of Guadalcanal Island, without enemy detection or attack" should have "affected fuel consumption no differently than routine flight operations anywhere." Of course those two days were far from "routine." TF-16 war diary. CTF-11 (Comcrupac) to Comsopac, Preliminary Report—Solomons Islands Operation (9 September 1942), copy in Hepburn report, 9–11. Maas memo AB *Watchtower*.

22. Carter, *Beans, Bullets and Black Oil*, 28.

23. President, Naval War College (8 December 1942). Zimmerman, 50.

24. Griffith, 252; Bates and Innis, 93–94; Morison, *United States Naval Operations*, 5:28. The *Enterprise*, reckoning her fuel in barrels, had 16,534 barrels on the eighth. Morison, *United States Naval Operations*, 5:28n, rendered that as 521,000 gallons; the correct total is 694,428. He erred by converting with 31.5, the standard for liquid measurement, whereas fuel oil is forty-two gallons per barrel. In 1952 Wright remarked: "It would surely not be safe to use their average daily consumption while cruising as a basis for computing battle requirements. Any officer who commanded task forces in the Pacific knows the constant worry that arose from 'How will I be fixed for fuel if I have to do the prolonged high speed steaming which will inevitably follow contact with enemy air or surface forces?'" Letter Wright to Wellborn (9 February 1952).

25. Dyer, 1:387–93.

26. *Dale* war diary. The TU-61.1.1 destroyers on 8 August had according to deck logs:

	Capacity (gallons)	On hand (gallons)	Percentage
Phelps	187,863	96,382	51%
Farragut	168,453	84,696	50%
Worden	168,453	72,850	43%
Macdonough	168,453	70,213	42%

27. The *Phelps* had 51 percent capacity, meaning eight days at fifteen knots, 2.2 days at twenty-five knots; *Gwin* 62 percent, 8.2 days at fifteen knots, 2.5 days at twenty-five knots. The *Grayson* (28 percent, 3.7 days at fifteen knots, 1.1 days at twenty-five knots) was the low destroyer, but the *Balch* (also TU-61.1.2) and *Sterett* (TU-61.1.3) were both at or under 40 percent.

28. CTF-11 report (9 September 1942); Dyer, 1:393; TF-16 war diary. The *Portland*, at 46 percent, had an endurance of about 3.9 days at twenty-five knots; the *Atlanta* (47 percent) for 3.1 days at twenty-five knots. The *Enterprise*, though down to 39 percent, was still capable of about 3.9 days at twenty-five knots. (In comparison the *Saratoga*'s 49 percent translated roughly to 3.3 days at twenty-five knots; the *Wasp*'s data is unknown.) At 60 percent the *North Carolina* enjoyed the greatest endurance of all, around 4.7 days at twenty-five knots. Reviewing Morison's volume 5, Vice Adm. Mahlon S. Tisdale commented: "We did not need to leave Admiral Turner's Force. We had plenty of fuel. . . . History will not support Admiral Fletcher's decision to abandon Admiral Turner's transport force." Letter Vice Adm. M. S. Tisdale, USN (Ret.), to Rear Adm. Charles

Wellborn Jr., USN (3 October 1950), in DNC, Office Files, box 20. Tisdale stated that Kinkaid in 1942 "had fought his Task Force probably more successfully than any other save only Spruance at Midway."

29. CTF-11 report (9 September 1942), letter Fletcher to Baldwin (8 July 1947). Record of Proceedings of an Investigation Conducted by Rear Adm. J. F. Shafroth, USN (hereafter *Wasp* investigation), Statement of Rear Adm. George D. Murray, U.S. Navy, Commander Task Force Seventeen on 15 September 1942, taken at Washington, D.C. (4 January 1943), in RG-38, Cincpac Flag Files.

30. Turner interview by Baldwin (10 October 1946). Messages 070602 Comsopac to CTF-61, CTF-62, and CTF-63; 042348 Comsopac to *Rainier*, *Kaskaskia*, and *Perkins*; and 051055 Comsopac to *Rainier*; all August 1942, CSCMF, roll 20.

31. Cincpac to Cominch (23 August 1942); Cominch Secret Information Bulletin No. 2; CTF-11 report (9 September 1942); Potter and Nimitz, 254.

32. Messages 050507 Gen (General) Roses to Comsopac Admin, and 051910 *Cimarron* to Comairsopac, August 1942, CSCMF, roll 20.

33. *Saratoga* war diary. Letter Vice Adm. Forrest Sherman to S. E. Morison (14 February 1949), in Morison Office Files, box 26. Morison, *United States Naval Operations*, 5:28, asserted, "In the carrier task force [Fletcher's] retirement request was greeted with dismay by senior officers, especially when they learned that the Australian Hudson's report of Mikawa's force had been received on board before 1900, and guessed that the Japanese Fleet was about to show its hand." The truth behind the second part of Morison's statement will be assessed in chapter 26, but there is no evidence whatsoever Noyes, Kinkaid, Ramsey, Davis, or Sherman, the "senior officers," disagreed in any way with Fletcher's request to withdraw the carriers. It will be seen Morison cited Sherman's letter detailing his fervent advice to Noyes early on the morning of 9 August to ask Fletcher's permission to strike enemy ships at Savo, but he chose not to mention the passage quoted above, where Sherman endorsed Fletcher's recommendation to withdraw the carriers.

34. Maas memo AB *Watchtower*; Dyer, 1:391.

35. Maas memo AB *Watchtower*; letter Fletcher to Baldwin (8 July 1947); Pederson lecture (13 January 1944).

CHAPTER 26. THE SAVO DISASTER

1. Maas diary. Bates and Innis charged, 96, that Fletcher withdrew at 1200 on 8 August; Morison, *United States Naval Operations*, 5:58, said that as of 0100, 9 August, Fletcher still had not received permission from Ghormley to "execute the retirement he had been virtually pursuing for twelve hours." Indeed the carriers made their closest approach, twenty-five miles, to the Guadalcanal coast at 1300 and again at 1700.

2. Stahl, 21, wrote this incident took place "around 1600," and that he saw a dispatch noting, "Seven cruisers headed toward us at high speed." No such signal arrived and the timing of the warning is well attested to 1837. Others also recalled the sighting report coming much earlier than it in fact did.

3. The plane was a Lockheed Hudson from No. 32 RAAF Squadron flown by Sergeant William J. Stutt, who was unfairly blamed for the delay in forwarding the sighting report to Sopac. Not receiving an acknowledgment, he flew back to Milne Bay, but headquarters did not radio the sighting for more than five hours. Warner and Warner with Seno, *Disaster in the Pacific*, chapter 1.

4. Message 071930 August 1942 Comsowespac to Cincpac, CSCMF, roll 20.

5. Conversations with Thomas Newsome; letter Fletcher to Baldwin (8 July 1947).

6. Letter Fletcher to Baldwin (8 July 1947). Lee, 334; Altemus diary. Hepburn report, 371, 461–62; Dyer, 1:360–69; Loxton, chapter 15. Warner and Warner, 234, charged that on the afternoon of the eighth Turner and Crutchley (and the *Saratoga*, but strangely not Fletcher) knew of the sighting.

7. Maas diary.

8. Messages 080947 Comsowespacfor to all CTFs, 081020 Comsowespac to Cincpac, 081130 Comsowespacfor to Cincpac, 081233 Comairsopac to CTF-61, 081055 CTF-62 to Comairsopac, and 081554 Comairsopac to CTG-63.5, August 1942, CSCMF, roll 20. The sighting at 1101 was made by another Hudson commanded by FO Mervyn Willman. The forwarding of his message by air headquarters was even slower than Stutt's (Warner and Warner, 17).

9. Message 081141 August 1942 Comsopac to CTF-61, CSCMF, roll 20. Ghormley, "Tide Turns," 93; Callaghan conference notes (28 July 1942). The c. 1949 memo in the Morison Office Files, box 27, asserted that "Ramsay" (presumably Donald Ramsey, Hepburn's assistant) bitterly denounced Fletcher's recommendation as a disgraceful way to "hang" responsibility on his superior. "Ramsay" urged Morison "not to hold Ghormley responsible for anything related to the withdrawal even though he approved it." Because he exercised only "strategical command," Fletcher, the tactical commander, "didn't need to ask his permission to retire." That is highly debatable.

10. Messages 081141 Comsopac to CTF-61; 080800 Comsopac to CTF-61; 081232 Comsopac to *Platte*, *Kaskaskia*, *Perkins*, and *Clark*; all August 1942, CSCMF, roll 20.

11. For the general movements of TF-62 on 8–9 August, see Comamphibforsopac war diary, Comamphibforsopac stafflog, and CTG-62.6 (Rear Adm. V. A. C. Crutchley, RN), Operation "Watchtower"—The Capture and Occupation by United Nations Forces of Tulagi and Guadalcanal (13 August 1942), copy in Hepburn report, 55–86. Letter Rear Adm. Richmond Kelly Turner to Rear Adm. Charles Wellborn (20 August 1950) with review of Morison's volume 5. Bates and Innis, 92, blamed Fletcher for, "significantly enough," not making "CTF 62 an information addressee for the message he sent Comsopacfor requesting approval for retiring the carriers." That is incorrect. Turner certainly was an information addressee as shown in the original copy in the Cincpac Secret and Confidential Message File and also in the Hepburn report, 659, which Bates and Innis used.

12. Comamphibforpac Administrative History, 47. Turner stated therein that he received Fletcher's message "about noon on 8 August," and that Fletcher "carried out his notice and left the vicinity at approximately 1500 on 8 August." Later the same account noted the carriers left "about noon of 8 August." All of this was much earlier than the actual withdrawal of the carriers.

13. Morison, *United States Naval Operations*, 5:31, referred to the possible Rekata seaplanes as "big bombers." However, message 150155 July 1942 Cincpac to PacFlt, CSCMF, roll 18, noted that the converted seaplane tender *Kiyokawa Maru* (reported at Rabaul) had a dozen float planes, none of which were torpedo planes. The latest ONI estimates in June 1942 gave the regular seaplane tenders a complement of fourteen such float planes and the auxiliary seaplane tenders ten, each with a maximum bomb load of five hundred pounds. Aerial torpedoes weighed from eighteen hundred to two thousand pounds.

14. Message 090230 August 1942 CTG-61.2 to Comsopac and CTF-61 (info CTG-62.4 and CTG-62.6), sent at 1452, 9 August, by the *McCawley* on 2122 kilocycles but not actually received until after it was handed to Ghormley on 13 August and sent as 131418 August 1942, CNO TS Blue File.

15. Letter Turner to Wellborn (20 August 1950).

16. Crutchley report (13 August 1942). Turner explained that on the evening of 8 August, he weighed the Sowespac estimate of reinforcements to Shortland, the absence of sighting reports from McCain, and "the false information in the contact report received about 1820 Love." He concluded, "After lengthy discussion" with Crutchley "the chances of attack that night were small." Memorandum, Rear Adm. R. K. Turner to Cincpac, Comment on Hepburn Report (c. May 1943), copy in Hepburn report.

17. Thomas unpublished manuscript, 23; Vandegrift, 128–29.

18. Messages 081418 CTF-62 to TF-62; and 081405 CTF-62 to Comsopac, CTF-61, and Comairsopac (info Cominch and Cincpac); both August 1942, copies in Hepburn report, 659, also 650.

19. For Savo island, see Hepburn report; Morison, *United States Naval Operations*, volume 5, chapter 2; Bates and Innis; Japan, *Senshi Sōsho*, 49:463–96; Gatacre, 169–80; Frank, chapter 4; Warner and Warner; Loxton.

20. Gatacre, 175.

21. In addition to the sources cited in note 11, see Rear Adm. V. A. C. Crutchley, Night Action off Savo Island (9 August 1942)—Remarks by CTG-62.6 (11 August 1942) and CTF-62 to CTG-62.6, Night Action of Savo Island, August 8–9, 1942 (12 August 1942) and Comcru TF-18 (Rear Adm. Norman Scott) to Cominch, Report of action, Tulagi-Guadalcanal, 6–10 August 1942 (13 August 1942). Cominch Secret Information Bulletin No. 2 noted Turner provided "no standing orders or doctrine covering the situation." The Yoke ships stayed at anchor.

22. Crutchley report (11 August 1942).

23. Comamphibforsopac staff log; Comtransdiv 8 (Commander, Transport Division; Capt. George B. Ashe) Sopac, USS *Neville* to Comamphibforsopac, Report of Operations in Tulagi-Gavutu Area (12 August 1942). Messages 081924 CTF-62 to CTG-62.6 and 62.1, and 081941 CTF-62 to CTF-61, August 1942, copies in Hepburn report, 659–60.

24. Cincpac to Cominch (23 August 1942); Hepburn report, 34; President, Naval War College (8 December 1942); Cominch Secret Information Bulletin No. 2.

25. TF-16 war diary. Lt. Cdr. Leonard J. Dow, TF-16 communications officer, related to Buaer (29 September 1942): "The night of [8–9 August] about 2 o'clock in the morning, we received a message on the transport circuit that there was a night action going on to westward and that the situation was obscure. Outside of that single message there was no indication of any action at all. They apparently did not break radio silence to tell us what was going on." Kinkaid memoir, 284.

26. Letter F. P. Sherman to Morison (14 February 1949).

27. Acquainted with the excellent night fighting tactics of the British carriers, the *Wasp* Air Group lacked aerial radar and hence any true night attack capability. Sherman would likely have desired his planes over Lunga at first light (0547) to attack ships or chase them toward New Georgia. Departing at 0500, the *Wasp* strike should have got to Savo before 0600 and overtaken Mikawa north of New Georgia an hour later and 130 miles northwest. The outbound leg would have been 260–75 miles. To reduce their return flight to two hundred miles, the carriers would need by 0830 to be at least fifty miles northwest of the launch point. Gaining such distance to westward could have been tricky. The northeast wind would force the flattops to run nearly opposite the Point Option course every time they conducted air operations—4 June all over again. A simultaneous *Saratoga* search 275 miles west and northwest could have discovered Mikawa's ships just ahead of the *Wasp* strike group. A second strike wave, from the *Enterprise*, might also have scored. Again, though, the carriers would need to work steadily northwest at a great cost of fuel in order to retrieve all the planes. Just to attack Mikawa, everything described here must have gone without a hitch. Swift cruisers and destroyers proved difficult targets, so any strikes might have been inconclusive. Yet even a gesture of revenge would certainly have saved some sorely needed face. Letter F. P. Sherman to Morison (14 February 1949); Pratt, *The Marine's War*, 30.

28. Letter Bates to Morison (1 February 1949), Morison Office Files, box 26; Bates and Innis, 323–24; Morison, *United States Naval Operations*, 5:58, citing letter (14 February 1949) from F. P. Sherman. Loxton, 252, stated Fletcher knew of Savo well before dawn and rejected pleas by the "Air Group Commander" to attack. He cited (301n31) Capt. H. G. Bradshaw, USN (Ret.), a torpedo plane pilot "embarked in *Saratoga*." In fact Bradshaw served in the *Wasp* and relayed what he heard of Sherman's entreaties to Noyes. Kinkaid's memoir, 283, stated Fletcher "was completely uninformed regarding the surface actions in Iron Bottom Sound during their progress."

29. S. E. Morison talk with Wright (12 November 1943); letter Wright to Wellborn (9 February 1952); Dyer, 1:395; letter Fletcher to Baldwin (8 July 1947). Letter George Clapp to Lundstrom (22 December 1997) and conversation 4 June 2001; Maas diary, 9 August 1942; Dyer, 1:395. Most likely Fletcher read message 081827 August 1942 CTF-44 to Comsowespac, Australian Commonwealth Naval Board: "*Canberra* damaged night action heavily on fire. Following received from USS *Patterson*. Begins. *Canberra* is abandoning ship. Have entire crew on board will destroy her," Hepburn report, 95.

30. TF-16 war diary.

31. Dyer, 1:395.

32. CTF-11 report (9 September 1942).

33. Letter F. P. Sherman to Morison (14 February 1949).

34. Message 082138 August 1942 Radio Canberra to Any or All USN Ships, CSCMF, roll 20; *Saratoga* war diary; Maas diary; Japan, *Senshi Sōsho*, 49:458–61.

35. TF-16 and *Saratoga* war diaries; Japan, *Senshi Sōsho*, 49:460–61.

36. Messages August 1942: 090050 Fletcher to Ghormley, Comsopac Message File; 090245 Comsopac to CTF-44, CTF-63, CTF-61, and CTF-62, CSCMF, roll 20; Maas diary.

37. Messages 090100 Comsopac to CTF-61 and CTF-63, 090218 Comsopac to CTF-63, 090310 Comsopac to Cincpac, August 1942, CSCMF, roll 20; 090315 August 1942 Fletcher to Comsopac, Greybook, 639.

38. Bates and Innis, 326, 321; Capt. George L. Russell, Memorandum for Admiral, Admiral Hepburn's Report on the Loss of the USS *Vincennes*, USS *Quincy*, USS *Astoria*, HMAS *Canberra*, August 9, 1942 near Savo Island—Comment upon (31 July 1943), in Hepburn report.

39. Message 090359 August 1942 Cincpac to Comsopac, Comsopac war diary. Following the recollections of Vice Adm. George Russell, Buell's *Master of Sea Power*, 221–22, described King learning of Savo on 12 August. Russell confused that with a later occasion. Fletcher's original message 090315 in the CNO TS Blue File microfilm clearly was received on the ninth.

40. Messages 090544 Comsopac to Any and All USN Ships, 090620 Fletcher to Comsopac, August 1942, CSCMF, roll 20; 090750 August 1942 Comsopac to CTF-61, CTF-62, and CTF-63, Greybook, 640.

41. Comamphibforsopac war diary and staff log; Comamphibforsopac report (22 February 1943); Comtransdiv 8 report (12 August 1942).

42. Message 090815 August 1942 (not sent until 12 August) CTF-62 to Comsopac, CNO TS Blue File and Comsopac war diary. Morison, *United States Naval Operations*, 5:17; letter Turner to Wellborn (20 August 1950); Comsopac to Cominch, Preliminary Report Watchtower Operation (16 August 1942), copy in Hepburn report, 31–32. The Allies did not know the exact composition of Mikawa's force until after mid October 1942 from prisoners taken in the Battle of Cape Esperance (Hepburn report, 30).

43. Letter Crutchley to Turner (10 August 1942), copy in Morison Office Files, box 26. Conference Notes [Cominch-Cincpac meetings in San Francisco] (8 September 1942); letter Nimitz to Ghormley (8 October 1942), Nimitz Papers.

44. Twining, 71; Comamphibforpac Administrative History, 48; Morison, *Two-Ocean War*, 168–69.

45. Turner and others made much of a message he sent McCain on the afternoon of 7 August, noting the scheduled search for 8 August did not cover the sector 290–318 degrees from Malaita. Turner conceded MacArthur's planes from New Guinea handled that particular sector, the upper Solomons around Bougainville, but asked McCain to "consider morning search necessary for adequate cover." Two B-17s flying the normal search 750 miles northwest from Espíritu Santo would only go as far as Vella Lavella and part of Choiseul, short of the waters Turner wanted examined. The TF-63 search (McCain's Op-Plan 1-42 of 25 July 1942, which Turner had since 27 July) was weighted to the north to prevent a surprise from that direction. The only planes that could have covered the sector that Turner desired were the *Mackinac*'s PBYs in southeast Malaita, hence his mention of that point of origin.

Turner's caution was fully justified. That was indeed where Mikawa was sighted the morning of 8 August. Unfortunately there is no contemporary evidence that his message, another *McCawley* transmission on 2122 kilocycles, ever reached McCain in time. Comsopac did not get it. On 20 October 1948, three years after McCain's death, Rear Adm. Matthias B. Gardner, his former chief of staff, recalled to Bates that two B-17s from Espíritu Santo flew the special search to 315 miles from Malaita (eight hundred miles from Espíritu

Santo) that morning but were still sixty miles short of Mikawa. No contemporary source confirms this search, which would have had four B-17s flying essentially the same mission, except that two proceeded fifty miles ahead of the lead pair. If McCain *had* received Turner's message and thought it worth reallocating resources, he would certainly have used the *Mackinac*'s PBYs that were in the best position to complete the task. Turner memo to Hepburn (1943); Morison, *United States Naval Operations*, 5:24–25; Bates and Innis, 99. Twining, 71, was very critical of what he perceived as a slur Turner cast on McCain for not making this search.

46. Comamphibforpac Administrative History, 47; Turner interview by Baldwin (10 October 1946).

47. Hepburn report, 39; Turner memo to Hepburn (1943), part of Hepburn report, 273.

48. Bates and Innis, 89–90; Twining, 70–71.

49. Twining, 62; Gatacre, 179.

50. Maas memo CC Watch-Tower (c. August 1942), Maas Papers; President, Naval War College (8 December 1942); Bates and Innis, 322; Turner memo (1943), part of Hepburn report, 272; message 201005 August 1942 Comamphibforsopac to Tutuila, CSCMF, roll 22.

51. Letter Turner to Col. James Webb (20 August 1942), Turner Papers, box 1; Twining, 57–59, 66–68; Dyer, 1:408. Turner's original withdrawal order (081418) did state that all boats that could not be retrieved before sailing were to be left behind with their crews (Hepburn report, 659).

52. Conference Notes [Cominch-Cincpac meetings in San Francisco] (8 September 1942); Russell memo (31 July 1943).

53. Russell memo (31 July 1943). Hepburn's itinerary, Appendix C of his report, shows that he was in San Francisco from 28 to 30 March 1943 before traveling east to Corpus Christi and then Washington, D.C., to complete his report. Dyer, 1:395.

54. Crutchley report (13 August 1942).

CHAPTER 27. COVERING CACTUS

1. Dyer, 1:396–98.

2. Message 110650 August 1942 Vandegrift to Comamphibforsopac, Greybook, 695.

3. Messages August 1942: 101006 Comsopac to Comsowespac, Greybook, 621; 102147 Cincpac to Comsopac, Greybook, 644; 110206 Comsopac to Fletcher, Greybook, 645.

4. Letter Ghormley to Nimitz (11 August 1942), Nimitz Papers; message 100122 August 1942 Comsopac to *Long Island*, CSCMF, roll 21.

5. Pederson lecture (13 January 1944).

6. Pederson lecture (13 January 1944). Messages August 1942: 091414 Comairsopac to CTF-61, CSCMF, roll 20; 110200 CTF-61 to CTF-63, CSCMF, roll 21; 120316 Comsopac to Comsowespacfor, Greybook, 647.

7. Basic sources for TF-61 are the following war diaries: *Saratoga* (which includes the daily air task group orders), Comcru TF-11, Desron One, *Minneapolis*, TF-16, Comcru TF-16, Desron Six, *Enterprise*, Comcru TF-18, Desron Twelve, *Platte*, *Kaskaskia*, *Cimarron*. The Comairsopac war diary detailed the daily search missions. Bell, *Condition Red*, 28. Messages August 1942: 090732 Comsopac to CTF-61, CSCMF, roll 20; 110150 CTF-61 to Comsopac, CSCMF, roll 21.

8. Kamada Minoru kindly identified this particular submarine by consulting records in the War History Office in Tokyo. SRH-012, volume 4, part 2, 384, RG-457; message 140159 August 1942 Cincpac to Comsopac, CTF-61, CTF-62, and CTF-63 (info Comsowespac), CSCMF, roll 21.

9. Messages 120130 CTF-61 to Comsopac (sent as 140414 Comsopac to Cincpac), 100007 Comsopac to Cincpac, 150119 Cincpac to Comsopac, 180207 Comsopac to Cincpac, August 1942, CSCMF, roll 21.

10. Greybook, 823; message 112209 August 1942 Cincpac to Comsopac, Greybook, 646.

11. Messages August 1942: 101220 CTF-62 to CTF-61, CSCMF, roll 21; 111400 CG 1st Marine Division (Mardiv) to Comairsopac, Comsopac war diary; 120216 Comsopac to CTF-63, CNO TS Blue File; 121119 Comairsopac to Comsopac, CSCMF, roll 21.

12. The *Dewey* returned to TF-11, *Ellet* and *Monssen* to TF-16, and *Buchanan* to TF-18.

13. Message 130307 August 1942 Cincpac Intel. Bull., CSCMF, roll 21; Japan, *Senshi Sōsho*, 49:512–13.

14. *Saratoga* war diary; message 132246 August 1942 CTF-61 to TF-61, CSCMF, roll 21.

15. Messages 130012 Comsopac to CTF-62, 140910 Comsopac to CTF-61, August 1942, CSCMF, roll 21. CO USS *Cimarron* to Comserforpac, Pertinent Information on Performance of as Task Force Oiler (30 September 1942), RG-313, Cincpac Secret Correspondence, box 4900.

16. Message 150412 August 1942 Fletcher to Comsopac, CSCMF, roll 21.

17. Messages August 1942: 142210 CTF-62 to Comsopac, Comsopac war diary; 150746 Comsopac to CTF-63, Greybook, 650; 130240 CTG-2.6 to Comairsopac, CSCMF, roll 21; 131600 Comsopac to Cincpac, CNO TS Blue File; 140011 Cincpac to Comsopac, 140402 Comairsopac to Comsopac, 150816 Comsopac to CTF-61, CSCMF, roll 21.

18. Message 160200 August 1942 Comairsopac to Comsopac, CSCMF, roll 21; Japan, *Senshi Sōsho*, 49:521, 533.

19. Messages 170835 CTG-2.6 to CTF-62, 170539 Comairsopac to *McFarland*, 170946 Comsopac to Comsowespacfor, 200910 CTF-62 to Comsopac, August 1942, CSCMF, roll 21; 161146 August 1942 Comsopac to Cominch, Greybook, 652.

20. Japan, *Senshi Sōsho*, 49:446–51, 508–9; Ugaki, 177–78.

21. Japan, *Senshi Sōsho*, 49:542–43, 43:599–600, 637–40.

22. Japan, *Senshi Sōsho*, 49:515, 543–44; Ugaki, 181–83.

23. Messages 112209 August 1942 Cincpac to Comsopac, Greybook, 646; 052138 November 1942 Opnav to Cincpac, CSCMF, roll 30.

24. Messages August 1942: 062035 Cincpac to Comsopac, Greybook, 638; 112030 Cominch to Cincpac, Greybook, 646; 121750 Cominch to Cincpac, Greybook, 647; Greybook, 823; 122337 Cincpac to Cominch, Greybook, 648.

25. SRMN-009, Cincpac Fleet Intelligence Summaries, 62; message 150003 August 1942 Cincpac to Cominch, CSCMF, roll 21; TF-17 war diary; 162111 August 1942 Comsopac to Cincpac, Comsopac war diary; 180225 August 1942 Cincpac to Comsopac, CNO TS Blue File; 171007 August 1942 CTF-61 to Comcarpac, CSCMF, roll 21.

26. Message 160443 August 1942 Cincpac Intel. Bull., CSCMF, roll 21; Greybook, 826.

27. Japan, *Senshi Sōsho*, 49:517–21; Ugaki, 179–81; Tanaka Raizō, "The Struggle for Guadalcanal," in Evans, *The Japanese Navy in World War II*, 160–62.

28. Japan, *Senshi Sōsho*, 49:521–24.

29. Messages August 1942: 171152 Comsopac to CTF-61, Comsopac Message File; 172047 Cincpac to Comsopac, Greybook, 654.

30. Comcru TF-18 war diary; Maas diary (18 August 1942); Japan, *Senshi Sōsho*, 49:519–20.

31. Maas diary (15 August 1942); undated memo in Maas Papers. Maas wrote Capt. Spencer Lewis was "very able; quiet; but knows what it is all about. Understands employment of aviation, operations of task forces. *Should be an Admiral. This is a must!* 4.0." Capt. Dewitt Ramsey was "very able, tactful, diplomatic, put *Sara* in improved condition immediately. Well liked and *respected*. Should be an Admiral *at once*. 4.0."

32. Messages August 1942: 180916 Comsopac to CTF-61, CTF-62, CTF-63, and CTF-44, Comsopac war diary; 181302 Comsopac to CTF-61, CSCMF, roll 21.

33. Message 182115 August 1942 Comairsopac to Any or all units, CSCMF, roll 21; Japan, *Senshi Sōsho*, 49:534; Comairsopac war diary.

34. TF-16 war diary; message 190145 August 1942 Cincpac Intel. Bull., CSCMF, roll 21. Messages 190315 CTF-62 to Guadalcanal and 190947 CG Cactus to Comsopac, August 1942, CSCMF, roll 21. Fletcher did not receive high-level intelligence summaries (messages 150325 Comsopac to Cincpac and 150901 Cincpac to Comsopac, August 1942, CSCMF, roll 21).

35. *Saratoga* war diary; Japan, *Senshi Sōsho*, 49:534–35.

36. *Saratoga* war diary; Lundstrom, *First Team Guadalcanal*, 96–97.

37. Messages August 1942: 200722 Comsopac to CTF-61 and CTF-44, CSCMF, roll 22; 192231 Comairsopac to CG Cactus, CSCMF, roll 21; 200910 CTF-62 to Comsopac, CSCMF, roll 22; 192320 Comsopac to CTF-61, CTF-62, and CTF-63, Comsopac war diary; 200235 Cincpac Intel. Bull., CSCMF, roll 22; 200041 Cincpac to Comsopac, Comsopac Message File; 200247 Cincpac to Comsopac, CSCMF, roll 22; Frank, 149.

38. Cincpac to Cominch, Solomon Islands Campaign—Action of 23–25 August (24 October 1942).

39. Tanaka, in Evans, 164–66; Japan, *Senshi Sōsho*, 49:537–39.

40. Ugaki, 185–86; Japan, *Senshi Sōsho*, 49:539–40, 544–45; 7th Cruiser Division war diary, in NHC microfilm JD16.

41. *Saratoga* war diary; message 202013 August 1942 CG Cactus to Comsopac, CSCMF, roll 22.

42. Messages 202140 *Mackinac* to Comairsopac, 202250 Comsopac to CTF-61, 202345 CG Cactus to Comsopac, August 1942, CSCMF, roll 22; *Saratoga* war diary; CTF-44, Operation Watchtower, Narrative of events subsequent to the withdrawal to Nouméa of the Amphibious Force after the Capture and Occupation of Tulagi and Guadalcanal [16 August–3 September 1942]; Comcru TF-18 war diary.

43. Message 210044 August 1942 21V37 to 55V3, CSCMF, roll 22; *Saratoga* war diary; Lundstrom, *First Team Guadalcanal*, 98–99; Japan, *Senshi Sōsho*, 49:549.

44. Messages 180809 Comcrupac to TF-61, 200041 Cincpac to Comsopac, August 1942, CSCMF, roll 22; *Saratoga* war diary.

45. Wright's group included *Minneapolis* and *New Orleans* from TF-11, *San Francisco* and *Salt Lake City* from TF-18, and destroyers *Selfridge*, *Lang*, *Patterson*, *Worden*, *Maury*, and *Benham* (Comcru TF-11 war diary).

46. Messages August 1942: 210257 Cincpac Intel. Bull., 210445 Comsowespac to all CTFs, 210250 Cactus to Transdiv 11, Transdiv 12, and *McFarland*, CSCMF, roll 22; 210426 Comsopac to CTF-61 and CTF-63, Comsopac war diary; 210702 CTF-62 to *Fomalhaut*, CSCMF, roll 22.

47. Comcru TF-11 war diary; *Minneapolis* war diary. Messages August 1942: 211050 Comsopac to CTF-61, CSCMF, roll 22; 211156 Comsopac to Cincpac, Comsopac war diary; 211021 CG Cactus to Comsopac, CSCMF, roll 22.

48. Japan, *Senshi Sōsho*, 49:549–52; Ugaki, 186–87; Boyd and Yoshida, *The Japanese Submarine Force and World War II*, 94–95. Message 211842 August 1942 Comdesdiv 7 to Comdesron 4 and CTF-62, CSCMF, roll 22.

49. Message 211120 August 1942 Fletcher to Comsopac, Greybook, 807.

50. *Saratoga* war diary; Lundstrom, *First Team Guadalcanal*, 100–101; Comcru TF-18 war diary.

51. Messages 220251 Cincpac Intel. Bull.; 220241 Comsopac to CTF-61, CTF-62, CTF-63, and *Mackinac*; 220900 Fletcher to Comsopac; all August 1942, CSCMF, roll 22. On *I-122*, see also Bob Hackett and Sander Kingsepp, *Sensuikan!* in http://www.combinedfleet.com/sensuikan.htm.

52. Message 220910 August 1942 Comsopac to CTF-61, Greybook, 808.

53. Japan, *Senshi Sōsho*, 49:536, 553–56; Ugaki, 187–88; 7th Cruiser Division war diary, in NHC microfilm JD16.

54. Greybook, 829; Cincpac report (24 October 1942). Cincpac's general message 190305 August 1942 (Comsopac war diary) stressed, "Carriers and all other ships are prime objectives for destructive attack," but "we cannot expect to inflict heavy losses on the enemy without ourselves accepting the risk of punishment." Frank, *Guadalcanal*, 204–5, postulated this "extraordinary message" reflected Nimitz's extreme dissatisfaction with Fletcher. "Since common sailors and junior officers were not in a position to choose when to accept or provoke battle, the object of this prod is plain." However, this was a low priority all-fleet bulletin just to encourage those "common sailors and junior officers" to greater effort. If Nimitz truly wanted to "prod" Fletcher he could employ much less subtle means directly to Fletcher. F. C. Sherman diary (24 August 1942); Cominch Secret Information Bulletin (1943); Frank, 205.

55. Between 9 and 23 August the following bombardments took place:

11 August "feint" bombardment of Lunga by sub *RO-34*

12 August destroyers *Yūzuki* and *Oite* briefly shelled Lunga

13 Augustsub *I-123* shelled Lunga, *I-122* shelled Tulagi

19 Augustdestroyers *Kagerō*, *Hagikaze*, and *Arashi* shelled Lunga and Tulagi

20 August*Kagerō* shelled Tulagi and Guadalcanal

22 Augustdestroyer *Kawakaze* attacked destroyers *Blue* and *Henley* off Tulagi

Japan, *Senshi Sōsho*, 49:512–13, 534, 552.

56. A total of 1,029 Japanese troops reached Guadalcanal between 9 and 23 August: 113 special landing force sailors on the night of 16–17 August from the *Oite* and 916 soldiers of the Ichiki Detachment's First Echelon from destroyers on the night of 18–19 August. Japan, *Senshi Sōsho*, 49:520, 533.

57. Herbert C. Merillat, 71–72.

CHAPTER 28. THE BATTLE OF THE EASTERN SOLOMONS I

1. Sources on the Battle of the Eastern Solomons: CTF-61 (Comcrupac) to Comsopac, Preliminary Report of Actions, August 23–24, 1942 (6 September 1942), with Second Endorsement by Comairsopac and Tabular Record of Combat Reports. Cincpac to Cominch, Solomon Islands Campaign, Action of 23–25 August 1942 (24 October 1942), with enclosed action reports of ships and squadrons, including: CO USS *Saratoga* to Cincpac, Report of Action Against Enemy (Japanese) Forces in Solomon Islands Area on August 24, 1942 (10 September 1942), including group and squadron reports; Tactical Situation and Chronological History of Events—August 24, 1942, Fighter Net Radio Log and Radar Plot for Engagement against Japanese on August 24, 1942; Commander, *Saratoga* Air Group, Narrative of Operations on August 23, 1942, and the Morning of August 24, 1942 (5 September 1942); Commander, *Saratoga* Air Group to CO, USS *Saratoga*, Narrative Report of Action with Enemy on August 24, 1942, in Solomon Islands Area (29 August 1942); CTF-11 to Cincpac, Endorsement of the *Saratoga*'s Report of Action against Enemy (Japanese) Forces in the Solomon Islands Area on August 24, 1942 (24 September 1942); CO USS *Enterprise* to Cincpac, Action of August 24, 1942, including Air Attack on USS *Enterprise*, Report of (5 September 1942); CTF-16 to Cincpac, Report of Action 24 August 1942 (9 September 1942); Comcru TF-16 to Cincpac, Report of Action, 24 August 1942 (27 August 1942); Endorsement CTF-61 to Cincpac, Action of August 24, 1942, including Air Attack on USS *Enterprise*, Report of (25 September 1942). Task Force 16 Chronological Order of Events 0500–2400, August 24, 1942.

CTF-44, Operation Watchtower, Narrative of events subsequent to the withdrawal to Nouméa of the Amphibious Force after the Capture and Occupation of Tulagi and Guadalcanal [16 August–3 September 1942].

War diaries: *Saratoga*, Comairsopac, TF-16, *Enterprise*, Comcru TF-11, Comcru TF-18, Comcru TF-16, Comdesron One, Comdesron Six, Comdesron Twelve, *Minneapolis*. Carrier Operations, lecture by Cdr. Oscar Pederson to Army and Navy Staff College (4 November 1943), Pederson Papers.

Combat Narratives, Solomon Islands Campaign III: The Battle of the Eastern Solomons 23–25 August 1942 (1943). Morison, *United States Naval Operations*, 5:79–107, Japan, *Senshi Sōsho*, 49:556–91; Frank, 159–93, Lundstrom, *First Team Guadalcanal*, 102–64.

2. Basic sources for Fletcher's decisions and actions in the Battle of the Eastern Solomons include his Preliminary Report (6 September 1942) with map of contacts, *Saratoga* war diary, the *Saratoga*'s Tactical Situation and Chronological History of Events, TF-16 war diary, TF-16 Chronological Order of Events 0500–2400 (24 August 1942), and Pederson lecture (4 November 1943).

3. Twining, 78, recalled Schindler bringing the strawberries, but mistook the date as 12 August. Message 221921 August 1942 Cincpac to all CTFs, Comsopac Message File.

4. The messages from search planes cited here are in the Comairsopac war diary, task force and carrier war diaries, and in CSCMF. James Sawruk identified the individual PBY plane commanders.

5. TF-16 war diary.

6. Message 230156 August 1942 Comsopac to CTF-61, CSCMF, roll 22. Destroyer fuel is ascertained from the figures in their deck logs.

7. TF-16 war diary.

8. TF-61 preliminary report; Lee, 339; Commander, *Saratoga* Air Group report (5 September 1942); Laing report; *Saratoga* war diary.

9. Messages August 1942: 230159 Comairsopac to *Mackinac*, 230309 Radio Canberra to any and all U.S. ships, 230315 Comsopac to Comsowespacfor, CSCMF, roll 22; 230642 General MacArthur to Comsopac, CNO TS Blue File; 230331 Radio Nouméa to Cactus, 230456 Comairsopac to Comsopac, CSCMF, roll 22.

10. Messages 230440 Comsopac to CTF-61, 230601 Comsowespacfor to Comairsopac, 230613 Comsowespac to all CTFs, August 1942, CSCMF, roll 22.

11. Yokoi, Toshiyuki, "The Admiral That Davy Jones Didn't Want," in Gluck, *Ukiyo,* 11.

12. Message 230345 August 1942 Cincpac Intel. Bull., CSCMF, roll 22; CTF-11 to Cincpac, First Endorsement (24 September 1942) of CO *Saratoga* report (10 September 1942).

13. Comcru TF-18 war diary, TF-16 war diary, TF-16 Chronological Order of Events.

14. Frank, 165. Morison, *United States Naval Operations*, 5:83, noted the seven destroyers with *Wasp* at noon 23 August had from 68,885 to 104,794 gallons, averaging 84,824 gallons. As usual he did not explain what these figures meant in terms of capacity and actual steaming at different speeds. The overall average was 55 percent. The low destroyer was the *Stack* (about 6.7 days at fifteen knots, 1.9 days at twenty-five knots). CO *Enterprise* report (5 September 1942).

15. Greybook, 832.

16. Messages 230709 Comsowespac to Cincpac, 231140 Comsowespacfor to Cincpac, August 1942, CSCMF, roll 22.

17. Messages 230816 CG Cactus to CTF-61 and CTF-62, 230835 *Mackinac* to CTF-63, 231040 CG Cactus to CTF-61, August 1942, CSCMF, roll 22.

18. Japan, *Senshi Sōsho*, 49:558–59; Ugaki, 188–89.

19. Tanaka, in Evans, 165; Japan, *Senshi Sōsho*, 49:557–62.

20. Tanaka, in Evans, 166; Japan, *Senshi Sōsho*, 49:562–63; Ugaki, 188–89.

21. Lundstrom, *First Team Guadalcanal*, 106; TF-16 Chronological Order of Events.

22. TF-16 Chronological Order of Events.

23. Comairsopac war diary; I am again indebted to James Sawruk's knowledge of Airsopac's search operations.

24. Japan, *Senshi Sōsho*, 49:562.

25. Japan, *Senshi Sōsho*, 49:563–64, 566.

26. *Saratoga* Tactical Situation; TF-16 Chronological Order of Events; TF-61 preliminary report (6 September 1942). Comairsopac war diary, Sawruk research.

27. TF-61 preliminary report (6 September 1942).

28. TF-61 preliminary report (6 September 1942); *Saratoga* Tactical Situation.

29. Comairsopac war diary, Sawruk research.

30. Felt, oral history, 109; Commander, *Saratoga* Air Group report (5 September 1942); Lee, 341–50 (quote on page 350).

31. Lee, 350; TF-16 Chronological Order of Events; TF-61 preliminary report (6 September 1942). Both Fletcher and Ghormley complained of communication problems with regard to contact reports.

32. TF-61 preliminary report (6 September 1942). Gen. John Bell Hood, *Advance and Retreat*, 57, in Pederson Papers. Pederson lecture (4 November 1943).

33. Felt, oral history, 110. CTF-61 preliminary report (6 September 1942); CTF-11 First Endorsement (24 September 1942).

34. TF-16 Chronological Order of Events; CTF-11 First Endorsement (24 September 1942).

35. Lundstrom, *First Team Guadalcanal*, 113–14; Japan, *Senshi Sōsho*, 49:582.

36. TF-16 Chronological Order of Events; TF-16 war diary; CO *Enterprise* report (5 September 1942).

37. Lundstrom, *First Team Guadalcanal*, 114; CTF-61 preliminary report (6 September 1942). Japan, *Senshi Sōsho*, 49:582.

38. Japan, *Senshi Sōsho*, 49:545–47, 572.

39. Japan, *Senshi Sōsho*, 49:564.

40. CO *Saratoga* report (10 September 1942); CTF-61 preliminary report (6 September 1942).

41. CTF-61 preliminary report (6 September 1942), with plot of contacts that can be compared with Japanese positions shown in maps in *Senshi Sōsho*, volume 49.

42. Lundstrom, *First Team Guadalcanal*, 123–24. Japan, *Senshi Sōsho*, 49:567.

43. Japan, *Senshi Sōsho*, 49:567–68.

44. TF-16 Chronological Order of Events. Message 240223 August 1942 Cincpac Intel. Bull., CSCMF, roll 22. RG-457, SRMD-002.

45. CTF-61 preliminary report (6 September 1942); CO *Saratoga* report (10 September 1942).

46. CTF-61 preliminary report (6 September 1942); message 240355 August 1942 *Mackinac* to Comairsopac, CSCMF, roll 22.

47. TF-16 Chronological Order of Events; TF-16 war diary; CO *Enterprise* report (5 September 1942); CTF-61 preliminary report (6 September 1942); CO Saratoga report (10 September 1942).

48. Comairsopac war diary; CO Bombing Squadron Six to CO USS *Enterprise*, Report of Action, August 24, 1942 (31 August 1942); Japan, *Senshi Sōsho*, 49:575–76.

49. CO Bombing Squadron Six report (31 August 1942); Japan, *Senshi Sōsho*, 49:573; information from James Sawruk. Transmissions on the fighter net blocked the search-attack frequency. Voice radio messages were unreliable beyond one hundred miles. See CTF-16 to Cincpac, Communications Failures Due to Faulty Equipment (3 October 1942), and CO USS *Enterprise* to Cincpac, Carrier Aircraft Radio Communications (25 September 1942), in RG-38, Cincpac Flag File.

50. TF-16 Chronological Order of Events.

51. From deck logs: TF-11 destroyer fuel, 24 August:

	Capacity (gallons)	On hand (gallons)	Percentage
Phelps	187,863	70,261	37%
Farragut	168,453	84,949	50%
Worden	168,453	80,829	48%
Macdonough	168,453	83,836	50%
Dewey	168,453	66,448	39%
Bagley	152,094	70,530	46%

No figures are available for the *Patterson*, but her fuel state was very probably close to her sister *Bagley*, which also came out from Nouméa with Crutchley.

TF-16 destroyer fuel, 24 August:

	Capacity (gallons)	On hand (gallons)	Percentage
Balch	187,863	73,074	39%
Maury	147,625	54,178	37%
Benham	147,625	70,098	47%
Grayson	140,663	39,320	28%
Ellet	147,625	93,723	63%
Monssen	140,663	73,575	52%

52. CO *Enterprise* report (5 September 1942); TF-16 Chronological Order of Events. Second Endorsement, CTF-61 preliminary report (6 September 1942) by Comairsopac.

53. Japan, *Senshi Sōsho*, 49:569–71.

54. Lee, 353; TF-16 Chronological Order of Events; Pederson lecture (4 November 1943).

55. CO *Enterprise* report (5 September 1942); CO Saratoga report (10 September 1942).

56. For the attack on TF-16, see Lundstrom, *First Team Guadalcanal*, 125–50; combat air patrol messages in USS *Saratoga* Fighter Net Radio Log and Radar Plot for Engagement against Japanese on August 24, 1942, enclosure to CO *Saratoga* report (10 September 1942). Lee, 353.

57. Lee, 354; Glover, 38. Letter from Cdr. G. C. Slonim to "Jim," one of S. E. Morison's research assistants (c. 1949), in Morison Office Files, box 27.

58. Lee, 355; TF-16 Chronological Order of Events; message 240625 August 1942 Fletcher to Comairsopac and Comsopac, *CSCMF, roll 22; Japan, Senshi Sōsho*, 49:568–69.

CHAPTER 29. THE BATTLE OF THE EASTERN SOLOMONS II

1. TF-16 Chronological Order of Events; Comdesdiv Twenty-two to Cincpac, Reports of action of 24 August, 1942, and subsequent events in connection there with (30 August 1942).

2. Lee, 355; CO *Saratoga* report (10 September 1942).

3. CO *Enterprise* report (5 September 1942); message 240808 August 1942 CTF-61 to Comsopac, CSCMF, roll 22.

4. CO *Saratoga* report (10 September 1942); Lundstrom, *First Team Guadalcanal*, 153.

5. CTF-61 preliminary report (6 September 1942); Commander, *Saratoga* Air Group to CO, USS *Saratoga*, Narrative Report of Action with Enemy on August 24, 1942, in Solomon Islands Area (29 August 1942); Slonim letter to "Jim" (c. 1949), in Morison Office Files, box 27.

6. Torpedo Squadron Eight, Commander, to CO, USS *Saratoga*, Narrative Report of Action with Enemy on 24 August 1942 in Solomon Islands Area (27 August 1942); Commander, Bombing Squadron Three, to CO, USS *Saratoga*, Narrative Report of Action against Enemy on August 24, 1942, in Solomon Islands Area (27 August 1942).

7. CTF-61 preliminary report (6 September 1942); TF-16 Chronological Order of Events. Slonim, 80; Slonim letter to "Jim" (c. 1949), in Morison Office Files, box 27.

8. Message 241014 August 1942 CTF-61 to Comsopac, Greybook, 809.

9. TF-16 Chronological Order of Events; TF-16 war diary; CO *Enterprise* report (5 September 1942); CO *Saratoga* report (10 September 1942); Desron One war diary. Message 241005 August 1942 Guadalcanal to CTF-61, CSCMF, roll 22. Vandegrift ran low on fuel. That evening he had only enough aviation gasoline for "about one days operation of a carrier group plus marine planes" (message 241431 August 1942 Comairsopac to CTF-62 [info CTF-61 and Comsopac], CSCMF, roll 22). Commander, *Enterprise* Air Group, to Cincpac, Report of Action in the Solomon Islands Area, August 22–25, 1942 (2 September 1942). Felt, oral history, 111.

10. Comairsopac war diary; identification of PBYs from Sawruk; CTF-61 preliminary report (6 September 1942). Messages August 1942: 241221 Comsopac to CTF-61, 241300 Ghormley to Fletcher, 241400 Comsopac to Guadalcanal, CSCMF, roll 22; 241102 Comsopac to CTF-17, Greybook, 809.

11. Japan, *Senshi Sōsho*, 49:566.

12. Japan, *Senshi Sōsho*, 49:571.

13. Japan, *Senshi Sōsho*, 49:573–75; TF-61 preliminary report (6 September 1942).

14. VT-8 report (27 August 1942); VB-3 report (27 August 1942); Japan, *Senshi Sōsho*, 49:574–77, 583.

15. Japan, *Senshi Sōsho*, 49:573–74.

16. Japan, *Senshi Sōsho*, 49:573–74. Pederson lecture (4 November 1943).

17. Ugaki, 190–92; Japan, *Senshi Sōsho*, 49:577.

18. Japan, *Senshi Sōsho*, 49:584–86.

19. Comcru TF-18 war diary; Capt. Forrest Sherman to Cincpac, Movements of USS *Wasp*, August 25, 1942 (14 November 1942).

20. Messages 241305 August 1942 Radio Guadalcanal to CTF-61, Comsopac war diary; 241355 August 1942 Guadalcanal to CTF-61, CSCMF, roll 22; Japan, *Senshi Sōsho*, 49:585–86; message 241350 August 1942 Comsopac to Comsowespacfor, in MacArthur Papers, Sopac message file, message no. 75.

21. Message 241449 August 1942 Comairsopac to CTF-61, CSCMF, roll 22; Lundstrom, *First Team Guadalcanal*, 158.

22. Comairsopac war diary, Sawruk research. SRMN-009, Cincpac Fleet Intelligence Summary, 24 August 1942, 72; message 242125 August 1942 Cincpac to Comsopac, CSCMF, roll 22.

23. Tanaka, in Evans, 167–69. Japan, *Senshi Sōsho*, 49:586–88.

24. Forrest Sherman letter to Cincpac (14 November 1942), NHC; Lundstrom, *First Team Guadalcanal*, 158–60.

25. *Saratoga* war diary, TF-16 war diary.

26. *Saratoga* war diary, Comcru TF-11 war diary, TF-16 war diary.

27. CTF-61 preliminary report (6 September 1942); message 250303 August 1942 Cincpac Intel. Bull., CSCMF, roll 22.

28. *Saratoga* war diary; TF-16 war diary; message 250646 August 1942 CTF-61 to Comsopac, Greybook, 659–60.

29. Japan, *Senshi Sōsho*, 49:583; Ugaki, 192–93; Boyd and Yoshida, 96–97.

30. Ugaki, 193–94.

31. CO *Enterprise* report (5 September 1942); CTF-16 letter to Cincpac (10 September 1942). In his First Endorsement (24 September1942) of CO *Saratoga* report (10 September 1942), Fletcher referred to his "report of Communications of September 17, 1942," which cannot now be located.

32. Lundstrom, *First Team Guadalcanal*, 162–64; CTF-61 Second Endorsement (25 September 1942) of CO *Enterprise* report (5 September 1942).

33. CTF-11, First Endorsement (24 September 1942) of CO *Saratoga* report (10 September 1942); CTF-16 letter to Cincpac (10 September.1942).

34. Comcrupac letter to Cincpac (24 September 1942); CTF-61 Second Endorsement (25 September 1942) of CO *Enterprise* report (5 September 1942); CO *Enterprise* report (5 September 1942).

35. Slonim letter to "Jim" (c. 1949), in Morison Office Files, box 27; CTF-61 preliminary report (6 September 1942); message 030600 September 1942 Comsopac to Cincpac, CSCMF, roll 23; Pederson lecture (4 November 1943); RG-457, SRH-036, Radio Intelligence in World War II Tactical Operations in the Pacific Ocean Areas, January 1943, 256–57.

36. Layton interview by Pineau and Costello (11 May 1983), 36; RG-457, SRH-12, Combat Intelligence Unit, Traffic Intelligence Summary, 24 August 1942, 800–801.

37. Cincpac to Cominch, Solomon Islands Campaign—Action of 23–25 August—Preliminary Report (27 September 1942).

38. Cincpac report (24 October 1942); Cominch Secret Intelligence Bulletin No. 2.

39. Potter and Nimitz, *Great Sea War*, 259, said Kondō's depleted Support Force lost ninety planes as well as the *Ryūjō*. In truth, counting the *Ryūjō* group, the Japanese lost sixty-four carrier planes (thirty-two fighters, twenty-four dive bombers, and eight torpedo planes) on 24 August.

40. The strangest wartime interpretation of the Eastern Solomons is Fletcher Pratt's officially sponsored *The Navy's War*, 227, 231. Pratt placed Kinkaid in charge and did not even mention Fletcher. He noted severe criticism for Kinkaid "not pursuing the Japs to the death." Kinkaid bristled over being blamed for Fletcher's decisions (Wheeler, *Kinkaid of the Seventh Fleet*, 292).

41. Slonim letter to "Jim" (c. 1949), in Morison Office Files, box 27; Morison, *United States Naval Operations*, 5:102–3, 106.

42. Morison, *United States Naval Operations*, 5:106; Cincpac report (27 October 1942).

CHAPTER 30. THE RIGHT OF THE LINE

1. General sources for the movements of TF-61 and its components in late August and early September 1942 are the war diaries of the *Saratoga*, Comcru TF-11, Comcru TF-18, Desron One, Desron Twelve, and TF-17.

2. Messages 0249Z/25 Radio Honolulu to any USN ship, 250620 Comsopac to CTF-17, August 1942, CSCMF, roll 22.

3. Messages August 1942: 251235 Cominch to Cincpac, Sopac Message File; 252205 Cincpac to Cominch, Greybook, 660; 252241 Cincpac to Cominch, Greybook, 658; 271935 Cincpac to Comsopac, CSCMF, roll 22; 251732 Comsopac to CG Defense Force Samoa, CNO TS Blue File.

4. Comairsopac war diary; TF-16 war diary. Messages August 1942: 260239 Cincpac to Comsopac, 260342 Comsopac to Cincpac, CNO TS Blue File; 260750 Comsopac to CTF-61, Sopac Message File; 260639 CTF-16 to Comsopac, CNO TS Blue File; 261812 Comsopac to CTF-16, Greybook, 660.

5. Messages 260332 Comsopac to CTF-17, 260345 CTF-62 to all CTFs, August 1942, CSCMF, roll 22.

6. *Saratoga* war diary; Rear Adm. D. C. Ramsey statement (16 February 1943), *Wasp* investigation.

7. Messages August 1942: 250646 CTF-61 to Comsopac, Greybook, 659–60; 261930 CTF-61 to Comsopac, Greybook, 810; 270132 Comsopac to CTF-61 and CTF-17, 270152 Comsopac to *Phoenix*, CSCMF, roll 22.

8. *Saratoga* war diary; Comairsopac war diary; Lundstrom, *First Team Guadalcanal*, 165–68.

9. Message 271026 August 1942 Comsopac to CTF-61, CTF-62, and CTF-63, Greybook, 662; Vice Adm. R. L. Ghormley statement (5 January 1943), *Wasp* investigation.

10. *Saratoga* war diary; messages 280445 August 1942 Cincpac Intel. Bull., CSCMF, roll 22; 281111 August 1942 Comairsopac to Radio Guadalcanal, CNO TS Blue File; Comcru TF-18 war diary.

11. Message 281045 August 1942 CG 1st Mardiv to Comsopac, CSCMF, roll 22. Japan, *Senshi Sōsho*, 83:21–28; Ugaki, 193, 197–98; Tanaka, 169–74.

12. Laing report; TF-17 war diary; Murray statement (4 January 1943), *Wasp* investigation. *Saratoga* war diary; messages 282251 CTF-61 to Comsopac, 282259 CTF-61 to *Phoenix*, August 1942, CSCMF, roll 22.

13. Messages 290709 Comsowespacfor to Cincpac, 290955 CTF-62 to *WW Burrows*, August 1942, CSCMF, roll 23; Tanaka, 174.

14. TF-61 Op-Ord 4-42 (29 August 1942) and TF-61 Op-Ord 5-42 (29 August 1942), in Op-Ord File.

15. Messages August 1942: 281240 Cominch to Cincpac, 290310 Comsopac to Cominch, Greybook, 666; 300015 Cincpac to Cominch, in MacArthur Papers, Sopac message file, message no. 80; 302123 Cincpac to Cominch, Greybook, 667.

16. Messages August 1942: 291642 Comsopac to CTF-61, Greybook, 684; 300542 Comsopac to *Cimarron* and *Guadalupe*, CSCMF, roll 23.

17. Messages 300519 Cactus to Comsopac, 301111 CTU-62.2.4 to CTF-62, August 1942, CSCMF, roll 23; 011315 September 1942 Cominch to Cincpac, Greybook, 2:862.

18. Reports on the torpedoing of the *Saratoga* include: Cincpac to Cominch, Solomon Islands Campaign—Torpedoing of *Saratoga*, *Wasp*, and *North Carolina* (31 October 1942); CO USS *Saratoga* to Cincpac, Action Report on Torpedoing of USS Saratoga, 31 August 1942 (10 September 1942), First Endorsement CTF-11 (18 September 1942); CTG-11.4 (Comdesron One) to Cincpac, Report of Action of Japanese submarine and Task Force 11 on 31 August 1942 (7 September 1942), CTF-11 First Endorsement (18 September 1942) to Comdesron One report.

19. CO *Saratoga* report (10 September 1942), Comdesron One report (7 September 1942); Japan, *Senshi Sōsho*, 83:65; Boyd and Yoshida, 98; Green diary; Lee, 360. In his 1966 interview with Walter Lord, Fletcher recalled suffering his wound at Midway, but all the evidence shows it occurred on 31 August 1942 when the *Saratoga* was torpedoed.

20. Lee, 360–61; message 302005 August 1942 All U.S. ships to Comsopac, Sopac Message File; Comdesron One report (7 September 1942); CO *Saratoga* report (10 September 1942); Stern, 59–60.

21. Roger L. Bond, oral history, 108. Bond joined the ship in 1943 as a quartermaster. Stern, 93–94.

22. Lee, 361; Glover, 38; CO *Saratoga* report (10 September 1942); Comdesron One report (7 September 1942). The *I-26* escaped after four hours of attacks by destroyers, although the *Monssen* was certain that her last attack at 0950 had finished the sub (message 012004 September 1942 *Monssen* to CTF-11, CSCMF, roll 23).

23. CO *Saratoga* report (10 September 1942); Cincpac report (31 October 1942); message 302340 August 1942 CTF-61 to Comsopac, CNO TS Blue File.

24. Messages August 1942: 302140 Comsopac to CTF-17, CTF-18, and CTF-61, 302355 CTF-18 to Comsopac, CSCMF, roll 23; 302123 Cincpac to Comsopac, Greybook, 687; 310242 Comsopac to CTF-16, CTF-17, CTF-18, and CTF-63, Greybook, 665. Crutchley's TF-44 was to comprise the *Australia*, *Hobart*, *Phoenix*, and six destroyers. Messages August 1942: 310602 Comsopac to *Guadalupe* and *Cimarron*, CSCMF, roll 23; 310950 Comsopac to Comairsopac, Sopac Message File; 311022 Comsopac to CTF-18, 311107 Comairsopac to Comsopac, 310402 Comairsopac to Cincpac, CSCMF, roll 23.

25. Rear Adm. Leigh Noyes statement (14 January 1943), *Wasp* investigation; TF-17 war diary; messages 310930 August 1942 CTF-61 to Comsopac, Greybook, 668; 010330 September 1942 Comsopac to CTF-61, CSCMF, roll 23.

26. *Saratoga* war diary. Messages September 1942: 010722 Comsopac to CTF-61, CSCMF, roll 23; 011025 CTF-11 to Cincpac, CNO TS Blue File. Stern, 60.

27. Message 012331 September 1942 Cincpac to Cominch, Greybook, 863.

28. Laing report; Cincpac report (31 October 1942); Ghormley statement (5 January 1943), Noyes statement (14 January 1943), *Wasp* investigation; Comcrupac letter to Cincpac (24 September 1942).

29. Ramsey statement (16 February 1943), *Wasp* investigation.

30. Letter Wright to Wellborn (9 February 1952) in DNC, Office Files, box 20; Cincpac report (31 October 1942); Murray statement (4 January 1943), Sherman statement (28 January 1943), *Wasp* investigation; message 072145 October 1942 Cincpac to CTF-1, CTF-11, CTF-16, CTF-17, CTF-62, CTF-64, and Comsopac, CSCMF, roll 26.

31. Morison, *United States Naval Operations*, 5:112; Cominch Secret Battle Experiences Bulletin No. 2.

32. Message 020924 September 1942 CTG-61.2 to Comsopac, CSCMF, roll 23; Murray statement (4 January 1943), *Wasp* investigation; Cincpac report (31 October 1942).

33. Cincpac report (31 October 1942); Ramsey statement (16 February 1943), Sherman statement (28 January 1943), *Wasp* investigation.

34. Messages September 1942: 020722 Comsopac to CTF-61, CSCMF, roll 23; 041302 Comsopac to CTF-11, Sopac Message File. Noyes statement (14 January 1943), *Wasp* investigation.

35. Messages September 1942: 052052 CTF-11 to Comsopac, 060550 Comsopac to Cincpac, Sopac Message File; 061325 Cincpac to Comsopac, CSCMF, roll 23; 062233 Cincpac to Cominch, CNO TS Blue File; 070148 Comsopac to CTF-61, CSCMF, roll 23; 070452 Comsopac to CTF-62, Comsopac war diary; 091016 Comsopac to CTF-18, CTF-17, CTF-62, CTF-63, and CTF-64, CNO TS Blue File.

36. Messages September 1942: 062246 CTG-2.9 to Comsopac, CNO TS Blue File; 080342 Comsopac to CTF-11, Sopac Message File; 110659 CTF-11 to Comsopac, 111030 Comsopac to CTF-11, CSCMF, roll 24.

37. For Sopac carrier operations to mid September 1942, see Lundstrom, *First Team Guadalcanal*, 202, 220–29.

38. Message 030736 September 1942 Comsopac to CTF-17, CSCMF, roll 23; TF-17 war diary; message 070217 September 1942 CTF-17 to Comsopac, CSCMF, roll 23; Ghormley statement (5 January 1943), *Wasp* investigation.

39. Noyes statement (14 January 1943), letter Turner to Noyes (9 September 1942), letter Noyes to Ghormley (9 September 1942), *Wasp* investigation. Several marine sources somehow misconstrued this exchange

between Noyes and Turner to blame Fletcher for trying to block the introduction of the grounded *Saratoga* planes in defense of Cactus. See Griffith, 111–12, and Sherrod, *History of Marine Corps Aviation in World War II*, 88.

40. Noyes statement (14 January 1943), *Wasp* investigation.

41. Sherman statement (28 January 1943), *Wasp* investigation.

42. Messages September 1942: 201322 Comsopac to CTF-17, Greybook, 882; 202147 Cincpac to Comsopac, 201755 Cominch to Cincpac, CSCMF, roll 25.

43. Ghormley statement (5 January 1943), Noyes statement (14 January 1943), Sherman statement (28 January 1943), *Wasp* investigation; Rear Adm. Leigh Noyes, Memo for Cincpac (5 October 1942).

44. Cominch Secret Battle Experience Bulletin No. 2; Capt. R. G. Tobin statement (17 February 1943), *Wasp* investigation.

45. Letter Comairpac (Halsey) to Cincpac (9 October 1942); Sherrod, 90.

CHAPTER 31. THE CLEAN SWEEP

1. *Saratoga* war diary. The conference minutes of the 7–9 September Cominch-Cincpac meetings first noted that Fletcher was to report to King for temporary duty for "about one month," but that was crossed out and replaced by "two weeks." Letter Nimitz to King (12 October 1942), in Admiral's Personal Letters, 1942, Nimitz Papers.

2. Conference Minutes, 7–9 September 1942. Messages September 1942: 010235 Cominch to Cincpac, CSCMF, roll 23; 141807 and 142007 Bupers to Comairpac, 110340 Com 12 to Com 14, CSCMF, roll 24. DSM citations in citation file, NHC. For the ceremony, see *New York Times* (16 September 1942), where Halsey is called "Fighting Bill." Halsey and Bryan, 108, wrongly placed the ceremony on 12 September in the absent *Saratoga*.

3. Notes on Conference at Palmyra, September 25, 1942, in Admiral's Personal Letters, 1942, in Nimitz Papers.

4. They left the next day in the battleship *Pennsylvania* and reached San Francisco on 4 October. The officers had orders to report back to NAS Alameda on 27 October, the enlisted men to San Francisco on 21 October, before returning to Pearl. Interviews of George Clapp and Norman Ulmer by Lundstrom.

5. Message 280258 September 1942 Com 14 to Com 12, CSCMF, roll 25; letter McCain to Nimitz (30 September 1942), in Commander, North Pacific Area (Comnorpac) Folder, Nimitz Papers; Conference Minutes (9 September 1942).

6. Letter Nimitz to Ghormley (8 October 1942), in Admiral's Personal Letters, 1942, Nimitz Papers. Messages October 1942: 070021 Cincpac to Cominch, CSCMF, roll 26; 110045 Cincpac to CTF-16 (info CTF-17), CSCMF, roll 27. Kinkaid wrote his wife on 8 October: "I am glad it has come out this way because there are a lot of aviators in the offing and there is some inclination to push them ahead of us ordinary mortals" (Wheeler, 266). Messages 071614 Cominch to Cincpac and 092207 Cincpac to Cominch, October 1942, CSCMF, roll 26.

7. Letter Nimitz to King (12 October 1942); message 110046 October 1942 Cincpac to CTF-16 and 17, CSCMF, roll 27.

8. Letter Nimitz to King (12 October 1942); message 260826 October 1942 Cincpac to Comairpac, CSCMF, roll 29; extract of letters to Mrs. Nimitz (27 October 1942), Nimitz Papers; Whitehill memo (14 August 1949), King Papers, NWC. Cincpac's First Endorsement (6 April 1943) in the *Wasp* investigation. Letter Noyes to Sherman (12 April 1950) in F. P. Sherman Papers.

9. Messages October 1942: 160440 Comsopac to Cincpac, 170243 Cincpac to Comsopac, CNO TS Blue File; 160937 Cincpac to Cominch, 161245 Cominch to Cincpac, Greybook, 2:895; 181350 Comsopac to Cincpac, Greybook, 2:896; Greybook, 2:1096; extract of letters to Mrs. Nimitz (17 October 1942), Nimitz Papers; 180244 October 1942 Cincpac to CTF-16, CSCMF, roll 28.

10. Messages 230019 Cincpac to CTF-64, 242357 Cincpac to Bupers with text of 232307 Bupers to Cincpac, October 1942, CSCMF, roll 28.

11. Interview of Rear Adm. Harry Smith by Dr. Stephen Regan (13 July 1986), courtesy of Dr. Regan.

12. Whitehill memo (14 August 1949). Cominch-Cincpac conference 11–13 December 1942, Personnel Matters (11 December, 1942). Letter Fletcher to Nimitz (22 January 1943), in Admiral's Personal Letters, 1943, Nimitz Papers. Layton interview by Pineau and Costello (11 May 1983).

13. For an example of how the *Lexington* received credit for the *Yorktown*'s achievements, see Cdr. C. G. Moore, Memorandum for Admiral Brown (1 March 1943), which stated, "It has been established beyond peradventure of a doubt [likely from Ted Sherman himself] that *Lexington* aircraft were largely, if not wholly, responsible for inflicting such heavy damage on the enemy carrier *Shokaku* that that vessel was withdrawn from service for many months." Moore served in the office of the CNO. Brown Papers. The president's itinerary in the Roosevelt Library at Hyde Park noted his 2 October 1942 meeting with King and Forrestal and revealed the only time during the whole war Fletcher met Roosevelt was in August 1944 in the Aleutians, e-mails 5 and 6 November 2002 from Raymond Teichman at Hyde Park.

14. F. C. Sherman diary, entry on 9 November 1942, which covered the period 12 October through 9 November; *Saratoga* war diary; messages 270400 Com 12 to Com 14 reporting Sherman's flight to Pearl and 282109 Cincpac to TF-11 reorganizing the task force under Ramsey's command, October 1942, CSCMF, roll 29.

15. Message 242239 October 1942 Cincpac to Bupers, CSCMF, roll 28.

16. Reynolds, *Towers*, 428. Nothing pertaining to the substitution of Ramsey for Sherman appears in this exhaustive biography of Towers, based on Towers's private diary and extensive personal papers. Given such rich sources, it is reasonable to expect that, had Towers influenced Nimitz on such an important matter, some hint would have appeared in his papers.

17. *Seattle Times* (22 November 1942); letter Fletcher to Nimitz (22 January 1943). Messages October 1942: 301745 Cominch to Cincpac, CSCMF, roll 29; 051617 Admiral Fletcher to Cincpac and 092215 Cincpac to Secnav, CSCMF, roll 26. Interview of Harry Smith (13 July 1986) by Regan. In March 1943 Lewis rose to rear admiral and served as chief of staff to Vice Adm. H. Kent Hewitt, Eighth Fleet commander during the Sicily and Salerno landings. In August 1944 he took over one of the amphibious task groups that invaded Southern France.

18. For Sopac carrier operations in October and November 1942, see Lundstrom, *First Team Guadalcanal*, chapters 14, 16, 18–26.

19. Reynolds, *Towers*, 408; F. C. Sherman diary (9–16 November 1942).

20. CTF-16 to Cincpac, Operations of Task Force Sixteen in the Action for the Defense of Guadalcanal 12–15 November 1942 (23 November 1942); CO USS *Enterprise* to Cincpac, Report of Action 13–14 November 1942 (19 November 1942); F. C. Sherman diary (17 November 1942); letter Halsey to Nimitz (17 November 1942), Comsopac Folder, Nimitz Papers.

21. F. C. Sherman diary (19–20 November 1942). On 23 November Kinkaid wrote his wife: "I hate to leave my present job because I feel I know it well and have had considerable success in it" (Wheeler, 291).

22. Message 230612 November 1942 Comsopac to all CTFs, Comsopac war diary; F. C. Sherman diary (20 and 25 November 1942). The text of Kinkaid's orders included: "You have commanded carrier task forces operating in this area with skill and effectiveness. You inflicted great damage upon the enemy in repeated engagements. . . . I desire to pay full tribute to your superb work" (Wheeler 295).

23. Wheeler, 295–97, 300–301. Halsey had independently recommended Kinkaid for a DSM for Santa Cruz, but it was never awarded. In 1946 Kinkaid tried to resurrect that DSM (actually a gold star in lieu of a second DSM) but the navy only rewrote the citation for his second DSM to include Santa Cruz and the Naval Battle of Guadalcanal with the Eastern Solomons (Wheeler, 291–92). Fletcher only received the one DSM for Coral Sea and Midway and no additional U.S. Navy decorations for the rest of the war.

24. Letter Nimitz to McCain (19 March 1943), in Admiral's Personal Letters, 1943; letter Nimitz to Halsey (18 December 1942), Comsopac Folder; both in Nimitz Papers. The last non-aviator regularly detailed to lead a carrier task force into action was Rear Adm. Robert C. Giffen, whose TF-18 in January and early February 1943 contained two escort carriers. Giffen suffered the loss of the *Chicago* in the Battle of Rennell Island, 29–30 January 1943. From 29 June to 7 July 1944, non-aviator Rear Adm. Wilder D. Baker, the cruiser commander, led TG-58.4 in strikes on Saipan after Rear Adm. William K. Harrill became medically disabled.

CHAPTER 32. WAR ON THE PERIPHERY

1. Commandant, Thirteenth Naval District, Administrative History of the Thirteenth Naval District, 4 volumes.

2. Morison, *Two-Ocean War*, 182; undated memo (1942) in Maas Papers.

3. Letter Fletcher to Nimitz (undated), letter Nimitz to Fletcher (14 August 1943), in Admiral's Personal Letters, 1943, Nimitz Papers.

4. Comcrupac to Cincpac (24 September 1942), Comairpac to Cincpac (9 October 1942); Cincpac to Task Force Commanders, Pacific Fleet, etc., Operations of Carrier Task Forces (9 December 1942), in RG-38, Cincpac Flag Files.

5. Comairpac to Cincpac, Operations of Carrier Task Forces (14 April 1943); Comcrupac to Cincpac (24 September 1942); Comairpac to Cincpac (9 October 1942).

6. CTF-16 to Cincpac, Operations of Carrier Task Forces (8 January 1943). Letter Vice Adm. H. S. Duckworth to Lundstrom (25 March 1972); H. M. Dater memo, talk with Rear Adm. H. S. Duckworth (18 January 1951), in Duckworth Papers.

7. Reynolds, *Fast Carriers*, 72–73.

8. Ramsey left to become chief of Buaer in place of John McCain. Duckworth wrote Clark Reynolds (10 January 1965): "I have the greatest admiration for the fighting & professional ability of 'Ted' Sherman—there was none better. He seemed to be able to think out most of the answers before the questions were asked. But he had the greatest negative personality I have ever known. No one liked him & it worked against him in the long run" (Duckworth Papers). Letter Duckworth to Lundstrom (4 August 1972). Reynolds, *Fast Carriers*, 73–78, 80–87.

9. Letters Duckworth to Lundstrom (25 March 1972, 4 August 1972); Reynolds, *Fast Carriers*, 87–88.

10. Weapons Systems Evaluation Group Staff Study No. 4, Operational Experiences of Fast Carrier Task Forces in World War II (15 August 1951), 17, 151–61; Reynolds, *Fast Carriers*, 88–109.

11. Dyer, 2:631–32; Reynolds, *Towers*, 440.

12. Reynolds, *Fast Carriers*, 95; Reynolds, *Towers*, 442.

13. Reynolds, *Towers*, 447–48; message 212225 November 1943 Cincpac to Comcenpacfor (Commander, Central Pacific Force) (info Cominch and CTF-50), CNO TS Blue File; WSEG Staff Study No. 4, 161.

14. Reynolds, *Towers*, 399.

15. Cominch-Cincpac Conferences, Minutes, 25–27 September 1943; Wheeler, 340–41, 343–45; Cincpac, Administrative History of the North Pacific Area, (1945); Hayes, 668–76; letter Fletcher to Nimitz (4 December 1943), in Admiral's Personal Letters, 1944, Nimitz Papers. For operations in the North Pacific Area, see also Hutchison, *World War II in the North Pacific*.

16. Letters Nimitz to Fletcher (7 January 1944 and 10 February 1944), Comnorpac Folder, Nimitz Papers. Morison, *United States Naval Operations*, 7:66, wrongly gave the date as 2 February. Morison concluded, "During the rest of the war the Aleutians sector offers little of interest to the military or the naval historian" and dealt with the following nineteen months of Comnorpac's combat operations in less than a paragraph. Hopkins, *Nice to Have You Aboard*, 114–15.

17. Letters Nimitz to Fletcher (22 June 1944), Fletcher to Nimitz (8 August 1944), Comnorpac Folder, Nimitz Papers; letter Roosevelt to Fletcher (9 August 1944), Fletcher Papers; Norpac Administrative History.

18. Vice Adm. John L. McCrea, oral history, 318–21.

19. Norpac Administrative History, 284–88.

20. Letter Fletcher to Nimitz (16 December 1944), High Ranking Officers Folder, Nimitz Papers. Nimitz sent Fletcher a Christmas present to which Fletcher replied on 30 January 1945 in a letter headed "Dear Chester," in which he wrote: "I think I can state positively that this is the only present that I ever received from a Fleet Admiral and naturally I am very grateful to be remembered by you." In May 1945 Nimitz thoughtfully sent Fletcher a press release regarding the USS *New Mexico*, which he personally annotated: "Dear Frank Jack—As an old C.O. of this gallant ship I think you will be pleased to read this. Aloha, CW Nimitz." Both documents in Fletcher Papers.

21. Minutes of Pacific Conference [Cominch-Cincpac], 24–26 November 1944. For the General Board, see Albion, *Makers of Naval Policy 1798–1947*, 78–93; Furer, 107–8.

22. Reynolds, *Towers*, 494–95; Minutes of Pacific Conference [Cominch-Cincpac], 24–26 November 1944. Fitch's response is interesting because Calhoun was his roommate at Annapolis and had helped him with his studies. Calhoun, though, was not "one of the boys" and was disliked by Fitch and other members of the class of 1906 for his know-it-all personality. Conversation 24 January 2003 with John C. Fitch, Admiral Fitch's son.

23. Russell, *Project Hula*; Norpac Administrative History; Hayes, 682–84.

24. Norpac Administrative History; Hutchison, 185.

25. Norpac Administrative History. Folder: World War II—Japanese Surrender Aboard USS *Panamint*, Robert T. Hartmann Papers, box 21. Hartmann was Fletcher's public relations officer. United States Naval Emergency Occupation, Ominato Guard District Area, Commander North Pacific Force and Area Aboard The USS *Panamint* (AGC-13) (9 September 1945), copy courtesy of Ralph Wilhelm.

26. DSM citation in Citation File, NHC. Washington, D.C., *Evening Star* (29 November 1945), copy in Officer Biographical File, NHC. Letter Air Marshal Robert Leckie, RCAF, to Fletcher (23 January 1947), and citation of Companion of the Bath in Fletcher Papers.

27. Furer, 166; Reynolds, *Towers*, 533–34; letter Forrestal to Fletcher (13 February 1947), Fletcher Papers.

CONCLUSION. "AN EXCELLENT, SEA-GOING, FIGHTING NAVAL OFFICER"

1. Letter Nimitz to King (29 May 1942), Nimitz Papers.

2. Pratt, "Campaign in the Coral Sea," 361; Cant, *America's Navy in World War II*; Pratt, *The Navy's War*; transcript of Layton interview by Pineau and Costello (11 May 1983), Layton Papers; *Battle Stations!*; Karig and Purdon, *Battle Report Pacific War*.

3. Berry, 58; Henry I. Shaw Jr., *First Offensive*, 48; Griffith, 8–9, 138; Morison, *United States Naval Operations*, 5:182–83.

4. Memorandum, Maj. R. D. Heinl Jr., Officer-in-charge, Historical Section, to Brig. Gen. W. E. Riley (9 January 1948), Morison Office Files, box 18; Berry, 58.

5. Pfitzer, *Samuel Eliot Morison's Historical World*, 172–74, 242–43; Morison, *United States Naval Operations*, 1:vii.

6. Letter Murphy to Rear Adm. C. C. Hartman (7 September 1951). An unidentified senior officer in Opnav wrote in response to Murphy's criticisms: "This makes disturbing reading to me and shows that we need a more critical review of Morison's work in the future. His work should be factually correct at least with fewer 'smart aleck' observations of his own. Abstracts from this may be shown *when the statements are checked*," memo "To 29 from 02" (10 September 1951).

7. Letter Spruance to Bates (19 June 1946), Bates Papers, series I, box 8; letter Bates to Adm. R. C. Giffen (18 February 1947), Bates Papers, series I, box 1; letter Bates to McMorris (26 May 1948), Bates Papers, series I, box 2. Vice Adm. David C. Richardson, oral history, 103; Pfitzer, 242–43.

8. Pratt, *Fleet Against Japan*, 53; Richardson, oral history, 102–3.

9. Letter Bates to Adm. Jesse Oldendorf (15 April 1947), Bates Papers, series I, box 1; letter Fletcher to Spruance, undated (c. 1947), copy in Fletcher Papers; letter Fletcher to Morison (1 December 1947), Fletcher Papers; Letter Fletcher to Wellborn (22 August 1950), Fletcher Papers; letter Fletcher to Smith (12 August 1964), in Smith Papers; letter Dyer to Lundstrom (19 January 1977). Fletcher did help Thaddeus V. Tuleja, author of *Climax at Midway* (1960), and later Walter Lord and Gordon Prange.

10. Fleet Adm. C. W. Nimitz, Statement on Command at Midway (8 March 1946), in RG-38, Action Reports, box 37; message 202013 June 1942 Cincpac to Cominch, CSCMF, roll 16. Nimitz's comments on Griffith's *Battle of Guadalcanal* appear on the dust jacket.

11. Letter Smith to Buckmaster (23 April 1966), copy in Pederson Papers. Butcher, "Admiral Frank Jack Fletcher, Pioneer Warrior or Gross Sinner?"

12. Jones, *Campbell Brown's Civil War*, 212.

13. Hughes, *Fleet Tactics*, 93.

14. Ulysses S. Grant, *The Personal Memoirs of U. S. Grant,* 87.

15. Letter Murphy to Hartman (7 September 1951). Sun-tzu, *The Art of War*, 18.

16. Ewing, *Thach Weave*, 168–70. Thach was McCain's operations officer in 1944–45 in the fast carriers and spent time with Mitscher in mid 1944. It must be said if Thach praised McCain's receptivity to new ideas, they were mainly Thach's own ideas, although he had to prove his case to McCain. Letter Lt. Cdr. Richard Best to Lundstrom (15 May 2000).

17. Stephens, *The Fighting Admirals*, 14–15.

Bibliography

DOCUMENTS

The principal unpublished sources for this reassessment of Adm. Frank Jack Fletcher as a carrier commander are official U.S. naval documents and personal papers. Most are held by the National Archives in two locations. Archives I in downtown Washington, D.C., contains most U.S. naval records prior to 1942. Archives II at College Park, Maryland, has the action reports, war diaries, operation orders, and administrative files divided between Record Groups 38 (RG-38, Chief of Naval Operations) and 313 (RG-313, Flag Files). RG-457 comprises the radio intelligence materials released by the National Security Agency. The Operational Archives Branch of the Naval Historical Center in the Washington Navy Yard contains the invaluable Cincpac Greybook (War Plans, Cincpac Files, Captain Steele's "Running Estimate and Summary"), interviews, tactical publications, biographical files, selected Japanese documents, and also important personal papers cited below. Operational dispatches, perhaps the most important of the new sources examined for this study, unfortunately cannot be found in one location. RG-38 at Archives II has on microfilm the voluminous the Cincpac Secret and Confidential Message Files from 1940 to 1942. However, certain high level (so-called Aidac or Sealed Secret) dispatches must be sought in such places as in RG-38 Commander in Chief U.S. Fleet (Cominch) 00 File, the Cincpac Greybook, and in Commander, South Pacific Area's administrative correspondence in the Flag Files (RG-313) in Archives II.

PERSONAL PAPERS

Ashford, Rear Adm. William H., Joyner Library, East Carolina University.

Barnes, Dr. Harry Elmer, American Heritage Center, University of Wyoming–Laramie.

Bates, Rear Adm. Richard W., Naval War College.

Bauer, Lt. Col. Harold W., via the Nimitz Museum.

Brown, Vice Adm. Wilson, Nimitz Library, U.S. Naval Academy.

Crace, Adm. John G., RN, Imperial War Museum.

Douglas, Capt. Archibald H., Naval War College.

Duckworth, Vice Adm. H. S., via John Duckworth.

Dyer, Vice Adm. George C., Naval Historical Center and Library of Congress.

Fitch, Adm. Aubrey W., Hoover Institution, Stanford University, via John C. Fitch.

Fitz-Gerald, Rear Adm. Phillip H., USN (Ret.), via Kenneth Crawford.

Fletcher, Adm. Frank Jack, American Heritage Center, University of Wyoming–Laramie.

Frederickson, Harry A., via James C. Sawruk.

Ghormley, Vice Adm. Robert L., via Jeffrey Barlow.

Graybar, Dr. Lloyd J., Naval Historical Center.

Halsey, Fleet Adm. William F., Jr., Library of Congress and Virginia Historical Society.

Hartmann, Robert T., Gerald R. Ford Presidential Library.

Kimmel, Rear Adm. Husband E., American Heritage Center, University of Wyoming–Laramie.

King, Fleet Adm. Ernest J., Naval Historical Center, Naval War College, and Library of Congress.

Kinkaid, Adm. Thomas C., Naval Historical Center.

Layton, Rear Adm. Edwin T., Naval War College.

Maas, Maj. Gen. and Congressman Melvin J., Minnesota Historical Society.
MacArthur, General of the Army Douglas, MacArthur Memorial.
McCain, Vice Adm. John S., Hoover Institution, Stanford University.
Moan, Capt. Floyd E., via James C. Sawruk.
Morison, Rear Adm. Samuel Eliot, Naval Historical Center.
Nimitz, Fleet Adm. Chester W., Naval Historical Center.
Pederson, Rear Adm. Oscar, National Museum of Naval Aviation.
Potter, Elmer B., Naval Historical Center.
Prange, Gordon, via Robert J. Cressman.
Regan, Stephen D., via Dr. Regan.
Register, Lt. Francis R., via Brandon Wood.
Roosevelt, Franklin Delano, Franklin D. Roosevelt Library, Hyde Park.
Sherman, Adm. Frederick C., in Biographical File, Officer Bio Files, Naval Historical Center.
Sherman, Adm. Forrest P., Naval Historical Center.
Smith, Vice Adm. William Ward, via Col. William W. Smith Jr., U.S. Army (Ret.).
Spruance, Adm. Raymond A., Naval War College.
Stark, Adm. Harold R., Naval Historical Center.
Thomas, Gen. Gerald C., Marine Corps Historical Center.
Tuleja, Thaddeus V., via Dr. Tuleja.
Turner, Adm. Richmond Kelly, Naval Historical Center.

INTERVIEWS AND CORRESPONDENCE

Arnold, Rear Adm. Murr E., USN (Ret.), *Yorktown*.
Altemus, John P., VF-5 *Saratoga*.
Beaver, Floyd, Flag *Lexington*.
Bennett, Capt. Vane M., USN (Ret.), *Yorktown*.
Best, Lt. Cdr. Richard H., USN (Ret.), VB-6 *Enterprise*.
Biard, Capt. Forrest R., USN (Ret.), Flag *Yorktown*, Hypo.
Bond, Roger L., *Saratoga*.
Boo, Frank W., Flag *Yorktown*, *Saratoga*.
Caldwell, Vice Adm. Turner F., USN (Ret.), VS-5 *Yorktown*, *Enterprise*.
Clapp, George E., Flag *Yorktown*, *Saratoga*.
Duckworth, Vice Adm. H. S., USN (Ret.), *Lexington*.
Dyer, Vice Adm. George C., USN (Ret.), Bureau of Navigation, *Indianapolis*.
Fields, Lt. Col. Wallace, USAF (Ret.), 19th Bomb Group.
Fitch, John C., son of Adm. Aubrey W. Fitch.
Green, Capt. Frank O., USN (Ret.), VF-5 *Saratoga*.
Greenbacker, Capt. John E., USN (Ret.), *Yorktown*.
Grow, Rear Adm. Bradford E., USN (Ret.), Flag *Wasp*.

Hollis, Hollis C., Flag *Yorktown*, *Saratoga*.

Ishikawa, Shirō, IJNS *Shōhō*.

Kerr, Raymond W., Flag *Yorktown*, *Saratoga*.

Layton, Rear Adm. Edwin T., USN (Ret.), Cincpac.

Leonard, Rear Adm. William N., USN (Ret.), VF-42 *Yorktown*.

Loxton, Commo. Bruce, RAN (Ret.) *HMAS Canberra*.

Newsome, Thomas I., Flag *Yorktown*, *Saratoga*.

Pederson, Rear Adm. Oscar, USN (Ret.), VF-42 *Yorktown*, Flag *Saratoga*.

Richardson, Vice Adm. David C., USN (Ret.), VF-5 *Saratoga*.

Schindler, Vice Adm. Walter G., USN (Ret.), Flag *Yorktown*, *Saratoga*.

Showers, Rear Adm. Donald M., USN (Ret.), Hypo.

Smith, Capt. Joseph G., USN (Ret.), VS-2 *Lexington*.

Smith, Col. W. W., Jr., U.S. Army, son of Vice Adm. William W. Smith, USN.

Ulmer, Norman W., Flag *Yorktown*, *Saratoga*.

Vejtasa, Capt. Stanley W., USN (Ret.), VS-5 *Yorktown*.

Weschler, Vice Adm. Thomas R., USN (Ret.), *Wasp*.

Wilhelm, Ralph V., *Portland*.

ORAL HISTORIES

Biard, Capt. Forrest R., U.S. Naval Institute.

Bond, Roger L., U.S. Naval Institute.

Carmichael, Kenneth E., Naval Security Group, National Archives, RG-457.

Dyer, Vice Adm. George C., U.S. Naval Institute.

Edwards, Capt. Frederick A., U.S. Naval Institute.

Felt, Adm. Harry Donald, U.S. Naval Institute.

Layton, Rear Adm. Edwin T., U.S. Naval Institute.

Loughlin, Rear Adm. Charles E., U.S. Naval Institute.

McCrea, Vice Adm. John L., U.S. Naval Institute.

Pollard, Lt. Joseph P., Medical Corps, Naval Historical Center.

Richardson, Vice Adm. David C., U.S. Naval Institute.

Rundle, Raymond A., Naval Security Group, National Archives, RG-457.

Stroop, Vice Adm. Paul D., U.S. Naval Institute.

Thach, Adm. John S., U.S. Naval Institute.

Train, Rear Adm. Harold C., Columbia University.

Weschler, Vice Adm. Thomas R., U.S. Naval Institute.

PUBLISHED SOURCES

Abercrombie, Capt. Laurence A., and Fletcher Pratt. *My Life to the Destroyers*. New York: Henry Holt, 1944.

Agawa, Hiroyuki. *The Reluctant Admiral: Yamamoto and the Imperial Navy*. Tokyo: Kodansha, 1979.

Albion, Robert Greenhalgh. *Makers of Naval Policy 1798–1947.* Annapolis, Md.: Naval Institute Press, 1980.

Ashworth, Norman. *How Not To Run An Air Force! The Higher Command of the Royal Australian Air Force During the Second World War.* 2 vols. Fairbairn, Australia: Air Power Studies Centre, 2000.

Barde, Robert E. *The Battle of Midway: A Study In Command.* Ann Arbor, Mich.: University Microfilms, 1972.

Barker, Chris A. *Teakwood Decks* [USS *Colorado*]. Independence, Mo.: privately printed, 1985.

Bartsch, William H. *December 8, 1941: MacArthur's Pearl Harbor.* College Station: Texas A&M University Press, 2003.

———. "Operation Dovetail: Bungled Guadalcanal Rehearsal, July 1942." *Journal of Military History* (April 2002): 443–76.

Bath, Alan Harris. *Tracking the Axis Enemy: The Triumph of Anglo-American Naval Intelligence.* Lawrence: University Press of Kansas, 1998.

Battle Stations! Your Navy in Action. New York: W. H. Wise & Co., Inc., 1946.

Beach, Capt. Edward L. *Salt and Steel: Reflections of a Submariner.* Annapolis, Md.: Naval Institute Press, 1999.

Beatty, Vice Adm. Frank. "The Background of the Secret Report." *National Review* (December 13, 1966): 1261–72.

Beaver, Floyd. *Chief . . . One Sailor's Personal History of World War II 1939–1945.* Mill Valley, Calif.: privately printed, n.d.

Bell, Capt. Frederick J. *Condition Red: Destroyer Action in the South Pacific.* New York: Longmans, Green, 1944.

Belote, James H., and William M. Belote. *Titans of the Seas.* New York: Harper and Row, 1975.

Benson, Robert Louis. *A History of U.S. Communications Intelligence during World War II: Policy and Administration.* Fort Meade, Md.: National Security Agency, 1997.

Berry, Henry. *Semper Fi, Mac: Living Memories of the U.S. Marines in World War II.* New York: Arbor House, 1982.

Biard, Capt. Forrest R. "The Pacific War Through the Eyes of Forrest R. 'Tex' Biard." *Cryptolog* (Winter 1989): 2–27.

Bland, Larry I., ed. *The Papers of George Catlett Marshall.* Vol. 2, *"We Cannot Delay" July 1, 1939–December 6, 1941.* Baltimore: Johns Hopkins University Press, 1986.

Boyd, Carl, and Akihiko Yoshida. *The Japanese Submarine Force and World War II.* Annapolis, Md.: Naval Institute Press, 1995.

Bradford, James C. *Quarterdeck and Bridge: Two Centuries of American Naval Leaders.* Annapolis, Md.: Naval Institute Press, 1997.

Brodhurst, Robin. *Churchill's Anchor: The Biography of Admiral of the Fleet Sir Dudley Pound OM, GCB, GCVO.* Barnsley, South Yorkshire: Leo Cooper, 2000.

Brown, Vice Adm. Wilson. "Aide to Four Presidents." *American Heritage* (February 1955): 66–96.

Brownlow, Donald Grey. *The Accused: The Ordeal of Rear Admiral Husband Edward Kimmel, U.S.N.* New York: Vantage, 1968.

Budiansky, Stephen. *Battle of Wits: The Complete Story of Codebreaking in World War II.* New York: Free Press, 2000.

———. "Too Late For Pearl Harbor." U.S. Naval Institute *Proceedings* (December 1999): 47–51.

Buell, Dr. Harold L. "Death of a Captain." U.S. Naval Institute *Proceedings* (February 1986): 92–96.

Buell, Thomas B. *Master of Sea Power: A Biography of Fleet Admiral Ernest J. King.* Boston: Little, Brown, 1980.

———. *The Quiet Warrior: A Biography of Admiral Raymond A. Spruance.* Boston: Little, Brown, 1974. Reprint, Annapolis, Md.: Naval Institute Press, 1987.

Buranelli, Prosper. *Maggie of the Suicide Fleet: As Written from the Log of Raymond D. Borden Lt. U.S.N.R.* Garden City, N.Y.: Doubleday, Doran, 1930.

Butcher, Lt. Cdr. M. E. "Admiral Frank Jack Fletcher, Pioneer Warrior or Gross Sinner?" *Naval War College Review* (Winter 1987): 69–79.

Calhoun, C. Raymond. *Tin Can Sailor: Life Aboard the USS Sterett, 1939–1945.* Annapolis, Md.: Naval Institute Press, 1993.

Campbell, John. *Naval Weapons of World War Two.* London: Conway, 1985.

Cant, Gilbert. *America's Navy in World War II.* New York: John Day, 1943.

Carter, Rear Adm. Worrall Reed. *Beans, Bullets and Black Oil: The Story of Fleet Logistics Afloat in the Pacific during World War II.* Washington, D.C.: GPO, 1952.

Chambers, John Whiteclay, II. *The Oxford Companion to American Military History.* New York: Oxford University Press, 1999.

Churchill, Winston S. *The Second World War: The Grand Alliance.* Boston: Houghton Mifflin, 1951.

Clark, Adm. J. J. "Jocko," with Clark G. Reynolds. *Carrier Admiral.* New York: David McKay, 1967.

Clemens, Martin. *Alone on Guadalcanal: A Coastwatcher's Story.* Annapolis, Md.: Naval Institute Press, 1998.

Coletta, Paolo E. *Admiral Marc A. Mitscher and U.S. Naval Aviation: Bald Eagle.* Lewiston, N.Y.: Edwin Mellen, 1997.

———. *American Secretaries of the Navy, 1775–1972.* 2 vols. Annapolis, Md.: Naval Institute Press, 1980.

———. *Patrick N. L. Bellinger and U.S. Naval Aviation.* Lanham, Md.: University Press of America, 1987.

———, ed. *United States Navy and Marine Corps Bases, Overseas.* Westport, Conn.: Greenwood, 1985.

Coulthard-Clark, Chris. *Action Stations Coral Sea: The Australian Commander's Story.* North Sydney: Allen and Unwin, 1991.

Craven, W. F., and J. L. Cate. *The Army Air Forces in World War II.* Vol. 1, *Plans and Early Operations (January 1939 to August 1942).* Chicago: University of Chicago Press, 1948.

———. *The Army Air Forces in World War II.* Vol. 4, *The Pacific: Guadalcanal to Saipan (August 1942–July 1944).* Chicago: University of Chicago Press, 1950.

Cressman, Robert J. *"A Magnificent Fight": The Battle of Wake Island.* Annapolis, Md.: Naval Institute Press, 1995.

———. *That Gallant Ship: U.S.S. Yorktown [CV-5].* Missoula, Mont.: Pictorial Histories, 2000.

Cressman, Robert J., Steve Ewing, Barrett Tillman, Mark Horan, Clark Reynolds, and Stan Cohen. *"A Glorious Page in Our History": The Battle of Midway 4–6 June 1942.* Missoula, Mont.: Pictorial Histories, 1990.

Cunningham, W. Scott, with Lydel Sims. *Wake Island Command.* Boston: Little, Brown, 1961.

Custer, Joe James. *Through the Perilous Night: The Astoria's Last Battle.* New York: Macmillan, 1944.

Dorris, Lt. Donald Hugh. *A Log of the Vincennes.* Louisville, Ky.: Standard Printing, 1947.

Dulin, Robert O., Jr., William H. Garzke Jr., Charles Haberlein Jr., Robert Egan, Dr. David Mindell, and William Jurens. *The Loss of the USS Yorktown (CV-5): A Marine Forensic Analysis.* N.p.: Society of Naval Architects and Marine Engineers, 1999.

Dull, Paul S. *A Battle History of the Imperial Japanese Navy (1941–1945).* Annapolis, Md.: Naval Institute Press, 1978.

Duncan, Francis. *Rickover: The Struggle for Excellence.* Annapolis, Md.: Naval Institute Press, 2001.

Dyer, Vice Adm. George C. *The Amphibians Came To Conquer: The Story of Admiral Richmond Kelly Turner.* 2 vols. Washington, D.C.: GPO, 1971.

Evans, David C., ed. *The Japanese Navy in World War II*. Annapolis, Md.: Naval Institute Press, 1986.

Evans, David C., and Mark R. Peattie. *Kaigun: Strategy, Tactics, and Technology in the Imperial Japanese Navy 1887–1941*. Annapolis, Md.: Naval Institute Press, 1997.

Ewing, Steve. *Thach Weave: The Life of Jimmie Thach*. Annapolis, Md.: Naval Institute Press, 2004.

Feldt, Eric. *The Coast Watchers*. Melbourne: Oxford University Press, 1946.

Forrestel, Vice Adm., E. P. *Admiral Raymond A. Spruance, USN: A Study in Command*. Washington, D.C.: Naval History Division, Department of the Navy, 1966.

Frank, Pat, and Joseph D. Harrington. *Rendezvous at Midway: USS Yorktown and the Japanese Carrier Fleet*. New York: John Day, 1967.

Frank, Richard B. *Guadalcanal*. New York: Random House, 1990.

Friedman, Norman. *U.S. Battleships: An Illustrated Design History*. Annapolis, Md.: Naval Institute Press, 1985.

———. *U.S. Carriers: An Illustrated Design History*. Annapolis, Md.: Naval Institute Press, 1983.

———. *U.S. Cruisers: An Illustrated Design History*. Annapolis, Md.: Naval Institute Press, 1984.

———. *U.S. Destroyers: An Illustrated Design History*. Annapolis, Md.: Naval Institute Press, 1982.

Fuchida, Mitsuo, and Masatake Okumiya. *Midway: The Battle That Doomed Japan*. Annapolis, Md.: Naval Institute Press, 1955.

Fuquea, David C. "Task Force One: The Wasted Assets of the United States Pacific Battleship Fleet, 1942." *Journal of Military History* (October 1997): 707–34.

Furer, Rear Adm. Julius Augustus. *Administration of the Navy Department in World War II*. Washington, D.C.: Naval History Division, Department of the Navy, 1959.

Gannon, Michael. *Pearl Harbor Betrayed*. New York: Henry Holt, 2001.

Gatacre, Rear Adm. G. G. O. *Reports of Proceedings*. Manly, NSW: Nautical, 1982.

Gay, George. *Sole Survivor*. Naples, Fla.: privately printed, 1979.

Gill, G. Hermon. *Royal Australian Navy*. 2 vols. Canberra: Australian War Memorial, 1957, 1968.

Gillison, Douglas. *Royal Australian Air Force 1939–1942*. Canberra: Australian War Memorial, 1962.

Glover, Adm. Cato D. *Command Performance With Guts*. New York: Greenwich, 1969.

Gluck, Jay, ed. *Ukiyo: Stories of the "Floating World" of Postwar Japan*. New York: Universal Library, 1964.

Goldstein, Donald M., and Katherine V. Dillon. *The Pearl Harbor Papers: Inside the Japanese Plans*. Washington, D.C.: Brassey's, 1993.

Grant, Ulysses S. *The Personal Memoirs of U. S. Grant*. New York: Viking Penguin, 1999.

Graybar, Lloyd J. "American Pacific Strategy after Pearl Harbor: The Relief of Wake Island." *Prologue* (Fall 1980): 134–50.

Great Britain. Ministry of Defence. Naval Historical Branch. *War With Japan*. 6 vols., 4 parts. London: HMSO, 1995.

Great Britain. Naval Intelligence Division. Geographical Handbook. *Pacific Islands*. 4 vols. London: HMSO, 1943–45.

Griffith, Brig. Gen. Samuel B., II. *The Battle for Guadalcanal*. Philadelphia: J. P. Lippincott, 1963.

Grossnick, Roy A. *U.S. Naval Aviation 1910–1995*. Washington, D.C.: Naval Historical Center, 1997.

Gwyer, J. M. A., and J. R. M. Butler. *Grand Strategy*. Vol. 3, June 1941–August 1942. 2 parts. London: HMSO, 1964.

Hailey, Foster. *Pacific Battle Line*. New York: Macmillan, 1944.

Halsey, Fleet Adm. William F., and Lt. Cdr. J. Bryan III. *Admiral Halsey's Story*. New York: Whittlesey House, McGraw-Hill, 1947.

Hara, Capt. Tameichi. *Japanese Destroyer Captain.* New York: Ballantine Books, 1961.

Harrington, Daniel F. "A Careless Hope: American Air Power and Japan, 1941." *Pacific Historical Review* (1979): 217–38.

Hata, Ikuhiko, and Yasuho Izawa. *Japanese Naval Aces and Fighter Units in World War II.* Annapolis, Md.: Naval Institute Press, 1989.

Hayes, Grace Person. *The History of the Joint Chiefs of Staff in World War II: The War Against Japan.* Annapolis, Md.: Naval Institute Press, 1982.

Heinl, Lt. Col. Robert D., Jr. *The Defense of Wake.* Washington, D.C.: Historical Section, U.S. Marine Corps, 1947.

———. "'We're Headed for Wake.'" *Marine Corps Gazette* (June 1946): 35–38.

Holbrook, Heber A. *The History and Times of the U.S.S. Portland.* Dixon, Calif.: Pacific Ship and Shore, 1990.

Holmes, W. J. *Double-Edged Secrets: U.S. Naval Intelligence Operations in the Pacific during World War II.* Annapolis, Md.: Naval Institute Press, 1979.

Hone, Thomas C., Norman Friedman, and Mark D. Mandeles. *American and British Aircraft Carrier Development 1919–1941.* Annapolis, Md.: Naval Institute Press, 1999.

Hone, Trent. "The Evolution of Fleet Tactical Doctrine in the U.S. Navy, 1922–1941." *Journal of Military History* (October 2003): 1107–49.

Hopkins, Capt. Harold. *Nice to Have You Aboard.* London: George Allen and Unwin, 1964.

Hough, Lt. Col. Frank O., Maj. Verle E. Ludwig, and Henry I. Shaw, Jr. *History of U.S. Marine Corps Operations in World War II.* Vol. 1, *Pearl Harbor to Guadalcanal.* Washington, D.C.: GPO, 1958.

Hoyt, Edwin P. *How They Won the War in the Pacific: Nimitz and His Admirals.* New York: Weybright and Talley, 1970.

Hughes, Capt. Wayne P., Jr. *Fleet Tactics: Theory and Practice.* Annapolis, Md.: Naval Institute Press, 1986.

Hutchison, Kevin Don. *World War II in the North Pacific: Chronology and Fact Book.* Westport, Conn.; Greenwood, 1994.

Isely, Jeter A., and Philip A. Crowl. *The U.S. Marines and Amphibious War.* Princeton, N.J.: Princeton University Press, 1951.

Isom, Dallas Woodbury. "The Battle of Midway: Why the Japanese Lost." *Naval War College Review* (Summer 2000): 60–100.

Japan. Self Defense Force. War History Office. *Senshi Sōsho.* Vol. 38, *Chūbu Taiheiyo Hōmen Kaigun Sakusen,* part 1 (Central Pacific Naval Operations to May 1942). Tokyo: Asagumo Shimbunsha, 1970.

———. *Senshi Sōsho.* Vol. 43, *Middowē Kaisen.* Tokyo: Asagumo Shimbunsha, 1971.

———. *Senshi Sōsho.* Vol. 49, *Nantohomen Kaigun Sakusen, 1 Gato Dakkai Sakusen Kaishimade* (Southeast Area Naval Operations, 1, To the Beginning of Operations to Recapture Guadalcanal). Tokyo: Asagumo Shimbunsha, 1971.

———. *Senshi Sōsho.* Vol. 83, *Nantohomen Kaigun Sakusen, 2 Gato Tesshumade* (Southeast Area Naval Operations, 2, To the Withdrawal from Guadalcanal). Tokyo: Asagumo Shimbunsha, 1975.

Jentschura, Hansgeorg et al. *Warships of the Imperial Japanses Navy 1869–1945.* London: Arms and Armour Press, 1977.

Johnston, Stanley. *Queen of the Flat-Tops: The U.S.S. Lexington and the Coral Sea Battle.* New York: E. P. Dutton, 1942.

Jones, Terry L., ed. *Campbell Brown's Civil War: With Ewell and the Army of Northern Virginia.* Baton Rouge: Louisiana State University Press, 2001.

Karig, Capt. Walter, and Cdr. Eric Purdon. *Battle Report Pacific War: Middle Phase*. New York: Rinehart, 1947.

Kennedy, David M. *Freedom from Fear: The American People in Depression and War, 1929–1945*. New York: Oxford University Press, 1999.

Kenney, George C. *General Kenney Reports*. New York: Duell, Sloan, and Pearce, 1949.

Key, David M., Jr. *Admiral Jerauld Wright: Warrior Among Diplomats*. Manhattan, Kans.: Sunflower University Press, 2001.

Kimball, Warren F., ed. *Churchill and Roosevelt: The Complete Correspondence*. 3 vols. Princeton: Princeton University Press, 1984.

Kimmel, Rear Adm. Husband E. *Admiral Kimmel's Story*. Chicago: Henry Regnery, 1955.

King, Fleet Adm. Ernest J., and Cdr. Walter Muir Whitehill. *Fleet Admiral King: A Naval Record*. New York: W. W. Norton, 1952.

Lacroix, Eric, and Linton Wells, II. *Japanese Cruisers of the Pacific War*. Annapolis, Md.: Naval Institute Press, 1997.

Lamar, H. Arthur. *I Saw Stars*. Fredericksburg, Tex.: Admiral Nimitz Foundation, 1985.

Larkins, William. *U.S. Naval Aircraft 1921–1941*. New York: Orion Books, 1988.

Layton, Rear Adm. Edwin T. "America Deciphered Our Code." U.S. Naval Institute *Proceedings* (June 1979): 98–99.

———. "24 *Sentai*—Japan's Commerce Raiders." U.S. Naval Institute *Proceedings* (June 1976): 53–61.

Layton, Rear Adm. Edwin T., with Capt. Roger Pineau, and John Costello. *"And I Was There": Pearl Harbor and Midway—Breaking the Secrets*. New York: William Morrow, 1985.

Leahy, Fleet Adm. William D. *I Was There*. New York: Whittlesey House, 1950.

Lee, Clark. *They Call It Pacific*. New York: Viking, 1943.

Leutze, James. *A Different Kind of Victory: A Biography of Admiral Thomas C. Hart*. Annapolis, Md.: Naval Institute Press, 1981.

Linzey, Capt. Stanford E. *God Was at Midway*. San Diego: Black Forrest, 1999.

Lord, Walter. *Incredible Victory*. New York: Harper and Row, 1967.

Love, Robert William, Jr., ed. *The Chiefs of Naval Operations*. Annapolis, Md.: Naval Institute Press, 1980.

Loxton, Bruce, with Chris Coulthard-Clark. *The Shame of Savo: Anatomy of a Naval Disaster*. Annapolis, Md.: Naval Institute Press, 1994.

Ludlum, Stuart D. *They Turned the War Around at Coral Sea and Midway: Going to War with Yorktown's Air Group Five*. Bennington, Vt.: Merriam, 1997.

Lundstrom, John B. "A Failure of Radio Intelligence: An Episode in the Battle of the Coral Sea." *Cryptologia* (April 1983): 97–118.

———. *The First South Pacific Campaign: Pacific Fleet Strategy December 1941–June 1942*. Annapolis, Md.: Naval Institute Press, 1976.

———. *The First Team: Pacific Air Combat from Pearl Harbor to Midway*. Annapolis, Md.: Naval Institute Press, 1990.

———. *The First Team and the Guadalcanal Campaign: Naval Fighter Combat from August to November 1942*. Annapolis, Md.: Naval Institute Press, 1994.

———. "Frank Jack Fletcher Got a Bum Rap." Pts. 1 and 2. *Naval History* (Summer 1992): 21–27; (Fall 1992): 22–28.

MacDonald, Scot. *Evolution of the Aircraft Carrier*. Washington, D.C.: Office of the Chief of Naval Operations, 1964.

Macintyre, Capt. Donald. *Fighting Admiral: The Life of Admiral of the Fleet Sir James Somerville, G.C.B., G.B.E., D.S.O.* London: Evans Brothers, 1961.

Mahnken, Thomas C. *Uncovering Ways of War: U.S. Intelligence and Foreign Military Innovation, 1918–1941.* Ithaca, N.Y.: Cornell University Press, 2002.

Manchester, William. *Goodbye, Darkness: A Memoir of the Pacific War.* Boston: Little, Brown, 1980.

Marder, Arthur J. *Old Friends, New Enemies: The Royal Navy and the Imperial Japanese Navy, Strategic Delusions 1936–1941.* Oxford: Oxford University Press, 1981.

Marder, Arthur J., Mark Jacobsen, and John Horsfield. *Old Friends, New Enemies: The Royal Navy and the Imperial Japanese Navy, The Pacific War 1942–1945.* Oxford: Oxford University Press, 1990.

Mason, John T., Jr. *The Pacific War Remembered: An Oral History Collection.* Annapolis, Md.: Naval Institute Press, 1986.

McCain, John. *Faith of My Fathers.* New York: Random House, 1999.

Mears, Lt. Frederick. *Carrier Combat.* New York: Doubleday, Doran, 1944.

Merillat, Capt. Herbert L. *The Island: A History of the Marines on Guadalcanal.* Boston: Houghton Mifflin, 1944.

Merillat, Herbert Christian. *Guadalcanal Remembered.* New York: Dodd, Mead, 1982.

Miller, Edward S. *War Plan Orange: The U.S. Strategy to Defeat Japan, 1897–1945.* Annapolis, Md.: Naval Institute Press, 1991.

Miller, John, Jr. *Guadalcanal: The First Offensive.* Washington, D.C.: GPO, 1949.

Miller, Nathan. *War At Sea: A Naval History of World War II.* New York: Scribner, 1995.

Miller, Thomas G., Jr. *The Cactus Air Force.* New York: Harper and Row, 1969.

Millett, Allan R. *In Many a Strife: General Gerald C. Thomas and the U.S. Marine Corps 1917–1956.* Annapolis, Md.: Naval Institute Press, 1993.

Mitchell, John H. *On Wings We Conquer.* Springfield, Mo.: G. E. M., 1990.

Morison, Rear Adm. Samuel Eliot. *History of United States Naval Operations in World War II.* Vol. 1, *The Battle of the Atlantic September 1939–May 1943.* Boston: Little, Brown, 1947.

———. *History of United States Naval Operations in World War II.* Vol. 3, *The Rising Sun in the Pacific.* Boston: Little, Brown, 1948.

———. *History of United States Naval Operations in World War II.* Vol. 4, *Coral Sea, Midway and Submarine Actions May 1942–August 1942.* Boston: Little, Brown, 1949.

———. *History of United States Naval Operations in World War II.* Vol. 5, *The Struggle for Guadalcanal August 1942–February 1943.* Boston: Little, Brown, 1949.

———. *History of United States Naval Operations in World War II.* Vol. 7, *Aleutians, Gilberts and Marshalls June 1942–April 1944.* Boston: Little, Brown, 1951.

———. *Two-Ocean War: A Short History of the United States Navy in the Second World War.* Boston: Little, Brown, 1963.

Morton, Louis. *Strategy and Command: The First Two Years.* Washington, D.C.: GPO, 1962.

Murray, Williamson, and Allen R. Millett. *A War to be Won: Fighting the Second World War.* Cambridge, Mass.: Harvard University Press, 2000.

Newcomb, Richard F. *Savo: The Incredible Naval Debacle off Guadalcanal.* New York: Holt, Rinehart and Winston, 1961.

Orita, Zenji. *I-Boat Captain.* Canoga Park, Calif.: Major Books, 1976.

Parker, Frederick D. *A Priceless Advantage: U.S. Navy Communications Intelligence and the Battles of Coral Sea, Midway, and the Aleutians.* Fort Meade, Md.: National Security Agency, 1993.

Parshall, Jonathan, David D. Dickson, and Anthony Tully. "Doctrine Matters: Why the Japanese Lost at Midway." *Naval War College Review* (Summer 2001): 139–51.

Parshall, Jonathan, and Anthony Tully. *Shattered Sword: The Untold Story of the Battle of Midway*. Dulles, Va.: Potomac Books, 2005.

Peattie, Mark R. *Sunburst: The Rise of Japanese Naval Air Power, 1909–1941*. Annapolis, Md.: Naval Institute Press, 2001.

Pfitzer, Gregory M. *Samuel Eliot Morison's Historical World*. Boston: Northeastern University Press, 1991.

Potter, E. B. *Bull Halsey*. Annapolis, Md.: Naval Institute Press, 1985.

———. *Nimitz*. Annapolis, Md.: Naval Institute Press, 1976.

Potter, E. B., and Chester W. Nimitz. *The Great Sea War: The Story of Naval Action in World War II*. New York: Bramhall House, 1960.

Prados, John. *Combined Fleet Decoded: The Secret History of American Intelligence and the Japanese Navy in World War II*. New York: Random House, 1995.

Prange, Gordon W. *At Dawn We Slept: The Untold Story of Pearl Harbor*. New York: McGraw-Hill, 1981.

———. *Miracle at Midway* New York: McGraw-Hill, 1982.

Pratt, Fletcher. "Campaign in the Coral Sea." *Harper's Magazine* (March 1943): 356–68.

———. *Fleet Against Japan*. New York: Harper and Brothers, 1946.

———. "The Knockout at Midway." *Harper's Magazine* (August 1943): 246–53.

———. *The Marine's War*. New York: William Sloane Associates, 1948.

———. "The Mysteries of Midway." *Harper's Magazine* (July 1943): 133–45.

———. *The Navy's War*. New York: Harper and Brothers, 1944.

Regan, Stephen D. *In Bitter Tempest: The Biography of Admiral Frank Jack Fletcher*. Ames: Iowa State University Press, 1994.

Reynolds, Clark G. *Admiral John H. Towers: The Struggle for Naval Air Supremacy*. Annapolis, Md.: Naval Institute Press, 1991.

———. *Famous American Admirals*. New York: Van Nostrand Reinhold, 1978.

———. *The Fast Carriers: The Forging of an Air Navy*. New York: McGraw-Hill, 1968.

———. "U.S. Carriers and the Fleet-in-Being Strategy of 1942." In *The Battle of the Coral Sea 1942, Conference Proceedings 1992*, edited by the Australian National Maritime Museum, 54–64. Sydney: Australian National Maritime Museum, 1993. Also published as "The U.S. Fleet-in-Being Strategy of 1942." *Journal of Military History* (January 1994): 103–19.

Richardson, James O., and George C. Dyer. *On the Treadmill to Pearl Harbor: The Memoirs of Admiral J. O. Richardson*. Washington, D.C.: Naval History Division, Department of the Navy, 1973.

Robinson, Douglas H., and Charles L. Keller. *"Up Ship!" U.S. Navy Rigid Airships 1919–1935*. Annapolis, Md.: Naval Institute Press, 1982.

Russell, Richard A. *Project Hula: Secret Soviet-American Cooperation in the War Against Japan*. Washington, D.C.: Naval Historical Center, 1997.

Sawachi, Hisae. *Middowē Kaisen Kitoku*. Tokyo: Bungei; Shunjū 1986.

Schom, Alan. *The Eagle and the Rising Sun: The Japanese-American War 1941–1943*. New York: W. W. Norton, 2004.

Shaw, Henry I., Jr. *First Offensive: The Marine Campaign for Guadalcanal*. Washington, D.C.: Marine Corps Historical Center, 1992.

Shaw, Norman W. *Screened Her Going Down*. Albany, N.Y.: Fort Orange, 1984.

Sherman, Adm. Frederick C. *Combat Command: The American Aircraft Carriers in the Pacific War*. New York: E. P. Dutton, 1950.

Sherrod, Robert. *History of Marine Corps Aviation in World War II*. Washington, D.C.: Combat Forces, 1952.

Shōkaku-kei Kūbō. Gakken Pacific War Series. Tokyo: Gakushu Kenkyusha, 1997.

Simpson, B. Mitchell, III. *Admiral Harold R. Stark: Architect of Victory 1939–1945*. Columbia: University of South Carolina Press, 1989.

Slonim, Capt. Gilven M. "A Flagship View of Command Decisions." U.S. Naval Institute *Proceedings* (April 1958): 80–89.

Smith, Michael. *The Emperor's Codes: Bletchley Park and the Breaking of Japan's Secret Ciphers*. London: Bantam, 2000.

Smith, Richard K. *First Across! The U.S. Navy's Transatlantic Flight of 1919*. Annapolis, Md.: Naval Institute Press, 1973.

Smith, William Ward. *Midway: Turning Point of the Pacific*. New York: Thomas Y. Crowell, 1966.

Spector, Ronald H. *Listening to the Enemy: Key Documents on the Role of Communications Intelligence in the War with Japan*. Wilmington, Del.: Scholarly Resources, 1988.

Stahl, Cdr. Robert B. "Back to Savo Island—Fifty Years Later." *Shipmate* (July–August 1992): 19–22.

Standard Oil Company. *Ships of the Esso Fleet in World War II*. [New York]: Standard Oil Company (New Jersey), 1946.

Stephens, Martin. *The Fighting Admirals. British Admirals of the Second World War.* Annapolis, MD: Naval Institute Press, 1991.

Stern, Robert C. *The Lexington Class Carriers*. Annapolis, Md.: Naval Institute Press, 1993.

Stillwell, Paul, ed. *Air Raid: Pearl Harbor!: Recollections of a Day of Infamy*. Annapolis, Md.: Naval Institute Press, 1981.

Straczek, J. H. *Royal Australian Navy: Ships, Aircraft and Shore Establishments*. Sydney: Naval Public Affairs, 1996.

Strange, Rear Adm. Hubert Ellis. *A Full Life: An Autobiography*. Hyattsville, Md.: privately printed, 1980.

Stringer, Harry R. *The Navy Book of Distinguished Service*. Washington, D.C.: Fassett, 1921.

Sun-tzu. *The Art of War*. Translated by John Minford. New York: Viking, 2002.

Sweetman, Jack. *The Landing at Veracruz: 1914*. Annapolis, Md.: Naval Institute Press, 1968.

Tanabe, Yahachi. "I Sank the *Yorktown*," U.S. Naval Institute *Proceedings* (May 1963): 59–65.

Taylor, Theodore. *The Magnificent Mitscher*. Annapolis, Md.: Naval Institute Press, 1991.

Trimble, William F. *Admiral William A. Moffett: Architect of Naval Aviation*. Washington, D.C.: Smithsonian Institution Press, 1994.

Tuleja, Thaddeus V. *Climax at Midway*. New York: W. W. Norton, 1960.

Turnbull, Archibald D., and Clifford L. Lord. *History of United States Naval Aviation*. New Haven, Conn.: Yale University Press, 1949.

Twining, Gen. Merrill B. *No Bended Knee*. Novato, Calif.: Presidio, 1996.

Ugaki, Matome. *Fading Victory: The Diary of Admiral Matome Ugaki 1941–1945*. Pittsburgh: University of Pittsburgh Press, 1991.

Underwood, Jeffery S. *The Wings of Democracy: The Influence of Air Power on the Roosevelt Administration, 1933–1941*. College Station: Texas A&M University Press, 1991.

U.S. Congress. *Pearl Harbor Attack: Hearings before the Joint Committee on the Investigation of the Pearl Harbor Attack*. 79th Congress, 1st Session. 38 parts. Washington, D.C.: GPO, 1946.

U.S. Naval War College (Capt. Richard W. Bates). *The Battle of the Coral Sea May 1 to May 11 Inclusive, 1942: Strategical and Tactical Analysis.* Newport, R.I.: Naval War College, 1947.

——— (Commo. Richard W. Bates). *The Battle of Midway Including the Aleutian Phase June 3 to June 14, 1942: Strategical and Tactical Analysis.* Newport, R.I.: Naval War College, 1948.

——— (Commo. Richard W. Bates and Cdr. Walter D. Innis). *The Battle of Savo Island August 9, 1942: Strategical and Tactical Analysis.* Newport, R.I.: Naval War College, 1950.

U.S. Navy. *Building the Navy's Bases in World War II.* 2 vols. Washington, D.C.: GPO, 1947.

U.S. Navy. Bureau of Navigation. *Navy Directory of the U.S. Navy and U.S. Marine Corps Officers.* Washington, D.C.: GPO, 1920–1942.

U.S. Navy. Bureau of Navigation/Bureau of Naval Personnel. *Register of Commissioned and Warrant Officers of the U.S. Navy and Marine Corps.* Washington, D.C.: GPO, 1906–1947.

Urwin, Gregory J. W. *Facing Fearful Odds: The Siege of Wake Island.* Lincoln: University of Nebraska Press, 1997.

Van Deurs, Rear Adm. George. *Wings for the Fleet.* Annapolis, Md.: Naval Institute Press, 1966.

Vandegrift, A. A., as told to Robert B. Asprey. *Once a Marine.* New York: W. W. Norton, 1964.

Warner, Denis, and Peggy Warner, with Sadao Seno. *Disaster in the Pacific: New Light on the Battle of Savo Island.* Annapolis, Md.: Naval Institute Press, 1992.

Wheeler, Gerald E. *Kinkaid of the Seventh Fleet: A Biography of Admiral Thomas C. Kinkaid, U.S. Navy.* Washington, D.C.: Naval Historical Center, 1995.

Wickland, John J., Jr. *All the Queen's Men* [USS *New Mexico*]. N.p.: Goretske Enterprises, 1992.

Wildenberg, Thomas. *All The Factors of Victory: Adm. Joseph Mason Reeves and the Origins of Carrier Air Power.* Washington, D.C.: Brassey's, 2003.

———. *Destined for Glory: Dive Bombing, Midway, and the Evolution of Carrier Air Power.* Annapolis, Md.: Naval Institute Press, 1998.

———. *Gray Steel and Black Oil: Fast Tankers and Replenishment at Sea in the U.S. Navy, 1912–1992.* Annapolis, Md.: Naval Institute Press, 1996.

Wiley, Adm. Henry A. *An Admiral from Texas.* Garden City, N.Y.: Doubleday, Doran, 1934.

Willis, Ron L., and Thomas Carmichael. *United States Navy Wings of Gold from 1917 to the Present.* Atglen, Pa.: Schiffer Military History, 1995.

Willmott, H. P. *The Barrier and the Javelin: Japanese and Allied Pacific Strategies February to June 1942.* Annapolis, Md.: Naval Institute Press, 1983.

Wilson, Eugene E. *Slipstream: The Autobiography of an Air Craftsman.* New York: Whittlesey House, 1950.

Wiper, Steve. *Omaha Class Cruisers. Warship Pictorial # 6.* Tucson, Ariz.: Classic Warships Publishing, 1999.

———. *USS Minneapolis CA-36. Warship Pictorial # 2.* Tucson, Ariz.: Classic Warships Publishing, 1997.

Worthington, Rear Adm. Joseph M. "A Destroyer at Midway." *Shipmate* (January 1965): 4–8.

Wukovits, John F. *Devotion to Duty: A Biography of Admiral Clifton A. F. Sprague.* Annapolis, Md.: Naval Institute Press, 1995.

Zehnpfennig, Gladys. *Melvin J. Maas: Gallant Man of Action.* Minneapolis, Minn.: T. S. Denison, 1967.

Zimmerman, Maj. John L. *The Guadalcanal Campaign.* Washington, D.C.: GPO, 1949.

Index

A

B

C

D

G

I

J

K

L

M

N

O

P

Q

R

S

U

V

W

X

Y

Z

About the Author

John B. Lundstrom is a Curator Emeritus of History of the Milwaukee Public Museum, where he worked for thirty-seven years. He received his master's degree in 1974 from the University of Wisconsin-Milwaukee. The author of four other books on the Pacific War, all published by the Naval Institute Press, he is a recipient of The Hook Contributor's Award (1988), the Samuel Eliot Morison Award for Naval Literature (1995), and the National Museum of Naval Aviation's Admiral Arthur W. Radford Award (1997). He is currently completing a book on a Minnesota regiment's experiences in the Civil War and planning more writing projects on various aspects of the Pacific War.

The Naval Institute Press is the book-publishing arm of the U.S. Naval Institute, a private, nonprofit, membership society for sea service professionals and others who share an interest in naval and maritime affairs. Established in 1873 at the U.S. Naval Academy in Annapolis, Maryland, where its offices remain today, the Naval Institute has members worldwide.

Members of the Naval Institute support the education programs of the society and receive the influential monthly magazine *Proceedings* and discounts on fine nautical prints and on ship and aircraft photos. They also have access to the transcripts of the Institute's Oral History Program and get discounted admission to any of the Institute-sponsored seminars offered around the country.

The Naval Institute also publishes *Naval History* magazine. This colorful bimonthly is filled with entertaining and thought-provoking articles, first-person reminiscences, and dramatic art and photography. Members receive a discount on *Naval History* subscriptions.

The Naval Institute's book-publishing program, begun in 1898 with basic guides to naval practices, has broadened its scope to include books of more general interest. Now the Naval Institute Press publishes about seventy titles each year, ranging from how-to books on boating and navigation to battle histories, biographies, ship and aircraft guides, and novels. Institute members receive significant discounts on the Press's more than eight hundred books in print.

Full-time students are eligible for special half-price membership rates. Life memberships are also available.

For a free catalog describing Naval Institute Press books currently available, and for further information about subscribing to *Naval History* magazine or about joining the U.S. Naval Institute, please write to:

Member Services
U.S. Naval Institute
291 Wood Road
Annapolis, MD 21402-5034
Telephone: (800) 233-8764
Fax: (410) 571-1703
Web address: www.navalinstitute.org